ART FUNDAMENTALS

Theory and Practice

TENTH EDITION

ART FUNDAMENTALS

Theory and Practice

TENTH EDITION

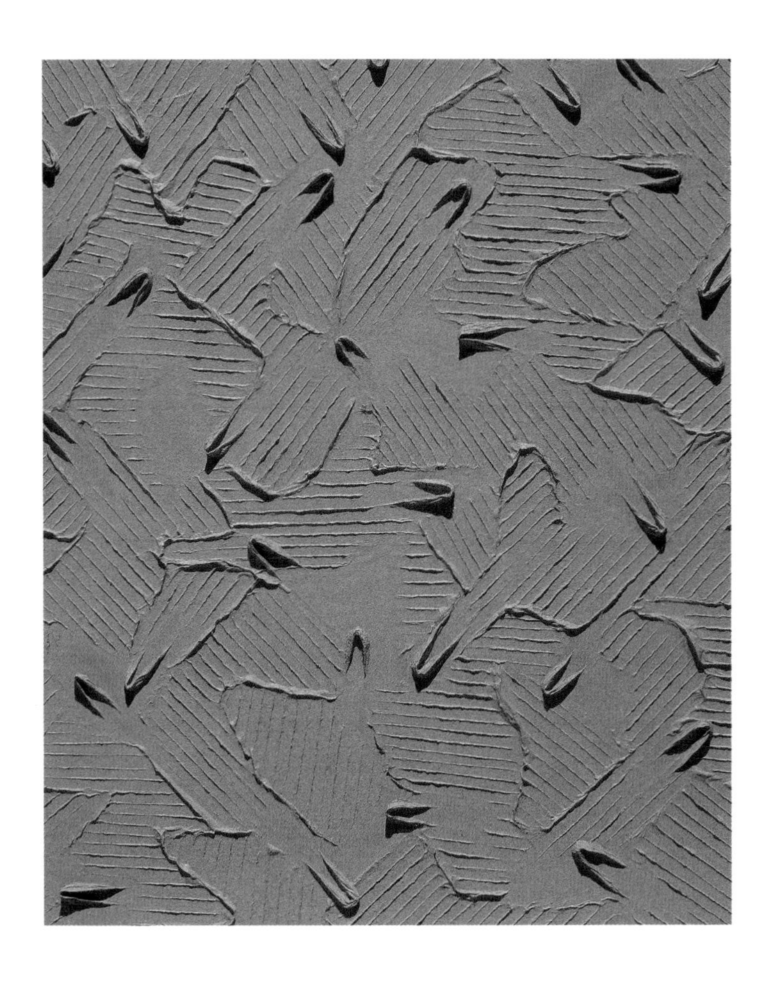

Otto G. Ocvirk
Robert E. Stinson
Philip R. Wigg
Robert O. Bone
David L. Cayton

School of Art
Bowling Green State University

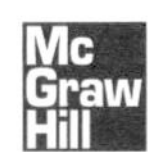

Boston Burr Ridge, IL Dubuque, IA Madison, WI New York San Francisco St. Louis
Bangkok Bogotá Caracas Kuala Lumpur Lisbon London Madrid Mexico City
Milan Montreal New Delhi Santiago Seoul Singapore Sydney Taipei Toronto

The McGraw·Hill Companies

Mc Graw Hill **Higher Education**

Published by McGraw-Hill, an imprint of The McGraw-Hill Companies, Inc., 1221 Avenue of the Americas, New York, NY 10020. Some ancillaries, including electronic and print components, may not be available to customers outside the United States.

This book is printed on acid-free paper.

1 2 3 4 5 6 7 8 9 0 DOW/DOW 0 9 8 7 6 5

ISBN 0-07-286233-5

Publisher: *Lyn Uhl*
Editor in Chief: *Emily Barrosse*
Director of Development: *Lisa Pinto*
Development Editor: *Margaret Manos*
Editorial Assistant: *Elizabeth Sigal*
Executive Marketing Manager: *Suzanna Ellison*
Managing Editor: *Melissa Williams*
Production Editor: *Anne Fuzellier*
Senior Designer: *Kim Menning*
Interior Designer: *Glenda King*
Cover Designer: *Joan Greenfield*
Photo Research Coordinator: *Natalia Peschiera*
Photo Researcher: *Emily Tietz*
Art Editor: *Emma Ghiselli*
Lead Media Producer: *Shannon Gattens*
Media Project Manager: *Michele Borrelli*
Production Supervisor: *Richard DeVitto*
Supplement Producer: *Louis Swaim*

Library of Congress Cataloging-in-Publication Data

Art fundamentals: theory & practice / Otto G. Ocvirk. [et al.].—10th ed.
p. cm.
Includes bibliographical references and index.
ISBN 0-07-286233-5 (softcover : acid-free paper)
1. Art—Technique. 2. Art. I. Ocvirk, Otto G.

N7430.A697 2005
701'.8—dc22 2005047998

Cover and title page:
Seo-Bo Park, *Ecriture No. 940110,* 1994. Mixed media with Korean paper, 26 × 18 in. (65.3 × 46 cm). Courtesy of Jean Art Gallery, Seoul, Korea.

www.mhhe.com

Preface ix
Acknowledgments xiv

CHAPTER ONE
Introduction 2
THE VOCABULARY OF INTRODUCTORY TERMS 3
THE NEED AND SEARCH FOR ART 5
THE INGREDIENTS OF ART 10
The Three Basic Components of a Work of Art 11
Subject 11
Form 11
Content 12
Savoring the Ingredients 15
THE INGREDIENTS ASSEMBLED 18
Two-Dimensional Media and Techniques 20
The Two-Dimensional Picture Plane 22
The Picture Frame 22
Positive and Negative Areas 22
The Art Elements 24

CHAPTER TWO
Form 26
THE VOCABULARY OF FORM 28
FORM AND VISUAL ORDERING 29
The Seven Principles of Organization 31
Harmony (1) 31
Variety (2) 47
Balance (3) 50
Proportion (4) 56
Dominance (5) 62
Movement (6) 63
Economy (7) 65
Space: Result of Elements/Principles 66
FORM UNITY: A SUMMARY 67

CHAPTER THREE
Line 68
THE VOCABULARY OF LINE 70
LINE: THE ELEMENTARY MEANS OF COMMUNICATION 70
THE PHYSICAL CHARACTERISTICS OF LINE 74
Measure 74
Type 74
Direction 74
Location 76
Character 77
THE EXPRESSIVE PROPERTIES OF LINE 78
LINE AND THE OTHER ART ELEMENTS 79
Line and Shape 79
Line and Value 81
Line and Texture 81
Line and Color 81
THE SPATIAL CHARACTERISTICS OF LINE 84
LINE AND REPRESENTATION 84

CHAPTER FOUR
Shape 88
THE VOCABULARY OF SHAPE 90
INTRODUCTION TO SHAPE 91
THE DEFINITION OF SHAPE 91
THE USE OF SHAPES 95
Shape Dimensions 96
The Illusions of Two-Dimensional Shapes 96
The Illusions of Three-Dimensional Shapes 97
Shape and Principles of Design 100
Balance 101
Direction 101
Duration and Relative Dominance 103
Harmony and Variety 104
Shapes and the Space Concept 104
SHAPE AND CONTENT 104

CHAPTER FIVE
Value 110
THE VOCABULARY OF VALUE 112
INTRODUCTION TO VALUE RELATIONSHIPS 112
DESCRIPTIVE USES OF VALUE 113
EXPRESSIVE USES OF VALUE 114
Chiaroscuro 116
Tenebrism 119
Printmaking Techniques and Value 119
Decorative Value 121

CONTENTS

COMPOSITIONAL FUNCTIONS OF VALUE 121
Value Patterns 123
Open and Closed Compositions 125

CHAPTER SIX
Texture 126
THE VOCABULARY OF TEXTURE 128
INTRODUCTION TO TEXTURE 129
TEXTURE AND THE VISUAL ARTS 129
THE NATURE OF TEXTURE 131
TYPES OF TEXTURES 131
Actual Texture 131
Simulated Texture 133
Abstract Texture 134
Invented Texture 135
TEXTURE AND PATTERN 136
TEXTURE AND COMPOSITION 137
Relative Dominance and Movement 137
Psychological Factors 138
TEXTURE AND SPACE 138
TEXTURE AND ART MEDIA 139

CHAPTER SEVEN
Color 140
THE VOCABULARY OF COLOR 142
THE CHARACTERISTICS OF COLOR 143
Light: The Source of Color 143
Additive Color 144
Subtractive Color 145
Artist's Color Mixing 146
The Triadic Color System 147
Neutrals 148
The Physical Properties of Color 148
Hue 149
Value 149
Intensity 150
Developing Aesthetic Color Relationships 152
Complements and Split-Complements 152
Triads 153
Tetrads 154
Analogous and Monochromatic Colors 154
Warm and Cool Colors 154
Plastic Colors 155
Simultaneous Contrast 156
Color and Emotion 161
Psychological Application of Color 161
The Evolution of the Color Wheel 163
The Origins of Color Systems 163
The Discovery of Pigment Primaries 163
The First Triadic Color Wheel 163
American Educators 163
The Ostwald Color System 163
The Munsell Color System 163
The Subtractive Printing System (Process Color System) 165
Color Photography 166
Color Computer Printing 167
The Discovery of Light Primaries 167
THE ROLE OF COLOR IN COMPOSITION 168
COLOR BALANCE 168
Color and Harmony 170
Color and Variety 171

CHAPTER EIGHT
Space 176
THE VOCABULARY OF SPACE 178
INTRODUCTION TO SPACE 179
SPATIAL PERCEPTION 179
MAJOR TYPES OF SPACE 179
Decorative Space 179
Plastic Space 180
Divisions of Plastic Space 180
SPATIAL INDICATORS 181
Sharp and Diminishing Detail 181
Size 182
Position 182
Overlapping 183
Transparency 183
Interpenetration 184
Fractional Representation 184
Converging Parallels 185
Linear Perspective 186
Major Systems of Linear Perspective 188
Perspective Concepts Applied 195
The Disadvantages of Linear Perspective 198
Other Projection Systems 200
Intuitive Space 200

THE SPATIAL PROPERTIES OF THE ELEMENTS 202
Line and Space 202
Shape and Space 204
Value and Space 204
Texture and Space 206
Color and Space 206
RECENT CONCEPTS OF SPACE 207
The Search for a New Spatial Dimension 207
Plastic Images 209
Pictorial Representations of Movement in Time 210
Motion Pictures 213
Video 214
The Computer and Art 215

CHAPTER NINE
The Art of the Third Dimension 218
THE VOCABULARY OF THE THIRD DIMENSION 220
BASIC CONCEPTS OF THREE-DIMENSIONAL ART 221
Sculpture 222
Other Areas of Three-Dimensional Art 223
Architecture 225
Metalwork 225
Glass Design 226
Ceramics 227
Fiberwork 227
Product Design 227
THE COMPONENTS OF THREE-DIMENSIONAL ART 228
Materials and Techniques 228
Subtraction 229
Manipulation 229
Addition 229
Substitution 230
The Elements of Three-Dimensional Form 230
Shape 230
Value 232
Space 234
Texture 236
Line 236
Color 237
Time (The Fourth Dimension) 237
Principles of Three-Dimensional Order 238
Harmony and Variety 238
Balance 240
Proportion 240
Economy 241
Movement 242
Installations 243

CHAPTER TEN
Content and Style 246
INTRODUCTION TO CONTENT AND STYLE 248
NINETEENTH-CENTURY ART 248
Neoclassicism (c. 1750–1820) 248
Romanticism 250
Beginning of Photography 255
Realism 255
Technological Developments in Photography 256
Impressionism 258
Post-Impressionism 262
Photographic Trends 266
EARLY-TWENTIETH-CENTURY ART 267
Expressionism 267
French Expressionism: The Fauves 267
German Expressionism 268
Sculpture in the Early 1900s 270
Expressionism in the United States 272
Expressionism in Mexico 272
Color Photography and Other New Trends 273
Cubism 274
Futurism 276
Abstract Art 278
Abstract Art in Europe 278
Abstract Art in the United States 279
Abstract Sculpture 280
Abstract and Realist Photography 281
Fantastic Art 284
Dadaism 284
Individual Fantasists 286
Surrealist Painting 287
Surrealist Sculpture 289
Surrealism and Photography 290
LATE-TWENTIETH-CENTURY ART 291
Abstract Expressionist Painting 291
Abstract Expressionist Sculpture 298
Abstract Expressionism and Photography 301
Kinetic Sculpture 302
Pop Art and Assemblage 302
Happenings and Performance or Action Art 306
Op Art 309
Minimalism 310

Environmental Art and Installations 312
Postmodernism 316
New Realism (Photorealism) 317
Process and Conceptual Art 319
Neo-Expressionism 320
Feminist Art 322
Other Trends: Neo-Abstraction, Film Stills, Photography 325
Neo-Abstraction 325
Film Stills 326
Photography 327

NEW GLOBAL ART 330

Chronological Outline of Western Art 333
Glossary 338
Bibliography 343
Index 345

The foundations or fundamentals course presents a unique challenge to the instructor. It is a course profoundly based in *doing*—in the experience of exploring art elements and media on a level of practical curiosity. At the same time, foundations has a history and language that successful students will learn and master—as a way of avoiding common pitfalls, if nothing else.

The original text that set the standard for introduction to art courses across the country, *Art Fundamentals* has guided generations of students through both the essential elements of art and the rich and varied history of their uses.

The tenth edition features a broader array of media and represents more diverse artists than the previous edition, particularly from the late twentieth century, including many new women artists and artists from non-Western cultures. New sections have been added on video art, contemporary photography, and global art, and many of the computer-aided illustrations in the text have been updated. In addition, the entire manuscript has been reviewed and refreshed for readability.

This edition of *Art Fundamentals* expands the wealth of study materials available to students and faculty by offering a free student *Core Concepts in Art* CD-ROM bound in the back of each new copy of the textbook purchased from McGraw-Hill, and a complete Online Learning Center.

CORE CONCEPTS IN ART, VERSION 3.0

This CD-ROM, designed for McGraw-Hill by leading instructional designer Bonnie Mitchell, of Bowling Green State University, offers a wealth of resources for art students. Updated and expanded, *Core Concepts* offers teachers and students hundreds of interactive exercises, over an hour of narrated video, and text-specific, chapter-by-chapter pedagogical resources such as images for study and reference, quizzes, and more. Exercises meant to encourage students to investigate the CD-ROM appear at the end of each chapter in the text. Please see A Guide to the CD-ROM on the following page for more detailed information.

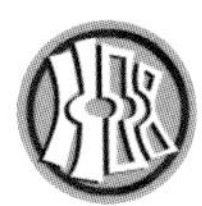

Students can interact with the formal elements and principles of art by working through more than seventy exercises that illustrate fundamental principles such as line, shape, color, and texture.

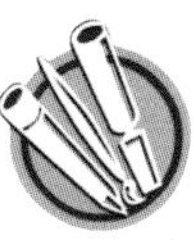

Students are invited to tour a variety of art studios. In extensive narrated video segments, this section illustrates techniques for working in a variety of media—from bronze to paint to film.

Study resources correlated to each chapter in *Art Fundamentals* include key terms, chapter summaries, and self-correcting study quizzes.

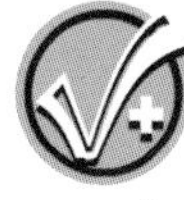

The Study Skills section provides broad, practical advice on adjusting to the rigors of college work.

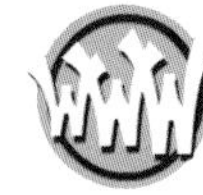

The Research and the Internet section introduces students to the research process—from idea generation, to organization, to researching on- and off-line—and includes guidelines for incorporating sources for term papers and bibliographies.

www.mhhe.com/artfundamentals10

The student section of the Online Learning Center contains study materials such as quizzes, key terms, flashcards, and crossword puzzles for each chapter in the book, plus a link to McGraw-Hill's Art Supersite, where students can research career opportunities. The instructor section includes sample student projects and links to multiple professional resources.

Also available for instructors are a set of high-quality art image slides; *The McGraw-Hill Guide to Electronic Research in Art* (ISBN 0-07-232956-4), and *The McGraw-Hill Museum-Goer's Guide* (ISBN 0-07-038731-1).

Together the various teaching and learning materials help reinforce the principles and elements of design with practical exercises, self-guided tutorials, interactive examples, and assignable student projects.

A Guide to *Core Concepts in Art* CD-ROM, Version 3.0

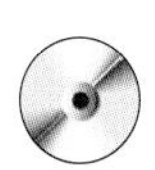

GETTING STARTED

System Requirements

In order to run this CD-ROM properly, please make sure that your computer meets the minimum system requirements:

WINDOWS

- Intel Pentium II 200
- 128 MB RAM (64 MB available RAM)
- Windows 95/98, 2000, XP, or NT 4.0+
- 4x (or better) CD-ROM drive
- SVGA or higher monitor with 800x600 resolution running 16-bit color

MACINTOSH OSX

- G3 running 10.1 or better
- 128 MG of available RAM
- Color monitor with 800x600 resolution running 16-bit color

MACINTOSH CLASSIC

- Power Macintosh 180 (G3 recommended)
- 128 MG of available RAM
- System 8.6 or later
- 4x (or better) CD-ROM drive
- Color monitor with 800x600 resolution running 16-bit color
- Sound capability

QuickTime Requirements

QuickTime is required to run the program. You can click the InstallQuicktime.html file on this CD-ROM, which will bring you directly to the Apple QuickTime website, where you can download the program. The website is www.apple.com/quicktime/download.

Starting the CD-ROM

Follow these steps to install the CD-ROM and begin working with the program:

WINDOWS

1. Insert the CD into the CD-ROM drive.
2. Double click on My Computer on your desktop.
3. Double click on the CD-ROM drive, most commonly called the D:/drive.
4. Double click on the Start_HerePC.exe file from the CD-ROM.

MACINTOSH

1. Insert the CD into the CD-ROM drive.
2. Double click on the "Launching the Imagination" CD-ROM.
3. Double click on the Start_Here (OSX) or Start_Here (Classic) file from the CD-ROM. Use Start_Here (OSX) for Macintosh 0SX 10.1 or higher, and Start_Here (Classic) for System 9.2 or lower.

If you need help installing this program, please call 1-800-331-5094 between 9am and 5pm EST.

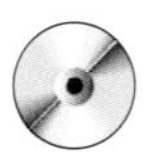

CD-ROM CONTENTS

The five icons on the main menu correspond to the five components of the *Core Concepts in Art* CD-ROM.

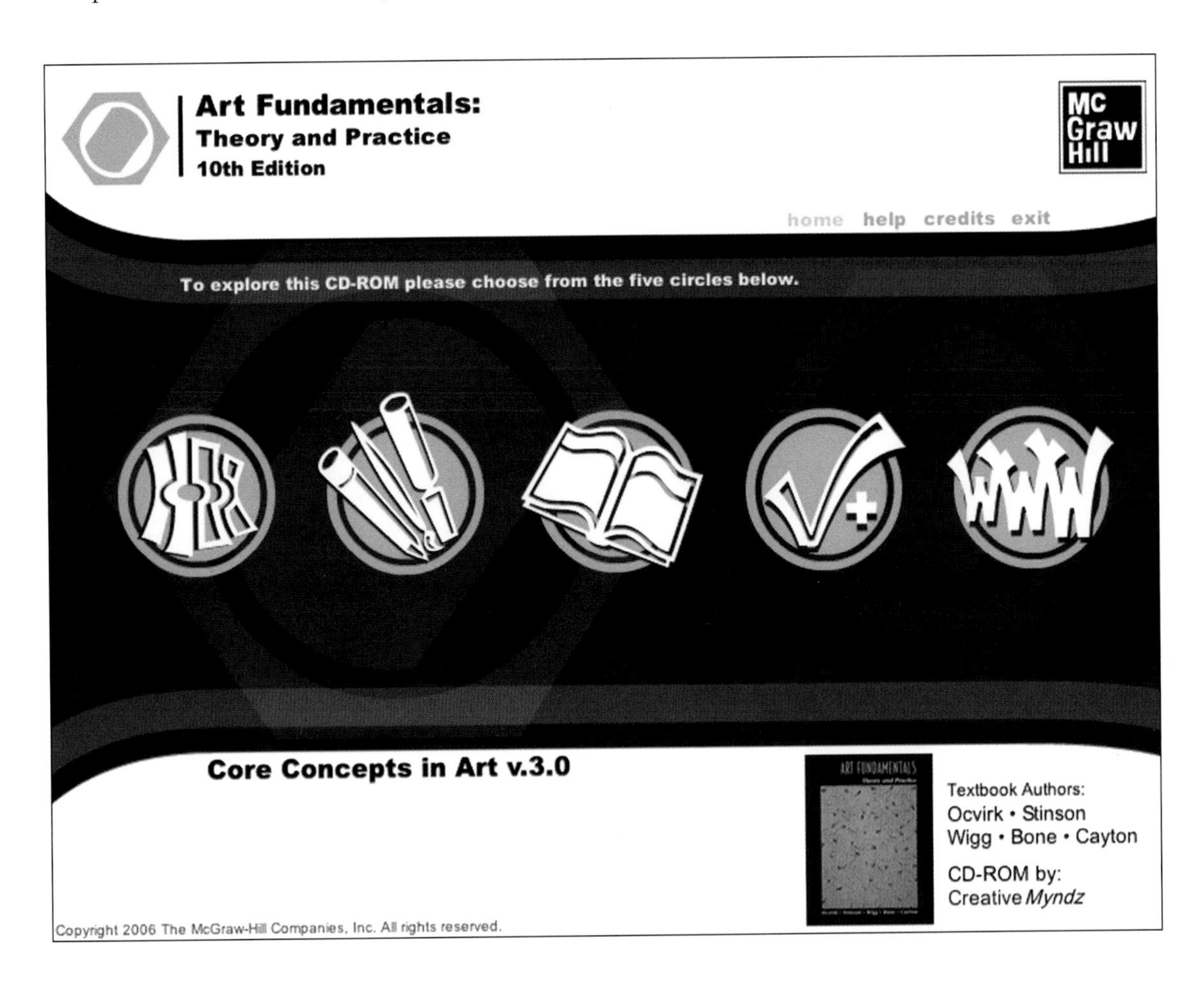

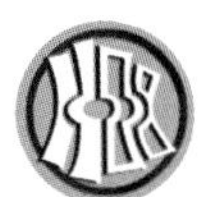

Elements and Principles of Art

Explore the elements of 2D, 3D, and time design through interactive exercises and animated demonstrations. Experiment with the principles of unity and variety, pattern and rhythm, balance, scale and proportion, emphasis and focal point, and illusion of space.

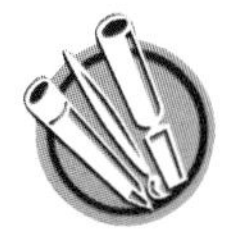

Art Techniques

Observe techniques for painting, sculpture, printmaking, glass, jewelry, photography, and new media in a series of video demonstrations.

Chapter Resources

Review the content of each chapter in *Art Fundamentals,* Tenth Edition, in this section of the CD-ROM.

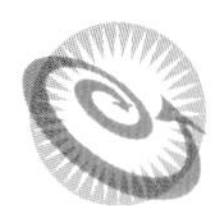

More extensive chapter review materials are also available at the McGraw-Hill **Online Learning Center** (www.mhhe.com/artfundamentals10), which can be launched from the Internet Resources section.

Study Skills Primer

Applicable to all your courses, this primer offers tips on study and organizational skills. It also includes advice on documenting sources.

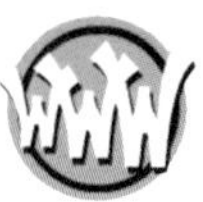

Internet Resources

This section is helpful if you are new to using the Internet for research. It offers basic "how-to's" on using the Web, along with an introduction to computer terminology and netiquette.

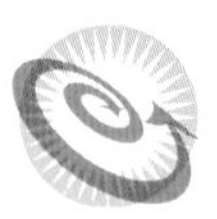

You can also access the McGraw-Hill **Online Learning Center** through a link in this section.

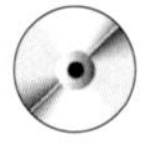

EXPLORING ELEMENTS, PRINCIPLES, AND TECHNIQUES

The following screen shots are examples of the types of demonstrations and interactive exercises found in the CD-ROM. For a guide to correlating the CD-ROM with this text, see the "Investigate the CD-ROM: Questions to Ask Yourself" feature at the end of every chapter.

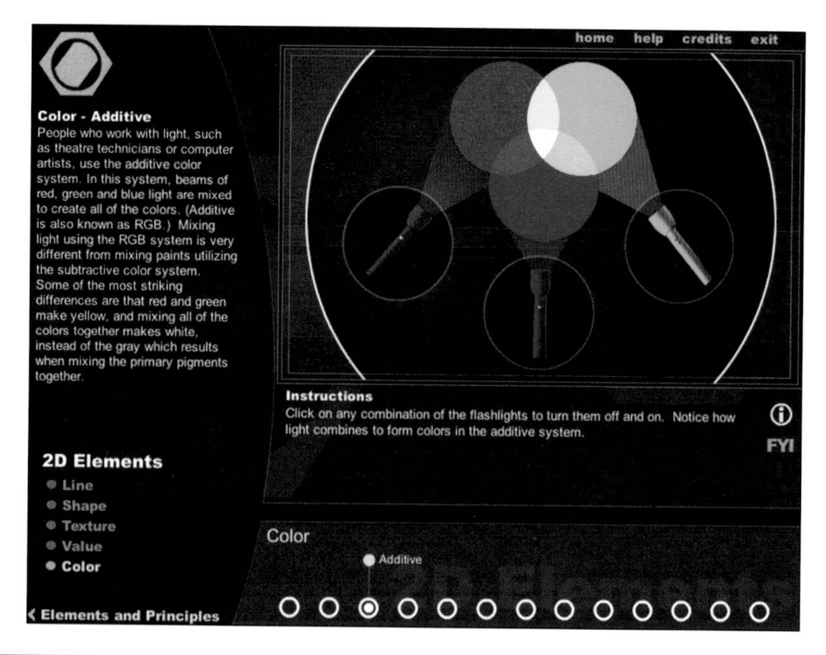

An interactive activity that allows you to experiment with additive color, found in "Elements and Principles of Art"

An interactive activity that allows you to experiment with positive and negative space, found in "Elements and Principles of Art"

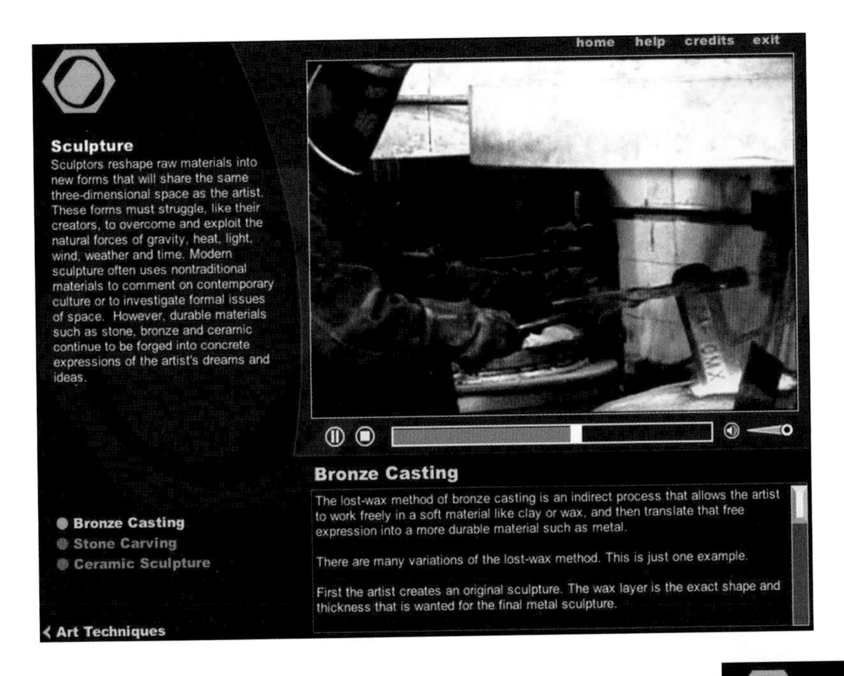

A video demonstration of the lost-wax method of bronze casting, found in "Techniques"

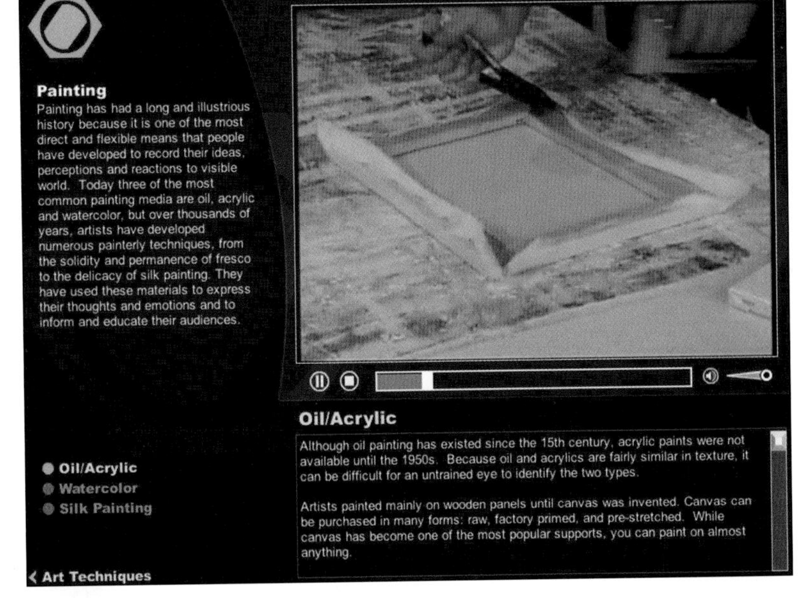

A video demonstration of painting with oils and acrylics, found in "Techniques"

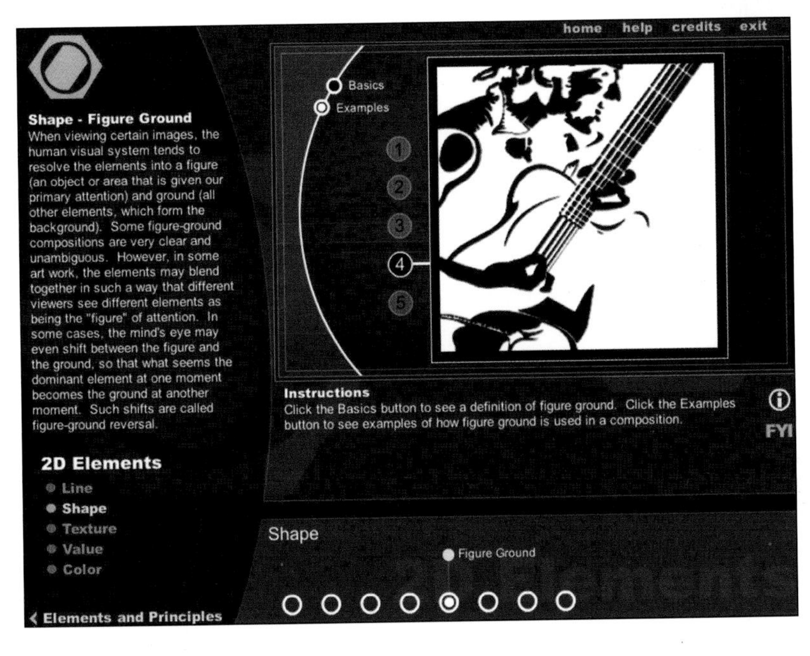

An interactive activity that allows you to experiment with positive and negative space, found in "Elements and Principles of Art"

ACKNOWLEDGMENTS

We owe a debt of gratitude to our publisher, McGraw-Hill, and its Higher Education staff for their excellent support. We would like to thank the many artists, museums, galleries, and art collectors for providing us with permissions and materials. We are especially indebted to the efforts and insights of the many reviewers whose comments and criticisms have guided this recent revision. Foremost among these is Sally Packard of the University of North Texas, who suggested image and text revisions throughout the book. Other reviewers whose opinions helped shape this edition are:

Lynda E. Andrus
Kansas State University

Roger Baer
Iowa State University

Stephanie Bowman
Pittsburg State University

D. Duane Chapman
Glenville State College

Tom Coaker
University of Arizona

Pat Conant
Westfield State College

Jennifer Costa
Illinois Central College

James A. J. Davies II
Rockingham Community College

Herb Goodman
Louisiana State University

Christopher Johns
Louisiana State University

Janice Kmetz
University of Minnesota, Duluth

Mark Nisenholt
Lakehead University

Elaine Oehmich
Appalachian State University

Teresa Paschke
Iowa State University

Carolyn Quinn-Hensley
Mesa State College

Linda Vanderkolk
Purdue University

Michelle Wiebe Zederayko
George Brown College

ART FUNDAMENTALS

Theory and Practice

TENTH EDITION

CHAPTER ONE

Introduction

THE VOCABULARY OF INTRODUCTORY TERMS

THE NEED AND SEARCH FOR ART

THE INGREDIENTS OF ART

The Three Basic Components of a Work of Art

Subject

Form

Content

Savoring the Ingredients

THE INGREDIENTS ASSEMBLED

Two-Dimensional Media and Techniques

The Two-Dimensional Picture Plane

The Picture Frame

Positive and Negative Areas

The Art Elements

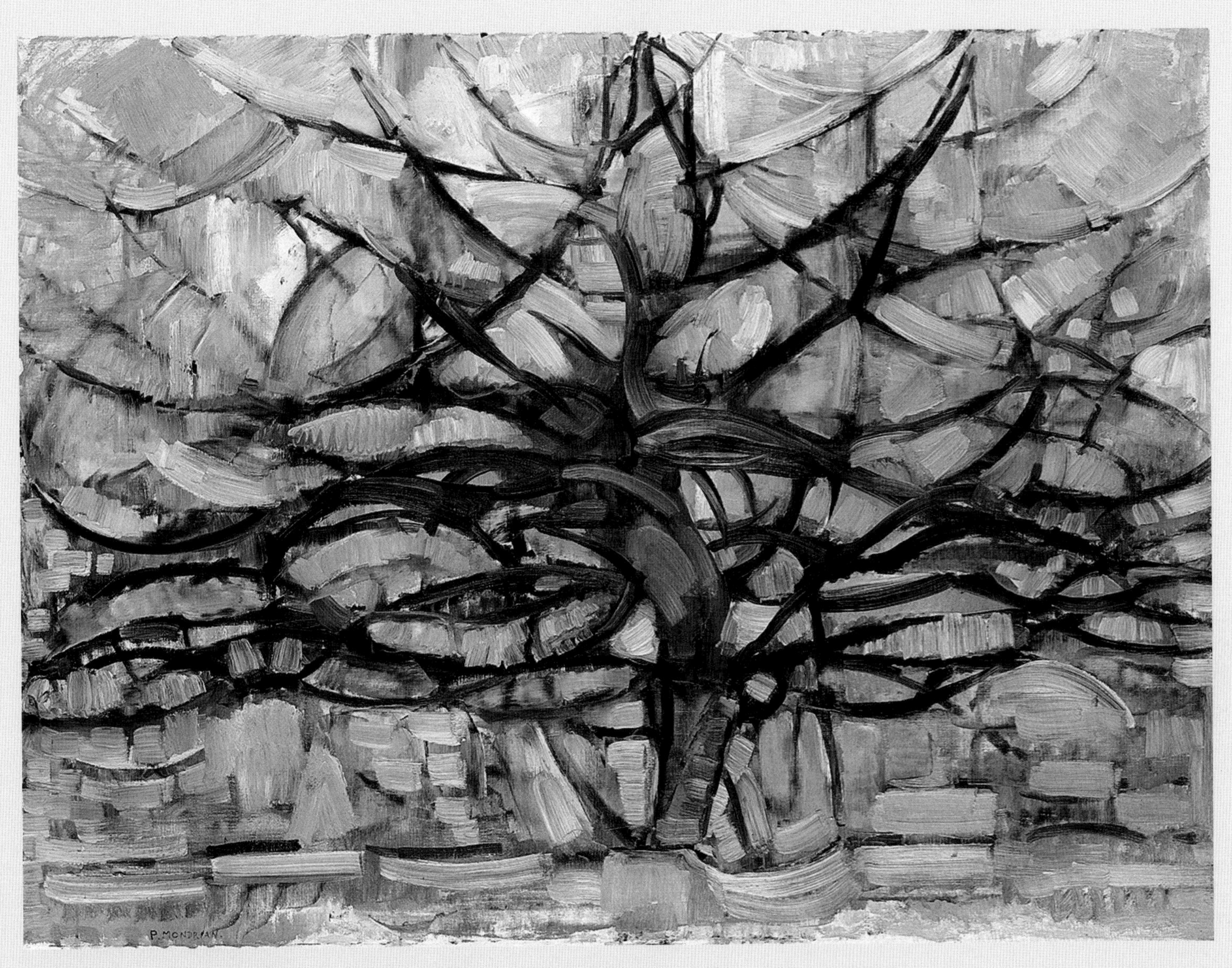

Piet Mondrian, *The Grey Tree,* 1911. Oil on canvas, 30½ × 42⅞ in. (79.7 × 109.1 cm). © 2005 Mondrian/Hotzman Trust c/o HCR International Warrenton Virginia.

THE VOCABULARY OF **INTRODUCTORY TERMS**

Art — The formal expression of a conceived image or imagined conception in terms of a given medium. —Sheldon Cheney

abstraction
1. The selection, simplification, and/or rearrangement of the representation of natural appearance. 2. Nonrepresentational work arranged simply to satisfy artists' needs for organization or expression. In varying degrees, abstraction is present in all works of art.

aesthetic, aesthetics
Traditionally a branch of philosophy concerned with the theory of the "beautiful," aesthetics is now a compound of the philosophy, psychology, and sociology of art. As such, aesthetics is no longer solely confined to determining what is beautiful in art, but attempts to discover the origins of the art experience and the relationship between art and other aspects of culture. In this book, the term *aesthetics* refers to the concern with artistic qualities of form, as opposed to descriptive form or the mere recording of facts.

conceptual perception
Creative vision derived from the imagination.

content
The essential meaning and significance of a work of art. Content refers to the sensory, subjective, psychological, or emotional properties a work of art contains, as opposed to its descriptive aspects alone.

craftsmanship
Aptitude, skill, or quality workmanship in the use of tools and materials.

decorative
Ornamenting or enriching but, more importantly in art, emphasizing the two-dimensional nature of an artwork or any of its elements. Decorative art emphasizes the essential flatness of a surface.

descriptive (art)
A type of art that is based on adherence to actual appearances.

design
The underlying plan on which an artwork is based. In a broader sense, *design* may be considered synonymous with the term **form.**

elements of art
Line, shape, value, texture, and color—the basic ingredients the artist uses to produce imagery. The use of these elements produces the visual language of art.

expression
1. The manifestation of thought, emotion, or quality of meaning in artistic form. 2. In art, *expression* is synonymous with the term **content.**

form
1. The organization and arrangement of visual elements that develop unity in an artwork. 2. The total appearance or organization of an artwork.

graphic art
1. Two-dimensional art forms, such as drawing, painting, and printmaking. 2. The two-dimensional use of the elements of art. 3. May also refer to the techniques of commercial art as used in the layout and production of newspapers, books, magazines, and Web pages.

mass
1. In graphic art, a shape that appears to stand out three-dimensionally from the space surrounding it or appears to create the illusion of a solid body of material. 2. In the plastic arts, the physical bulk of a solid body of material. (See **plastic art.**)

medium, media (pl.)
The materials and means used to bring an artwork into existence.

naturalism
The approach to art that attempts a description of things as they appear in nature. Pure naturalism would contain no personal interpretation introduced by the artist.

negative area
The unoccupied or empty space in an artwork defined by the positive elements created by the artist. (See **positive area(s).**)

nonobjective, nonrepresentational art
A type of art that is entirely imaginative and not derived from anything visually perceived by the artist, and consequently not associated by the observer with any previously experienced natural object.

objective art
Art that is based on physical actuality, optical perception, and the appearance of things as they are. Such art tends to appear natural or real.

optical perception
Things as seen through the eye.

organic unity
A condition in which the components of an artwork—that is, subject, form, and content—form an interdependent whole.

picture frame
The outermost boundary of the picture plane.

picture plane
The actual flat surface on which the artist executes a pictorial image. In some cases, the picture plane acts merely as a transparent plane of reference to establish the illusion of forms existing in a three-dimensional space.

plane
1. An area that is essentially two-dimensional, having height and width. 2. A flat or level surface. 3. A two-dimensional surface having a positive extension and spatial direction or position.

plastic art
1. The use of the elements of art to create the illusion of the third dimension on a two-dimensional surface. 2. Three-dimensional art forms, such as architecture, sculpture, and ceramics.

positive area(s)
The portion of an artwork in which the art elements (shape, line, etc.), or their combination, produce the subject—nonrepresentational or recognizable images. (See **negative area.**)

realism, Realism (art movement)
The style of art that creates an impression of visual actuality without going to extremes of detail, while attempting to relate and interpret universal meanings that lie beneath surface appearances. As a movement, it relates to painters like Honoré Daumier in nineteenth-century France and Winslow Homer in the United States in the 1850s.

representational art
A type of art in which the subject is presented through the visual art elements so that the observer is reminded of actual objects. (See **naturalism** and **realism.**)

space
The interval, or measurable distance, between points or images.

style
A specific artistic character or dominant trend of form noted during a period of history or during an art movement. Style also refers to the expressive use of media that gives an artwork individual character.

subject
The persons, things, signs, or ideas represented in an artwork that express the artist's inspiration or intention.

subjective (art, shape, color, etc.)
That which is derived from a personal viewpoint, bias, or emotion.

technique
The manner with which an artist uses tools and materials to achieve an expressive effect.

three-dimensional
Possessing a dimension of depth, in addition to having the dimensions of height and width.

two-dimensional
Possessing the dimensions of height and width.

unity
The result of bringing the elements of art into the appropriate ratio between harmony and variety to achieve a sense of oneness.

volume
A measurable area of defined or occupied space.

THE NEED AND SEARCH FOR ART

Art Fundamentals: The two words that form the title of this book should make our purpose fairly clear. We probably think we know what is meant by the word *art,* but, as we will see, there are many interpretations.

As to *fundamentals,* we mean the basics of art. But even these are in dispute today. We could apply the word to the fundamental urge to create art that has persisted among humans since the earliest recesses of history. Witness the paintings and carvings of prehistory (figs. 1.1 and 1.2). The cave paintings may have been done to ensure success in hunting—a form of magic. But why the figure carvings? Perhaps to serve as fertility fetishes. In any case, and whatever the

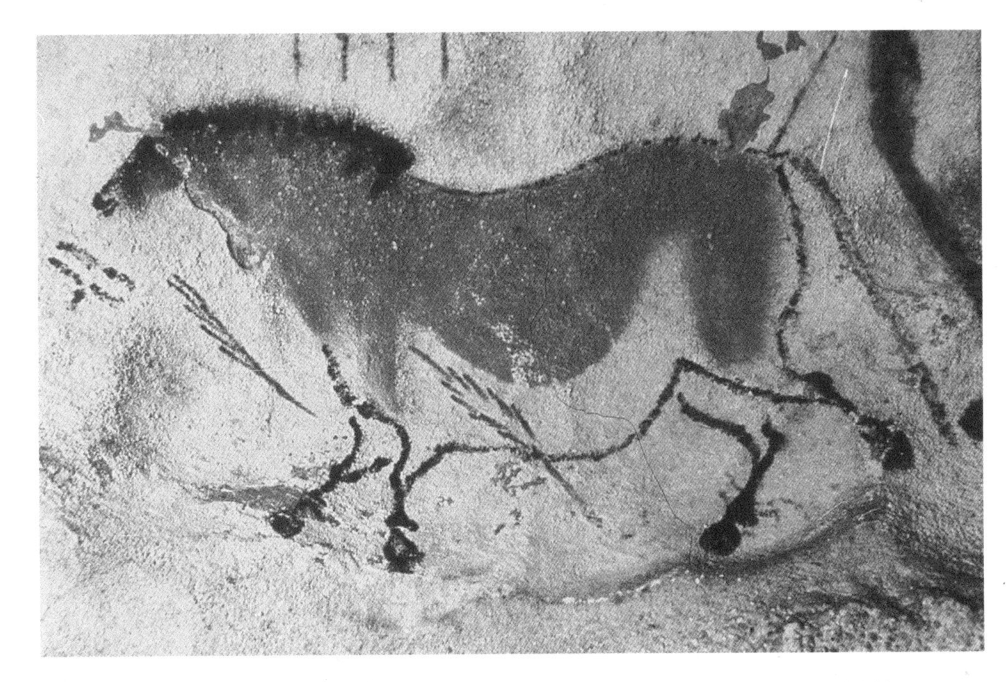

1.1 ***Running Horse Attacked by Arrows.*** **Paleolithic cave painting, c. 15,000–10,000 B.C., Lascaux, France.** In the context of fine art, one meaning of the word *fundamental* is the essential or basic urge to create art. Erich Lessing/Art Resource, NY.

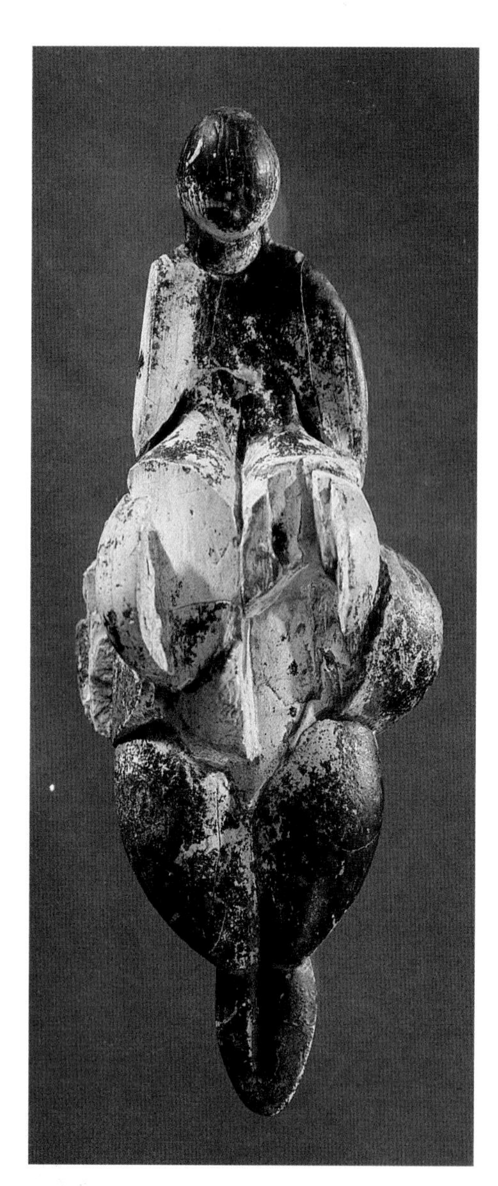

1.2 ***Venus of Lespugue,* carving from the Aurignacian period.** Possibly used as a magical fertility fetish, the *Venus of Lespugue* was carved from a mammoth tusk during the Aurignacian period. Scala/Art Resource, NY.

motivation, this is surely a preeminent form of magic—the magic of the ability to create art.

Since those remote times, the techniques and aims of art have enlarged, so that today we have a boundless variety of different approaches to art. As these **"styles"** have proliferated, they have provoked countless attempts to define art. A few of these definitions follow. While all of them have been challenged, each one contains some essence of what may be thought of as art: the formal expression of a conceived image in terms of a given medium (Cheney), the making of a form produced by the cooperation of all the faculties of the mind (Longman), significant form (Bell), eloquence (Burke), the unexpected inevitability of formal relations (Fry), a unified manifold that is pleasure-giving (Mather), a diagram or paradigm with a meaning that gives pleasure (Lostowel), that which gives pleasure apart from desire (Thomas Aquinas), objectified pleasure (Santayana).

Notice that several of these definitions stress "pleasure" as a component of art, although some art seems to have no intention of arousing pleasure. Nevertheless, these attempts at definition exemplify a recurring desire to decipher the real nature of art and prove that it is different things for different people. If a definition were attempted today, it would need to be awkwardly all-encompassing. Whatever art is, it can be a relaxant or a stimulant. For the artist, it can also produce frustration—but in most cases, finally, a sense of achievement.

Before investigating the ingredients of art in the next section, let's consider some historical attitudes toward art. One such attitude deals with the appreciation of the "beautiful." Known as **aesthetics,** this area of study is complex and has never been totally resolved, particularly as it relates to the definition of beauty. Ever troublesome, definitions of beauty have changed with the times, radically over the past several generations. In some art circles today, beauty is considered obsolete. Historically, various cultures have had their own concepts of beauty, many of which would not correspond to our tastes, and since the nineteenth century, changes in the arts have repeatedly confounded the public. What does the public like and expect in art? Three things: a familiar subject, a recognizable subject, and a sentimental or "pleasant" subject. For many people, these constitute beauty in art. But what if a work meets all three guidelines but is poorly executed? What if a work lacks the expected criteria but is expertly executed? Some artists have created great works on unpleasant subjects, and many artists have produced inferior works on cherished subjects. Certainly not all people, even of similar backgrounds, would agree on the "beauty" of a given subject, much less its interpretation.

Beauty, whatever it may be, is not necessarily sought by today's artists. For example, Process and Conceptual artists are much more concerned with the "how" (the **technique** used to create the work) than the "what" (the final product). Although such artists might consider their art beautiful (though they would probably not use that word), many members of the public may find it to be an alien, unrecognizable kind of beauty. Perhaps "beauty" is due for a new definition—if one can be found!

An artwork's "fingerprint," or recognizability, exists in its style. Some styles are individual and unique, whereas others have been continued by generations of artists. Regardless of style and the time or place of its creation, art has always been produced when an artist has had something to say and has chosen a particular way of saying it. Over the years, artists have been variously praised, neglected, misunderstood, and criticized. The amount of art being created today is unrivaled, and to provide some insight into the subject, many books have been written. Some have been intended for casual, enjoyable viewing;

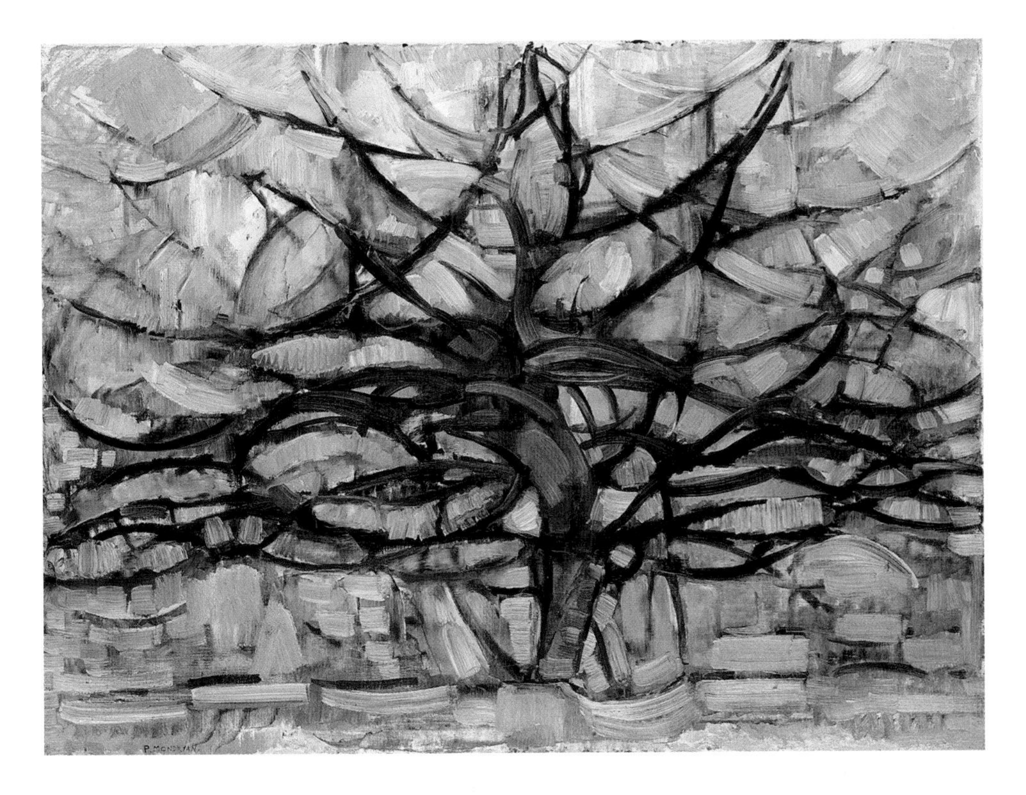

1.3 Piet Mondrian, *The Grey Tree,* 1911. Oil on canvas, 31½ × 42⅞ in. (79.7 × 109.1 cm). In this work, we see the beginnings of the abstraction that marked Mondrian's progress through figs. 1.4 and 1.5 to the purity of his mature style (see fig. 1.6). © 2005 Mondrian/Hotzman Trust c/o HCR International Warrenton Virginia.

1.4 Piet Mondrian, *The Trees,* 1912. Oil on canvas, 37 × 27⅞ in. (94 × 70.8 cm). This painting is another in Mondrian's gradual abstract progression in the tree series to his final classical purism in fig. 1.6. It is a step away from the greater realism of fig. 1.3, toward the greater abstraction of fig. 1.5. Carnegie Museum of Art, Pittsburgh; Patrons Art Fund. Acc. 61.1 © 2005 Mondrian/Holtzman Trust c/o HCR International Warrenton Virginia. Photographer: Peter Harholdt.

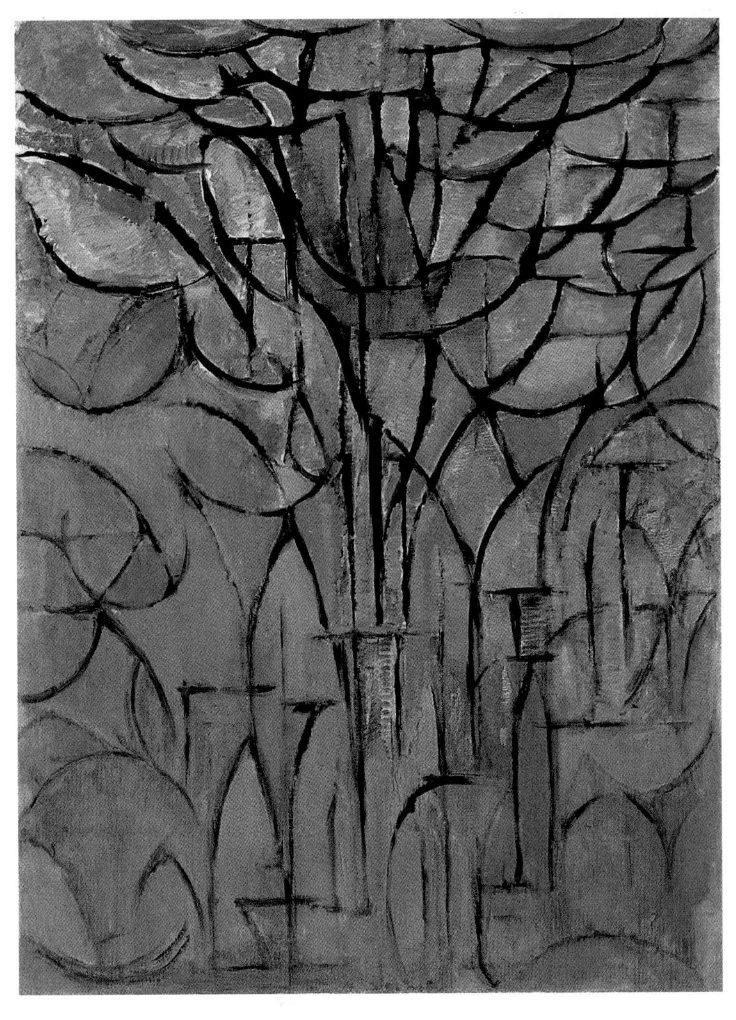

some for the general artistic enlightenment of the layperson; some for coffee-table display; and some for an introduction to the practice of art. Apparently, many people want to engage with art, but if what they see is not meaningful to them, this may add to their inhibitions. One source of these difficulties may be the enormous diversity of our world. Sophisticated printing and distribution techniques have made more art of the past and present available to us than ever before. Radio, air travel, television, and global interactive communications have contributed to a great mixing of cultures. This is a far cry from the insularity of societies before the twentieth century; in those days, people may have had a better understanding and greater acceptance of what they saw because they saw so little.

Throughout history, drawing, painting, printing, and sculpture have been the bellwether of social change and discovery. For example, we can trace Piet Mondrian's style in a chronological examination of his works (figs. 1.3, 1.4, 1.5, and 1.6). His final style, the one best

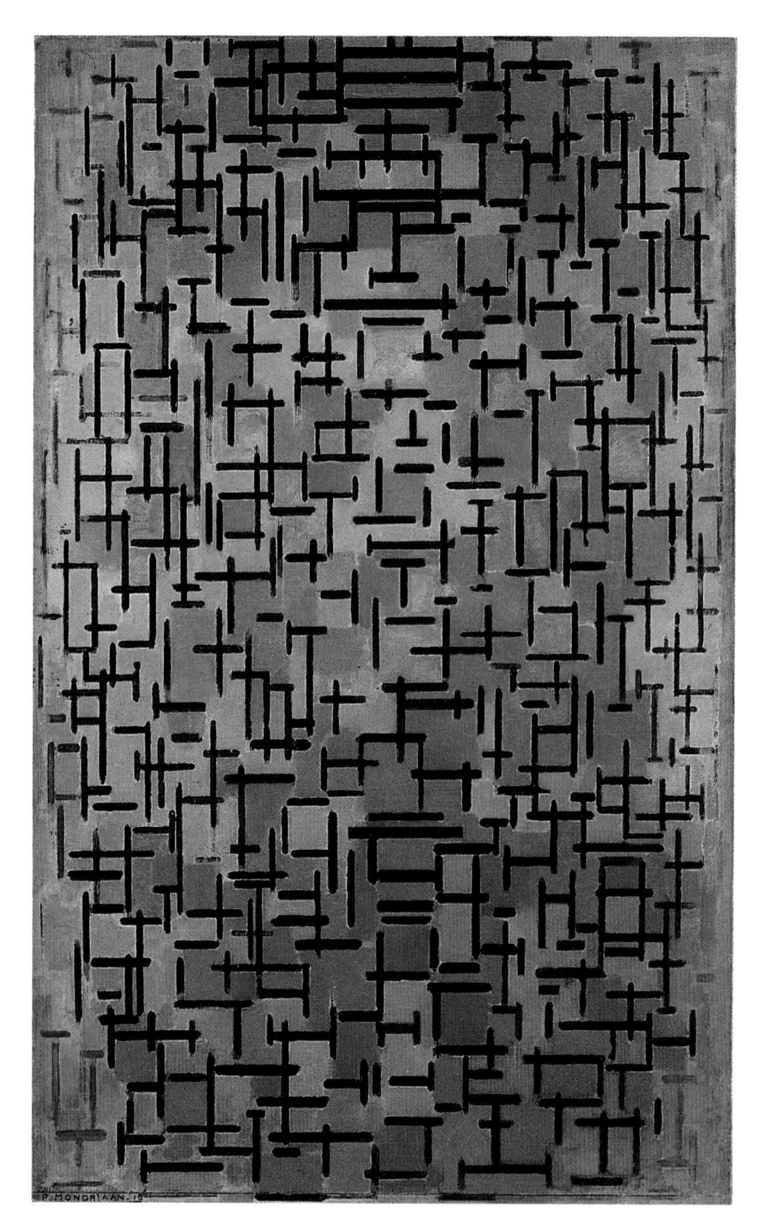

1.5 **Piet Mondrian, *Composition,* 1916. Oil on canvas and wood strip, 47¼ × 29½ in. (120 × 74.9 cm).** As a follow-up to figs. 1.3 and 1.4, this later work is even closer to the severity of Mondrian's final style in fig. 1.6. Solomon R. Guggenheim Foundation, New York (FN 4/9.1229). © 2005 Mondrian/Holtzman Trust c/o HCR International Warrenton Virginia.

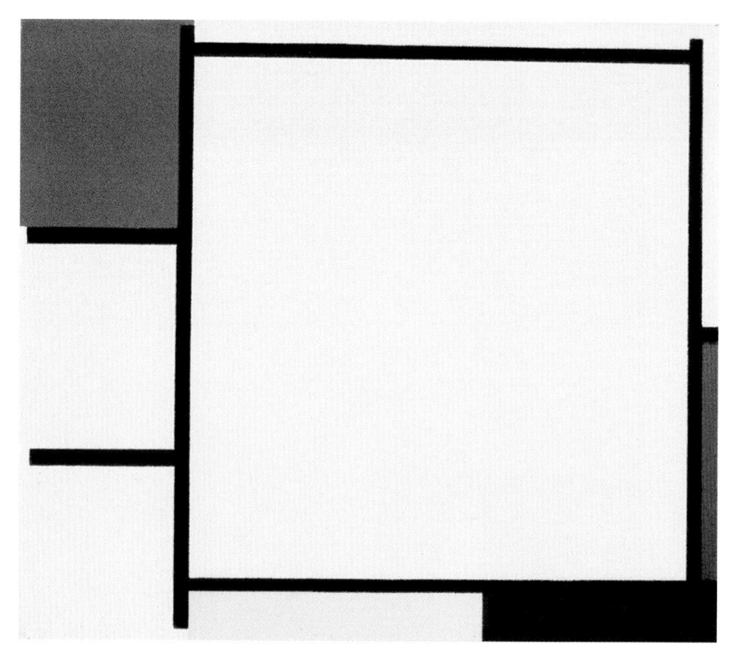

1.6 **Piet Mondrian, *Composition with Red, Blue, Yellow, Black, and Gray,* 1922. Oil on canvas, 16½ × 19⅛ in. (41.9 × 48.6 cm).** The primary colors divided by block lines, all in a two-dimensional grid, are typical of Mondrian's later work. This is the style that has generated so much influence through the years. Toledo Museum of Art. Toledo, OH. Purchased with funds from the Libbey Endowment, Gift of Edward Drummond Libbey. (1978.44) © 2005 Mondrian/Holtzman Trust c/o HCR International Warrenton Virginia.

known, remains influential in a wide variety of applications (figs. 1.7, 1.8, and 1.9), and it has seeped into our attitudes about modern life. Similarly, other artists have subtly altered our vision. Many of the artists included in this book have changed our world.

In order to appreciate the many forms of art to which we have access today, we should learn the basics from which these art forms have grown. We can do this by examining the factors involved in producing artworks and the principles that govern those factors. We can avoid the pitfalls of favoring one style over another by learning to evaluate art by examining its structure. Analyzing structure may sound cold when applied to artistic creation, but structure is at the core of all the arts, including music, dance, and literature. Without structure the expression would not come through, and the work would lack interest.

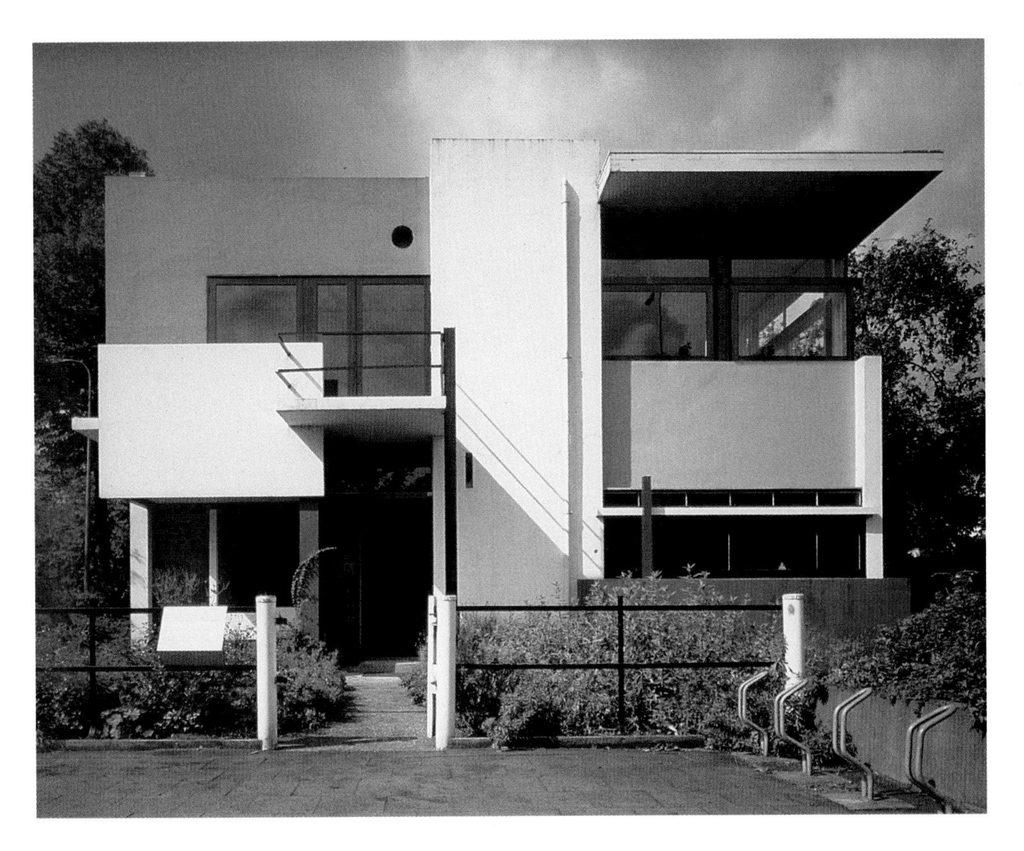

1.7 Gerrit Rietveld and Truus Schröder, *Rietveld-Schröder House,* 1920–24. Rietveld (architect and designer) and Schröder (client and codesigner) were members, along with Mondrian, of the de Stijl group in Holland—a fact that probably accounts for the similarities in style. © Nathan Willock/Architectural Association Slide Library, London.

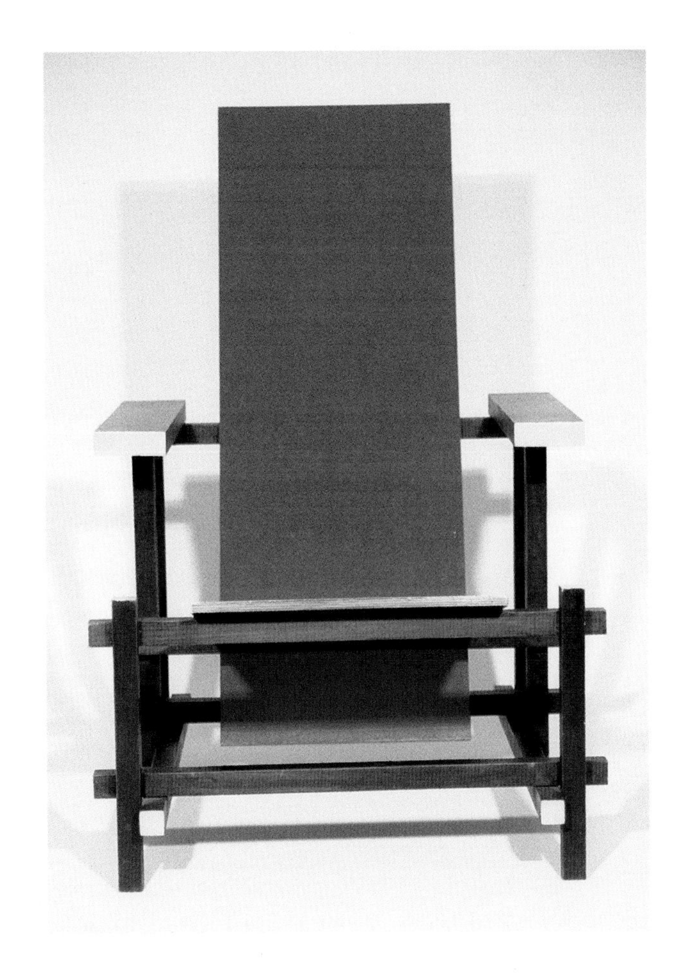

1.8 Gerrit Rietveld, *Red/Blue Chair,* designed 1918 (made c. 1950 by G. van de Groenekan). Pine, ebonized and painted, 34⅞ × 23⅝ × 29¾ in. (88.4 × 60 × 75.5 cm). The relationships between horizontals and verticals and the juxtapositions of color within an asymmetrical grid are features shared by this chair and the paintings of Piet Mondrian. Toledo Museum of Art, Toledo, OH. Purchased with funds from the Florence Scott Libbey Bequest, in memory of her father, Maurice A. Scott (1985.48); © 1998 Beeldrecht Amsterdam.

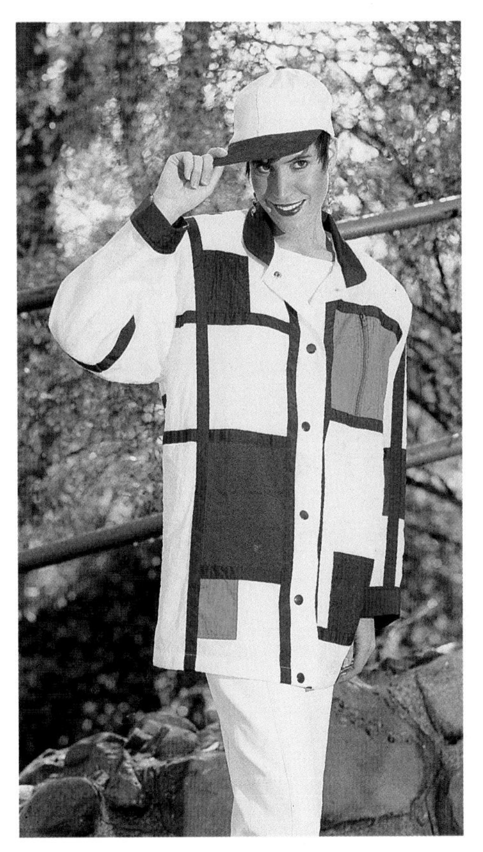

1.9 From the Deerskin catalog, a lightweight color block jacket. The influence of Mondrian on commercial products is clearly evident in this design. Courtesy of The Deerskin Companies, Upper Saddle River, NJ.

THE INGREDIENTS OF ART

Subject, form, and content may be considered the basic components of a work of art. However, these components are sometimes difficult to identify, differentiate, and define in certain works.

Traditionally, the subject of a work of art has been a person, object, event, or theme. Today, subject can also refer to a particular configuration of the art elements and sometimes to a record of the energy and movement of the artist. The modernist subject can no longer be understood simply from the work's appearance or organization. This can create confusion, indeed, for someone who is trying to write about art!

The definition of content, too, has changed from its original meaning. Conventionally, content referred to a work's total message as developed by the artist and interpreted by the viewer. Today, however, we often find that the content derives from an artist's private experiences. These experiences may be so personal that an observer cannot understand the message without additional information about the artist's intentions. The definitions of subject, form, and content that follow are traditional. However, as you look at the illustrations in the book, you will recognize the contemporary blurring of these definitions. With that in mind, works that defy your usual understanding will become more meaningful.

Beyond the basic components of subject, form, and content are certain principles of organization—harmony, variety, balance, movement, proportion, dominance, and economy. Although we may quarrel about the observance of these principles in certain works, no one can argue with their constituent elements: line, shape, value, texture, and color. Artists deal with these elements either alone or in combination. They may be the guiding forces for organization and interpretation and as a conse-

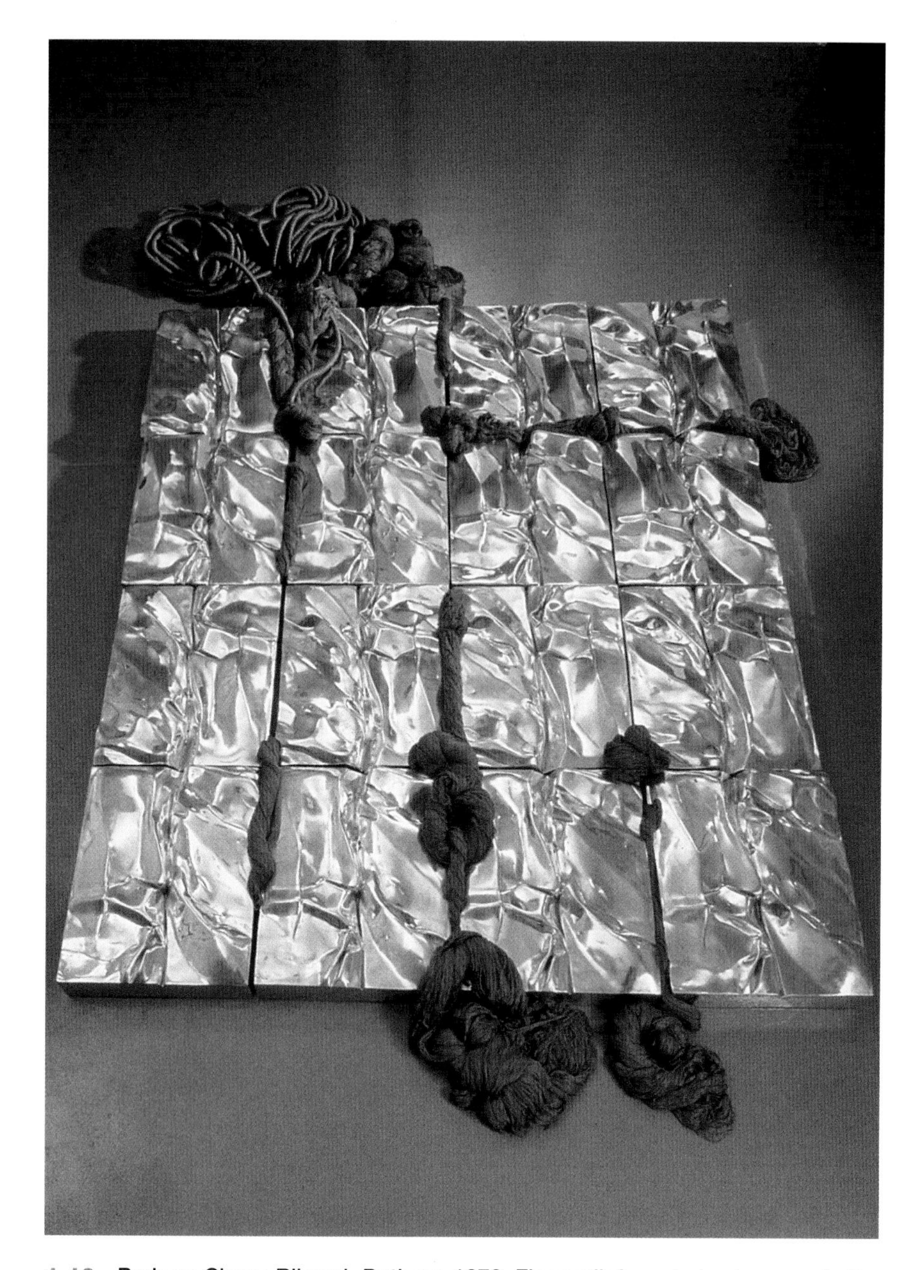

1.10 **Barbara Chase-Riboud, *Bathers,* 1973. Floor relief, cast aluminum and silk in 16 pieces, 400 × 400 × 12 cm.** Barbara Chase-Riboud does not limit her image to a superficial presentation of subject, bathers. She reveals deeper formal meanings with the repetition of cast undulating surface folds and the contrast of metal against flowing silk coils. Courtesy of the artist and Jernigan Wicker Fine Arts, CA.

quence, they give content an opportunity to appear. Thus, to summarize, in art we have the motivation (subject), the substantiation (form), and communication (content).

The Three Basic Components of a Work of Art

Subject

A **subject** is a person, a thing, or an idea. A person or thing may be recognizable to the average observer, but an idea may not be. In **abstract** or semi-abstract works, the subject may be somewhat perceivable, but in **nonobjective** works, the subject is the idea behind the form of the work, and it communicates with those who can read the language of form (fig. 1.10). The subject is important only to the degree that the artist is motivated by it and thus is only a starting point. The way a subject is presented or formed to give it **expression** is the important consideration.

Music, like art, deals with subjects and makes an interesting comparison. In the visual arts, the subject is often a particular thing viewed and reproduced by the artist. But at other times, art presents a "nonrecognizable" subject—an idea rather than a thing. Likewise, music sometimes deals with recognizable sounds—thunderstorms and birdsongs in Beethoven's *Pastoral* Symphony or taxi horns in Gershwin's *An American in Paris.* While represented rather abstractly, these are the musical equivalents of recognizable subjects in an artwork. By way of contrast, Beethoven's Fifth Symphony and Gershwin's Concerto in F are strictly collections of musical ideas. In the medium of dance, choreography often has no specific subject, but dancing in Copland's ballet *Rodeo* is, to a degree, subject oriented. In all of the arts, subjects obviously should be judged not alone but by what is done with them (fig. 1.11).

Form

The term **form** has various meanings in discussions of art. When applied to sculpture, form refers to the essence of the sculpture as expressed in its total organization. A sculpture's appearance is a result of the use of the elements of line, texture, color, shape, and value and their relationship to the principles of harmony and variety. Form does not refer exclusively to the sculpture's shape, although a

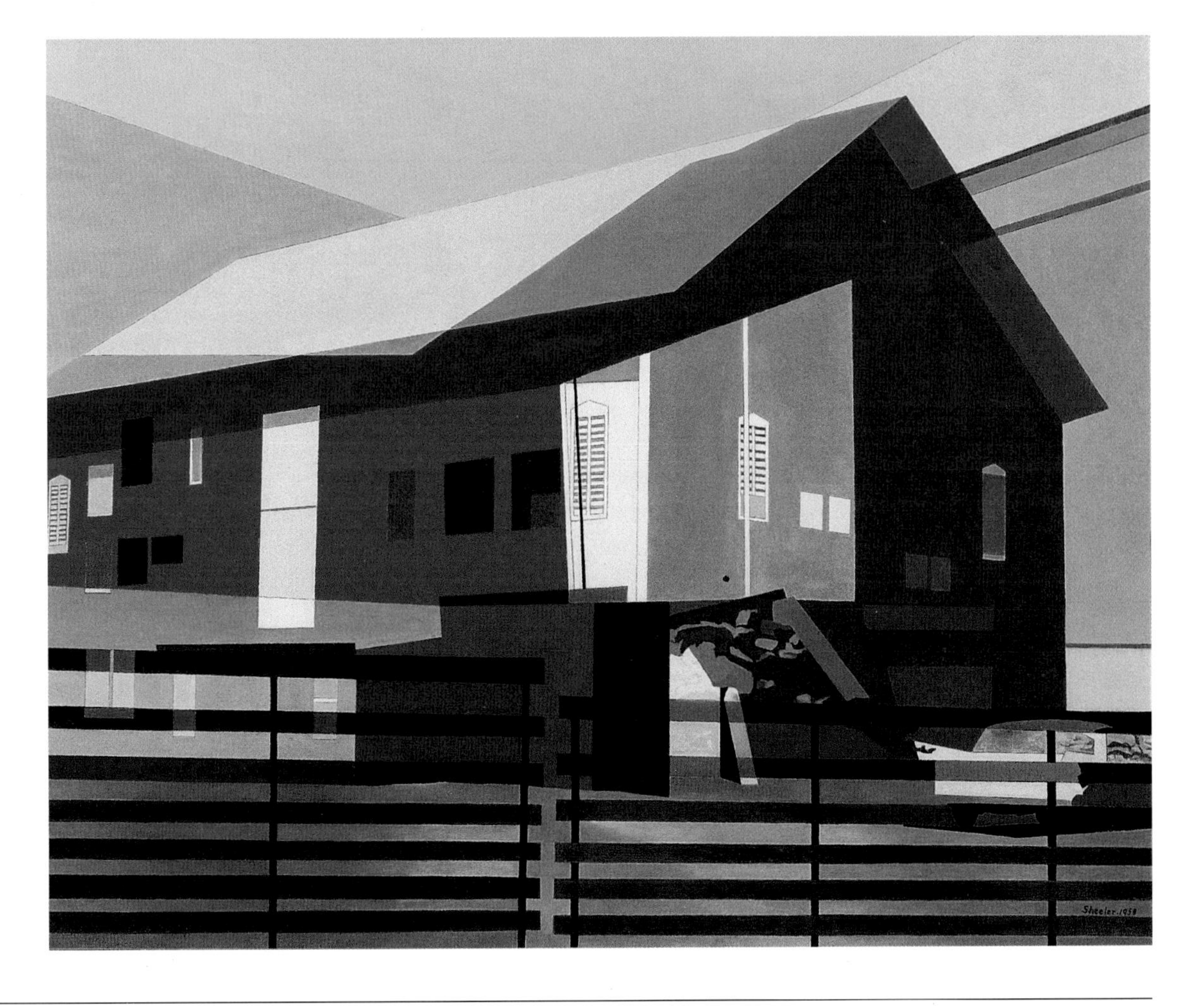

1.11 Charles Sheeler, *Composition around Red (Pennsylvania),* 1958. Oil on canvas, 26 × 33 in. The subject—a man-made structure—is clear enough. However, a work of art should be judged not by its subject alone but rather by how that subject is treated. Montgomery Museum of Fine Arts. The Blount Collection of American Art.

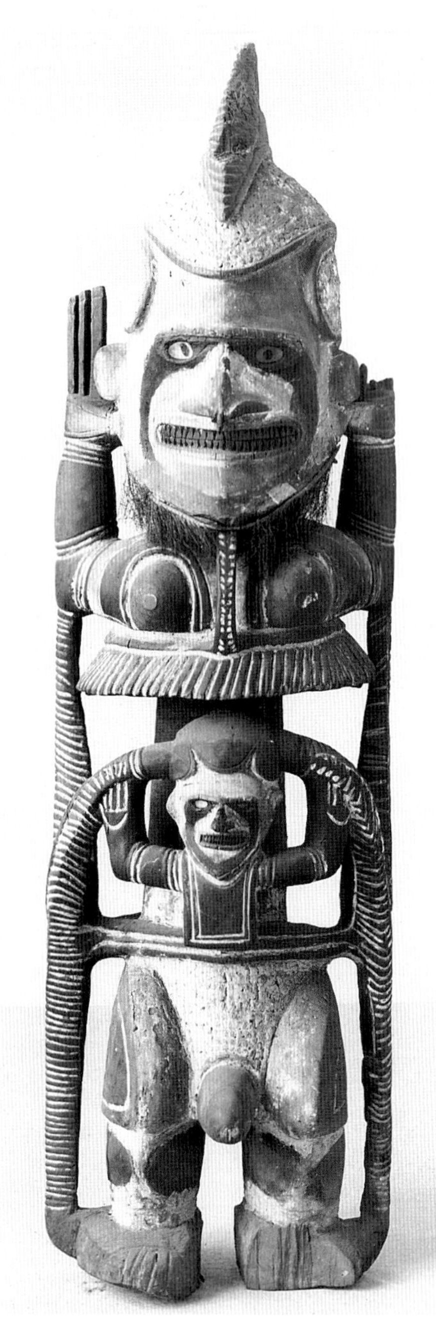

1.12 Uli figure, New Zealand. Painted wood figure, 59 in. (152 cm) high. To illustrate the different meanings of the term *form,* we may say that the forms in this piece of sculpture are the open and solid individual shapes, or that the form of the work consists of the total assembly of those individual parts. Hamburgisches Museum für Völkerkunde.

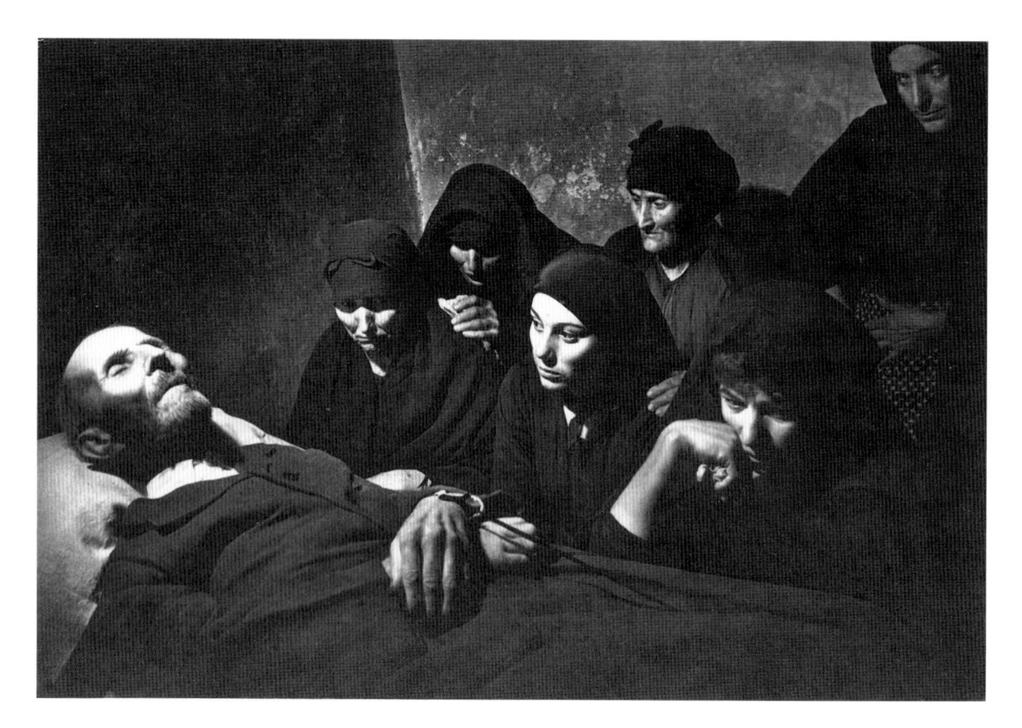

1.13 W. Eugene Smith, *Spanish Wake,* 1951. Photograph. The emotional factor in the content of this photograph is quite evident (and with this particular subject would probably always be so). However, the artist-photographer has enhanced the content with his handling of the situation.

shape is the result of form (fig. 1.12). On the other hand, sculptors may speak of "forms" when referring to the shapes suggested by cavities or protuberances.

Even in two-dimensional work, formal organization involves all the visual devices available in the material of the medium. Using these devices, effective artists arrange and manipulate their materials to convey what is being expressed. Some artists arrange intuitively, others logically. With experience, however, all artists develop a personal feeling for organization and form.

Form is so central to the creation and understanding of art that we devote an entire chapter to it. The principles of formal order are flexible and creative, not dogmatic rules; every work is original and has its own unique problems. Thus, an artist employs the principles of form to create meaning in structure.

Content

The emotional and intellectual message of an artwork is its **content,** a statement, expression, or mood found in the work by the observer, ideally attuned to the artist's intentions. For example, the photographer W. Eugene Smith suggests meanings through his subject and the associated symbols of death in figure 1.13. In this work, form expresses meaning through the somber use of blacks and grays, the restriction of texture, and the emphasis of low diagonals. For some people, content is confined to associations aroused by familiar objects or ideas. This obviously limits those observers to art that expresses familiar experiences. A broader and more meaningful experience does not rely solely on the subject of the image but can be subtly reinforced by the form. This content born of form can be found in abstract as well as **realistic** works.

Although all visual artworks require *some* degree of abstraction, a great degree of abstraction is sometimes difficult to understand and appreciate. "Abstraction" often imposes itself on the artist during the creative process, although

Development toward Abstraction

Object from Nature	Naturalism	Realism	Semiabstract	Abstraction (objective)	Abstraction (nonobjective)
	Fully representational. (very objective)	Representational but emphasizing the emotional. (more subjective)	Partly representational but simplified and rearranged.	*Based* on a subject but visually appears nonobjective.	Nonrepresentational, started without *any reference to subject* and assuming artistic value resides in ***form*** and ***content*** completely.

1.14 Development leading toward abstraction. Abstraction is a relative concept because it is present in varying degrees in all works of art, from full representation to complete nonobjectivity.

this effect is not always foreseen while the work is in progress. Abstraction usually involves reordering and emphasis—in short, the route taken to arrive at a certain result. It is a stripping down to expressive and communicative essentials. The end result is not always appreciated by observers conditioned to expect a literal copying of a subject (fig. 1.14).

The simplification that results from abstraction does not mean a less profound outcome than with realistic works; instead, these simplifications allow the deeper meaning to emerge. If an observer's expectation is too literal, the content of an artwork is easily misinterpreted. In the case of nonobjective or nonliteral abstraction, the "objective" is the content, as in all art (see fig. 6.6). The content in such work is generally subjective and sometimes totally invented, and a subject, if one exists (although normally it does not) is unseen. We often see the term *abstract* used comprehensively for all art that is both derivative and nonderivative. We think a distinction should be made. In truth, *abstract* is more often a verb than a noun.

The development of the content of an artwork generally follows a certain course. The artist is motivated by feelings about a subject (the "what"). That subject may or may not be a **representational** likeness. The artist then manipulates the artistic elements (line, shape, etc.) to create the kind of form (the "how") that will result in the desired content (the "why"). The content expresses the artist's feelings (fig. 1.15). In this process, the artist attempts to make all parts of the work mutually interactive and interrelated—as they are in a living organism. If this is achieved, we can call it **organic unity,** containing all that is necessary in relationships that seem inevitable.

A television set provides an illustration of organic unity because it has a complex of parts intended to function together, like the organs in the human body. A TV set contains the minimum number of parts necessary to function, and these parts work only when properly assembled with respect to one another. When all the parts are activated, they become organically unified. Likewise, art seeks this sense of reciprocal "wholeness."

The works of some contemporary artists challenge this tradition of wholeness. In their works, distinctions between subject, form, and content are blurred, lost, or "muddied" because these ingredients are sometimes treated as identical. This break with tradition requires a shift in our thinking. In Conceptual art (a style; most art is conceptual, to some degree), the concept is foremost, the form is considered negligible, and the content and subject seem to be one. In Process art (another style), the act of producing is the subject of the artwork, reducing form and content to one entity. (See the "Process and Conceptual Art" section in Chapter 10.) Art can be quite puzzling if the aims of the artist are not understood by the viewer.

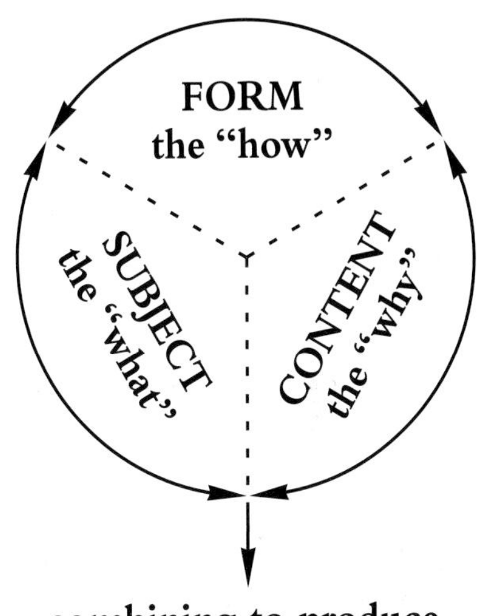

1.15 This diagram illustrates the interrelationship of subject, form, and concept as described on pages 11–15. Subject is not always the starting point. In some instances, artists start by exploring color or shape (the elements) and discover meaning as they work. The components' positions on the diagram and their degree of importance may be changed. And, though the content is revealed by the form, it might, in some instances, be the motivating force. Whatever the evolution, progression, or emphasis of the components—subject, form, and content—organic unity is the desired end.

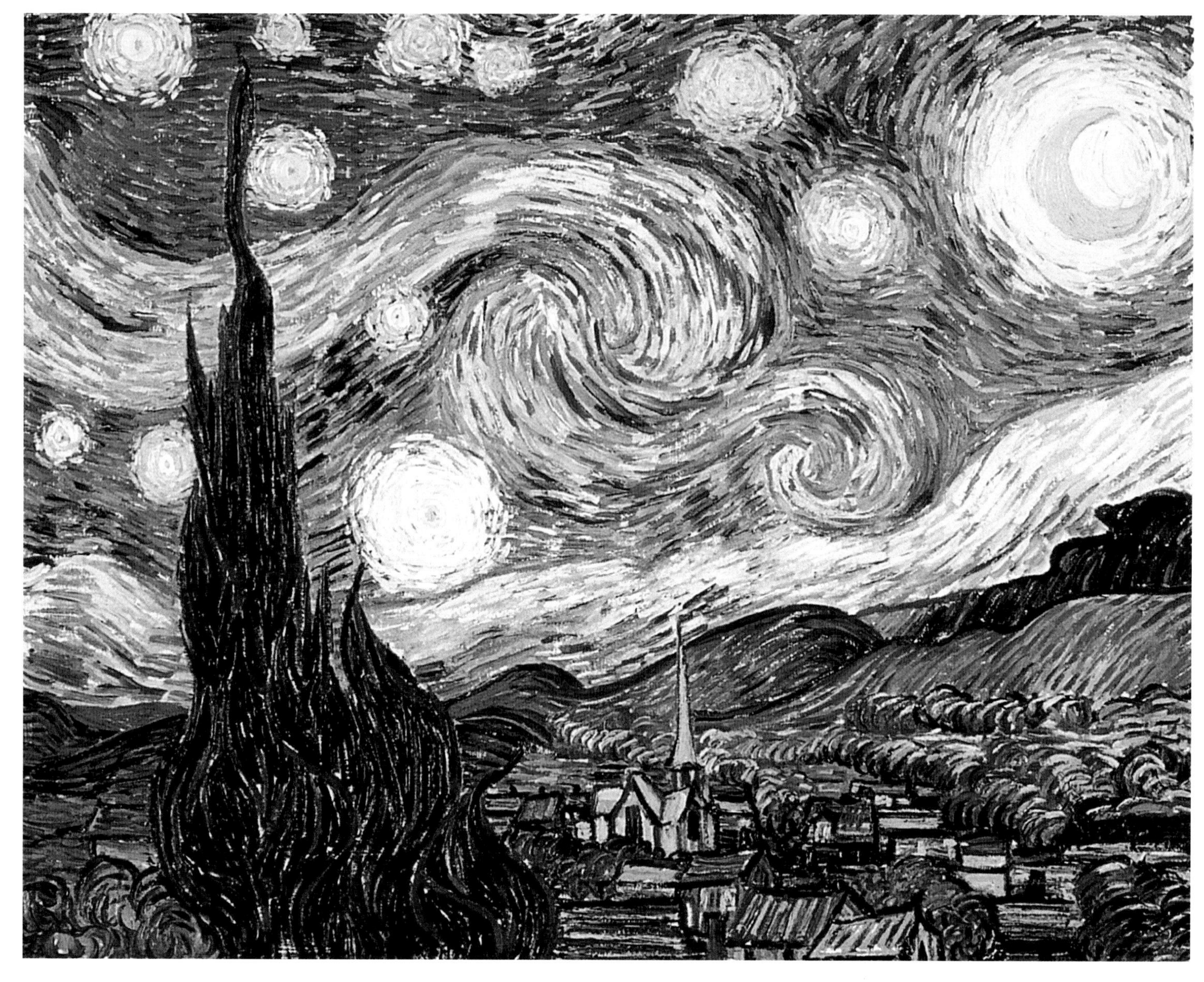

1.16 Vincent van Gogh, *The Starry Night,* 1889. Oil on canvas, 29 × 36¼ in. (73.7 × 92.1 cm). Surveying the landscape is a fairly common experience, but few (if any) of us see landscapes with the perception and intensity of van Gogh. The Museum of Modern Art, New York. Acquired through the Lillie P. Bliss Bequest. Photograph © 1998 The Museum of Modern Art, New York.

Even conventional styles of art sometimes scramble the roles of the components. Sometimes content or form may function as the precipitating force, thereby taking priority over the subject in the scheme of things. Also, in some cases, the developing form may mutate into a subject and/or content altogether different from that originally conceived.

When art is recognizable, faithfully representing familiar items such as houses, flowers, people, trees, it may be thought of as recording the "real" world. The artist who works in this manner could be called a "perceptual" artist because he or she records only what is perceived. But in art, the "real" can supersede mere appearances; the reality in art can also include things seen and, more importantly, includes our reactions to those things (fig. 1.16). Artists who are more concerned with responses than with commonplace perceptions are legitimately called "conceptual" because they are idea oriented.

Creativity emanates from ideas born in the mind. For the artist, a creative idea may be an all-encompassing plan, a unique set of relationships, an attitude to be conveyed, or a solution to a visual problem. In the artist's mind, the idea occurs as imagery. It may be an inspiration that arrives as a "bolt from the blue," or it may be the end product of much thoughtful effort, as reflected in notes, sketches, and repeated overhauls of the artwork.

All such creative enterprise is occasionally obstructed by mental blocks, but these seem to afflict the fledgling artist most. For the beginner, the idea may be conceived at a pedestrian level, being equated with subject ("I don't know what to do!"). In such situations, the familiar object or experience is the best starter, supplemented by brainstorming. In art, an idea is of value only when converted into visual reality; sometimes this is the problem, sometimes not, depending on the fertility of one's imagination.

Savoring the Ingredients

All art is illusory to some extent, and some artworks are more successful than others at drawing us out of ordinary existence into a heightened state of awareness. Frames, stages, exaggerated costumes and gestures, cosmetics, concert halls, and galleries all serve to emphasize the idea that when we enter the artwork, we are transported from the everyday world to a world of "greater" values. By channeling this illusion, art enlarges our awareness.

When, in being **subjective,** the artist reaches beyond appearances and uses unfamiliar ways to find unexpected truths, the results can be distressing for observers. Especially following changes in art styles, artists have been accused of being incompetent charlatans. Much of what we value in art today was once decried in this way. Acceptance of the new comes about when enough time has passed for it to be reevaluated. At that point, the new begins to lose its abrasiveness. Thus, there is no need to feel embarrassed or defiant about an artwork that seems "far out"; instead, we need to strive for continued exposure, thought, and study (fig 1.17). Each of us has a unique capacity to appreciate the beautiful and expressive, as evidenced by the aesthetic choices we make every day. Furthermore, we can enlarge our sensitivity and taste, making them more inclusive.

One way to extend our responses to art is to attempt to see the uniqueness in things. The author Gertrude Stein wrote, "Rose is a rose is a rose." A literal interpretation might lead us to expect all roses to be identical, but we know that every rose has different characters, even with identical breeding and grooming. Every object is ultimately unique, be it a chair, a tree, or a person. The artist sees and experiences the subtle differences in things. By exposing these differences, the artist makes the ordinary seem distinctive, the humdrum exciting (fig. 1.18).

Perception is the key. When an artist views an object—a tree branch, for example—and is inspired to try to reproduce the original as seen, he or she is using and drawing inspiration from **optical perception.** However, another artist seeing the same branch may find that it evokes a crying child or a rearing horse. When the imagination triggers and suggests additional images, the artist is using **conceptual perception.**

Leonardo da Vinci, in his *Treatise on Painting,* recorded an experience with conceptual perception while studying clouds. "On one occasion above Milan, over in the direction of Lake Maggiore, I saw a cloud shaped like a huge mountain made up of banks of fire." Elsewhere, he recommends staring at stains on walls as a source of inspiration. Following Leonardo, author and painter Victor Hugo reported finding many of his ideas for drawings by studying the blots made by coffee stains on tablecloths.

Another way to enlarge our sensitivity to the visual arts is by ridding ourselves of the expectation that all forms of art should follow the same rules. Photography might serve as an example. For instance, we can judge a work of art by how closely it can be made to look like something, and it is true that skillful artists do create amazing resemblances. But the artist loses when the battle with the camera is fought by photography's rules. An artist can be proud of the ability to reproduce appearances, but most artists regard this skill as less important. If making look-alikes were the key to art, then why would photographers not be content to simply point and shoot? Instead, they look for the best view, blur the focus, use filters, alter lighting, and make adjustments in developing (fig. 1.19). Photographers become artists when they explore beyond obvious appearances. So, too, do **plastic** and **graphic** artists.

People associate visual art with literature when they hope it will tell a story in a **descriptive** manner. Many artworks contain elements of storytelling, but artists have no obligation to narrate. "Picture stories" succeed as art because of their formal characteristics (fig. 1.20). The visual arts and literature do share certain elements. For the author, objects or things are nouns; for the visual artist, representational subjects are nouns. Nouns are informative but are not poetic by themselves; they need verbs, adjectives, and so on to establish action, moods, and meaning. Similarly, the visual artist's "subject-nouns" rarely inspire, except occasionally by association. For the visual artist, the "verbs" are the combined effect of the elements and their principles; by manipulating these, he or she can achieve a poetic effect like that found in literature.

In adapting ourselves to the rules peculiar to art, we must place our own taste on trial. This means accepting the possibility that what is unfamiliar or disliked may not necessarily be badly executed or devoid of meaning. Conversely, we should not automatically accept what we like; in both cases,

THE WRAPPING UP

Here's what it takes to wrap the German Reichstag as Christo and Jeanne-Claude did:

The German Reichstag
- Total perimeter: 1,520.3 feet
- Width (north-south): 314.9 feet
- Length (east-west): 445.2 feet
- Height of the four towers: 139.4 feet
- Height at roof: 105.5 feet

The Materials
- Yarn for weaving: 43,836 miles
- Silver polypropylene fabric: 119,603 square yards
- Width of the original woven fabric: 5 feet
- Number of fabric panels: 70
- Length of thread: 807.8 miles
- Window anchors: 110
- Roof anchors: 270

Visits to Germany by the Christos
- 1976–95: 54
- Members of Parliament visited: 352
- Number of presidents of the Bundestag involved: 6

The Workforce
- Monitors: 1,200 in four 6-hour shifts
- Professional climbers: 90
- Professional helpers: 120 in two shifts
- Office staff (Berlin): 17
- Office staff (New York): 2

The Costs
- Rope: $72,000
- Fabric metalization: $72,000
- Sewing: $1,080,000
- Structural engineering and construction: $1,080,000
- Documentation of building condition: $72,000
- Air cushions and covering of cages: $216,000
- Steel construction: $2,160,000
- Steel weights: $180,000
- Insulation and dismantling: $1,368,000
- Monitors and security: $1,296,000
- Rents, further wages, transportation: $324,000

Total cost to Christo and Jeanne-Claude:
$13,000,000 of their own money. The work of art was entirely financed by the artists, as they have done for all their projects, through the sale of preparatory studies, drawings, collages, and scale models, as well as early works and original lithographs. The artists do not accept sponsorship of any kind.

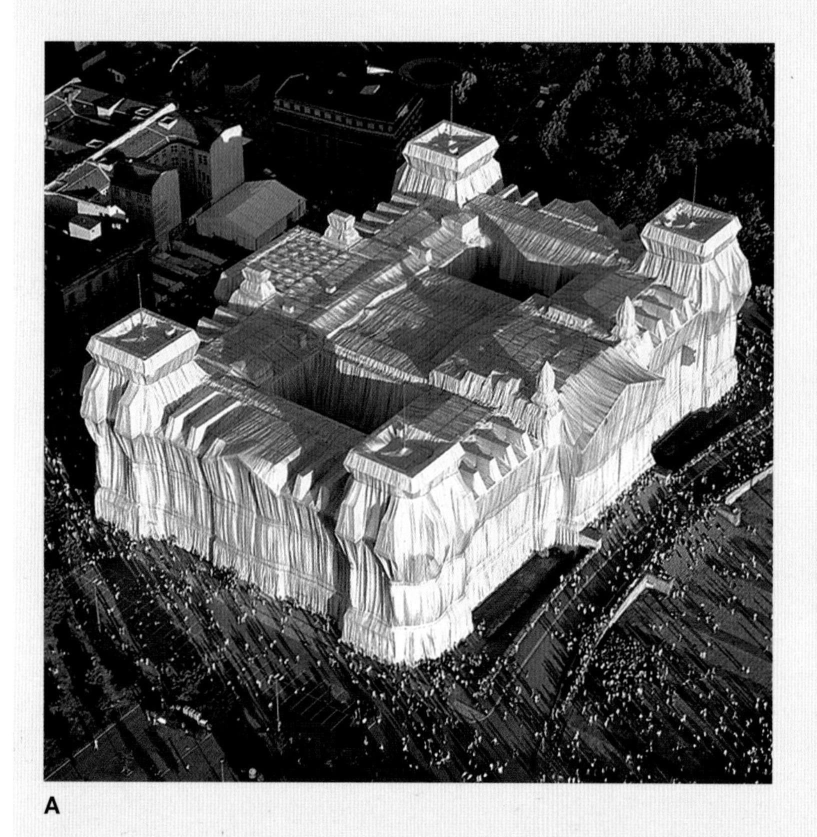

A

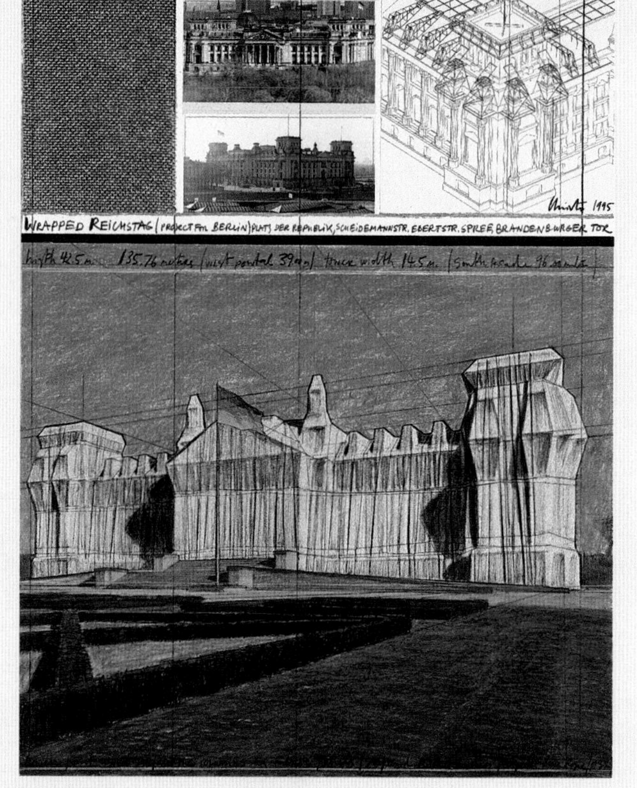

B

1.17 **(A) The realized work: Christo and Jeanne-Claude, *Wrapped Reichstag, Berlin*, 1971–95. (B) Preparation work (drawings) before the project was realized: Christo, *Wrapped Reichstag, Project for Berlin*.** Wrapping the Reichstag in aluminum-coated fabric and rope was the culmination of Christo and Jeanne-Claude's long-held dream. Photographs: Wolfgang Volz.

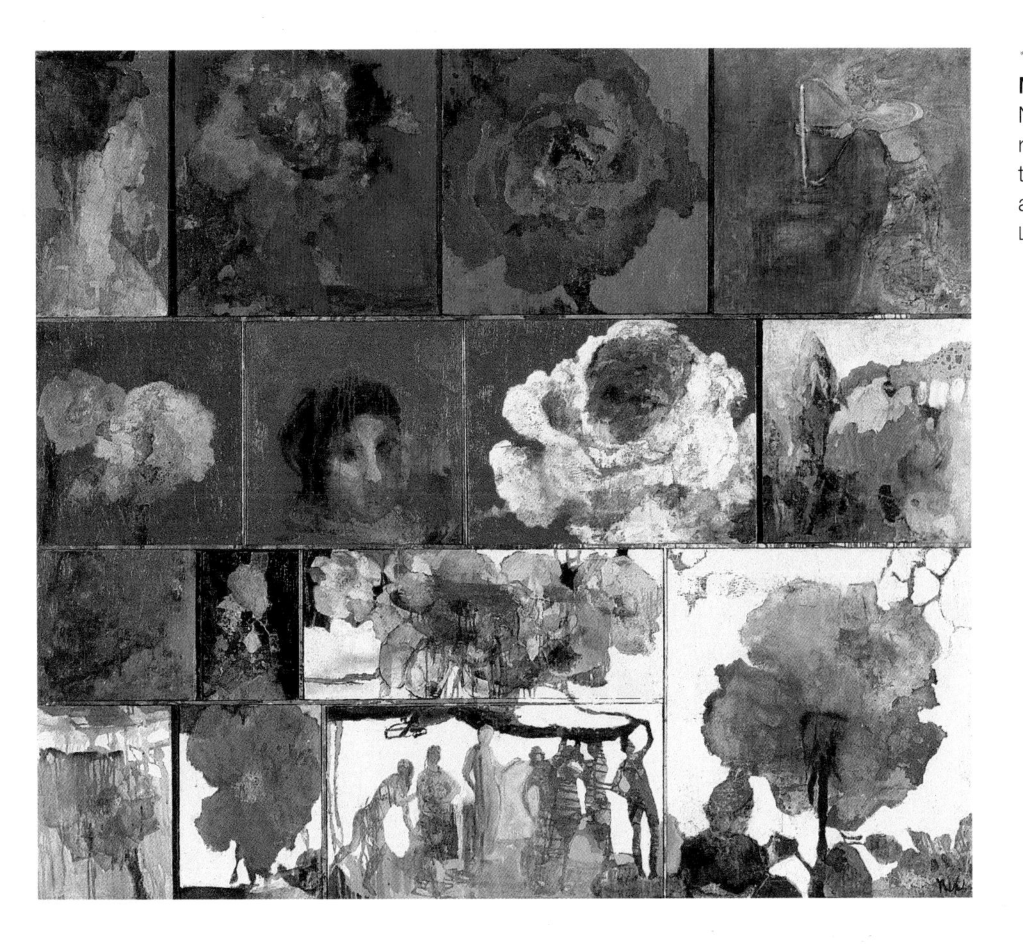

1.18 Patricia Nix, *La Primavera,* 1992–94. Mixed media on canvas, 72 × 80 in. Patricia Nix's *La Primavera* presents roses as a repeated theme, but subtle differences in texture, color, and treatment keep them fresh and unique. From the collection of Ivan Blinoff, London. Courtesy of the artist.

1.19 Minor White, *Cobblestone House, Avon, New York,* 1958. Gelatin silver print. Photographers may have the edge on other visual artists when it comes to recording objective reality, but photographer-artists are not satisfied with obvious appearances and use complex technical strategies to achieve their goals. The Art Museum, Princeton University, Princeton, NJ. The Minor White Archive. (© 1982 Trustees of Princeton University.)

open-mindedness is required. Artists and critics are rarely unanimous about artworks or their creators. Even with training, people's tastes, like Stein's roses, do not turn out to be identical. Art is always open to question.

One of the dividends we gain by a better understanding of the visual arts is that it puts us in touch with perceptive people. We always benefit from contact, however indirect, with the creations of genius. Einstein exposed relationships that have reshaped our view of the universe. Mozart created sounds that, in an abstract way, summed up the experiences and feelings of humankind. Though not always of equal magnitude, artists expand our frames of reference, revealing new ways of seeing and responding to our surroundings. When we view artworks knowledgeably, we can be on the same wavelength with the artist.

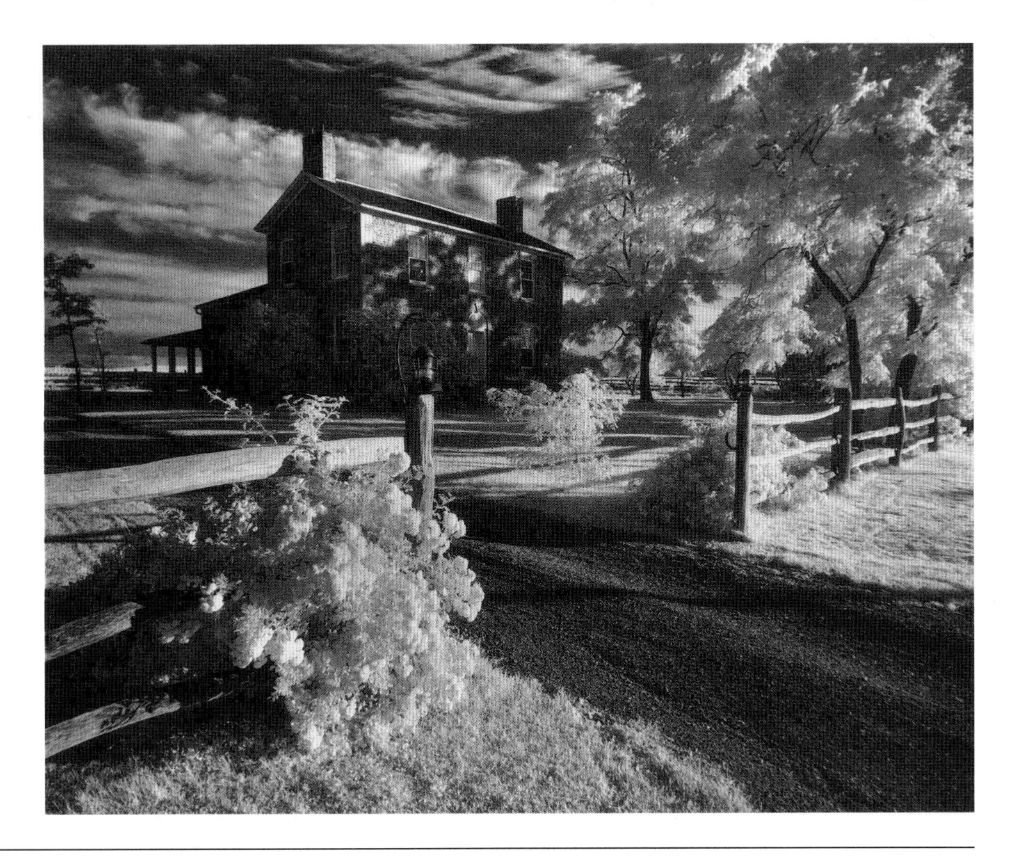

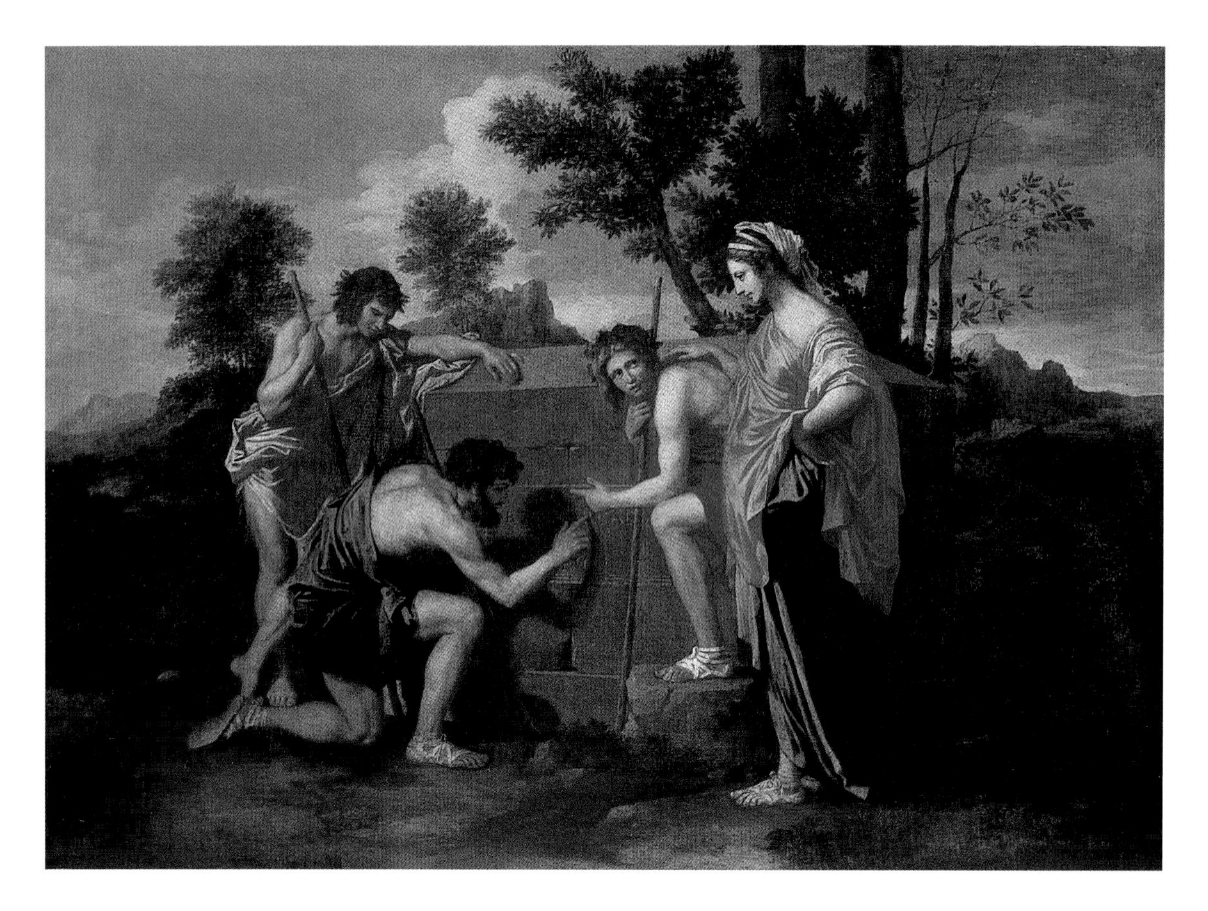

1.20 Nicolas Poussin, ***Et In Arcadia Ego (Shepherds of Arcadia),*** **c. 1650–65.** This painting could be called a "picture story" because it derives from a classical mythological tale. It could have been merely a factual statement about a moment in that myth, but Poussin's concern for design enhances the meaning of the tale.
Louvre, Paris, France/The Bridgeman Art Library.

THE INGREDIENTS ASSEMBLED

We have mentioned some of the means by which an artist's emotions may be brought to the surface. You have been introduced to the components, elements, and principles involved in making visual art. You now have an idea of how all these factors enter into the expression of the artist's feelings. You have been given some advice on the attitudes to develop in order to share the artist's feelings. Now, let's consider how these matters fit into developing a hypothetical work of art.

Any construction project requires structural elements. Under the supervision of the contractor, these are assembled and put together until an edifice of some kind results. The corresponding structural **elements of art** are **line, shape, value, texture,** and **color.** In making a work of art, the artist is not only the contractor but also the architect; he or she has the vision, which shapes the way the elements are brought together. Whereas a building contractor adheres to blueprints, an artist has the advantage of infinite flexibility in structuring the work. For example, in painting, the raw elements can be manipulated to produce either a **two-dimensional** effect (circle, triangle, or square) or a **three-dimensional** effect (sphere, pyramid, or cube). In a 2D effect, the elements and whatever they produce seem to lie flat on the **picture plane,** but when the elements create a 3D effect, that **plane** seems to imply a space.

Other terms are used in discussing art to describe the conditions found in any imagery. For instance, while **decorative** is a term we usually associate with ornamentation, it is also used to describe the effects produced by the elements of art when they remain flat. Line is decorative if it does not leap toward or away from the viewer dramatically in the format. The same is true of the other art elements. When they are of this nature collectively, we call the relatively flat space created by them "decorative." On the other hand, if the elements make us feel that we could enter the picture and weave our way around and behind the art elements, the space implied is said to be "plastic."

The term *plastic* has clear implications for sculpture, because we can (we must!) move about the piece. Any **mass,** whether actual (as in a statue) or implied (as portrayed in drawing or painting), can be called plastic. Mass is anything that has cohesive, homogeneous bulk, implying a quality of weightiness. **Volume,** on the other hand, is an area of defined containment. An empty room has volume in its dimensions, but no mass. A brick has mass within its volume. Mass and volume indicate the presence of three dimensionality in art.

A distinction must be made between plastic art and graphic art. The graphic arts—drawing, painting, printmaking, photography—generally exist on a flat surface and only create the illusion of the third dimension. In contrast, the plastic arts—sculpture, ceramics, architecture—are tangible and occupy space in three dimensions. Nevertheless, the art elements that create 2D effects in graphic arts share the same properties as the art elements that create a 3D reality in the plastic arts.

An artist must begin with an idea that will eventually develop into the concept of the finished artwork. The idea may be the result of aimless doodling, a thought that has suddenly struck the artist, or a notion that has been growing in his or her mind for a long time. In order to become tangible, this idea must be developed in a **medium** (clay, oil paint, watercolor, etc.). The artist controls the medium but is controlled by it as well. The elements of form, with their intrinsic meanings, emerge through the medium. The image may be a nonobjective or objective image; in either case, the meaning derives from the form created by the elements.

In developing an artwork, the artist composes formal structures while exploring interesting and communicative presentations of an idea. During this process, **abstraction** occurs, even in work that is realistic—elements are simplified, changed, added, eliminated, and edited (fig. 1.21). This process happens with an awareness, and within the parameters, of the principles of the artwork.

As the creative process unfolds (not always directly, neatly, or without stress or anguish), the artist fervently hopes to reveal an organic unity. As stated earlier, this term refers to the fulfillment of everything that is being sought in the work. In this fulfillment, every part not only fits but also contributes to the

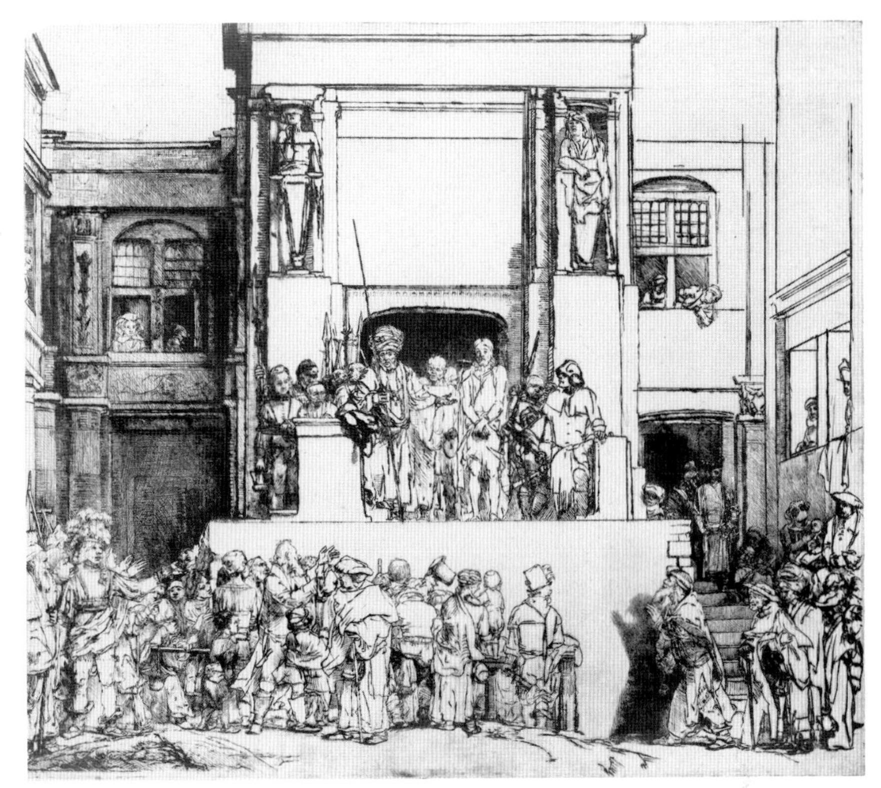

A

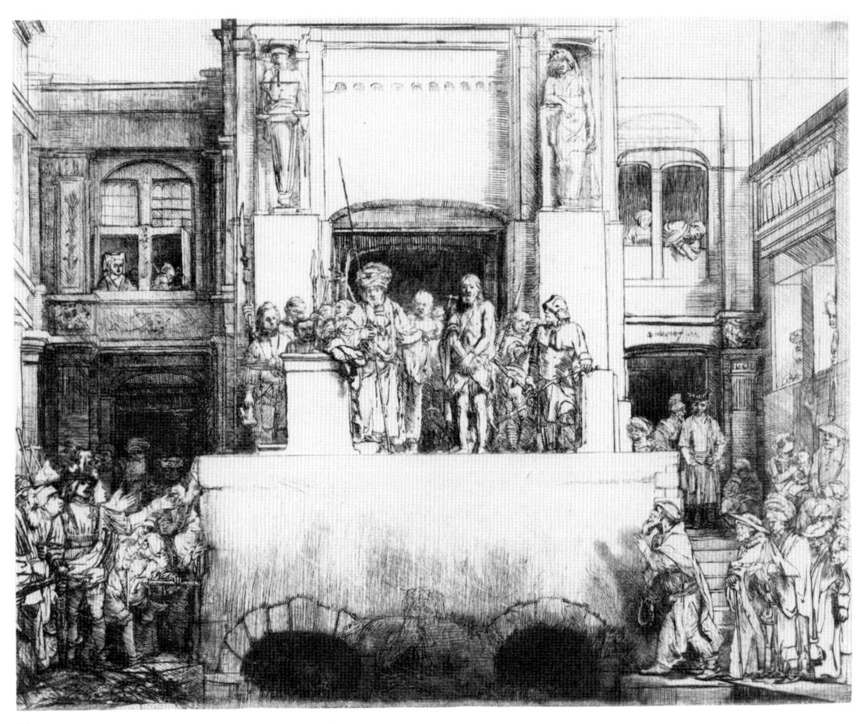

B

1.21 Rembrandt Harmenszoon van Rijn, *Christ Presented to the People,* last state 1606–9, print (etching). Rembrandt searched for the most interesting and communicative presentation of his idea. In doing so, he made dramatic deletions and changes, which in this case involved scraping out a portion of the copper plate. Figure 1.21A is the first version of the work, and figure 1.21B is the last. Metropolitan Museum of Art, New York. Gift of Felix M. Warburg and his family, 1941.

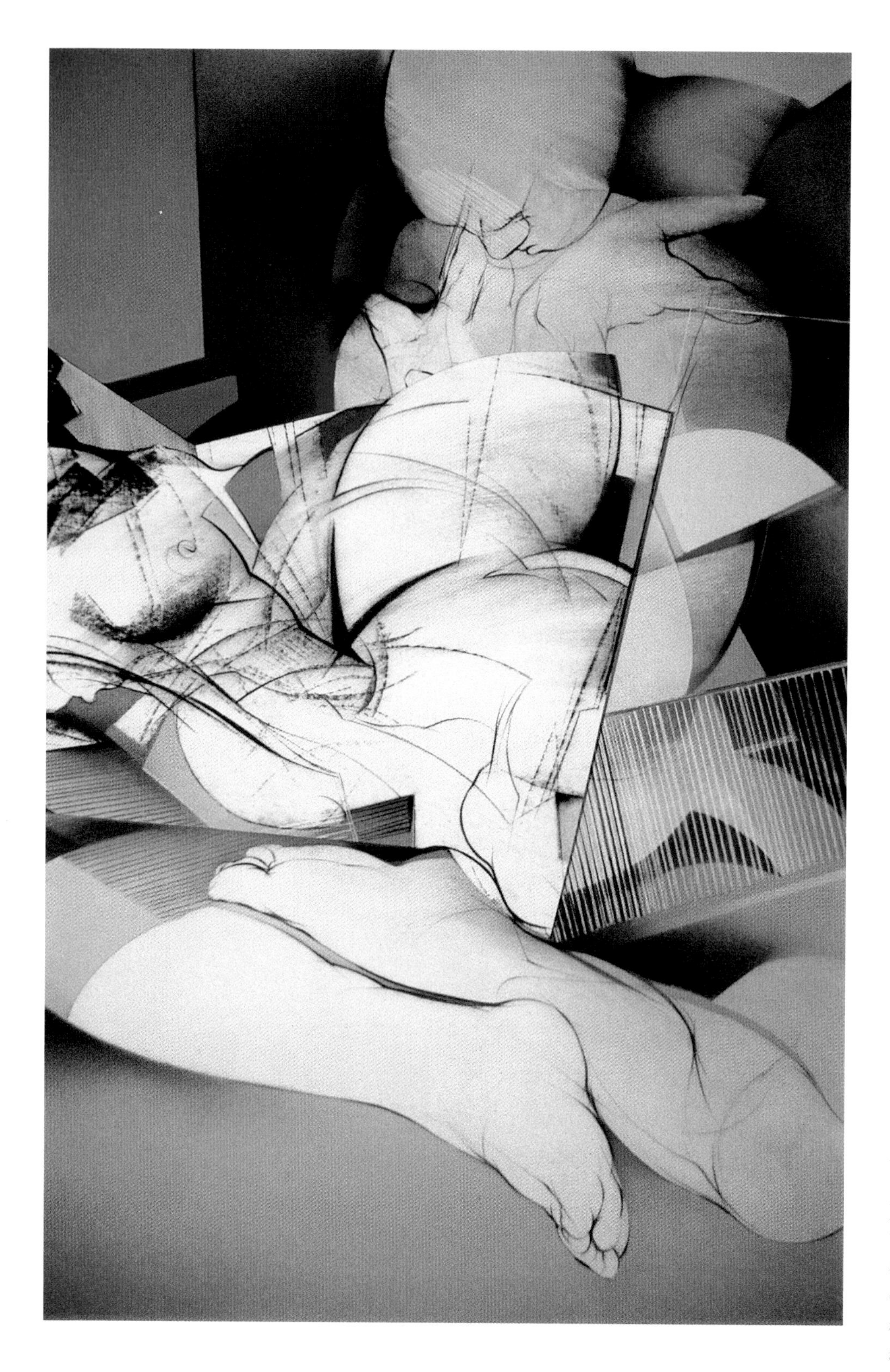

1.22 Thomas Hilty, *Meditation,* 1996. Charcoal, pastel, and conté on museum board, 28 × 40 in. (71.12 × 101.6 cm). This drawing shows the artist's characteristic use of mixed media. He has skillfully blended and rubbed the materials to produce the effect of expressive and varied surfaces. Courtesy of the artist.

overall content, or meaning. At this point, however arduous or circuitous the artist's route, the work is finished—or is it? Having given the best of themselves, artists are never sure of this! Perhaps the perspective of a few days, months, or even years will give the answer. And if the work is finished, and it has organic unity, is it guaranteed to be judged a "great work of art"? The ingredients assembled in organic unity do not guarantee it, but they do help give the work a vital completeness.

Two-Dimensional Media and Techniques

Media are the materials used in making an artwork, and techniques control their application. Artists derive much stimulation for creative expression from their interaction with their materials and the various techniques. In two-dimensional media, certain processes, many of them developed over centuries, have become common or traditional. Painters are attracted by the smell and feel of fresh plaster resisting the brush in fresco and secco painting. Oils and watercolors provide different tactile excitements than gouache and tempera, as do wet and dry surfaces. For the draftsman, the difference between a heavy pressure and a light touch can be just as compelling as the textural quality of the drawing surface. Graphite, charcoal, colored pencils, pastels, and chalk can all be blended or erased (fig. 1.22). Inks, whether applied by brush, quill, pen, or bamboo stick, are exciting in how they react to dry and dampened surfaces.

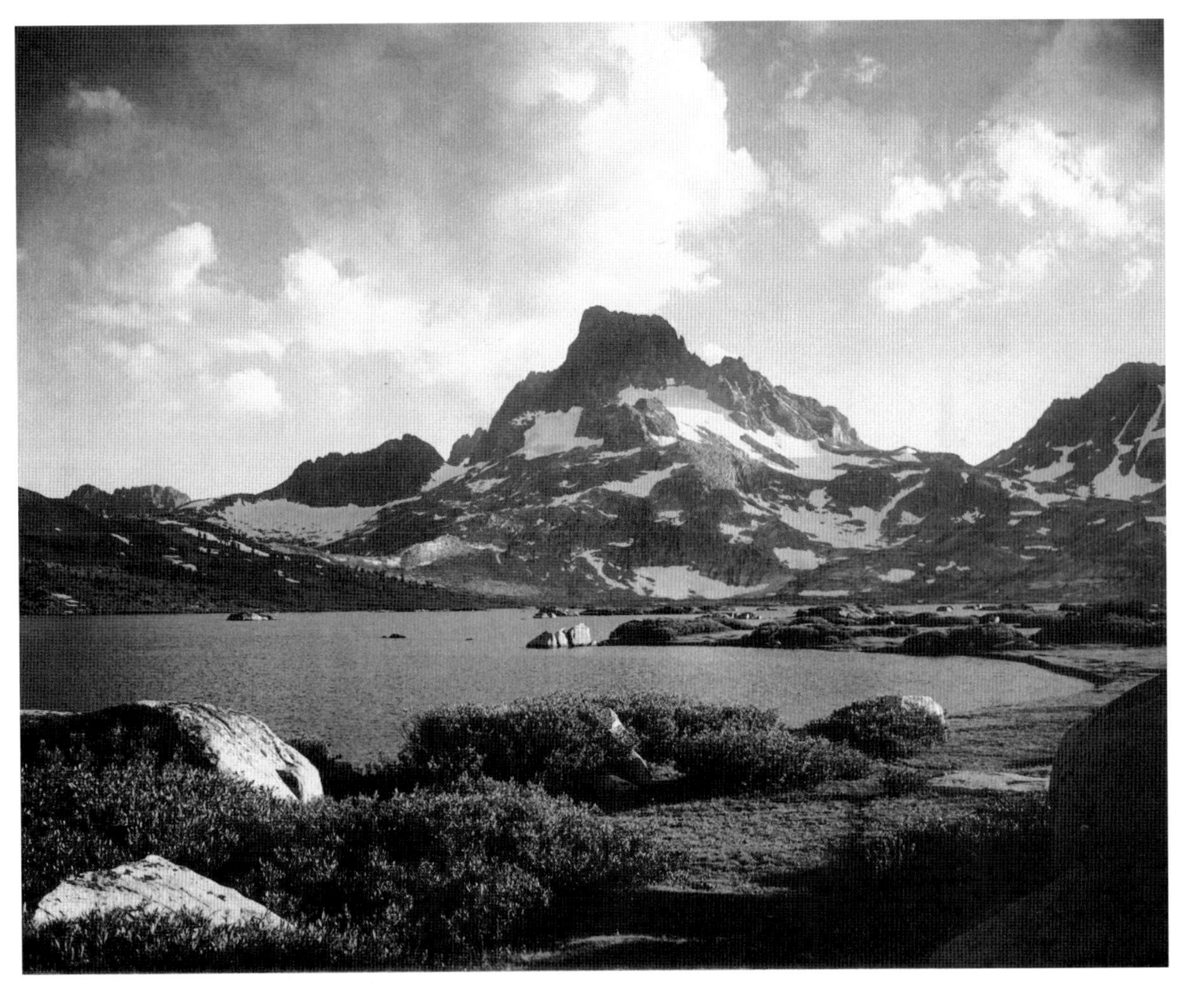

1.23 Ansel Adams, ***Banner Peak and Thousand Island Lake, Sierra Nevada, California,*** **1923. Panchromatic glass.** The invention and development of photography added an important new medium to the repertoire of artists. The accomplishments of such photographers as Ansel Adams rank with those of well-known painters, sculptors, and architects. Courtesy of the Ansel Adams Publishing Rights Trust/CORBIS.

For printmakers (see Chapter 5), watching the physical surface change is intriguing. In lithography, the drawing comes to life as water magically resists the application of ink; intaglio plates are etched in acid until the topography reveals the image below the plate's surface. In woodcuts and wood engraving, the nature of the wood provides a unique texture. Serigraphic images can be flat in decorative color and surface quality or resolve into transparency and overlapping texture.

Nineteenth- and twentieth-century artists benefited from numerous advances in scientific technology. One of the great breakthroughs was the development of photography. Although a camera is not as flexible as a paintbrush, photographic innovations have broadened the artist's vision. Photographic artists such as Edward Steichen, Alfred Stieglitz, and Ansel Adams (fig. 1.23) are recognized today alongside many of our important painters and sculptors. Creative filmmaking, xerography, and employment of other photographic media have all been absorbed into the artist's repertoire.

Today we are flooded with new media and new techniques. Some are extensions of traditional approaches, whereas others, like digital-generated imagery, are without precedent. Traditional painting media have been augmented by acrylics, enamels, lacquers, preliquified watercolors, and roplex. Drawing media include new types of chalk, pastels, crayons, inks, and drawing pens. The sculptor's arsenal has been augmented by welding, plastics, composition board, aluminum, and stainless steel. Printmakers now use paper, light-sensitive polymer plates, and presensitized metal. Although most of the artworks we see are static (lacking movement), new art forms today incorporate movement in their imagery;

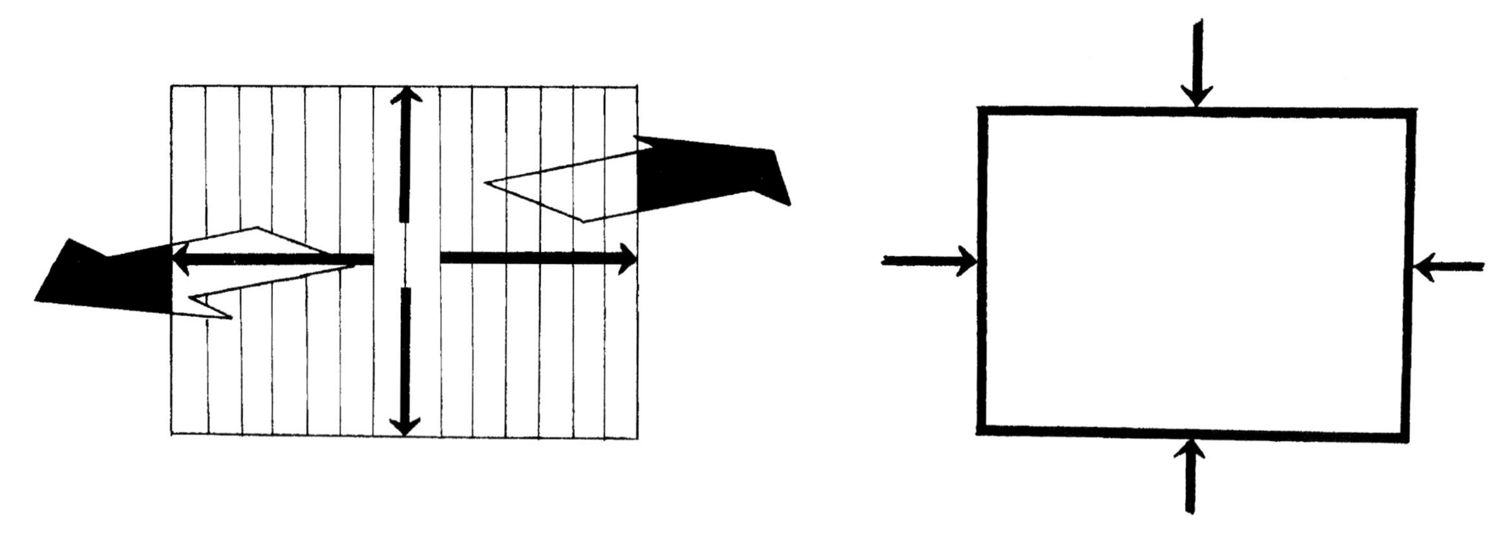

1.24A The picture plane. Movement can take place on a flat surface, as indicated by the vertical and horizontal arrows. The vertical lines represent an imaginary plane through which a picture is seen. The artist can also give the illusion of advancing and receding movement in space, as shown by the two large arrows.

1.24B The picture frame. The picture frame represents the outermost limits, or boundary, of the picture plane. These limits are represented by the edges of the canvas or paper on which the artist works, or by the margin drawn within these edges.

think of video, holography, virtual reality, computer-generated action, and performances that mix dance, drama, sound, and light and even include the audience. Very often, traditional and nontraditional media and techniques are combined.

The Two-Dimensional Picture Plane

There are many ways to begin a work of art. Artists who work with two-dimensional art generally begin with a flat surface. The flat surface is the picture plane on which artists execute their pictorial images. This working area could be a piece of paper, a canvas, a board, or a plate. This flat surface may represent a picture plane, or it may represent an imaginary plane of reference on which an artist can create spatial illusions. The artist may manipulate forms or elements so that they seem flat on the picture plane, or extend them so that they appear to exist in front of or behind the picture plane (fig. 1.24A). In this way, the picture plane is used as the basis for judging the space in the picture. In three-dimensional art, on the other hand, the artist begins with a material—metal, clay, stone, glass, and so on—and works on its total form in the surrounding space of the real world, with no limitations except for the outermost contour (see Chapter 9).

The Picture Frame

Used by artists of all cultures, defined boundaries around the working area, or picture plane, are called the **picture frame** (fig. 1.24B). The picture frame should be clearly established at the beginning of a pictorial organization. Once its shape, size, and proportion are defined, all of the art elements and their employment will be influenced by it. Thus, the pictorial artist's problem is to organize the elements of art within the picture frame on the picture plane.

The proportions and shapes of frames used by artists vary. Squares, triangles, circles, and ovals can all be used as frame shapes, but the most popular frame is the rectangular shape, which offers infinitely varying proportions of two-dimensional **space** (figs. 1.25, 1.26, 1.27; see fig. 2.25). Traditionally, many artists selected the proportions of their picture frames on the basis of geometric ratios. (See the "Proportion" section in Chapter 2.) These classical rules suggest dividing surface areas into mathematical proportions of two-to-three or three-to-five, rather than into equal relationships. The results are visually pleasing. Most artists, however, rely on their instincts rather than on mathematical proportions. After the picture frame has been established, the direction and movement of the elements of art should harmonize with this shape. Otherwise, they will tend to disrupt the unity of the picture.

Positive and Negative Areas

All of the areas in a picture should contribute to its **unity.** Those areas that contain the artist's assertion of elements are called **positive areas.** Positive areas may depict recognizable objects or non-representational elements. The unoccupied spaces are termed **negative areas** (fig. 1.28). The negative areas are as

1.25 Esphyr Slobodkina, *Composition in an Oval,* c. 1953. Oil on gesso board, 32½ × 61½ in. (82.5 × 156.2 cm). Slobodkina has used an unusual frame shape to emphasize an angular abstract painting. Now used less frequently, such frame shapes were employed more often in the past with traditional religious subjects. Grey Art Gallery. New York University Art Collection. Gift of Mr. and Mrs. Irving Walsey, 1962.

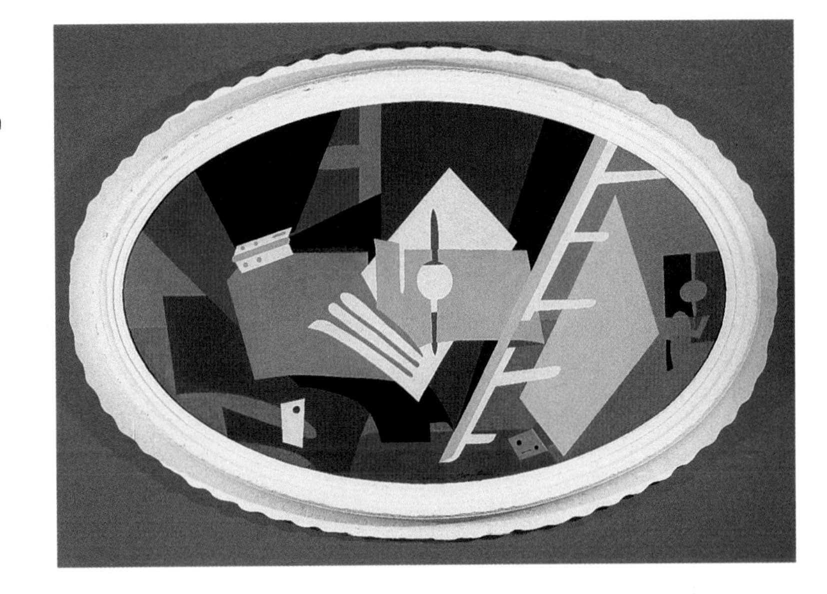

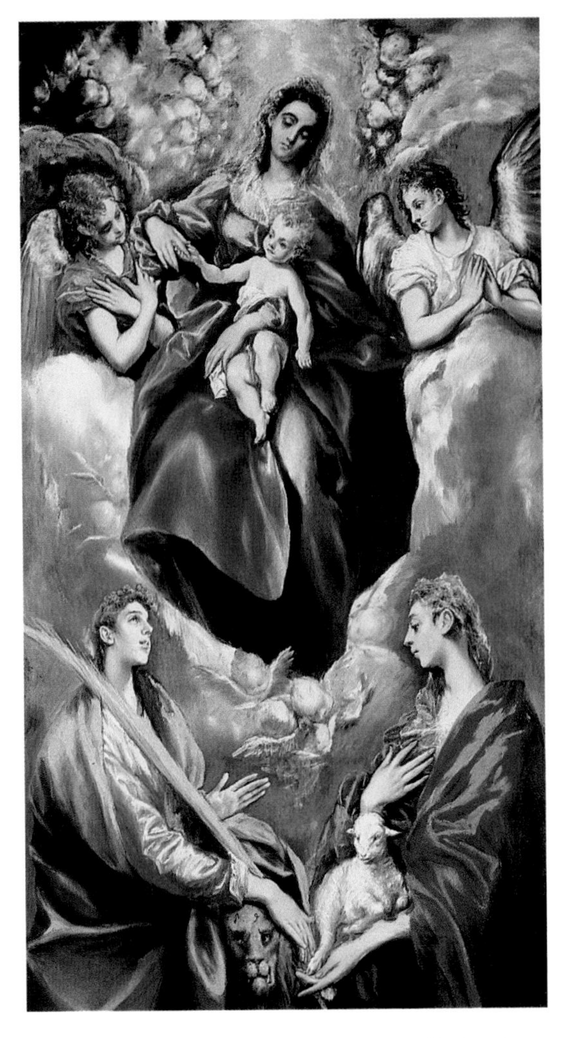

1.26 El Greco, *Madonna and Child with Saint Martina and Saint Agnes,* c. 1597–99. Oil on canvas, 6 ft 4⅛ in. × 3 ft 4½ in. (1.94 × 1.03 m). The rectangular frame shape, by its proportions, offers the artist a pleasing and interesting spatial arrangement. Here, El Greco has elongated his main shapes to repeat and harmonize with the vertical character of the picture frame. Widener Collection. © 1997 Board of Trustees. National Gallery of Art, Washington.

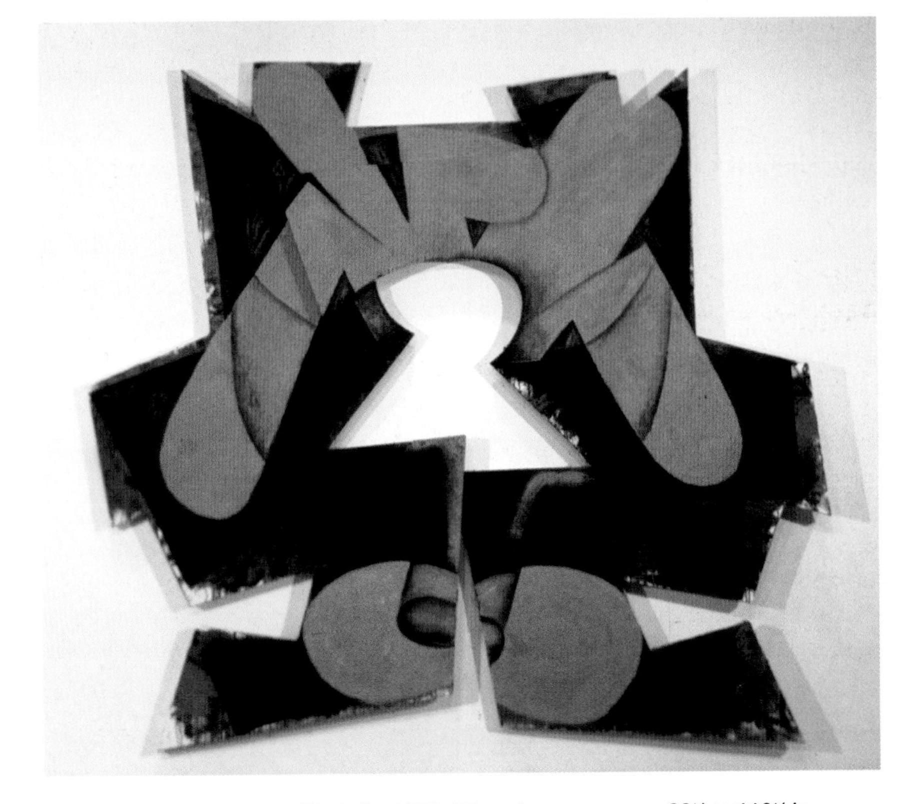

1.27 Elizabeth Murray, *Keyhole,* 1982. Oil on two canvases, 99½ × 110½ in. Murray uses the picture plane as physical space. The shapes that make up the picture plane contribute movement and a 3D element to her paintings. This potentially chaotic aspect of her work is kept under control by the flattened, abstracted shapes that she uses in her imagery. © Elizabeth Murray, Courtesy PaceWildenstein, New York; Courtesy Paula Cooper Gallery, New York; Courtesy the Collection of Agnes Gund.

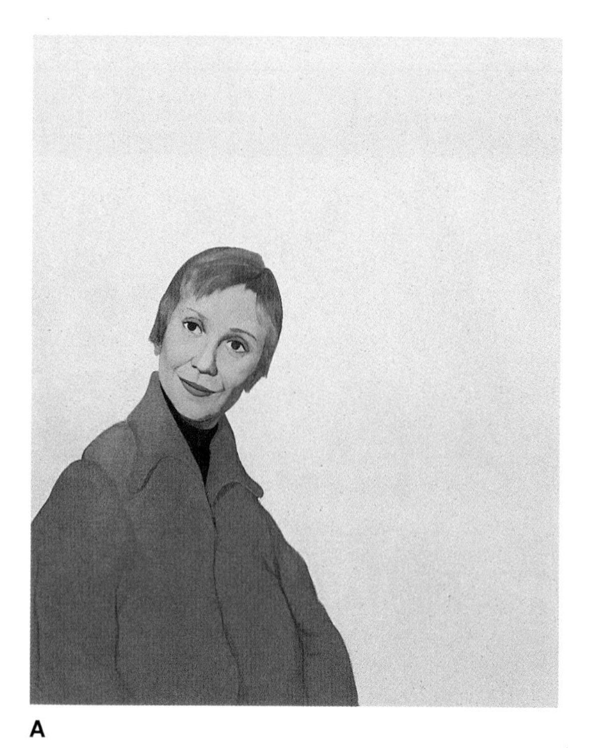

A

B

1.28 John Currin, *The Moved Over Lady,* 1991. Oil on canvas, 46 × 38 in. (116.8 × 96.5 cm). The subject in this painting represents a positive shape that has been enhanced by careful consideration of the negative areas, or the surrounding space. In figure 1.28B, the dark area indicates the negative shape and the white area the positive shape. Andrea Rosen Gallery, New York. Photograph: Fred Scraton.

important to total picture unity as the positive areas, which seem more explicit. Negative areas are those portions of the picture plane that continue to show through after the positive areas have been placed in a framed space (fig. 1.29).

The traditional terms *figure* and *ground* refer to the positive and negative areas of a picture. Thus, foreground positions have been considered positive, while background areas have been considered negative. The term *figure* probably derives from the human form, which was the central subject in art, traditionally occupying a position in front of the remaining background (fig. 1.30; see fig. 1.28). In recent times, painters use the term *field* to mean positive and *ground* to mean negative. They speak of a color field on a white ground, or of a field of shapes against a ground of contrasting value.

Recognizing both positive and negative areas is important to beginning artists. Inexperienced artists tend to direct their attention to positive forms while neglecting the surrounding areas. As a result, their pictures often seem overcrowded, busy, and confusing.

When the artist's tool touches the picture plane, leaving a mark, two things happen. First, the mark divides the picture plane to some extent. Generally the mark is seen as a positive image, leaving the remainder to be perceived as a negative area. Second, the mark may seem to take a position in front of, or at some distance behind, the picture plane. Each of these results will continue to be important to the artist as the work develops.

The Art Elements

The artist employs various media to implement the art elements: line, shape, value, texture, and color. These elements are the fundamental, essential constituents of any artwork. The basic elements are so indispensable to art fundamentals that each will be examined individually in the chapters that follow.

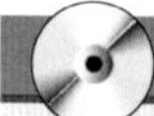

INVESTIGATE THE CD-ROM **Questions to Ask Yourself**

Throughout history, humans have felt the need to make art and incorporate it into everyday life.

While checking out the accompanying CD-ROM, answer these questions:

1. What medium of art appeals to you most? Why?
2. What particular aspect of that medium do you especially like?
3. Do other media also share this aspect? If so, which ones?
4. If you were to begin making an artwork right now, how would you start and what would you do?

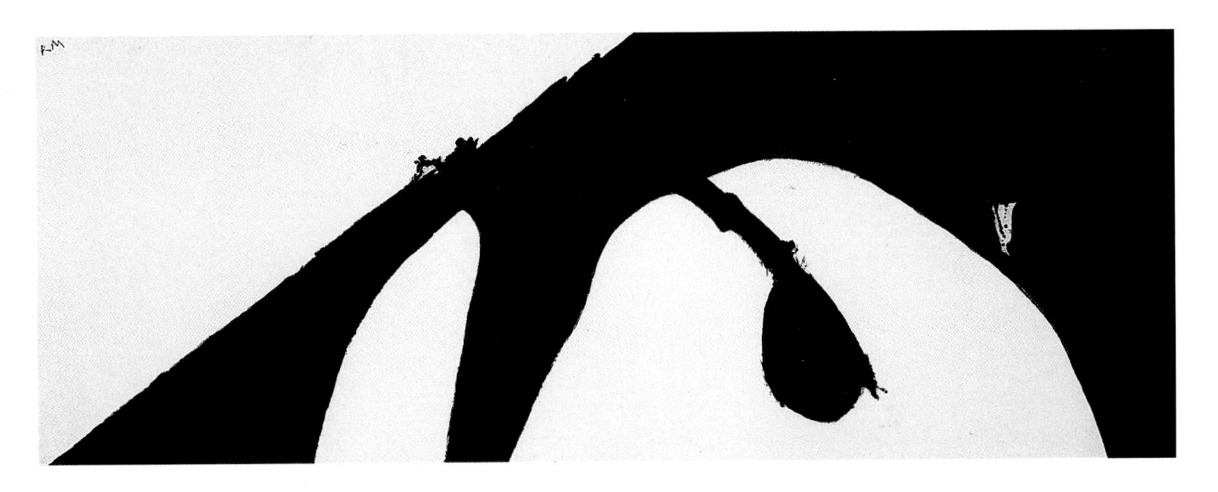

1.29 Robert Motherwell, *Africa,* 1965. Acrylic on Belgian linen, 81 × 222½ in. In this nonfigurative or nonobjective work, some areas have been painted and others not. It is very simple, perhaps deceptively so. To the viewer, the darks seem to be the positive shapes, although after some looking, the effect may be reversed. The Baltimore Museum of Art. Gift of the Artist. BMA 1965.012. © Dedalus Foundation, Inc./ Licensed by VAGA, New York, NY.

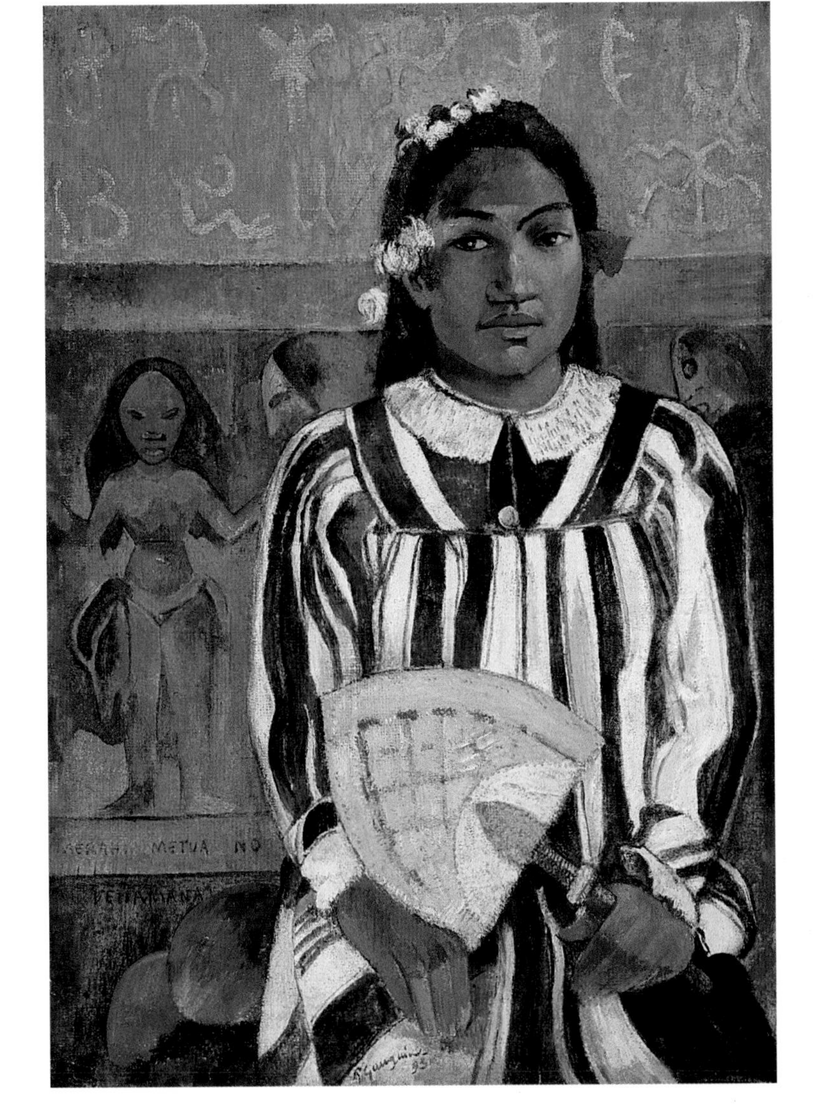

1.30 Paul Gauguin, *Ancestors of Tehamana,* 1893. Oil on canvas, 30⅛ × 21⅛ in. (76.3 × 54.3 cm). Items in the foreground (generally toward the bottom of the picture plane) are traditionally considered positive areas, whereas unoccupied spaces in the background are negative areas. This traditional view does not always apply, however, as can be seen by looking at other illustrations in this book. Art Institute of Chicago. Gift of Mr. and Mrs. Charles Deering McCormick, 1980.613. Photo © Art Institute of Chicago.

CHAPTER TWO

Form

THE VOCABULARY OF FORM

FORM AND VISUAL ORDERING

The Seven Principles of Organization

Harmony (1)
Variety (2)
Balance (3)
Proportion (4)
Dominance (5)
Movement (6)
Economy (7)

Space: Result of Elements/Principles

FORM UNITY: A SUMMARY

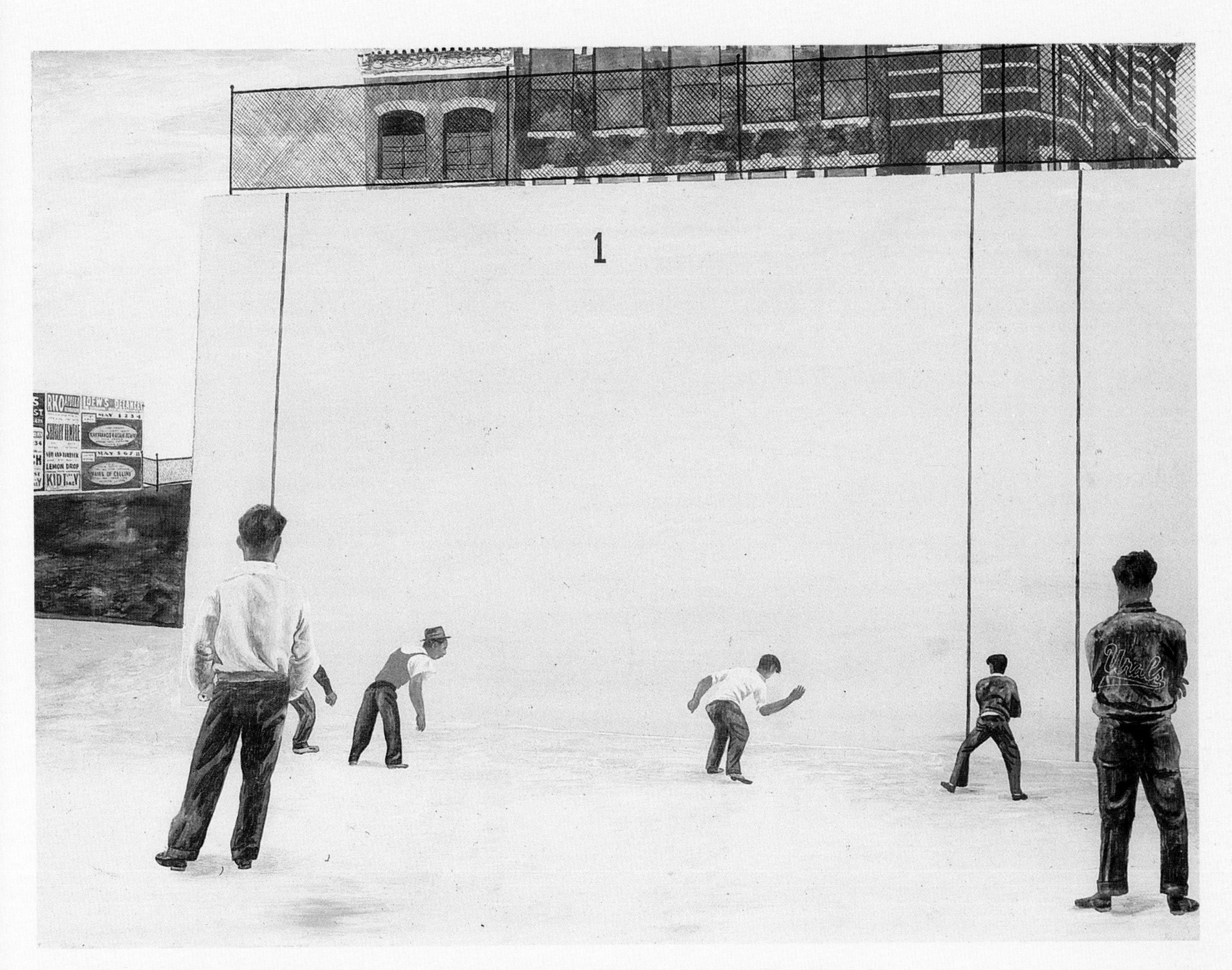

Ben Shahn, *Handball,* 1939. Tempera on paper over composition board, 22¾ × 31¼ in. (57.8 × 79.4 cm).

THE VOCABULARY OF **FORM**

Form—1. The arrangement of elements in an artwork according to the principles that foster unity. 2. The total appearance or organization.

academic
Art that conforms to the traditions and conventions practiced in art academies. Academic art stresses standards, set procedures, and rules.

allover pattern
The repetition of design units in a recognizably systematic arrangement over an entire surface.

approximate symmetry
The use of similar imagery on both sides of a central axis. The imagery on one side resembles that on the other but is varied to prevent monotony.

asymmetry
Having unlike, or noncorresponding, appearances—"without symmetry." An example: a two-dimensional artwork that, without any necessarily visible or implied axis, displays an uneven distribution of parts throughout.

balance
A sense of equilibrium achieved through implied weight, attention, or attraction, by manipulating the visual elements within an artwork.

closure
A concept derived from Gestalt psychology describing the mental relationships that develop while incomplete information is grasped as a complete, unified whole; the artist provides visual suggestions that the observer brings to final recognition.

composition
The total arrangement of all the elements in an artwork. Sometimes interchangeable with the terms *design* and *form.*

concept
1. A comprehensive idea or generalization. 2. An idea that brings diverse elements into a basic relationship.

design
The underlying plan on which an artwork is based. In a broader sense, *design* may be considered synonymous with the term *form.*

dominance
The principle of visual organization that certain elements are more important than others in a particular composition or design. Some features are emphasized, and others are subordinated.

economy
The distillation of the image to the basic essentials for clarity of presentation.

Gestalt (Gestalt psychology)
A German word for "form"; an organized whole in experience. Around 1912, the Gestalt psychologists promoted the theory that explains psychological phenomena by their relationships to total forms, or Gestalten, rather than by their parts.

golden mean, golden section
1. Golden mean—"perfect" harmonious proportions that avoid extremes; the moderation between extremes. 2. Golden section—a traditional system for harmonious proportion expressed by dividing a line or an area into two sections such that the smaller part is to the larger as the larger is to the whole. The ratio developed is 1:1.6180, or roughly 8:13.

harmony
The pleasing quality achieved by different elements of a composition interacting to form a whole. Harmony is often accomplished through repetition of the same or similar characteristics.

interpenetration
The interlocking movement of planes, objects, or shapes within a specified area of space.

motif
A design unit that is repeated often enough in the total composition to make it a significant or dominant feature. Motif is similar to a theme in a musical composition.

movement
Eye travel directed by visual design in a work of art.

pattern
1. Any artistic design serving as a model for imitation. 2. A repeated element and/or design that is usually varied and produces interconnections and obvious directional movements.

principles of organization
Seven principles that guide the use of the elements of art in achieving unity: harmony, variety, balance, proportion, dominance, movement, and economy.

proportion
The comparative size relationship between the parts of a whole. For example, the size of the Statue of Liberty's hand relates to the size of her head. (See **scale.**)

radial
Emanating from a center.

repetition
The use of the same visual effect a number of times in the same composition. Repetition may produce the dominance, harmony, pattern, or rhythm.

rhythm
A sense of movement achieved by the repetition of visual units; the use of measured accents.

scale
Size relative to human dimensions or another standard unit of measure. For example, the Statue of Liberty's scale is apparent when she is seen next to an automobile. (See **proportion.**)

symmetry
The mirrorlike repetition of appearances on both sides of an imaginary central axis.

transparency
A visual quality in which a distant image or element can be seen through a nearer one.

unity
The result of bringing the elements of art into the appropriate ratio between harmony and variety to achieve a sense of oneness.

variety
Differences achieved by opposing, contrasting, changing, elaborating, or diversifying elements in a composition to add individualism and interest; the counterweight of **harmony** in art.

FORM AND VISUAL ORDERING

A work of art always has three essential components: subject, form, and content. These components may vary in degree of emphasis, but their interdependence is so great that no single one can exist without the others, nor can it be fully understood in isolation from the others. The entire artwork should be more important than any one of its components. In this chapter, we explore the component **form** in order to investigate the structural principles of visual order (see fig. 2.1).

When we see images, we take an active part in forming or ordering what we see. An object is reduced to elements. A chair might be seen as a black shape, a wall as a gradient of white, and a floor as a red field. In this case, the eye and mind can organize the different areas of color into a unified whole. Our minds instinctively create order out of the chaos. This instinct for order is the basis of our appreciation of form.

In like manner, artists form a visual order. With their materials they arrange the elements—lines, shapes, values, textures, and colors—to reveal the structure of their plan. These elements need to be controlled and integrated, and artists manage to do this by using the principles of organization: **harmony, variety, balance, proportion, dominance, movement,** and **economy.** These principles inform the artist and, if the

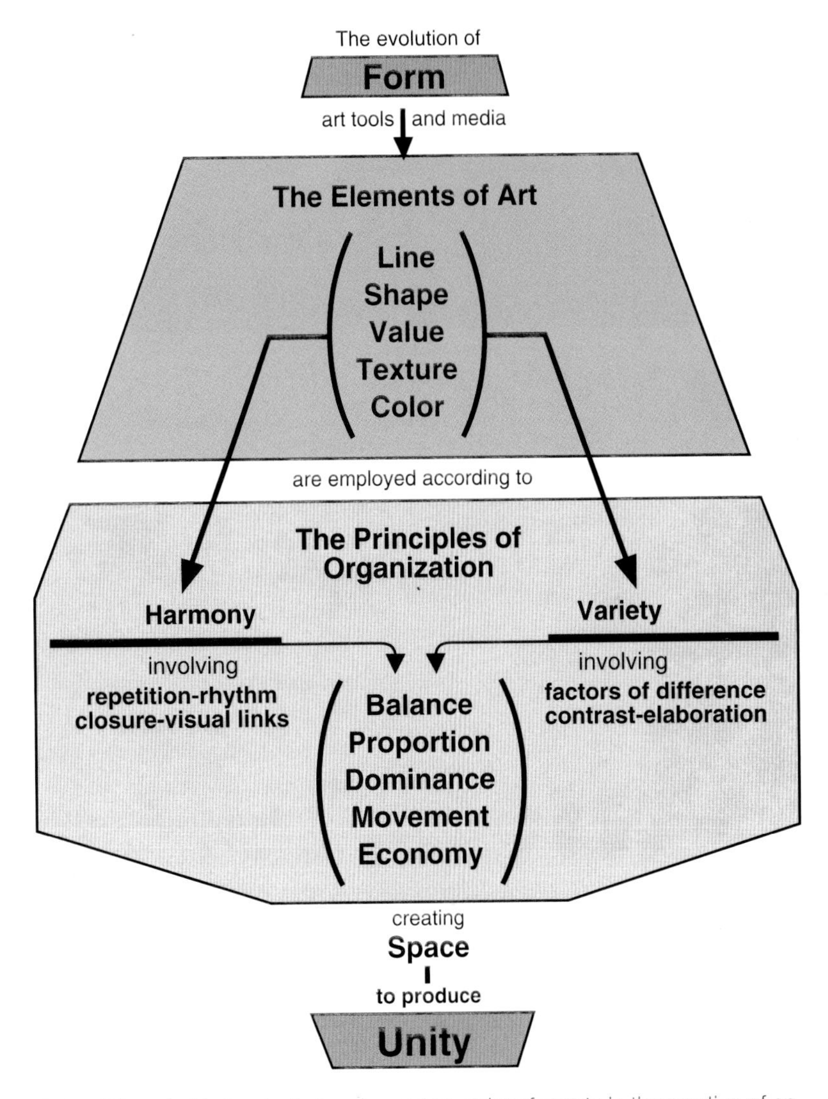

2.1 Although this is a logical and common order of events in the creation of an artwork, artists often alter the sequence.

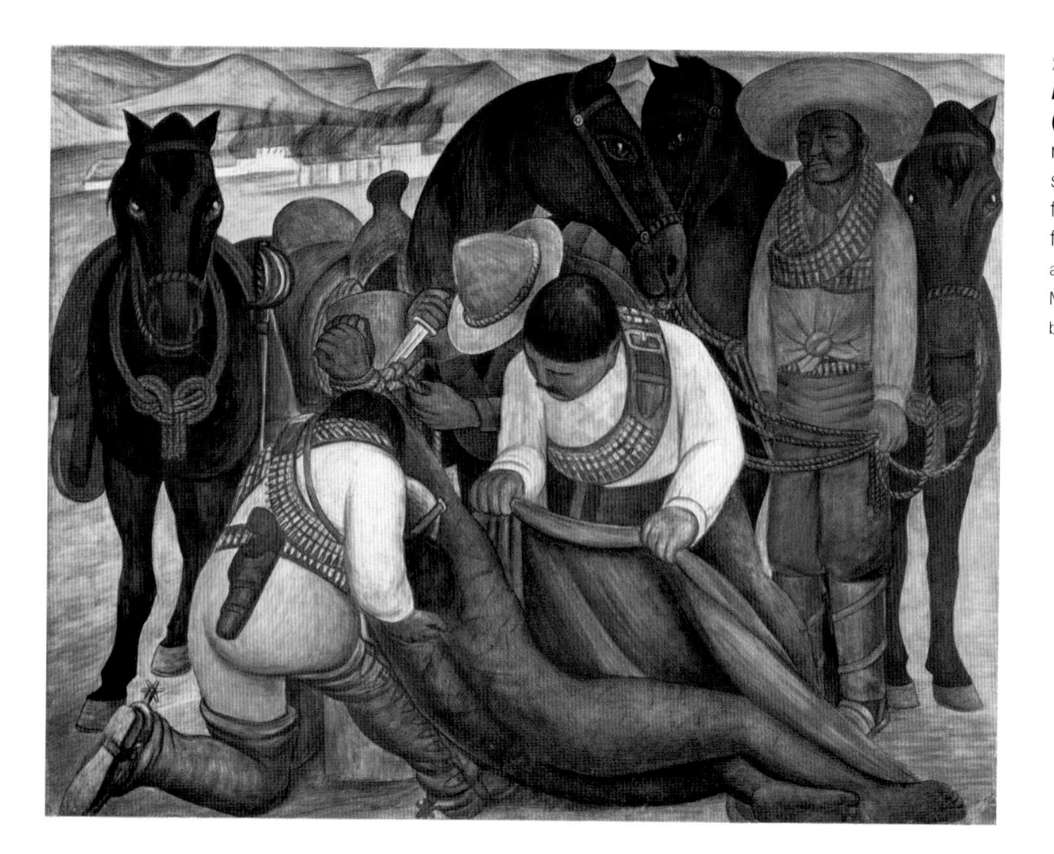

2.2 Diego Rivera, *The Liberation of the Peon,* 1931. Fresco, 6 ft 2 in. × 7 ft 11 in. (1.88 × 2.41 m). Here we see a political artist making use of appropriate and expected subject material. Without the effective use of form, however, the statement would be far less forceful. Philadelphia Museum of Art, PA. Gift of Mr. and Mrs. Herbert Cameron Morris. © Philadelphia Museum of Art/Corbis Media. Reproduction authorized by National Institute of Fine Art and Literature of Mexico.

artist's plan is successful, the sum total equals **unity.** Unity means oneness: the organization of parts that fit into a whole and become vital to it.

Form results from the complete state of the work. The artist produces this overall condition using the elements of art structure, subject to the principles of organization. The artist's plan is usually a mix of intuition and intellect. Ideally, the plan will effectively communicate the artist's feeling, even though the plan may change as the work progresses. The plan can be variously termed **composition** or **design** (fig. 2.2).

In this chapter, we deal with *how* the elements are organized. The individual characteristics of each element are so integral to this organizational process that they cannot be separated from it. But, for the sake of clarity, we will discuss the elements individually in the chapters that follow. If the *how* of organization is as important as *what* is being organized, which should we address first? This is a problem of the chicken or the egg. We must know about the individual elements in order to use them to harmonize a work. For example, the properties of line include length, width, character, direction, and so on. While an artist may use line to unify a work, the resulting harmony is actually created by the "relatedness" of all of those properties. Thus, as we shall see in this chapter, the principles of organization can be applied to the individual characteristics of each element, and the individual characteristics of each element can be tools of analysis in understanding how the principles of organization bring unity to a composition. In view of this interconnectedness, these principles of organization should be reviewed again and again after each of the following chapters to see how each element and its attributes can be used to achieve harmony, variety, balance, proportion, dominance, movement, and economy.

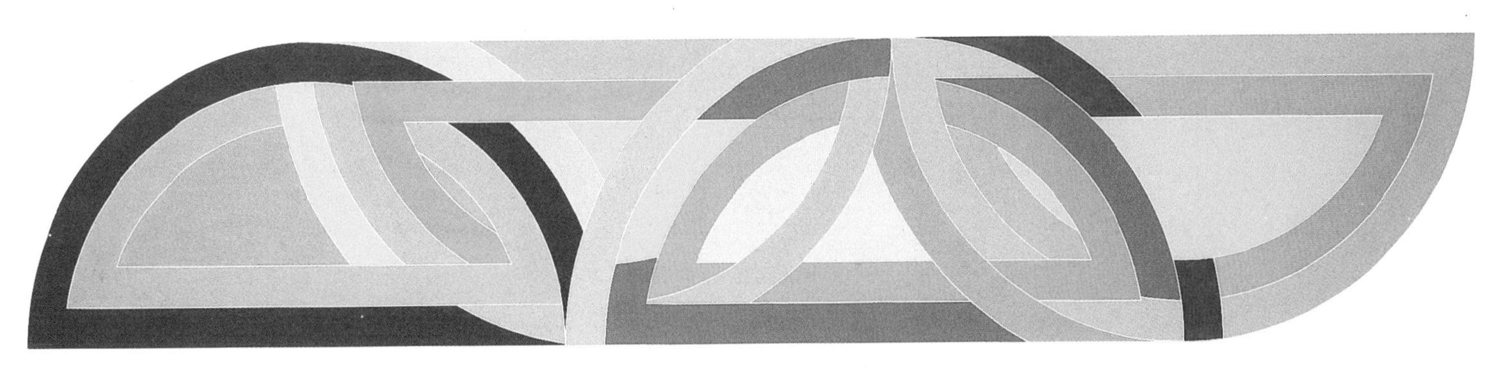

2.3 Frank Stella, *Damascus Gate Stretch Variation,* 1968. Acrylic on canvas, 60 × 300 in. (152.4 × 763.9 cm). Stella has harmonized the painting through his inventive use of the curve and straight-edged shapes; he has provided variety by using contrasting colors and shape sizes. Collection Walker Art Center, Minneapolis. Gift of Mr. and Mrs. Edmond R. Ruben, 1969. © 2005 Frank Stella/Artists Rights Society (ARS), NY.

The Seven Principles of Organization

As mentioned before, the principles of organization—(1) harmony, (2) variety, (3) balance, (4) proportion, (5) dominance, (6) movement, and (7) economy—are flexible guides; they are not laws with only one possible interpretation. These principles help organize the elements of art into some kind of action. The principles of organization help in finding certain solutions, but they are not ends in themselves, so merely following them does not guarantee results. Artworks are unique expressions of personal experience and feeling, and should be judged in their totality. In other words, the application of the principles is intuitive and their interpretations are subjective.

Organization in art consists of developing a unified whole out of diverse parts. This is done by relating contrasts through similarities. For example, an artist might use two opposing kinds of lines, vertical and horizontal, in a composition. Because both the horizontal and vertical lines are already straight, this likeness relates them. Unity and organization in art are dependent on a dualism of similarity and contrast—a balance between harmony and variety (fig. 2.3). As you read the rest of this chapter, we encourage you to spend some time exploring the related activities on the accompanying CD-ROM.

Harmony (1)

We may think of harmony as a factor of cohesion—relating various parts together. On a picture surface, the artist accomplishes this harmonizing of opposing forces by giving the different parts some common element: color, texture, value, for example. The continued introduction of the same element throughout the composition reconciles the underlying opposition. **Rhythm** is also established when visual units are repeated regularly. Whether created by **repetition** or rhythm, harmony becomes boring or monotonous when carried to extremes. But, properly introduced, harmony is a necessary ingredient of unity.

Musical composition is quite similar to the construction of visual artwork. For instance, harmony in music occurs when the component notes fit together in producing a sound. Of course, sometimes composers intentionally introduce discord (notes that sound awkward together) to be resolved later in the composition. Discord can also occur in art when unrelated parts are put together.

Music making involves the efforts of at least two identities: the composer and the performer. The composer (the creator) provides the musical blueprint (the score) and the key signature (what notes go together); the performer (the interpreter) follows these guidelines, with some latitude for individual interpretation. The score indicates the tempo, order, and duration of the notes and the rests and the degree of loudness to be produced. This is not unlike a visual art product; the artwork is like a score, suggesting the speed and direction of eye movement, providing pauses (rests) and, in a sense, the volume and tempo (loud or soft colors and clashing or gently related lines and shapes). In the visual arts, the artist/creator lays out the guidelines, and the interpretation is performed through the viewer's eyes and mind. The viewer thus connects with the artist through the execution of the artwork. A knowledgeable and sensitive viewer is a necessity.

If relationships are essential to harmony, what relates one part of the artwork to the other parts? A common element or motif—a repeated color, texture, or value, or a common configuration of line or shape—can be the connecting force. Rhythm is also present when regulated units are repeated. At all

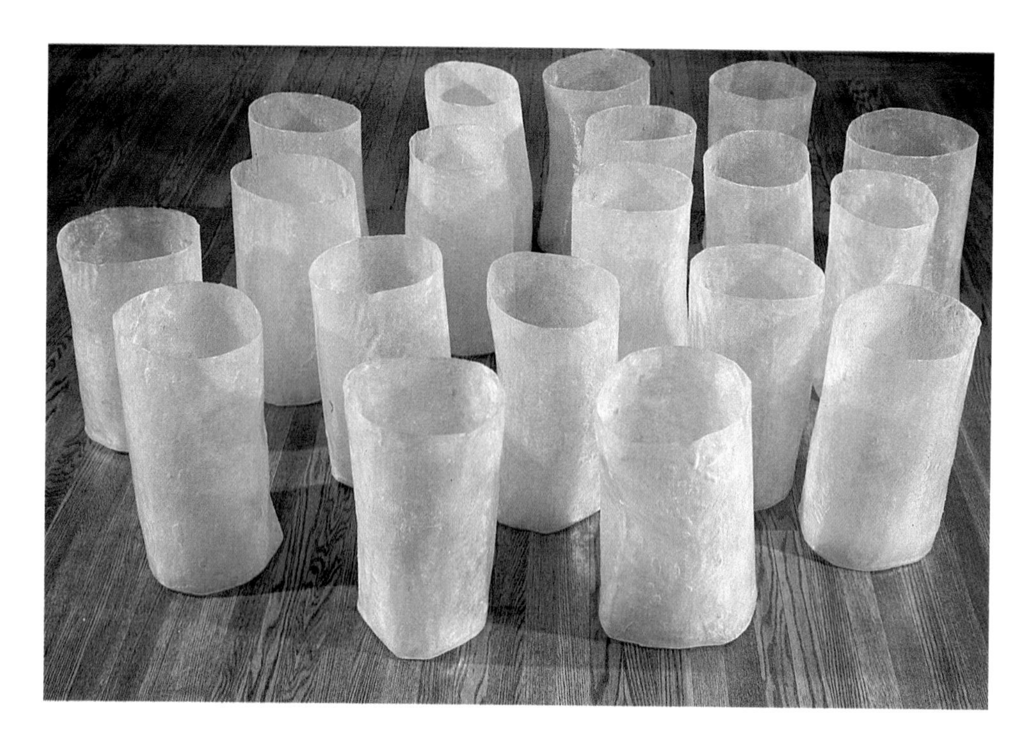

2.4 **Eva Hesse (1936–1970) © Estate of Eva Hesse. *Repetition 19, III.* (1968). Nineteen tubular fiberglass units, 19 to 20¼ high × 11 to 13¾ diameter (48 to 51 cm high × 27.8 to 32.3 cm diameter).** This work, as the title implies, exploits the repetitive dimensions of identical "can forms." These are then given variety by distorting the basic shapes. Gift of Charles and Anita Blatt. (1004.1969.a-s) The Museum of Modern Art, New York, NY, U.S.A. Digital image © The Museum of Modern Art/Licensed by SCALA/Art Resource, NY.

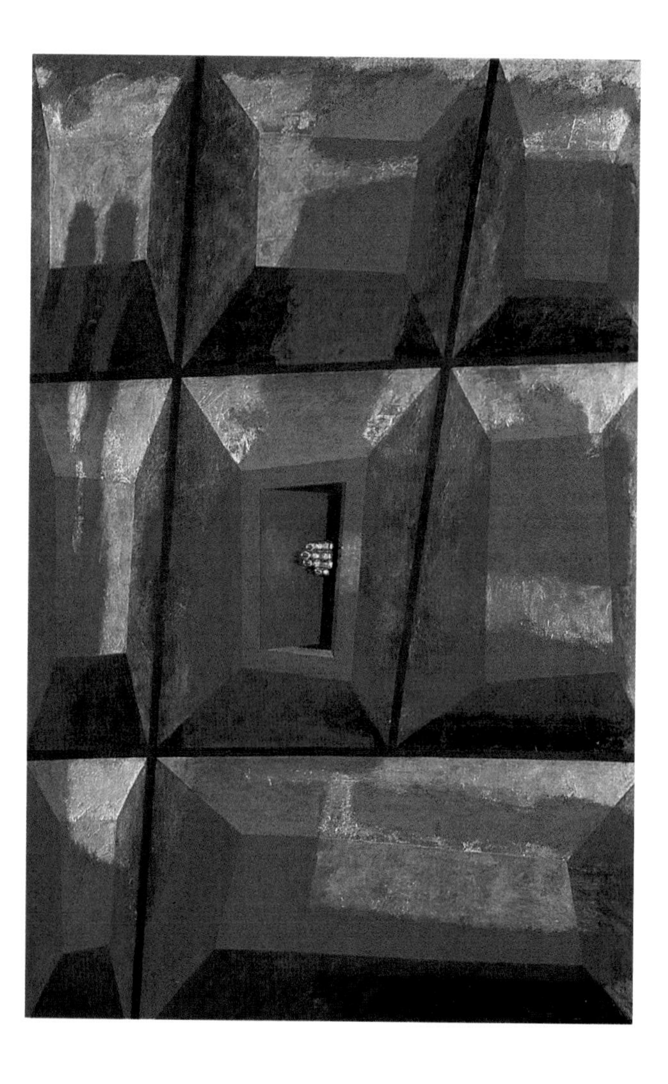

2.5 **Pauline Gagnon, *Secret Little Door,* 1992. Mixed media on canvas, 48 × 72 in.** Repetition is introduced in this image by the theme of architectural surface and shape. But, by repeating those items in differing ways, the artist creates variety and a potentially monotonous composition is greatly enlivened. Courtesy of the artist and Jain Marunouchi Gallery.

events, harmony is a necessary ingredient in the broader coalescence of unity. In art, as in music, if the parts fit, harmony is achieved.

Repetition

Repetition, needless to say, means that certain things are repeated. In art these things include the elements of art, characteristics of those elements, and designs produced by combinations of the elements. The relationships created by repetitive resemblances give artwork a degree of harmony. The repetitions need not be exact duplicates but, instead, can be similarities and near likenesses. Repetitions hammer home, through emphasis, a condition desired by the artist. Carefully handled repetition can use similarities as links to induce the eye travel of the observer. Furthermore, as those similarities are reduced, the *least* related elements also achieves an emphasis, drawing attention to the dissimilarities. Emphases of any kind hold our attention, if only briefly. Repetitive similarities are like our genetic predisposition to resemble our parents, expressing relatedness. Harmonious relatedness is similarly established in art through repetition (figs. 2.4, 2.5, and 2.6).

Pattern A concept important to the discussion of repetition is **pattern.** At the most elementary level, any arrangement or design may be seen as a pattern that may function as the model for imitation or the template for making things. Examples include the pattern a dressmaker uses when making a skirt,

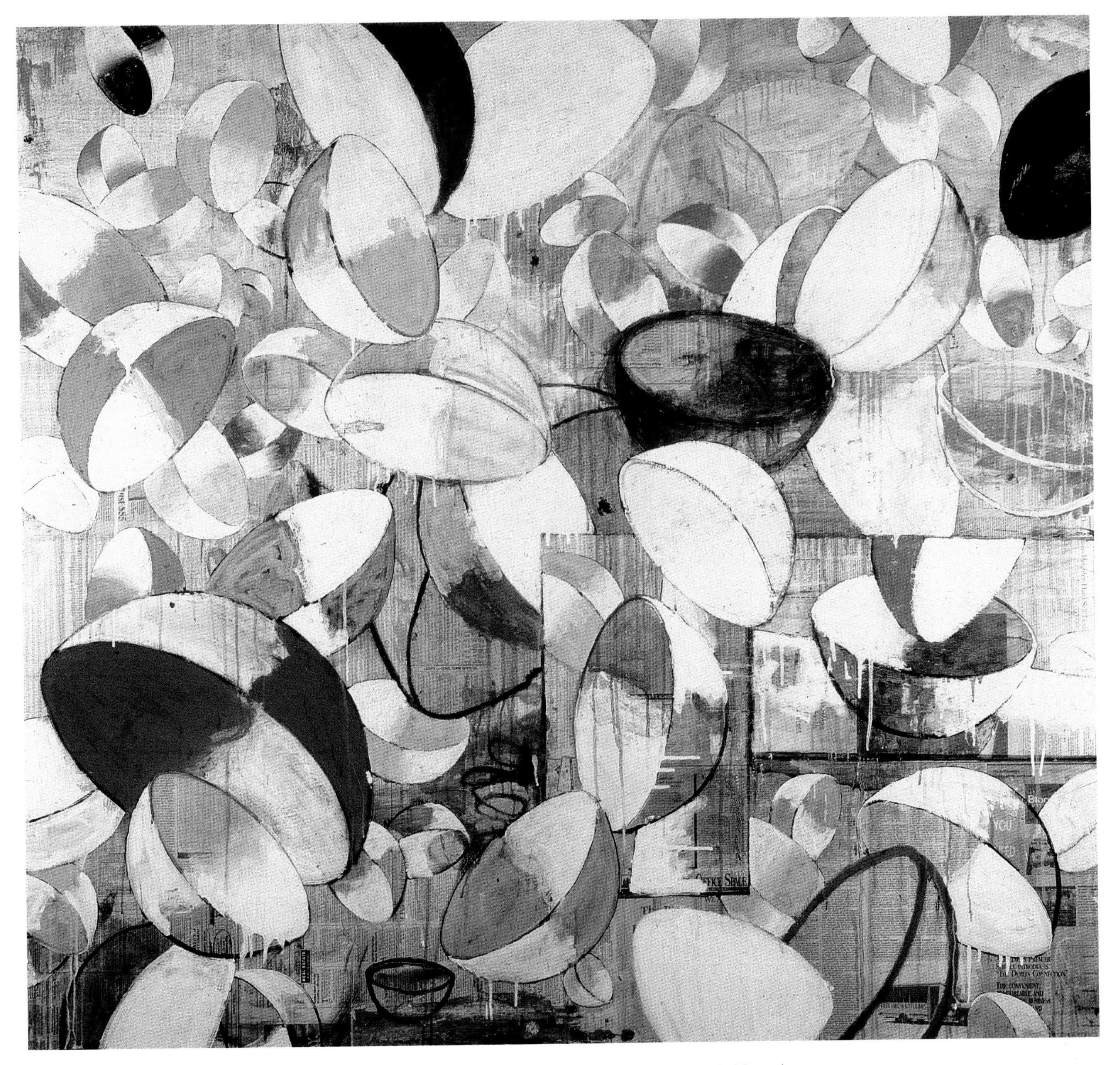

2.6 Paul Manes, *Eiso*, 1995. Oil on canvas, 60 × 66 in. (152.4 × 167.6 cm). The visual units in Manes's painting are ovoid saucer shapes. The repetition of this shape creates harmony. Variety develops out of differences in the shape's size and color. Courtesy of Paul Rogers/9W Gallery, New York, NY.

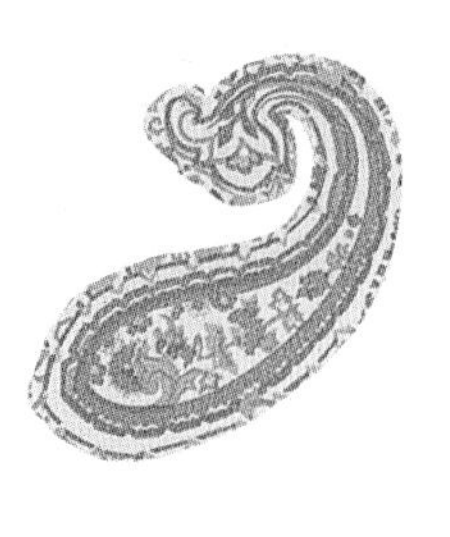

A

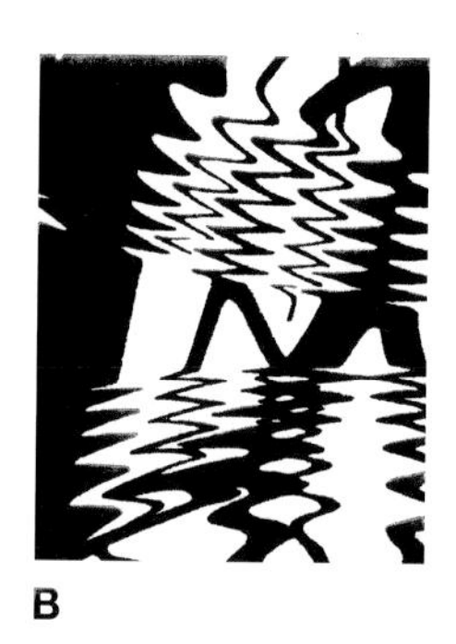

B

2.7 (A) The basic pattern is the universally and immediately recognizable paisley shape (see fig. 2.9). (B) A pattern created by an arrangement of lines and positive and negative shapes based on an abstraction of tree reflections (see fig. 2.8).

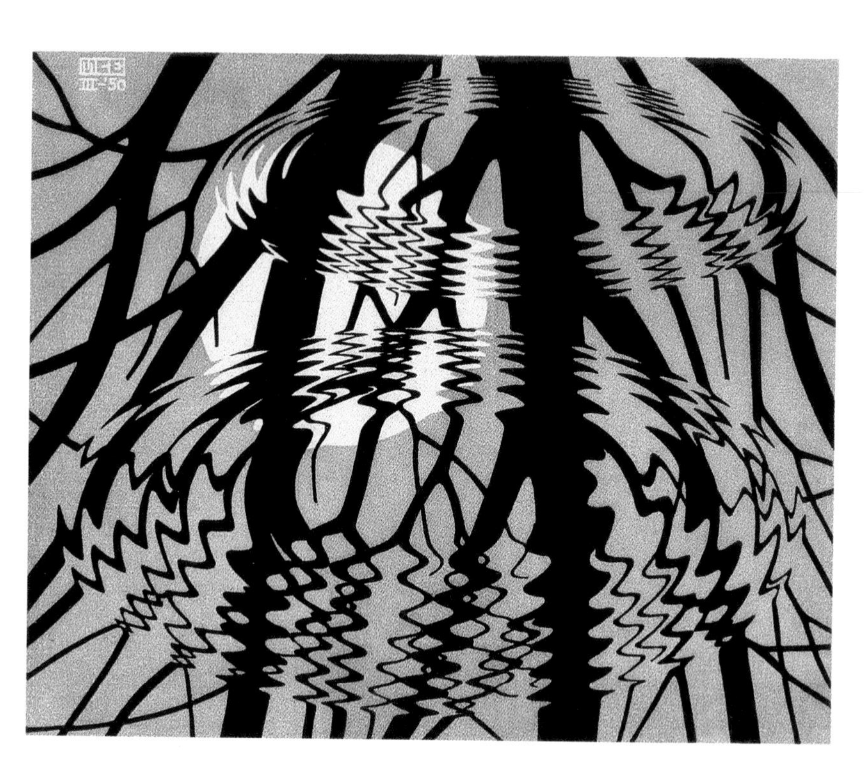

2.8 **M. C. Escher, *Rippled Surface*, 1950.** Although the subject is trees, the distinctive pictorial characteristic of this work is the pattern produced by the rippling reflections of the trees—a pattern that is developed, though not identically, in all areas of the work, creating unity. The Gemeentemuseum, The Hague.

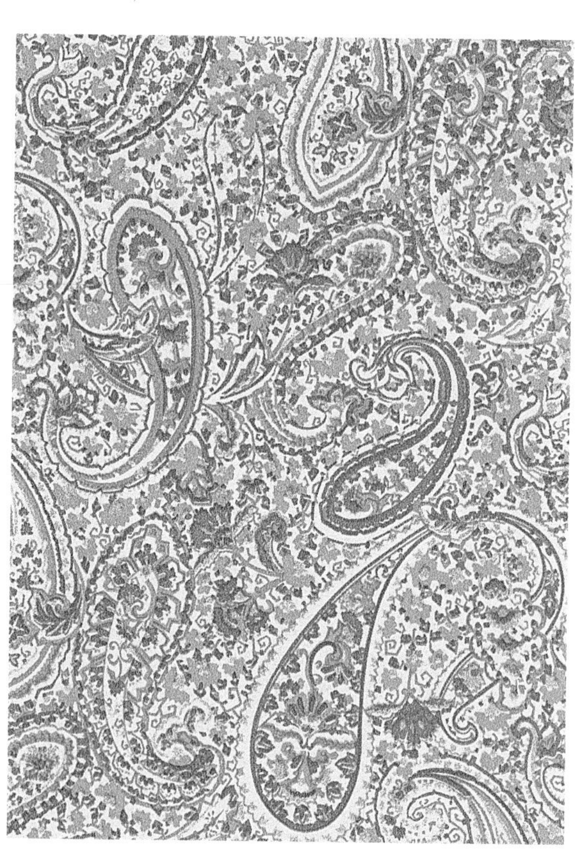

2.9 **Paisley pattern, 1992. Wallcovering.** The paisley is repeated casually to achieve a pattern of more or less irregular design. Courtesy of Fashion Wallcoverings, Distributors, Cleveland, OH.

the pattern a moldmaker uses for casting a machine part, or the drawings an artist uses while developing an artistic design. On the next level, pattern is the formation of characteristics that is created when the basic pattern is repeated; these are patterns within patterns.

These repetitions may be composed of any arrangement of elements, from simple marks to complex relationships of line, shape, value, texture, or color. They may be totally invented, as in a paisley or geometric pattern, or suggested by objects, like tree branches and/or their spaces (figs. 2.7A, B). The repetitive nature of patterns can create harmony and rhythm with intervals and marks that flow, connect, and punctuate. They serve to direct eye movement from one part of the artwork to another. The resulting organization may appear casual when the repetitions are irregular, as in the reflected tree pattern and wallcovering pattern in figures 2.8 and 2.9, or controlled when regulated repetitions are used (fig. 2.10). At all events, the individual units, patterns, or repetitions become part of a new organization, creating an **allover pattern.**

Motif **Motif** is a concept closely related to pattern. Once the basic unit, tile, or original pattern (model) is created and repeated, it is referred to as a motif. The smallest repeating design unit in a roll of wallpaper is the motif. The

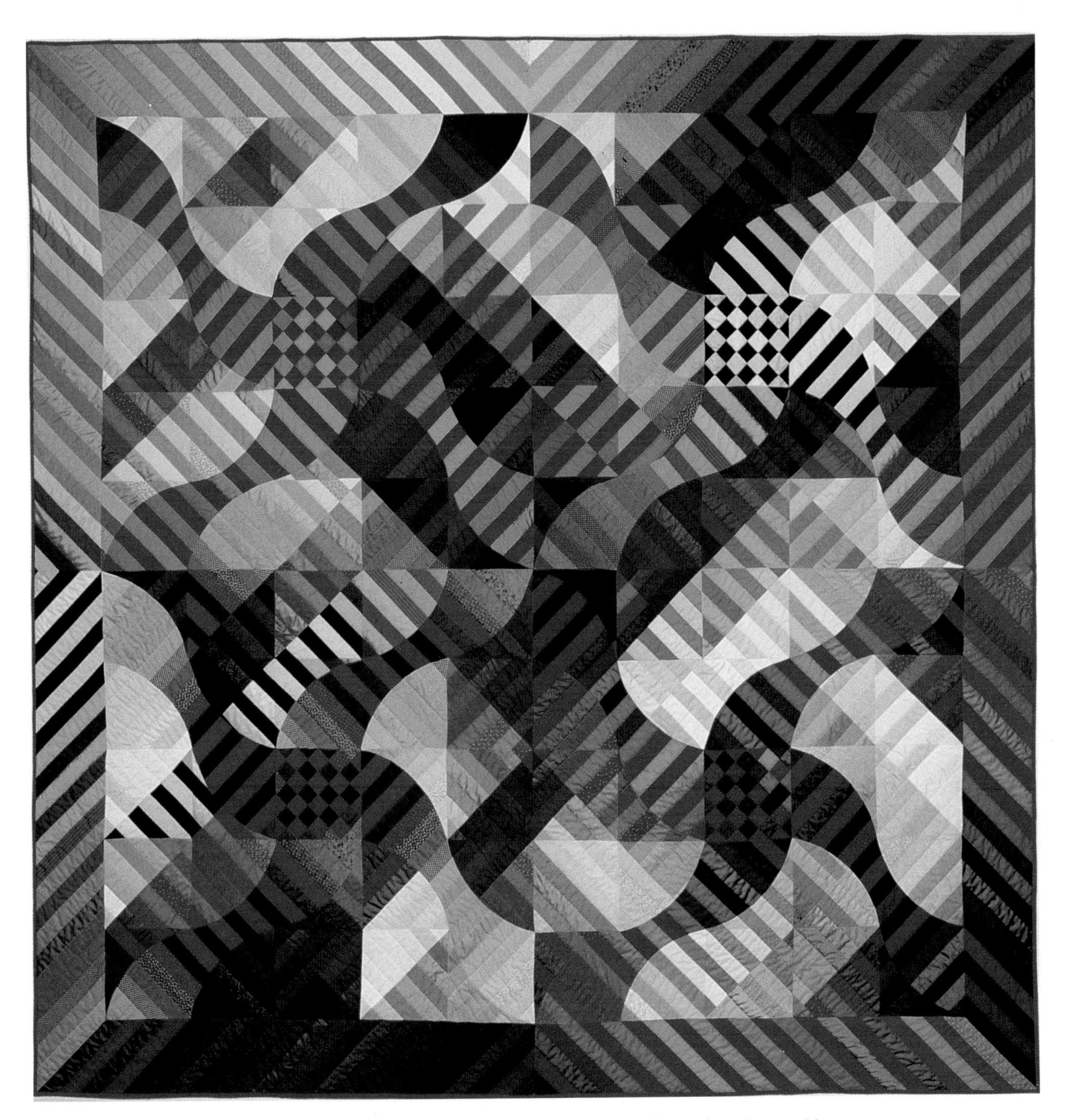

2.10 Michael James, *Rhythm/Color: Spanish Dance,* 1985. Somerset Village, Massachusetts, machine-pieced cotton and silk, machine quilted. 100 × 100 in. (254 × 254 cm). Using traditional quilting techniques, Michael James has repeated the basic design unit four times. However, the unusual allover pattern becomes more important than the repeating motif after color, value, and texture are changed within the units to accentuate and emphasize new space relationships. Collection of the Newark Museum, Newark, New Jersey. Photograph by David Caras.

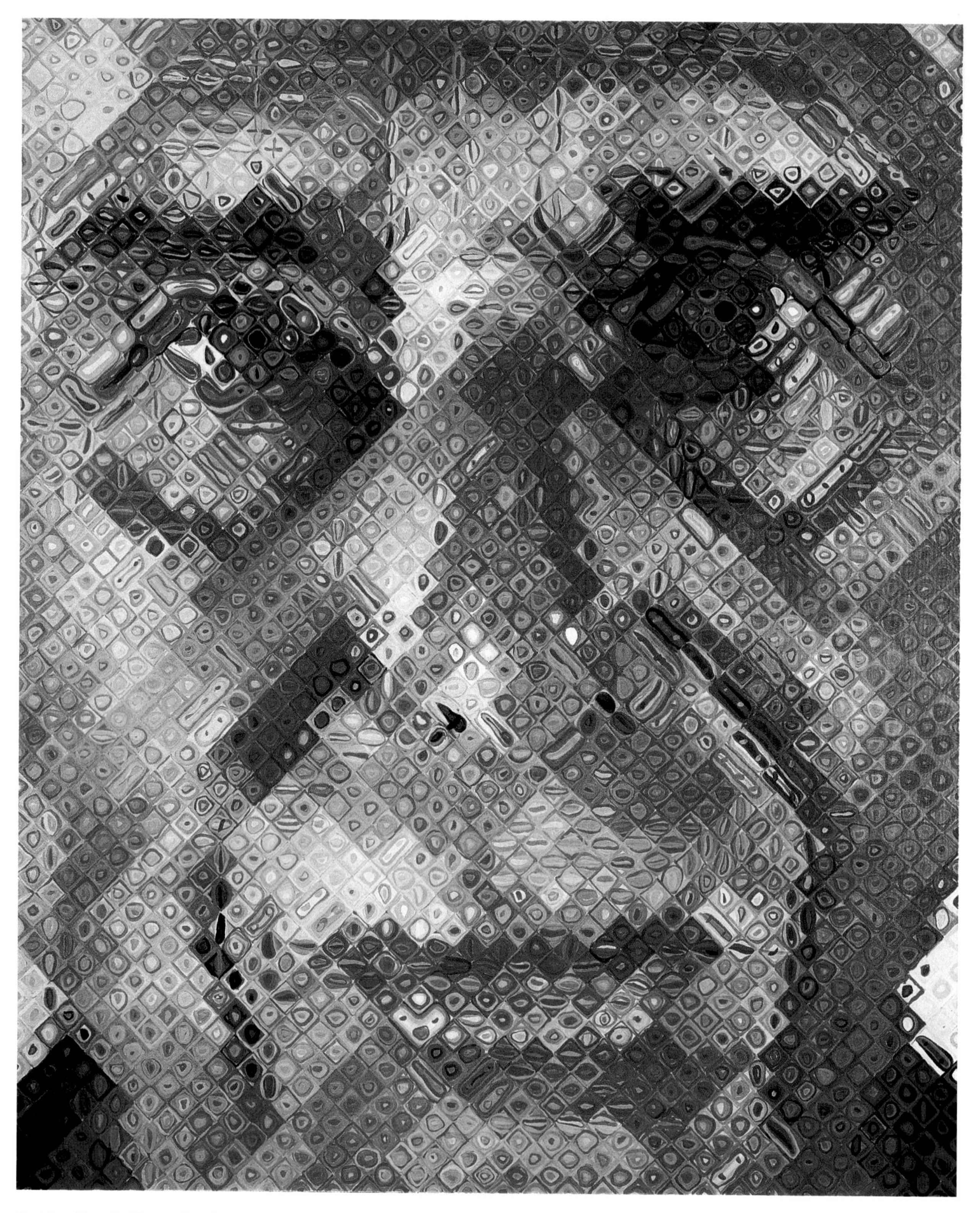

2.11 Chuck Close, *Paul III*, 1996. Oil on canvas, 102 × 84 in. (259.1 × 213.4 cm). A very interesting allover pattern emerges as a larger-than-life portrait. Because of the changing treatment in color and value, the allover pattern dominates the repeating motif or design unit—a diamond with a series of internal circles. Image © The Cleveland Museum of Art, Mr. and Mrs. William H. Marlatt Fund, 1977.59. Photograph by Ellen Page Wilson, courtesy Pace Wildenstein.

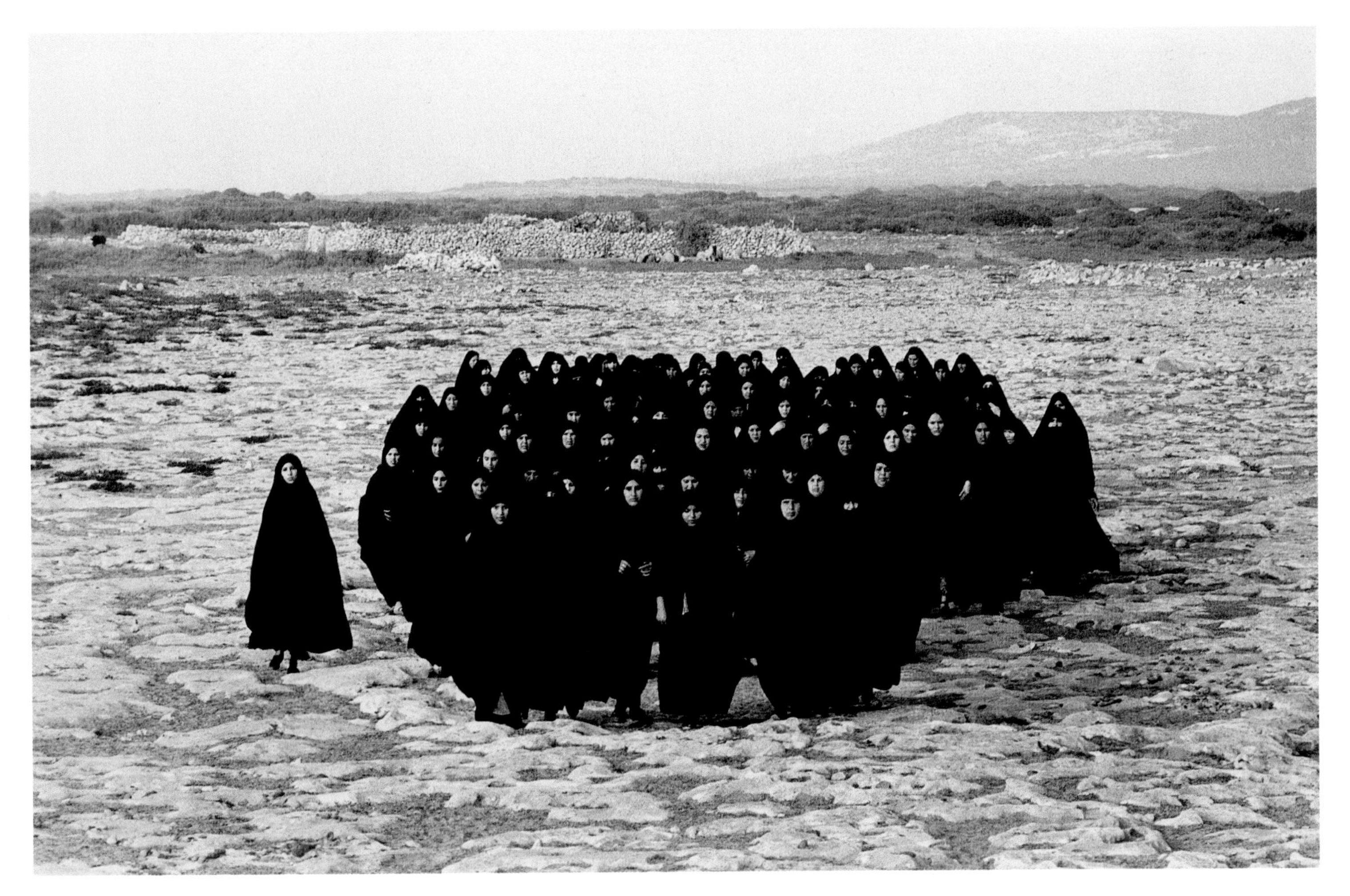

2.12 Shirim Neshat (b. 1957), *Untitled (Rapture),* 1999. Gelatin silver print, Sight 43¼ × 68¼ in. (109.86 × 173.36 cm). This video still shows a mass of women walking to the sea. The chador-covered woman is the "motif" repeated in the image. This motif is underscored by the simple palette, the horizontal gradients of sand and sea, as well as the women's shadows and flapping chadors. The extremely spare arrangement creates a high degree of abstraction. Whitney Museum of American Art, New York; Purchase, with funds from Kathryn Fleck in honor of Maxwell L. Anderson 2000.106.

continued repetition of this design unit defines the wall and creates an allover pattern for the room. Motifs are easy to find in the work of Pop artist Andy Warhol, who created allover patterns with his soup can artworks (see fig. 10.91). Allover patterns don't always have to be predictable. An artist who doesn't want such a repetitive image might choose to create an irregular pattern design (see figs. 2.8 and 2.9). For instance, quiltmakers often rotate their motifs, changing their color, value, texture, and placement. This allows them to further accent variations and bring about a new pattern of diagonals, squares, or diamonds that seem to emerge from the allover pattern (fig. 2.10; see also fig. 7.23). In a similar manner, Chuck Close has established the repeating design unit of the diamond with a series of internal circles but, because he changes color and value in each cell, the allover pattern is a portrait of Paul III (fig. 2.11).

Studio artists often find the obvious and continuous repetition of a motif in an allover pattern too monotonous. For them, a subtler use of motif would treat it more like a repeated idea, theme, or pattern of notes in music. For example, the "ta-ta-ta-TUM" in Beethoven's Fifth Symphony is repeated but constantly changes in terms of tempo, pitch, volume, and the voice of the instrument playing it. Shirim Neshat, in *Rapture,* uses the shrouded image of the female figure in much the same way (fig. 2.12). It is not repeated over and over exactly alike but rather is introduced as a theme, constantly changing and accented in differing ways.

Sometimes the theme develops for an artist over a long series of work. Consider 30 paintings by an artist, each

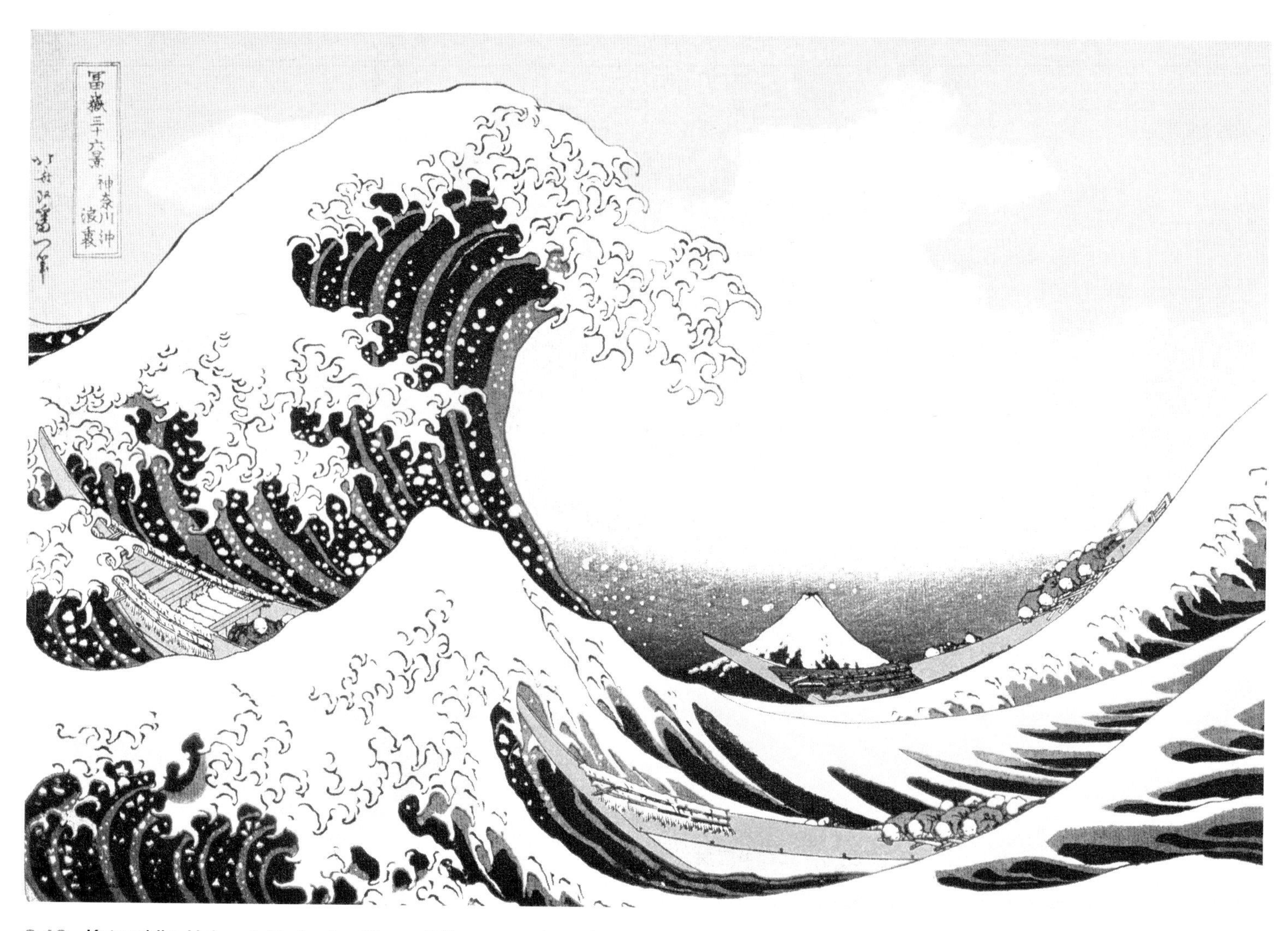

2.13 Katsushika Hokusai, *Under the Wave off Kanagawa* (from the series "The Thirty-Six Views of Fuji"), 1829–33. Colored woodblock print, 10½ × 15 in. (26.7 × 38.1 cm). Hokusai has given us a dramatic sense of the rhythmic surging of the sea in this print. Takahashi Collection. Sakamoto Photo Research Laboratory/Corbis Media.

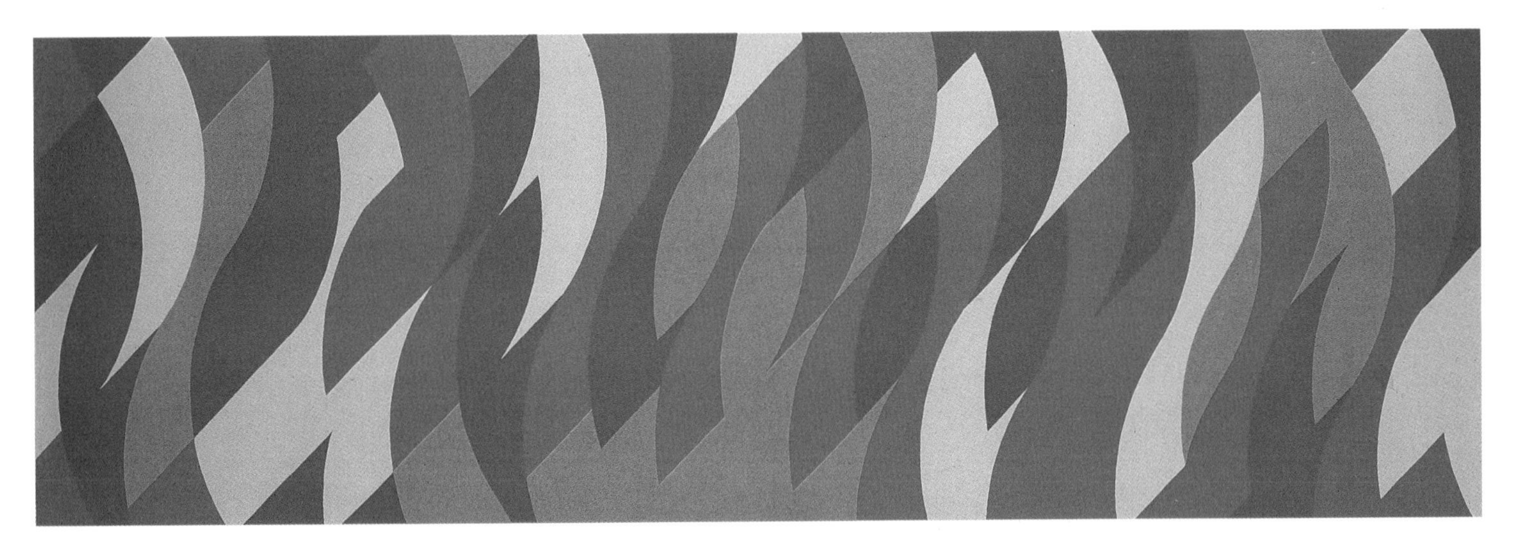

2.14 Bridget Riley, *Evoë 1*, 1999–2000. Oil on linen, 6 × 19 ft. (194 × 580 cm). Shapes related in color, value, and curving edges create a dramatic sweep across the composition. Interest is added to the rhythmic movement and ordered beat by changing the size and type of shape and the diagonal accents. Courtesy Karsten Schubert, London. © 2000 Bridget Riley. All rights reserved. Photograph by Prudence Cumming, London.

dealing with a cat in some different attitude or position. In each individual painting, the cat would be the subject. But, within a consideration of the total series, the cat may be seen as the artist's repeating theme or motif. Two examples from a larger series may be seen in the Impressionist artist Claude Monet's *Waterloo Bridge* paintings (see figs. 7.24 and 7.25) and the work of Piet Mondrian (see figs. 1.3 through 1.6).

Rhythm

One attribute of repetition is the ability to produce rhythm. Rhythm results from repeated beats, sometimes regular, sometimes more eccentric. Walking, running, dancing, wood chopping, and hammering are all human activities with recurring measures. Rhythm in art derives from reiterating and measuring similar or equal parts. This reiteration is a synonym for repetition. The repetition of elements and motifs, if strategically placed and suitably accented, will result in rhythm (fig. 2.13). The rhythm of visual movement may be smoothly flowing or it may be less regular and even jerky, as dictated by the artist (much like a musical composition). Depending on how they are used, repetition and rhythm can confer on an artwork both excitement and harmony. A gentle rhythm in a quiet landscape suggests peace, whereas an active rhythm, as in a stormy landscape, suggests violence. The type of rhythm will depend on horizontal or vertical lines versus diagonal lines, regular or irregular shapes, and smooth or fast transitions through which the eye is guided. Bridget Riley charges her image *Evoë 1* with rhythmical order (fig. 2.14), combining several rhythmical measures to create unity. She ties the picture together by repeating curvilinear shapes, relating their direction, and using colors of modified value and intensity.

In art, just as in music, rhythmic variation—in size (quarter or whole notes) or volume (loudness or softness)—draws our attention, but another aspect of rhythm may be overlooked: the intervals of silence between repeating units. When a drummer taps out a beat, the recognizable rhythmic pattern is due to the variation in the negative spaces or intervals of silence between the beats. Applied to the visual arts, an example of this variation in spacing can be seen in the sculpture of Alexander Calder (see fig. 9.35) or in the placement and intervals between the heads in Andrew Stepovich's *Carnival* (see fig. 5.20).

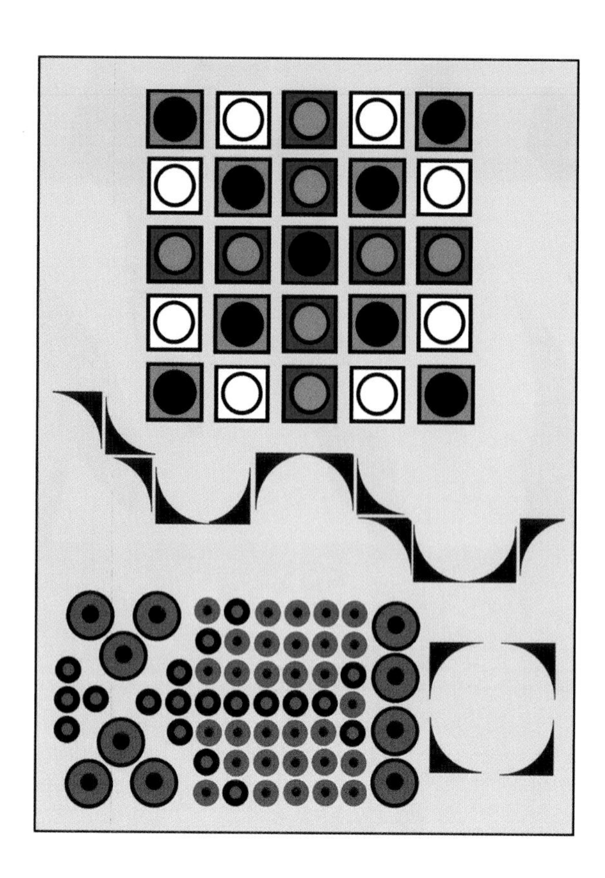

2.15 Examples of closure. Top: The total configuration is more important than the individual components. An X, a central cross, and a squared outer circular shape are recognized before the individual circles used. Center and lower right: Similar shapes optically join to form a green serpentine object and a circle in a green square. Bottom left: Similar shapes help form red arrows.

Closure or visual grouping

In the early part of the twentieth century, Max Wertheimer, a German **Gestalt** psychologist, began to investigate how the viewer sees form, pattern, configuration, or shape in terms of group relationships rather than as individual items. He discovered that several factors, such as nearness and size, help relate objects visually. We will be referring to the mental process of assembling these together to create pattern as **closure.** The principle of closure suggests that people tend to see incomplete patterns or information as complete or unified wholes. This "closure tendency" occurs when an artist provides a minimum of information or visual clues, and the observer provides the closure or imposes an understanding of the patterns with final recognition. For example, in the upper example in figure 2.15, some viewers will see an X formed by the black circles, and others will see a + created by the blue squares. By application of this principle, the four dark triangles with concave hypotenuses would seem to create a complete green circle (bottom right illustration in fig. 2.15). Cover up one triangle or move them farther apart, as in figure 2.16B, and the circle is destroyed. Admittedly, with closure there are many principles at work, like the rule of proximity (relative nearness joins objects visually) and the rule of similarity (visual elements may join optically if they resemble one another in size or shape; see illustration in fig. 2.15, bottom left). For Wertheimer, this visual ordering helped explain how artists organize structure and create pattern in their work. With the concept of closure, the whole (the collective pattern or organization) is greater than its individual parts. In practice, this simply means that in figures 2.16A, B, and C, as circles, rectangles, and triangles move closer together, it becomes easier to see a developing circular grouping in the upper half and a lower horizontal line. The new grouping becomes more important than any one individual part (triangle, circle, or rectangle).

How do images interact visually as they are moved or placed closer and closer together? In the diagram shown in figure 2.16A, when separate images are evenly spaced throughout the area, each is experienced individually. But as we begin to pull some of those shapes nearer together, as in figure 2.16B, they begin to join together as visual units. As enough shapes come together, we have growing awareness of a circular form and a horizontal linear development. In the final image, all of the various shapes have a harmonious relationship because of their spacing (fig. 2.16C). All of the individual shapes (circles, rectangles, and squares of many sizes) have become related. Harmonizing may be aided by similarities—of color, related surface, or shape type—but here shapes are dissimilar to illustrate the effects of spacing by itself. The relationship is in fact psychological, whereby all the different individual images become part of something even greater in our minds. We see the larger group rather than the individual parts involved in its creation. With variation of the negative intervals between shapes, the new grouping can appear dense in one location while fading away in another. The same shapes that create a circle in one location can be made to suggest a serpentine movement in another (center example, fig. 2.15). It is not always necessary to create recognizable shapes through closure. For instance, a group of value—or color-related shapes may appear to move across a composition as its controlling value pattern (see fig. 2.54). In this case, the shapes come together visually to form a new grouping. Relatedness in color, value, texture, shape, direction, or linear quality can also help this happen.

In addition to positive images, closure can make negative areas identifiable.

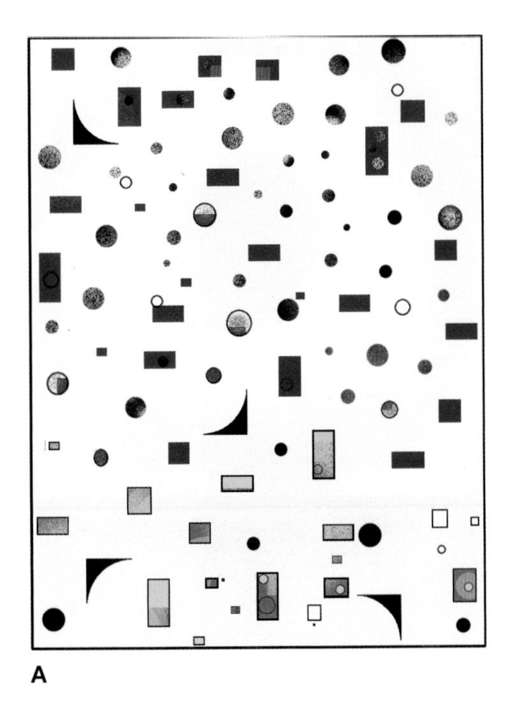

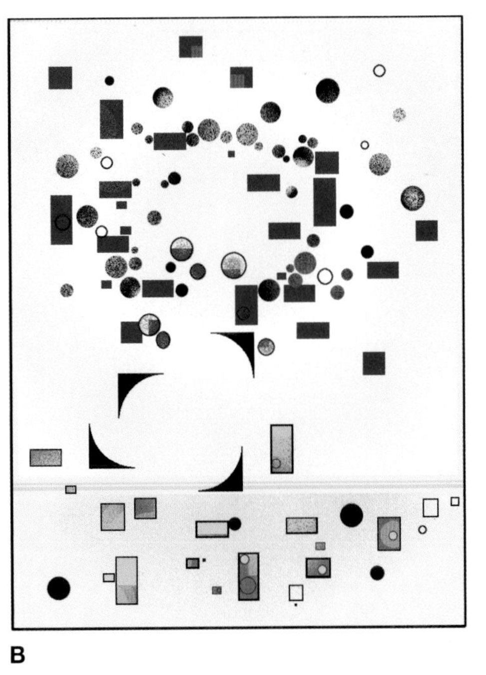

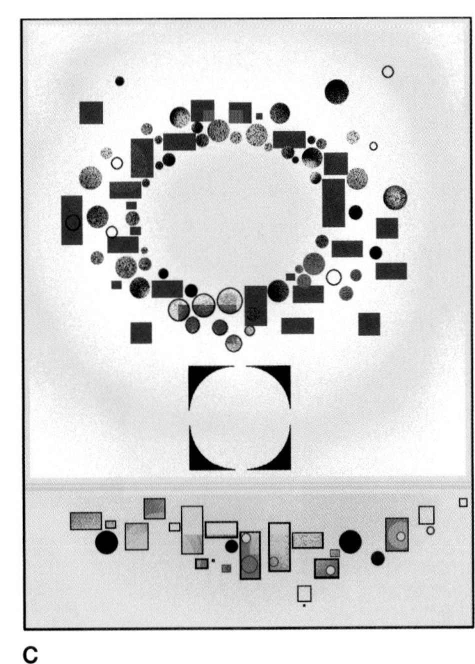

2.16 (A) Individual shapes without any implied organization. (B) Individual shapes moving closer together and beginning to establish a visual grouping. (C) Shapes close together with closure suggesting patterns of an oval, a circle, and a horizontal bar. For more information see the accompanying CD-ROM.

Notice, in the center image of figure 2.16C, how the four black triangular corner shapes cause the negative area to become important. It is difficult to see the background only as negative area surrounding the black shapes. Instead, the missing sections of the black shapes are filled in, and we are forced to see the central area as a circle. As shapes are moved around, explore the relationship of their placement—the negative interval. Discover how the mind fills in missing information. Determine at what point shapes begin to join visually. Can a third shape be made to join a grouping of two? Is more or less space needed between the units as a third joins the unit? Try to determine at what point the most tension is created in the spacing between units. At certain spacing intervals, unrelated elements, shapes, or images enter harmonious relationships as parts of an implied grouping.

Visual linking

Just as closure unifies shapes that share an implied relationship, bringing the elements so close together that they physically touch suggests other ways of unifying a composition. When this occurs, the shared space itself becomes the cohesive factor.

Connections—shared edges Shapes sharing a common edge (contacting, touching, butting together) are often united, because the sharing imposes common relationships that draw them together. For example, such shapes tend to appear to be on the same limited space plane or share a similar spatial or pictorial depth. The Cubists and some contemporary artists like Gunther Gerzso (fig. 2.17) have used this idea successfully.

A way to unite compositions dealing with flat or limited space is by using shapes of the same size and related color or value. This technique, however, is not always the easiest way to develop an illusionistic or three-dimensional space. This is difficult because shapes with a shared edge and contrasting values limit the ability to create a spatial reference (fig. 2.18A, left). Changing the sizes of shapes with shared edges makes it easier to see those shapes pass behind or in front of each other (fig. 2.18A, right).

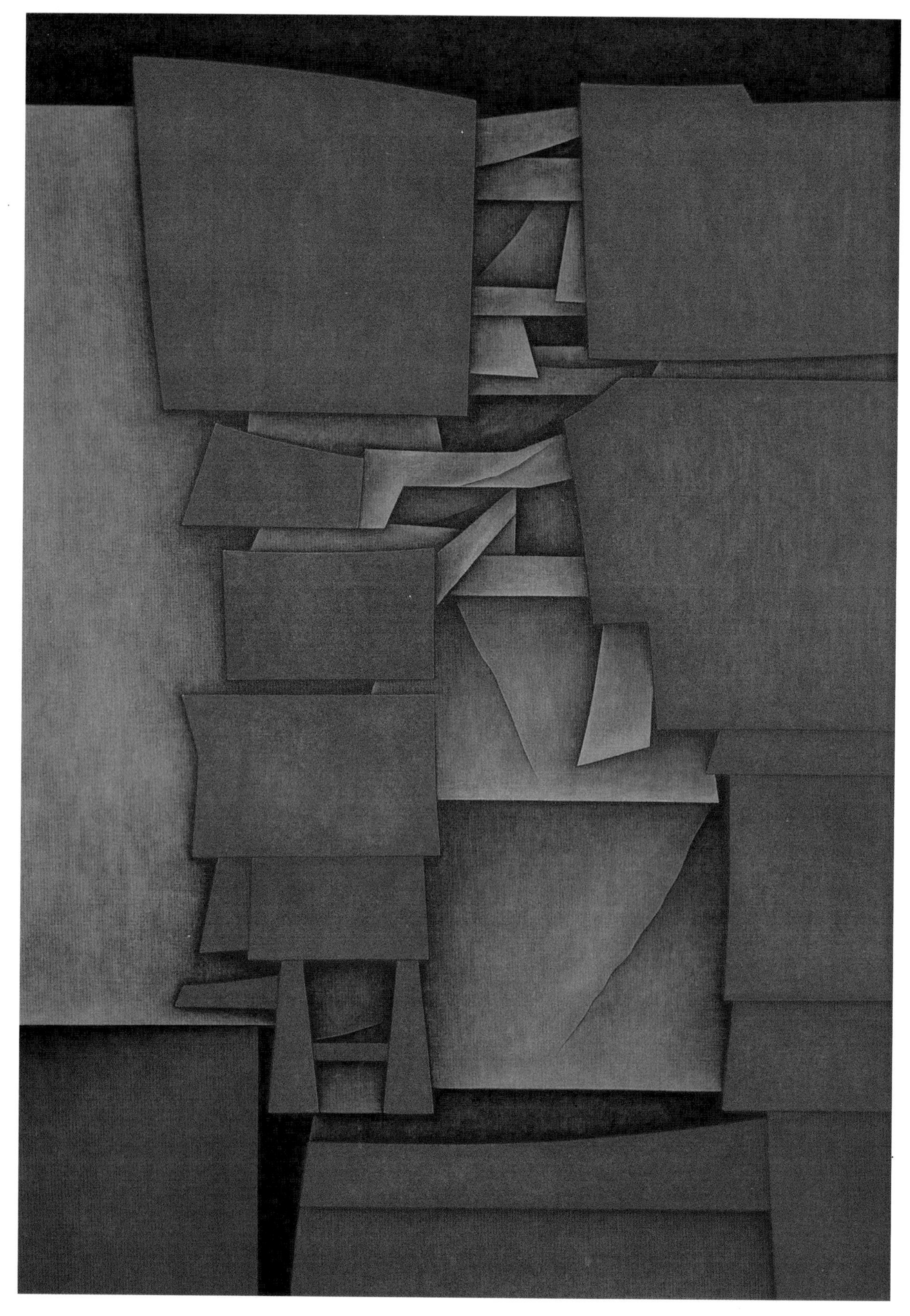

2.17 Gunther Gerzso, *Personage in Red and Blue,* 1964. Oil on fabric, 39⅜ × 28¾ in. (100.33 × 73 cm). In this painting, shapes are united by shared edges as well as similar color and textural development. Though the sense of space is shallow, it is heightened by the contrast of value. Collection Jacques and Natasha Gelman, courtesy of Centro Cultural/Arte Contemporáneo, A. C., Mexico. Photograph: Jorge Contreras Chacel.

When shapes with a common border share a similar value level or color, the dividing edge where they merge is often obscured or lost altogether—visually they become one new shape (fig. 2.18B, left). Even with decorative relationships, there is a danger with sharing edges. Two shapes seem to meet and retain their individual character when the common dividing edge is rather nondescript, because when the edge begins to suggest something recognizable, the suggested image becomes a positive shape. A specific spatial reference is created that forces the remaining shared shape to become a negative area (fig. 2.18B, right). Differences in value or texture further exacerbate the situation. M. C. Escher explored this phenomenon, using it to his advantage when he made patterns of dark ducks fly through patterns of light ducks (fig. 2.19). As the ducks fly farther away from the central part of the image, the detail becomes more and more distinct. As that same shape system is tracked backward, it looks less and less like ducks and takes on the imagery of the landscape.

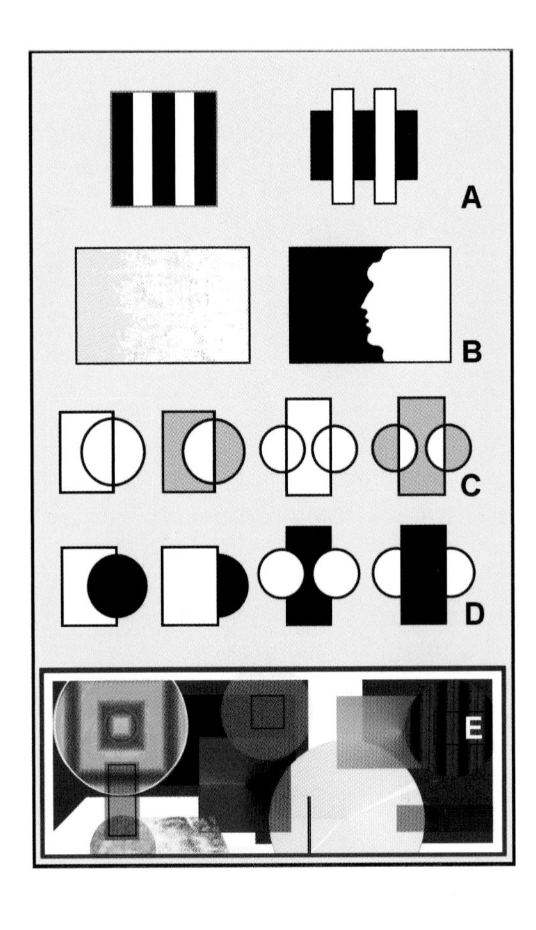

2.18 (A) Shapes, which deny and imply space, are related by shared edges. (B) Dissolved and altered spatial references involving shared edges. (C) Shapes related by overlapping edges. The new shapes, defined by value change, create little spatial reference. (D) Spatial reference created by overlapping shapes. (E) Shapes related by transparency.

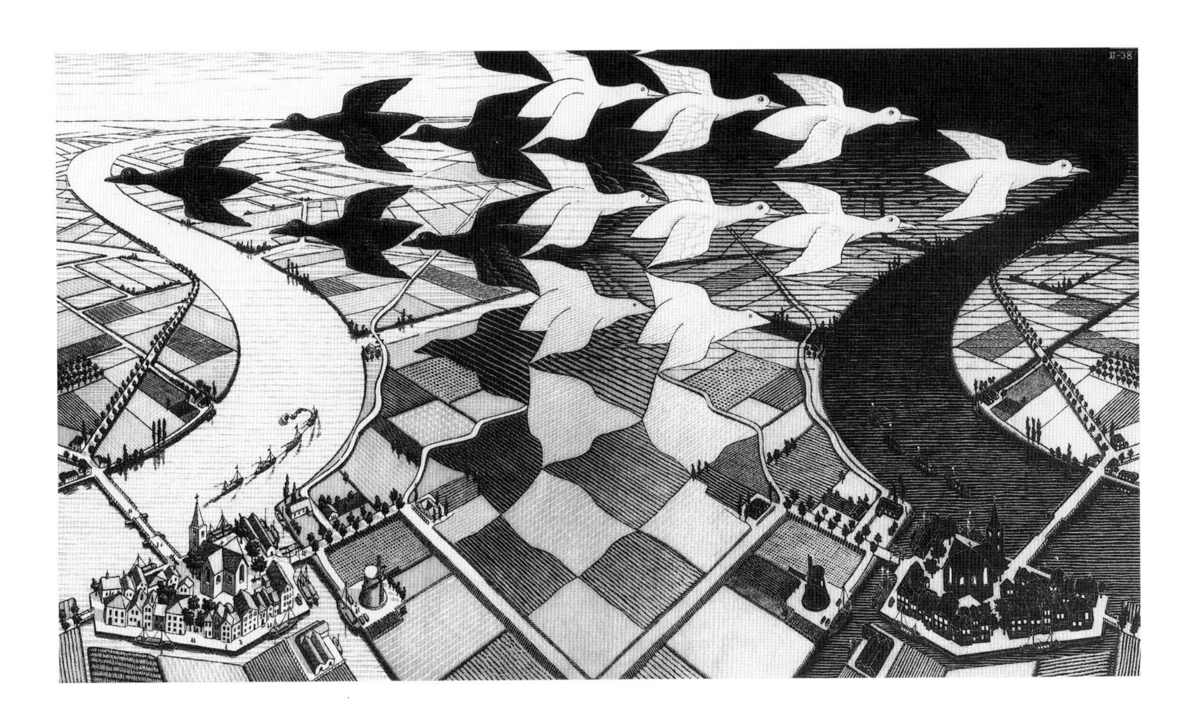

2.19 M. C. Escher, *Day and Night,* 1938. Woodcut in two colors, 15½ × 26¾ in. (39.3 × 67.9 cm). This is an example of shapes sharing mutual edges, with one image (light ducks), appearing to change into another (dark ducks). The Gemeentemuseum, The Hague.

Overlapping With overlapping, the areas involved are also drawn together by a common relationship, and the shared item is a bit more involved than a simple edge; it becomes a shared area. As long as the color, value, texture, and so on are the same or related, the overlapping of the areas tends to unite the items involved (fig. 2.18C). However, the space defined may be shallow and rather ambiguous—one time the circle is seen on top; the next time the square is seen on top. The Futurists often achieved this effect by overlapping multiple views of the same object (fig. 8.51). Unrelated objects can be harmonized in this fashion. Overlapping does not always mean limited space or cohesive relationships, because a deeper space may be caused by visual separation or difference in treatment. The object overlapped can be seen as the receding object (fig. 2.18D). Color and value choices can exaggerate or minimize the spatial effect of overlapped shapes. With a more figurative application, independent symbolic information can not only overlap but even occupy the same shared physical space. In this manner, entirely different symbols or image areas can even be brought into a plausible harmonious context. If we study Sam Haskins's photo *Apple Face,* 1973, the face is quite believably contained within the shape of the apple (fig. 2.20).

Transparency **Transparency** is another way an artist can add harmony to images that occur in the same area. When a shape or an image is seen through another, the relating visual devices that create harmony and unite those areas include the shared area itself, the layers of space they all pass through, and the surface treatment of all the images (highlights, shading, color, texture). Like simple overlapping, this technique tends to limit the visual depth that the artist may introduce and serves as another relating harmonious device (see figs. 2.18E and 8.9).

Interpenetration When several images not only share the same area but appear to pass through each other, they are brought into an harmonious relationship not only by the common location but also by the physical depth of the space in which they all appear (see fig. 8.10). Whether shallow or deep, illusionistic or stylized, the space itself pulls the various images into a visual harmony. Notice that in figure 2.21 there are two series of shapes. Some seem to plunge toward the left end and the rest toward the right end of the composi-

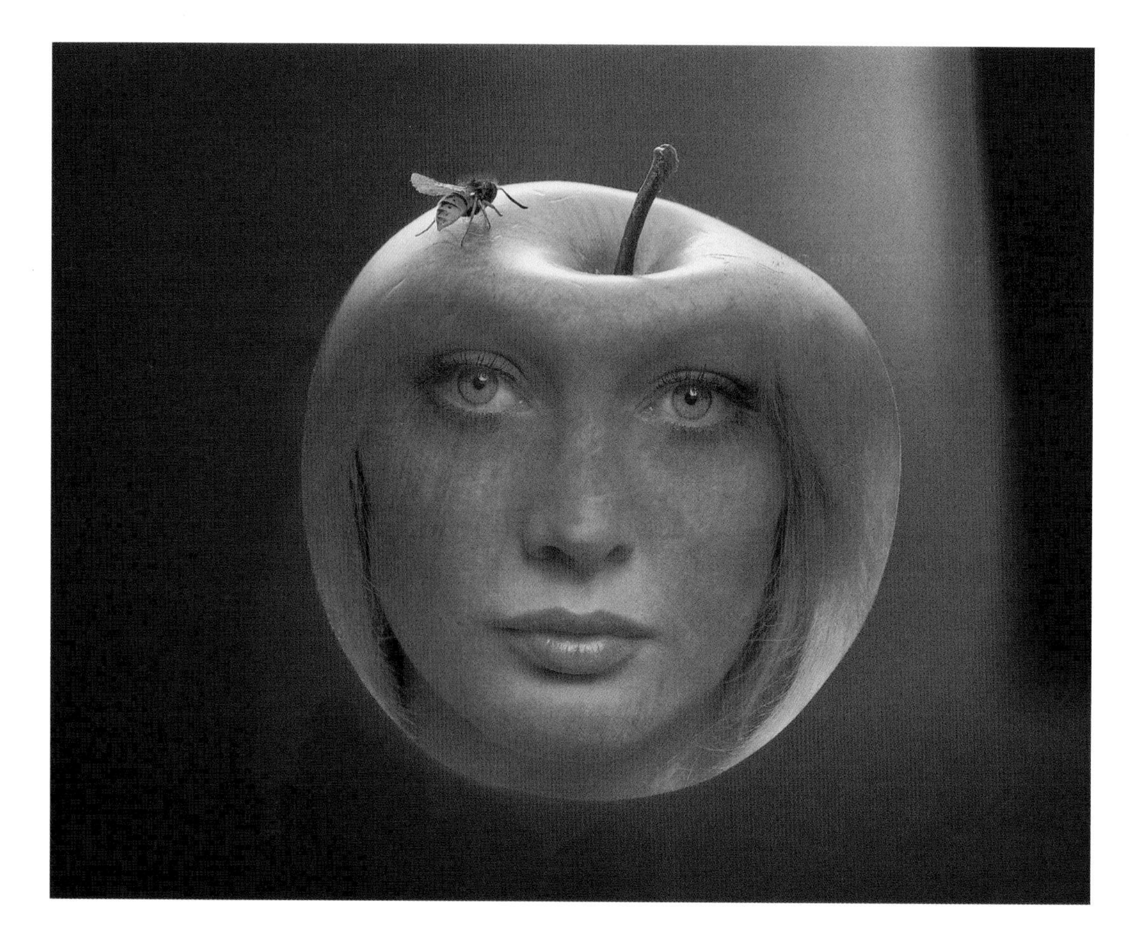

2.20 **Sam Haskins, *Apple Face,* from the book HASKINS POSTERS, 1973. Photograph.** In this image, two distinctly different naturalistic images convincingly share the same shape and space. © Sam Haskins Partnership. (Website URL: www.haskins.com)

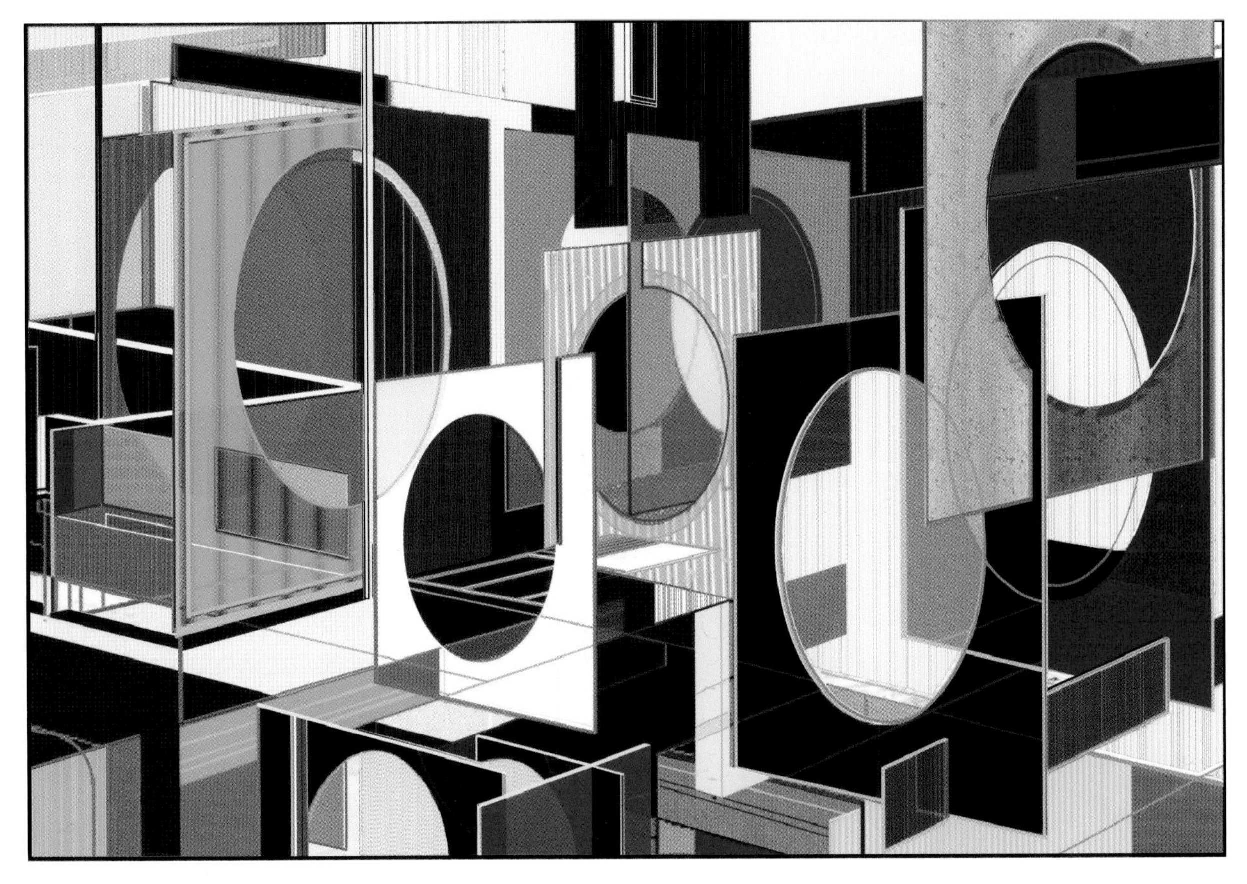

2.21 Clouret Bouchel, *Passing Through,* 2001. Digital imagery, 7 × 10½ in. (17.8 × 26.7 cm). This is an example of interpenetration, with lines, shapes, and planes passing through one another. Courtesy of the artist.

tion. Even though the two areas are in different colors, the sharing of the internal space created by **interpenetration** of shapes helps unify this work.

Extensions (implied and subjective edges, lines, or shapes) Like the invisible lines of a surveyor that map out and organize the cities, roads, and contours of the land, the extended edges in a composition help the artist organize and bring all parts of that structure into an harmonious relationship. While we have seen harmony achieved by concepts where there are jointly shared edges, shared areas of overlapping shapes, similar transparency of surface, or even the relating of forms passing through each other, these inherently relate items that are relatively close to each other. However, the concept of extensions—implied edges, lines, or shapes—provides the artist with another system of visual alignment. By simply extending the edge of a shape across the composition, the artist establishes new objects, images, or shapes in locations some distance away. Placing new shapes along the implied extended edge links distant shapes, thereby harmonizing the areas. Artists often use such placement to integrate an entire composition and create space by implied tension.

Extensions reveal "hidden" relationships. They harmonize by relating directional forces, creating movement, and repeating predictable intervals between units. The directional impulse of these invisible, implied extensions suggests—subconciously sometimes—an expectation that something will be discovered in a new area and pull the eye toward this new location. These impulses integrate a work as they wind through the composition along contours of information (figs. 2.22A, B).

As an element in its own right, line draws all sectors of an arrangement together (see figs. 3.9 and 3.10). This line may be clear and dominant, or less emphasized, fading away to a dissolved contour (see figs. 5.20 and 5.21). As strong indicators of direction, new lines introduced anywhere along the extension of a first line influence the original and new lines by implied direction. Invisible linear extensions (subjective lines) are exceedingly strong devices for relating compositional areas, and designers usually rely on them in the form of grid systems for the layout and organization of blocks of type, logos, and graphic information (fig. 2.23).

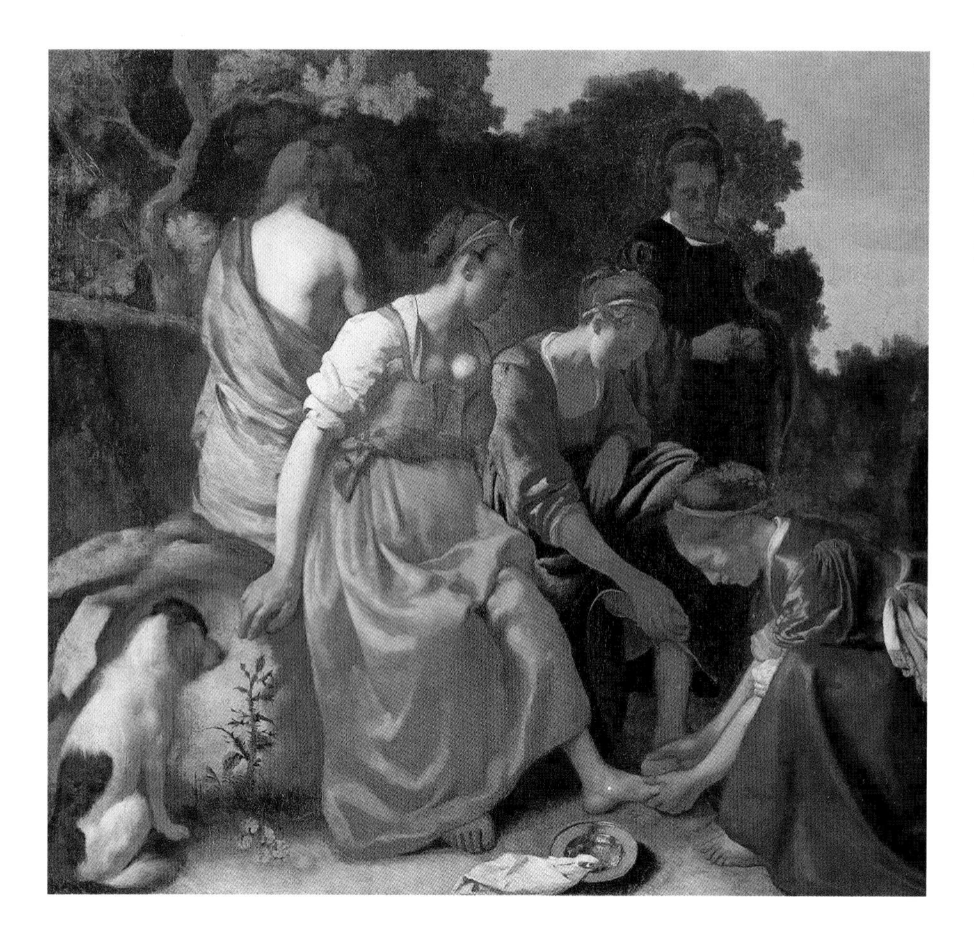

2.22A Johannes Vermeer, *Diana and the Nymphs*, c. 1655–56. Oil on canvas, 33½ × 41 in. (97.8 × 104.6 cm). Here, Vermeer uses extended edges to interlock the images, find the location for new forms, relate shapes, and create directional movement across the painting. Royal Cabinet of Paintings, Mauritshuis. The Hague, Netherlands, Scala/Art Resource.

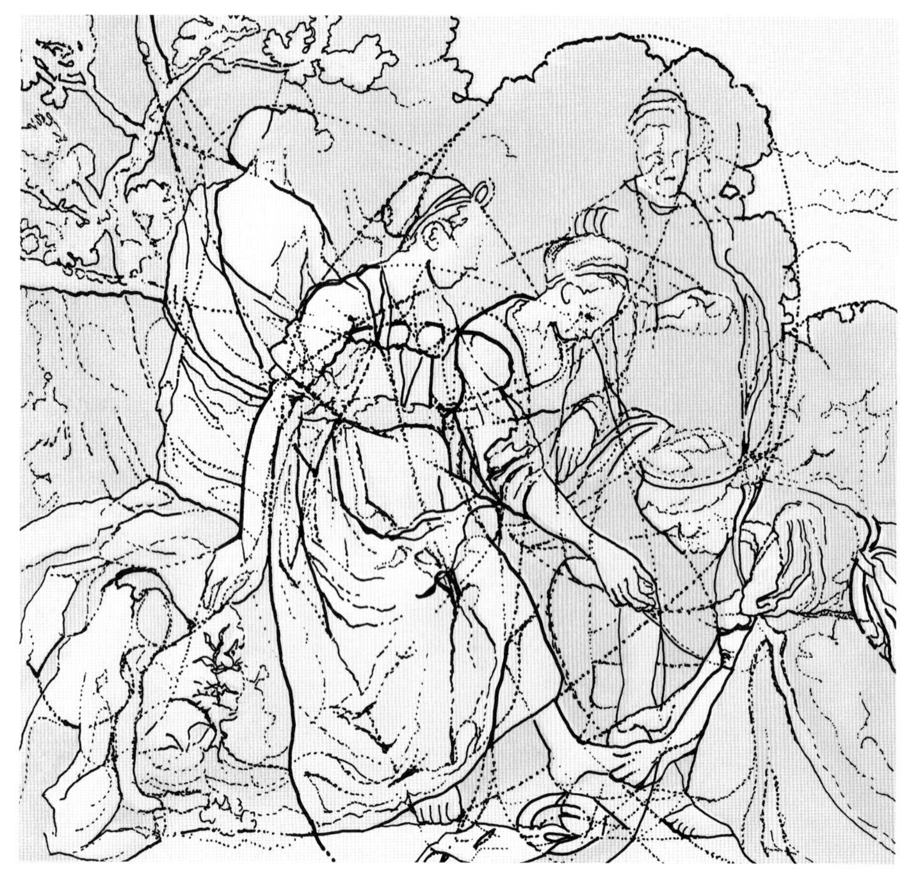

2.22B This overlay shows some of the extended edges with solid lines of various weights and their extensions by dots and dashes. Notice how the implied direction is often interrupted or disguised by subtle changes.

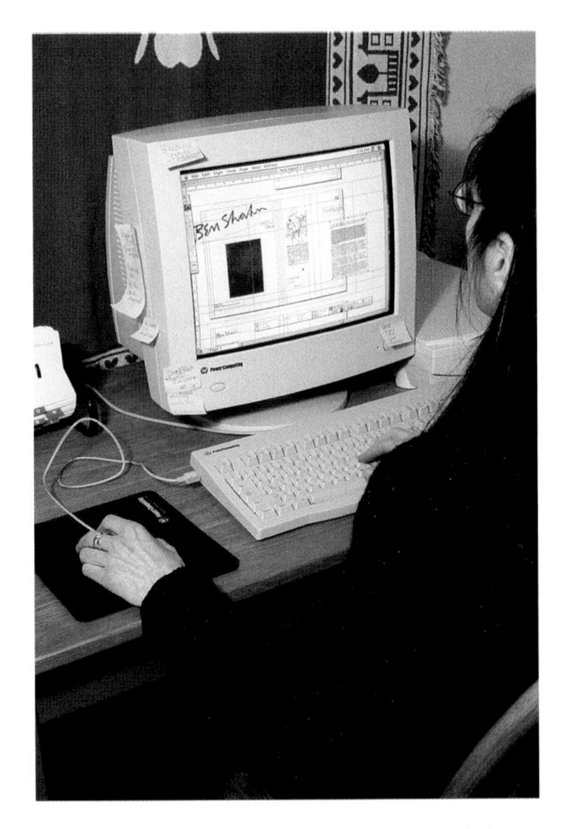

2.23 Designers often use a grid system to help with the layout and organization of text and visual information. The system can be applied to one image or made to relate a whole corporate campaign. © Erv Schowengerdt.

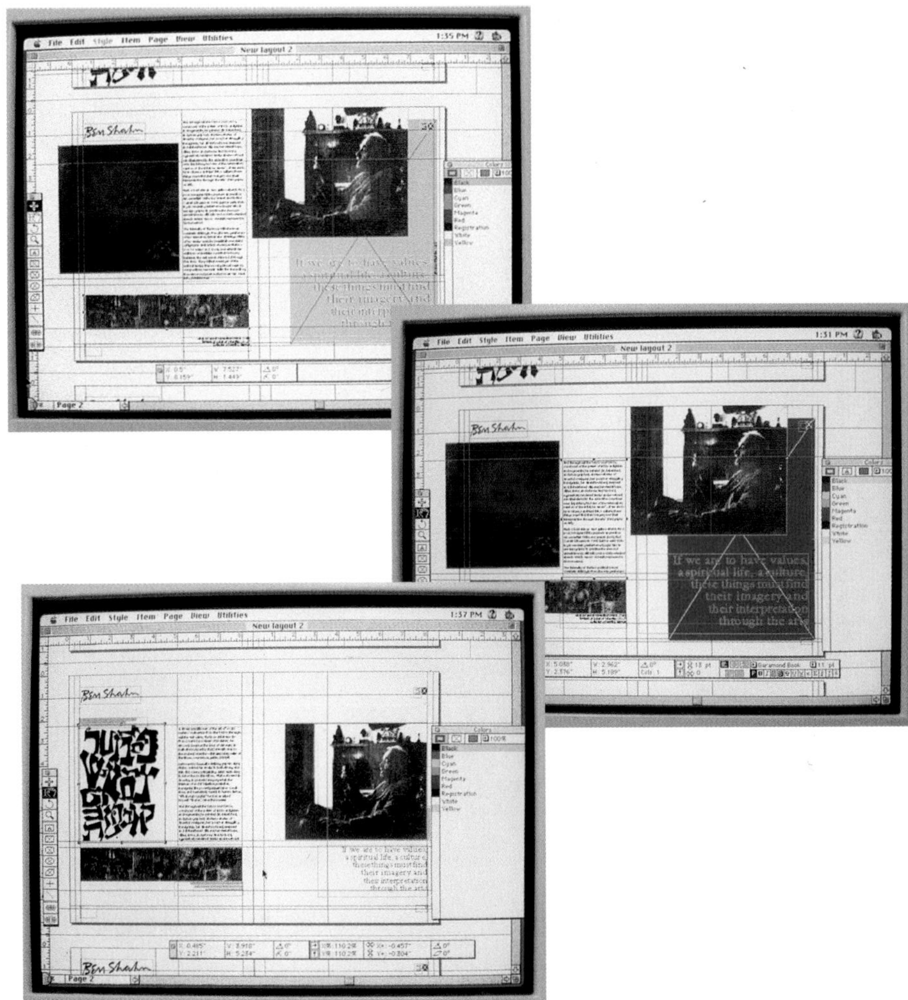

Like line, shape can create a strong directional movement and act as an organizational tool, creating cohesive (harmonious) relationships with other shapes. Shape can create directional force or visual movement in two ways: (1) when the shape points in a general direction (for example, a long triangle points in the direction of the narrow end), it directs the viewer across the composition; and (2) when the outside edges of that pointing shape can be extended by hidden lines, they will direct the viewer in two other directions. These implied or subjective edge extensions may be used to locate new shapes or objects all across the composition that can be harmonized by the same directional force. Irregular shapes can also be brought into harmonious relationship and into group patterns (closure) much more quickly by moving them around until their invisible extended edges intersect or align. A grouping of shapes in one part of the composition can create tension or subconscious closure with other groupings or individual shapes some distance away. The use of subjective edges allows movement to be controlled and directed anywhere, rotating volumes in space and returning the viewer to the picture plane (see the implied circle and serpentine movement in the center portion of figure 2.15).

While many concepts used to create harmony do tend to limit the depth of pictorial space, the unifying concepts of extension may be applied equally well to plastic space, decorative space development, and any degree of abstraction. The implied lines may cross over areas enclosed by other images and shapes as well as across open areas of color and texture. Because extensions are such an important tool of organization, great care must be taken that their use does not become too obvious. Therefore, artists delight in hiding directional forces by interrupting them with countermovements, accents, and subtle misalignments.

Variety (2)

Variety is the counterweight to harmony, the other side of organization essential to unity. While an artist might bring a work together with harmony,

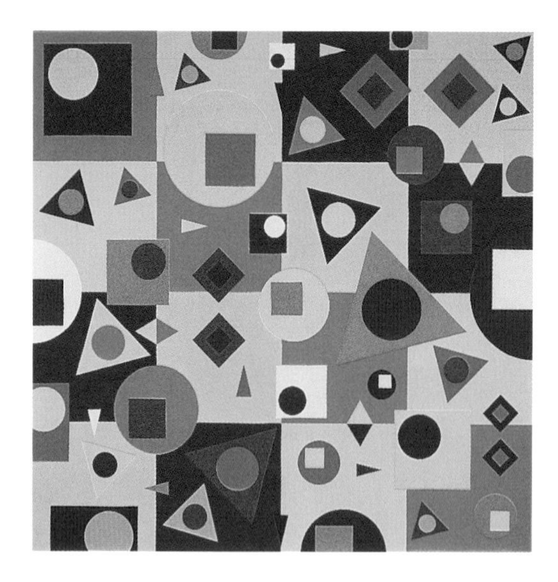

2.24 Franklin Jonas, *Geostructure 1*, 1998. Acrylic on linen, 200 × 200 cm. The balance between harmony and variety can be tipped to favor either principle or order depending on the artist's intention. Franklin Jonas pushes his balance strongly in the direction of variety. In this painting, Jonas varies the shape size, direction, and color with a personal vigor. He arouses an initial curiosity in his viewer that, after greater reflection, provides enduring vitality. Courtesy of the artist. Photo by Kerry Bowman.

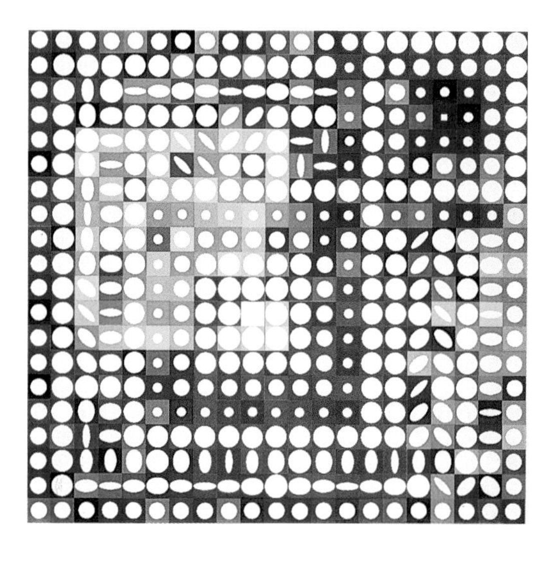

2.25 Victor Vasarely, *Orion*, 1956–62. Paper on paper mounted on wood, 6 ft 10½ in. × 6 ft 6¾ in. (2.09 × 2 m). While harmony is provided through the recurring use of circles, the artist achieves interest through the variety of the same shapes: Some are tipped; some are larger or smaller than the norm; and some are emphasized by contrast with their backgrounds. Hirshhorn Museum and Sculpture Garden, Smithsonian Institution, Washington, D.C. Gift of Joseph H. Hirshhorn, 1966. Photograph by Lee Stalsworth. © 2001 Artists Rights Society (ARS), New York/ADAGP, Paris.

it is variety that imparts individuality. Variety arouses the viewers' curiosity and holds their attention. If an artist achieves complete equality of visual forces, the work will be balanced, but it may also be static, lifeless, and unemotional. Visually, boredom indicates an overly harmonious composition. By adding variation to the visual forces, the artist introduces essential ingredients (such as diversion or change) for sustaining attention.

Visual interest, then, results directly from adding variety to the pictorial components. Variety causes visual separation—a pulling apart of related elements or images, differentiating and disassociating the components. This separation is achieved by the use of contrast and elaboration.

Contrast

Contrast occurs when the elements are repeated in a way that makes them appear unrelated—a few wide lines in an area of narrow ones. Dissimilarities are more exaggerated by contrast when opposing elements and/or their parts are juxtaposed or placed in proximity, such as red marks against green or extreme dark against extreme light. As these contrasts are heightened, the areas involved become less harmonious but more visually exciting (fig. 2.24). It is through the introduction of increasing contrasts that an area, image, or shape is made to become dominant.

Elaboration

Elaboration is another way to introduce variety and dissimilarity to areas that lack visual interest. Elaboration adds detail and embellishment. The enhancement of the surface with subtle or contradictory information attracts attention. Though elaboration and contrast may sound like repetition, the intent is not to increase relatedness but, quite the opposite, to gradually introduce visual difference or opposition. Notice how M. C. Escher added more and more detail to the duck shapes as they move away from the center, making them stand apart from the opposite-colored area, which is slowly becoming background (see fig. 2.19). Artists rework areas persistently to elaborate their expression until a satisfactory resolution is reached. Surfaces enriched by extensive changes impart the artist's concept with dramatic strength and purposeful meaning.

Picture surfaces become more exciting as variations are introduced. In music, the higher the pitch, the greater the number of vibrations. Similarly, in art, as contrasts are introduced, the "pitch," or excitement is increased; reduction in contrast lowers the "vibration." The frequency of contrasts in an artwork might also be compared to contrasts of volume in a musical composition. In art, contrasts are necessary to give some parts greater emphasis than the rest. However, if contrast is overused, the excessive variety causes a feeling of visual chaos. But something just short of that point can be quite exciting!

One of the most difficult concepts to grasp is that of applying harmony and variety at the same time and by using the same element. Consider the use of shape. In *Orion*, Victor Vasarely uses circles as a unifying device to create a harmonious

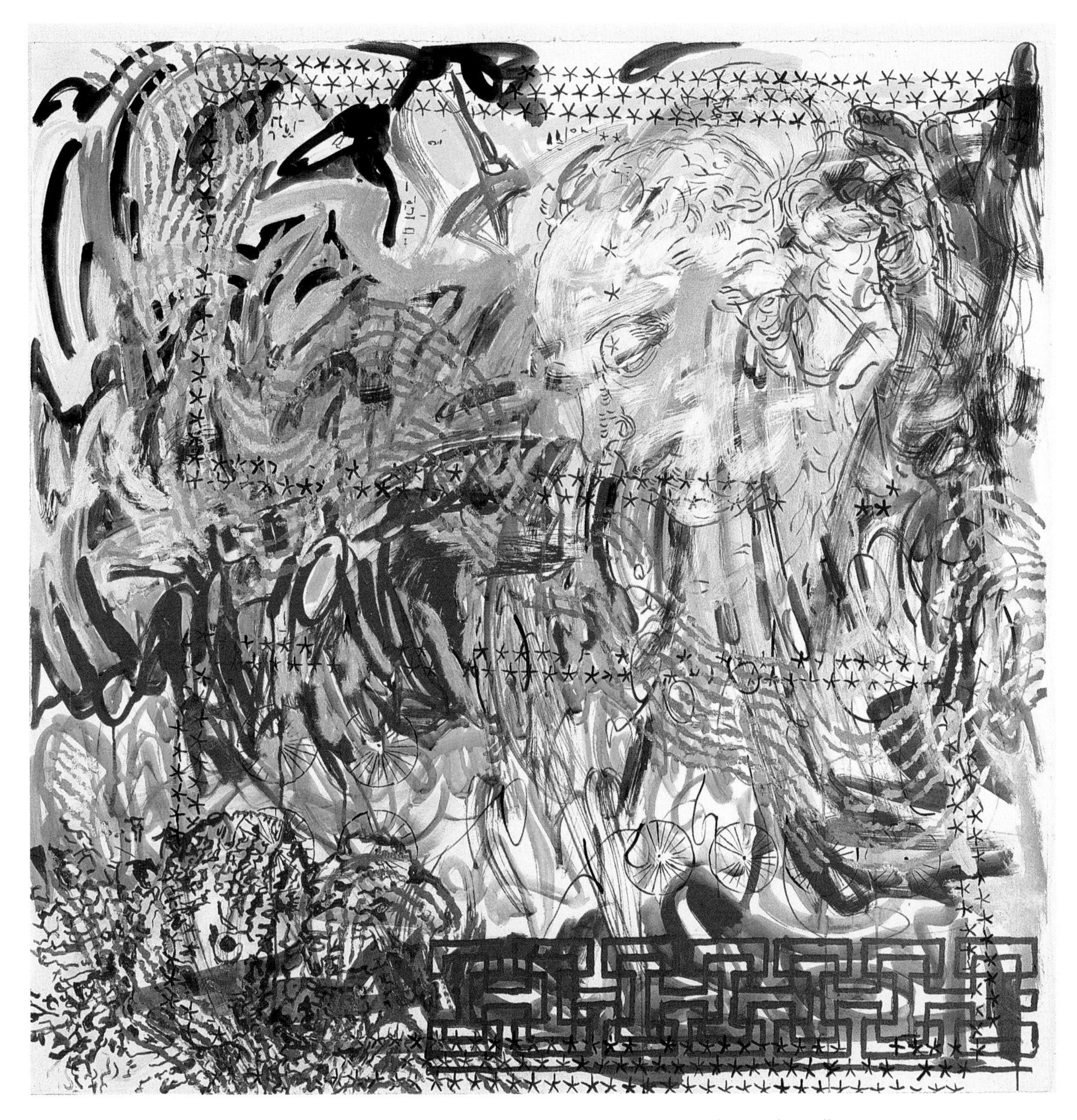

2.26 Nancy Graves, *Perfect Syntax of Stone and Air,* 1990. Watercolor, gouache, and acrylic on paper, 48½ × 48⅜ in. (123.2 × 122.9 cm). So many colored brush strokes and black linear symbols are used that some degree of harmony is sure to exist, but variety is by far the dominant theme because of the array of colors and patterns. Gerald G. Peters Gallery. © 1998 Nancy Graves Foundation/licensed by VAGA, New York, NY.

relationship (fig. 2.25). However, to avoid monotony, the artist seeks all the different ways that circles can be introduced by changing their size, point of view, and angle. Thus, he introduces variety by way of circular shapes, the very element used to create harmony. The same thing could be done with any of the elements. Red, for example, could be used to make a series of shapes relate, providing harmony. Changing the red's character, by making it lighter or darker or changing its brilliance or intensity, could vary the design while adding interest. Again, variety and harmony are developed by the thoughtful use of the same basic component.

Harmonious means seem necessary to hold contrasts together. However, the ratio of shared similarities to shared differences does not have to be equal; harmony might outweigh variety, or variety might outweigh harmony (figs. 2.25 and 2.26). Whatever ratio of harmony and variety that arises, it will influence the other principles of organization. A sensitive use of harmony and variety will help to create space and will have a bearing on the development of balance, movement, proportions, dominance, and economy.

Balance (3)

We deal with balance on a daily basis. Gravity is universal and we feel it intuitively. Walking, standing on one leg, or tipping back in a chair, all reveal our need for balance. When we are off balance, we have a strong fear that we will fall over, that gravity will pull us down. We spend our lives under gravity's influence. Similarly, in art we have strong expectations about gravitational forces. Most artworks are viewed in a vertical orientation—in terms of top, sides, and bottom. Gravity could then affect the visual components. For example, a ball placed high in the pictorial field produces a sense of tension between the ball and the baseline of the picture plane. There is the expectation that gravity will cause that ball to drop—a tension is created (fig. 2.27A). A ball placed low or on the baseline provides a sense of peace or resolution, gravity having acted on the ball (fig. 2.27B). Our comprehension of a particular image includes our estimate of its mass and weight, which affect the resulting balance in a composition. For example, if the ball in figure 2.27A becomes a hot-air balloon, a large negative area under that shape will tend to support or balance it—we may even have the sensation of the balloon lifting up from that area (fig. 2.27C). If the image becomes a lower-positioned bowling ball, its symbolic weight seems to make the composition bottom-heavy—gravity's force seems to be pulling the bowling ball down to a still position on the lane at the picture's bottom (fig. 2.27D). What we know of the weight of actual objects (here a ball, a balloon, and a bowling ball) influences how we judge balance on a picture surface. If we were to replace the objects with nonobjective entities, their psychological weight would be created by their shape, value, and color, and our view of their balance again would change. Whether objective or nonobjective components are used, the influence of psychological weight/balance and its compositional adjustment are endless.

Artists often offset their pictorial works with a mat—an area between the picture's edge and a picture frame (structured of wood, metal, and so on). Even here, psychological factors can affect the visual weight and balance. If a mat with two-inch top, sides, and bottom were used, the bottom would have the illusion of being pinched or smaller than the other sides. This is an optical illusion that may make the artwork appear to be unstable or rising on the wall. To compensate, the bottom measurements are generally made wider than the top width so that the mats seem stabilized or balanced.

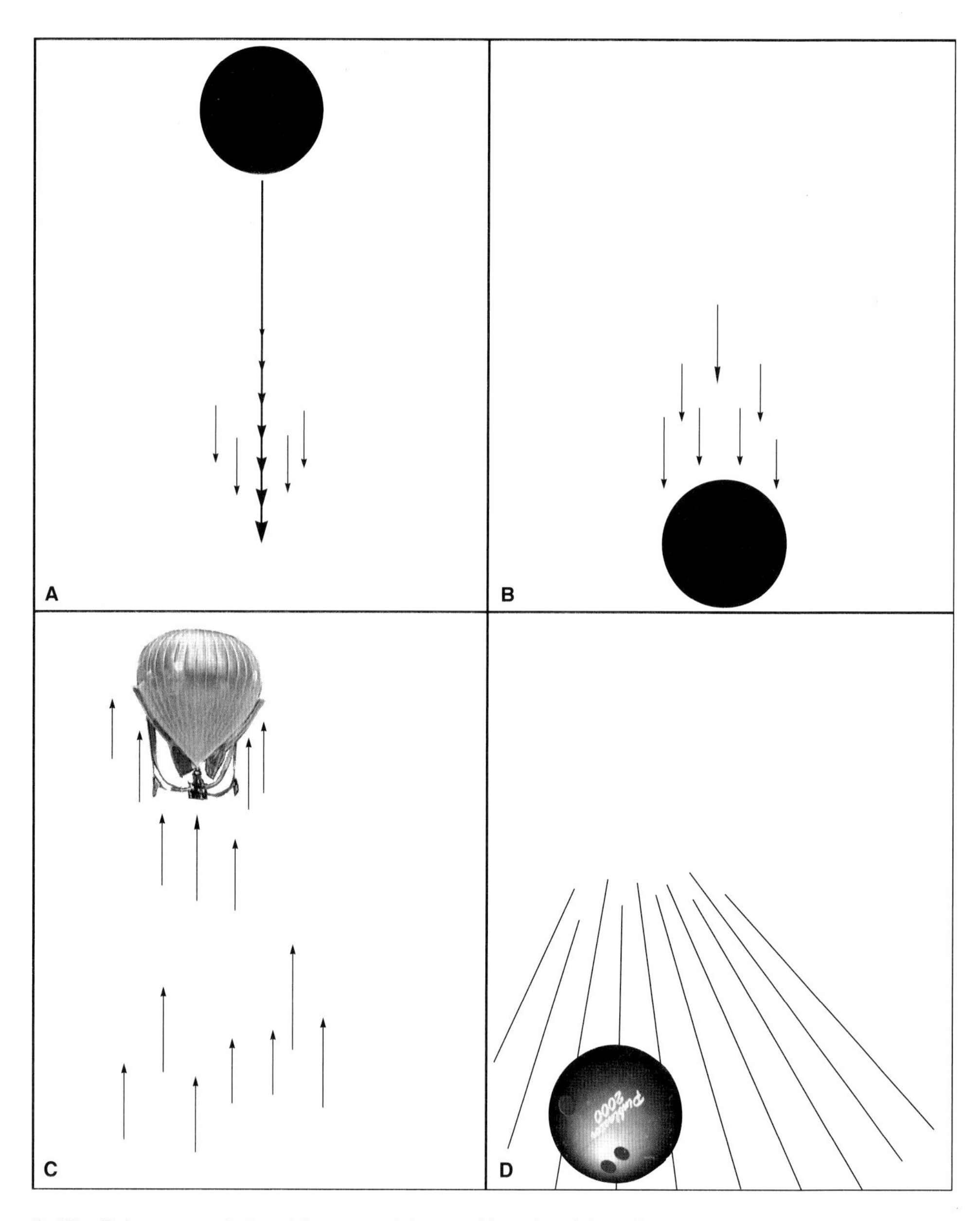

2.27 Balance: gravitational forces and the resulting pictorial tensions.

Balance is so fundamental to unity that it is impossible to consider the principles of organization without it. At the simplest level, balance implies the gravitational equilibrium of a single mark on a picture plane. Try placing a single colored shape on a white surface anywhere *but* in the center. The final location will involve a balance between the object and the amount of open space around it. Balance can also refer to the gravitational equilibrium of pairs or groups of units (such as lines or shapes) that are arranged on either side of a central axis. Such balancing can be illustrated with representations of weighing scales that have beams poised on centering points (fig. 2.28). When we apply this concept to art, balance does not result from the actual physical weighing process, but from the visual judgment of the observer, based on his or her past experience and intuitive grasp of the principles of physics.

Figure 2.28 provides examples of three types of balancing scales. These illustrate ways of imagining pictorial and/or three-dimensional balance. In the first two rows of scales, the forces are balanced horizontally, left and right, with respect to the supporting balance beam. The scale shows a line of one physical dimension balancing or counterbalancing a line with equal physical characteristics. Such balance can also exist between lines, shapes, and values that have been modified. A second type of weighing scale, in which forces are balanced vertically, is also illustrated in figure 2.28. The third weighing device shown in the figure points out not only horizontal and vertical balance, but also the balance of forces distributed around a center point. This is a **radial** weighing scale.

In picture making, balance refers to the optical equilibrium felt among all parts of the work. The artist balances forces horizontally, vertically, and diagonally in all directions and positions (fig. 2.29). Several factors, when combined with the elements, contribute to balance

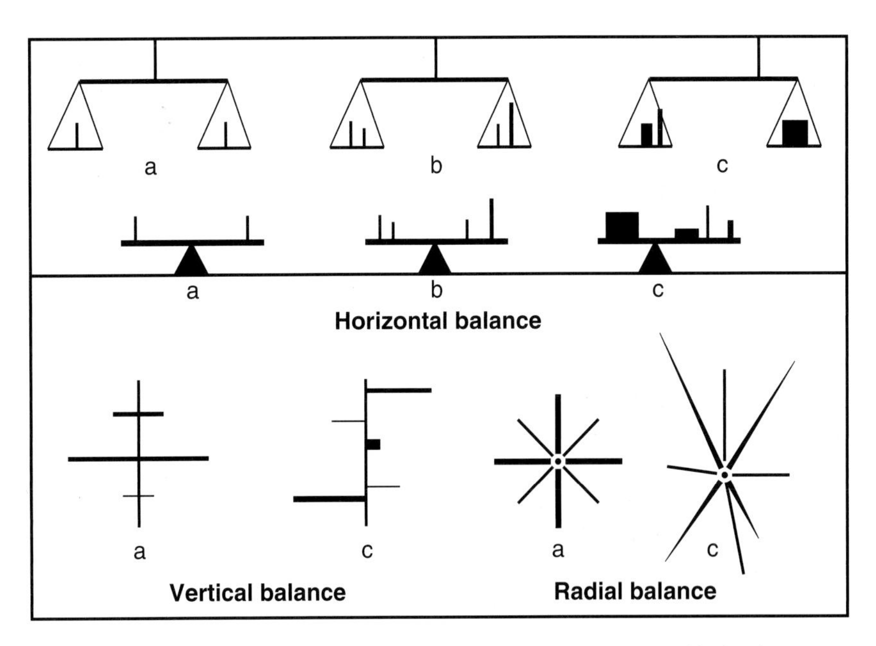

2.28 Using simple elements, these diagrams illustrate three types of balancing studies: horizontal, vertical, and radial. Also illustrated are (a) symmetry, (b) approximate (near) symmetry, and (c) asymmetry (see pages 52–56).

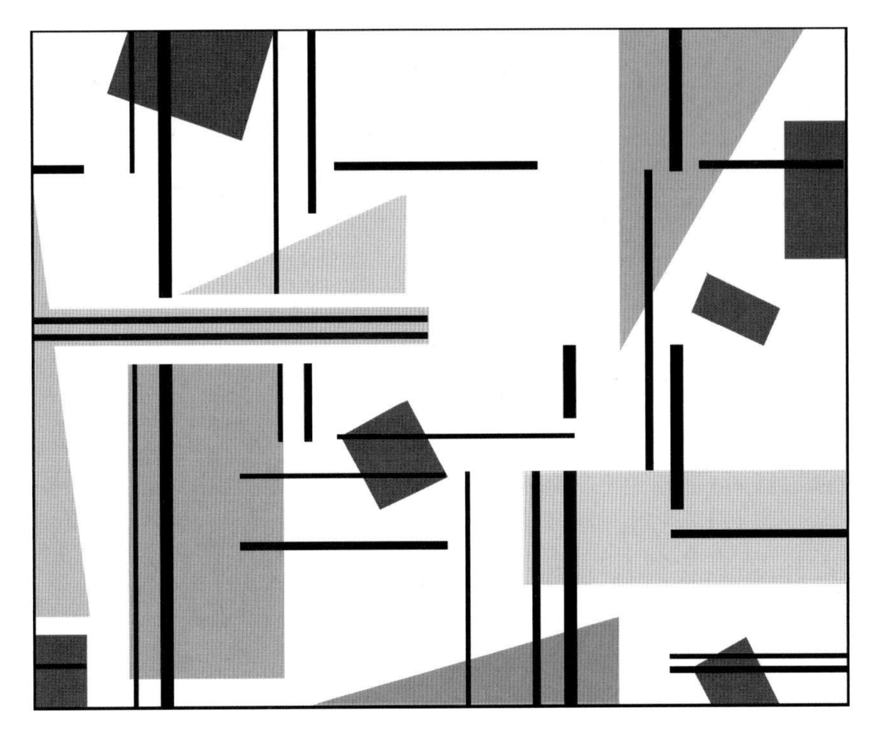

2.29 Here, all the chief forms of balance—horizontal, vertical, and diagonal—are combined. For additional information see the CD-ROM.

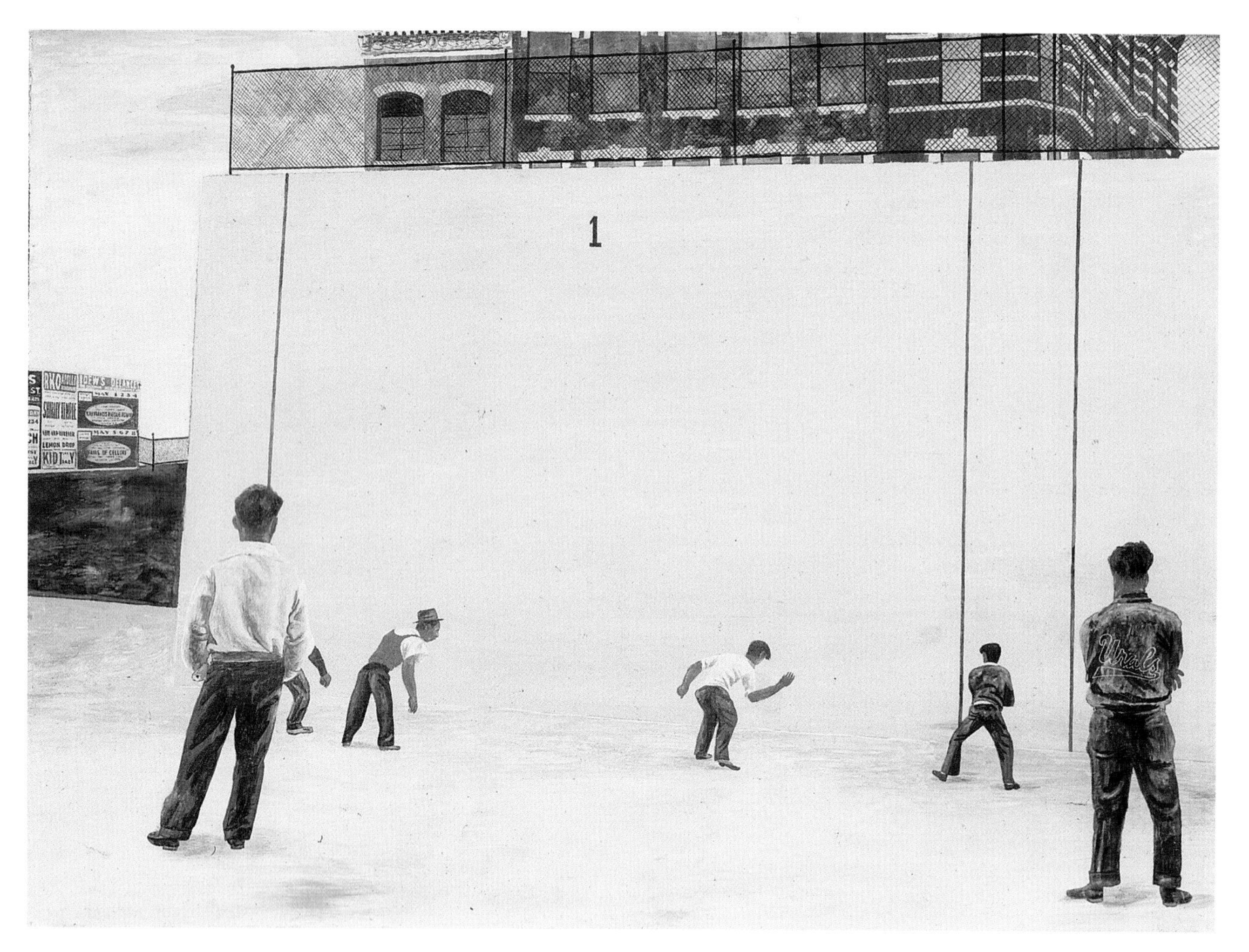

2.30 **Ben Shahn, *Handball,* 1939. Tempera on paper over composition board, 22¾ × 31¼ in. (57.8 × 79.4 cm).** Collectively, the figures and buildings may be seen as representative forces that the artist sets in a supporting, controlled balance and tension. The Museum of Modern Art, New York, Abby Aldrich Rockefeller Fund. Photo © 1998 Museum of Modern Art. © Estate of Ben Shahn/Licensed by VAGA, New York, NY.

in a work of art. These factors or variables are position or placement, size, proportion, character, and direction of the elements. Of these factors, position plays the lead role. If two shapes of equal physical qualities are placed near the left side of a picture frame, the work will appear out of balance with the right side. Such shapes should be positioned to contribute to the total balance of all the picture parts involved. Similarly, the other factors can put a pictorial arrangement in or out of balance according to their use.

As the eye travels over the picture surface, it pauses momentarily at the significant picture parts—areas of increased contrast of size, color, texture, and so on. These points of interest represent moving and directional forces that counterbalance one another and may be termed *moments of force.* In seeking balance, the artist should recognize that the varied elements create the moments of force, and that their discriminating placement will result in controlled tension. In the painting *Handball,* Ben Shahn creates tension between the two figures in the foreground and the numeral 1 at the top of the wall (fig. 2.30). These forces together support one another. The darker values of the building above the large wall are counterbalanced by those of the building at left and of the figures in the lower portion of the painting.

Symmetrical balance

A symmetrical image displays a portion on one side of the format that is repeated on the other side. It is a mirror view, the simplest form of artistic balance (fig. 2.31). If we have two people of equal weight on a centered teeter-totter equidistanced from each other, symmetrical balance is achieved. If those same persons had identical shapes, *pure* **symmetry** would be present. In an artwork, of course, the teetering persons could be replaced by any images.

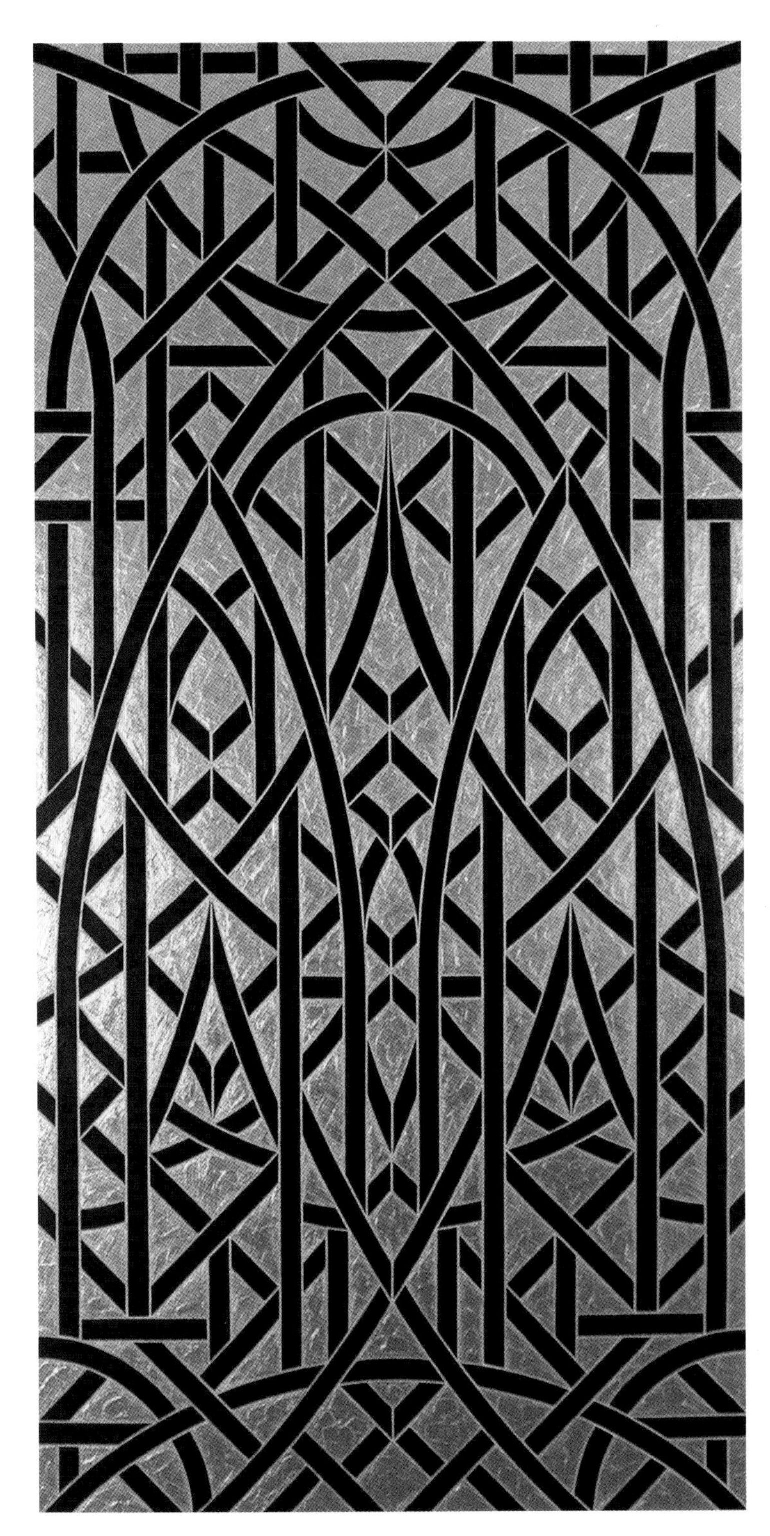

2.31 Valerie Jaudon, *Big Springs,* 1980. Gold leaf and oil on canvas, 96 × 48 in. (243.8 × 121.9 cm). The repetitious nature of this symmetrical work is counterbalanced and relieved by the active interlacing linear pattern. The composition is divided equally on either side of a subtle vertical axis.

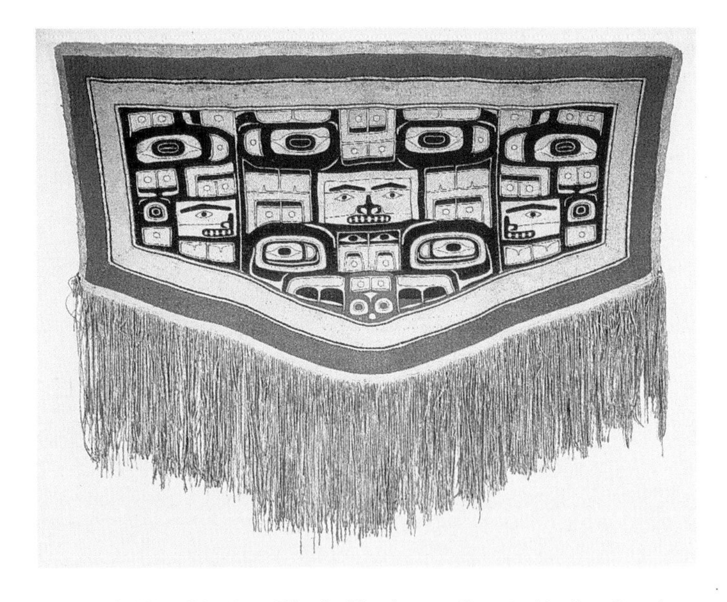

2.32 Chilkat Blanket, Tlingit, Northwest Coast, Alaska. Dyed wool and cedar bark fibers, 69 in. (175.2 cm). A formal, symmetrical product that relies on shape, size, and arresting imagery. The frontality of the center section draws the spectator into the composition. Adolph Gottlieb Collection, Brooklyn Museum.

Symmetrical works can be confrontational; they can stare directly at us in an intimidating manner. This frontality captures our attention, but its hold on us is usually short-lived because of the static quality of the composition. However, secondary features may tend to alleviate this somewhat. Because of the nature of symmetry, unity can be readily achieved, but the artist is challenged to maintain our interest with details (fig. 2.32; see also fig. 4.29).

Approximate symmetrical balance

The potentially boring qualities of symmetry can be reduced by deviations from its repetitive nature. Balance is still the goal, and the solution is similar, but the artistic components, instead of being identical, are different; they are, however, still positioned in the same manner. The apparent weights of the components must still balance out. The differences add variety, thereby producing more interest, but at the loss of some harmony. The image, though, is still fairly static. **Approximate symmetry** requires more sensitivity from the artist regarding the various weights of the components. Nevertheless, the monotony of pure symmetry is somewhat relieved (figs. 2.33 and 2.34).

Radial balance

Another type of arrangement, called radial balance, can create true or approximate symmetry. In radial balance, forces are distributed around a central point. The rotation of these forces results in a visual circulation, adding a new dimension to what might otherwise be a static, symmetrical balance. Pure radial balance opposes identical forces, but interesting varieties can be achieved by modifying the spaces, numbers, and directions of the forces (figs. 2.35 and 2.36; see also fig. 10.62). In a modified form, the principle of repetition is still stressed so that its unifying effect can be utilized. Radial balance is widely used in the applied arts. For instance, jewelers often use radial patterns for stone settings on rings, pins, necklaces, and brooches. Architects

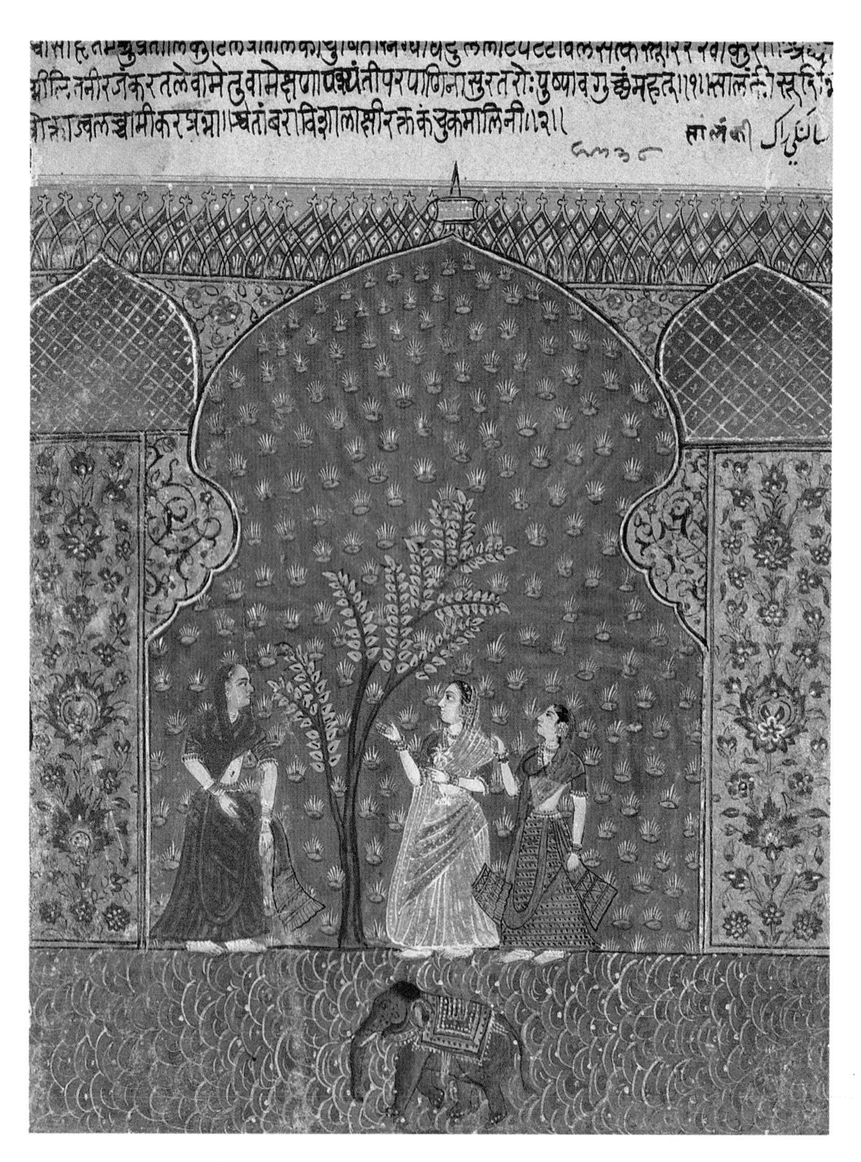

2.33 Ragamala, *Salangi Raga* (*Three Females under a Tree*), c. 1580–90. Indian (Deccan, probably Ahmadnagar). Colors and gilt on paper, 10$\frac{15}{16}$ × 8$\frac{3}{4}$ in. (27.79 × 22.23 cm). This image has approximate symmetry. While the format is symmetrical, the central image is rendered asymmetrical by modifying the positions of the trees, figures, and elephant. The vertical axis is still retained. The Metropolitan Museum of Art, Rogers Fund, 1972. (1972.285.1) Photograph © 1978 The Metropolitan Museum of Art.

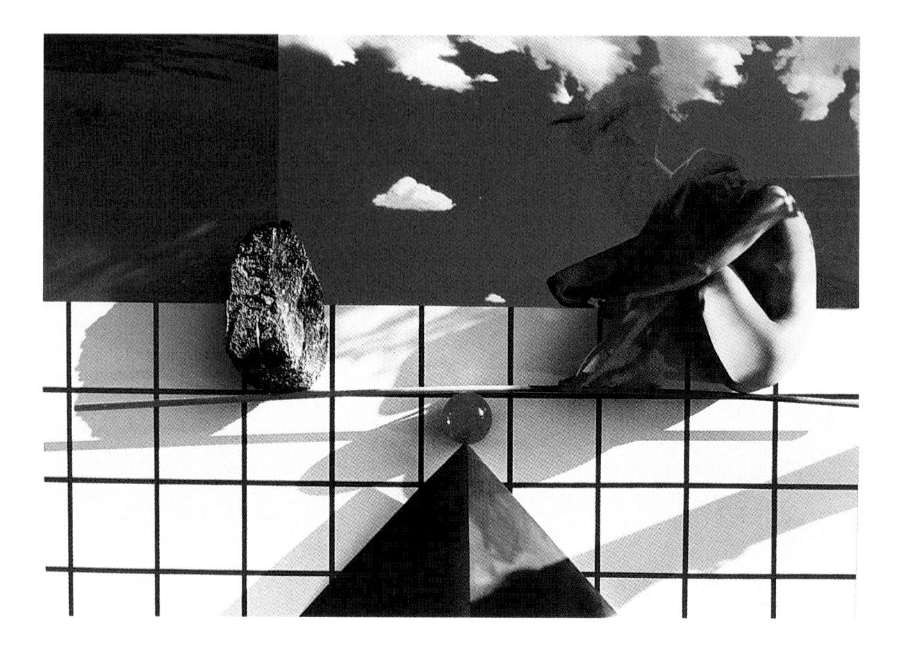

2.34 Masoud Yasami, *Balancing Act with Stone II*, 1992. Edition of 50, Ilfochrome, 3 ft 4 in. × 5 ft (1.02 × 1.52 m). Approximate symmetry could be said to be the subject as well as the form of this composition. Courtesy of Masoud Yasami (American, 1949–).

feature radial balance in quatrefoils and rose windows, where the panes of glass are arranged radially like petals of flowers. Plates and vessels of all kinds evolve on the potter's wheel in a radial manner, frequently giving evidence of this genesis. In two-dimensional work, the visual material producing the radial effect can be either nonobjective or figurative.

Asymmetrical (occult) balance

Balance created through **asymmetry** achieves the visual control of contrasts through a felt equilibrium between parts of a picture. For example, felt balance might be achieved between a small area of strong color and a large empty space. Particular parts can contrast, provided that they contribute to the allover balance of the total picture. There are no rules for achieving asymmetrical balance; there is no center point and no dividing axis. If, however, the artist can establish the opposing forces and their tensions so that they balance each other within a total concept, the result will be

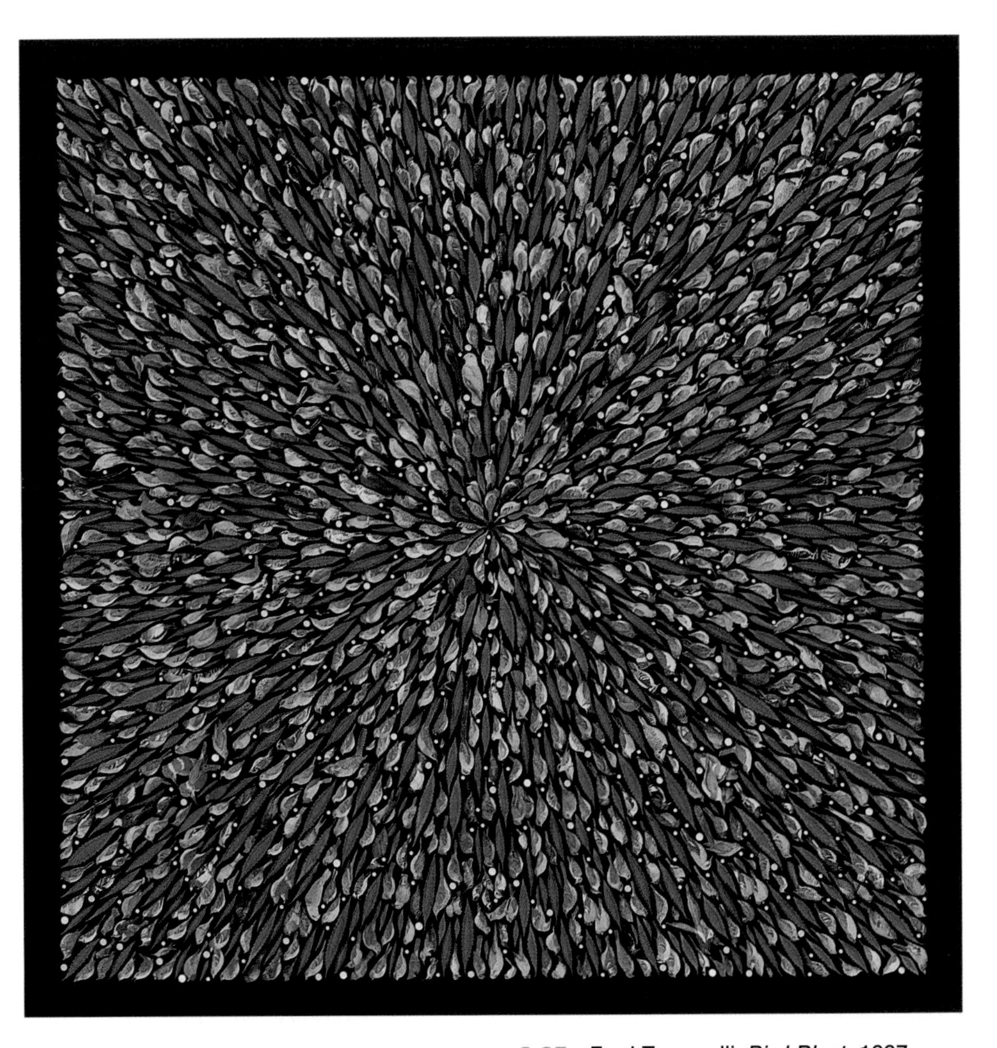

2.35 Fred Tomaselli, *Bird Blast,* 1997. Pills, hemp leaves, photocollage, acrylic, resin on wood panel, 60 × 60 in. (152.4 × 152.4 cm). With radial balance, there is frequently a divergence from some (usually central) source. Here, too, the linear development of the red leaves and the birds seems to explode from the center of the composition. Gift of Douglas S. Cramer. The Museum of Modern Art, New York, NY. U.S.A. Digital image © The Museum of Modern Art/Licensed by SCALA/Art Resource, NY.

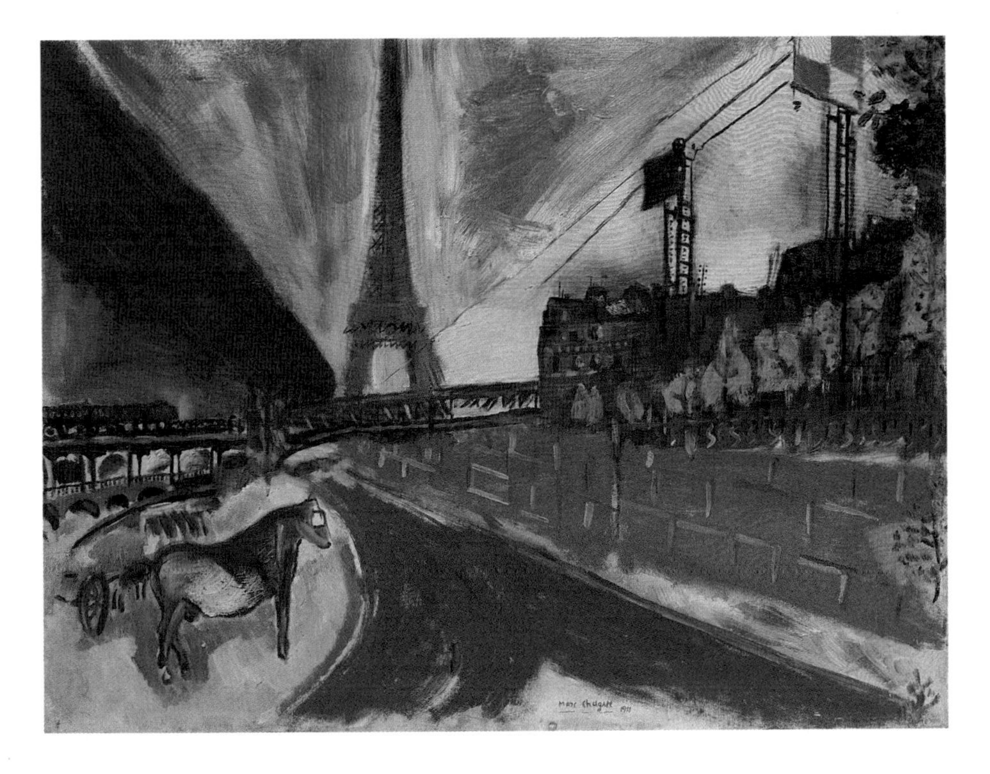

2.36 Marc Chagall, *Le Pont de Passy et la Tour Eiffel,* 1911. Oil on Canvas, 23¾ × 32 in. (60 × 80 cm). The equilibrium in this painting is centered where the radiating diagonal edges and lines come together under the railroad bridge. The Metropolitan Museum of Art, Robert Lehman Collection, 1975. (1975.1.161) Photograph © The Metropolitan Museum of Art © 2005 Artists Rights Society (ARS), New York/ADAGP, Paris.

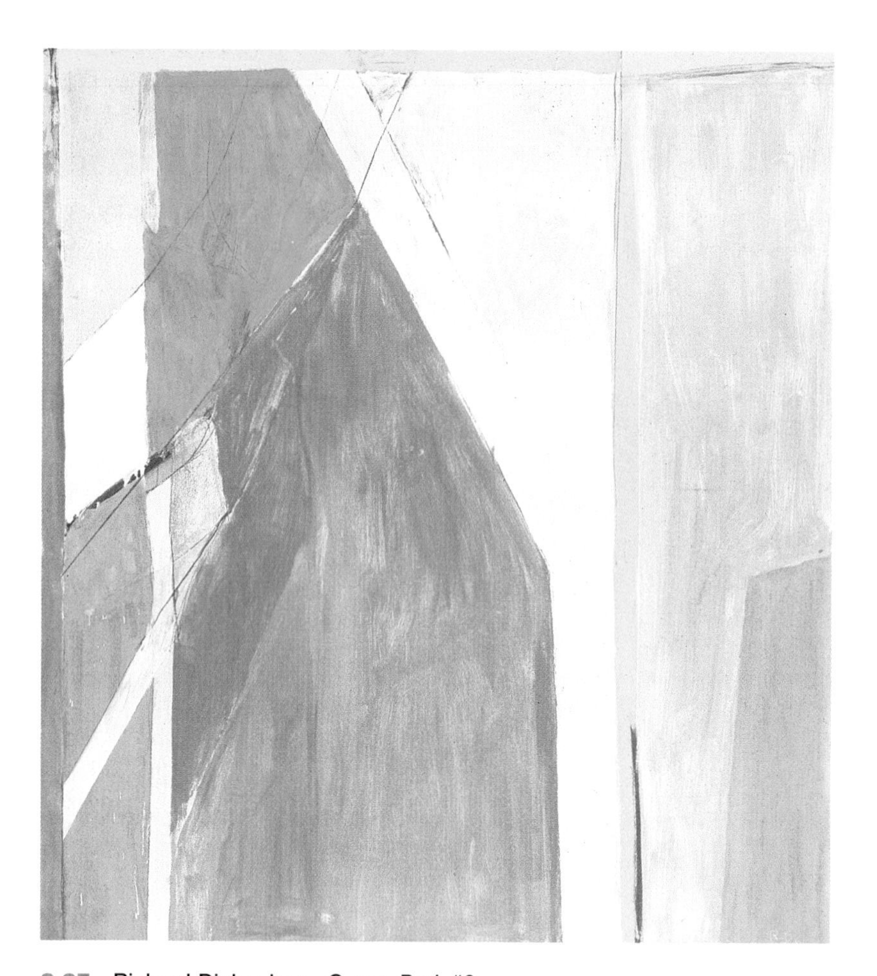

2.37 Richard Diebenkorn, *Ocean Park #9,* **1968. Oil on canvas, 84 × 78 in. (213.5 × 198.1 cm).** Relying on a felt balance, Diebenkorn uses a large open bluish-gray area to balance smaller but more active areas at the top and side. Linear information is balanced against brush textures, and horizontals and verticals are countered by strategically placed diagonals. Christie's Images.

vital, dynamic, and expressive. A picture balanced by contradictory forces (for instance, shape and open space) compels further investigation of these relationships and thus becomes an interesting visual experience (figs. 2.37 and 2.38).

Proportion (4)

Proportion deals with the ratio of individual parts to one another and to the whole. In works of art, the relationships of parts are difficult to compare with accuracy because proportion is often a matter of personal judgment. Proportional parts are considered in relation to the whole and, when related, the parts create harmony and balance. The term **scale** is used when proportion is related to size and refers to some gauge for relating parts to the whole. Often a "norm" or standard is established as a scale. For example, the human figure is a norm used by architects for scaling buildings as well as by artists for representing scale in artworks.

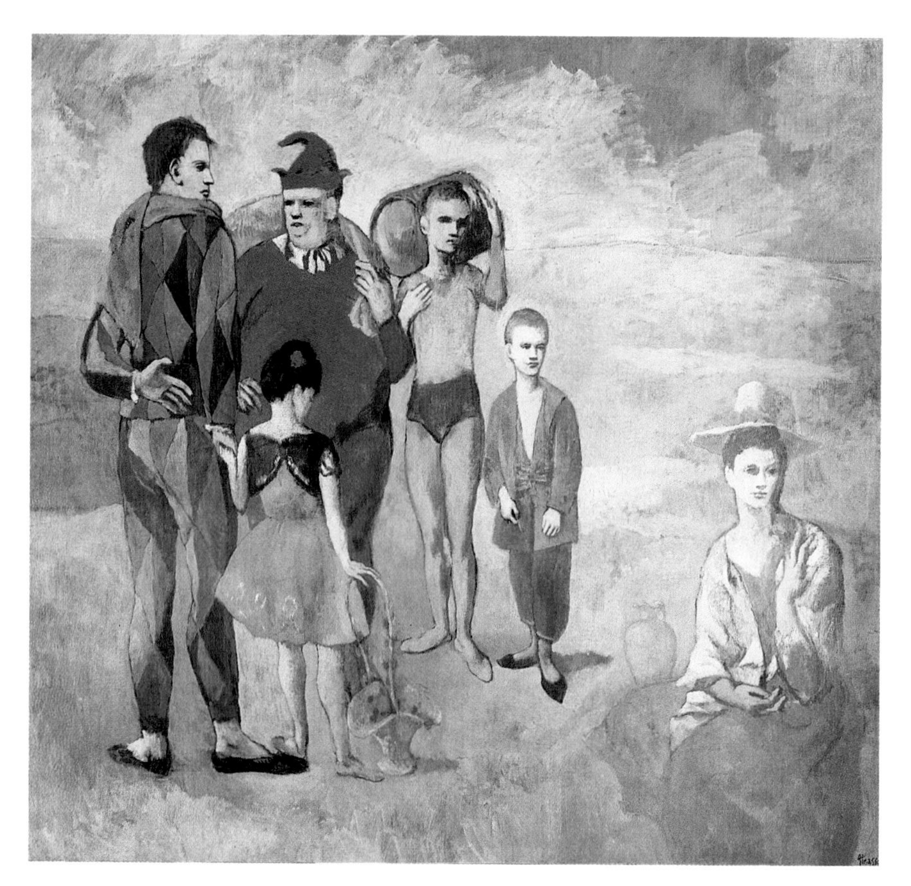

2.38 Pablo Picasso, *Family of Saltimbanques,* **1905. Oil on canvas, 6 ft 11¾ in. × 7 ft 6⅜ in. (2.13 × 2.30 m).** An intuitive balance is achieved through the juxtaposition of varying shapes and the continuous distribution of similar values and colors. Chester Dale Collection. © 1998 Board of Trustees, National Gallery of Art, Washington. Photo: B. Grove © 2005 Estate of Pablo Picasso/Artists Rights Society (ARS), New York.

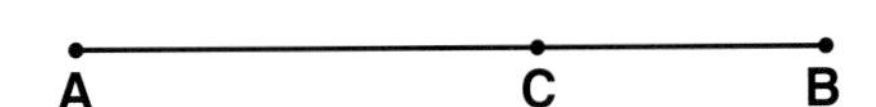

2.39 A line is here divided into a geometric relationship known as the mean and extreme ratio. This is sometimes referred to as the golden mean or golden section.

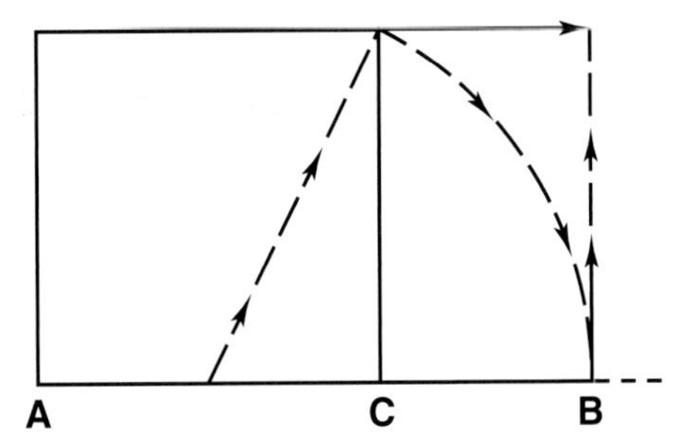

2.40A A golden rectangle may be found by extending the baseline of a perfect square in one direction. With a compass point fixed on the center of the square's baseline, draw an arc from the upper corner of the square down to the extended baseline. Having thus located the length of the new rectangle, draw a line upward to the line extended from the top of the square.

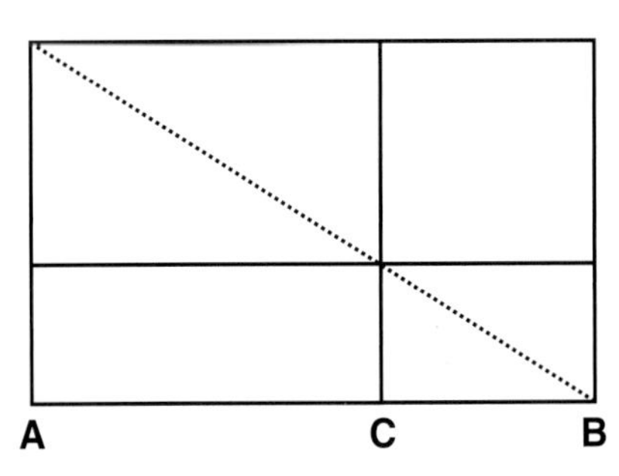

2.40B A diagonal line drawn across the new rectangle will cross the original square where the golden mean should be drawn parallel to the baseline. Measuring the sides of the golden rectangle will expose some interesting mathematical relationships. Comparing the original length of the square (AC) to the length of the new rectangle (AB) will reveal the same ratio as that of the length of the new addition (CB) to the original square (AC). That ratio will be 1 to 1.6180. (See the discussion of the Fibonacci Series in text.)

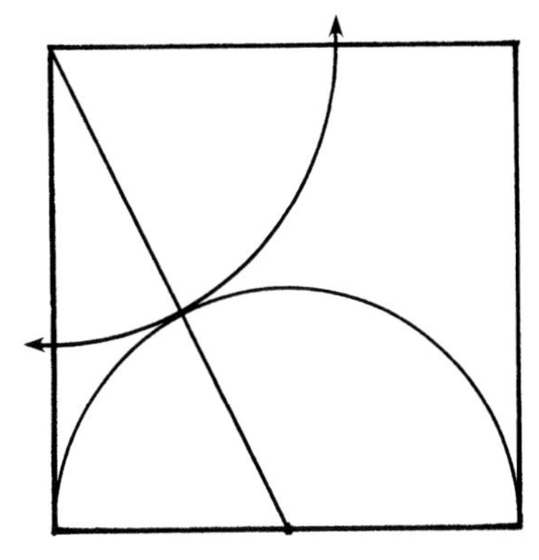

2.41A A golden mean may be achieved by projecting into a square as well as by projecting a square into a rectangle. From the center of the base of the square, draw a semicircle inside the square. Next draw a line from the center of the baseline to the square's upper corner. Where the diagonal crosses the first circle, establish a radius from the upper corner, and draw an arch to the top and side of the square.

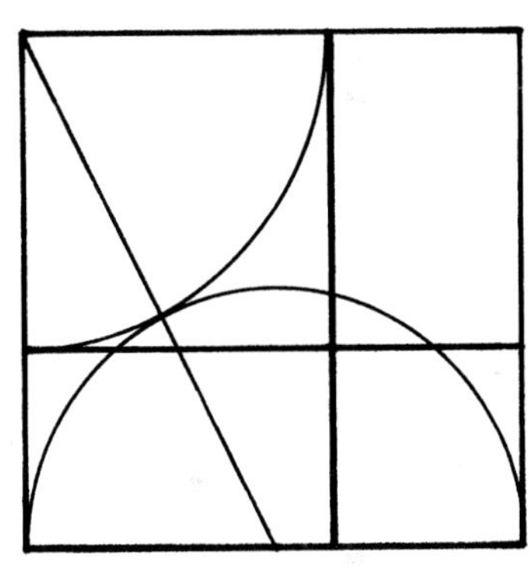

2.41B Lines drawn parallel to the top and side of the square from the points of intersection by the second arc will subdivide the square into golden rectangles with the mathematical ratio of 1:1.6180. This process may be done again from the opposite side or repeated in the new squares just created. This subdivision could continue on indefinitely revealing the same ratio of 1:1.6180. (See the discussion of Fibonacci Series in text.)

Artists have been seeking an ideal standard for proportional relationships since ancient times. Classical Greek philosophy expressed the view that mathematics was the controlling force of the universe and established the **golden mean,** sometimes called the **golden section,** to represent the ideal standard for proportion and balance in life and art. The Greek mathematician Euclid held that the golden mean was the "moderation of all things," a place between two extremes. The golden section, as it applies to works of art, states that a small part relates to a larger part as the larger part relates to the whole. It may be seen in a geometric relationship when a line is divided into what is called the mean and extreme ratio (fig. 2.39). When a line AB is sectioned at point C, AC is the same ratio to AB as CB is to AC; that is, AC:AB = CB:AC. This extreme and mean ratio has a numerical value of .6180. Any new unit will be this much smaller or larger than the original unit, making those units in a ratio of 1 to 1.6180. Applying this concept to geometry, the Greeks sought the most beautifully proportioned rectangle that could be created out of a square, and they arrived at what is referred to as the golden rectangle (figs. 2.40A, B; 2.41A, B).

Holding the human figure in highest esteem, the ancient Greeks devised special proportional standards for their figurative works. We can find these standards in their sculpture. The scale was based on certain canons, or mathematical rules, that established ideal relations of human parts. A figure, for example, was determined to be seven and one-half heads tall, and the distance from the top of the head to the chest was said to be one-quarter of the total height. The Greek sculptor Polyclitus is thought to have been the first to issue such a canon in the form of a written treatise (which has since been lost). The bronze copy of his sculpture of a spear bearer (the original is also lost) is sometimes called "the

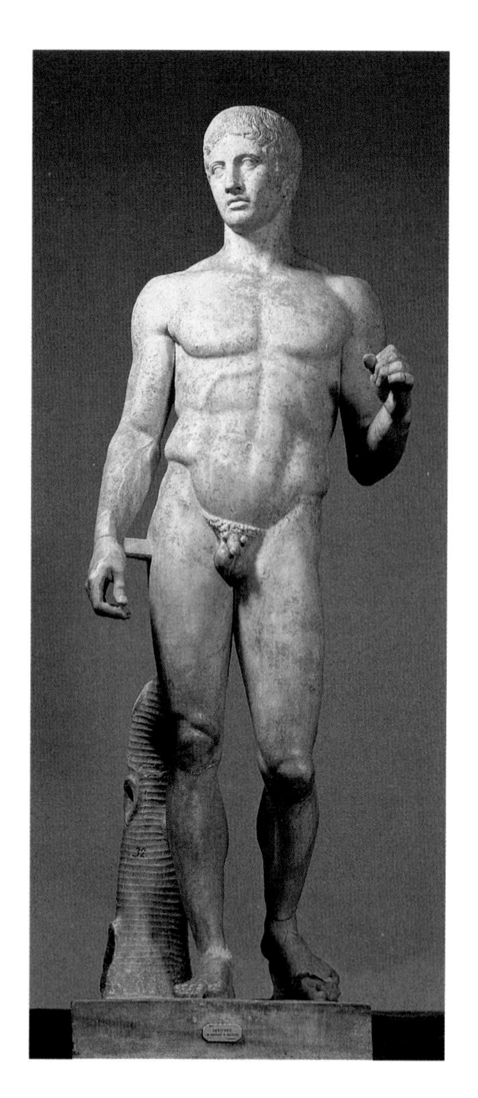

2.42 Polyclitus of Argos, *Doryphoros* (Roman copy), 450–440 B.C. Marble, 6 ft 11 in. (212 cm) high. Polyclitus wrote a theoretical treatise and demonstrated a new system of ideal proportions in a sculpture, which took the form of a young man walking with a spear (the spear is no longer extant). The Greeks called the figure "Doryphoros" (spear carrier). The Polyclitus style was characterized by harmonious and rhythmical composition, and it influenced Roman culture. Museo Archeologico Nazionale, Naples, Italy. Scala/Art Resource, New York.

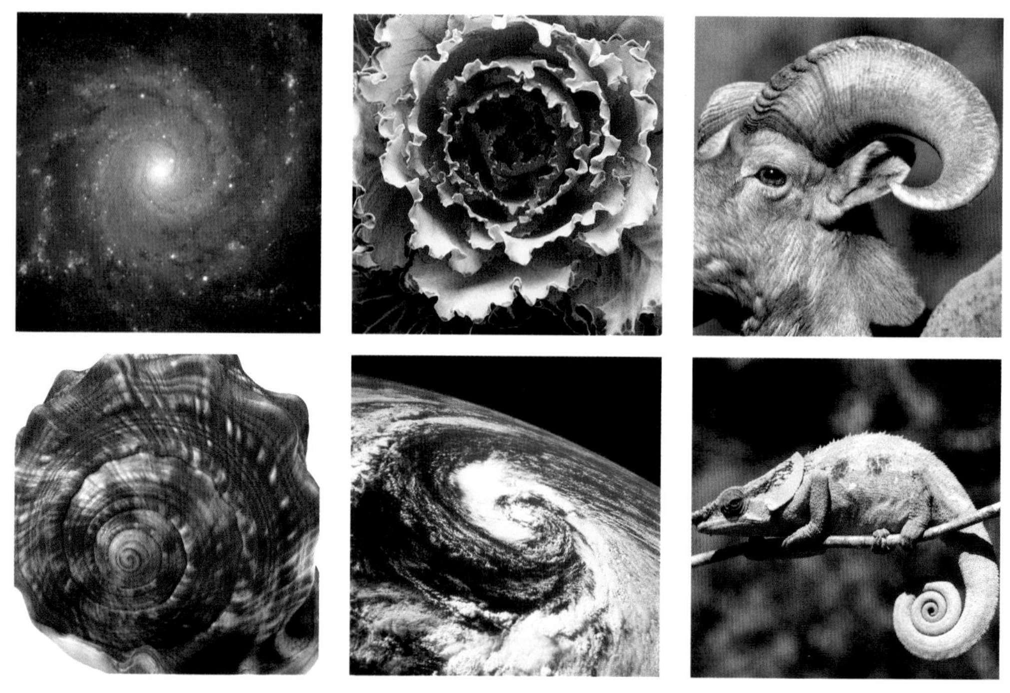

2.43 Examples of spiraling curves taken from nature. From top left to bottom left: © Gemini Observatory-GMOS Team. © C Squared Studios/Getty Images. © Brand X Pictures. © Nicole Duplaix/NGS/Getty Images. © StockTrek/Getty Images. © Brand X Pictures/Punch Stock.

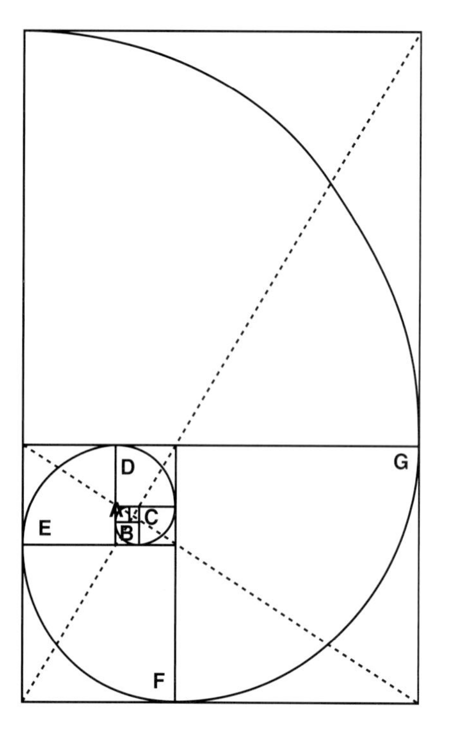

2.44A The spiraling curve is created by the continuing projection of the golden section and may be drawn with the aid of a compass. The inside corner of the square locates the compass point, which scribes an arc from corner to corner. This line is continued into the next square with a new compass point located on the inside center corner of that square. The process continues from square to square until the spiral is completed.

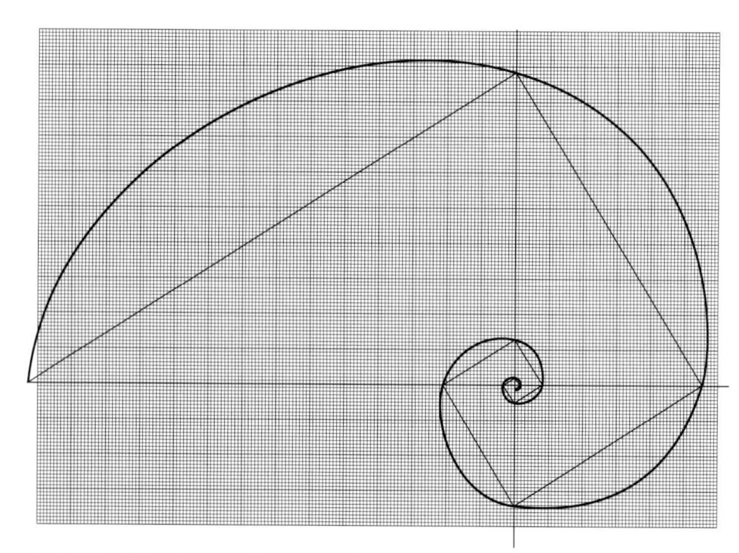

2.44B This diagram illustrates the same spiral, created by plotting the numbers from the Fibonacci Series (1, 1, 2, 3, 5, 8, 13, 21, 34, 55, 89, 144) on a horizontal and vertical axis.

canon," because it best demonstrates his standard for figure proportions (fig. 2.42). The idea of affording keenly pleasing proportional relationships extended into all areas of daily Greek life.

Historically, these ancient Greek ideals have had continuing effects, influencing generations of artists. Leonardo Fibonacci, a medieval mathematician of the thirteenth century, discovered a series of related numbers. The sequence was created by adding the two previous numbers to arrive at each new number: 0, 1, 1, 2, 3, 5, 8, 13, 21, 34, 56, and so on. Published in *Liber Abaci* (*Book of the Abacus*) in 1202, this sequence is called the Fibonacci Series and also demonstrates an increasing ratio of approximately 1:1.6180. Indeed, one may start with any number. Using 10 for example, one can multiply by 1.6180 to get the number 16. From that point, simply adding the previous two numbers will provide the next number (26, 42, 68, . . .), and consecutive numbers in the growing sequence will have the same ratio as the golden section.

Today, scientists recognize this relationship in nature. It is found in the expanding curve of the nautilus shell, the curve of a cat's claw, the spiral growth of a pine cone, the seed patterns in a sunflower's head, and the center of a daisy (fig. 2.43). Botanists study this spiral arrangement (called phyllotaxy) in leaves, scales, and flowers. This spiraling curve may be demonstrated in the continuing projection of the golden rectangle into progressively larger and larger units (figs. 2.44A, B).

During the Renaissance, artists like Leonardo da Vinci renewed interest in mathematically formulated proportional scaling. This can be found, for example, in Leonardo's drawing *Proportions of the Human Figure* (fig. 2.45).

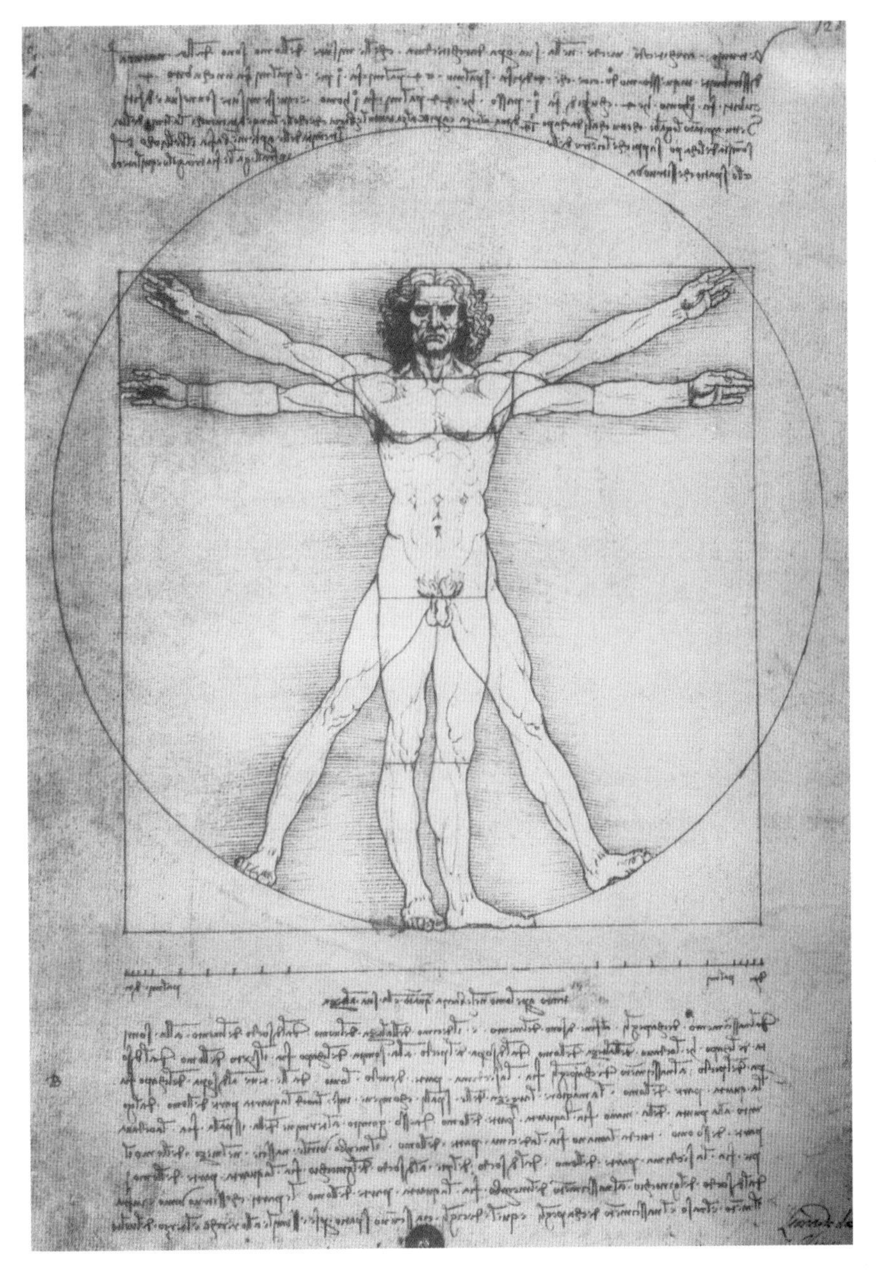

2.45 Leonardo da Vinci, *Proportions of the Human Figure* (after Vitruvius), c. 1485–90. Pen and ink, 13½ × 9¾ in. (34.3 × 24.8 cm). Here, Leonardo demonstrates his interest in human anatomy. By positioning a male figure within a circle and a square, Leonardo was investigating the proportional relationships of the head, body, arms, and legs. Note that the figure's height is equal to its outstretched arms and that the square's center is located where the legs join while the circle's center is the navel. Accademia, Venice, Italy. Corbis-Bettmann.

Modern artists also have composed pictures that conform with the frame shape of the golden rectangle. The French painter Georges Seurat is known for his scientifically measured use of the Post-Impressionistic technique of Pointillism and his use of light and simultaneously contrasted colors. He was also intrigued with the mathematical proportions of the golden rectangle. In the painting *Circus Sideshow* (*La Parade*), Seurat used subtle variations of golden rectangles and squares (figs. 2.46A, B). Notice how he strategically placed the softly rounded figures, the tree, the geometric forms, and the various decorative motifs at golden section points.

A

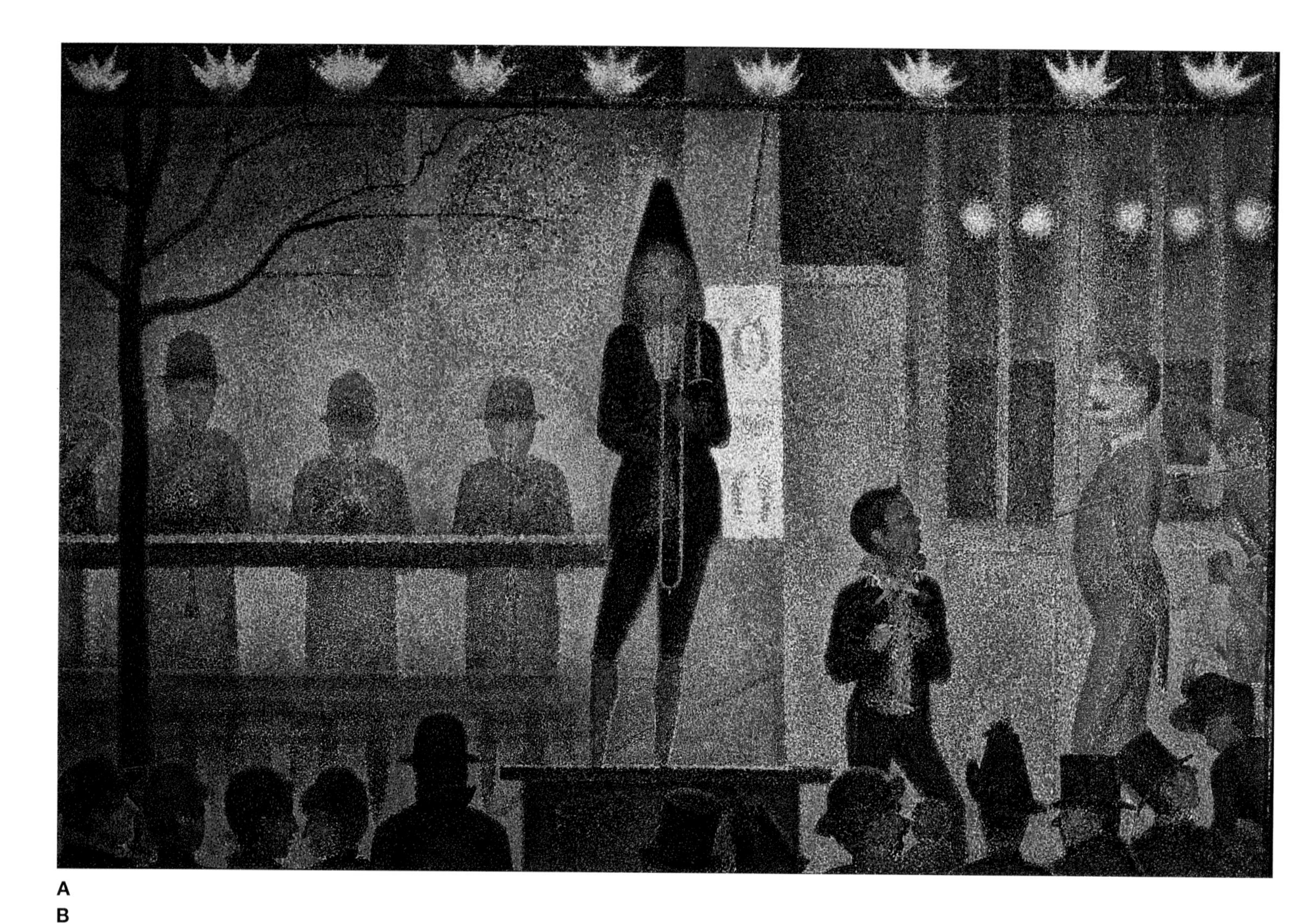

B

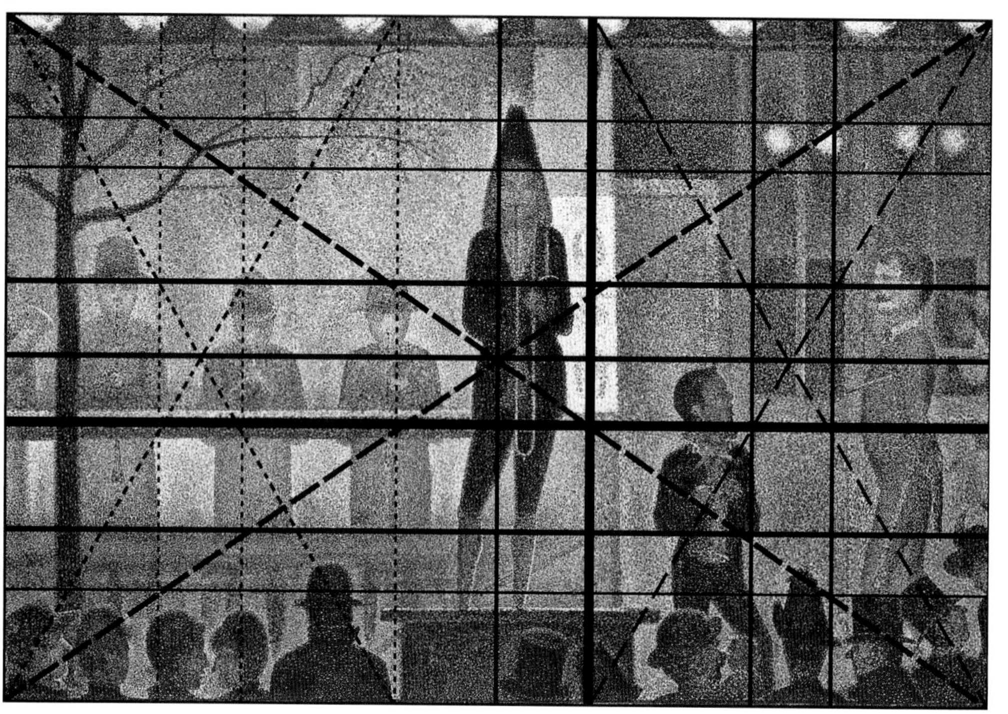

2.46 **Georges Seurat, *Circus Sideshow (La Parade)*, 1887–88. Oil on canvas, 39¼ × 59 in. (99.7 × 149.9 cm).** (B) When this Seurat painting is divided by a diagonal from upper left to lower right (large dashes), it crosses the large square where a golden rectangle would be subdivided by a heavy horizontal line. Smaller golden rectangles are created in the vertical rectangle on the right. These small rectangles may be further divided by intersecting diagonals. This could continue indefinitely. In addition, when the original square is established on the right side of the picture (small dotted lines) and a diagonal is drawn from lower left to upper right, the left side may be broken down into smaller golden rectangles that mirror those on the right side of the diagram. Notice how Seurat has used these lines and their intersections for the strategic placement of figures and imagery. The Metropolitan Museum of Art, Bequest of Stephen C. Clark, 1960. (61.101.17) Photograph © 1989 The Metropolitan Museum of Art.

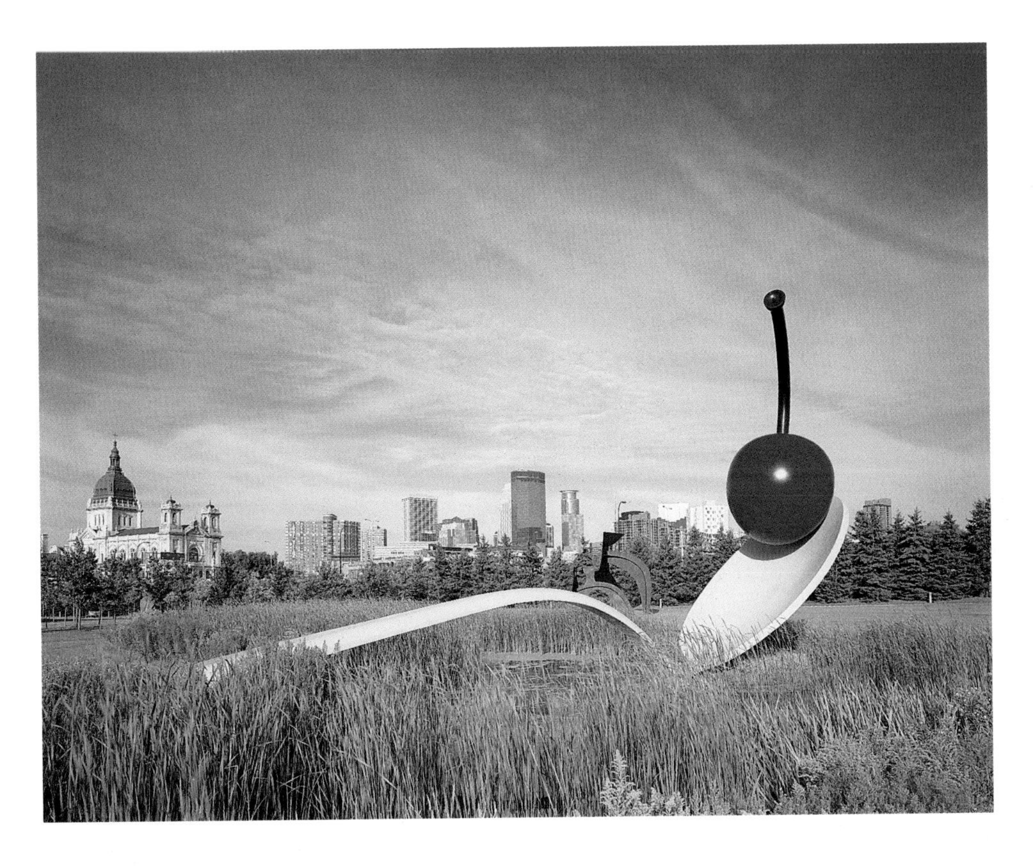

2.47 Claes Oldenburg and Coosje van Bruggen, *Spoonbridge and Cherry* (a fountain), 1985–88. Stainless steel, paint, and aluminum, 139 × 243⅓ × 63¾ in. (354 × 618 × 162 cm). These clearly recognizable objects far surpass the scale expected of them. Collection Walker Art Center. Minneapolis. Gift of Frederick R. Weisman in honor of his parents, William and Mary Weisman, 1988.

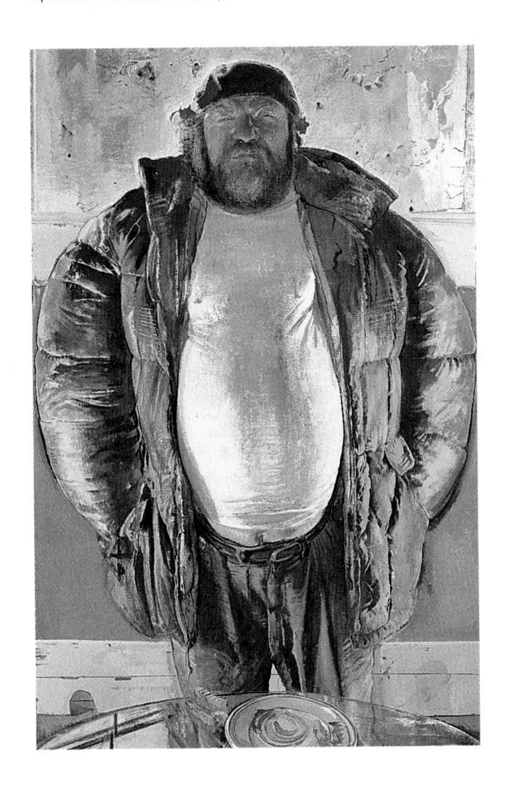

2.48 Jerome Paul Witkin, *Jeff Davies*, 1980. Oil on canvas, 6 × 4 ft (1.83 × 1.22 m). If there was ever a painting in which one subject dominated the work, this must be it. Most artworks do not need this degree of dominance, but Witkin evidently wanted a forceful presence—and he got it. Palmer Museum of Art, Pennsylvania State University. Gift of the American Academy and Institute of Arts and Letters (Hassam and Speicher Purchase Fund).

Most artists seek balance and logical proportions. The dimensions of the images reproduced in this book reinforce this claim. Some artists choose to disregard the essentials of proportions, that is, harmonious and balanced relationships, in order to emphasize the extremes of scale. When a very large shape is placed alongside a much smaller one in an artwork, the effect is disproportionate. A spectator may register some dismay when confronted with extreme examples of disproportionate scale. Common objects become unsettling when made monumental (fig. 2.47). When making judgments in determining proportions, most artists will rely on an educated intuition and adjust and readjust the sizes of their elements so that they seem to fill the whole work of art.

Still, many artists find a need for enlarging and/or diminishing the sizes of certain elements to aid the expression of an idea or as a means of creating emphasis or dominance. When using changes in scale for emphasis, the artist will find that he or she can harness and sustain the observer's attention. In the Jerome Witkin painting *Jeff Davies* (fig. 2.48), the artist uses enlargement as a means of emphasizing the presence of his figure. The subject, a large, physically imposing man, is presented with a bulky torso in simple, light values, surrounded by the darker forms of the head, arms, jacket, and pants. The artist has positioned the white torso in the center of the composition for primary attention and has sized the figure's image so that it seems to burst the limits of the painting's format. Witkin's exaggerated enlargement and relative scaling came from his perceptions of the actual figure he was to represent. The result is an overpowering portrait.

Another way artists have used inordinate proportion or scaling is to indicate rank, status, or importance of religious, political, military, and social personages. *Hierarchical scaling* is a term used to describe this system, whereby figures of

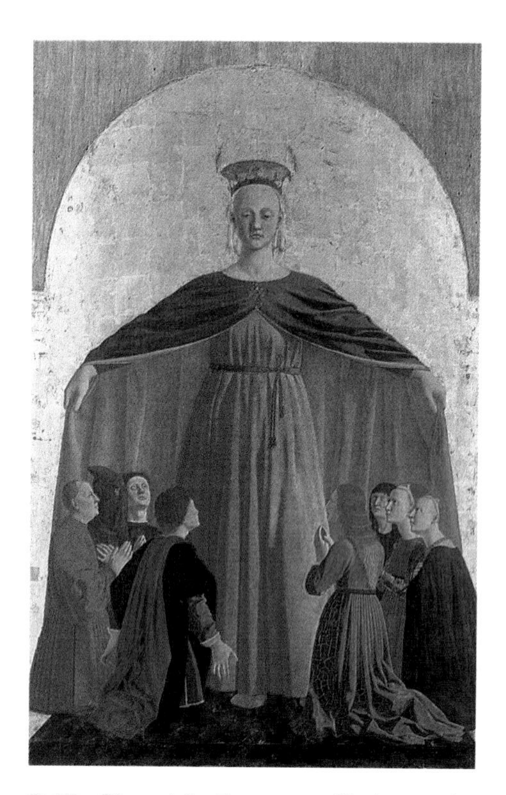

2.49 Piero della Francesca, *Madonna of Mercy* (center panel of triptych), 1445–55. Oil and tempera on wood, height about 4 ft 9 in. (1.44 m). The figure of Mary extends her arms to make a shelter of her cape for the smaller figures at her feet. The positioning of the worshipful figures who surround the central columnar form helps to give a sense of depth to the scene. The artist's use of hierarchical scaling also strengthens the feeling of the maternal and merciful power of the Madonna. Italian Civic Museum, Sansepolcro, Italy/SuperStock.

greatest importance are made larger in size according to their status. In the painting *Madonna of Mercy,* Piero della Francesca doubled the size of his Madonna figure in order to elevate her to a lofty object of reverence (fig. 2.49). The proportions in this painting, and other works like it, are subjective in their intent rather than representational (fig. 2.50).

The physical size of the work in comparison to human scale can also be utilized for expressive purposes. The artist Chuck Close tends to overwhelm us with paintings of enormous human heads (fig. 2.51). Resulting from their overall size—the portraits range from five to eight feet in height—there is a proportional enlargement of facial details, such as hairs and skin pores. The view of the artist in his studio illustrates the overpowering scale of these enlargements (see fig. 2.11). The heads, at first heroic, become intimidating and, in some respects, sordid.

To summarize: Artists use scaling to create emphasis and expressive effects and to suggest spatial positions, as we will show in later chapters.

Dominance (5)

Any work of art that strives for interest must exhibit differences that emphasize the degrees of importance of its various parts. These differences result from compositional considerations within the medium. A musical piece, for example, can use crescendo; a dramatic production can use a spotlight. The means by which differences can be achieved, in fact, are many. Substituting the term *contrast* for *difference,* we see that the following, among others, can be used to achieve dominance: (1) isolation or sep-

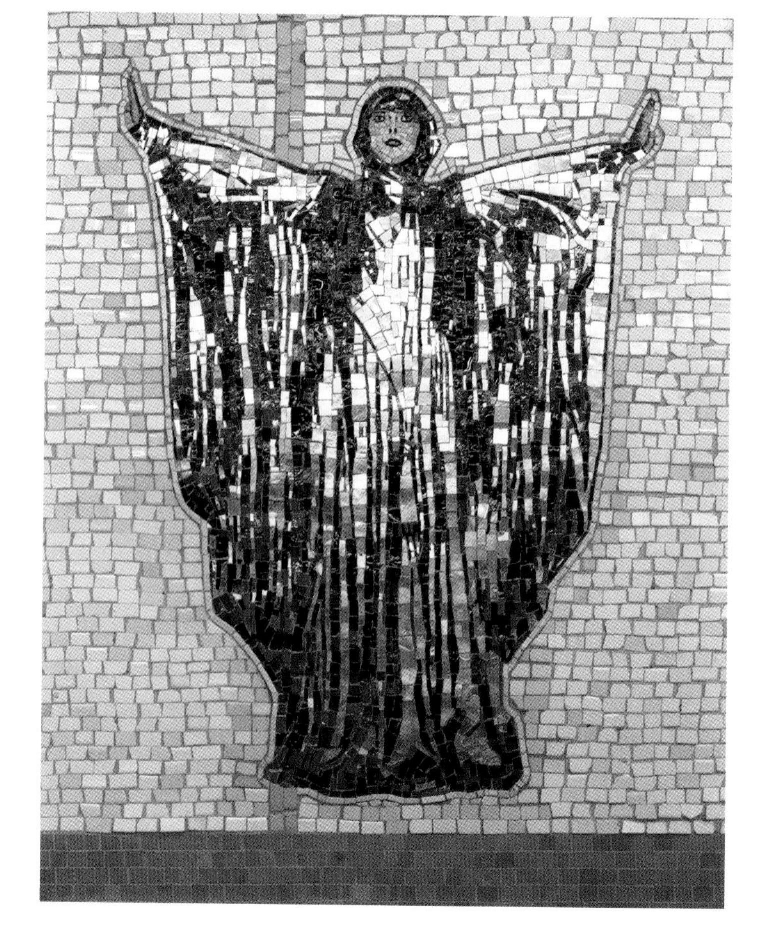

2.50 Nancy Spero, *Artemis, Acrobats, Divas and Dancers,* 1999–2000. Glass and ceramic mosaic. Comparing the *Madonna of Mercy* (fig. 2.49) from 1445–55 with the female figure in Spero's *Artemis, Acrobats, Divas and Dancers* reveals a variety of ways to impart dominance. Even though the *Madonna* was made for a sacred space, while Spero's *Artemis* resides in the profane space of a New York City subway stop, both use centrality to establish dominance. Francesca's *Madonna* also uses scale relationships within the painting to establish her importance. Staring directly at the viewer, Artemis spreads her arms in a gesture of independence, using her cape as an extension of her body. Gazing downward, the Madonna also spreads her arms but to envelop her dependents in a gesture of protection, making her cloak a refuge. While different, each pose expresses dominance. Public commission for MTA Arts for Transit, New York, NY. © Nancy Spero. Courtesy Galerie Lelong, New York.

aration of one part from others; (2) placement—"center stage" is most often used, but another position can be dominant, depending on the surroundings; (3) direction—a movement that contrasts with others draws attention; (4) scale—larger sizes normally dominate; and (5) character—a significant difference in general appearance is striking. Contrasts in color, value, and texture can also help to produce dominance.

The artist uses contrast to call attention to the significant parts of the work, thereby making them dominant. Artwork neglecting dominance seems to imply that everything is of equal importance; such art creates a confusing image that gives the viewer no direction and fails to communicate. In one sense, all parts are important, because even the secondary parts produce the norm against which the dominant parts are contrasted.

Regarding dominance, artists have two problems. First, they must see that each part has the necessary degree of importance; and second, they must incorporate these parts, with their varying degrees of importance, into the rhythmic movement and balance of the work. In doing this, artists find that they must use different methods to achieve dominance. One significant area might derive importance from its change in value, whereas another might rely on its busy or exciting shape (figs. 2.52, 2.53, and 2.54; see also fig. 5.12).

We witness the basic order created by variations in dominance (and in hierarchy, more generally) at every level of our lives—the celebrity pecking order in the entertainment field; the hierarchy of political, ecclesiastical, and civic organizations; the atomic system; the solar system—all in very different ways.

Movement (6)

Many observers do not realize that, in looking at an artwork, they are being "taken for a ride" or, more accurately, a tour. The tour director is, of course, the

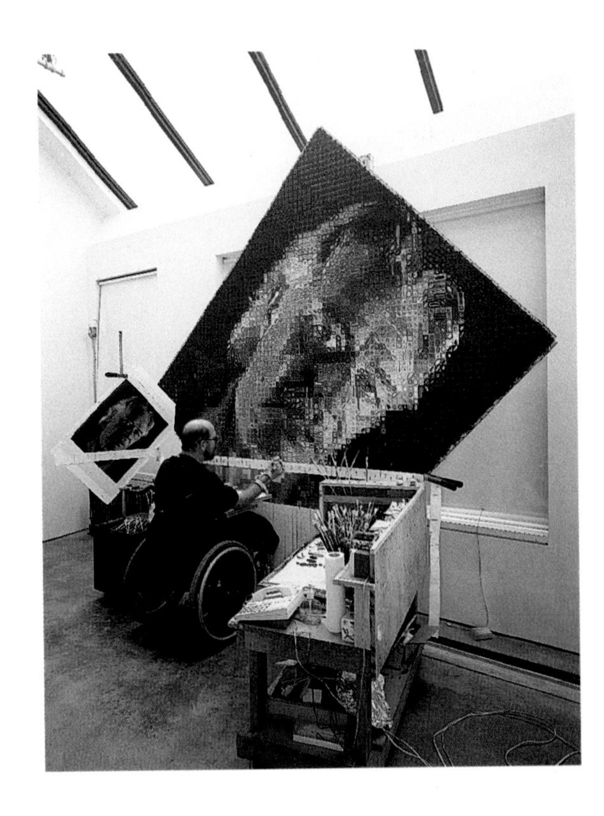

2.51 Chuck Close working on *John*, 1992. Oil on canvas, 100 × 84 in. The colossal size of the heads in Close's painting requires an examination and interpretation of every textural and topographical feature of the model's face. Courtesy of Pace Wildenstein. Photograph by Bill Jacobson.

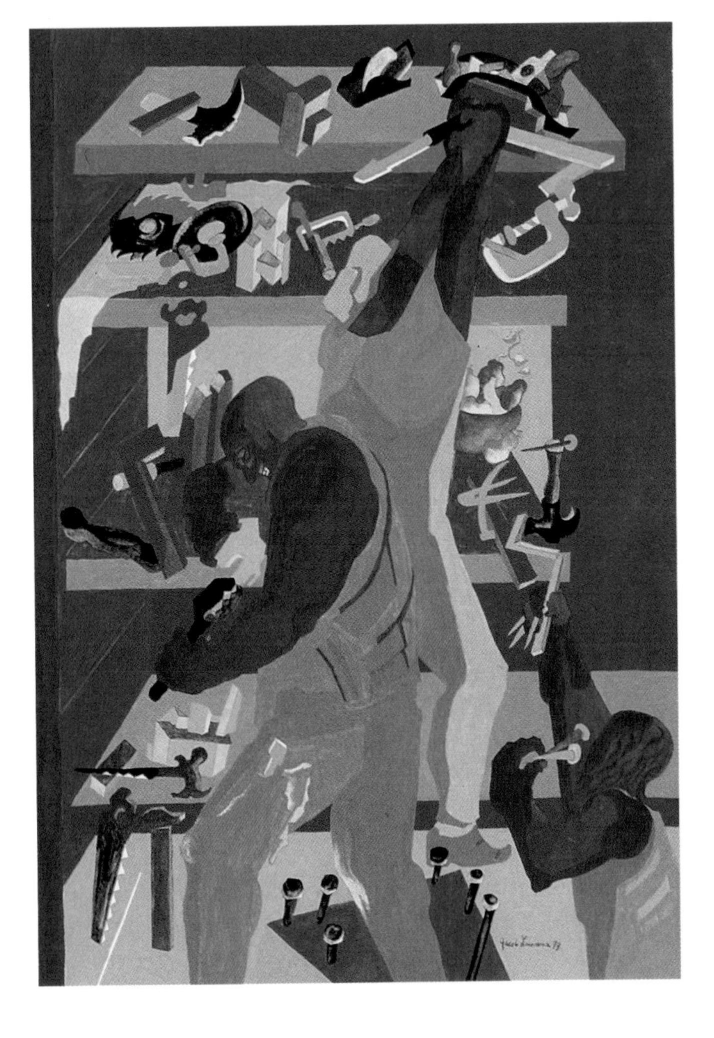

2.52 Jacob Lawrence, *Builders in the Workshop*, 1993. Gouache on paper, 28½ × 19 in. (72.3 × 47.7 cm). The human figures here become the focal points, or optical units of greatest importance, because of their size and activity. The dominant area is where the two central figures merge. The other figure directs attention toward the center, and the tables and tools are less dominant still. © The Estate of Gwendolyn Lawrence/Artists Rights Society (ARS), New York.

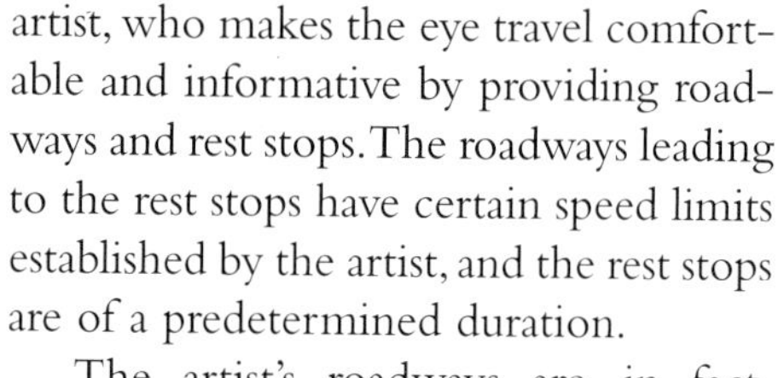

artist, who makes the eye travel comfortable and informative by providing roadways and rest stops. The roadways leading to the rest stops have certain speed limits established by the artist, and the rest stops are of a predetermined duration.

The artist's roadways are, in fact, transitions between the rest stops, or optical units. The eye movements dictated by these transitions are produced by the direction of lines, shapes, shape edges (or contours), and motifs that, in their similarity, cause us to relate them to one another. The lines, shapes, and shape contours are generally pointed at one another in the same general direction. They may be touching but are normally interrupted by gaps over which the eyes skip as they move about. Sometimes "leaps" are necessary, requiring strong directional thrusts and attractions.

The optical units that direct us contain vital information. In a work such as the *Mona Lisa,* the figure is such a dominant unit that little eye movement is required, although there is secondary material of considerable interest (see fig. 5.8). In other works, there may be several units of great interest that are widely separated, and it thus becomes critical that the observer's vision be directed to them. There is usually some hierarchy in these units, with some calling for more attention than others.

2.53 Poteet Victory, *Symbols of Manifest Destiny,* 1999. Oil and mixed media on canvas, 60 × 40 in. (152.4 × 101.6 cm). In this work, the yellow-orange striped rectangle becomes dominant because of the contrast of light against dark and warm color against cool color. Courtesy of the artist.

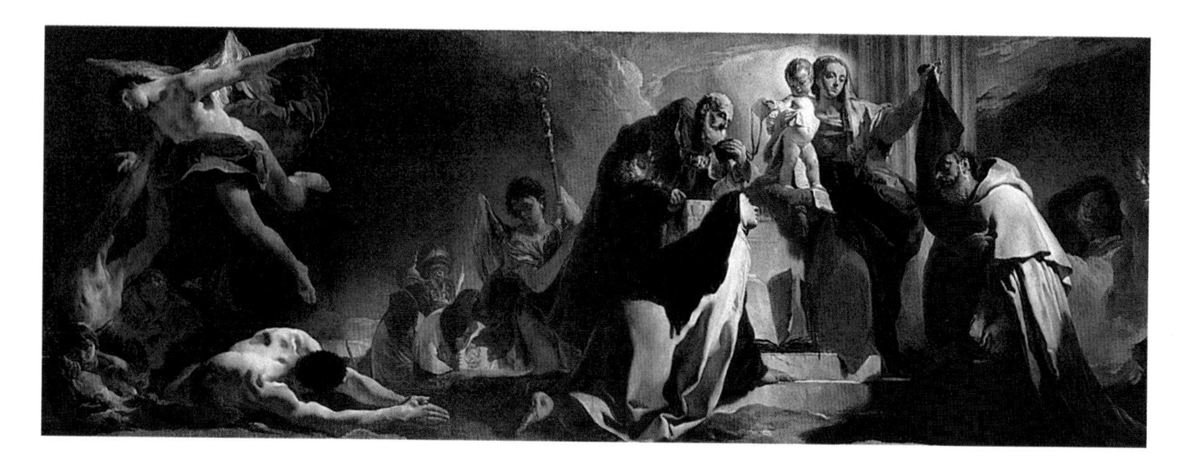

2.54 Giambattista Tiepolo, *Madonna of Mt. Carmel and the Souls in Purgatory,* c. 1720. Oil on canvas, 82⅝ × 256 in. (210 × 650 cm). The movement weaves its way through this work because the lighting gives the figures dominance. Scala/Art Resource, New York.

Kinetic, or moving sculpture exists, but most sculpture and picture surfaces are static. Any animation in such works must come from an illusion of movement created by the artist through the configuration of their parts. The written word is read from side to side, but a visual image, whether two-dimensional or three-dimensional, can be read in any direction. The movement of one's eyes is dictated by the artist who must ensure that all areas are exploited with no static or uninteresting parts. The movement should be self-renewing, constantly being drawn back into the work (fig. 2.55; see also the "Pictorial Representations of Movement in Time" section in Chapter 8, p. 210).

In pictures, the spatial positioning of the elements also causes movement. Historically the illusion of movement into the space of the work has been founded on linear perspective. Perspective is effective, but not necessary. There is also "intuitive" space, which can deny perspective by using certain artistic devices covered in the chapter on space. Some art, as in sculpture, and particularly kinetic sculpture, even incorporates the element of time into its movement; there will be more on this later, as well (see the "Movement" section in Chapter 9, p. 210).

Economy (7)

Very often, as a work develops, the artist will realize that the solutions to various visual problems are resulting in unnecessary complexity. This problem is frequently characterized by broad aspects of the work deteriorating into fragmentation. This process may be a necessary part of the developmental phase of the work, but it may result in resolutions that lack unity.

The artist can sometimes restore order by returning to essentials, eliminating elaborate details, and relating the particulars to the whole. This sacrifice is not easily made or accepted because, in returning to essentials, interesting discoveries and effects must often be surrendered for legibility and a more direct expression. Economy has no rules but rather must be an outgrowth of the artist's instincts. If something works with respect to the whole, it is kept; if disruptive, it may be reworked or rejected.

Economy is sometimes associated with the term *abstraction*. Abstraction implies an active process of selecting the essentials that strengthen both the conceptual and organizational aspects of the artwork. In some measure, the artistic style dictates the kind of abstraction and the degree of abstraction, though all art requires abstraction to some extent (fig. 2.56).

Economy is easy to detect in many contemporary art styles. The early modernists Pablo Picasso and Henri Matisse were among those most influential in the trend toward economical abstraction; another artist who used economy effectively was Milton Avery (fig. 2.57; see also fig. 4.7). The hard-edged works of Ellsworth Kelly, the "field" paintings of Barnett Newman and Morris Louis, and the analogous color canvases of Ad Reinhardt all clearly feature economy (see figs. 7.14, 10.76, and 10.101). Two sculptors of the Minimalist style (which itself bespeaks economy), Beverly Pepper and Donald Judd, make use of severely

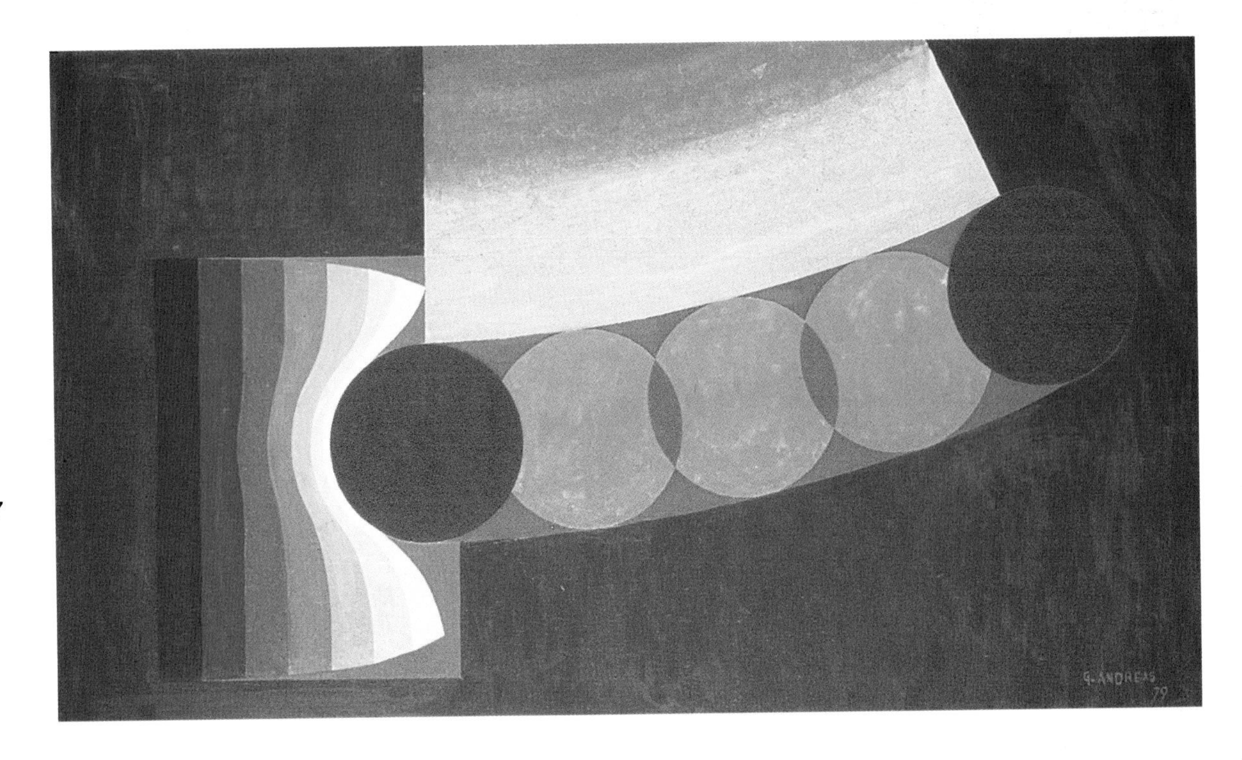

2.55 George Andreas, *Energy,* 1979. Oil on canvas, 31 × 54 in. (78.7 × 137.2 cm). The swing of the circles and their subsequent rebounding generate a sweeping pendulumlike movement. Courtesy of the artist and Andreas Galleries.

2.56 **Tom Wesselmann, *1960 Judy Trying on Clothes,* 1997. Alkyd oil on cut-out aluminum, 58½ × 72½ in.** Wesselmann has reduced the image to the few details he considers crucial, thereby practicing economy. Collection of the artist. Photograph by Jim Strong, Inc. © Estate of Tom Wesselmann/ Licensed by VAGA, New York, NY.

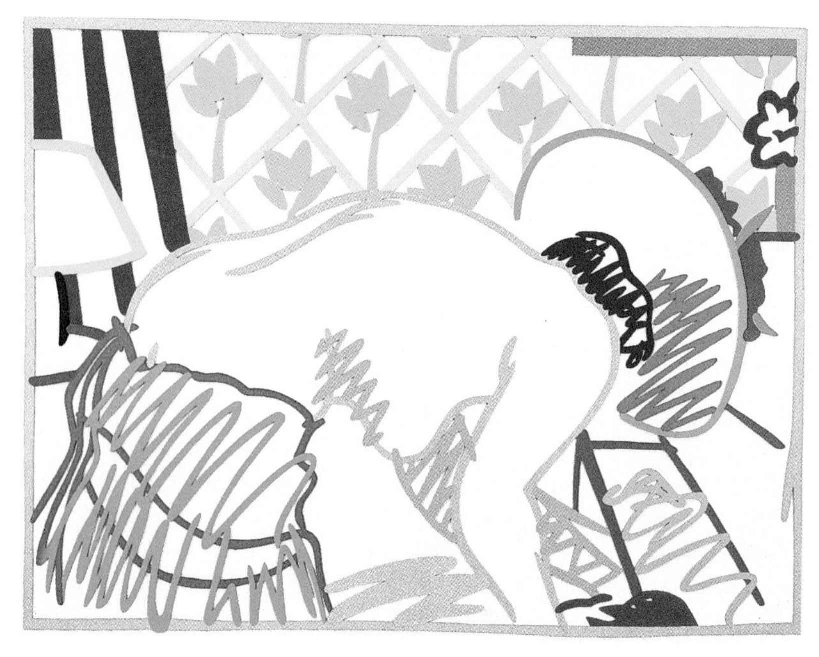

2.57 **Milton Avery, *Seated Blonde,* 1946. Oil, charcoal on linen, 52 × 33¾ in. (132.1 × 85.7 cm).** Avery has simplified the complex qualities of the surface structures of his two figures, reducing them to shapes and flat color. Through the use of economy, the artist abstracted the figures to strengthen their distance and isolation. Walker Art Center, Minneapolis, MN. Gift of Mr. and Mrs. Roy R. Neuberger, New York, NY, 1952. © 2005 Milton Avery Trust/Artists Rights Society (ARS), NY.

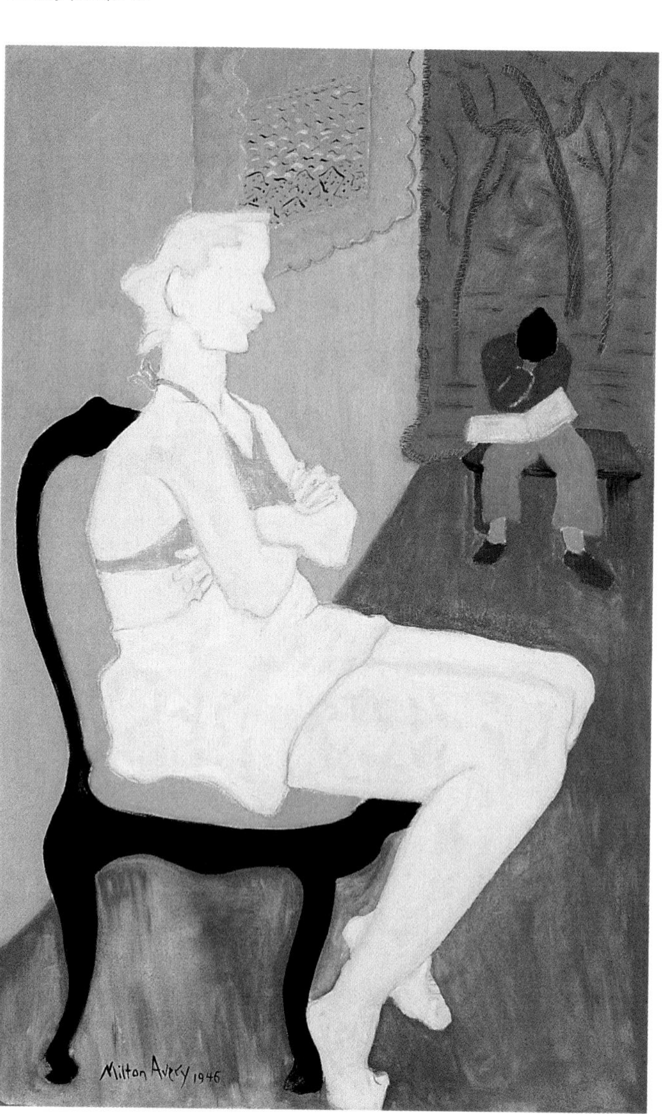

limited geometric forms (see figs. 9.40 and 9.41). They have renounced illusionism, preferring instead to create three-dimensional objects in actual space that excludes all excesses. The absence of elaboration results in a very direct statement.

In economizing, one flirts with monotony. Sometimes embellishments must be preserved or added to avoid this pitfall. But if the result is greater clarity, the risk may be well worth it.

Space: Result of Elements/Principles

The artist is always concerned about space as it evolves in an artwork. The authors have taken the position that space is not an element (that is, not one of the **principles of organization**) but rather a by-product of the elements as they are put into action and altered by the various principles of organization. Other people regard space as an element in its own right. However we may classify space, the **concept** of space is unquestionably important—so much so, that many chapter sections in the text and the entire contents of Chapter 8 are devoted to the subject.

If we follow the order in our diagram (see fig. 2.1), we see that a medium is necessary for the creation of an element and that, once an element (a line, for example) becomes visible, it automatically creates a spatial position in contrast with its background.

An artist, when considering space in a work, looks for consistency of relationships. Nothing can throw an artwork out of kilter like a jumbled spatial order. An artist who begins with one kind of space, say, a flat, two-dimensional representation of a figure, should continue to develop 2D concepts in the succeeding stages of the artwork. Consistency contributes immeasurably to unity.

Our familiarity with space comes, in part, from the exploration of outer space. Of course, we personally become acquainted with space, on a less exalted level, as we move from point to point in the performance of our normal daily duties. As we do this we are unconsciously aware of the distance between these points and even of the limit of our vision, the horizon. In transferring nature's space to the canvas, the painter faces problems that have been dealt with in various ways in different historical periods. The artist must use the art elements to produce the illusion of the spatial phenomena he or she wants represented in the artwork. Quite often the effect sought has the observer viewing the frame as a window into the space, terminating at some point or continuing to infinity. Such space is called three-dimensional because all of this is condensed into a picture surface. These surfaces have their actual limits, but the illusion of depth gives a further dimension of 3D space.

FORM UNITY: A SUMMARY

Artists select a picture plane framed by certain dimensions. They have their tools and materials and with them begin to create elements on the surface. As they do so, spatial suggestions appear that may conform to the artist's original conception; if not, a process of adjustment begins. The adjustment accelerates and continues as harmony and variety are applied to achieve balance, proportion, dominance, movement, and economy. As the development continues, artists depend on their intellect, emotions, and instincts in ratios varying from artist to artist and from work to work. The result is an artwork that has its own distinctive form. If the work is successful, its form has unity—all parts belong and work together.

A unified artwork develops like symphonic orchestration in music. The musical composer generally begins with a theme that is taken through a number of variations. Notations direct the tempo and dynamics for the performers. The individual instruments, in following these notations, play their parts in contributing to the total musical effect. In addition, the thematic material is woven through the content of the work, harmonizing its sections. A successful musical composition sounds eloquent, with every measure perfected.

The musical elements just mentioned have their counterparts in art. In every creative medium, be it music, art, dance, poetry, prose, or theater, the goal is unity. For the creator, unity results from the selection of devices peculiar to the medium and the use of certain principles to relate them. In art, an understanding of the principles of form-structure is indispensable. In the first chapters of this book, we can begin to see the vast possibilities in the creative art realm. Through study of the principles of form-organization, we can develop an understanding that becomes, through persistent practice, natural and instinctive.

The art elements—line, shape, value, texture, and color—on which form is based can do little in isolation. They join forces in the total work. Their individual contributions can be studied separately, but in the development of a work, the ways in which they relate to one another are paramount. Because each element makes an individual contribution and has an intrinsic appeal, the elements are discussed separately in the following five chapters. It is necessary to do this for **academic** reasons. As you study each element in turn, please keep the others in mind. In the end, you must consider all the elements both individually and collectively. The task is great, but necessary for that one vital ingredient—unity.

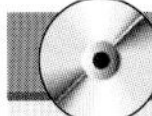

INVESTIGATE THE CD-ROM **Questions to Ask Yourself**

The quest for wholeness is a primary motivation in all art.

As you review this chapter on the CD-ROM, think about an artwork that you particularly like, and answer these questions:

1. How does this artwork achieve wholeness?
2. What is it about this artwork that you like?
3. What does this tell you about your own quest for wholeness in life?

CHAPTER THREE

Line

THE VOCABULARY OF LINE

LINE: THE ELEMENTARY MEANS OF COMMUNICATION

THE PHYSICAL CHARACTERISTICS OF LINE

- Measure
- Type
- Direction
- Location
- Character

THE EXPRESSIVE PROPERTIES OF LINE

LINE AND THE OTHER ART ELEMENTS

- Line and Shape
- Line and Value
- Line and Texture
- Line and Color

THE SPATIAL CHARACTERISTICS OF LINE

LINE AND REPRESENTATION

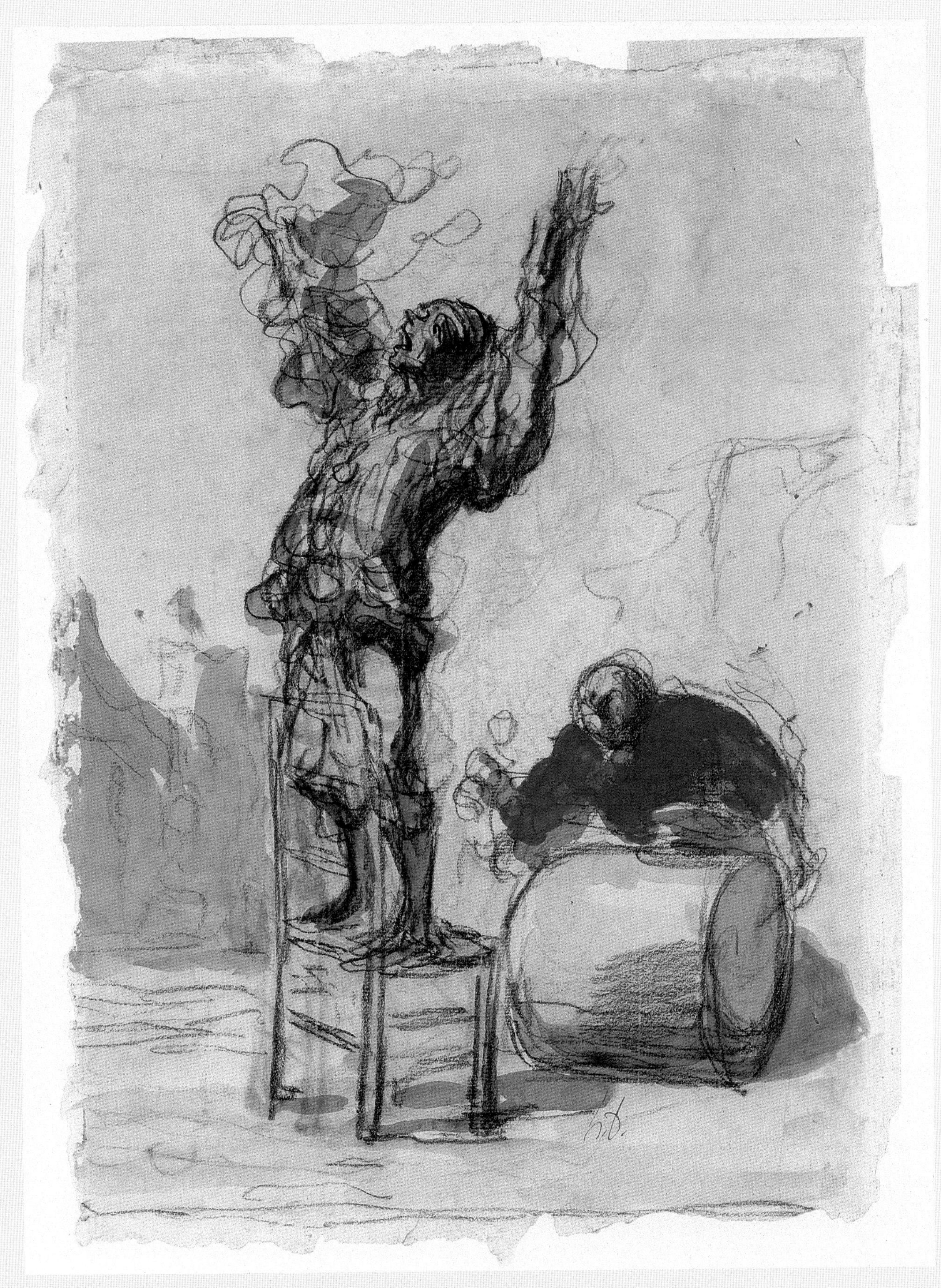

Honoré Daumier, *Street Show*, 1865–66. Black chalk and watercolor on laid paper, 14⅜ × 10¹⁄₁₆ in.
The Metropolitan Museum of Art, Rogers Fund, 1927. (27.152.2) Photograph © The Metropolitan Museum of Art.

THE VOCABULARY OF **LINE**

Line — The path traced by the point of a tool, instrument, or medium as it moves across an area. A line is visible when it contrasts in value with its surroundings. Three-dimensional lines may be made using string, wire, tubes, solid rods, and the like.

calligraphy
Elegant, decorative writing. Lines in artworks that possess qualities found in writing may be called "calligraphic" and are generally flowing and rhythmical.

contour
The line that defines the edges of an object or a drawn or painted shape. The "outline" contours also may be marked by the variations of tones, textures, or colors.

cross-contour
A line that defines the surface undulations between, or up to, the outermost edges of shapes or objects.

expression
1. The manifestation of a thought, emotion, or quality of meaning through artistic form.
2. In art, *expression* is synonymous with the term *content.*

hatching
Repeated strokes of an art tool producing clustered lines (usually parallel) that create values. In "cross-hatching," similar lines pass over the hatched lines in a different direction, usually resulting in darker values.

implied line
Implied lines (subjective lines) are those that dim, fade, stop, and/or disappear. The missing portion of the line is implied to continue and is visually completed by the observer as the line reappears.

representation(al) art
A type of art in which the subject is presented through the visual art elements so that the observer is reminded of actual objects. (See **naturalism** and **realism** in the Glossary.)

LINE: THE ELEMENTARY MEANS OF COMMUNICATION

Line is the most familiar of the art elements; we use it every day. In art, line is the primary element in sketching and drawing, and is often employed in preparation for larger works. The term *line* is used in connection with many other situations: the checkout line, the prison or shopping lineup, the football line, the line of sight, the gas line, and so on. These everyday expressions imply something that is strung out or stretched a certain distance. You have undoubtedly stood in line for something and found your impatience turn to relief as you reached the front. Your line may have been a single line (narrow) or two abreast (wider). Sometimes lines become straggly, like the line to get in to a movie—but this had better not happen in a military parade, where a perfect formation is required. Standing lines often exhibit differences in width because of the different sizes of the people in the line or because people are bunched together.

Art lines and "people lines" have things in common. Theoretically, a line is an extended dot; so, if only one person shows up, a dot is made. But, as other people are added, with their different dimensions and positions, the line's characteristics change. In art, these line variations are called "physical characteristics," and the artist can use them to imply meanings as well as to produce appearances.

Lines are everywhere: the lines the artist makes with crayons, pens, and pencils have counterparts in the phenomena in nature. We can perceive lines in the cracks in a sidewalk, the annular rings of a tree, or a series of pebbles in alignment; and linear masses such as spider webs and tree limbs may also be seen as lines.

The artist can use line as a graphic device to indicate visual structures or as a mark symbolizing something observed; line is a ready means for recording reactions to observations (fig. 3.1). Linear designs in the form of ideograms and letters are a means of written communication, but the artist can use lines in a more broadly communicative manner. Line operates in different ways in the visual arts. For example, line can describe an edge, as on a piece of sculpture; or it

3.1 **Pat Steir, *Inner Sanctum Waterfall*, 1992. Oil on linen, 104 × 136.4 in. (246.4 × 346.7 cm).** Subjective in approach, Pat Steir uses line to create the waterfall's power and movement in this private place. Courtesy of Ani and David Kasparian, New Jersey.

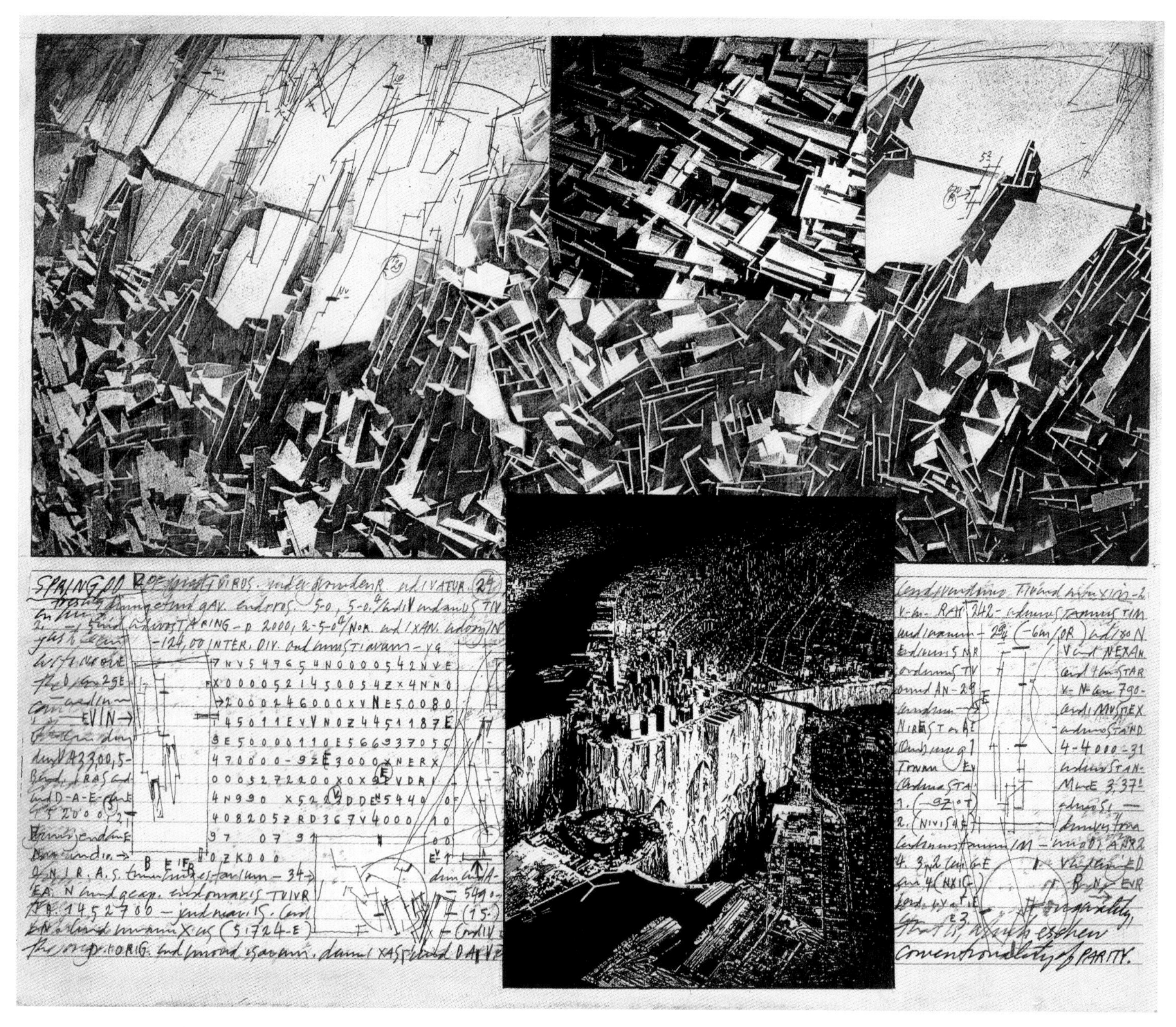

3.2 Lebbeus Woods, *Terrain 10,* 1999. Sanded paper collage with electrostatic print, ink, pencil, pastel and colored pencil, 23⅜ × 19⅜ in. Woods combines abstract mark, text, and realistic rendering in this image. In the top half of the image, line is used to create the illusion of planes, alluding to natural and architectonic forms. In the top right and left of the image, the line disintegrates into mark where no modeling or value is used. The bottom half of the image employs writing/documentation and a realistic rendering of Manhattan in an altered landscape. The text functions as line and mark and balances the light areas on the top. The central positioning of the cityscape draws the viewer's attention by its realistic rendering, extreme dark and light values, and tightly rendered mark. Notice how this area is echoed in the top middle of the image to balance the white of the values. Courtesy Henry Urbach Architecture, New York.

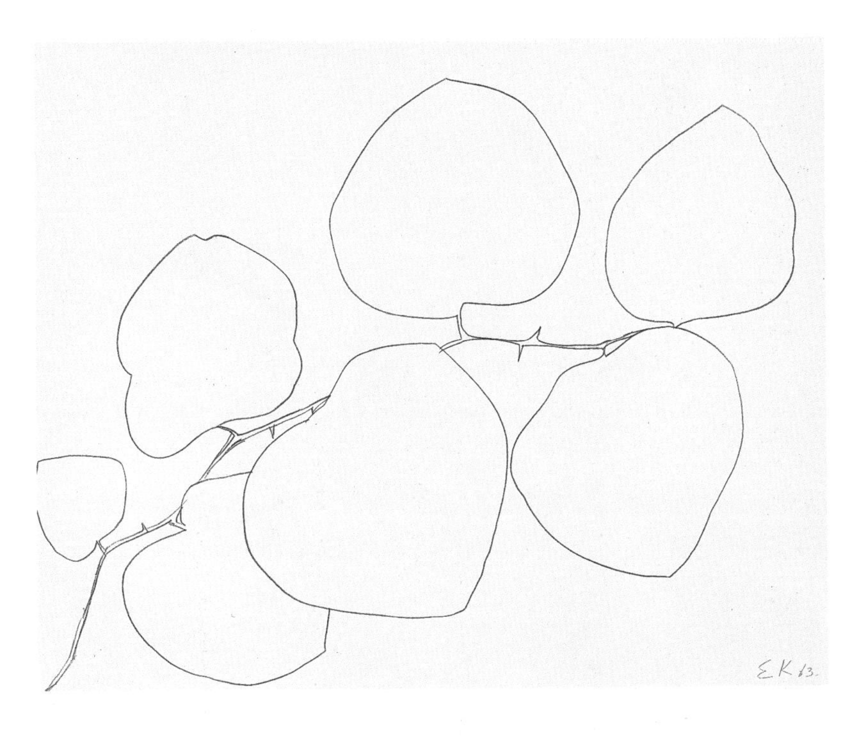

3.3 Ellsworth Kelly, *Briar,* 1963. Graphite on paper, 22⅝ × 28⅜ in. (57 × 72 cm). Line becomes contour as it encircles an object, giving it a distinctive, and often recognizable, shape. Whitney Museum of American Art, New York. Purchase, with funds from the Neysa McMein Purchase Award. 65.42. Photograph by Geoffrey Clements © 2000: The Whitney Museum of American Art.

3.4 Henri de Toulouse-Lautrec, *Jane Avril,* first plate from *Le Café Concert,* 1893. Lithograph, printed in black, 10½ × 8⁷⁄₁₆ in. (26.7 × 21.4 cm). The lines in this image seem to have been drawn with great freedom, communicating the graceful action of the subject. Gift of Abby Aldrich Rockefeller. (167.1946) The Museum of Modern Art/Licensed by SCALA/Art Resource, NY.

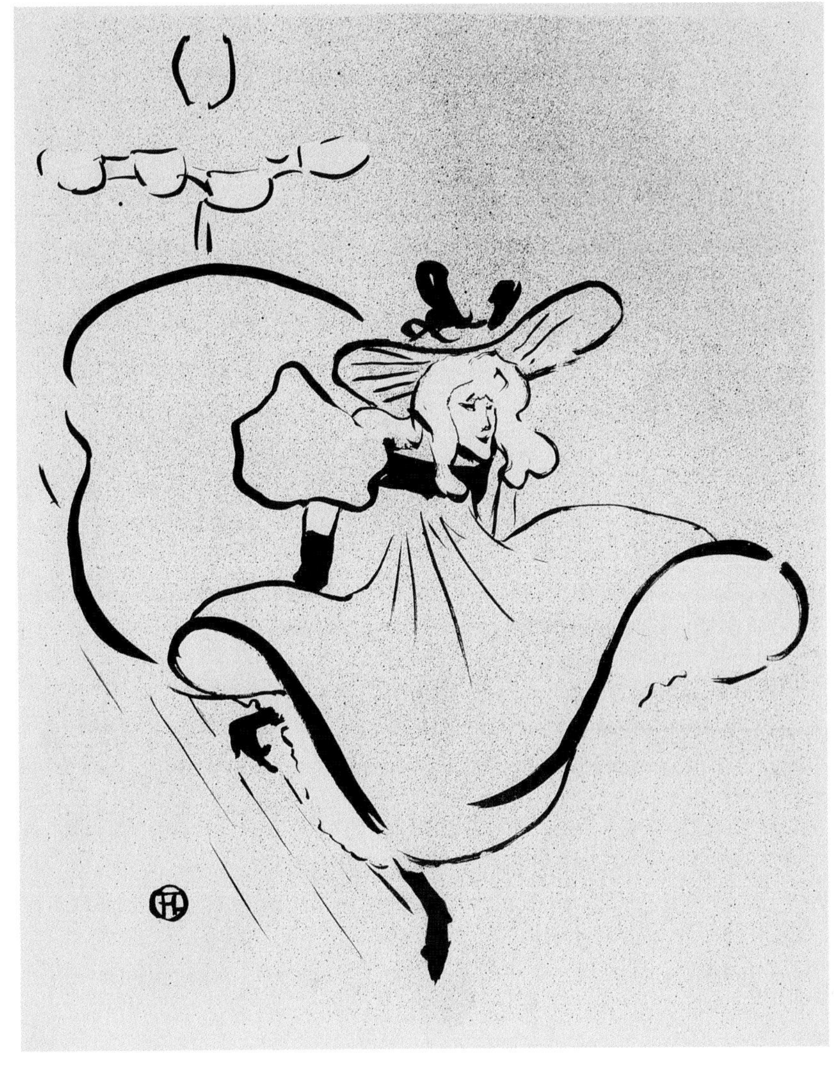

may mark a meeting of areas where value, textural, or color differences do not blend in a drawing (fig. 3.2); or it may be the contour defining the limits of a shape (fig. 3.3).

Although an artist most often draws clear and positively laid down graphic lines, he or she may occasionally use a broken **implied line** for variation in application to suggest spatial change, movement, or animation. These lines seem to fade, stop, and/or disappear and then reappear as a continuation or an extension of an edge or a direction. In the lithograph by Henri de Toulouse-Lautrec (fig. 3.4), the line of the dancer's skirt above her foot is implied to continue, and the shapes in the highest portion of the print have implied lines that the spectator must complete.

In three-dimensional art, actual lines can be created with wire, tubes, solid rods, and the like. Artists like Richard Lippold, Alexander Calder, and Kenneth Snelson have devoted their entire careers to creating sculpture in such materials (see figs. 9.26, 9.34, and 9.36).

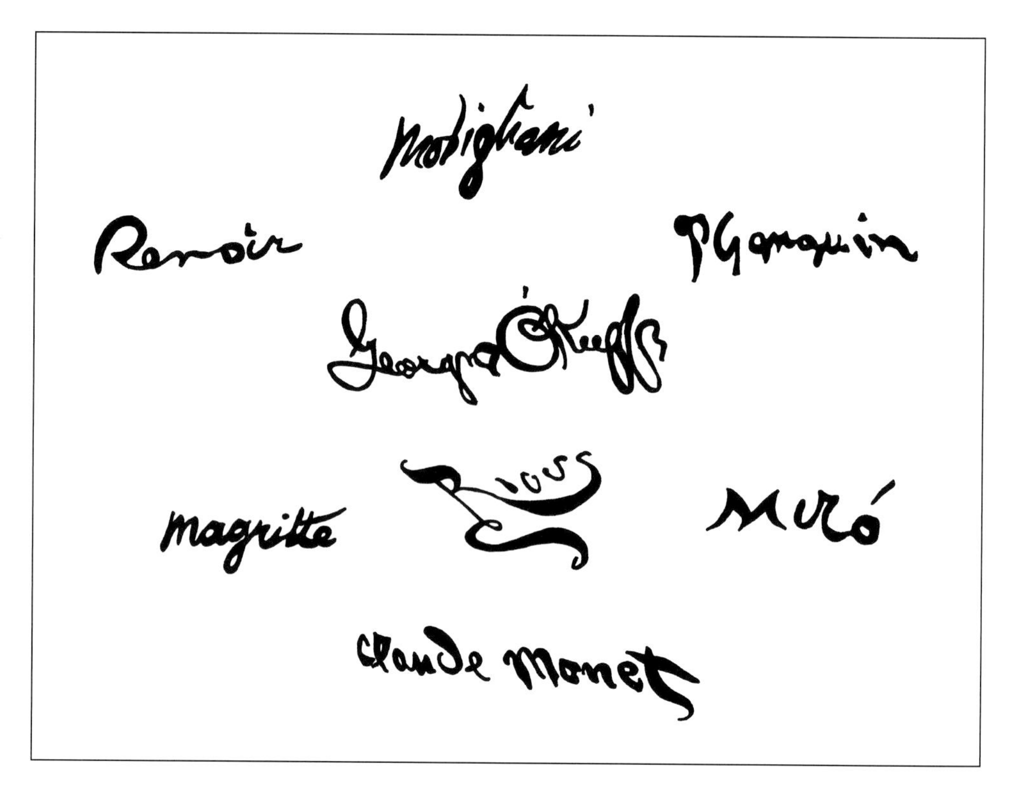

3.5 The illustrated signatures of famous artists often have, to some degree, the character of calligraphy, perhaps due to their profession.

Linear-type materials used sculpturally add an extra dimension to lines as they literally move throughout space. They may seem flat or actually swoop and swirl in space. Such explorations of space are a relatively new development.

Calligraphic lines in graphic art also seem to swoop and swirl, sometimes suggesting but never actually dipping into three dimensions. A calligraphic line is personal in nature, individualistic like handwriting; it is flowing and rhythmical, and intriguing to the eye as it enriches an artwork. In comparing the **calligraphy** of figure 3.5 with examples of drawn figures 3.6 and 3.7, one can see the shared qualities of grace and elegance. In addition, line performs several functions at the same time, including the expression of value and texture, thus illustrating the impossibility of making a real separation between the elements of art structure (see figs. 3.17 and 3.19).

Lines express feelings and nervous energy. The artist's selection of lines can imply certain meanings. Through the choice of line, the subject may be altered or enhanced, and the work becomes an interpretation of that subject. Line meanings also operate in conjunction with the other art elements.

THE PHYSICAL CHARACTERISTICS OF LINE

The physical characteristics of line are many. Lines may be straight or curved, direct or meandering, short or long, thin or thick, zigzag or serpentine. These characteristics have built-in associations that the artist can command. When we say that a person is a "straight arrow," we mean that he or she is straightforward and reliable; a "crooked" person, on the other hand, is devious and untrustworthy. In most cases, we have adjectives that fit the various kinds of lines we see; these meanings, like the word associations cited above, make for line's subtle power of psychological suggestion.

Measure

Measure refers to length and width of line. A line may be of any length and breadth. An infinite number of combinations of long and short, thick and thin lines can—according to their use—divide, balance, or unbalance a pictorial area.

Type

There are many different kinds of lines. If the line continues in only one direction, it is straight; if changes of direction gradually occur, it is curved; if those changes are sudden and abrupt, an angular line is created. Taking into consideration the characteristic of type as well as measure, we find that long or short, thick or thin lines can be straight, angular, or curved. The straight line, in its continuity, ultimately becomes repetitious and, depending on its length, either rigid or brittle. The curved line may form an arc, reverse its curve to become wavy, or continue turning within itself to produce a spiral. Alterations of movement become visually entertaining and physically stimulating if they are rhythmical. A curved line is inherently graceful and, to a degree, unstable (see figs. 3.4 and 3.25). The abrupt changes of direction in an angular line can create excitement and confusion (fig. 3.8). Frequently, our eyes have difficulty adapting to an angular line's unexpected deviations of direction. Hence, the angular line is full of challenging interest.

Direction

A further complication of line is its basic direction; a line's direction does not depend simply on the component

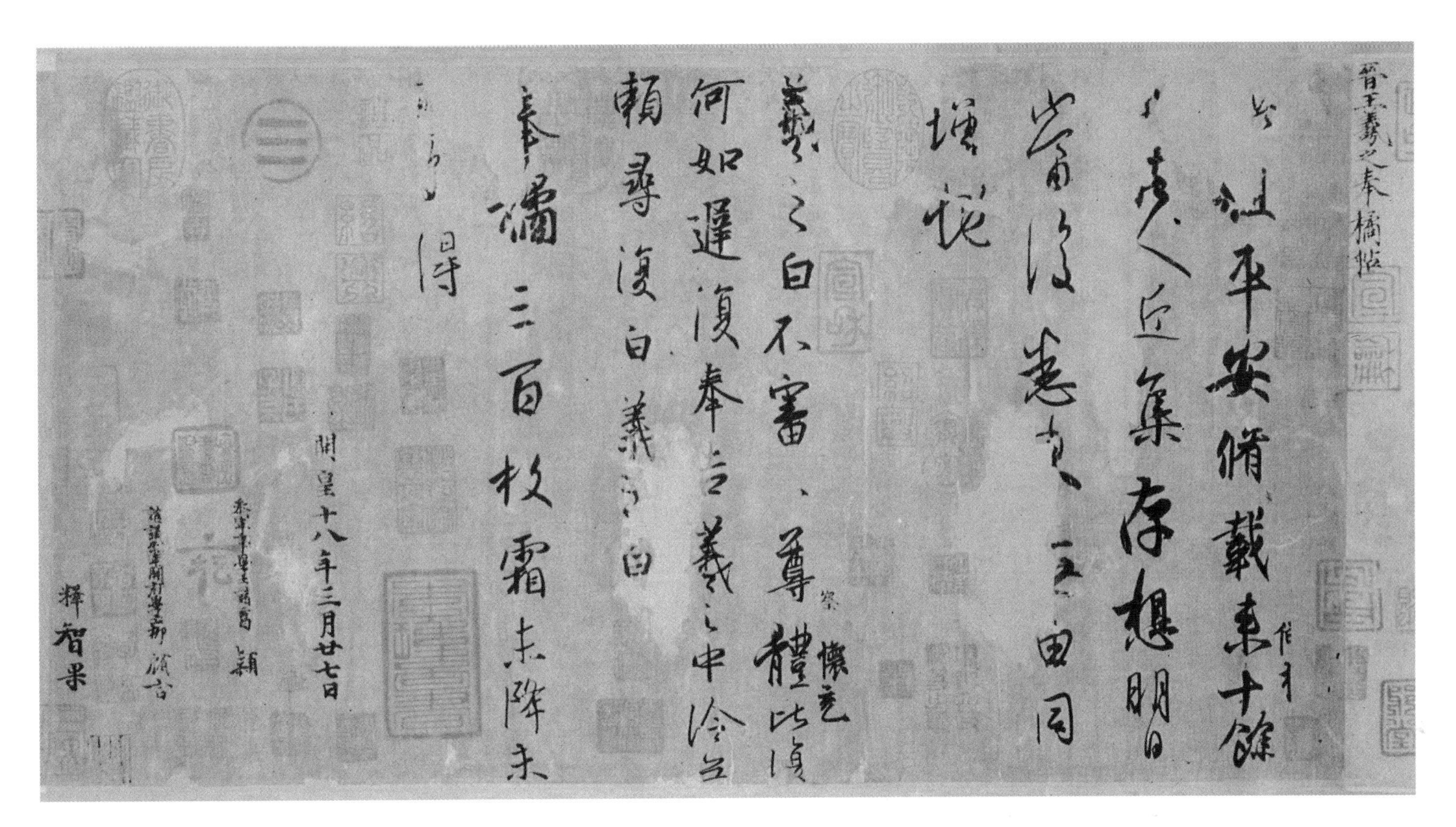

3.6 **Wang Hsi-chih, from Three Passages of Calligraphy: "Ping-an," "Ho-ju," and "Feng-chu," Eastern Ch'in dynasty, fourth century (A.D. 321–379),** ***Calligraphy.*** **Ink on paper.** Certain meanings intrinsic to line arise from their character. These meanings are the product of the medium, the tools used, and the artist's method of application. Calligraphy is esteemed in China as an art form equal to painting. Created with brush and ink on paper (the Chinese invented paper), the lively, abstract ideographs of Chinese calligraphy appear to leap upward and outward, "like a dragon leaping over heaven's gate." National Palace Museum, Taipei, Taiwan, Republic of China.

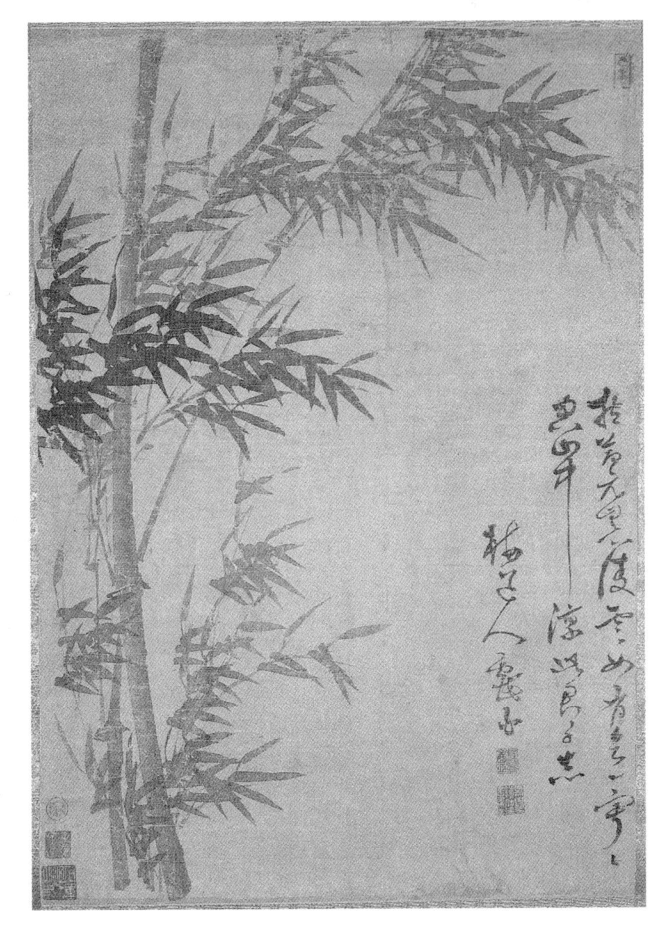

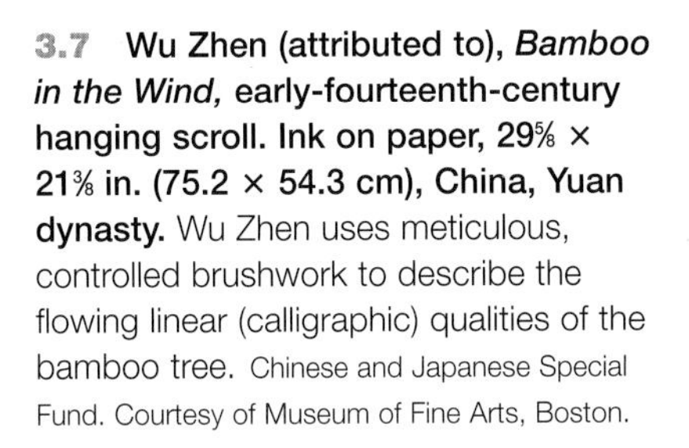

3.7 **Wu Zhen (attributed to),** ***Bamboo in the Wind,*** **early-fourteenth-century hanging scroll. Ink on paper, 29⅝ × 21⅜ in. (75.2 × 54.3 cm), China, Yuan dynasty.** Wu Zhen uses meticulous, controlled brushwork to describe the flowing linear (calligraphic) qualities of the bamboo tree. Chinese and Japanese Special Fund. Courtesy of Museum of Fine Arts, Boston.

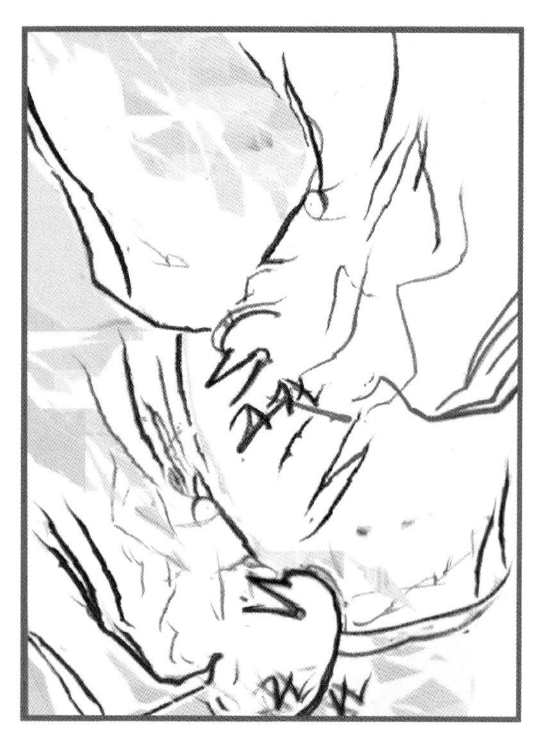

3.8 Clouret Bouchel, *Fight or Flight.* 9¼ × 12½ in. The abrupt changes of direction in the diagonal angular lines in this drawing create the excitement and tension of combat. Courtesy of the authors.

3.9 Mel Bochner, *Vertigo,* 1982. Charcoal, conté crayon, and pastel on canvas, 9 ft × 6 ft 2 in. (2.74 × 1.88 m). Line, the dominant element in this work, is almost wholly diagonal, imparting a feeling of intense activity and stress. Albright-Knox Art Gallery, Buffalo, NY. Charles Clifton Fund, 1982. © Mel Bochner.

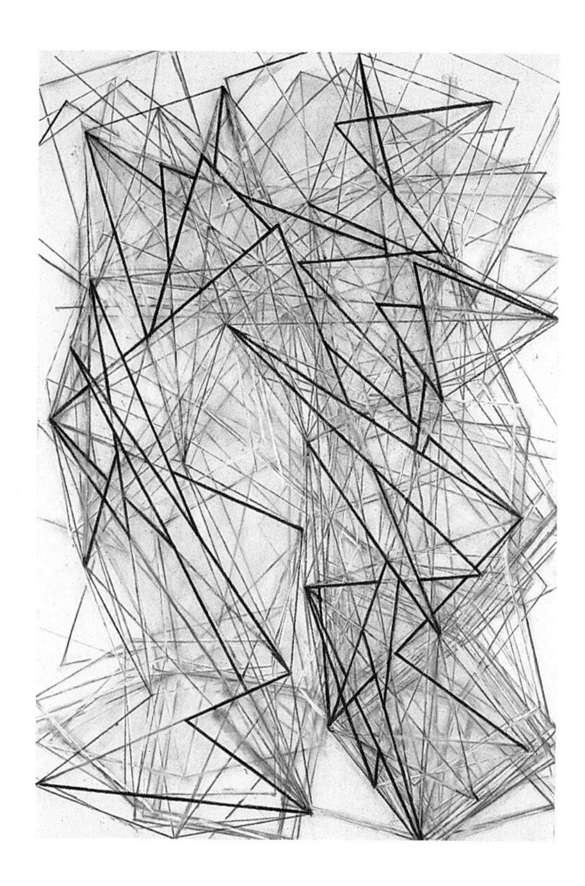

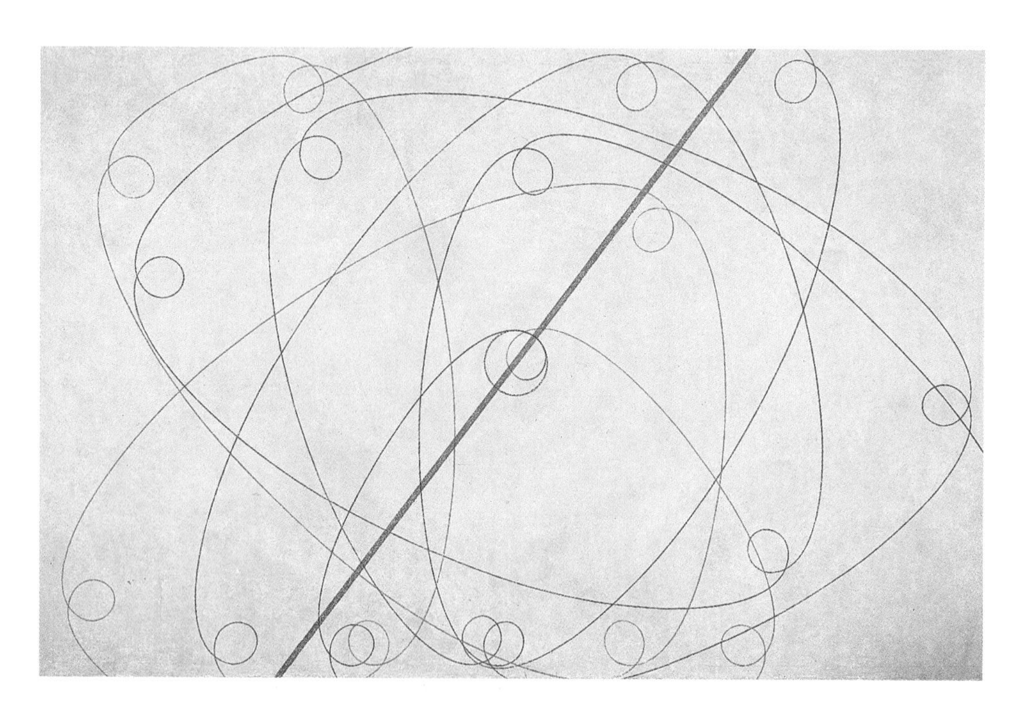

3.10 Dorothea Rockburne, *Continuous Ship Curves, Yellow Ochre,* 1991. Fresco pigment and watercolor stick, 10 ft × 15 ft 7 in. (3.05 × 4.75 m). The ever-changing directions of the continuous lines in Dorothea Rockburne's painting control the movement of the eye as they loop about and traverse the pictorial composition. Courtesy of André Emmerich Gallery, a Division of Sotheby's, on behalf of © 2005 Dorothea Rockburne/Artists Rights Society (ARS), NY.

movements within it. That is, a line can be a zigzag type but take a generally curved direction. Thus, the line type can be contradicted or reaffirmed by its basic movement. A generally horizontal direction could indicate serenity and stability, whereas a diagonal direction would probably imply agitation and motion (fig. 3.9). A vertical line generally suggests poise and aspiration. The direction of line is very important, because in large measure it controls the movements of our eyes while we view a picture. Our eye movements can facilitate the continuity of relationships among the various properties of the element (fig. 3.10).

Location

The control exercised over the measure, type, or direction of a line can be enhanced or diminished by its specific location. According to its placement, a line can serve to unify or divide, balance or unbalance a pictorial area. A diagonal line might be soaring or plunging, depending on its high or low position relative to the frame. The various attributes of line can act in concert toward one goal or can serve separate roles of expression and design. A fully developed work, therefore, may use all the physical properties of line, although it is also possible that fewer can be used successfully. This is true largely because of the dual role of these properties. For instance, unity in a work might be achieved by repetition of line length at the same time that variety is being created through difference in the lines' width, medium, or other properties.

Character

Along with measure, type, direction, and location, line possesses character, a term largely related to the medium with which the line is created. Different media can be used in the same work to create greater interest. Monotony can result from the consistent use of lines of the same character unless the unity so gained is balanced by the variation of other physical properties. Varied instruments, such as the brush, pen, stick, or finger, have distinctive characteristics that the artist can exploit (fig. 3.11). The artist is the real master of the situation, and it is the artist's ability, experience, intention, and mental and physical condition that determine the effectiveness of line character. Whether the viewer sees lines of uniformity or accent, certainty or indecision, tension or relaxation depends on decisions the artist makes.

The personality or emotional quality of the line is rooted in the nature of the medium chosen. In Rembrandt's sketch *Nathan Admonishing David,* the expressive qualities created by the soft brush lines of ink, juxtaposed with the precise and firm lines of the pen, can be clearly seen (fig. 3.12).

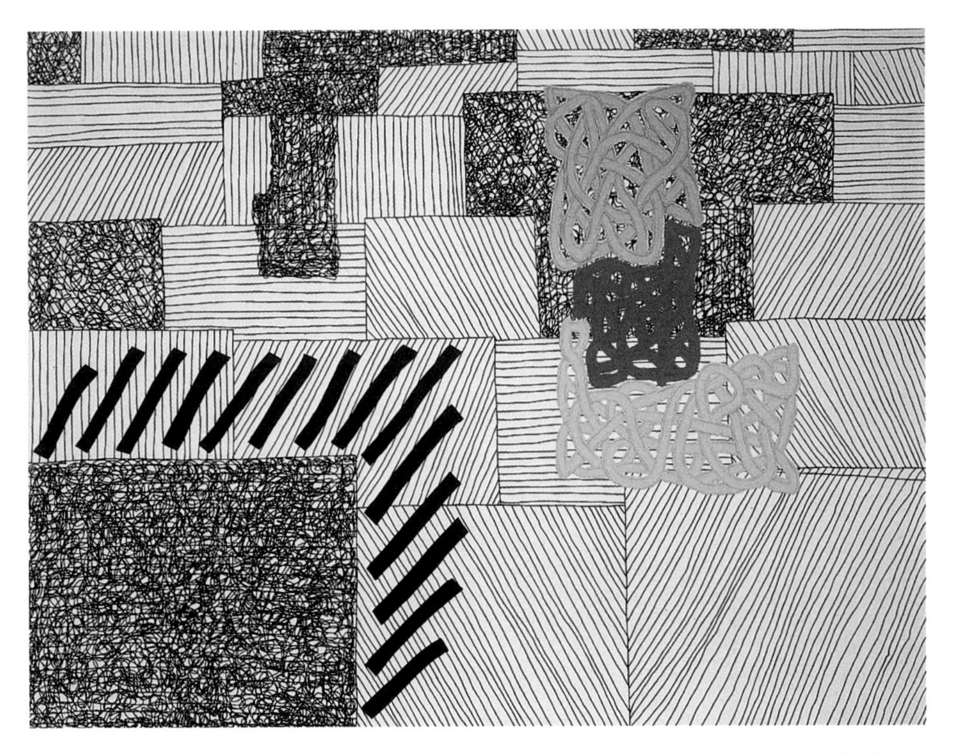

3.11 Jonathan Lasker, *The Artistic Painting,* 1993. Oil on canvas, 90 × 120 in. (228.6 × 304.8 cm). The unique character of the line work in this piece is enhanced by the careful choice of tools, color, and shape. Collection Fonds Cultural National, Luxembourg (Sammlung des zukünftigen Musée d'Art Moderne Grand-Duc Jean). Courtesy of Sperone Westwater, New York.

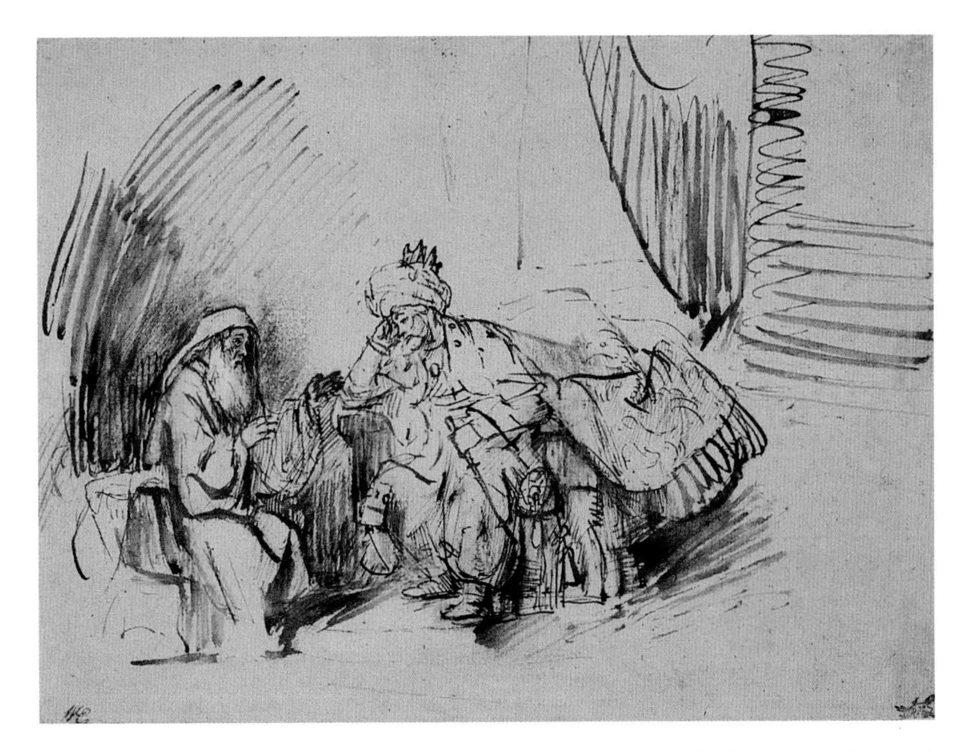

3.12 Rembrandt Harmenszoon van Rijn, *Nathan Admonishing David,* no date. Pen and brush with bistre, 7⁵⁄₁₆ × 9⁵⁄₁₆ in. (18.6 × 23.6 cm). The crisp, biting lines of the pen contrast effectively with broader, softer lines of the brush. © Metropolitan Museum of Art, New York. Bequest of Mrs. H. O. Havemeyer, 1929. The Havemeyer Collection.

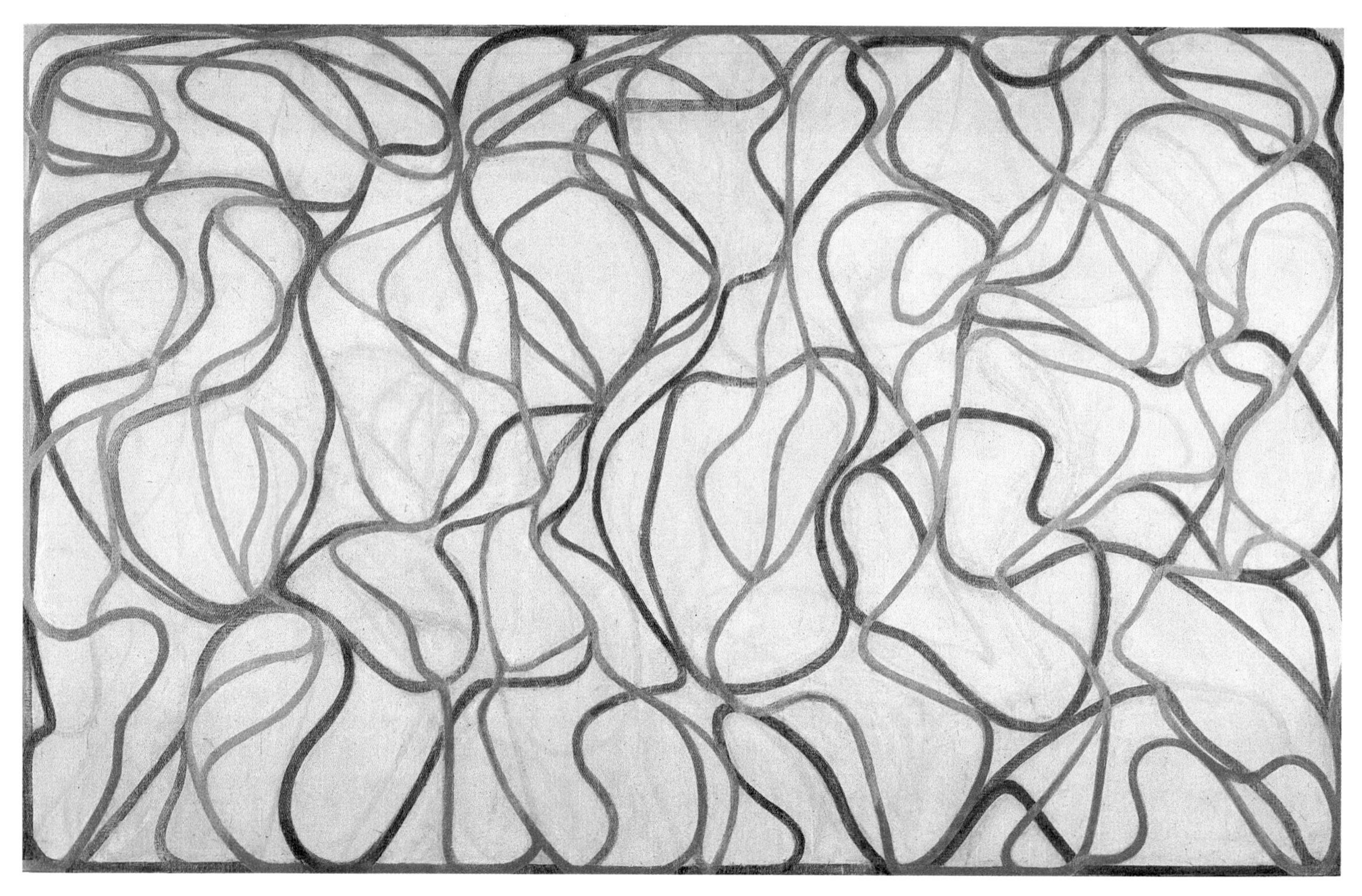

3.13 Brice Marden, *Study for the Muses* (Eaglesmere Version), 1991–97. Oil on linen, 83 × 135 in. Brice Marden presents a weblike network of lines that seem to wander in space. This artist, however, works, reworks, and calculates the lines as he engages in spatial exploration using subtle changes in value, color, and trailing line. Courtesy of Matthew Marks Gallery, New York. MART.PA.2683. © 2005 Brice Marden/Artists Rights Society (ARS), NY.

THE EXPRESSIVE PROPERTIES OF LINE

The qualities of line can be described in terms of feelings—somber, tired, energetic, brittle, alive, and the like. However, in a work of art, as in the human mind, such feelings are rarely so clearly defined. An infinite number of conditions of varying subtlety can be communicated by the artist. The spectator's apprehension of these qualities is also a matter of feeling, which means that the spectator must be receptive and perceptive and have a reservoir of experience to draw upon.

Through composition and **expression,** individual lines come to life as they play their roles. Some lines are dominant and some subordinate, but all are integrally important to the work of art. Although lines may be admired separately, their real beauty lies in the relationships they establish in the form (fig. 3.13). This form can be representational or nonrepresentational, but recognition and enjoyment of the work are heightened when the work is understood on the abstract level. A preoccupation with subject can blind us to the work's expressive art qualities, and the resulting lack of organizational soundness may confuse us about the artist's intentions. Organization brings the artist's intentions to the forefront. The composition also influences our thoughts and feelings

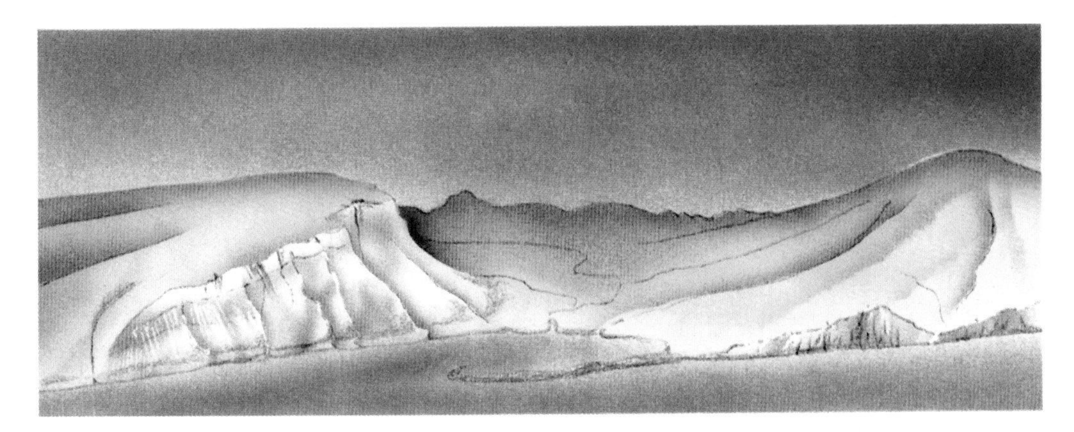

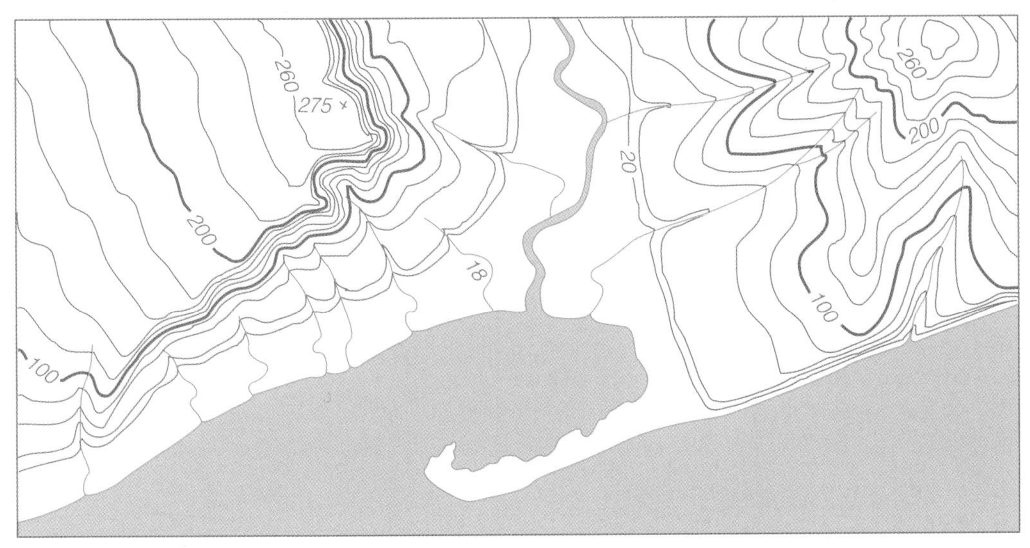

3.14 The lines on a topographical map indicate the various elevations of the earth's surface. In a similar way, the artist uses cross-contours to show the configuration of the subject.

regarding the image depicted, regardless of whether the subject matter has been a part of our past experience.

LINE AND THE OTHER ART ELEMENTS

Line has physical characteristics that are closely related to the other art elements. Line can possess color, value, and texture, and it can create shape. Some of these factors are essential to the very creation of line, whereas others enter as needed. These properties might be thought of separately, but nevertheless they cooperate to give line intrinsic appeal, such that line is admired for its own sake. Artists often exploit this appeal by creating pictures where the linear effects dominate all the other effects. On the other hand, some works seem absent of line, depending entirely on other elements.

Line and Shape

To create shape, line traces the continuous edge of a figure, object, or mass. A line that describes an area in this manner is called a **contour.** Whereas contour lines generally describe the extremities of shapes or masses, **cross-contours** provide information about the nature of the surfaces contained within those edges, somewhat in the manner of a topographical map (fig. 3.14). If one imagines an ant, saturated with ink, crawling around one's face and leaving a trail, one can see that it has described the features of that face by cross-contour (fig. 3.15). An artist can use modulated lines—that is, thick and thin, irregular and curved—to enhance cross-contours; he or she can even vary the pressure when producing the line so that its darkest portion would seem to advance and the lightest to recede. Lines, massed together, can be varied in spacing from narrow to wide to produce a similar advancing and/or receding effect. Contour lines also have the capacity to separate shapes, values, textures, and colors (fig. 3.16).

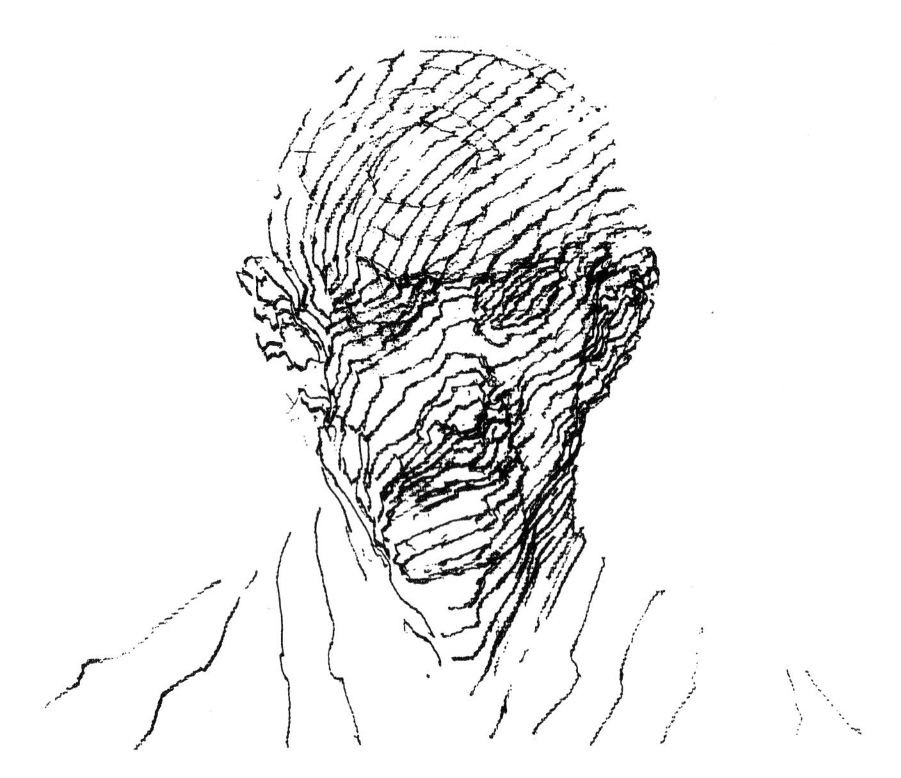

3.15 Harold Tovish, *Contour Drawing,* 1972. Pencil, 19 × 25 in. (48.3 × 63.5 cm). The cross-contours illustrate the dips and swells of features. This technique can be used to describe the surface of any subject being interpreted. Courtesy of the artist.

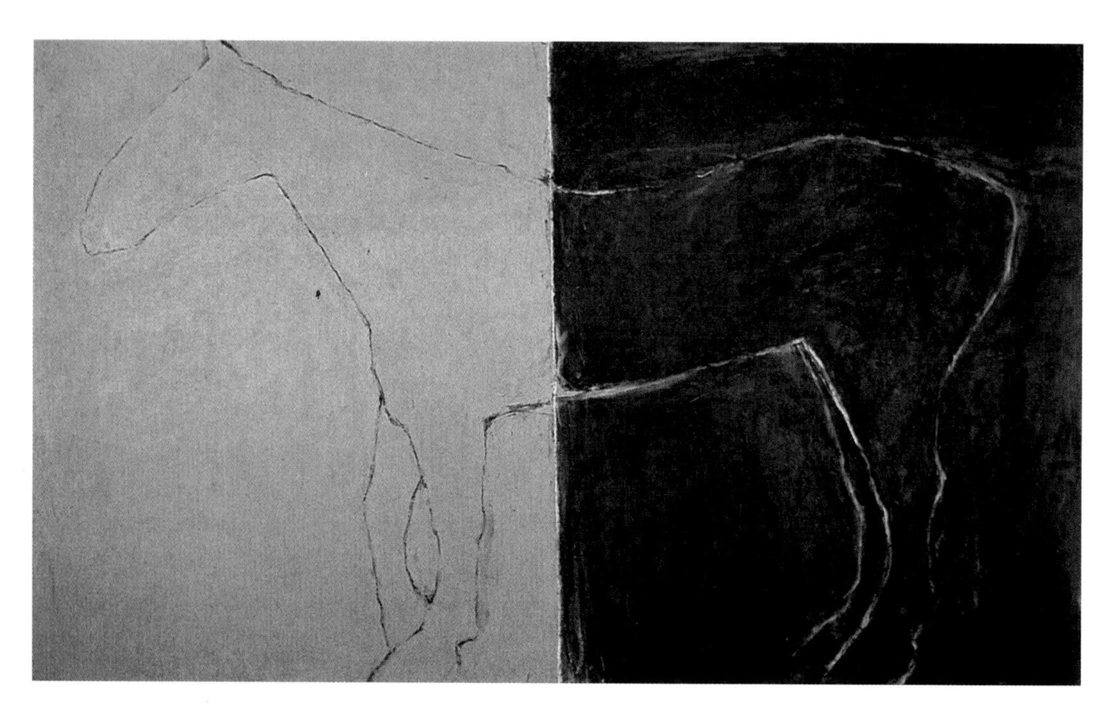

3.16 Susan Rothenberg, *United States,* 1975. Acrylic and tempera on canvas, 9 ft 6 in. × 15 ft 9 in. (2.90 × 4.80 m). The line describing the horse in this painting is called a contour. Susan Rothenberg is a contemporary artist who is noted for her series of horses done in a manner that might be referred to as Minimalist-Abstract. Collection of Mr. and Mrs. Frank Rothman. Courtesy of Sperone Westwater, New York, on behalf of the artist. © 2005 Susan Rothenberg, Artists Rights Society (ARS), NY.

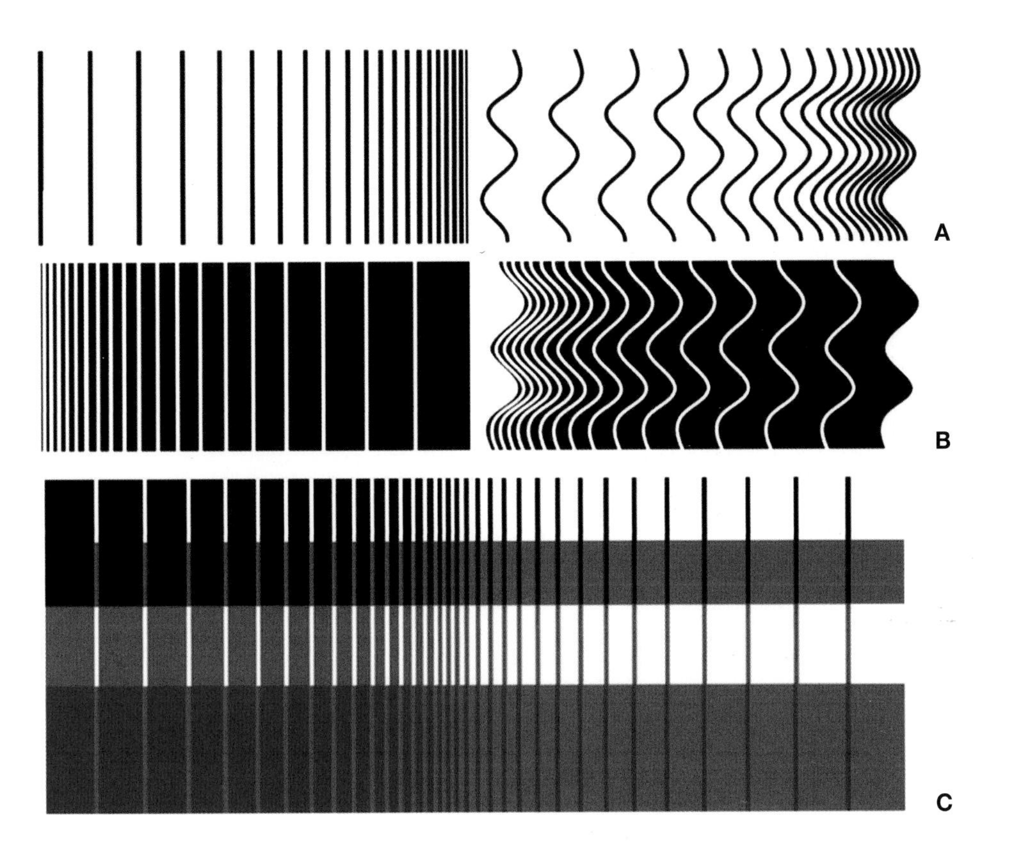

3.17 Group lines produce value. (A) Darker areas are created as lines (straight or irregular) are drawn more closely together. (B) Dark values appear as the width of the line increases but the spacing between remains constant. (C) Lines act as a transition between dark and light, dark and a color, a color and white, and two different colors.

A series of closely placed lines creates textures and toned areas. The relationships of the ends of these linear areas establish boundaries that transpose the areas into shapes.

Line and Value

The contrast in lightness and darkness that a line exhibits against its background is called value. Usually, a line will use a value different from its surroundings to be visible. Groups of lines create areas that can differ in value. Lines can be thick, thin, or any width in between. Wide, heavy lines appear dark in value, while narrow lines appear light in value. Value changes also can be controlled by varying the spaces between the lines. Widely spaced lines appear light, and closely spaced lines appear dark (fig. 3.17). Value differences can also result from mixtures of media or from variations in the amount of pressure exerted. Parallel lines and cross-hatching are examples of groups of lines that create areas of differing value (fig. 3.18). Sometimes, when **hatching** is used to produce value, the strokes will also define the direction of a surface at any given point.

Line and Texture

Groups of lines can combine to suggest the texture of a surface (fig. 3.19). This apparent texture can result from the inherent characteristics of individual media and tools, and these distinctive characteristics can be enhanced or diminished by the manner of handling. Brushes with a hard bristle, for instance, can make either sharp or rough lines, depending on hand pressure, amount of medium carried, and quality of execution. Brushes with soft hairs can produce smooth lines if loaded with thin paint and can produce thick blotted lines if loaded with heavy paint. Similar variations of line are inherent in all tools and media (fig. 3.20).

Line and Color

The introduction of color to a line increases expressive potential. Color can accentuate other line properties. A hard line combined with an intense color produces a forceful or even harsh effect. This effect would be considerably muted if the same line were created in a neutral color. Different colors are identified with different emotional states. Thus, the artist might use red as a symbol of passion or anger, yellow to suggest cowardice or warmth, and so forth (see the "Color and Emotion" section in Chapter 7, p. 161).

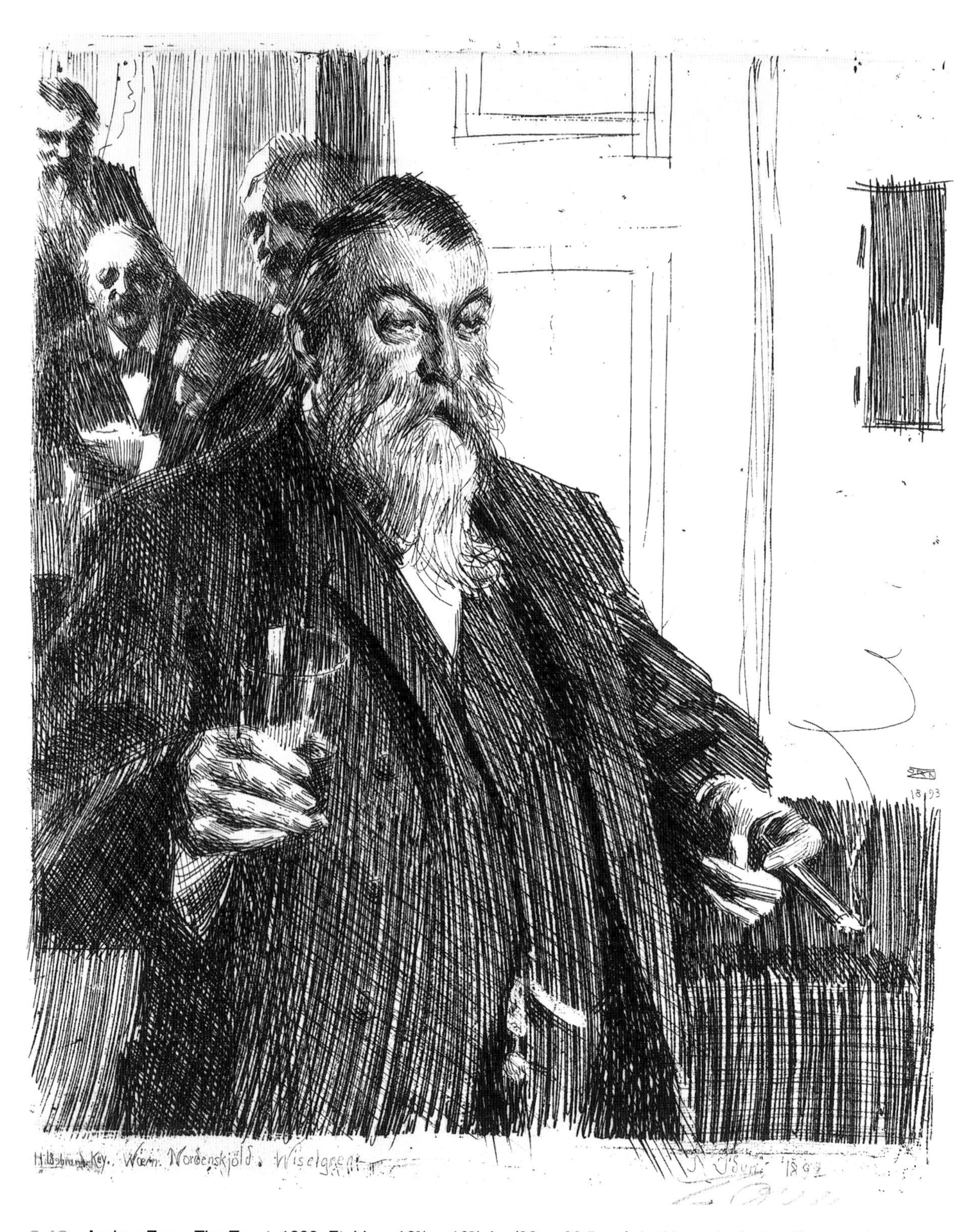

3.18 Andres Zorn, *The Toast*, 1893. Etching, $12\frac{5}{8} \times 10\frac{7}{16}$ in. (32 × 26.5 cm). In this work, Andres Zorn used hatching and cross-hatching to create degrees of value: darks where lines are densely drawn and lighter values where more paper can be seen. Kupferstichkabinett, Staatliche Kunstsammlungen, Dresden. Photo Deutsche Fotothek, Dresden.

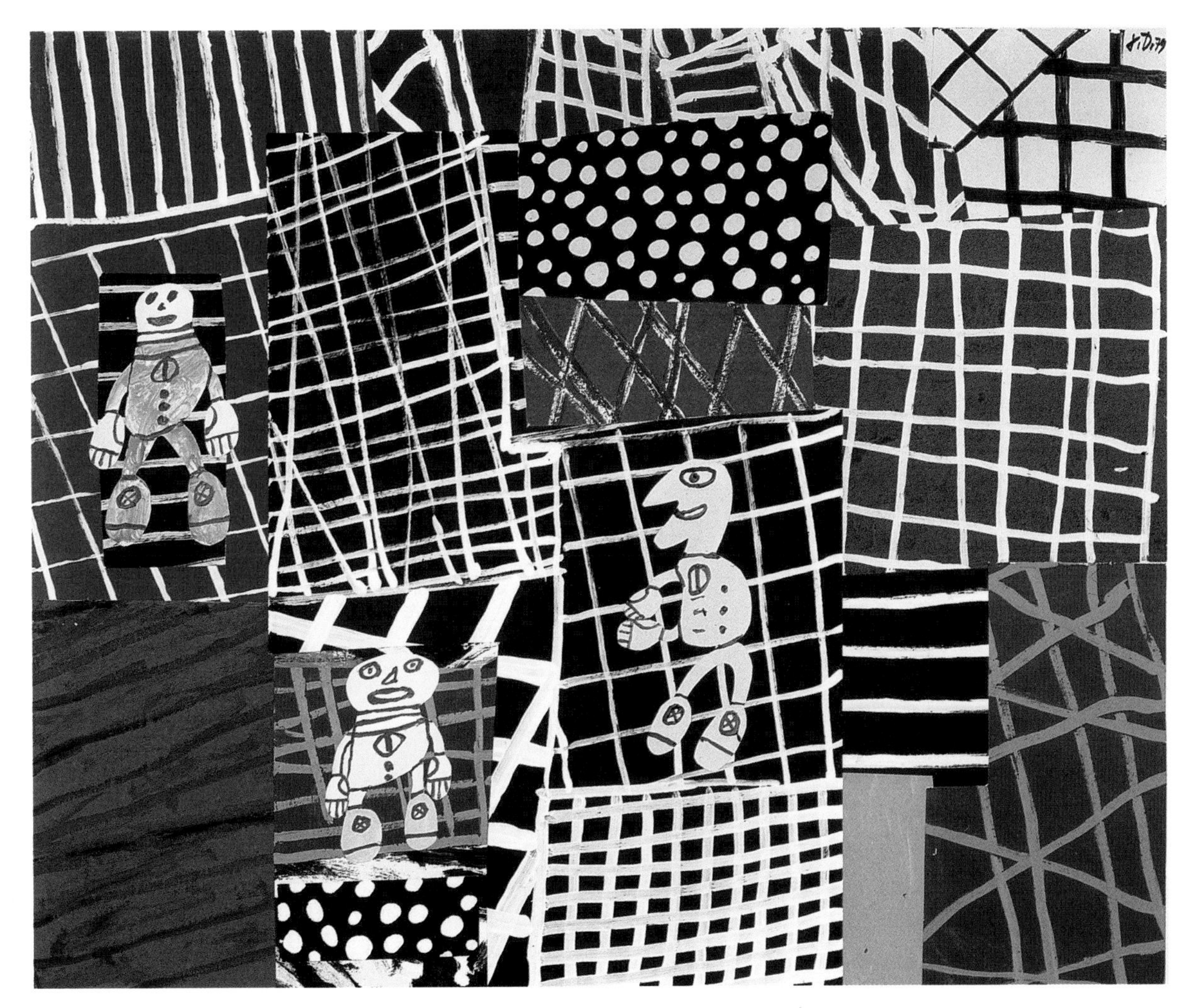

3.19 Jean Dubuffet, *Urgence,* 1979. Acrylic on canvas-backed paper with collage, 22½ × 27½ in. (57.15 × 69.85 cm). In this painting/collage, Jean Dubuffet creates diverse textures by varying his many line combinations. Collection Donald Rubin. Courtesy of Jonathan Novak Contemporary Art, Los Angeles. © 2005 Artists Rights Society (ARS), New York/ADAGP, Paris.

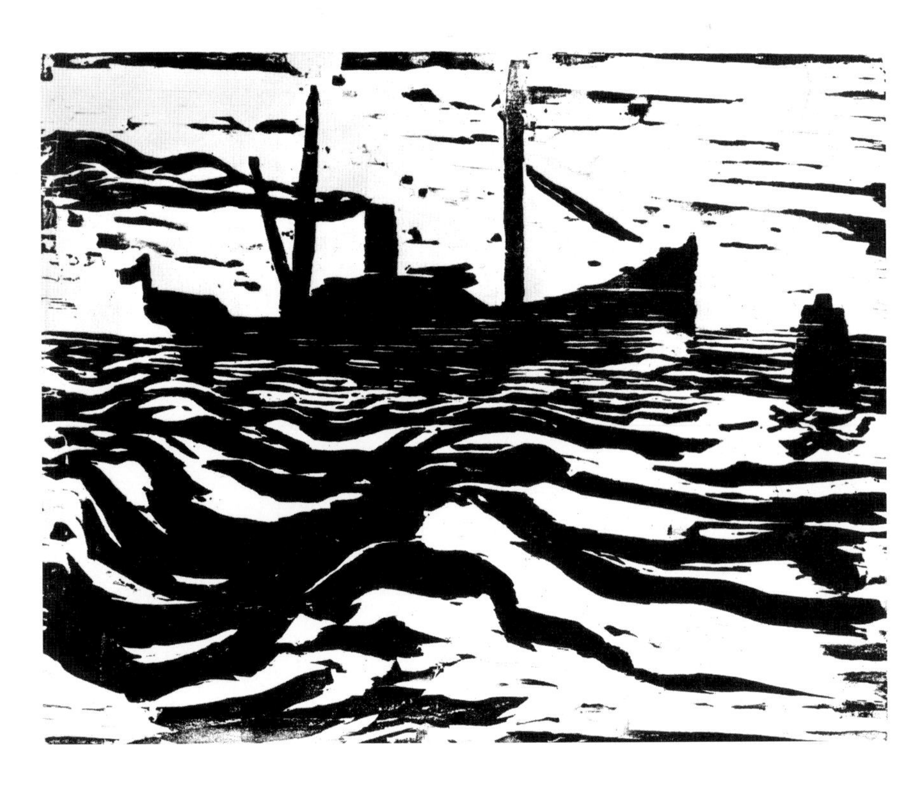

3.20 Emil Nolde, *Fischdampfer* (*Fishing Boat*), 1910. Print (woodcut), 11¾ × 15⅝ in. (29.84 × 39.37 cm). When knives and gouges are used to cut the wood, the lines and textures created are different from those produced by another medium. Nolde-Stiftung Seebüll, Germany. Inventory number Ho41. Photograph by Kleinhempel, Hamburg.

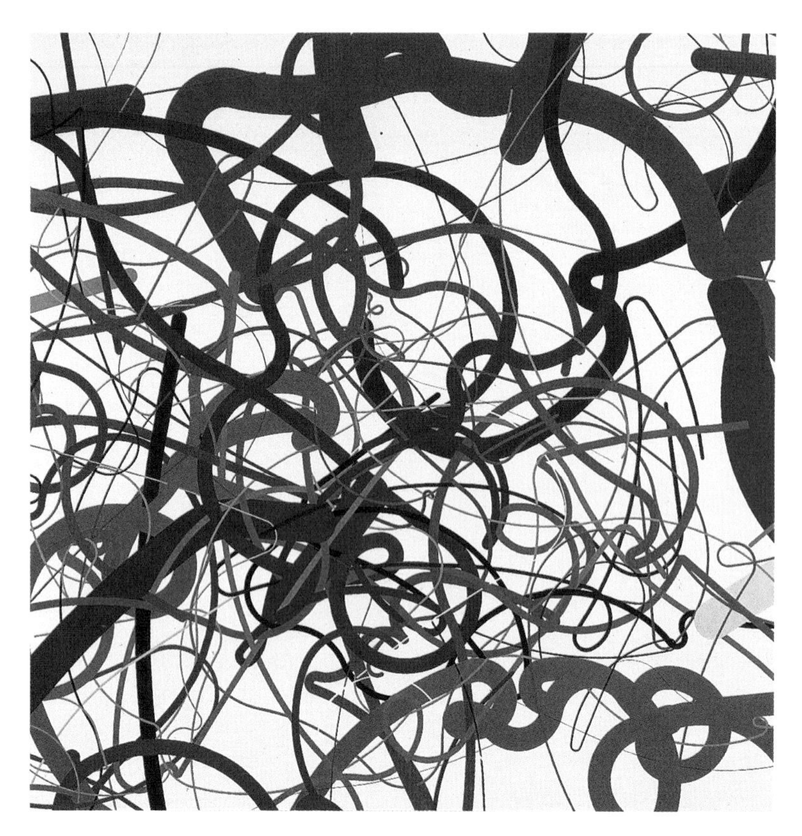

3.21 Zdenek Sykora, *Line No. 50,* 1988. Oil on canvas, 59 × 59 in. (149.8 × 149.8 cm). Variations in the continuous curvilinear lines within this painting create illusions of open space. These variations include changes in the physical properties of the measure, direction, location, and character of the lines, as well as changes in value and color. Courtesy of Prague National Gallery.

THE SPATIAL CHARACTERISTICS OF LINE

All the physical characteristics of line contain spatial properties that are subject to control by the artist. Mere position within a prescribed area suggests space. Value contrast can cause lines to advance and recede (fig. 3.21). An individual line with varied values throughout its length may appear to writhe and twist in space. Because warm colors generally advance and cool colors generally recede, the spatial properties of colored lines are obvious. Every factor that produces line has something to say about a line's location in space. The artist's job is to use these factors to create spatial order (fig. 3.22).

LINE AND REPRESENTATION

Line creates representation on both abstract and realistic levels. In general, we have dealt primarily with abstract definitions, but it is easy to see that the application can be observed equally in a realistic context. For example, we have discussed the advancing and receding qualities of value in a line. If a particular line is drawn to represent the contours of a piece of drapery, the value contrast, as it changes in measure and direction, might describe the relative spatial position of the folds of the drapery (fig. 3.23). An artist drawing a linear portrait

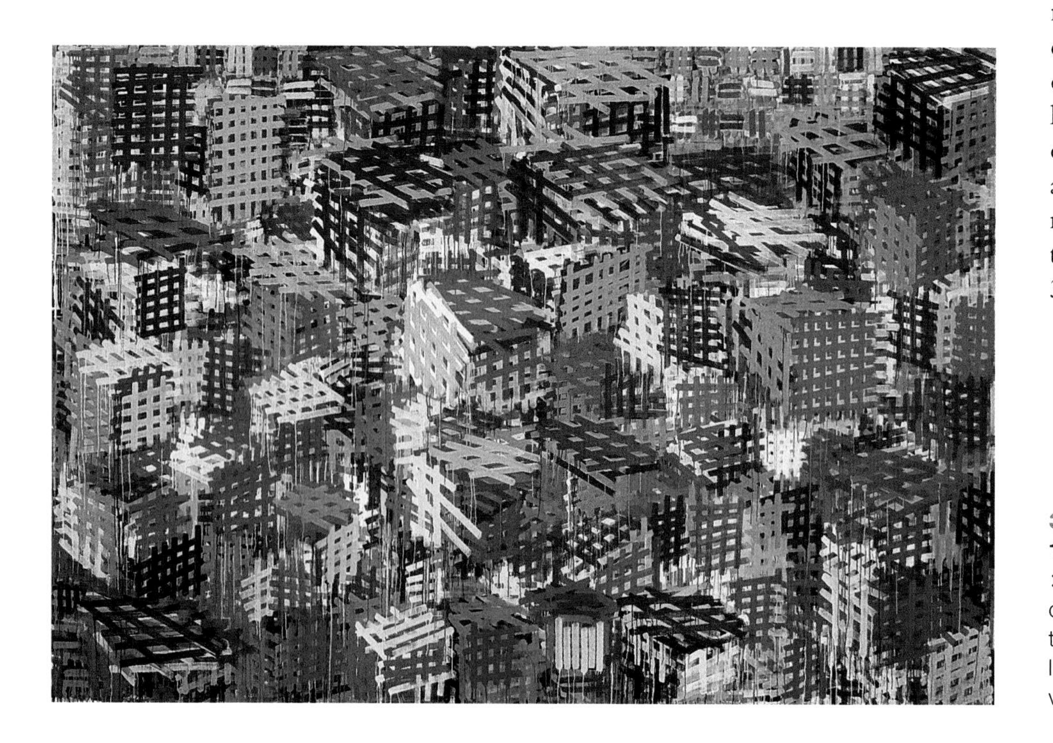

3.22 Denyse Thomasos, *Urban Jewels,* 1995. Acrylic on canvas, 10 × 16 ft (304.8 × 487.68 cm). The spatial illusion, of such obvious importance in this example, is largely the product of the physical properties of the lines strengthened by contrasting areas of value and color. Lennon, Weinberg, NY.

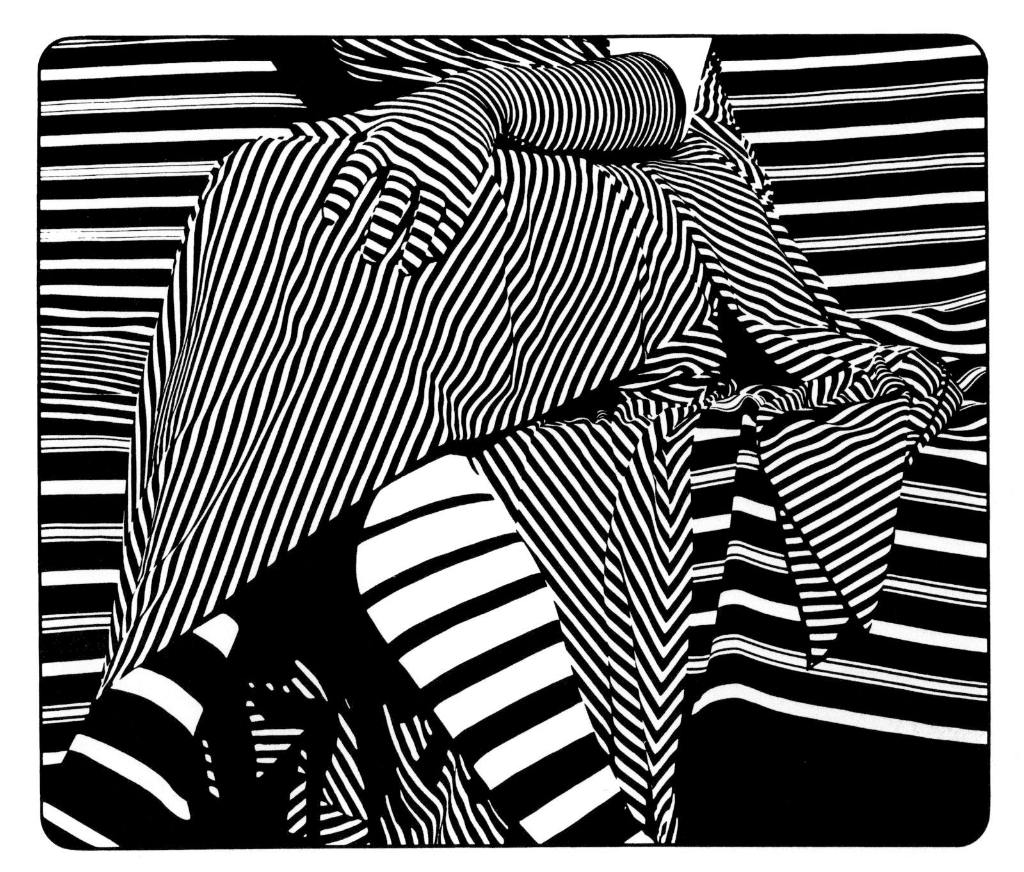

3.23 J. Seeley, *Stripe Song,* 1981. Print (photo silkscreen), 22 × 30 in (81.9 × 76.2 cm). Seeley is an acknowledged master of the high-contrast image. Combining the undeniable visual appeal of Op art with the implicit realism of the photographic image, the artist's black-and-white linear abstractions are boldly decorative, highly complex, and a delightful treat for the eye. © Seeley/Licensed by VAGA, New York, NY.

of a person might use line properties to suggest a physical presence (fig. 3.24). The artist might also be able to convey—either satirically or sympathetically—much information about the character of the sitter. Thus, line in **representational art** has many objective and subjective implications. All are the result of the artist's manipulation of its physical properties.

In its role of signifying ideas and conveying feelings, line moves and lives, pulsating with significant emotions. In visual art, line becomes a means for transcribing the nervous energy of ideas and emotions. It describes the edges or contours of shapes, it diagrams silhouettes, it encompasses spaces and areas—all in such a way as to convey meaning.

Line is not used exclusively to express deep emotion. Often, it depicts the facts alone: the lines drawn in an architect's

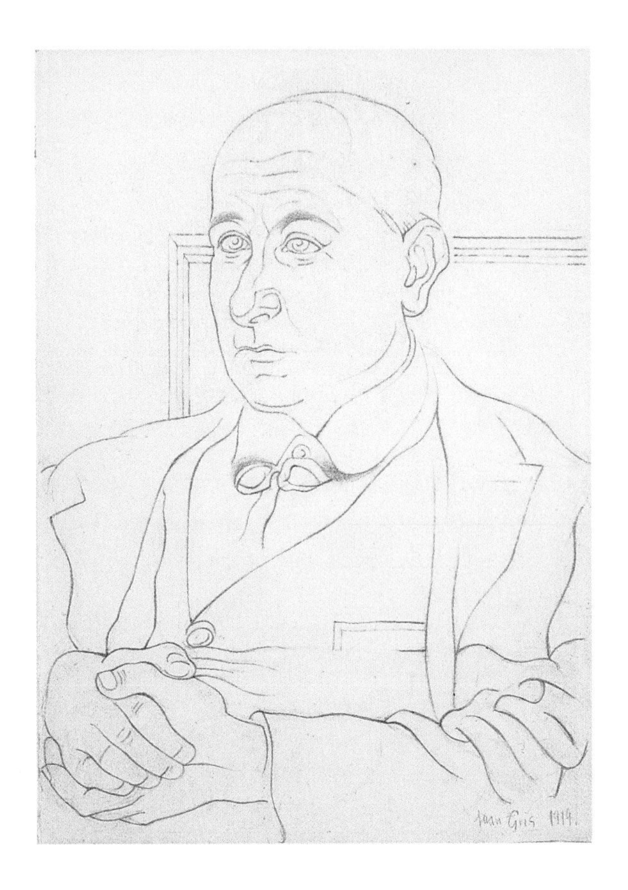

3.24 Juan Gris (José Victoriano González), *Portrait of Max Jacob,* 1919. Pencil on sheet, 14⅜ × 10½ in. (36.5 × 26.7 cm). This drawing, done entirely in line, describes the physical presence as well as the psychological character of the sitter. Gift of James Thrall Soby. The Museum of Modern Art, New York, NY, U.S.A. Digital image © The Museum of Modern Art/Licensed by SCALA/Art Resource, NY.

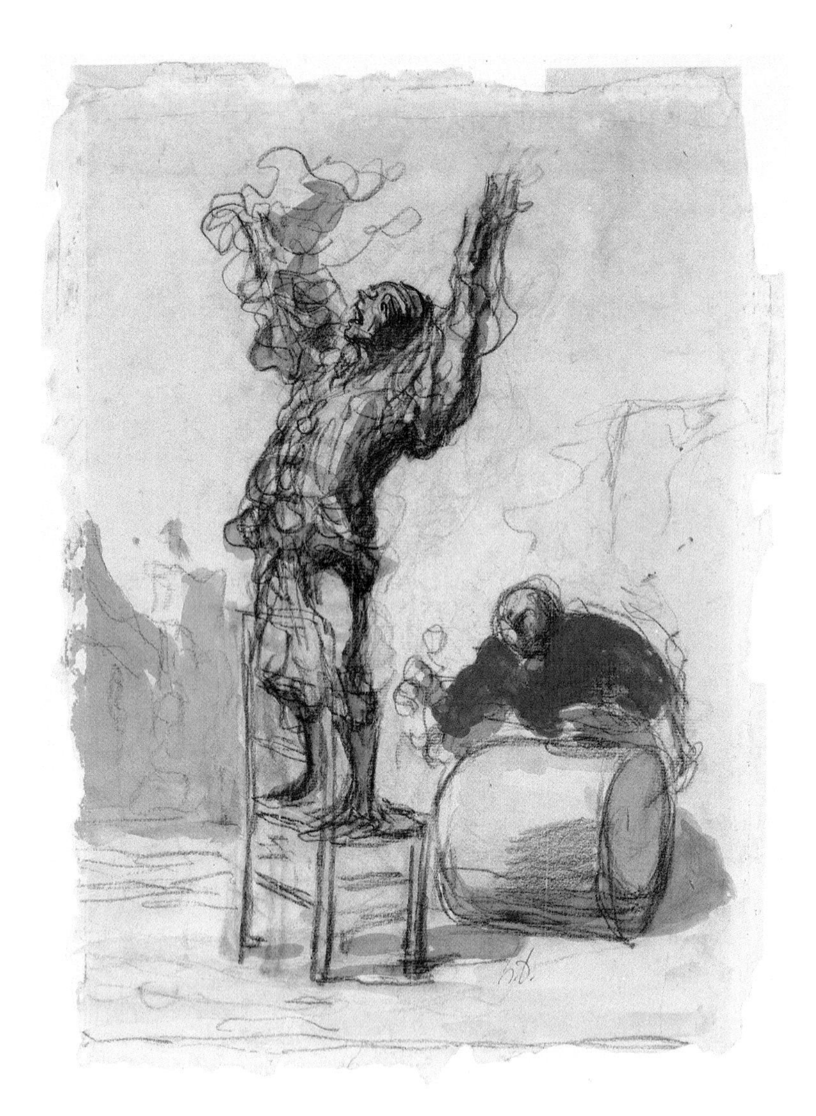

3.25 Honoré Daumier, *Street Show*, 1865–66. Black chalk and watercolor on laid paper, 14⅝ × 10⅟₁₆ in. (36.8 × 25.4 cm). Though subjects are often static and immobile, Daumier used the excitement of gestural line to interpret the gyrations of the dancer and the frenzied beating of the drummer. The Metropolitan Museum of Art, Rogers Fund, 1927. (27.152.2) Photograph © The Metropolitan Museum of Art.

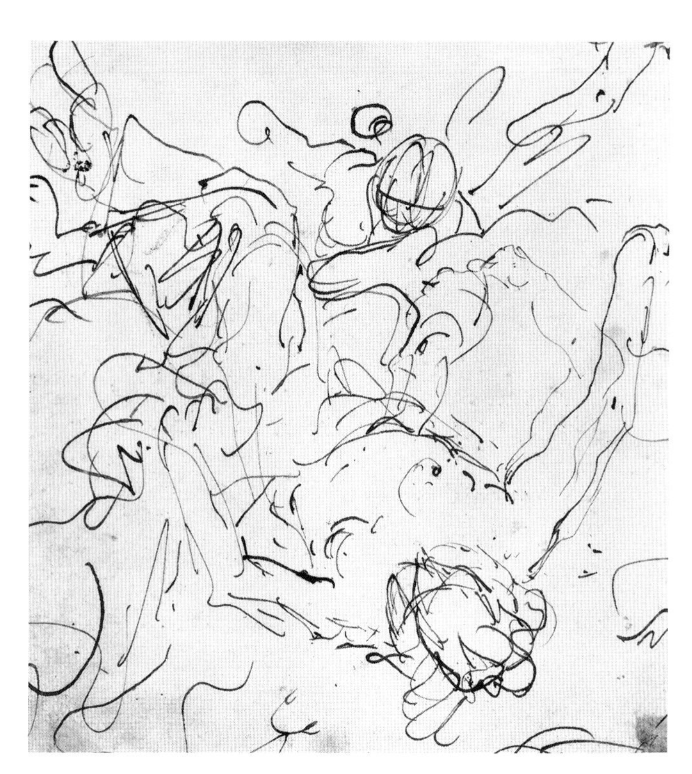

3.26 Giovanni Battista Tiepolo, *Study for Figure of Falsehood on the Ceiling of the Palazzo Trento-Valmarana, Vicenza*, no date. Pen and brown ink, 6⅜ × 6 in. (16.2 × 15.4 cm). This gestural drawing clearly illustrates the dramatic action of drawing as an activity. Artists often try to sustain this effect beyond the initial stage of a sketch. Princeton University Art Museum. Bequest of Dan Fellows Platt, Class of 1895 x1948-863.

plan for a building or an engineer's drawings of a bridge; the lines drawn on maps to represent rivers, roads, or contours; or the lines drawn on paper to represent words. Such use of line is primarily utilitarian, a neutral way of communicating ideas to another person.

And yet, in addition to its ability to describe facts with precision, line can express action in a "gestural" sense. The gesture in graphic work implies the past, present, and future motion of the drawn subject. Gestural drawing in any medium displays lines that are free, quick, and seemingly without inhibition. If preserved in the work, the gesture captures the spirit and animation of the subject. This spirit is intrinsic to both animate and inanimate subjects—a towel casually thrown over a chair has a unique spirit resulting from the way it falls, its weight and texture, and the surface it touches. Obviously this gestural concept applies even more conspicuously to living subjects that are capable of movement (fig. 3.25). Many paintings are preceded by and based on the artist's initial gestural response (fig. 3.26).

Whichever the emphasis—expression of human emotions, depiction of action, or communication of factual information—line is an important element for the artist to use (fig. 3.27).

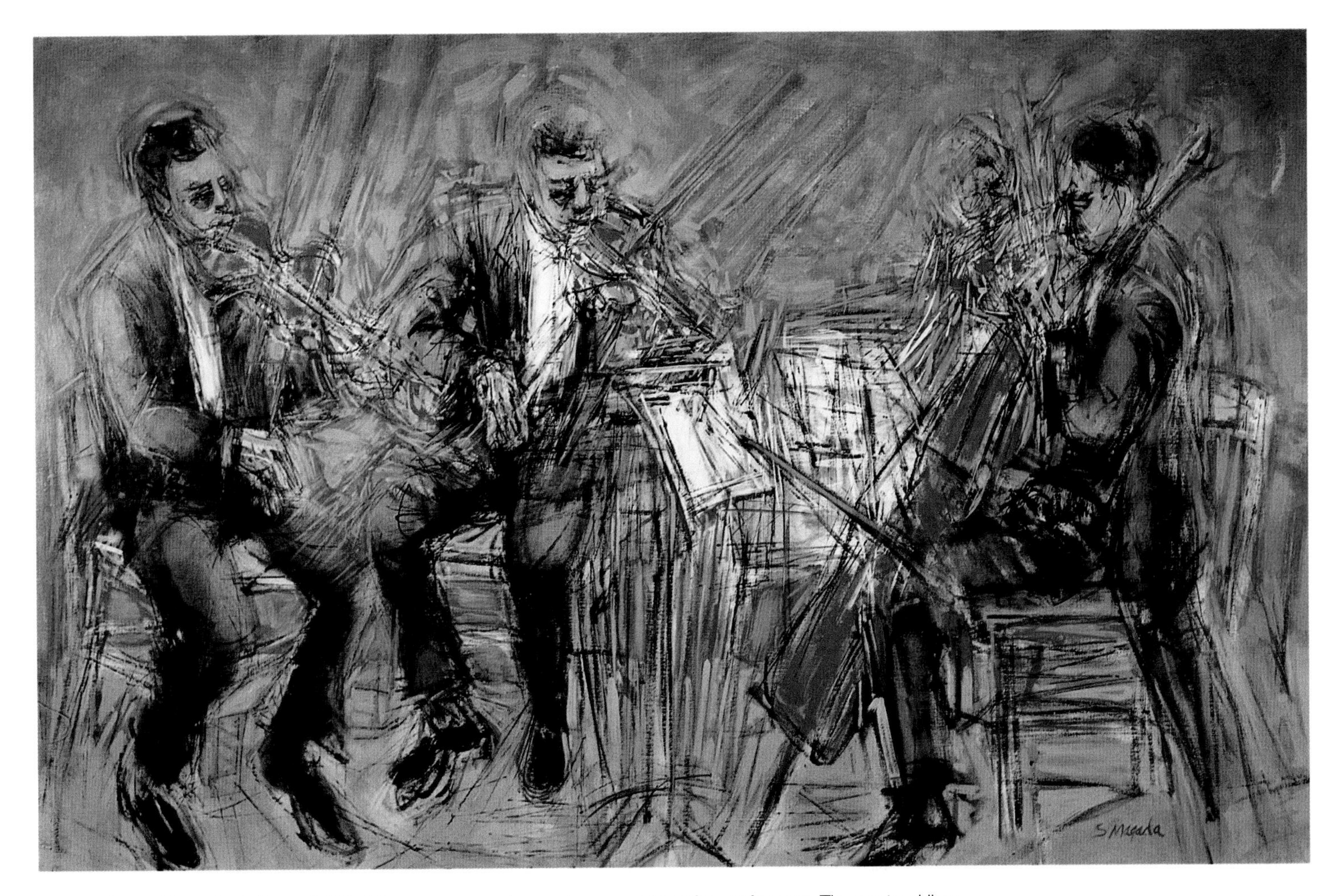

3.27 Steve Magada, *Trio*, c. 1966. Oil on canvas, size and present location unknown. The gestural lines in this work successfully evoke the movements of the performers. Photograph courtesy of Virginia Magada.

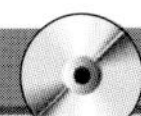

INVESTIGATE THE CD-ROM **Questions to Ask Yourself**

Line expresses the "mood of the hand."

As you review the CD-ROM on the subject of line, answer the following questions:

1. What kinds of lines especially appeal to you?
2. What is it that you like about these lines?
3. How does it feel when you draw these lines?

CHAPTER FOUR

Shape

THE VOCABULARY OF SHAPE

INTRODUCTION TO SHAPE

THE DEFINITION OF SHAPE

THE USE OF SHAPES

Shape Dimensions

The Illusions of Two-Dimensional Shapes

The Illusions of Three-Dimensional Shapes

Shape and Principles of Design

Balance

Direction

Duration and Relative Dominance

Harmony and Variety

Shapes and the Space Concept

SHAPE AND CONTENT

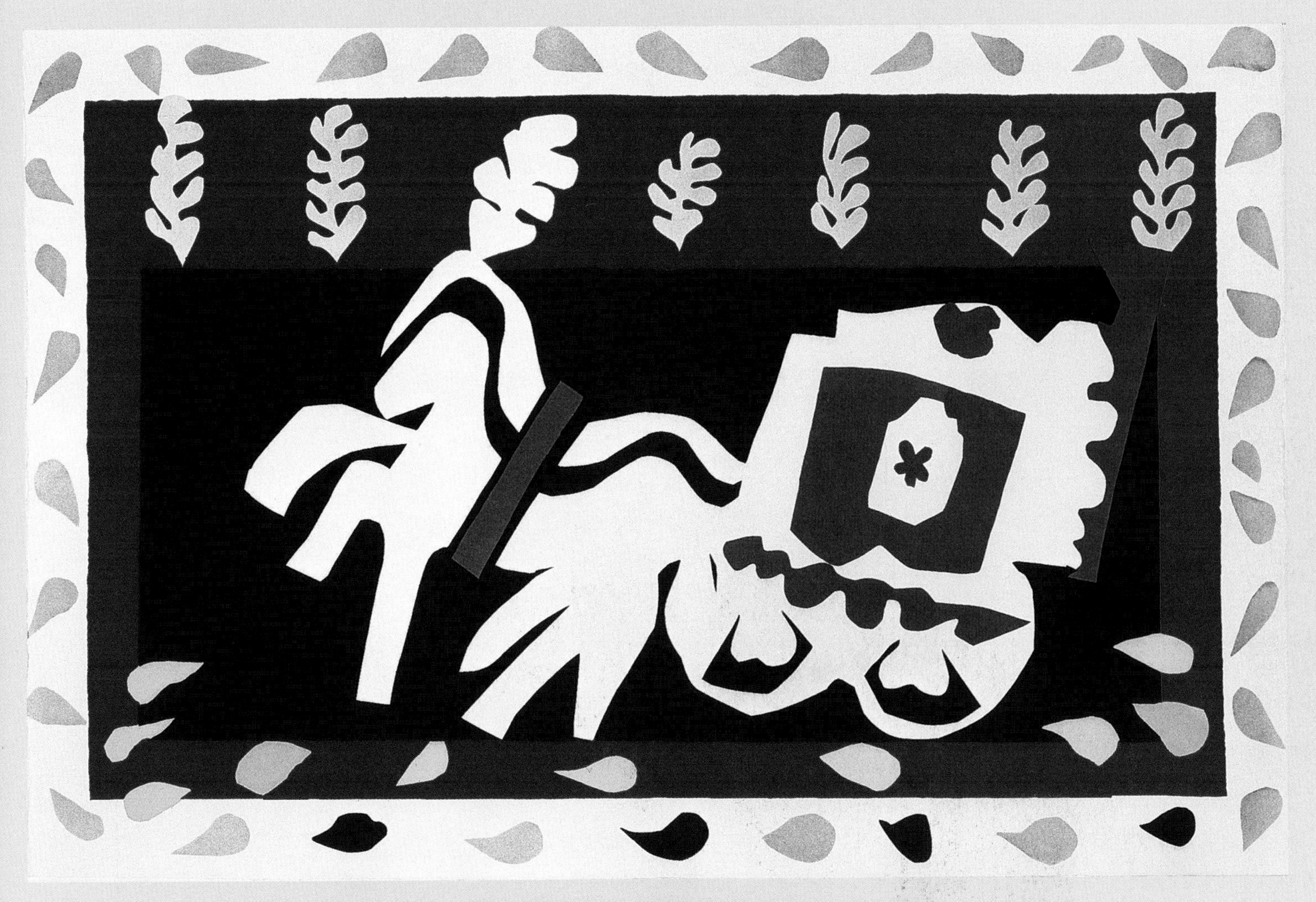

Henri Matisse, *The Burial of Pierrot,* Plate VIII from *Jazz,* 1947. Pochoir (stencil printing), 16¼ × 25⅛ in. (41.2 × 63.5 cm). École des Beaux-Arts, Paris, France.

THE VOCABULARY OF **SHAPE**

Shape — An area that stands out because of a defined or implied boundary or because of differences of value, color, or texture.

actual shape
A clearly defined or positive area (as opposed to an implied shape).

amorphous shape
A shape without clear definition: formless, indistinct, and of uncertain dimension.

biomorphic shape
An irregular shape that resembles the freely developed curves found in living organisms.

Cubism
The name given to the painting style invented by Pablo Picasso and Georges Braque between 1907 and 1912, which incorporates multiple views of objects to simulate their three-dimensionality while acknowledging the two-dimensional surface of the picture plane. Signaling the beginning of abstract art, Cubism is a semi-abstract style that continued a trend away from representational art initiated by Cezanne in the late 1800s.

curvilinear
Stressing the use of curved lines, as opposed to rectilinear, which stresses straight lines.

decorative (shape)
Ornamenting or enriching but, more importantly in art, stressing the two-dimensional nature of an artwork and its elements. Decorative art emphasizes the essential flatness of a surface.

equivocal space
A condition, usually intentional on the artist's part, in which the viewer may, at different times, see more than one set of relationships between art elements or depicted objects.

geometric shape
A shape that appears related to geometry; usually simple, such as a triangle, rectangle, or circle.

implied shape
A shape that does not physically exist but is suggested by dots, lines, areas, or their edges. (See **Gestalt** in the Glossary.)

kinetic art
From the Greek word *kinesis,* meaning "motion," art that includes the element of actual movement.

mass
1. In graphic art, a shape that appears to stand out three-dimensionally from the space surrounding it or that appears to be a solid body of material. 2. In the plastic arts, a physical bulk of material. (See **plastic (shape), three-dimensional,** and **volume.**)

nonrepresentational art
Artwork encompassing nonrecognizable imagery, ranging from pure abstraction (nonrecognizable but derived from a recognizable object) to nonobjective art (not a product of abstraction, but derived from the artist's mind).

objective
That which is based, as nearly as possible, on physical actuality or optical perception, tending to appear natural or real.

perspective
Any graphic system used to create the illusion of three-dimensional images and/or spatial relationships on a two-dimensional surface. There are several types of perspectives: See atmospheric, linear, and projection systems in Chapter 8.

planar
Having to do with planes.

plane
1. An area that is two-dimensional, having height and width. 2. A flat or level surface. 3. A two-dimensional surface having a positive extension and spatial direction or position.

plastic (shape)
1. The use of shape to create the illusion of the third dimension on a two-dimensional surface. 2. Three-dimensional art forms, such as architecture, sculpture, and ceramics. (See **mass, three-dimensional,** and **volume.**)

rectilinear shape
A shape whose boundaries consist of straight lines.

subjective
That which is derived from the mind, reflecting a personal viewpoint, bias, or emotion.

Surrealism
A style of art, influenced by Freudian psychology, that emphasizes fantasy and is said to be revealed by the subconscious through the use of automatic techniques (rubbings, doodles, blots, cloud patterns, and the like). Originally a literary movement that grew out of Dadaism, Surrealism was established by a literary manifesto written by André Breton in 1924.

three-dimensional
Possessing, or creating the illusion of possessing, the dimension of depth, as well as the dimensions of height and width.

two-dimensional
Possessing the dimensions of height and width, especially with reference to the flatness of the picture plane.

volume
A measurable area of defined or occupied space. (See **mass, plastic (shape),** and **three-dimensional.**)

INTRODUCTION TO SHAPE

As artists begin their work, they usually have some preliminary vision of it in terms of line and/or shape. Quite often things begin with a sketch utilizing lines that may soon materialize into defined shapes. Some works, however, are intended to be purely linear; but even in such cases, as multiple lines crisscross each other, the spaces between them appear as shapes. Such spaces may be thought of as "voids" or open shapes.

Shapes are the building blocks of art structure. Edifices of brick, stone, and mortar are intended by the architect and mason to exhibit beauty of design, skilled craftsmanship, and structural strength. The artist shares these same goals in creating a picture. Bricks and stones, however, are tangible objects, whereas pictorial shapes exist largely in terms of the illusions they create. The challenge facing the artist is to use the infinitely varied illusions of **shape** to make believable the fantasy inherent in all art. In other words, an artwork is never the real thing, and the shapes producing the image are never real animals, buildings, people; they are the artist's subjects, if indeed the artist uses subjects at all. The artist might be stimulated by such objects and, in many cases, might reproduce an object's appearance fairly closely. The alterations of surface appearance required to achieve compositional unity may result in a semifantasy (fig. 4.1). On the other hand, the artist may use shapes that are not intended to represent anything or that, even though representational at the outset, may eventually lead to a final work where copied appearances are almost eliminated. This could be called pure fantasy, because the final image is entirely the product of the artist's imagination. Capable artists, whatever degree of fantasy they employ, are able to convince us that the fantasy is a possible reality. Any successful work of art, regardless of medium, plunges the sensitive observer into the realm of the imagination. In the visual arts, shapes play an important part in achieving this goal.

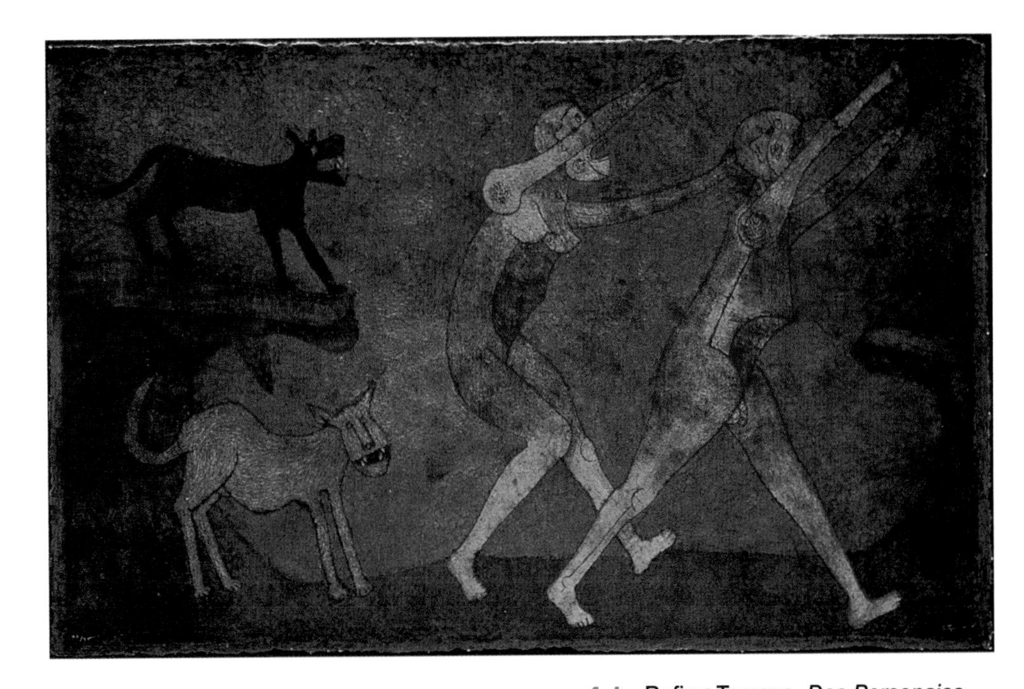

4.1 Rufino Tamayo, *Dos Personajes Atacados por Perros*, 1983. (Edition of 75) Mixografia on handmade paper, 60 × 90 in. (152.4 × 228.6 cm). Tamayo has created an air of fantasy by semi-abstracting the people and dogs, creating an image of distance and ritualized terror. Courtesy of Remba Gallery, Hollywood, CA.

THE DEFINITION OF SHAPE

We can begin to define shape in art as a line enclosing an area. Such a line is called outline or contour. However, even when we have only a few elements of form to go by, as illustrated in figure 4.2, our minds adjust to read a visible effect of shape. Apparently, we have an instinctive ability to fill in incomplete patterns and shapes. This principle, first put forward by the German Gestalt psychologists in the early twentieth century, suggests that our minds tend to "see" organized wholes, or forms, as a totality (*Gestalt* is the German word for "form") before perceiving the individual parts. Our minds also tend to find shapes in approximately related elements, such as the four dots perceived as a square. Thus we read the diagrams in figure 4.2 as shapes, even though no contours have been drawn. The last drawing, where

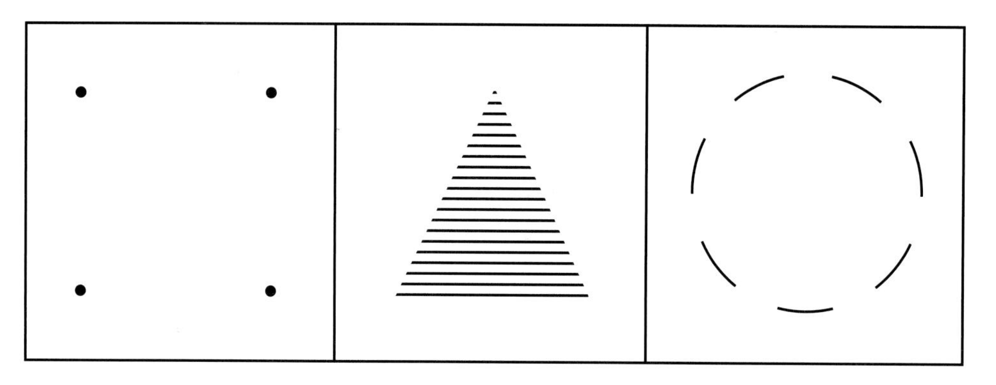

4.2 The spectator automatically infers fully drawn shapes from those suggested by the dots and lines.

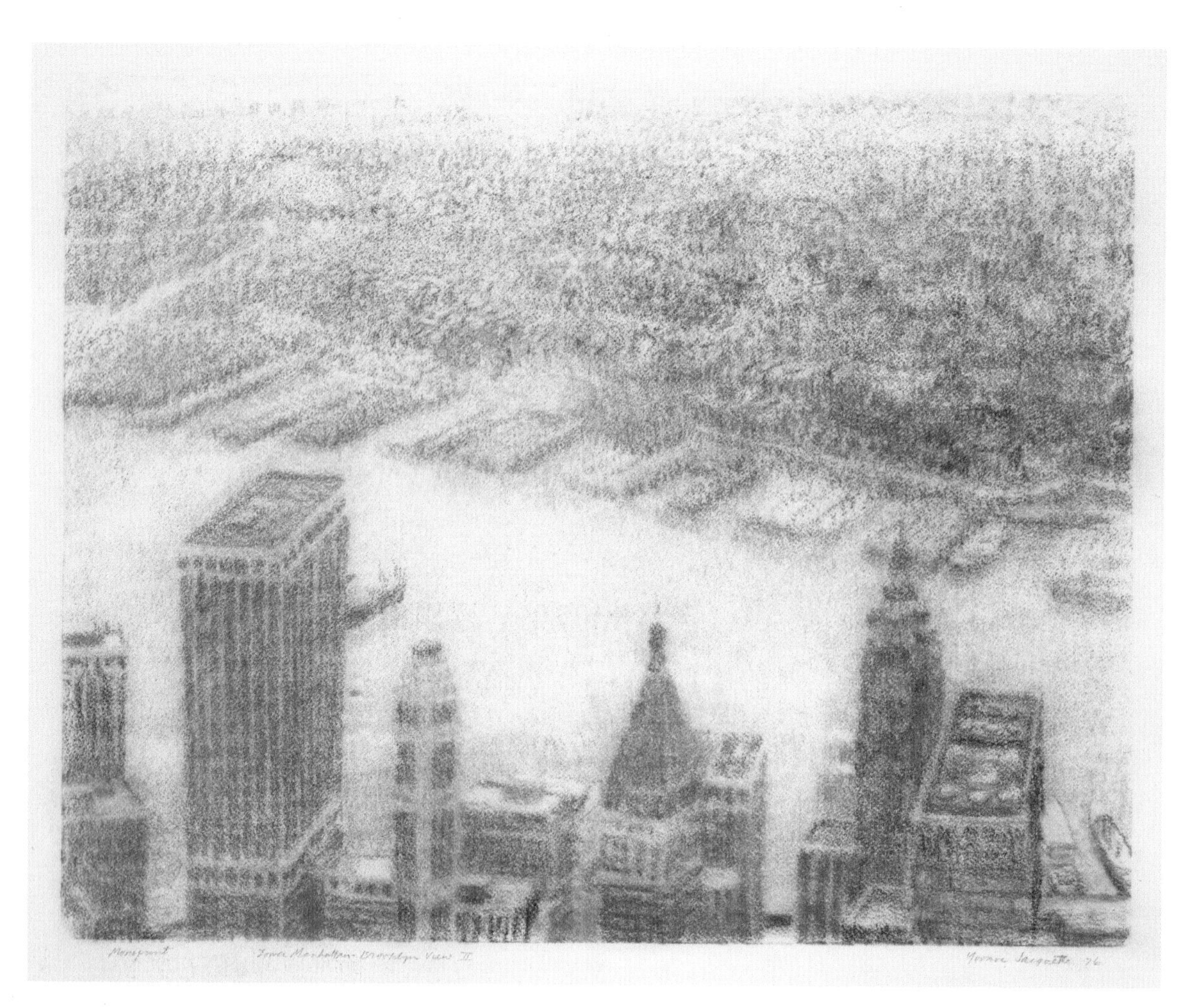

4.3 Yvonne Jacquette, American, Unknown, *Lower Manhattan—Brooklyn Bridge View II,* 1976. Pastel monotype on off-white wove paper, 45.8 × 58.6 cm. This pastel by Jacquette is similar to Monet's paintings from the nineteenth century. She notes that van Gogh and Seurat have influenced her soft, atmospheric style. A winter landscape, seen through flurries of snow, lends itself well to the blurred contours and high-key palette in this drawing. Gift of Anne Marie Davidson, 1989.482.12. Reproduction, The Art Institute of Chicago.

4.4 Anthony Caro, *Odalisque,* 1984. Steel, 6 ft 5 in. × 8 ft 1 in. × 5 ft 4 in. (1.96 × 2.46 × 1.63 m). Despite the irregularity and complexity of the contours, lighting, and color of these sculptural shapes, the edges of contours read more clearly than is often the case in the graphic arts. The Metropolitan Museum of Art, Gift of GFI/Knoll International Foundation, 1984. (1984.328.a–d) Photograph © 1985 The Metropolitan Museum of Art.

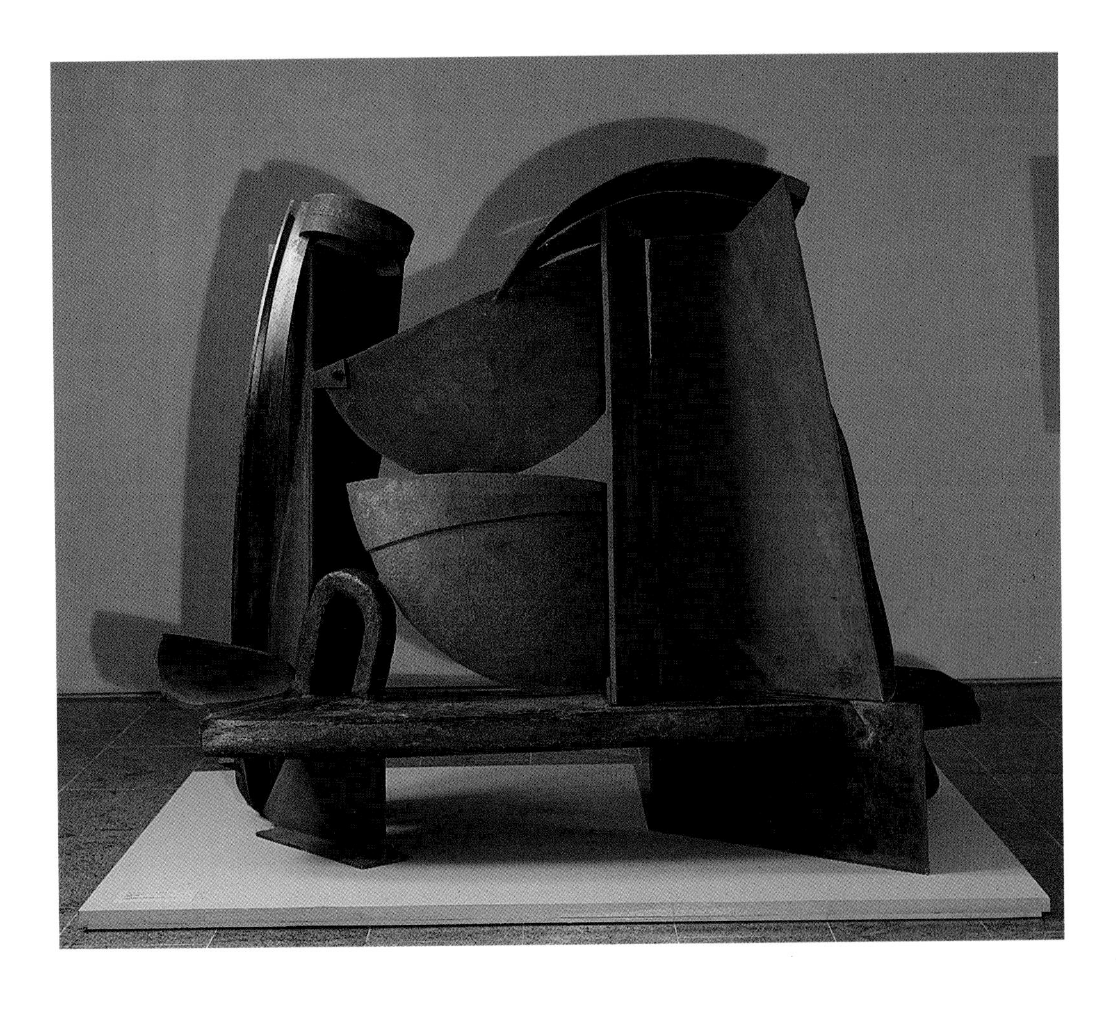

gaps and dashes are mentally filled in to form a circle, comes closest to illustrating our first definition of a shape as being a line enclosing an area. But Gestalt theory causes us to question our first definition, because closure is not always a necessary condition for forming a shape.

Other definitions of shape may round out our understanding of this element. Among these are any visually perceived area of value, texture, color, or line, or any combination of these elements. In pictorial art, shapes are flat, or two-dimensional. In the three-dimensional forms of art (sculpture, architecture, environmental design, and so on), shapes are more often solid masses. When three-dimensional artists do their initial drawings, they must be aware that the picture does not completely describe their 3D, or plastic, intentions and in reality offers only one view of the proposed 3D work. The picture plane conditions the use and characteristics of all shapes and other elements on it, as already discussed in Chapter 2.

Actual shapes in pictorial art have exact limits, as in the case of geometric shapes; or there may be **implied shapes,** as illustrated by the preceding diagrams. In addition, they may be **amorphous**—that is, so vague or lacking in shape that their edges cannot be determined (fig. 4.3). Shapes in the **plastic** arts, however, are defined, because of the very nature of the materials from which they are created. Their edges, or outer contours, are the determining factor, no matter what their degree of irregularity (fig. 4.4).

Shapes can vary endlessly, ranging in type from objective to subjective, from geometric to biomorphic, and from implied to amorphous. They may differ in size, position, balance, color, value, and texture according to the function they need to fulfill in the work of art. Shapes also can be static, stable, active, or lively, and seem to contract or expand, depending on how the artist uses them.

There are different names for categories or families of shape, depending on whether they are imaginary (**subjective**) or derived from observable phenomena (**objective**). The configuration of a shape gives it a character that distinguishes it from others. When the shapes used by an artist imitate those formed by natural forces (stones, puddles, leaves, clouds) they are called by various terms in addition to objective, such as naturalistic, representational, or realistic, depending on the context of

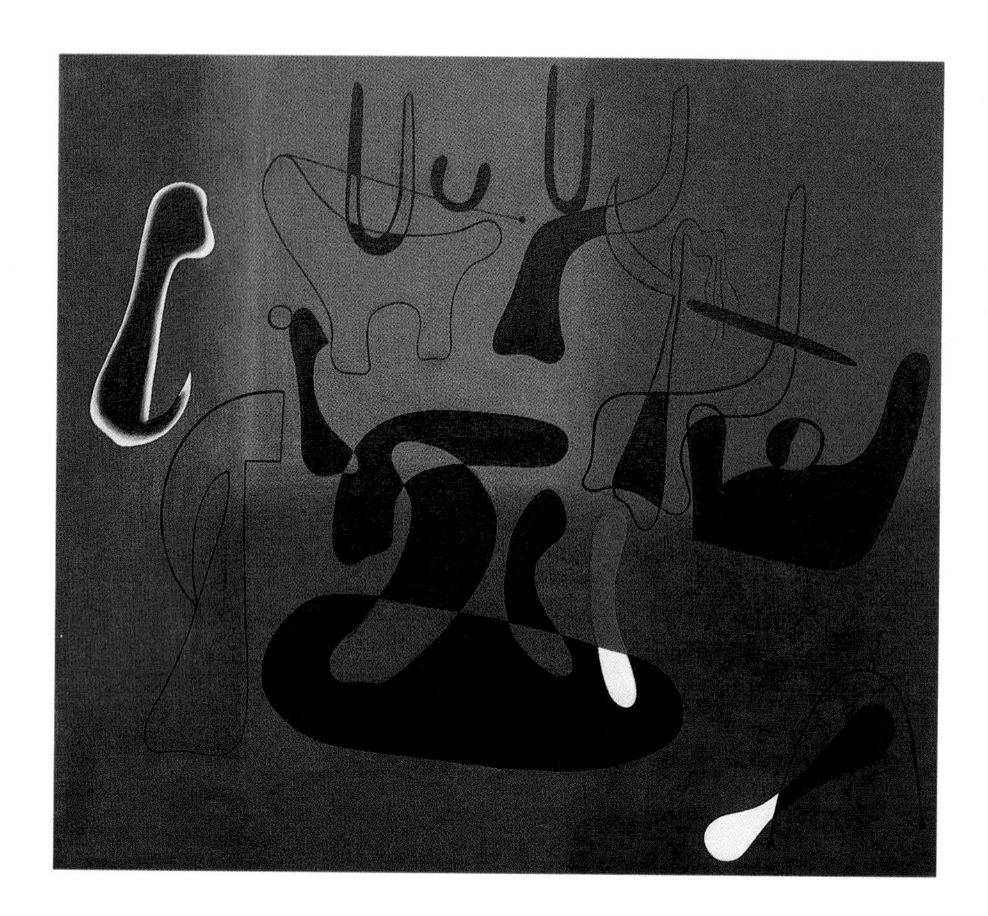

4.5 Joan Miró (1893–1983) © ARS, NY. *The Painting,* 1933. Oil on canvas, 68½ × 6'5¼ (174 × 196.2 cm). Some shapes in this work seem to be veiled references to unlikely creatures and deserve the term *biomorphic* because of their organic configuration. Loula D. Lasker Bequest (by exchange). (229.1937) The Museum of Modern Art, New York, NY, U.S.A. Digital image © The Museum of Modern Art/Licensed by SCALA/Art Resource, NY.

their use. When they seem to have been contrived by the artist, they are also given various names in addition to subjective and abstract. Among these are the terms **nonrepresentational** and nonobjective. The distinction between these opposed shape families is not always easily made, because the variations are so vast. Hence, several specific terms have evolved to attempt an explanation.

Natural objects generally seem rounded. We see this in the fundamental organisms encountered in biological studies (such as amoebas, viruses, and cells). Such shapes are normally referred to as organic, but, because organic shapes are often curved, the term **biomorphic** was coined in early-twentieth-century art to describe the irregular rounded shapes in art that suggest life (fig. 4.5; see figs. 10.80 and 10.83).

With the great interest aroused by abstract art (beginning around 1910), the

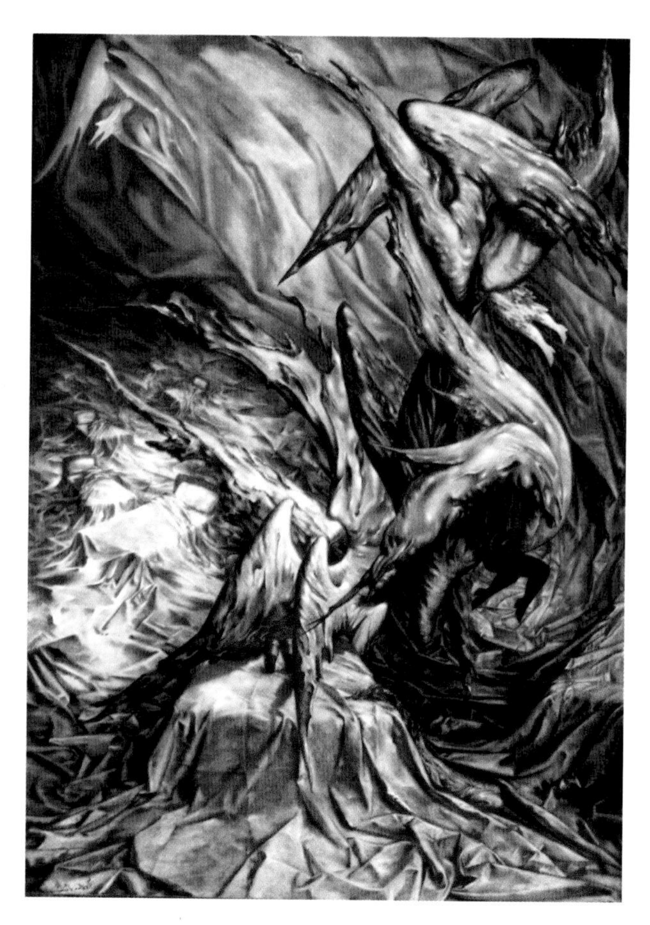

4.6 Dorothea Tanning, *Guardian Angels,* 1946. Oil on canvas, 35 × 57½ in. Here, Tanning combines a realistic rendering of form with the fantastic. Like other Surrealists, Tanning was interested in the inner psychic life of human beings. Courtesy New Orleans Museum of Art. © 2005 Artists Rights Society (ARS), New York/ADGP, Paris.

increasing awareness of the microscopic world through science, and the growth of Freudian psychology, the biomorphic shape became a key component in **Surrealism.** Surrealist artists' interests in the mystic origins of being and in the exploration of subconscious revelations, such as in dreams, attracted them strongly to organic or biomorphic shapes (fig. 4.6). Other artists (Matisse and Braque are examples) abstracted organic forms in a less symbolic and primarily decorative manner (fig. 4.7; see also fig. 4.17).

Rectilinear (straight-lined) shapes, called **geometric** because they are based on the standardized shapes used in mathematics, contrast with biomorphic shapes. The precisionist, machinelike geometric shapes appealed to artists working in **Cubism,** who used them in their analytical dissection and reformulation of the natural world (fig. 4.8).

From these examples, it is clear that, however shapes are classified, each shape or combination of shapes can display a particular personality according to its physical employment and our responses to it.

4.7 Henri Matisse, *The Burial of Pierrot,* Plate VIII from *Jazz,* 1947. Pochoir (stencil printing), 16¼ × 25⅛ in. (41.2 × 63.5 cm). Matisse abstracted organic forms for the purpose of decorative organization. École des Beaux-Arts, Paris, France. © 2005 Succession H. Matisse, Paris/Artists Rights Society (ARS), New York. Bridgeman-Giraudon/Art Resource, NY.

THE USE OF SHAPES

Artists use shapes to suggest a physical form they have seen or imagined and to give certain visual qualities or content to a work of art.

Shape is also used:

1. To achieve order, harmony, and variety.
2. To create the illusion of mass, volume, and space on the surface of the picture plane.
3. To increase the viewer's span of interest.

The last item in this list requires further clarification. While the arts of music, theater, and dance evolve in time, the visual arts are usually fixed in time. This means that the length of time an observer

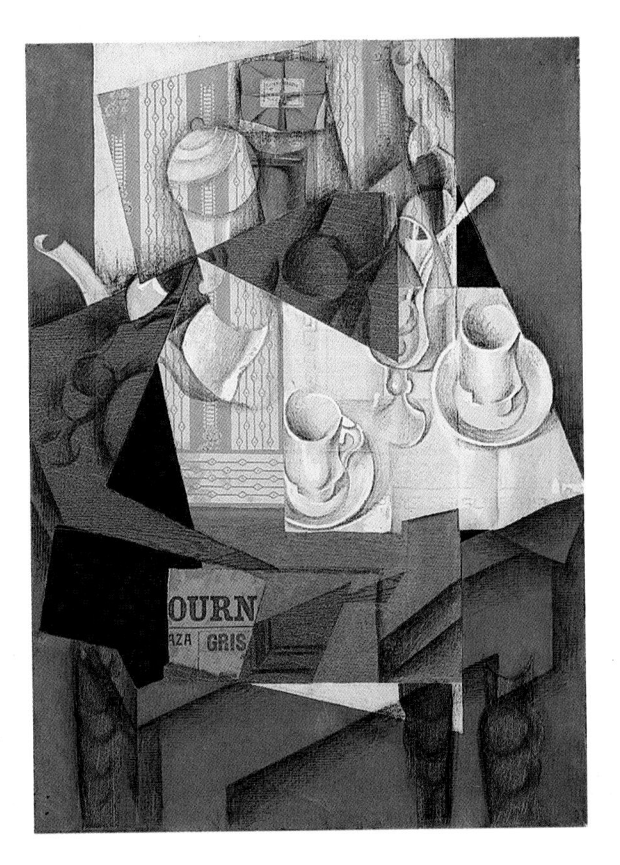

4.8 Juan Gris (José Victoriano González), *Breakfast,* 1914. Cut-and-pasted paper, crayon, and oil over canvas, 31⅞ × 23½ in. (80.9 × 59.7 cm). Gris, a Cubist, not only simplified shapes into larger, more dominant areas but also gave each shape a characteristic value, producing a carefully conceived light–dark pattern. He also made use of open-value composition, where the value moves from one shape into the adjoining shape, as we see in this example. The Museum of Modern Art, New York, NY. U.S.A. Acquired through the Lillie P. Bliss Bequest. Digital image © The Museum of Modern Art/Licensed by SCALA/Art Resource, NY.

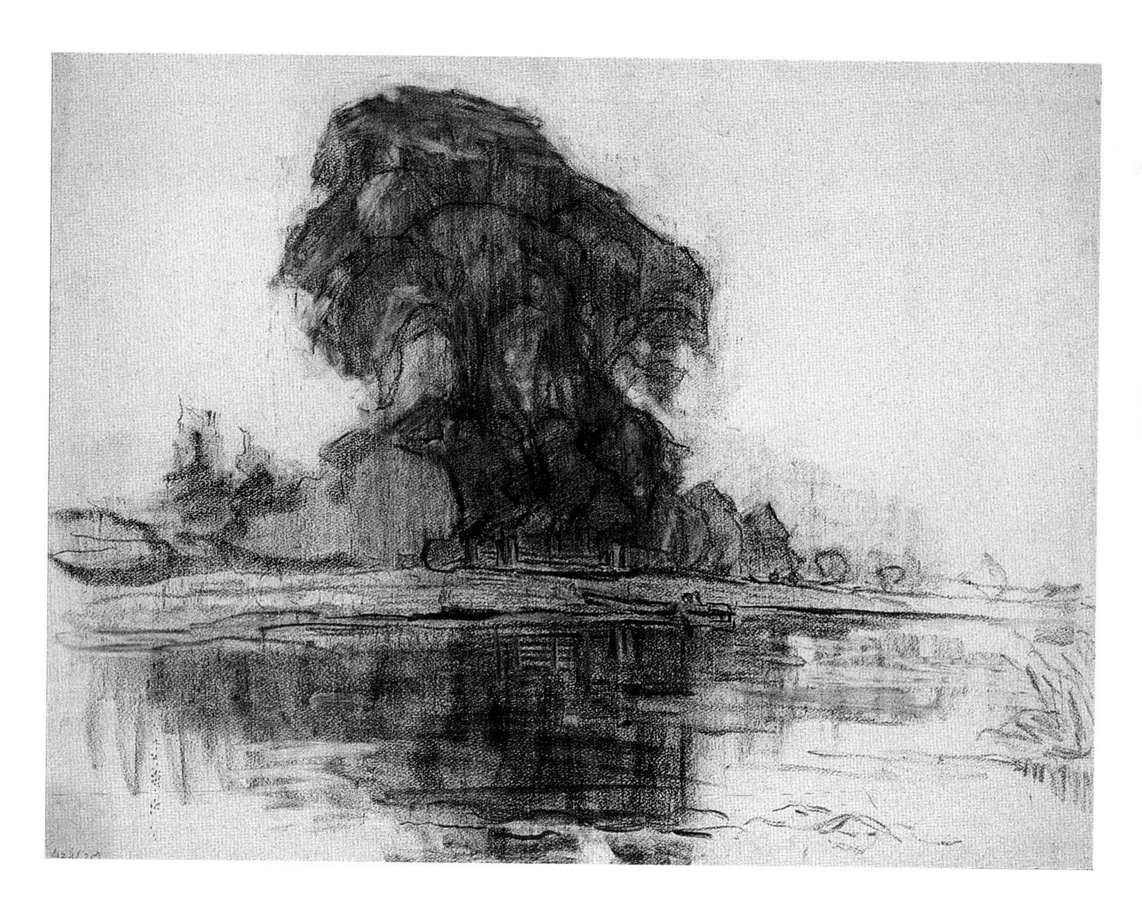

4.9 Piet Mondrian, ***Landzicht Farm: Compositional Study,*** **c. 1915. Charcoal on blue/grey paper, 18⅜ × 24½ in. (46.7 × 62.2 cm).** In this work, Piet Mondrian uses outer contours to establish the larger simplified planar shapes. They, in turn, are broken into smaller organic planes that provide more and more detail. Edward E. Ayer Endowment in memory of Charles L. Hutchinson, 1962.105., The Art Institute of Chicago © 2005 Mondrian/Holtzman Trust, c/o HCR International Warrenton Virginia.

concentrates on a visual artwork is by comparison usually limited. This is particularly true of pictorial arts, but it is not quite as true of plastic art, especially its **kinetic** forms. Mobiles, for example, are a form of sculpture in motion; their constantly changing relationships of shapes may hold the viewer's attention longer than immobile forms of art.

Shape Dimensions

We have already defined shapes as having either two- or three-dimensional identities. In order to use shape(s) successfully in works of art, we must further consider these dimensional aspects. Some people, for example, make a distinction between shape that is **two-dimensional** and shape that is **three-dimensional** (referred to as **mass** and/or **volume**) and consider them to be two separate elements. However, the authors have always considered shape, whether two-dimensional or three-dimensional, to be one element of form.

The Illusions of Two-Dimensional Shapes

Foremost among shapes and probably the most useful is the two-dimensional **plane.** In pictorial artworks, the flat surface on which artists work is called the picture plane. In addition to being a working surface, a planar shape can be used to summarize vastness or intricate areas in nature. In sketching trees, for example, an artist can utilize a large, simple **planar** shape to represent the overall image of the tree. Further, individual clumps of foliage can be indicated by small varied shapes (fig. 4.9). The use of the plane creates economical, stable, and readily ordered units that are useful not only for preliminary sketches but also for finalizing the organization of an artwork. Beyond this, planes are useful in creating the illusion of three-dimensionality on the two-dimensional picture plane, whether they have the appearance of objects or are abstract.

The use of the plane can vary from the flat or **decorative** appearance on a picture plane to the appearance of occupying space. Artists use all kinds of shapes, from geometric to organic, to achieve both of these effects. A rectilinear shape—that is, a geometric shape whose boundaries consist of straight lines—might appear flat when lying on the surface of the picture plane, but even a simple overlapping of two or more rectilinear shapes can impart a sense of depth. The addition of contrasts in size, color, value, and texture to these planes can establish a more definitive impression of depth (fig. 4.10).

Curvilinear planes, those planar shapes made up of circles, ovals, or irregular organic attributes, can also create depth or, through their curving nature, suggest movements in depth. When

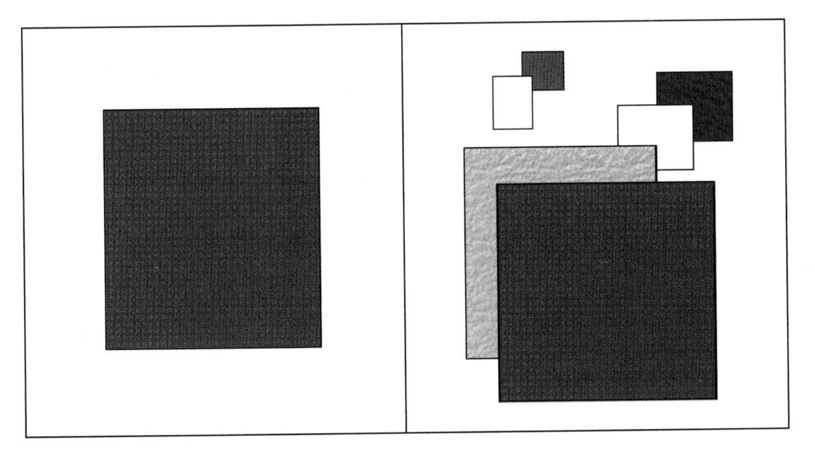

4.10 Rectilinear planes can suggest the illusion of depth in a number of ways.

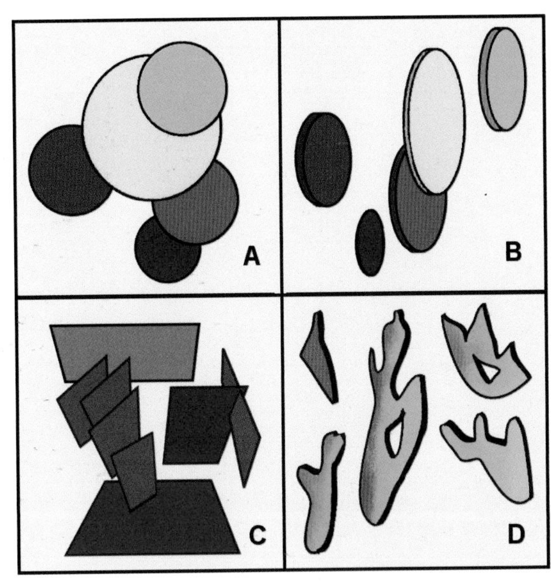

4.11 The diagrams illustrate how differently shaped and positioned planes can create illusions of depth: (A) curvilinear or circular planes overlapped to suggest shallow space; (B) curvilinear planes placed on edge and tilted to suggest an effect of greater depth—note how the circles become elliptical in shape; (C) straight-edged or rectilinear planes positioned so that they float in deep space (see fig. 4.10 for a shallower effect); (D) irregular shapes creating a sense of depth.

In diagrams B, C, and D, the illusion of depth is accentuated by thickening the nearest edges of the planes. Variations of value, size, texture, and color further enhance or diminish the illusion of depth.

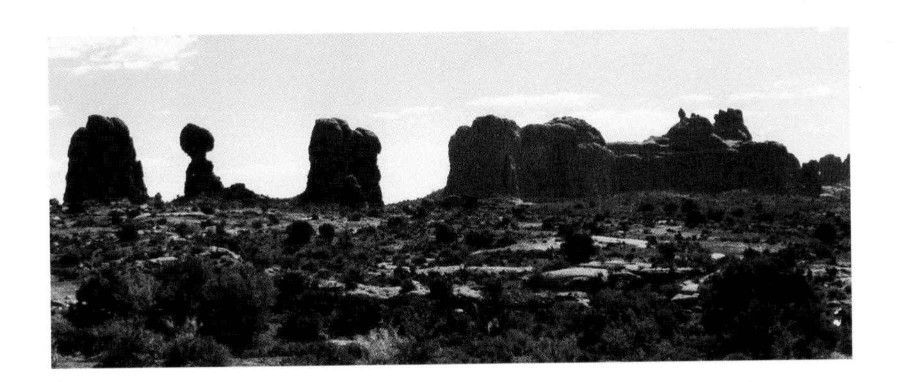

A

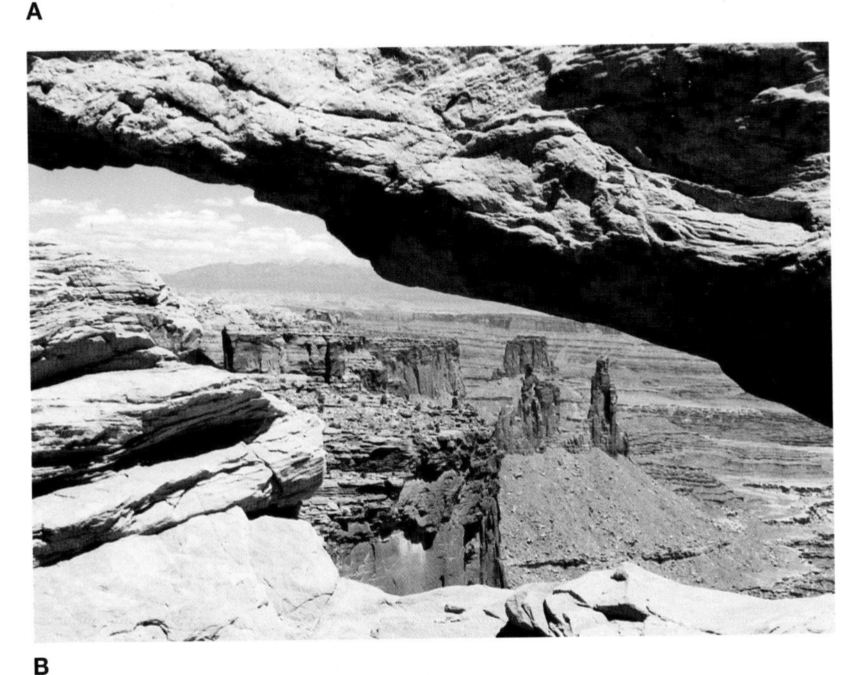

B

4.12 Masses and volumes: Arches and Canyonlands national parks, Utah. In figure 4.12A, mountainous rock formations and their valleys represent mass and volume. Figure 4.12B illustrates a close-up view of a gigantic rock formation (mass) with an enormous hole (volume).

curvilinear, rectilinear, or other irregular planes are given a foreshortened appearance by tilting them and making the near end look larger than the distant one, we have a more pronounced statement about depth than occurs in the decorative use of planes (figs. 4.11A–D).

The Illusions of Three-Dimensional Shapes

When we use the term *mass* to describe shapes in the picture plane, we mean that they have the appearance of solid three-dimensional bodies. If a 3D shape is a void or an area of definable containment, it occupies a certain amount of measurable space and is called a volume. Rocks and mountains are masses, while holes and valleys are volumes; cups are masses, while the areas they contain are volumes (figs. 4.12A, B). When beginning to paint or draw 3D shapes, we should select the

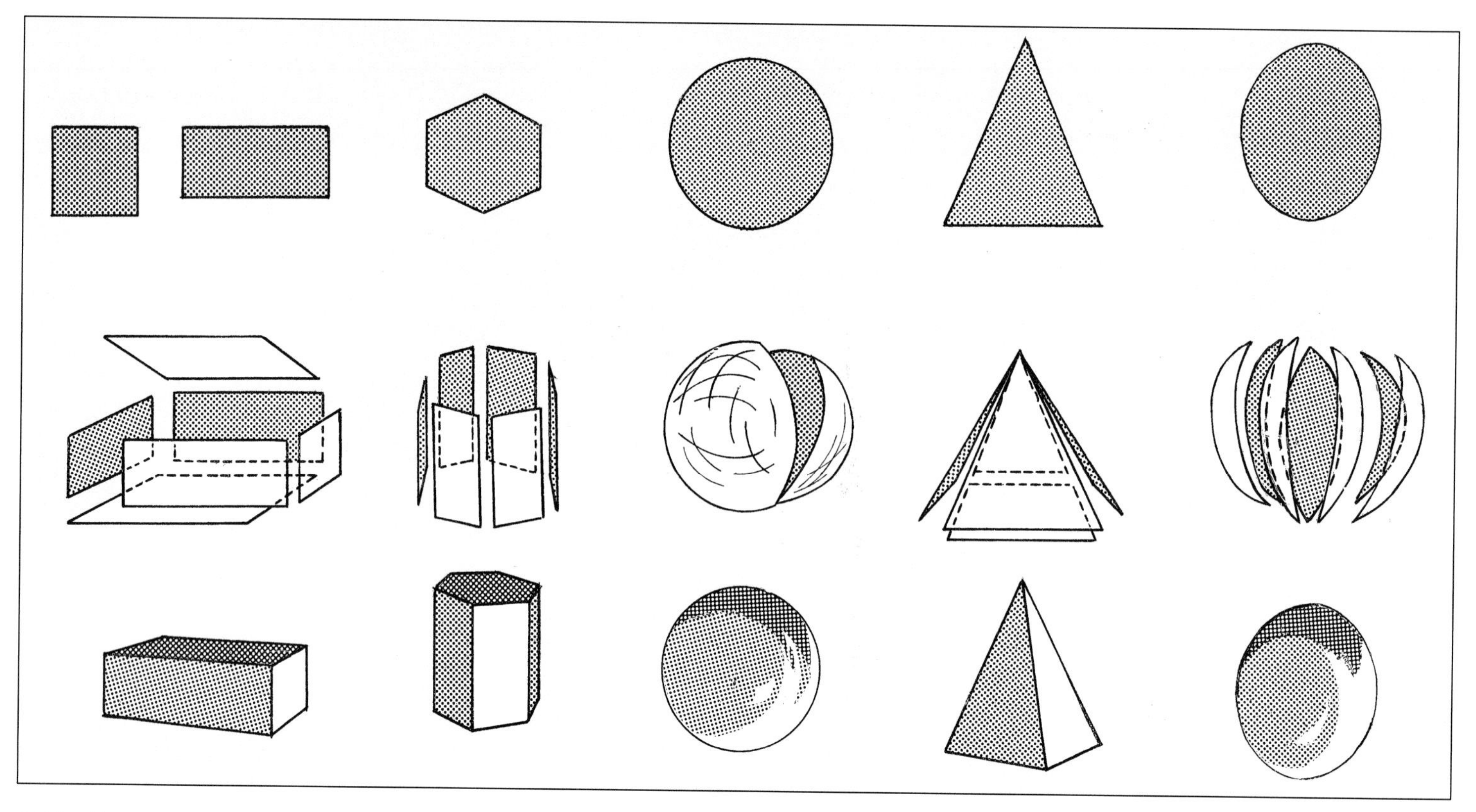

4.13 Planes and their three-dimensional equivalents.

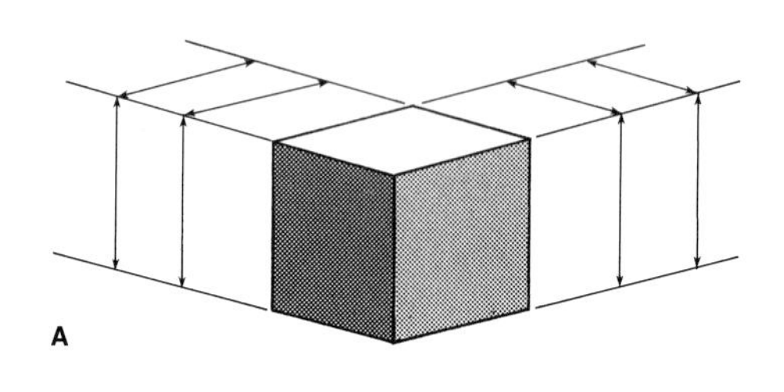

4.14A A combination of planes that show parallel edges in depth creates the illusion of mass (shape).

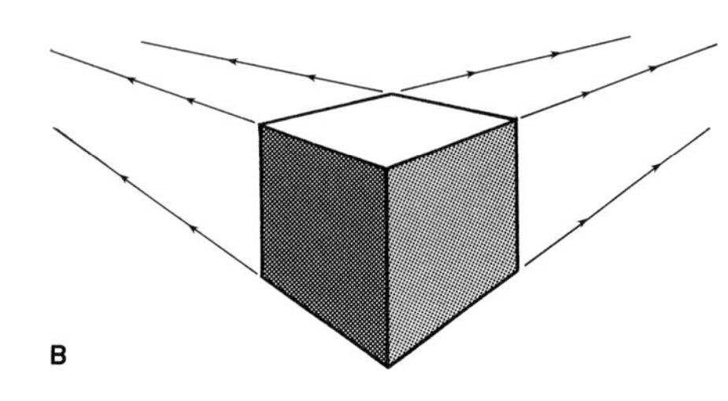

4.14B A combination of planes that show converging edges in depth (moving *away* from the viewer) creates the illusion of mass (shape).

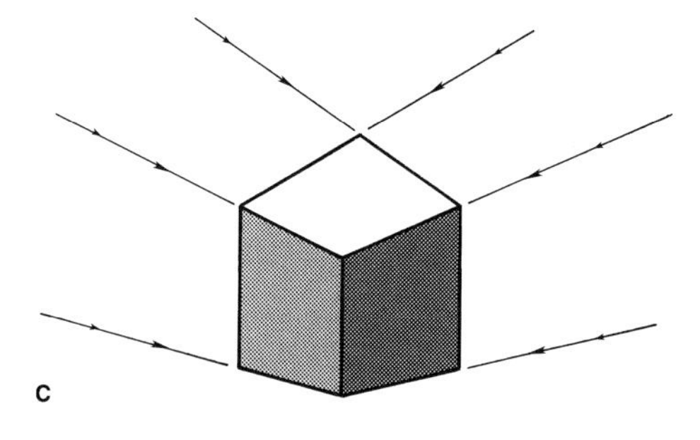

4.14C A combination of planes with edges converging *toward* the viewer creates the illusion of mass (shape). (This is the reverse effect of the shape in figure 4.14B.)

kind(s) of shape(s) we wish to portray—geometric, organic, or irregular—just as we did in working with their 2D counterparts. Because geometric shapes, such as the square/rectangle, are the most basic 2D shapes, let us look at the development of their 3D equivalents—the cube/rectangular solid.

To produce the illusion of masses or volumes on the picture plane, the artist arranges two or more flat or curvilinear planes in relation to one another to give them an appearance of solidity, as shown in figure 4.13. The planes that constitute the sides of these illusionary 3D objects could be detached from the parent mass and tilted back at any angle. In fact, such planes do not have to be closed or joined at the corners in order to afford an appearance of solidity—the Gestalt effect again. As we see in this diagram, there is no limit to the number of shapes that can be shown in three dimensions, but the rectangular solid is probably the

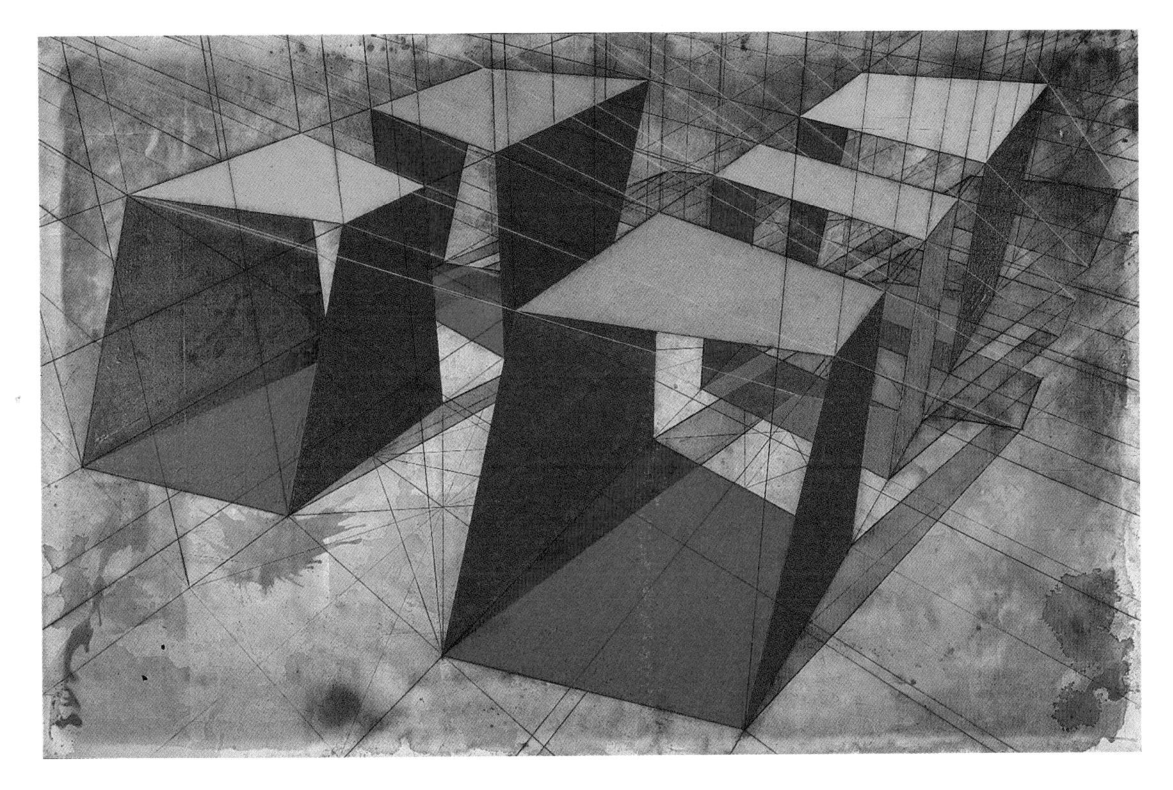

4.15 **Ron Davis, *Parallelepiped Vents #545,* 1977. Acrylic on canvas, 9 ft 6 in. × 15 ft (2.90 × 4.57 m).** While the strict order of linear perspective is not observed here, a sense of space is achieved by other means under the control of the artist's instincts. Los Angeles County Museum of Art, CA. Gift of the Eli and Edythe Broad Fund. Photography © 2001 Museum Associates/LACMA.

simplest. Spheres, pyramids, and hexagonal and ovoidal solids all have their counterparts in planar shapes, such as circles, triangles, hexagons, and ovoids.

Juxtaposing planes without connecting them makes the arrangement of planes seem less substantial than the mass, but it shows the development of the planes and is more flexible in the pictorial exploration of volume and space. Presenting the planes in this way highlights the importance of the edges' functions as the planes combine to form the illusion of mass and its depth. In figure 4.14A, the diagram shows planes that have parallel-angled edges. They establish a directional movement (usually away from a central location—an edge/corner). This combination of planes seems to provide solidity, whereas any plane on its own would appear relatively flat.

In the next example of a mass, figure 4.14B, the planes appear to tilt or tip, taking on an added feeling of dimension—depth illusion—as they appear to recede from the spectator. These planes are the converging sides of the mass. When several converging planes are juxtaposed and touching, the spatial illusion of mass and depth is greater than that provided by the use of parallel-edged planes. This occurs because the illusion of the converging planes receding in depth more closely relates to our optical perception. Under normal conditions, one may expect the size of the planes to appear to diminish as they move away from the viewer. The use of planes with converging sides is not limited to this situation; for instance, equivocal (ambiguous or uncertain) planes also occur when the traditional application is reversed, as in figure 4.14C. This is certainly true of **equivocal space** in this example, in which "now you see it and now you don't" or, more accurately, "now you see it and now you see it another way." This is typical of equivocal art situations. Initially, figure 4.14C is seen as a solid block, though not in perspective. After another inspection, the white plane may be seen as an advancing "ceiling" and other planes as retreating to a corner. Such ambiguities can add challenge, spice, and interest to the viewing. The artist can use this application of converging edges advancing to exaggerate and distort shape definitions and impart decorative qualities to the image; however, the individual planes in isolation remain relatively plastic.

Review figures 4.13 to 4.14C, and you will find examples of 3D shapes that have planes with parallel, advancing, and receding converging edges. Artists enjoy the freedom of creating imaginative shapes in three dimensions unencumbered by the restrictions of formulae and mechanical processes. Ron Davis, in his painting *Parallelepiped Vents #545,* employs flat planes, shapes with parallel edges, shapes with converging edges receding, and shapes with converging edges advancing (fig. 4.15). Al Held creatively employs the same types of shape-edge development in his painting *B/WX* (see fig. 8.41).

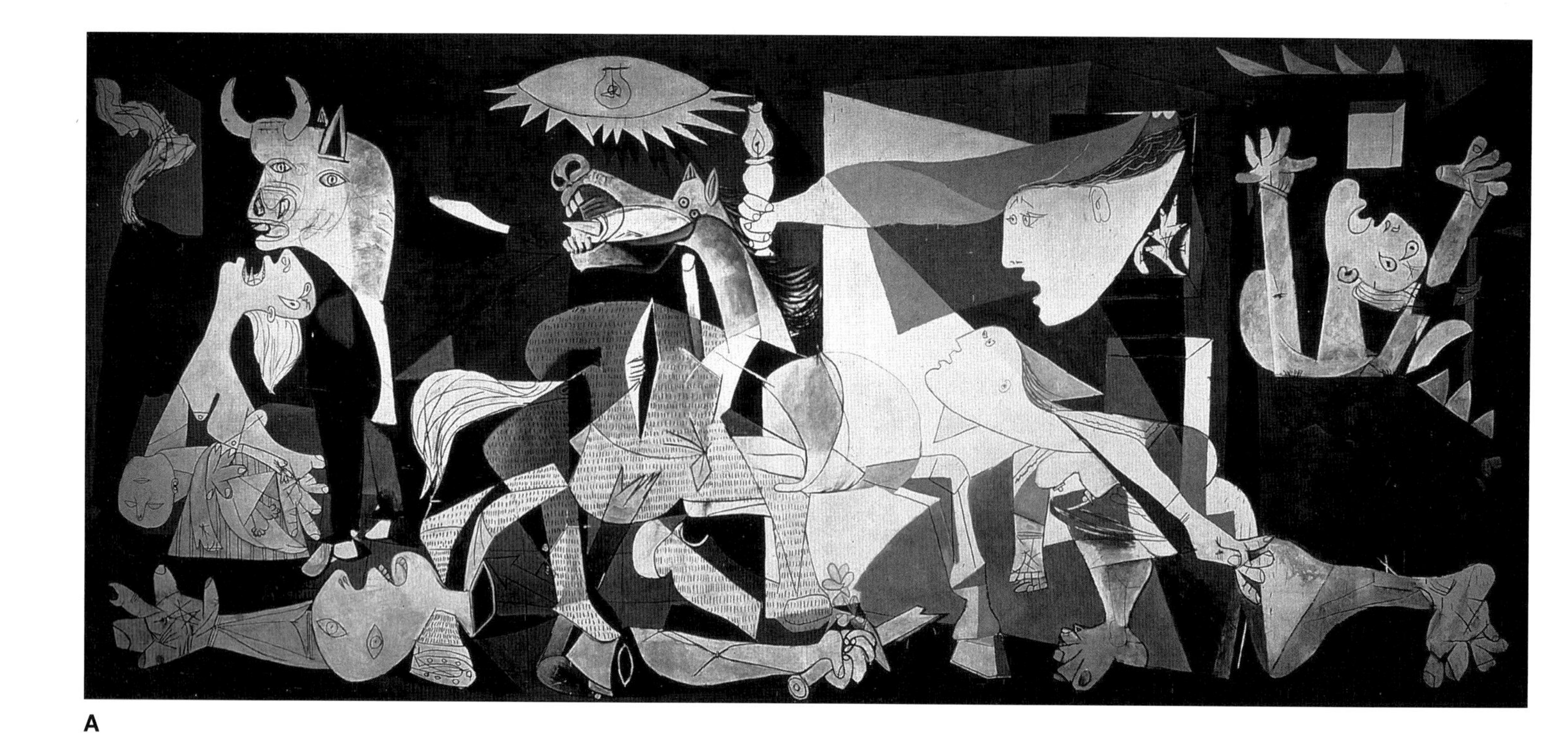

A

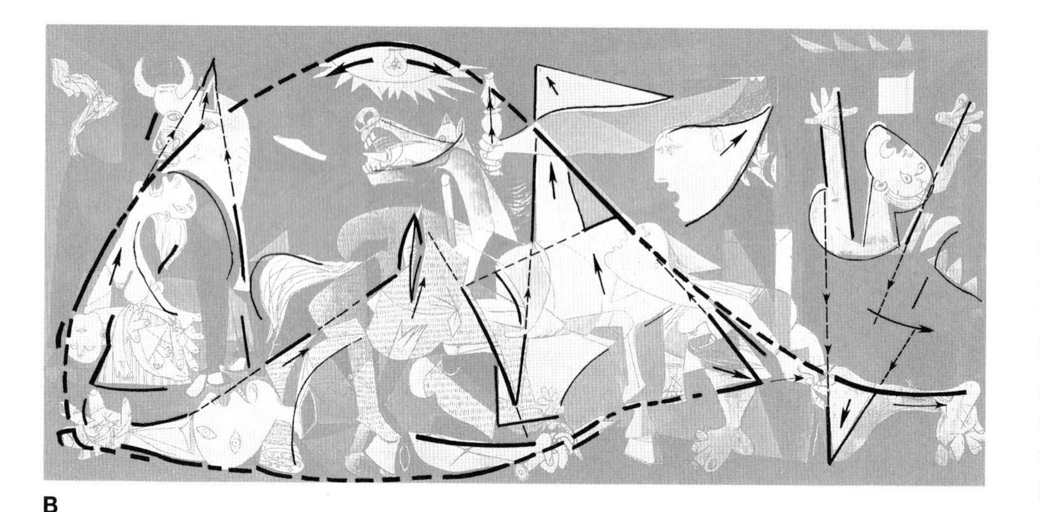

B

4.16 Pablo Picasso, *Guernica,* 1937. Oil on canvas, 11 ft 5½ in. × 25 ft 5¼ in. (3.49 × 7.75 m). The linear diagram (B) overlaying Picasso's *Guernica* is one of several possible interpretations of the way shape is used as a directional device. The arrows in the middle of shapes indicate their major directional thrust. The thick solid lines show the edges where a felt direction seems to line up with a corresponding shape edge across a space (indicated by broken lines). These create the major shape directions in the overall composition. Secondary shapes, related in a similar way, are shown by middleweight lines. The lighter lines show curving shape edges counteracting the straighter and more broadly arced edges of the design. Museo del Prado, Madrid, Spain. Photo: Centro de Arte Reina Sofia, Madrid/Giraudon, Paris/SuperStock.

The creation of 3D shapes and their depth through the use of converging edges (receding and/or advancing) preceded the development of linear perspective but is closely related to it. Because of linear perspective's importance to the creation of space, it will be discussed further in Chapter 8, "Space." The parallel-edge shape concepts that have been presented are closely related to the system of **perspective** used in mechanical drawings. Within this chapter we are primarily concerned with the illusions of shape and depth created by graphic artists. Other artists employ actual 3D shapes in their art, but this is more appropriately discussed in Chapter 9, "The Art of the Third Dimension."

Shape and Principles of Design

Artists who wish to create order or unity and increase their viewers' attention spans have to conform to certain principles of order or design. In observing these principles, they are often forced to alter shapes from their natural appearance. In this respect, shapes are the building blocks of art structure. Just as in the case of line, our first element of artistic form, shapes have multiple purposes in terms of visual manipulation and emotional effect. These purposes vary depending on the artist and the viewer.

The principles determining the ordering of shapes are common to the other elements of form. In their search for significant order and expression, artists modify the elements until:

1. The desired degree and type of balance are achieved.
2. The observer's attention is controlled in terms of both direction and duration.
3. The appropriate ratio of harmony and variety results.
4. The space concept achieves consistency throughout.

While space is a result of the use of the elements, and harmony and variety have already been discussed (pp. 31–56), the concepts of balance, direction, and duration, as they regard shape, warrant additional discussion at this point.

Balance

As artists seek compositional balance, they work with the knowledge that shapes have different visual weights depending on how they are used. Although this principle was treated in Chapter 2, it may be helpful to reexamine balance in particular regard to shape by reusing the example of the seesaw, or weighing scale, as depicted in figure 2.28. We see that placing shapes of different sizes at varying distances from the fulcrum controls the sense of balance or imbalance. Because no actual weight is involved, these sensations are intuitive, or felt, as a result of the various properties composing the art elements. For example, a dark value adds weight to a shape, while substituting a narrow line for a wider line reduces apparent weight.

The seesaw shows how a few basic elements can operate along only one plane of action. Developed artworks, on the other hand, contain many diverse elements working in many directions. The factors that control the amounts of directional and tensional force generated by the various elements are placement, size, accents or emphasis, and general shape character (including associative equivalents to be discussed under "Duration and Relative Dominance," p. 103). The artist manipulates these elements until the energy of their relationships results in dynamic tension.

Direction

Artists can generate visual forces that direct our eyes as we view the work. They devise pathways to encourage transition from one pictorial area to another. There are several ways of facilitating this; one way is to use shapes pointing in specific directions (shorter shapes generally obstruct the visual pathways). Second, artists often extend or "aim" edges so that they imply connections with the edges of other shapes or suggest related movements in a certain direction (figs. 4.16A, B). A third solution is the use of intuitive space (see Chapter 8, p. 200), an implied perspective that tilts shapes with reference to the picture plane and directs our eyes along three-dimensional routes; we can observe this in figures 4.11B, C, and D. The direction of the eyes along these paths should be rhythmic, providing pleasurable viewing and unification of the work. The character of the rhythm may be jerky, sinuous, swift, or slow, depending on the artist's intentions (fig. 4.17). The control of direction helps us to see things in the proper sequence and according to the degree of emphasis the artist planned for them.

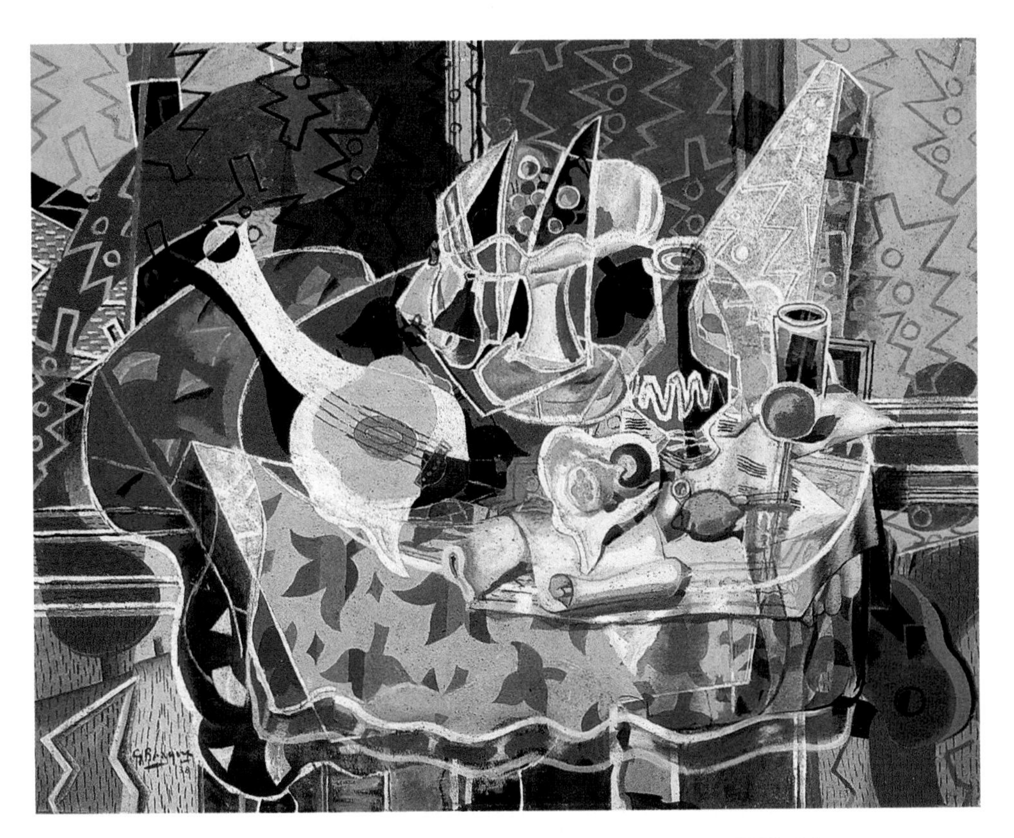

4.17 Georges Braque, *Still Life with Fruit and Stringed Instrument*, 1938. Oil on canvas, 45 × 58 in. (114.3 × 147.3 cm). The shapes of white line or light value define the designed pathways of eye travel. The visual tension and rhythmic movement results from the placement, size, soft accent, and general character of the shapes involved. Gift of Mary and Leigh Block, 1988. 141.6. Photograph © 2005 Artists Rights Society (ARS), New York/ADGP, Paris.

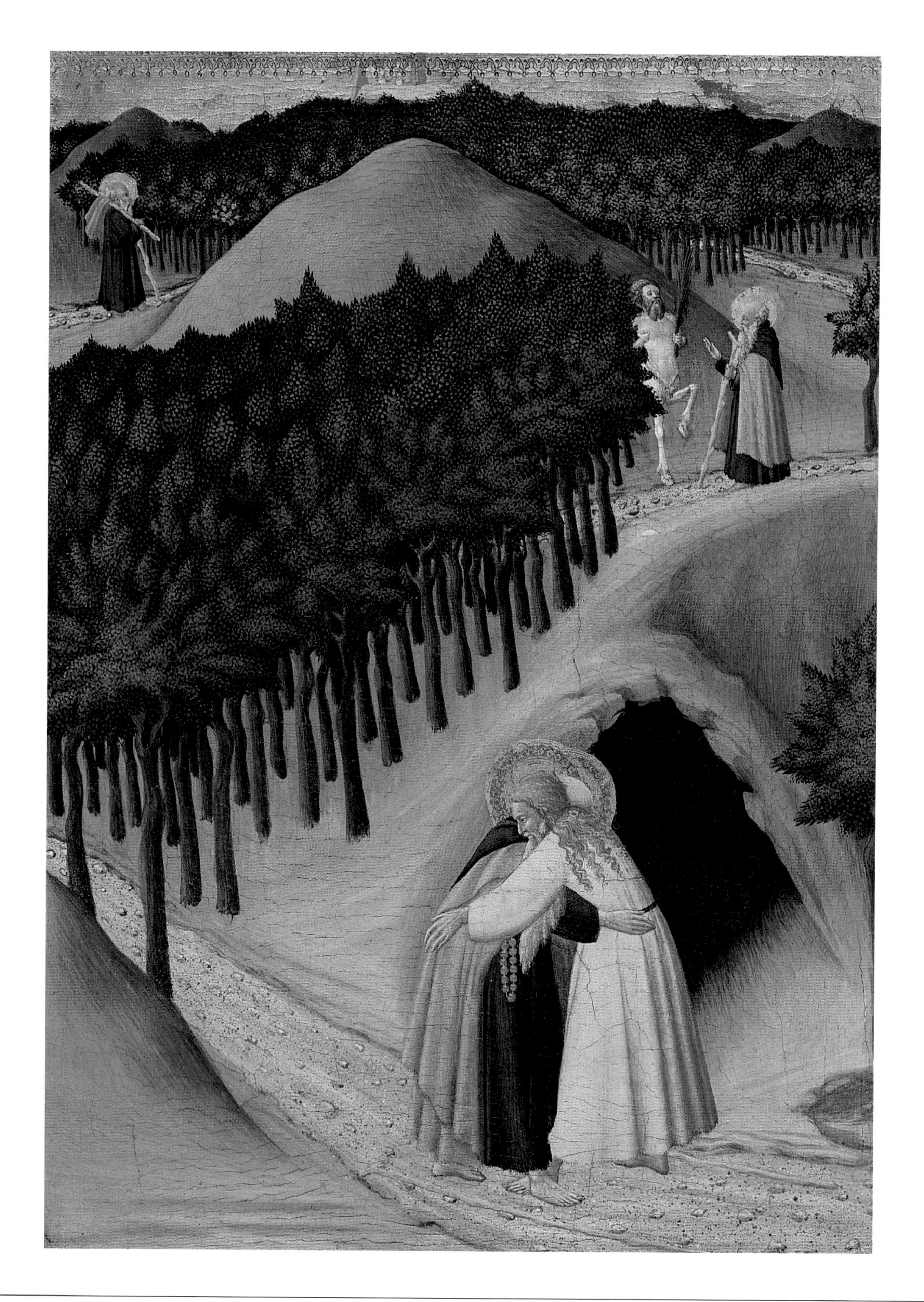

Duration and Relative Dominance

The unifying and rhythmic effects provided by eye paths are modified by the number and duration of pauses in the eye journey. If the planned pauses are of equal length, the viewing experience is monotonous. The artist, therefore, attempts to organize pauses so that their durations are related to the importance of the sights the viewer will see on the eye journey (fig. 4.18). The duration of a pause is determined by the pictorial importance of the area. While shapes create transitions, they are also focal points in a picture. In a work depicting the Crucifixion, for example, we would expect an artist to make the figure of Christ particularly significant (fig. 4.19). In the case of the illustration shown, this dominance is achieved by the size of Christ's body. The effect of a shape's size can be further modified by manipulations of value, location, color, or any combination of these elements. Artists develop dominance on the basis of their feelings, and they reconcile the demands of design principles with those of relative dominance. The degree of dominance is usually in direct proportion to the amount of visual contrast. This is true of both representational and abstract works (see figs. 4.19 and 4.20). The idea of relative dominance is similar to the hierarchy of organizations that have a dominant figure and other figures with diminishing responsibilities.

Other aspects also tend to influence the attention given to shapes or other elements. The contrasts between Christ's T shape, the ovals in the right and left foreground, the arch tops in the background, and the differences in value and color from his figure, all serve to increase the dominance of the crucified Christ in Ismael Rodríguez Rueda's painting *El Sueño de Erasmo*. Playing a diminished role, but adding to the coherence of the painting, is the repetition of the similar head shapes in the figures and the touches of yellow, red, and green in parts of the painting (fig. 4.19). In an abstract work of art, such as the Birchman digital image (fig. 4.20), an oval shape may receive more attention because it is highly focused. Of course, size remains the principal device used for dominance. At other times, artists use the appeal of associative factors, weighing them in the balance of relative dominance and forcing them to operate for the benefit of the total organization.

4.18 Sassetta, workshop of, *The Meeting of Saint Anthony and Saint Paul,* c. 1440. Tempera on panel, 18¾ × 13⅝ in. (47.6 × 34.6 cm). In this painting by the Italian artist Sassetta, episodes in a journey are indicated by contrasts of value, and eye paths are provided that lead from figure to figure. This painting also illustrates how late-Gothic artists used shallow space in compositions prior to the full development of perspective. Samuel H. Kress Collection. © Board of Trustees, National Gallery of Art, Washington.

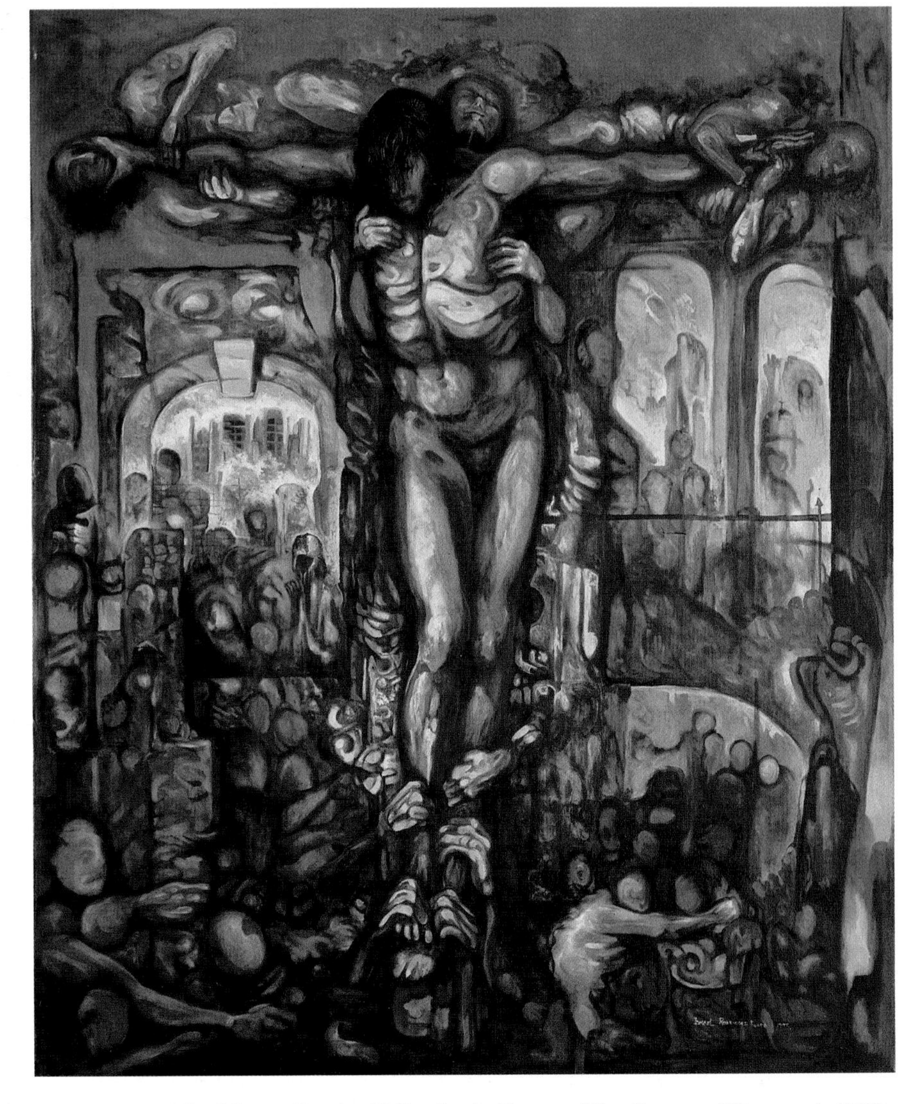

4.19 Ismael Rodríguez Rueda, *El Sueño de Erasmo* (*The Dream of Erasmus*), 1995. Oil on canvas, 39⅓ × 47½ in. (100 × 120 cm). The figure of Christ is made dominant by its size and centrality of location. Courtesy of Ismael Rodríguez Rueda.

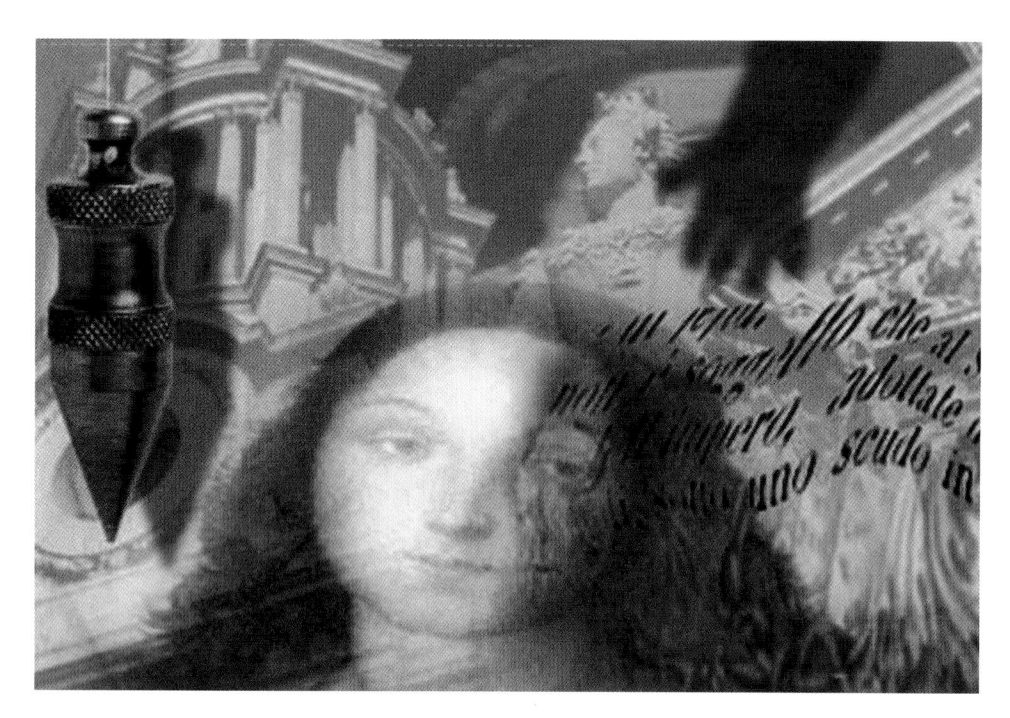

4.20 Fred Birchman, *Plum*, 1998. Digital image. Birchman uses dominance in this digital image in an interesting way. The plumb bob in the foreground is highly focused and casts a shadow. Even though the images behind the plumb bob are distorted and unfocused, they maintain their place because they remain recognizable and form a planar and scalar relationship to the plumb bob. Courtesy of Fred Birchman.

Harmony and Variety

Harmony ensures that all things seem to belong together. Shapes and other elements can achieve this by sharing a likeness. With repetition, these parts form a family, sharing certain characteristics. A family of shapes could be mostly rectilinear (composed of straight edges), curvilinear (curved edges), or another similar type. An artist can enhance a shape likeness by additional common likenesses of value, texture, or color. The likeness need be not identical but merely sufficient to suggest a relationship. A stress on shape harmony can result in a relatively peaceful situation, but overstressing harmony may curtail our interest.

Variety is the other side of the coin. Enough differences must exist to make for challenging viewing. These differences attract and hold our attention for the period thought necessary by the artist. If the artwork consists of mostly gently flowing shapes, the introduction of angular shapes will produce sharp accents and, of course, the reverse would also be true. Although the presence of some differences is essential, excessive differences may be out of tune with the total concept; some reconciliation with harmony is necessary. If agitation and disruptive effects are sought, shape variety is the answer. Remember: repetitive shapes for harmony; contrasting shapes for variety.

Shapes and the Space Concept

Regarding space, the sculptor may have an advantage over the two-dimensional artist who confronts a flat working surface. The flat surface must be converted into a "window" in which shapes appear to advance and retreat. Artists deal with this illusion of space in different ways in different cultures—sometimes extending its depth, sometimes compressing it. In either case, shapes are an important factor.

Shapes are often perceived as planes, independent of or part of objects, tilted or upright, and often, although not always, flat. Shapes may appear to be ground surfaces, walls, tabletops and sides, and the like. Frequently, shapes are seen in perspective appearing to recede from us, resulting in different depths of space. Shapes may twist and bend in space or overlap and may be seen through and penetrate each other, causing new spatial relationships.

The artist must be consistent with his or her space; a mix does not ordinarily work well. One challenge is balancing the spatial forces. In two-dimensional art, one form of balance depends on the apparent weights of the elements. To give an appearance of three dimensions, the thrust and recession of the elements in space must balance; otherwise, the picture plane will appear twisted. Equalization of the spatial forces depends on adjustments in size and position and variations of value and color. When making these adjustments, the artist coaxes the shapes to take their position in space.

SHAPE AND CONTENT

Whereas the physical effects created by artists are relatively easy to define, the qualities of expression, or character, provided by shapes in a work of art are numerous and varied. In some cases, our responses to shapes are commonplace; in others, our reactions are complex because our own personality traits (for example, shyness, aggressiveness, awkwardness, poise, and so forth) influence our interpretation of a shape. Artists, naturally, make use of such expressive possibilities in developing their works of art, although much of their work is done instinctively.

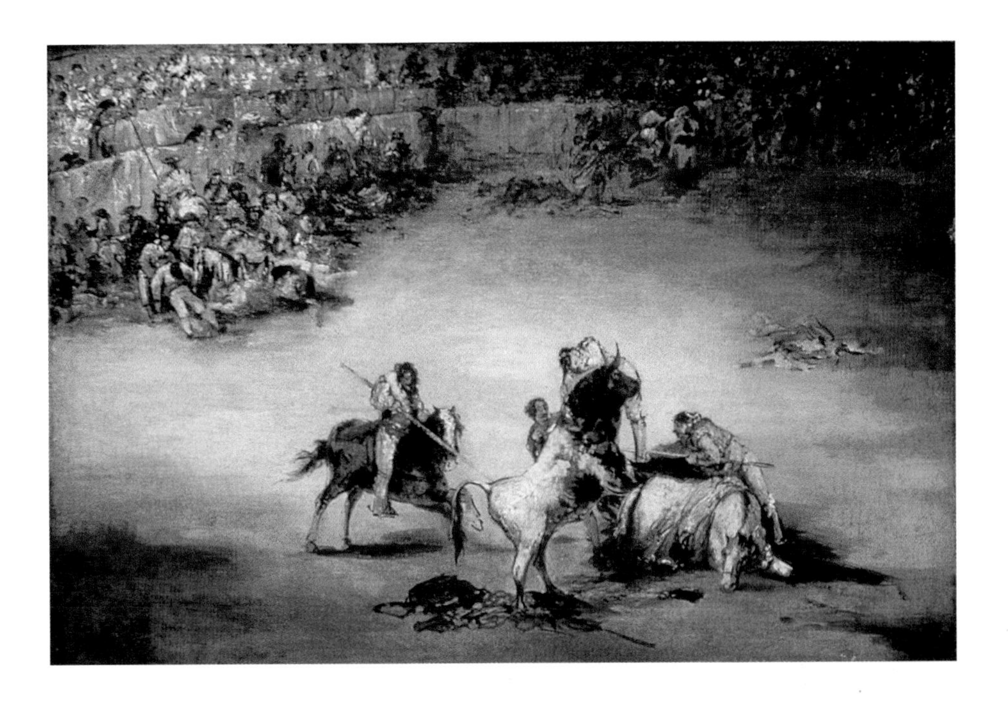

4.21 Francisco Goya, *The Bullfight,* c. 1824. Oil on canvas, 24¾ × 36½ in. (63 × 93 cm). While it is a straightforward exercise to recognize the picador in this painting, this should only be a starting point for understanding the blood and tragedy that Goya found in the bull ring. Toledo Museum of Art, Toledo, Ohio. Purchased with funds from the Libbey Endowment. Gift of Edward Drummond Libbey.

It is uncommon that an architect shapes a building to suggest a natural form. On the other hand, sculptors and pictorial artists have often used natural forms in their respective media. Nevertheless, they are not always interested in using shapes to represent known objects. Artists seem to prefer to present what they imagine to be real rather than what they perceive to be real. Particularly in the twentieth century, numerous movements were based on the nonrepresentational use of shapes—from the abstract movement of the early 1900s, to the conceptual movement of the seventies and eighties, to the "Neo-Geo" of the nineties.

Thus, conception and imagination have always been parts of artistic expression. It is usually a matter of degree as to how much artists use their imagination and how much they use their perceptual vision. By trying to say something through the use of subject and form, artists find that they cannot make their points without editing the elements (or "grammar") of form/expression. So, while the work of artists devoted to representing actual appearances might seem to be natural, comparison with the original subject in nature will show considerable disparities (figs. 4.21 and 4.22). Artists, therefore, go beyond literal copying and try to transform object shapes into their own language of form (figs. 4.23, 4.24, and 4.25; see fig. 4.5).

Just as the configuration of a shape distinguishes it from other shapes, so does configuration also give shape content and expressive meaning. Many of

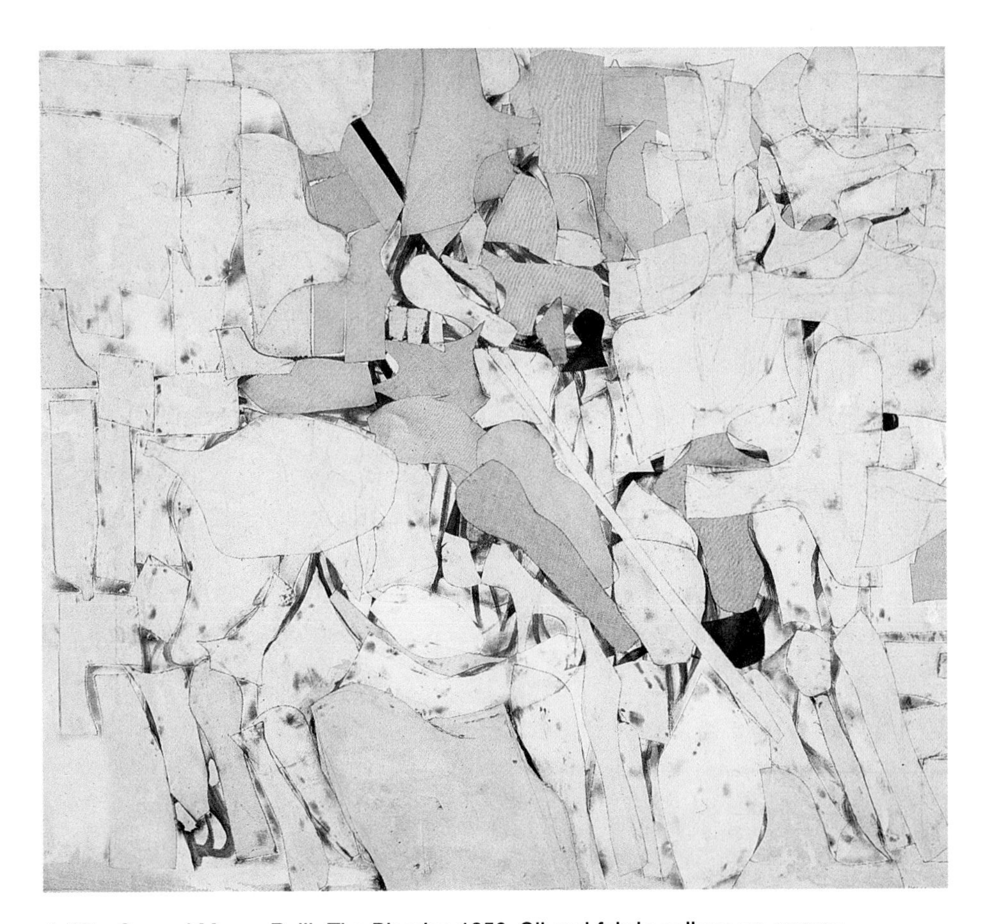

4.22 Conrad Marca-Relli, *The Picador,* 1956. Oil and fabric collage on canvas, 3 ft 11¼ in. × 4 ft 5 in. (1.20 × 1.35 m). Artists differ in their responses to subject matter. It is often a matter of degree as to how much artists use their imaginations and how much their visual perceptions vary. Such differences are apparent if one contrasts the use of the picador in figures 4.21 and 4.22. Hirshhorn Museum and Sculpture Garden, Smithsonian Institution, Washington, D.C. Gift of Joseph H. Hirshhorn, 1966. Photograph by Lee Stalsworth.

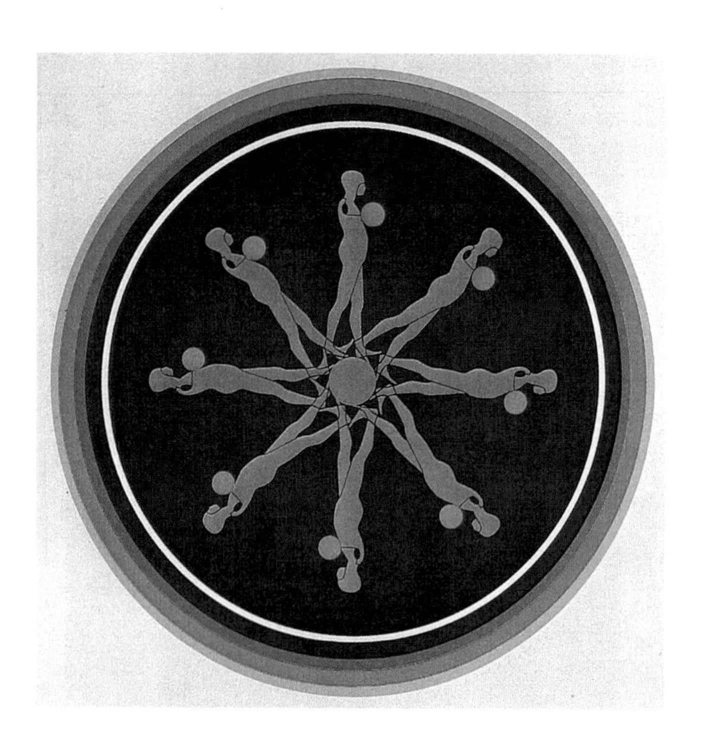

4.23 Ernest Trova, *Untitled,* from the series *Index,* 1969. Serigraph, sheet 15 × 12½ in. (15.2 × 31.7 cm). Trova takes the use of the human figure beyond literal interpretation. It becomes a personal symbol reinforcing the circular format as a radial design unit. Courtesy of the artist.

the abstract artists of the twentieth century seem to have been influenced by machinery, for example, in stylizing pristine, clear-cut shape relationships. Our reactions to these, or the meanings we find in them, vary with our own psychological attitudes. In figure 4.26, Charles Sheeler abstracts patterns from shadows to create shapes that establish compositional movement. While people may accept the abstract shapes in Sheeler's artworks because of their recognizability, they may react adversely to those in Albers's paintings (see fig. 4.25). While both artists use similar shapes, the differences in the relationships among these shapes change their meanings. They differ in color and treatment of value—one flat and the other blended. In other examples, shape extremities become important; thus, the terms *soft edge* and *hard edge* are simply another way of

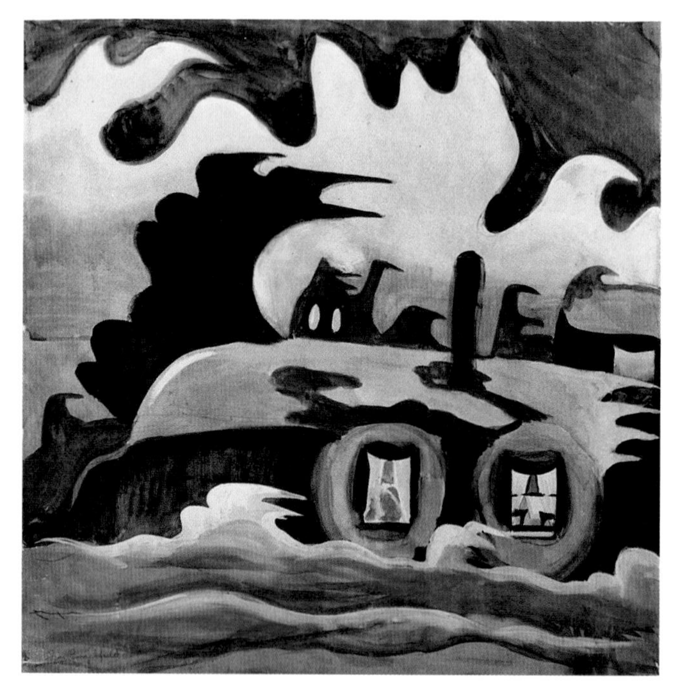

4.24 Charles Burchfield, *The Night Wind,* (Salem, Ohio, January) 1918. Watercolor and gouache on paper, 21½ × 21⅞ in. (54.4 × 55.5 cm). The shapes used by Burchfield in this painting are partly psychological and partly symbolic. The approaching storm seems to evoke human emotions, such as the onset of depression or anger. Gift of A. Conger Goodyear. The Museum of Modern Art, New York, NY. U.S.A. Digital image © The Museum of Modern Art/Licensed by SCALA/Art Resource, NY.

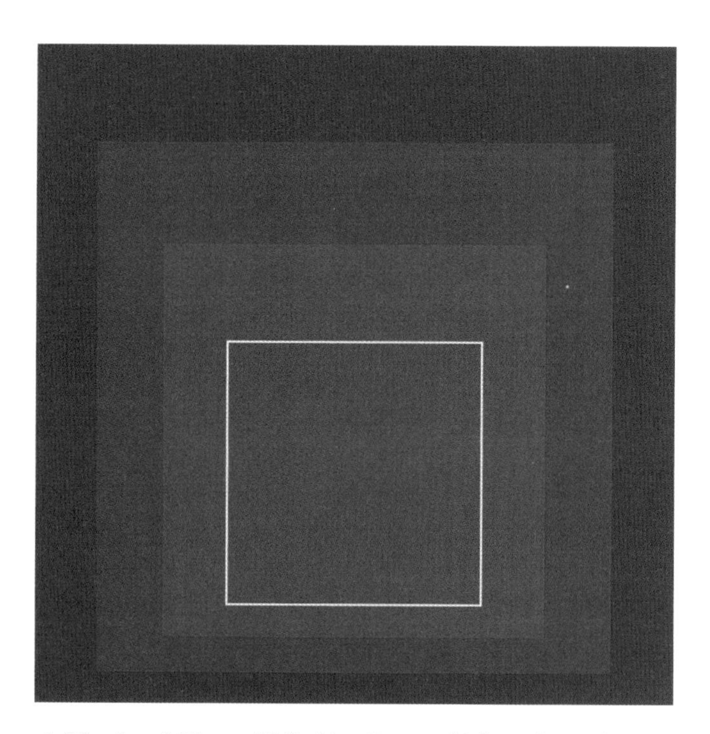

4.25 Josef Albers, *White Line Square IX,* from the series *Homage to the Square,* 1966. Colored lithograph, 21 × 21 in. (53.3 × 53.3 cm). The meaning of the squares in this picture lies not in their resemblance to a real object but in their relationship to one another. © 1966 Josef Albers and Gemini G.E.L., Los Angeles, CA. © 2005 the Josef and Anni Albers Foundation/Artists Rights Society (ARS), New York.

calling shape edges fuzzy and indistinct as opposed to clear-cut and sharply defined (figs. 4.27, 4.28, and 4.29). In addition, colors, values, textures, and the application of particular media affect the way an artwork impresses us. The student has only to glance around a class where everyone is working on the same exercise to see the variety of personal ways the work is done; it is amazing to see the differences in style and content that can result from the same assignment. How much more can we expect, in terms of endless expressive potential, in the case of trained artists?

All the principles involved in ordering shapes are of little value until one becomes aware of the various meanings that can be revealed through relationships made possible by the language of art. Much of this awareness, of course, comes through practice, as in learning any language.

Artists usually select their shapes to express an idea, but they may initially be motivated by the psychological associations of shape, as in the Miró and Burchfield paintings (see figs. 4.5 and

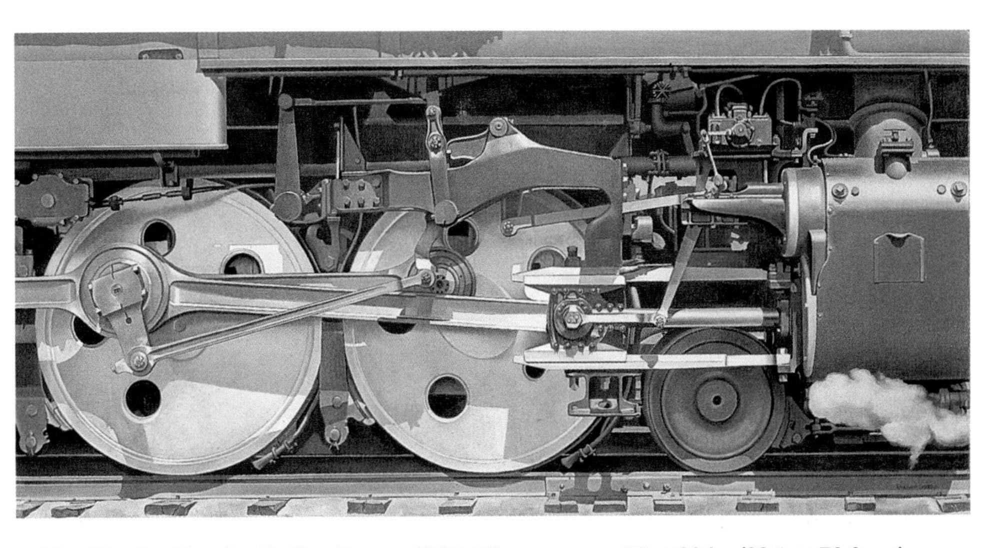

4.26 Charles Sheeler, *Rolling Power,* 1955. Oil on canvas, 15 × 30 in. (38.1 × 72.6 cm). While commenting on the abstract quality of his images, Sheeler remarked, "I had come to feel that a picture could have incorporated in it the structural design implied in abstraction and be presented in a wholly realistic manner." Smith College Museum of Art, Northampton, MA. Purchased, Drayton Hillyer Fund, 1940. Courtesy of Smith College Museum, Northampton, MA.

4.27 Helen Frankenthaler, *Madame Butterfly,* 2000. Woodcut print, triptych: 41¼ × 79 in. (104.8 × 200.7 cm). Many shapes are not meant to represent or even symbolize. Here, for example, the shape extremities, the softly changing values of the larger shapes, and the brown wood-grained ground act against the horizontal violet and white components and the outer frame shape. The artist provokes a momentary feeling of excitement within an otherwise quiet mood. Printed and published by Tyler Graphics Ltd., 2000. © Helen Frankenthaler/Tyler Graphics Ltd. Photograph by Steven Sloman.

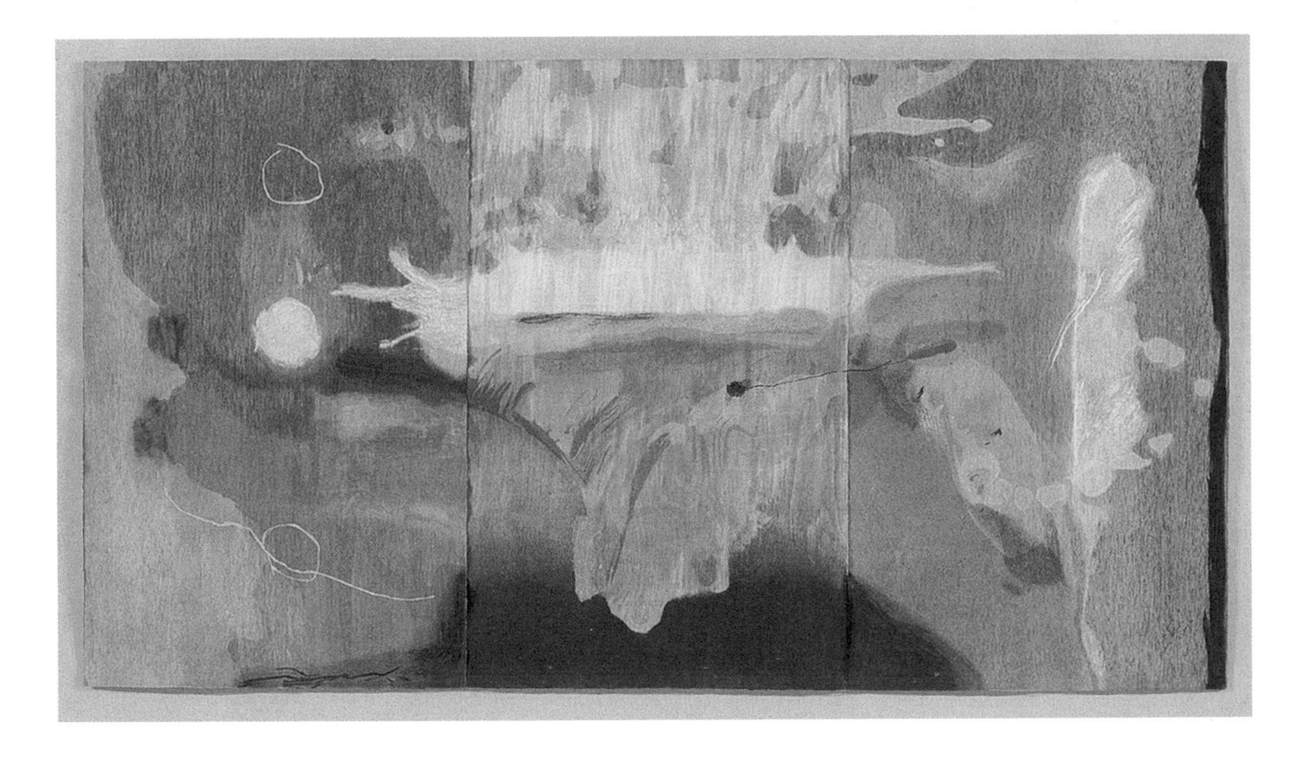

4.28 **Fernand Léger, *Three Women* (*Le Grand Déjeuner*), 1921. Oil on canvas, 6 ft ¼ in. × 8 ft 3 in. (183.5 × 251.5 cm).** The Cubist painter Léger commonly used varied combinations of geometric shapes in very complex patterns. Here, because of his sensitive design, he not only overcomes a dominant, hard-edged feel but also imbues the painting with an air of femininity.

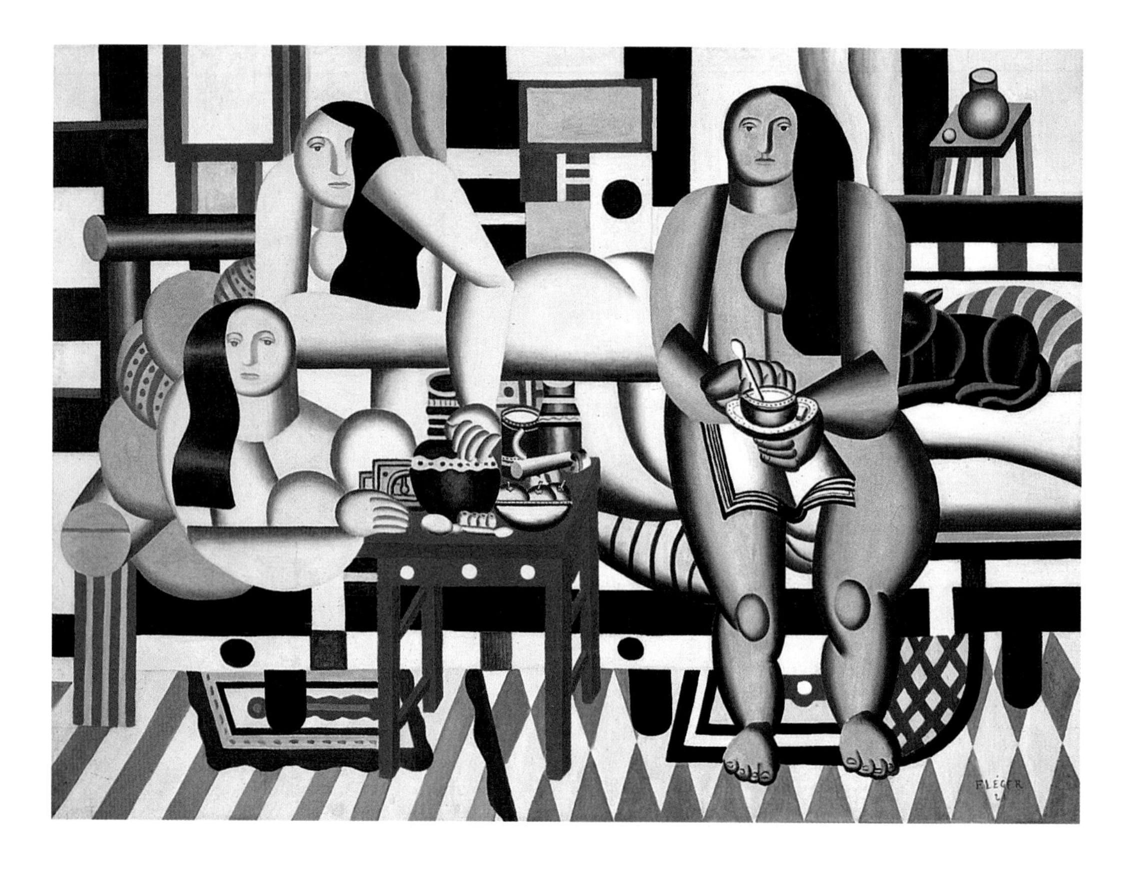

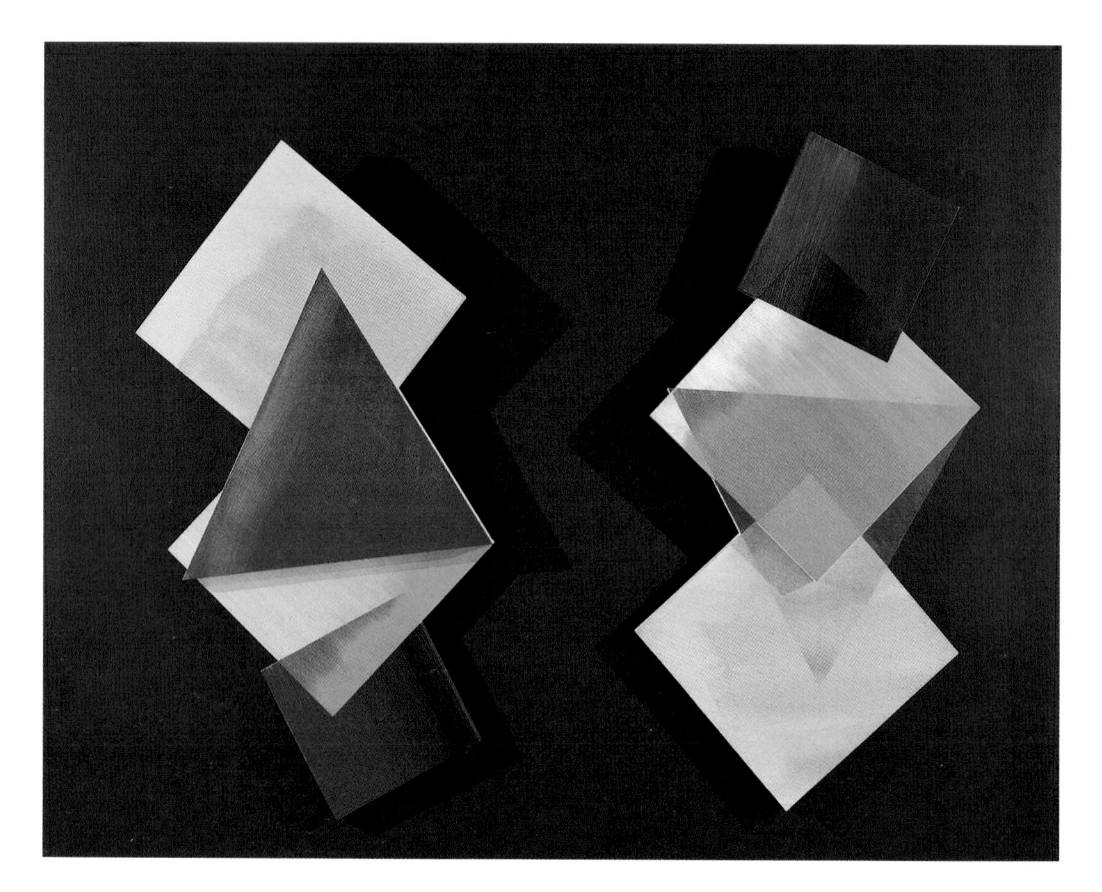

4.29 **Dorothea Rockburne, *Mozart and Mozart Upside Down and Backward,* 1985–87. Oil on gessoed linen, hung on blue wall, 89 × 115 × 4 in. (226.06 × 292.1 × 10.16 cm).** In this painting, Dorothea Rockburne is representative of the Neo-Abstractionist painters who leaned toward the geometric abstraction of the 1950s. Though based on a seemingly simple scheme, on closer examination this piece reveals a labyrinth of interlocking rectilinear shapes.

4.24). Shapes suggest certain meanings, some readily recognizable, others less clear. The standard meanings conveyed by squares, for instance, are perfection, stability, solidity, symmetry, self-reliance, and monotony. Although squares may have different meanings for different people, many common sensations are shared when viewing them (see fig. 4.25). Similarly, circles may suggest self-possession, independence, and/or confinement; ovals might suggest fruitfulness and creation; and stars could suggest reaching out. Most shapes possess distinctive meanings; however, meaningfulness depends on the complexity of their context and the insight of those who observe them (figs. 4.27 and 4.28). How different are our reactions to the biomorphic shapes of the Surrealists when compared to the hard-edged shapes of the geometric Abstractionists (see figs. 4.5 and 4.29)? We know we are sensitive to shape meaning, as demonstrated by the psychologist's use of the familiar Rorschach (inkblot) test, which is designed to aid in evaluating emotional stability. This test indicates that shapes provoke emotional responses on different levels. Thus, the artist might use either abstract or representational shapes to provoke a desired response. By using the knowledge that some shapes are inevitably associated with certain objects and situations, the artist can set the stage for a pictorial or sculptural drama.

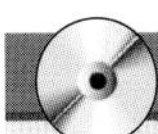

INVESTIGATE THE CD-ROM **Questions to Ask Yourself**

As an image is defined, it attains shape.

While reviewing this chapter on the CD-ROM, think about an artwork that you particularly like, and answer these questions:

1. What kinds of shapes are in the artwork?
2. What are some of the uses of shape in art, and which ones are at play in this artwork?
3. How do these shapes help us to understand the meaning of the artwork?
4. What kinds of interesting changes could be made to change the meaning of the artwork?

CHAPTER FIVE

Value

THE VOCABULARY OF VALUE

INTRODUCTION TO VALUE RELATIONSHIPS

DESCRIPTIVE USES OF VALUE

EXPRESSIVE USES OF VALUE

- Chiaroscuro
- Tenebrism
  - *Printmaking Techniques and Value*
- Decorative Value

COMPOSITIONAL FUNCTIONS OF VALUE

- Value Patterns
- Open and Closed Compositions

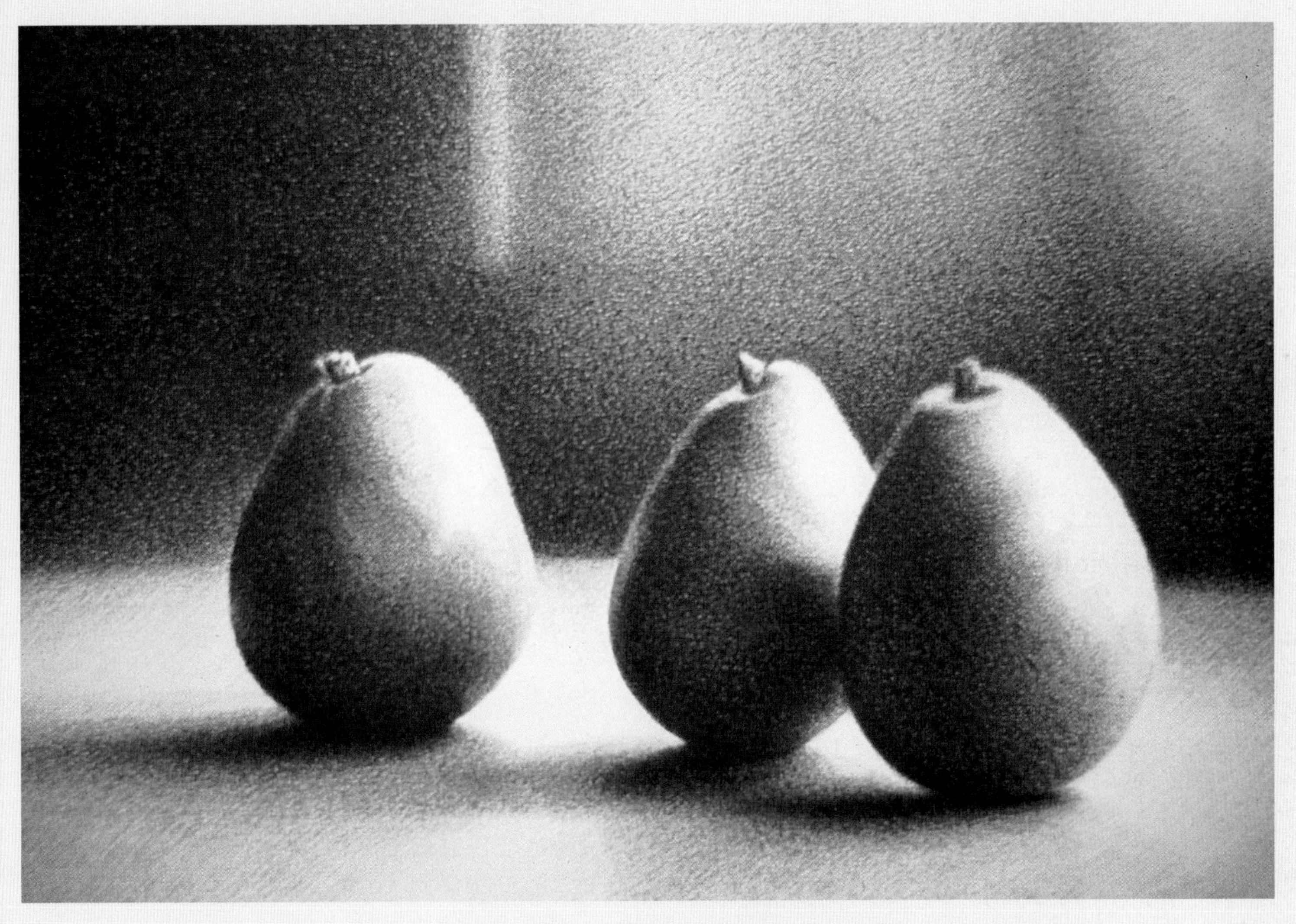

Martha Alf, *Pears Series 11 #7,* 1978. 4B pencil on bond paper, 11 × 14 in. Newspace Gallery, Los Angeles.
Photograph by George Hoffman.

THE VOCABULARY OF **VALUE**

Value — 1. The relative degree of light or dark. 2. The characteristic of color determined by the quantity of light reflected by the color.

achromatic value
Relating to differences of light and dark, without regard for hue and intensity.

cast shadow
The dark area that occurs on a surface as a result of something being placed between that surface and a light source.

chiaroscuro
1. Distribution of light and dark in a picture. 2. A technique of representation that blends light and shade gradually to create the illusion of three-dimensional objects in space or atmosphere.

chromatic value
The relative degree of lightness or darkness demonstrated by a given color.

closed-value composition
Composition in which values are limited by the edges or boundaries of shapes.

decorative value
Value stressing the essential flatness of a surface.

high-key value
A value that has a level of middle gray or lighter.

highlight
The portion of an object that, from the observer's position, receives the greatest amount of direct light.

local value
The relative lightness or darkness of a surface, seen in the objective world, that is independent of any effect created by the degree of light falling on it.

low-key value
Any value that has a level of middle gray or darker.

open-value composition
Composition in which values cross over shape boundaries into adjoining areas.

plastic value
Value used to create the illusion of volume and space.

shadow, shade, shading
The darker value on the surface of an object that gives the illusion that a portion of it is turned away from or obscured by the source of light.

shallow space
The illusion of limited depth. With shallow space, the imagery moves only a slight distance back from the picture plane.

tenebrism
A technique of painting that exaggerates or emphasizes the effects of **chiaroscuro.** Larger amounts of dark value are placed close to smaller areas of highly contrasting lights—which change suddenly—in order to concentrate attention on important features.

value pattern
The arrangement or organization of values that control compositional movement and create a unifying effect throughout a work of art.

INTRODUCTION TO VALUE RELATIONSHIPS

Value is a term commonly used to indicate worth, and the worth and certainly the success of an artwork are enhanced by an artist who makes good use of lights and darks. In art, lights and darks are referred to as **value.** We can readily experience the phenomenon of value when the sun rises and sets, gradually altering the values of the objects that surround us. This chapter is primarily concerned with **achromatic values** consisting of white, black, and the limitless degrees of gray, disregarding other terms sometimes used for value such as *tone, brightness,* and even *color.*

All the other elements of art form possess value. An examination of the value scale in figure 5.1 indicates that there are **low-key values** (middle value to black) and **high-key values** (middle value to white). Some artworks lean toward low-key values (often with lighter accents), while others take the opposite path. The "key" selected usually sets the mood of the work.

For the graphic arts, the particular value of a line is the result of the medium used and the pressure the artist exerts on the medium. For example, the degree of value of a pencil line is determined by the hardness of the graphite and the force with which it is used (see fig. 1.22). Value is also created by placing lines of the same or different qualities (wet or dry, pencil or chalk, or direct or blended) alongside or across from each other to produce generalized areas of value. These lines may be so delicate that they are barely noticeable or so aggressive that they reveal the energy driving the artist. Value, however applied, will create distinguishable shapes (figs. 5.2 and 5.3). The values of line are also used to simulate textures, including the **shadows** and **highlights** peculiar to a particular surface, or to produce abstract textures. The values in abstract textures depart to some degree from the values of the objects being represented and may even be totally the artist's invention.

In addition to draftsmen, printmakers have traditionally worked entirely with achromatic values. Still today, many artists and photographers prefer this approach. Rich darks and sparkling lights can be a visual delight.

Painters have discovered that the effects of a particular color may be entirely dependent on its **chromatic value**—the lightness or darkness of a color. A standard yellow, for example, is of far greater lightness than a standard violet, although both colors may be modified to a point that they become virtually equal in value. A common weakness in painting is the disregard for the pattern created by the value relationships of the colors. Black-and-white photographs of paintings can reveal these relationships very clearly.

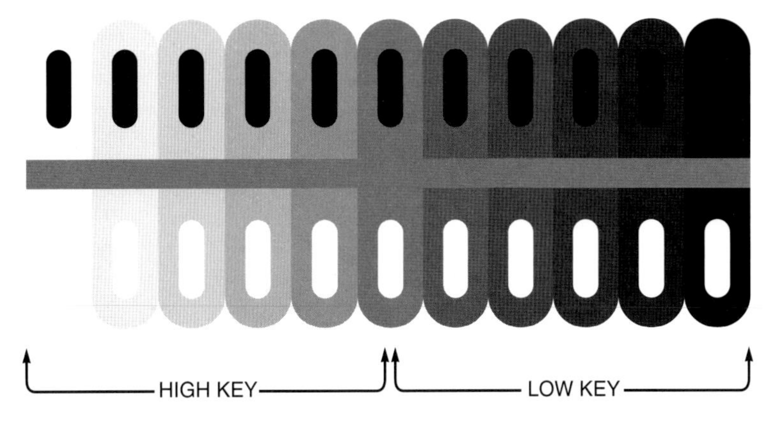

5.1 This value scale shows a gradation from light to dark. The value is also seen against middle gray and black and white. Regardless of media or technique, compositions that use values from white to middle gray are referred to as high key, while low-key images would include dark values—middle grays to black. Small amounts of contrasting value are often necessary to make either low or high key exciting.

DESCRIPTIVE USES OF VALUE

Applications of value enrich artistic readings of objects, shapes, and space (fig. 5.3). When artists describe images using only the naturally occurring values of those objects, they are working with **local value.** However, the descriptive uses of value can be broadened to encompass psychological, emotional, and dramatic expression. Painters use value to translate the effect of light playing about the earth and its inhabitants. We perceive objects in terms of the patterns that occur when those objects are exposed to light rays. Under normal circumstances, objects do not receive light from all directions at once. Usually, a

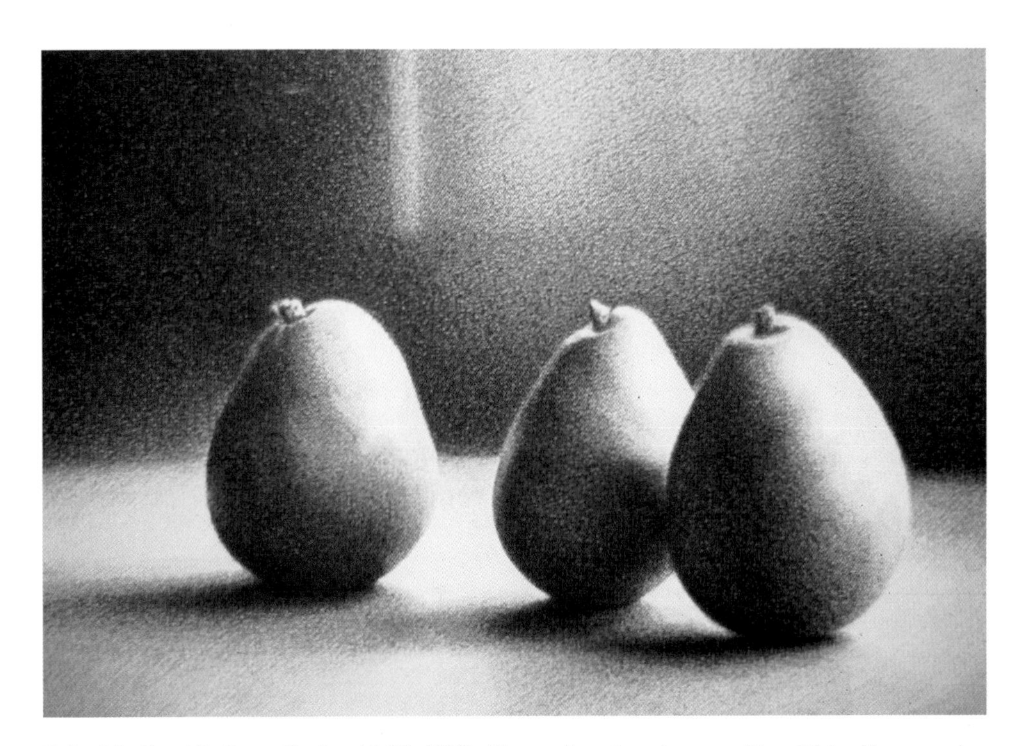

5.2 Martha Alf, *Pears Series 11 #7,* 1978. 4B pencil on bond paper, 11 × 14 in. At a casual glance, these values appear blended by rubbing drawing materials, but close examination reveals that Martha Alf created this image using delicately drawn lines so fine that they are not recognized as individual lines. Rather, the marks combine to produce areas of strong highlights and shadow that define the pears and their surroundings. This results in crisp and sparkling surfaces. Newspace Gallery, Los Angeles. Photograph by George Hoffman.

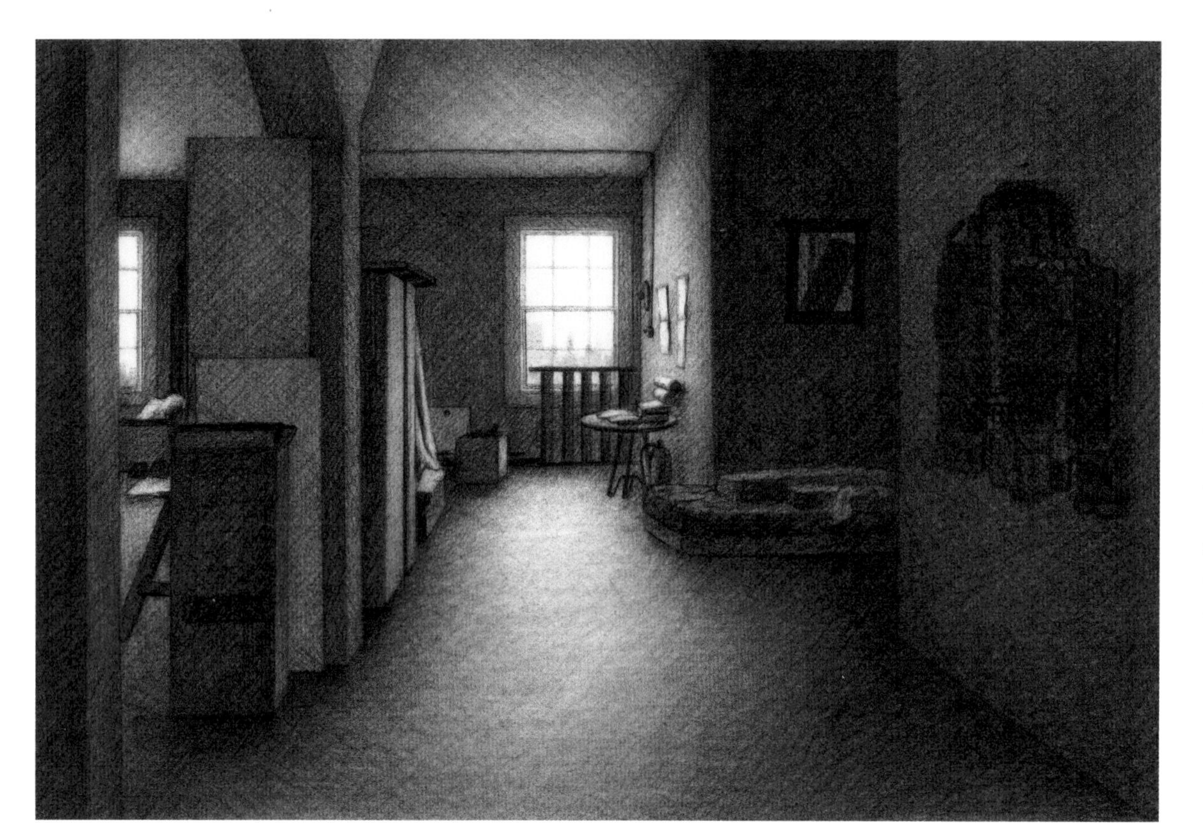

5.3 Susan Kraut, American, born 1945, *Untitled,* 1979. Charcoal, with stumping and erasing, on ivory laid paper, 325 × 459 mm. The degree of line concentration indicates the value of the subject; where tightly bunched shadows are suggested, the forms of the interior are defined. Though defined with strong contrasts and refined shapes, the overall darkness and minimal use of highlights creates a thoughtful mood. Jalane and Richard Davidson Collection, 2001.689. Photograph by Robert Lifson. Reproduction, The Art Institute of Chicago.

solid object gets more light from one side than another because that side is closer to the light source and thus intercepts the light and casts shadows on the other side (fig. 5.4A).

Light patterns vary according to the surface of the object receiving the light. A spherical surface exhibits an even gradient from light to dark; a surface with intersecting planes shows sudden contrasts of light and dark values. Each basic form has its own basic highlight and shadow pattern. Evenly flowing tone gradation evokes a sense of a gently curved surface. An abrupt change of tone indicates a sharp or angular surface (see fig. 5.4A).

Cast shadows are the dark areas that occur on an object or a surface when a shape is placed between it and the light source. The nature of the shadow created depends on the size and location of the light source, the size and shape of the interposed body, and the character of the surfaces where the shadows fall. Although cast shadows offer definite clues to the circumstances of a given situation, they only occasionally give an ideal indication of the true nature of the forms (fig. 5.4B). The artist normally uses shadows to aid in description, to enhance the effectiveness of the design pattern, and to contribute to the mood or expression.

Many artists use value to create representational imagery, sometimes employing chiaroscuro (see below), which gives special emphasis to light and shadow. In addition, other artists like Anne Dykmans and realist painters such as Richard Estes and Philip Pearlstein draw inspiration from photography and cinema for their artworks (fig. 5.5; see figs. 10.112 and 10.113). When an artist uses value to create the illusion of volume and space, it can be called **plastic value.**

EXPRESSIVE USES OF VALUE

The type of expression sought by the artist ordinarily determines the balance between light and dark in a work of art. A preponderance of dark areas creates an atmosphere of gloom, mystery, drama, or menace, whereas a composition that is basically light will produce the opposite effect. Artists are not bound to duplicate the cause and effect of light and shadow exactly, because this may create a monotonous effect. They often revise the shapes of highlights and shadows to produce desired degrees of unity and contrast with adjacent areas in the

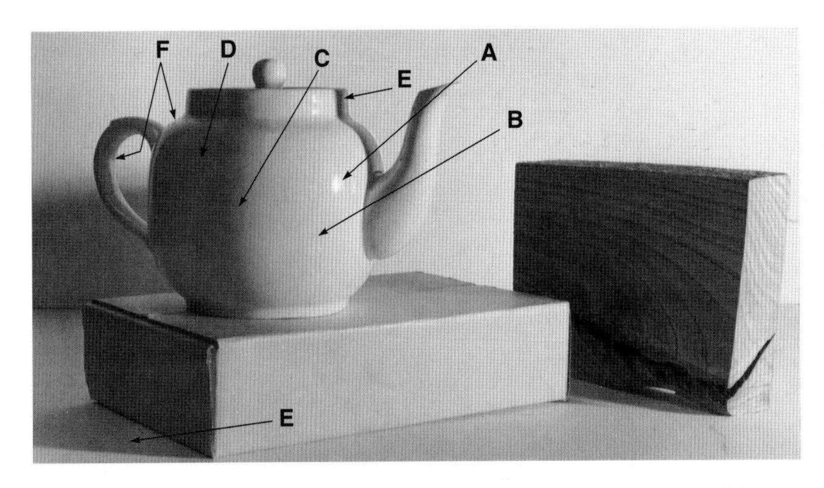

5.4A Russell F. McKnight, *Light and Dark,* 1984. Photograph. A solid object receives more light on one side than the other because of its proximity to a light source. As the light is blocked out, shadows occur. Curved surfaces exhibit a gradual change of value, whereas angular surfaces give sharp changes: (A) highlight; (B) light; (C) shadow edge; (D) shadow core; (E) cast shadow; and (F) reflected light. Courtesy of the artist.

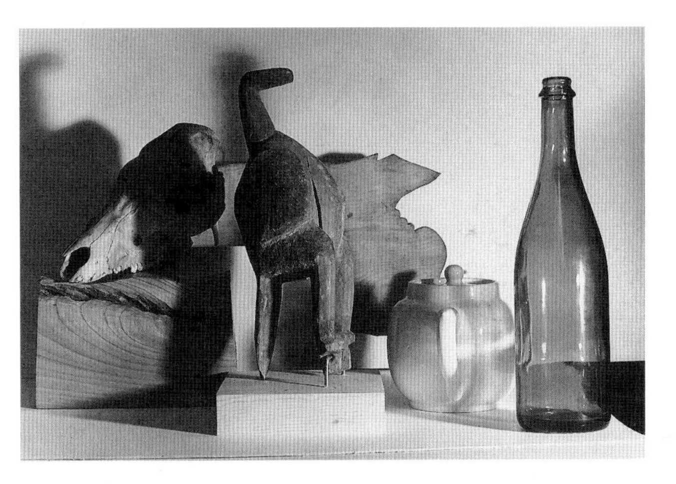

5.4B Russell F. McKnight, *Shadows,* 1984. Photograph. Light can cast overlapping shadows that tend to break up and hide the true character of object forms. When the shapes of shadows are not factored into the composition, results are often disorganized, as in this experiment. Courtesy of the artist.

5.5 Anne Dykmans, *Trois Fois,* 1986. Etching, mezzotint and aquatint, 13¾ × 19½ in. (34.9 × 49.53 cm). This is fairly straightforward portrayal of the benches, including cast shadows of an undisclosed source. The background is made moody because of the shielding. One might initially expect this to be a photograph. Courtesy Stone and Press Galleries, New Orleans, LA.

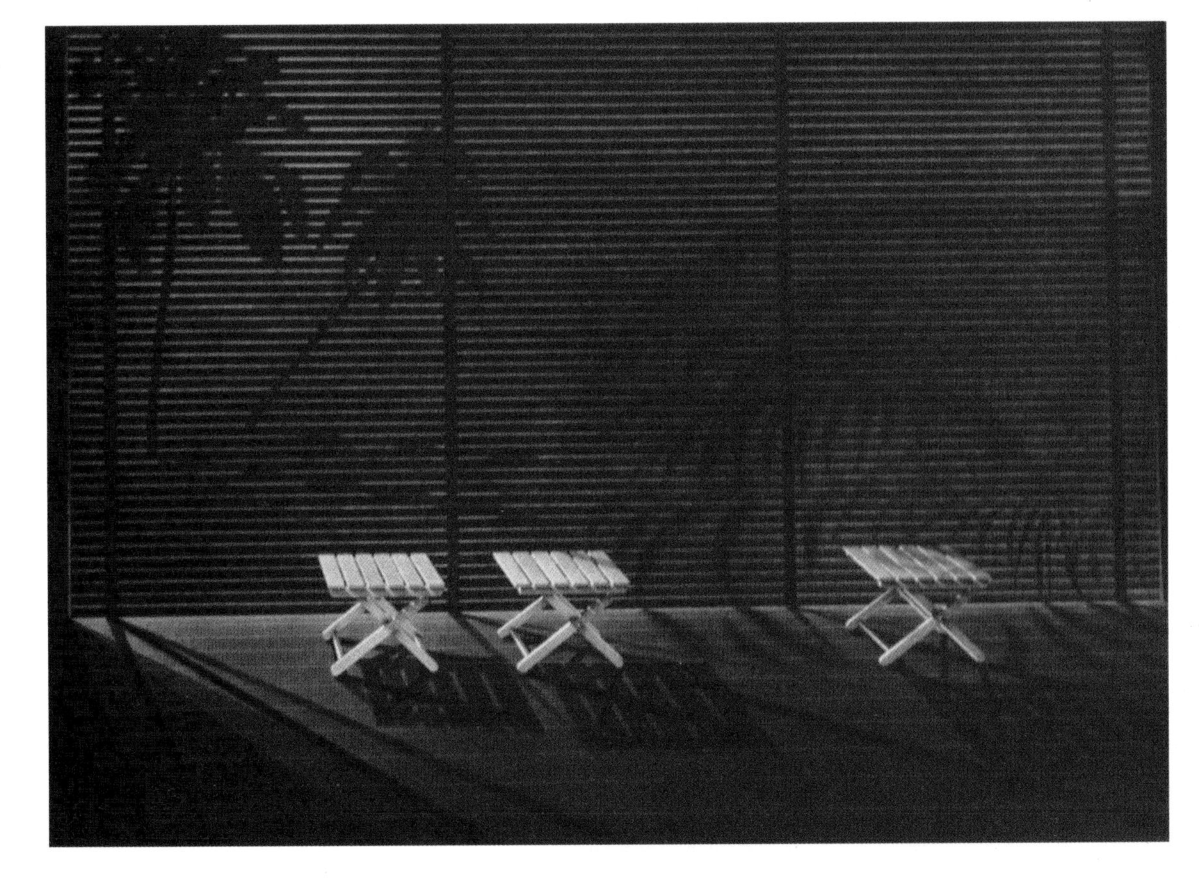

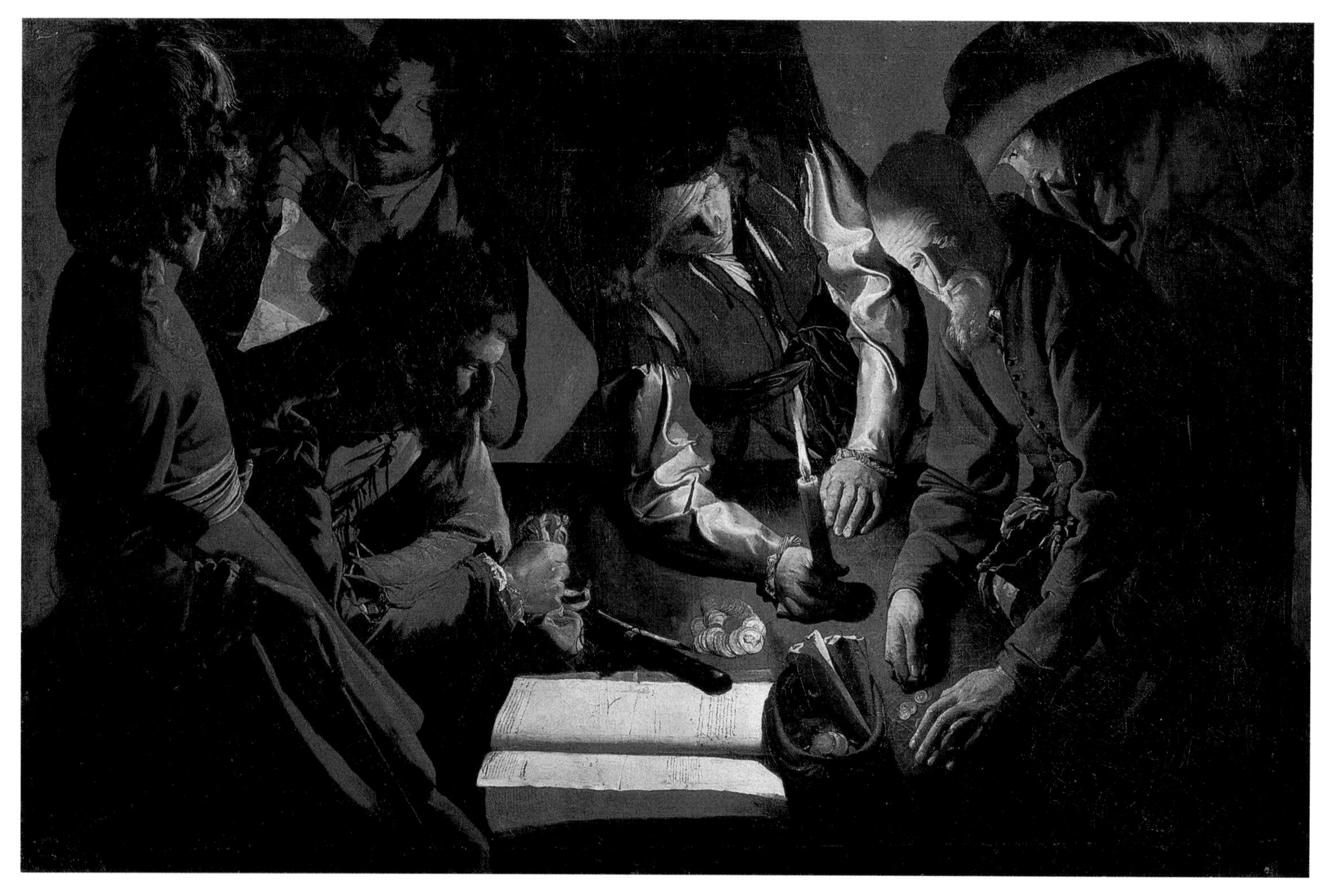

5.6 Georges de La Tour, *The Payment of Taxes*, c. 1618–20. Oil on canvas. In a complex composition, La Tour has used strong candlelight and its highlights and shadows to produce the atmosphere of a quiet drama. Multiple figures provide the opportunity for combining natural and invented shadows, which reinforce the structural movement. Lviv State Picture Gallery, Ukraine/The Bridgeman Art Library.

composition. In summary, lights and shadows exist in nature as the by-products of strictly physical laws. Artists can adjust and take liberties with lights and shadows to create their own visual language (fig. 5.6).

Chiaroscuro

Chiaroscuro refers to the technique of representation that makes subtle use of contrasting lights and darks. The term also alludes to the way artists handle atmospheric effects to create the illusion that the objects are surrounded on all sides by space. **Chiaroscuro** developed mainly in painting, beginning with Giotto (1266–1337), who used darks and lights for modeling while expressing shape and space in terms of line (fig. 5.7). The early Florentine masters Masaccio, Fra Angelico, and Fra Filippo Lippi carried chiaroscuro a step further by expressing spatial structure and volume in even, graded tonalities (see figs. 1.27 and 8.17A). Later, Leonardo da Vinci employed even bolder contrasts in light and dark, but always with soft value transitions (fig. 5.8). Thereafter, the great Venetian painters, such as Titian, completely subordinated line and suggested compositional unity through an enveloping atmosphere of dominant tonality (fig. 5.9). More recently, artists such as Jack Beal continue to apply the same techniques (fig. 5.10).

5.7 **Giotto, *The Kiss of Judas,* Scrovegni Chapel, Padua, 1304–6. Fresco, 7 ft 7 in. × 6 ft 7½ in. (2.31 × 2.02 m).** Although line and shape predominate in Giotto's works, some early attempts at modeling with chiaroscuro value can be seen. Photo: Arena Chapel, Cappella Degli Scrovegni, Padua/SuperStock.

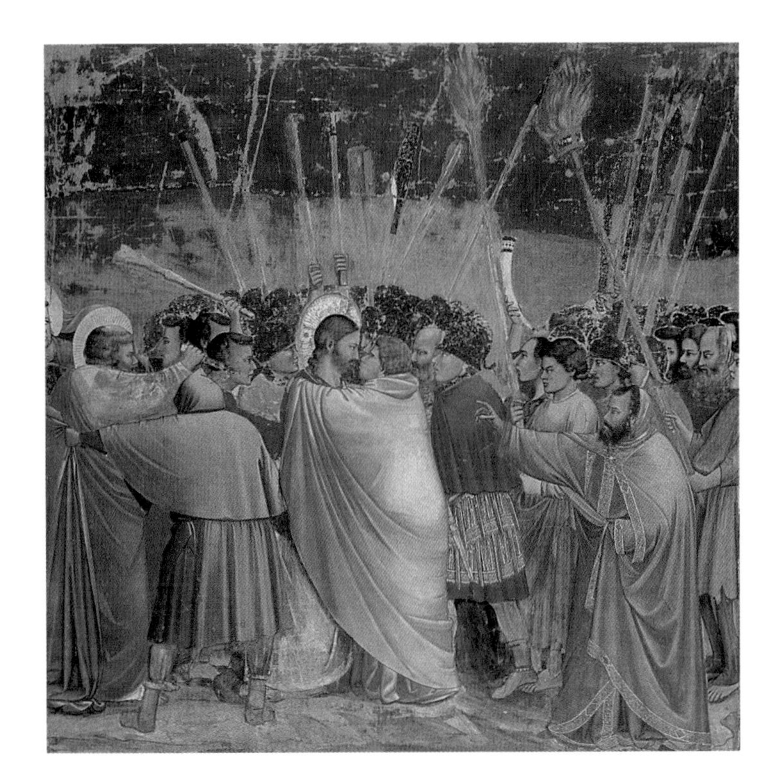

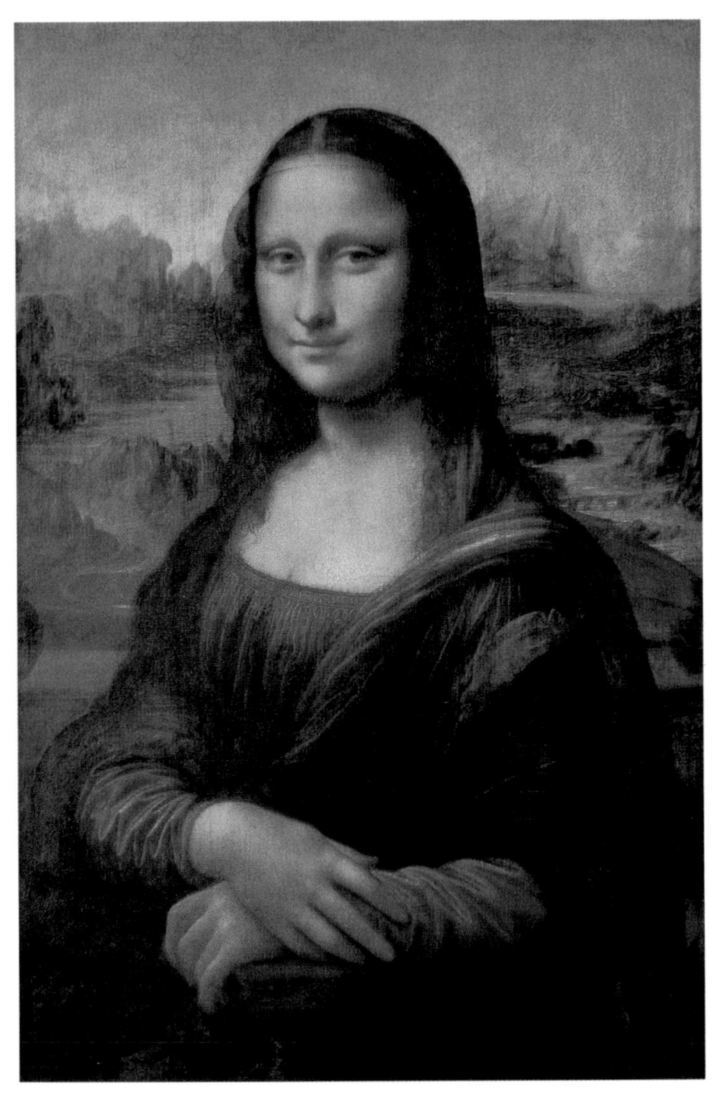

5.8 **Leonardo da Vinci, *Mona Lisa,* 1503–6. Oil on panel, 30½ × 21 in. (76.2 × 52.5 cm).** While exploring chiaroscuro, Leonardo extended the value range set by previous artists; he also developed a technique known as *sfumato,* which featured soft blending and subtle transitions from light to dark. Louvre, Paris, France/The Bridgeman Art Library.

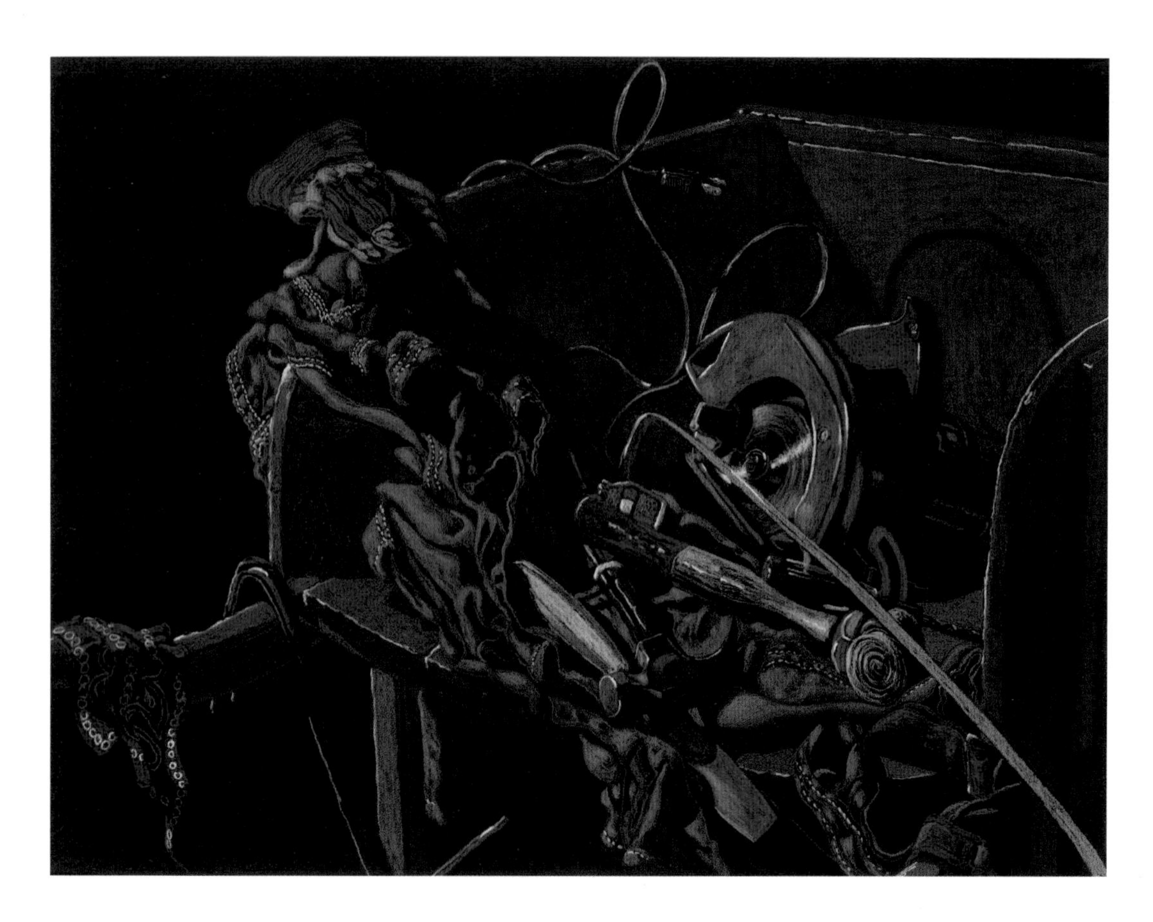

5.9 Jack Beal, American, born 1931, *Still Life with Tools,* 1979. Pastel on black wove paper, 75.9 × 101.7 cm (sheet). Beal transforms ordinary tools into mysterious objects with his tenebristic use of pastel. The objects in the wheelbarrow seem to glow, elevated from their prosaic origins. Jalane and Richard Davison Collection, 1990.511.2. Reproduction, The Art Institute of Chicago.

5.10 Titian (Tiziano Vecellio), *The Entombment of Christ,* 1559. Oil on canvas, 4 ft 6 in. × 5 ft 8⅞ in. (1.37 × 1.75 m). The Venetian master Titian subordinated line (contrasting edges with value) and enveloped his figures in a total atmosphere that approaches tenebrism. Museo del Prado, Madrid, Spain. Photo: Scala/Art Resource, NY.

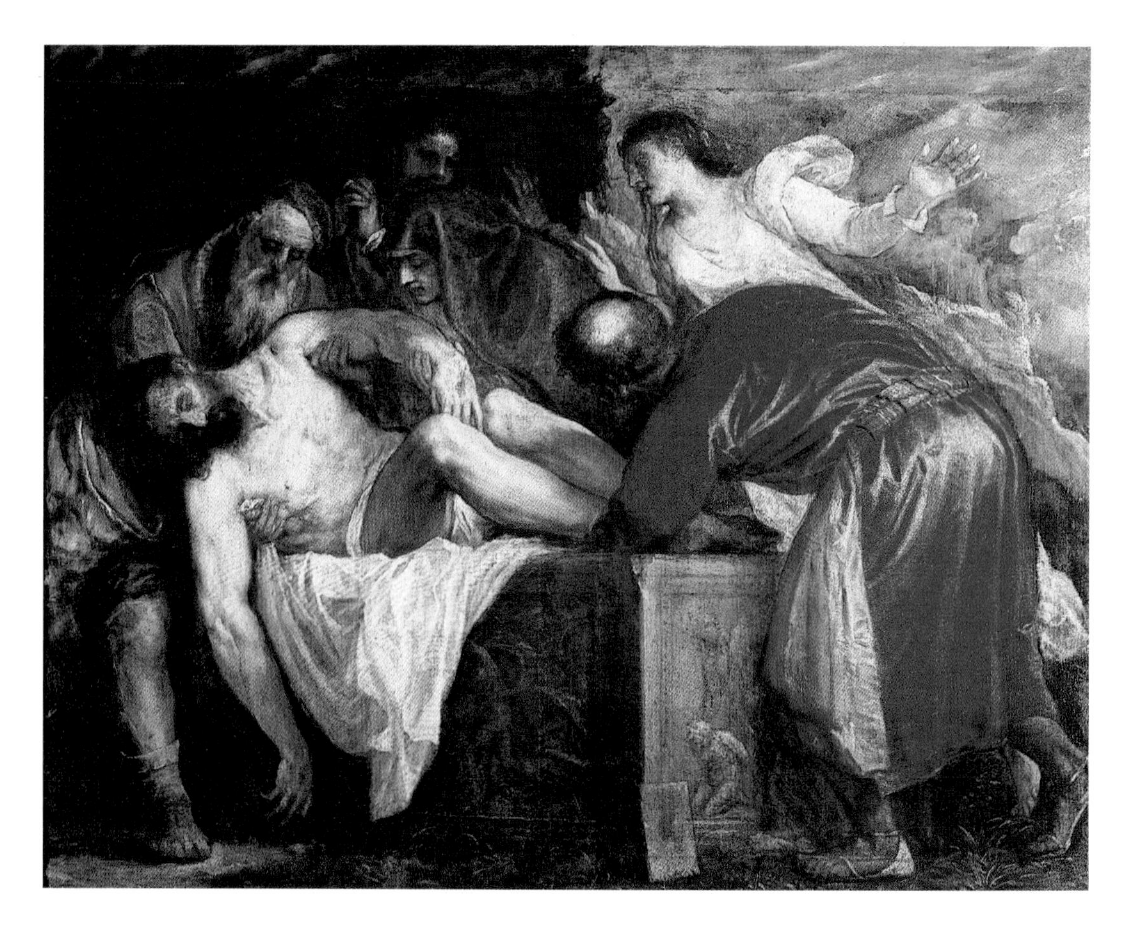

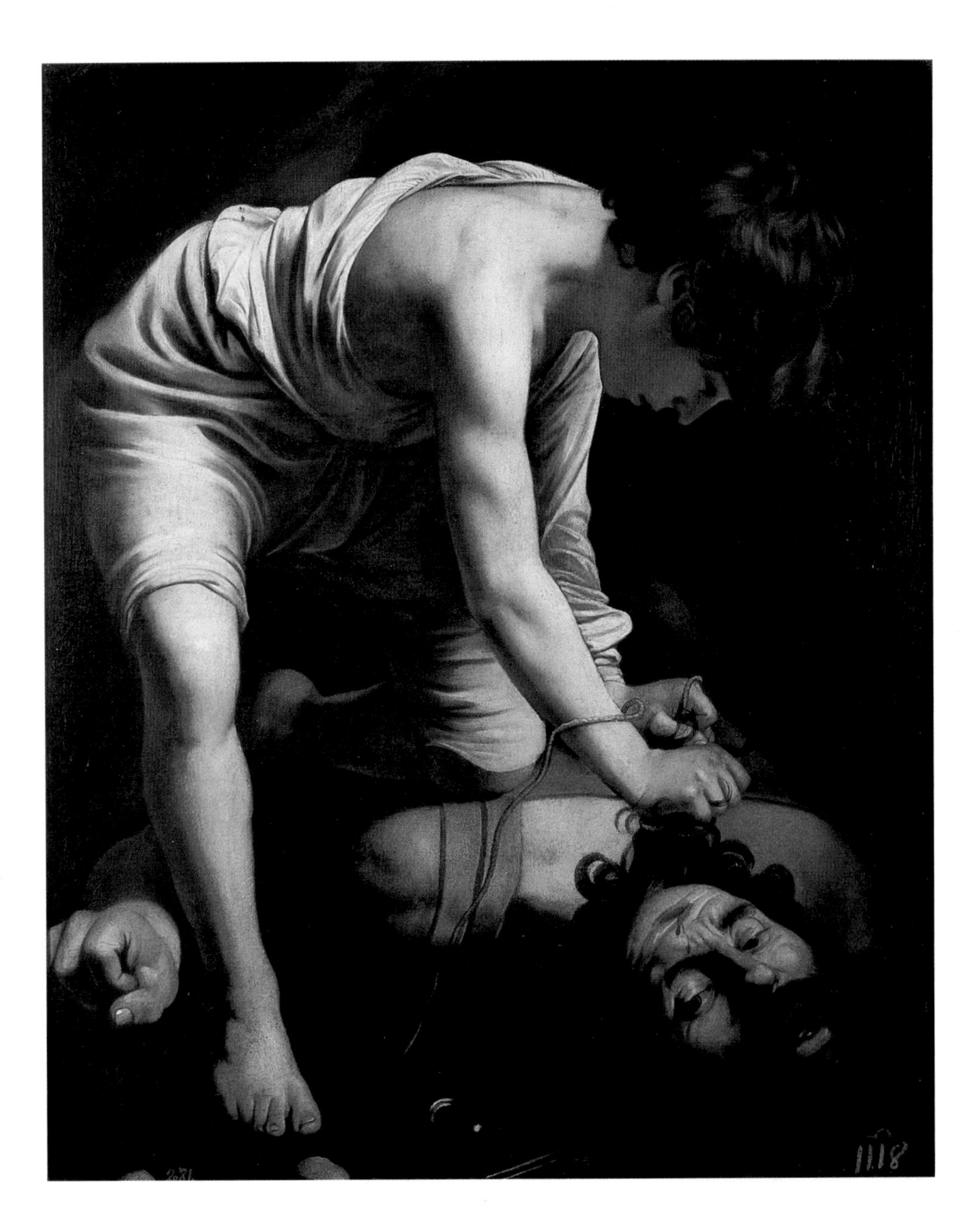

5.11 Michelangelo Merisi, called Caravaggio, *David Victorious over Goliath,* 1599–1600. Oil on canvas, 44 × 36 in. (110 × 91 cm). Caravaggio was essentially the leader in establishing the dark manner of painting in the sixteenth and seventeenth centuries. Several of the earlier northern Italian painters, however, such as Correggio, Titian, and Tintoretto, show a strong tendency toward compositions using darker values. The Prado Museum, Madrid, Spain/The Bridgeman Art Library.

Tenebrism

Extreme chiaroscuro is called **tenebrism.** The first tenebrists were an international group of painters who, early in the seventeenth century, were inspired by the work of Michelangelo Merisi da Caravaggio (fig. 5.11). Caravaggio based his chiaroscuro on Correggio's work and instituted the so-called dark manner of painting in western Europe. Rembrandt adapted the technique and perfected the manner, which he learned from migratory artists of Germany and southern Holland (fig. 5.12). The dark manner made value an instrument of the characteristic exaggeration we find in Baroque painting. The strong contrasts lent themselves to the highly dramatic, even theatrical, feelings of the period.

Later, this dark manner devolved into the pallid, muddy monotone that pervaded much of nineteenth-century Western painting. The tenebrists and their followers were fascinated by peculiarities of lighting, particularly the way that lighting affected mood or emotional expression. They deviated from ordinary lighting conditions by placing the implied light sources in unexpected locations, creating unusual visual and spatial effects. In the hands of masters such as Rembrandt, these effects were revelations; in lesser hands, they were mere tricks and visual sleight-of-hand.

Printmaking Techniques and Value

Rembrandt was a printmaker, known for his intaglio prints or etchings, which were achromatic but employed a strong contrast of light and dark (see figs. 1.21A, B). Intaglio printing involves a metal plate that the artist has cut into or etched using acid. Ink is rubbed into the crevices of the plate, which is then wiped so that only those crevices contain the ink. Under the pressure of a press, the ink is then forced out of the plate onto the printing paper.

Woodcut, or relief, prints by artists from this same period were printed in black and white from single blocks cut with gouges or knives. In an attempt to achieve subtle shading or chiaroscuro effects, artists began to explore the use of multiple blocks, printing gray tones under the final black-and-white block.

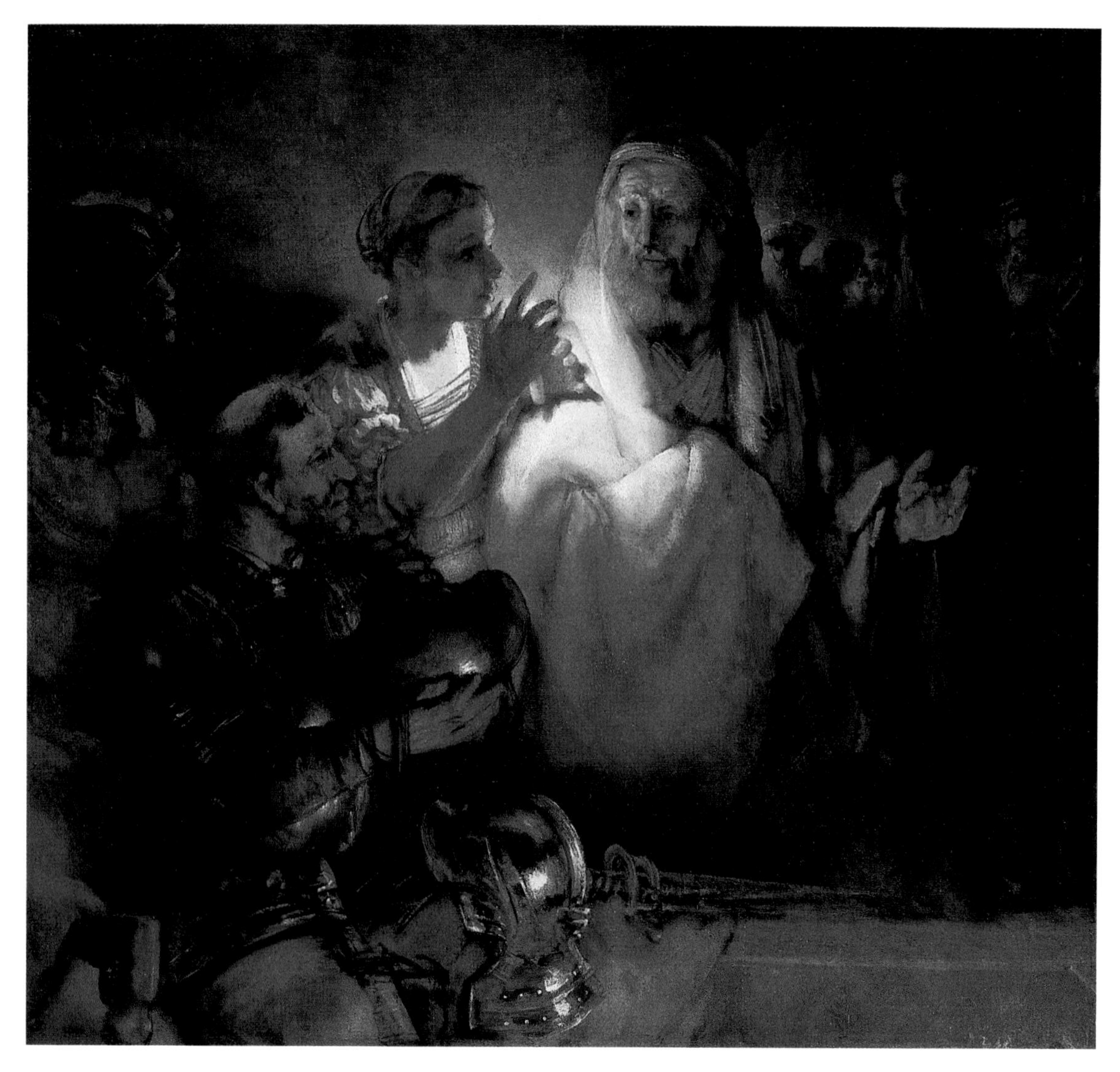

5.12 **Rembrandt van Rijn, *The Denial of St. Peter,* 1660. Oil, 154 × 169 cm.** Rembrandt often used invented and hidden light sources that deviated from standard conditions to enhance the mood or emotional expression. The spotlight effect predates the invention of dramatic stage lighting. Collection Rijksmuseum Amsterdam.

This experimentation soon led to colored blocks, and the use of color in printmaking remains popular today (see fig. 4.27).

Lithography, developed in the early nineteenth century, used achromatic values drawn by oil crayon on a slab of limestone (later replaced by metal plates). Chemically treated and washed in water, the stone would allow the application of ink in only the drawn areas. When the inked stone, which was covered with paper, passed through a press with a scraper bar, the pressure of the press forced the ink to transfer to the paper (see fig. 3.4).

Screen printing, also known as silk screen and serigraphy, became popular because of its speed of printing. It is capable of black-and-white images but has been more often used to print colored images. With screen printing, ink is forced through a screen onto the printing paper by pressure applied to a squeegee. The preparation of the screen determines the ink pattern (fig. 2.56).

Whether the artist is creating colored or black-and-white prints, the use

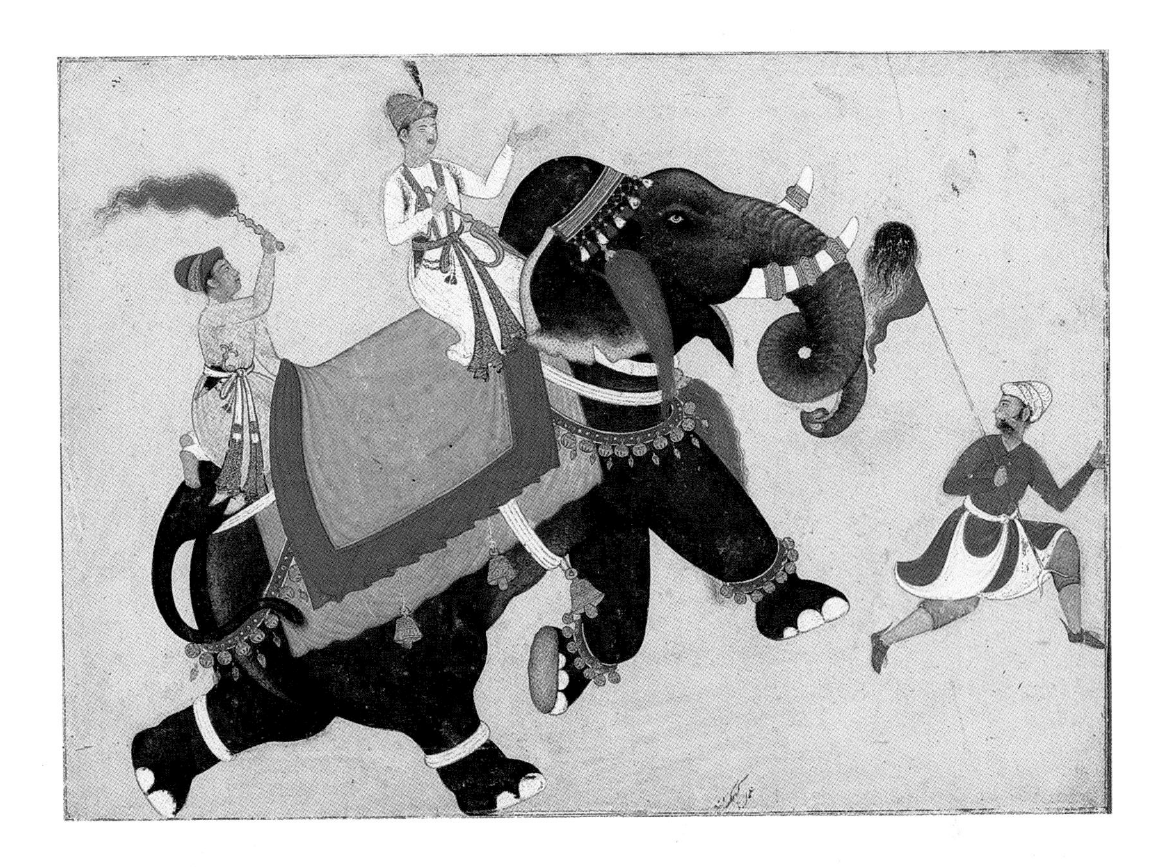

5.13 Signed: Khem Karan, *Prince Riding an Elephant*, Mughal, period of Akbar, c. 1600. Opaque watercolor and gold on paper, 12¼ × 18½ in. (31.2 × 47 cm). Historically, South Asian artists have usually disregarded the use of light (illumination) in favor of decorative value compositions. The Metropolitan Museum of Art, Rogers Fund, 1925. (25.6B.4) Photograph © 1988 The Metropolitan Museum of Art.

of value to organize and create successful images remains fundamental in all four of these basic printmaking techniques. Many prints use combinations of these techniques. For more information on printmaking tools and processes, see the accompanying CD-ROM.

Decorative Value

Art styles that stress **decorative** effects usually ignore conventional light sources or neglect representation of light altogether. If light effects appear, they are often selected for their contribution to the total form of the work. The neglect of natural lighting, or "staged" lighting, is characteristic of the artworks of children and of primitive and prehistoric tribes, traditional East Asians, and certain periods of Western art, notably the Middle Ages. Many contemporary artworks are completely free of illusionistic lighting. An artwork that thus divorces itself from natural law tends to be more concerned with pictorial invention, imagination, and form. Such works do not necessarily sacrifice emotional impact, but the emotions speak primarily through the forms and are consequently less extroverted.

A trend away from illumination values grew during the nineteenth century, partly because of growing interest in Middle Eastern and East Asian art forms (fig. 5.13). This trend was given a scientific interpretation when the naturalist painter Edouard Manet observed that multiple light sources tended to flatten object surfaces. He found that this light condition neutralized the plastic qualities of objects, thereby minimizing gradations of value, as can be seen by comparing figures 5.14A and B. As a result, he laid his colors on canvas in flat areas, beginning with bright, light colors and generally neglecting shadow (fig. 5.15). Some critics have claimed this to be the basic technical advance of nineteenth-century painting, because it paved the way for nonrepresentational uses of value and helped revive interest in the shallow-space concept.

COMPOSITIONAL FUNCTIONS OF VALUE

The revived concept of shallow space is illustrated in the works of the early Cubists and their followers. In those paintings, space is given its order by the arrangement of flat planes abstracted from the subject matter. In the initial stages of this trend, the planes were shaded individually and semi-illusionistically, without giving an indication of any one light source. Later, each plane took on a characteristic value and, in combination with others, produced a carefully conceived **shallow space.** Eventually, this shallow space was developed through attention to the

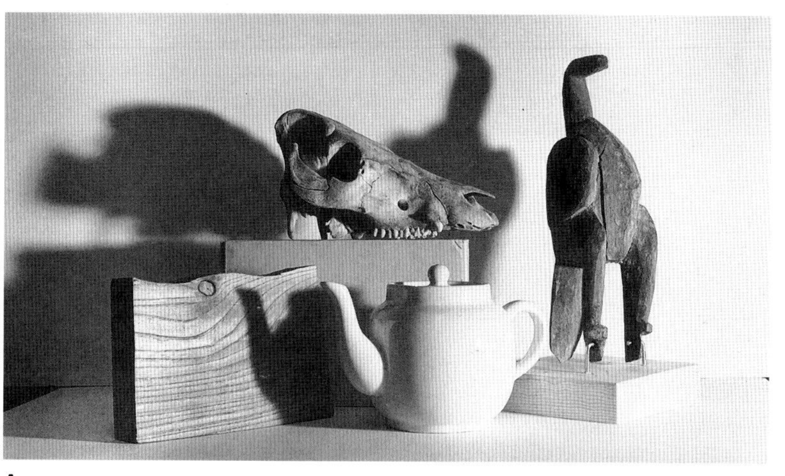

A

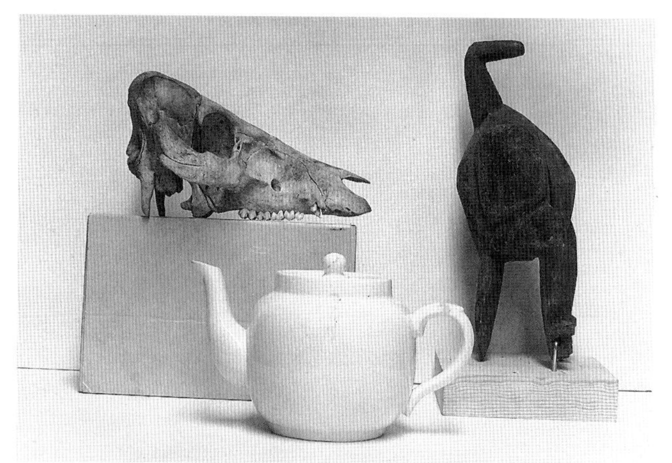

B

5.14 Russell F. McKnight, *Effect of Light on Objects,* 1984. Photograph. Figure 5.14A demonstrates how light from one source emphasizes the three-dimensional qualities of an object and gives an indication of depth. The cast shadows also give definite clues to the descriptive and plastic qualities of the various objects. The photograph in figure 5.14B shows the group of objects under illumination from several light sources. This form of lighting tends to flatten object surfaces and produces a decorative effect. Courtesy of the artist.

5.15 Edouard Manet, *The Dead Toreador,* probably 1864. Oil on canvas, $29\frac{7}{8} \times 60\frac{3}{8}$ in. (75.9 × 153.4 cm). Manet, a nineteenth-century naturalist, was one of the first artists to break with traditional chiaroscuro, making use, instead, of flat areas of value. These flat areas meet abruptly, unlike the blended edges used by artists previous to Manet. This was one of the great technical developments of nineteenth-century art. Widener Collection. © 1998 Board of Trustees, National Gallery of Art, Washington, D.C.

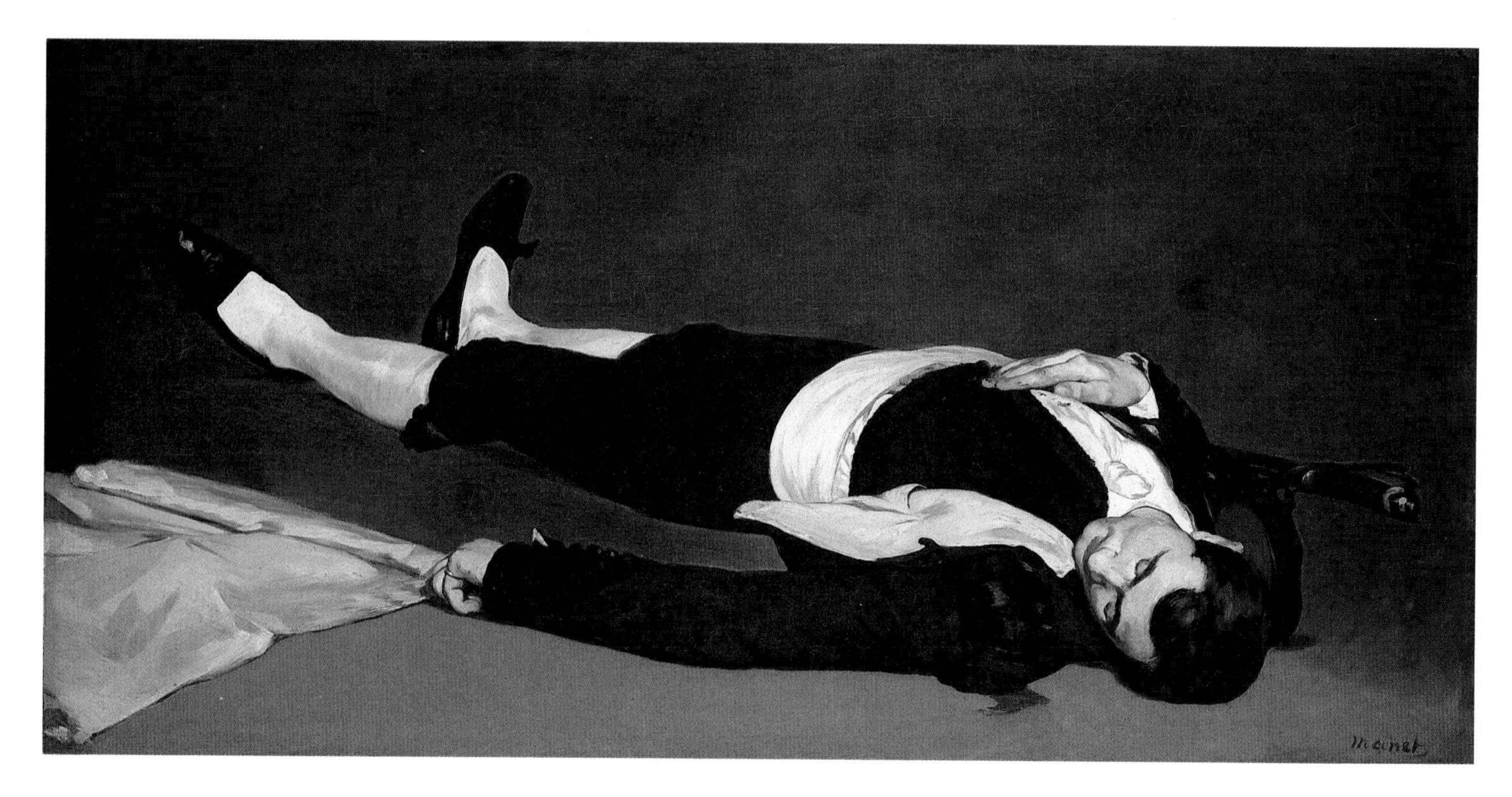

advancing and receding characteristics of value itself (see fig. 4.8). The explorations of these early-twentieth-century artists helped focus attention on the intrinsic significance of each and every element. Value was no longer merely a technique of superficial transcription. Today, artists think of value as a vital and descriptive participant in pictorial organization. An artist can strengthen underlying compositional structure by controlling contrast of value; it is instrumental in creating relative dominance, indicating deep or two-dimensional space, establishing mood, and producing spatial unity (fig. 5.16).

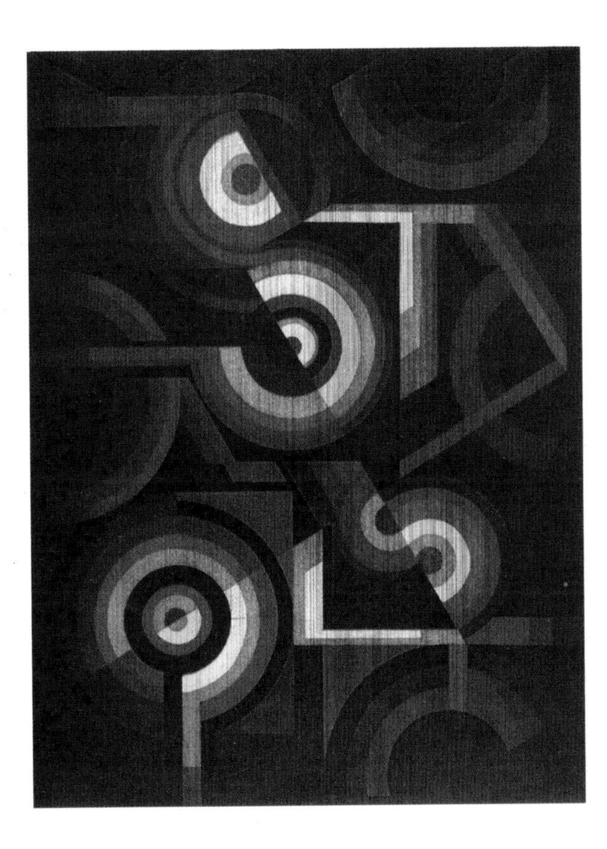

5.16 Jisik Shin, *Lunar Image I*, 1990. Print (etching), 11⅞ × 15¾ in. (30 × 40 cm). Absent of the need for any three-dimensional illusion of imagery, the light and dark contrasts in this etching create a dynamic two-dimensional value pattern. Courtesy of the artist.

Value Patterns

Artists have long examined possible variations for a composition's value pattern—its underlying movement and ground system—by making small studies of the value structure called thumbnail sketches. We can think of these **value patterns** as the compositional skeleton that supports the image. When properly integrated into the final work, the movement, tension, and structure of the value pattern explored in the sketches reinforce the subject. The value pattern should neither distract from the image nor separate itself as an overpowering entity or an isolated component. The advantage of small-scale preliminary value studies is that they allow an artist to quickly explore compositional variations before selecting a final solution. In figures 5.17, 5.18, and 5.19, for example, Nicolas Poussin and Barry Schactman develop large rhythmical dark shapes across the bottom while intermingling smaller receding toned shapes in the middle areas.

Such small studies may be difficult to relate to the final work because of scale. In small drawings, the areas of value may look exciting because they are drawn with rapid, sketchy strokes. But when enlarged, these small strokes may become flat shapes that no longer have the same visual appeal. The new, enlarged shapes

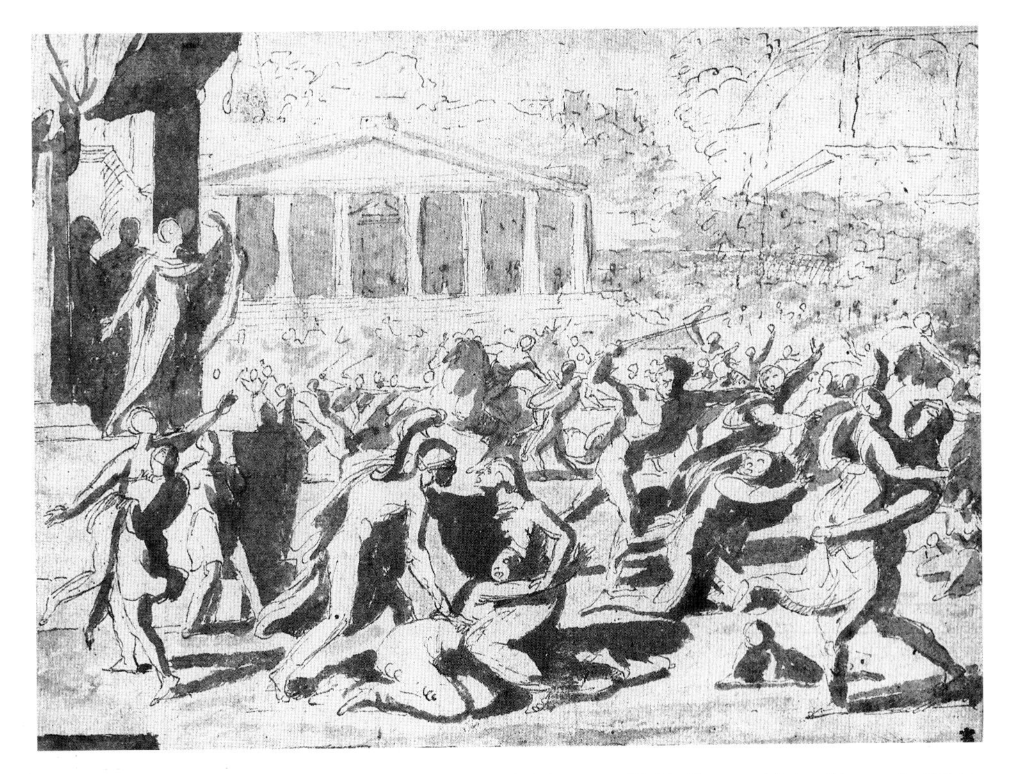

5.17 Nicolas Poussin, study for *Rape of the Sabines*, c. 1633. Pen and ink with wash, 6½ × 8⅞ in. (16.4 × 22.5 cm). Preparatory, or "thumbnail", sketches give the artist the opportunity to explore movement, ground systems, value structure, and compositional variations. In Poussin's sketch, it seems likely that the artist was striving for rhythmical movement within the horizontal thrust of the composition. Devonshire Collection, Chatsworth, England. Reproduced by permission of the Trustees of the Chatsworth Settlement. (Photograph from Courtauld Institute of Art, London.)

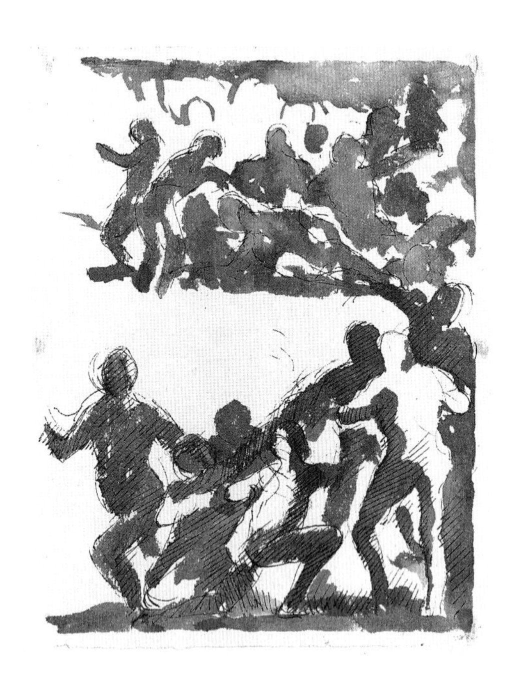

5.18 Barry Schactman, *Study after Poussin,* 1959. Brush and ink with wash, 10 × 7⅞ in. (25.4 × 20 cm). By using thumbnail sketches, artists can quickly position subjects in several locations before arriving at the final composition. Collection of Yale University, New Haven, CT. Transfer from Yale Art School.

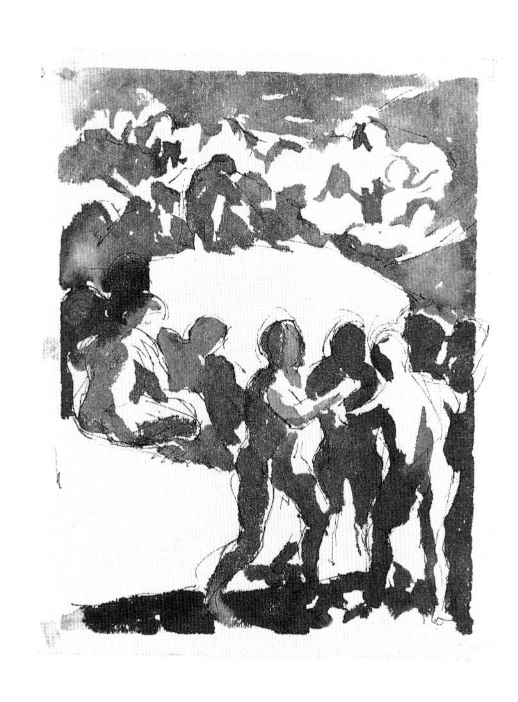

5.19 Barry Schactman, *Study after Poussin,* 1959. Brush and ink with wash, 10 × 7⅞ in. (25.4 × 20 cm). Loose, rapid sketches can also be used to explore value patterns, color structure, and movement. Yale University Art Gallery, New Haven, CT. Transfer from Yale Art School.

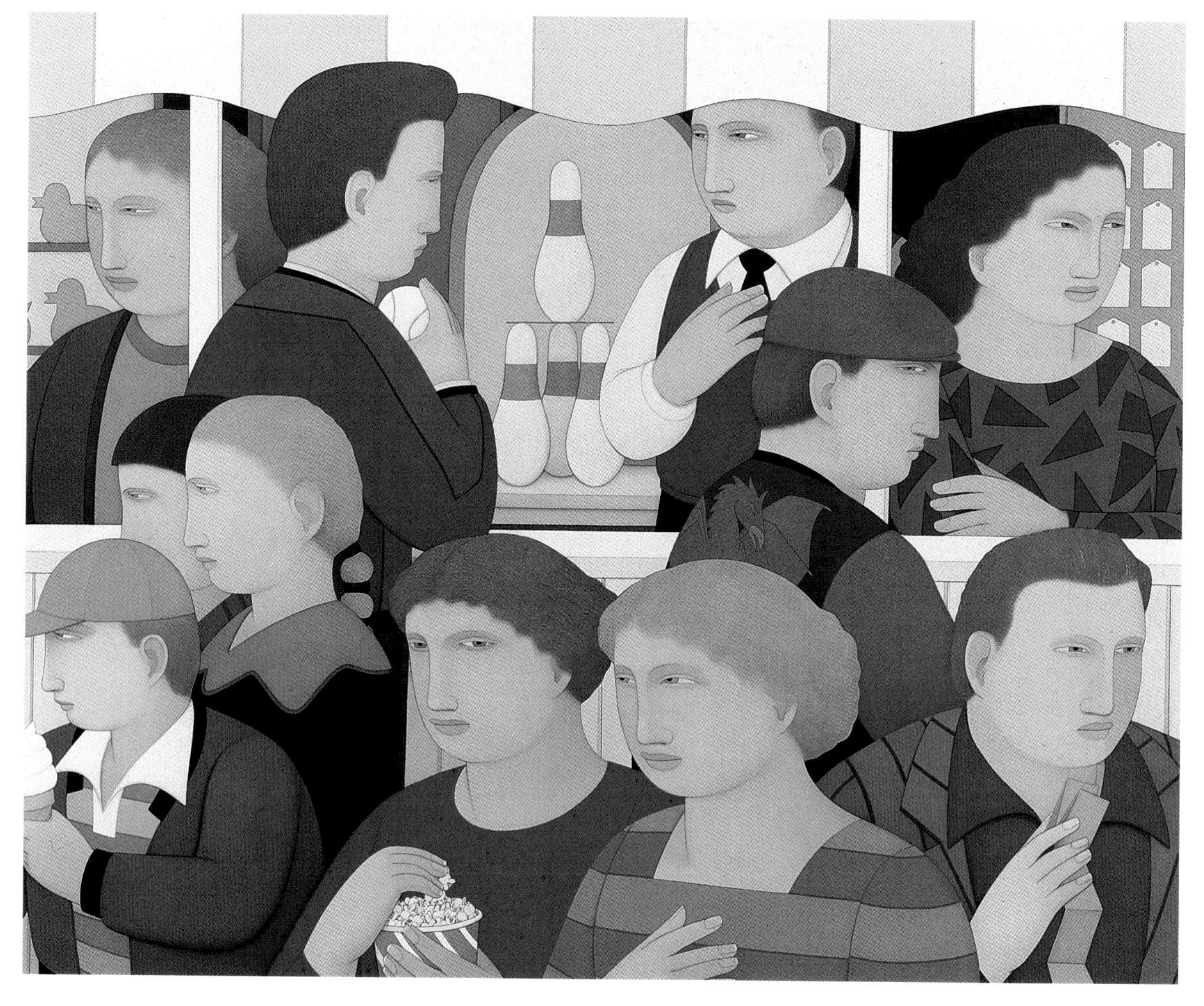

5.20 Andrew Stevovich, *Carnival,* 1992. Oil on linen, 4 × 5 ft (1.22 × 1.52 m). In this painting, a closed-value composition, the color values lie between prescribed and precise limits, usually object edges or contours. Courtesy of Adelson Galleries, New York.

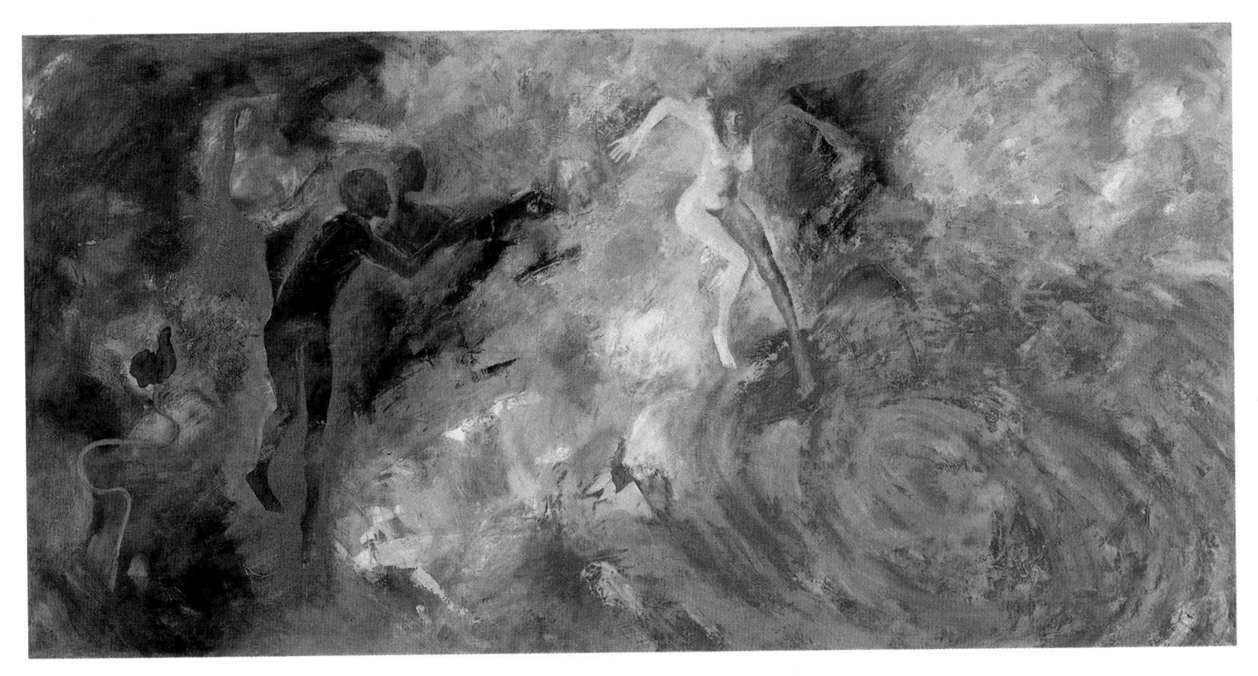

5.21 **Mary Frank, *At the Point of Waking,* 1991–92. Oil on board, 48 × 96 in.** The figures in this painting are simultaneously separated and absorbed by the swirling atmosphere. The images coalesce and fade, sharing boundaries with paint strokes. By limiting her palette to complements (blue and orange) and their dark and light values, Frank more easily allows color and mark to become figure and form.
Private Collection, Courtesy DC Moore Gallery, NYC.

of value will then require elaboration of detail before the proper relationship of value and mood is established.

Open and Closed Compositions

While integrating the value structure and the image, the artist should be aware of two approaches for developing the value pattern—closed-value or open-value compositions. In **closed-value** compositions, values are limited by the edges or boundaries of shapes (fig. 5.20). This serves to clearly identify and, at times, even isolate the shapes (see fig. 5.16). In **open-value** compositions, values can cross over shape boundaries into adjoining areas. This helps to integrate the shapes and unify the composition (fig. 5.21; see fig. 4.8). With both open- and closed-value compositions, the emotive possibilities of value schemes are easy to see. The artist may employ closely related values for hazy, foglike effects (see fig. 4.5). Sharply crystallized shapes may be created by dramatically contrasting values (see figs. 5.2 and 5.6). Thus, value can run the gamut from decoration to violent expression. It is a multipurpose tool, and the success of the total work of art is in large measure based on the effectiveness with which the artist has made value serve these many functions.

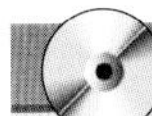

INVESTIGATE THE CD-ROM **Questions to Ask Yourself**

The principles of value add gradation and subtlety in artwork.

As you review this chapter on the CD-ROM, compare two prints that you particularly like, and answer the following questions:

1. How has each artist used value?
2. How do the uses of value in each artwork compare and contrast?
3. How could you change the use of value in one of these prints, and what would be the effect of this change?
4. How does value affect the mood of an artwork?

CHAPTER SIX

Texture

THE VOCABULARY OF TEXTURE

INTRODUCTION TO TEXTURE

TEXTURE AND THE VISUAL ARTS

THE NATURE OF TEXTURE

TYPES OF TEXTURE

- Actual Texture
- Simulated Texture
- Abstract Texture
- Invented Texture

TEXTURE AND PATTERN

TEXTURE AND COMPOSITION

- Relative Dominance and Movement
- Psychological Factors

TEXTURE AND SPACE

TEXTURE AND ART MEDIA

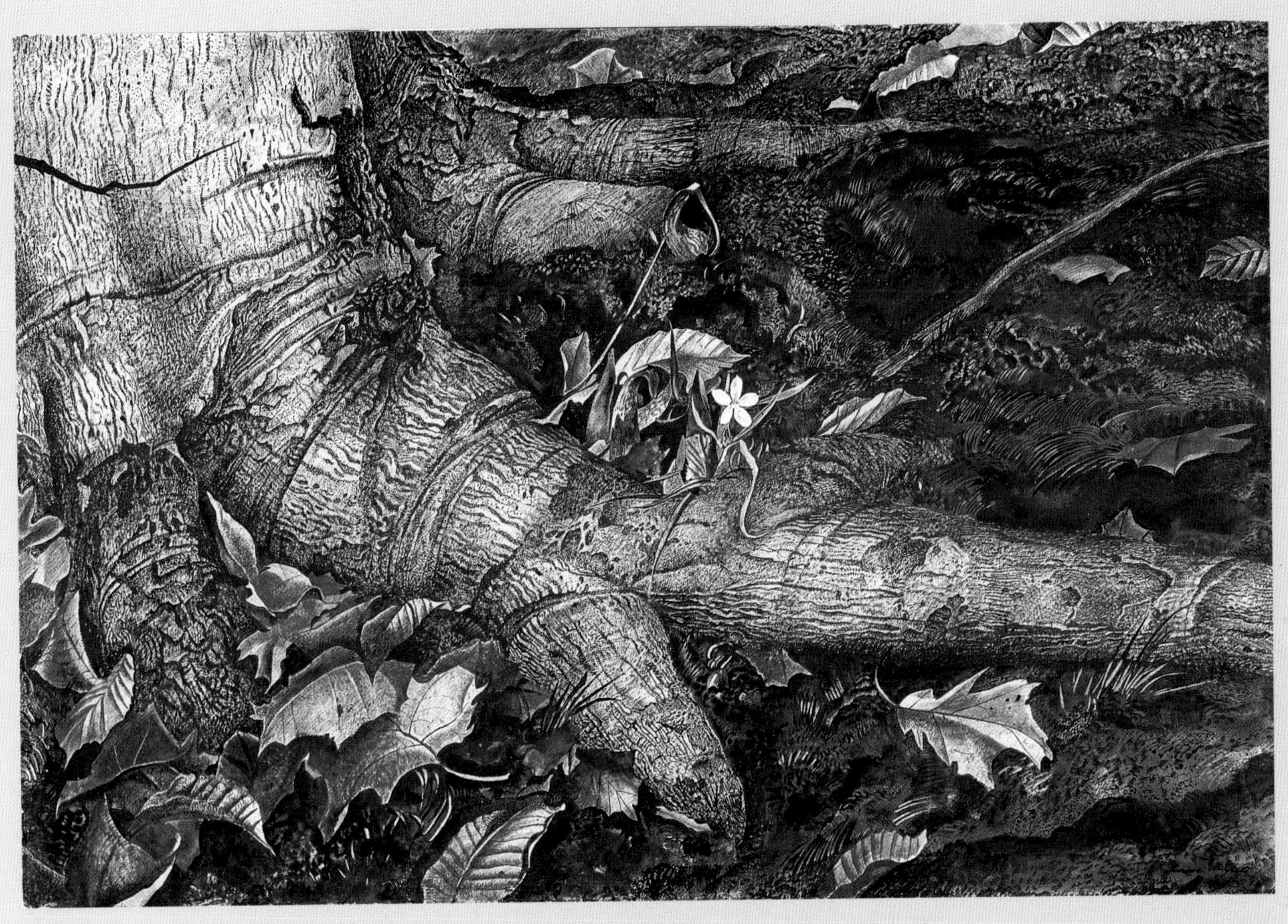

Andrew Newell Wyeth, *Spring Beauty,* 1943. Drybrush watercolor on paper, 20 × 30 in. (50.8 × 76.2 cm).
Sheldon Memorial Art Gallery, University of Nebraska, Lincoln, Nebraska. The F. M. Hall Collection 1944. H-247.

THE VOCABULARY OF **TEXTURE**

Texture — The surface character of a material that can be experienced through touch or the illusion of touch. Texture is produced by natural forces or through an artist's manipulation of the art elements.

abstract texture
A texture derived from the appearance of an actual surface but rearranged and/or simplified by the artist to satisfy the demands of the artwork.

accent
Any stress or emphasis given to elements of a composition that makes them attract more attention than the other features around them. Accent can be created by a brighter color, darker tone, greater size, or any other means by which a difference is expressed.

actual texture
A surface that can be experienced through the sense of touch (as opposed to a surface visually simulated by the artist).

assemblage
A technique that combines actual items in a display.

atmospheric perspective
The illusion of depth produced in graphic works by lightening values, softening details and textures, reducing value contrasts, and neutralizing colors in objects as they recede.

collage
A technique of picturemaking in which real materials possessing actual textures are attached on the picture plane surface, often in combination with painted or drawn passages.

genre painting
Picture subjects that concern everyday life, domestic scenes, family relationships, and the like.

invented texture
A created texture whose only source is in the imagination of the artist. Generally a decorative pattern, it should not be confused with **abstract texture.**

natural texture
Texture created as the result of nature's processes.

paint quality
The textural character of applied paint. Interest is created by the ingenuity in handling paint for its intrinsic character.

papier collé
A visual and tactile technique in which scraps of paper are pasted to the picture surface. In addition to the texture of the paper, the use of printed matter can add richness and pattern similar to an artist's invented texture.

pattern
1. Any artistic design (sometimes serving as a model for imitation). 2. A repeated element and/or design that is usually varied and produces interconnections and directional movements.

simulated texture
A convincing copy or translation of an object's texture in any medium.

tactile
A quality that refers to the sense of touch.

trompe l'oeil
Literally, "deceives the eye"; a painting technique that copies nature with such exactitude as to be mistaken for the real thing.

INTRODUCTION TO TEXTURE

Texture is an experience that is always with us. Whenever we touch something, we feel its texture. By concentrating on your hands and fingers holding this book, you will realize that you are experiencing **texture.** If your fingers are against the open side, they will feel the ridged effect of the stacked pages; if on the surface of a page, its smoothness. By looking around the room where you sit, you will find many textures. In fact, everything has a texture, from the hard glossiness of glass through the partial roughness of a lampshade to the soft fluffiness of a carpet. If your room happens to contain a painting or an art reproduction, the work most likely illustrates textures that can be seen and not felt—but that are made to look as if they could be felt.

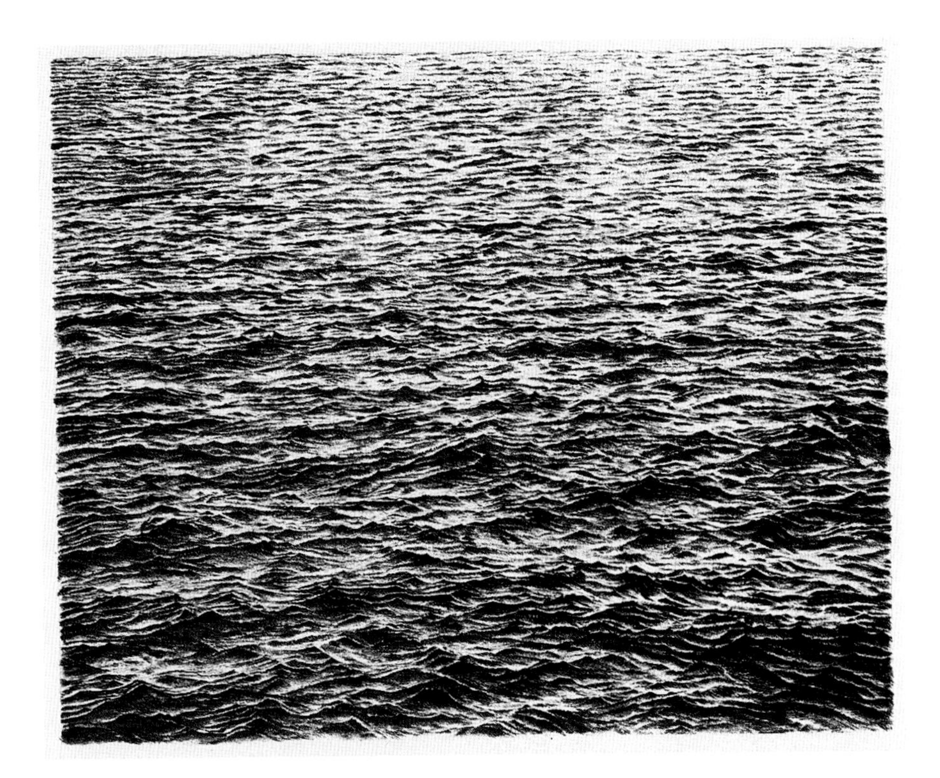

6.1 Vija Celmins, *Drypoint–Ocean Surface,* 1983. Drypoint, 26⅛ × 20⅛ in. Celmins skillfully manipulates her medium to create a photographic image of water. She gives the image a feeling of serenity and emotional peace. © 1983, Vija Celmins and Gemini G.E.L., Los Angeles, California.

TEXTURE AND THE VISUAL ARTS

Texture is unique among the art elements because it activates two sensory processes. It is more intimately and dramatically known through the sense of touch, but we also can see texture and thus, indirectly, predict its feel. In viewing a picture, we may recognize objects through the artist's use of characteristic shapes, colors, and value patterns. But we may also react to the artist's rendering of the surface character of those objects. In such a case, we have both visual and **tactile** experiences (fig. 6.1).

Whether the artist is working in the two-dimensional or three-dimensional field, our tactile response to the work is always a concern (fig. 6.2). Sculptors become involved with the problem of texture by their choice of material and the type and degree of finish they use. If they wish, sculptors can recreate the textures that are characteristic of the

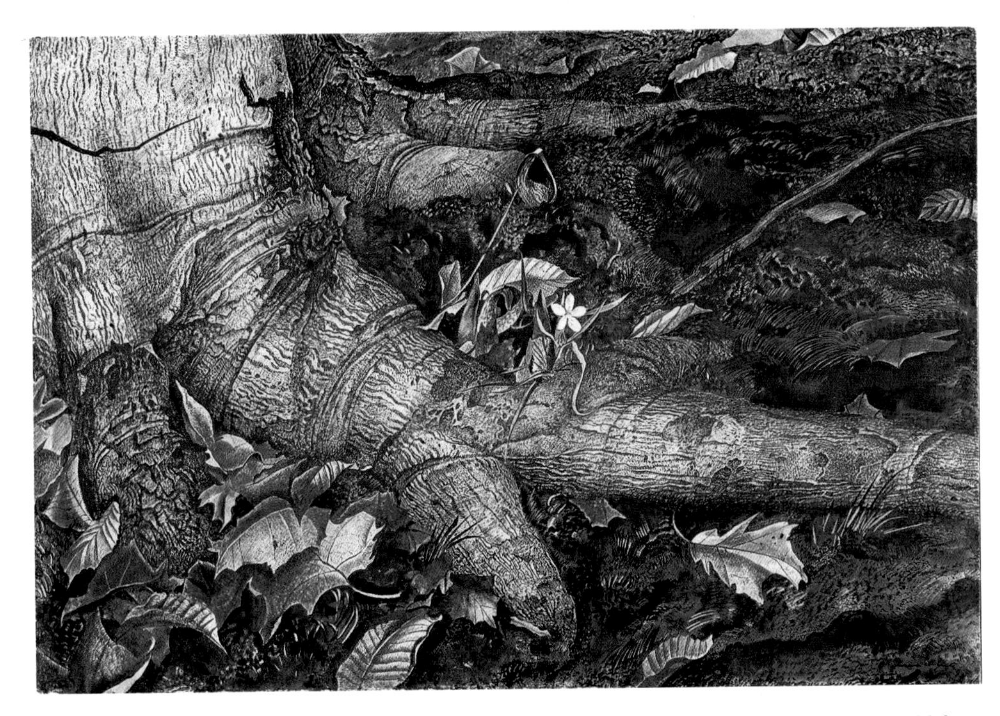

6.2 Andrew Newell Wyeth, *Spring Beauty,* 1943. Drybrush watercolor on paper, 20 × 30 in. (50.8 × 76.2 cm). Skillful manipulation of the medium can effectively simulate actual textures. Sheldon Memorial Art Gallery, University of Nebraska, Lincoln, Nebraska. The F. M. Hall Collection 1944. H-247.

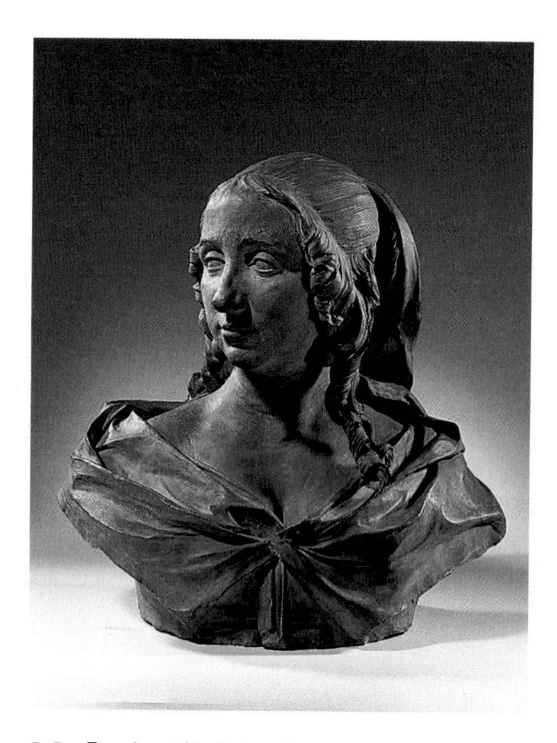

6.3 Rombout Verhulst, *Bust of Maria van Reygersberg,* Leiden, 1663. Terracotta, 45 cm high. In this work, Rombout Verhulst has united the sober realism of the period to the skillful rendering of details such as hair and clothing. The sensitivity of his modeling of flesh brings out the expressive and malleable qualities of the clay. Courtesy of Rijksmuseum, Amsterdam.

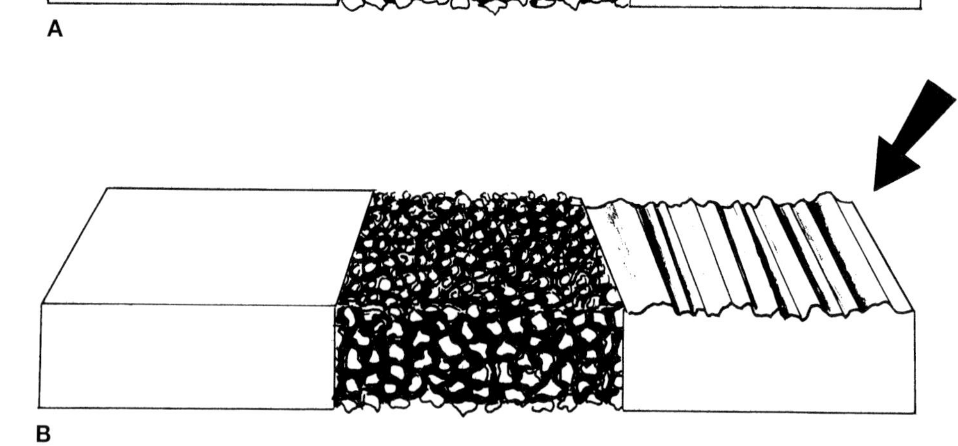

6.4 (A) A cross section of three materials. On the left is a hard, smooth substance; in the middle is cinderblock; and on the right is weathered wood. The texture of the three upper surfaces can be clearly seen and could be felt if stroked. (B) The same cross section showing its upper plane. The arrow indicates the light source. The texture is defined by the highlights and shadows formed by this illumination. The material to the left, being smooth, produces no shadows (if glossy, it would show reflections). In the cinderblock, shadows are cast among the small stones. The undulations in the weathered wood have shadows on the left side and highlights on the right. The nature of the texture in materials is defined by light and shadow patterns.

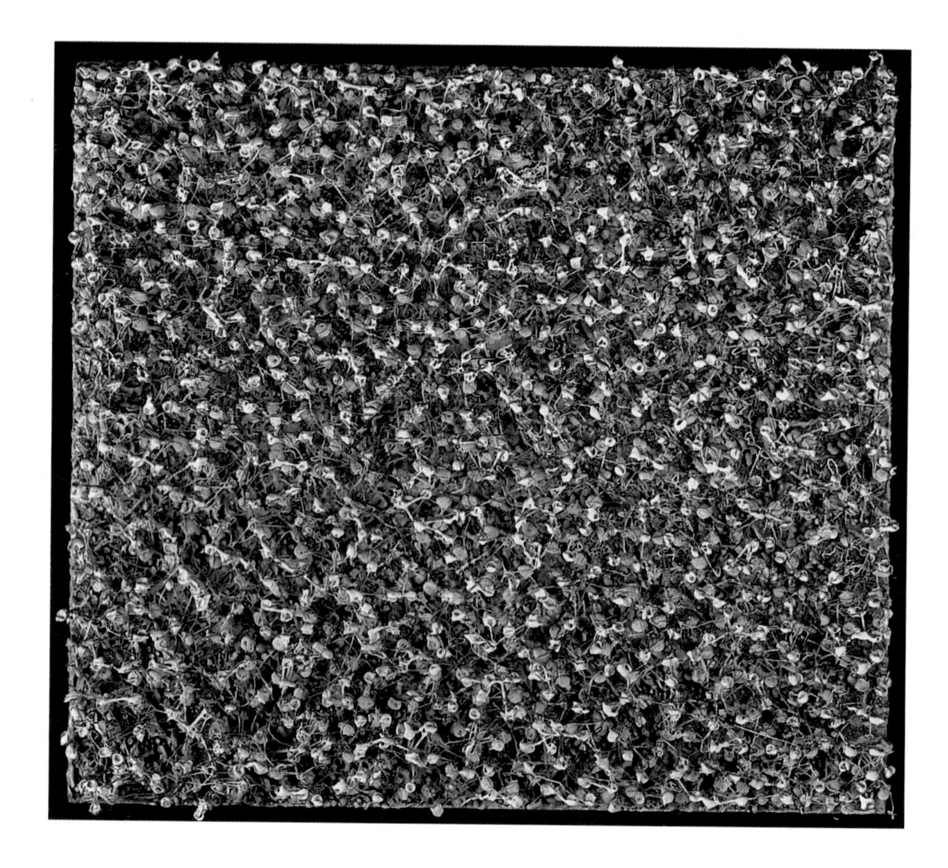

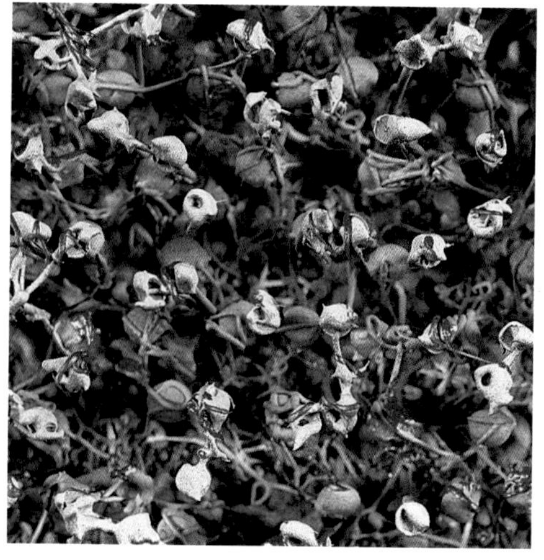

6.5 Gary Lawe, *I Remember Being Free,* 1998. Lucite, acrylic, encaustic, and nails, 24 × 30 in. (61 × 76 cm). The admixture of nails with the varied paint media is used to create an actual textured surface that is rich in its inherent visual and tactile qualities. Courtesy of the artist Gary Lawe and the Don O'Melveny Gallery, West Hollywood.

subject being interpreted. By cutting into the surface of the material, they can suggest the exterior qualities of hair, cloth, skin, and other textures (fig. 6.3).

THE NATURE OF TEXTURE

The sense of touch helps to inform us about our immediate surroundings. Our language, through such words as *smooth, rough, soft,* and *hard,* demonstrates that touch can tell us about the nature of objects. Texture is really surface, and the feel of that surface depends on the degree to which it is broken up by its composition. This determines how we see it and feel it. Rough surfaces intercept light rays, producing lights and darks. Glossy surfaces reflect the light more evenly, giving a less broken appearance (figs. 6.4A, B).

TYPES OF TEXTURE

The artist can use four basic types of texture: actual, simulated, abstract, and invented.

Actual Texture

Actual texture is the "real thing"; it is the way the surface of an object looks and feels. Generally, the emphasis is on the way it feels to the touch, but we can get a preliminary idea of the feel by viewing the object (fig. 6.5). Historically, **actual texture** has been a natural part of three-dimensional art, but it has rarely been present in the graphic arts. An exception might be the buildup of paint on Seo-Bo Park's *Ecriture* or van Gogh's *Starry Night,* in which the pigment has been applied in projecting mounds or furrows for its intrinsic **paint quality** (fig. 6.6; see fig. 1.16). The usual artistic application of actual texture involves attaching a textured object or a natural texture to the working surface. When this is done, the texture simply represents itself, although a texture may sometimes be used out of context by displacing an expected texture. The adhering of textures in two-dimensional art probably began in the early twentieth century. In 1908, Picasso pasted a piece of paper to a drawing. This is the first known example of **papier collé.** Artists later expanded this practice to include the use of tickets, portions of newspapers, menus, and the like.

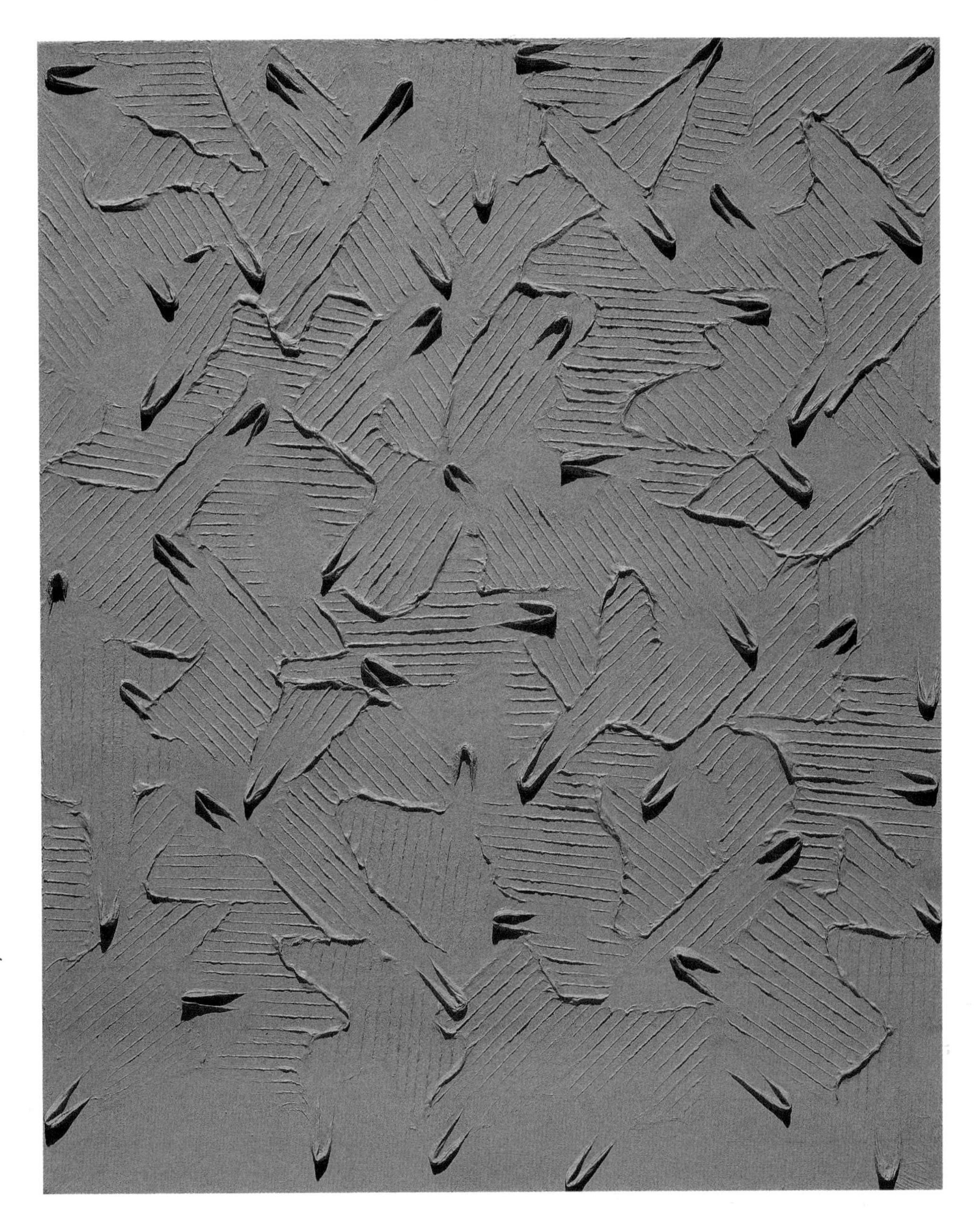

6.6 Seo-Bo Park, *Ecriture No. 940110,* 1994. Mixed media with Korean paper, 26 × 18 in. (65.3 × 46 cm). The massing of paint is clearly evident, particularly in the central portion. Some shapes seem to have been effected by a comblike instrument. Courtesy of Jean Art Gallery, Seoul, Korea.

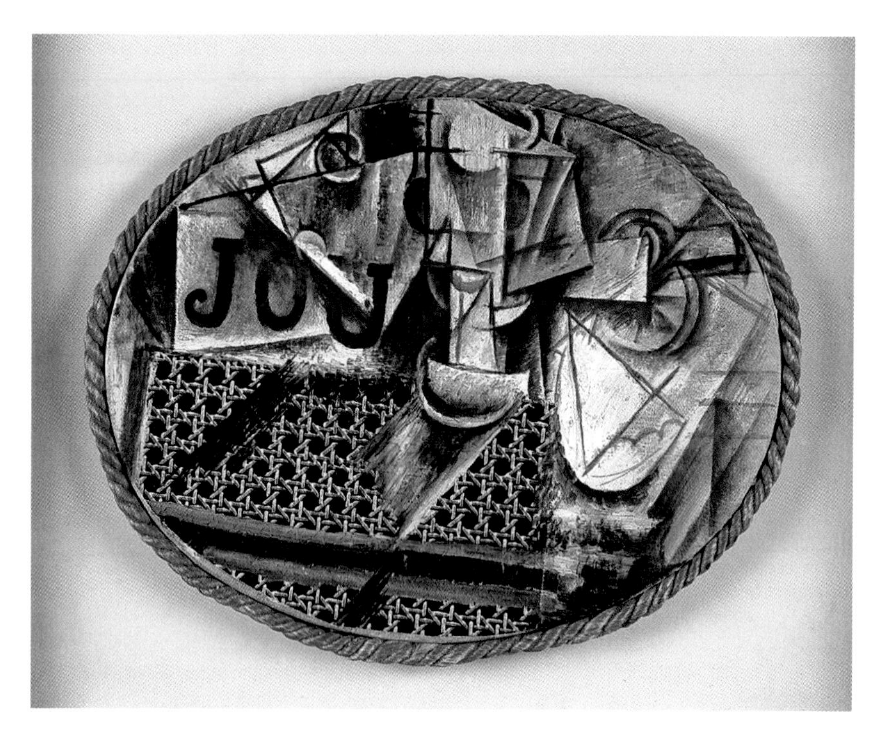

6.7 Pablo Picasso, *Still Life with Chair Caning,* 1912. Oil on pasted oilcloth, rope, oval 10⅝ × 13¾ in. (27 × 34.9 cm). With this work, Picasso pioneered the development of the papier collé and collage forms—art created by fastening actual materials with textural interest to a flat working surface. These art forms may be used to simulate natural textures but are usually created for decorative purposes. Musée Picasso, Paris, France. © 2005 Estate of Pablo Picasso/Artists Rights Society (ARS), NY. Bridgeman-Giraudon/Art Resources, NY.

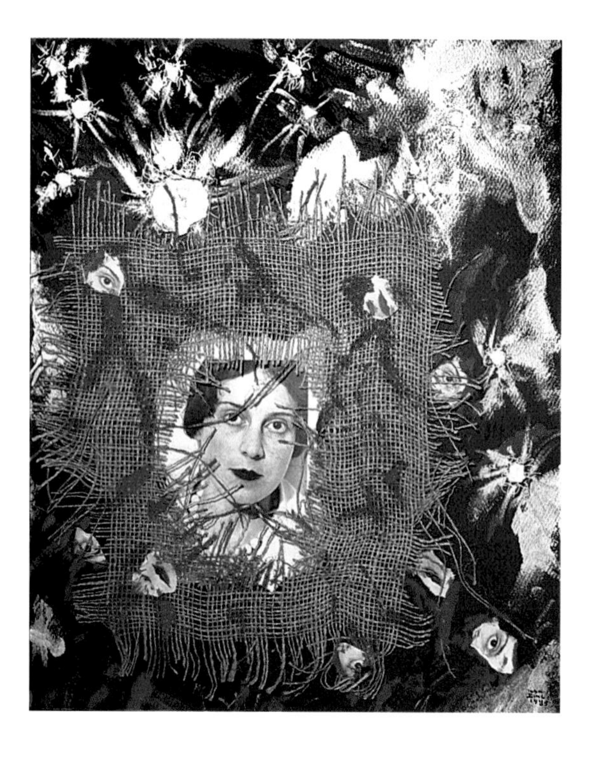

6.8 Ilse Bing, *My World,* 1985. Mixed media, 14 × 17 × 3¾ in. (35.6 × 43.2 × 9.5 cm). The inspiration behind the use of burlap in this artwork stems ultimately from the first collages of Picasso and Braque—then a revolutionary, but now a fairly commonplace, technique. © Ilse Bing, courtesy of Edwynn Houk Gallery, New York.

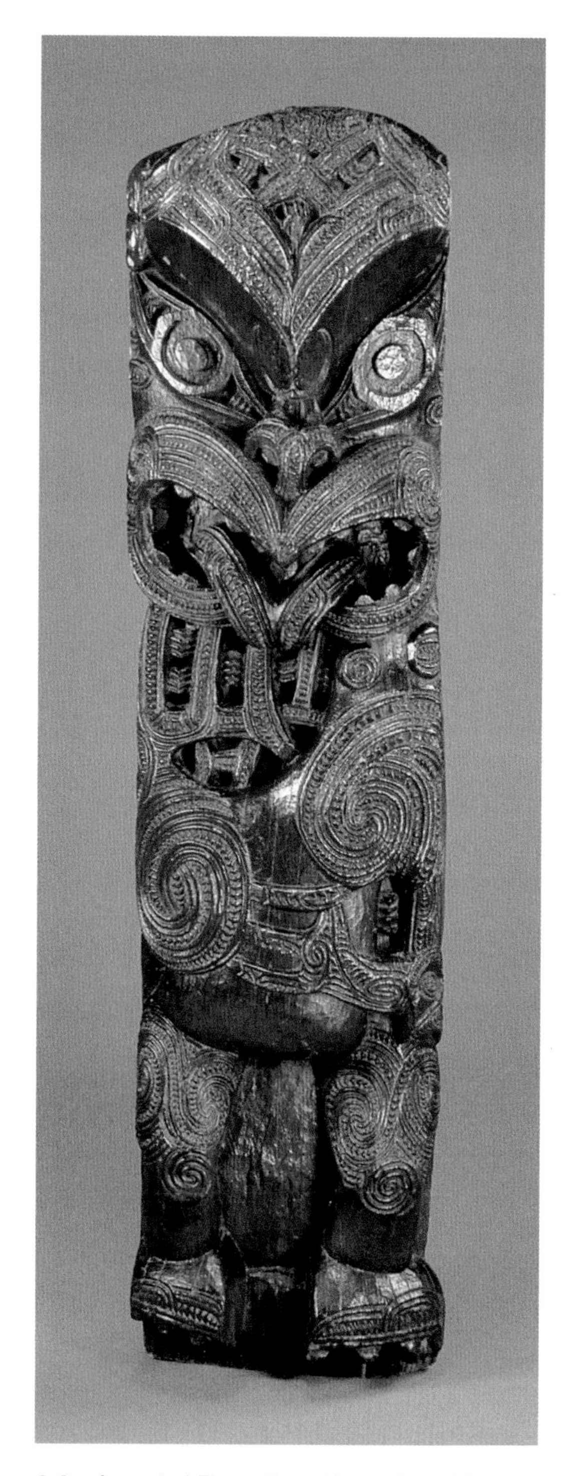

6.9 *Ancestral Figure from House Post,* Maori, New Zealand, c. 118–129. Wood, 43 in. (109.22 cm) high. The Maori shallow relief figure from New Zealand, representing a tribal ancestor, has incorporated curving or spiral bands of invented textural pattern. The decorative treatment relates to the tattooing that embellished the tribal members' bodies, including their faces. The carving functioned as one of the wall planks in their meeting house. © Boltin Picture Library.

Papier collé soon led to **collage,** an art form where actual textures, in the form of rope, chair caning, and other articles of greater substance than paper, were employed. Sometimes artists used these in combination with simulated textures (fig. 6.7). The use of papier collé and collage leads to an uncertainty that can be perplexing. The problem created by mixing objects and painting is: What is real—the objects, the artistic elements, or both? Do the painted objects have the same reality as the genuine objects? Whatever the answers, the early explorations of the Cubists (the style of Picasso and Braque, about 1907–12) stimulated other artists to explore new attitudes toward art and made them much more conscious of surface (fig. 6.8). An interest in **pattern** arising out of texture can be found in the work of artists from every culture (fig. 6.9). In the art of today, we find many forms of surface applications. Aside from the familiar texture of manipulated paint, we also find aggregates (sand, gravel, and so on) mixed into the paint to make the surface smoother or rougher, for whatever reason (see fig. 6.5).

Actual textures play important roles in the fairly recent development called **assemblage.** If any distinction can be made between collage and assemblage, it is that assemblages usually include rather bulky individual items that are displayed three-dimensionally, rather than simply on a wall (fig. 6.10). These objects, of course, possess actual texture in their own right (see figs. 10.89 and 10.90).

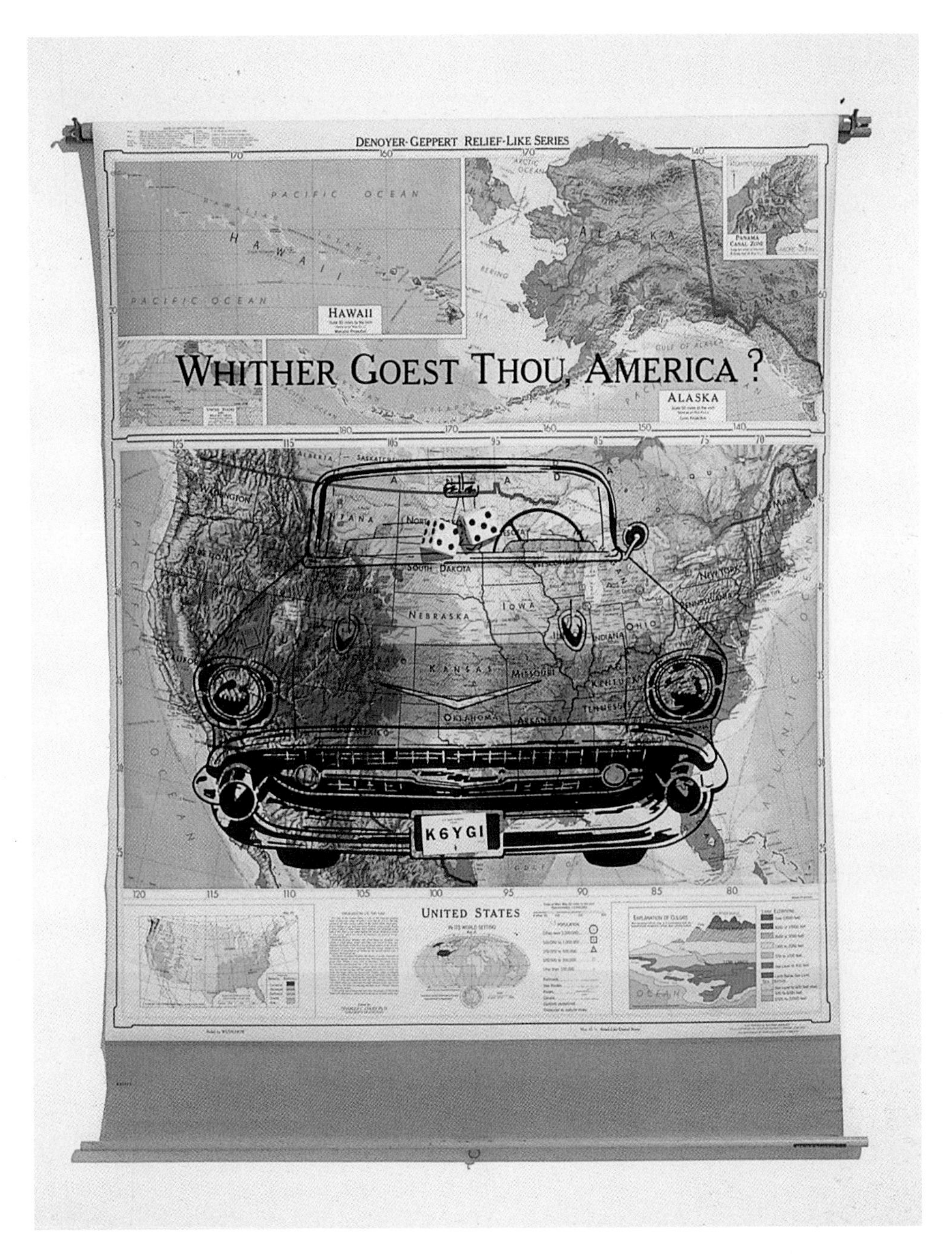

6.10 **Alexis Smith, *Pair o' Dice,* 1990. Mixed-media collage, 85.5 x 67 x 3 in.** *Pair o' Dice* is in part homage to Jack Kerouac's book *On the Road.* Upon a large map, Smith superimposes a drawing of an automobile from the era of Kerouac's book and an actual pair of dice. In this collage she visualizes the American desire to constantly move using Kerouac's query, "Whither Goest Thou, America?" Collection of Morrison and Foerster, CA. Courtesy of Margo Leavin Gallery.

Simulated Texture

A surface character that looks real but, in fact, is not is said to be **simulated texture.** Every surface has characteristic light and dark features as well as reflections. When these are skillfully reproduced in the artist's medium (as in the case of the seventeenth-century Dutch painters), they can often be mistaken for the surfaces of real objects. Simulation is

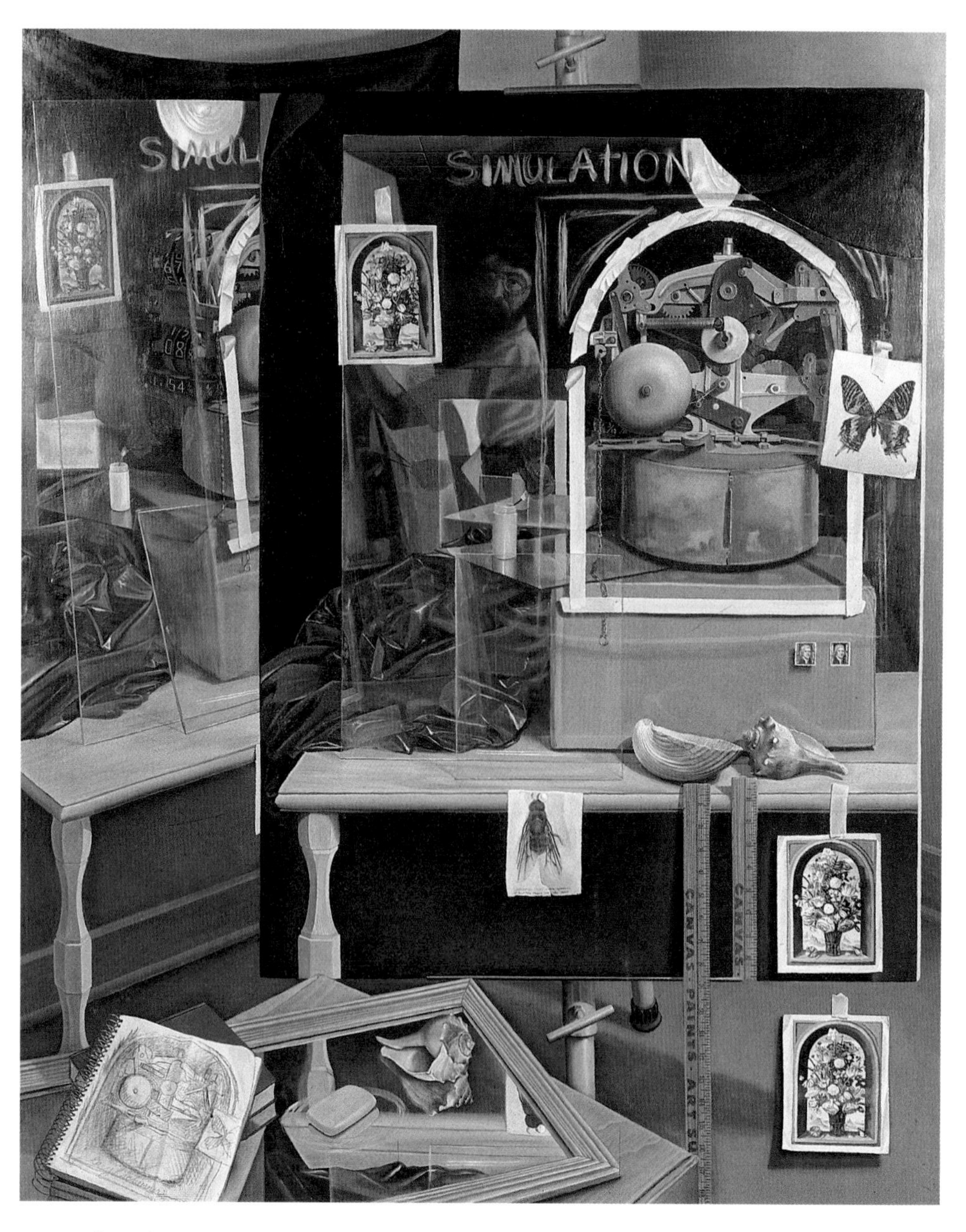

6.11 Gary Schumer, *Simulation,* 1979. Oil on canvas, 3 ft 6½ in. × 4 ft 4½ in. (1.08 × 1.33 m). As the title implies, the artist is concerned with the simulation of natural textures. Courtesy of Owens Corning Collection, Toledo, OH.

a copying technique, a skill that can be quite impressive in its own right; but it is far from being the sum total of art.

Simulated textures are useful for making things identifiable; moreover, we experience a rich tactile enjoyment when viewing them. The Dutch and Flemish artists produced amazing naturalistic effects in still-life and **genre paintings.** We share their evident relish as we look from one textural detail to another. Interior designers employ this concept when painting "faux" (fake) surface treatments of imitation stone or marble-veined wall texture. Simulated textures are often associated with **trompe l'oeil** paintings, which attempt to "fool the eye" (fig. 6.11; see fig. 6.1).

Simulated texture can serve to illustrate the dual character of texture. Imagine an artist painting a picture that includes a barn door. The door is so weathered and eroded that its wood grain stands out prominently; it would feel rough if stroked. The roughness results from the ridges and valleys formed by exposure to the elements. These ridges and valleys can be felt but are visible only because they are defined by light and shadow. In rendering (or simulating) the door's texture, the artist copies the highlights and shadows from a photograph (fig. 6.12) and, if performed with skill, this technique works like a feat of magic. The copied door appears to be rough but is, in fact, smooth, as can be confirmed by stroking the surface of the work.

Abstract Texture

Very often artists may be interested in using texture, but, instead of simulating textures, they **abstract** them. Abstract textures usually display some hint of the original texture but have been modified to suit the artist's particular needs. The result is usually a simplified version of the original, emphasizing pattern. Abstract textures normally appear in works where the degree of abstraction is con-

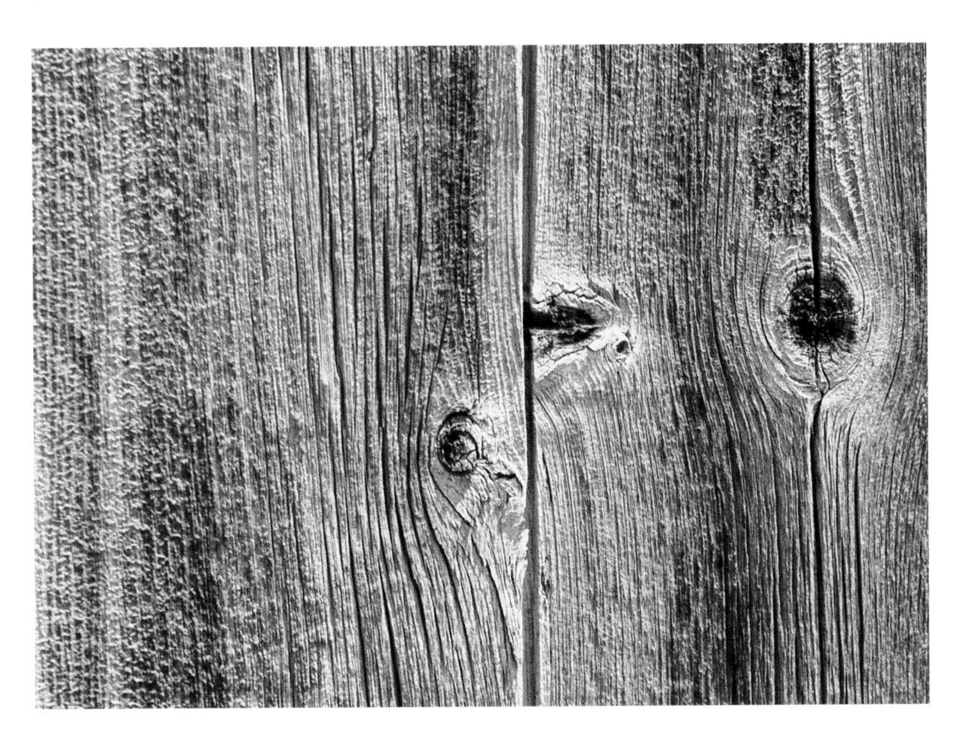

6.12 A close-up of a wooden barn door shows a detailed view of its grain. The wood has been so eroded by the weather that the grain and knots stand out. If you were to touch the actual surface of the door it would feel rough, but if you stroke the surface of the photographic reproduction on this page it feels perfectly smooth. The picture is, in fact, a simulation of the textured barn door. Courtesy of the authors.

sistent throughout. In these works they function in a decorative way; obviously there is no attempt to fool the eye, but they serve the role of enrichment in the same way that simulated textures do. Besides helping the artist to simplify his or her material, abstract textures can be used to **accent** or diminish areas (relative dominance) and to control movement. They can be a potent compositional tool (fig. 6.13).

Invented Texture

Invented textures are textures without precedent; they do not simulate nor are they abstracted from reality; they are purely the creation of the artist's imagination. In some settings, **invented textures** may suggest that they function as another type of texture, but such references are not generally intended by the artist. Invented textures usually appear in abstract works, as they are entirely nonobjective. It is sometimes difficult to distinguish abstracted from invented textures, because an artist with the same level of skill as the simulator (but probably with more imagination) can invent

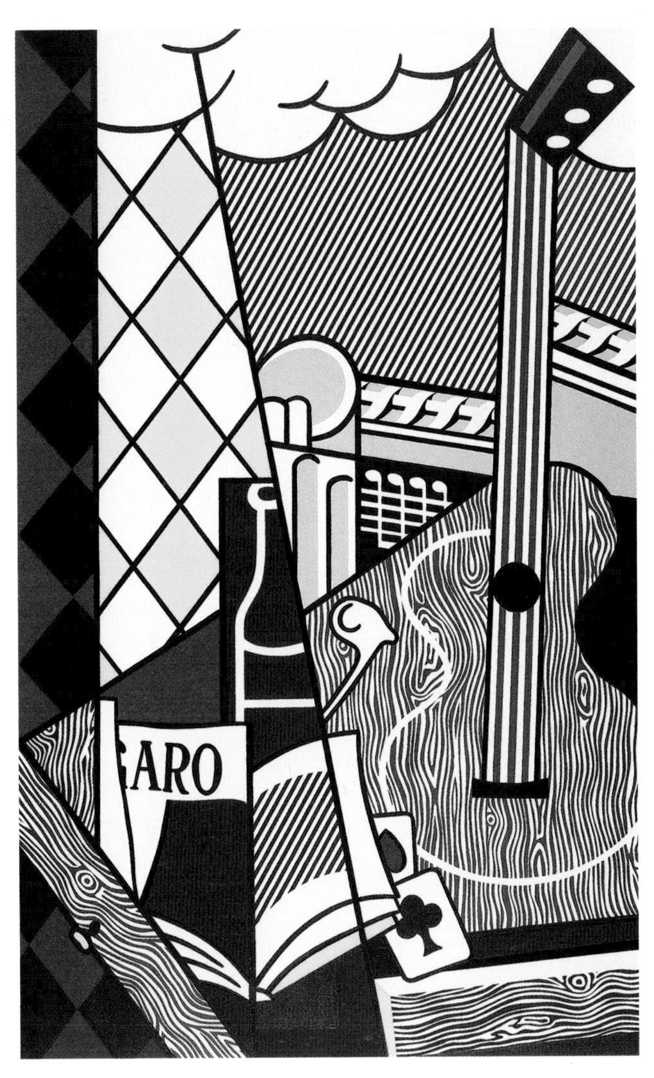

6.13 Roy Lichtenstein, *Cubist Still Life with Playing Cards*, 1974. Oil and magna on canvas, 96 × 60 in. (243.8 × 152.4 cm). The wood grain in this work is not abstracted beyond recognition; it is clearly derived from wood, though simplified and stylized. © Estate of Roy Lichtenstein.

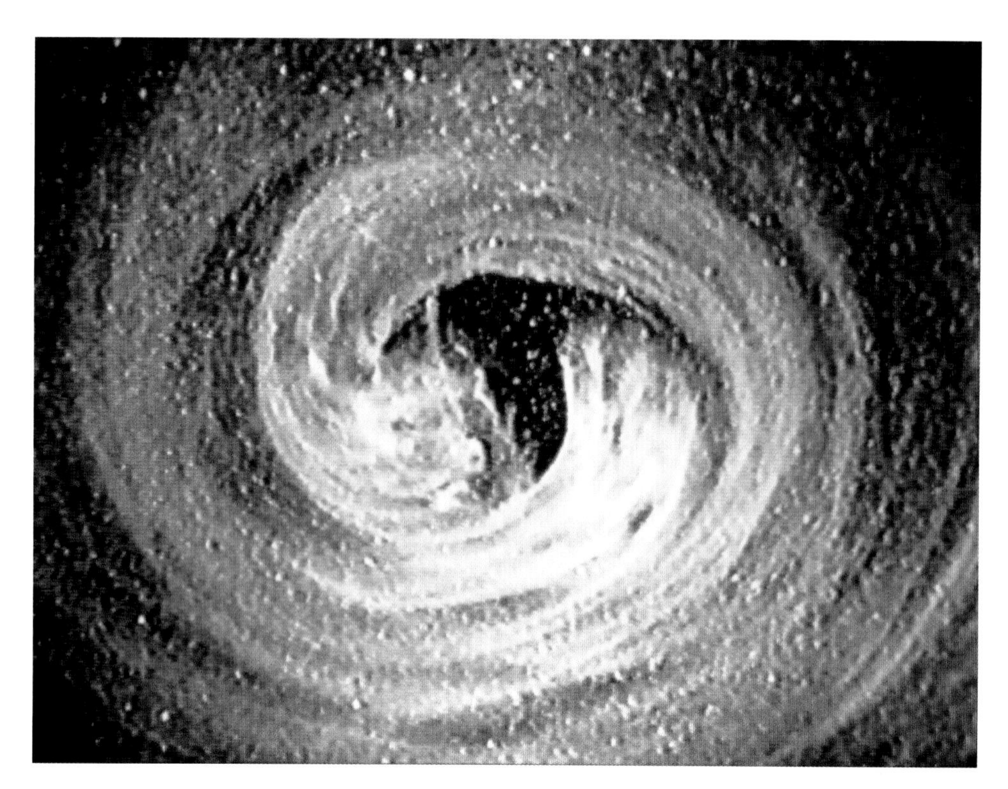

6.14 **Brian Fridge, *Vault Sequence No. 10,* 2000. Black and white silent video, 4 minutes, DVD, edition 2 of 5.** *Vault Sequence* is a seven-minute video of the inside of the artist's refrigerator freezer. Through the medium of video the artist creates invented texture. The time-based aspect of this medium creates images that would otherwise not be seen. The video camera's eye reveals mini-universes. Courtesy of Brian Fridge, the Modern Art Museum of Fort Worth, and Dunn & Brown Contemporary.

a texture and make it appear to have a precedent where none exists (fig. 6.14). In such a case it is difficult to know how to classify the texture; although the texture is created, and not re-created, it still seems to be derived from some source. When invented texture is used in a realistic or semirealistic work, it is probable that the invention has some resemblance to a subject's texture. In contrast, there are invented textures in which such references to the objective world are not intended. These textures would most likely show up in abstract works in which the viewer might not know whether they were invented or abstracted. Usually the uses of invented textures are much the same as those cited for abstract textures. And, in the hands of a Surrealistic artist, it is possible that invented textures could be inserted in an unlikely context for a surprise or shock effect (see figs. 4.5 and 10.63).

TEXTURE AND PATTERN

Because texture is interpreted by lights and darks, there is a fine line between texture and pattern (which is created in a similar way). For example, a printed paisley pattern on a silk tie does not have an exaggerated texture; according to the dictionary, it is essentially a design (see fig. 2.9). This implies that pattern is concerned not with surface feel but rather with appearance. Pattern serves the artist mainly as ornament, independent from any tactile possibilities. But there is an overlap, because texture can create pattern (figs. 6.15A–C).

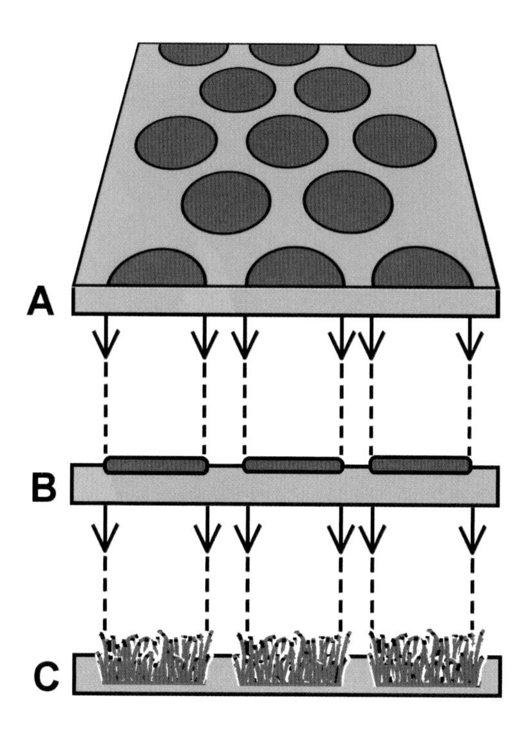

6.15 This figure illustrates the differences and similarities between pattern and texture. (A) Design with a light-and-dark allover pattern with no texture. (B) Cross section of design A, assuming it to be a piece of wallpaper. The dark spots are ink; the ink sits on the surface and penetrates the material, creating a smooth texture. (C) Cross section of design A, assuming it to be a piece of carpet. The pattern comes from color changes and tufted areas (texture). Thus we have both pattern and texture in example C.

Pattern usually suggests a repetition, sometimes at random and sometimes controlled. A planter sows corn seeds at regular intervals in a field. As the corn grows, the stalks produce the effects of both pattern and texture. An aerial view of the field shows the pattern primarily, but when the viewer comes closer, the texture becomes more visible (figs. 6.16

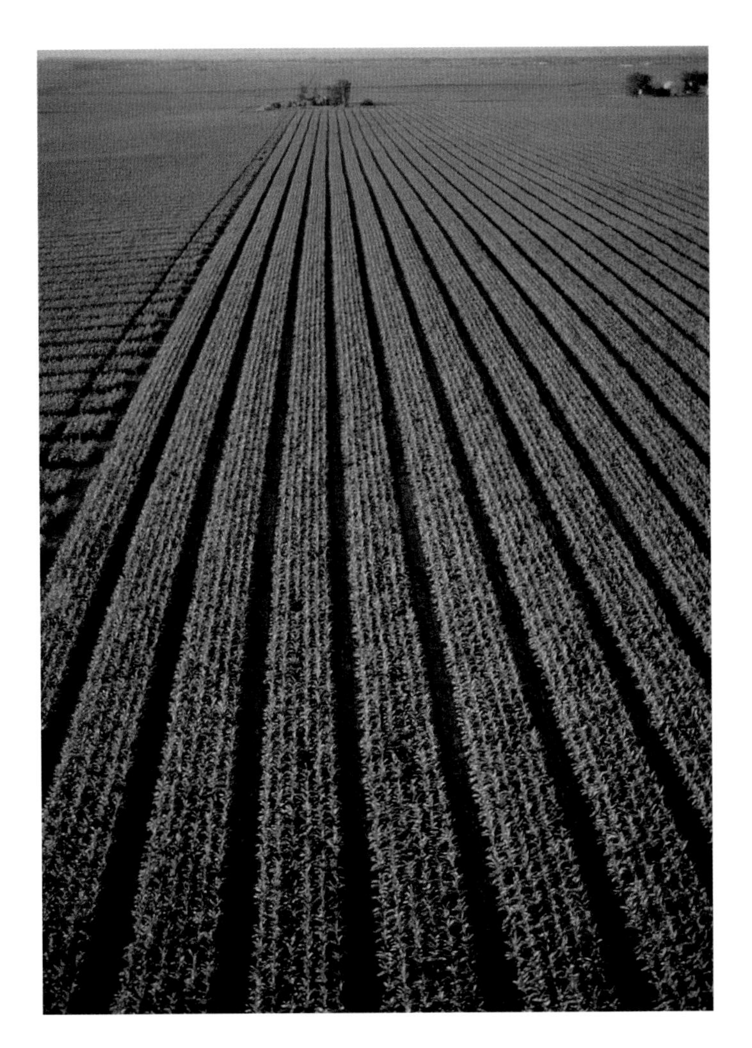

6.16 In this photograph of a cornfield, we have examples of both pattern and texture. The rows of corn and the gaps between them create a striped pattern, while the massed stalks produce a texture. © Craig Aurness/CORBIS West Light.

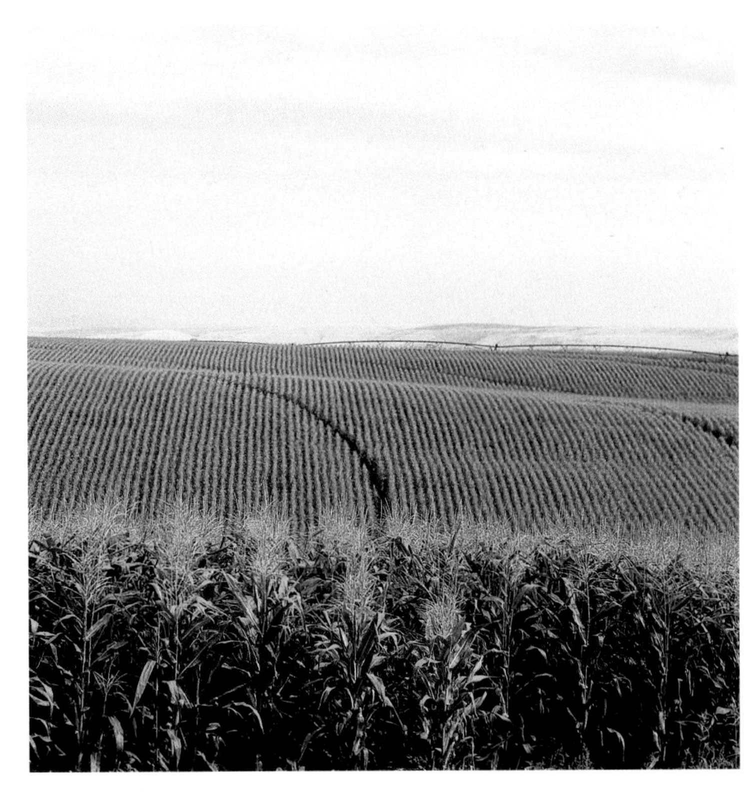

6.17 The individual cornstalks, with their leaves and husks, can be clearly seen in this low-altitude view of a field. In the foreground, the corn, taken as a whole, appears as a huge three-dimensional texture. In the distant view over the top of the field, the corn forms patterned rows. © Royalty-Free/Corbis.

and 6.17). Unless smooth like glass or steel, texture is identified with a three-dimensional disruption of a surface. Consider the contrast between a pane of glass and a shag carpet; the smoothness of glass might be regarded as a texture of sorts, but there is no doubt as to the carpet's texture. Pattern, in contrast, is generally thought of as a design in two-dimensional (or flat) terms and does not always involve texture.

TEXTURE AND COMPOSITION

The emphasis and emotional associations of texture influence composition as a whole.

Relative Dominance and Movement

The sense of touch aside, texture is seen as variations of light and dark. These variations, apart from their ability to stimulate our sense of touch, are often exciting and attractive. In drawing our attention, these textural areas may create a problem if they compete with other parts of the artwork. If the textural area is too strong in its hold on the spectator, other areas, possibly more important ones, may not get the attention they deserve; the texture must then be diminished. On the other hand, if an area is "dead," or not attractive, a texture can be added or emphasized to make it come to life.

Our attention is constantly being maneuvered about the surface of an artwork by (among other things) the degree of emphasis given to the various areas of that surface. The movement of our eyes is directed from one attractive area to another, passing over or through the "rests" (or deemphasized areas). The control of textures obviously can be a part of the directional thrusts that move through the work; texture shares this role

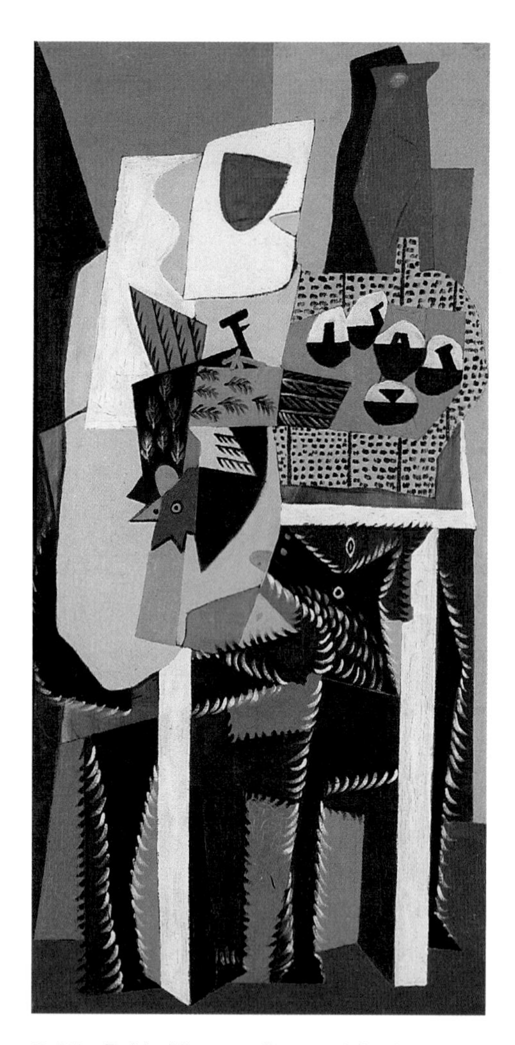

6.18 Pablo Picasso, *Dog and Cock,* 1929. Oil on canvas, 60⅞ × 30⅛ in. (154.6 × 76.5 cm). Abstract texture can be a compositional tool that is important for capturing and directing attention. Clearly the abstracted white fur of the dog attracts us and creates movement. Yale University Art Gallery, New Haven, CT. Gift of Stephen Carlton Clark, B.A. 1903. © 2005 Estate of Pablo Picasso/Artists Rights Society (ARS), New York.

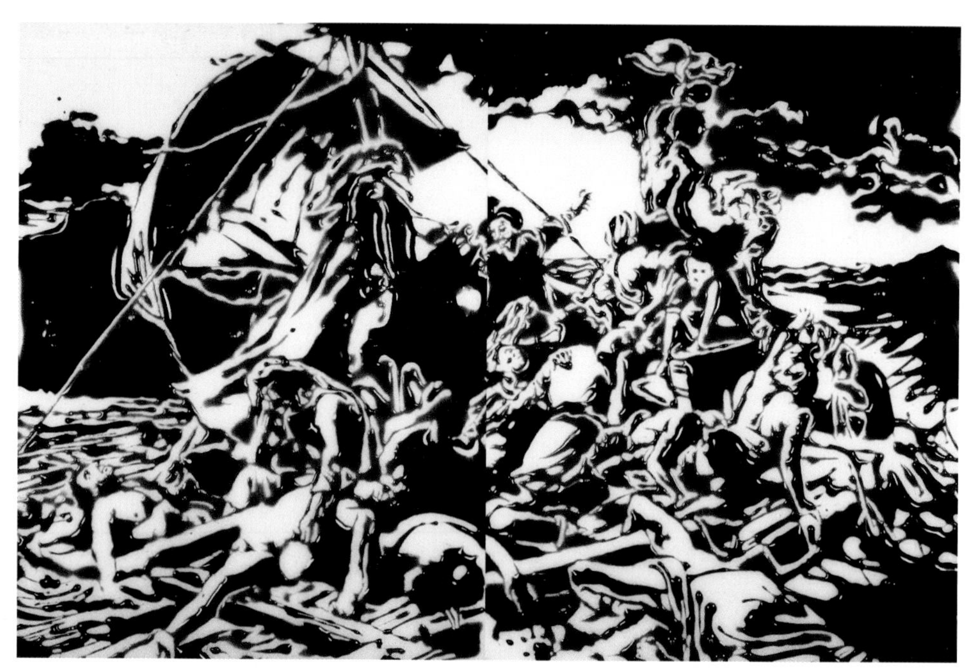

6.19 Vik Muniz, born 1961, *The Raft of the Medusa,* 1999. Pictures of Chocolate. Two chromogenic color prints, Overall: 80 × 125 in. (203.2 × 317.5 cm); Panel (each): 80 × 62½ in. (203.2 × 158.8 cm). In *The Raft of the Medusa,* Muniz photographed a painting from 1819 by the French Romantic painter Théodore Géricault. The original painting was based on an event of Géricault's time. Muniz then drew over his initial photograph with chocolate syrup and photographed it again for the final image. The medium used to create the texture of the photograph obscures Géricault's original imagery. The resultant image and the visceral quality of the medium cause the viewer to question and analyze the layers of meaning presented by Muniz. Whitney Museum of American Art, New York; Purchase, with funds from Anne and Joel Ehrenkranz 2000.144a-b. © Vik Muniz/Licensed by VAGA, New York, NY.

with the other art elements. The abstract textures in Picasso's *Dog and Cock,* for example, draw our eyes to the more significant parts of the painting (fig. 6.18).

Psychological Factors

Textures can provoke psychological or emotional responses in us that may be either pleasant or unpleasant. In doing this, the textures are usually associated with environments, events, objects, or persons from our experience. Textures can also have symbolic meanings. When we say a person is "slippery as a snake" or "a roughneck," tactile sensations are being linked to personality traits. Similarly, textures can be used as supplementary psychological devices in art. The artist can also use textures to stimulate our curiosity, shock us, or make us reevaluate our perceptions (fig. 6.19).

TEXTURE AND SPACE

Texture can also help to define space. The character of the texture of plant life, for example, differs with distance (see fig. 8.4). When textures appear blurred and lack strong contrasts, they make objects seem distant, but if they are sharp and have strong contrasts, the objects appear to move forward. This is one of the principles of **atmospheric perspective,** a commonly used technique in representational painting. A less traditional artist might use textures

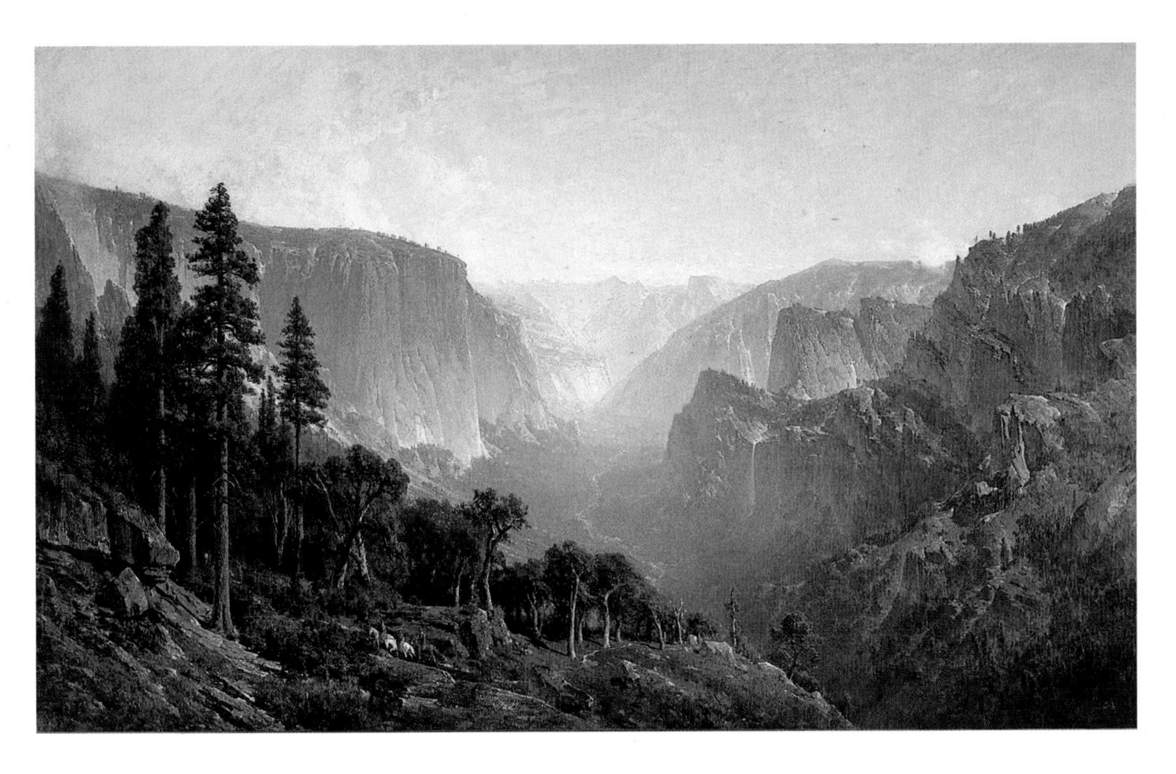

6.20 Thomas Hill, *Yosemite Valley (from below Sentinel Dome as Seen from Artist's Point),* 1876. Oil on canvas, 72 × 120 in. (182.88 × 304.8 cm). The foreground areas move forward because of their greater textural contrasts and clarity, while other areas are thrust into space by grayness and only the faint suggestion of details. The Oakland Museum Kahn Collection 68.133.1. Photograph by M. Lee Fatherree.

from far to near and produce controlled variations or surprising contradictions (fig. 6.20).

TEXTURE AND ART MEDIA

Most of this discussion has dealt with the graphic arts, but textural possibilities are perhaps even more pronounced in making other kinds of artworks. The architect balances the smoothness of steel and glass with the roughness of stone, concrete, and brick (see figs. 9.8 and 9.9). The ceramist works with glazes, aggregates in the clay, and various incised and impressed textures (see fig. 9.12). Jewelers, using different techniques, show concern for texture when making raised ware, pins, necklaces, brooches, or bracelets (see fig. 9.10). Printmakers use textures that are transferred onto paper after being etched into the printing plate (see fig. 5.16). Sculptors manipulate the textures of clay, wood, metal, and other natural and artificial materials (see fig. 9.4). From this we can see that texture is involved in all art forms, as it is in many life experiences—however unconscious of it we may be.

INVESTIGATE THE CD-ROM **Questions to Ask Yourself**

Texture connects to our minds through vision and to our bodies through touch.

As you review this chapter on the CD-ROM, think about the element of texture in artworks that you particularly like, and answer the following questions:

1. What kinds of texture particularly appeal to you? Do all the artworks you like have these textures, or do they show other textures as well?
2. How has the artist created these textures?
3. If you made an artwork right now, what kind of texture would it have? What does this say about the way you are feeling right now?

CHAPTER SEVEN

Color

THE VOCABULARY OF COLOR

THE CHARACTERISTICS OF COLOR

- Light: The Source of Color
  - *Additive Color*
  - *Subtractive Color*
- Artist's Color Mixing
  - *The Triadic Color System*
  - *Neutrals*
- The Physical Properties of Color
  - *Hue*
  - *Value*
  - *Intensity*
- Developing Aesthetic Color Relationships
  - *Complements and Split-Complements*
  - *Triads*
  - *Tetrads*
  - *Analogous and Monochromatic Colors*
  - *Warm and Cool Colors*
  - *Plastic Colors*
  - *Simultaneous Contrast*
  - *Color and Emotion*
  - *Psychological Application of Color*
- The Evolution of the Color Wheel
  - *The Origins of Color Systems*
  - *The Discovery of Pigment Primaries*
  - *The First Triadic Color Wheel*
  - *American Educators*
  - *The Ostwald Color System*
  - *The Munsell Color System*
  - *The Subtractive Printing System (Process Color System)*
  - *Color Photography*
  - *Color Computer Printing*
  - *The Discovery of Light Primaries*

THE ROLE OF COLOR IN COMPOSITION

COLOR BALANCE

- Color and Harmony
- Color and Variety

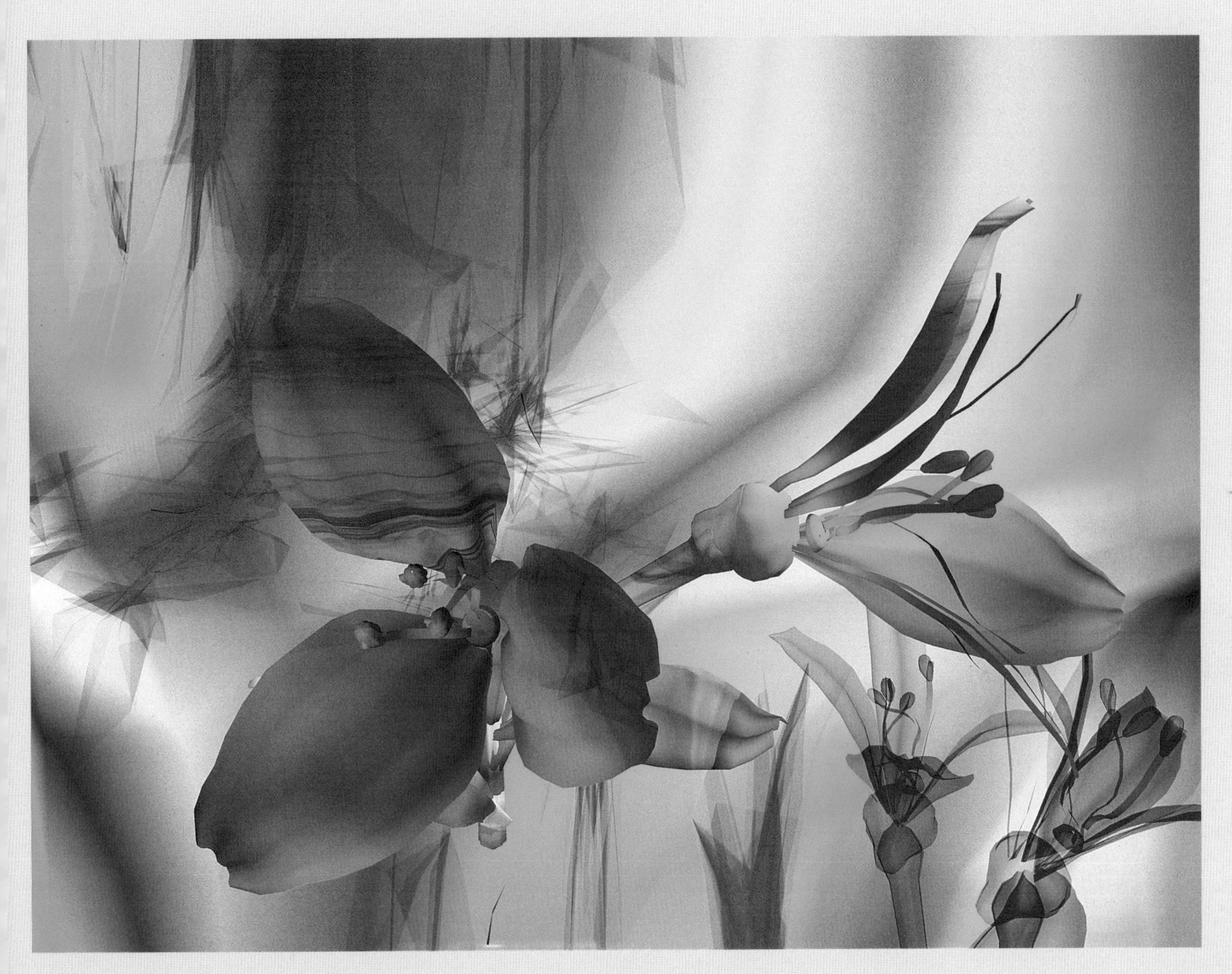

Charles Csuri, *Wondrous Spring,* 1992. Computer image, 48 × 65 in. (121.9 × 165.1 cm). Courtesy of the artist.

THE VOCABULARY OF **COLOR**

Color — The visual response to different wavelengths of sunlight identified as red, green, blue, and so on; having the physical properties of hue, intensity, and value.

academic
Art that conforms to established traditions and approved conventions as practiced in art academies. Academic art stresses standards, set procedures, and rules.

achromatic
Relating to differences of light and dark; the absence of hue and its intensity.

additive color
Color created by superimposing light rays. Superimposing the three primary color lights—red, blue, and green—produces white. The secondaries are cyan, yellow, and magenta.

analogous colors
Colors that are closely related in hue. They are usually adjacent to each other on the color wheel.

chroma
1. The purity of hue or its freedom from white, black, or gray. 2. The intensity of hue.

chromatic
Pertaining to the presence of color.

chromatic value
The relative degree of lightness or darkness demonstrated by a given color.

color tetrad
Four colors, equally spaced on the color wheel, containing a primary and its complement and a complementary pair of intermediates. This has also come to mean any organization of color on the wheel forming a rectangle that could include a double split-complement.

color triad
Three colors spaced an equal distance apart on the color wheel forming an equilateral triangle. The twelve-color wheel is made up of a primary triad, a secondary triad, and two intermediate triads.

complementary colors
Two colors directly opposite each other on the color wheel. A primary color is complementary to a secondary color, which is a mixture of the two remaining primaries.

high-key color
Any color that has a value level of middle gray or lighter.

hue
Designates the common name of a color and indicates its position in the spectrum or on the color wheel. Hue is determined by the specific wavelength of the color in a ray of light.

intensity
The saturation, strength, or purity of a hue. A vivid color is of high intensity; a dull color is of low intensity.

intermediate color
A color produced by a mixture of a primary color and a secondary color.

local (objective) color
The color as seen in the objective world (green grass, blue sky, red barn, and the like).

low-key color
Any color that has a value level of middle gray or darker.

monochromatic color
A color that has only one hue but has the complete range of value of that color from white to black.

neutralized color
A color that has been grayed or reduced in intensity by being mixed with any of the neutrals or with a complementary color.

neutrals
1. The inclusion of all color wavelengths will produce white, and the absence of any wavelengths will be perceived as black. With neutrals, no single color is noticed—only a sense of light and dark or the range from white through gray to black. 2. A color altered by the addition of its complement so that the original sensation of hue is lost or grayed.

pigments
Color substances that give their color property to another material by being mixed with it or covering it. Pigments, usually insoluble, are added to liquid vehicles to produce paint and ink. Colored substances dissolved in liquids that give their coloring effects by being absorbed or staining are referred to as dyes.

primary color
The preliminary hues that cannot be broken down or reduced into component colors. The basic hues of any color system that in theory may be used to mix all other colors.

secondary color
A color produced by a mixture of two primary colors.

simultaneous contrast
When two different colors come into direct contact, the contrast intensifies the difference between them.

spectrum
The band of individual colors that results when a beam of white light is broken into its component wavelengths, identifiable as hues.

split-complement(s)
A color and the two colors on either side of its complement.

subjective
1. That which is derived from the mind reflecting a personal viewpoint, bias, or emotion. 2. A subjective color tends to be inventive or creative.

subtractive color
The sensation of color that is produced when wavelengths of light are reflected back to the viewer after all other wavelengths have been subtracted and/or absorbed.

tertiary color
Color resulting from the mixture of all three primaries in differing amounts or two secondary colors. Tertiary colors are characterized by the neutralization of intensity and hue. They are found on the color wheel on the inner rings of color leading to complete neutralization.

value (color)
1. The relative degree of light or dark. 2. The characteristic of color determined by light or dark or the quantity of light reflected by the color.

THE CHARACTERISTICS OF COLOR

Color, the most universally appreciated element, appeals to children and adults instantly. An infant reaches out for brightly colored objects, and children watch in fascination as yellow magically becomes green with the addition of blue. The average person finds color exciting and attractive. This person may question art for many other reasons but seldom objects to the use of color, provided that it is harmonious in character. In fact, a work of art can frequently be appreciated for its color style alone.

Color is one of the most expressive elements because it affects our emotions directly. When we view a work of art, we do not have to rationalize what we are supposed to feel about its color; instead, we have an immediate emotional reaction to it. Pleasing rhythms and harmonies of color satisfy our aesthetic desires. We like certain combinations of color and reject others. In representational art, color identifies objects and creates illusionistic space. The study of color is based on scientific theory—principles that can be observed and easily systematized. We will examine these basic characteristics of color relationships to see how they help to give form and meaning to the subject of an artist's work.

Light: The Source of Color

Color begins with and is derived from light, either natural or artificial. Where there is little light, there is little color; where the light is strong, color is likely to be intense. When the light is weak, such as at dusk or dawn, it is difficult to distinguish one color from another. Under bright, strong sunlight, as in tropical climates, colors seem to take on additional intensity.

Every ray of light coming from the sun is composed of waves that vibrate at different speeds. The sensation of color is aroused in the mind by the way our sense of vision responds to the different wavelengths. This can be demonstrated by observing the way a beam of white light passes through a triangle-shaped piece of glass (a prism) and then reflects off a sheet of white paper. The rays of light bend, or refract, as they pass through the glass at different angles (according to their wavelengths) and then reflect off the white paper as different colors. We see these colors as individual stripes in a narrow band called the **spectrum.** The colors easily distinguishable in this band are red, orange, yellow, green, blue, blue-violet, and violet (scientists use the term *indigo* for the color artists call *blue-violet*). These colors also blend gradually so that we can discern several intermediate colors between them (figs. 7.1 and 7.2).

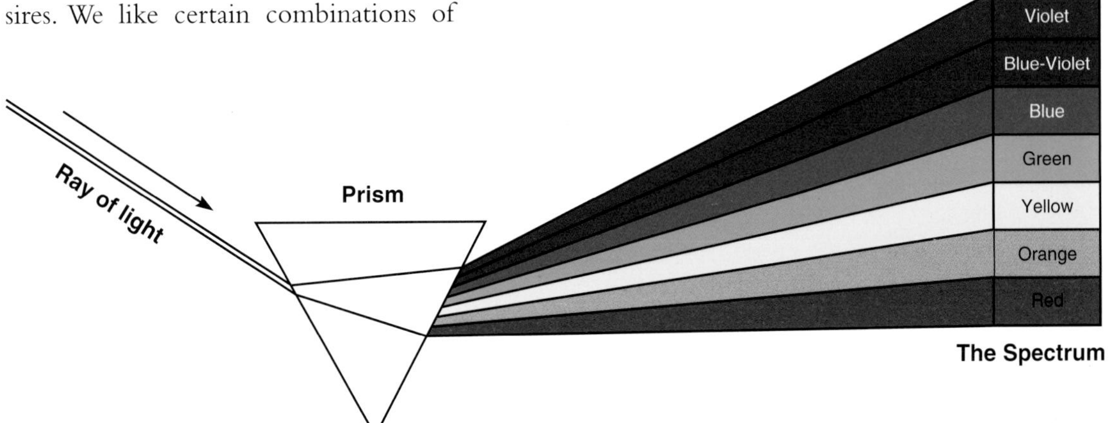

7.1 The rays of red have the longest wavelength, and those of violet the shortest. The angle at which the rays are bent, or refracted, is greatest at the violet end and least at the red end.

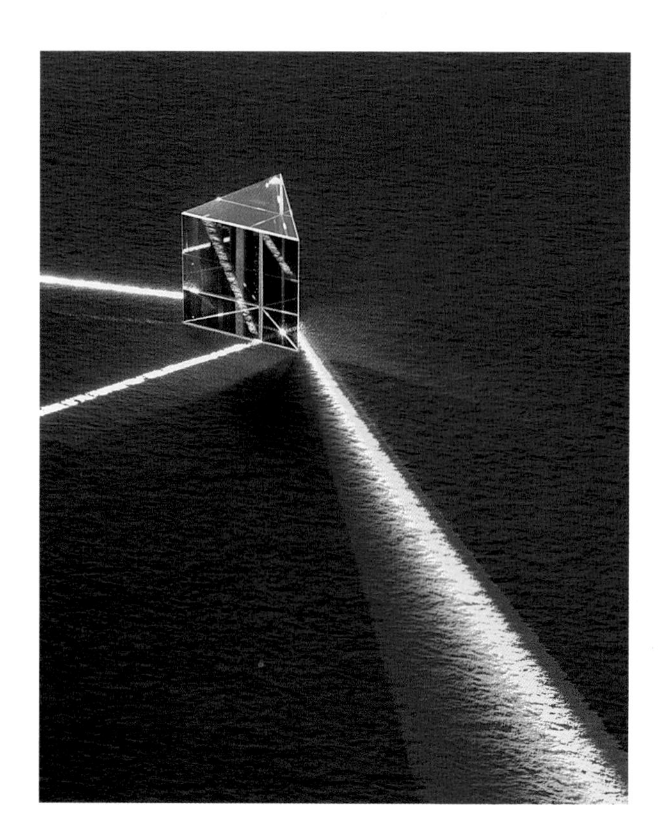

7.2 A beam of light passes through a triangular-shaped piece of glass (prism). The rays of light are bent, or refracted, as they pass through the glass at different angles (according to their wavelengths), producing a rainbow array of hues called the spectrum. © David Parker, SPL/PhotoResearchers, Inc.

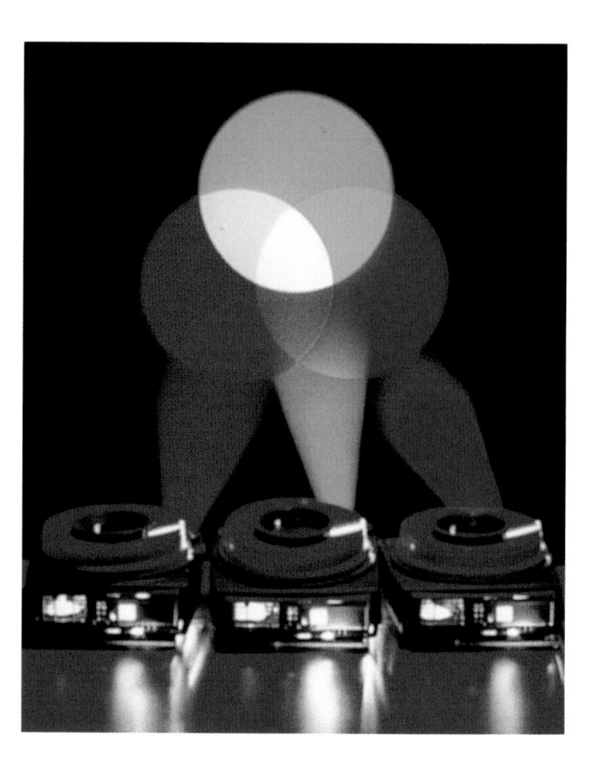

7.3 The projected additive primary colors—red, blue (a color named by industry and scientists that is actually closer to violet), and green—create the secondary colors of cyan, yellow, and magenta when two are overlapped. When all three primaries are combined, white light is produced. © Eastman Kodak Company.

Additive Color

The colors of the spectrum are pure, and they represent the greatest intensity (brightness) possible. If we could collect all these spectrum colors and mix them in a process reversed from the one described in the previous paragraph, we would again have white light. When artists or physicists work with rays of colored light, they are using **additive color.** When rays of the additive primaries red, blue, and green are overlapped, the secondary colors are created. Where red and blue light overlap, magenta is produced; where red and green light overlap, yellow is produced; where green and blue light overlap, cyan is produced. Where red, blue, and green light rays overlap, white light is produced—demonstrating that white light may be created by the presence of all color wavelengths (fig. 7.3).

The television industry uses this additive color mixing process. The modern color monitor is made up of small triplet phosphor units of red, blue, and green. Seen in 525 horizontal lines, the units are illuminated singly or in various combinations to produce the sensation of every color possible. Each image is made up of two scans of alternate lines—odd-numbered lines, then even. This takes place at a rate of 60 scans per second. At viewing distance, the lines and stripes of glowing colored phosphors cannot be distinguished as the eye merges them into a sharp image in full color.

Like television, the computer is another important tool that uses additive color mixing. It is employed by the artist to explore and create color images (fig. 7.4). In addition, computer-generated models can provide the illusion of three-dimensional space and scale. They allow the viewer to move about in the image, trying multiple spacing and color relationships. In a computer model, the artist is able to explore the additive color effects of stage lighting on characters and props before building the actual set. An old accountant's saying states, "If you want to count green pigs, shine a green spotlight upon them." With additive color stage lighting, things are not always what they may seem to be either.

A reddish stage light will make the object take on that color, and if green is projected on the opposite side, interesting qualities may be created by the highlight and shadows of the natural contours. Where the two spotlights overlap, a new color (yellow tones) may be seen. Though a bit garish in this instance, additive color stage lighting that is appropriate to the image can do much to heighten the emotional response of the audience.

Increasingly, an artist needs to be familiar with the additive color system. In addition to computer art, it is used in theater, video production, computer animation graphics, the neon sign industry, slide and multimedia presentations, laser light shows, and landscape and interior lighting. In each case, artists and technicians work with light and create color by mixing the light primaries—red, blue, and green.

Subtractive Color

Because all the colors are present in a beam of daylight, how are we able to distinguish a single color as it is reflected from a natural object? Any colored object has certain physical properties, called color quality or pigmentation, that enable it to absorb some color waves and reflect others. A green leaf appears green to the eye because the leaf reflects only the green waves in the ray of light. An artist's **pigments** have this property and, when applied to the surface of an object, give it the same characteristic. The artist may also alter the surface pigmentation of an object through the use of dyes, stains, and chemical treatments.

Regardless of how the surface pigmentation is applied or altered, the sensation of color is created when the surface absorbs all the wavelengths except those of the color perceived. When the work is experienced through reflected light, we are dealing with **subtractive color** rather than actual light rays or additive color. With an area of white, all the light wavelengths of color are reflected back to the viewer—none is subtracted by the white. However, when a color covers the surface, only the wavelengths of that color are reflected back to the viewer—all others are subtracted or absorbed by the pigment. As a result, the sensation of that specific color is experienced. Furthermore, the total energy subtracted (not reflected) is equal to the reflected color's opposite or complement (see fig. 7.22).

Therefore, in theory, when a color is physically mixed on the palette with its complement, they should cancel each other out, and the mixture should absorb *all* wavelengths. In theory, the area should appear black—no reflected light. In theory, the mixing of a color—blue, for instance—and its complement—in this case, orange (yellow and red)—involves the mixture of all three primaries to appear black. Notice that the result here is the opposite of additive

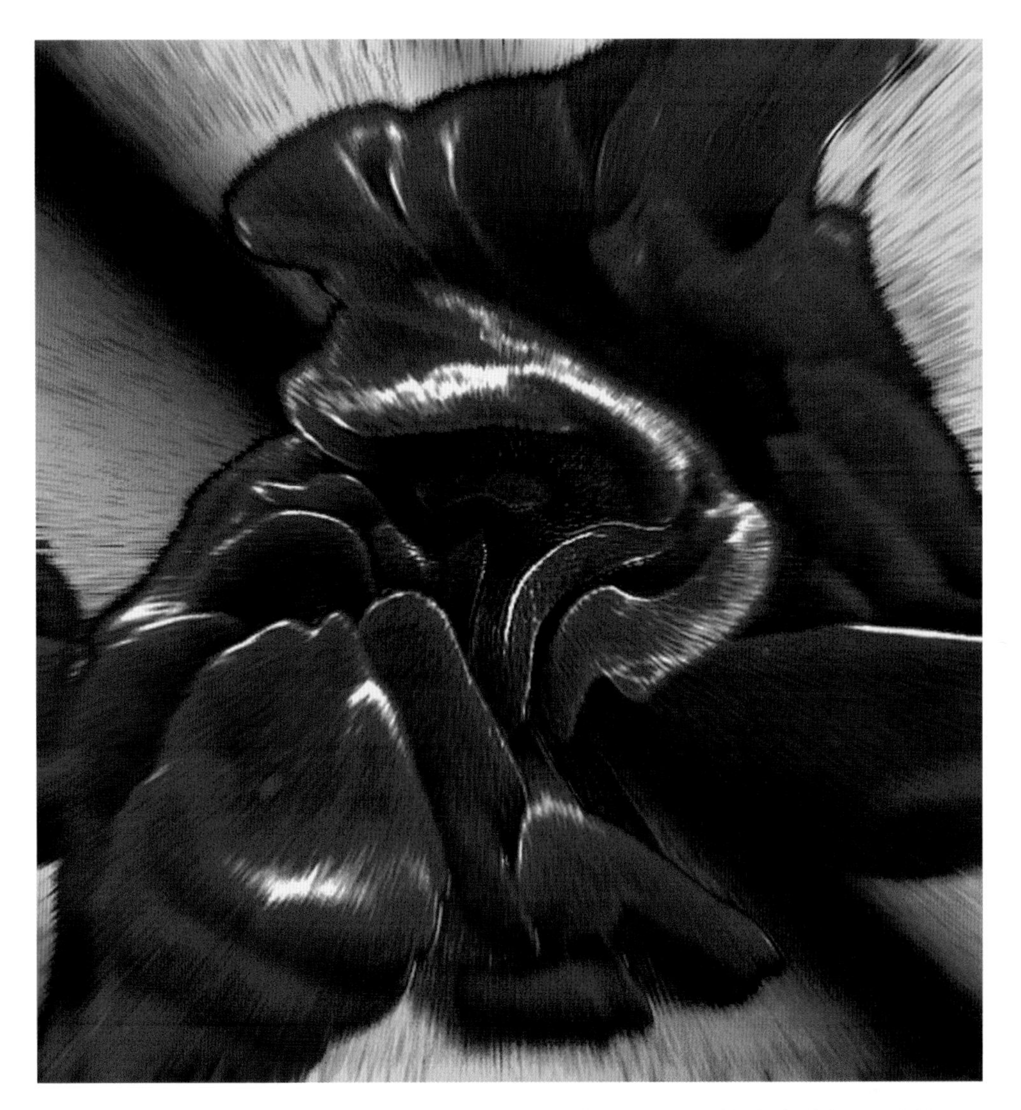

7.4 Bettina Pousttchi, *Vera Naturelle,* 1999. Digital photograph behind plexiglass, 49.99 × 57.48 in. In this digital print, Pousttchi examines the relationship between nature and science. She uses technology to generate the image creating a sensuous, organic form that is familiar but not identifiable. Courtesy Buchmann Galerie Berlin.

color mixing, which produces white by mixing all the light primaries.

However, in actual practice on the palette, the mixture of all three primaries (yellow, red, and blue) does not result in black but in a neutralized dark gray—hinting at an uncertain color that feels rather "muddy." This occurs because of adulterants and imperfections in pigments, inks, and dyes and the fact that the surface may not perfectly absorb all wavelengths except for those being reflected. In addition, the pigment may reflect more than just one dominant color and/or a certain amount of white.

The theory of subtractive color, then, helps to explain how we perceive color, as an image reflects only the wavelength of the color seen, while absorbing all other wavelengths. We will see later that photographers, printers, and some artists use a subtractive color system comprising a special set of primaries (see "The Subtractive Printing System (Process Color System)," p. 165). But, for the following sections when we discuss color, we will be concerned with the painter's palette and the hues made visible by reflected light.

Artist's Color Mixing

As previously mentioned, the spectrum contains red, orange, yellow, green, blue, blue-violet, and violet, with hundreds of subtle color variations, all at their greatest intensity. This range of color is available in pigment as well. Beginning artists are likely to use only a few simple, pure colors and may not realize that simple colors can be varied. But many colors can be created by mixing two other colors.

In traditional processes, three colors cannot be created from mixtures; these are the hues red, yellow, and blue, known as the **primary colors** (fig. 7.5). When these primaries are mixed in pairs, in equal or unequal amounts, they can produce all of the possible colors.

Mixing any *two* primaries in more or less equal proportions produces a **secondary color:** Orange results from mixing red and yellow; green is created by mixing yellow and blue; and violet occurs when red and blue are mixed (see fig. 7.5).

Intermediate colors are mixtures of a primary color with a neighboring secondary color. Because a change in the proportion of primary or secondary color used will change the resultant hue, many subtle variations are possible. For example, between yellow, yellow-green, and green, more yellow will move green toward yellow-green (fig. 7.6). If we study the theoretical progression of mixed color from yellow to yellow-green to green and so on, we discover a

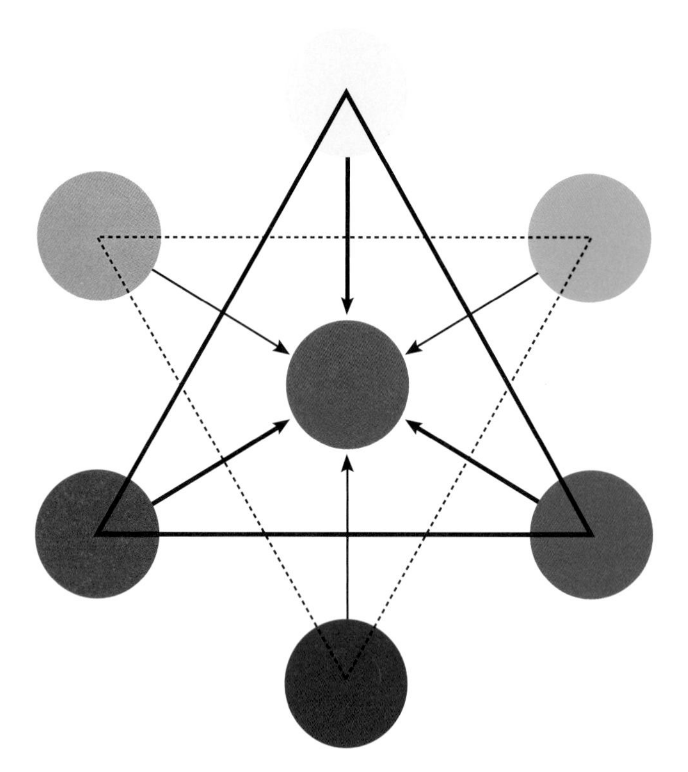

7.5 A primary triad is shown in solid line. When the yellow, red, and blue of the primary triad are properly mixed together, the resulting color is neutralized gray. A secondary triad is connected by dotted lines. When secondary colors are also properly mixed together, the resulting color is gray. Triadic color intervals are of medium contrast.

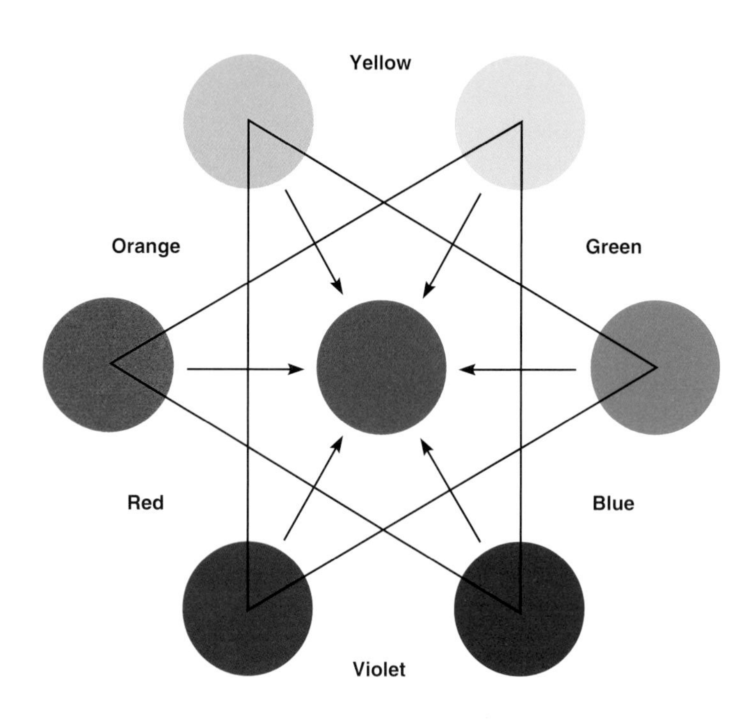

7.6 Intermediate colors. When the colors of the intermediate triads are mixed together in even proportions, the resulting color is usually a neutralized gray. Uneven mixtures produce tertiary colors, found in figure 7.7.

natural order that may be presented as a color wheel (fig. 7.7). Our ability to differentiate subtle variations allows us to see a new color at each position. Note that the primaries, secondaries, and intermediates are found on the outer ring with the hues at spectrum intensity.

Tertiary colors are infinite in number. They are created by mixing any two secondary colors or through the neutralization of one color by its complement. In practical terms, this involves the intermixing of all three primaries in varying proportions, creating the browns, olives, maroons, and so on found on the inner rings of the color wheel. Though we have presented only two inner rings, we could have shown numerous rings as possible steps from a hue to complete neutralization in the center (fig. 7.7). This is more fully explained in the coming section "Intensity."

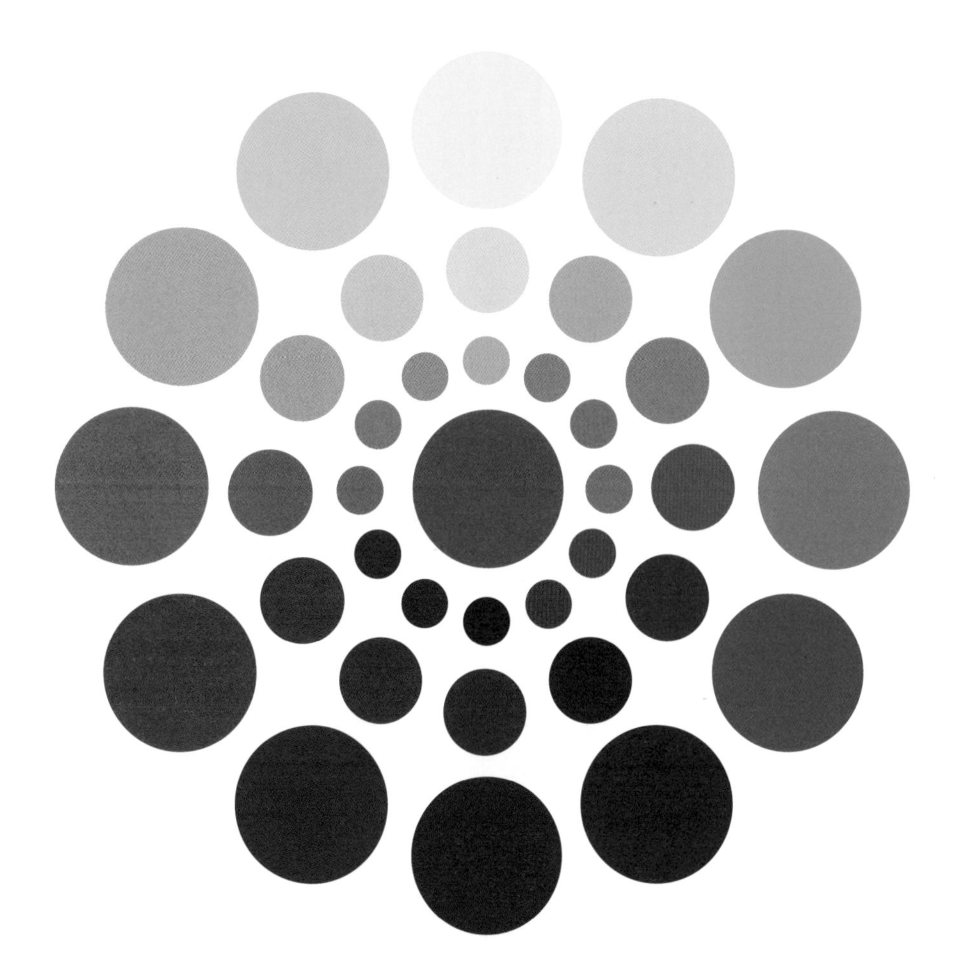

7.7 This color wheel includes the primary, secondary, and intermediate hues, or the "standard" hues; of course, the number of possible hues is infinite. As one moves from a hue to its opposite on the color wheel, the smaller circles indicate the lessening of intensity due to the mixing of these opposites, or complementaries. The inner circles are the location of the tertiary hues—those hues result from the mixture or neutralization of one primary by its complement. This results in mixing three primaries. The features of tertiary colors are a loss of intensity and a neutralization of hue. Complete neutralization occurs in the center circle.

The Triadic Color System

The system of **color triads** is a way to organize color in theory. The color illustrations are created by inks and should be used as guides rather than absolutes. The actual mixing of pigments will reveal, for instance, that each manufacturer's "red" is different or that the color of your green depends on what you use as primaries. Lemon yellow mixed with ultramarine blue will create a different green than one that uses cadmium yellow and cobalt blue. Color mixing experiments will disclose much about opacity, staining power, and the adulterants added in by the manufacturers.

With the triadic color system, the three primary colors are spaced equally on a wheel, with yellow usually on the top because it is closest to white in value. These colors form an equilateral triangle called a primary triad (see fig. 7.5). The three secondary colors are placed between the primaries from which they are mixed; evenly spaced, they create a secondary triad composed of orange, green, and violet (see fig. 7.5). Intermediate colors placed between each primary and secondary color create equally spaced units known as intermediate triads (see fig. 7.6). The placement of all the colors results in a twelve-color wheel. The colors change as we move around the color wheel, because the wavelengths of the light rays that produce these colors change. The closer together colors appear on the color wheel, the closer are their hue relationships; the farther apart, the more contrasting they are in character. The hues directly opposite each other afford the greatest contrast and are known as **complementary colors** (see fig. 7.15).

The complement of any color is based on the triadic system. For example, the complement of red is green—a theoretical mixture of equal parts of the remaining points of the triad, yellow and blue. Thus, the color and its complement are made up of the three primary triadic colors; the complement of yellow is created by mixing blue and red, resulting in violet. If the color is a "mixed" secondary hue (orange, say), we can find its complement by knowing what primaries created the color (red and yellow); the remaining member of the triad (blue) will be the mixed color's complement.

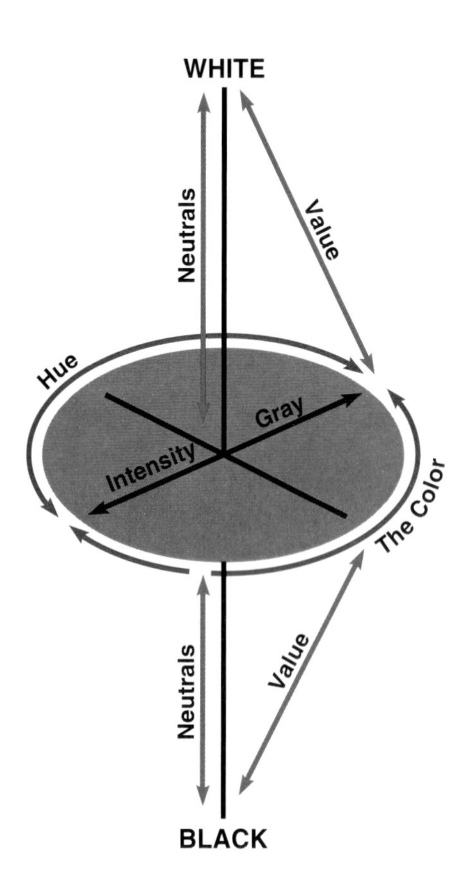

7.8 This diagram demonstrates the three physical properties of color. We can see all the color variations as existing on a three-dimensional solid (a double cone). As the colors move around this solid, they change in hue. When these hues move upward or downward on the solid, they change in value. As all of the colors on the outside move toward the center, they become closer to the neutral values, and there is a change in intensity (see also fig. 7.9).

Neutrals

Not all pigments contain a perceivable color. Some, like black, white, and gray, do not look like any of the hues of the spectrum. No color quality is found in these examples; they are **achromatic.** They differ merely in the quantity of light they reflect. Because we do not distinguish any one color in black, white, and gray, they are also called **neutrals.** These neutrals actually reflect varying amounts of the color wavelengths in a ray of light.

One neutral, white, can be thought of as the presence of all color, because it occurs when a surface reflects all of the color wavelengths to an equal degree.

Black, then, is usually called the absence of color, because it results when a surface absorbs all the color rays equally and reflects none of them. Absolute black is rarely experienced except in such places as deep caves and the like. Therefore, most blacks will contain some trace of reflected color, however slight.

Any gray is an impure white, because it is created by only partial reflection of all the color waves. If the amount of light reflected is great, the gray is light; if the amount reflected is little, the gray is dark. The neutrals are indicated by the *quantity* of light reflected, whereas color is concerned with the *quality* of light reflected.

The Physical Properties of Color

Regardless of whether the artist works with **chromatic** paints, dyes, or inks, every color used must be described in terms of three physical properties: **hue, value,** and **intensity** (figs. 7.8 and 7.9).

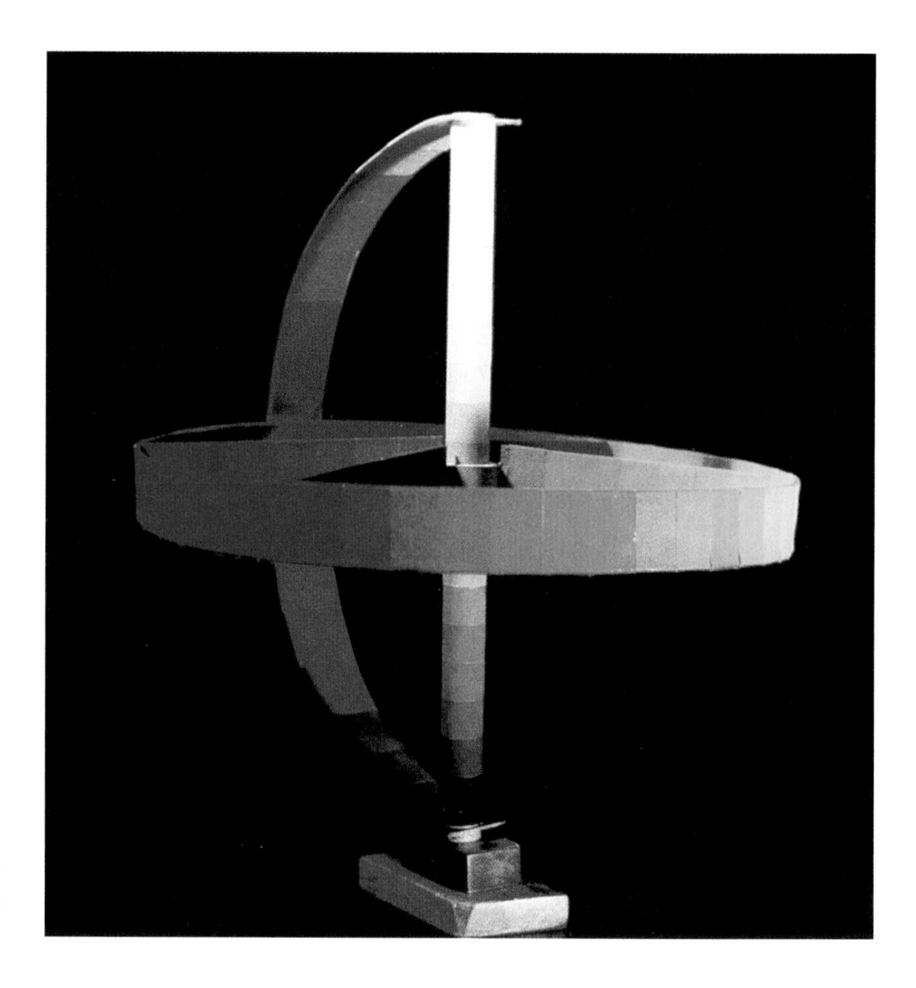

7.9 A three-dimensional model illustrating the three main characteristics of color (see also fig. 7.8). Photograph courtesy of Ronald Coleman.

Hue

Hue is the generic color name—red, blue, green, and so on—given to the visual response for each range of identifiable wavelengths in visible light (fig. 7.10; see fig. 7.1). Hue designates a color's position in the spectrum or on the color wheel. Every color actually exists in many subtle variations, although they all continue to bear the simple color names. Many reds, for example, differ in character from the theoretical red of the spectrum, yet we recognize the redness of the hue in all of them. In addition, a color's hue can be changed by adding it to another hue; this actually changes the wavelength of light. There are an unlimited number of steps (variations) that may be created by mixing any two colors—between yellow and green, for example. Yet, for the sake of clarity, artists recognize the hues as identified on the twelve-step color wheel.

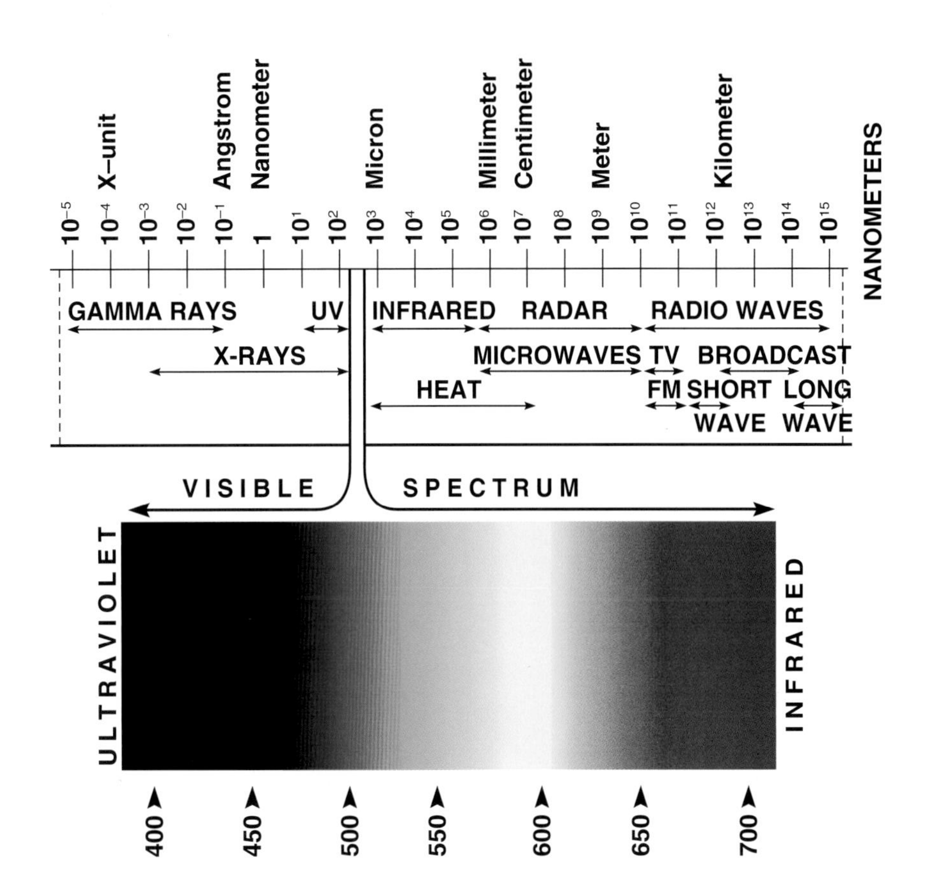

7.10 The electromagnetic spectrum. The sun, being the most efficient source of light, sends radiation to the earth in a series of waves known as electromagnetic energy. This may be likened to throwing a pebble into the middle of a pond. Waves radiate from that point and can be measured from the crest of one ripple to the crest of the next ripple. Similarly, waves from the sun range from mere atmospheric ripples—gamma rays, which measure no more than 6 quadrillionths of an inch (0.000000000000006 in.)—to the long, rolling radio waves, which stretch 18½ miles from crest to crest.

The wavelengths visible to the human eye are found in only a narrow range within this electromagnetic spectrum; their unit of measure is the "nanometer" (nm), which measures one billionth of a meter from crest to crest. The shortest wavelength visible to mankind measures 400 nm—a light violet. The sensations of yellow, orange, and red are apparent as the waves lengthen to between 600 and 700 nm. Contained in a ray of light but invisible to the human eye are infrareds (below reds) and ultraviolets (above violets): see figure 7.1.

Value

A wide range of color value variations can be produced by adding black or white to a hue. This indicates that colors have characteristics other than hue. The property of color known as **chromatic value** distinguishes between the lightness and darkness of colors or the quantity of light a color reflects. Many value steps can exist between the darkest and lightest appearance of any one hue. When a hue is mixed with varying amounts of white, the colors produced are known as tints. Shades are produced when a hue is mixed with black. Value changes may also be made when we mix the pigment of one hue with the pigment of another hue that is darker or lighter; this mixing will also alter the color's hue. The only dark or light pigments available that would not also change the hue are black and white or a gray.

Each of the colors reflects a different quantity of light as well as a different wavelength. A large amount of light is reflected from yellow, whereas a small amount of light is reflected from violet. Each color at its maximum intensity has a normal value that indicates the amount of light it reflects. It can, however, be made lighter or darker than normal by adding white or black, as previously noted. We should know the normal value of each of the colors in order to use them effectively. This normal value can be most easily seen when the colors of the wheel are placed next to a scale of neutral values from black to white (fig. 7.11). On this scale (and in the color wheel), all colors that are above middle gray are called **high-key colors.** All colors that are below middle gray are referred to as **low-key colors.** Whether a color remains low or high key is up to the artist. As noted, a low-key violet may be lightened with white. That adjustment may raise violet's value level until it corresponds to the value

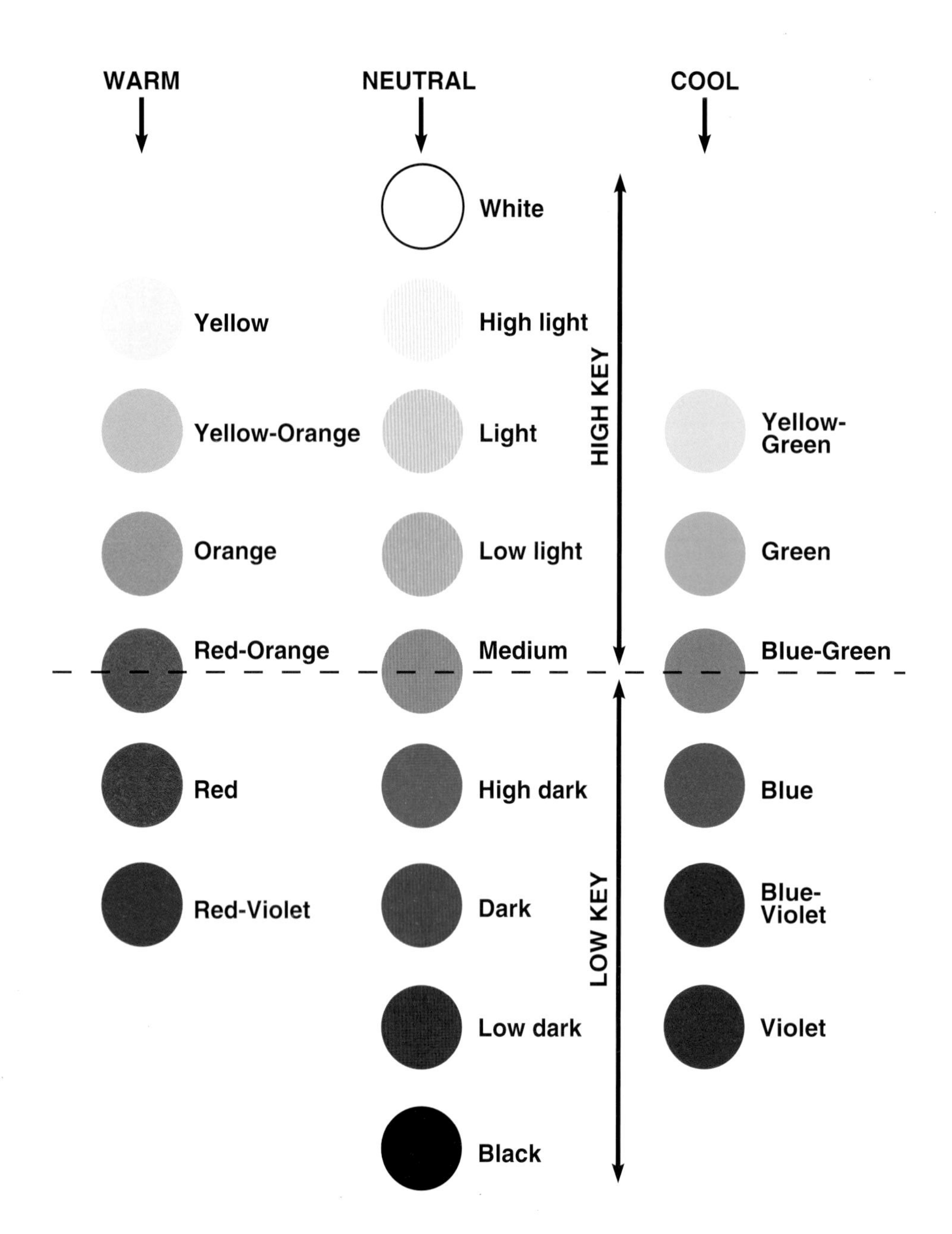

7.11 Color values. This chart indicates the relative normal values of the hues at their maximum intensity (purity or brilliance). The broken line identifies those colors and neutrals at the middle (50 percent) gray position. All neutrals and colors above this line are high key, and any below it are low key. Warm colors are found on the yellow and red side, while cool colors are found with the greens and blues.

level of gray for any color along the neutral scale; violet could be made equal in value to yellow-orange by checking the gray scale. Similarly, a high-key color such as yellow may be adjusted with enough black that it becomes a low-key color. Regardless of how the value level is obtained, color can be used to create a value pattern in the organization of a work. A wise artist once said, "Color gets all the glory . . . but value does all the work!" While many artists work intuitively using only color and its brilliance, the most insightful also understand and employ color's value as a compositional tool.

Intensity

The third property of color, intensity (also sometimes called saturation or **chroma**), refers to the quality of light in a color. Intensity distinguishes a brighter appearance from a duller one of the same hue; that is, it differentiates a color that has a high degree of saturation or strength from one that is grayed, neutralized, or less intense. The saturation point, or the purest color, is actually found in the spectrum produced by a beam of light passing through a prism. The artist's pigment that comes closest to resembling this color is said to be at maximum intensity. The purity of the light waves reflected from the pigment produces the variation in brightness or dullness of the color. For example, a pigment that reflects only the red rays of light is an intense red, but if any of the complementary green rays are also reflected, the red's brightness is dulled or neutralized. If the green and red rays are equally absorbed by the reflecting surface, the resulting effect is a neutral gray. Consequently, as a color loses its intensity, it tends to approach gray.

There are several ways to change the intensity of a color. To *increase* a color's intensity, an old technique involved an underpainting in the color's complement. For example, when a red object was painted on top of a green underpainting, any green wavelengths that might have been reflected back were absorbed by the green underpainting—making the reflected red purer and more intense. Another common approach is to place one color next to its complement, which will appear to increase the color's intensity.

Other methods of change *lower* the intensity and require the mixing of pigments (fig. 7.12). This will automatically lower the intensity of the color being affected. Figure 7.12 shows the alteration of a hue (pigment) by adding a neutral

7.12 This diagram illustrates the way neutrals may be used to change the intensity of color. As white is added to bright red, the value gets lighter, but the resulting color is lowered in intensity. In the same way, the addition of black to bright red creates a dark red closer to the neutral scale because the intensity changes. When a neutral gray is added to the spectrum color, the intensity is lowered, but the value is neither raised nor lowered.

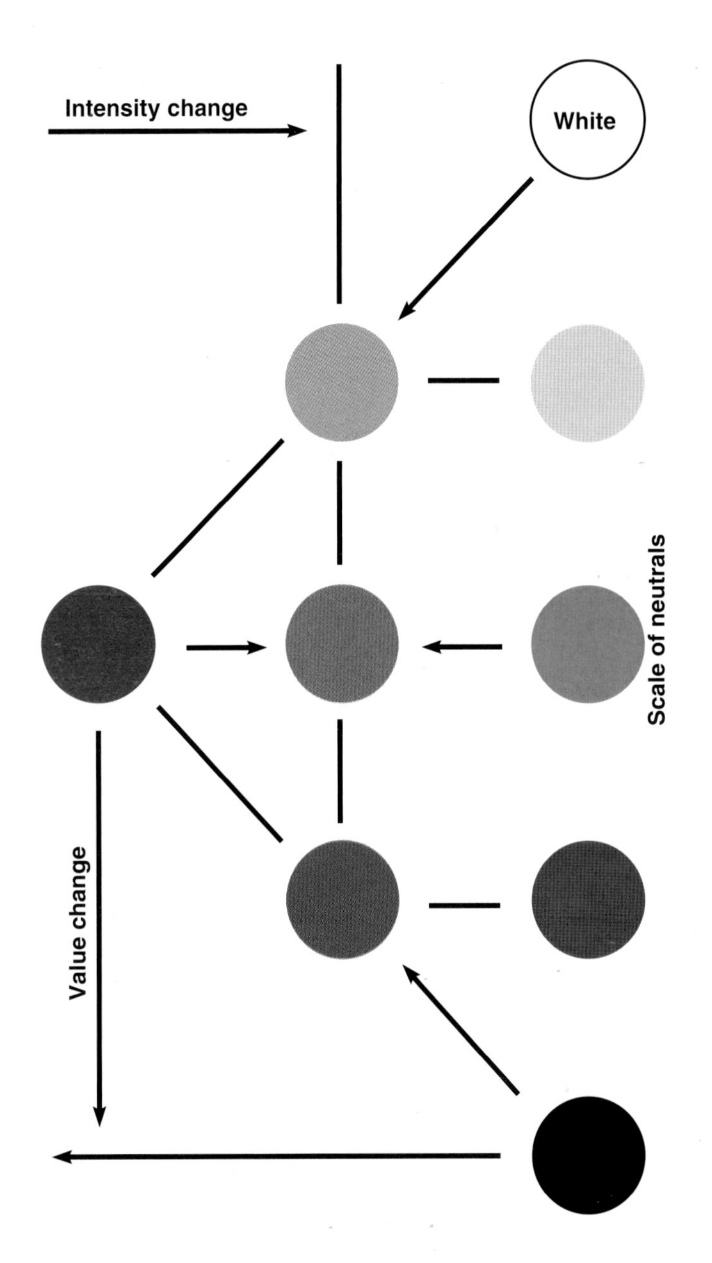

(black, white, or gray). As white is added to any hue, the color becomes lighter in value, but it also loses its brightness or intensity. In the same way, when black is added to a hue, the intensity diminishes as the value darkens. We cannot change value without changing intensity, although these two properties are not the same. The illustration also shows an intensity change created by mixing the hue (pigment) with a neutral gray of the same value. The resulting mixture is a variation in intensity without a change in value. The color becomes less bright as more gray is added, but it will not become lighter or darker in value. The most efficient way to change the intensity of any hue is to add the complementary hue. Mixing two hues that occur exactly opposite each other on the color wheel, such as red and green, blue and orange, or yellow and violet, actually results in the intermixing of all three primaries. In theory, when equal portions of the three primaries are used, a black should be created to absorb all wavelengths and not allow any colors to be reflected. However, because of impurities and an inability to absorb all the wavelengths, a neutral gray is actually produced. In the studio, some complements—blue to orange, for example—may give better grays than others. Note: The gray ink in these diagrams may appear darker and characterless compared to your experiments.

When the three primaries are used in the mixing of a new color, a tertiary color is produced and is characterized by a neutralization of intensity and hue. This occurs when complements are mixed. If the mixture has uneven proportions, the dominating hue creates the resulting color character. Though the hue's intensity has been neutralized to varying degrees relative to the amount of complement used, the resulting colors have a certain liveliness of character not present when a hue is neutralized with a gray pigment. Hundreds of tertiary colors may be observed in a neutralization scale from one color to its complement. These show incremental steps of the change of one hue created by adding more and more of its complement until complete neutralization occurs. Tertiary colors may also be created by mixing two secondary colors (not analogous) that share a common color. For example, yellow-orange and red-violet share red as a common hue. They will have the same character and appearance as those colors created by the neutralization of a color by its complement. On the color wheel, the tertiary colors of the same

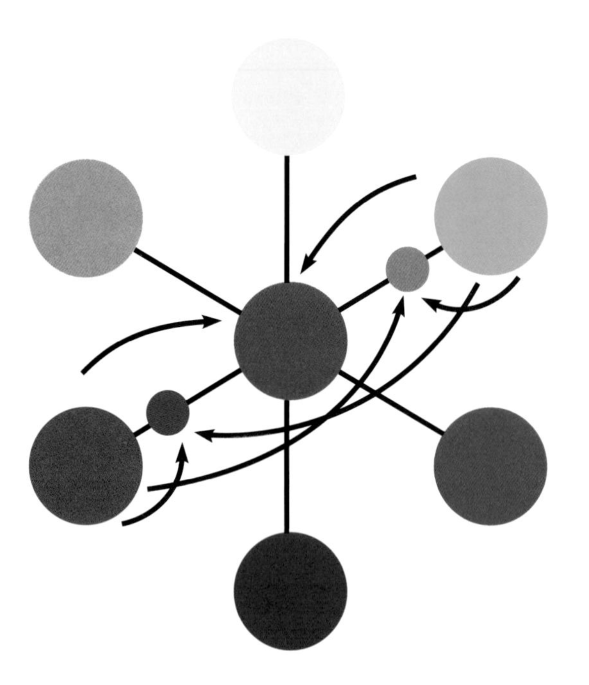

7.13 This diagram indicates change of intensity by adding to a color a little of its complement. For instance, by adding a small amount of green to red, a gray-red is produced. In the same way, a small amount of red added to green results in a gray-green. When the two colors are balanced (not necessarily in equal amounts), the resulting mixture is a neutral gray.

degree of neutralization create inner circles and appear as the browns (neutralized oranges), olives (neutralized greens), and so on. They are characterized by a loss of intensity and a neutralization of hue. They are not to be found on the outer circle with the secondary and intermediate colors (see fig. 7.7).

This neutralization also occurs with the mixing of any combination of hues that contain the three primaries. For example, yellow-orange (y+y,r) and yellow-green (y+y,b) added to red-violet (r+r,b) would actually mix four yellows with three reds and two blues—a reddish violet. Here, the resulting neutralization should have a reddish appearance.

It is difficult to change a color's intensity (by adding a little of its complement) without *also* changing its value level (fig. 7.13). If a small amount of green (lighter value) is added to red (darker value), the result is a loss of intensity and a lightening of value for the neutralized red. Conversely, when a small amount of red (darker value) is added to the green (lighter value), the green loses some of its intensity and becomes darker in value. This dual relationship, affecting the change of intensity and value, is perhaps most easily seen with yellow and violet. However, it occurs with every pair of complements except one—red-orange and blue-green. They are the only pair of complements that may be used to lower each other's intensity *without* changing the value level. This occurs because they begin with the same value level—middle gray.

Developing Aesthetic Color Relationships

When listening to music, we find a single note played for a long period of time rather boring. Once the composer begins to combine notes in chords, harmonic relationships of sound are created. Sounds combine in different ways, and some are better than others at creating harmonic effects. The same is true for an artist's colors. No color is important in itself; each is seen on the picture surface in a dynamic interaction with other colors. Because combinations and arrangements of color express content or meaning, any arrangement—objective or nonobjective—evokes sensations because of its presentation (see fig. 7.40). To develop a discerning eye, we need to study the inexhaustible supply of color combinations we find in nature, from the extravagant color relationships of a peacock's feather to the soft muted tonalities on the surface of a rock. This study can be followed by experiments and practice with these color schemes. There are no exact rules for creating sensations from color relationships, only some guiding principles.

The successful use of color depends on an understanding of some basic color relationships. A single color by itself has a certain character, creates mood, or elicits an emotional response, but that character can change when the color is seen with other colors in a harmonic relationship. Just as the musician can vary combined tones to form different harmonies, so too can the artist create different relationships (harmonies) among colors that may be closely allied or contrasting (fig. 7.14).

Complements and Split-Complements

Color organizations that result in the greatest contrast in hue occur when two colors that appear directly opposite each other on the color wheel (complementaries) are placed next to each other in a composition (fig. 7.15). When a color is seen, only that wavelength is being reflected; the wavelengths not reflected equal the color's complement. Therefore, when two complements are placed nearby, a vibrance occurs because of the great contrast. Each color tends to increase the apparent intensity of the other color, and, when used in equal amounts, they are difficult to look at for any length of time (see "Simultaneous Contrast," p. 156). This is overcome by reducing the size of one of the colors or introducing changes in the intensity or value level of one or both colors.

A subtle variation with slightly less contrast would be the **split-complement** system, which incorporates a color and the two colors on either side of its complement (fig. 7.15). This color scheme provides more variety than the straight complementary system, because the color is opposed by two colors closely related to the color's complement. Even greater variety or interest may be achieved by using an intensity change or selecting variations from the complete value range of any or all of the colors in this color scheme.

Triads

A triadic color organization is based on an even shorter interval between colors, giving less contrast between the colors. Here, three equally spaced colors form an equilateral triangle on the color wheel; triads are used in many combinations. A primary triad, using only primary colors, creates striking contrasts (see fig. 7.5). With the secondary triad, composed of orange, green, and violet, the interval between hues is the same, but the contrast is softer. This effect

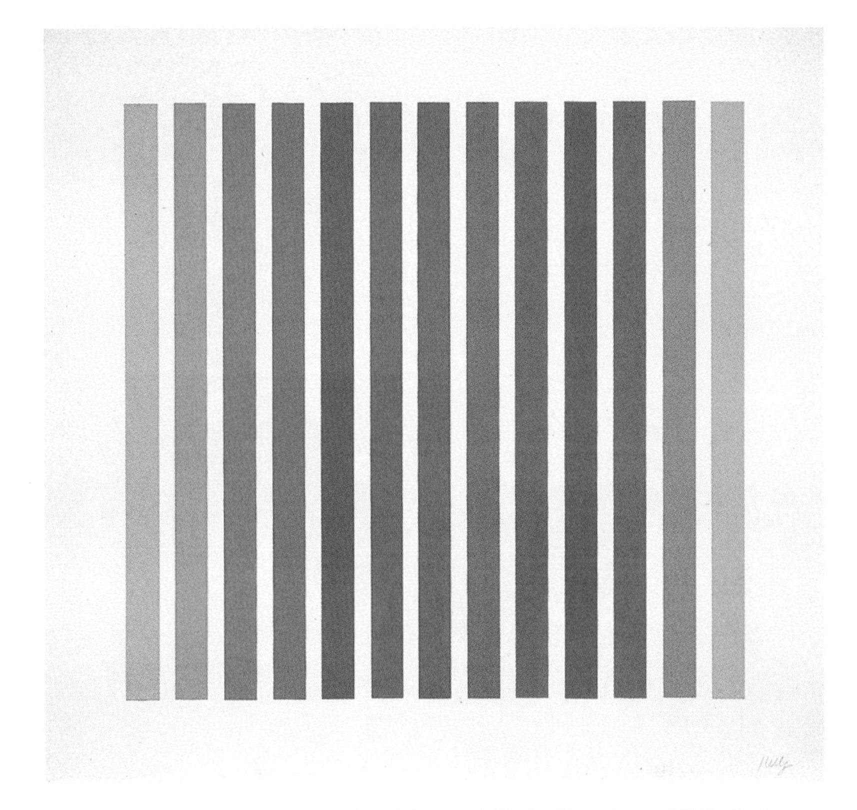

7.14 Ellsworth Kelly, *Spectrum,* 1972. Collage on paper, 45 × 48 in. (114.3 × 121.9 cm). In this color study, Kelly has employed all the contrasting colors in the spectrum. The addition of white to each color brought them into a harmonious relationship by raising their value level and lowering their intensity.

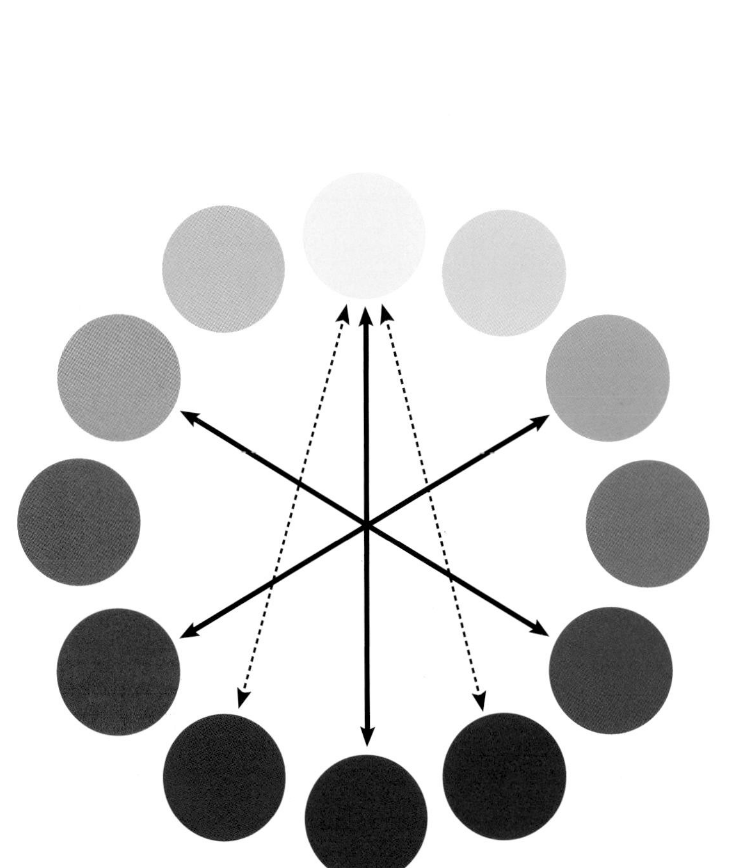

7.15 Complementary colors are shown connected by solid lines. They are of extreme contrast. An example of split-complementary colors (yellow, red-violet, and blue-violet) is shown by dotted lines. Though yellow is used, the idea may be applied to any color and would include the color on either side of the hue's complement. Split-complements are not quite as extreme in contrast as complements.

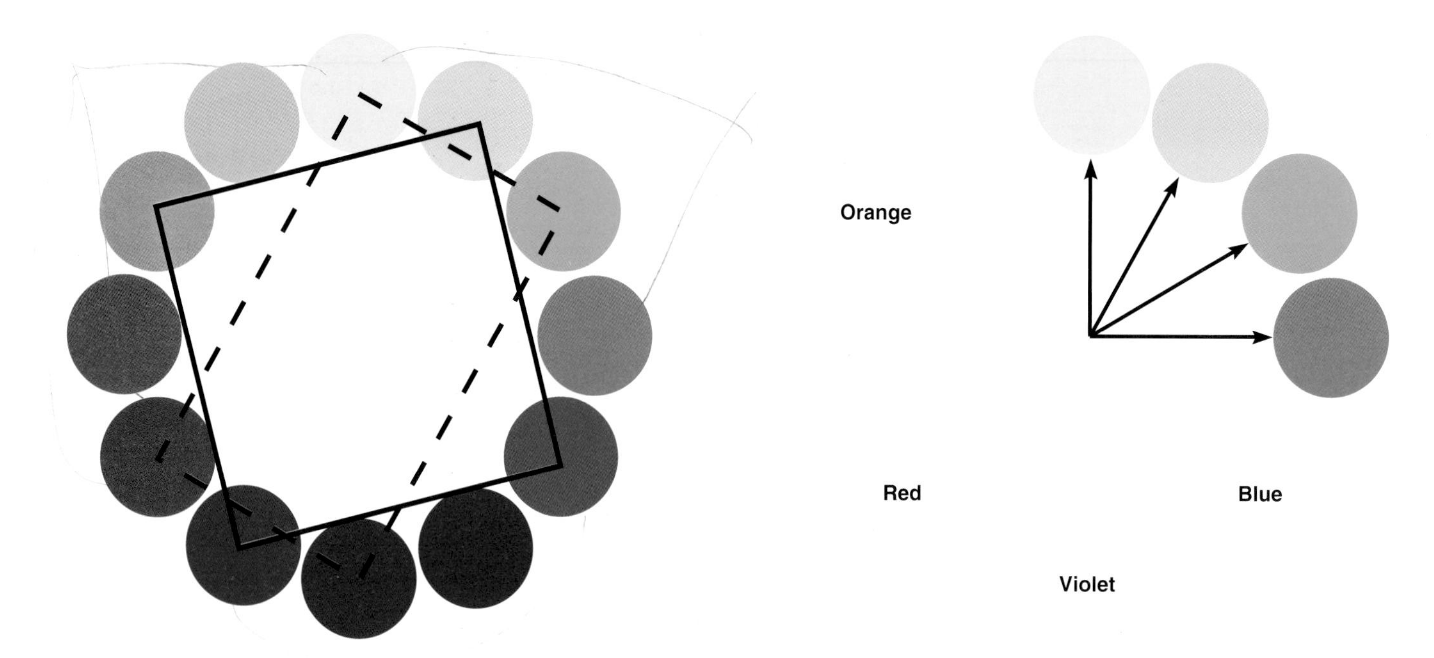

7.16 Color tetrad intervals (squares and rectangles). The color tetrad is composed of four colors equally spaced to form a square. A more casual relationship would have a rectangle formed out of two complements and their split-complements. The rectangle or square may be rotated to any position on the color wheel to reveal other tetrad color intervals.

7.17 Analogous colors (close relationships).

probably occurs because any two hues of the triad share a common color: Orange and green both contain yellow; orange and violet both contain red; and green and violet both contain blue. Intermediate color schemes may be organized into two intermediate triads (see fig. 7.6). Here, too, as we move farther away from the purity of the primaries, the contrast among the two triads is softer.

Tetrads

Another color relationship is based on a square rather than an equilateral triangle. Known as a **color tetrad,** this system is formed when four colors are used in the organization. They are equally spaced around the color wheel and contain a primary, its complement, and a complementary pair of intermediates (fig. 7.16). A tetrad has also come to mean, in a less strict sense, any organization of color forming a "rectangular structure" that could include a double split-complement. This system of color harmony is potentially more varied than the triad because of the additional colors present. If you avoid the temptation of using all the colors in equal volumes, the increased variety will be even more interesting.

Analogous and Monochromatic Colors

Analogous colors are those that appear next to each other on the color wheel. They have the shortest interval and therefore the most harmonious relationship, because three or four neighboring hues always contain one common color that dominates the group (fig. 7.17). Analogous colors not only are found at the spectrum intensity levels (outer ring of the color wheel) but may also include colors made by neutralization (intensity changes) and value changes of any of these related hues (fig. 7.18). On the other hand, **monochromatic color** schemes use only one hue but explore the complete range of tints (value levels of hue to white) and shades (value levels to black) for that color (see fig. 7.35). Even with thousands of variations of tints and shades of one color, this scheme is potentially the most monotonous. However, monochromatic studies are a useful test of the artist's understanding of the value range of that hue.

Warm and Cool Colors

Color "temperature" may be considered as another way to organize color schemes. All of the colors can be classified into one of two groups: "warm" colors or "cool" colors. Red, orange, and yellow are associated with the sun or fire and thus are considered warm. Any colors containing blue, such as green, violet, and blue-green, are associated with

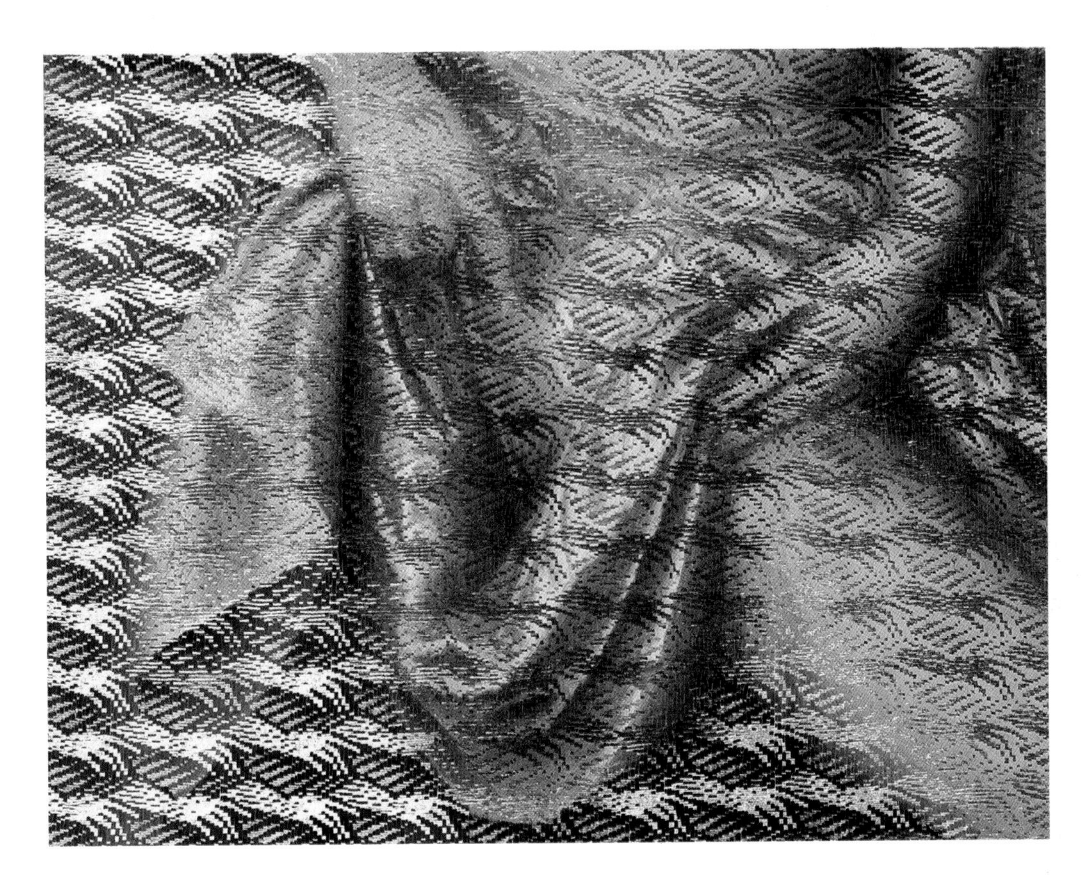

7.18 Lia Cook, *Point of Touch: Bathsheba,* 1995. Linen, rayon, oil paint and dyes, 46 × 61 in. (116.84 × 154.94 cm). Cook employs analogous colors, containing a common hue, to develop the illusion of hands holding folds of fabric on a pattern of changing hand images. Collection of Oakland Museum of California. © Lia Cook.

air, sky, earth, and water; these are called cool. This quality of warmth or coolness in a color may be affected or even changed by the hues around or near it. For example, the coolness of blue, like its intensity, may be heightened by locating blue near a touch of its complement, orange.

Plastic Colors

Colors may also be organized according to their ability to create compositional depth. Artists are able to create the illusion of an object's volume or flatten an area by using color. This ability to model a shape comes from the advancing and receding characteristics of certain colors. For example, a spot of red on a gray surface seems to be in front of that surface; a spot of blue, similarly placed, seems to sink back into the surface. In general, warm colors advance and cool colors recede (fig. 7.19). The character

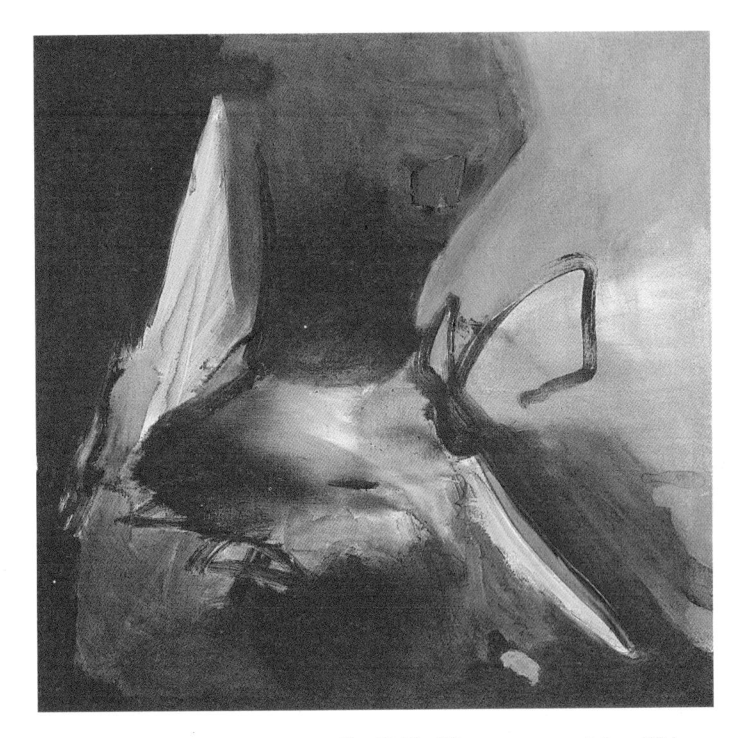

7.19 Emily Mason, *Upon a Jib,* 1989. Oil on canvas, 54 × 52 in. (137.2 × 132.1 cm). Like a sail filling with air, the large red and yellow shapes of this painting billow toward the viewer while the blues and greens seem to poke holes in the surface or recede. Courtesy of the artist and David Findlay, Jr. Fine Art, New York © Licensed by VAGA, New York.

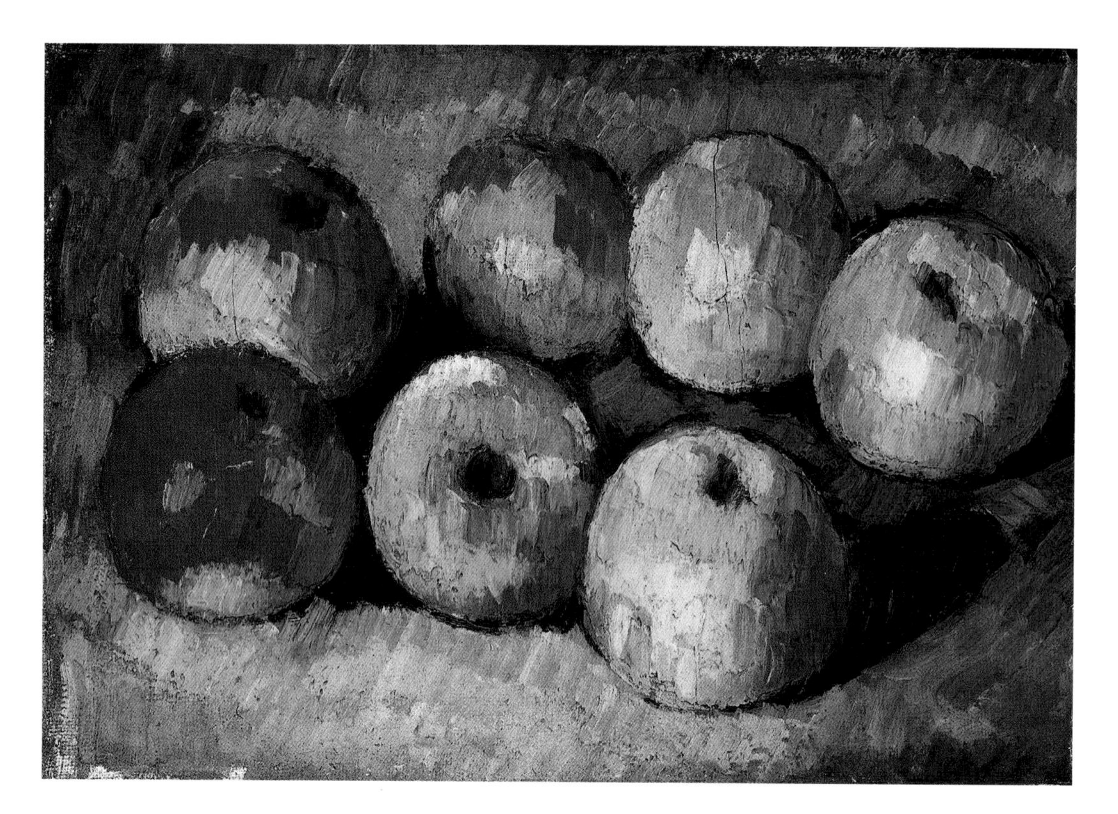

7.20 **Paul Cézanne, *Still Life with Apples*, 1875–77. Oil on canvas, 7½ × 10¾ in. (19 × 27.3 cm).** Cézanne used brushstrokes and change of color as a means of modeling form. Rather than merely indicating an adjustment in value, warm colors made the shapes come forward while cool colors forced outer edges to recede. By kind permission of the Provost and Fellows of King's College, Cambridge, England (Keynes Collection).

of such effects, however, can be altered by differences in the value and/or intensity of the color.

These spatial characteristics of color were fully developed by the French artist Paul Cézanne in the latter part of the nineteenth century. He admired the sparkling brilliancy of the Impressionist artists of the period but thought their work had lost the solidity of earlier painting. Consequently, he began to experiment with expressing the bulk and weight of forms by modeling with color. Previous to Cézanne's experiments, the traditional **academic** artist had modeled form by changing values in monotone (one color). The artist then tinted these tones with a thin, dry local color that was characteristic of the object being painted. Cézanne discovered that a change of color on a form could serve the purpose of a change of value, while imparting new effectiveness of expression. He modeled the form by placing warm color on the part of the subject that was to advance and adding cool color where the surface receded (fig. 7.20). Cézanne felt that this rich color and its textural application expressed the actual structure of a solid object. Later, modern artists realized that Cézanne's advancing and receding colors could also create those backward and forward movements in space that give liveliness and interest to the picture surface (see fig. 7.33). However, this is only a tool, and there is no single correct way to employ it.

Paul Gauguin, for example, often applied the same principles *in reverse* to flatten the spatial qualities in a pictorial organization. By placing cool colors in the foreground, he makes it appear to recede. By painting the background in warm colors, he causes it to advance. This combination flattens the pictorial space, making it more decorative than plastic (fig. 7.21). Likewise, abstract artists use the color relationships to create balance, movement, and space, giving content to a painting even though no actual objects are represented (see fig. 10.76). Line, value, shape, and texture are greatly influenced by the ability of color to create space and meaning.

Simultaneous Contrast

An artist may mix a color on a palette, only to find that it appears entirely different when juxtaposed with other colors on the canvas. Why does a red-violet appear to change color when placed beside a violet? During the early part of the nineteenth century, a French chemist, M. E. Chevreul, wanted to discover why the Gobelins tapestry works was having trouble with complaints about the color stability of certain blues, browns, light violets, and blacks. As director of tints and dyes, Chevreul discovered that the problem was not a question of the dyestuffs but rather a phenomenon of color contrast. The appearance of these colors varied depending on which color they were placed

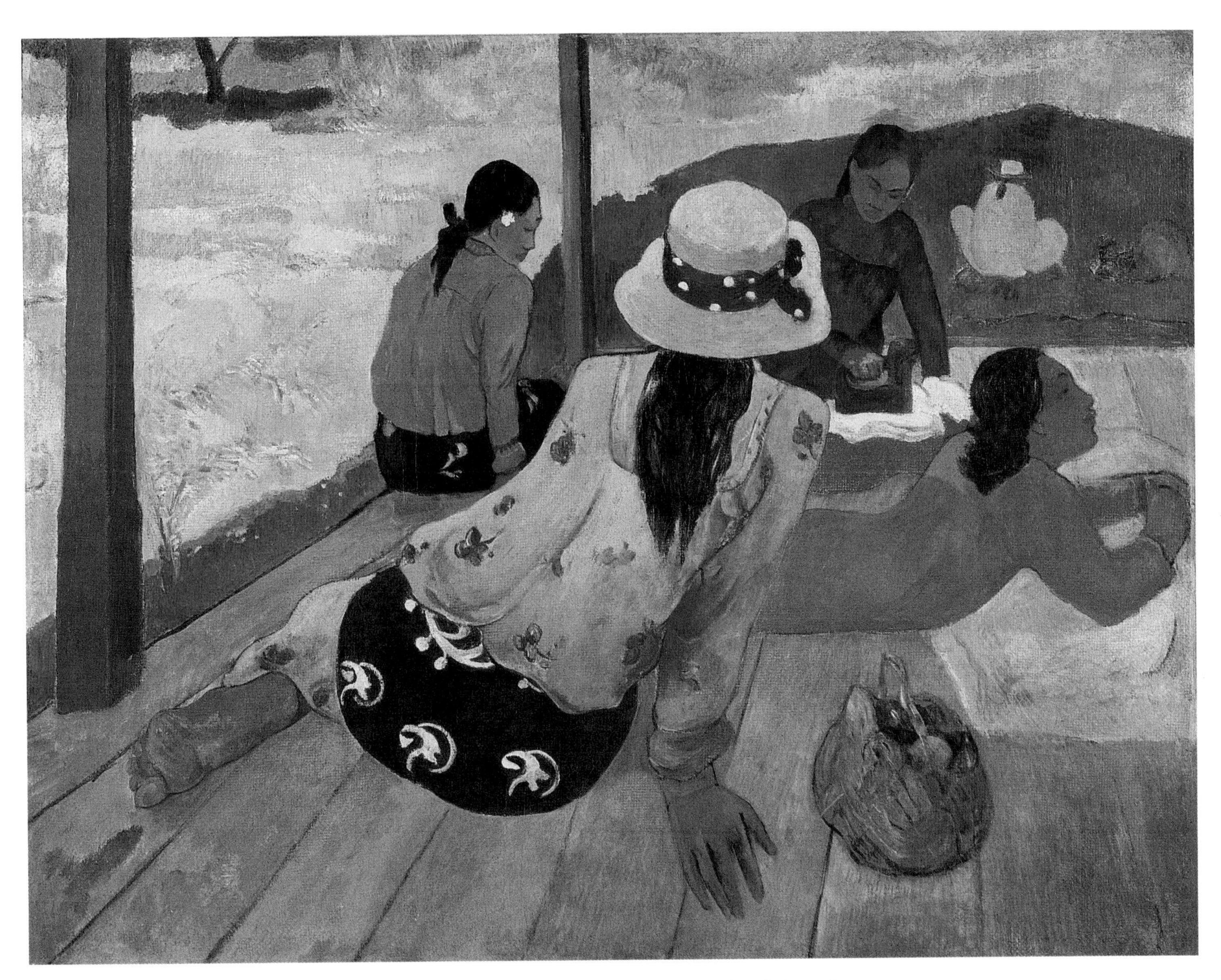

7.21 Paul Gauguin, *The Siesta*, c. 1891–92. Oil on canvas, 34¼ × 45⅝ in. (87 × 115.9 cm). Gauguin has used the nature of plastic color to reverse the spatial effect and make it shallow. Cool blues, blue-violets, and neutralized reds, surrounded by dark greens, push the foreground back, while warm yellows and yellow-greens pull the background forward, flattening the pictorial space. The Metropolitan Museum of Art, The Walter H. and Leonore Annenberg Collection. Partial gift of Walter H. and Leonore Annenberg, 1993 (1993.400.3). Photograph © 1994 The Metropolitan Museum of Art.

beside. These discoveries were the starting point for the *Law of Simultaneous Contrast of Colors,* published in 1839. With this publication, Chevreul became the "technical prophet" of two schools of painting that followed—Impressionism and Post-Impressionism. Both groups of painters often juxtaposed complements that increased the intensity of each through simultaneous contrast. Another early student of these principles, Eugène Delacroix, once said, "Give me mud and I will make the skin of a Venus out of it, if you will allow me to surround it as I please."

The effect of one color on another is explained by the rule of **simultaneous contrast.** According to this rule, whenever two different colors come into direct contact, their similarities seem to decrease, and their dissimilarities seem to increase. In short, contrast intensifies the difference between colors. This effect is most extreme, of course, when the colors are directly contrasting in hue, but it occurs even if the colors have some degree of relationship. For example, a

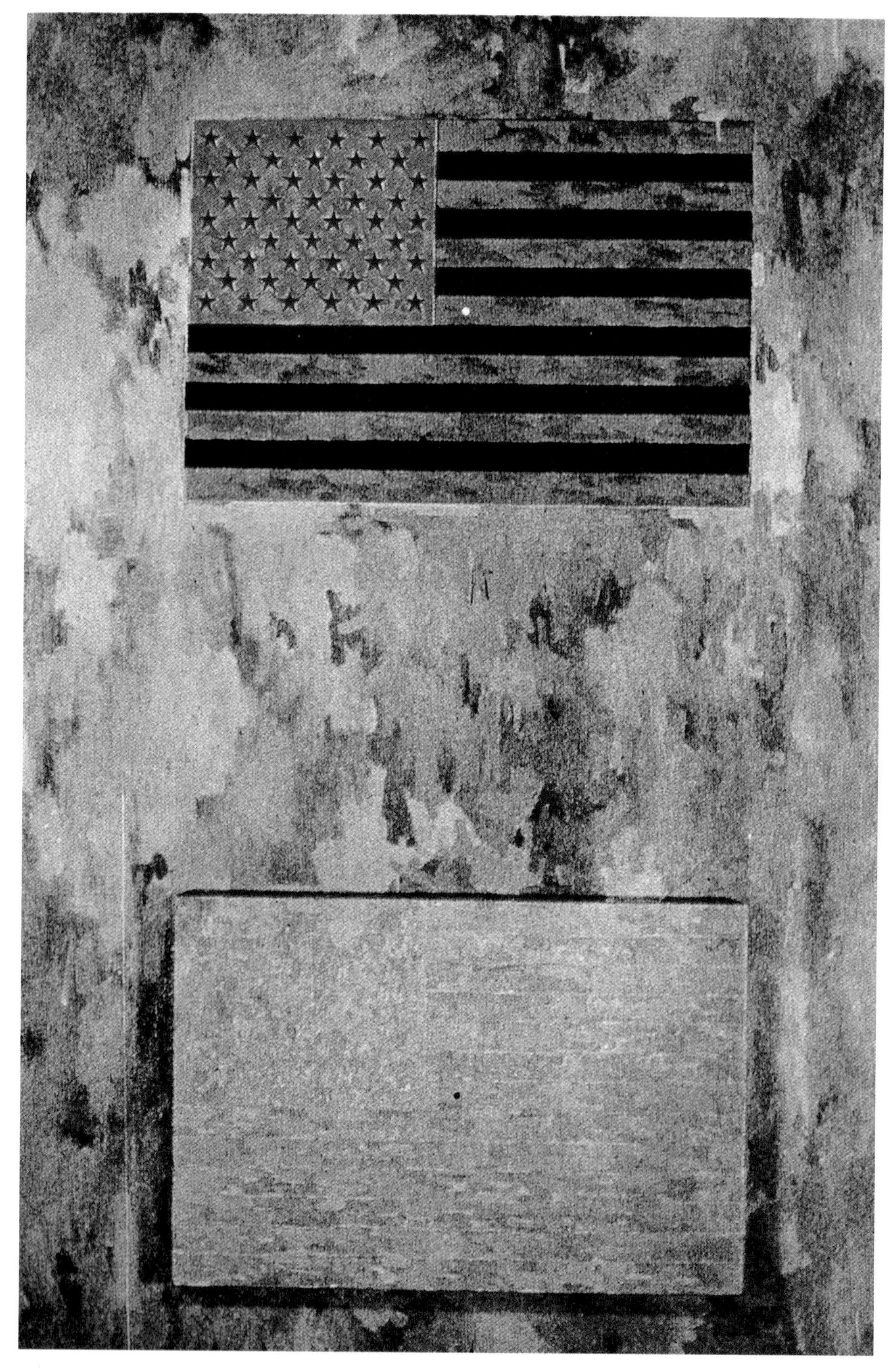

7.22 Jasper Johns, *Flags,* 1965. Oil on canvas with raised canvas, 6 × 4 ft (1.83 × 1.22 m). With this painting, Johns wanted the viewer to experience an afterimage. This occurs when the retina's receptors are overstimulated and are unable to accept additional signals. They then project the wavelengths of the complementary color. Stare at the white dot on the upper flag for forty seconds. Shift focus to the dark dot on the lower flag, and an afterimage will be seen in red, white, and blue.

yellow-green surrounded by green appears more yellow, but if surrounded by yellow it seems more strongly green. The contrast can be in the characteristics of intensity and value as well as of hue. A grayed blue looks brighter if placed against a gray background and will tend to make the gray take on an orange cast; it looks grayer or more neutralized against a bright blue background. The most striking effect occurs when complementary hues are juxtaposed: Blue is brightest when seen next to orange, and green is brightest when seen next to red. When a warm color is seen in simultaneous contrast with a cool color, the warm hue appears warmer and the cool color cooler. A color always tends to bring out its complement in a neighboring color. If a green rug is placed against a white wall, the eye may make the white take on a very light red or warm cast. A touch of green in the white may be necessary to counteract this. When a neutralized gray made up of two complementary colors is placed next to a strong intense color, it tends to take on a hue that is opposite the intense color. When a person wears a certain color of clothing, the complementary color in that person's complexion is emphasized.

Some of these conditions of imposed "color" may be explained by the theory that the eye (and mind) seeks a state of balanced involvement with the three primaries. More than a psychological factor, this seems to be a physiological function of the eyes' receptors and their ability to receive the three light primaries—some combination of all three is involved in most mixed colors. And, as our eyes flash unceasingly about our field of vision, all the primaries and all receptors are repeatedly activated. The mind seems to function with less stress when all three receptor systems are involved concurrently. Within the area of vision, any combination of primaries may cause this without necessarily having to be of equal proportions.

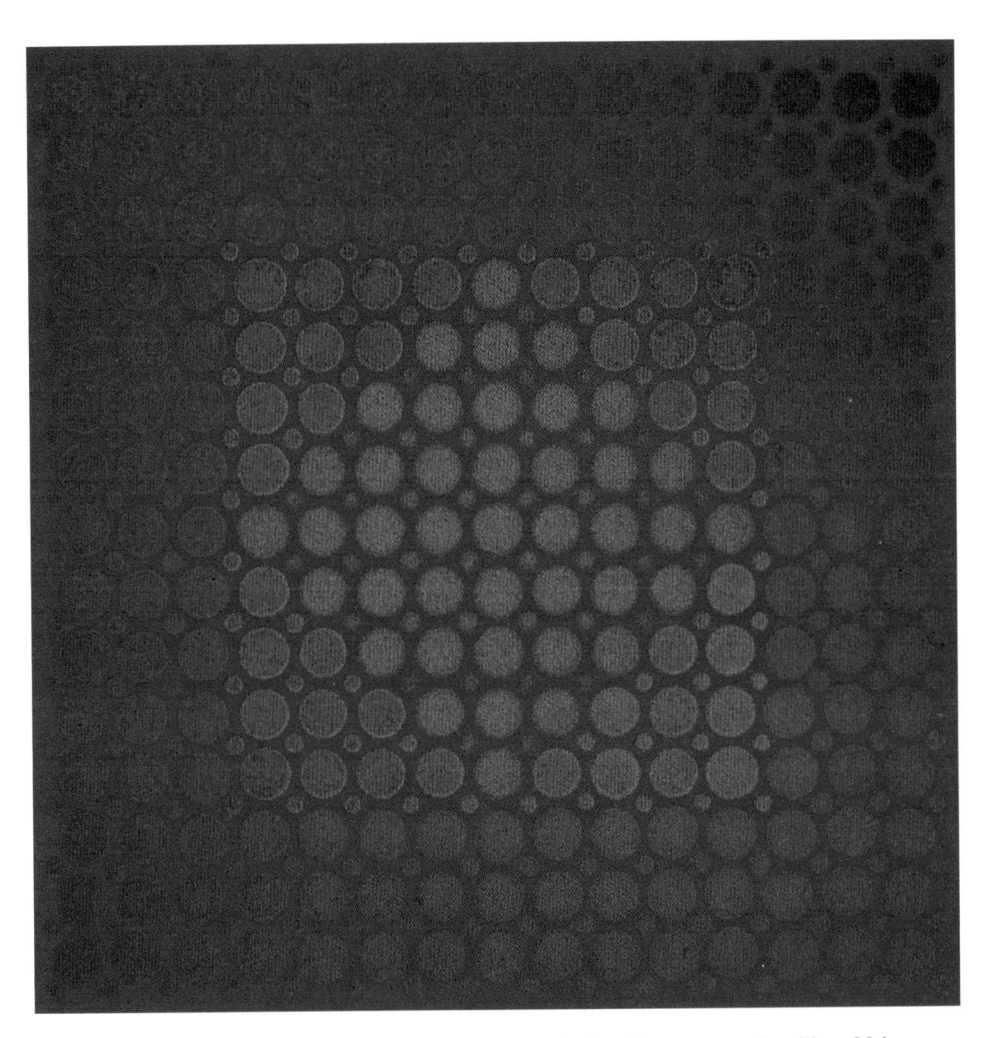

7.23 Richard Anuszkiewicz, *Injured by Green,* 1963. Acrylic on masonite, 36 × 36 in. (91.4 × 91.4 cm). This use of simultaneous contrast, using a consistent pattern of two dot sizes, builds intensity toward the center by the juxtaposition of red and its complement. The central green becomes a diamond shape. Collection of the Noyes Museum of Art, Oceanville, New Jersey. © Richard Anuszkiewicz/Licensed by VAGA, New York, NY.

However, if one or more primaries are missing, the eye seems to try to replace the missing color or colors. If we stare at a spot of intense red for several seconds and then shift our eyes to a white area, we see an afterimage of the same spot in green, its complement. The phenomenon can be noted with any pair of complementary colors (fig. 7.22). Though we seem to desire the three primaries visually, our optic function may get overstimulated under certain conditions. Large volumes of clashing full-intensity complements can make us uneasy. Museum guards at an Op Art show were said to have asked for reassignment, complaining of visual problems ranging from headaches to blurred focus. In figure 7.23, Richard Anuszkiewicz refers in the title *Injured by Green* to the unsettling optical fatigue and pulsating colors created by simultaneous contrast.

The condition of balanced stimulation of the color receptors is much easier to experience when the three primaries are physically mixed together. The colors produced are less saturated or intense and seem easier to experience physically. This would explain why tertiary colors, neutralized—sometimes

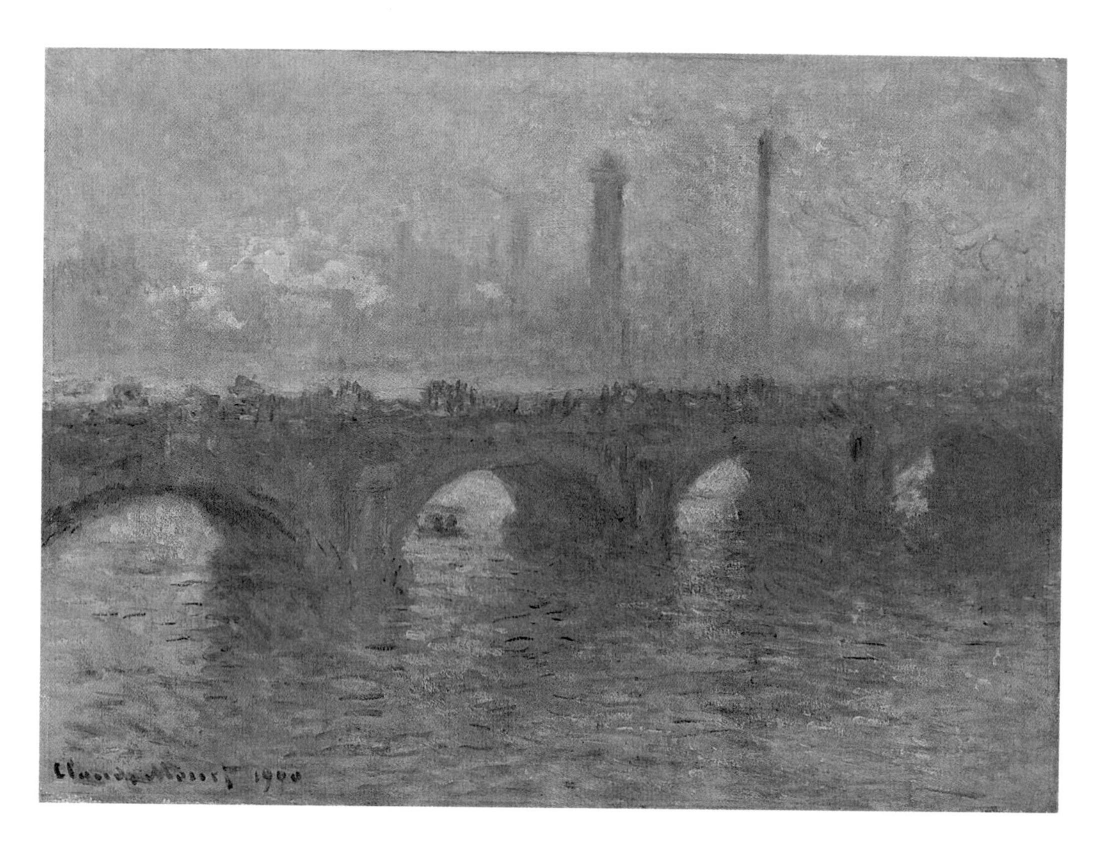

7.24 Claude Monet, *Waterloo Bridge, Grey Weather,* 1900. Oil on canvas, 65.4 × 92.4 cm. The Impressionist Monet painted almost 100 views of the Waterloo Bridge during three trips to London. Painting the view from his room in the Savoy Hotel, he studied the characteristics of light at different times of the day and in differing weather conditions. As a result, the hues, values, and intensities are markedly affected, as we can see by comparing this painting with figure 7.25. Gift of Mrs. Mortimer B. Harris, 1984.1173. The Art Institute of Chicago. All rights reserved.

7.25 Claude Monet, *Waterloo Bridge, Sunlight Effect,* 1903. Oil on canvas, 65.7 × 101 cm. In giving the impression of a passing moment, the artist has deliberately sacrificed detailed architectural information for the effect of sunlight, color, and atmosphere playing on that form. This also applies to figure 7.24. Mr. and Mrs. Martin A. Ryerson Collection, 1993.1163. The Art Institute of Chicago. All rights reserved.

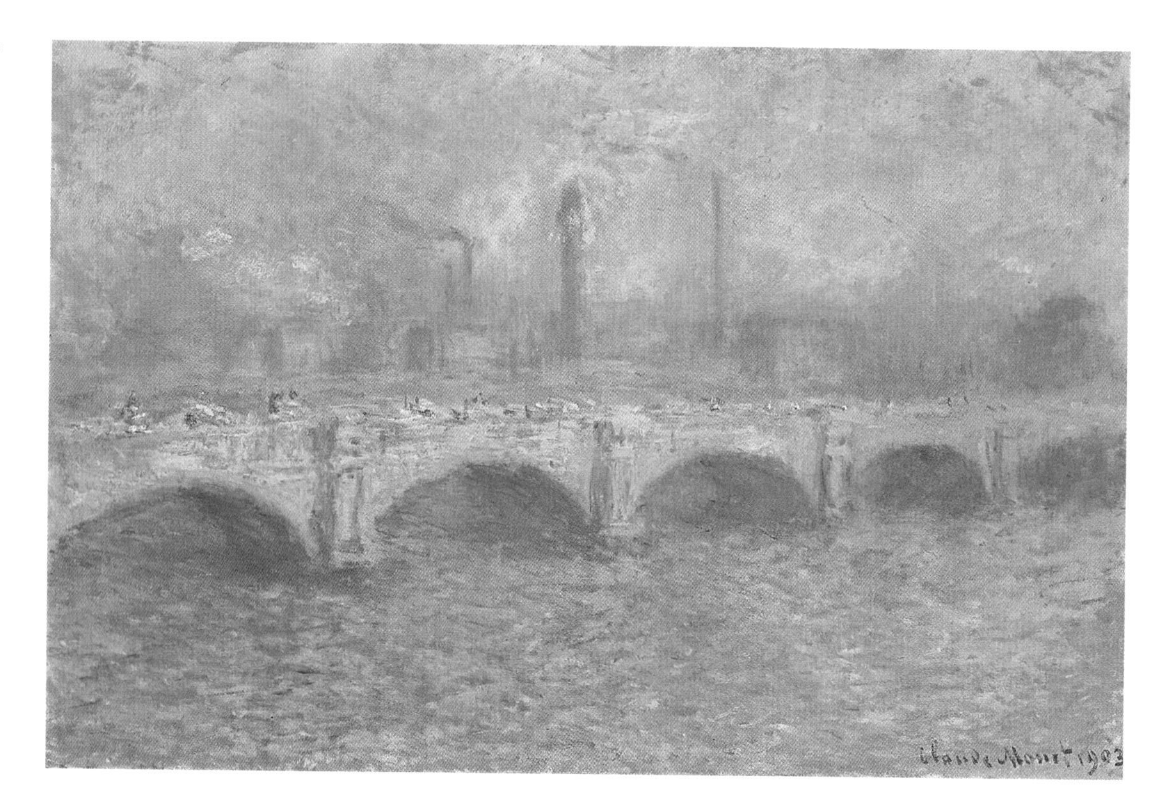

nearly to the loss of hue—are thought of as being more relaxing. Hues such as blues and greens seem to be easier on the eye and mind when lightened with white; white would add more wavelength to the reflected light and thus stimulate additional combinations of receptors. Hues that have been muted, neutralized, or lightened in value will appear to recede compared to their most saturated or intense states. Intense blue walls will make a room appear smaller than a very light tint of the same blue.

Try some experiments to apply the principles of simultaneous contrast in practice. See if the same color placed in the center of two related colors can be made to appear as two different hues, however subtle or different. Further, try making two subtle variations in color appear to be the same by changing their surrounding colors. Investigate the eye's battle to focus or find edges when adjoining shapes or areas are closely related in value level or intensity and become difficult to see. Black lines will give greater clarity to the image but may also tend to flatten the areas. This may also work for "pulsating" edges that occur when the eye has the greatest struggle for edge definition—when complements are placed together. Greater contrast in value or intensity levels will also help with the visual problem of edge resolution or separation of image.

All these changes in appearance make us realize that no one color can be used for itself alone; rather, each must be considered in relation to the other colors present. For this reason, many artists find it easier to develop a color composition globally rather than try to finish one area completely before going on to another.

Color and Emotion

Color may also be organized or employed according to its ability to create mood, symbolize ideas, and express emotions. Color, as found on the canvas, can express a mood or feeling in its own right, even though it may not be descriptive of the objects represented. Reds are often thought of as being cheerful and exciting, whereas blues can impart dignity, sadness, or serenity. Also, different values and intensities in a color range affect emotional impact. A wide value range (strongly contrasting light or dark hues) gives vitality and directness to a color scheme; closely related values and low intensities create feelings of subtlety, calmness, and repose (figs. 7.24 and 7.25).

Colors can evoke emotions that are personal and reinforced by everyday experiences. For example, some yellows look acidic and bitter, almost forcing a pucker, like a sour lemon. Other colors carry with them associations given by the culture. Our speech is full of phrases that associate abstract qualities like virtue, loyalty, and evil with color: "true blue," "dirty yellow coward," "red with rage," "seeing red," "virgin white," "green with envy," and "gray gloom." In some cases, these feelings seem to be universal because they are based on shared experiences. Every culture understands the danger of fire (reds) and the great vastness, mystery, and consistency of the heavens and the seas (blues). Blues can imply reliability, fidelity, loyalty, and honesty, while reds also suggest danger, bravery, sin, passion, or violent death. However, not all color has the same meaning in every culture. On pre-Columbian artifacts, priest-kings are shown in self-bloodletting rituals, and victims are sacrificed to the sun, with red symbolizing renewal and rebirth by allowing the life of the sun to continue. For other cultures, green rather than red is the sign of regeneration, hope, and life. Many color associations can be traced back historically. For example, purple has signified royalty since the ancient Greeks and Romans. Because of the expense of extracting a purple dye from 10,000 tiny shellfish, which is what was required to produce a gram of color, only royalty could afford it. However, even when dye became more affordable, the tradition (and the significance) remained. In China, ancient potters created the technology of glazing ware with very unusual glazes. Among the glazes was a very deep copper red that was so beautiful that the very best ware in every kilnload was immediately carried away to the emperor himself.

Psychological Application of Color

Research has shown that light, bright colors make us feel joyful and uplifted; warm colors are generally stimulating; cool colors are calming; while cool, dark, or somber colors are generally depressing. Medical facilities, trauma centers, and state correctional facilities are often painted in light blues or "institutional greens" because of the calming effect. Winter skiing lodges are adorned in warm yellows, knotty pine, oranges, and browns to welcome those coming in from subzero temperatures. Stories abound of the use of motivating color and sports programs. One visiting team was furious and refused to use the assigned locker room because the "powder-puff pink" walls implied they were "sissies." In another incident, the home team's locker room was painted bright red to keep them keyed up and on edge during halftime, while light-blue surroundings in the visitors' locker room encouraged the opponent to let down and relax. It has been shown in some work situations that bright intense colors encourage worker productivity, whereas neutralized or lighter hues slow down the workforce.

We are continually exposed to the application of color's emotive power. In a supermarket, the meat section is sparkling white to assure us of its cleanliness and purity. To encourage us to purchase the product, the best steaks are garnished with parsley or green plastic trim to make them appear redder and more irresistible. Bright yellow and

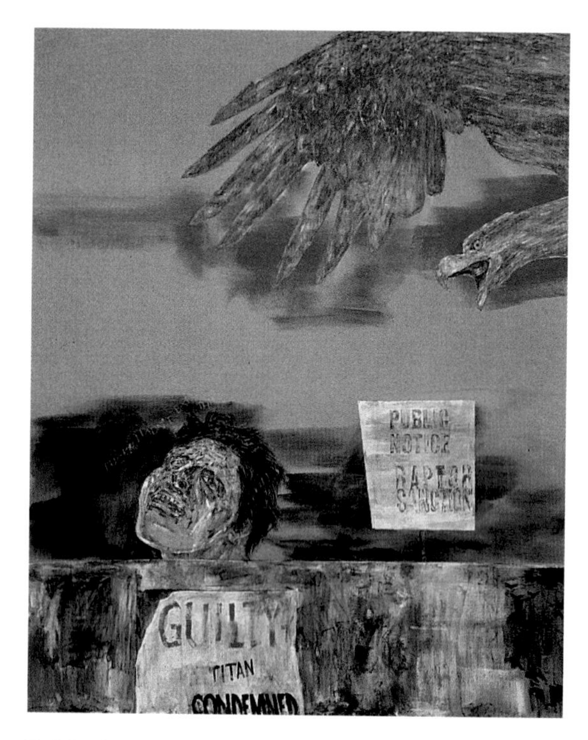

7.26 **Leon Golub, *Prometheus II,* 1998. Acrylic on linen, 119 × 97 in. (302.3 × 246.4 cm).** Leon Golub often deals with psychological color, expressing personal issues through metaphors. A bloody red announces the daily vulture attack, while deep gloomy colors remind us of death and pain. Prometheus, a Titan, was chained to a rock by the Greek god Zeus for stealing fire from Mount Olympus. Courtesy of Ronald Feldman Fine Arts, New York.

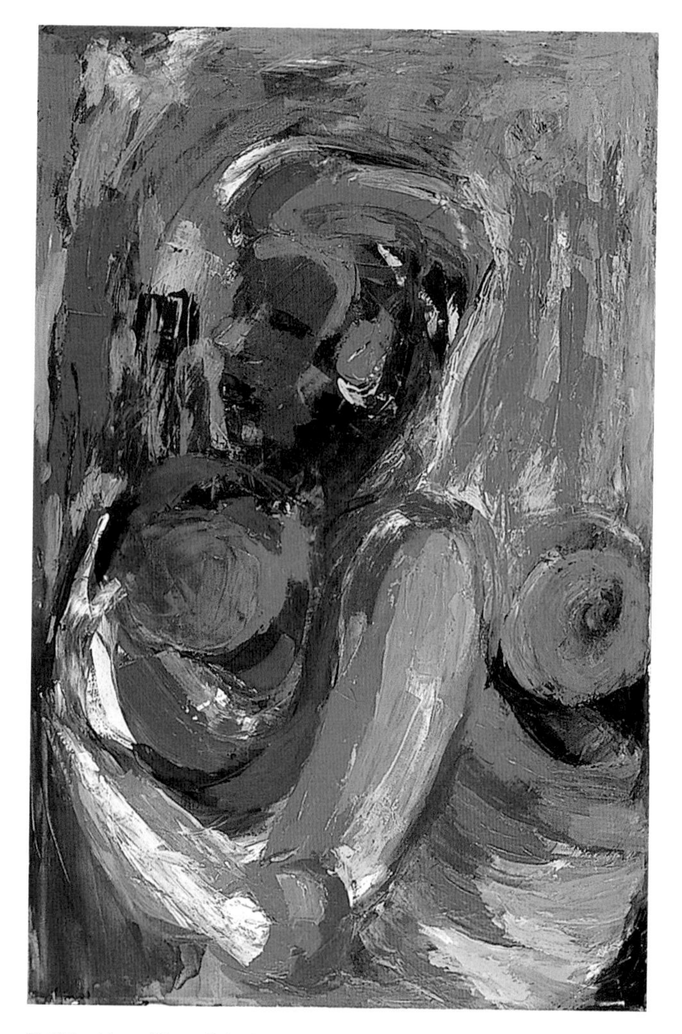

7.27 **Uwa Hunwick, *Lya-Ibeji,* 2003. Acrylic, 36 × 24 in.** Hunwick uses pure chroma, mostly complementary color, and active brushwork in this dynamic composition. Her color choices integrate the figure of the painting with the environment, creating a sense of strength and identity in the subject. © Uwa Hunwick.

orange cereal boxes use contrasting lettering (often complementary) to scream for our attention. Extremely small spaces are rarely painted dark or bright warm colors that would make them feel even smaller. Instead, the space is made to appear larger by light cool colors.

With artists, an angry exchange, a love letter, a near miss in traffic may all subconsciously influence a choice of color. The power of color to symbolize ideas becomes a tool. It enriches the metaphor and makes the work stronger in content and meaning. Many artists have evolved a personal color style that comes primarily from their feelings about the subject rather than being purely descriptive. John Marin's colors are essentially suggestive, with little expression of form or solidity (see fig. 8.43). Frequently delicate and light in tone, they are in keeping with the medium in which he works (watercolor). The color in the paintings of Vincent van Gogh is often vivid, hot, intense, and applied in snakelike ribbons of pigment (see fig. 1.16). His uses of texture and color express the intensely personal style of his work. In the work of Leon Golub, color becomes a personal symbol. Anything but delicate and saccharin, Golub's color sets a gloomy mood and helps to express his feelings about the inevitability of pain, aging, indignity, and death (fig. 7.26). An emotional approach to color appealed particularly to the Expressionist painters, who used it to create an entirely subjective treatment having nothing to do with objective reality (see fig. 10.31). Contemporary artists like Uwa Hunwick continue to interpret their environment in terms of personal color selection (fig. 7.27). We cannot avoid the emotional effects of color because they impact our senses directly as a psychological and physiological function of sight itself.

The Evolution of the Color Wheel

In this book, the arrangement of the color wheel is based on a subtractive system of artist pigments using red, yellow, and blue as primaries. This triadic primary system has evolved over many centuries.

The Origins of Color Systems

Sir Isaac Newton investigated the physical nature of color around 1660. Having separated color into the spectrum—red on top and violet on the bottom—he was the first to conceive of it as a color wheel. Ingeniously, he twisted what was a straight-line spectrum, joined the ends, and inserted purple, a color leaning to red-violet and not found in the spectrum. This red-violet he saw as a transition between violet and red. Newton's wheel contained seven colors, which he related to the seven known planets and the seven notes of the diatonic scale in music (the standard major scale without chromatic half-steps)—red corresponding to note C, orange to D, yellow to E, green to F, blue to G, indigo to A, and violet to B.

The Discovery of Pigment Primaries

Around 1731, J. C. Le Blon recognized the primary characteristic of the pigments of red, yellow, and blue and their ability to create orange, green, and violet. To this day, his discovery remains the basis of pigment color theory.

The First Triadic Color Wheel

The first wheel in full color and based on the three-primary system was published around 1766. It appeared in a book titled *The Natural System of Colours* by Morris Harris, an English engraver. In the first decade of the nineteenth century, Johann Wolfgang von Goethe began placing the colors, with their triangular arrangements, around a circle. In addition, Philipp Otto Runge created the first color solid (a three-dimensional color organization) by exploring tints, tones, and shades of color.

American Educators

In the United States, many educators advanced the red, yellow, and blue primary color wheels. Most noted among them was Louis Prang, who published *The Theory of Color* in 1876. Modern-day scholars like Johanness Itten, Faber Birren, and Joseph Albers have done much to explore the relationship between color and expression. Their research has also clarified the historical development of the triadic color system and how colors interact, each affecting the perception of the other.

The Ostwald Color System

A distinguished German chemist and physicist, Wilhelm Ostwald, developed a color system around 1916 related to psychological harmony and order. Created from pigment hues technically available at the time, it used red, yellow, sea green, and blue, with the secondaries orange, purple, turquoise, and leaf green. The colors were placed in a circle and expanded by mixing neighboring colors into a 24-hue system—capable of further expansion. Complements were placed opposite each other—blue opposite yellow, for example. Strict rules for standardizing colors for industrial application were used. A three-dimensional model placed each color on the apex of a triangle and black and white on the other two points. The color harmonies were based on mathematical relationships that doubled the tonal color change at each step from white to black, providing an even progression in the steps. This system concentrated on value changes, with intensity being controlled by and limited to the initial point of the triangle. The system was never fully adopted for industrial application.

The Munsell Color System

Around 1936, the American artist Albert Munsell formulated a system to show the relationships between different color tints and shades based on hue, value, and intensity. This system was an attempt to give names to the many varieties of hues that result from mixing different colors with each other or with the neutrals. American industry adopted the Munsell system in 1943 as its material standard for naming different colors. The system was also adopted by the United States Bureau of Standards in Washington, D.C.

In the Munsell system, the five basic hues on the color wheel are red, yellow, green, blue, and purple (violet). The mixture of any two of these colors that are adjacent on this color wheel is called an intermediate color. For example, the mixture of red and yellow is the intermediate color yellow-red. The other intermediate hues are green-yellow, blue-green, purple-blue, and red-purple.

To clarify color relationships, Munsell devised a three-dimensional color system that classifies the different shades or variations of colors according to the qualities of hue, value, and intensity (or chroma). His system is in the form of a tree. The many different color tones are adhered to transparent plastic vanes that extend from a central trunk like tree branches. The column nearest the center trunk shows a scale of neutral tones that begin with black at the bottom and rise through grays to white at the top. The color tone at the outer limit of each branch represents the most intense hue possible at each level of value (fig. 7.28).

The most important part of the Munsell color system is the color notation, which describes a color in terms of a letter and numeral formula. The hue is indicated by the notation found on the inner circle of the color wheel. The

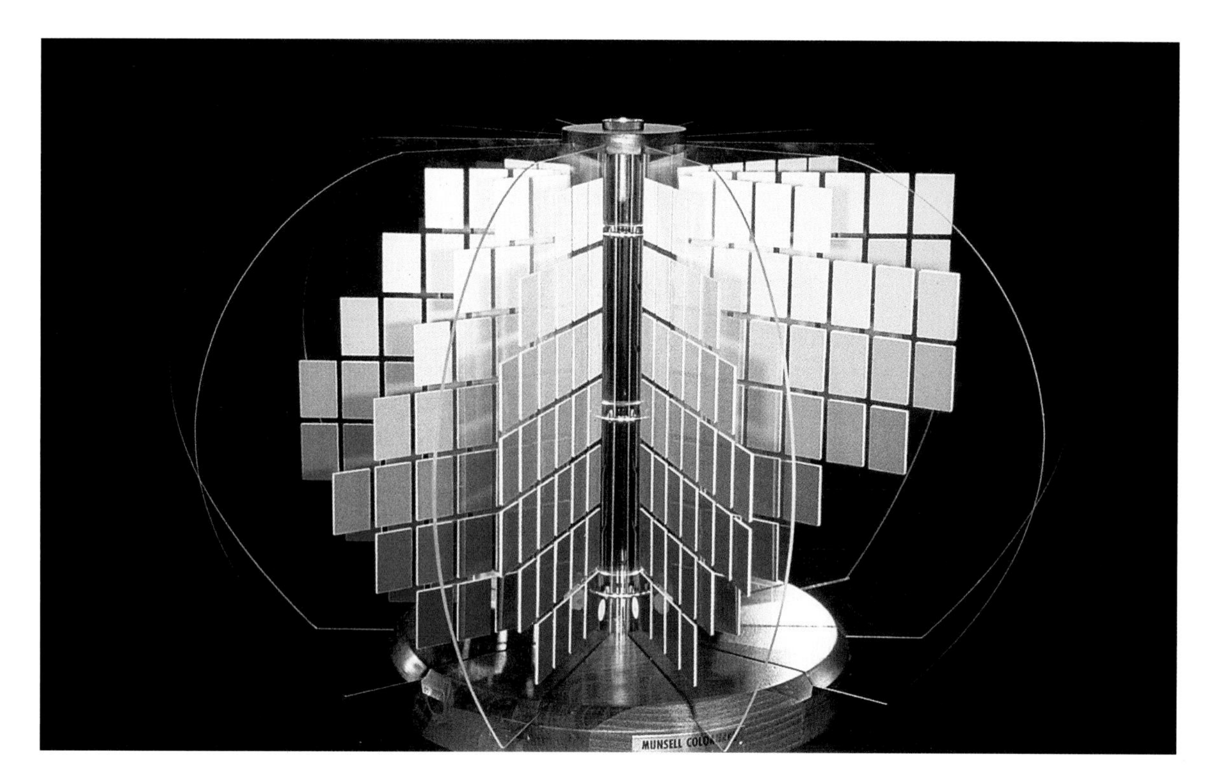

7.28 Munsell color tree, 1972. Clear plastic chart 10½ × 12 in. (26.7 × 30.5 cm); base size 12 in. (30.5 cm) diameter; center pole size 12⅝ in. (32.1 cm) high; chip size ¾ × 1⅜ in. (1.9 × 3.5 cm). The Munsell system in three dimensions. The greatest intensity of each hue is found in the color vane farthest from the center trunk. The value of each vane changes as it moves up and down the tree. The center trunk changes only from light to dark. The colors change in hue as they move around the tree. Courtesy of Macbeth, New Windsor, NY.

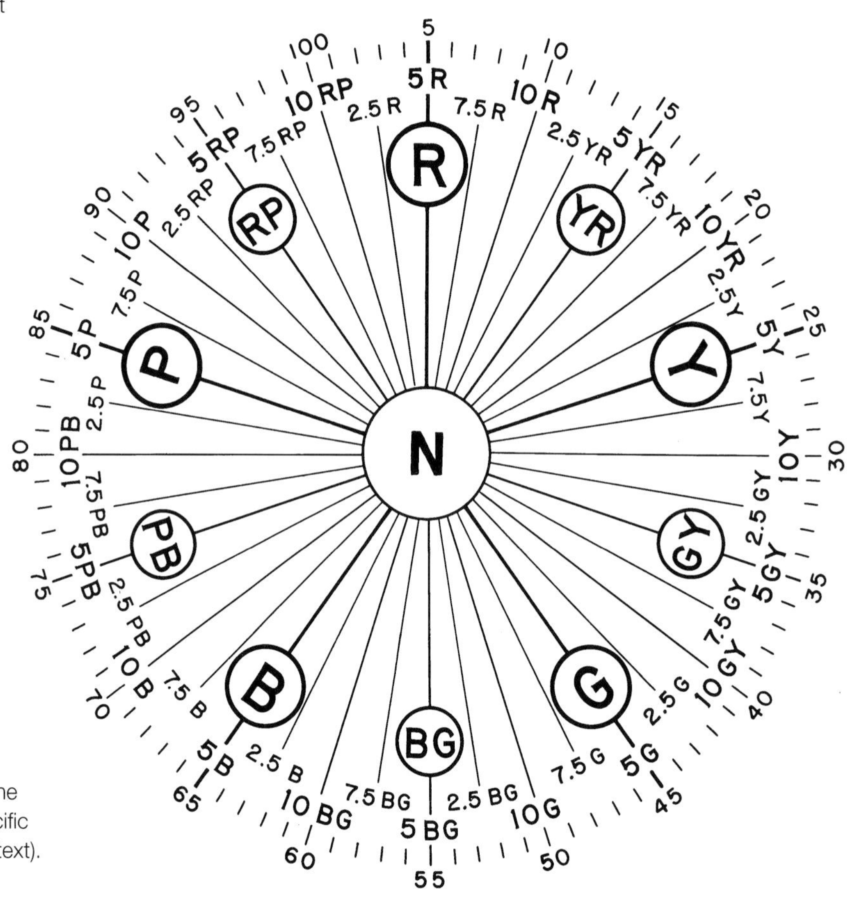

7.29 Munsell color wheel. This diagram shows the relationships of the hues on the wheel in terms of a specific type of notation (as explained in the text). Courtesy of Macbeth, New Windsor, NY.

value of the colors is indicated by the numbers on the central trunk, as shown in figure 7.29. The intensity, or chroma, is shown by the numbers on the vanes that radiate from the trunk. These value and intensity relationships are expressed by fractions, with the number on top representing the value and the number on the bottom indicating the intensity (chroma). For example, $^{5Y}\frac{8}{12}$ is the notation for a bright yellow.

It is interesting to compare the Munsell color wheel with the one used in this book (fig. 7.29; see fig. 7.7). Munsell places blue opposite yellow-red and red opposite blue-green, whereas we place blue opposite orange and red opposite green.

The Subtractive Printing System (Process Color System)

We have already discussed how we experience color by reflected light. A colored object reflects only the wavelengths of that color while absorbing all others (see "Subtractive Color," p. 145). By taking the reflected wavelengths and passing them through specific camera filters, photographers and printers have learned how to isolate individual wavelengths and photograph them. They found that when light passed through a sheet of clear glass, all the color wavelengths passed through. When a red-colored glass was used, only the wavelengths of red were allowed to pass through, all others being absorbed; the blocked wavelengths equaled red's opposite or the additive light complement of red, which was cyan. Thus, a red glass camera filter blocked all exposure on black-and-white film except for the shades of red that were recorded as gray to black shapes on the negative. The wavelengths removed by the filter (equaling red's complement cyan) were also recorded as transparent areas on the negative. When a photosensitive printing plate was exposed through the negative film, the transparent areas allowed exposure of the plate, making it printable—revealing the levels of cyan. Where the negative was opaque black (from recording the red wavelengths), the unexposed printing plate remained white and unprintable.

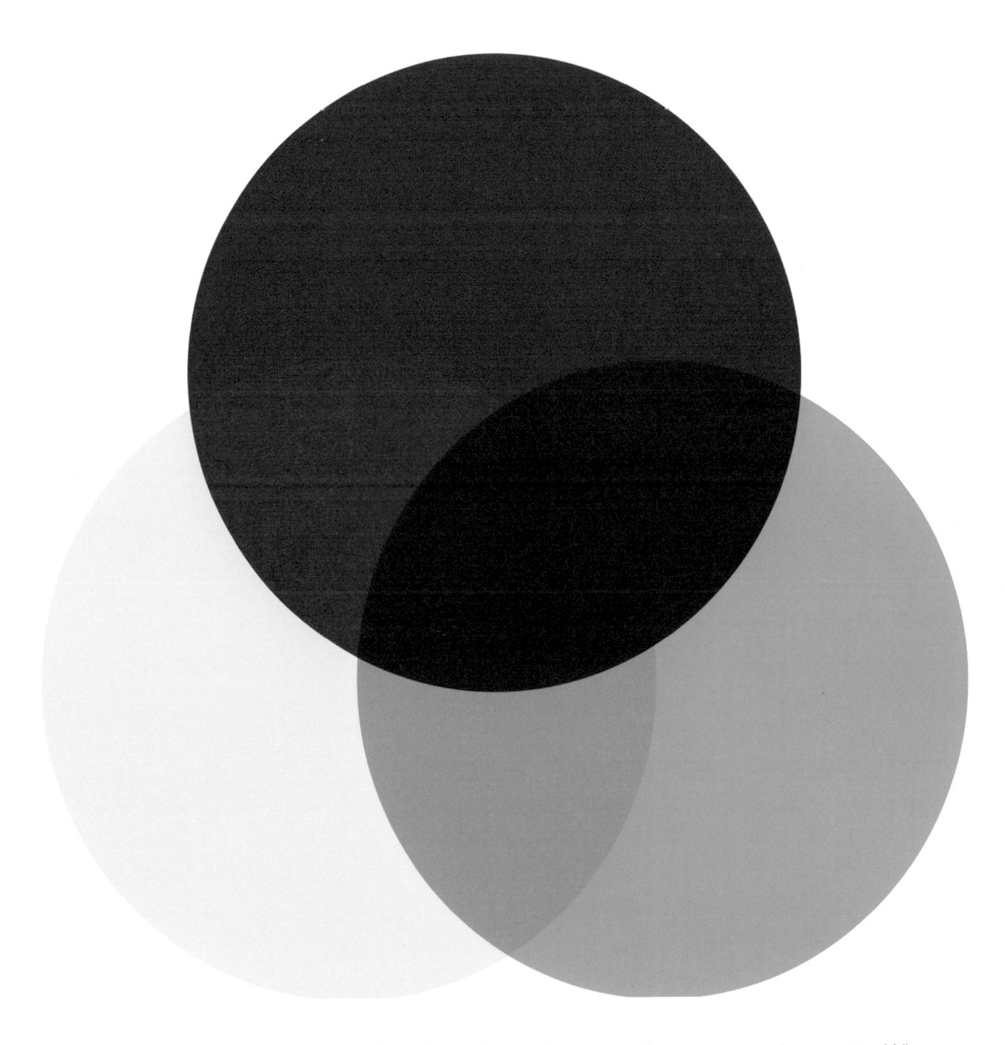

7.30 The primary colors of the subtractive color system are yellow, cyan, and magenta. Where they are mixed they produce red, blue (a color named by industry and scientists that is actually closer to violet), and green. When all three are combined, they produce black. Notice that the subtractive color primaries are the additive secondary colors and that the subtractive secondary colors are the additive primary colors.

When this process was completed using a green filter, a printing plate for the value levels of magenta was created. Similarly, photographing through a filter named "blue"—actually on the violet side—produced a plate printing in the value ranges of yellow.

Using these techniques to produce printing plates, printers and photographers have created a special color organization with the primary colors of magenta, yellow, and cyan (fig. 7.30). Notice that these primaries are the secondary colors in the additive (light) system (see fig. 7.3), and they aren't the primary colors of red, yellow, and blue familiar to the studio artist. In this system, red is a mixed color! Artists who work with dyes, color printing for photography, transparent inks, and the printing industry will need to become familiar with the subtractive primaries of magenta, yellow, and cyan.

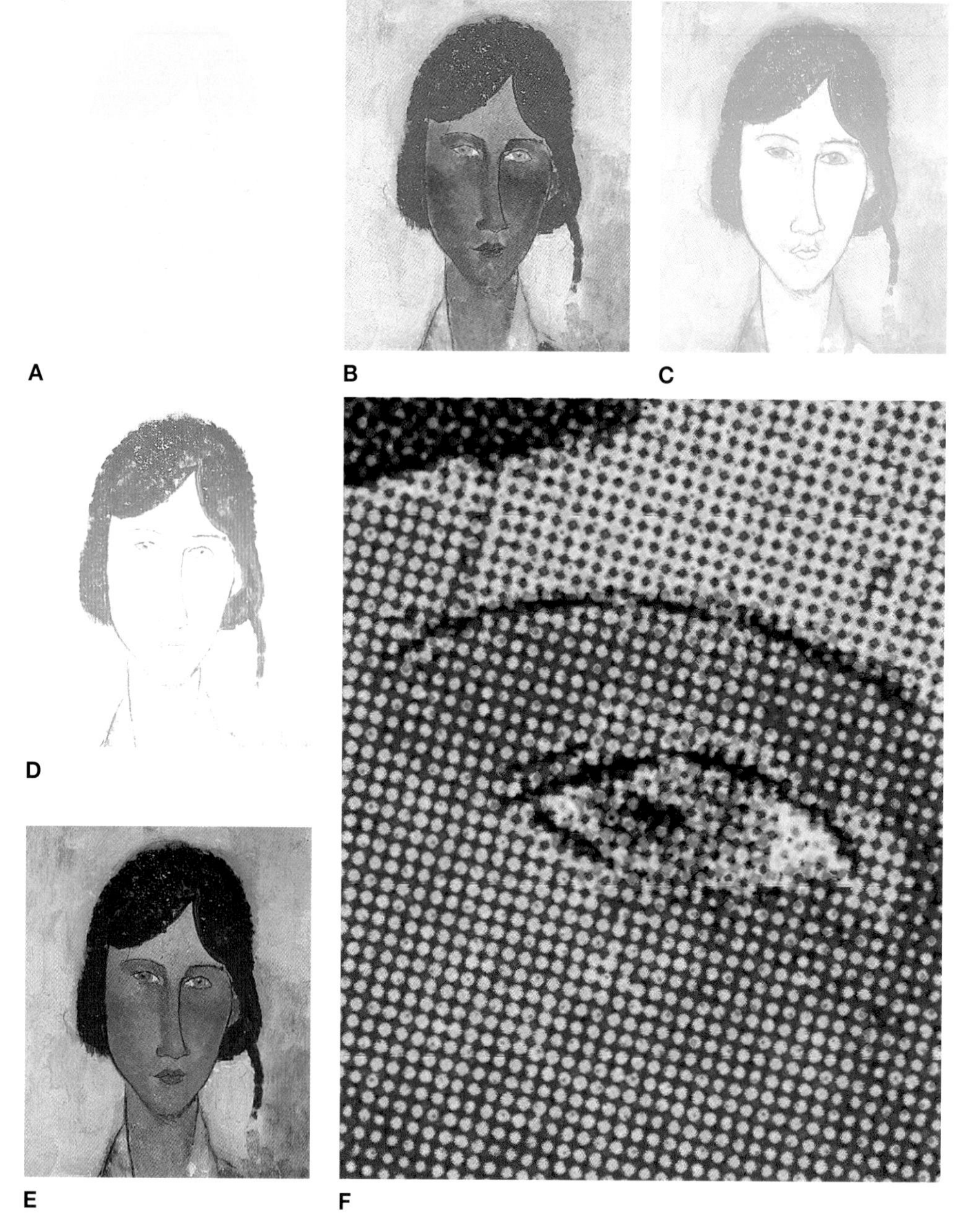

7.31 These illustrations show the yellow (A), magenta (B), cyan (C), and black (D) printing plates used in the four-color printing process. When layered together, they produce the full color image (E), a detail of Modigliani's *Gypsy Woman with Baby.* An enlargement shows the dots printed from each plate and the colors created where the yellow, magenta, cyan, and black inks overlap (F). © National Gallery of Art, Washington/SuperStock.

The printing industry has applied these subtractive primaries to the four-color printing process and has made great advances in color reproduction. Several existing techniques came together to make this process possible:

1. Monochrome photography provided images in black, white, and a full value range of unbroken grays.
2. Halftoning was invented, which allowed all the shades of gray to be printed by one shade of ink—black on white paper. This was done by translating grays into networks of tiny black-and-white dots of differing sizes for different values.
3. It was discovered that photographing a colored image through various colored filters and adding halftoning could create a printing plate with the proper range of value for each of the primaries—magenta, yellow, and cyan (fig. 7.31 A–C).

When the printing plates for cyan, magenta, and yellow are layered together, all the colors and value ranges possible are created. Where the magenta and yellow overlap, red (a pigment primary for the artist's palette) is created as a secondary color. Where the magenta is decreased and the yellow increased, the color swings more toward orange—and so on, depending on the adjustment of the two colors. Similarly, the other subtractive color mixing secondary colors are created by overprinting the remaining primaries: Cyan plus magenta produces blue, and cyan plus yellow produces green. Overprinting cyan, magenta, and yellow creates something close to black, but that is usually heightened by printing the fourth plate in black to add definition (fig. 7.31 D–F).

Color Photography

Color photographers also use magenta, cyan, and yellow. Instead of artists' pigment, they develop color using dyes and gelatin emulsions. Colored film contains three layers of emulsion that respond to blue, red, and green light. When the exposed film is developed, a multilayered negative results. Light-sensitive silver halide compounds are converted to metallic compounds by the developer. In the process, they oxidize and combine with "coupler" compounds to produce dyes. Each layer forms one of the three dyes that are the subtractive primaries—yellow, magenta, and cyan. A yellow image is formed on the blue-sensitive layer; a magenta image forms on the green-sensitive layer; and a cyan image is created on the red-sensitive layer. Next, the silver is bleached out of each layer, leaving only the appropriate colored dye on the correct layer. Color negatives, positive color transparencies (slides), and color printers all involve this same basic process (fig. 7.32).

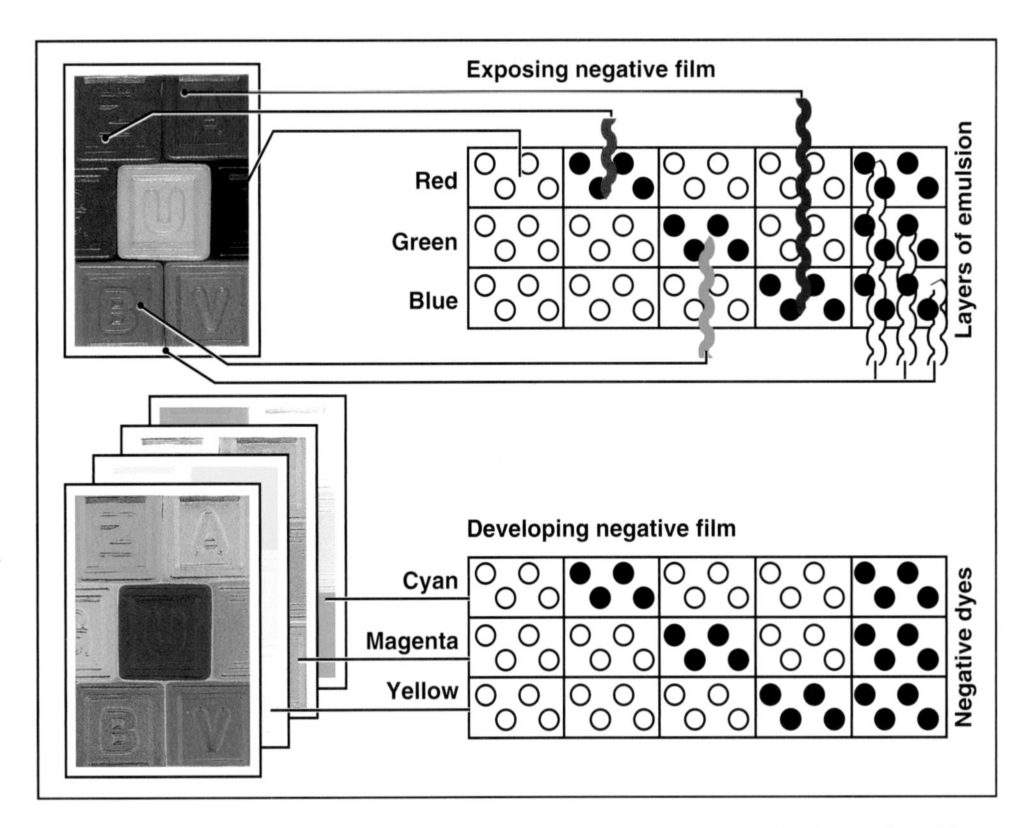

7.32 When color negative film is exposed, the blue-, green-, and red-sensitive layers of emulsion (color spots) record latent images (gray dots) that can be developed into black-and-white negatives. Colors that are mixtures of the primaries are recorded on several layers. Blacks do not expose any of the emulsion, while white light is recorded in all layers. Each color thus leaves a corresponding negative black-and-white impression.

When exposed color negative film is developed, a black-and-white negative image is produced in each emulsion layer (black dots). During this development, a colored dye is combined with each black-and-white negative image. The dyes are cyan, magenta, and yellow. Once the silver is bleached out, the three layers (colored dots) show the subject in superimposed negative dye images. Photograph by Bob Coyle/© McGraw-Hill Higher Education.

Color Computer Printing

Electronic imagery—drawn by hand, imported by scanning, or created by digital camera—requires a computer printer to produce a paper image. Most printers employ a CYMK ink system, which is an acronym for cyan, yellow, magenta (the subtractive color mixing system primaries in ink form), and black. "K" is used to denote black to avoid the confusion of black with blue. Because the computer images are created on the color monitor, each of these colors is in turn printed on paper simulating the illumination of the pixels on the monitor. The eight basic colors are produced by printing the primaries either alone or in various combinations: "black" (requiring all the primaries), red, green, blue, cyan, magenta, and yellow. "White" is a result of the color of the paper stock being used. Cyan and magenta produce "blue" (a color closer to violet); yellow and cyan produce green; and magenta and yellow produce red.

Printers now have the capacity of printing colored detail so fine that it is difficult to see without magnification. This is determined by the size of the dot pattern. Color printers are capable of more than 300 dots per inch. Hundreds of dots of varied colors can be printed in a small area. The closeness of the dots of color, the variety of colors printed, and their concentration in an area produce virtually any color and/or value the artist desires.

Many color printers now have programs that allow the artist to greatly alter the mood and appearance of the finished image. Increasing the percentage of any of the primaries or their value levels may dramatically change the intensity, mood, and spirit of the presentation. By using additive light, the color printer can become an interesting tool for color manipulation. The final image is printed using the subtractive printing system primaries of cyan, yellow, and magenta, followed by black.

(See the CD-ROM for illustrations using standard relationships of CYMK inks and illustrations of how the images have been affected by changing the percentages of CYMK.)

The Discovery of Light Primaries

Paralleling early developments with pigment was the discovery around 1790 of the red, green, and blue light primaries.

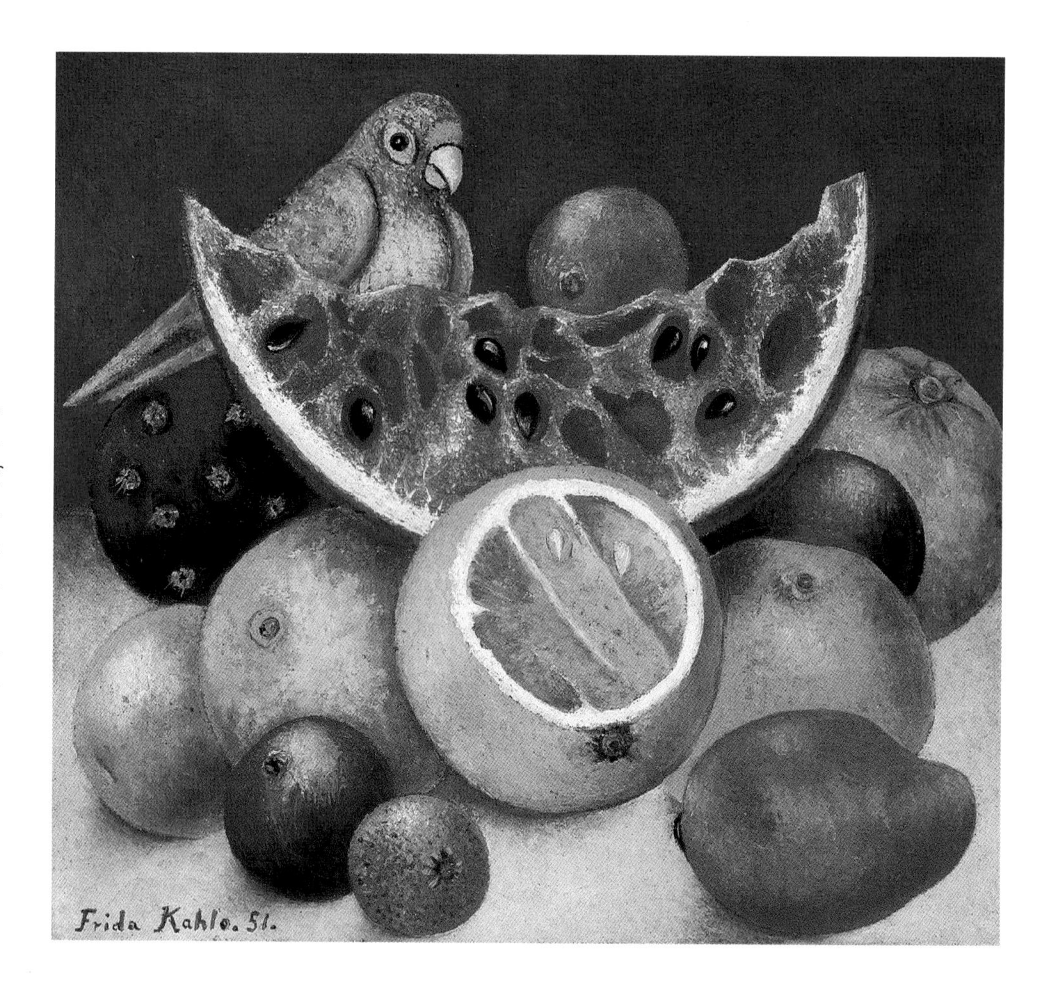

7.33 Frida Kahlo, *Still Life with Parrot*, 1951. Oil on masonite, 9½ × 10¼ in. (24.1 × 26 cm). This still life is painted in local color—color that simulates the hues of the objects in nature. Art Collection, Harry Ransom Humanities Research Center, University of Texas at Austin. Reproduction authorized by National Institute of Fine Art and Literature of Mexico.

These concepts were explored by scientists Hermann von Helmholtz of Germany and James Clerk Maxwell of Great Britain. Some additive-light primary systems have been represented as circles, but they should not be confused with color systems designed for artists' pigment. Space does not permit discussion of all the color systems that have evolved.

THE ROLE OF COLOR IN COMPOSITION

When painting was seen as a purely illustrative art, the description of appearances was considered color's most important function. For a long period in the history of Western art, color was seen as arising from the object being represented. In painting, color that is used to indicate the natural appearance of an object is known as **local (objective) color** (fig. 7.33). Yet an expressive quality is achieved when the artist depicts objects in colors other than their conventional local color. An entirely **subjective color** treatment can be substituted for local color. The colors used and their relationships are invented by the artist for purposes other than mere representation (fig. 7.34). This style of treatment may even deny color as an objective reality; that is, we may have purple cows, green faces, or red trees. When colors are subjectively applied, as in much of contemporary art, an understanding of their use becomes critical to an understanding of their meaning.

In artistic composition, color serves several purposes. These purposes are not separate and distinct, but instead frequently overlap and interrelate. We have seen that color can be used in the following ways:

1. To give spatial quality to the pictorial field.
   a. Color can supplement, or even substitute for, value differences to give plastic quality.
   b. Color can create interest through the counterbalance of backward and forward movement in pictorial space.
2. To create mood and symbolize ideas.
3. To serve as a vehicle for expressing personal emotions and feelings.
4. To attract and direct attention as a means of giving organization to a composition.
5. To accomplish aesthetic appeal by a system of well-ordered color relationships.
6. To identify objects by describing the superficial facts of their appearance.

COLOR BALANCE

Any attempt to base the aesthetic effect of color pattern on certain fixed color harmonies will probably not be successful. The effect depends as much on how we distribute our color as on the relationships among the hues themselves. All good color combinations have some similarities and some contrasts, and the

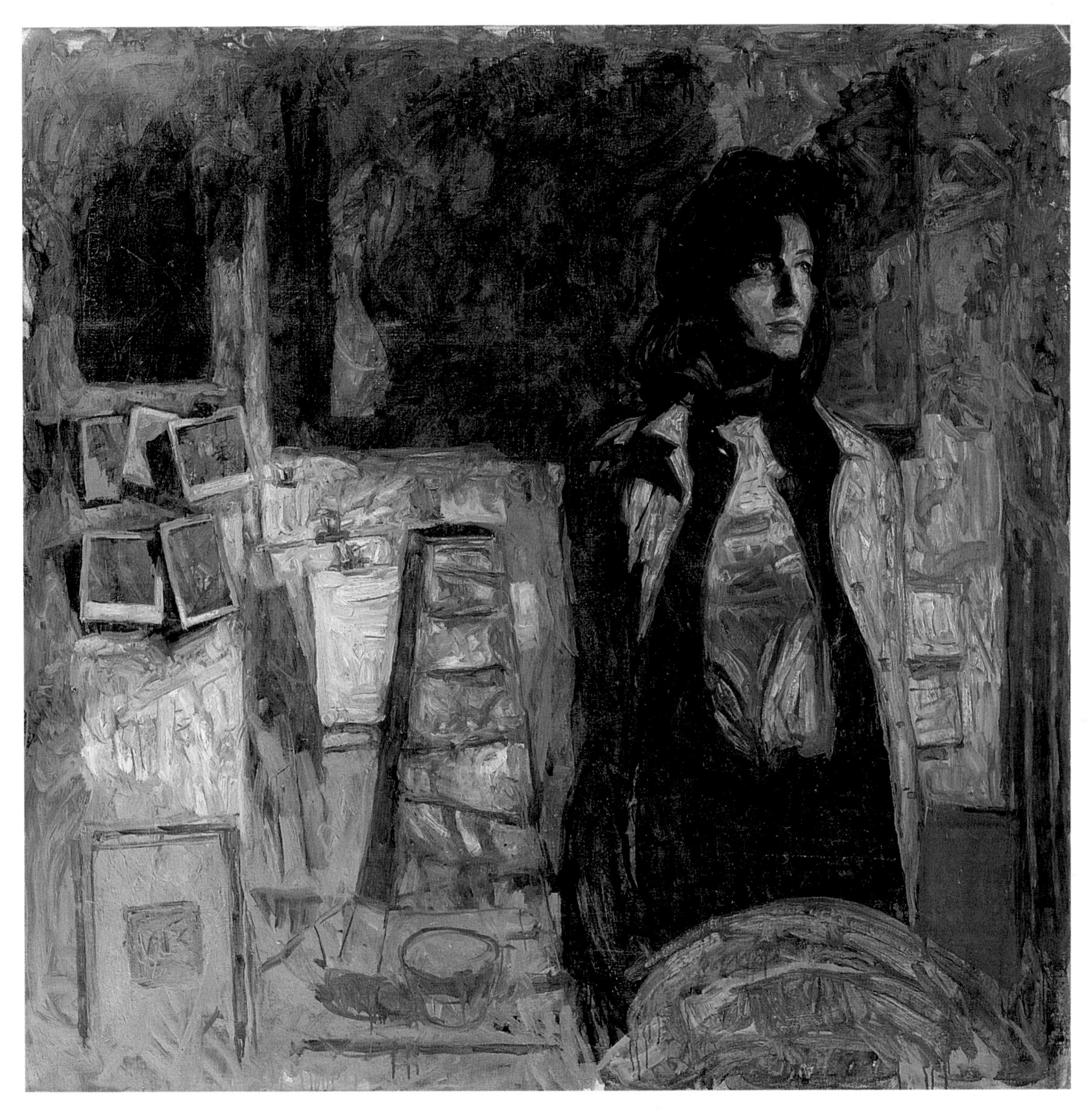

7.34 Gilles Marrey, *1997*, 1998. Oil on canvas, 55 × 56 in. (140 × 142 cm). The subjective or invented color relationships in this painting may not be as obvious as a "blue horse," but they effectively set up the mood and mystery within this painting. © Caldwell Snyder Gallery, NY.

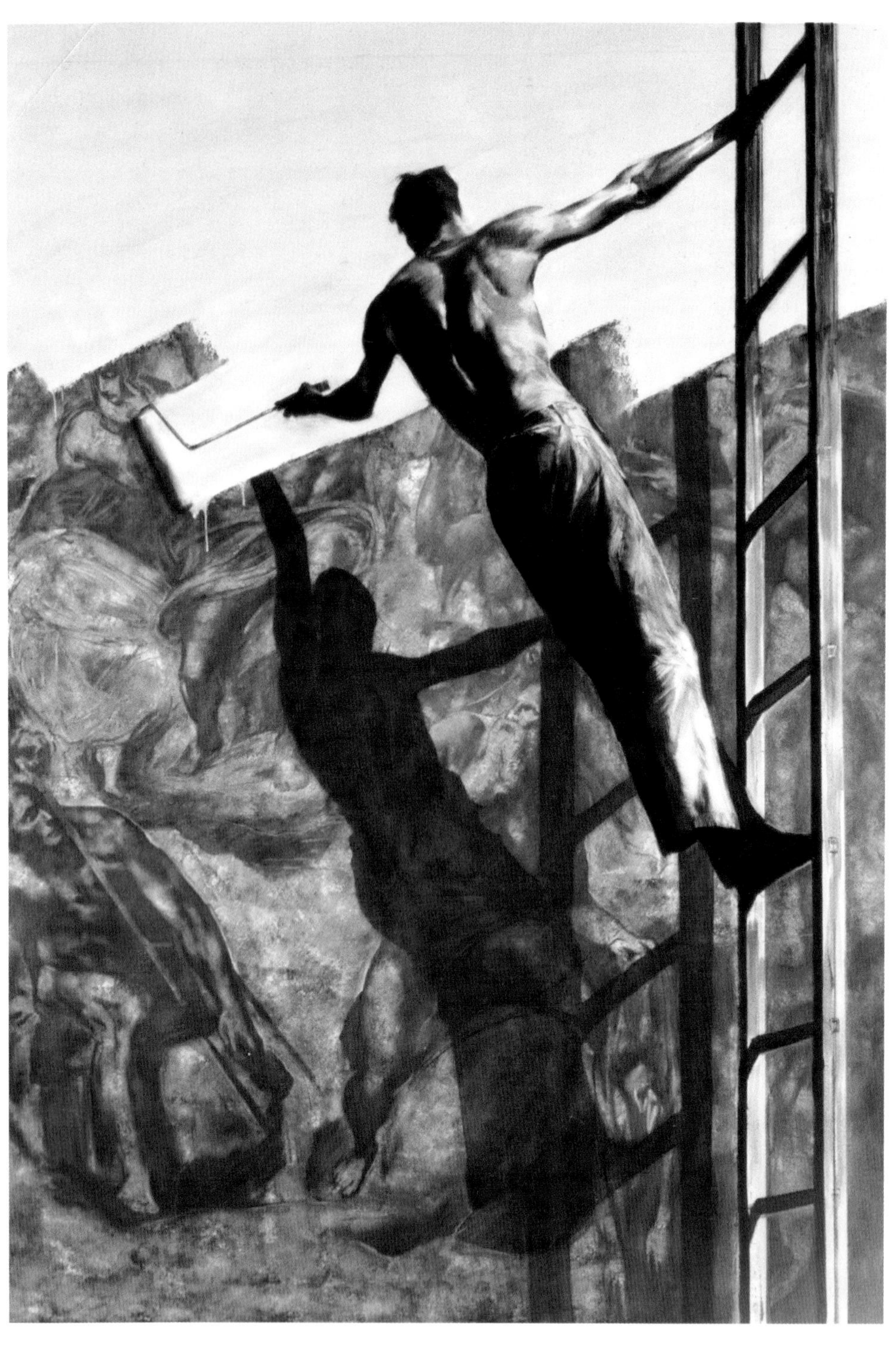

7.35 Mark Tansey, *Triumph over Mastery II*, 1987. Oil on canvas, 98 × 68 in. The harmony and serenity of Tansey's monochromatic palette is deceptive for the viewer. Only close inspection reveals its picture within a picture structure. The figure in the image is rolling paint over Michelangelo's *Last Judgment.* Courtesy Gagosian Gallery, New York.

basic problem remains the same as in all aspects of form organization: variety in unity. Harmonious relationships must exist between the various hues, but these relationships must be made alive and interesting through variety.

Color and Harmony

Let us look first at how to harmonize the color relationships. The pleasing quality of a color pattern frequently depends on the amount or proportion of color used. A simple way to create harmony and balance is to repeat a color in differing values and intensities (fig. 7.35) while controlling its placement in different parts of a composition. This one hue can also be a harmonizing factor if a little of it is mixed with every color used (see fig. 7.14). A similar effect can be created by glazing over a varicolored pattern with a single transparent color, which becomes the unifying hue. In general, equal amounts of different colors are not as interesting as a color arrangement where one color, or one kind of color, predominates (see fig. 10.50). Such a unified pattern is found when all warm or all cool colors are used in combination. Again, however, a small amount of a complementary color or a contrasting neutral can add variety to the color pattern (see fig. 4.15). As a rule, where warm and cool colors are balanced against each other in a composition, it is better to allow one temperature to dominate (see fig. 7.19). The dominance of any one color in a pattern can be because of its hue, value, or intensity; when the hue intervals are closely related, as in analogous colors, greater related areas may become dominant. However, when color dominance is not enough to pull an organization together and the image is still difficult to understand, the image can be made readable by the character of the surrounding areas (fig. 7.36).

A wide range of color may also be harmonized by bringing all the colors to

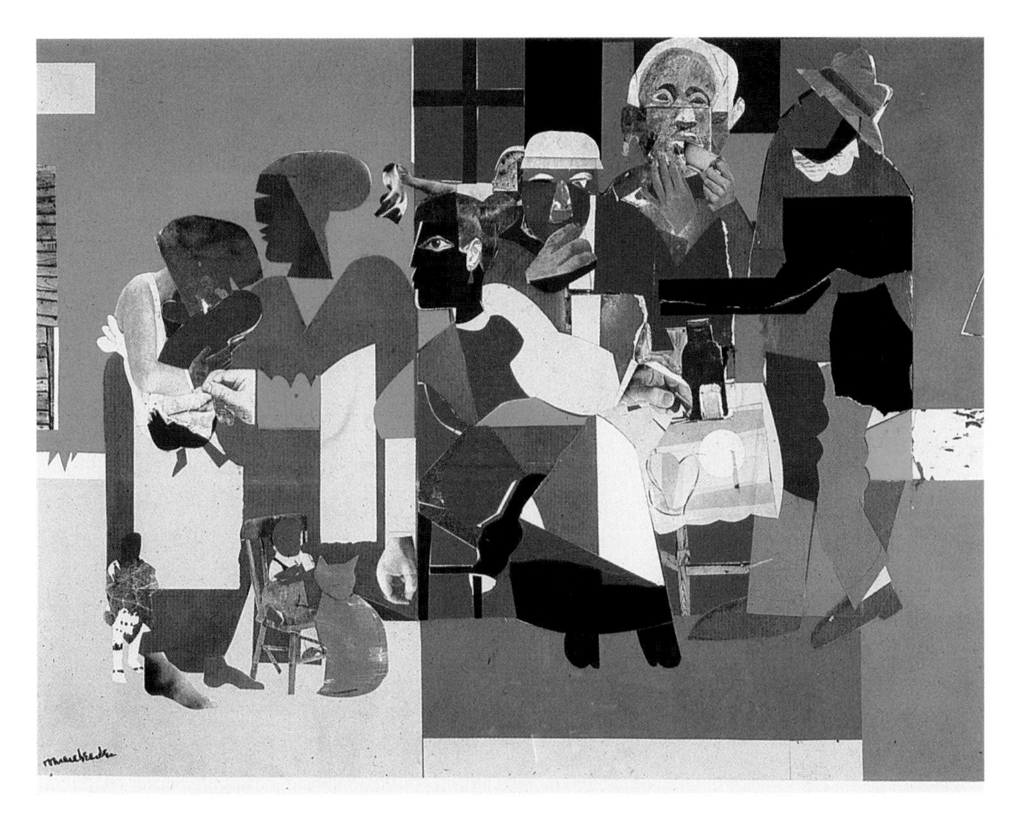

7.36 Romare Bearden, *Family Dinner,* 1968. Collage on board, 30 × 40 in. (76.2 × 101.6 cm). Though the analogous blues, blue-greens, and greens are the dominant hues in this painting, we understand the meaning of the work because of the contrast of the dark shapes, their symbolic character, and the recognizable human features.

a similar value level or making their intensity levels correspond. Where the basic unity of a color pattern has been established, strong contrasts of color hue, value, or intensity can be used in small accents; their size, then, prevents them from disturbing the basic unity of the color scheme (fig. 7.37). Low-key or high-key compositions benefit greatly from such contrasting accents, which add interest to what might otherwise be a monotonous composition (see figs. 4.19 and 10.10).

7.37 Fernando Pomalaza, *Past and Present,* 1999. Mixed media on canvas, 18 × 26 in. (101.6 × 137.2 cm). In this painting, the basic color unity has been established by the warm ochers and browns, but small accents of contrasting value, hue, and intensity add visual interest and prevent it from becoming monotonous. Courtesy of the artist and Jain Marunouchi Gallery.

Color and Variety

In an attempt to become overly harmonious, we are often confused by color schemes in which all of the tones become equally important, because we cannot find a dominant area on which to fix our attention. It is sometimes necessary to develop hue combinations that depend on strong contrast or a variety of

7.38 **Joan Mitchell, *Untitled,* 1992. Oil on canvas, 110¼ × 78¾ in. (280 × 200 cm).** Characterized by aggressive brushwork, Joan Mitchell's painting has a variety of highly contrasting colors and values: Large areas of dark are balanced by even larger areas of light value; blues are countered by smaller oranges, green by pink, and yellowish white by touches of violet. Reference MITC–0436. Courtesy of the artist's estate and the Robert Miller Gallery.

colors (figs. 7.38 and 7.39). With this type of color scheme, the hue intervals are farther apart, the greatest possible interval being that between two complementary colors. Color schemes based on strong contrasts of hue, value, or intensity have great possibilities for expressive effect. In the contrasting color scheme, the basic problem is to unify the contrasts without destroying the general strength and intensity of expression. These contrasts can sometimes be controlled by the amount of opposing color used (fig. 7.39; see also fig. 7.20). In this situation, a small, dark spot of color, through its lower value, can dominate a large, light area. At other times, a spot of intense color, though small, can balance a larger amount of a grayer, more neutralized color (see fig. 7.34). Also, a small amount of warm color usually dominates a larger amount of cool color, although both may be of the same intensity (see fig. 7.21).

Complementary colors, which are vying for our attention through simultaneous contrast, can be made more attractive if one of them is softened or neutralized. Another commonly used method of slightly softening exaggerated

7.39 **Norman Sunshine, *Double Fugue (diptych),* 2000. Oil on canvas, 60 × 96 in. (152.4 × 243.8 cm).** This still-life painting presents two visual units, similar in image and shape placement. A unique vantage point is complemented by the highly contrasting use of color and value and their differing treatment in both units. Private collection. Photograph courtesy of Neuhoff Gallery, New York. Photograph by Michael Korol.

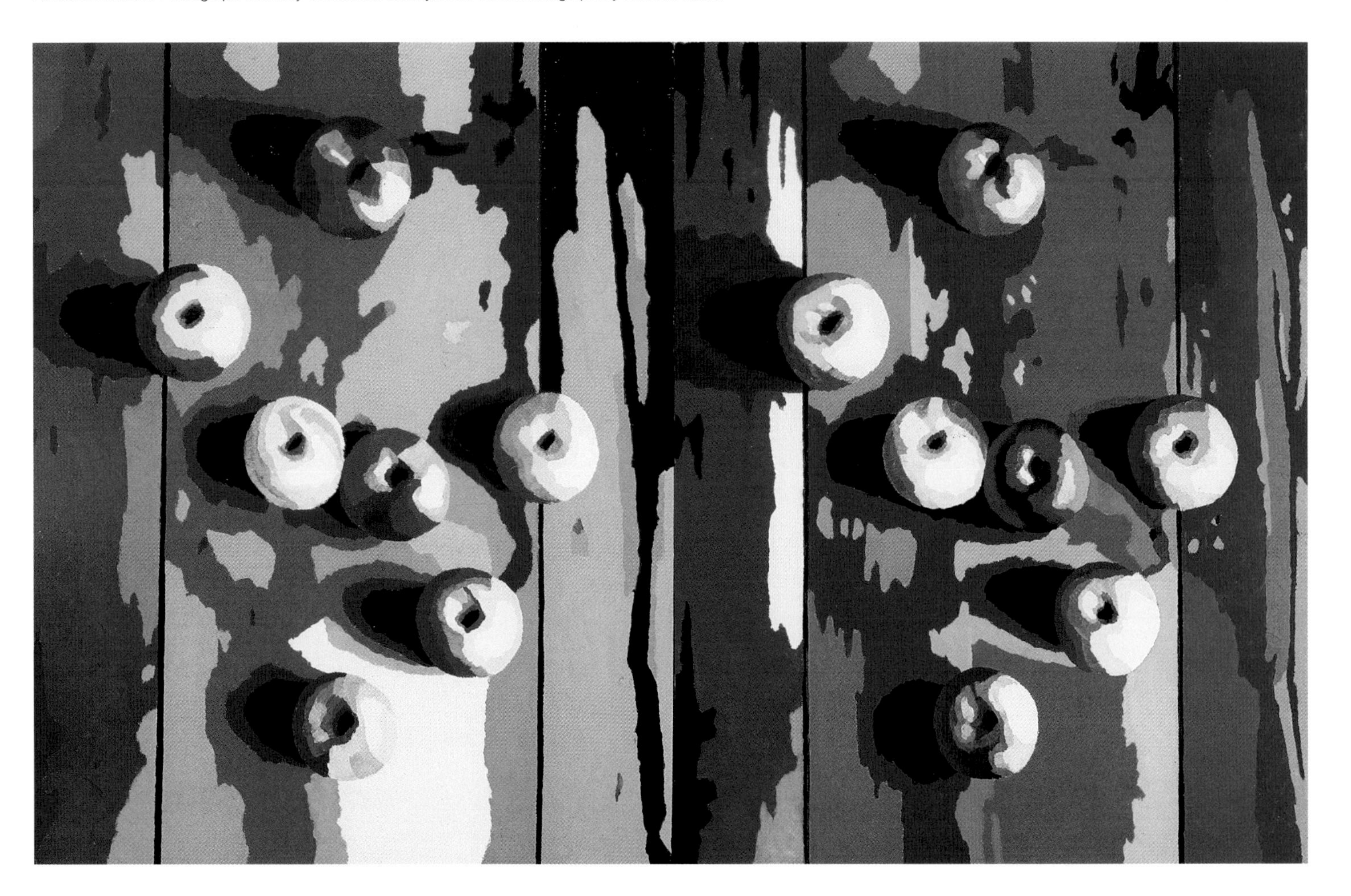

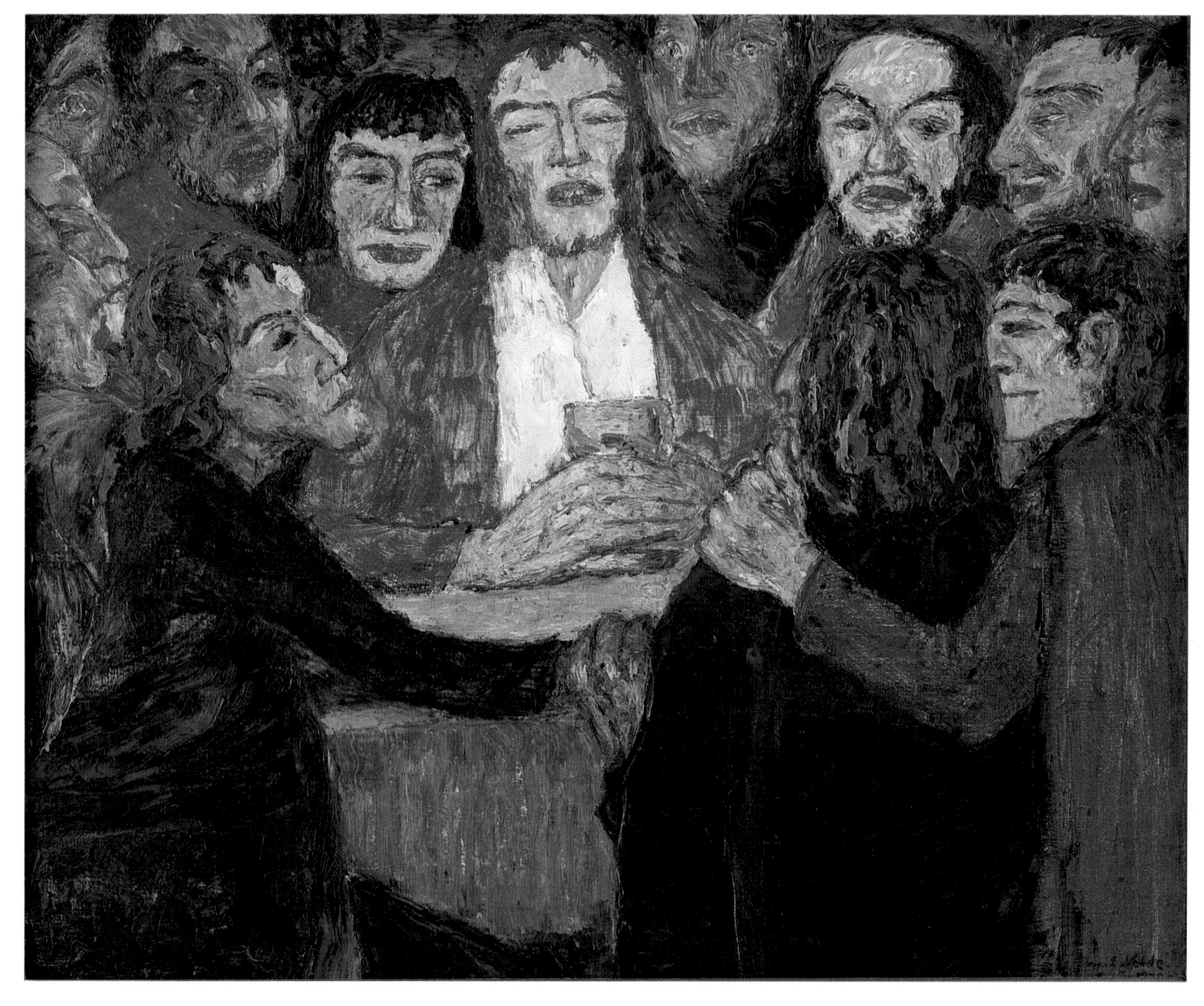

7.40 **Emil Nolde, *The Last Supper,* 1909. Oil on canvas, 33⅞ × 42⅛ in. (86 × 107 cm).** The Expressionists usually employed bold, clashing hues to emphasize their emotional identification with a subject. Intense feeling is created by the use of complementary and near-complementary hues.
Courtesy of the Statens Museum for Kunst, Copenhagen.

contrasts is to separate all or a part of the colors by a neutral line or area. Absolute black or white lines are the most effective neutrals for this purpose because they are so positive in character themselves. They not only tie together the contrasting hues but also enhance their color character because of value contrast. The lead outlines between the brilliant colors of stained-glass windows are an example of this unifying character. Likewise, the modern painters Georges Rouault and Max Beckmann found black effective in separating highly contrasting colors (see figs. 10.29 and 10.35). A similar unifying effect can be brought about by using a large area of neutral or light gray or a **neutralized color** as a background for clashing contrasts of color (fig. 7.38, see fig. 2.12).

Finally, we should remember that artists frequently produce color combinations that defy these guiding principles but are still satisfying to the eye. Artists use color as they do the other elements of art structure—to give a highly personalized meaning to the subject of their work. We must realize that there can be brutal color combinations as well as refined ones. These brutal combinations are satisfying if they accomplish the artist's purpose of exciting us rather than calming us. Some German Expressionist paintings show how these brutal, clashing color schemes can be used purposefully (fig. 7.40). No exact rules exist for arriving at pleasing color relationships, but we have discussed some guiding principles. With this foundation, every artist can build his or her own language of color in dynamic interaction with each work.

INVESTIGATE THE CD-ROM **Questions to Ask Yourself**

Color reflects the light of the universe, reaching our innermost feelings.

As you review this chapter on the CD-ROM, think about the use of color in an artwork that you particularly like, and answer these questions:

1. How has the artist used color?
2. What colors or combinations of color particularly appeal to you? Why do you think this is so?
3. Now try to imagine changing colors in the artwork. What colors would you change? How would this change the meaning of the artwork?
4. How would you feel in a world without color?

CHAPTER EIGHT

Space

THE VOCABULARY OF SPACE

INTRODUCTION TO SPACE

SPATIAL PERCEPTION

MAJOR TYPES OF SPACE

- Decorative Space
- Plastic Space
  - *Divisions of Plastic Space*

SPATIAL INDICATORS

- Sharp and Diminishing Detail
- Size
- Position
- Overlapping
- Transparency
- Interpenetration
- Fractional Representation
- Converging Parallels
- Linear Perspective
  - *Major Systems of Linear Perspective*
  - *Perspective Concepts Applied*
  - *The Disadvantages of Linear Perspective*
- Other Projection Systems
- Intuitive Space

THE SPATIAL PROPERTIES OF THE ELEMENTS

- Line and Space
- Shape and Space
- Value and Space
- Texture and Space
- Color and Space

RECENT CONCEPTS OF SPACE

- The Search for a New Spatial Dimension
- Plastic Images
- Pictorial Representations of Movement in Time
  - *Motion Pictures*
  - *Video*
  - *The Computer and Art*

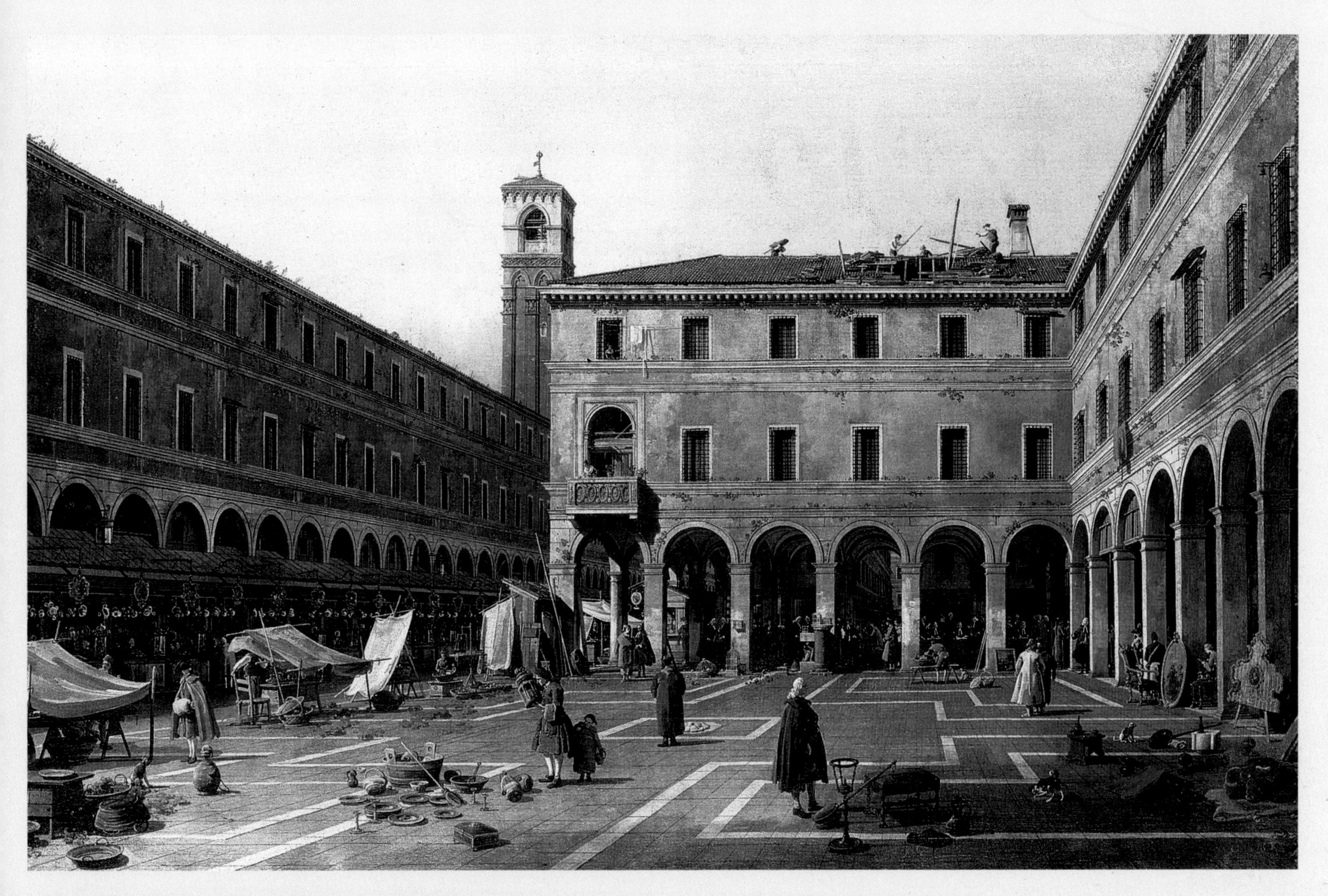

Antonio Canaletto, *Campo di Rialto,* c. 1756. Oil on canvas, 119 × 186 cm. Bildarchiv Preussicher Kulturbesitz/Art Resource, NY.

THE VOCABULARY OF **SPACE**

Space — The interval, or measurable distance, between points or images.

atmospheric perspective
The illusion of deep space produced in graphic works by lightening values, softening details and textures, reducing value contrasts, and neutralizing colors in objects as they recede (see **perspective**).

decorative space
Ornamenting or enriching but, more importantly in art, stressing the two-dimensional nature of an artwork or any of its elements. Decorative art (space) emphasizes the essential flatness of a surface.

four-dimensional space
An imaginative treatment of forms that gives a sense of intervals of time or motion.

fractional representation
A pictorial device (used notably by the Egyptians) in which several spatial aspects of the same subject are combined in the same image.

infinite space
Pictorial space in which the picture frame acts as a window through which objects can be seen receding endlessly.

interpenetration
The movement of planes, objects, or shapes through each other, locking them together within a specific area of space.

intuitive space
The illusion of space that the artist creates by instinctively manipulating certain space-producing devices, including overlapping, transparency, interpenetration, inclined planes, disproportionate scale, fractional representation, and the inherent spatial properties of the art elements.

isometric projection
A technical drawing system in which a three-dimensional object is presented two-dimensionally; starting with the nearest vertical edge, the horizontal edges of the object are drawn at a 30-degree angle and all verticals are projected perpendicularly from a horizontal base.

linear perspective
A system used to depict three-dimensional images on a two-dimensional surface; it develops the optical phenomenon of diminishing size by treating edges as converging parallel lines. They extend to a vanishing point or points on the horizon (eye level) and recede from the viewer (see **perspective**).

oblique projection
A technical drawing system in which a three-dimensional object is presented two-dimensionally, the front and back sides of the object are parallel to the horizontal base, and the other planes are drawn as parallels coming off the front plane at a 45-degree angle.

orthographic drawing
Graphic representation of two-dimensional views of an object, showing a plan, vertical elevations, and/or a section.

perspective
Any graphic system used in creating the illusion of three-dimensional images and/or spatial relationships on a two-dimensional surface. There are several types of perspectives—atmospheric, linear, and projection systems.

plastic (space)
1. The use of the elements to create the illusion of the third dimension on a two-dimensional surface. 2. Three-dimensional art forms, such as architecture, sculpture, and ceramics.

shallow space
The illusion of limited depth. With shallow space, the imagery appears to move only a slight distance back from the picture plane.

three-dimensional (space)
Possessing, or creating the illusion of possessing, the dimension of depth, as well as the dimensions of height and width.

transparency
A visual quality in which a distant image or element can be seen through a nearer one.

two-dimensional (space)
Possessing the dimensions of height and width, especially when considering the flat surface or picture plane.

INTRODUCTION TO SPACE

Today, the mention of space makes us think of spaceships, a space station, the solar system, and the infinite cosmos beyond. Artists, too, have been interested in an unending deep space, but one, paradoxically, to be found right here on earth. As will soon be seen, artistic devices can give the illusion of this kind of infinite space. On the other hand, the artist may choose to limit the degree of space we see; we frequently find this kind of limit in the art of the Near and Far East. Space can be shrunk almost to the level of the picture plane, but not quite, because any element placed in a pictorial area immediately takes on some apparent depth in space. All of this is, of course, pure illusion in pictorial art, but it is not illusion for three-dimensional artists such as sculptors, jewelers, and architects, who produce objects that have their own space. **Space,** thus, concerns all artists, and they must find ways of dealing with it in a consistent manner.

Some people consider space as a genuine element in **two-dimensional** art, whereas others see it as a "product" of the elements. In this text, space is conceived of as a product rather than an element, being instead created by the elements. Space, as discussed in this chapter, is limited to the graphic fields—that is, such two-dimensional surface arts as drawing, painting, printmaking, and so forth. **Three-dimensional** space concepts are discussed in Chapter 9.

SPATIAL PERCEPTION

Our conceptions of space are conditioned by our experience of the world. Vision is perceived through the eyes but experienced by the mind. Visual experience involves the whole pattern of nerve and brain response to what we see. Our eyes perceive the world around us as we continually shift our focus of attention. In the process, we use two different types of vision: stereoscopic and kinesthetic. Having two eyes set slightly apart from each other, we receive two slightly different views of our visual field at the same time. The term *stereoscopic* refers to our ability to mentally combine these two slightly different views into one image. This process enables us to experience vision three-dimensionally and makes it possible for us to judge distances.

With kinesthetic vision we experience space by combining the movements of our eyes and bodies with our perceptions of the visual field. We traverse object surfaces with our eyes in order to recognize them. Likewise, our eyes travel while viewing an artwork, as we attempt to organize its separate parts to be seen as a whole. Furthermore, objects close to the viewer require more ocular movement than those farther away, and this kinesthetic eye activity adds spatial perception to our vision.

MAJOR TYPES OF SPACE

Two types of space can be suggested by the artist: **decorative space** and **plastic space.**

Decorative Space

Decorative space lacks real depth as we know it and is confined to the flatness of the picture plane. As the artist adds art elements to that plane (or surface), the illusion created appears flat or limited. In fact, a truly decorative space is difficult to achieve; any art element when used in conjunction with others will seem to advance or recede. The term *decorative space,* though sometimes useful in describing essentially flat pictorial effects, is hardly accurate because decorative space is so limited in depth (fig. 8.1; see fig. 5.15).

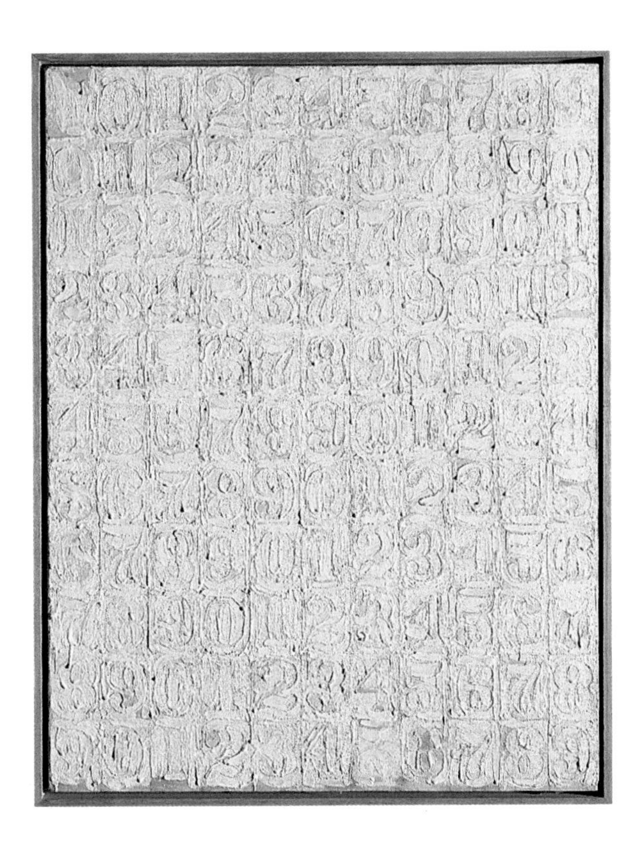

8.1 Jasper Johns, *White Numbers,* 1955. Encaustic on linen, 28 × 22 in. (71.1 × 55.9 cm). Though the heavy application of pigment casts shadows, in this decorative treatment there is no pictorial illusion of space, and the images appear very shallow on the picture's surface.

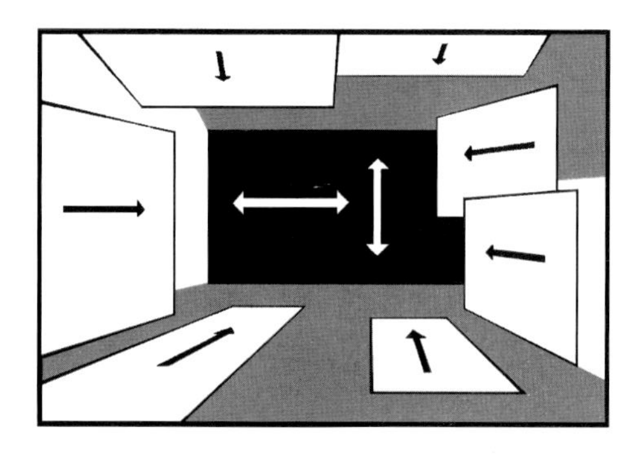

8.2 **Shallow space.** As a variation on the concept of shallow space, artists occasionally define the planes that make up the outer limits of a hollow boxlike space behind the picture plane. The diagram shows this concept, although in actual practice, a return to the picture plane would be made through objects occupying the space defined. The back plane acts as a curtain that prevents penetration into deep space.

Plastic Space

The term *plastic* applies to all spatial imagery other than decorative. Since artwork arises from our experiences of the world, it is natural that it should explore space.

Divisions of Plastic Space

Artists locate their images in plastic space according to their needs and feelings, and infinite range of depth is possible. As a result, analytical categorizations of depth are not specific or fixed but must remain general and adjustable to include broad conceptual areas.

Shallow Space

A concentration on the picture surface usually limits the depth of a composition. Varying degrees of limited space are possible. Limited space (or **shallow space**) can be compared to the feelings one might experience if confined to a box or stage. The space is limited by the placement of the sides or walls. For consistency, any compositional objects or figures that might appear in such stagelike confines should be narrowed in depth or flattened (fig. 8.2). In the modern painting *Cabinet Makers* by Jacob Lawrence, the figures have been flattened and placed in a confined room (fig. 8.3).

Asian, Egyptian, and European medieval painters used comparatively shallow space in their art. Early Renaissance paintings were often based on the shallow sculptures that were popular then. Many modern artists have elected to use shallow space because it allows more positive control than deep space and is more in keeping with the flatness of the working surface. Gauguin, Matisse, Modigliani, and Beckmann are typical advocates of the concept of limited space (see figs. 7.21 and 4.7). For these artists, not having to create the illusion of deep plastic space allows more control of the placement of decorative shapes as purely compositional elements.

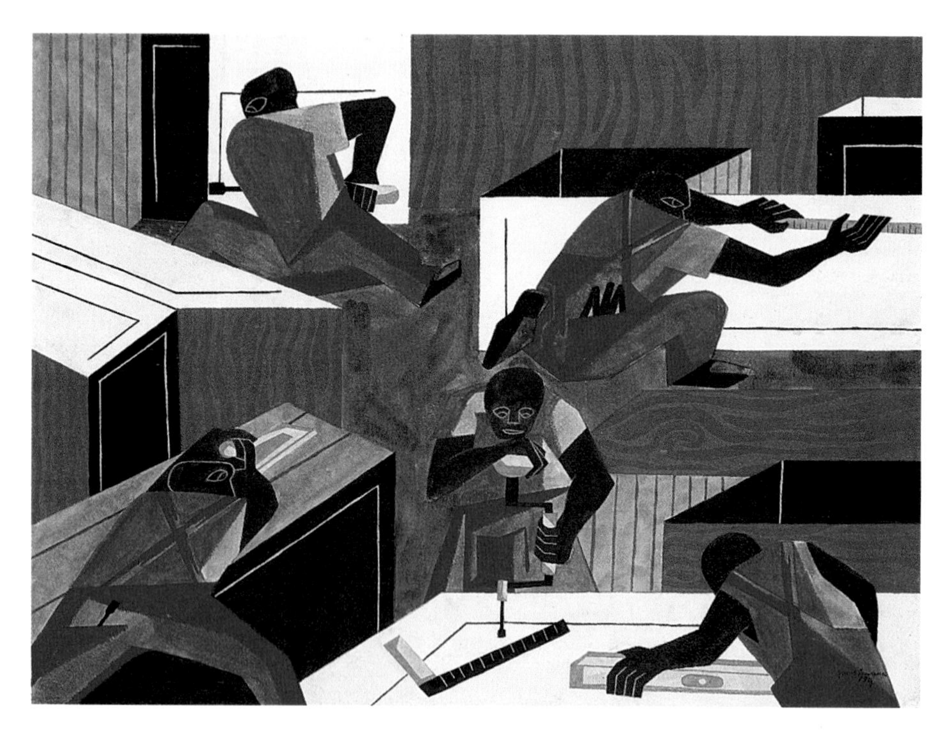

8.3 **Jacob Lawrence, *Cabinet Makers*, 1946. Gouache with pencil underdrawing on paper, 21¾ × 30 in. (55.2 × 76.2 cm).** The use of shapes with solid colors and values, generally lacking in traditional shading, creates an overall feeling of flatness. In addition, a stagelike effect arises from the shallow space. Hirshhorn Museum and Sculpture Garden, Smithsonian Institution, Washington, D.C. Gift of Joseph H. Hirshhorn, 1966. Photograph by Lee Stalsworth.

Deep and Infinite Space

An artwork that emphasizes deep space denies the picture plane except as a starting point where the space begins. The viewer seems to be moving into the far distances of the picture field. This spatial feeling is similar to looking through an open window over a landscape that rolls on and on into infinity. This infinite quality is produced by certain relationships of art form: size, position, overlapping images, sharp and diminishing details, converging parallels, and perspective are traditional methods of indicating deep spatial penetration (see fig. 6.20).

Infinite spatial concepts, allied with atmospheric perspective, dominated Western art from the beginning of the Renaissance (about 1350) to the middle of the nineteenth century. During this period, generations of artists,

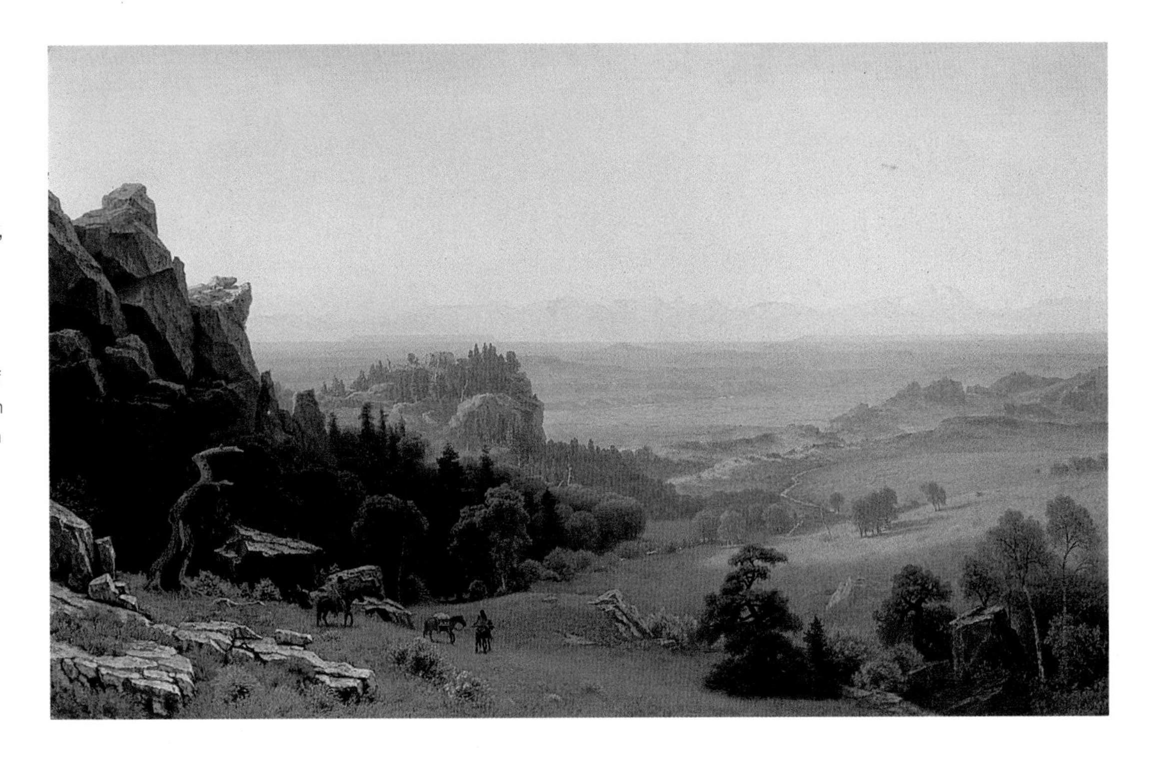

8.4 Albert Bierstadt, *View from the Wind River Mountains, Wyoming,* 1860. Oil on canvas, 30¼ × 48¼ in. (76.8 × 122.6 cm). Nineteenth-century American landscape painting, which aimed at the maximum illusion of visual reality, emphasized the concept of infinite space. Diminishing sizes of objects and hazy effects of atmospheric perspective give the viewer a sense of seeing far into the distance. Gift of Mrs. Maxim Karolik for the Karolik Collection of American Paintings 1815–1865, Museum of Fine Arts, Boston, MA (47.1202).

such as Botticelli, Ruisdael, Rembrandt, and Bierstadt, to name only a few, developed and perfected the deep-space illusion that seems to accord with visual reality (fig. 8.4). Present-day art is largely dominated by the shallow-space concept, although many other contemporary artists work with strongly recessed fields. Any space concept can be valid as long as its elements are consistent in relation to the spatial field chosen.

SPATIAL INDICATORS

Artistic methods of representing space are so interdependent that attempts to isolate and examine all of them here would be impractical and inconclusive and might leave the reader with the feeling that art is based on a formula. Thus, we will confine this discussion to basic spatial concepts.

Our comprehension of space, which comes to us through objective experiences, is enlarged, interpreted, and given meaning by the use of our intuitive faculties. Spatial order develops when the artist senses the right balance and the best placement, then selects vital forces to create completeness and unity. Obviously, then, this process is not a purely intellectual one but a matter of instinct or subconscious response (see fig. 5.9).

Because the subjective element plays so large a part in controlling space, we can readily see that emphasis on formula here, as elsewhere, can quell the creative spirit. Art is a product of human creativity and is always dependent on individual interpretations and responses. Space, like other qualities in art, may be either spontaneous or premeditated but is always the product of the artist's will. If an artist has the impassioned will to make things so, they will usually be so, despite inconsistency and defiance of established principles. Therefore, the methods of spatial indication discussed in the following pages are those that have been used frequently and that guarantee one effect of space, though not necessarily one that is always exactly the same. These traditional methods are presented merely to give the student a conception of the conventional spatial forces (see fig. 4.15).

Sharp and Diminishing Detail

Because we do not have the eyes of eagles, and because we view things through the earth's atmosphere, we are not able to see near and distant planes with equal clarity at the same time. A glance out the window confirms that close objects appear sharp and clear in detail, whereas those at great distances seem blurred and lack definition. Artists have long known of this phenomenon and have used it widely in illusionistic work. In recent times they have used this method and other traditional methods of space indication in works that are otherwise quite abstract. Thus, in abstract and nonobjective conceptions, sharp lines, clearly defined shapes and

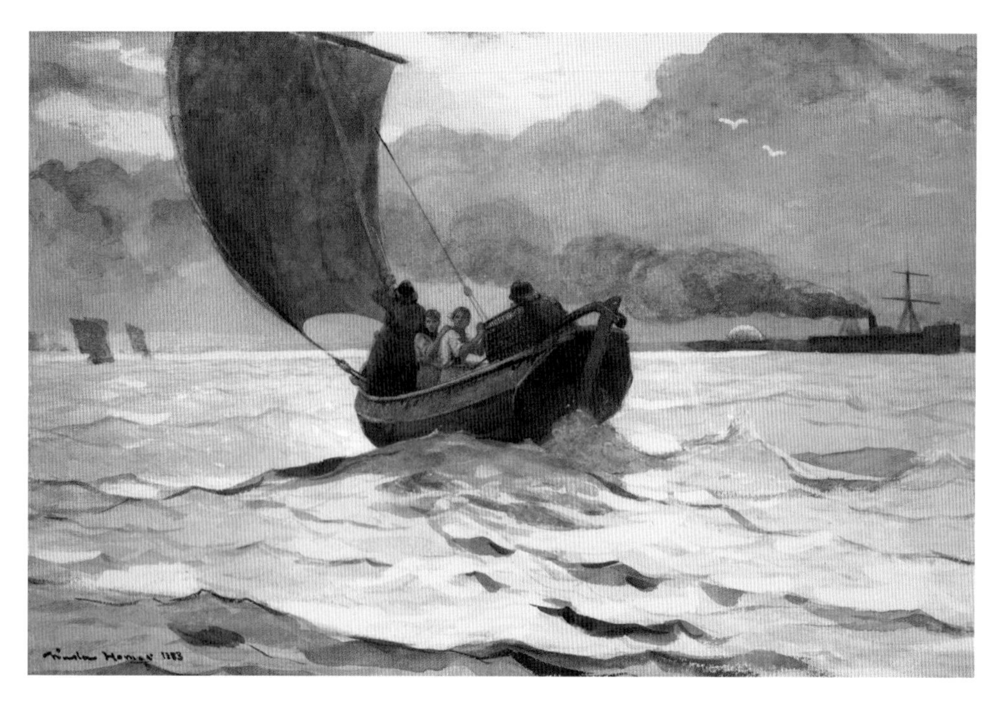

8.5 Winslow Homer, *Returning Fishing Boats,* 1883. Watercolor and white gouache over graphite on white paper, 13 × 19⅝ in. (40.3 × 62.9 cm). The horizon line in this painting separates the space into a ground plane below and a sky plane above. The smaller size and higher position of the distant boats help to achieve the spatial effect. Courtesy of the Fogg Art Museum, Harvard University Art Museums, Anonymous Gift. Photograph by Katya Kallsen. © President and Fellows of Harvard College, Harvard University.

values, complex textures, and intense colors are associated with foreground, or near, positions. Hazy lines, indistinct shapes, grayed values, simple textures, and neutralized colors are identified with background locations. These characteristics are often included in the definition of **atmospheric perspective** (see fig. 8.4).

Size

We usually interpret largeness of scale in terms of nearness. Conversely, a smaller scale suggests distance. If two sailboats are several hundred feet apart, the nearer boat appears larger than the other. Ordinarily we interpret this difference in scale not as one large and one small image (although this could play a part in our perception), but as vessels of approximately the same size placed at varying distances from the viewer (fig. 8.5). Therefore, if we are to use depth scale as our guide, an object or a human figure assumes a scale that corresponds to its distance from us, regardless of all other factors (fig. 8.6; see fig. 10.22). This concept of space has not always been prevalent. In some styles of art, largeness indicates importance, power, and strength, rather than spatial location (see figs. 8.12 and 2.49).

Position

Artists and observers customarily assume that the horizon line, which provides a point of reference, is at eye level.

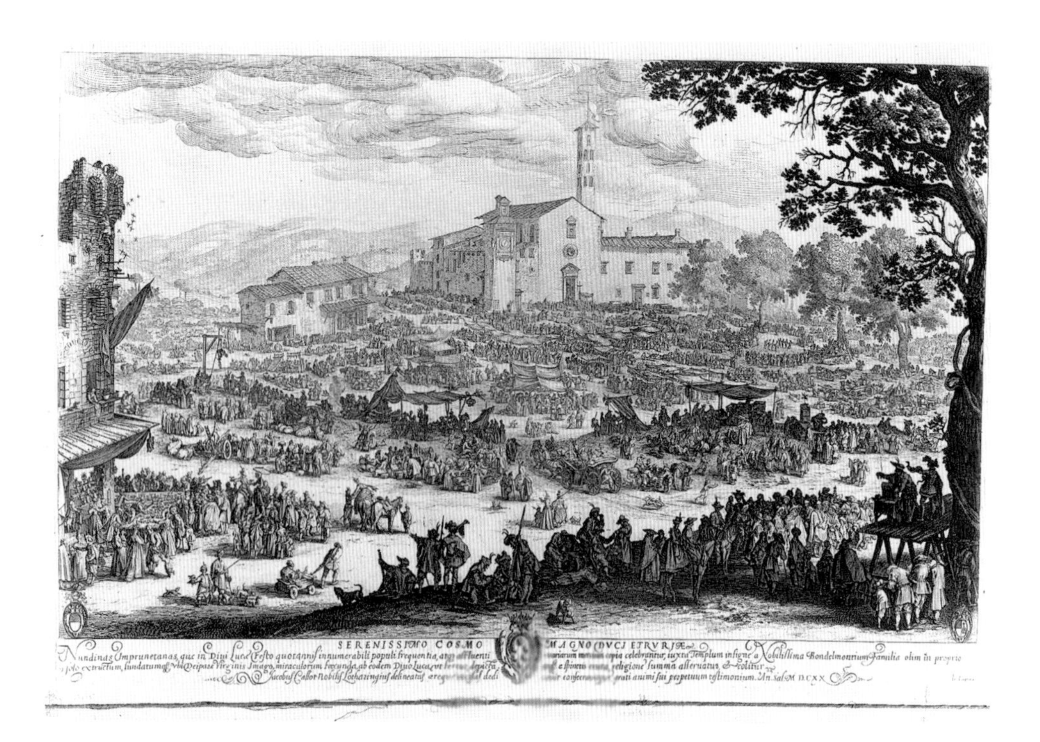

8.6 Jacques Callot, *The Great Fair at Imprunita,* 1620. Etching, 16¹⁵⁄₁₆ × 26 in. In Callot's print, note how the figures gradually get smaller as they recede into the background areas. This, combined with the artist's use of linear perspective with the buildings, gives the viewer a strong sense of depth. The Metropolitan Museum of Art, Harris Brisbane Dick Fund, 1917 (17.3.2645).

Thus, the position of objects is judged in relation to that horizon line. The bottom of the picture plane is seen as the closest visual point, and the rise up to the horizon line indicates the receding of space (see fig. 8.5). Evidence suggests that this manner of seeing is instinctive (resulting from continued exposure to the objective world), for its influence persists even in viewing greatly abstracted and nonobjective work (fig. 8.7). The alternative, of course, is to see the picture plane as entirely devoid of spatial illusion and to register the distances between visual elements as simply what is actually measurable across the flat surface. It is difficult to perceive a picture in this way even when we discipline ourselves to do so, because it requires us to divorce ourselves entirely from all the intuitions about space we form through our experience.

8.7 Placement of squares. A line across the picture plane reminds us of the horizon that divides ground plane from sky plane. Consequently, the lower shape seems close and the intermediate shape more distant, while the upper square is in a rather ambiguous position as it touches nothing and seems to float in the sky.

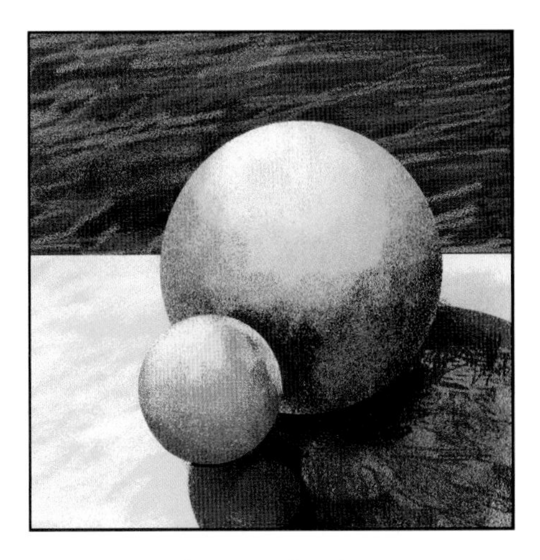

8.8 Larger objects usually advance more than smaller ones, but as an indicator of space, overlapping causes the object being covered to recede regardless of size.

Overlapping

Another way of suggesting space is by overlapping planes or volumes. If one object covers part of the visible surface of another, the first object is assumed to be nearer. Overlapping is a powerful indication of space, because once used, it takes precedence over other spatial signs. For instance, a ball placed in front of a larger ball appears closer than the larger ball, despite its smaller size (fig. 8.8).

Transparency

The overlapped portion of an object is usually obscured from our view. If, however, that portion is visible through the overlapping plane or object, the effect of **transparency** is created. Transparency, which tends to produce a spatial relationship of closeness, is clearly evident in the triangles in the painting by Leonardo Nierman (fig. 8.9). It is also found in the works of the Cubists and other artists who are interested in exploring shallow space (see figs. 4.8 and 10.41).

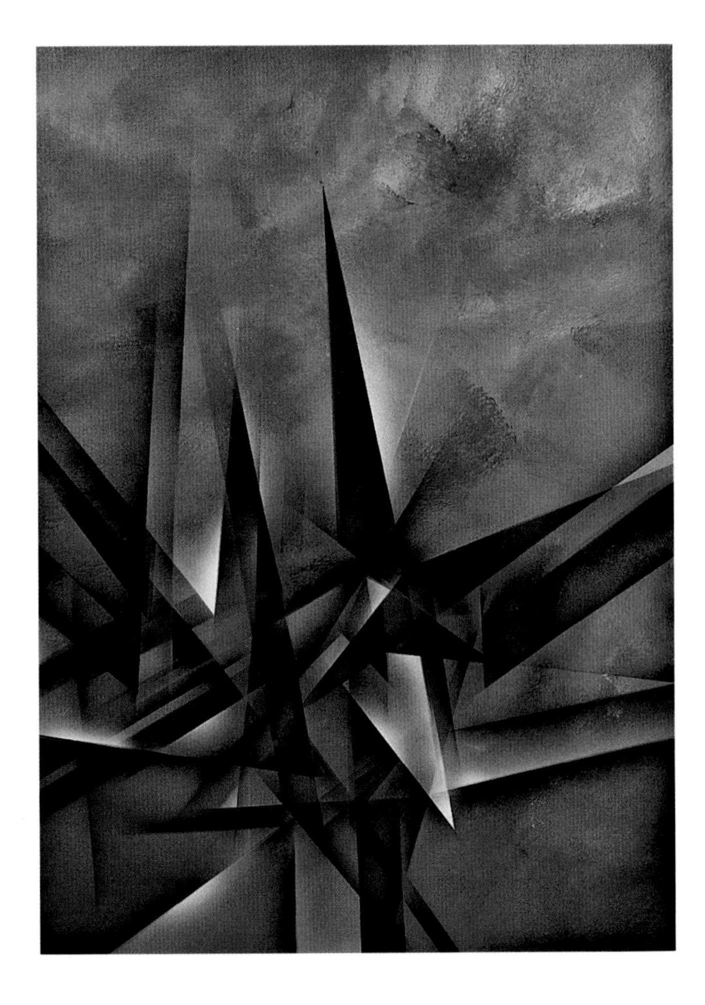

8.9 Leonardo Nierman, *Broken Star,* 1991. Mixed media on masonite, 32 × 24 in. The precise, hard-edged geometric shapes in this work are a legacy of Cubism. However, notice that the implied triangular shapes overlap, remain transparent, and create a shallow space that contrasts with the deeper space behind. Courtesy of the artist.

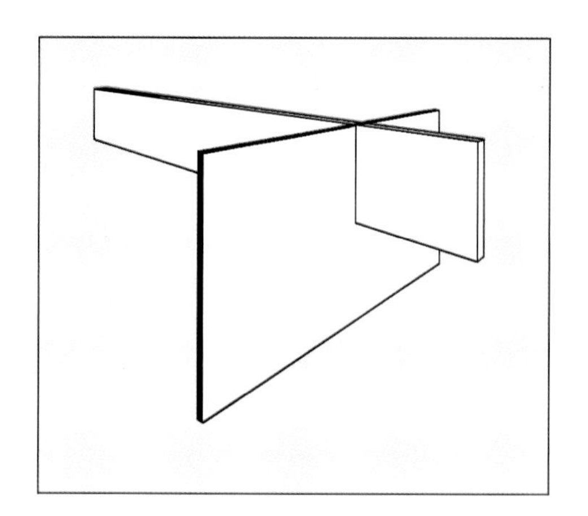

8.10 Interpenetrating planes. The passage of one plane or volume through another automatically gives depth to a picture.

Interpenetration

Interpenetration occurs when planes or objects pass through each other, emerging on the other side. The spatial positioning of the planes and objects involved can create the illusion of either shallow or deep space (figs. 8.10 and 8.11; also see fig. 2.21).

Fractional Representation

Fractional representation can best be understood by studying the treatment of the human body by Egyptian mural artists. Here we can find, in one figure, the profile of the head with the frontal eye visible, the torso seen front-on, and a side view of the hips and legs. This

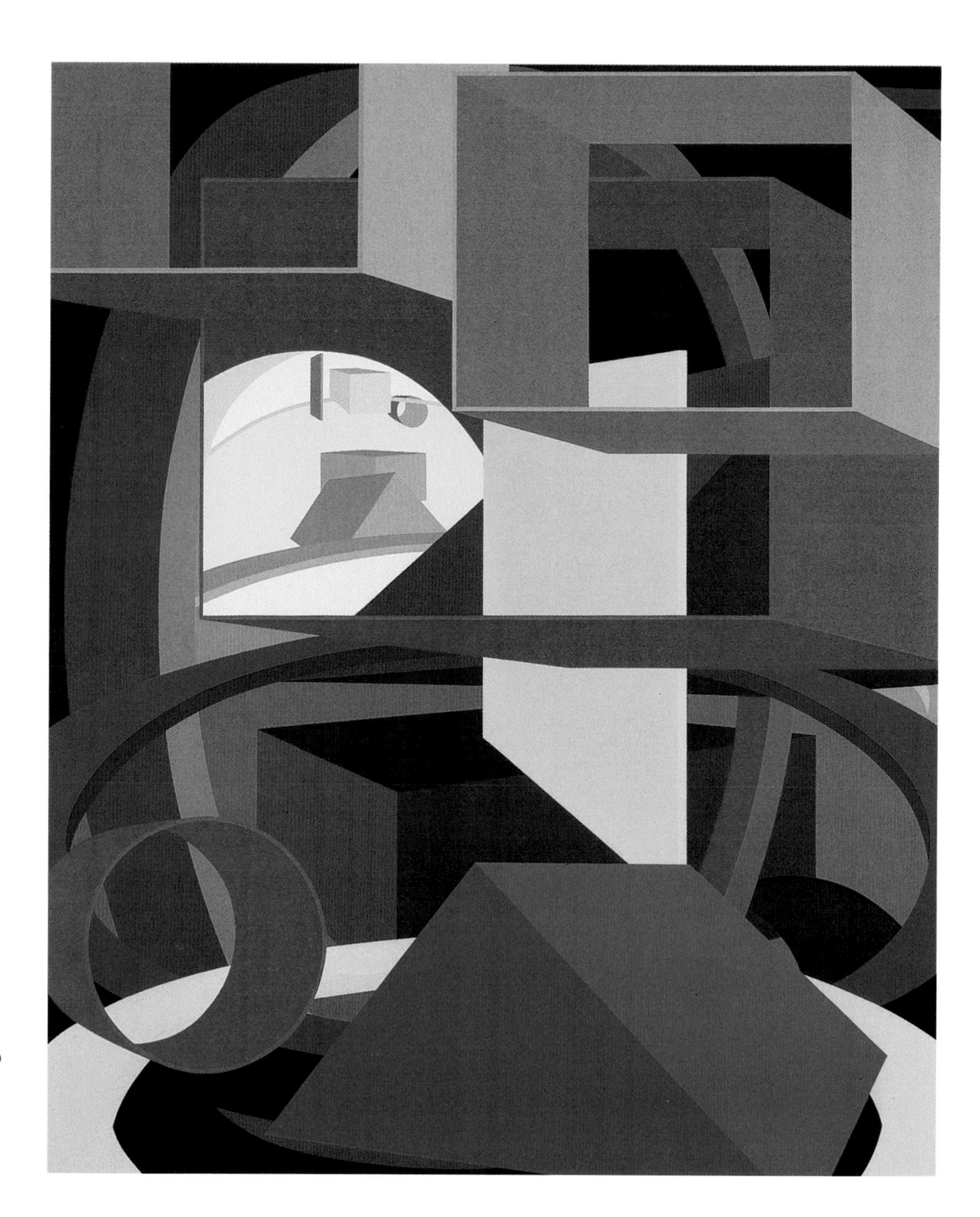

8.11 Al Held, *Quattro Centric XIII*, 1990. Acrylic on canvas, 5 × 6 ft (1.52 × 1.83 m). The effects in this work are quite subtle and do not follow any formal technique for generating space. Areas of overlapping and interpenetration contribute strongly to the overall sense of depth. Al Held/Licensed by VAGA, New York, NY.

combines the most representative aspects of the different parts of the body (figs. 8.12 and 8.13). **Fractional representation** is a spatial device revived in the nineteenth century by Cézanne, who used its principles in his still-life paintings (see "Plastic Images," p. 209). It was employed by many twentieth-century artists, most conspicuously Pablo Picasso. The effect is flattening in Egyptian work but plastic in the paintings by Cézanne because it is used to move us "around" the subjects.

Converging Parallels

The space indicated by converging parallels can be illustrated using a rectangular plane such as a sheet of paper or a tabletop. By actual measurement, a rectangle possesses one set of short parallel edges and one set of long parallel edges (fig. 8.14). If the plane is arranged so that one short edge (A) is viewed head-on, the corresponding parallel edge (B) will appear to be shorter. Because these parallel edges appear to be of different

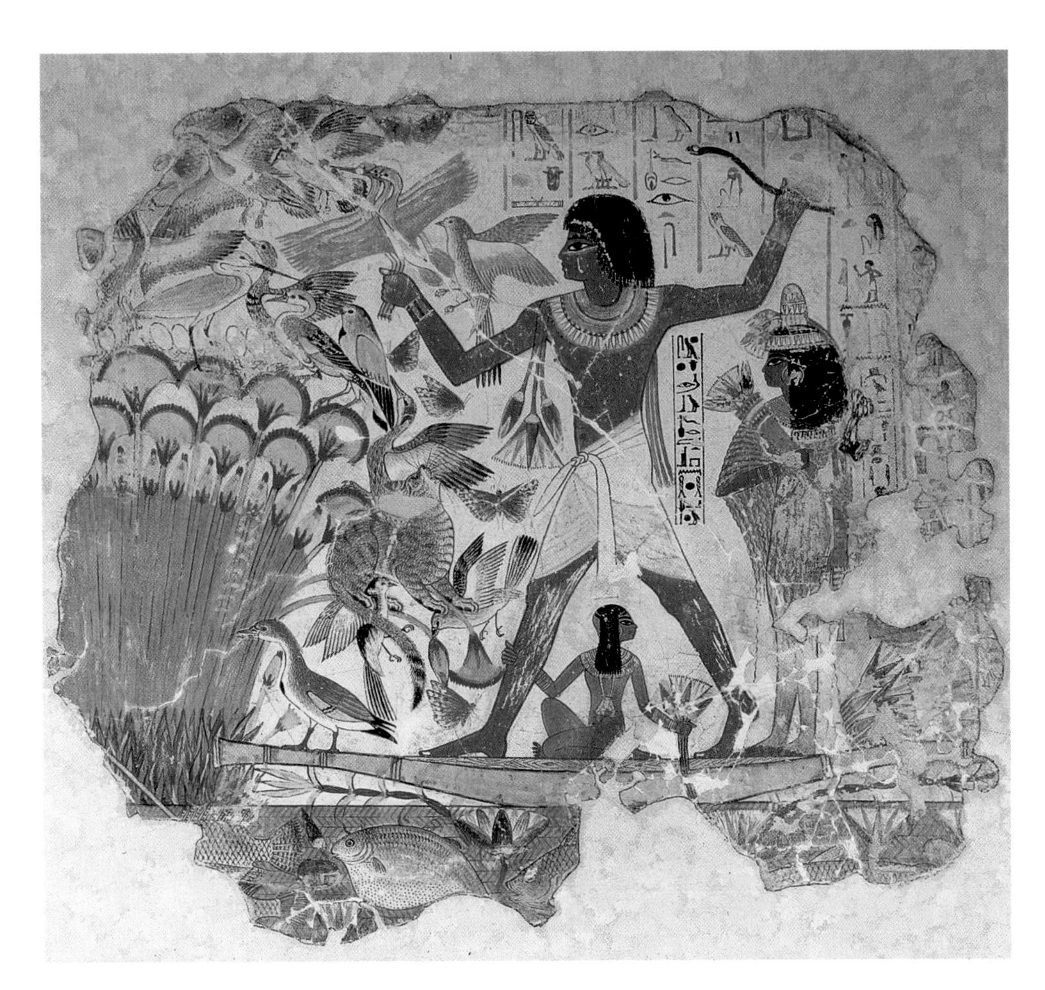

8.12 Nebamun hunting birds, from the tomb of Nebamun, Thebes, Egypt, c. 1400 B.C. This work illustrates the Egyptian concept of pictorial plasticity: Various representative views of the figure are combined into one image (fractional representation) and are kept compatible with the flatness of the picture plane. The arbitrary positioning of the figures and their disproportionate scale add to this effect. Fragment of a fresco secco. Courtesy of the British Museum, London.

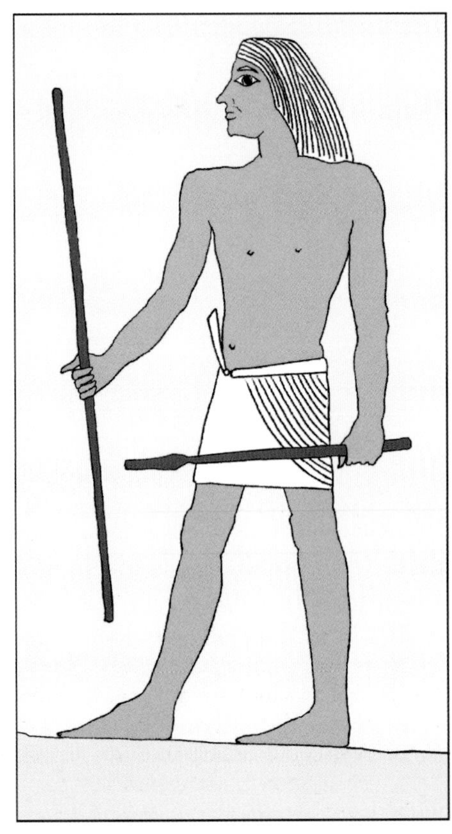

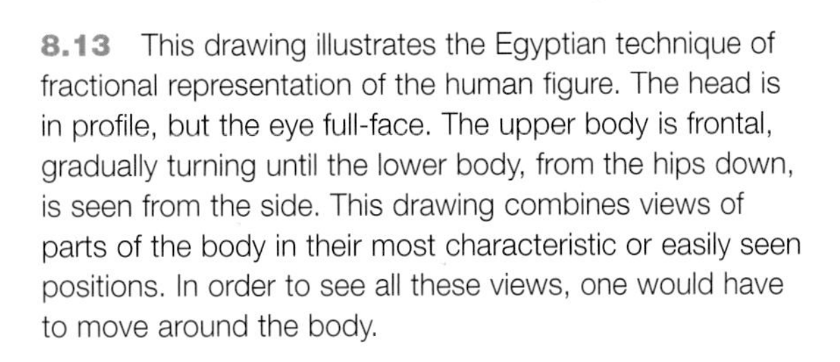

8.13 This drawing illustrates the Egyptian technique of fractional representation of the human figure. The head is in profile, but the eye full-face. The upper body is frontal, gradually turning until the lower body, from the hips down, is seen from the side. This drawing combines views of parts of the body in their most characteristic or easily seen positions. In order to see all these views, one would have to move around the body.

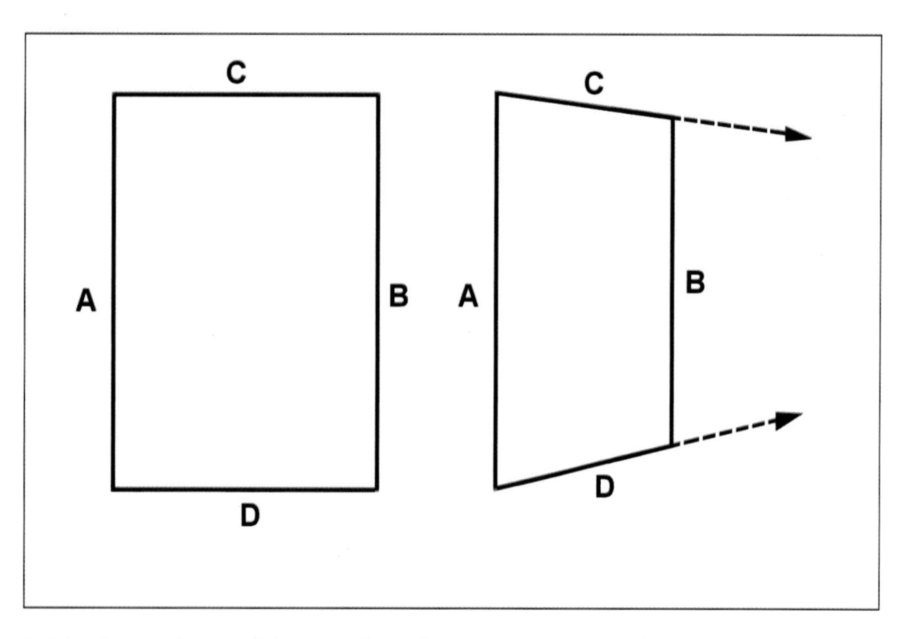

8.14 Converging parallels can make a shape appear to recede into the pictorial field.

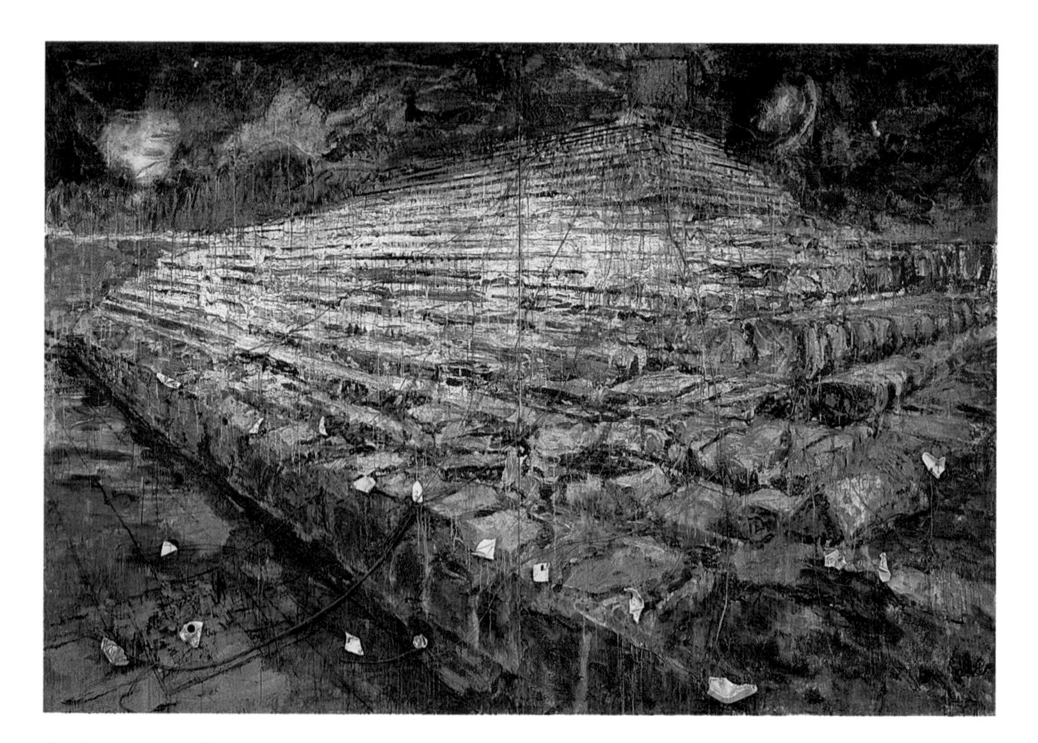

8.15 **Anselm Kiefer, *Osiris und Isis/Bruch und Einung*, 1985–87. Mixed media, 150 × 220½ in. (381 × 560 cm).** Kiefer uses perspective to help him intensify the viewer's confrontation with scale in his enormous canvas. San Francisco Museum of Modern Art. Purchased through a gift of Jean Stein, by exchange, the Mrs. Paul L. Wattis Fund, and the Doris and Donald Fisher Fund.

lengths, the pair of parallel edges (C and D) that connect them seem to converge as they move back into space. Either set of lines, even in the absence of the other set, would continue to indicate space quite forcefully. This principle of converging parallels is found in many works of art that do not necessarily abide by the rules of **perspective.** The principle is closely related to perspective, but the degree of convergence is a matter of subjective or intuitive choice by the artist. It need not be governed by fixed vanishing points or other systematic rules governing the rate of convergence (fig. 8.15).

Linear Perspective

Linear perspective is a system for accurately representing sizes and distances of known objects in a unified visual space. Based on optical perception, it incorporates the artist's/viewer's judgments about concepts of scale, proportion, placement, and so on by applying spatial indicators such as size, position, and converging parallels. A general understanding of perspective occurred during the revival of interest in ancient Greco-Roman literature, philosophy, and art in Renaissance Italy. This spirit swept Europe during the fourteenth and fifteenth centuries—the era that brought this spatial system to a point of high refinement. Linear perspective focuses attention on one view, a selected portion of nature, seen from one position at a particular moment in time. The use of eye level, guidelines, and vanishing points gives this view mathematical exactitude (figs. 8.16A, B).

It is generally believed that perspective was developed by the Florentine architect Filippo Brunelleschi (1377–1446) and was quickly adapted to painting by his contemporary, Masaccio (1401–1428) (see fig. 8.16A). Employing their knowledge of geometry (an important subject in the classical education), Renaissance artists conceived a method

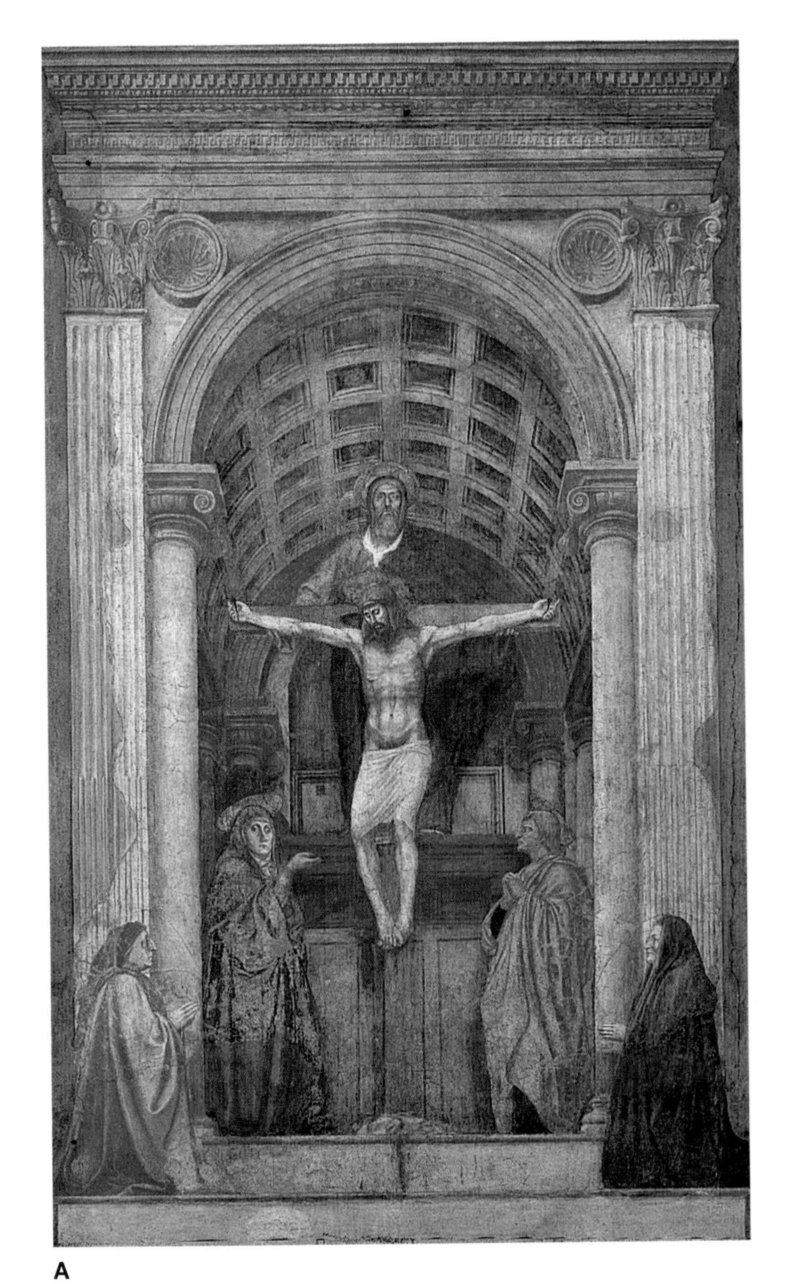
A

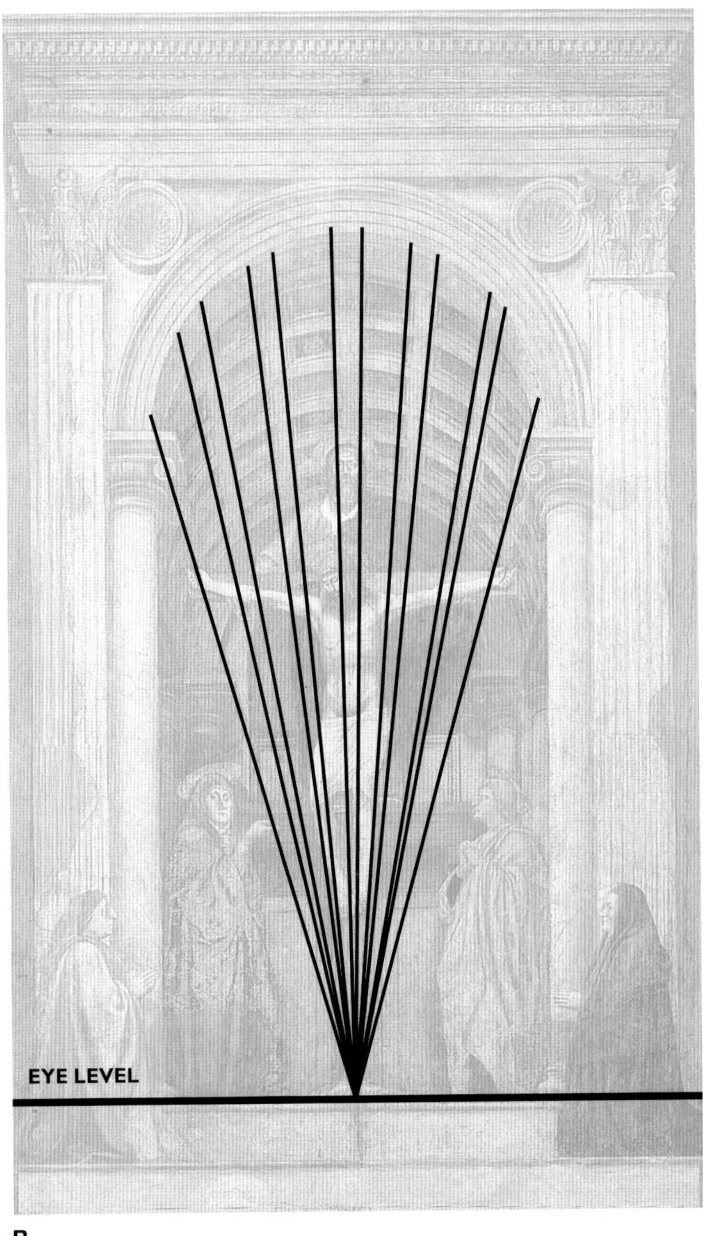

B

8.16 Masaccio, *Trinity with the Virgin, St. John and Donors,* 1427. Fresco at Santa Maria Novella, Florence, Italy, 21 ft 10 in. × 10 ft 5 in. (6.65 × 3.18 m). According to some art history experts, Masaccio's fresco is the first painting created in correct geometric perspective. The single vanishing point lies at the foot of the cross, as indicated by the overlay in figure 8.16B. Photo SCALA/Art Resource, New York.

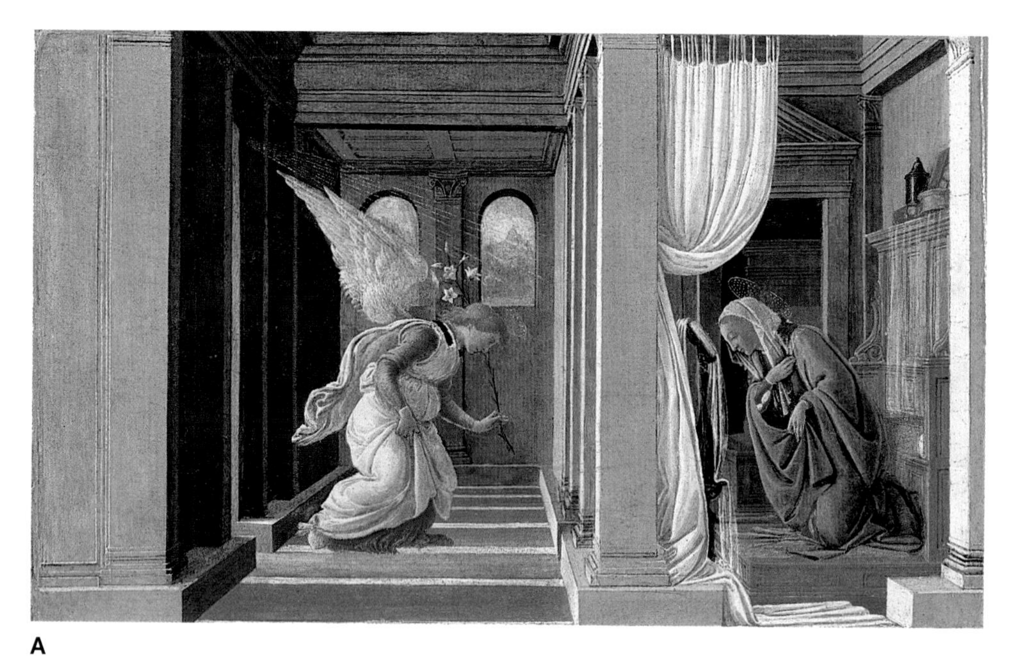

A

Left viewing field

Right viewing field

SKY PLANE
(ceiling)

GUIDELINES (orthogonal)

EYE LEVEL

GROUND PLANE (floor)

B

Vanishing point (VP)

Viewer's location point

8.17 Sandro Botticelli, *Annunciation,* c. 1490. Tempera and gold on panel, 7½ × 12⅜ in. (19.1 × 31.4 cm) (painted surface). In the tradition of much art of the Renaissance period, perspective in the form of receding planes creates space and directs our attention to the vanishing point (see fig. 8.17B). The Metropolitan Museum of Art, Alfred Stieglitz Collection, 1949 (49.70.121) Photograph © The Metropolitan Museum of Art.

of depicting objects, both animate and inanimate, in a space more realistic than any other that had appeared in Western art since the Romans. In their concept, the perspective drawing of shapes (fig. 8.17A) makes the picture plane akin to a view through a window, the picture frame acting as a window frame.

In figure 8.17B, imaginary sightlines or "orthogonals," called guidelines, are extended along the edges of the room's architectural planes to a point behind the angel's head. The guidelines converge at a point on the eye level that is called the vanishing point (infinity). By convention, the eye level is synonymous with the horizon line (where the sky and ground meet) that is often seen in landscapes (see figs. 8.4 and 8.5). While the eye level represents the elevation of the observer's/painter's eyes, it also demarcates upper and lower divisions called ground plane (floor) and sky plane (ceiling). A vertical axis that can be seen through the vanishing point, behind the angel's head, establishes the location of the artist or viewer. This is known as the viewer's location point. Changing this point will drastically alter the view of the room (figs. 8.18A, B).

Major Systems of Linear Perspective

There are three major systems of linear perspective: one-point, two-point, and three-point. Each system is related to the way the artist views the subject or scene. Perspective is based on the theoretical assumptions that the artist maintains a fixed position and, in theory, views the subject with one eye (fig. 8.19). The Renaissance painter's approach imagined rays of light emanating from one fixed point (the artist's eye) to every point on the object being drawn. These rays passed through a glass screen—representing the artist's canvas—between the artist and the object. The collection of points where the lines passed through the glass comprised the naturalistic view the artist wanted to recreate on the canvas. These devices acted as portable camera obscuras (see the "Beginning of Photography" section in Chapter 10, p. 255).

In reality, viewers casually move their eyes and head as they move their focus from object to object within the image. While these movements increase the viewer's ability to understand the subject, such changes of viewpoint to some extent violate the concepts of linear perspective.

Assuming a minimum of movement, the artist can view his or her subjects in one of three ways:

1. By taking a position directly in front of the image; the whole front plane of the subject is made to appear flat or parallel to the picture plane (one-point).
2. By moving so that an edge—instead of the whole flat plane—is closest and centrally located; all planes will then appear to recede, because the top and bottom edges converge to vanishing points on either side (two-point).
3. By assuming a position very much above or below the subject, the sides as well as the top and bottom edges converge to distant points (three-point).

In each of these examples, the subject is thought of as stationary and the artist as changing position. But the same concepts could be applied to subjects that can be altered or repositioned; for instance, a small box could be moved to each of the three locations relative to the artist's viewpoint, which meanwhile remains stationary.

One-Point Perspective

One-point perspective is used when the artist views a flat surface or facing plane directly, or front-on. This flat plane will be drawn parallel to the picture plane and the horizon line. In this system, the artist first establishes the horizon line,

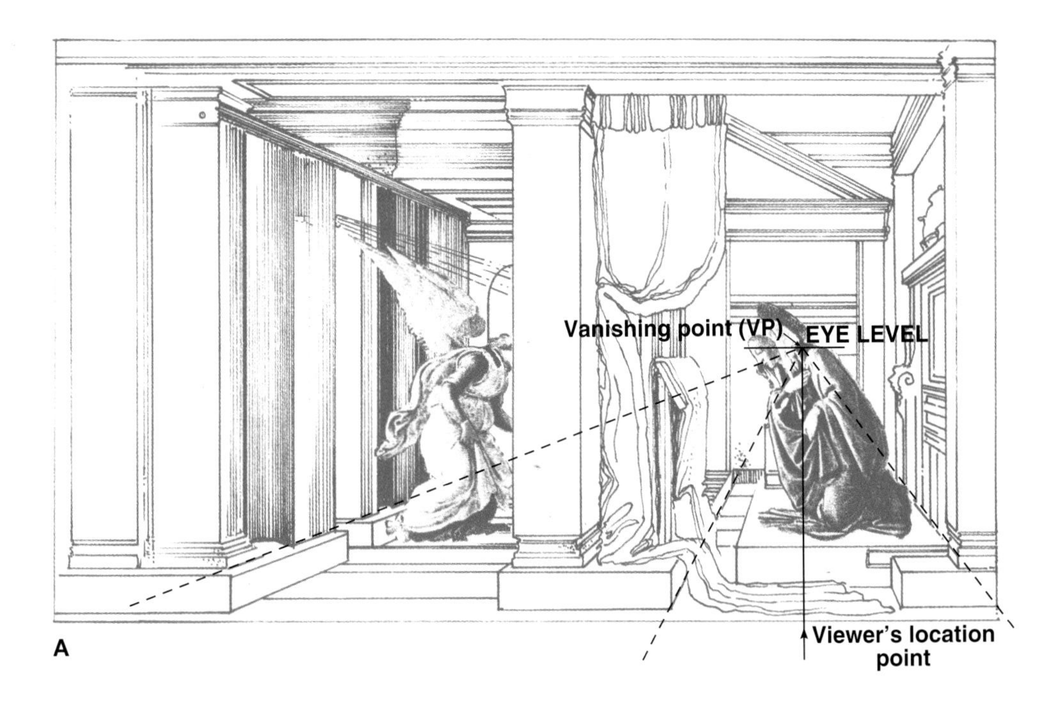

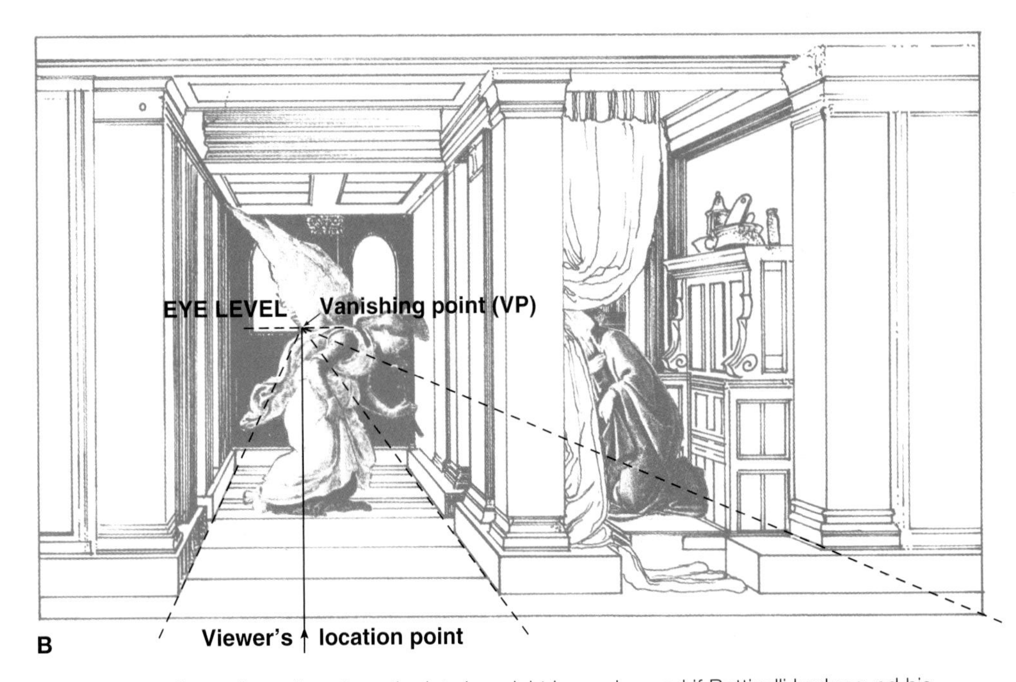

8.18 These illustrations show how the interior might have changed if Botticelli had moved his location point left or right and up or down (see fig. 8.17A). Figure 8.18A indicates what Botticelli would have seen by moving to the right and standing directly in front of the Madonna. Figure 8.18B depicts the view he would have had by moving to the left, past the angel, and moving up a ladder one or two steps. Notice how the architectural elements change with each view, obscuring important parts of the image.

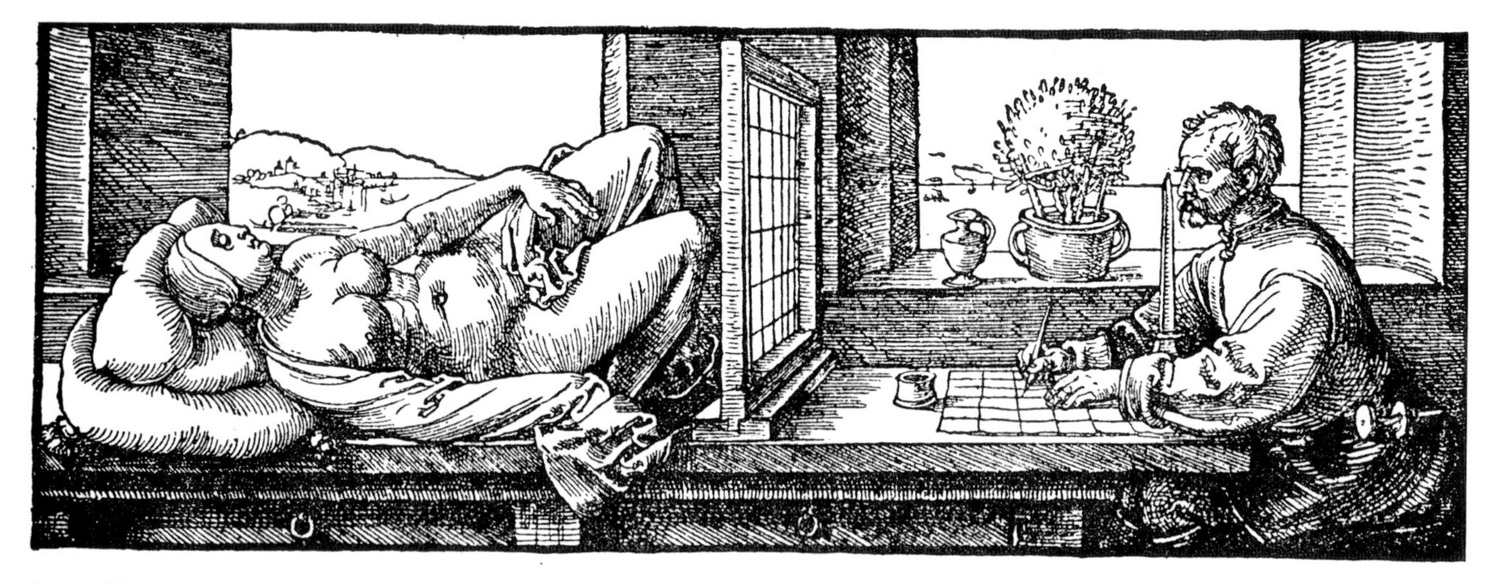

8.19 **Albrecht Dürer, *Draftsman Drawing a Nude,* c. 1525. Woodcut.** This woodcut illustrates an early approach to recording the effects of perspective and foreshortening from a fixed view. In "Underweysung der Messing (Instruction in Proportion)" (Nurenberg, 1527) (appeared only 3rd ED., 1538). Private collection/Foto Marburg/Art Resource, New York.

8.20 With one-point perspective, the whole front or back plane of the subject is made to appear flat or parallel to the picture plane.

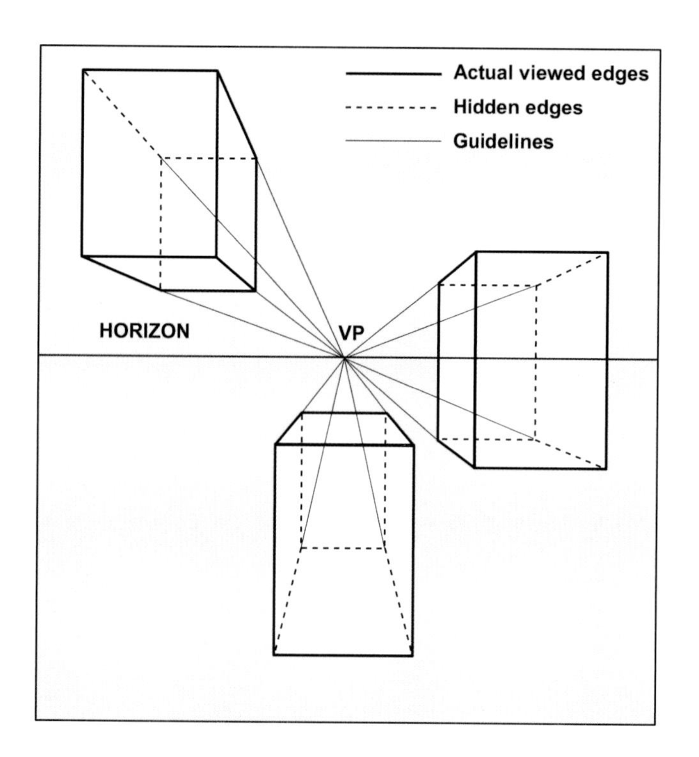

which represents the eye level (fig. 8.20). The horizon line is placed low on the page if the artist is close to the ground, high on the page if the artist is on a ladder, or centered if the artist is standing. Next, the artist chooses a vanishing point, usually centered on the horizon line. To make the composition less static, the vanishing point can be placed slightly to the right or left of center, so that the picture is not divided too symmetrically. In either case, the vanishing point represents a position directly in front of the viewer and at eye level.

After the vanishing point on the horizon line is established, the artist begins with the frontal plane of the geometric solid—that portion closest to the viewer. Guidelines drawn from the four corners of the front plane to the vanishing point establish the solid's side planes. The solid's sides will appear to diminish in size as they recede in depth toward the horizon. In one-point perspective, all guidelines recede to the same vanishing point. Lines defining the original flat plane or any planes behind and parallel to it are horizontals or verticals, at right angles to each other, and remain constant and geometrically measurable. The lines forming these planes are parallel to the ground plane or perpendicular to it and establish their spatial location. Notice that the three geometric solids in figure 8.20 are located fairly close to the vanishing point. In reality, when viewing such solids, one sees the sides as foreshortened. The farther from the vanishing point the solids are, the more distorted their side planes should seem to appear. Far right and left locations are no longer truly frontal and would be drawn more correctly in a two-point perspective view. However, artists often employ such distortions for compositional and/or conceptual advantage.

Subjects with a flat frontal view, like the end of a room, hallways, long frontal views of the interior and exterior of buildings, streets, and lines of trees, lend themselves well to one-point perspective pictures, as seen in Canaletto's *Campo di Rialto* (fig. 8.21).

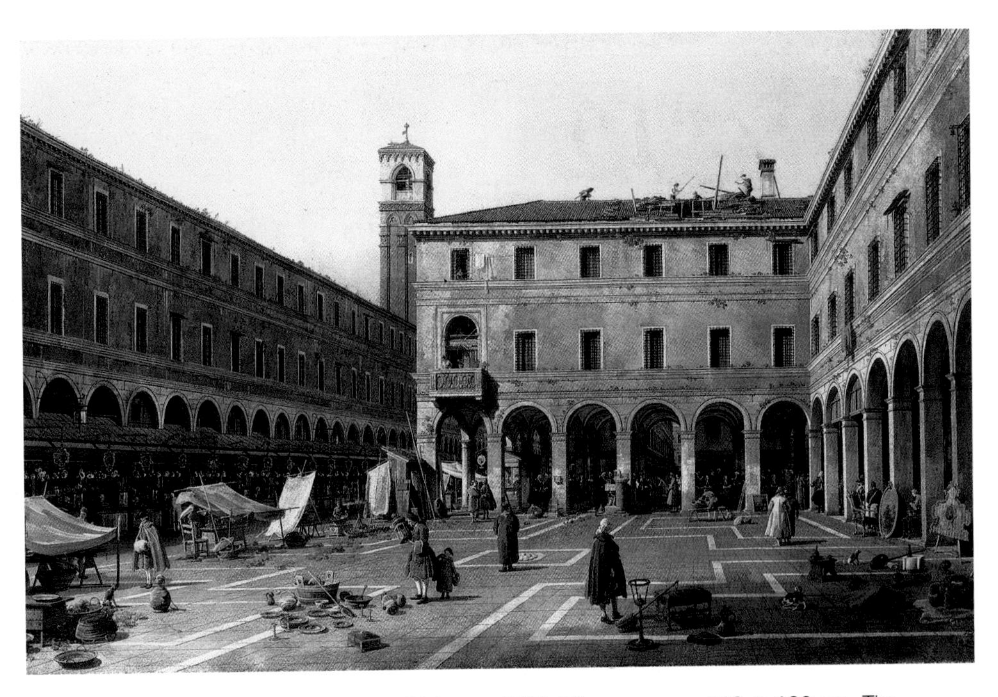

8.21 Antonio Canaletto, *Campo di Rialto,* c. 1756. Oil on canvas, 119 × 186 cm. The appearance of planes and volumes in space determined by the systematic procedures of linear perspective is well illustrated in this painting by an eighteenth-century Venetian artist. It is in one-point perspective and shows the day-to-day business of Venice's center. Bildarchiv Preussicher Kulturbesitz/Art Resource, NY.

Two-Point Perspective

Two-point perspective is most often employed when the artist views a leading edge instead of a flat plane (fig. 8.22). This will cause the geometric solid to appear to be at an angle to the lines of sight or, in other words, to appear to be at angular positions in depth on the surface of the picture plane. The artist begins by establishing the horizon line, as in one-point perspective, its placement in the drawing being relative to the height of the artist's viewing position. Next, vanishing points are located on the horizon line at the extreme left and right ends. In reality, the vanishing points are near the edge of our field of view, and, for the convenience of drawing, they are often located as far apart as possible. Now, the artist draws the closest portion of the box—the vertical edge—as a vertical line. From the top and bottom corners of this vertical, guidelines are extended back to both sets of vanishing points, tentatively establishing the side, top, and/or bottom planes of the geometric solid. These planes will appear to diminish as they recede toward the vanishing points.

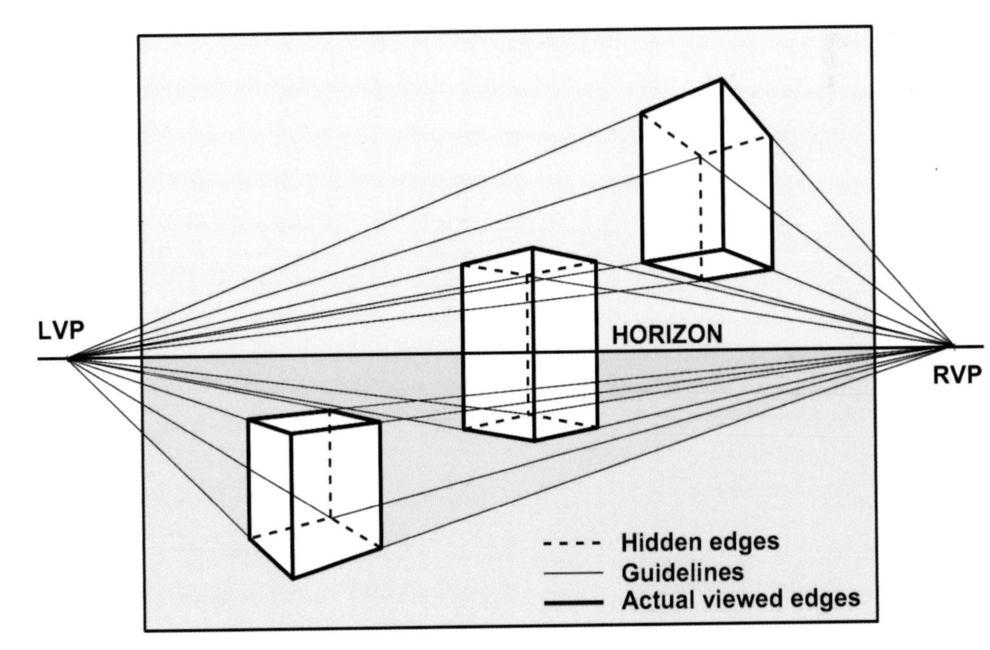

8.22 With two-point perspective, one vertical edge is closest, and all top and bottom edges recede and converge at the left or right vanishing point.

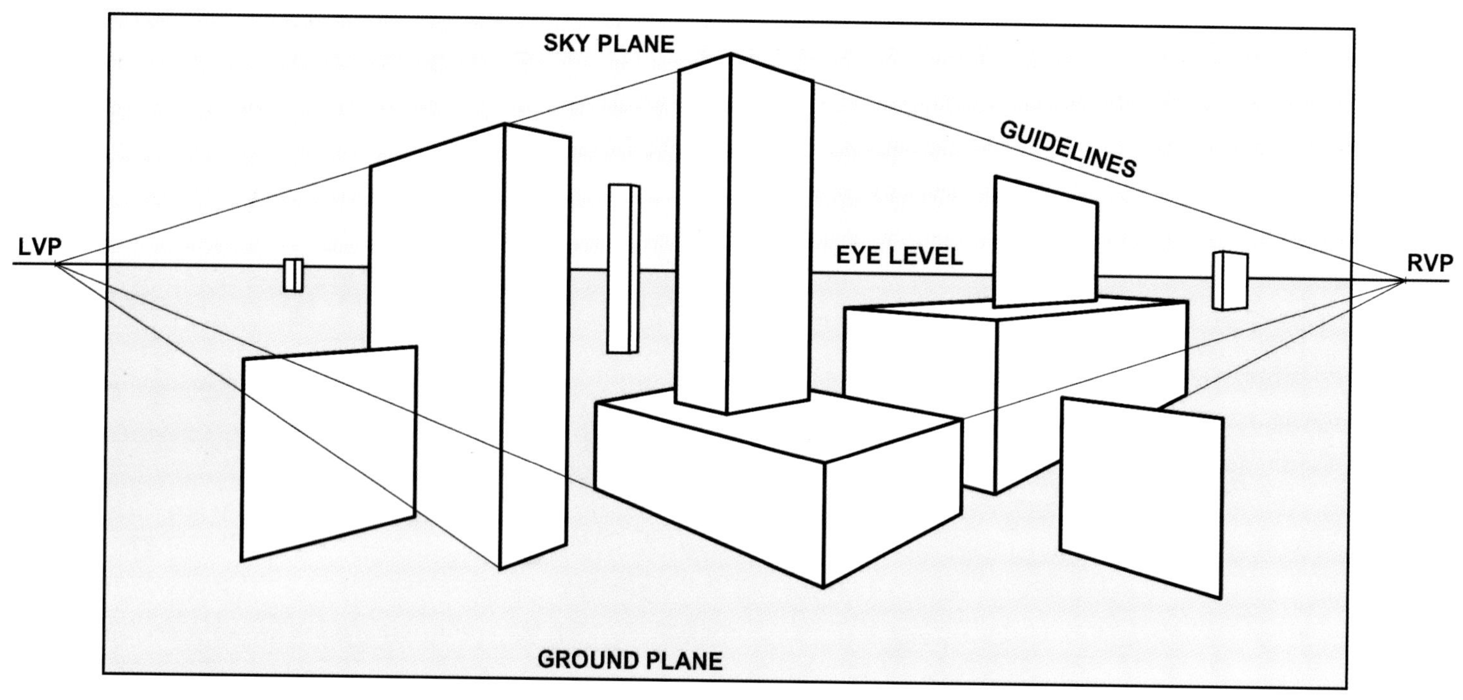

8.23 A drawing showing the essential difference between planes and three-dimensional shapes. Planes are shapes having only two dimensions (height and width), whereas three-dimensional shapes, which are made up of planes, have the effect of solidity (height, width, and depth). The component planes (sides) of 3D shapes may be detached and inclined at any angle. The drawing is also an example of two-point perspective. Object edges are shown as heavy lines, orthogonals (guidelines) as lighter lines. Vanishing points (left vanishing point and right vanishing point) show where object edges converge at the eye level or horizon line, which represents infinity. The eye level divides the picture plane into areas that stand for the ground and the sky.

With two-point perspective, all lines except those that are vertical will return to the vanishing points. The verticals indicate the height of the volumes, remain parallel, and are perpendicular to the ground plane. Only the verticals may be measured and never converge.

Notice in figure 8.23 that multiple solids and planes create a sense of deep space. In addition, the vanishing points are placed outside the picture plane. An artist has control over how much distortion of the objects is desired. Placing the vanishing points *inside* the edges of the picture frame will increase the exaggerated appearance of the shapes. Placing the vanishing points farther apart eliminates the distortion that occurs when they are close together. Unlike with flies, with multiple lenses and 360-degree vision, our field of vision makes us particularly aware of objects in the central 60 degrees, with some additional peripheral awareness of 20 to 30 degrees on either side. On the outer edges of our visual awareness we may only sense movement or images without color. With this in mind, the length of horizon line drawn on the paper can represent the width of our visual field. Ordinarily, the vanishing points may be placed beyond the ends of the drawn horizon line, as far as a distance equal to approximately one-quarter of its width. The horizon line should be extended to the vanishing points, which may be outside the pictorial area and possibly off the page. But, for compositional reasons, an artist might choose to work with only a portion of the complete field of view. In such a case, the distance between vanishing points will remain unchanged, but the depicted space can be located anywhere along the horizon line. In any case, the location of the vanishing points is only a tool and can be used to exaggerate (placed extremely close), represent naturally (appropriately located), or distort by nearly eliminating the receding quality of the image (spaced extremely far apart). Each effect may be exactly what the artist needs at some point.

Two-point perspective is most often employed to depict objects—usually in architectural settings—at an angle to the lines of sight or when the artist wishes them to appear at angular positions in depth on the picture plane, as we can see in the Hopper painting and in Callot's drawing (fig. 8.24; see fig. 8.6).

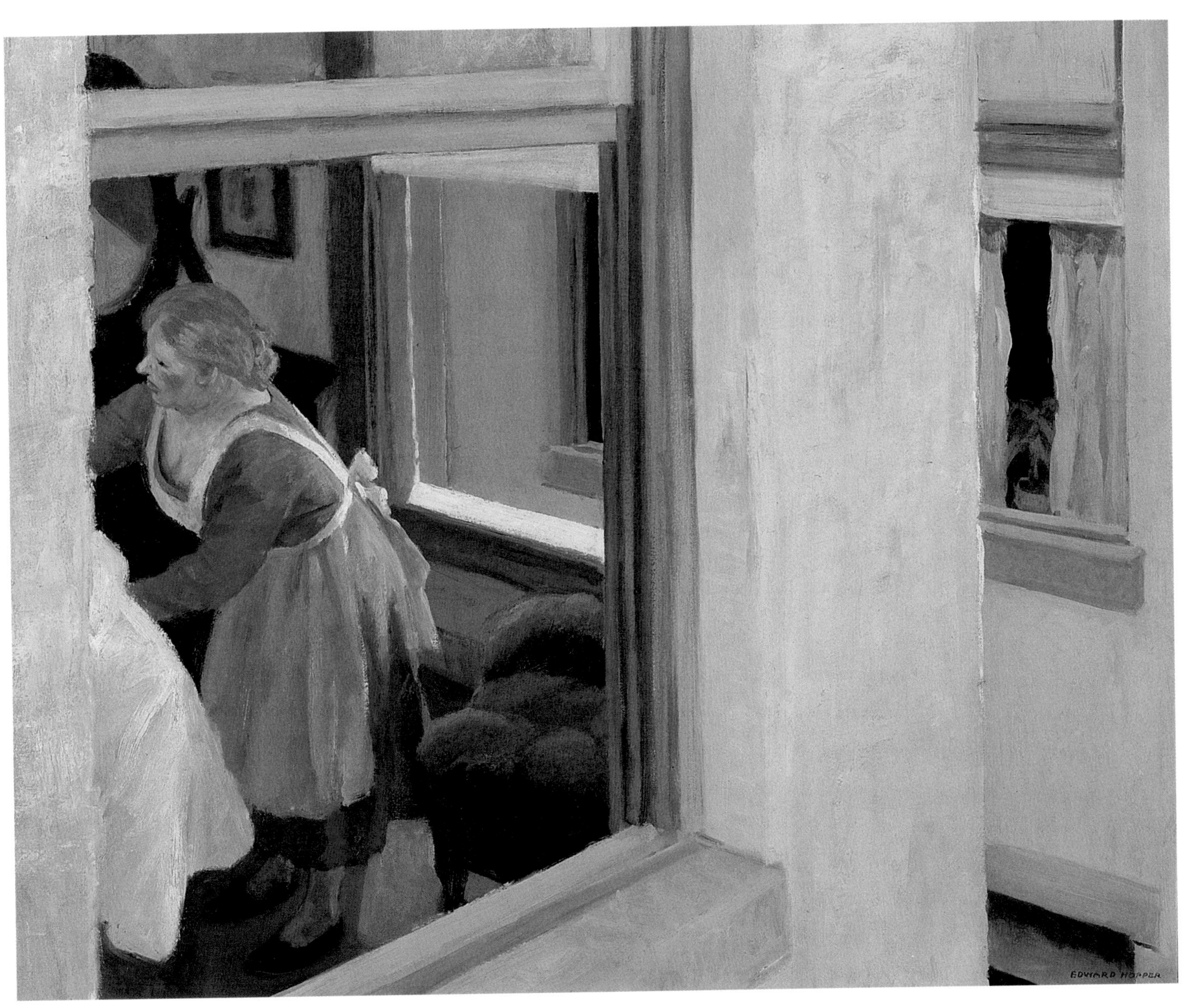

8.24 Edward Hopper, *Apartment Houses,* 1923. Oil on canvas, 25½ × 31½ in. (64.8 × 80 cm). This unusual interior with layers of space revealed through windows is painted in two-point perspective. The perspective is used to direct the viewer back and forth into the picture plane. Pennsylvania Academy of the Fine Arts, Philadelphia. John Lambert Fund. Acc. No. 1925.5.

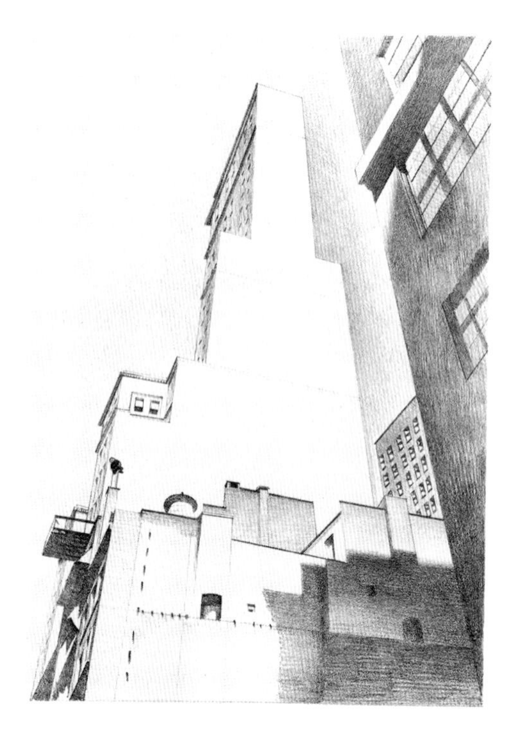

8.25 Charles Sheeler, *Delmonico Building*, 1926. Lithograph, 9¾ × 6⅞ in. (24.7 × 17.4 cm). This painting makes use of three-point perspective—a "frog's-eye view." Fogg Art Museum. © President and Fellows, Harvard University Art Museums, Boston, MA. Gift of Paul J. Sachs.

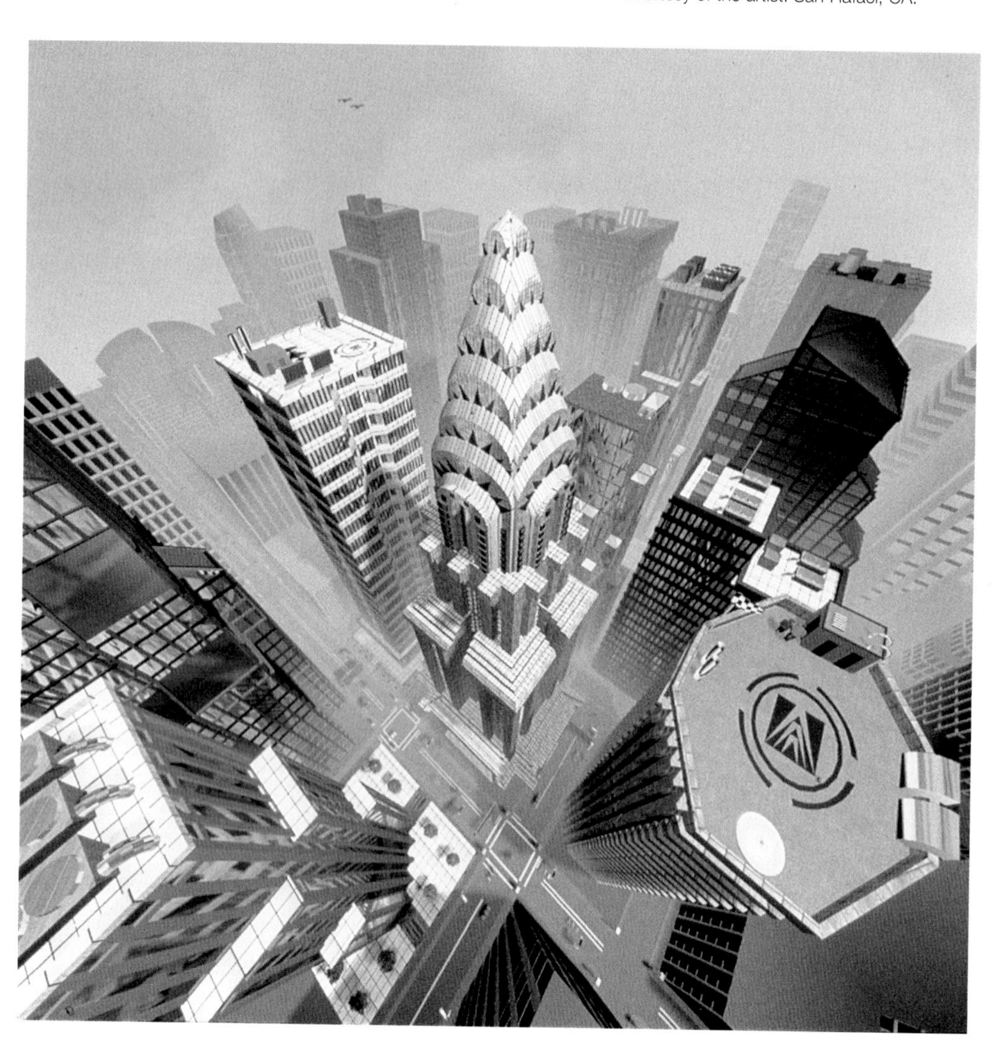

8.26 Gene Bodio, *New City*, 1992. Computer graphic created using Autodesk 3D Studio–Release 2. This is a "bird's-eye view" generated by a computer. Though not strictly in three-point perspective, the picture is an unusual variation in the depiction of three-dimensional objects in space. Courtesy of the artist. San Rafael, CA.

Three-Point Perspective

Three-point perspective is used when an artist views an object from an exaggerated position—lying on the ground and looking up at a tree or looking down from the sky into the center of the city. These are sometimes referred to as a "frog's-eye view" (fig. 8.25) and a "bird's-eye view" (fig. 8.26), respectively.

The artist begins by locating the horizon line, which indicates the location of the viewer's eyes, and fixing the left vanishing point (LVP) and the right vanishing point (RVP) at the appropriate locations on the horizon line (fig. 8.27). Keep in mind that the closer together the vanishing points are placed, the greater the exaggeration or distortion of your image. Usually the horizon line will be relatively high or low on the picture plane. Next, a third point, called the vertical vanishing point (VVP), is located along an axis perpendicular to the horizon line at a point representing the viewer's location point. The location of

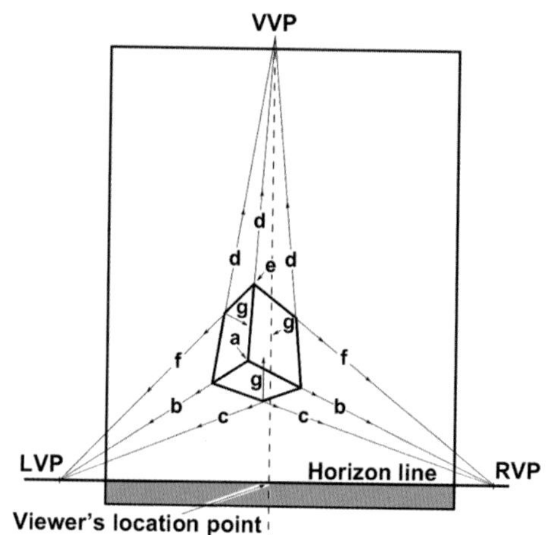

8.27 With three-point perspective, a vantage point is assumed far above or below the subject. This will cause the sides, as well as the top and bottom edges, to converge to one of the three distant vanishing points.

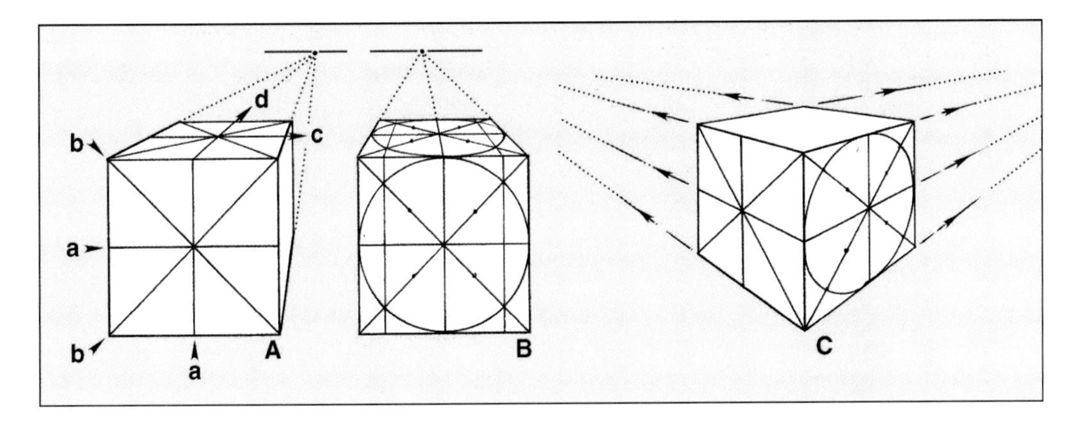

8.28 Subdividing a plane. These diagrams illustrate how to find the perspective center of a plane by crossing diagonals from corner to corner (A). To draw a circle on the same plane, divide each half of the diagonals into thirds. Draw the circle so that it passes through the outside "third" marks (closest to the corners) on the diagonals. The circle should also touch the middle points on the sides of the square. This concept may be applied to one- and two-point perspective (B and C).

the VVP also controls the distortion of the object—the farther away from the horizon line the third point is located, the less exaggerated the image will be. The image in figure 8.27 is started by fixing the nearest corner (a) of what will become a rectangular solid that seems to be floating overhead. From this point, guidelines (b) are extended to the RVP and to the LVP. This locates the leading front edges of the bottom plane. The width of both edges should be indicated, and from those points new guidelines should be extended (c) again to the RVP and the LVP. This completes the bottom plane and locates all four corners. The "verticals" (d) should now be drawn up and away from the three closest corners; but because there are no verticals in three-point perspective, these lines will have to converge to the VVP. Once the "verticals" are drawn, it should be decided how long the rectangular solid must be by gauging its length on the closest, or center, "vertical" edge (a–e). After marking this point (e), guidelines (f) are extended from it to the RVP and to the LVP. In certain cases the hidden back edges (g) could be added. This completes the drawing of the edges and defines the geometric solid as seen from below in three-point perspective.

Only in three-point perspective are the vertical (height) lines, as well as those receding to the left and right vanishing points, spatially indicated. All three guideline systems converge at vanishing points. They are neither perpendicular nor parallel to one another but at oblique angles (see fig. 8.25).

Perspective Concepts Applied

Whether using one-, two-, or three-point perspective, the artist is working with a system that allows the development of items of known size and their placement at various distances into the picture plane. A one-point cube, as illustrated in figure 8.28A, shows a whole flat frontal plane (the closest part) and a receding top plane. The center of any front plane—square or rectangular—may be found by mechanically measuring the horizontal and vertical lengths and dividing them in half. Lines (a) drawn from those points parallel to the verticals and horizontals will divide the plane into quarters. However, this type of measurement works only on flat, frontal planes found exclusively with one-point perspective. It will not work on any plane with converging sides—one-, two-, or three-point—because the sides get smaller as they move away from the viewer, and their changing ratio is not measurable on a ruler. Notice, on the front plane, that diagonals (b) drawn from corner to corner pass through the exact center found by mechanical measurement. The same type of diagonal lines drawn from corner to corner on the receding plane pass through the perspective center of the converging top plane. Lines drawn through this point parallel to the front edge (c) or to the vanishing point (d) create the equal division of the four edges of the receding plane. This concept of corner-to-corner diagonals may be applied to cubes or rectangles in one-, two-, and three-point perspective to locate the perspective centers on any receding plane.

Using the center point of a cube's front square, we can draw a circle with a compass that should fit into the square perfectly (fig. 8.28B). Notice that when the diagonals are divided in thirds from the center, the circle crosses the diagonal lines on approximately the outer third mark. With a compass, try to draw a circle that fits into the top receding plane. It cannot be done, because even though we know that it is a circle, it will appear as an ellipse. The appropriate ellipse can be drawn on the top receding plane when it passes through the third marks on the diagonals and touches the square on the center points of each side. This system may be applied to any receding plane—vertical or horizontal—in one-, two-, or three-point perspective (fig. 8.28C).

Figure 8.29A shows the changing ellipses that could be located in a very tall rectangle. Occasionally, an artist must draw the appropriate ellipse for the top and bottom of anything cylindrical relative to its position above or below the horizon line. Notice that the ellipses farther away from the horizon line are less distorted and that they flatten as they get closer to the horizon line. Ellipses do not always have to be horizontal or vertical. Observe the ellipse drawn on the diagonal plane (fig. 8.29B). It is drawn using the same diagonal system for finding the center of the diagonal plane. In addition, the concept may be applied to drawing arches, bridges, and so on (fig. 8.29C). Although only the upper halves of the ellipses are shown in the arch, it will be necessary to know the basic cube or rectangle they were found in and the perspective centers of their shapes.

Once a square or rectangle is created it may be easily turned into a pyramid, cylinder, or cone by finding the perspective center for the top and bottom planes of the new shapes (figs. 8.30A–D). For a pyramid (A), simply draw lines from the top plane's perspective center to the four corners on the bottom plane. For the cylinder (B), it will be necessary to first draw the proper ellipse on the top and bottom planes—as described earlier. Then draw vertical lines from the outermost limits of both ellipses. Also note that a second pyramid (C) and cone (D) can be drawn with only the establishment of the bottom plane. Find the perspective center of those planes and, from their points, draw lines perpendicular to the bottom planes at any desired length. Then, from the end of this line, draw the lines to the four corners for a pyramid and to the outer-edge points on an ellipse for a cone.

The system for finding the perspective center of a receding plane can be used to project known distances back or

8.29 When seen from the side, a perfect circle looks like an ellipse. The ellipse flattens as it moves closer to the horizon line (A). It may be applied to an inclined plane (B) or used to create arches, tunnels, and so on (C).

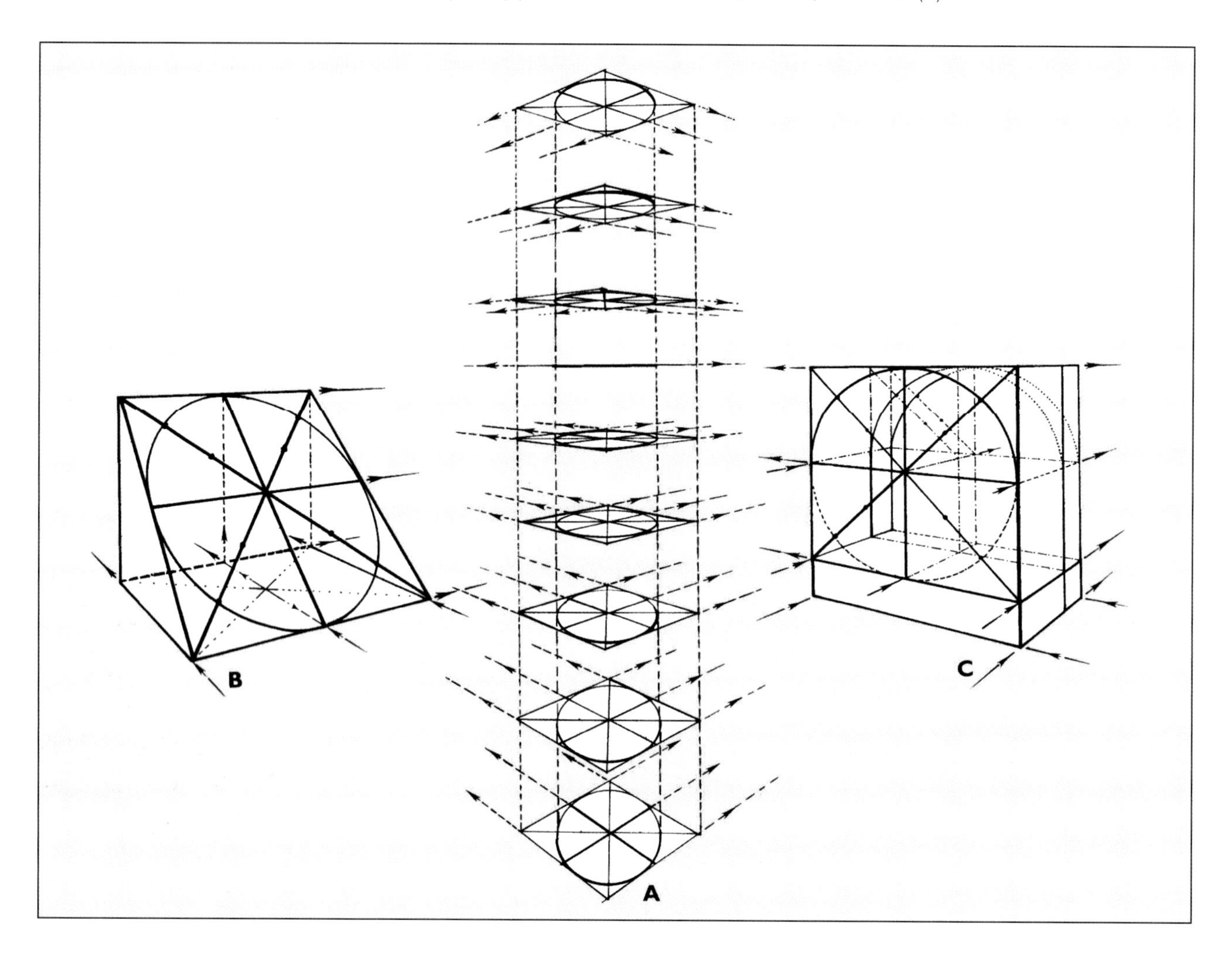

sideways into space at the proper diminishing rate or ratio. If a telephone company plants seven poles equally spaced down the road, how does an artist know exactly where they should be drawn on the picture plane? Study figure 8.28A, covering up one-half of the illustration. Note that the diagonal lines stop at the center point. In the portion covered up, they continue on toward the upper and lower corners. Therefore, if the perspective center (vertical or horizontal plane) can be found, a known shape (half a unit) can be projected into a space on the opposite side of the center mark by continuing the diagonals until they cross an extension of the top or bottom edge.

To draw the telephone poles equally spaced in perspective, simply draw the first pole and then extend guidelines from the top and bottom to the vanishing point (fig. 8.31). Draw the second pole any distance you desire from the first and parallel to it touching the top and bottom guidelines. Next, find the center of the second pole either by measuring or by dividing the shape between the poles with diagonal lines. The point where the diagonals cross may be projected to the second pole by drawing a guideline from that point to the vanishing point. Now, remembering that diagonals cross on the midpoint, draw lines from the top and bottom of the first pole through the midpoint found on the second pole, extending them until they touch the guidelines. Where they do, extend another vertical, and it will locate the next pole at a perspective unit equal to the one just projected. A single diagonal line may be used to project through the center point on the new pole to find the location of the next pole. This process may be repeated as often as necessary until the number of poles desired has been reached. Spacing may be projected horizontally as well as vertically. The same procedure has been applied to the guardrail poles in the lower right corner of figure 8.31. In addition, horizontal projection may be

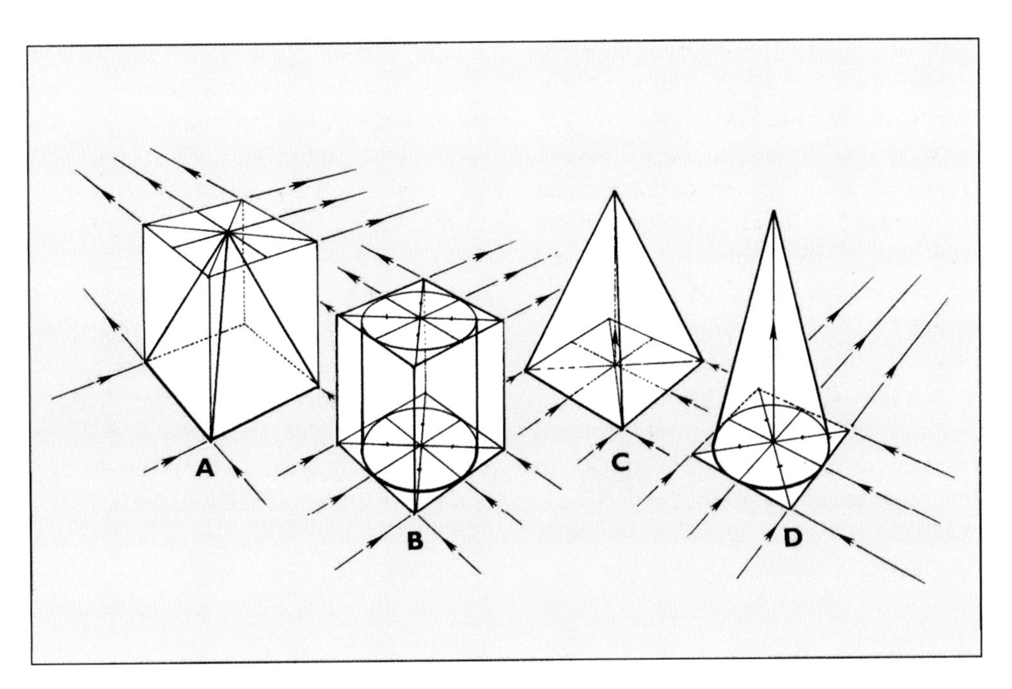

8.30 The concept of locating a plane's perspective center and the correct ellipse to indicate a circle can be extended to create pyramids, cylinders, and cones.

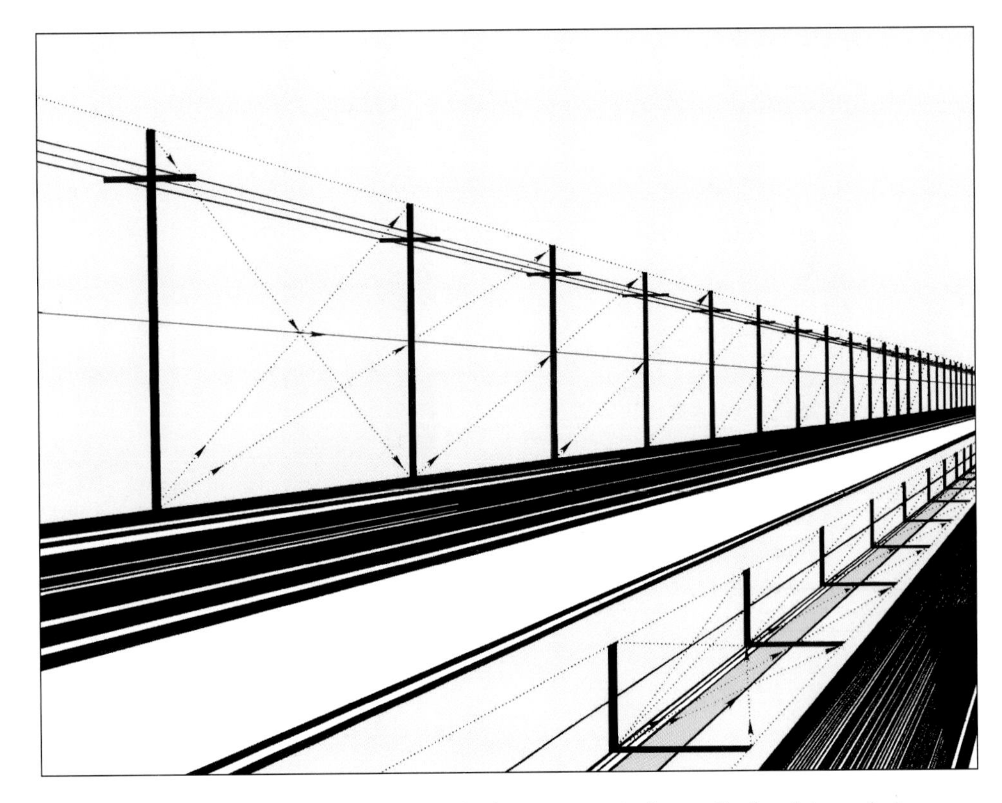

8.31 Telephone poles showing vertical projection systems. A given unit—the distance between two telephone poles—may be projected. Extending a diagonal guideline from a corner through the midpoint of the next pole to the appropriate top or bottom guideline reveals the location of the next pole. Units may be projected on a vertical or horizontal plane.

applied to locate floor tiles, windows, or any architectural components with consistent spacing (fig. 8.32).

A perspective drawing may also have several vanishing points other than those located on the horizon line (fig. 8.33). Multiple vanishing points are often used when it is desirable to show an angular or spatially receding plane within a perspective drawing, such as on a gable or truss-roofed house or a door opening at an angle. In this case, the roof is located first, and its edges are extended back to their new vanishing point. Then, any additional images that would be drawn on that receding plane—for example, shingles and skylight windows—must be extended to that new point. A point may also be located as a source of light with all cast shadows being indicated by guidelines projected from it to the ground plane. As a further complication, an artist may encounter situations where houses and other objects are not parallel to each other. One-, two-, and possibly three-point perspective systems may be used in the same drawing.

The Disadvantages of Linear Perspective

Linear perspective has been a traditional drawing device used by artists for centuries. During that time, the system has evolved and undergone modifications in attempts to make it more flexible or more realistic in depicting natural appearances. Some of these include multiple perspectives, with more than three vanishing points, and, at other times, the use of multiple eye levels. Linear perspective has been most popular during periods of scientific inquiry and reached its culmination in the mid-nineteenth century. Despite its seeming virtue of accurately depicting natural appearances, the method has certain disadvantages that, in the opinion of some artists, outweigh its usefulness. Briefly, the liabilities of linear perspective are as follows:

1. It can never depict a shape or mass as it is known to be.
2. It can portray appearances from only one position in space.
3. The necessary recession of parallel lines toward common points readily leads to monotonous effects.
4. The reduction of scale within a single object, resulting from the convergence of lines, is a type of distortion (see fig. 8.14; this diagram indicates that a rectangular shape depicted in perspective becomes a trapezoid and leaves spatial vacuums above C and below D).

These disadvantages are mentioned only to suggest that familiar modes of vision are not necessarily best in every

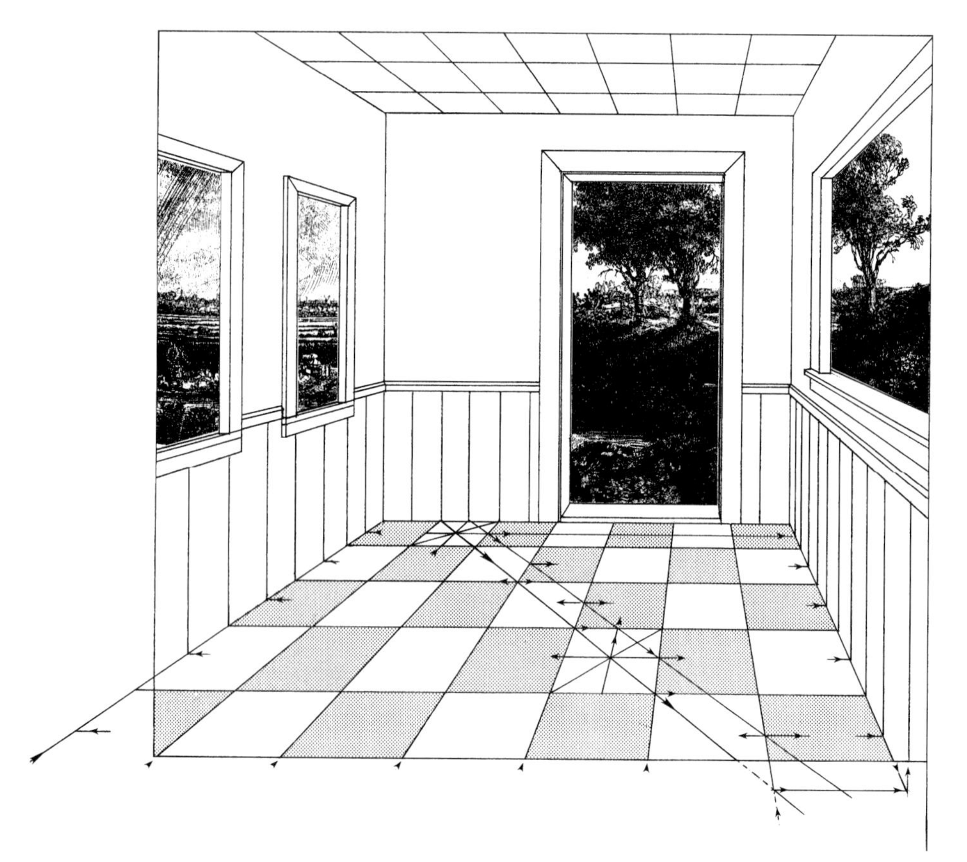

8.32 A room interior. Because horizontals and verticals in one-point perspective may be measured, all tile spacing was marked on the back edge of the floor. From the vanishing point, floor lines were extended through each of these points toward the viewer. After establishing the first row of tiles, a diagonal line was extended from corner to corner of one tile and beyond. Where the diagonal crossed each floor line, a horizontal line was drawn, thereby defining a new row of tiles. A second line, passing through the center of the edge of each tile, located points that were projected onto both walls to identify wallboard spacing and window widths.

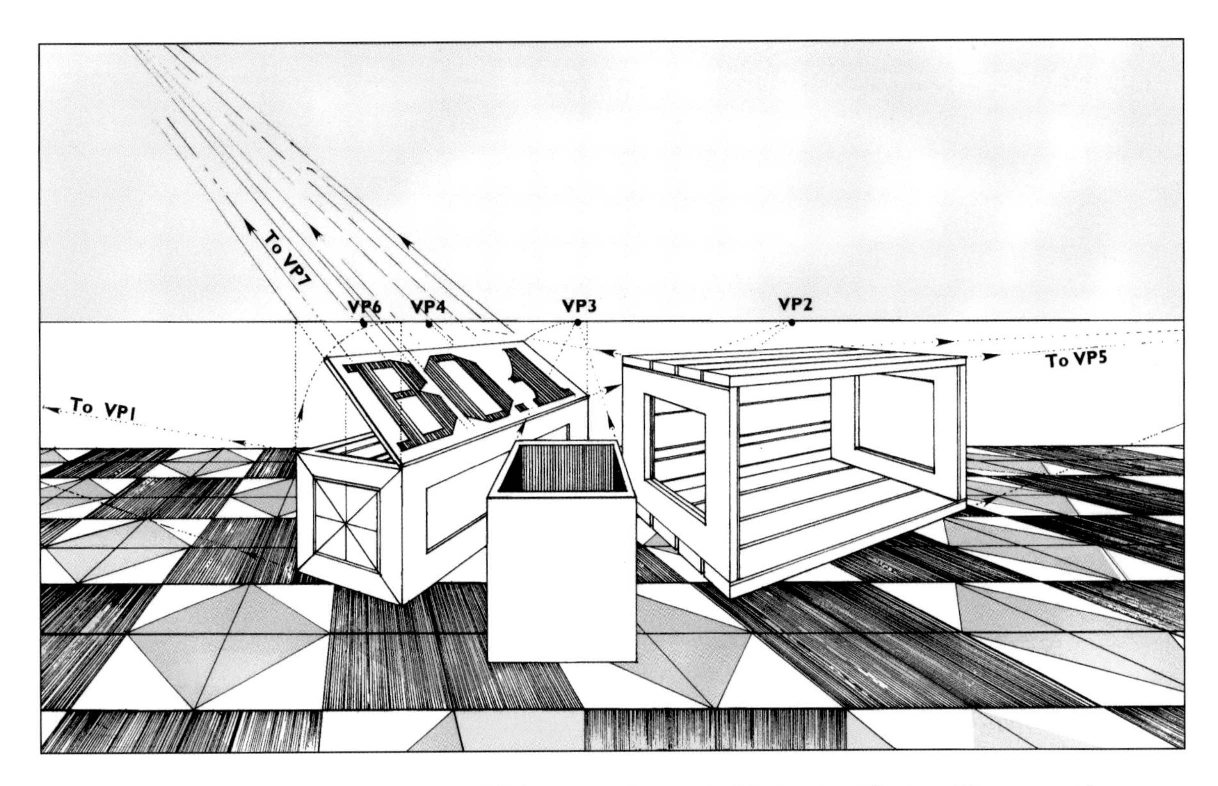

8.33 Seven in one. Seven vanishing points (VPs) were used to create this drawing. VPs 1 and 2 were used for the left box. VP 3 was used to create the center cube. VPs 4 and 5 were used for the open crate on the right. VP 6 was used for the floor tiles. VP 7 was used to define the inclined plane of the box lid and its lettering.

work of art. At times, an intuitive use of perspective can be more expressive than systematic formulas for indicating pictorial depth (see fig. 8.38).

Artists can become prisoners of the system they use. Because of its inflexible rules, perspective emphasizes accuracy of representation—an emphasis that tends to make the presentation more important than what is being represented. If, however, artists see perspective as an aid rather than an end in itself, as something to be used when and if the need arises in creating a picture, it can be very useful (see fig. 8.15). Many fine works of art ignore perspective or show "faults" in the use of the system. In such a case, the type of spatial order created by traditional perspective is not compatible with the aims of the artist (fig. 8.34). Perspective, like any tool, should be learned by artists because it extends the range of conceptual expression.

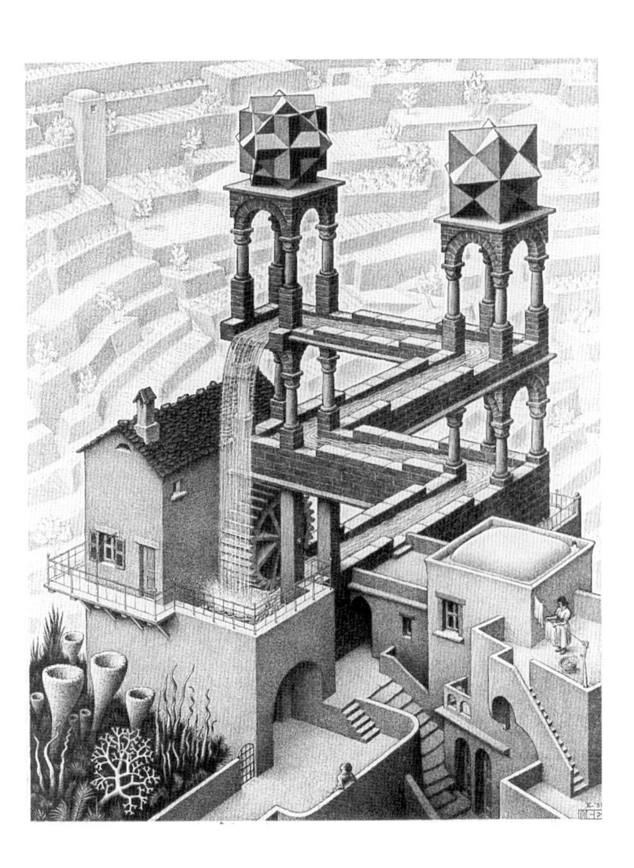

8.34 M. C. Escher, *Waterfall*, 1961. Lithograph, 15 × 11 in. (380 × 300 cm). From his early youth, Escher practiced the graphic technique of perspective and for many years strived to master that skill. Later he found ideas he could communicate by extending his perspective technique, and he became fascinated with visually subverting our commonsense view of the three-dimensional world. In this print, Escher knew it was impossible to see multiple stories of the same building on one level. Yet, the water flows downhill from the first floor to the third. The Gemeentemuseum, The Hague.

Other Projection Systems

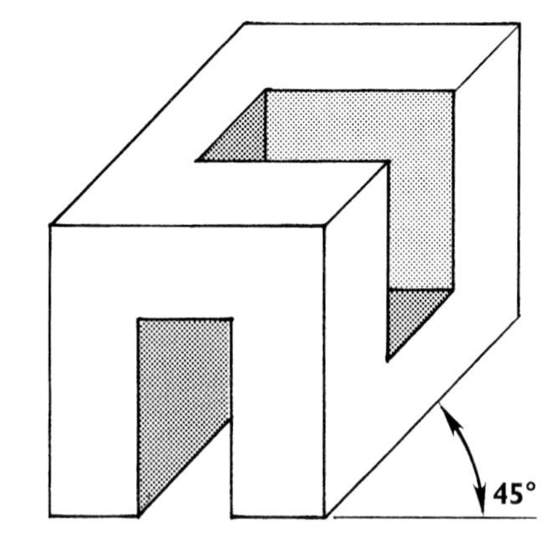

8.35A Oblique projection. This system for showing spatial relationships makes use of a flat frontal shape with nonconverging side planes drawn at a 45-degree angle from the front plane.

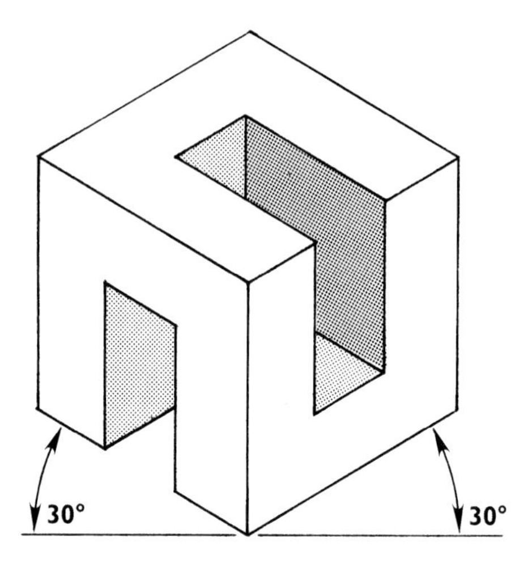

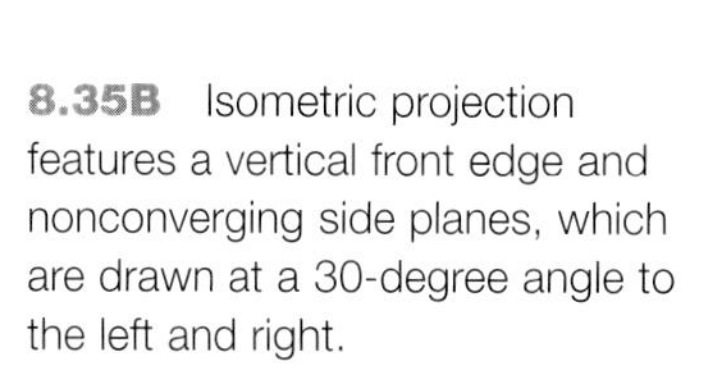
8.35B Isometric projection features a vertical front edge and nonconverging side planes, which are drawn at a 30-degree angle to the left and right.

Other systems to depict objects spatially have been developed. These methods use parallel projecting lines (nonconverging). Because these systems present a stable and consistently measurable image that does not diminish as it recedes, designers, architects, and technical engineers use them for ease of drawing. They do, however, tend to "flatten" out objects when compared to traditional perspective systems that use vanishing points.

Oblique projection looks at first glance to be related to one-point perspective, for both present a flat frontal view that is always parallel to the picture plane (fig. 8.35A). For engineering and architectural applications, the front plane is always drawn at full scale. However, with oblique perspective, all left- or right-side edges that would have converged at a singular vanishing point are drawn parallel. They come off the front plane at a 45-degree angle. This type of nonconverging parallel edges on receding planes is also seen in Asian art.

Isometric projection may be compared to two-point perspective in appearance. Both begin with a vertical frontal edge. Like oblique perspective, isometric work does not have any converging receding edges (fig. 8.35B). All edges that intersect at the vertical move away at a 30-degree angle, both to the left and to the right. For ease of drawing, all three dimensions of the object use the same measurement system (scale); there is no diminishing ratio on the receding planes. Artists often prefer this system to oblique perspective because all three faces are visible at the same time with less apparent distortion. No side of the image is drawn parallel to the viewer (picture plane). This system is used for technical illustration and drafting.

Orthographic drawing is perhaps less understood as a system for identifying objects in a spatial setting, but engineers and architects use it to present blueprints and schematic layouts (see fig. 8.47). With this system, all sides of the rectangular (geometric) object are drawn parallel or perpendicular to a base line, and the measurements are scaled to an exact ratio. Artists, engineers, industrial designers, and architects employ this system.

The reverse perspective seen in East Asian art is a dramatic contrast to the linear perspective of the West. Ancient canons prescribed convergence of parallel lines as they approach the spectator. This type of presentation closes the space in depth so that the picture becomes a stage and the spectator becomes an actor-participant in an active spatial panorama that rarely loses its identification with the picture plane (fig. 8.36A, B). Similar space concepts have been employed in the West during various historical periods. Ideas on pictorial space usually agree with the prevailing mental climate of the society that produces the art. In this sense, space is a form of human expression.

Intuitive Space

The same planes and volumes that create illusions of space in linear perspective can also be used to produce **intuitive space,** which is independent of strict rules and formulas. Intuitive space is thus not a system but a product of the artist's instinct for manipulating certain space-producing devices. The devices that help the artist to control space include overlap, transparency, interpenetration, inclined planes, disproportionate scale, and fractional representation. In addition, the artist may exploit the inherent spatial properties of the art elements. The physical properties of the art elements tend to thrust forward or backward; this can be used to define items spatially. By marshaling these spatial forces in any

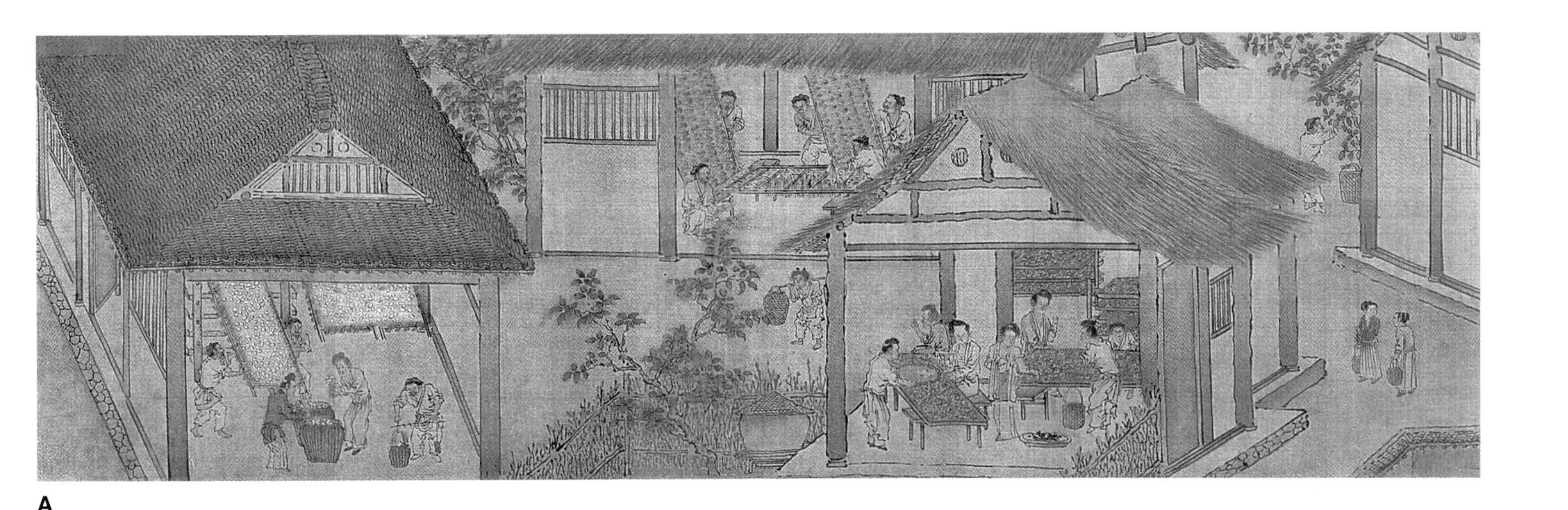

A

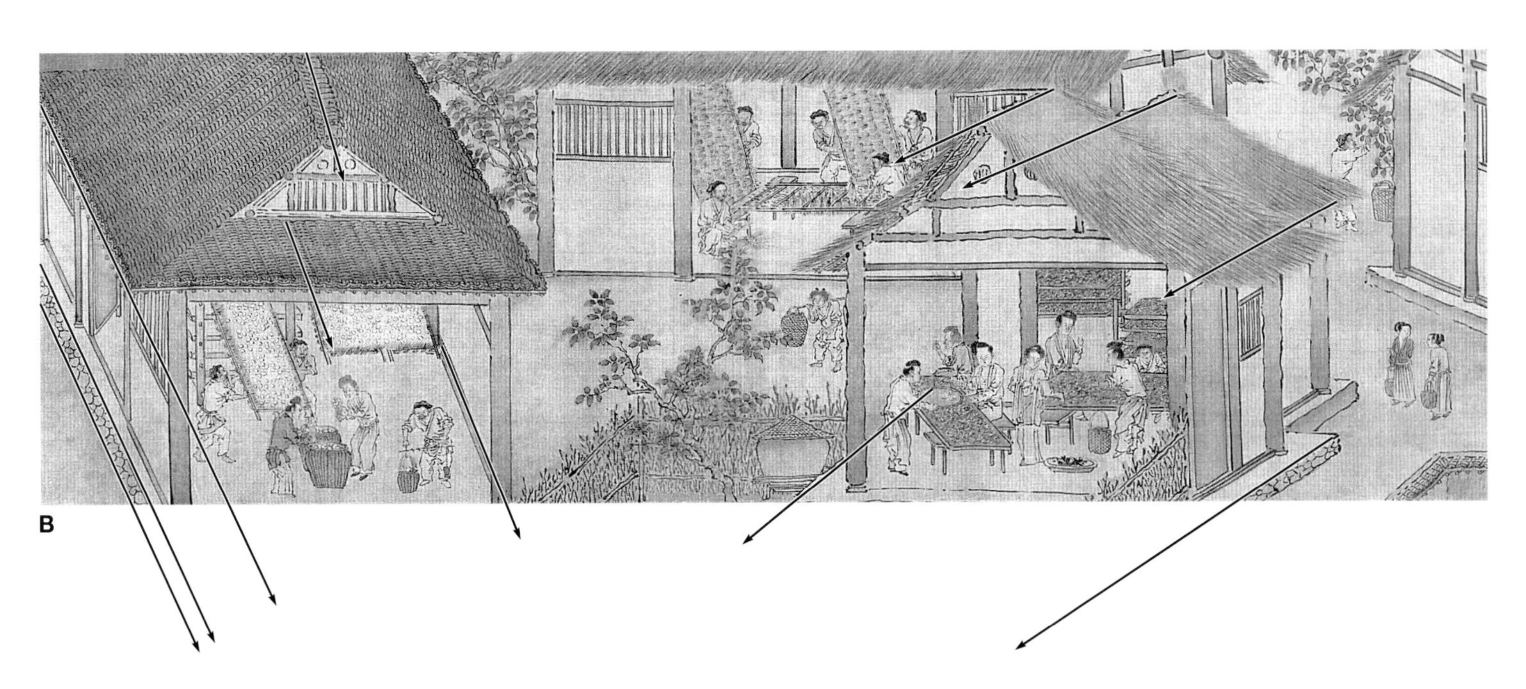

B

8.36 Attributed to Liang Kai, *Sericulture* (detail), Chinese, early thirteenth century, Southern Song dynasty. Handscroll, ink, and light color on paper, 26.5 × 98.5 cm. (A) This Chinese artist, following his own (Asian) concept of space as moving forward toward the observer, employs—from a Western point of view—a kind of reverse perspective. (B) A simple analysis of the *Sericulture* detail shows that if the lines defining the buildings are extended back toward the horizon line, they will never meet as they would in the linear perspective of Western artists. However, if they are extended forward, following the Asian concept of space, they seem to converge. As a result, the near edge of the buildings is narrower than the back—which is characteristic of East Asian perspective.

combination as needed, the artist can impart a sense of space to the pictorial image while adjusting relationships (fig. 8.37). The space derived from this method is readily sensed by everyone; judged by the standards of linear perspective, however, it may seem strange, even distorted. Nevertheless, intuitive space has been the dominant procedure during most of the history of art; it rarely implies great depth, but it makes for tightly knit imagery within a relatively shallow spatial field (fig. 8.38).

THE SPATIAL PROPERTIES OF THE ELEMENTS

The spatial effects that arise from using the elements of art structure must be recognized and controlled. Each of the elements possesses inherent spatial qualities, but the interrelationship between elements yields the greatest spatial feeling. The artist can achieve many types of spatial experiences by manipulating the elements—that is, by varying their position, number, direction, value, texture, size, and color. The resultant spatial variations are endless (see fig. 3.22).

Line and Space

Line, by its physical structure, implies continued direction of movement. Thus line, whether moving across the picture plane or deep into it, helps to indicate spatial presence. Because, by definition, a line must be greater in length than in width (or else it would be indistinguishable from a dot or a shape), it tends to emphasize one direction. The extension of this dominant direction in a single line creates continuity, moving the eye of the observer from one unit or general area to another. Line can be a transition that unifies the front, middle, and background areas.

In addition to direction, line contains other spatial properties. Long or short, thick or thin lines, and straight, angular, or curved lines take on different spatial positions and movements in contrast with one another. The indications of three-dimensional space mentioned earlier in this chapter are actively combined with the physical properties of line. A long thick line, for instance, appears larger (a spatial indication) and hence closer to the viewer than a short thin line. Overlapping lines establish differing spatial positions, especially when they are set in opposite directions (that is, vertical against horizontal). A diagonal line seems to move from the picture plane into deep space, whereas a vertical or horizontal line generally appears

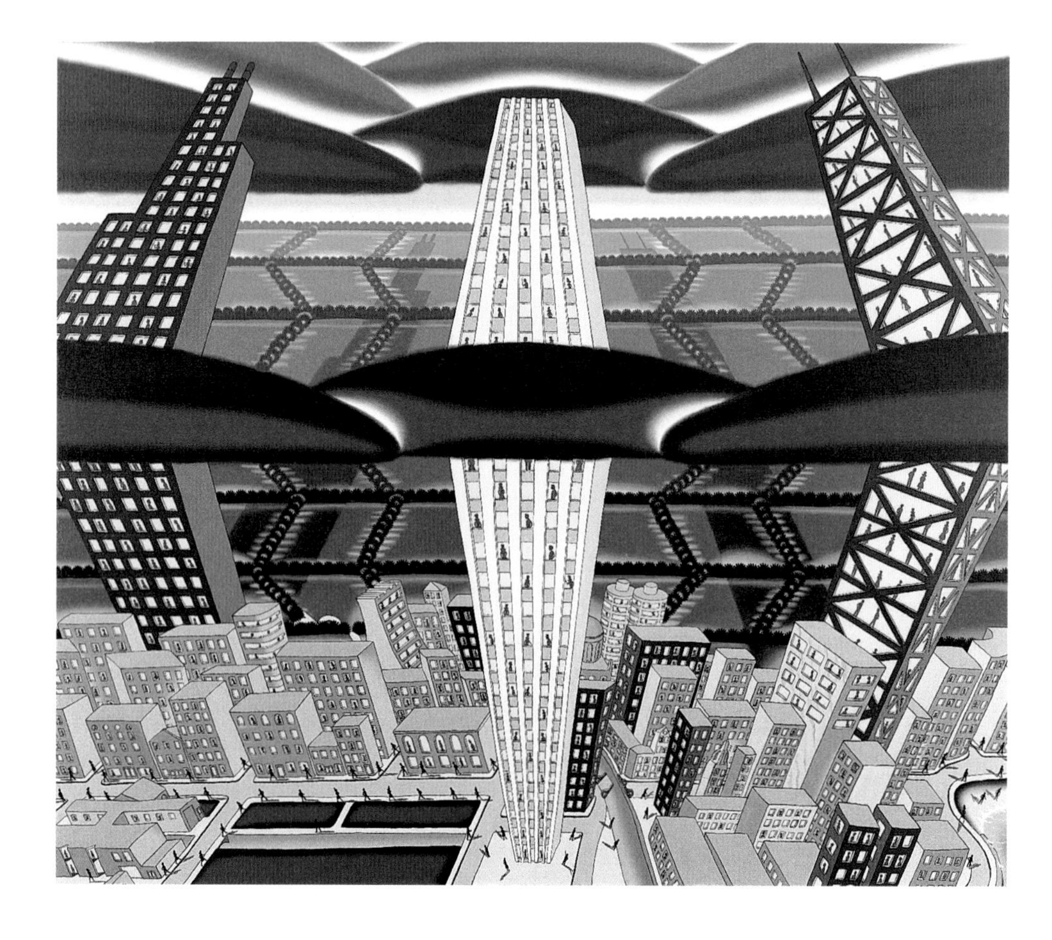

8.37 Roger Brown, *Land of Lincoln*, 1978. Oil on canvas, 5 ft 11½ in. × 7 ft (1.82 × 2.13 m). Certain contemporary artists employ individualistic devices to create unusual spatial effects. This painting by Roger Brown shows multiple viewpoints that seem to project backward and forward in a scale of unusual proportions.

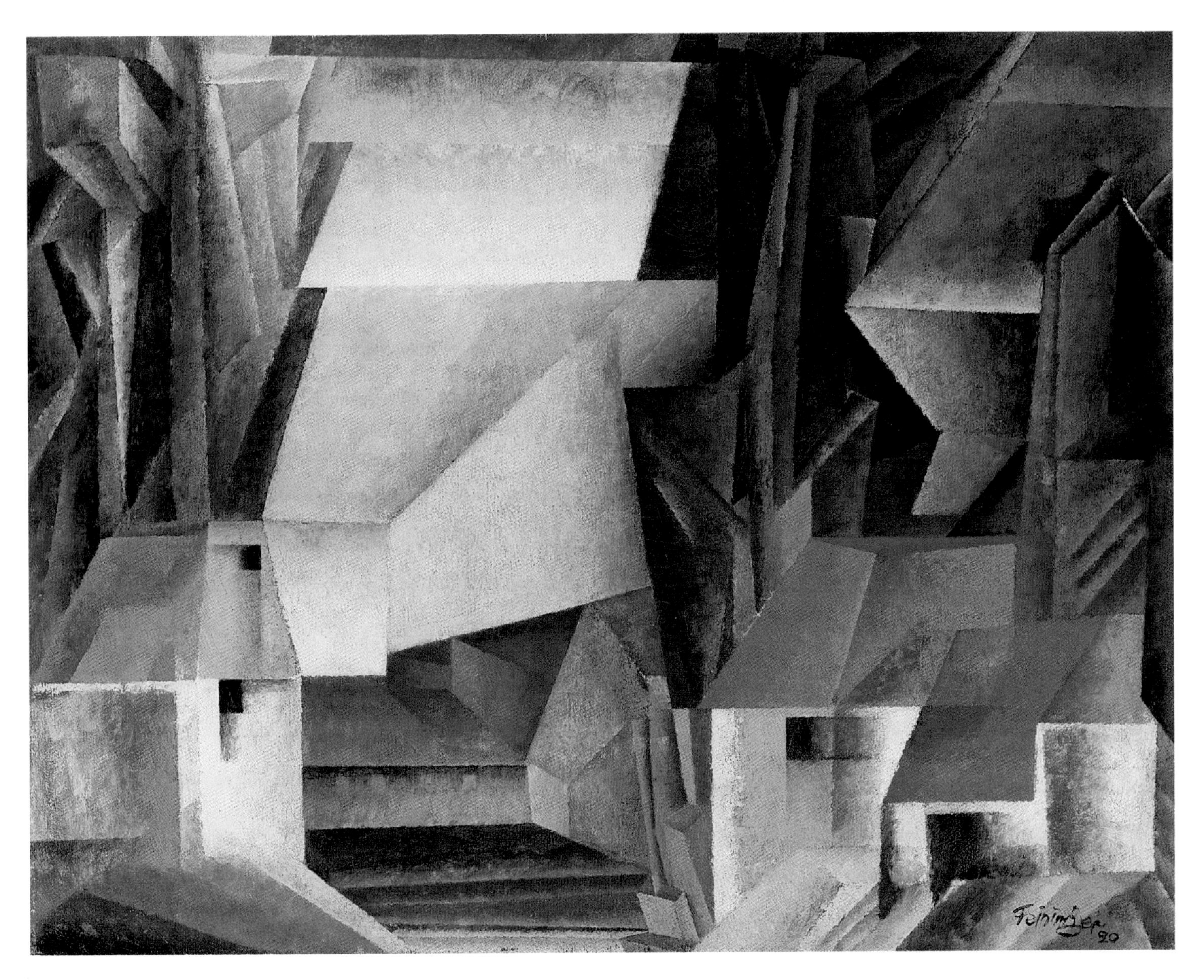

8.38 Lyonel Feininger, *Hopfgarten,* 1920. Oil on canvas, 25 × 32¼ in. In this painting, the artist has used intuitive methods of space control, including overlapping planes and transparencies, as well as planes that interpenetrate one another and incline into space.
The Minneapolis Institute of the Arts. Given in memory of Catharine Roberts Seybold by her friends and family.

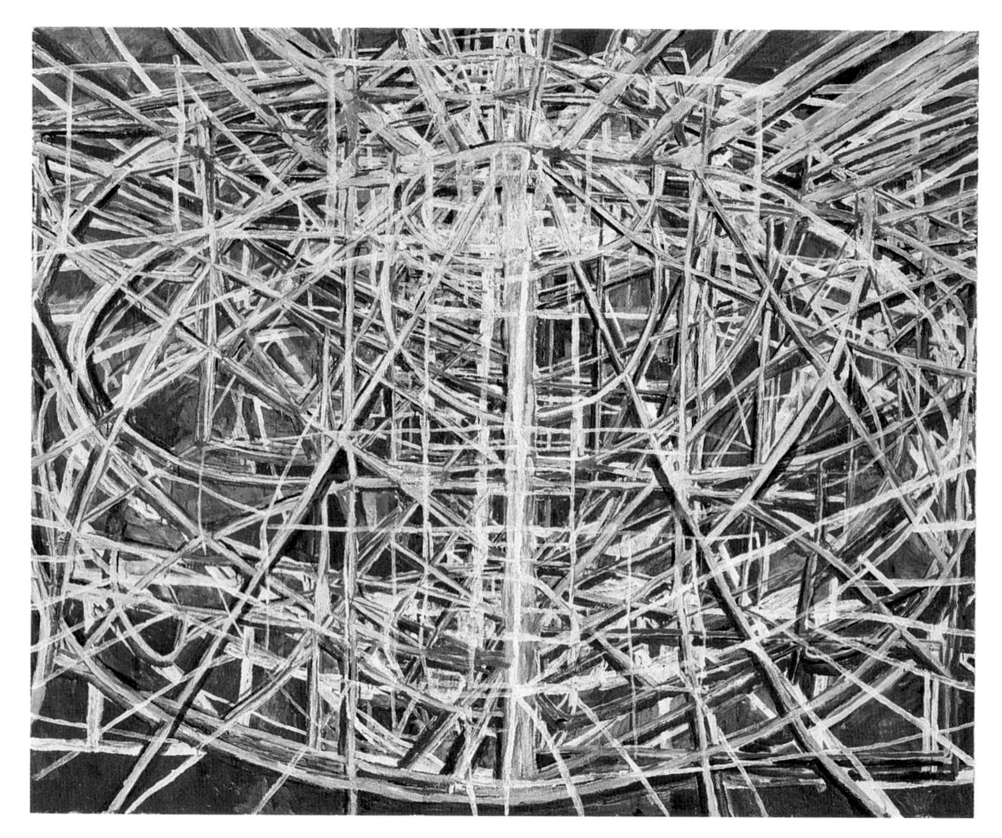

8.39 **Terry Winters, *Image Location*, 1997. Oil, alkyd resin, mica, and graphite on linen, 96 × 120 in. (243.8 × 304.8 cm).** Individual lines overlap, converge, and define their own space while collectively creating a relatively deep visual labyrinth. Courtesy of Matthew Marks Gallery, New York, NY. TW97.015.

comparatively static (fig. 8.39). In addition, the plastic qualities of overlapping lines can be increased by modulating their values. Lines can be lightened to the point that they disappear or become "lost," only to reappear (become "found") and grow darker across the composition. This missing section or implied line can also help control compositional direction or movement. The modulated plastic illusion invariably suggests change of position in space.

The spatial indication of line convergence that occurs in linear perspective is always in evidence wherever a complex of lines occurs. The spatial suggestions arising out of this principle are so infinitely varied that particular effects are usually the product of the artist's intuitive explorations. Wavy, spiral, serpentine, and zigzag line types adapt to all kinds of space through their unexpected deviations of direction and accent. They seem to move back and forth from one spatial plane to another. Unattached single lines define their own space and may have plastic qualities within themselves (fig. 8.39). Lines also clarify the spatial dimensions of solid shapes (see fig. 8.41 and fig. 3.9).

Shape and Space

Shape may refer to planes, solids, or volumes, all of which occupy space and are therefore entitled to consideration in this chapter. A plane, although physically two-dimensional, may create the illusion of three-dimensional space (see figs. 4.10 and 4.11). The space appears two-dimensional when the plane seems to lie on the picture surface (see fig. 4.10). The space appears three-dimensional when its edges seem to converge at a point toward the front or the back of the picture plane (fig. 8.40).

Solids, volumes, and masses automatically suggest three dimensions. Such shapes express the space in which they must exist and become an actual part of it. Planes, solids, and volumes can be made distant by diminishing their size in comparison to others in the foreground and by neutralizing their value, color, intensity, and detail (fig. 8.41). This treatment relates back to the indications of space outlined earlier in this chapter.

Value and Space

The plastic effect of value can be used to control pictorial space. When a light source is assumed to be in front of a work, the objects in the foreground appear light. The middle and background objects become progressively dark as they move away from the picture plane (see fig. 10.1). When the light source is located at the back of the work, the order of values is reversed (see fig. 6.20). The order of value change is consistent in gradation from light to dark or dark to light.

In the natural world, foreground objects are seen with clarity and great contrast, while distant objects are ill defined and gray. Therefore, neutral grays, when juxtaposed with blacks or whites, generally take a distant position (see fig. 8.4).

Cast shadows are sometimes helpful in describing plastic space, but they may be spatially confusing and even injurious to the design if not handled judiciously (see figs. 5.4A and 5.6).

Value-modeling can be abstract in the sense that it need not follow the objective natural order of light and dark. Many artists totally ignore this natural order, using instead the inherent spatial position that results from the contrast of dark and light (fig. 8.42).

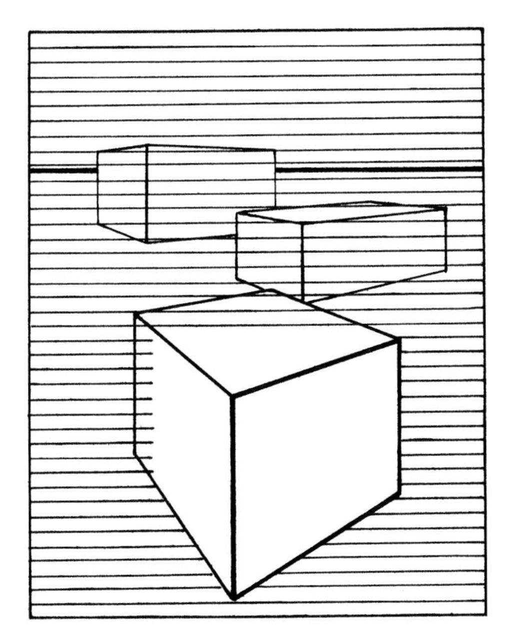

8.40 Planes and solids in space. The relationship of planes in this diagram describes an effect of solids or volumes that in turn seem to occupy space. The size, overlapping, and placement of these volumes further increase the effect of solidity. The horizontal shaded lines indicate an imaginary position for the picture plane, causing the near volume to project into the observer's space, or in front of the picture plane.

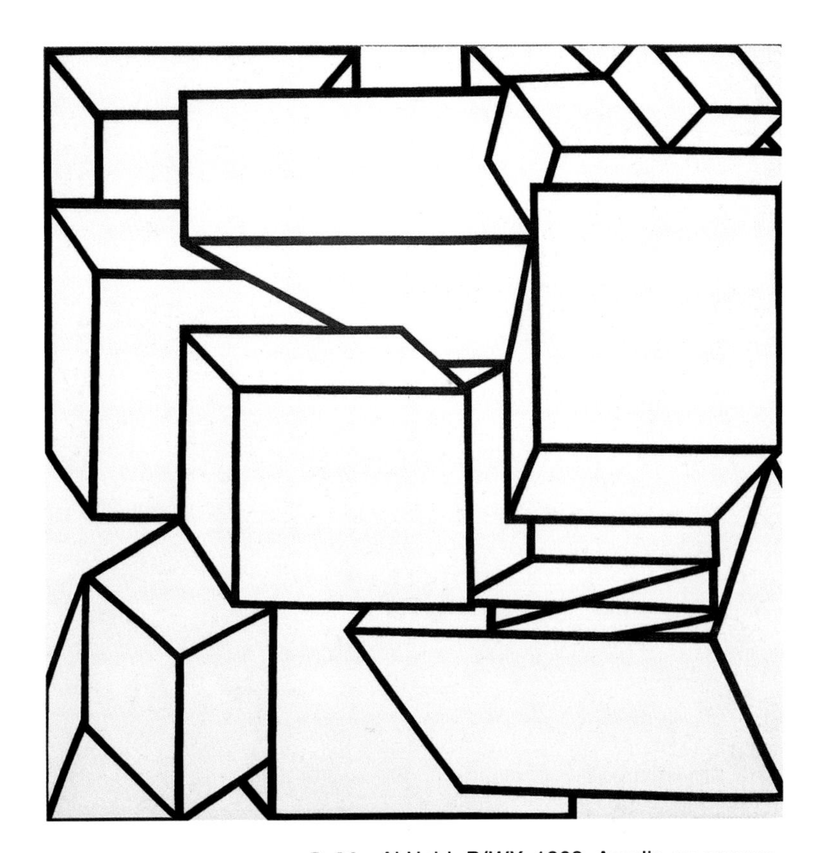

8.41 Al Held, *B/WX,* 1968. Acrylic on canvas, 9 ft 6 in. × 9 ft 6 in. (2.90 × 2.90 m). Although the physical properties of the lines in this work are consistent throughout, their arrangement causes the enclosed shapes to be seen in different spatial positions. This is somewhat similar to the program of Op Art. Albright-Knox Art Gallery, Buffalo, NY. Gift of Seymour H. Knox, 1969. © Al Held/Licensed by VAGA, New York, NY.

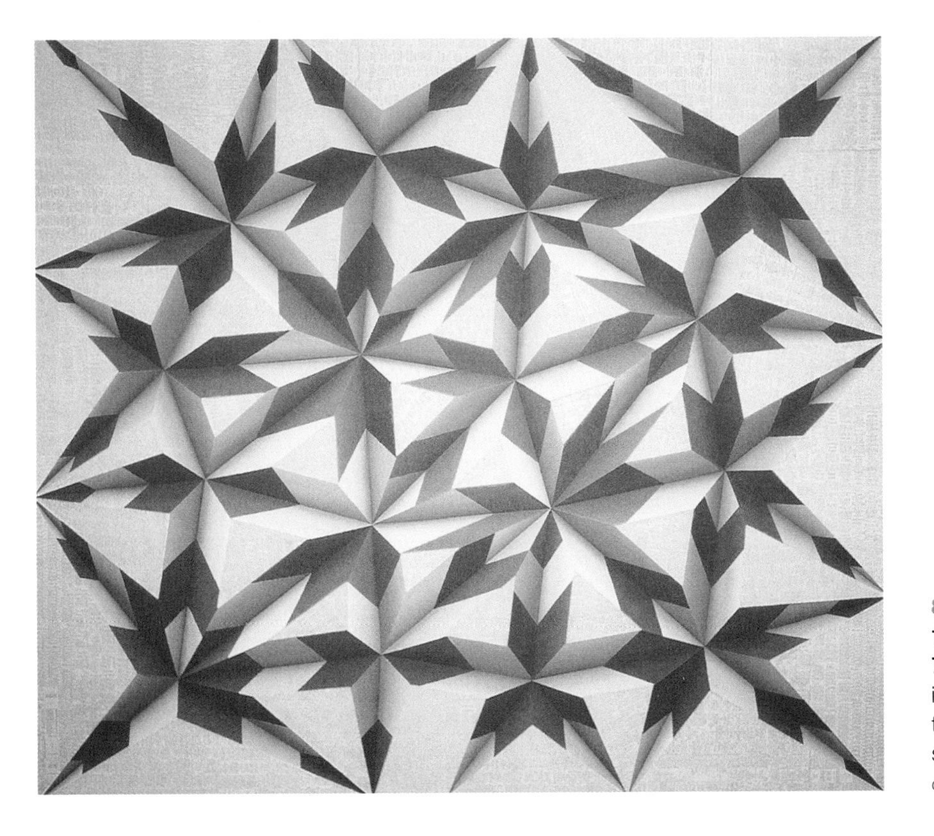

8.42 Tony King, *Map: Spirit of '76,* 1976. Acrylic and newspaper on canvas, 7 × 8 ft (2.13 × 2.44 m). The format, with its papier collé surface, is perfectly flat, but the use of light and dark values creates a strongly three-dimensional illusion. Courtesy of Owens Corning Collection, Toledo, OH.

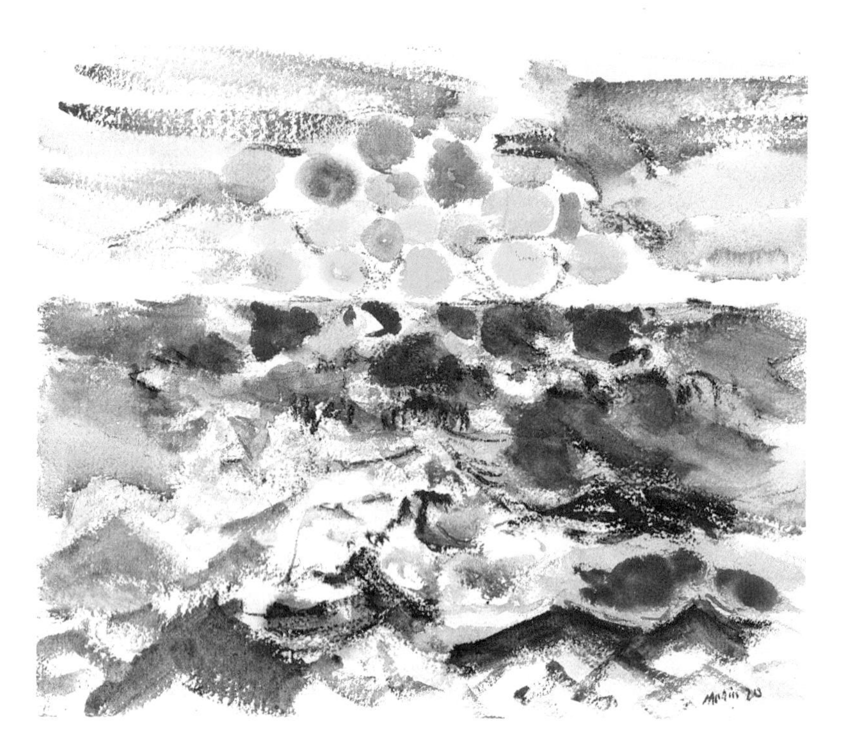

8.43 John Marin, *Sun Spots,* 1920. Watercolor and charcoal on off-white wove paper, 16½ × 19¾ in. (41.9 × 50.2 cm). Marin used the watercolor medium to exhibit a free, loose style of painting. His play of color—sea against sunspots—helps to create tremendous spatial interaction. The Metropolitan Museum of Art, Robert Lehman Collection, 1975 (1975.1.74). Photograph © 1991, The Metropolitan Museum of Art, all rights reserved.

8.44 Hans Hofmann, *The Gate,* 1959–60. Oil on canvas, 6 ft 3⅛ in. × 4 ft ½ in. (1.9 × 1.23 m). The large receding areas of cool greens and blues in this painting unify the color scheme. The smaller areas of warm yellows and reds give balance to the total color pattern. Spatial contrast is softened and the composition is harmonized by the lower intensity of the colors used. Solomon R. Guggenheim Museum, New York, NY. 62.1620. Photograph by David Heald. © Estate of Hans Hofmann/ Licensed by VAGA, New York, NY.

Texture and Space

Because of the surface enrichment that texture produces, it is tempting to think of this element purely in terms of decorative usefulness. Actually, texture can have the plastic function of describing the depth position of surfaces. Generally speaking, sharp, clear, and bold textures advance, while fuzzy, dull, and minuscule textures recede. When modified through varied use of value, color, and line, texture significantly contributes to the total pictorial unity.

Texture is one of the visual signs used to produce the decorative surface so valued in contemporary art. The physical character of texture is related to allover patterned design and therefore operates effectively on decorative surfaces. When patterned surfaces are repeated and distributed over the entire pictorial area, the flatness of the picture plane becomes vitally important. Many works by Pablo Picasso utilize surface textures to preserve the flatness of the picture plane (see fig. 6.18).

Color and Space

One of the outstanding contributions of modern artists has been their reevaluation of the plastic potentialities of color. Color is now integrated directly into the form of the picture in a positive and direct manner in order to model the various spatial planes of surface areas (see the "Plastic Colors" section in Chapter 7, pp. 155–56). Since the time of Cézanne, a new awareness of the spatial characteristics of color has arisen in art. Prior to that, space was considered as deriving from the picture plane and receding from it. Later, John Marin and others dealt with the spaces on or in front of the picture plane chiefly through the use of color (fig. 8.43). Hans Hofmann, the abstractionist, often used colors to advance shapes seemingly beyond the picture plane. He controlled the degree to which they advanced or receded by contrasts of value, intensity, and hue (fig. 8.44).

Analogous colors, because they are closely related, create limited spatial movement; contrasting colors enlarge the space and provide varied accents or focal points of interest. Both exploit the limitless dimensions of space.

RECENT CONCEPTS OF SPACE

Every great period in the history of art has espoused a particular concept of space. These spatial preferences reflect basic conditions within the civilization that produced them. Certain fundamental attitudes toward space seem to recur in varied forms throughout recorded history. When a new spatial approach is introduced, the public may resist it at first. Eventually, however, it becomes the standard lens through which people view things. During their period of influence, these conventions are the norm for people and gradually condition them to expect art that conforms to certain general principles. The acceleration of change prompted by modern science has now produced new concepts that are without precedent. Today, artists are looking for ways to understand and interpret these ever-widening horizons, and, as they do, their explorations are met by characteristic resistance from the public (fig. 8.45).

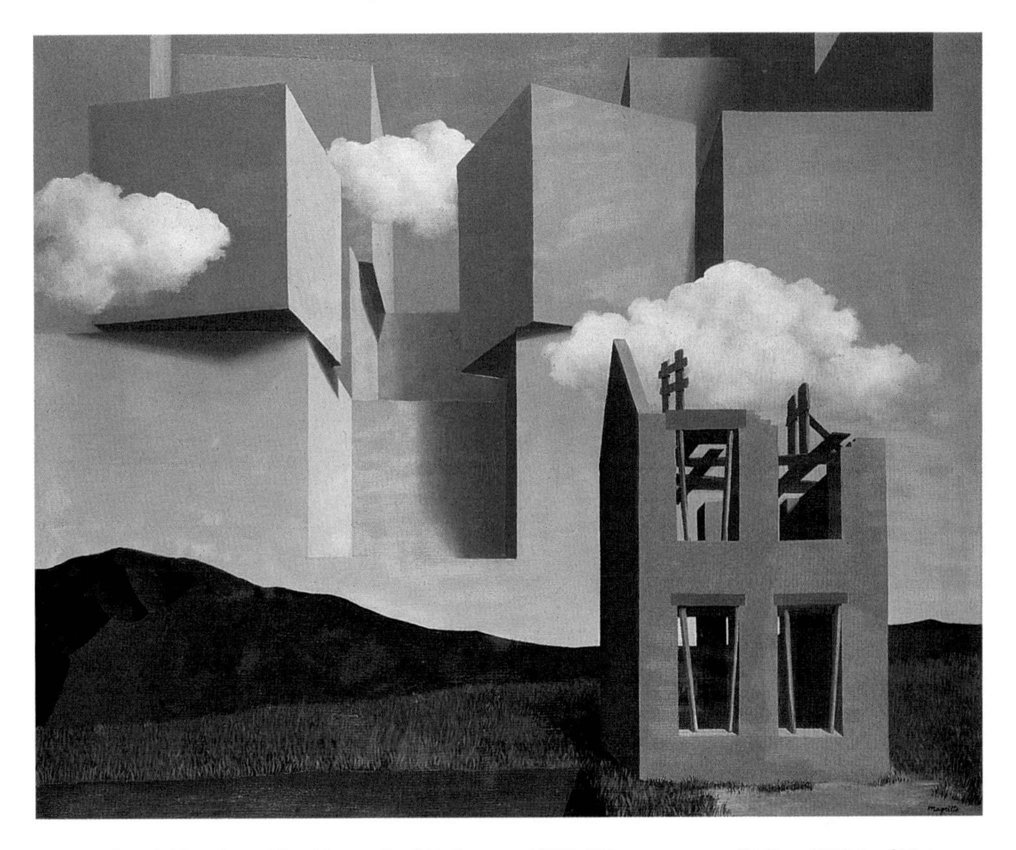

8.45 René Magritte, *The Unmasked Universe*, 1932. Oil on canvas, 29.5 × 35.8 in. (75 × 91 cm). On close inspection, one can see that this work is deliberately inconsistent in its use of space. As a Surrealist, Magritte often created ambiguous and unexpected effects to titillate our senses.

The Search for a New Spatial Dimension

Artists of the Renaissance, conditioned by the outlook of the period, set as their goal the optical, scientific mastery of nature. They sought to accomplish this by reducing nature, part by part, to a static geometric system. By restricting their attention to one point of view, artists were able to develop perspective and represent some of the illusionary distortions of actual shapes as seen by the human eye.

Modern artists, equipped with new scientific and industrial materials and technology, have extended the search into nature initiated by the Renaissance. They have probed nature's inner and outer structure with microscope, camera, video, and telescope. Automobiles, airplanes, and spacecraft have given them the opportunity to see more of the world than their early predecessors knew existed. The radically changed environment of the artist has brought about a new awareness of space. It has become increasingly evident that space cannot always be described from the one point of view characteristic of Renaissance artists, and the search continues for a new graphic vocabulary to describe visual discoveries. Because one outstanding feature of the modern world is motion, contemporary artistic representation must move, at least illusionistically. Motion has become a part of space, and this space can be grasped only if a certain period of time is allotted to cover it. Hence, a new dimension is added to spatial conception—the **fourth dimension,** which combines space, time, and motion and presents an important artistic challenge. This challenge is to discover a practical method for representing things in motion from every viewpoint on a flat surface. In searching for solutions to this problem, artists have turned to their own experiences as well as to the work of others.

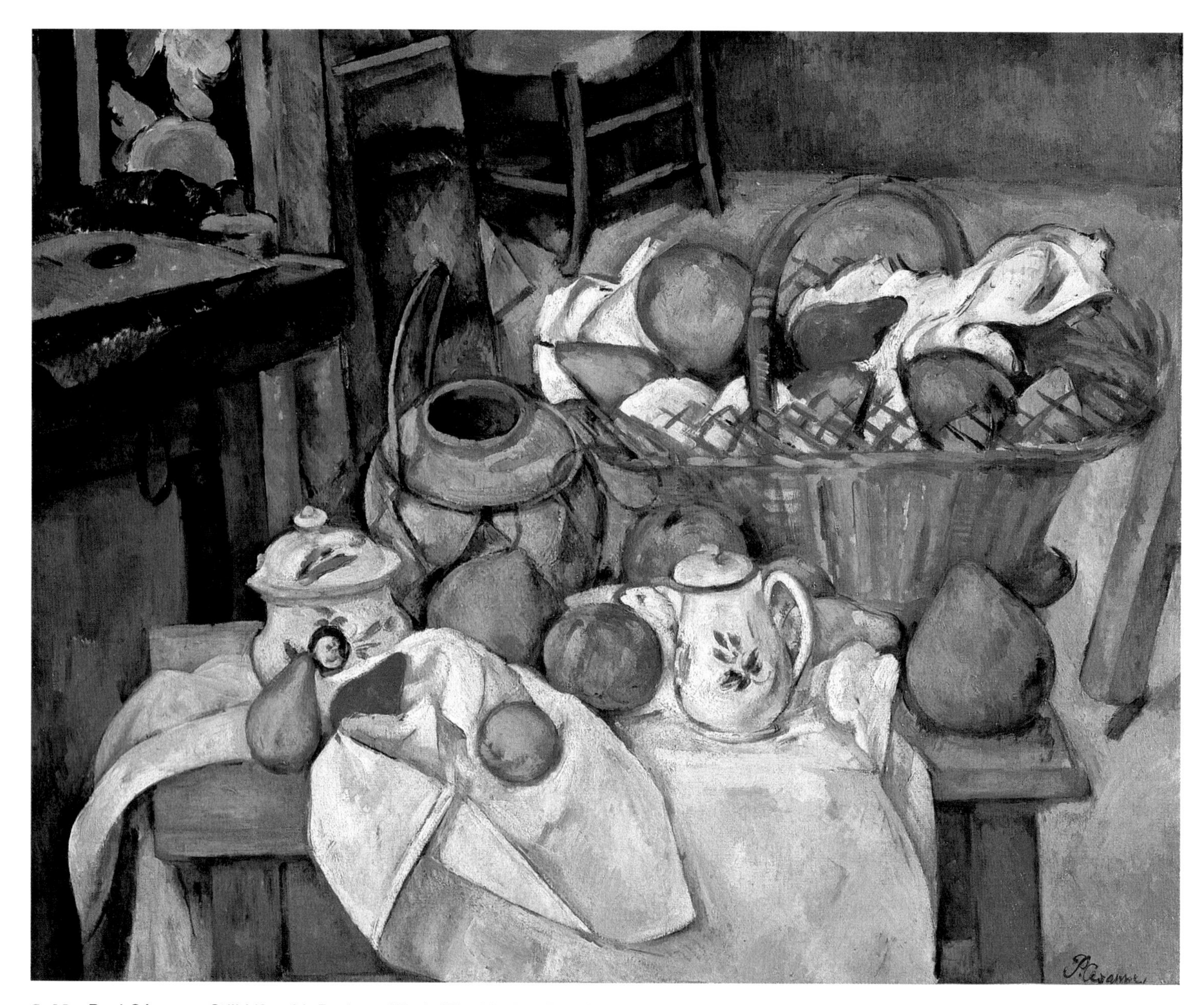

8.46 **Paul Cézanne, *Still Life with Basket of Fruit (The Kitchen Table),* c. 1888–90. Oil on canvas, 25⅝ × 31⅞ in. (65.1 × 81 cm).** Cézanne was concerned with the plastic reality of objects as well as with their organization into a unified design. Although the pitcher and sugar bowl are viewed from a direct frontal position, the rounded jar behind them is painted as if it were being seen from a higher location. The handle of the basket is shown as centered at the front, but it seems to become skewed into a right-sided view as it proceeds to the rear. The left and right front table edges do not line up and are thus viewed from different vantage points. Cézanne combined these multiple viewpoints in one painting in order to present each object with a more profound sense of three-dimensional reality. Musée d'Orsay, Paris, France. Photo © Erich Lessing/Art Resource, New York.

Plastic Images

Paul Cézanne, the nineteenth-century Post-Impressionist, was an early pioneer in the attempt to express the new dimension. His aim was to render objects in a manner more true to nature. This nature, it should be pointed out, was not the Renaissance world of optical appearances; instead, it was a world of forms in space, conceived in terms of a plastic image (fig. 8.46). In painting a still life, Cézanne selected the most characteristic viewpoint of all his objects; he then changed the eye levels, split the individual object planes, and combined all of these views in the same painting, creating a composite view of the group. Cézanne often shifted his viewpoint of a single object from the right side to the left side and from the top to the bottom, creating the illusion of looking around it. To see these multiple views of the actual object, we would have to move around it or revolve it in front of us; this act would involve motion, space, and time.

The Cubists adopted many of the pictorial devices used by Cézanne. They usually showed an object from as many views as suited them. Objects were rendered in a type of orthographic drawing, divided into essential views that could be drawn in two dimensions, not unlike the Egyptian technique previously cited (see "Fractional Representation," pp. 184–85, and figs. 8.12 and 8.13). The basic view (the top view) is called a plan. With the plan as a basis, the elevations (or profiles) were taken from the front and back, and the sections were taken from the right and left sides (fig. 8.47). The juxtaposition of these views in a painting showed much more of the object than would normally be visible. The technique seems a distortion to the lay spectator conditioned to a static view, but within the limits of artistic selection, everything is present that we would ordinarily expect to see (fig. 8.48).

In the works of the Cubists, we find that a picture can have a life of its own and that the creation of space is not essentially a matter of portrayal or rendering. The Cubists worked step-by-step to illustrate that the more a painted object departs from straightforward optical resemblance, the more systematically could the full three-dimensional nature of the object be explored. Eventually, they developed the concept of the "synthetically" designed picture. Instead of analyzing a subject, they began by developing large, simple geometric shapes, divorced from a model. Subject matter suggested by the shapes was then imposed or synthesized into this spatial system (see fig. 4.8).

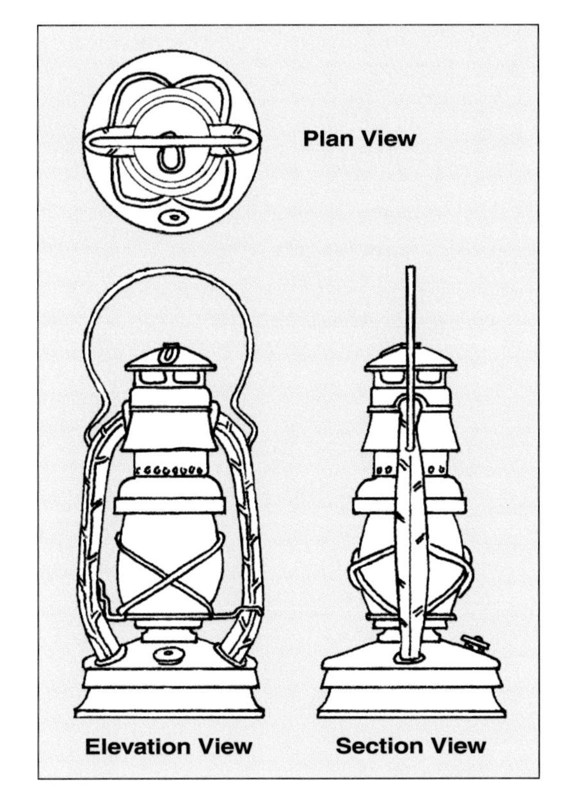

8.47 **Tom Haverfield, *Kerosene Lamp*, c. 1960. Pen and ink, 9 × 12 in. (22.9 × 30.5 cm).** In this work, objects are rendered in a type of orthographic drawing that divides them into essential views able to be drawn in two dimensions. Courtesy of the artist.

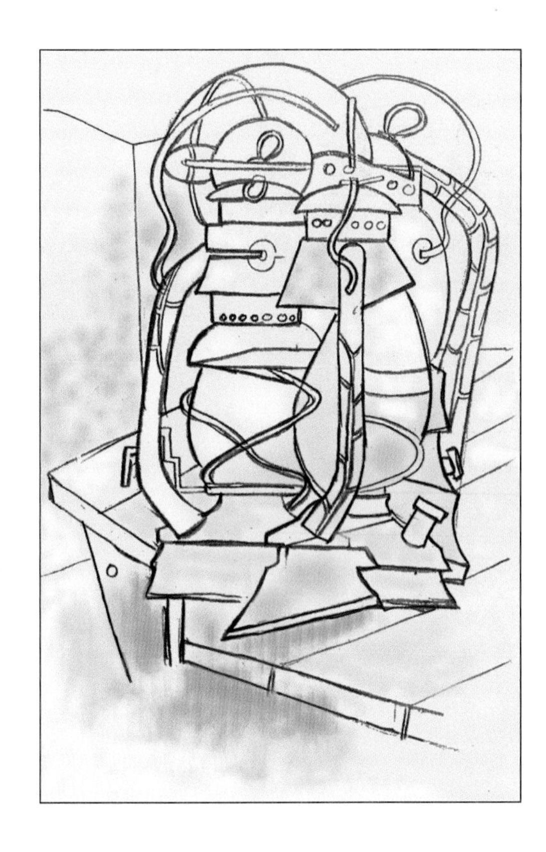

8.48 **Tom Haverfield, *Kerosene Lamp II*, c. 1960. Pencil on paper, 14 × 18 in. (35.6 × 45.7 cm).** The juxtaposition of orthographic views illustrates all the physical attributes and different views of the object in one drawing. Such a composite drawing shows much more of an object than could normally be visible. Courtesy of the artist.

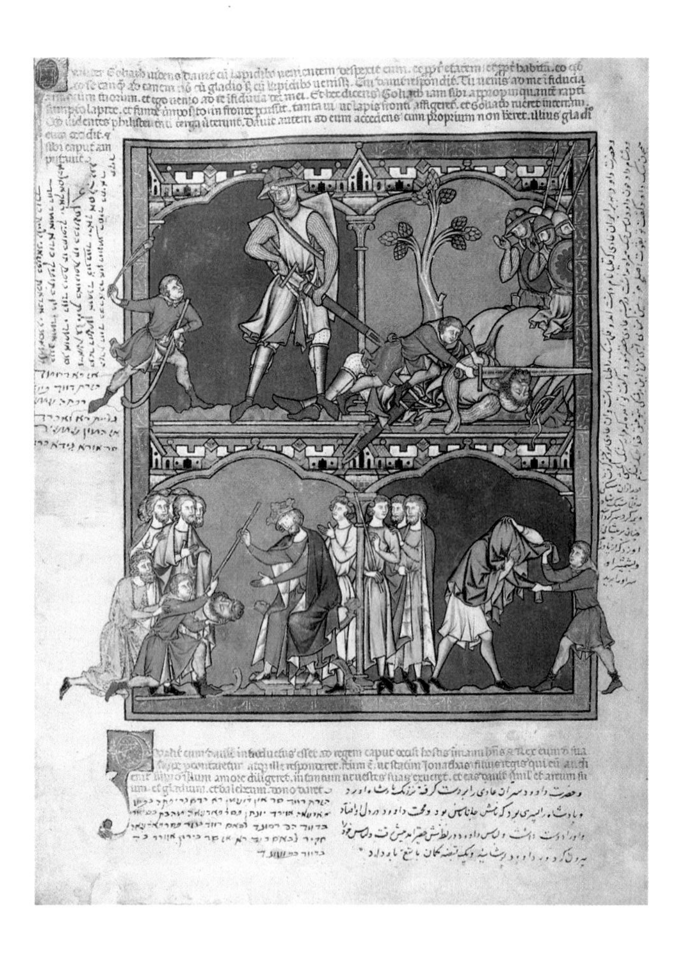

8.49 Unknown, *David and Goliath,* c. 1250. Manuscript dimensions: 15⅝ × 11¾ in. (39 × 30 cm). The element of time passing is present here but in a conventional episodic manner. The order of events proceeds in a style similar to that of a comic strip. Pierpont Morgan Library, New York, M.638 f.28v./Art Resource, New York.

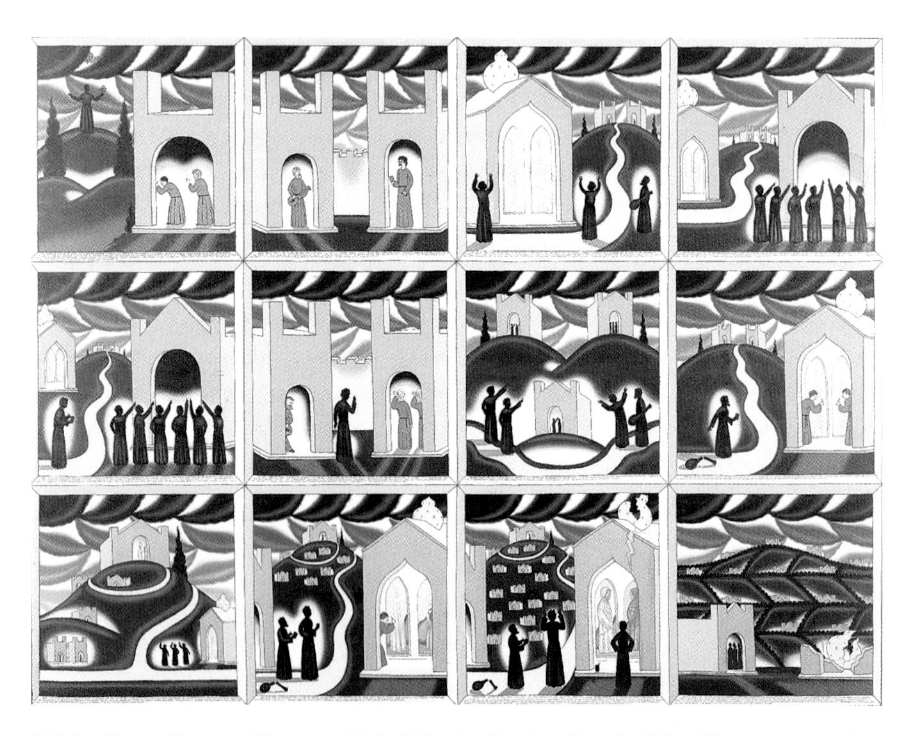

8.50 Roger Brown, *Giotto and His Friends (Getting Even),* 1981. Oil on canvas, 6 ft × 8 ft ⅜ in. (1.83 × 2.45 m). Contemporary artist Roger Brown has used the historical technique of segmental narrative. Each segment of the work is a portion of an unfolding story. © The School of the Art Institute of Chicago and the Brown Family.

Pictorial Representations of Movement in Time

From time immemorial, artists have grappled with the problem of representing movement on the stationary picture surface. In the works of prehistoric and primitive humans, the efforts were not organized but were isolated attempts to show a limited phase of observed movement.

In an early attempt to convey an impression of movement, Greek sculptors organized the lines in the draperies of their figures to accent a continuous flowing direction. By following these linear accents, the eye of the observer readily moves smoothly over the figure's surface.

The artists of the medieval and early Renaissance periods illustrated biblical stories by repeating a series of still pictures. The representation of the different phases of the narrative (in either a sequence of several pictures or a sequence within a single work) created a visual synopsis of the subject's movement, the time period, and the space covered. These pictures are antecedents of modern comic-strip and motion-picture techniques, whose individual frames, when projected at speed, provide the illusion of movement (figs. 8.49 and 8.50; see fig. 8.37).

Another representational means that artists have used to suggest movement superimposes a series of views of a stationary figure or its parts within a single pictorial arrangement. This technique in essence catalogs the sequence of position of a moving body, indicating the visible changes. Twentieth-century artists explored the possibility of fusing these changing figure positions by filling out the pathway of its movement. Figures are seen not in fixed positions but as abstract moving paths of action. The subject in Marcel Duchamp's *Nude Descending a Staircase, No. 2,* is not the human body but rather the type and degree of energy the human body emits as it passes through space. This painting signals important progress in the pictorialization of motion, because the plastic forces are functionally integrated with the composition (fig. 8.51).

The Futurists (see the "Futurism" section in Chapter 10, p. 276) were devoted to motion for its own sake. They included not only the shapes of figures and objects and their pathways of movement but also their backgrounds. These features were combined in a pattern of kinetic energy. Although this form of expression was not entirely new, it provided a new type of artistic adventure—simultaneity of figure, object, and environment (figs. 8.52 and 8.53). Motion pictures, which were a part of the culture during the period, almost certainly influenced these artists (see the following discussion of motion pictures). Contemporary artists continue to experiment with the concept of movement, subject, and surroundings (figs. 8.54, 8.55, and 8.56).

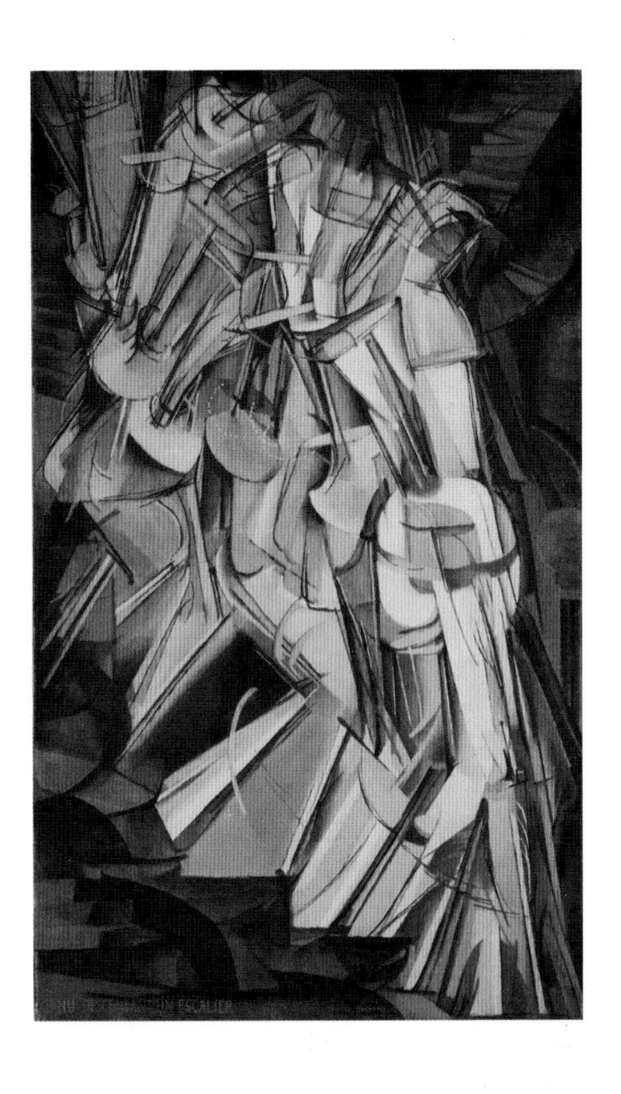

8.51 Marcel Duchamp, *Nude Descending a Staircase, No. 2,* 1912. Oil on canvas, 58 × 35 in. (147.3 × 88.9 cm). The subject of Duchamp's painting is not the human body but rather the type and degree of energy a body emits as it passes through space. Philadelphia Museum of Art, PA. Louise and Walter Arensberg Collection. Photo: Corbis Media. © 2005 Artists Rights Society (ARS), New York/ADAGP, Paris/Estate of Marcel Duchamp.

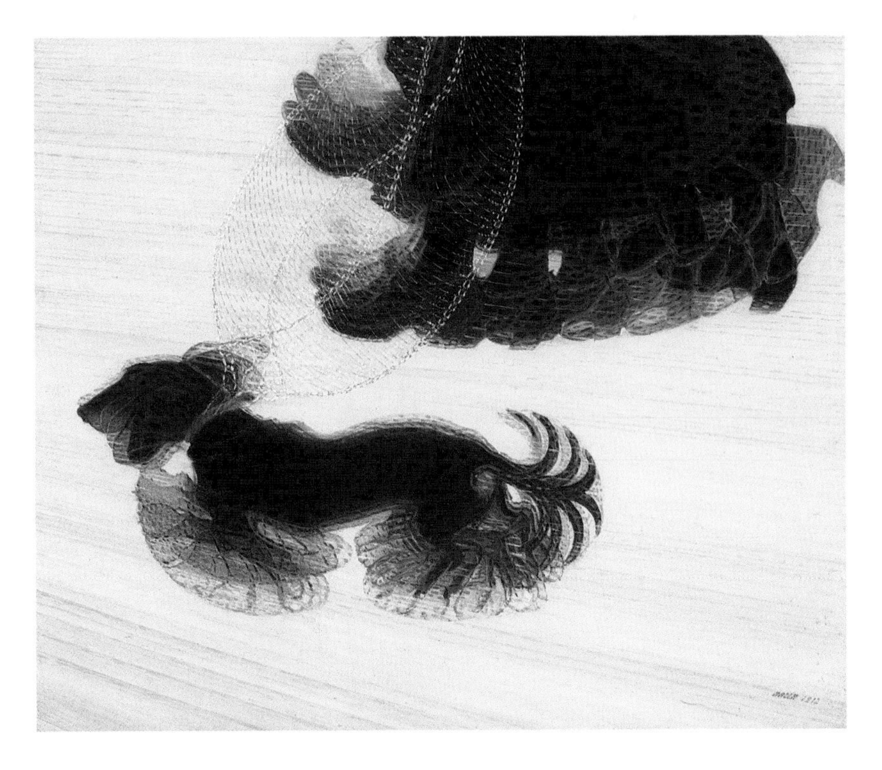

8.52 Giacomo Balla, *Dynamism of a Dog on a Leash,* 1912. Oil on canvas, 35⅜ × 43¼ in. (89.9 × 109.9 cm). To suggest motion as it is involved in time and space, Balla invented the technique of repeated contours. This device soon became commonly imitated in newspaper comic strips, thereby becoming a mere convention. Albright-Knox Art Gallery, Buffalo, NY. Bequest of A. Conger Goodyear and Gift of George F. Goodyear, 1964. © 2005 Artists Rights Society (ARS), New York/SIAE, Rome.

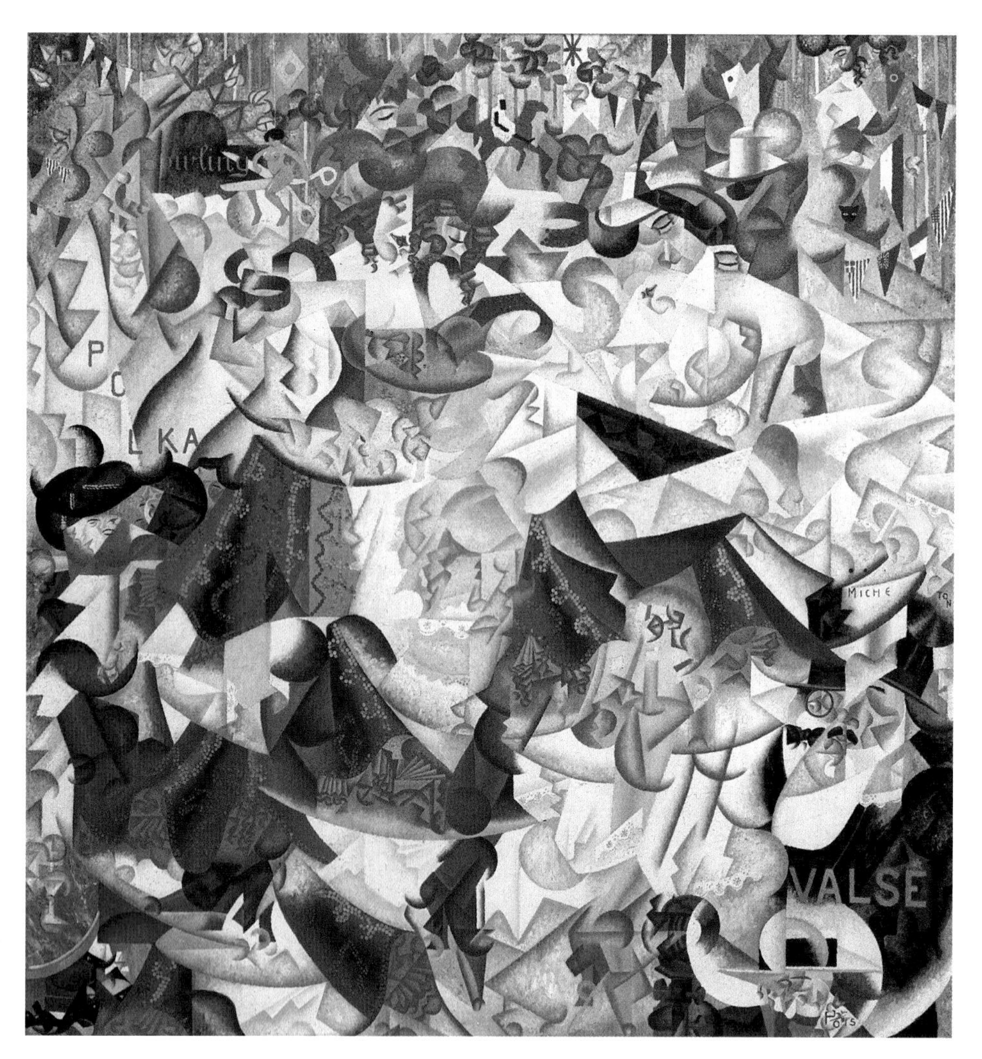

8.53 Gino Severini, ***Dynamic Hieroglyphic of the Bal Tabarin,*** **1912. Oil on canvas with sequins, 63⅝ × 61½ in. (161.6 × 156.2 cm).** The works of the Futurists were devoted to motion for its own sake. They included not only the shapes of figures and objects and their pathways of movement but also their backgrounds. These features were combined in a pattern of kinetic energy. © 2005 Artists Rights Society (ARS), New York/ ADGP, Paris. The Museum of Modern Art, New York, NY. U.S.A. Acquired through the Lillie P. Bliss Bequest. Digital image © The Museum of Modern Art/Licensed by SCALA/Art Resource, NY.

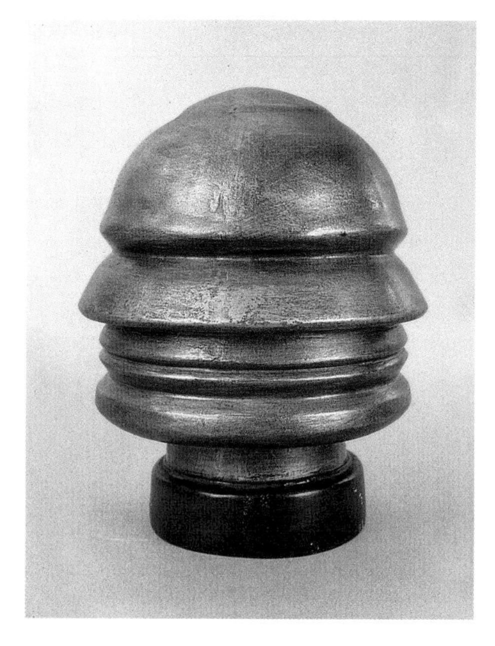

8.54 Renato Bertelli, ***Continuous Profile of Mussolini,*** **1933 (later manufactured by Ditta EFFEFFE, Milan, with Mussolini's approval). Bronzed terra-cotta, 11¾ in. high × 9 in. in diameter (29.8 cm high × 22.9 cm in diameter).** Bertelli, following the influence of the Futurists, explored the concepts of simultaneity and continuous movement in portraiture. Mussolini recognized the appeal to "modernity" and organized the mass distribution of the sculpture. Courtesy of The Mitchell Wolfson Jr. Collection, The Wolfsonian–Florida International University, Miami Beach, Florida. Photograph by Bruce White.

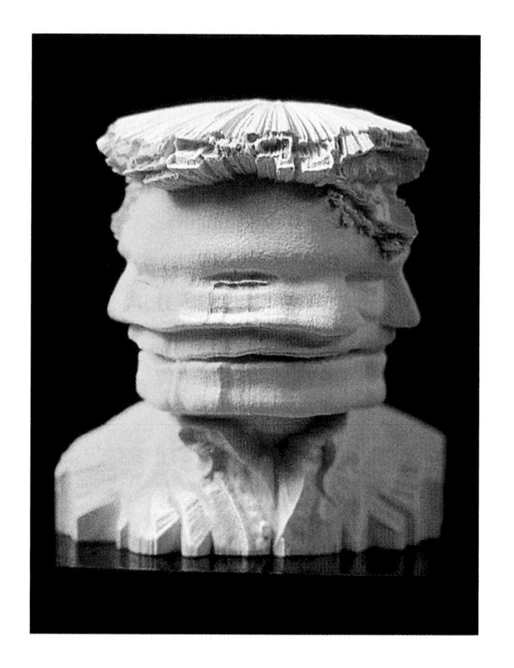

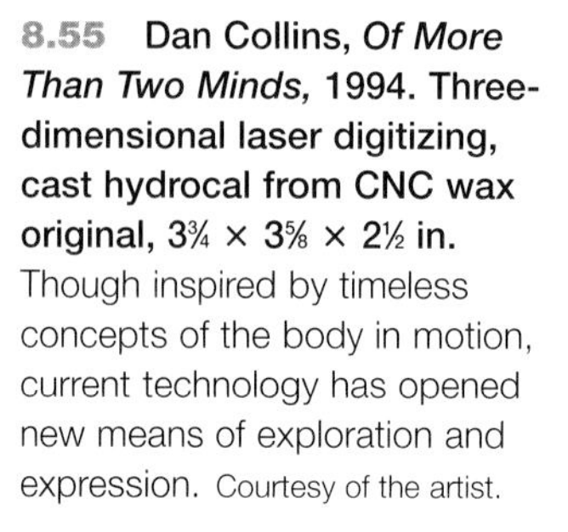

8.55 Dan Collins, ***Of More Than Two Minds,*** **1994. Three-dimensional laser digitizing, cast hydrocal from CNC wax original, 3¾ × 3⅝ × 2½ in.** Though inspired by timeless concepts of the body in motion, current technology has opened new means of exploration and expression. Courtesy of the artist.

The exploration of space in terms of the four-dimensional space–time continuum is in its infancy. As research reveals more of the mysteries of the natural world, artists will continue to absorb and interpret them according to their individual experiences. It is reasonable to assume that even more revolutionary concepts will emerge in time, producing great changes in art styles. The important point to remember is that distortions and unfamiliar forms of art expression do not occur in a vacuum; they usually represent earnest efforts to apprehend and interpret our world in terms of the latest frontiers of understanding.

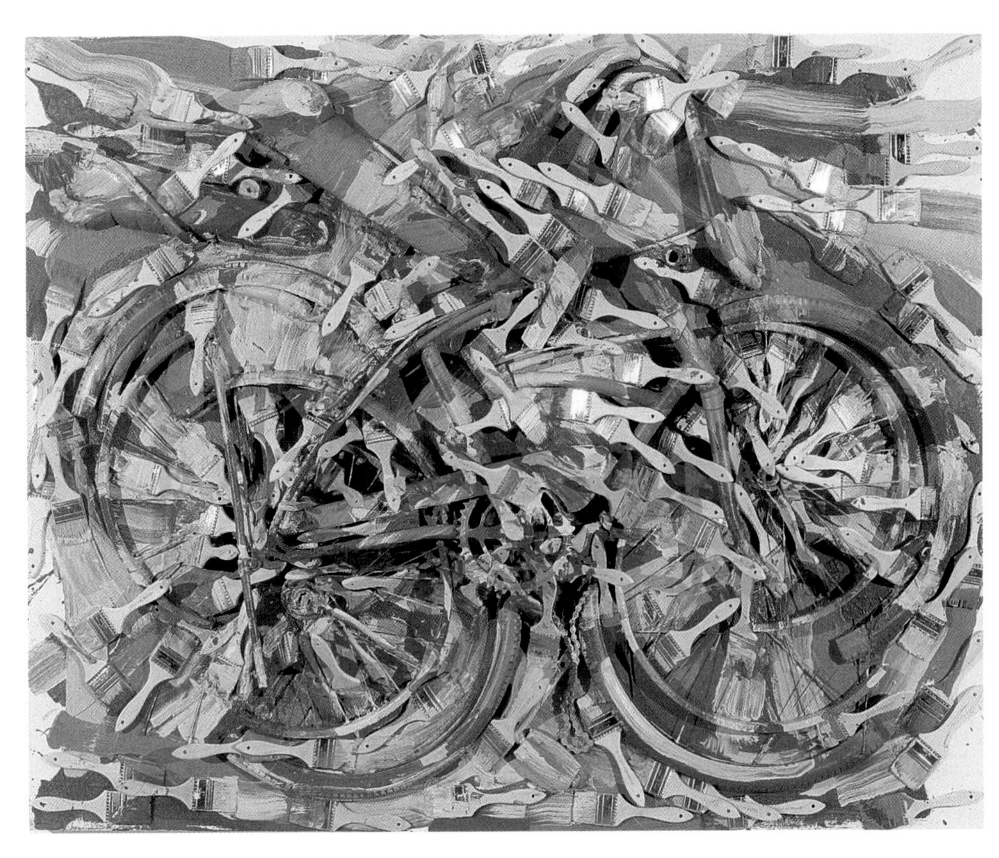

8.56 Arman, *Lava Bike*, 1991. Bicycle, brushes, acrylic paint on canvas, 48 × 60 × 12½ in. (121.9 × 152.4 × 31.8 cm). Fluid motion, speed, and environment are presented in new ways with modern materials and in a new, shallow three-dimensional format. Courtesy of the artist. © 2005 Artists Rights Society (ARS), New York/ADAGP, Paris.

Motion Pictures

Modern scientific study of the optics of an object in motion began around 1824 and paralleled the discovery and development of photography. Among the pioneers to link photography with the study of motion were Coleman Sellers, an engineer, and the English American, Eadweard Muybridge, a photographer who used a Zoetrope, a drumlike wheel, to roll into view individual photographs that projected as animated images. Muybridge, clearly the investigative leader, is known for his photographs of animals and people in motion (fig. 8.57). He drew worldwide acclaim from his extensive public lectures and book publications. The French painter Jean Louis Ernest Meissonier was known to be one of his correspondents.

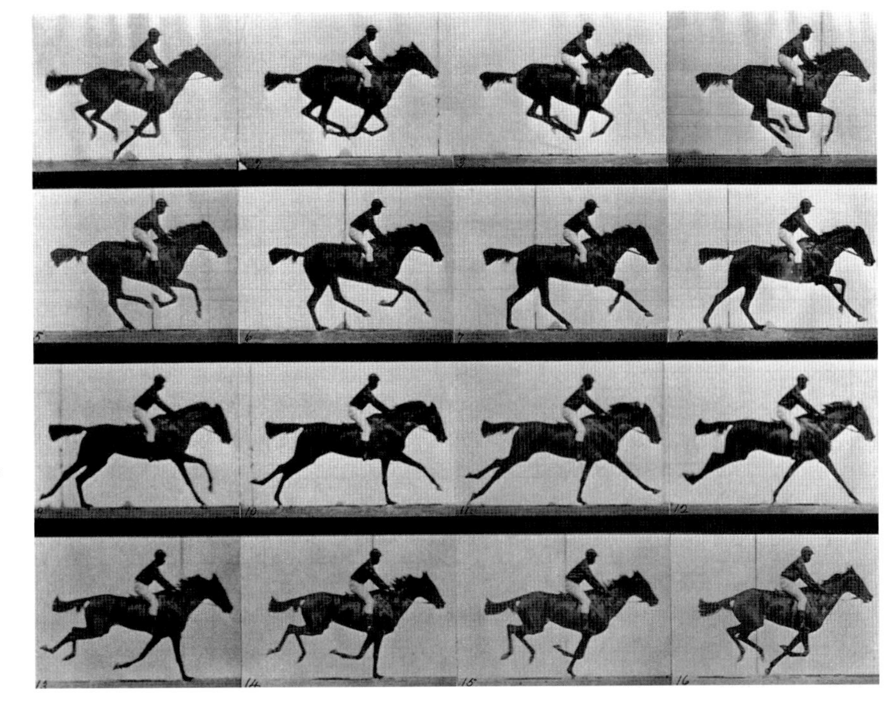

8.57 Eadweard Muybridge, *A Horse's Motion Scientifically Considered.* Engravings after photographs, c. 1875. An American rancher friend and supporter of Muybridge encouraged his studies of horses in motion, which proved that at some point in midgallop all four hooves leave the ground (note the top row, numbers 2, 3, and 4). The photographer took the series with some of the earliest fast-action cameras and went on to influence Manet (see fig. 10.14), Degas, and later artistic students of motion. Hulton Deutsch Collection/Corbis.

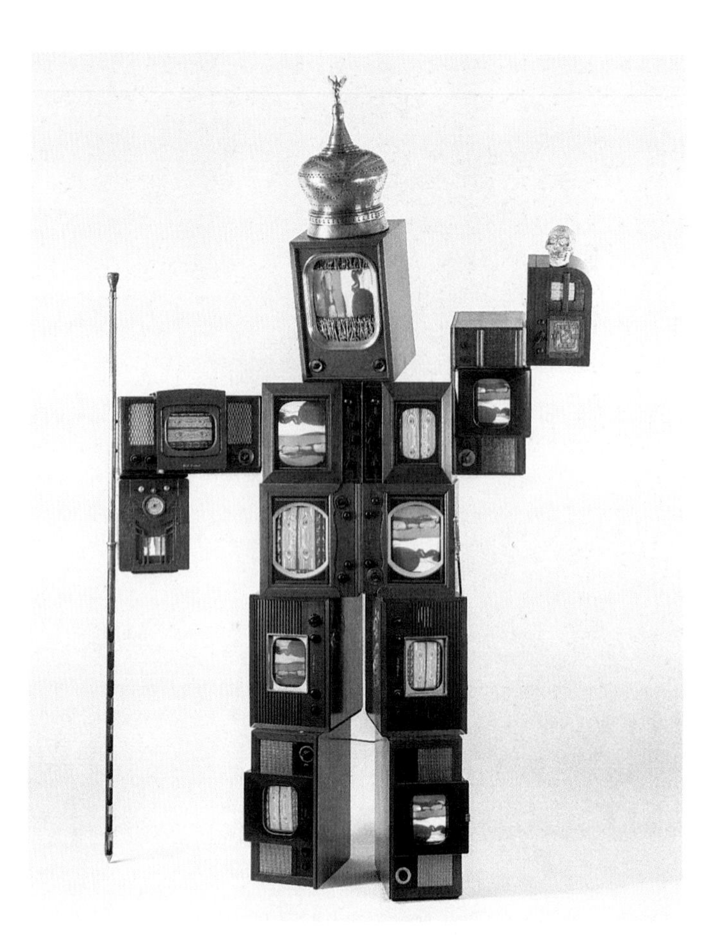

8.58 Nam June Paik, *Hamlet Robot,* 1996. 2 radios, 24 TVs, transformer, 2 laser disk players, laser disks, crown, scepter, sword, and skull. 144 × 88 × 32 in. Nam June Paik's portrait of Hamlet is a video sculpture programmed with a kaleidoscopic mix of contemporary audio and visual technology. Courtesy Carl Solway Gallery, Cincinnati, OH, from the collection of The Chrysler Museum of Art, Norfolk, VA. Photograph by Chris Gomien.

Throughout the entertainment motion-picture industry, art house films have been viewed as escapism from the Hollywood-type productions. The more serious, realistic, lifelike films have come mostly from Europe. Some, like the Surrealistic film *The Andalusian Dog* of 1929, which was created by the painter Salvador Dalí and the Spanish director Luis Buñuel, were personal and emotional accomplishments.

In 1923, Eastman Kodak developed 16mm fireproof celluloid film, and in the 1960s, 8mm film—along with portable cameras, projectors, and other user-friendly equipment—was available so that artist-designers, teachers, students, home users, and professionals of modest means could practically view, produce, and create films. Moreover, these improvements in picture taking and viewing have expanded the use of film from a product for the entertainment industry to one for any inspired individual.

Video

Television, the first of the truly electronic systems, extends the senses of vision (video) and hearing (audio). It instantaneously transmits still or moving images with accompanying sounds, either over electrical transmission lines or by electromagnetic radiation waves (radio waves). The most important constituent of the parts for transmission are the scanner, which breaks the image into a sequence of signals, and the picture tube, or the kinescope, which modulates the electrical impulses of the signals into beams of electrons that strike the receiver's screen, producing light and a continuous picture.

Somewhat like the motion-picture camera, the television camcorder is a portable TV camera and, in addition, a videotape recorder. The camcorder has given individual artists a practical means for creating programs that offer direct action of human thoughts and movements. Art museums and galleries are currently featuring shows that have installations of TV receivers, monitors, and motion-picture screens glowing with artistic images of every imaginable human expression or action. The receivers and screens are positioned for the utmost viewing and, in some installations, seemingly as if they were paintings, drawings, prints, or sculptures. Their sizes and scale are varied for compatible viewing.

The Korean-born artist Nam June Paik is the first artist to use television video monitors as an art form. Actually, Paik uses not only the monitor screen but also the receiver's cabinet and its parts to build a sculptured form (fig. 8.58). He has produced numerous performance works, along with rewired TVs and multimonitor sculptures, in almost every possible arrangement. They include giant walls of television sets: *Information Wall* in 1992 with 429 monitors; *Megatron* in 1995, which included 215 monitors with eight-channel color video and two-channel sound; and a blinking, flashing lights show using laser beams, TV sets, and a waterfall at the Guggenheim in 2000. They were brilliant displays!

Early contact with Nam June Paik and other sound and video artists encouraged Bill Viola to continue creating video artworks and installations in the 1970s. He has since become a pioneer in the use of video and the exploration of the moving image in artworks that reflect art history, spirituality, and conceptual issues. The work illustrated in figure

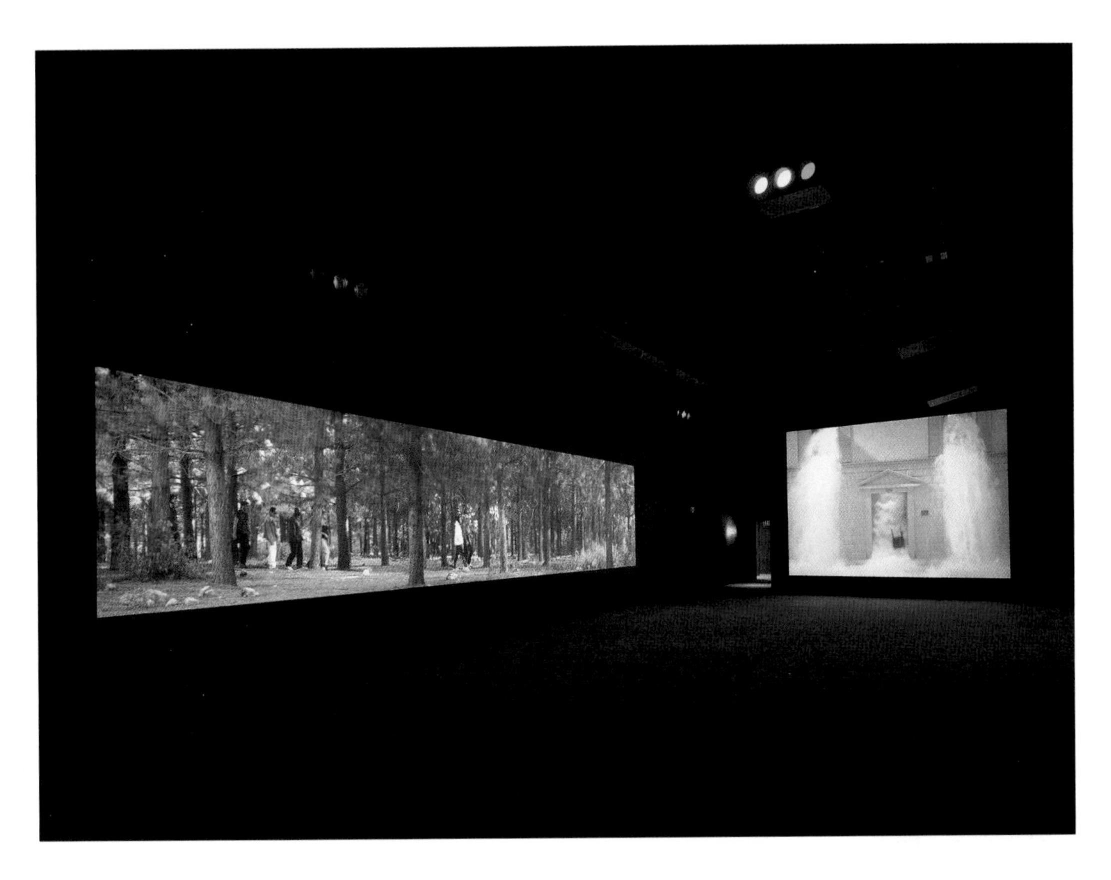

8.59 **Bill Viola, *Going Forth by Day,* 2002. Video and sound installation with 7 projectors, 10 speakers, sub-woofer, 7 amps, 6 equalizers, cables, speakers and projector mounts and 2 servers. Dimensions vary with installation.** *Going Forth by Day* is a video installation inspired by the Egyptian Book of the Dead and the great fresco paintings of the Italian Renaissance. It comprises five panels that examine cycles of birth, death, and rebirth. The "panels"—actually state-of-the-art high definition video projections seen directly on the walls of a space—are approximately 35 minutes long and play simultaneously on continuous loops. The suite of works is an epic about nature's cycles and the flow of time. Commissioned by the Deutsche Bank in consultation with the Solomon R. Guggenheim Foundation for the Deutsche Guggenheim Berlin, 2004, 2004.59. Photograph by David Heald © The Solomon R. Guggenheim Foundation, New York.

8.59, commissioned by a museum in Berlin, is a culmination of this expertise. Viewers enter the work architecturally, with all five image-sequences playing simultaneously on every wall of one large gallery. Once inside, they stand at the center of an image-sound world. Each panel tells a story that is part of a larger narrative cycle. Viewers are free to move around and watch each panel individually or to experience the piece as a whole.

The Computer and Art

Bill Viola's work is a good example of the degree to which the computer has become a tool in the field of art today (fig. 8.59). In his case the computer, no doubt, aided in the conceptualizing during the planning phase, the scriptwriting, the editing of audiovisuals, and the control of the presentation. But we do not call it "computer art" as such.

Computer art can be traced back to 1962, when Ivan Sutherland introduced Sketchpad, a computer-based drawing program utilizing a light pen and a mainframe computer. During the course of the 1960s, other computer scientists—engineers and mathematicians—demonstrated various properties of computer programming by creating drawings using the computer in conjunction with ink plotters and other printing devices. George Nees's show in Stuttgart in 1965 of his computer-generated drawings is often credited with being the first exhibition of "computer art." A 1968 exhibition in London titled "Cybernetic Serendipity" is considered to be the first to draw widespread international attention to the potentials of computer-based computation in art.

After the introduction of the personal computer around 1979, the focus of computer art shifted from printed output to the animation of graphics onscreen. To represent 3D perspective pictures realistically in films, hardware and software developers had to find ways to achieve high resolution and the realistic lighting of moving scenes. The result is that effects such as the penetration, melting away, or shape changing of objects are now common in films and advertising. This development and improvement of computer graphics during the past generation rivals or even exceeds in scope the transformation of painting during the Italian Renaissance.

In its early stages, "computer art" was looked down on as the hobby of technicians. But the boundaries of science, technology, and art are blurring, and now more artists are engaging in computer art. In the 1990s, artists began using computing power to try new procedures and practices, including interactive installations and the programming of art over networks. One such new media artist is Yael Kanarek (b. 1967). Since 1995, Kanarek has maintained an online journal called *World of Awe* (www.worldofawe.net), a multimedia narrative about a traveler in search of a

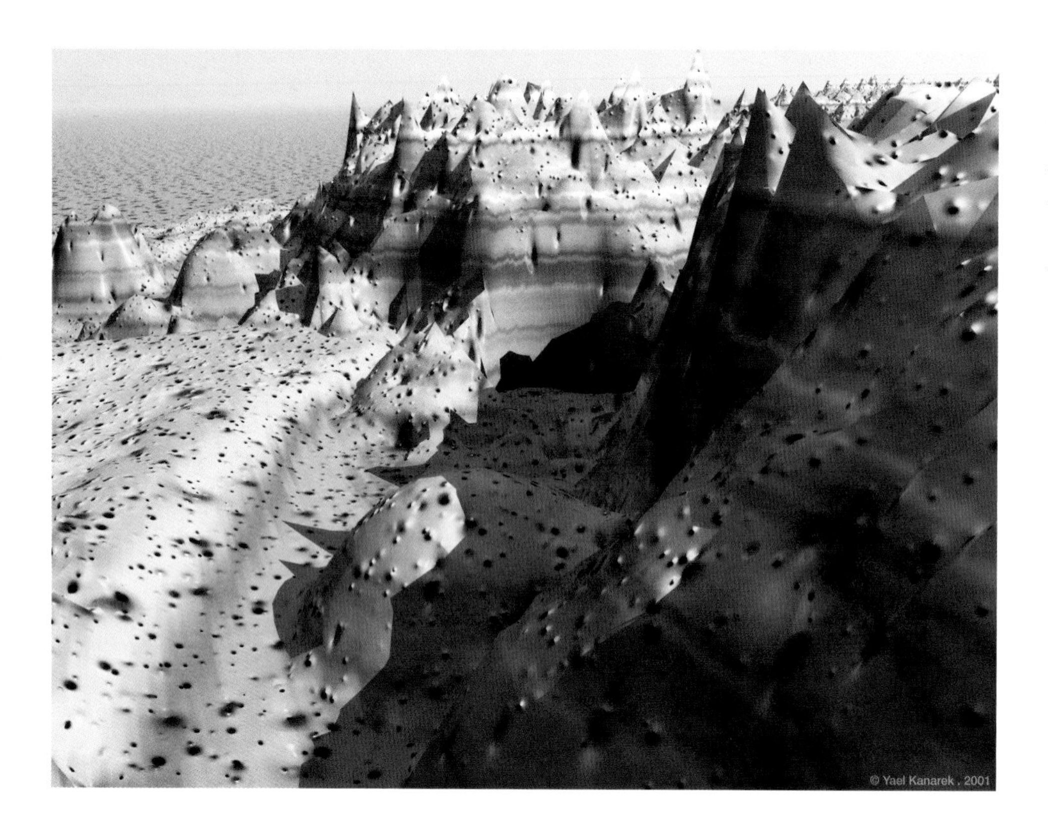

8.60 Yael Kanarek, Digital landscape in the sunset/sunrise desert terrain of *World of Awe,* 2000. *World of Awe* is a Web-based, imaginary reality combining text and imagery. The graphical user interface evolves continuously, presenting a journal that includes landscape drawings, love letters, travelogs, and unique navigation features. © Yael Kanarek.

8.61 Sheriann Ki-Sun Burnham, *Nomad,* 1996. Iris print, 22¼ × 22¼ in. (56.5 × 56.5 cm). While encouraging the evolution of innovative graphic directions, the newest technology aids the artist in the investigation of texture, pattern, transparent layering, and the integration of the visual complexities within the layers. Courtesy of the artist.

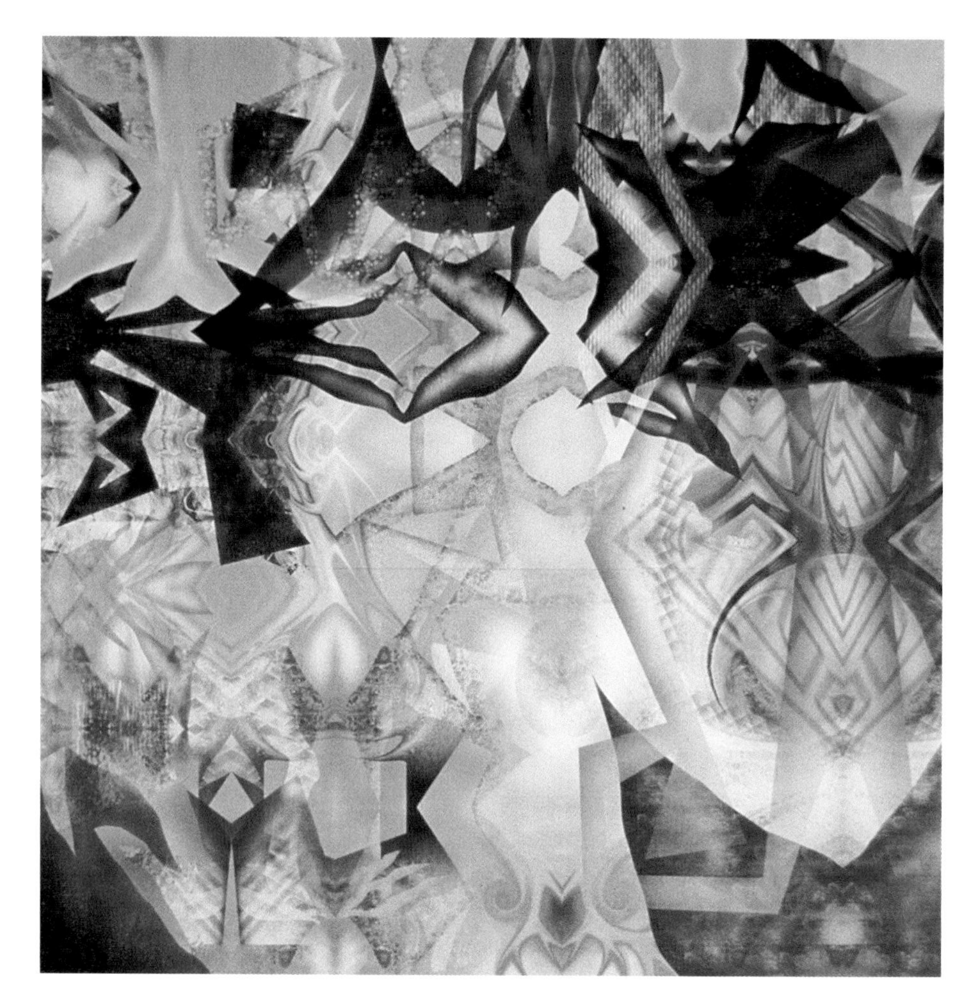

lost treasure. This Web-based artwork has expanded over the years, evolving into a network of projects and collaborations online, in galleries, and in performance spaces (fig. 8.60).

The computer has become an integral part of telecommunications. With the use of coaxial cable, fiber-optic cable, and twisted-pair cable, two-way transmission can take place between different computers (terminals), which in turn use the television, movie, and telephone systems. Computers have opened a new era of multimedia for communications, information gathering, and processing, which are changing the world like nothing before them. And indeed, computers have provided multimedia users access to writing processors and research and entertainment resources, as well as tools for creative artistic development, including motion explorations.

Multimedia may already be one of the most powerful educational and entertainment tools that a computer facilitates. First, as its name suggests, multimedia combines many different groups of varying media into a single unifying force. It combines such media as text, still and moving graphics (animation), and spoken and instrumental sounds into a single group. Second, these may be joined with the communication media: television (including cable and video), telephone (modem and Internet), and the movies (film and video).

Finally, because computers have become powerful enough to process almost any type of data that can be stored on a CD-ROM, programmers have added a seemingly endless group of program titles, among which many are available for ready use by artist-designers. This software has become more user-friendly with the means and tools for fantastic development. Some of the most frequently used software programs include paint programs (drawing and painting), image manipulation, 3D modeling, animation, digital video (motion sequences), and video compression. Many artists create their own software so that they can control the most implicit specialized areas.

Artists today are taking advantage of the many technological advances of our age. The many facets of multimedia generate images that are preparatory, simulative, or final art products. By these means, the human scene as it evolves in time, space, and action has become an inspiration for study and creativity in many exciting forms (fig. 8.61).

Involving combinations of various art forms, multimedia naturally leads to collaborations between artists of different disciplines. Jack Ox (b. 1948) and David Britton began working together in 1998 to try to create visualizations that interpret complex interactive data (fig. 8.62). Ox had twenty years of experience producing 2D work. Britton came to the project with software experience in animation and computer gaming. They created a "virtual color organ" capable of visualizing musical compositions.

Today, the use of technology and the computer are embedded in artistic practice. For artists around the world, the digital workbench has become a place where art is made.

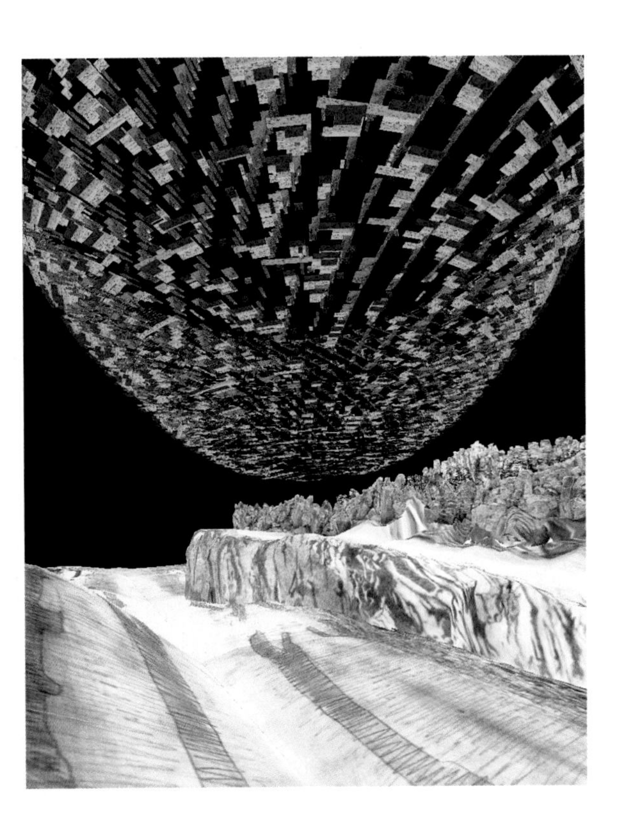

8.62 Visualization of *Im Januar am Nil* composed by Clarence Barlow, 1984, 2001. "Im Januar am Nil" is a visualization of a Clarence Barlow composition for small chamber orchestra. Barlow's unusual spiraling temporal pattern, although difficult to apprehend by ear, becomes visible when translated into 3D computer images. After the music is finished, viewers can move through the image and interact with different parts that evolved during the course of the musical performance. © Jack Ox and David Britton. It was realized in the 21st C. Virtual Color Organ™. For the full story: www.jackox.net.

INVESTIGATE THE CD-ROM **Questions to Ask Yourself**

The appearance of depth in space is a constant concern in pictorial arts.

As you review this chapter on the CD-ROM, think about how space is expressed in a painting or drawing that you particularly like, and answer these questions:

1. What kind of space has the artist created? What devices did the artist use to create this space?
2. If you wanted to change the kind of space in this artwork, what other changes would you have to make to which other elements?
3. Now try to imagine changing the fourth dimension of time in this artwork. Does this change the space in the artwork? If so, describe what changes. If not, explain why nothing changes.

CHAPTER NINE

The Art of the Third Dimension

THE VOCABULARY OF THE THIRD DIMENSION

BASIC CONCEPTS OF THREE-DIMENSIONAL ART

- Sculpture
- Other Areas of Three-Dimensional Art
  - *Architecture*
  - *Metalwork*
  - *Glass Design*
  - *Ceramics*
  - *Fiberwork*
  - *Product Design*

THE COMPONENTS OF THREE-DIMENSIONAL ART

- Materials and Techniques
  - *Subtraction*
  - *Manipulation*
  - *Addition*
  - *Substitution*
- The Elements of Three-Dimensional Form
  - *Shape*
  - *Value*
  - *Space*
  - *Texture*
  - *Line*
  - *Color*
  - *Time (the Fourth Dimension)*
- Principles of Three-Dimensional Order
  - *Harmony and Variety*
  - *Balance*
  - *Proportion*
  - *Economy*
  - *Movement*
  - *Installations*

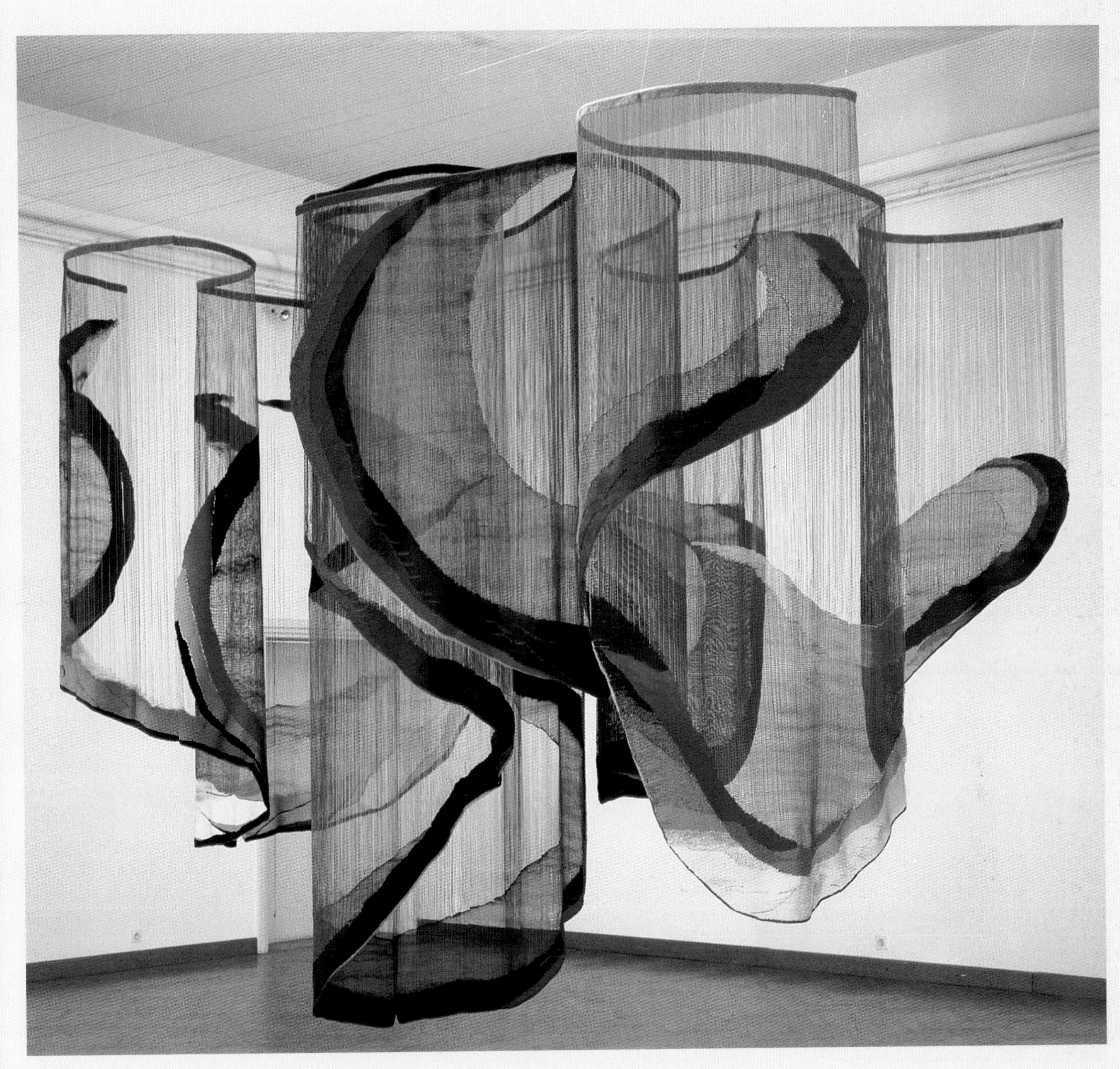

Eta Sadar Breznik, *Space,* 1995. Woven rayon, 157½ × 137⅞ × 137⅞ in. Ljubljana, Slovenia. Photo © Boris Gaberšček.

THE VOCABULARY OF THE THIRD DIMENSION

Three-dimensional — Possessing, or creating the illusion of possessing, the dimension of depth as well as the dimensions of height and width.

addition
A sculptural term that means building up, assembling, or putting on material.

atectonic
Characterized by considerable amounts of space; open, as opposed to massive (or tectonic), and often with extended appendages.

Bauhaus
Originally a German school of architecture that flourished between World War I and World War II. The Bauhaus attracted many leading experimental artists of both two- and three-dimensional fields.

casting
A sculptural technique in which liquid materials are shaped by being poured into a mold.

glyptic
1. The quality of an art material like stone, wood, or metal that can be carved or engraved. 2. An art form that retains the color and the tensile and tactile qualities of the material from which it was created. 3. The quality of hardness, solidity, or resistance found in carved or engraved materials.

installations
Interior or exterior settings of media created by artists to heighten the viewers' awareness of the environmental space.

manipulation
The sculptural technique of shaping pliable materials by hands or tools.

mass (third dimension)
1. In graphic art, a shape that appears to stand out three-dimensionally from the space surrounding it or that appears to create the illusion of a solid body of material. 2. In the plastic arts, the physical bulk of a solid body of material.

mobile
A three-dimensional moving sculpture.

modeling
The sculptural technique of shaping a pliable material.

patina
1. A natural film, usually greenish, that results from the oxidation of bronze or other metallic material. 2. Colored pigments and/or chemicals applied to a sculptural surface.

relief sculpture
An artwork, graphic in concept but sculptural in application, utilizing relatively shallow depth to establish images. The space development may range from very limited projection, known as "low relief," to exaggerated space development, known as "high relief." Relief sculpture is meant to be viewed frontally, not in the round.

sculpture
The art of expressive shaping of three-dimensional materials. "Man's expression to man through three-dimensional form" (Jules Struppeck; see Bibliography).

shape (third dimension)
An area that stands out from the space next to or around it due to a defined or implied boundary or because of differences in value, color, or texture.

silhouette
The area between or bounded by the contours, or edges, of an object; the total shape.

substitution
In sculpture, replacing one material or medium with another (see also **casting**).

subtraction
A sculptural term meaning the carving or cutting away of material.

tectonic
The quality of simple massiveness; lacking any significant extrusions or intrusions.

void
1. An area lacking positive substance and consisting of negative space. 2. A spatial area within an object that penetrates and passes through it.

volume (third dimension)
A measurable area of defined or occupied space.

BASIC CONCEPTS OF THREE-DIMENSIONAL ART

In the preceding chapters, our examination of art fundamentals has been limited mostly to the graphic arts. These art disciplines (drawing, painting, photography, printmaking, graphic design, and so on) have two dimensions (height and width), existing on a flat surface and generating sensations of space mainly through illusions created by the artist. This chapter deals with the unique properties of **three-dimensional** artwork and the creative concepts that evolve from these properties.

In three-dimensional art, the added dimension is that of actual depth. This depth results in a greater sense of reality and, as a consequence, increases the physical impact of the work. A graphic work is usually limited to a two-dimensional format that is bounded by a geometrically shaped picture frame, but a three-dimensional work is limited only by the outer extremities of its multiple positions and/or views. The 3D format, although more complicated, offers freer range to the artist and greater viewing interest to the spectator than the 2D format.

Because actual depth is fundamental to 3D art, one must be in the presence of the artwork to fully appreciate it. Words and graphic representations of 3D art are not substitutes for actual experience. Two-dimensional depictions are flat, rigid, and representative of only one viewpoint; however, they do serve as a visual shorthand for actual sensory experiences. In this book, we can use only 2D descriptions, by way of text and photographic reproductions, as the most convenient means of conveying the 3D experience. But we emphatically encourage readers to put actual observation into practice.

Practicing artists and art authorities designate the 3D qualities of objects in space with such terms as form, shape, mass, and volume. The term *form* can be misleading here, because its meaning differs from the definition applied in early chapters—the inventive arrangement of all the visual elements according to principles that will produce unity. In a broad structural sense, form is the sum total of all the media and techniques used to organize the 3D elements within an artwork. In this respect, a church is a total form and its doors are contributing shapes; similarly, a human figure is a total form, while the head, arms, and legs are contributing shapes. However, in a more limited sense, form may refer just to the appearance of an object—to a contour, a shape, or a structure. **Shape,** when used in a three-dimensional sense, may refer to a positive or open negative area. In comparison, **mass** invariably denotes a solid physical object of relatively large weight or bulk. Mass may also refer to a coherent body of matter, like clay or metal, that is not yet shaped or to a lump of raw material that could be modeled or cast. Stone carvers, accustomed to working with **glyptic** materials, tend to think of a heavy, weighty mass (fig. 9.1); modelers, who manipulate clay or wax, favor a pliable mass. **Volume** is the amount of space the mass, or bulk, occupies, or the three-dimensional area of space that is totally or partially enclosed by planes, linear edges, or wires. Many authorities conceive of masses as positive solids and volumes as negative open spaces. For example, a potter who throws a bowl on a wheel adjusts the

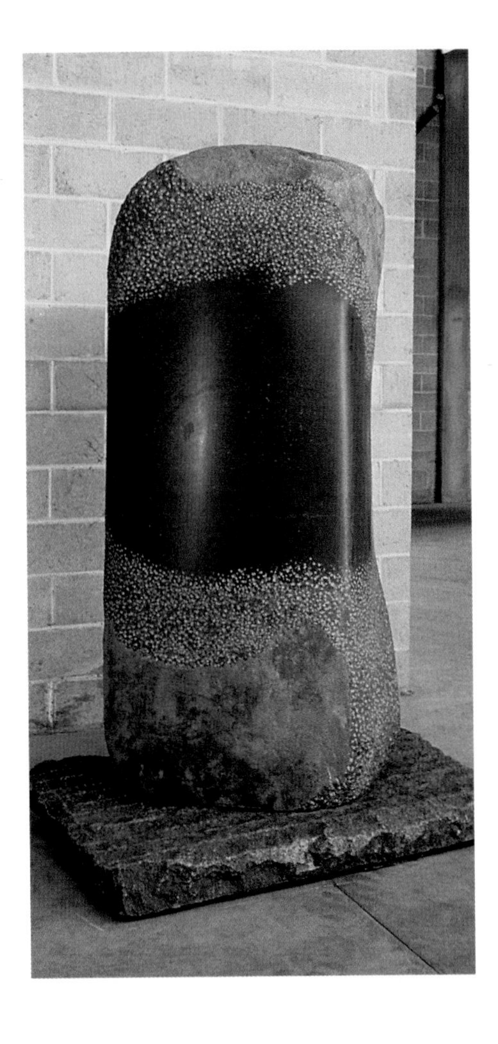

9.1 Isamu Noguchi, *The Stone Within,* 1982. Basalt, 75 × 38 × 27 in. (190.5 × 96.5 × 68.6 cm). The sculptor Noguchi has subtracted just enough stone in this work to introduce his concept of minimal form while preserving the integrity of the material and its heavy, weighty mass.

dimensions of the interior volume (negative interior space) by expanding or compressing the clay planes (positive mass). The sculptor who assembles materials may also enclose negative volumes to form unique relationships (fig. 9.2).

When we look more widely, most objects in our environment have 3D qualities of height, width, and depth and can be divided into natural and human-made forms. Although natural forms may stimulate the thought processes, they are not in themselves creative. Artists invent forms to satisfy their need for self-expression. In the distant past, most 3D objects were created for utilitarian purposes. They included such implements as stone axes, pottery, hammers, and knives, as well as objects of worship. Nearly all these human-made forms possessed qualities of artistic expression; many depicted the animals their creators hunted. These prehistoric objects are an early expression of the sculptural impulse.

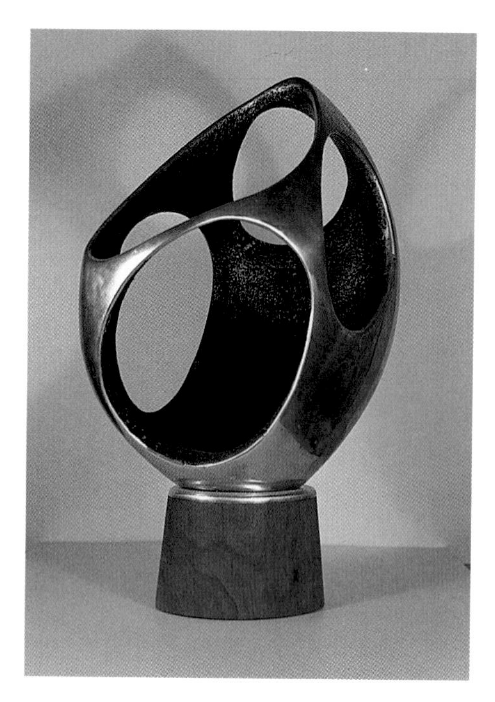

9.2 John W. Goforth, *Untitled,* 1971. Cast aluminum, 15¾ in. (40 cm) high with base.
The volume incorporates the space, both solid and empty, that is occupied by the work.
Collection of Otto Ocvirk. Courtesy of Carolyn Goforth.

Sculpture

The term *sculpture* has had varied meanings throughout history. The word derives from the Latin verb *sculpere,* which refers to the process of carving, cutting, or engraving. The ancient Greeks' definition of **sculpture** also included the **modeling** of such pliable materials as clay or wax to produce figures in relief or in the round. The Greeks developed an ideal standard for the sculptured human form that they considered the perfect physical organization—harmonious, balanced, and totally related in all parts. Beautiful proportions were a part of their concept of sculpture (see fig. 2.42).

Modern sculpture has taken on new qualities in response to the changing conditions of an industrialized age. Science and machinery have made sculptors more conscious of materials and technology and more aware of the underlying abstract structure in their art.

Sculpture is no longer limited to carving and modeling. It now includes any means of giving form to all types of 3D materials. These means include welding, bolting, riveting, gluing, sewing, machine-hammering, and stamping. In turn, the 3D artists have expanded their range of sculptural forms to include planar, solid, and linear constructions made of such materials as steel, plastic, wood, and fabric (fig. 9.3). The resulting sculptures are stronger (even though made of

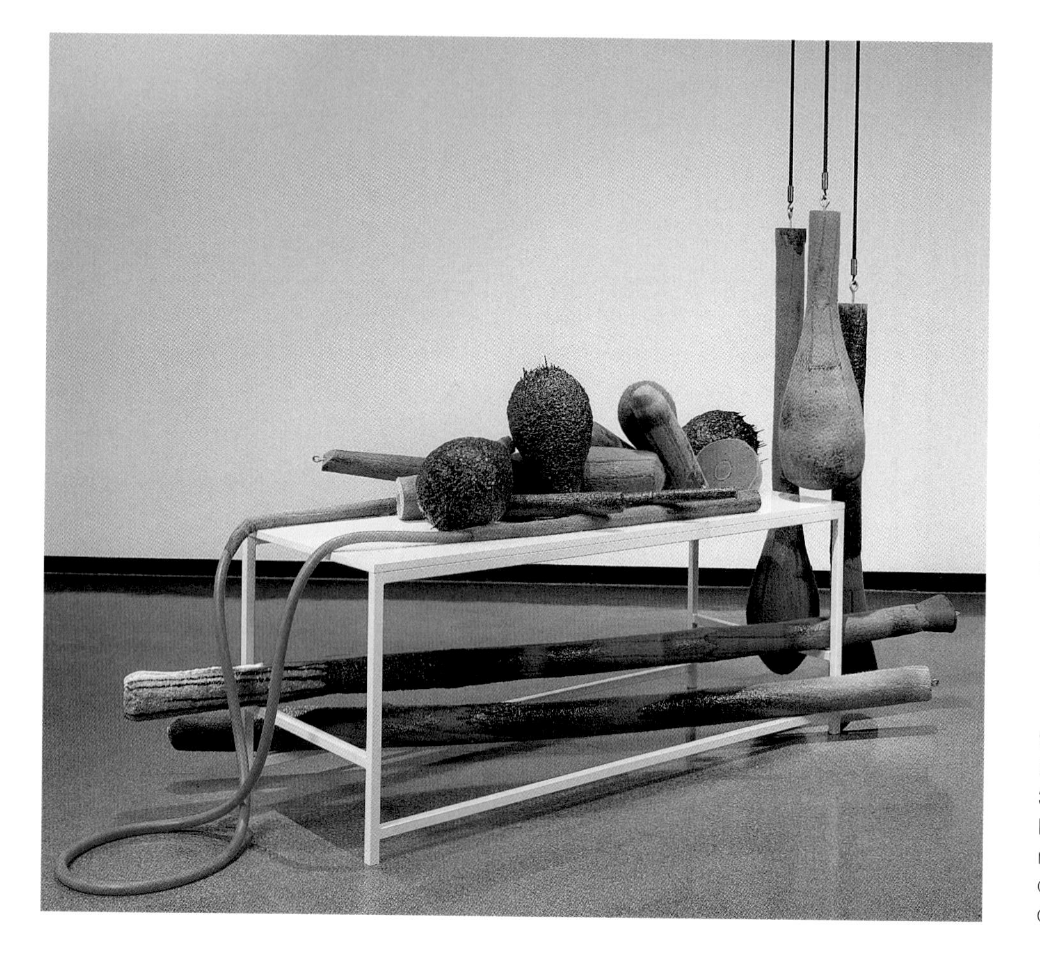

9.3 Joan Livingstone, *Seeped,* 1997–2000. Felt, stain, resin, pigment, and steel, 112 × 36 × 96 in. (284.5 × 91.4 × 243.8 cm).
Modern sculpture exploits every conceivable material that suits the intentions of the artist.
Courtesy of the artist and the SYBARIS Gallery, Royal Oak, MI. Photograph by Michael Tropea.

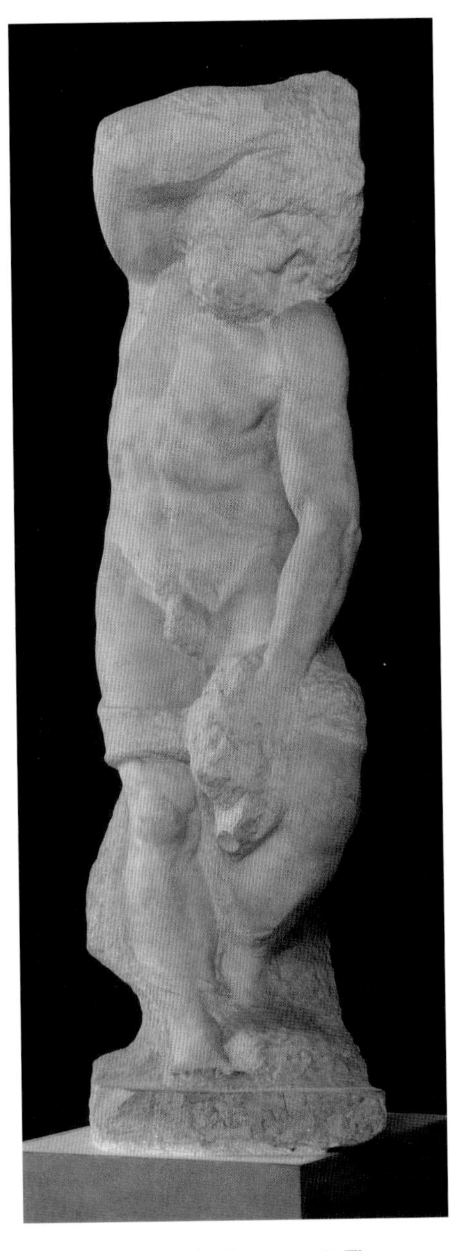

9.4 **Michelangelo Buonarroti, *The Bearded Captive,* c. 1516–27. Marble, 8 ft 8¼ in. (2.65 m) high.** Michelangelo created heavy, massive sculpture and enlarged the sizes of human body parts for expressive purposes. The tectonic composition was in keeping with the intrinsic nature of the stone. Accademia, Florence, Italy. © Arte & Immagine srl/Corbis.

lighter materials) and more open. They also have expanded spatial relationships. Three-dimensional forms like wire constructions and **mobiles** have changed the definition of sculpture that, prior to the nineteenth century, would have included only solid, heavy, and sturdy glyptic forms. In contrast, Michelangelo Buonarroti, an innovative sculptor of the Renaissance, thought in terms of massive materials and heavy figures (fig. 9.4).

The diversity of newfound materials and techniques has led to greater individual expression and artistic freedom. Sculptors experiment with new theories and have found new audiences and new markets.

Other Areas of Three-Dimensional Art

The bulk of this book has addressed works of pure or fine art that have no practical function. But sensitivity to the sculptural (and/or artistic) impulse is not confined to the fine arts; it permeates all 3D structures. The same abstract quality of expressive beauty that is the foundation for a piece of sculpture can underlie such functional forms as automobiles, television receivers, telephones, industrial equipment, window and interior displays, furniture, and buildings (fig. 9.5). Artist-designers of these 3D products organize elements, shapes, textures, colors, and space according to the same principles of harmony, proportion, balance, and variety as are used in the fine arts. Although form principles can be applied to such useful objects, the need for utility often restricts the creative latitude of the artist.

The architect Louis Sullivan made the oft-repeated remark that "form follows function." This concept has influenced several decades of design, changing the appearance of tools, telephones, silverware, chairs, and a vast array of other familiar and less familiar items. Sometimes this concept is

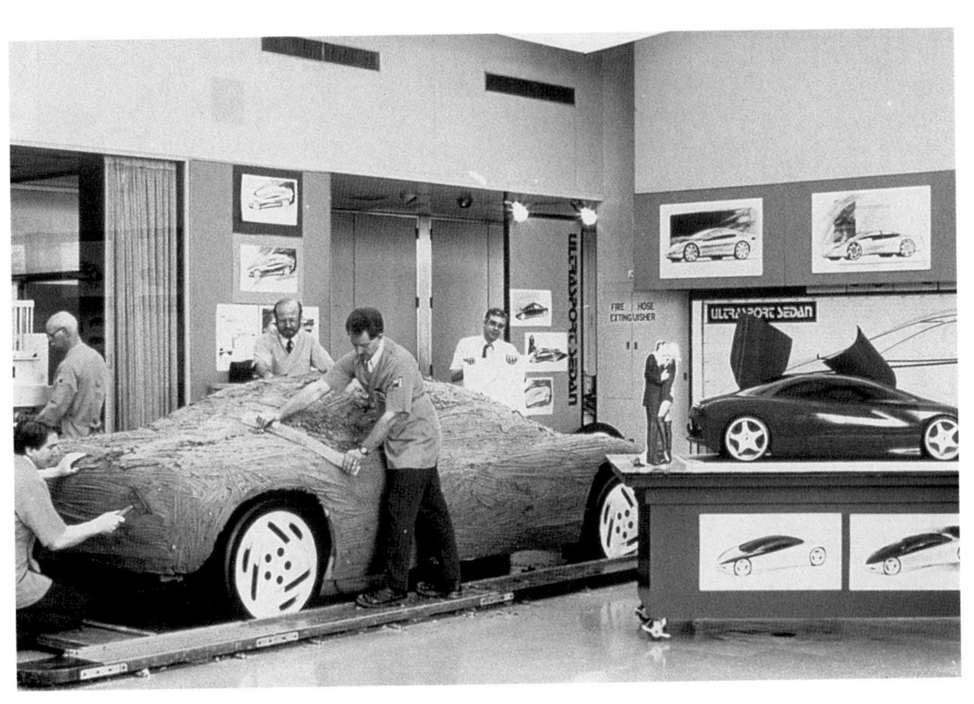

9.5 **Pontiac Protosport concept car, 2001 GM Corp. Mixed media, full scale.** New concepts in automotive design are determined by advances in technology, engineering, economics, and visual appearance. One of the stages of the design process is shown here as artisans model the basic form. 2001 GM Corp. Used with permission of the GM Media Archives.

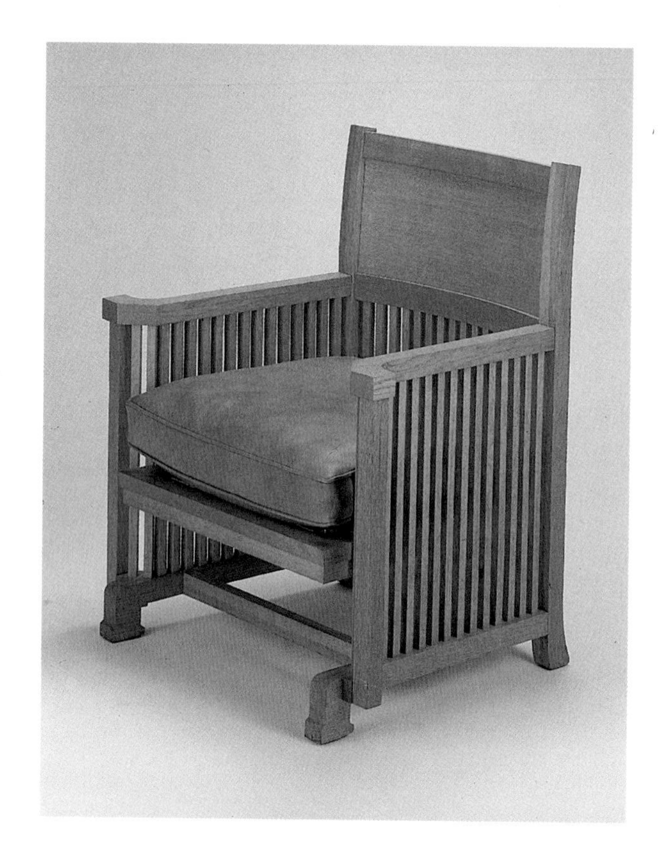

9.6 Armchair designed by Frank Lloyd Wright for the Ray W. Evans House, Chicago, IL, made by Neideken and Walbridge, c. 1908. Oak, 34¼ × 23 × 22½ in. (86.9 × 58.5 × 57.1 cm). To Wright, form and function were inseparable, so a chair, which is made for sitting, should be considered along with the whole architectural environment. Art Institute of Chicago. Gift of Mr. and Mrs. F. M. Fahrenwald, 1970.435. Photo © Art Institute of Chicago. All rights reserved. © 2001 Frank Lloyd Wright Foundation, Scottsdale, AZ, Artists Rights Society (ARS), NY.

9.7 Michael Coffey, *Aphrodite* (a rocking lounge chair), 1978. Laminated mozambique, 4 ft 6 in. × 7 ft 6 in. × 28 in. (137 × 229 × 71.1 cm). A useful household article can be transformed by the style of contemporary sculpture. Courtesy of the artist. Photograph by Rich Baldinger, Schenectady, NY.

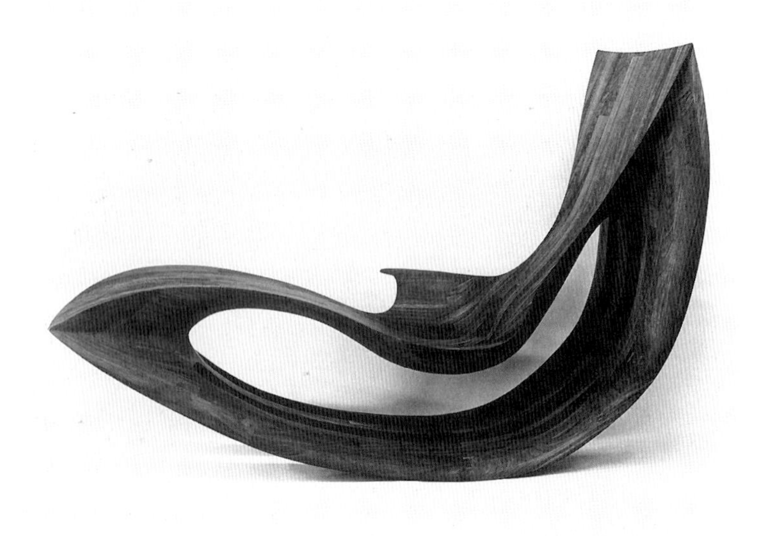

misapplied. The idea of streamlining is practical when applied to the design of such moving objects as trains and cars, because it has the function of reducing wind resistance. However, streamlining has less logical application in the design of spoons and lamps. Although streamlining is helpful in eliminating irrelevancies from design, even simplification can be overdone. The **Bauhaus** notion of the house as a "machine for living" helped architects rethink architectural principles, but it also introduced a cold and austere style against which there was an inevitable reaction.

Contemporary designers are very aware of the functional requirements of the objects they plan. Consequently, they design forms that express and aid function. However, they also know that these forms should be aesthetically pleasing. In order to meet all of these objectives, the creator of functional objects must apply the principles of fundamental order within the strictures of utilitarian need. Frank Lloyd Wright, the celebrated American architect, combined architecture, engineering, and art in shaping his materials and their environment. The unity of his ideas is expressed in the chair he designed for the Ray W. Evans House (fig. 9.6). The sophisticated design and formal balance that Wright incorporated into this ordinary object can be seen in his highly selective repetitions, proportional relationships, and refinement of details.

The balance that exists between design, function, and expressive content within an object varies with example. For instance, when designing his rocking lounge chair, Michael Coffey placed strong emphasis on expressive form without sacrificing the function of reclining comfort (fig. 9.7). At first glance, we are drawn in by the chair's dominant outer contour and by its open shape. This piece of furniture resembles a freely expressed contemporary sculpture. Expressive form follows function in a new and creative way.

Tremendous developments have taken place in the general areas of three-dimensional design where works are intended to serve some functional purpose.

Architecture

Recent technological innovations and new building materials have given architects greater artistic flexibility. Thanks to technical developments in steel and concrete, buildings can now be large in scale without projecting massive, weighty forms. With the advent of electric lighting, vast interior spaces can be illuminated. Because of air conditioning, buildings can be completely enclosed or sheathed in glass. Cantilevered forms can be extended into space. Free-form shapes can be created with the use of precast concrete. All of these structural improvements have allowed architects to think and plan more freely. Contemporary public buildings that demonstrate these developments include the National Assembly Building at Shere-e-Bangla Nagar, in Dhaka, Bangladesh (fig. 9.8); the Lincoln Center for the Performing Arts in New York; the Kennedy Center in Washington, D.C.; the Jefferson Westward Expansion Memorial in St. Louis; and the Los Angeles City Hall and Civic Center. In many ways architects today are "building sculptors," and their designs require a thorough grounding in artistic principles as well as an understanding of engineering concepts. Furthermore, computer-aided design has allowed for the structural engineering of highly idiosyncratic buildings that could otherwise not be calculated. This may be seen in Frank Gehry's Guggenheim Museum in Bilbao, Spain, and the proposed Guggenheim South Street Seaport project (fig. 9.9).

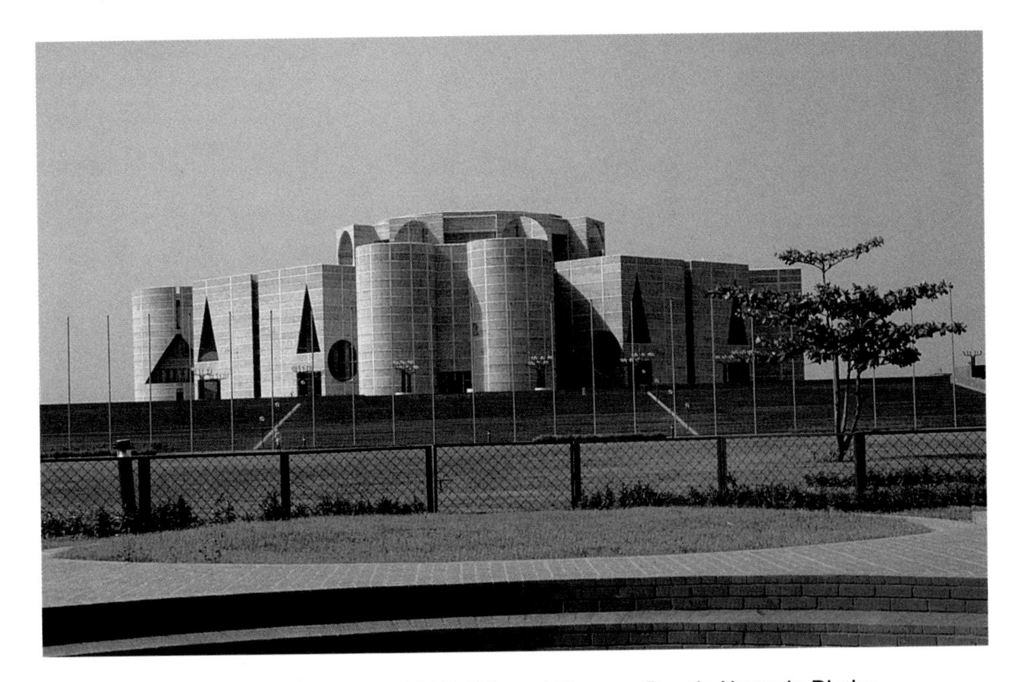

9.8 Louis I. Kahn, National Assembly Building at Shere-e-Bangla Nagar in Dhaka, Bangladesh, 1962–83. Poured concrete, wood, brick. Louis Kahn, an American architect, shows his unique use of geometry in a simple, massive sculpturelike structure. © Khaled Nowan/Architectural Association Slide Library, London.

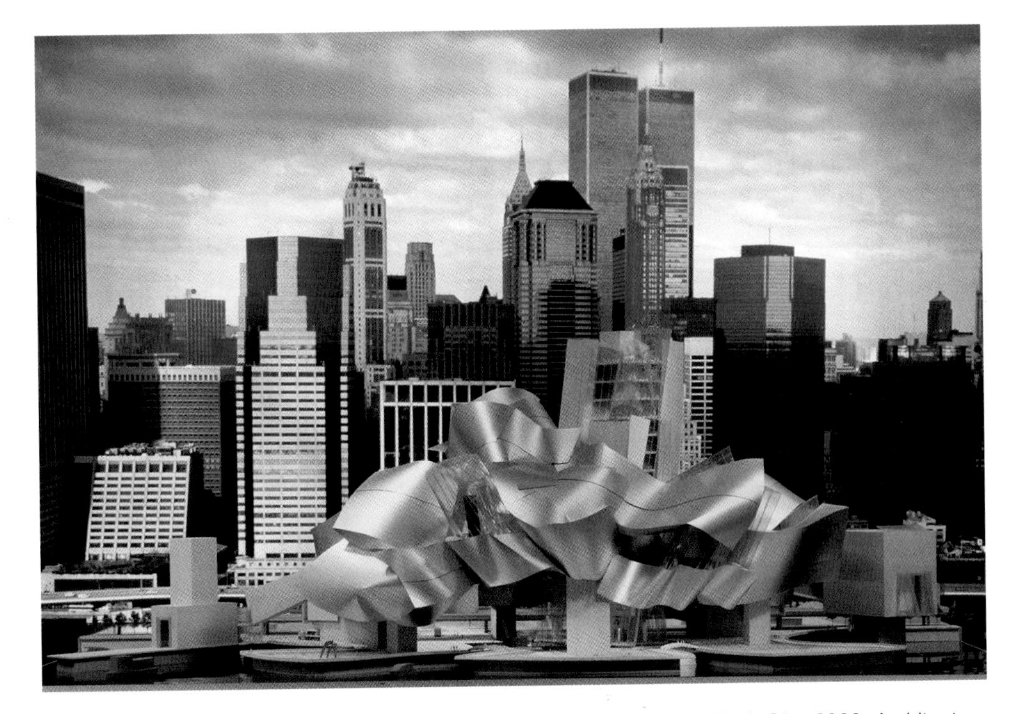

9.9 Frank Gehry, *Model for a New Guggenheim Museum in New York City,* 2000. Architect Frank Gehry proposed this free-flowing sculpturelike design to house art from the twentieth century. Frank O. Gehry & Associates. Photograph by David Heald. © Solomon R. Guggenheim Foundation, New York.

Metalwork

Most of the changes in metalworking (jewelry, decorative and functional ware, and so on) have been in concept rather than technique. Traditional techniques

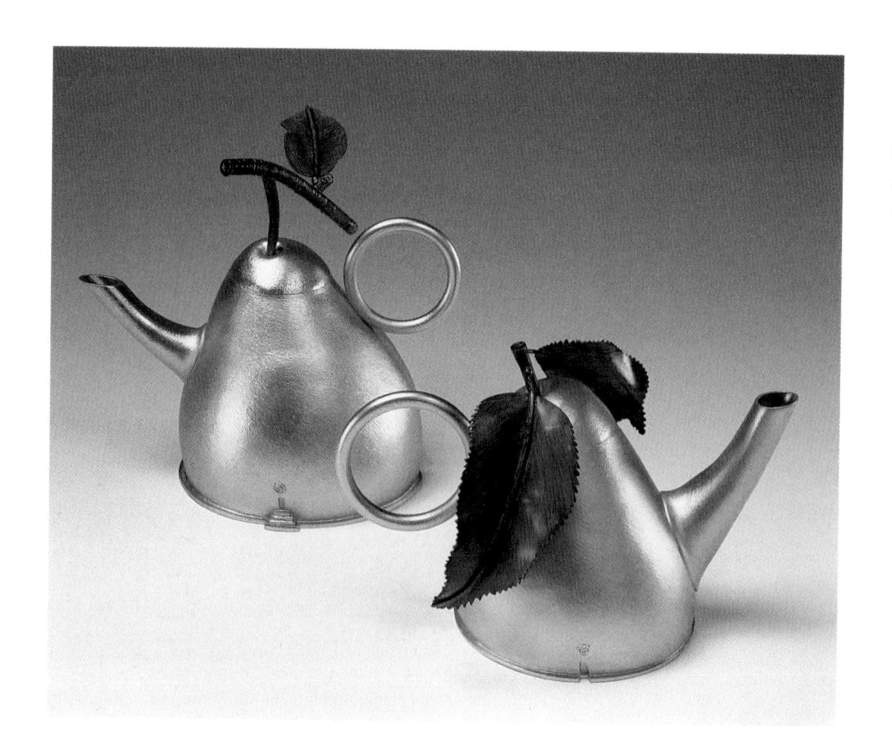

9.10 Marilyn da Silva, *The Golden Pair,* 1996. Copper, brass, 24K gold-plate, gesso, colored pencil, (each teapot) 3½ in. high × 6 in. wide × 2½ in. in diameter (8.9 × 15.2 × 6.4 cm). This pair of pears, as teapot dwellings, reflects the artist's use of personal symbolism in a sculptural approach to metalwork. Courtesy of the artist. Photograph by Philip Cohen.

9.11 Dale Chihuly, *Lakawanna Ikebana,* 1994. Blown glass, 18 ft. in diameter. These magnificent glass pieces are most unusual and creative in their scale, coloring, shape definition, and total environmental concept. Courtesy of the artist. From the Union Station Federal Courthouse, Tacoma, Washington. Photograph by Russell Johnson © Chihuly Studio.

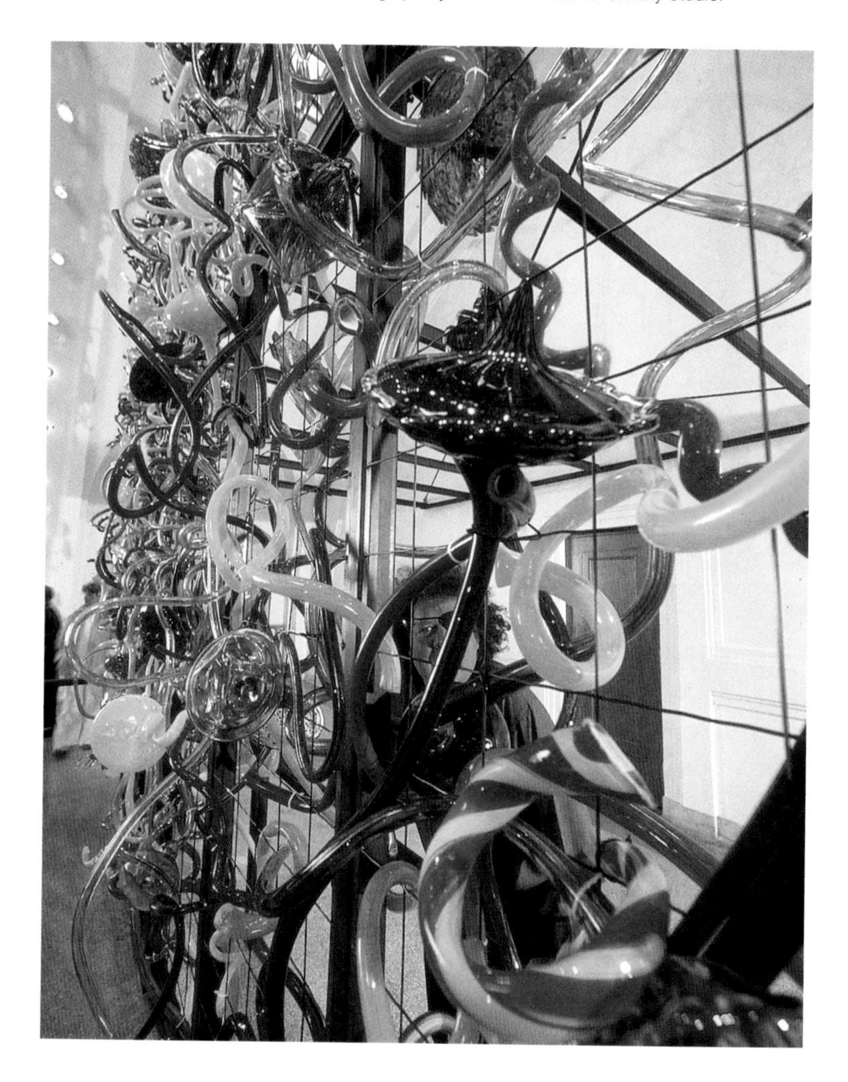

are still in use, although modern equipment has made procedures simpler and more convenient. To a large degree, fashion determines the character of metalwork, but it is safe to say that contemporary work is larger and more oriented toward sculpture than most work of the past. Constant cross-fertilization occurs among the art areas, and metalwork is not immune to these influences. The metalworker benefits from studying the principles of both two- and three-dimensional art (fig. 9.10).

Glass Design

Glassworking is similar to metalworking now that modern equipment has simplified traditional techniques. Designing glass objects, however, is very much an art form of recent times. Many free-form and figurative pieces have the look of contemporary sculpture. Colors augment the designs in a decorative, as well as an expressive, sense. Thus, the principles of art structure are integrated with the craft of the medium (fig. 9.11).

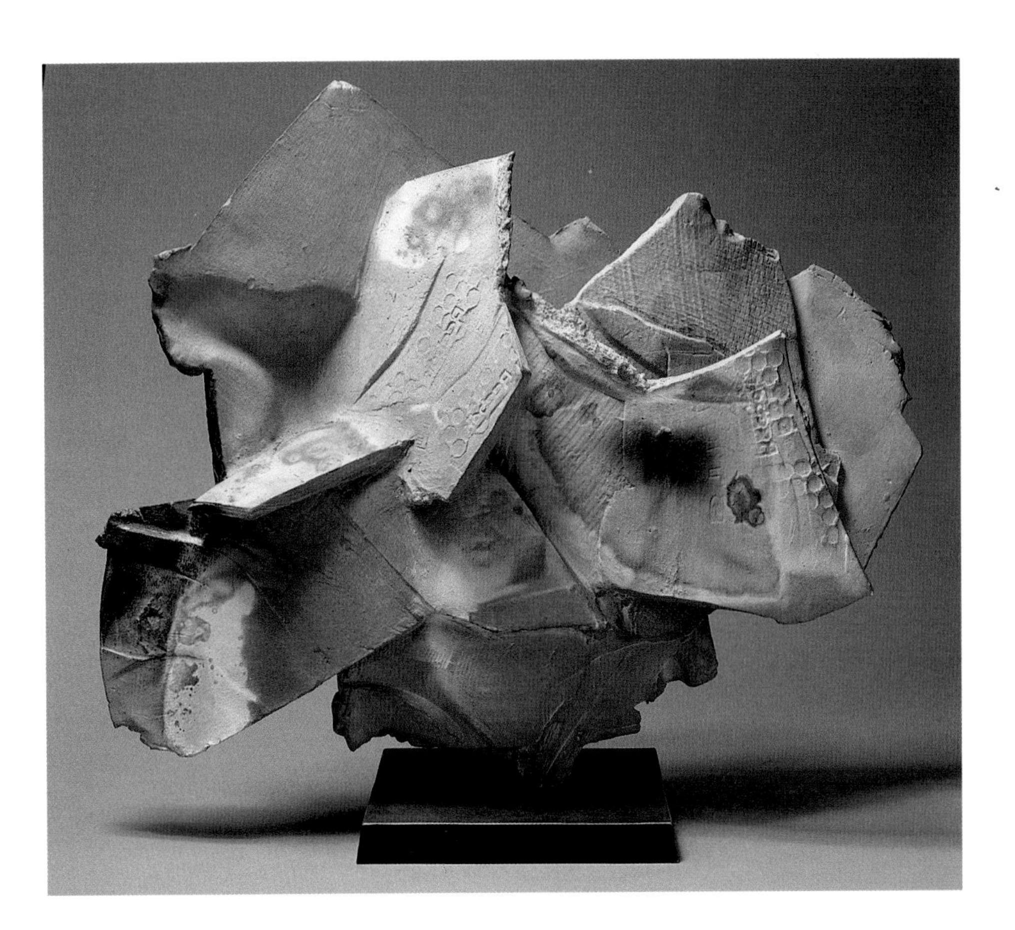

9.12 **Paul Soldner, *Pedestal Piece (907)*, 1990. Thrown and altered clay with slips and low-temperature salt glaze, 27 × 30 × 11 in. (68.6 × 76.2 × 27.9 cm).** The coloring resulting from the controlled firing process enhances the sculptural composition of the clay piece. Scripps College, Claremont, CA. Gift of Mr. and Mrs. Fred Marer, 92.1.154.

Ceramics

In recent years the basic shape of the ceramic object has become more sculptural as ceramic work has become, in many cases, less functional. The ceramist must be equally aware of three-dimensional considerations and of the fundamentals of graphic art, because individual surfaces may be altered by incising, painting with colored slips, fuming, or glazing (fig. 9.12).

Fiberwork

Fiberwork has undergone a considerable revolution recently. Three-dimensional forms are becoming increasingly more common, particularly as the traditional making by hand of rugs and tapestries has diminished. Woven objects now include a vast array of materials incorporated into designs of considerable scale and bulk. Traditional as well as contemporary concepts of fiberwork require an understanding of both 2D and 3D principles (fig. 9.13).

Product Design

A relative newcomer on the art scene, product design usually has commercial applications. The designer produces works based on function but geared to consumer appeal. To be contemporary in appearance and thus attractive to consumers, products must exploit all the design principles of our age. The designs of common objects in our daily environment are the products of the designer's training in these various principles.

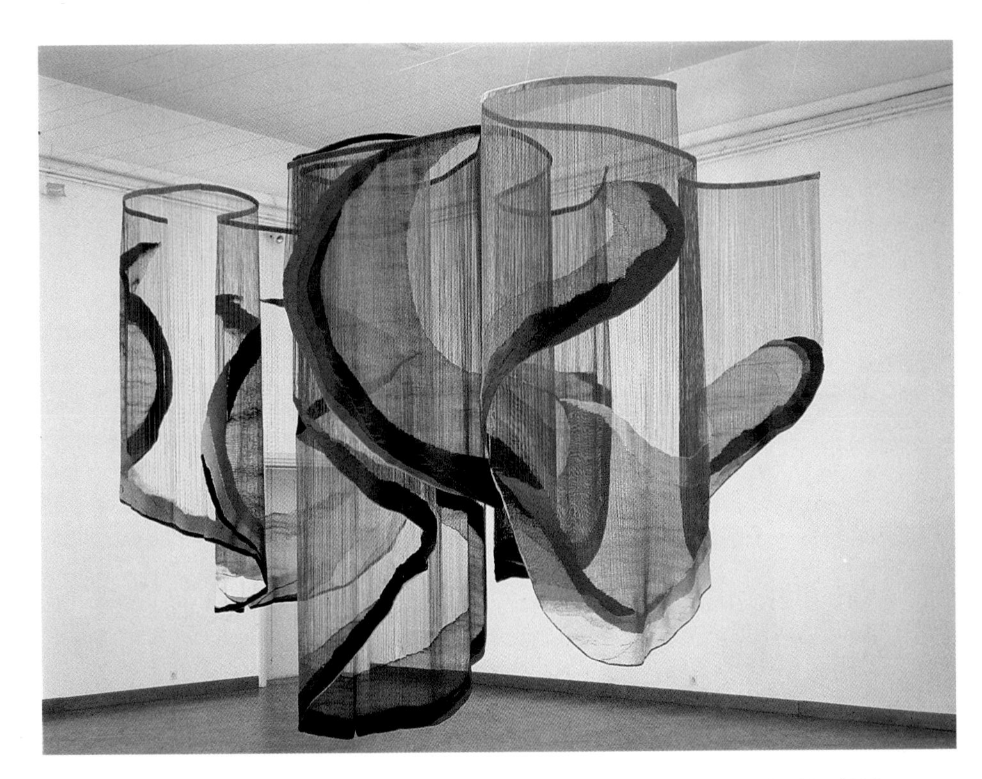

9.13 **Eta Sadar Breznik, *Space*, 1995. Woven rayon, 157½ × 137⅞ × 137⅞ in. (400 × 350 × 350 cm).** Contemporary textile design frequently goes beyond its largely two-dimensional traditions. Ljubljana, Slovenia. Photo © Boris Gaberšček.

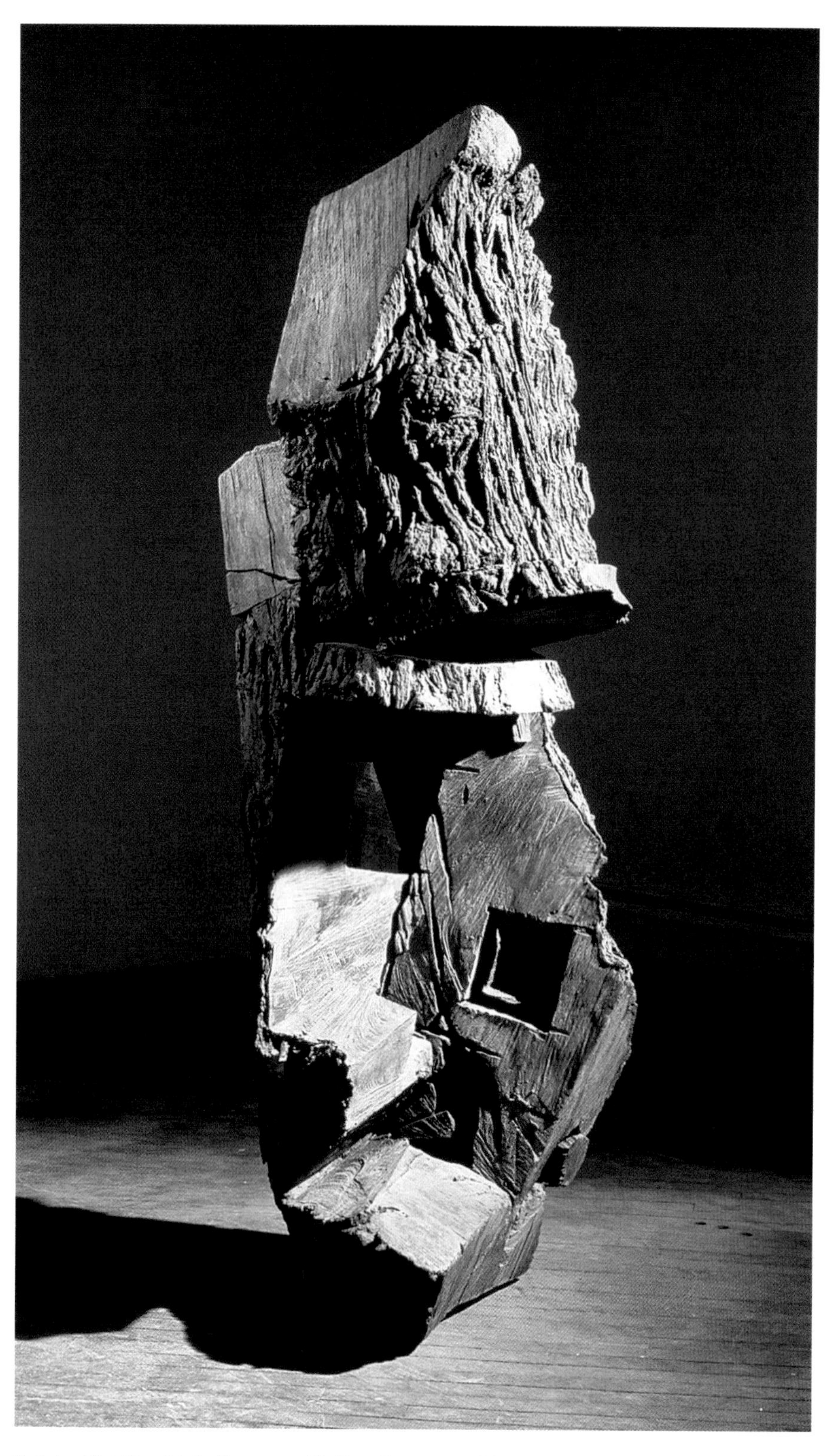

9.14 **Mel Kendrick, *Bronze with Two Squares,* 1989–90. Bronze (edition of three), 73 × 28 × 28 in. (185.4 × 71.1 × 71.1 cm).** This piece appears to be made of wood, but it is actually bronze that has been colored chemically to resemble weathered wood. The sculptor has to know his materials well to create this kind of *trompe l'oeil* effect. Courtesy of the artist.

THE COMPONENTS OF THREE-DIMENSIONAL ART

Subject, form, and content—the components of graphic art—function in much the same manner in the plastic arts. The emphasis placed on each of the components, however, may vary. For example, sculptors use the components for expressive purposes. Architects, ceramists, and metalsmiths, while expressive, may also interpret form for the sake of utility and ornamentation.

Formal organization is more complex in three-dimensional art than in the graphic arts. Materials developed in actual space through physical manipulation exist in a tactile, as well as in a visual, sense. The resulting complexities expand the content or meaning of the form.

Materials and Techniques

Materials and techniques also play larger roles in three-dimensional art than in the graphic arts. In the past 100 years the range of 3D materials has expanded from basic stone, wood, and bronze to steel, plastic, fabric, glass, laser beams (holography), fluorescent and incandescent lighting, and so on. Such materials have revealed new areas for free explorations within the components of subject, form, and content. But they have also increased our responsibilities for fully understanding 3D materials and their accompanying technologies. The nature of the materials puts limitations on the structures that can be created and the techniques that can be used. For example, clay modelers adapt the characteristics of clay to their concept. They manipulate the material with their hands, a block, or a knife to produce a given expression or idea. Modelers don't try to cut the clay with a saw. They understand the characteristics of their material and adapt the right tools and techniques to control it. They also know that materials, tools, and techniques are not ends in themselves but necessary means for developing a three-dimensional work (fig. 9.14).

The four primary technical methods for creating three-dimensional forms are **subtraction, manipulation, addition,** and **substitution.** Although each of the technical methods is developed and discussed separately in the following sections, many three-dimensional works are produced using combinations of the four methods.

Subtraction

Artists cut away materials capable of being carved (glyptic materials), such as stone, wood, cement, plaster, clay, and some plastics. They may use chisels, hammers, torches, saws, grinders, and polishers to reduce their materials (fig. 9.15). It has often been said that when carvers take away material, they "free" the image frozen in the material, and a sculpture emerges. The freeing of form by the subtraction method, although not simple, produces unique qualities characteristic of the artist's material.

Manipulation

Widely known as modeling, manipulation relates to the way materials are handled. Clay, wax, and plaster are common media that are pliable or that can be made pliable during their working periods. Manipulation is a direct method for creating form. Artists can use their hands to model a material like clay into a form that, when completed, will be a finished product. For additional control, special tools, such as wedging boards, wires, pounding blocks, spatulas, and modeling tools (wood and metal), are used to work manipulable materials (fig. 9.16).

Manipulable materials respond directly to human touch, leaving the artist's imprint, or are mechanically shaped to imitate other materials. Although many artists favor the honest autographic qualities of pliable materials, others—especially those in business and manufacturing—opt for the economics of quick results and fast change. Techniques and materials are important because both contribute their own special quality to the final form.

Because most common manipulable materials are not durable, they usually undergo further technical change. For instance, clay may be fired in a kiln (fig. 9.17) or cast in a more permanent material like bronze.

Addition

Methods of addition may involve greater technology and, in terms of (nonfunctional) sculpture, have brought about the most recent innovations. When using additive methods, artists add materials

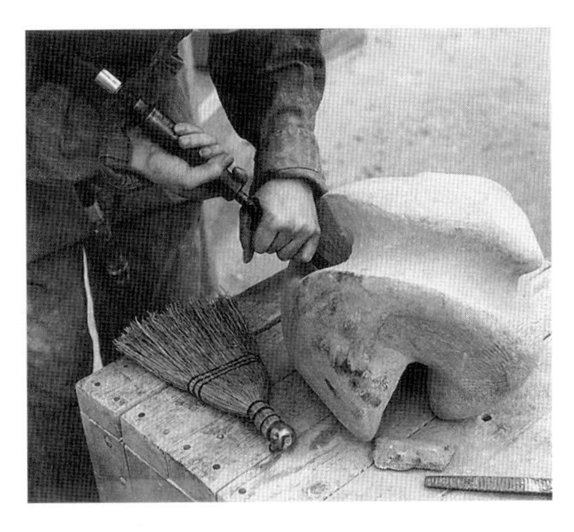

9.15 Subtracting stone. In the subtractive process, the raw material is removed until the artist's conception of the form is revealed. Stone can be shaped manually or with an air hammer, as above. Photograph courtesy of Ronald Coleman.

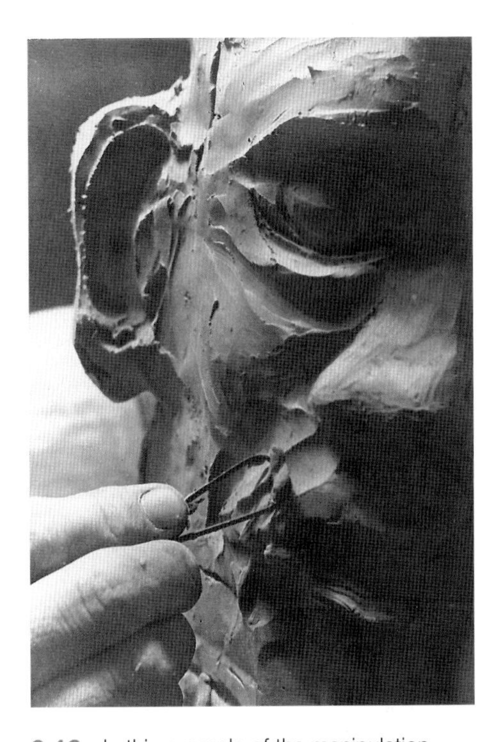

9.16 In this example of the manipulation technique, clay is removed with a loop tool. Clay may be applied to the surface with fingers, hands, or other tools. Photograph courtesy of Ronald Coleman.

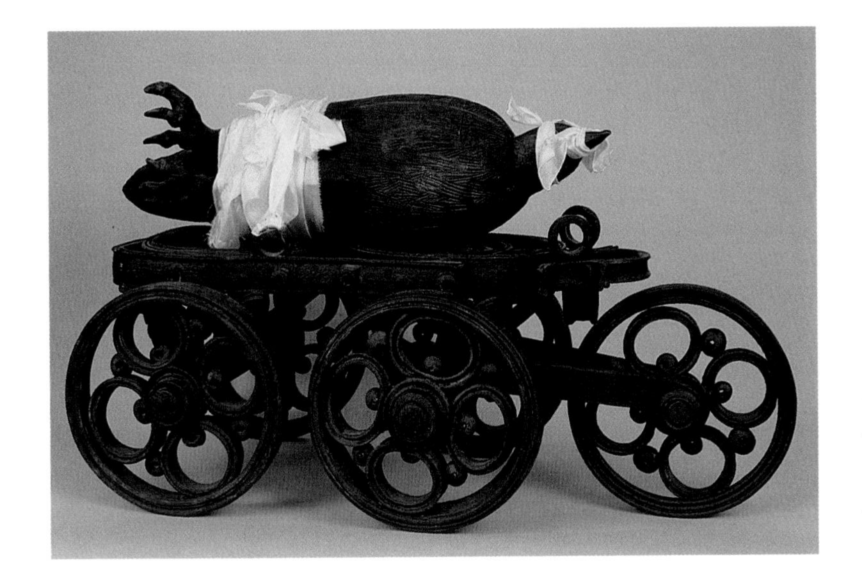

9.17 David Cayton, *One Dead Tern Deserves Another,* 1990. Ceramics, primitive firing, 18 in. (45.7 cm) high. This is an example of clay that has been fired in a primitive kiln: the heavy reduction firing has caused the clay surfaces to turn black. Courtesy of the artist. Photograph by Lynn Whitney.

that may be pliable and/or fluid, such as plaster or cement. They assemble materials like metal, wood, and plastic with tools (a welding torch, soldering gun, stapler, and so on) and fasteners (bolts, screws, nails, rivets, glue, rope, or even thread) (fig. 9.18; see fig. 9.3).

Because three-dimensional materials and techniques are held in high esteem today, the additive methods, with great range, freedom, and diversity, offer solutions to many 3D form challenges.

Substitution

Substitution, or **casting,** is almost always a technique for reproducing an original three-dimensional model. Sometimes an artist alters the substitution process to change the nature of the cast. Basically, in this technique, a model in one material is exchanged for a duplicate form in another material, called the cast, and this is done by means of a mold. The purposes of substitution are, first, to duplicate the model and, second, to change the material of the model, generally to a permanent one. For example, clay or wax can be exchanged for bronze (fig. 9.19), fiberglass, or cement. A variety of processes (sand casting, plaster casting, lost-wax casting, and so on) and molds (flexible molds, waste molds, piece molds, and so on) are used in substitution. Substitution is the least creative or inventive of the technical methods because it is imitative; the creativity lies in the original, not in the casting process.

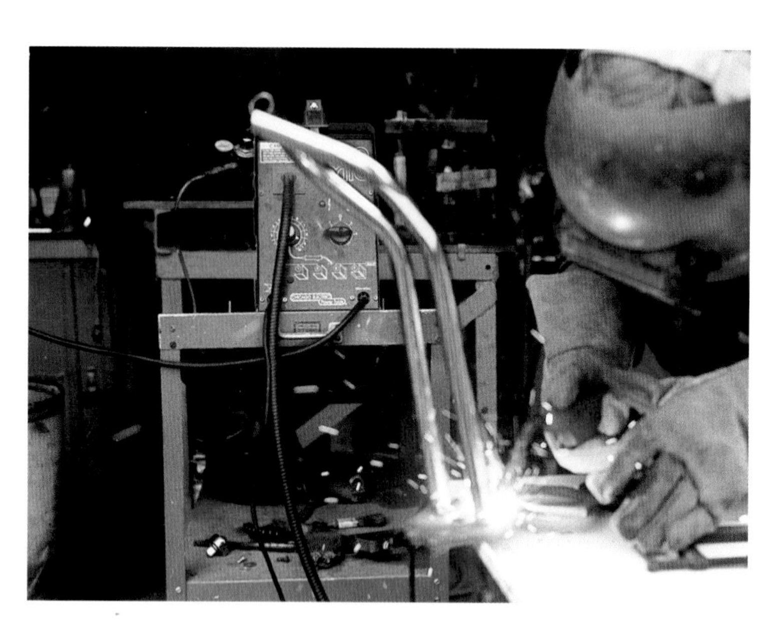

9.18 Welding. In the additive process, pieces of material are attached to each other, and the form is gradually built up. Welded pieces such as the one illustrated are often, though not always, more open than other sculptural techniques. Photograph courtesy of Ronald Coleman.

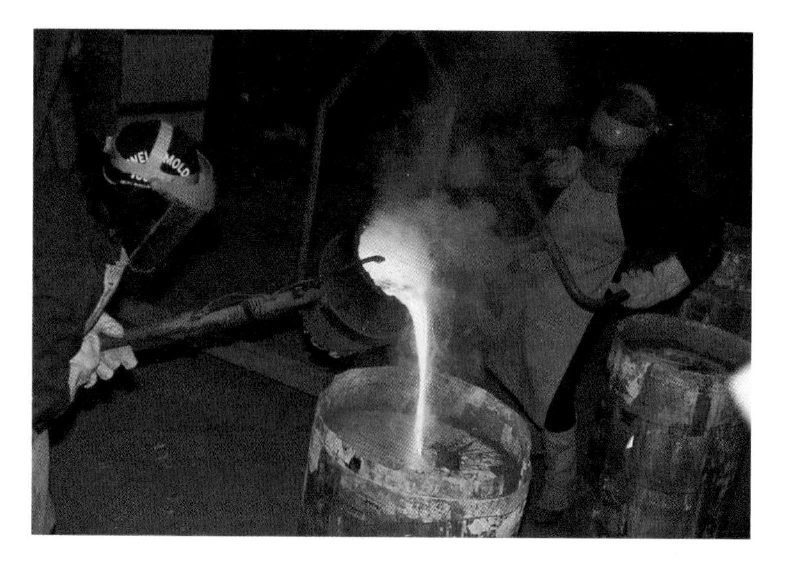

9.19 Substitution technique. In this illustration of the substitution process, molten metal is poured into a sand mold that was made from a model. Photograph courtesy of Ronald Coleman.

Besides acquiring a knowledge of three-dimensional materials and their respective techniques, artists must also be aware of the elements of form.

The Elements of Three-Dimensional Form

Three-dimensional form is composed of the visual elements: shape, value, space, texture, line, color, and time (the fourth dimension). The order of listing is different from that for two-dimensional art and is based on significance and usage.

Shape

The artist working in three dimensions instinctively begins with shape. Shape, a familiar element in the graphic arts, takes on expanded meaning in the plastic arts. It implies the totality of the mass or volume lying between its contours, including any projections and depressions. It may also include interior planes. We can speak of the overall space-displacing shape of a piece of sculpture or architecture, of the flat or curved shape that moves in space, or of a negative shape that is partially or totally enclosed. These shapes are gener-

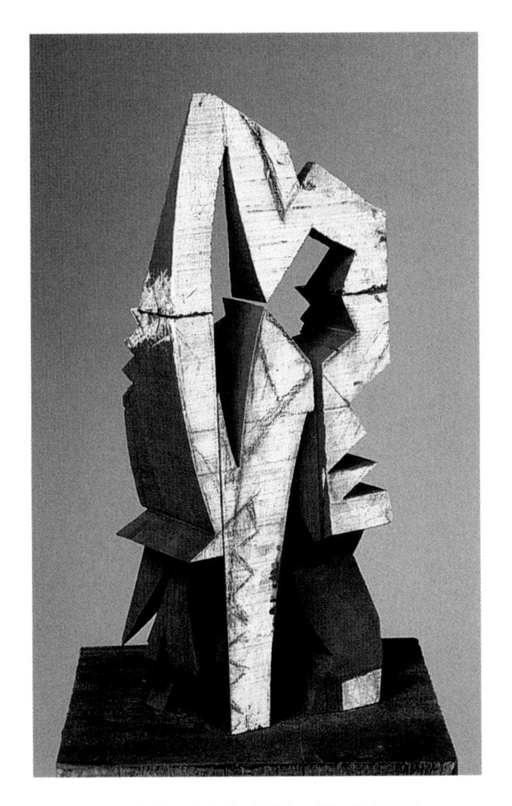

9.20 Mel Kendrick, *White Wall,* 1984. Basswood, Japan paint, 16 × 5 × 6½ in. (40.6 × 12.7 × 16.5 cm). The shape of this three-dimensional piece has edges that have been clearly defined. Courtesy of the artist.

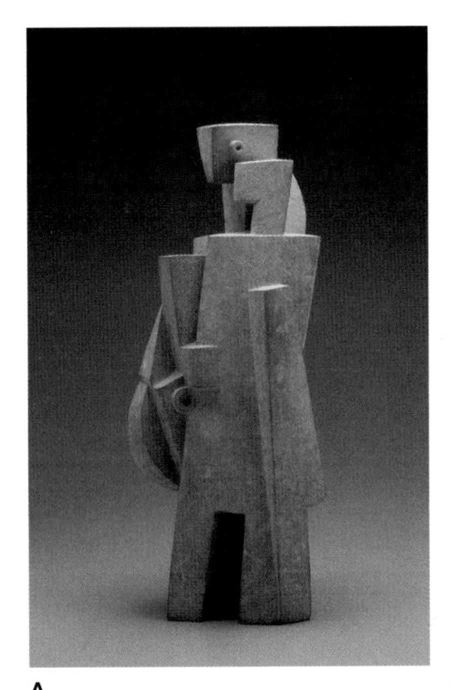

A

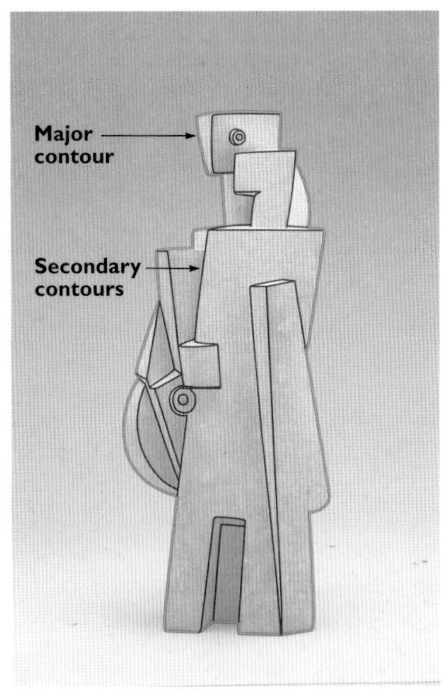

B

9.21 Jacques Lipchitz, *Man with Mandolin,* 1917. Limestone, 29¾ in. (75.6 cm) high. Exploring Lipchitz's work in the round from every position reveals the changing contours and makes the three-dimensional work exciting. In figure 9.21B, an isolated view of the image, the major contour surrounds the silhouette or the total visible area of the work. Secondary contours occur on internal edges. Yale University Art Gallery. Gift of The Société Anonyme Collection.

ally measurable areas limited by and/or contrasted with other shapes, values, textures, and colors. The three-dimensional artist can clearly define the actual edges of shape borders (fig. 9.20). Ill-defined edges often lead to viewers' confusion or monotony. Shape edges guide the eye through, around, and over the 3D surface.

In three-dimensional art the visible shape depends on the viewer's position. A slight change of position results in a change in shape. A major contour is the outer limit of the total 3D work as seen from one position (figs. 9.21A, B). Secondary contours are perceived edges of shapes or planes that move across and/or between the major contours. Some 3D works are constructed so that the secondary contours are negligible (fig. 9.22).

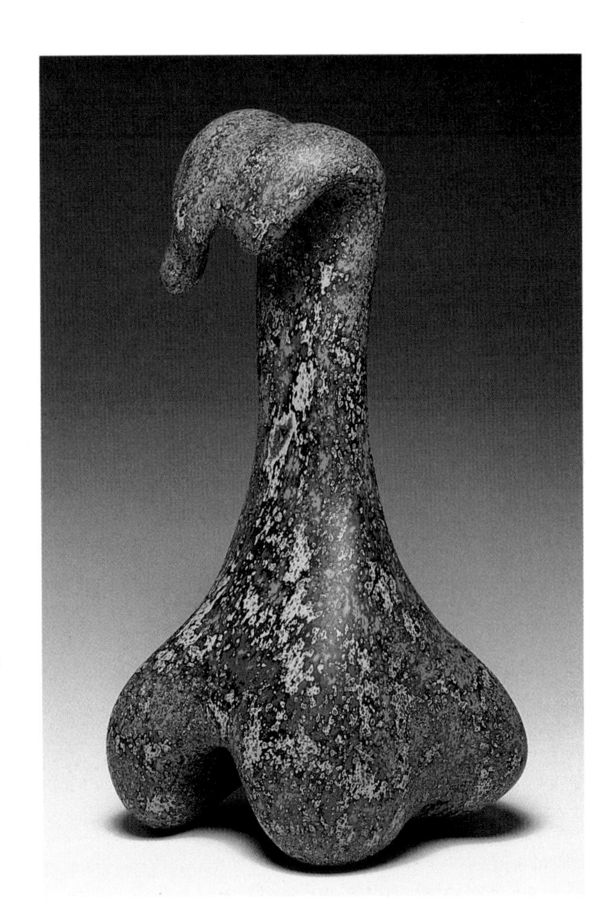

9.22 Ken Price, *Pacific,* 2000. Fired and painted clay, 21½ × 11¾ × 9½ in. (54.6 × 28.6 × 24.1 cm). The major contour of *Pacific* is its outermost edge. Secondary contours are nonexistent or, at best, minimal. © Ken Price, courtesy of L. A. Louver, Venice, California. Photograph by Brian Forrest.

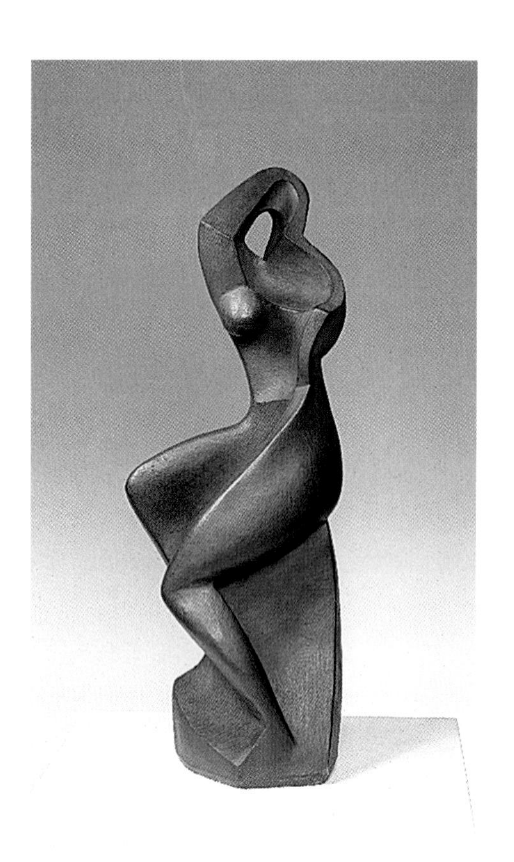

9.23 Alexander Archipenko, *Woman Doing Her Hair,* c. 1958. Bronze casting from plaster based on original terra-cotta of 1916, 21⅝ in. (55 cm) high. This is a significant example of sculptural form where the shape creates negative space, or a void. Archipenko was one of the pioneers of this concept. Courtesy of the Kunst Museum, Düsseldorf, Germany. Photograph by Walter Klein.

A shape might be a negative space—a three-dimensional open area that seems to penetrate through or be contained by solid material. Open shapes can be areas that surround or extend between solids. Such open shapes are often called **voids.** Alexander Archipenko and Henry Moore, prominent twentieth-century sculptural innovators, pioneered the use of void shapes (fig. 9.23; see figs. 9.25 and 10.79). Voids provided new spatial extensions for these artists; they revealed interior surfaces, opened direct routes to back sides of the sculpture, and reduced excessive weight. Void shapes should be considered integral parts of the total form. In linear sculpture, enclosed void shapes become so important that they often dominate the width, thickness, and weight of the materials that define them (fig. 9.24).

Value

As the artist physically manipulates three-dimensional shapes, contrasting values appear through the lights and shadows produced by the forms. Value is

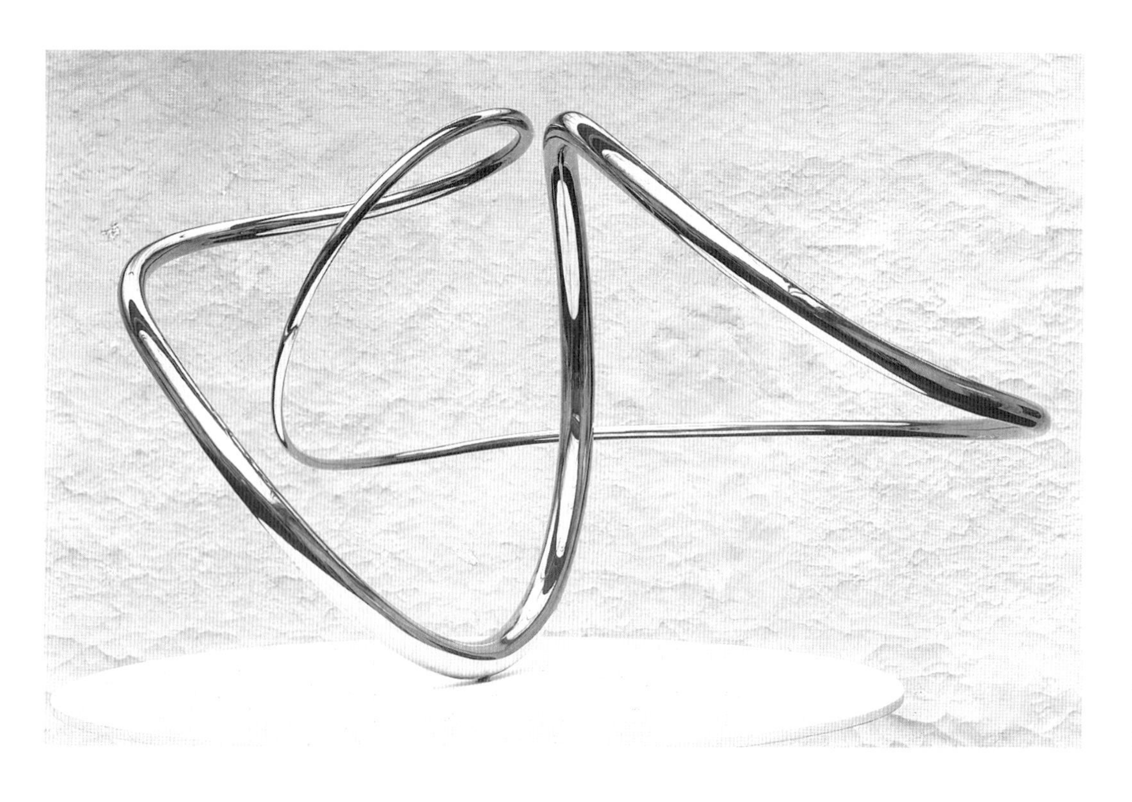

9.24 José de Rivera, *Brussels Construction,* 1958. Stainless steel, 3 ft 10½ in. × 6 ft 6¾ in. (1.18 × 2 m). The concept of attracting observers to a continuous series of rewarding visual experiences as they move about a static three-dimensional work of art led to the principle of kinetic or mobile art, as with this sculpture set on a slowly turning motorized plinth. Art Institute of Chicago. Gift of Mr. and Mrs. R. Howard Goldsmith, 1961.46.

the quantity of light actually reflected by an object's surfaces. Surfaces that are high and facing a source of illumination are light, while surfaces that are low, penetrated to any degree, or facing away from the light source appear dark. Any angular change of two juxtaposed surfaces, however slight, results in changed value contrasts. The sharper the angular change, the greater the contrast (fig. 9.25).

When any part of a 3D work blocks the passage of light, shadows result. The shadows change as the position of the viewer, the work, or its source of illumination changes. If a work has a substantial high and low shape variation and/or penetration, the shadow patterns are more likely to define the work, regardless of the position of the light source. Sculptors who create mobiles typify artists interested in continuously changing light and shadow. The intensity of light markedly changes the shadow effect as the object moves.

Value changes can also be affected by painting a 3D work. Light values strengthen the shadows, while dark values weaken them. The lighter values work best on pieces that depend on secondary contours; darker values are most successful in emphasizing the major contours. Thin linear structures depend more on background contrast and appear as strong dark or light **silhouettes** (fig. 9.26).

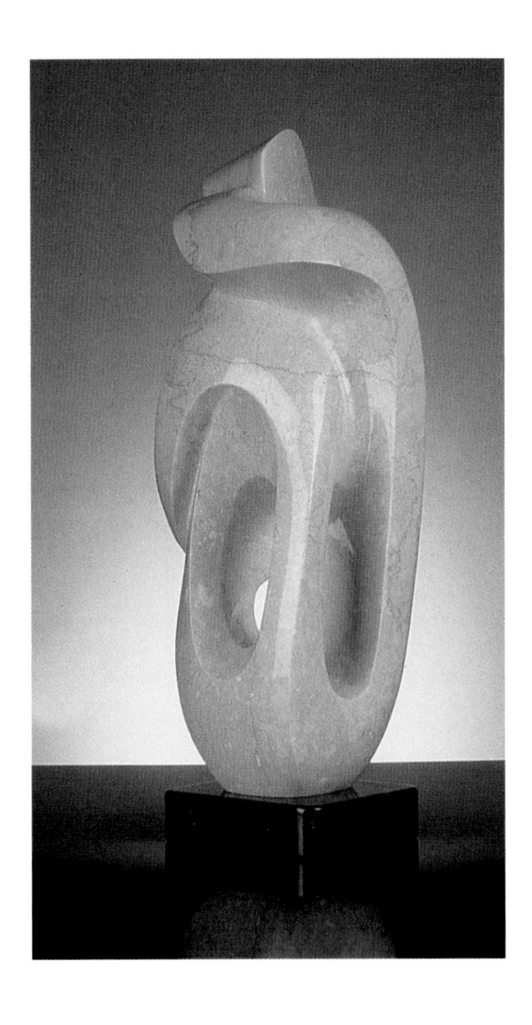

9.25 Julie Warren Martin, *Marchesa,* 1988. Italian botticino marble, 28 × 12 × 10 in. (71.1 × 30.5 × 25.4 cm). A piece of sculpture "paints" itself with values. The greater the projections and the sharper the edges, the greater and more abrupt the contrasts. From the Collection of Kirby and Priscilla Smith.

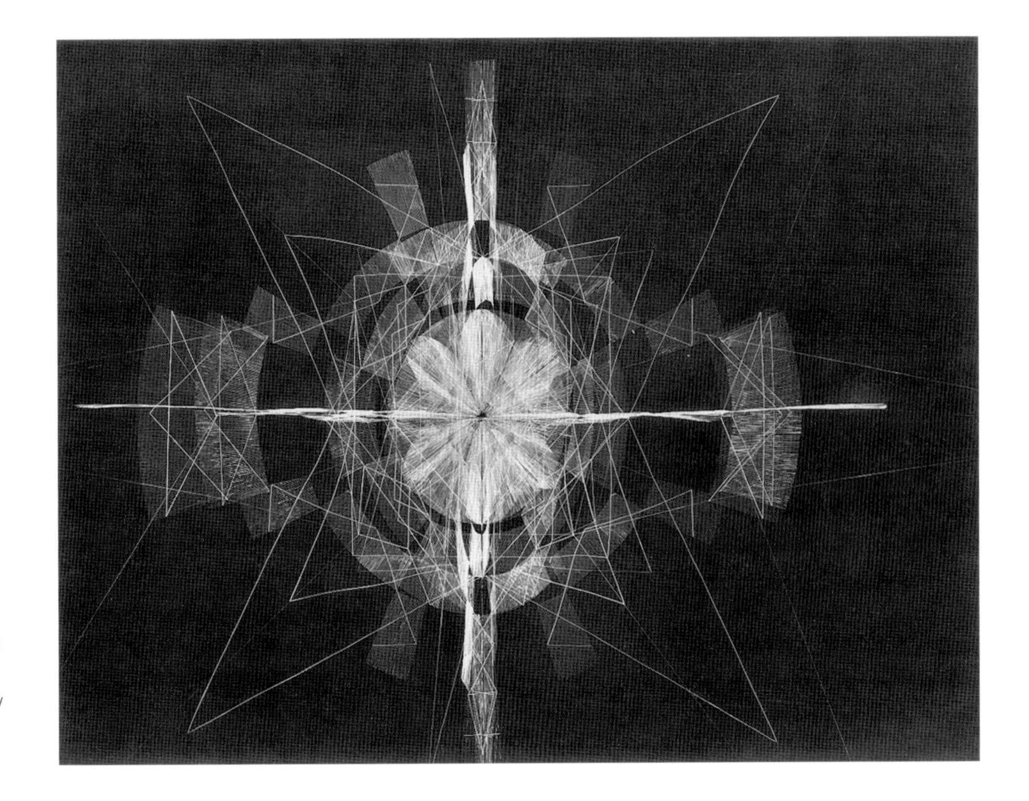

9.26 Richard Lippold, *Variation within a Sphere, No. 10, the Sun,* 1953–56. 22K gold-filled wire, 11 × 22 × 5½ ft (3.35 × 6.70 × 1.68 m). Development of welding and soldering techniques for use in sculpture made the shaping and joining of thin linear metals possible, as in this work by Lippold. Metropolitan Museum of Art, New York. Fletcher Fund, 1956. Photo © Metropolitan Museum of Art, all rights reserved.

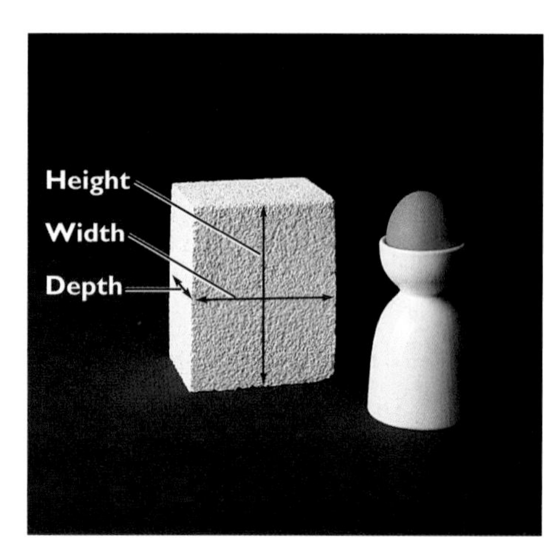

9.27 The rectangular and ovoid solids are examples of two minimal objects that can be formed from displaced, boundless space. The flat and rounded planes in these positions define their special characteristics and spatial intervals. Photograph: Lynn Whitney.

9.28 The figures show four bricks that have been arranged and rearranged to illustrate an increasing level of visual complexity within the third dimension—this is achieved by interactions between the *positive* objects and *negative* sculptural spaces. (A) Stacked bricks. (B) Separated bricks. (C) Crooked bricks. (D) Slanted bricks. (E) Crossed bricks. (F) An installation of bricks. Photographs: Lynn Whitney.

Space

Space may be characterized as a boundless extension of occupied areas. When artists use space, they tend to limit its vastness. They may mark off extensions in one, two, or three dimensions or as measurable distances between preestablished elements. Three-dimensional artists use objects to displace space and to control spatial intervals and locations. Rectangular and ovoid shapes control space effectively, because their weight is felt and established by the flat or rounded dimensions of the planes (fig. 9.27). The two shapes seen together create a spatial interval. Although the two solids illustrated are three-dimensional, their spatial indications are minimal. Greater interest and, in turn, greater spatial qualities could be added to the two shapes by manipulating their surfaces. If material were cut away, the space would move inward, and if material were added, the space would move outward.

In figure 9.28A, four bricks have been arranged in a very restricted manner to form a large, minimal rectangular solid. The individual bricks are distinguished only by the line of cracklike edges visible in the front and side planes. These linear edges are reminiscent of graphic linear renderings.

The four bricks illustrated in figure 9.28B are separated by indentations similar to the mortar joints used by masons. These gaps, although relatively shallow, nevertheless produce distinctively clearer and darker edges than those shown in figure 9.28A. Although the darker edges indicate greater three-dimensional variation than in the first stack of bricks shown, they still have decided spatial limitations. Many low-**relief sculptures** function in a similar way (fig. 9.29).

The bricks in figure 9.28C utilize even more space. They are positioned so that the planes moving in depth are contrasted with the front and side planes, moving toward and away from the viewer. The light that strikes the grouping produces stronger shadows and more interesting value patterns than are found in figure 9.28B. This arrangement can be compared to the qualities of high-relief sculpture. The play of deep shadows against the lights on projecting parts of a high-relief sculpture can in-

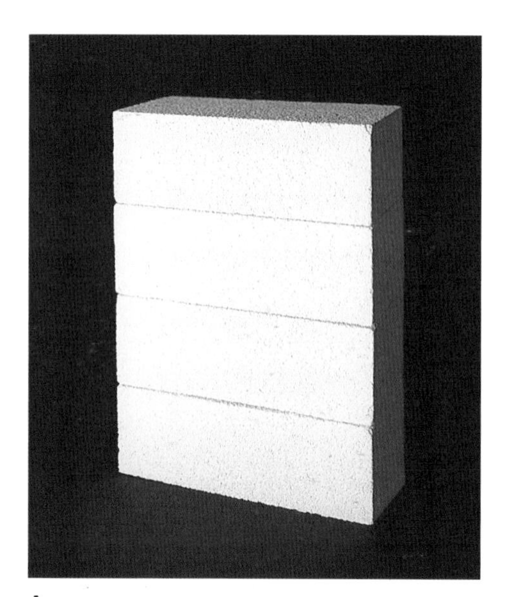

A

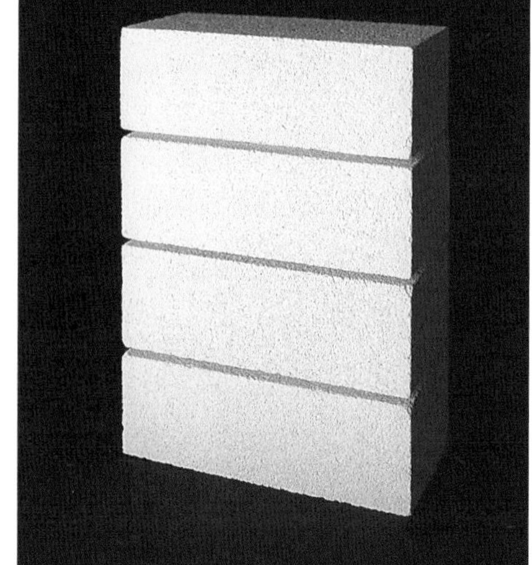

B

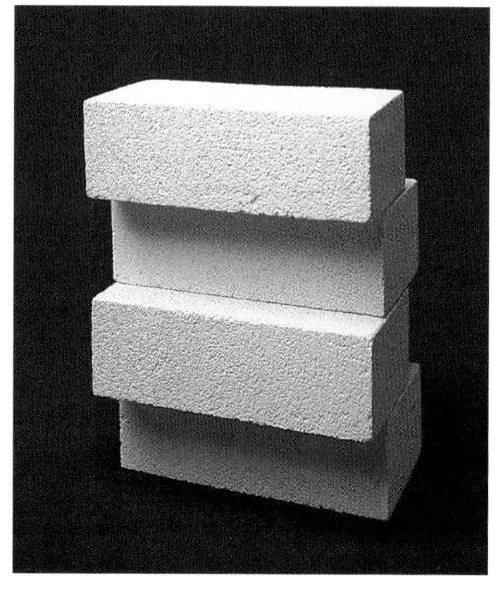

C

crease the work's expressive or emotional qualities (fig. 9.30).

Although the bricks are still in a compact and closed arrangement, their rotation in figure 9.28D makes possible new directions and spatial relationships. The work is becoming more spatially interesting as contrasts of movement, light, and shadow increase. In a way, this inward and outward play of bricks is similar to what the sculptor creates in a freestanding form. Such works are concerned no longer with simple front, side, and back views, but with multiple axes and multiple views. Although all the brick illustrations are actually freestanding, or in the round, the first two examples show surface characteristics closer in spirit to the condition of relief sculpture, as previously indicated. Some authorities use the terms *freestanding* and *sculpture in the round* interchangeably when referring to any three-dimensional work of art not attached to a wall surface (see fig. 9.25).

The variety of brick positions in figure 9.28E, particularly that of the diagonally tipped brick, creates far greater exploitation of space than other groupings. The void, or open space, emphasizes the three-dimensional quality of the arrangement by producing a direct link between the space on each side.

In figure 9.28F, the bricks are separated and achieve greater spatial independence in a manner similar to that of an architectural environment or an installation within a special space. Thus, we have seen the concept of the brick grow increasingly more complex in sculptural consideration and application.

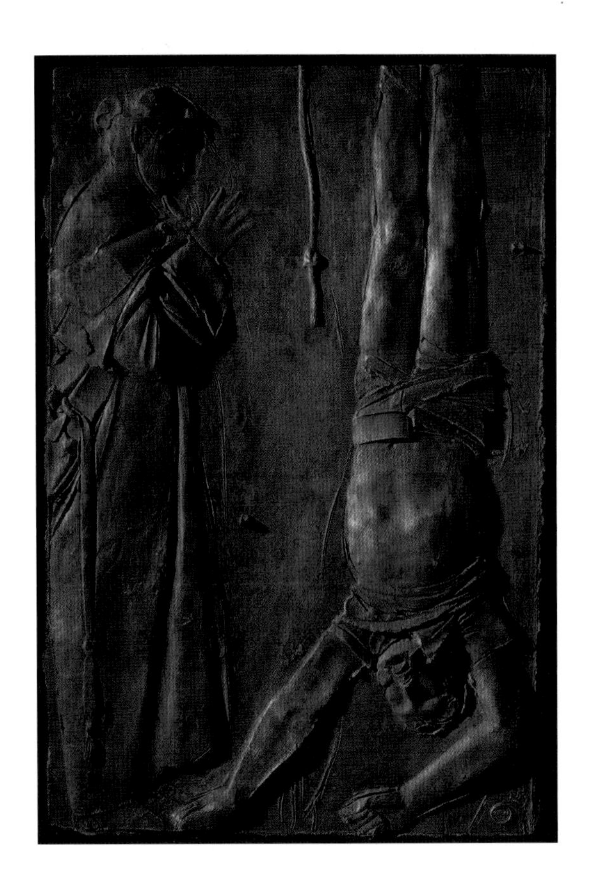

9.29 Giacomo Manzu, *Death by Violence,* 1950. Bronze cast from clay model, 36⅝ × 25¼ in. (93.5 × 64 cm). This is a study for one of a series of panels for the doors of St. Peter's (Vatican, Rome). The confining spatial limitations of relief sculpture are evident. To create a greater feeling of mass, Manzu used sharply incised modeling that is similar to the engraved lines of the printmaker's plate. The crisp incising creates sharp value contrasts that accentuate movement as well as depth. © David Lees/Corbis.

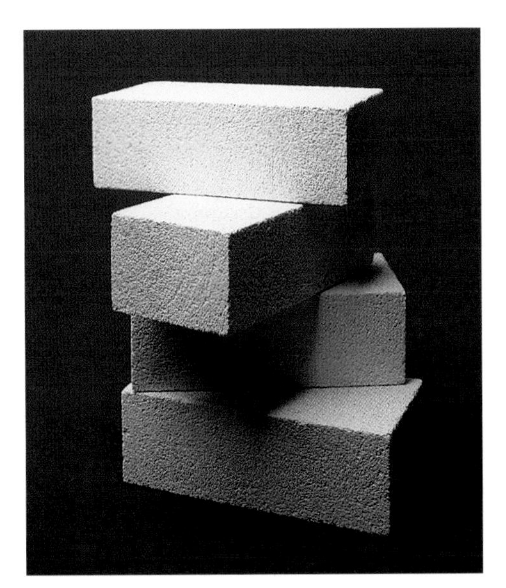

D

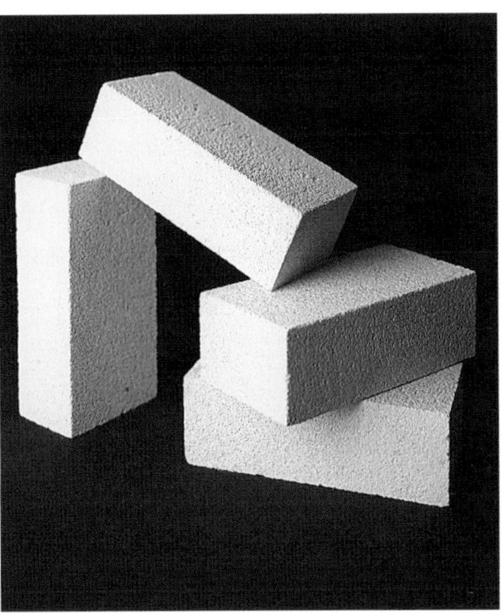

E

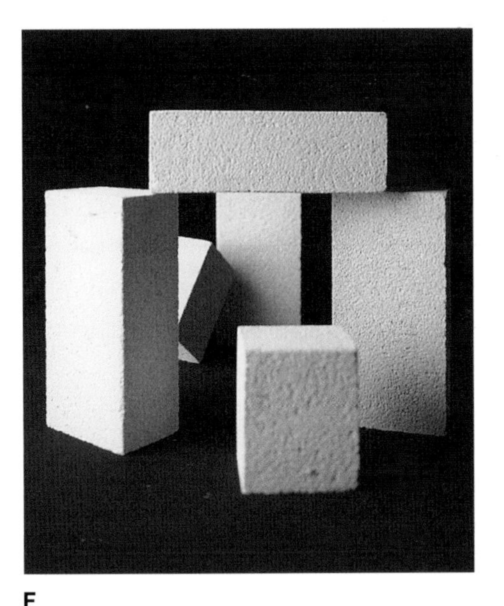

F

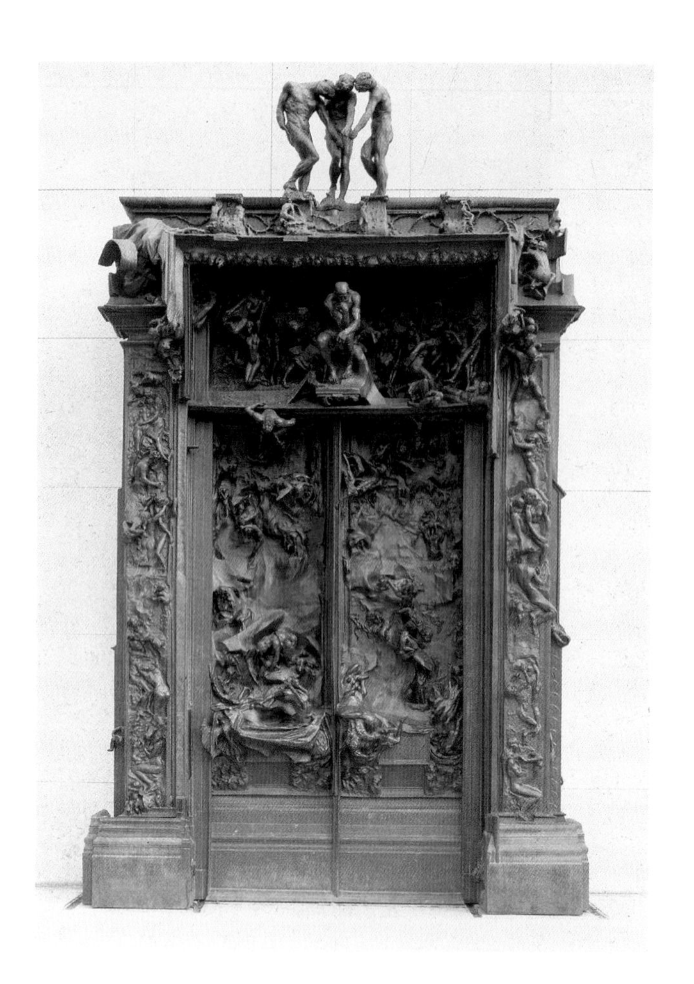

9.30 Auguste Rodin, *The Gates of Hell,* 1880–1917. Bronze, 20 ft 8 in. × 13 ft 1 in. (6.3 × 3.99 m). In this high relief, the forms nearly break loose from the underlying surface. Musée Rodin, Paris, France. Peter Willi/The Bridgeman Art Library.

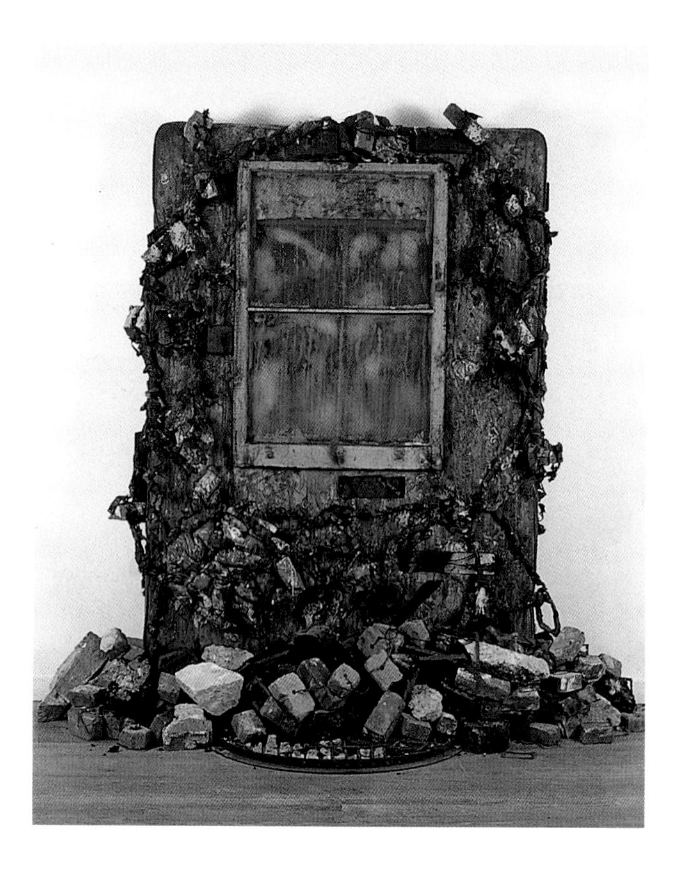

9.31 Nari Ward, *Blue Window Brick Vine,* 1993. Mixed media. Ward uses the texture of found objects (mattress, window, soda cans, bricks) to create a feeling of nature's reclamation of a human habitation. Because of its shallow depth (three inches), it functions much like a stage flat used for theater. © Nari Ward.

Texture

Textures enrich a surface, complement the medium, and enhance expression and content. Textured surfaces range from the rough media (fig. 9.31) to the contrasting hard glossiness of glass or polished marble (fig. 9.32). Certain surfaces are inherent to certain media, and, traditionally, these intrinsic textures are respected. Thus, the artist usually employs texture to characterize the distinctive qualities of the subject. The sleek suppleness of a seal, for example, seems to call for a polished surface, whereas the character of a rugged, forceful person calls for a rough-hewn treatment. However, artists sometimes surprise us with a different kind of treatment. The actual, simulated, and invented textures of graphic artists are also available to plastic artists and are developed from the textures inherent in the materials that plastic artists use.

Line

Line is a phenomenon that does not actually exist in nature or in the third dimension. It is primarily a graphic device used to indicate the meeting of planes or the outer edges of shapes. When two planes come together, they form an edge or an arris. This edge can appear to be a line when it is enhanced by a cast shadow or the different values of the two planes. The definition of line may also be broadened to include the main direction or axial thrust of a three-dimensional shape whose length is greater than its width. In addition, line can be used to refer to the thin shapes of contemporary linear sculpture comprising wires and rods. Development of welding and soldering techniques made possible the shaping and joining of thin linear metals in sculpture. Such artists as José de Rivera and Richard Lippold have expanded the techniques of linear sculpture (see figs. 9.24 and 9.26).

Incising line in clay or in any other soft medium is similar to the graphic technique of drawing. In three-

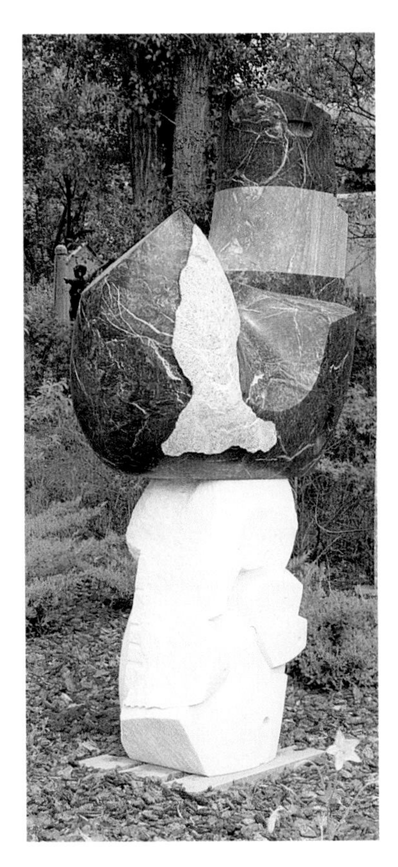

9.32 Michael Braden, *Nurse Log,* 1998. Persian travertine, Swedish verde, and Colorado yule marble, 7 ft 6 in. × 4 ft × 2 ft 4 in. (228.6 × 121.9 × 71.1 cm). This sculpture is enriched by the artist's choice of materials in contrasting colors and variegated graining. Lumina Gallery, New Mexico.

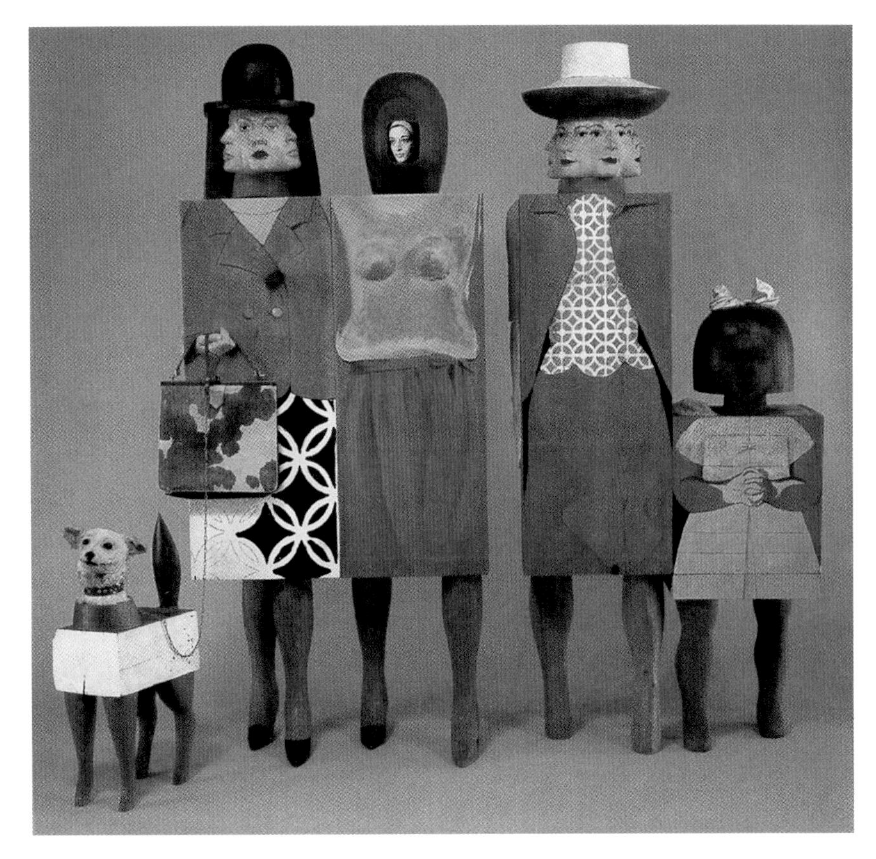

9.33 Marisol, *Women and Dog,* 1964. Wood, plaster, synthetic polymer, taxidermed dog head and miscellaneous items, 72¼ × 73 × 30[15]⁄16 in. (183.5 × 185.4 × 78.6 cm). This example of Pop Art reveals the willingness of some contemporary artists to use bright color to heighten the three-dimensional characteristics of form at the same time that it enriches surfaces. The form has its roots in earlier twentieth-century styles (Cubism, Constructivism), while the use of combine-assemblage tends to fuse the media of sculpture and painting into one.

dimensional art, incised lines are used to accent surfaces for interest and movement. The Italian Giacomo Manzu employed such lines to add sparkle to relief sculpture (see fig. 9.29).

Color

Color is an inherent feature of all materials. Sometimes it is pleasant, as in the variegated veining of wood or stone (fig. 9.32), but it can also be bland as in the flat chalkiness of plaster. Paint can be added when the material needs enrichment or when the surface requires color to bring out the form more effectively. Painted surfaces, as with any color application, can add expression and boost attractive qualities. The elements of value and color are so interwoven in sculpture that artists often use the two terms interchangeably. Thus, an artist may refer to value contrasts in terms of color, actually thinking of both simultaneously. Many times, the application of color is an attempt to capture the richness and form-flattering quality of the **patina** found on bronzes oxidized by exposure to the atmosphere. This approach subordinates color to the structure of the piece. On the other hand, in certain historical periods (for example, early Greek art) the application of bright color was commonplace. Some revival of this technique is evident in contemporary works. In every case the basic criterion for the use of color is compatibility with the form of the work (fig. 9.33).

Time (The Fourth Dimension)

Time is also an element of the spatial arts. Time is involved in graphic arts only insofar as contemplation and reflection on meaning are concerned, since the act of viewing a graphic work as a totality requires only a moment. However, in a plastic work, the work must turn or we must move around it to see it completely, thus adding a fourth dimension.

The artist wants the time required to inspect the work to be a continuum of rewarding visual variation. Each sequence or interval of the viewing experience brings out relationships that will lure the observer around the work, all the while extending the time spent on it.

In the case of kinetic sculpture, the artwork itself, not the observer, moves. Such works require time for their movements. Mobiles, for example, present a constantly changing, almost infinite series of views (fig. 9.34; see fig. 10.81).

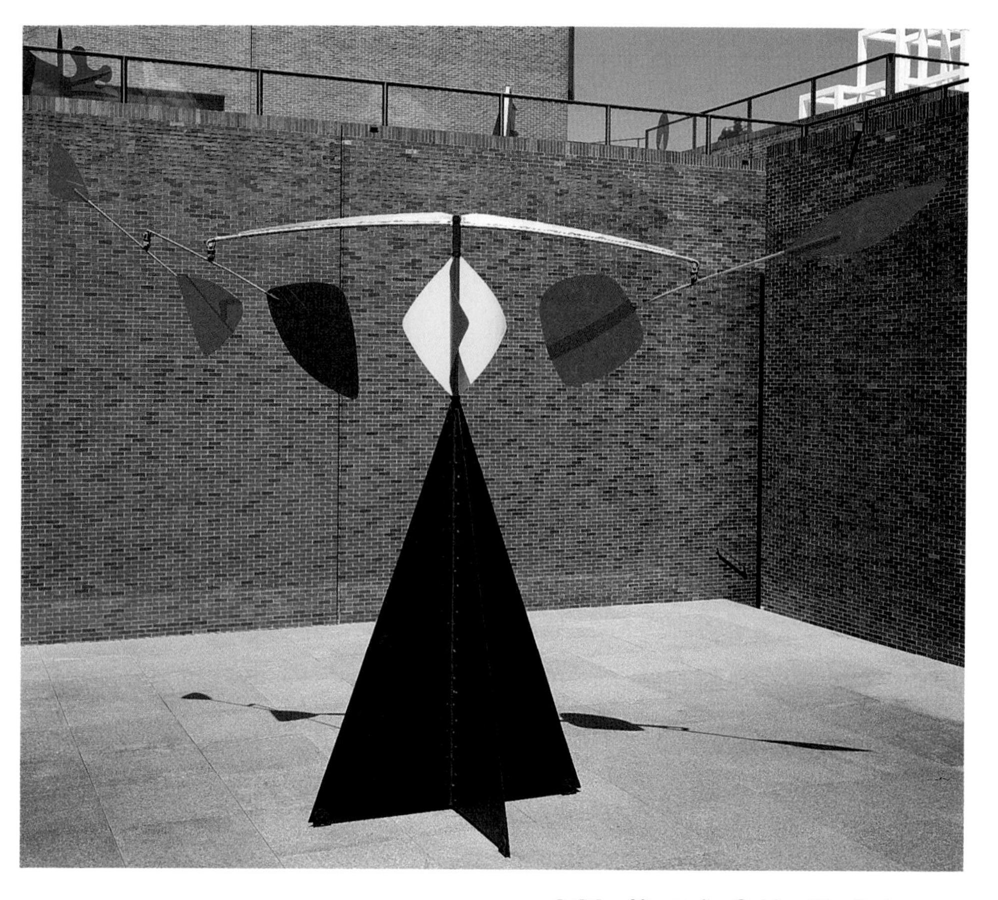

9.34 Alexander Calder, *The Spinner,* 1966. Aluminum, steel, paint, 235 × 351 in. This noted artist introduced physically moving sculptures called mobiles. In this mobile-stabile, movement requires time for the observation of the changing relationships, thereby introducing a new dimension to art in addition to height, width, and space. The result is a constantly altered, almost infinite series of views of parts of the mobile. Collection Walker Art Center, Minneapolis. Gift of Dayton Hudson Corporation, Minneapolis.

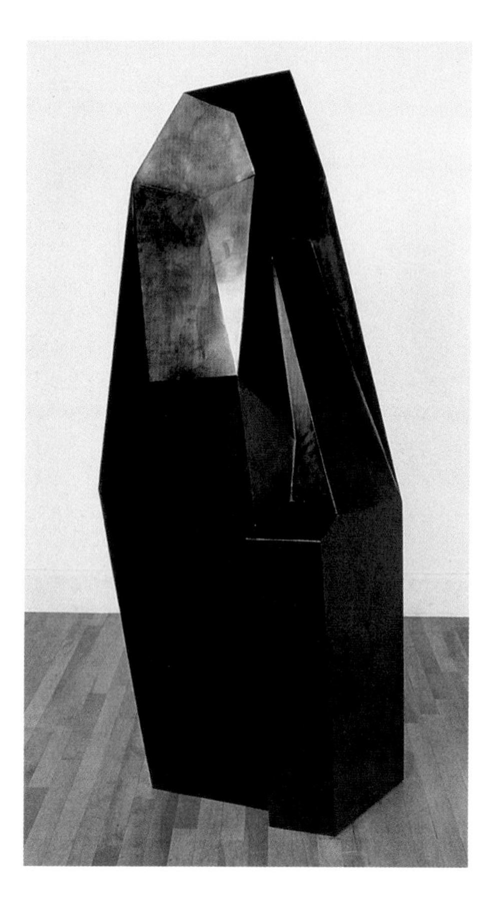

9.35 James De Woody, *Big Egypt,* 1985. Black oxidized steel, 72 × 30 × 30 in. (182.9 × 76.2 × 76.2 cm). In this example of a tectonic arrangement, James De Woody has cut planes that project in and out of his surfaces without penetrating voids or opening spaces. This is sometimes referred to as "closed" composition. Courtesy of the Arthur Roger Gallery, New Orleans, LA.

Principles of Three-Dimensional Order

Organizing three-dimensional art is the same as organizing two-dimensional art. However, three-dimensional forms, with their unique spatial properties, call for somewhat different applications of the principles.

Three-dimensional artists deal with forms that have multiple views. Composing is more complex. What might be a satisfactory solution for an arrangement with one view might be only a partial answer in the case of a work seen from many different positions. Adjustments are required in order to totally unify a piece. Compositionally, a three-dimensional work may be **tectonic** (closed, massive, and simple) with few and limited projections, as in figure 9.35, or **atectonic** (open, to a large degree), with frequent extensive penetrations and thin projections, as in figure 9.36. Both tectonic and atectonic arrangements can be found in nearly all 3D art, and each of these arrangements can be used individually to achieve different expressive and spatial effects.

Harmony and Variety

Harmony and variety have been cited as indispensable concerns in the creation of two-dimensional artworks; this is equally true in the realm of the third dimension, although its discernment is not always so obvious and its achievement somewhat different. In order to bring this to light, we will focus primarily on sculpture because it exists in the round. One must keep in mind that in order to fully view a three-dimensional work such as sculpture, the viewer must "circumnavigate" the work, which has an almost infinite number of aspects. The interest generated by the many views under the control of the sculptor produces a degree of variety, but this must be balanced by harmony for the benefit of the work's totality.

"Extensions" are an important consideration in producing harmony and in leading the viewer around a sculpture. These are actual and subjective lines or edges and shapes that suggest directions around the work. They imply connections with other such lines and shapes, thus creating a continuous movement encircling the work. The sculptor can calculate this movement to give a sense of rhythm that is either agitated or comparatively calm. Predictable rhythm incorporates proportional transitions that aid in giving flow to a work (fig. 9.37).

If there are areas considered significant, the sculptor may utilize closure by employing the proximity of certain shapes or lines to achieve a focus on those passages. Viewers must, however, be able to extricate themselves from these areas to facilitate the continuous movement sought. We must be reminded that, in sculpture, shapes may be seen as well-defined edges or as cavities and bulges, whereas lines may again be edges or scratches and extended cuts.

Some sculptors make use of transparent materials, such as glass, rather than opaque media. The superimposition of such material creates genuine transparency, unlike the illusions of two-dimensional art. This also can suggest space, albeit usually in a limited way. Architects, who are increasingly sculptural in their projects, sometimes make use of overlapping to produce harmony among the sections of their building structures. Additionally, in sculpture

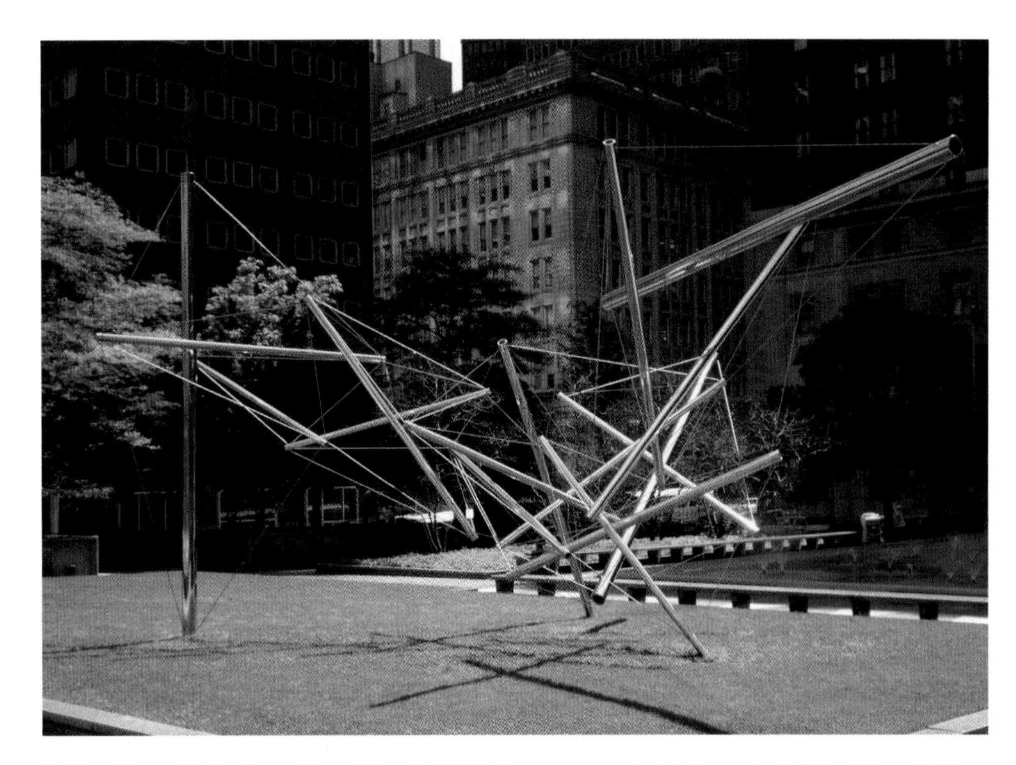

9.36 Kenneth Snelson, *Forest Devil*, 1977. Aluminum and stainless steel, 17 × 35 × 25 ft (5 × 10.5 × 7.5 m). Kenneth Snelson has developed sculptures that are "open," or atectonic. Collection Museum of Art, Carnegie Institute, Pittsburgh, PA. Courtesy of the artist.

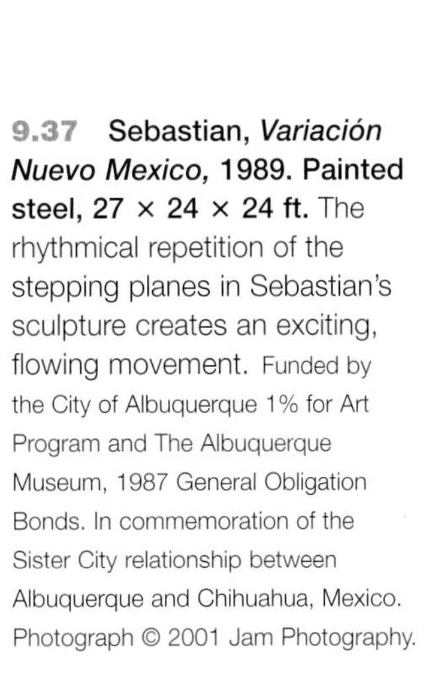

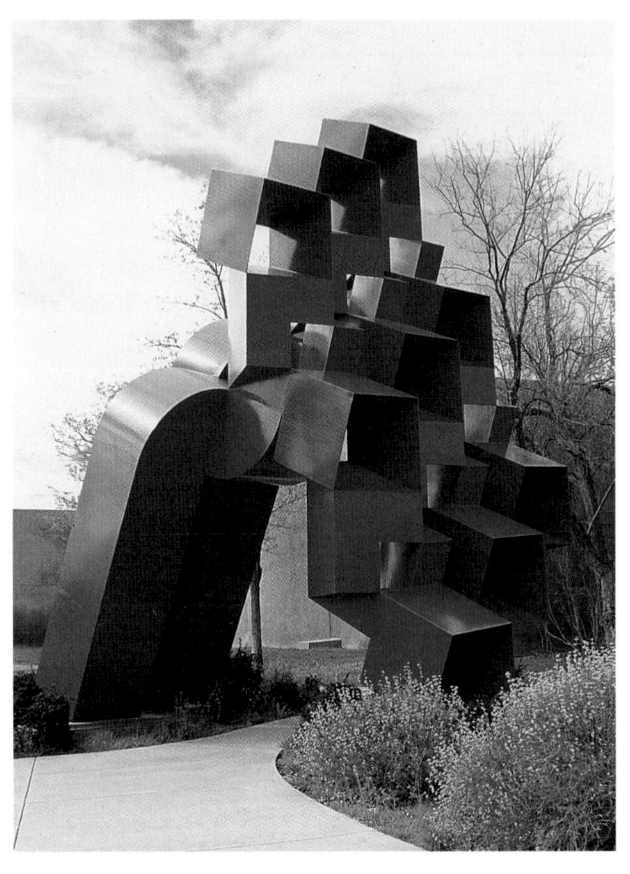

9.37 Sebastian, *Variación Nuevo Mexico*, 1989. Painted steel, 27 × 24 × 24 ft. The rhythmical repetition of the stepping planes in Sebastian's sculpture creates an exciting, flowing movement. Funded by the City of Albuquerque 1% for Art Program and The Albuquerque Museum, 1987 General Obligation Bonds. In commemoration of the Sister City relationship between Albuquerque and Chihuahua, Mexico. Photograph © 2001 Jam Photography.

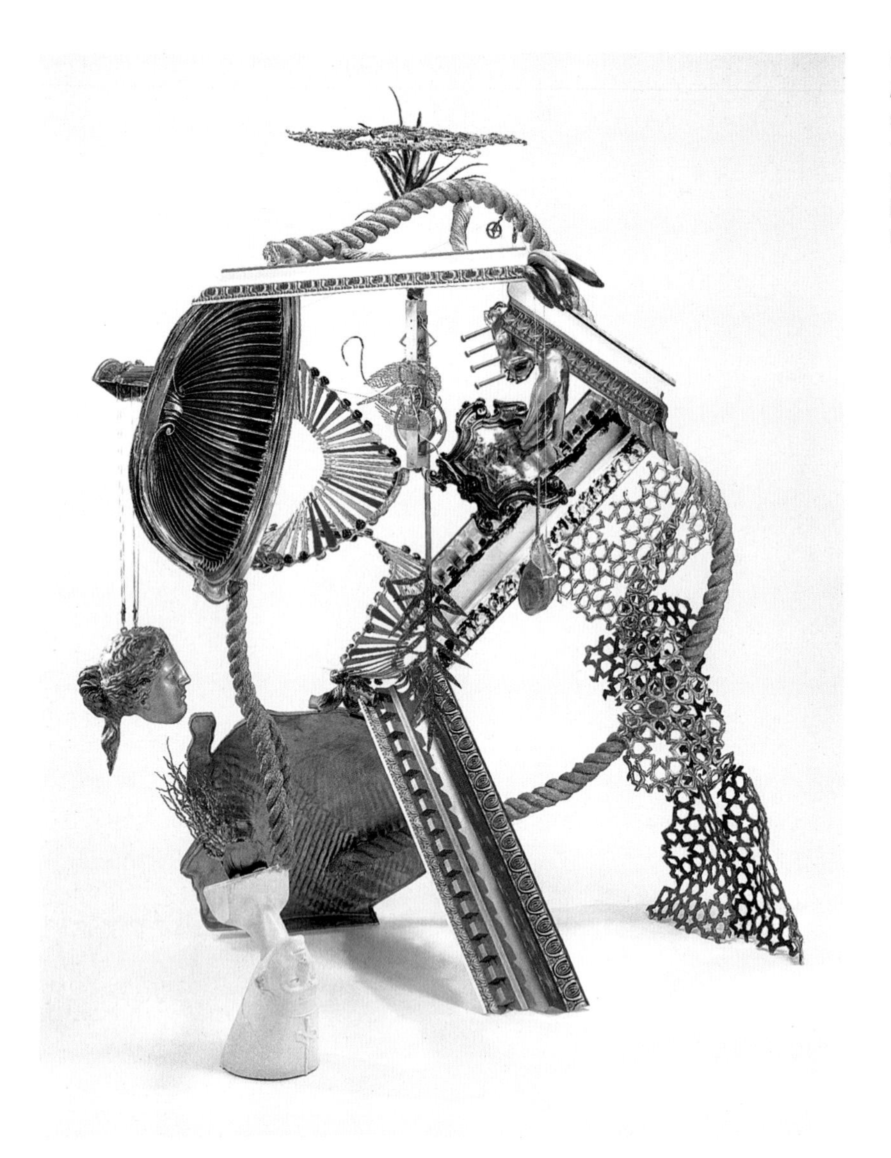

9.38 **Nancy Graves, *Unending Revolution of Venus, Plants, and Pendulum,* 1992. Bronze, brass, enamel, stainless steel, and aluminum, 97 × 71½ × 56½ in. (2.46 × 1.82 × 1.44 m).** In this sculpture, we see a variety of form parts. We also see an excellent example of an asymmetrically balanced sculpture. © Nancy Graves Foundation/Licensed by VAGA, New York, NY.

there are instances of "interpenetration" used to pull things together, notably in large metal sculpture pieces. Media that are related in color, in actual material or through painting of the surface, may also assist in achieving harmony in sculpture. All of the foregoing are means by which the three-dimensional artist may find harmony. Variety, as in two-dimensional work, is possible by reversing the means by which harmony is produced, the aim being to create greater interest (fig. 9.38). The ultimate goal is usually a precarious balance between harmony and variety. This goal is a concern of all 3D artists whatever the nature of the work.

It might be added, in returning to sculpture, that such work in low relief is closely related to 2D work, whereas high-relief sculpture is somewhat of a hybrid production, at times calling on some of the problems of harmony and variety encountered in sculpture in the round.

Balance

When considering balance and the extension of spatial effects in three-dimensional art, we need to examine some special conditions. For example, when balancing a 3D piece of work, the added dimension of depth affects its multiple views. While a sphere appears symmetrical from any view, a rectangular box may appear symmetrical from the front and back but not from the side or top when seen in conjunction with other views. The views that are seen in depth may project other types of balance. Three types of balance are possible in actual space: symmetrical (see fig. 9.41), asymmetrical (see fig. 9.38), and radial (fig. 9.39). Of the three, symmetrical and radial balance are considered formal and regular. Radial balance is spherical, with the fulcrum in the center. The parts that radiate from this point are usually similar in their formations. However, artists more commonly make use of asymmetrical balance because it provides the greatest individual latitude and variety.

Proportion

When we are viewing a three-dimensional work, the effect of proportion (the relationship of the parts to the whole) is crucial. Being in the presence of an actual 3D work that not only can be seen but also can be touched or caressed, stood on, walked on, or passed through puts special emphasis on the relation of the parts to the whole. These proportional relations must apply continually in a 3D artwork as we look at it from multiple views. We should get much the same sensation as we might by grasping that sculpture in our arms. Proportion is fundamental in determining the basic form, setting the standard for relationships and permeating the other principles.

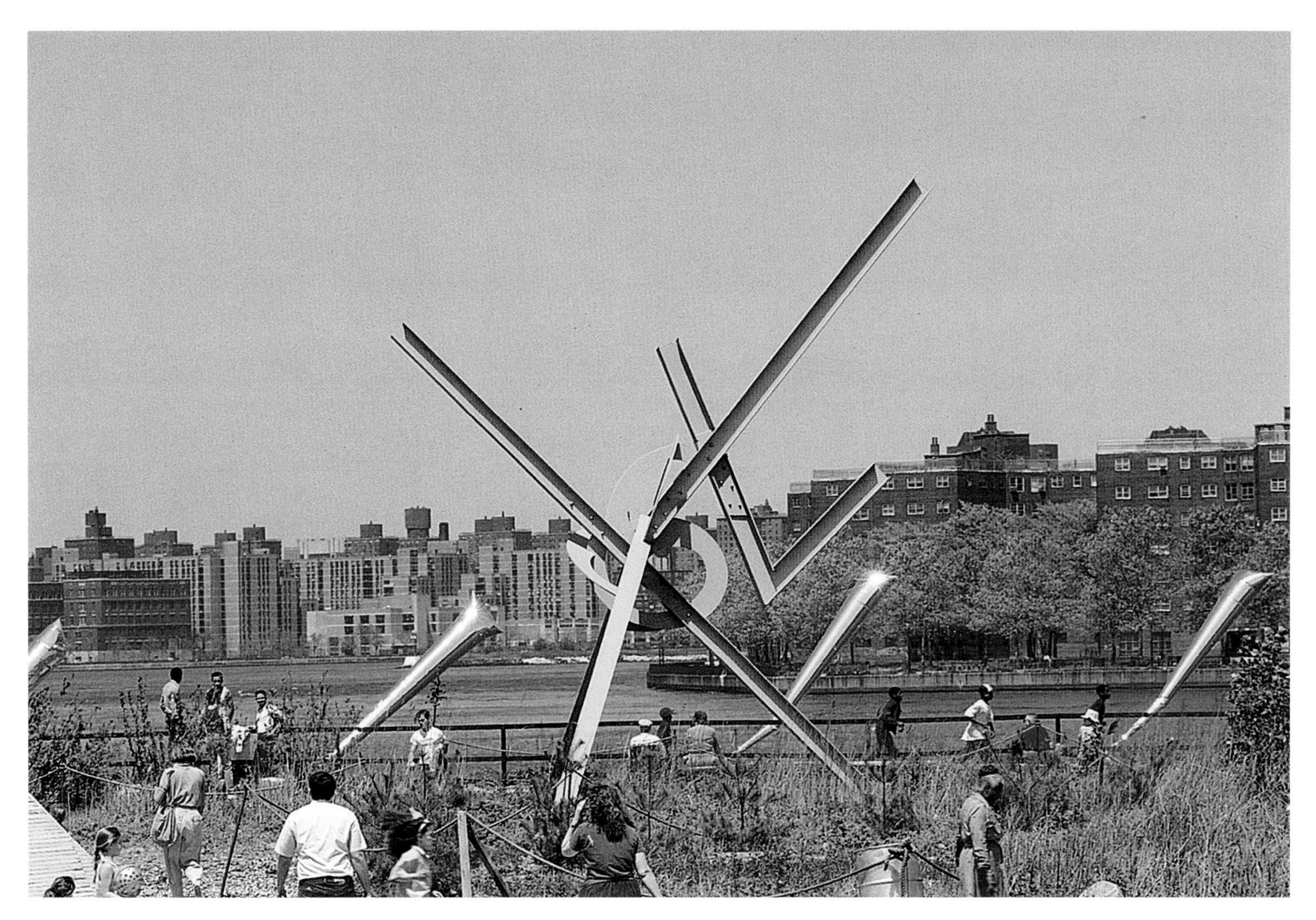

9.39 Mark di Suvero, *For Veronica,* 1987. Steel, 21 ft 9 in. × 35 ft. The center of this sculpture is the fulcrum identified by the contrasting rounded, curled parts. Most of the diagonal beams radiate in outwardly thrusting directions. The exception purposefully adds variety to an otherwise formal radial balance. The Rene and Veronica di Rosa Foundation, Napa, CA. Photograph Oil & Steel Gallery, Long Island City, NY.

Scale is most dramatic at the extremes, when 3D pieces are small enough to be held in the palm of the hand or when we stand in the presence of gigantic architecture, landscapes, or sculptures (see fig. 9.9). The actual size of a 3D work when compared to the physical measurement of the human figure is referred to as its scale. Small jewelry and/or miniaturized models, or maquettes, of automobiles, architecture, landscapes, and sculpture are considered small scale. Works made for public places are usually large scale. Religious temples, mosques, cathedrals, statehouses, malls, parks, 3D commercial displays, and sculpture sites are examples of large-scale works. These can be awe inspiring in their size and scope, especially when one is in their presence (see figs. 9.9 and 9.36).

The relationship that occurs when one actually experiences a three-dimensional work brings out a special feeling for tension, balance, and scale. The proportions determining the basic form set a standard and permeate the other principles. Repetitions and rhythms share in these proportional relationships.

Economy

Included within the group known as Primary Structurists or Minimalists are three-dimensional artists who emphasize

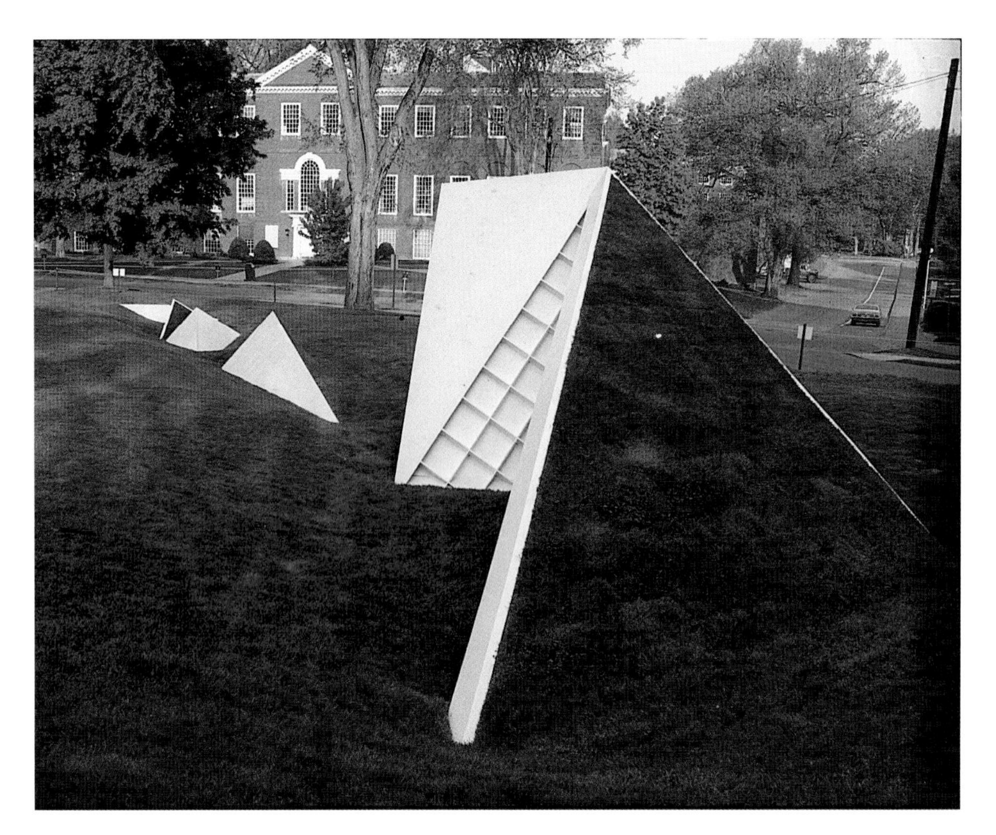

9.40 Beverly Pepper, *Thel*, 1977. Metal, paint, and earth, 15 ft high × 18 ft wide × 135 ft long. Beverly Pepper has created many artworks that represent nothing more than large-scale, starkly simple geometric shapes. In this group, she has repeated shapes that interact spatially and seem to grow out of the earth. Pepper's economic means unify this interesting arrangement. Site-specific installation at Dartmouth College. Photograph courtesy of Dartmouth College.

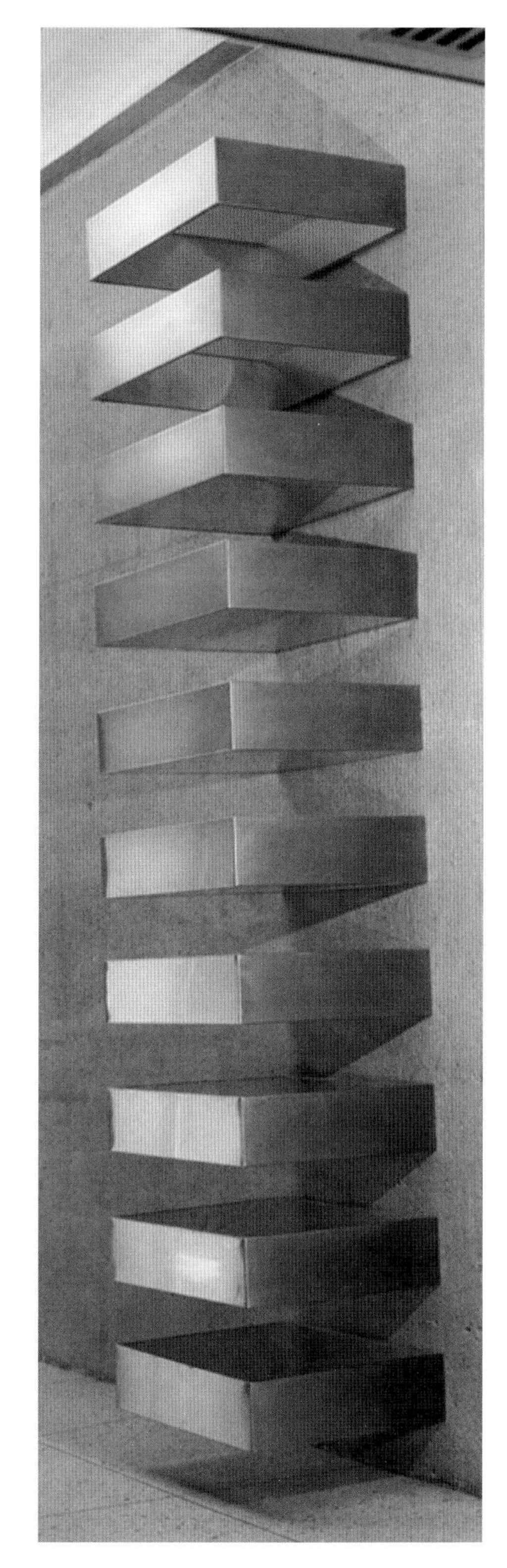

9.41 Donald Judd, *Untitled*, 1968. Brass, ten boxes, 6 × 27 × 24 in. (15.2 × 68.6 × 61 cm). Judd is primarily interested in perceptually explicit shapes, reflective surfaces, and vertical interplay.

the principle of economy in their works, because they, like their fellow painters, want to create stark, simple, geometric shapes. These Minimalists strip their shapes of any emotional, psychological, or symbolic associations and eliminate physical irrelevancies. For further emphasis, they also tend to make a feature of large size. Beverly Pepper has reduced her shapes to simple geometric forms (fig. 9.40), while Donald Judd aligns his primary shapes in vertical and horizontal rows, thereby interrelating economy with repetition and rhythm (fig. 9.41).

Movement

Two types of movements are used by three-dimensional artists. Implied movement, the most common type (fig. 9.42; see fig. 9.37), is illusory, but actual movement is special and involves the total work. Actual movements that take place in kinetic art can be set into motion by air, water, or mechanical devices. Alexander Calder, the innovator of mobile sculptures, at first used motors to drive his pieces but later used air currents generated by human body motion, wind, air conditioning, or heating (see figs. 9.34 and 10.81). George Rickey, a contemporary sculptor, works with wind and air propulsion (see fig. 10.87). Water has been used as a propellant in other 3D works. Jean Tinguely, Arthur Ganson (fig. 9.43), José de Rivera (see fig. 9.24), and Pol Bury (see fig. 10.86) propel their sculptures with motor drives. Computer-activated kinetics are

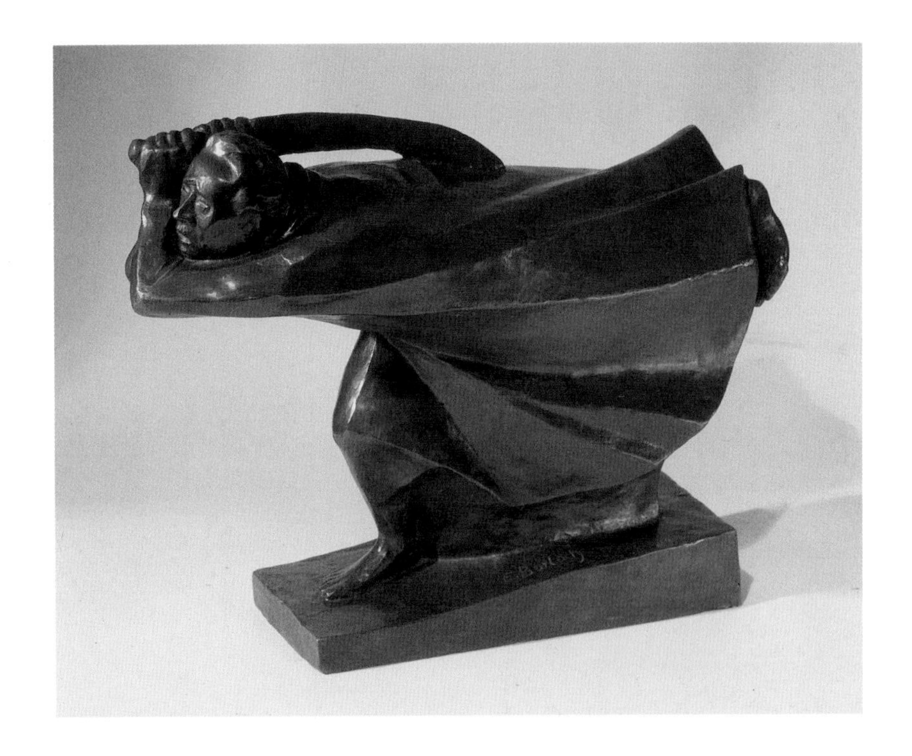

9.42 Ernst Barlach, *The Avenger,* 1914, later cast. Bronze, 17¼ × 22¾ × 8 in. (43.8 × 57.8 × 20.3 cm). This figure is not actually moving, but it does depict a powerful forward thrust. Movement is implied by the long sweeping horizontal and diagonal directions made by the edges of the robe, the projection of the head and shoulders, and the base plane. © The Ernst Barlach Foundation. Photo Tate Gallery, London/Art Resource, NY.

now being marketed. The principle of movement is inherently related to the art elements of time and space.

When properly combined, the principles of order produce vibrant forms. In the three-dimensional field, new conceptual uses of time, space, and movement have changed definitions and meanings that had endured for centuries. The prevailing thought of the past, that sculpture was a stepchild of the graphic arts, need no longer be true.

Installations

Artists turned toward **installations** during the 1960s. The work that has evolved is usually nonfigurative and ranges in size from the relatively small to

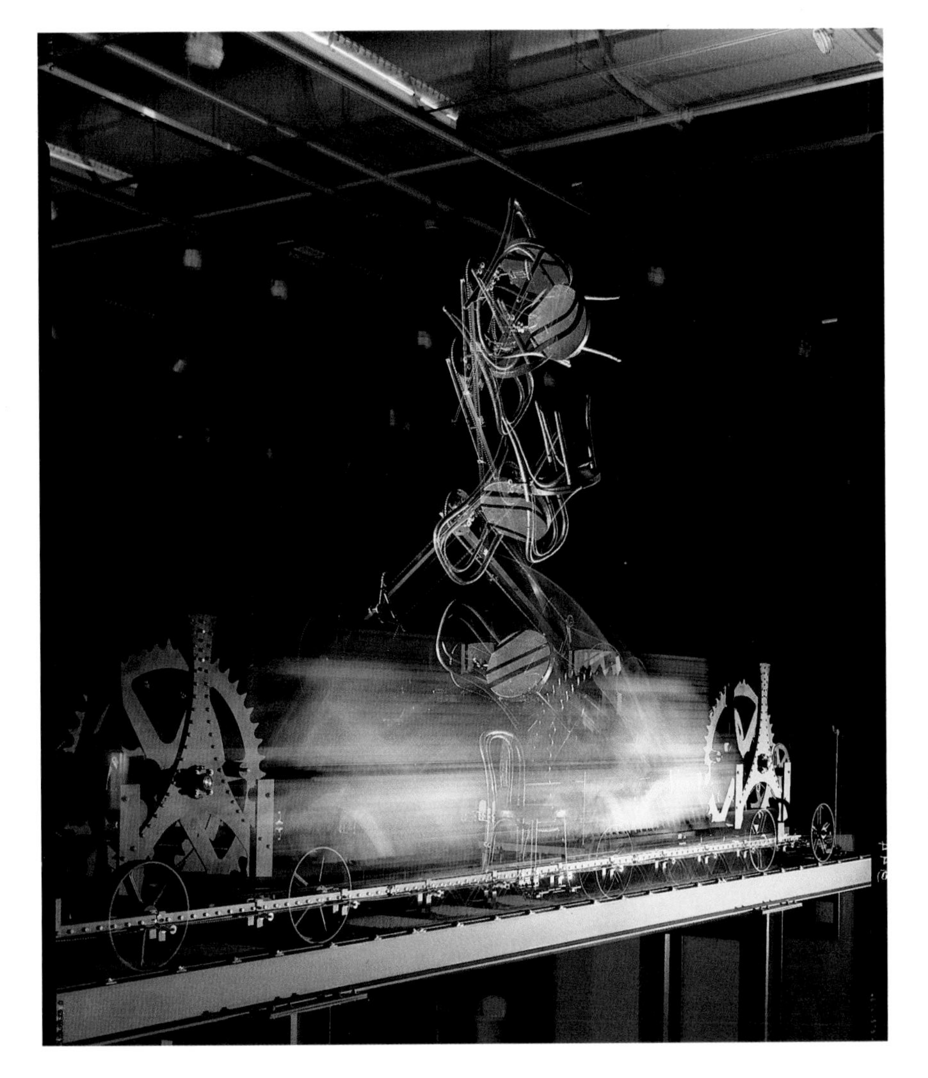

9.43 Arthur Ganson, *Machine with Chair* (time-lapse photograph of 1995 version), 1995. Steel (machine), fiberglass over foam (chair), motor, electronic switches and circuits, rubber. Track 30 ft long, machine 5 ft high, chair at highest point 13 ft from track. Like Jean Tinguely, Arthur Ganson has found the machine to be an instrument for the poet/artist. He produces some machine-driven sculptures that involve kinetic ironies, mechanical awareness, and a sense of time, space, and motion. Arthur Ganson is a sculptor at the Massachusetts Institute of Technology. Photograph by Henry Groskinsky.

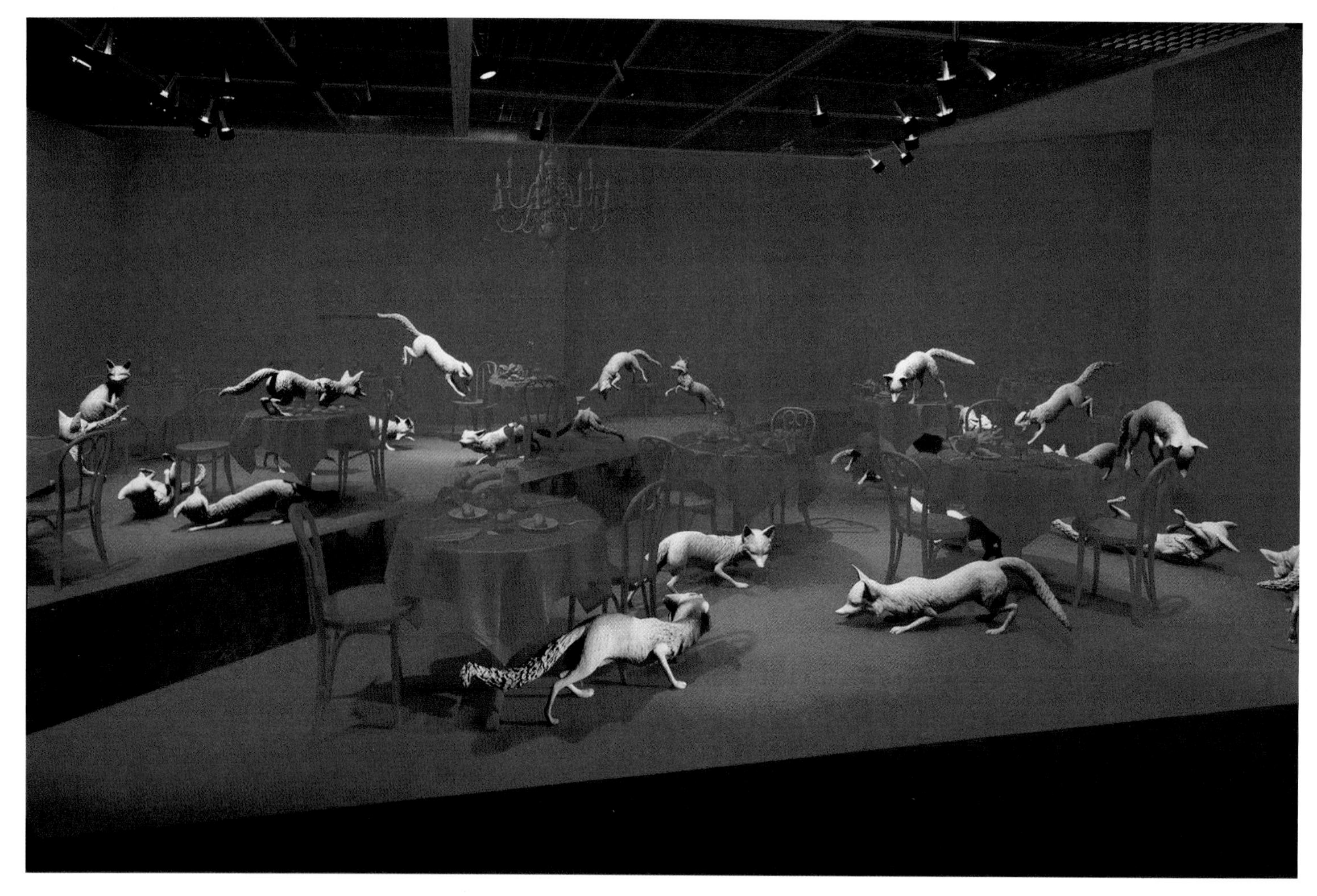

9.44 **Sandy Skoglund, *Fox Games*, 1990. Polyester resin sculptures, tables, chairs, painted tableware, painted bread, chandelier, cloth napkins and tablecloths. Approx. 30 × 30 × 12 ft high.** In this installation, Sandy Skoglund presents a personal environment of red tables and gray foxes, which confronts the viewer, causing them to see the spatial setting in a new way. This version was installed at the Denver Art Museum in Colorado in June of 1990. Denver Art Museum Collection, 1991.36. Photograph by Bill O'Connor. © Denver Art Museum. Sandy Skoglund, FOX GAMES © 1989.

the enormous. Materials that have been used include sheet metal, fiberglass, wood, bronze, steel, plastic, plaster, and stone, but actually any available materials are eligible. Outdoor installations may be simple but are frequently quite large and often sit in accessible civic locations. Most frequently, installations are placed indoors and are comprised of multiple pieces, often filling the floors and walls. The pieces may be simply but dominatingly placed or even haphazardly spread out.

One reasonable definition of an installation might be "setting in a place." This implies that one could create an installation by setting out dinnerware, installing a battery in a car, or placing a work of art on a wall. Obviously, this covers a limitless amount of ground, but here we refer to installations produced by artists and placed in interior or exterior situations. Works of this kind can be composed of any media or contrivance and be of any configuration. A principal intention of installation art is to heighten awareness of environmental space.

Though carefully thought out, some installations have been decried as inconsequential, dehumanized, or irrational, even provoking violent reactions. This is not surprising as installation is a new art form, and unusual styles of art have many times produced a general outcry. Richard Serra is an American sculptor whose minimalist installations have been controversial; his *Tilted Arc* was removed after public protests. One judge equated it with "garbage, and garbage causes rats." These criticisms are rebuffed by artists who believe that art should be given free rein, mindful that artworks have drawn widespread condemnations in the past, only to be revered with the passage of time.

Observers who are fond of the art world are frequently more accepting than others, who may be hostile or indecisive in their response. These people react in different ways, some perplexed, some overcome, some having their vision altered, and some delaying judgment. Despite the ridicule sometimes heaped on installation art, it is now a fixture of the art scene. Installations enhance viewer involvement and produce new outlooks on the spaces in which they are placed. Among significant artists in this area are Anne Hamilton, whose work is sensuous and monolithic; Sandy Skoglund (fig. 9.44); Rebecca Horn (fig. 9.45), whose arrangements of ordinary things evoke surreal feelings; and Richard Long, who specializes in arrangements of stone and wood.

Much of the public is curious about this kind of art; and, whatever the reactions, many artists are engaging in it. No matter what, installations require a great deal of laborious effort—no doubt, to its creators, a labor of love.

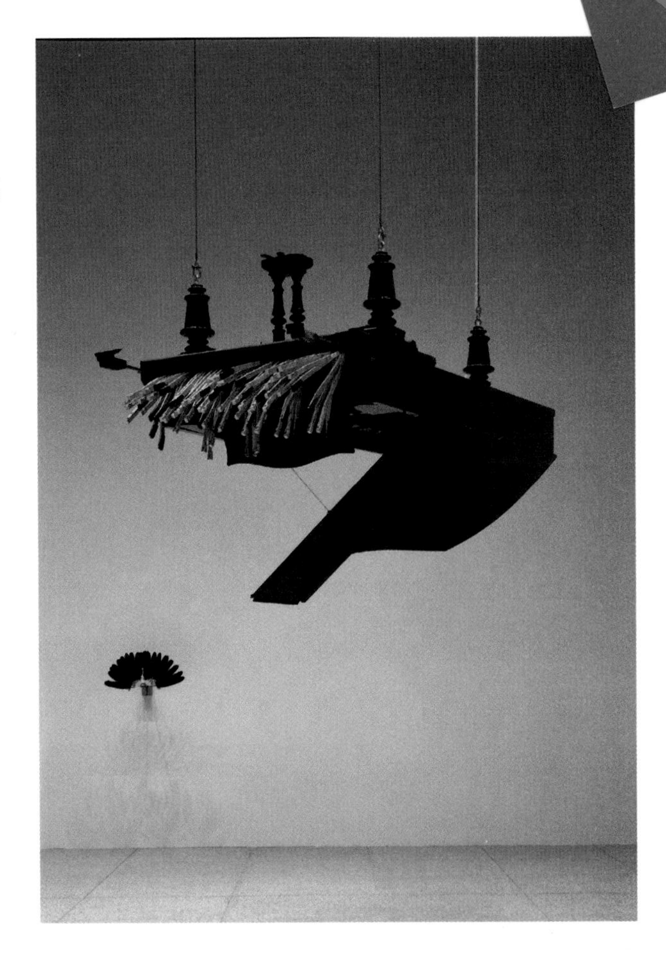

9.45 Rebecca Horn, *Concert for Anarchy,* Berlin 1994. Grand piano and mixed media, variable dimensions. Horn's use of a piano in defiance of gravity makes the space within her installation an intimidating and overwhelming three-dimensional setting. Photograph by Attilio Marazano. © Rebecca Horn. All rights reserved. © 2005 Artists Rights Society (ARS), New York/VG Bild-Kunst, Bonn.

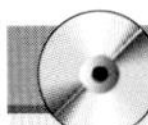

INVESTIGATE THE CD-ROM **Questions to Ask Yourself**

We live in three dimensions of space that form the context for all we know and do.

As you review this chapter on the CD-ROM, think about a building, sculpture, or object like a piece of jewelry or even a cup that you particularly like, and answer these questions:

1. What qualities of this building, sculpture, or object particularly appeal to you? What senses do you use to appreciate these qualities?
2. What would it be like if you could hold this building, sculpture, or object in the palm of your hand? Or the opposite, what would it be like if it were so big you could get inside it? How would the qualities that appeal to you change?
3. In your imagination, try changing the materials out of which the building, sculpture, or object is made. As you change the materials, what does this do to the building, sculpture, or object?
4. In your imagination, try changing other elements of the three-dimensional form. What effects do these changes have?

CHAPTER TEN

Content and Style

INTRODUCTION TO CONTENT AND STYLE

NINETEENTH-CENTURY ART

- Neoclassicism (c. 1750–1820)
- Romanticism
- Beginning of Photography
- Realism
- Technological Developments in Photography
- Impressionism
- Post-Impressionism
- Photographic Trends

EARLY-TWENTIETH-CENTURY ART

- Expressionism
  - *French Expressionism: The Fauves*
  - *German Expressionism*
  - *Sculpture in the Early 1900s*
  - *Expressionism in the United States*
  - *Expressionism in Mexico*
- Color Photography and Other New Trends
- Cubism
- Futurism
- Abstract Art
  - *Abstract Art in Europe*
  - *Abstract Art in the United States*
  - *Abstract Sculpture*
  - *Abstract and Realist Photography*
- Fantastic Art
  - *Dadaism*
  - *Individual Fantasists*
  - *Surrealist Painting*
  - *Surrealist Sculpture*
  - *Surrealism and Photography*

LATE-TWENTIETH-CENTURY ART

- Abstract Expressionist Painting
- Abstract Expressionist Sculpture
- Abstract Expressionism and Photography
- Kinetic Sculpture
- Pop Art and Assemblage
- Happenings and Performance or Action Art
- Op Art
- Minimalism
- Environmental Art and Installations
- Postmodernism
- New Realism (Photorealism)
- Process and Conceptual Art
- Neo-Expressionism
- Feminist Art
- Other Trends: Neo-Abstraction, Film Stills, Photography
  - *Neo-Abstraction*
  - *Film Stills*
  - *Photography*

NEW GLOBAL ART

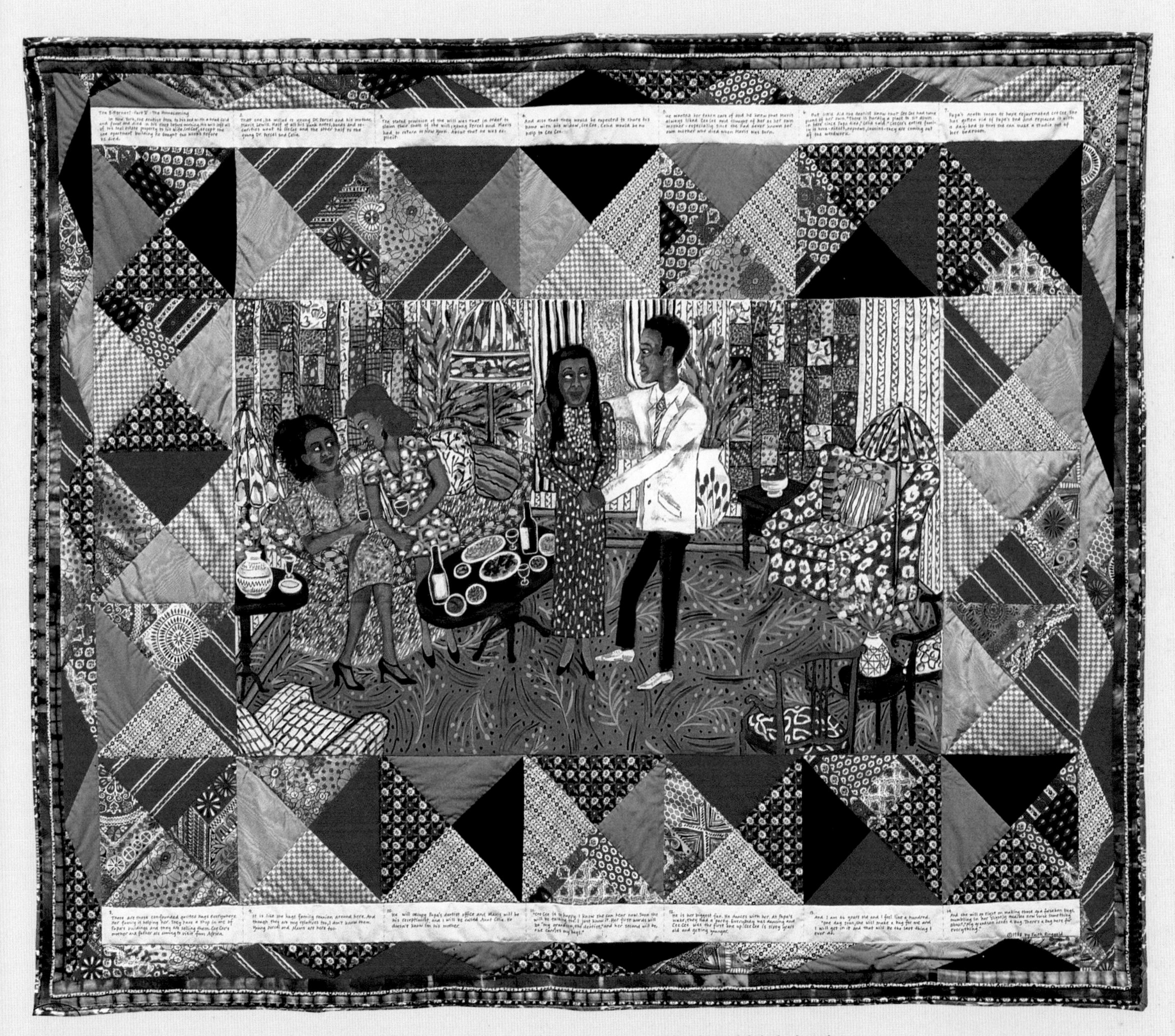

Faith Ringgold, *The Bitter Nest, Part V: Homecoming,* 1988. Acrylic on canvas with pieced fabric border, 76 × 96 in. (193 × 243.8 cm). Courtesy of the artist.

INTRODUCTION TO CONTENT AND STYLE

The term **content** refers to the expression, essential meaning, significance, or aesthetic value of a work of art. Content derives from the subjective, emotional properties we feel in a work of art, as opposed to our perception of its descriptive aspects alone. This chapter is also concerned with style, defined in the vocabulary for Chapter 1 as the specific artistic character and dominant trends of form noted during periods of history and art movements. Style also refers to the expressive use of media that gives an artist's work individual character.

The content, or meaning, of a work of art constantly undergoes interpretive revisions over time. We look at art from the past in ways that differ from viewers in the past. Personal experiences and thought shape the way we look at art today, just as they did in the past. To understand the art of the past, therefore, we must try to recover the historical influences that affected artists and what they had to say about their times. This is as true for us today as it was for viewers in the past simply because yesterday is today's history.

Our presentation here will usually discuss the characteristics of a style or movement first, rather than the specific content of the artists involved, because this can better offer clues as to how their expressive ends characterize the style. We will discuss only a few prominent exponents of each style because it is too broad a reach for a text devoted primarily to the theory and creation of artistic form to cover the history of art as well. Interested individual students must do this through classes specifically devoted to these subjects or through their own endeavors. We will, however, discuss how the gradual growth of knowledge about the art of other countries may have influenced artists in the Western countries presented in this book.

NINETEENTH-CENTURY ART

The stylistic movements of the nineteenth century in Europe contributed much to the character of art in the twentieth century. On the other hand, besides being influenced by the art of the nineteenth century, the twentieth century also reacted in large measure to all art of the past. Representing the appearance of the world around them inspired the work of painters and sculptors until about the middle of the 1800s. But the development of photography at about that time helped change this. By the end of the nineteenth century, partly because of photography and partly because of graphic techniques from the Renaissance, painters had so completely mastered the old problems of representation that many of them began to search for new expressive directions. Some painters turned to ancient styles or to those of the Middle Ages, while others were influenced by exotic arts from the Middle East, Far East, Africa, and the Americas. The cult of the "noble savage" promulgated in eighteenth-century France also helped to diminish European insularity. These ideas also influenced sculptors, albeit slightly later.

The proliferation of photography in popular journals and newspapers also exposed the European public to art from hitherto unknown places. These new opportunities displaced the noble, the religious, and the wealthy merchant classes as the only patrons of the arts. Artists no longer needed to rely on their patronage but, by the same token, had to find sources of income among the populace. So, while a wider audience created new venues for artists pursuing new directions, the loss of traditional patronage forced artists to advertise and sell their art like any other merchandise. Some artists, naturally, continued to cater to the tastes of the upper classes in order to prosper during the turmoil of the Industrial Revolution, with its poor classes, slums, and injustices. But artists who had the courage and means to assert their own inventiveness, who dared to fight the tide of convention and prejudice, became the leaders of an avant-garde. Drawing inspiration from prosaic subjects that seemed to them to have more universality, they pioneered new styles and ideas.

Sculptors as well as painters were affected by the cultural and social changes of their times. The spirit of nineteenth-century sculpture was primarily painterly, or additive, because clay modeling, an additive rather than a subtractive process, was dominant during that time. Painterly attitudes tended to diminish the regard for wood and stone sculpture. Diminished interest in these traditional materials and processes led to fewer innovations in those media. During the course of the nineteenth century, the authority of the European art academies gradually declined, and the conservative reluctance toward change diminished in sculpture as well as in painting. In sculpture, a preference lingered for allegorical subjects, which use the human figure to symbolize spiritual values drawn from mythology, religion, or philosophy. Sculpture also tended to be more conservative than painting because sculpture remained a public art, dependent on conservative patronage. The fidelity to nature possible in an additive process like clay modeling was also nurtured by the popularization of the photographic image. Full-size models built up in clay or plaster were copied by virtuoso stone carvers, who created some memorable works.

Neoclassicism (c.1750–1820)

The **Neoclassical** style originated in France, the recognized center of the arts in Europe since the seventeenth century. The founding in 1648 of the French Royal Academy of Arts and Letters by

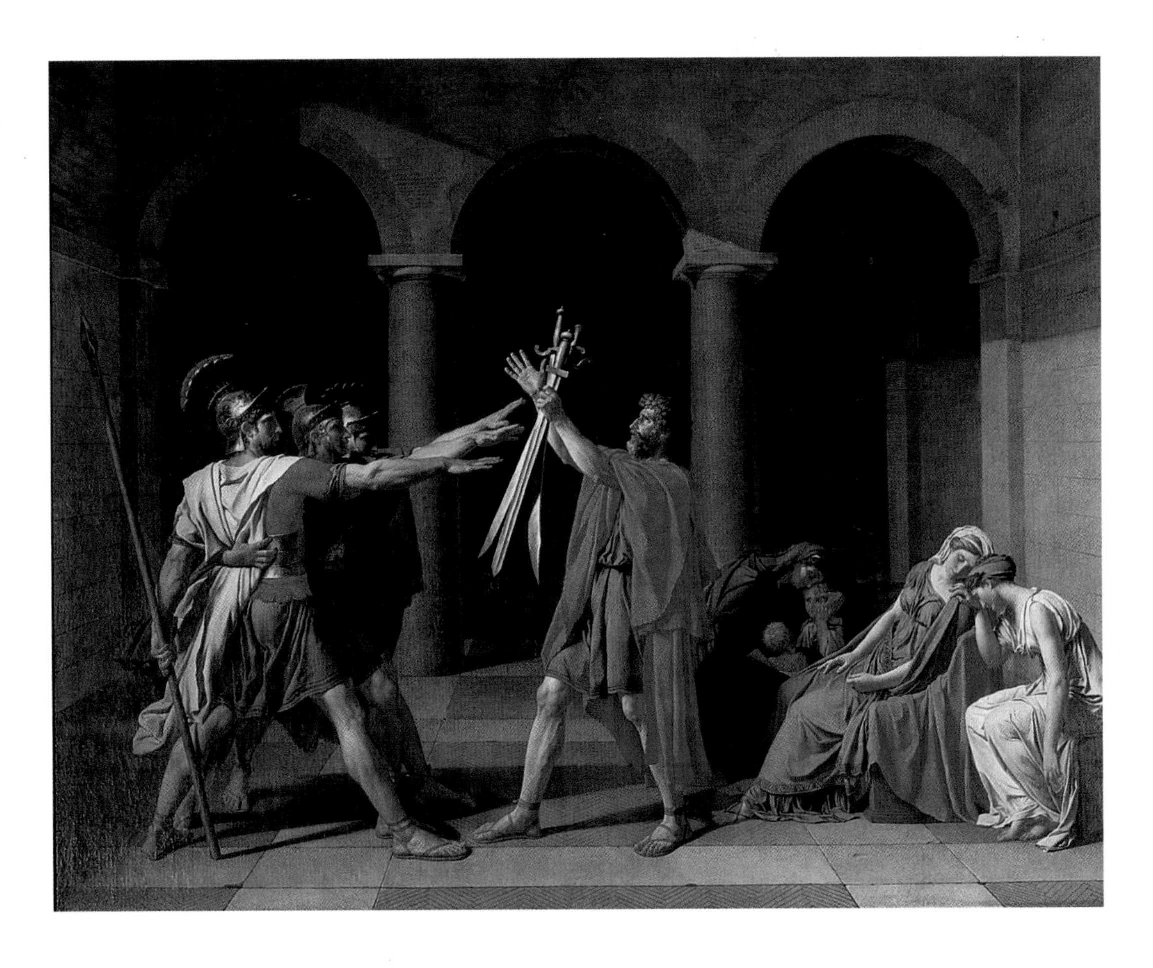

10.1 Jacques-Louis David, *The Oath of the Horatii,* 1786. Oil on canvas, approx. 14 × 11 ft (4.27 × 3.35 m). A cold, formal ordering of shapes, with emphasis on the sharpness of drawing, characterized the Neoclassical form of expression. Both style and subject matter are strongly influenced by ancient Greek and Roman sculpture. The Louvre, Paris, France. Photo: Lauros-Giraudon, Paris/SuperStock.

King Louis XIV, promoting rules for creating "correct" works of art, was at least part of the reason for the dominance of French art. Similar government-sponsored academies soon followed in other countries. Throughout the late eighteenth and nineteenth centuries, the approval of such government-sponsored institutions continued to be the principal factor in an artist's acceptance.

The characteristics of the Neoclassical style were forming by the middle 1700s, and the movement dated from that time until about 1820. A stimulus for the rise of Neoclassicism was the discovery in the 1730s and '40s of the ancient Roman ruins of Herculaneum and Pompeii. These towns had been covered in lava and ash left by the volcanic eruption of Mount Vesuvius in A.D. 79. Up to their discovery, Rome had been the only well-known city of antiquity. Now there were other "true" ancient cities. Archaeological research at these ruins led to the New or Neoclassical architectural style that spread across Europe to the Americas.

The Neoclassical revival in the arts of painting and sculpture was also influenced by the publication in 1764 of Johann Joachim Winckelmann's *The History of the Art of the Ancients.* This book definitively clarified the differences between Greek and Roman art for the first time.

The principal Neoclassical painter was Jacques-Louis David (1748–1825). His severely monumental style, as in *The Oath of the Horatii* (fig. 10.1), established the style for others in France, founded on the desire for moral, political, and social reforms among the masses. This attitude led to the French Revolution in 1789. David's classical style was furthered by his having won the Royal Academy's *Prix de Rome* (a scholarship for French artists to study in Rome), permitting him to make a closer study of Roman art. David rebelled against the Rococo, the style approved by the aristocracy during his youth, finding it immoral and artificial. The clearly readable horizontal composition of *The Oath of the Horatii* is classical in its restraint, unconscious of the chaos and excess of the revolution that was to follow. The clarity and realistic details seem to anticipate photography and foreshadow the concern with the two-dimensional nature of painting, which was to be so significant in the twentieth century. David was closely connected to the Napoleonic regime after the Revolution.

A later Neoclassicist, Jean-Auguste-Dominique Ingres (1780–1867), was in essence a doctrinaire follower of the

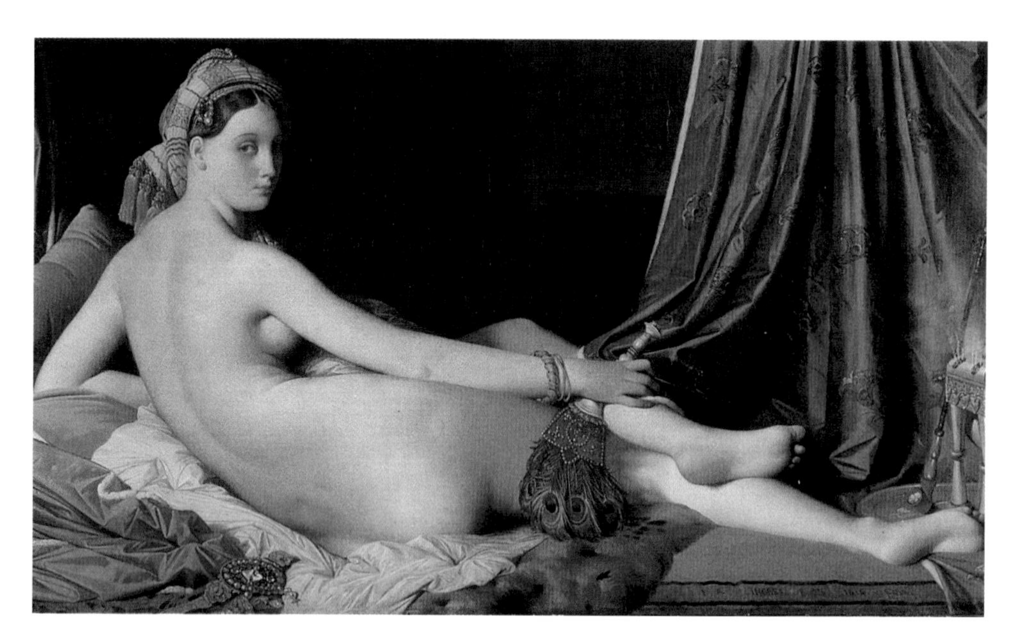

10.2 Jean-Auguste-Dominique Ingres, *La Grande Odalisque,* 1814. Oil, 35¼ × 63¾ in. (89.5 × 161.9 cm). Neoclassicist Ingres, while being a doctrinaire follower of Classical expression, often tended toward romantic subjects with their attendant sensual expression of content. *Odalisque* was a term meaning harem girl, or concubine, in a Turkish seraglio. The Louvre, Paris, France. Photo: Lauros-Giraudon, Paris/SuperStock.

movement. In his paintings of voluptuous nudes, that is, *La Grande Odalisque* (1814) (fig. 10.2), his compositions emphasize a soft, ornamental, linear manner, owing much to the High Renaissance manner of Raphael. He also had a romantic interest in exotic lands and people, which reflected the desire of society to escape from the growing materialism of the time. This aspect of Ingres and his followers predicted the replacement of Neoclassicism by the style called Romantic art.

The Italian-born Neoclassical sculptor Antonio Canova (1757–1822) was a virtuoso carver of hard materials, like marble, as in his statue *Perseus with the Head of Medusa* (c. 1808) (fig. 10.3). Most of Canova's sculptures, as here, illustrate mythological themes, thus connecting his work to the ancient roots of the West in Greece and Rome. Canova, like David, worked for Napoleon after the Revolution.

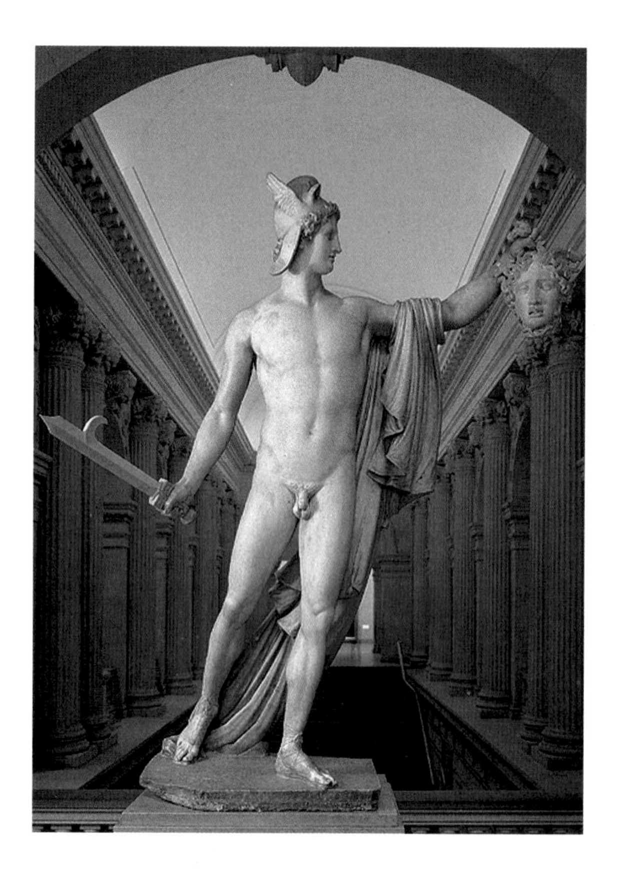

10.3 Antonio Canova, *Perseus with the Head of Medusa,* c. 1808. Marble, 7 ft 2⅝ in. (2.20 m) high. Although Canova was the best of the Neoclassical sculptors, his great technical facility lacked the streak of individualistic meaning that would have made his art truly outstanding. He repeated themes that were centuries old and hackneyed. The Metropolitan Museum of Art, Fletcher Fund, 1967. (67.110.1) Photograph © 1993 The Metropolitan Museum of Art.

Romanticism

Romantic art grew out of the literary trends that affected all of eighteenth-century Europe, called **Romanticism** or the Romantic movement. Romanticism became a philosophy and way of life. The poems, novels, and prose of writers like Shakespeare, Dante, Jean-Jacques Rousseau, Thomas Gray, George Gordon, Lord Byron, Johann Wolfgang von Goethe, and Sir Walter Scott, plus the Christian Bible, were common sources of subjects for Romantic artists. Contemporary news accounts and journals were also sources for the dramatic and exotic themes expressed in Romantic art. Accounts of faraway rebellions, in America and particularly in Greece against the Turks, offered exotic flavor, already popular in Neoclassical painting. The passionate convictions and emotionalism aroused by these events shattered the existing mode of intellectual certainty and formal order forever. A new age of concern for human individ-

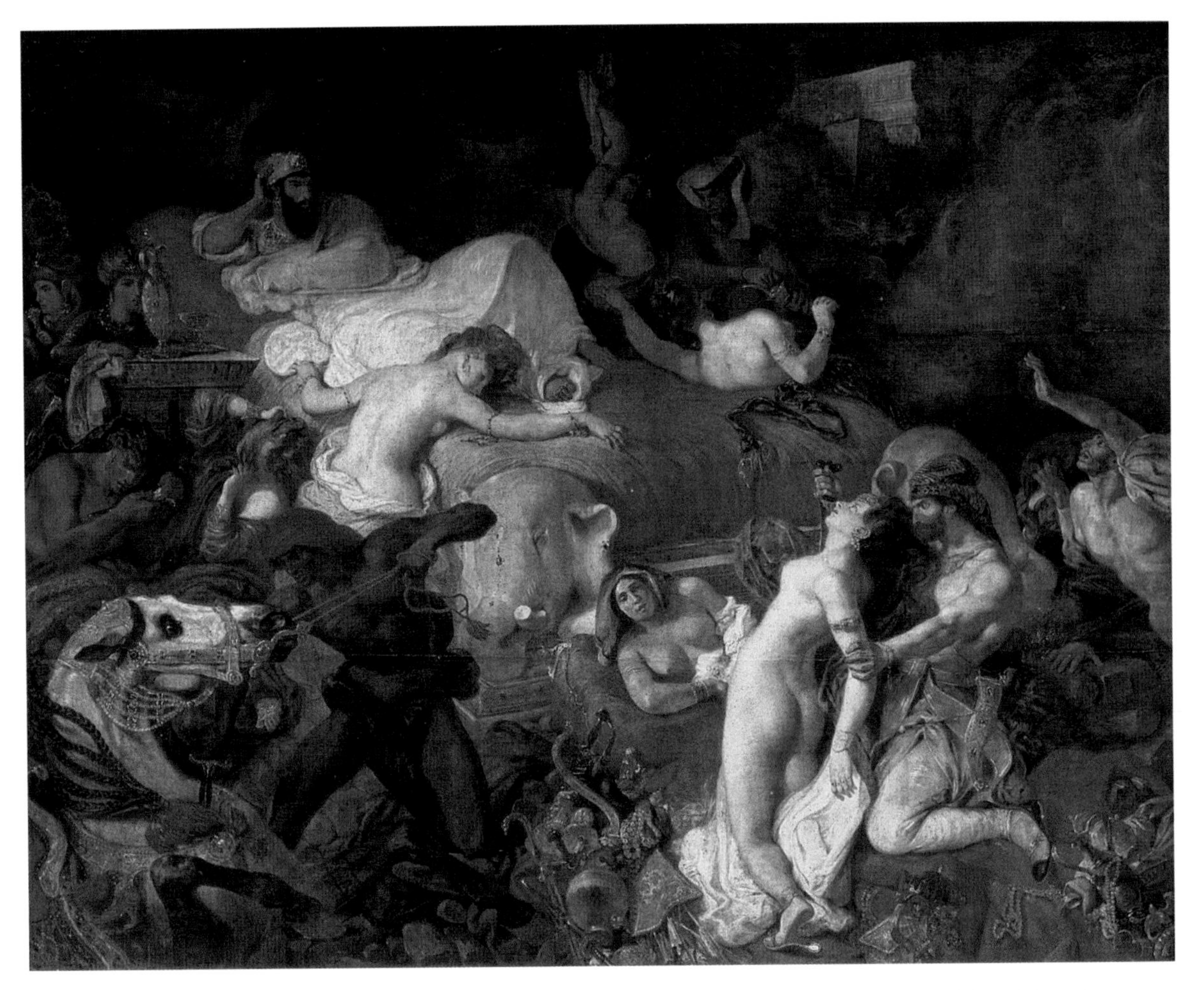

10.4 Eugène Delacroix, *The Death of Sardanapalus,* 1827. Oil on canvas, 145 × 195 in. (395 × 495 cm). Subject matter most common to the Romantic movement was composed of violent action, often in foreign settings. The exaggeratedly bold expression of violence, sensuality, and death is frequently found in Delacroix's work. Louvre, Paris, France/The Bridgeman Art Library.

uality began. The irrational, the macabre, the fantastic, the stormy and lyric moods of nature, animals, and humans became fit subjects for artistic expression. This romantic approach to art, in fact, reduced the emphasis on choice of subject, since any subject now became plausible. A new accent on form, artist's materials, and process now began, new emphases that were to gather importance in twentieth-century art.

Technically, Romantic artists exploited the excitement of diagonal compositions and the juicy, bold textures of oil paint. Bright, exciting hues and stirring contrasts of value to express emotions are typical of Romantic art. This was in obvious opposition to the Neoclassicists' reserved use of value and color, and insistence on linearity and formal composition.

Here, we will consider three important Romantic painters: the French artist Eugène Delacroix (1780–1867); the Spaniard Francisco Goya (1746–1828); and the English artist J. M. W. Turner (1774–1851).

Delacroix was the outstanding representative of Romantic painting in France. He was the leader of the faction preferring Rubens and the Venetian painters, as opposed to the Neoclassical painters, who preferred Nicholas Poussin (a classical painter of the 1600s). Trained as a Neoclassicist, Delacroix painted in a vigorous, active style that broke the formal boundaries of his background. A major example exhibiting Delacroix's expressive content is *The Death of Sardanapalus* (1827) (fig. 10.4). The exaggerated expression of violence, sensuality, and death is frequently found in his work.

The Spaniard Goya was the earliest of the nineteenth-century Romantic painters, emerging from the Spanish Rococo of the late 1700s. Of the same generation as J. L. David, he was not a

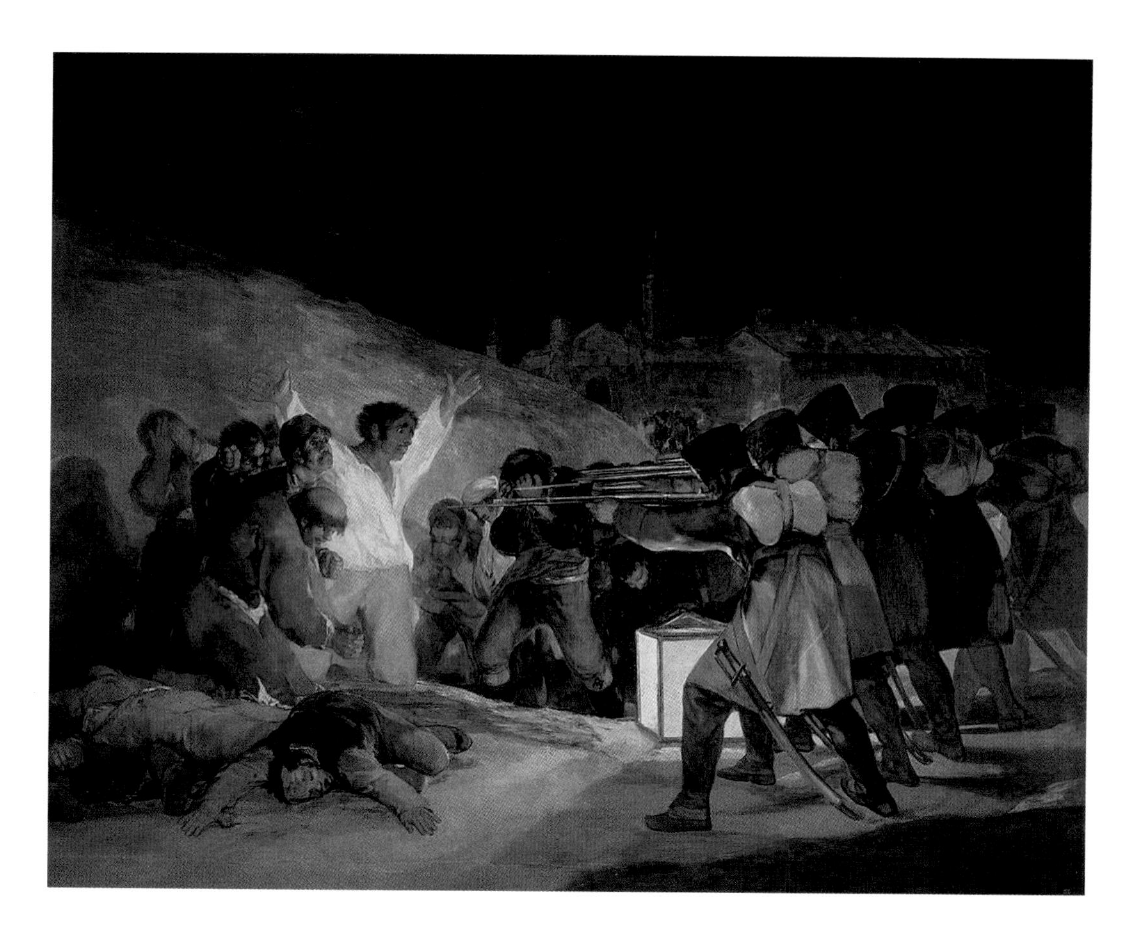

10.5 Francisco Goya, *The Third of May,* 1808. Oil on canvas, 8 ft 8 in. × 11 ft 8 in. (2.64 × 3.55 m). The romanticism of Goya is displayed in both his choice of subject matter and his dramatic use of light and dark values. Museo del Prado, Madrid, Spain. Photo: Erich Lessing/Art Resource.

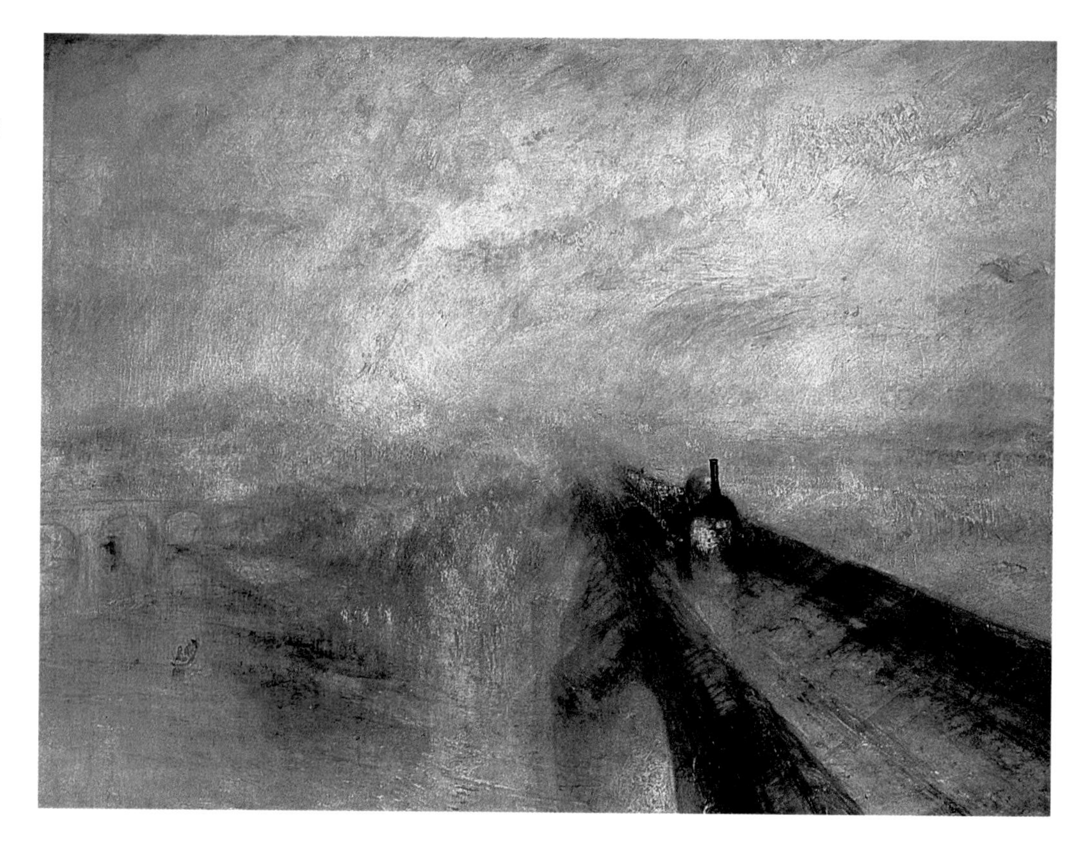

10.6 J. M. W. Turner, *Rain, Steam, and Speed—the Great Western Railway,* 1844. Oil, 90.8 × 121.9 cm. Historical themes and the clash of natural forces were frequently found in Turner's work. This illustration shows that Turner had ridden through a violent storm with the window open and was astonished at the power of the tempest and the speed of the new railway. National Gallery, London. Erich Lessing/Art Resource, NY.

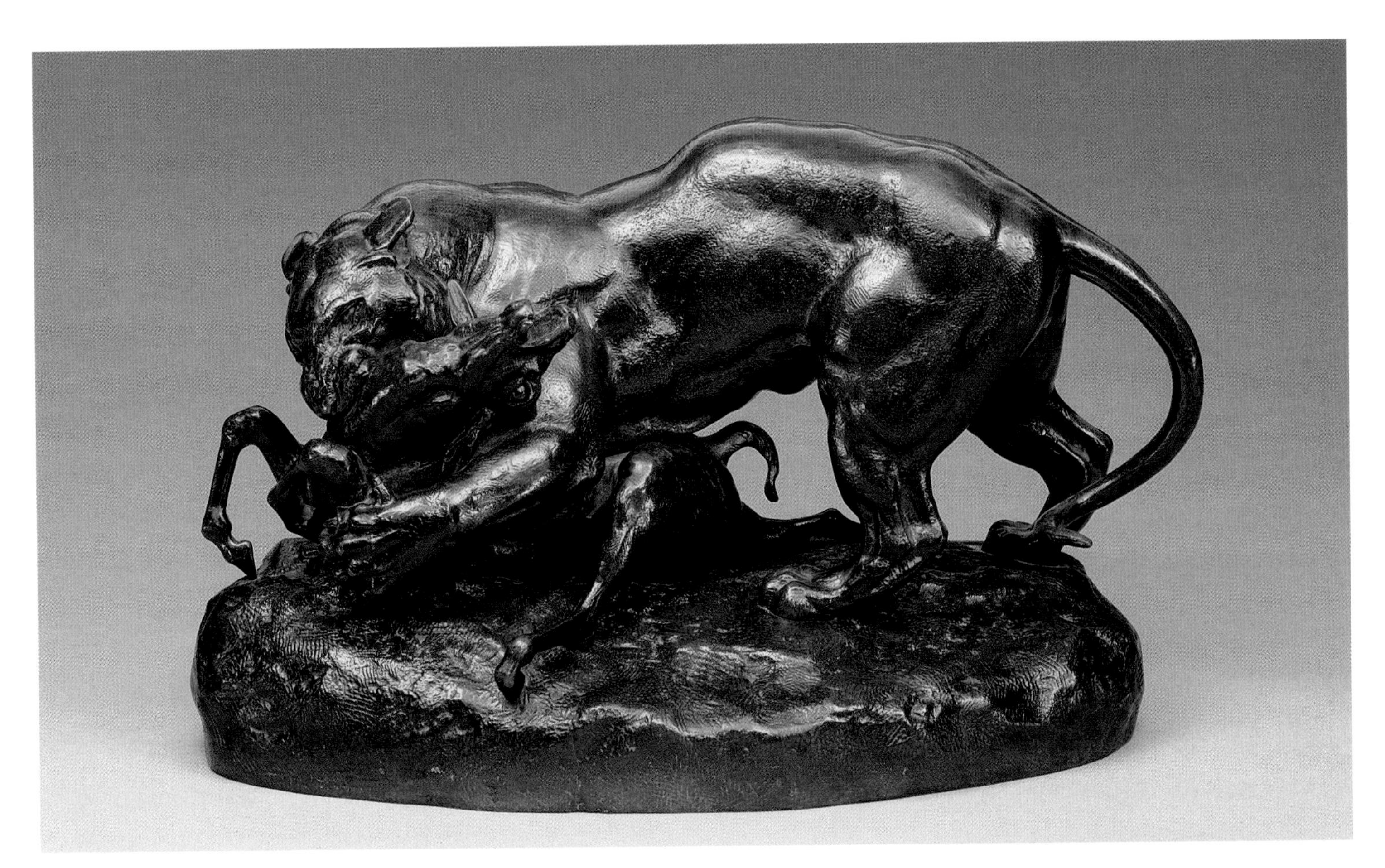

10.7 **Antoine Louis Barye, *Tiger Devouring an Antelope,* 1851. Bronze, 13 × 22½ × 11⅝ in. (33 × 57.2 × 29.5 cm).** Barye's emotionalized romantic form is similar in dynamism to the intense coloristic qualities of Romantic painters such as Delacroix and Turner. Philadelphia Museum of Art: The W. P. Wilstach Collection, bequest of Anna H. Wilstach, 1893.

Neoclassicist but went through a range of styles, from realism through the romantic to the fantastic. Goya's early work tends to be charming in its portrayal of court life, but there are hints of his psychological understanding of human follies and deeds (see fig. 4.21). After a serious illness in 1792 left him totally deaf, Goya's content became crueler, often incorporating nightmarish imagery. This is found in two famous print series: *Los Caprichos* (c. 1797–99) and the *Disasters of War* (c. 1813–20). These etchings express, in marvelous tones of black and white, the irrational behavior of human beings under duress. Two oil paintings express the bitterness felt by the Spanish against their French invaders; the second of these, *The Third of May* (1808) (fig. 10.5), is illustrated here. In it, Madrid civilians are massacred by French soldiers in reprisal for the ambush of French troops the day before. The content poignantly deals with the inhuman actions fomented by war.

Turner was England's outstanding Romantic landscape painter. His early landscapes were influenced by **classical** prototypes such as Claude Lorraine (1600–1682). But as time went on, mist, rain, fire, and sea foam became his favorite subjects. Turner became increasingly fascinated by the ability of oil paint to depict the moods and powers of nature as metaphors for human emotions (called the pathetic fallacy in literature). Turner's uneasiness about the Industrial Revolution and its effect on human beings is often hinted at, as in *Rain, Steam, and Speed—the Great Western Railway* (1844) (fig. 10.6). Here the dark mass of a locomotive pulling a line of cars expresses an ominous feeling of excitement as it hurtles out of the fog and mist of a storm. This work is from Turner's last decade, when his impressionistic technique was at its peak, a legacy inherited by the artists of the Impressionist movement, twenty-five years later.

French Romantic sculptor Antoine Louis Barye (1796–1875) appears more imaginative than Canova because of his employment of malleable materials such as clay and plaster (from which his bronzes were cast) (fig. 10.7). Yet, while Barye seems original in his dynamic,

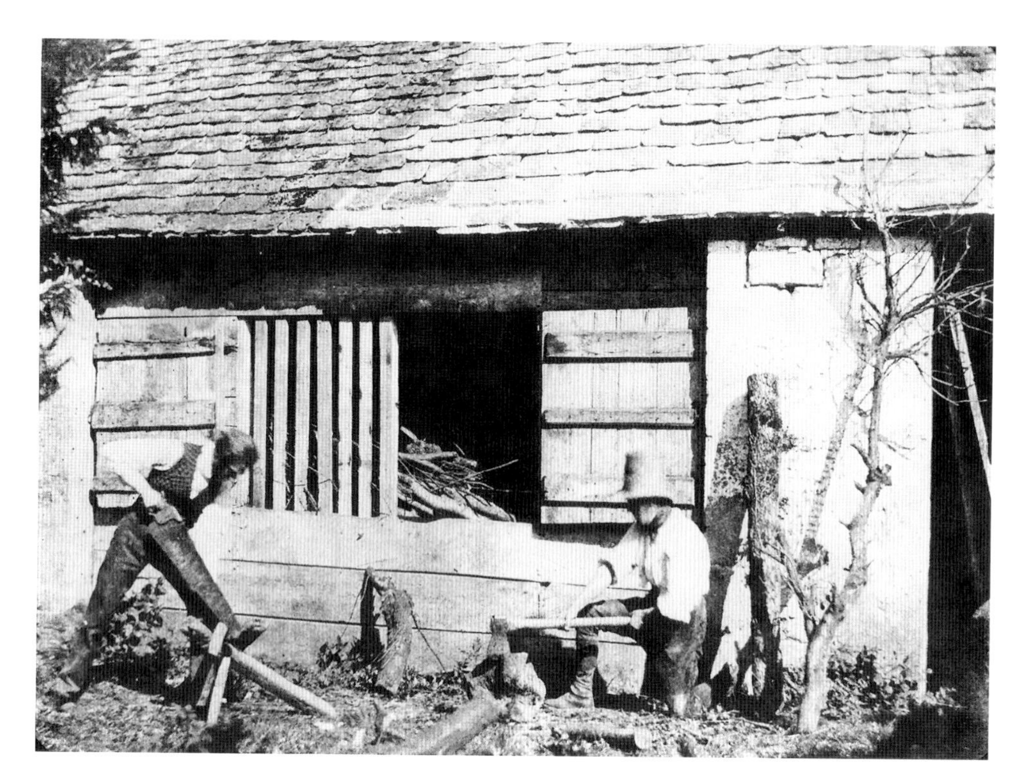

10.8 William Henry Fox Talbot, *Nicole & Pullen Sawing and Cleaving*, c. 1846. Salt paper print. This is an example of a photograph by one of the medium's earliest pioneers, the English aristocrat Fox Talbot. His system, using sensitized paper negatives from which many prints could be made (calotype), was one of the key foundations of modern photography. Because of the long exposure time needed, "action" shots like this would have involved posing motionless for some minutes. © The Royal Photographic Society of Great Britain, Bath, England.

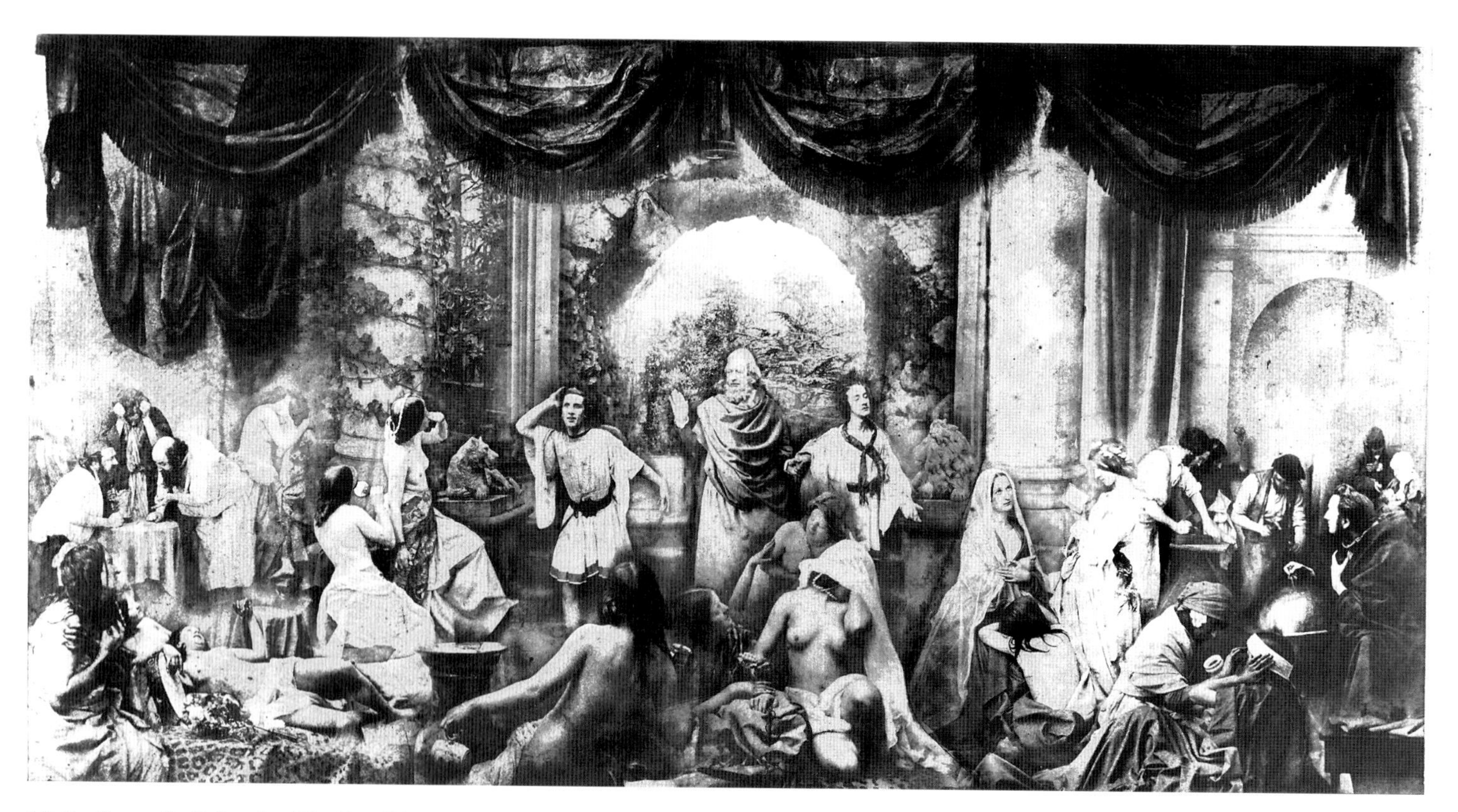

10.9 Oscar G. Rejlander, *The Two Ways of Life*, 1857. Gelatin silver print. A photographer trained as a painter, Rejlander tried to create a great mural out of hundreds of photographs. His approach to image manipulation is a Romantic one that is called "Pictorialism" in photography. Courtesy George Eastman House, Rochester, N.Y., Gift of the Royal Photographic Society of Great Britain, Bath, England.

monumental, and ferocious characterizations of animal life, his allegorical subjects and additive technique still conform to the traditional recommendations of the academies. Like Turner, Barye reworked the Romantic tradition of evoking human emotions by parallels with animal nature or the vagaries of the weather. This concept originated with the Dutch philosopher Baruch Spinoza in the 1600s. Turner's late paintings seem more innovative in technique, and therefore more original, than Barye's sculptures, which repeat older values and ways of thinking. However, both artists' overt expression of energy, as opposed to the restraint of classical works, defines our sense of Romantic art.

Beginning of Photography

The use of the camera to produce images emerged over a number of centuries. However, not until the mechanical inventions of the Industrial Revolution (usually dated in England around 1750–1850) was the way prepared for the invention and use of the photographic camera. We can trace the origins of the camera back to the camera obscura (Latin for "dark room") in the Renaissance (although it was already known in ancient Greece). The camera obscura was a lightproof room or box with a small hole in one side that could produce an inverted image of an outside scene or object on the surface opposite the hole. The example by Dürer (see fig. 8.19) shows a variation of the camera obscura by which artists could directly draw from the model to establish foreshortening and/or perspective. The late Renaissance artist Jacopo Pontormo (1494–1556) is believed to have added the first lenses to the camera obscura, providing the next step toward the picturemaking camera. The final step, the process of fixing an image on a light-sensitized surface, culminated between the 1830s and 1850s, making possible the imitation of natural appearances in a permanent image—the photograph. The efforts of, particularly, Louis J. M. Daguerre (1789–1851) and Joseph N. Niépce (1765–1833) (both of France), William Henry Fox Talbot (1800–1877) (of England), and others produced the first photographic images (fig. 10.8). By midcentury the camera image had evolved far enough that Oscar G. Rejlander (1813–1875) (fig. 10.9) could composite a colossal, romantic work out of numerous prints and exhibit it like a painting in the Salon des Beaux-Arts in 1857. This set in motion one style of photography, called **Pictorialism,** which was opposed by those who believed that there should be no additional manipulation of the image, in either the taking or the developing process. These were designated **Straight,** or sometimes **Realist,** photographers.

Realism

The art of the Romantics had been a reaction to the classicizing, pedantic formulas of Neoclassicism. The Realist movement arose in about 1850, partly as a reaction against the favoritism of academic circles that accepted only old, hackneyed themes, and partly as a reaction against the exotic, escapist, literary tendencies of Romanticism. The movement lasted until about 1870, when it began to be replaced by Impressionism.

The Realists were stimulated by the prestige of science, particularly the technological revolution epitomized by photography, but they opposed the kind of superficial pictorial Romantic-Realism embraced by Rejlander. At the same time, they eschewed surface appearances, such as those usually recorded by the camera, and sought instead a philosophical, expressive quality in their art. Yet they also tried to impart the real-life immediacy they found missing from the idealism of Neoclassical and Romantic art. Although the Realists believed their patrons shared their worldview, their art was not immediately accepted. Instead, because they chose to depict farmers and working-class people, the Realists were regarded as subversive by their potential, mostly urban, middle- and upper-class clientele. The most extreme form of Realist art is naturalism, a term invented by the writer Émile Zola near the end of the nineteenth century. Naturalism, according to Zola, attempts to present the world as it appears, much like a photograph. Naturalistic artists believed that this kind of description of things accorded best with the way most people regarded reality. Thus, naturalistic painters attempted to make a visual copy of the objective world, without investing their art with the more universal meanings associated with realism. The major difference between Realistic and naturalistic art, therefore, lies in the degree of significance placed on the specifics of detail, location, and time (e.g., the particularizing of weather conditions).

The most important Realists were the French painters Honoré Daumier (1808–1879) and Gustave Courbet (1819–1877). Daumier's expressive renderings of poor city workers, actors, tradespeople, political dissidents, and refugees best represent the Realist point of view, whereas Courbet's technique best represents the naturalistic approach to subject and form. During his lifetime, Daumier painted many oils expressing concern for the meager life of the poor, meanwhile laboring to produce hundreds of political cartoons and caricatures for two Parisian journals to earn his living (fig. 10.10). His caricatures mark the beginning of satirical political cartooning (see fig. 3.26).

Courbet was the instigator of the Realist style in painting. He too was a political activist and believed that artists should paint only what they could see and touch. "Show me an angel and I will paint one" is his famous statement in this regard. He was a master of both the technique of oil painting and composition,

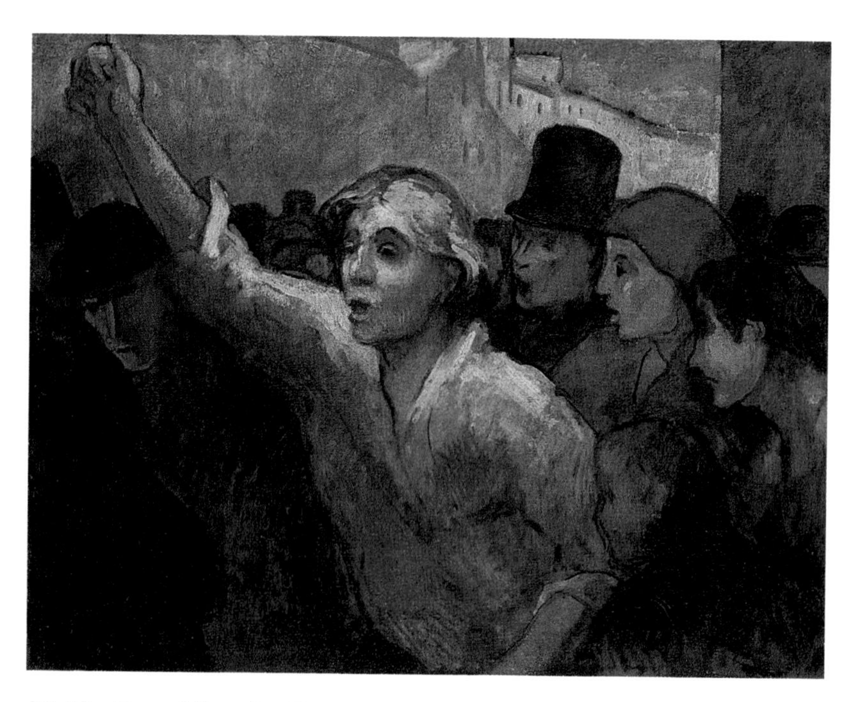

10.10 Honoré Daumier, *The Uprising*, c. 1852–58. Oil on canvas, 34 × 44 in. Influenced by a climate of scientific positivism, the artists of the Realist movement tried to record the world as it appeared to the eye, but they also wished to interpret it so as to record timeless truths. This painting by Daumier shows his broadly realist renderings of a political protest. Acquired 1925. The Phillips Collection, Washington, D.C.

10.11 Gustave Courbet, *Burial at Ornans*, 1849. Oil, 10 × 22 ft (3 × 6.7 m). Courbet was the leading early exponent of the naturalist leanings of some Realist painters. Critics harshly condemned him for painting "ugly" pictures of average people at their mundane activities. Collection the Louvre, Paris. Photo: AKG, Berlin/SuperStock.

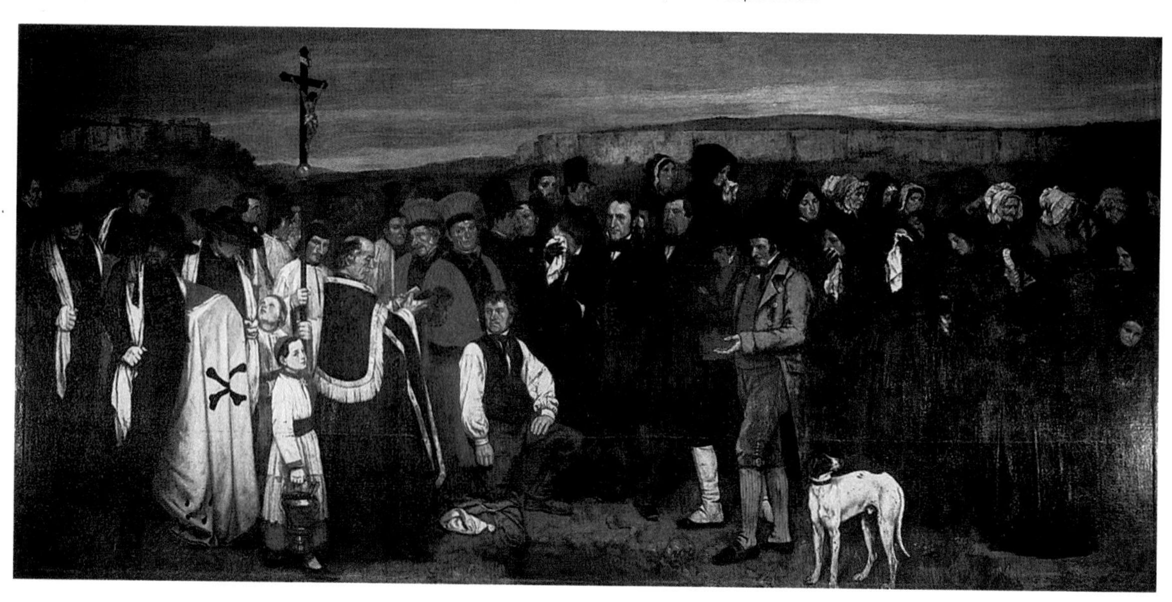

and created many memorable works, such as his *Burial at Ornans* (1849) (fig. 10.11), which the critical and public tastes of his time found doubly distasteful. Official art circles, critics, and the public, expecting idealistic renderings of noble subjects in formal compositions, were aghast at a funeral scene portraying a crowd of commoners. In the particularization of detail, location, and even time of day, which make the painting look almost photographic, Courbet comes close to Zola's dictum on naturalism.

Technological Developments in Photography

At the same time that the Realist style came into being, photography was also developing its own kind of artistic expression. Not yet able to escape the long-standing traditions of painting, Pictorialist photographers tried to replicate painterly effects of lighting and atmosphere. Technical experiments and research led to rapid improvements in cameras, lenses, and printing processes, enabling photographers to experiment with new ways of creating pictures.

Among some of the technical developments were the faster lenses invented in the 1840s, the "wet plate" (or collodion) process in 1851, and the "dry plate" process in 1871.

By the 1860s, such developments had reduced exposure time to a few seconds. Among other important inventions in the late 1890s and early 1900s were negative films to replace glass and metal plates, which also speeded the exposure process. In 1888, George Eastman (1854–1932) invented the first camera that could be mass-produced (the "Kodak"); from then on, amateurs could take pictures economically without having to process the film or make prints themselves. Thus, the widespread popularity of the medium was ensured.

Because of these technical developments, photography improved as an artistic medium, as well as a medium to record events objectively. Despite the size and amount of the equipment required, early photographers began to generate a notable record of human and natural phenomena around the world. For instance, by midcentury, cameras were recording the face of mass conflict, such as the Crimean War (1853–56) and the American Civil War (1861–65). Mathew Brady (c. 1823–96), originally a New York portrait photographer, organized a team of photographers to make a photographic record of the Civil War (fig. 10.12). Other photographers explored the ruins of ancient cities, contemporary foreign cities, nature, and, particularly, the American West (fig. 10.13). From such images, the public who could not actually travel themselves became familiar with exotic places and cultures past and present. Out of both the technical improvements and the photographic record cited came the first illustrations leading to photogravure (printing from an etched plate made from a photograph), which in its turn hastened the development of photojournalism. The expansion of photographic images in newspapers, magazines, and

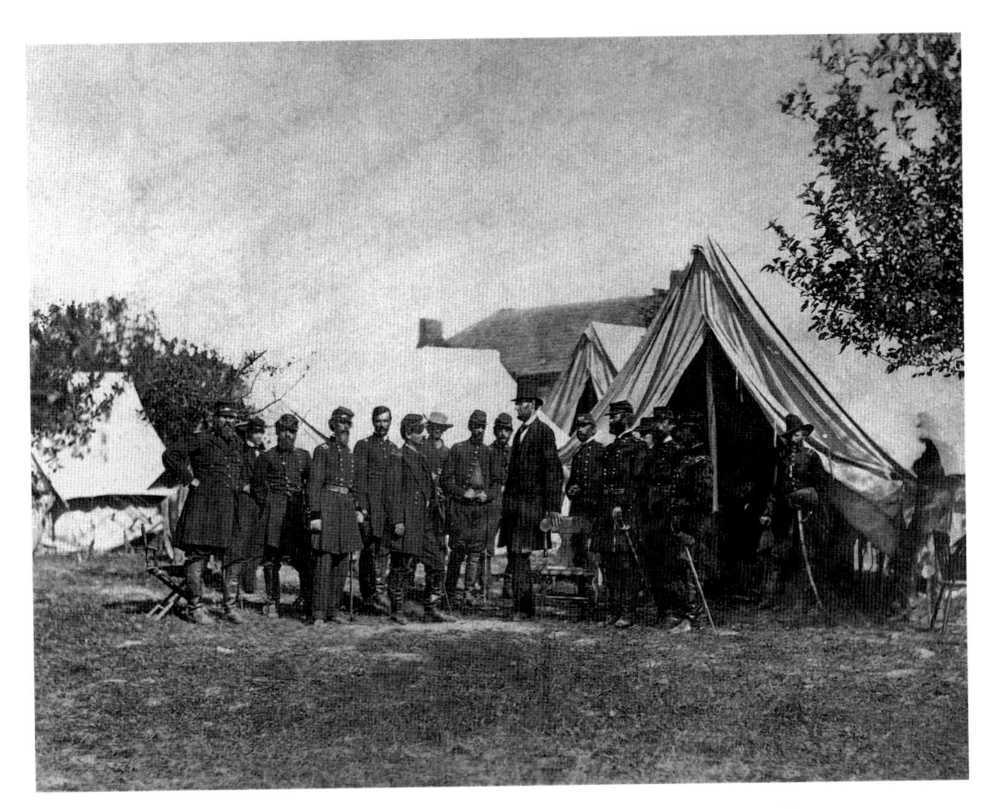

10.12 Alexander Gardner, *Lincoln Meeting McClellan after the Battle of Antietam*, Oct. 1, 1862. Photograph. Despite the bulky equipment needed in the "wet plate" process, by the 1860s photographers were busily documenting wars, nature, and exotic locations all over the world. Alexander Gardner was one of a troop of photographers assembled by Mathew Brady, who left us an amazing record of the American Civil War. Library of Congress/Corbis.

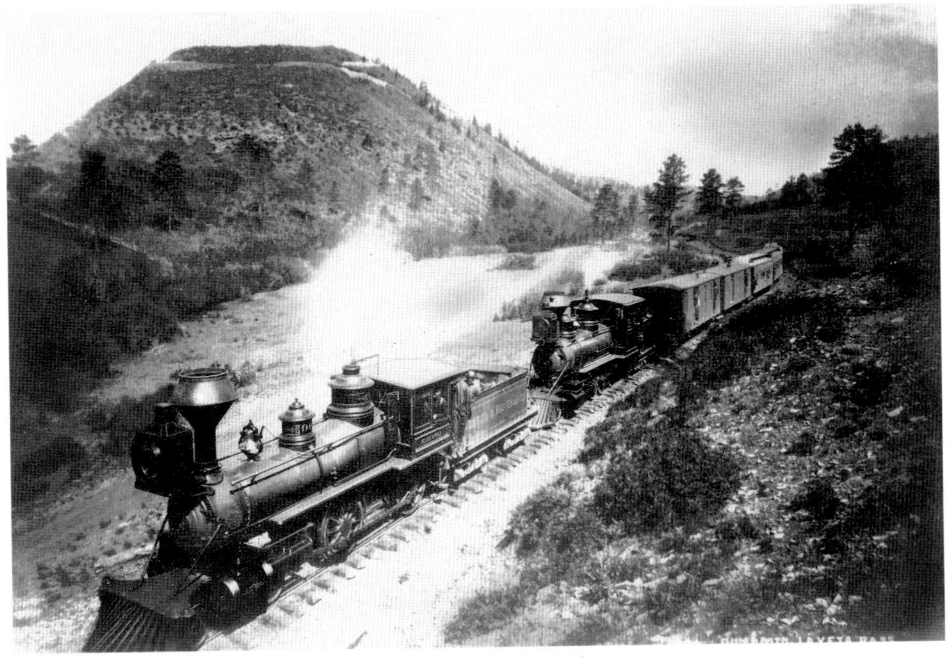

10.13 William Henry Jackson, *Dump Mountain La Veta Pass*, 1882. Photograph. After the Civil War, Jackson was interested in the expansion of the West as expressed through his photographs of the railroads. Courtesy of the Denver Public Library/Western History Collection; Call number WHJ.381.

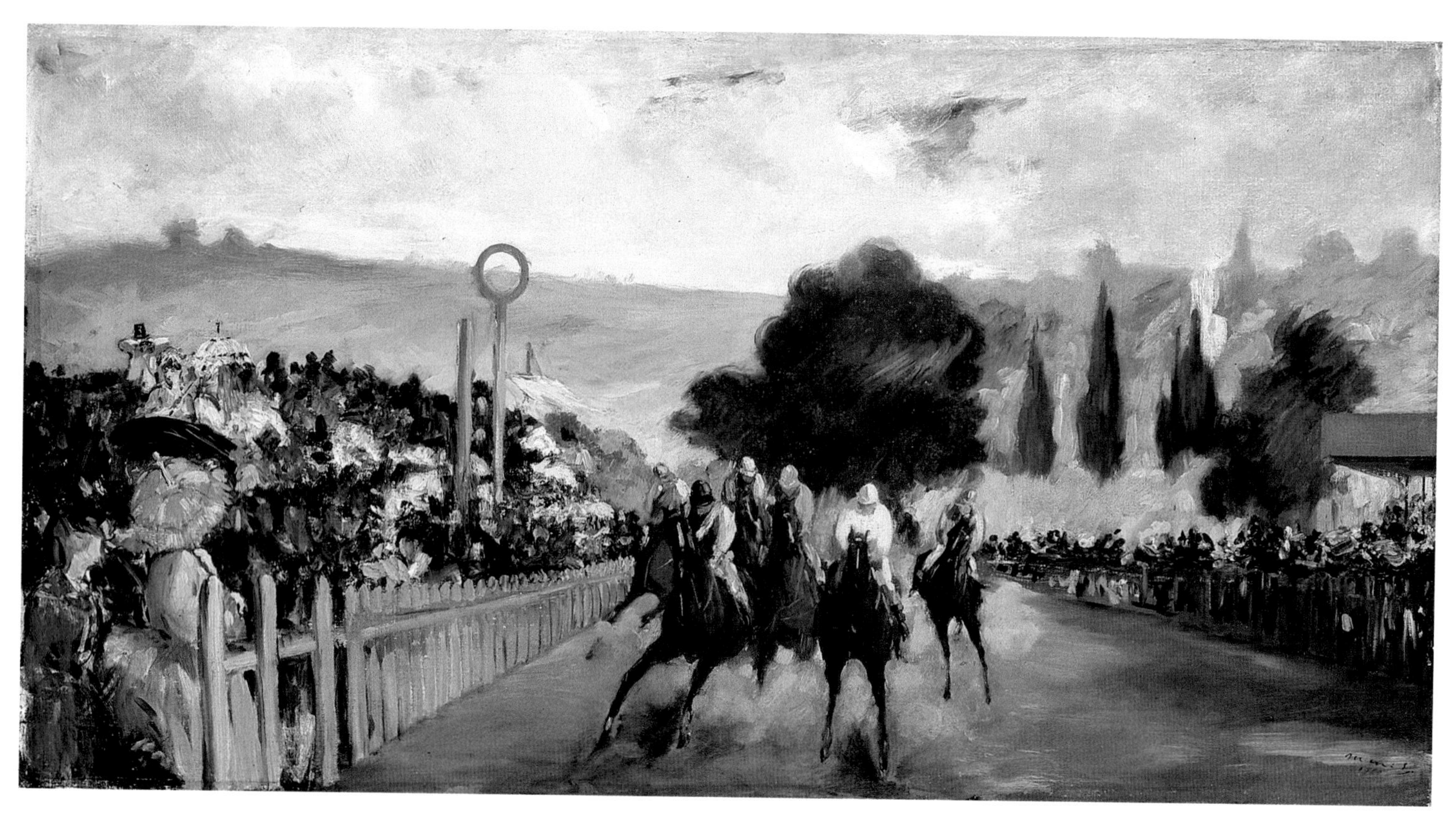

10.14 **Edouard Manet, *The Races at Longchamps,* 1866. Oil on canvas, 17¼ × 33½ in. (43.9 × 84.5 cm).** The artist Manet reveals the Impressionists' concern with capturing movement realistically, as part of their desire to render perceptual reality in a new way. Photographic studies like those of Muybridge may have benefited Manet. Art Institute of Chicago, Mr. and Mrs. Potter Palmer Collection 1922.424. Photo © 1998 Art Institute of Chicago.

journals included all kinds of topics. Photojournals gradually became a means of artistic expression in photography and helped to gain acceptance of and appreciation for the formal qualities of the medium.

Among other important discoveries were those in color photography. Daguerre had experimented with color, but little progress was made until James Clerk Maxwell demonstrated in 1860 that all color could be reduced to three primary colors. A decade later, Dr. Hermann Vogel discovered that dye colors could be made sensitive to light, and thus the sensitivity of silver emulsions could be extended into both panchromatic and orthochromatic areas of the spectrum.

Impressionism

In the 1860s, younger Realist painters such as Edouard Manet (1832–1883), Edgar Degas (1834–1917), and Pierre-Auguste Renoir (1841–1919) often painted outdoor subjects like picnics, café groups, and boaters.

Manet's *Olympia* of 1863 and the *Dead Toreador* of 1864 reveal his fascination with the manner in which reflected light tends to flatten surfaces, and these paintings represent the transition from the Realist style to **Impressionism** (see fig. 5.15). These works initiated new ideas about color, light, and, to a lesser degree, movement that became preoccupations of Impressionist painters. These early paintings excited a new concern for the actual surface of the painting. This change was profound for the modernist painters of the future who wanted their brushwork, scratches, and other markings to give the viewer the experience of the artwork itself as well as the sensations of the artist creating it. Manet's was the initial step whereby the physical form of the painting eventually

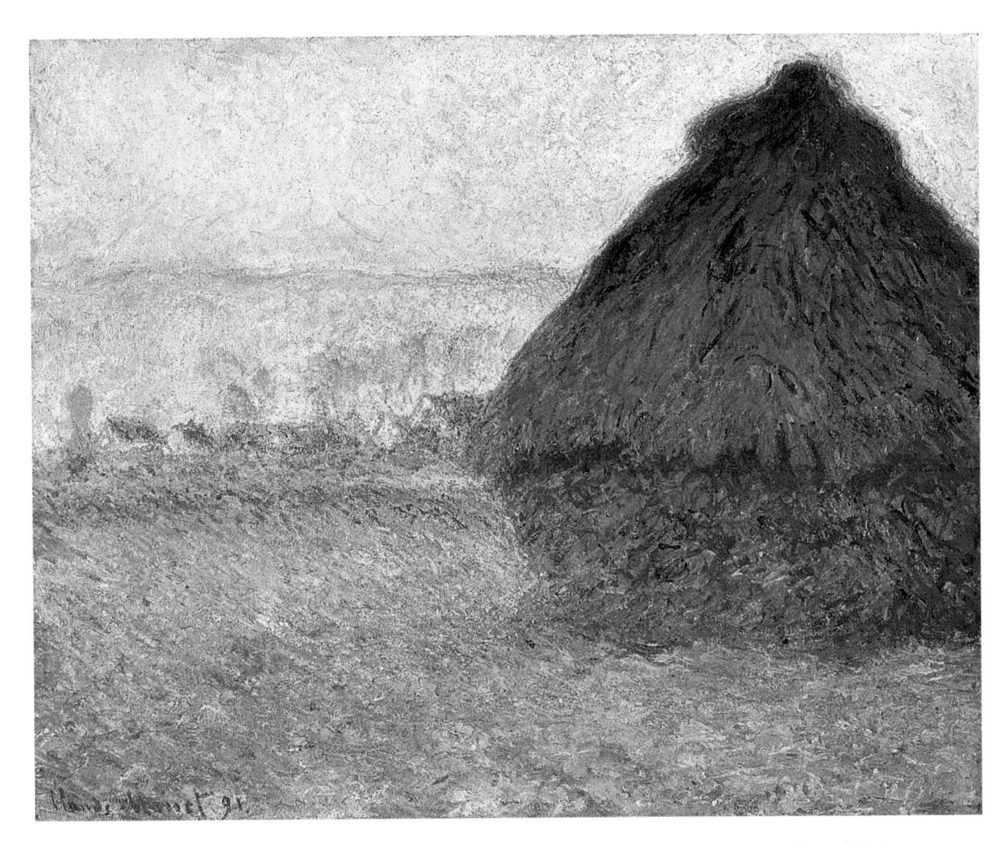

10.15 Claude Monet, *Haystack at Sunset*, 1880. Oil on canvas, 28⅞ × 36½ in. (73.3 × 92.6 cm). The selection of subject in this painting is typical of the Impressionist movement. The bright weather and the blazing colors at sundown offered an opportunity to express light and atmosphere through a scientific approach to the use of color. Juliana Cheney Edwards Collection. Courtesy of Museum of Fine Arts, Boston.

became its own subject and meaning in twentieth-century abstraction.

That photography had an impact on Manet and the other Impressionists is readily apparent. Manet's painting *The Races at Longchamps* (1866) (a racetrack near Paris), in which the horses almost seem to float, suggest he studied the stop-action photography of the Anglo-American photographer Eadweard Muybridge (1830–1904) (fig. 10.14; see also fig. 8.57). The manner in which Manet handled the sunlight scintillating from the clothing and parasols of some of the spectators shows that in his later work he had become a full-fledged Impressionist.

Claude Monet (1840–1926), Camille Pissarro, and Renoir took the lead in the Impressionist movement. Monet's painting *Impression—Sunrise* (1872) gave the movement its name. In this painting and succeeding ones, Monet (along with Manet) began to see, or paint, the world in terms of color and light rather in terms of depth and volume. The Impressionists' close relationship to photography is evidenced by the fact that their first independently arranged exhibit, in 1874, was held in the studio of the eminent Realist portrait photographer Nadar (Gaspard-Félix Tournachon [1824–1910]). Outgrowing Realism, the Impressionists wanted to find their own way of painting reality, and photography showed them a new way. From the somewhat lengthy exposures required of photographs, they learned that the use of blurring and partial obscuring of objects in their paintings was similar to the effects that bright sunlight or misty weather seemed to have on nature when they painted outdoors. Monet, who loved to paint outdoors, studied these effects in his series on haystacks (fig. 10.15), the Waterloo Bridge series (see figs. 7.24 and 7.25), and in his late garden series. In order to achieve the vibrating character of light, the Impressionists developed the techniques of juxtaposing complementary hues in large areas for greater brilliance and the interpretation of shadows as being composed of hues opposite those of the object casting shadows. They also revived the old technique of painting thick dabs that catch and reflect actual light from the surface called *tachiste* painting (from the French *la tache,* meaning "spot"). The Impressionists' use of complementary hues in the dabs of pigment, however, was the important breakthrough. When seen from a distance, these spots or dabs tend to form tones fused from the separate hues. Local color was very important to render the effects of sunlight, shade, shadows, and all kinds of weather conditions. Paintings of landscapes *en plein air,* or outdoors, directly from the subject to the canvas "wet-on-wet" (*alla prima*), became the Impressionists' favorite method of recording nature (see fig. 4.3).

The Impressionists also challenged traditional methods of composition. From photography they learned to place figures and objects at random, showing them from untraditional high angles or cut off as if they were snapshots at a moment in a continuous event. The Impressionists' discovery of the possibilities of unexpected angles of composition was also influenced by the introduction of Japanese block prints into France in the mid- to late 1800s. These prints often derived a dramatic decorative emphasis from high-angle views looking down on landscape subjects and figures. Compare, for instance, Camille Pissarro's *La Place du Théâtre Français* (fig. 10.16) to Utagawa Hiroshige's *Kintaikyo Bridge at*

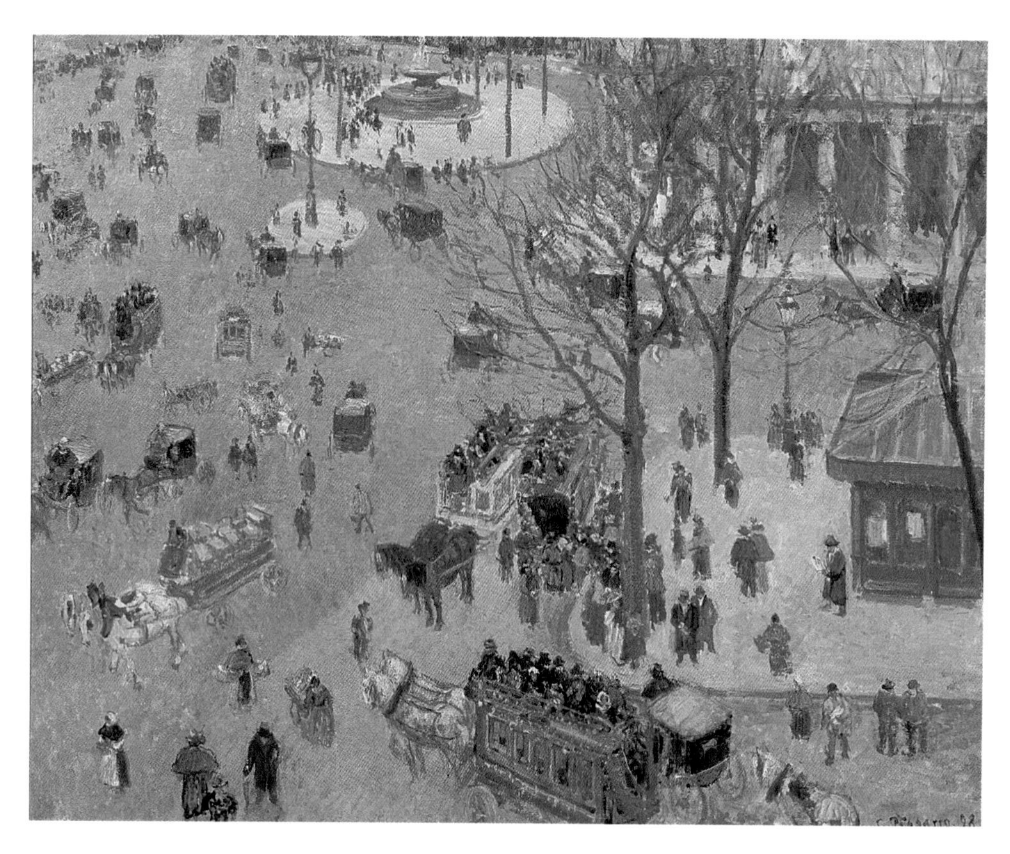

10.16 **Camille Pissarro, *La Place du Théâtre Français,* 1898. Oil on canvas, 28½ × 36¼ in. (72.4 × 92.1 cm).** In this painting, the Impressionist Pissarro shows a high-angle view of a Parisian street, a technique that was influenced by both Japanese prints and photography. Los Angeles County Museum of Art, CA. Jr. and Mrs. George Gard De Sylva Collection, M.46.3.2. Photo: Lauros-Giraudon, Paris/SuperStock.

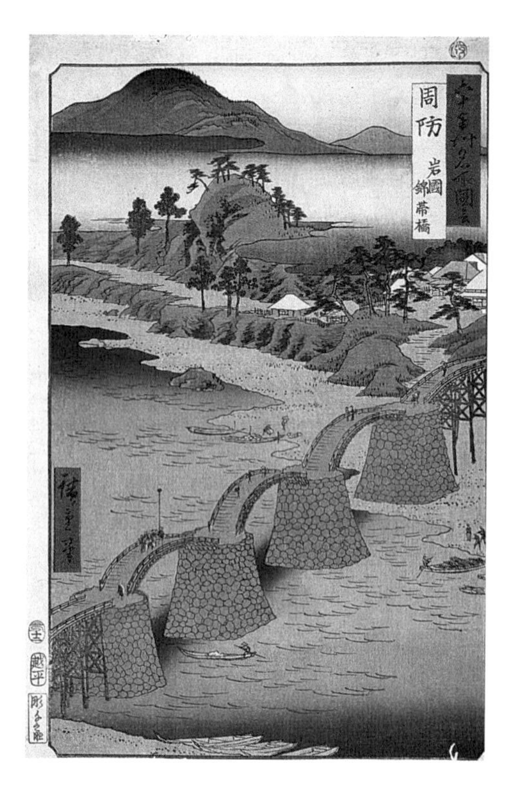

10.17 **Utagawa Hiroshige, Suö Province, *Kintaikyo Bridge at Iwakuni (No. 52),* mid-nineteenth century. Color woodblock print.** The high-angle view of this bridge from the artist's series, Landscapes at Celebrated Places in the Sixty-Odd Provinces of Japan, shows one aspect of Japanese art that influenced French Impressionism and Post-Impressionism in the 1800s. Courtesy Hiraki Ukiyo-E Foundation, Tokyo, and Hiraki Ukiyo-E Museum, Yokohama, Japan.

Iwakuni (No. 52) print (fig. 10.17). Sometimes found as mere wrapping paper on goods being shipped to Europe, these prints contained cropped images, resulting in curious truncated compositions. The resultant views seemed completely different from the arrangements that Western artists had conventionally used for almost 600 years.

Some of the coloristic and atmospheric effects that painters captured in pigments were not possible in photography as yet, but this began to change with the invention in 1906 of a commercially feasible color process; the color was not dependable, however, until the 1930s.

Pierre-Auguste Renoir was another Impressionist master. His *Luncheon of the Boating Party* (1881) shows him at his peak (fig. 10.18). Like Monet, whose career his somewhat parallels, he was enchanted by the capture of vibrant light and its effects.

Renoir kept a more human touch than Monet and Pissarro, especially in his paintings of nudes dappled by sunlight and shadow. In the 1890s, however, after study in Italy and in continuing devotion to the great figurative art of the masters, he turned away from Impressionism to seek a firmer rendering of figures, trying to reestablish monumentality in figurative painting.

Edgar Degas (1834–1917) is sometimes included as an Impressionist of movement or of "stop-action" painting (fig. 10.19). Degas, in fact, was well acquainted with photography, sometimes using photographs to achieve his high-angle views and the sense of motion in his ballet dancers and other subjects. He preferred working in his studio to painting out-of-doors, however. Degas also did some sculpture. His preference was for the use of clay and wax to cast small figures in bronze (such as his dancers), which are notable for their mobility and poise.

Two women painters connected with Impressionism were Berthe Morisot (1841–1895), a descendant of

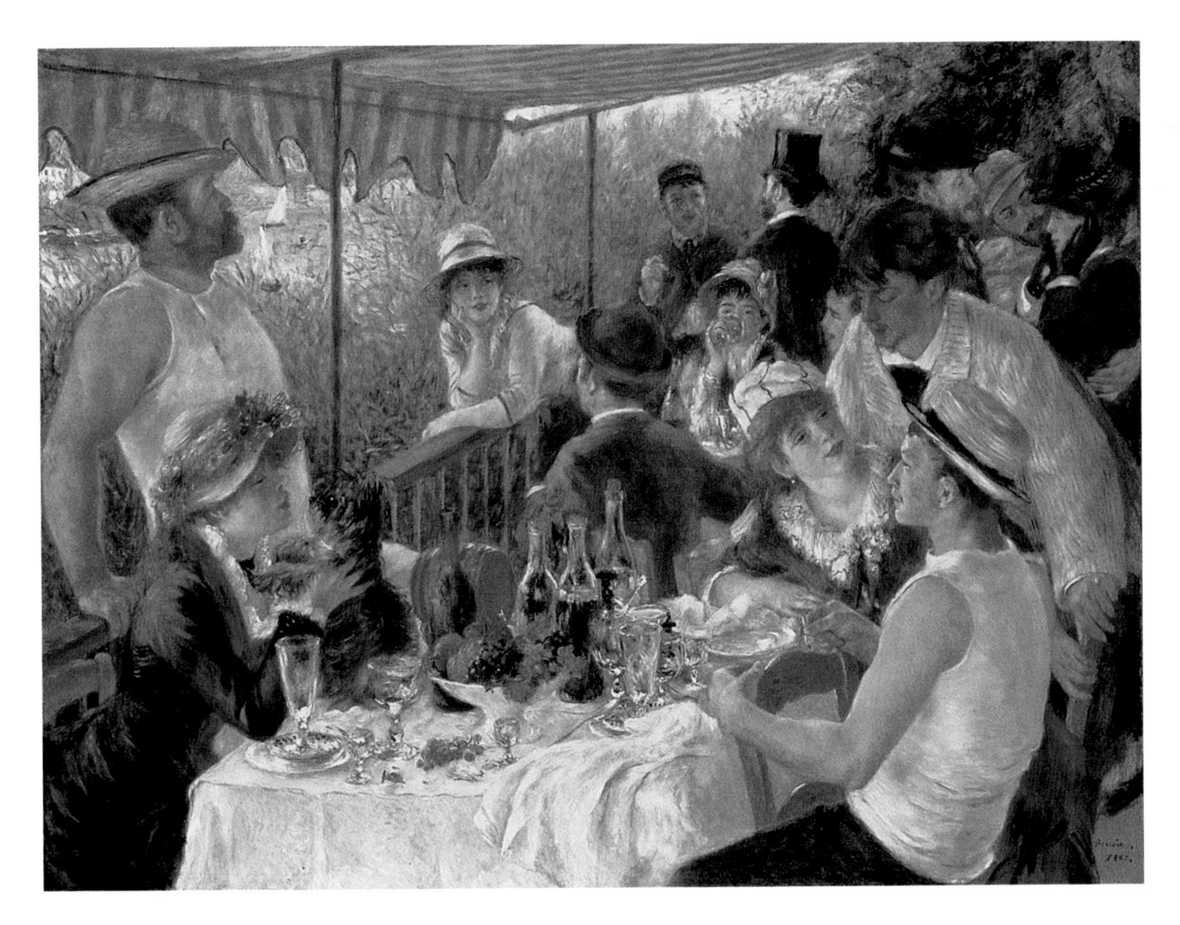

10.18 **Pierre-Auguste Renoir, *Luncheon of the Boating Party,* 1881. Oil on canvas, 51 × 68 in. (129 × 172 cm).** Renoir was enchanted by the capture of vibrant light and its effects. Acquired 1923. The Phillips Collection, Washington, D.C. © 2001 Artists Rights Society (ARS), New York/ADAGP, Paris.

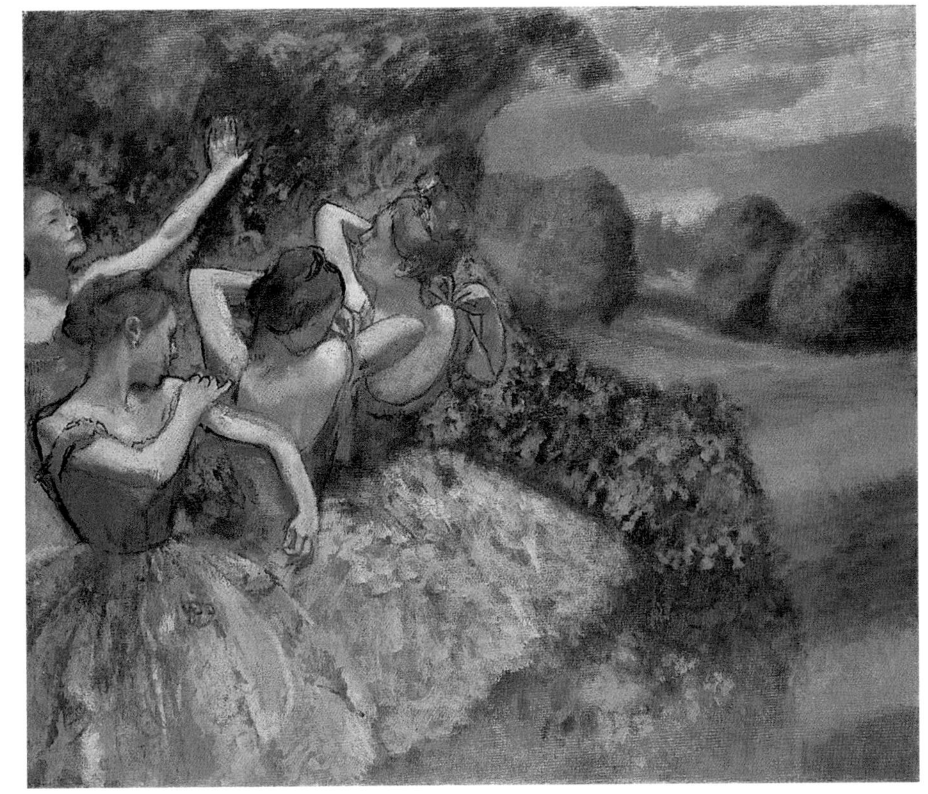

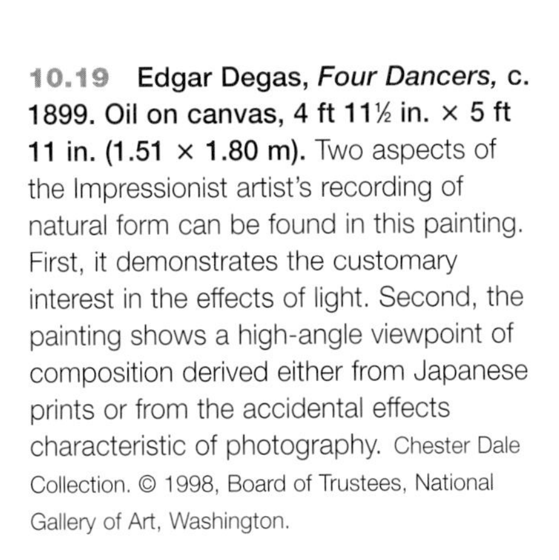

10.19 **Edgar Degas, *Four Dancers,* c. 1899. Oil on canvas, 4 ft 11½ in. × 5 ft 11 in. (1.51 × 1.80 m).** Two aspects of the Impressionist artist's recording of natural form can be found in this painting. First, it demonstrates the customary interest in the effects of light. Second, the painting shows a high-angle viewpoint of composition derived either from Japanese prints or from the accidental effects characteristic of photography. Chester Dale Collection. © 1998, Board of Trustees, National Gallery of Art, Washington.

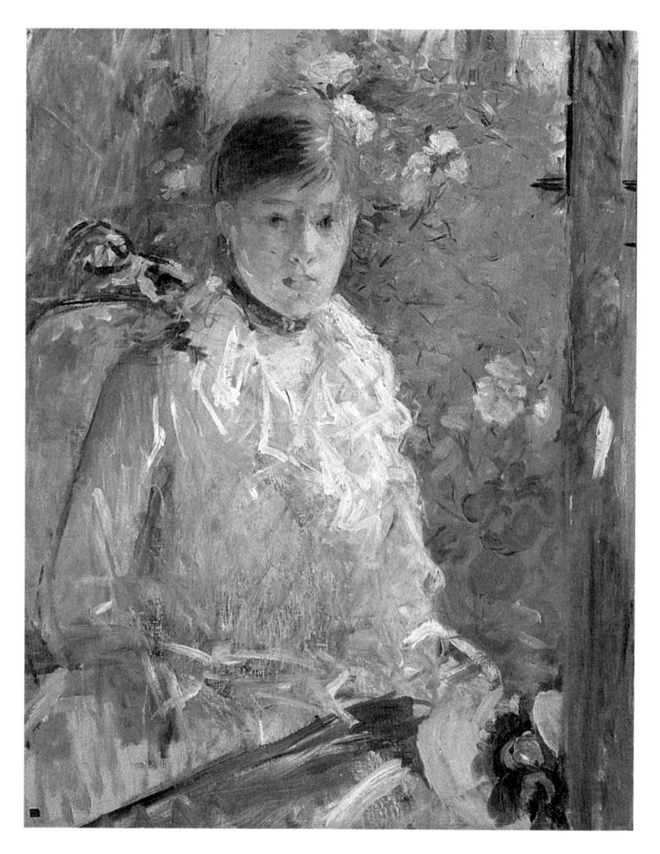

10.20 Berthe Morisot, *Young Girl by a Window,* 1878. Oil on canvas, $29\frac{15}{16} \times 24$ in. (76 × 61 cm). Morisot painted Impressionist figures with bold strokes and a lively, light palette. Musée Fabre, Montpellier, France.

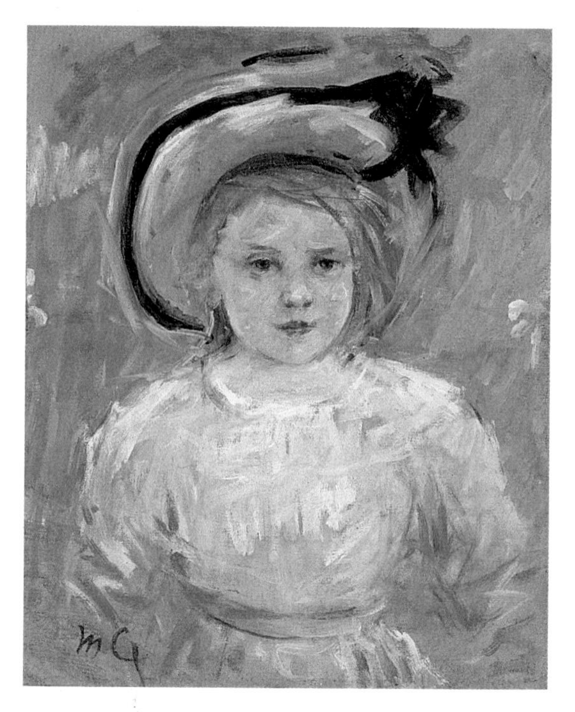

10.21 Mary Cassatt, *La Jeune Fille,* c. 1910. Oil on canvas, 42.5 × 36.8 cm. Mary Cassatt was an American who studied in Paris and was rumored to be Degas' only student. This painting shows one of her typical freely painted oils of children. Gift of Mrs. Henry C. Woods, 1964.1099, The Art Institute of Chicago.

the eighteenth-century French court painter Jean Honoré Fragonard (1732–1806) (fig. 10.20), and the American Mary Cassatt (1848–1926). Cassatt studied with Degas and concentrated on charming figures of women and children (fig. 10.21).

Post-Impressionism

By 1888, some painters associated with Impressionism began to feel that there were certain deficiencies in the style, causing them to follow other directions. The key innovations of the 1860s and '70s, such as the perceptual recording of light, color, and atmospheric effects, were now felt to be rote and superficial. But the principal flaw, which irritated most of these painters, was the loss of shape and design resulting from an acceptance of surface illusion alone whereby shapes and objects dissolved into obscure masses of color. The **Post-Impressionists,** as they were to be called, also objected to the way outdoor lighting affected the way they saw color. In strong sunlight, it was difficult to avoid making greens too raw, and there was a tendency to overload the canvas with yellows.

The most important Post-Impressionist artists were Georges Seurat (1859–1891), Paul Cézanne (1839–1906), Paul Gauguin (1848–1903), and Vincent van Gogh (1853–1890). From these pioneers stem the major directions and styles of the first sixty or so years of twentieth-century art. At the same time, their styles were each individualistic and completely different from one another. The ambiguous title given to these artists—Post-Impressionists—does not indicate this, nor does it point to their significance for the future of art.

The Post-Impressionists are classified together because they shared somewhat similar goals. They all sought such ends as: (1) a return to the structural organization of pictorial form; (2) an increased emphasis on the picture surface for the sake of pictorial unity and the unique patterns that might result; and (3) a more-or-less conscious exaggeration of natural appearances for emotionally suggestive effects. The latter is sometimes popularly called distortion. On the whole, Seurat and Cézanne illustrate the first of these aims; Gauguin, the second; and van Gogh, the third. Each, however,

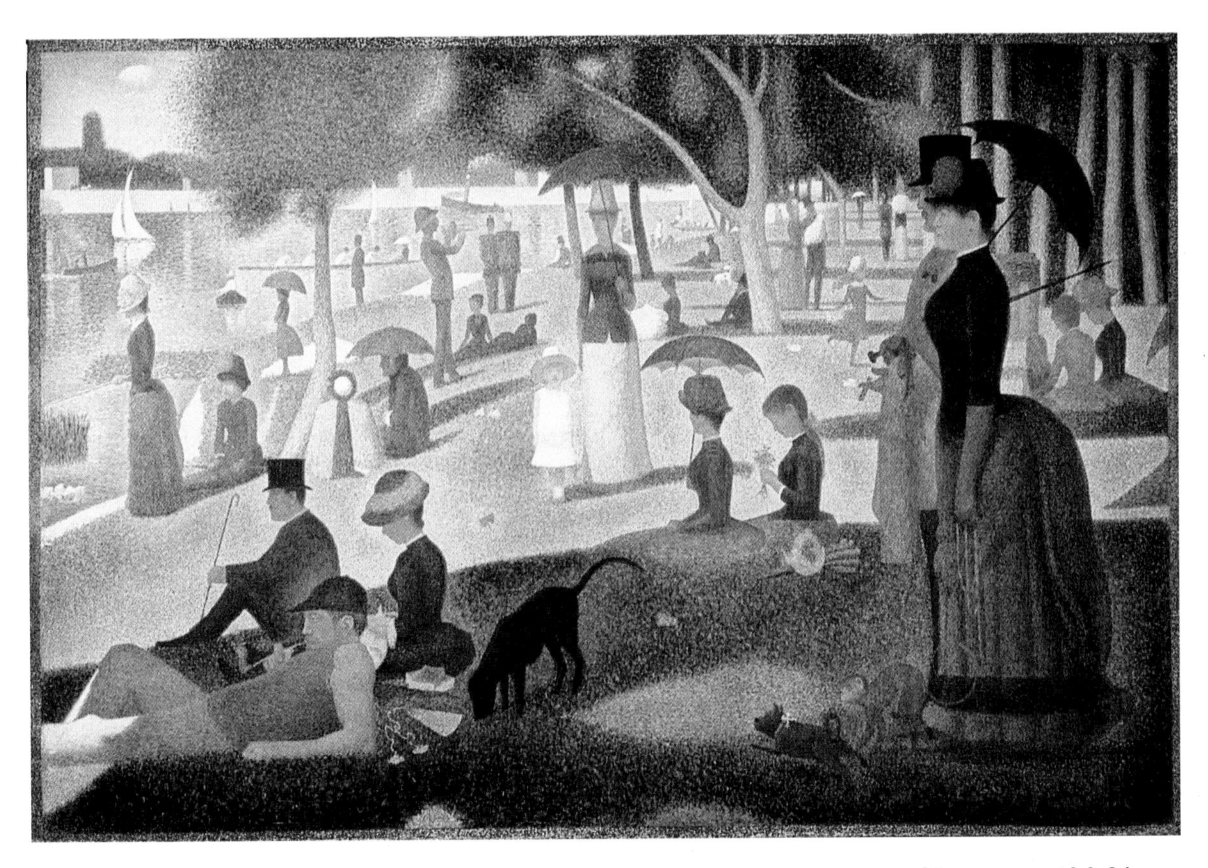

10.22 Georges Seurat, *Sunday Afternoon on the Island of La Grande Jatte,* 1884–86. Oil on canvas, 6 ft 9 in. × 10 ft 6 in. (2.06 × 3.2 m). Seurat is classified as a Post-Impressionist, but his technique set him apart from all other artists. He applied his color in a manner that he considered scientific, using dots of broken color that are resolved and harmonized by the eye of the observer. Though a remarkable achievement, "Pointillism" had only a brief stylistic life. Art Institute of Chicago. Helen Birch Bartlett Memorial Collection 1926.224. Photo © 1998 Art Institute of Chicago. All rights reserved.

incorporated some aspect of the others' objectives in his stylistic form.

In 1886, at the last Impressionist exhibit, Georges Seurat's masterpiece *Sunday Afternoon on the Island of La Grande Jatte* appeared (fig. 10.22). This painting, with its methodically dotted canvas, in many ways defines the moment when Impressionism began to be supplanted by Post-Impressionism. Although Seurat was trained in the academic manner at the École des Beaux-Arts and admired classical prototypes of the early Renaissance, the eighteenth century, and Ingres from his own century (see fig. 10.2), he came under the influence of Impressionism in the 1880s. From these influences he developed his own style, which he called Divisionism, but which others came to call Pointillism or Neo-Impressionism. His merged style is found in the *Grande Jatte.* In its interrelationship between people and object shapes, it is Classical, while in its textured pigment and use of precisely arranged complementary colors, it is Impressionist. Seurat's classical monumentality and reserve also contrast with the lighter-hearted mood of Impressionism. This combination foretells much about the abstract art of the following century.

Like Seurat, Paul Cézanne—by general agreement, the paramount artist of the Post-Impressionist movement—remains close in spirit to classicism. He, too, sought a way out of the haphazard organization and ephemeral forms of the Impressionists, seeing a work of art in terms of the interrelationship of all its parts. In this, he foreshadowed the Gestalt psychologists' theories a short time later (see Chapter 4, p. 91). While retaining the individual dabs of color of the Impressionists, Cézanne used them more as building blocks to structure his paintings, without becoming as rigidly precise as Seurat (see figs. 7.20 and 8.46).

Apparently lacking a natural aptitude for painting, Cézanne suffered many years of abuse by critics and the public before finding his own style. But gradually he taught himself to develop mass and space (such as *Still Life with Basket of Fruit;* see fig. 8.46) through the intensity of color, rather than the traditional method of dark and light values, while still respecting the flatness of his canvases. Cézanne's technique of painting thin, translucent, parallel strokes of the brush to develop form expresses in the

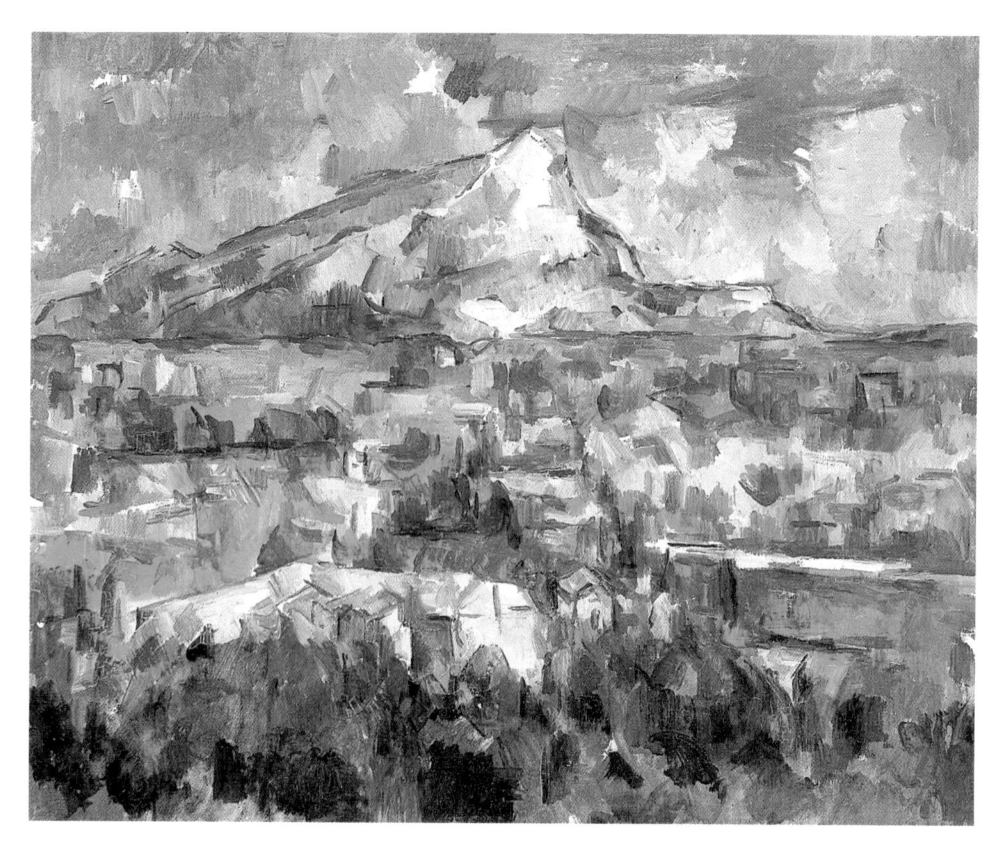

10.23 Paul Cézanne, *Mount Sainte-Victoire,* 1902–4. Oil on canvas, 27 × 35 in. Cézanne tried to show the essence of natural forms rather than describe them. This painting shows his style at its climax, in which depth is suggested but the planes into which the painting is divided tend to merge background and foreground two-dimensionally. Acc. No. 1936-1-1. Philadelphia Museum of Art, The George W. Elkins Collection. Photograph by Graydon Wood, 1994.

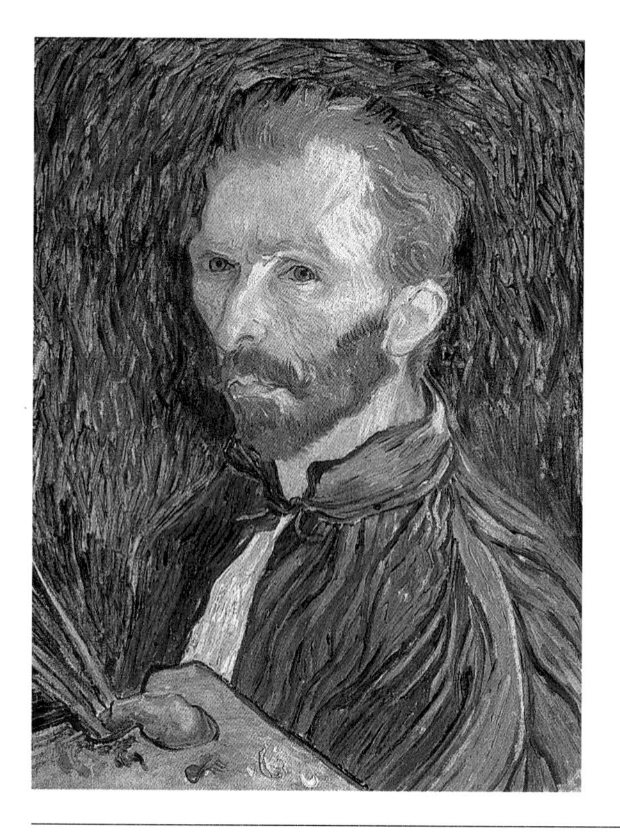

10.24 Vincent van Gogh, *Self-Portrait,* 1889. Oil on canvas, 22 × 17 in. (56 × 43 cm). As seen in this self-portrait, painted in the year before his death, the emotional content of van Gogh's style becomes one with the ribboned paint texture. It was applied by brush, palette knife, and possibly fingers. Collection of Mr. and Mrs. John Hay Whitney. Photograph © 2001 Board of Trustees, National Gallery of Art, Washington.

rich sonority of hue his emotional reaction to his subjects. By combining views of various objects and nature from different points in space and by using broken contours, Cézanne accounted for human eye movement while simultaneously relating things to each other and the two-dimensional painting surface.

Thus Cézanne conceived of reality as a totality of form and expression transformed by the artist's mind and hand as it was derived from the appearance of nature. In this way Cézanne became the first artist of modern times to consider the appearance of pictorial form more important than the representation of a subject (fig. 10.23). Due to the intellectual approach involved in his realization of form, Cézanne is a Classicist in spirit. Nevertheless, he was the forerunner of Cubism and abstraction in the twentieth century.

In comparison to the classical character of Cézanne's and Seurat's works, the paintings of Paul Gauguin display the invention of a vivid, symbolic world of decorative patterns (see figs. 1.30 and 7.21). These patterns owe part of their character to the gleanings Gauguin took from medieval carvings, mosaics, and manuscripts. He saw such carvings on roadside chapels while living in Brittany, France, during the 1880s. While his later themes (during the 1890s) were inspired by his travel to the island of Tahiti in the Pacific, Gauguin's work always demonstrates a gracefulness typical of French art despite the exotic mystery and menace of the Tahitian elements that he merged into his work. The brilliant color and free patterns of his decorative style, plus the otherworldly effect, inspired not only the Symbolists at the end of the 1800s but also the early-twentieth-century French Fauves.

The work of Vincent van Gogh, the fourth Post-Impressionist, represents the beginning of a new, highly charged subjectivity that we find in much of subsequent modern art. The character of Expressionism in the early 1900s owes a great deal to van Gogh's impetuous brush strokes and dramatic distortions of color and form. He was mostly self-taught as an artist, having turned to art after failures at other careers. It was van Gogh's sense of personal failure, however, that was the root of his impassioned style. The throbbing emotion revealed through his subject matter, be his portrait, landscape, or still life, goes far beyond the perceptual premises and final forms of the Impressionists (fig. 10.24, see also fig. 1.16).

Henri de Toulouse-Lautrec (1864–1901), a descendant of an ancient aristocratic family, is classifiable as both an Impressionist of movement and a Post-Impressionist of expressive color and psychological insight. His physical growth was stunted in childhood, and Lautrec's dwarfish appearance led to his estrangement from the high social strata of his family. To find solace for his appearance, Lautrec befriended the outcasts of Parisian society, where, after studying art, he sought his subjects in cabarets, circuses, and brothels. He rendered such people as he found in these places, with strong lines and raw color in such a way as to express his convivial acceptance of their society. Lautrec is noted for his inventive posters advertising cabaret performances. His fluid line, shape, and use of flat color capture the song and dance of Parisian nightclubs and suited the art of color lithography immensely (see fig. 3.4).

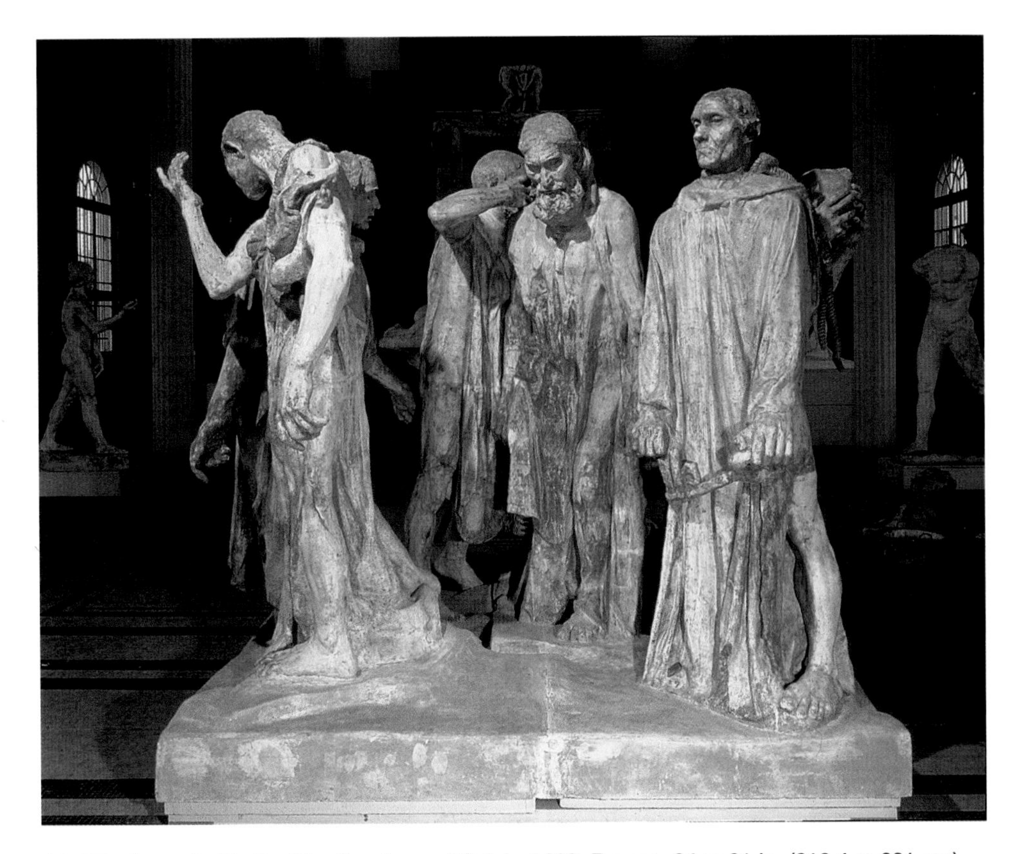

10.25 Auguste Rodin, *The Burghers of Calais,* 1888. Bronze, 84 × 91 in. (213.4 × 231 cm). The French port city of Calais commissioned this work in which the sculptor's content reaches a peak of psychological impact through gesturing figures standing on the same level as the observer. They have been mistaken for real people at night. Musée Rodin, Paris, France. Peter Willi/The Bridgeman Art Library.

There was no clearly defined Post-Impressionist movement among sculptors seeking revolutionary changes like those that were occurring in painting at the end of the 1800s. The closest representative perhaps is Auguste Rodin (1840–1917), the most active sculptor in late-nineteenth-century France. He looked to the future as well as to the past, and he was a link to exploiting form, materials, and expressive content for their own inherent sake. Nonetheless, Rodin remained basically a Realist who, by embracing Romantic, Realist, and Impressionist effects, predicted the early-twentieth-century Expressionists. In his search to suggest emotional states directly through sculptural form he was a Romantic. In his attack on the medium of clay and plaster (from which his many bronzes were cast), his gouged, irregular surface effects are similar to those of the Impressionists, particularly because of the way light falls on them. An emotional quality, something like that of van Gogh and Toulouse-Lautrec, results from these effects.

Rodin studied with Antoine Louis Barye but was even more influenced by Renaissance sculptors Donatello (c. 1386–1466) and Michelangelo (1475–1564). Rodin also held the great seventeenth-century sculptor Giovanni Lorenzo Bernini (1598–1680) in high regard and admired the carvings on Gothic cathedrals. While he repudiated the academic sculpture of his time, he did not hesitate to use similar themes, as in *The Gates of Hell* (see fig. 9.30), which are inspired by the emotional writings of Dante and Baudelaire. Rodin also tried to express the drama and emotive effects of movement in static sculpture, as in *The Burghers of Calais* (1888) (fig. 10.25). This commission by the port of Calais commemorated an incident in which citizens of the city offered themselves as hostages to English invaders to save the city itself. By actually placing these gesturing figures on ground level—removed from the traditional pedestal—Rodin imparts feelings of immediacy and sympathy. The *Gates of Hell* and *Burghers* were cast in bronze from preliminary models.

When Rodin worked in hard materials like marble, however, as in the *Danaide* (1885), he tried to restore sculptural values that he felt had been lost since the incomparable Michelangelo. In

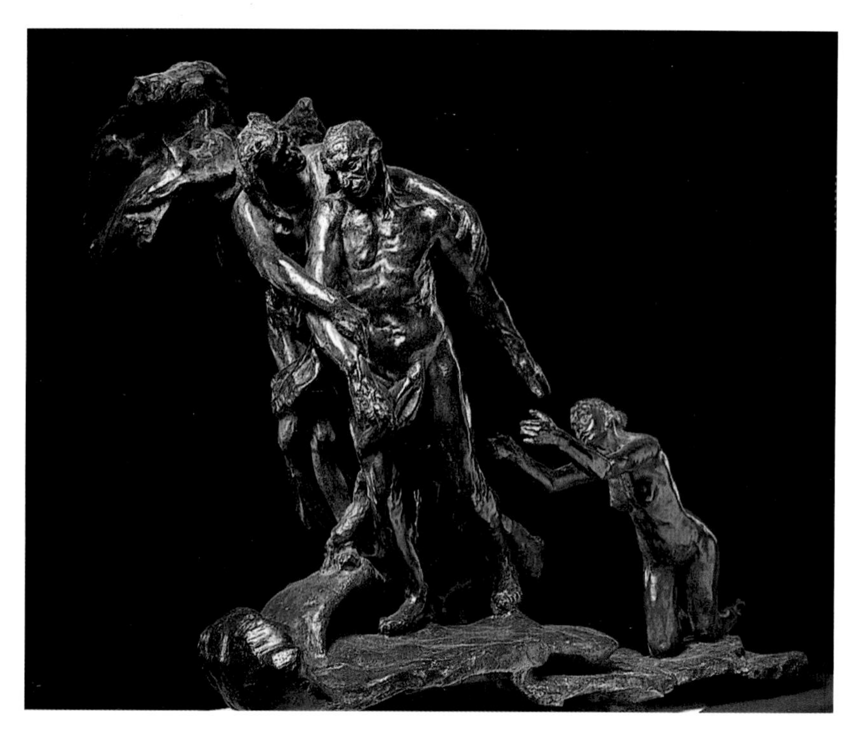

10.26 Camille Claudel, *Maturity* (*L'Age Mûr*), 1907. Bronze, 47⅝ × 70⅞ × 28¾ in. (121 × 180 × 73 cm). Sadly neglected for half a century, this sculptress was student, assistant, model, and mistress to Auguste Rodin. Her work had a more fluid style than Rodin's. Collection Musée Rodin, Paris. © 2005 Musée Rodin/DR. Artists Rights Society (ARS), New York/ADAGP, Paris. Photograph by Erik & Petra Hesmerg.

stone, Rodin tried to restore the values of heft and texture, the contrast between high polish and unfinished roughness, and the impression of the figure emerging from the block of stone. In other sketches and finished works, he created fragmentary human forms, suggesting humanity striving against fateful forces (see fig. 9.4). Moreover, in the unusual effects of torsion, dimension, fractional presentation, and potency of form Rodin helped pave the way to twentieth-century sculpture.

One of Rodin's assistants, Camille Claudel (1864–1943), has been restored to recognition after years of obscurity and is sometimes credited with being the source of some of Rodin's best ideas. Starting as his student, Claudel became Rodin's model and mistress. Her works on display at the Rodin Museum and in private collections indicate that, while less imaginative and monumental than Rodin, she was similarly adept at handling materials (fig. 10.26).

Photographic Trends

While certain Pictorialist photographers were working in an Impressionist or Post-Impressionist vein, others were following the **Symbolists,** whose style sought to achieve an ultimate reality through intuitive or inward spiritual experiences of the world. These photographers, like their counterparts in painting, worked directly from nature and yet, increasingly, made perception a way of studying composition and evoking expression. They also believed that there was something beyond the mere recording of a moment. Other Pictorialists did not approve of the fuzzy focus and film manipulation that their colleagues used to attain their effects. They began to experiment instead with the natural effects of light and atmospheric conditions, as had the Impressionist painters. The fusing of experimental Pictorialism with a Realist point of view, then, seems to have been influenced by the theories of both Post-Impressionism and, to some extent, Symbolism. Many of these modernist photographers grouped together, leading to the foundation in London in 1892 of the so-called Linked Ring. The Royal Photographic Society of England shortly after branched off from this early group, while various "Linked Ring" groups spread to the major cities of Europe. By the end of the nineteenth century, many of these photographers were advocating the artistic worth of the camera image through exhibits and documents. They called themselves Photo-Secessionists and likened themselves to painters who had held "secessionist" exhibits of their rejected works in defiance of the École des Beaux-Arts.

In great part due to the photographer Alfred Stieglitz (1864–1946), progressive modernism in art came to America. Stieglitz originally went to Germany to study engineering but soon became interested in photography as a career. His early work was Pictorialist with an affinity to late-nineteenth-century painting. In Germany, Stieglitz met the younger photographer Edward Steichen (1879–1923), who helped him found the Little Gallery of the Photo Secession at 291 Fifth Avenue in New York City in 1905. There Stieglitz exhibited avant-garde painting and sculpture from Europe, with Steichen's aid. While his photograph *The Terminal* (c. 1892) (fig. 10.27), created shortly after his return to the United States in 1890, displays an awareness of Impressionist "slices of life" under atmospheric conditions, it also indicates Stieglitz's experimentation with a Straight or Realist manner. Stieglitz strongly believed in the autonomous value of the camera image. In articles written for the New York Camera Club and in his magazine *Camera Work,* established in 1903, Stieglitz joined the

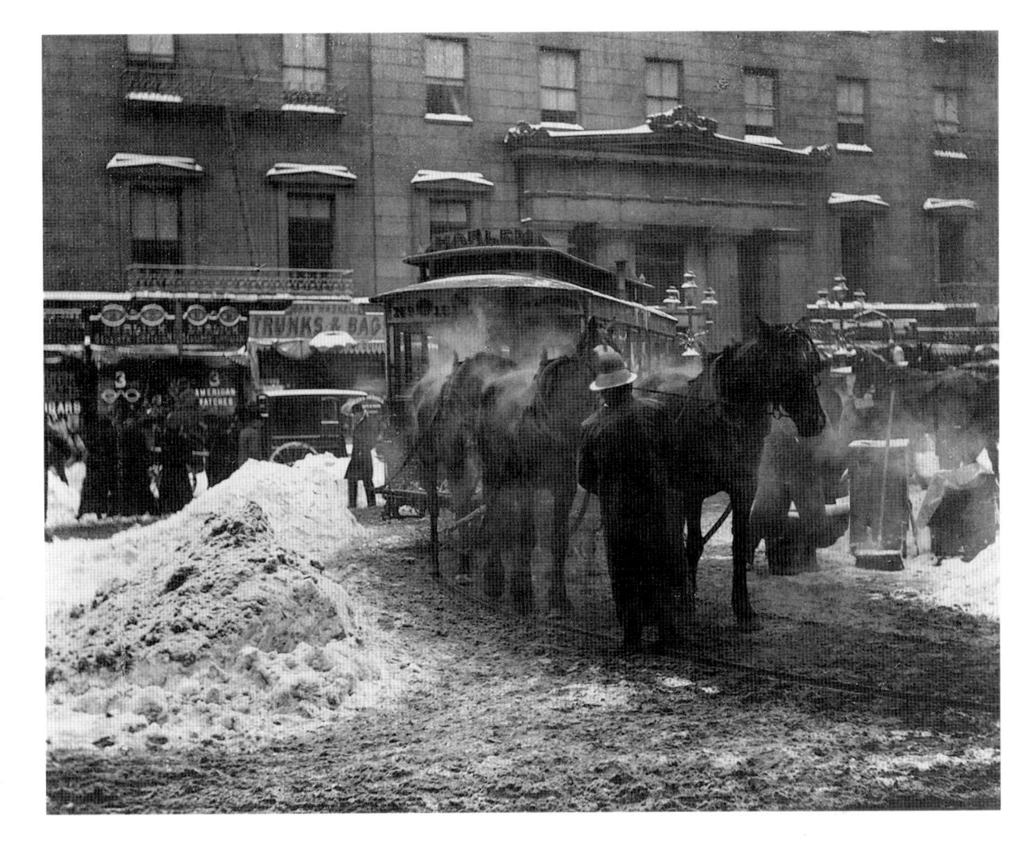

10.27 Alfred Stieglitz, *The Terminal*, c. 1892. Photogravure, 10 × 13¼ in. (25.4 × 33.7 cm). Stieglitz was probably the most influential photographer of the late 1800s and early 1900s and had a very important role in introducing avant-garde European and American art to the public in the United States. He was an artist with Pictorialist leanings at first who became one of the best Straight photographers. Here he recorded the atmospheric conditions of a cold morning in a memorable image. Art Institute of Chicago. The Alfred Stieglitz Collection, 1949.706. Photo © 1998 Art Institute of Chicago. All rights reserved.

Pictorialists in maintaining that their works should be displayed and regarded for their intrinsic artistic quality, like other art media. At 291 Fifth Avenue (the new name for the Little Gallery), Stieglitz exhibited photography as a unique form of art in its own right.

EARLY-TWENTIETH-CENTURY ART

Expressionism

Expressionism, perhaps the most significant phase in the evolution of newer art forms, came into being in France and Germany around 1910. The young artists of this movement were the first to forcefully declare outright their freedom to paint a subject in accord with their feelings. Expressionism is a form of art that tries to reveal the emotional essence rather than to show external appearance. These ideas were similar to those being put forward by the Photo-Secessionist groups.

In a sense, these artists were merely more-liberal Romantics. However, it had become possible to be more liberal only after the intervening period of change, driven by Impressionism and Post-Impressionism—a period that had introduced new ways of seeing and feeling. Thus, the early 1900s saw an even greater growth of this new awareness in art. Cézanne, Seurat, Gauguin, and van Gogh had opened the door through which hosts of young artists were to pass, eager to explore a new world of artistic sensation, diversion, and mystery. The shape of this new artistic world was illuminated by an explosion of color and an exciting style of drawing that ranged from the graceful curves of Henri Matisse to the bold slashings of Oskar Kokoschka.

French Expressionism: The Fauves

The members of the earliest Expressionist group were called **Les Fauves** (The Wild Beasts), a name applied to them by the French critic Louis Vauxcelles when he saw their first exhibit at the Salon d'Automne in 1905. Vauxcelles thought their paintings were wild due to their unnaturally bold coloring and use of exaggeratedly distorted figures. (Vauxcelles was later to name the Cubists in disparaging the work of Georges Braque as mere cubes.) Official French artistic circles and the general public were still expecting a more conservative traditional style, since they were as yet only dimly aware of the Impressionists and Post-Impressionists. But they could not for long ignore this host of new young painters, who threw Paris into a turmoil with group exhibitions, pamphleteering, and other forms of publicity. The Fauves lived up to their name for about seven years, however. By 1912 they had lost their original vigor and were considered rather sedate compared to newer movements that were evolving. While seeking to evoke the emotional essence of the subject, the Fauve manner was decorative, colorful, spontaneous, and intuitive. When this emotional excitement is communicated to the spectator, an Expressionist artwork can be called successful.

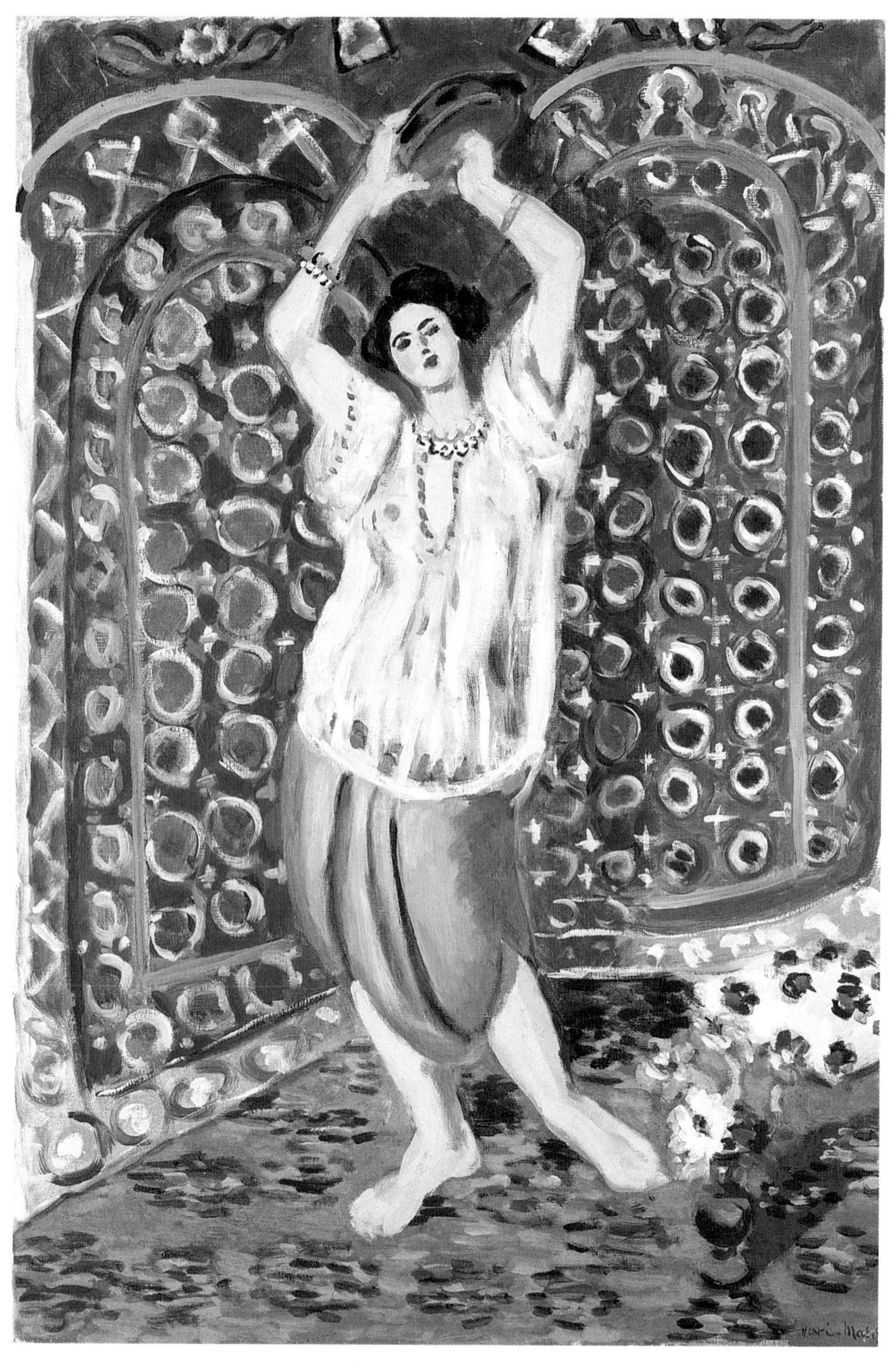

10.28 **Henri Matisse, *Odalisque with Tambourine (Harmony in Blue)*, 1926. Oil on canvas, 36¼ × 25⅝ in. (92.1 × 65.1 cm).** The Fauves, led by Matisse, tried to show the emotional essence of a subject rather than its external appearance. Matisse also exhibits the characteristically decorative, colorful, spontaneous, and intuitive qualities of this French Expressionist style. Norton Simon Art Foundation, Pasadena, CA © 2005 Succession H. Matisse/Artists Rights Society (ARS), New York.

In its colors, brilliance, and sophistication, the work of Henri Matisse (1869–1954), nominal leader of the Fauvist group, was largely influenced by Persian and Middle Eastern art (fig. 10.28; see also figs. 3.24 and 4.7). The Fauves as a group hunted exotic influences, searching for exciting patterns in the artifacts of museums. They were inspired by the work of the Byzantines, the Coptic Christians, and archaic Greek artists, as well as by the tribal art of Africa, Oceania, and Native Americans. The influence of African masks and sculpture is readily apparent in the stylized, impersonal faces in Matisse's paintings, as well as in the art of numerous other early-twentieth-century artists. Behind these impassive gazes lies a sense of mystery and unsettling enigma (see fig. 10.40).

The Expressionists Matisse and Amadeo Modigliani (1884–1920) shared a preference for strong, vibrant color and created charming, decorative forms notable for their classical restraint. Georges Rouault (1871–1958), on the other hand, was an exception among the French Fauve Expressionists; his work was harsh and dramatic. His paintings express a violent reaction to the hypocrisy and materialism of his time through characteristic use of thick, crumbling reds and blacks. His images of Christ are symbols of man's inhumanity to man, as his *Christ Mocked by Soldiers* (1932) reveals (fig. 10.29); his paintings of judges are comments on the crime and corruption of his time. Rouault's artistic comments on the French political and legislative leaders of the day were anything but complimentary.

German Expressionism

German artists of the early twentieth century felt that they, as prophets of new, unknown artistic values, must destroy the conventions that bound the art of their time. The foundation of painting in Europe for the next fifty years was partly provided by three groups of German

10.29 Georges Rouault, *Christ Mocked by Soldiers*, 1932. Oil on canvas, 36¼ × 28½ in. (92.1 × 72.4 cm). In this Expressionist contrast of clashing complements, the pattern is stabilized by heavy neutralizing lines of black reminiscent of medieval stained glass. © 2005 Artists Rights Society (ARS), New York/ADGP, Paris. The Museum of Modern Art, New York, NY. U.S.A. Given anonymously. Digital image © The Museum of Modern Art/Licensed by SCALA/Art Resource, NY.

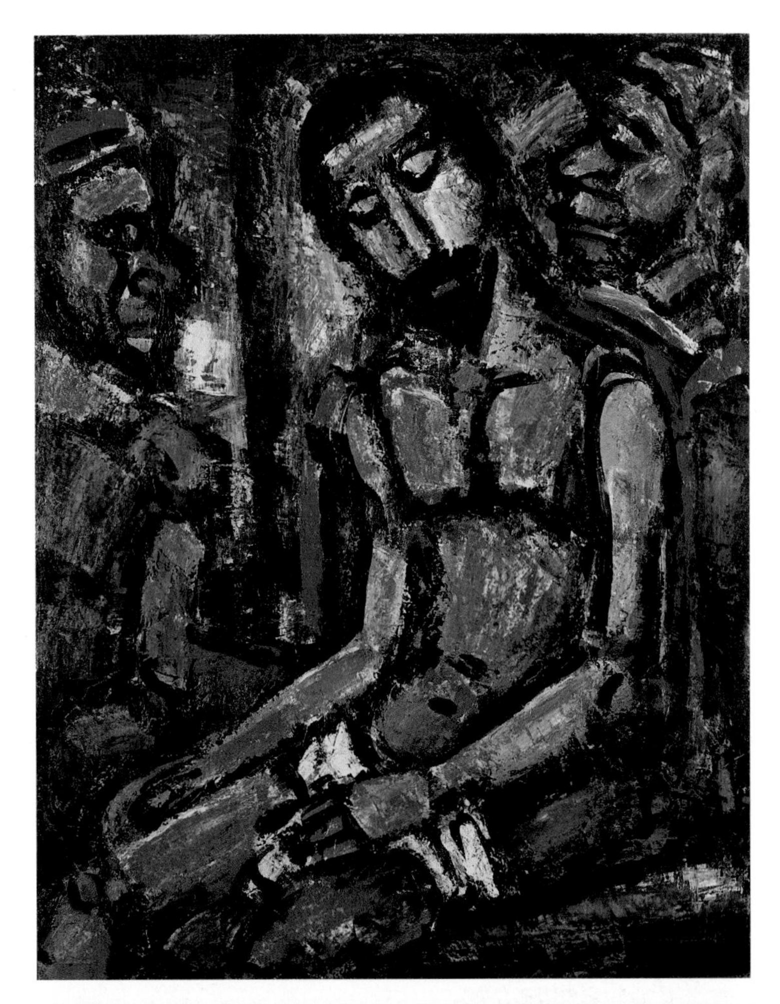

Expressionist artists. First among these was The Bridge (*Die Brücke*), founded in Dresden at the same time as the Fauves' exhibit at the Salon d'Automne (1905). Ernst Ludwig Kirchner (1888–1938) was the outstanding leader of The Bridge (fig. 10.30). Another important member who joined later was Emil Nolde (1867–1956). The Bridge died out with the opening of World War I in 1914 (see fig. 3.20).

The Blue Rider (*Der Blaue Reiter*), a second group founded in Munich, Germany, in 1911, was as much abstract as expressionist in style, and its primary artist was Wassily Kandinsky (1866–1944), whom we will consider later under European abstraction.

The New Objectivity (*Die Neue Sachlichkeit*) was the third group of Expressionists and was founded after World War I. Its artists, including George Grosz (1893–1959) and Otto Dix (1891–1969), chose as their principal themes the corruption and chaos left in Germany by World War I, the succeeding Weimar Republic, and the rise of Hitler's National Socialist regime resulting in World War II.

The Expressionism of The Bridge was the most typical of the German Expressionists. Its artists created images that had a vehemence, drama, gruesomeness, and fanaticism completely unlike the rationality of French art. They frequently identified with the religious mysticism of the Middle Ages, with the tribal arts of Oceania and Africa, and with the psychotic expression of the mentally ill. Some followed the manner of children, with a naive but direct emotional identification with the environment. For example, the art of Emil Nolde is similar in

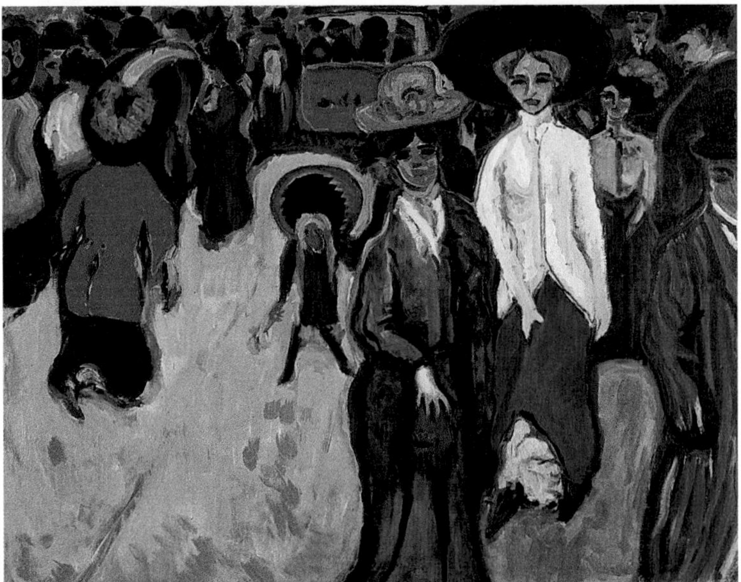

10.30 Ernst Ludwig Kirchner, *The Street*, 1909. Oil on canvas, 4 ft 11¼ in. × 6 ft 6⅞ in. (1.5 × 2 m). While creating a world of emotional intensity, bright colors and wraith or ghostlike figures without any apparent gravity show Fauve and some Cubist impact on this artist. © by Ingeborg & Dr. Wolfgang Henze-Ketterer, Wichtrach/Bern. © The Museum of Modern Art/Licensed by SCALA/Art Resource, NY.

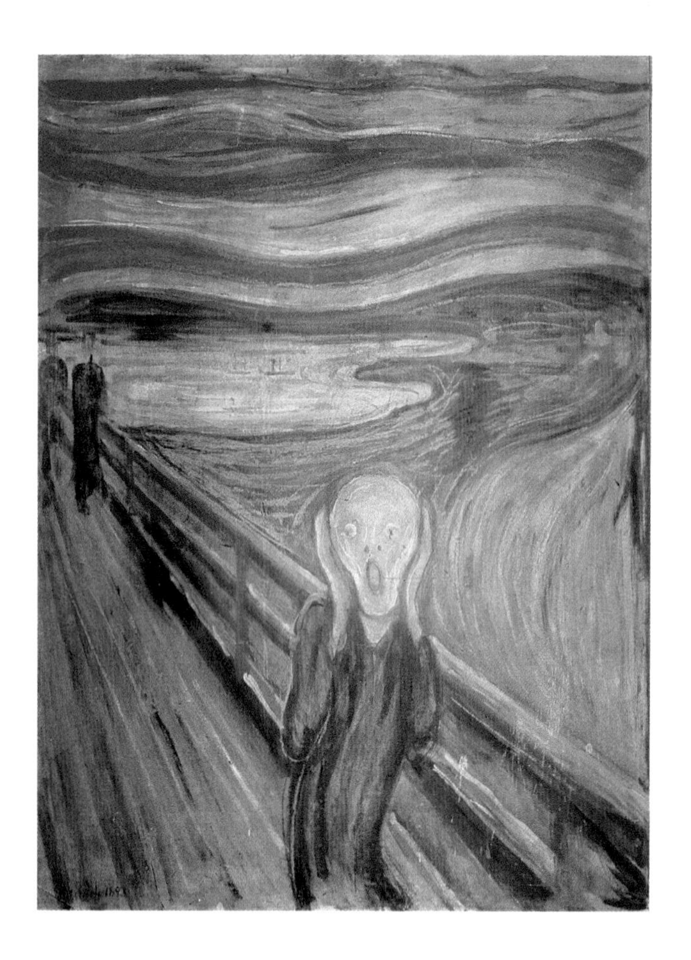

10.31 Edvard Munch, *The Scream* or *The Cry,* 1893. Oil and tempera on board, 35¼ × 28 in. (89.5 × 73.7 cm). The angst-ridden life of this artist is reflected in his emotional and distorted pictures. Childish terrors and medieval superstitions are interwoven in a form of frightful conditions. National Gallery, Oslo, Norway. Photo: Bridgemen Art Library, London/SuperStock. © 2005 The Munch Museum/The Munch-Ellingsen Group/Artists Rights Society (ARS), New York.

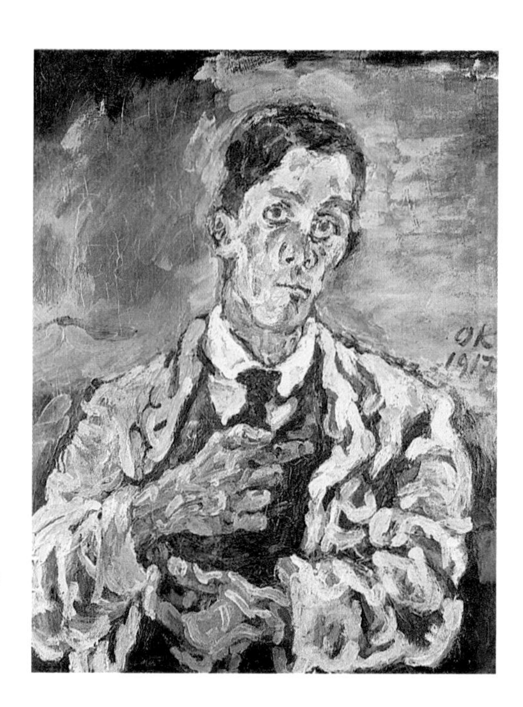

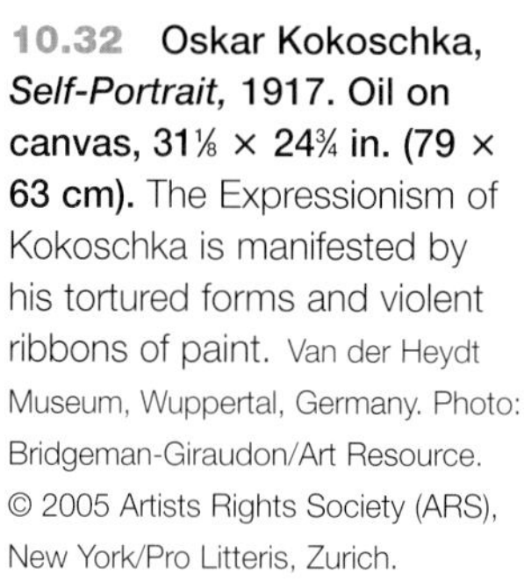

10.32 Oskar Kokoschka, *Self-Portrait,* 1917. Oil on canvas, 31⅛ × 24¾ in. (79 × 63 cm). The Expressionism of Kokoschka is manifested by his tortured forms and violent ribbons of paint. Van der Heydt Museum, Wuppertal, Germany. Photo: Bridgeman-Giraudon/Art Resource. © 2005 Artists Rights Society (ARS), New York/Pro Litteris, Zurich.

feeling to the mystic art of the Middle Ages (see figs. 3.20 and 7.40). The Norwegian Edvard Munch (1863–1944), a pioneer of Expressionism living in Germany, was introducing a style of emotional instability based on his own tragic childhood (fig. 10.31). Munch was also partly influenced by folk art, tales from the Middle Ages, and African tribal art. The Austrian Oskar Kokoschka (1886–1980) revealed that even in portraiture it was not the external likeness that counted but rather the emotional significance and mood of the artist and model (fig. 10.32). Kokoschka in his later years turned to an increasingly romantic kind of impressionist-abstraction in which he tried to infuse cities in different parts of the world with an emotional, personal character.

Following World War I, protests against Prussian jingoism and the failures of the Weimar Republic became the subject matter of the New Objectivity (or New Reality) painters George Grosz and Otto Dix (figs. 10.33 and 10.34). Max Beckmann (1884–1950), although not a part of any organized Expressionist group, followed a path close in spirit to the work of the New Objectivity. While his work similarly satirized the swampy, degraded underworld of political society, he modified Expressionism's emotional bite by way of a calming, geometric order, learned from Cubism. This quality gives his manner a certainty of execution that is reminiscent of the work of the old masters (fig. 10.35).

Sculpture in the Early 1900s

Although new concepts in art tended to arise earlier in painting than in sculpture until the 1950s, nevertheless a continuous interchange of ideas guaranteed that lines of development were parallel in the two groups.

By 1900, revolutionary changes were discernible as sculptors began to react to contemporary thought and experience rather than to ancient myth and legend. Sculpture then took three general directions: (1) the human figure was retained but simplified to express the essentials of structure and material; (2) forms were abstracted from nature, or new forms of a highly structural character were invented; and (3) experimentation with new materials produced new shapes and techniques.

While there were no exact parallels to Post-Impressionist painting in sculpture, the work of French sculptor Aristide Maillol (1861–1944) suggests a new economy in the totality of form and an accent on the inherent character of materials. These trends are similar to

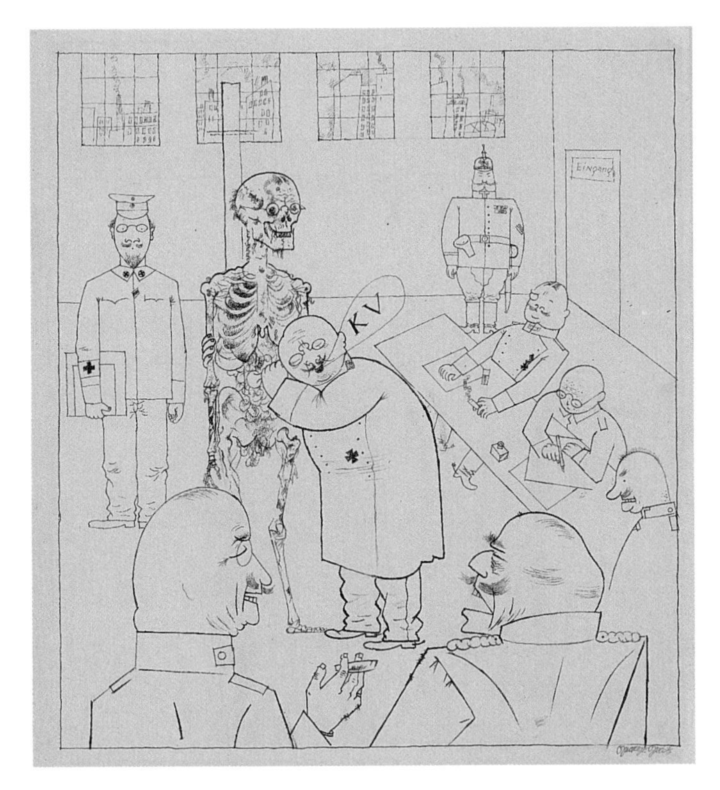

10.33 George Grosz, *Fit for Active Service,* 1916–17. Pen, brush and ink, 10 × 14⅜ in. (50.8 × 36.5 cm). In this work, characteristic German emotionalism is pressed into the service of satire. Expressionism, which shows moral indignation at its peak, now becomes an instrument of social protest, as the artist comments bitterly on his experiences of World War I. Niceties of color are ignored in favor of harsh, biting black lines.

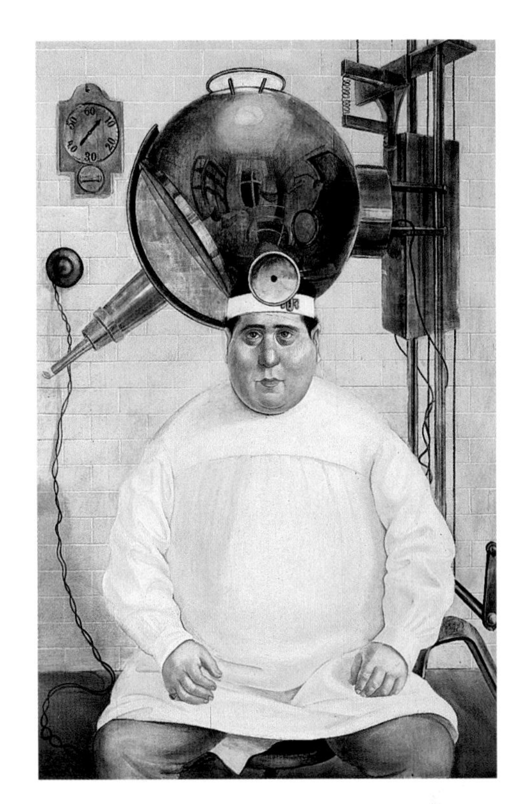

10.34 Otto Dix, *Dr. Mayer-Hermann,* 1926. Oil and tempera on wood, 58¾ × 39 in. (149.2 × 99.1 cm). The German Expressionists, with whom Dix is grouped, were highly critical of German society after World War I. Their paintings of people of that period were either tinged with satire or savage with invective.

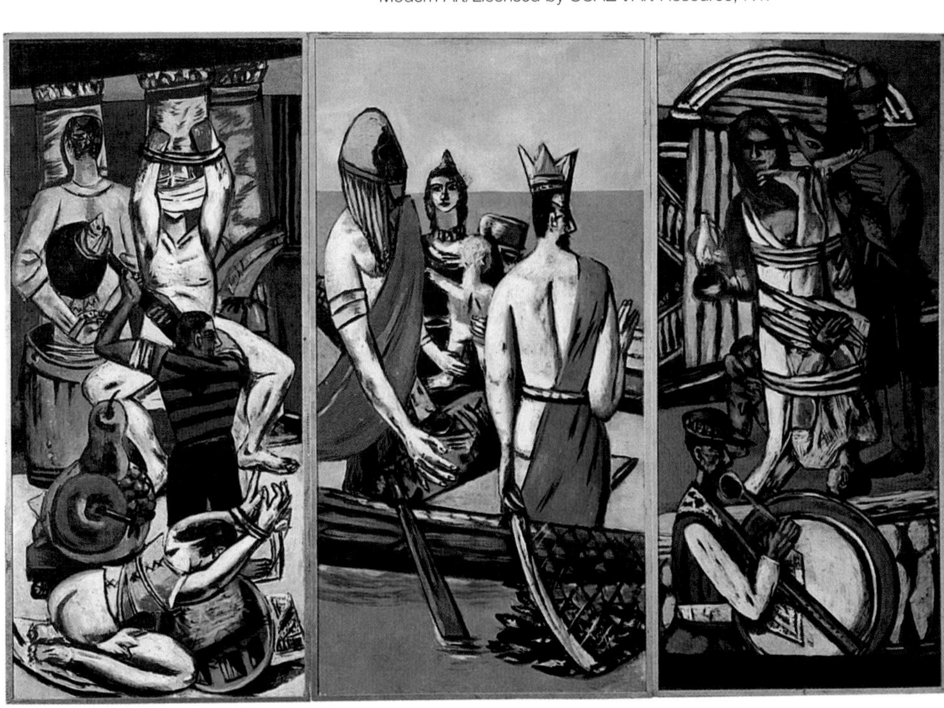

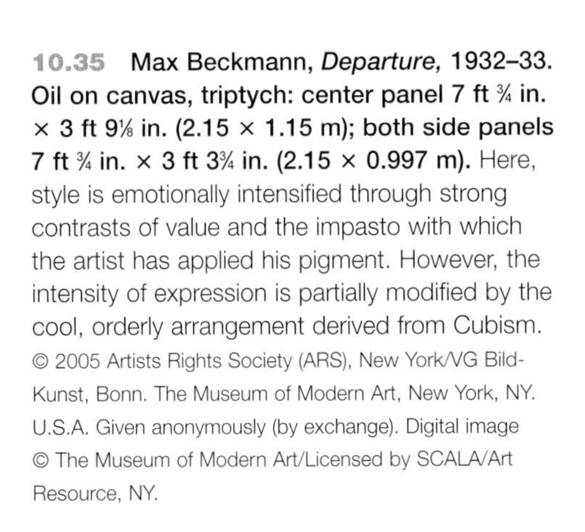

10.35 Max Beckmann, *Departure,* 1932–33. Oil on canvas, triptych: center panel 7 ft ¾ in. × 3 ft 9⅛ in. (2.15 × 1.15 m); both side panels 7 ft ¾ in. × 3 ft 3¾ in. (2.15 × 0.997 m). Here, style is emotionally intensified through strong contrasts of value and the impasto with which the artist has applied his pigment. However, the intensity of expression is partially modified by the cool, orderly arrangement derived from Cubism.

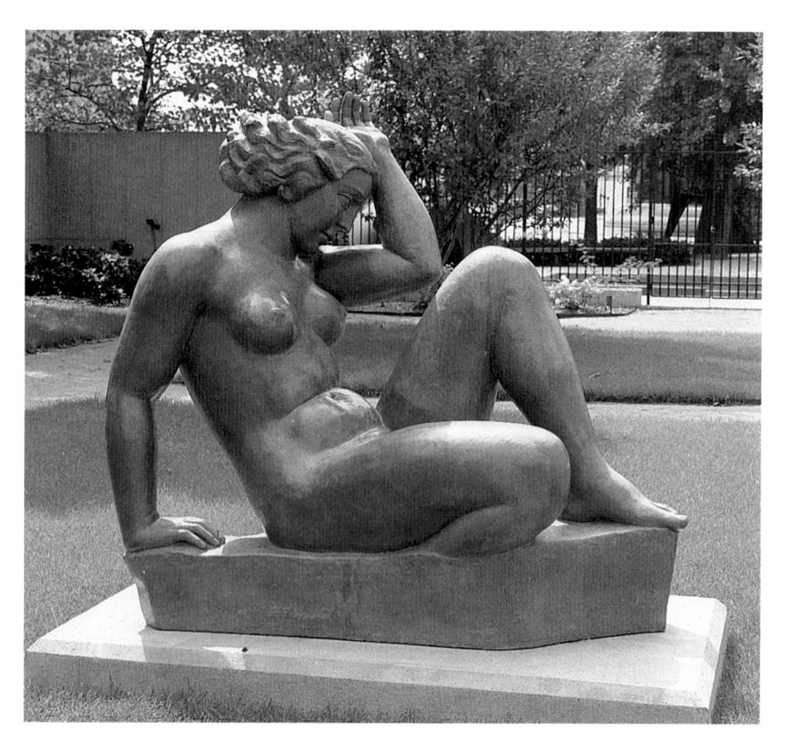

10.36 Aristide Maillol, *La Montagne*, 1937. Original plaster, posthumously cast in lead, 1979, 66½ in. (168.9 cm) high. Aristide Maillol combined classical serenity and repose with a sense of modern monumentality. Columbus Museum of Art, Ohio. Museum Purchase: Schumacher Fund and the Battelle Memorial Institute Foundation. © 2005 Artists Rights Society (ARS), New York/ADAGP, Paris.

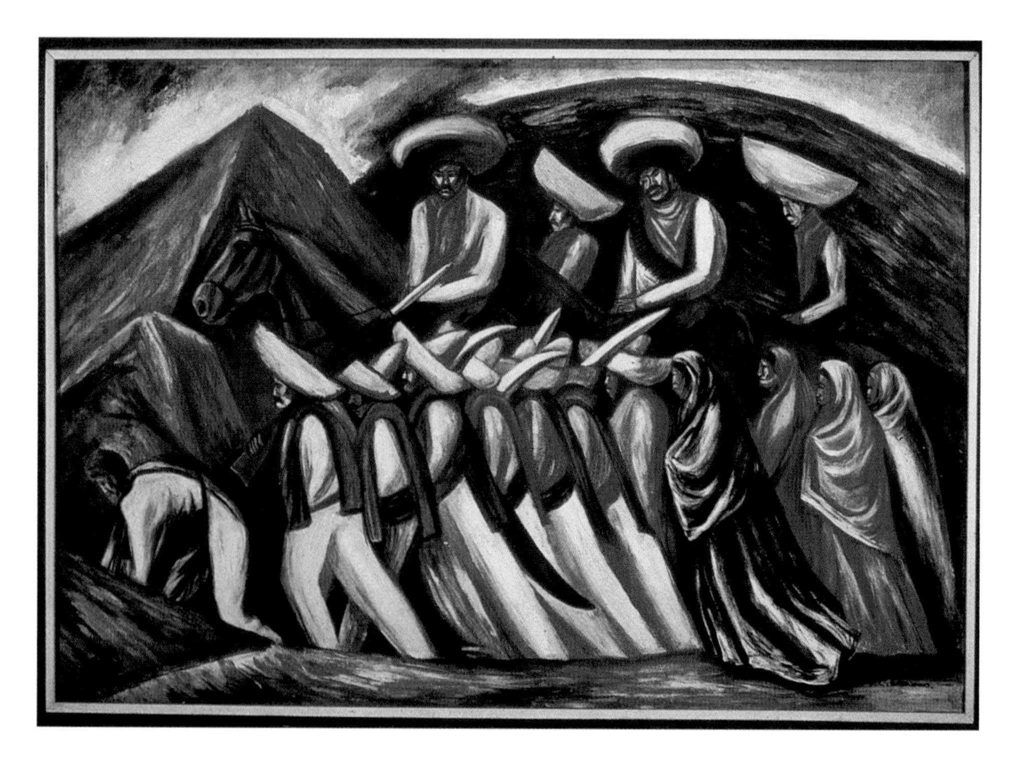

10.37 José Clemente Orozco, *Zapatistas*, date unknown. Oil on canvas. In this painting, the disciples of the leader, Zapata, are striving to improve the conditions of the underprivileged. This effort is seen in the thrusting figures. Private Collection/Index/Bridgeman Art Library. © Clemente V. Orozco.

the new synthesis of form in Post-Impressionist painting.

Maillol retained a classical sense of serenity while pioneering a simplification of figurative form similar to the goals of Cézanne and Seurat. He achieved sculptural monumentality by asserting the essential weight and mass of stone and bronze as sensuous volume. Maillol could accomplish this by breaking away from academic representations of human figures and using carefully exaggerated proportions (fig. 10.36).

Expressionism in the United States

The Expressionist style had adherents in the Americas as well as in Europe. The Great Depression of the 1930s influenced artists such as John Marin (1879–1953), Max Weber (1881–1961), and Ben Shahn (1898–1969), all of whom spent time in Paris either during World War I or shortly thereafter. They were affected by the two current styles of Fauvism and Cubism while in Paris. Social Realists like Ben Shahn returned home to face the Depression and make mournful and sometimes satirical comments on the American society of that time (see figs. 2.30 and 8.43). One of the earliest African American painters to be recognized, Jacob Lawrence (1917–2000), spoke in his art of the inequalities and injustices that blacks faced in America. Lawrence's style was Expressionist, but tempered by Cubism to make a more formal use of shallow space (see figs. 2.52, 4.24, 6.7, and 8.3).

It was also in this milieu that young experimental artists like Edward Hopper (1882–1967), Charles Burchfield (1893–1967), and Grant Wood (1892–1942)—among the best of the so-called Regionalists or Scene Painters—had to find their way (see figs. 8.24 and 4.24).

Expressionism in Mexico

During the 1920s and '30s, Mexico underwent an artistic renaissance. Many artists there found fruitful ground in an

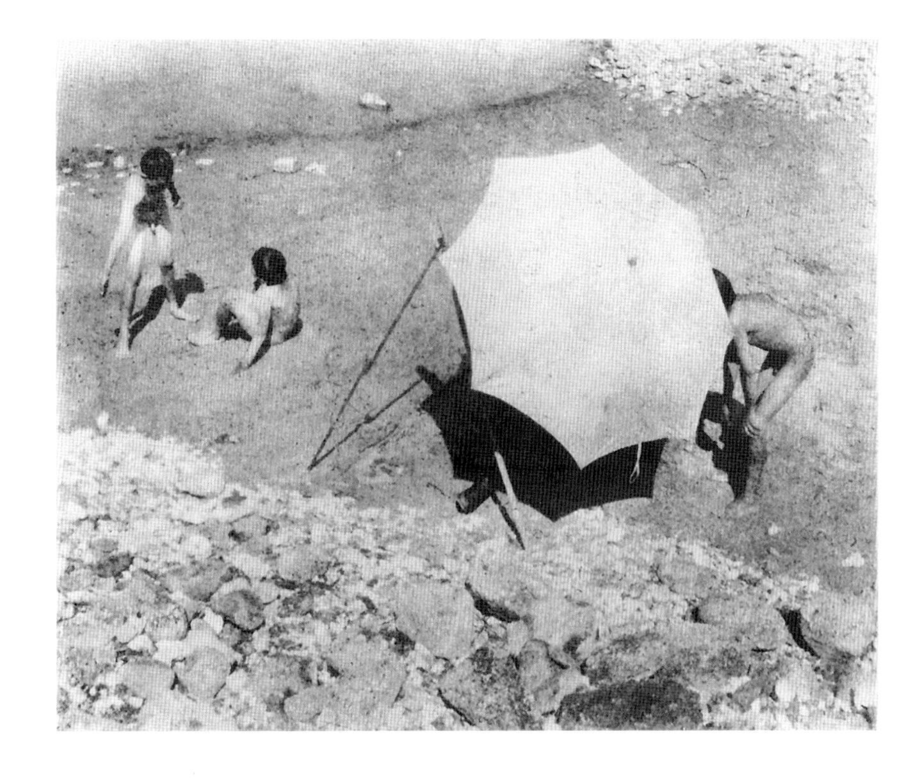

10.38 Heinrich Kuehn, *Der Malschirm* (*The Artist's Umbrella*), 1901. Hand-printed photogravure on heavy wove paper, 91½ × 11⅜ in. (23 × 28.9 cm). As late as 1910, the photographing of nudes in unusual settings was a rebellion against the vestiges of Victorian prudery. This, in itself, marks Kuehn as a modernist, but so does the use of a high-angled shot, which has the effect of flattening space. © Metropolitan Museum of Art, New York. The Alfred Stieglitz Collection, 1949. (49.55.193).

Expressionist style that identified with the problems of the Indian and mestizo (mixed) classes. José Clemente Orozco (1883–1949), whose art evolved during this period, became the greatest exponent of Expressionism in the Western Hemisphere. Inspired by the rapidly changing social order in Mexico, he produced work in a dark, tragic vision similar to that of Rouault in Europe (fig. 10.37).

Like the United States, Mexico also found its own brand of Social Realism in Diego Rivera (1886–1957), who painted government-sponsored murals about Mexican history influenced by Marxist doctrine. The paintings of Rivera's third wife, Frida Kahlo (1907–1954), also often consisted of politically pointed subjects with Marxist overtones, but in a semisurrealist/realist style (see figs. 2.2 and 7.33).

Color Photography and Other New Trends

In 1907, when the Lumière brothers made it commercially possible to create color images with the autochrome, photographers began to experiment. Although the process used in the autochromes—coating a plate with tiny grains of starch loaded with light spectrum colors—gave images with good color fidelity, some found the coarseness of these grains objectionable. Yet, interestingly, this graininess, in conjunction with the Pointillism of Seurat, was a major influence on the Fauve painters' method of working.

Another drawback to early experiments with color photography was the instability of the color dyes, which had a tendency to bleed into the layers of emulsion. In 1935, with Kodak's development of Kodachrome film, which left the dyes to the color process, more dependable and less grainy color images could be made. This film also made color film as simple to expose as black-and-white film, and it was soon being employed not only by photographers but also by movie-makers. With the introduction of the first 35-millimeter camera in 1925, the German Leica, a small versatile photographic instrument was made available. This type of camera soon became the favorite means for taking both black-and-white and color photographs. Eventually, newer color films increased the speed with which exposures could be made in weaker light, enabling cameras to stop fast action in color. Naturally, all these advancements led to the further growth of experimentation in photography, paralleling similar efforts in painting and sculpture to express a freedom from past ideas. Most professional photographers, however, continued using monochromatic photography, rather than color, and this remained the case until recent times. This was because of the more abstract quality of black-and-white images and the departure from ordinary appearances that they provide, not to mention the less reliable quality of color dyes used in color films and printing papers.

Painting and photography have had a long history of mutual influence, from Daguerre's first discovery in 1839 to the present day. We noted how the grainy texture of early autochromes influenced the Fauves; the German Expressionists were also indebted to photographers' experiments and contributed to them, too. Photography affected the New Objective portraits of painter Otto Dix, for example. Conversely, photographer Heinrich Kuehn (1866–1944) was influenced by the Expressionist painters to take unidealized shots of nude models in bright natural light, reminiscent of the Brücke artists (fig. 10.38).

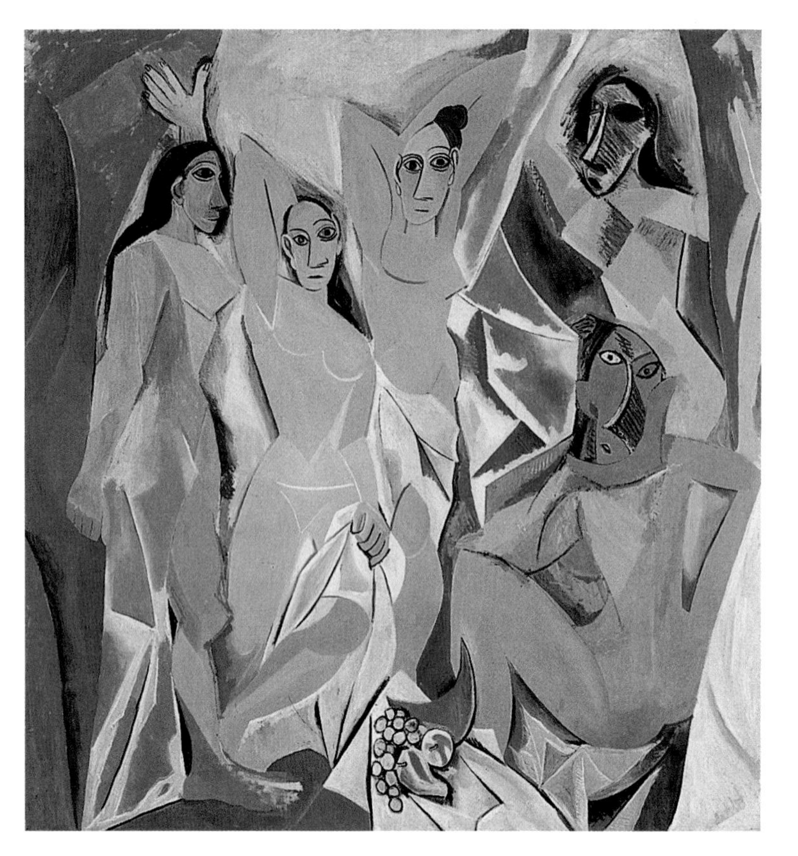

10.39 Pablo Picasso, *Les Demoiselles d'Avignon,* June–July 1907. Oil on canvas, 8 ft × 7 ft 8 in. (2.43 × 2.33 m). In this landmark painting, Picasso swept away practically all previous concepts of painting. This resulted, in part, from his exposure to African tribal sculpture. © 2005 Estate of Pablo Picasso/Artists Rights Society (ARS), New York. The Museum of Modern Art, New York, NY. U.S.A. Acquired through the Lillie P. Bliss Bequest. Digital image © The Museum of Modern Art/Licensed by SCALA/Art Resource, NY.

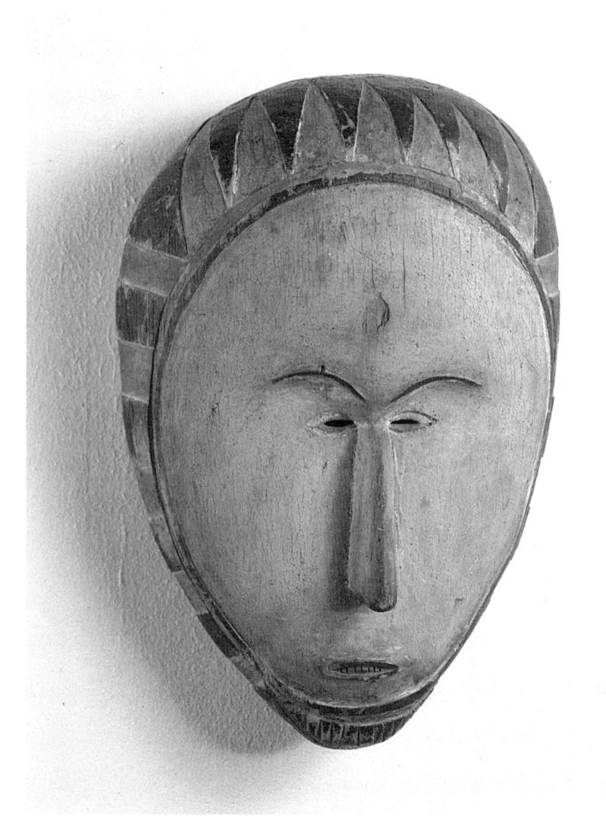

10.40 Fang tribal mask from Gabon, Africa. Painted wood, 19⅞ in. (48 cm) high. This mask is a typical example of African tribal arts that influenced so many of the early-twentieth-century artists such as Matisse, Modigliani, and Picasso. CNAC/MNAM/Dist. Réunion des Musées Nationaux/Art Resource, NY.

Cubism

Around 1906 in Paris, a new attitude toward the world emerged in the work of certain artists. Before Cézanne, European artists tended to see nature and objects in terms of material surfaces. Cézanne began a new trend by searching for a reality (the universal unvariables) that lay beneath these material things. He tried to observe and depict the basic structure of the world around him. This new way of seeing developed gradually over a period of about twenty-five years, paralleling the changes in science and photography. Cézanne stated, for instance, that the artist should seek the universal forms of nature in the cube, the cone, and the sphere. Artistic exploration founded directly on this concept evolved in the styles of certain Fauve Expressionists and finally resulted in a new approach to art, termed Cubism.

Among the most active of the young artists in the Fauve movement from 1903 to 1906 was the Spaniard Pablo Picasso (1881–1973) (see fig. 2.38). Because of his admiration for the work of Paul Cézanne and his desire to challenge Henri Matisse's leadership of the Fauves, Picasso began to look for new possibilities of form expression. He based his explorations on volumetric illusions and an analysis of spatial structure. Like Cézanne, Picasso had become dissatisfied with the contemporary emphasis on the external characteristics of objects and sought a method whereby he could express their internal structure. By 1907, in his painting *Les Demoiselles d'Avignon,* Picasso had begun to develop a style that showed the structure of objects in space by portraying many facets of them at the same time—a principle called **simultaneity** (fig. 10.39). Many of his ideas for this type of pictorial expression are traceable not only to the influence of Cézanne but also to the style characteristics found in such **primitive art** as archaic Greek sculpture and traditional African tribal sculpture. Compare the Fang tribal mask from Gabon, Africa (fig. 10.40), to the women's faces in Picasso's painting (see fig. 10.39), for example. In 1910–11, the sophistication of this style—called Analytical Cubism—culminated in such works as *Man with a Violin* (fig. 10.41; see also figs. 6.7 and 6.18 for Picasso's art after his Cubist period).

One of the most noticeable aspects of Analytical Cubist paintings by Picasso and his collaborator Georges Braque (1882–1963) is the cubelike rendering or geometric faceting of the people and objects they painted (see fig. 4.17). Another feature of these works is that different views from different positions in space—i.e., back, front, and high-angle views—are all superimposed simultaneously, thereby preserving a sense of the two-dimensional picture plane. By these methods, the Cubist artists, as well as their chief followers, tried to arrive at a more permanent order than that found in a standard representation of natural forms—an idea certainly stimulated by Cézanne. At the same time, Cubists set about reordering the traditional illusion of space in order to create a more stable form of spatial relationships, independent of the vagaries of light and the distorting effects of linear perspective. Between 1912 and 1914, Picasso was also experimenting with collages (influenced by Braque; see below) and constructions, which opened the way for a wide range of abstract sculptural forms.

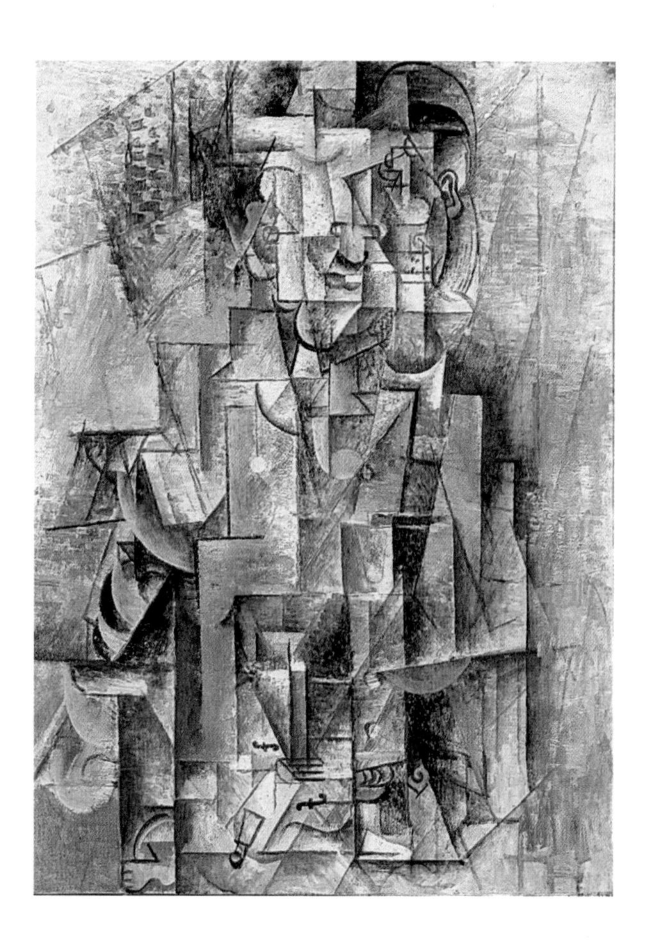

10.41 Pablo Picasso, *Man with a Violin*, 1911–12. Oil on canvas, 39⅜ × 29⅞ in. (10 × 7.59 m). The shapes in Picasso's facet-Cubist style are component planes coaxed forth from subject forms and freely rearranged to suit the artist's design concept. Some facets are retained in their original position, and certain elements of the figure are only fleetingly recognizable. Philadelphia Museum of Art, PA. Louise and Walter Arensberg Collection. 1950 © 2005 Estate of Pablo Picasso/Artists Rights Society (ARS), New York.

In his concern with arriving at a new aesthetic view of the structure of matter, Picasso often stripped away many aids to expression—in painting, complexity of color, for example. Moreover, in this process of reduction, he formulated an artistic language that put an end to the adherence to surface appearance that had been dominant since the time of the Renaissance. Paintings and sculptures began to emphasize image-making in its own right rather than as a means for imitating nature. Traditional renderings of natural appearances gave way to expressions of pure artistic form. This new value accorded to the art elements as builders of artistic form and expression in their own right required a new set of terms to explain what the artist was trying to achieve as the goal of art. "Abstract art" was the term principally used and applied to these new forms. Cubism, a semirepresentational art form, became the forerunner of all the later forms of abstraction, whether they were still partly representing (or symbolic of) nature or totally abstract. Thus, a gradual transformation occurred from the Post-Impressionists through the Cubists and the Futurists to the abstractions of Wassily Kandinsky and Piet Mondrian.

As the beginning of what became abstract art, Cubism was of major importance. It was introduced to the world not only in the works of Picasso but also in those of Georges Braque, a French artist who shared a studio with Picasso between 1910 and 1912. Braque added a uniquely expressive quality to the Cubist approach by attaching non-painted, textured materials to the surface of his canvases—a technique called *papier collé* (French for "pasted paper") or, more generally, collage (see fig. 6.7). But it is worth repeating that Louis Vauxcelles, while criticizing Braque's landscape exhibit of 1908, launched the name Cubism. However, despite his use of the new Cubist forms, Braque remained true to the tradition in French art of reason and charm in content. This contrasted with the more forceful, even brutal quality seen in Picasso's work. The sense of relaxed beauty in Braque's works executed during the peak of Cubist expression (1911–18) was engendered by his restrained manipulation of tasteful color and value patterns. The patterns were developed in terms of the finite volume of space, one of the chief Cubist idioms (see fig. 4.17 for Braque's

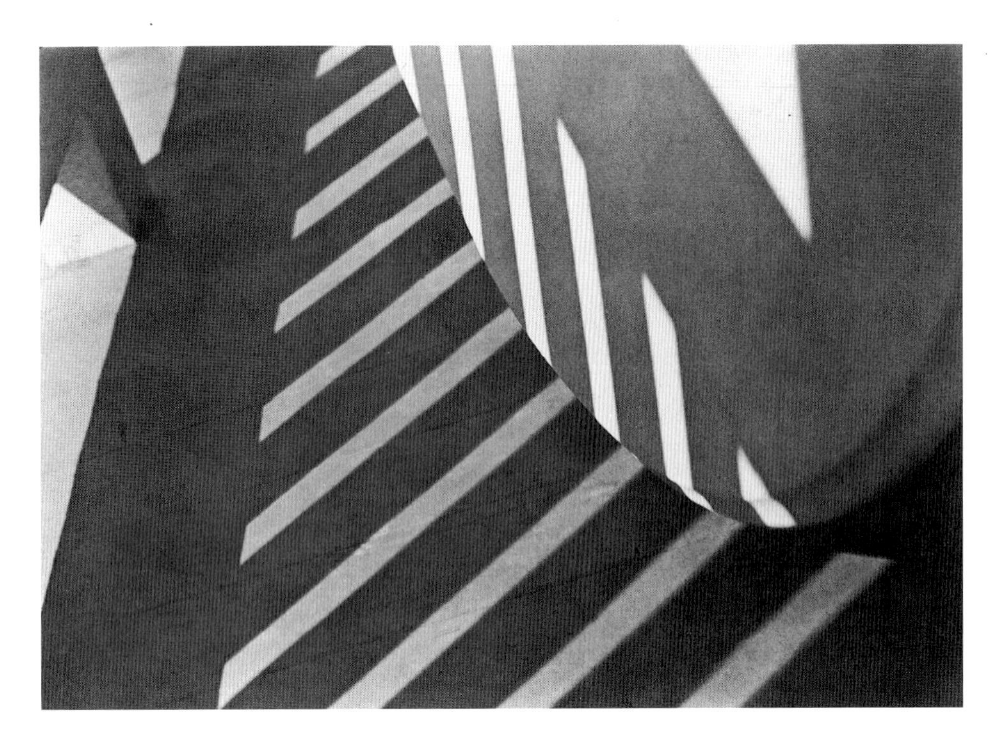

10.42 Paul Strand, *Abstraction, Porch Shadows, Twin Lakes, Conn.*, 1916. Satista print, 13 × 9 in. (33.2 × 23 cm). In this high-angle close-up, Paul Strand has created a handsome abstract shadow photograph with rich darks and brilliant whites. Art Institute of Chicago. The Alfred Stieglitz Collection, 1949.885. Photo © 1997 Art Institute of Chicago, all rights reserved. © 191 Aperture Foundation, Inc./Paul Strand Archive.

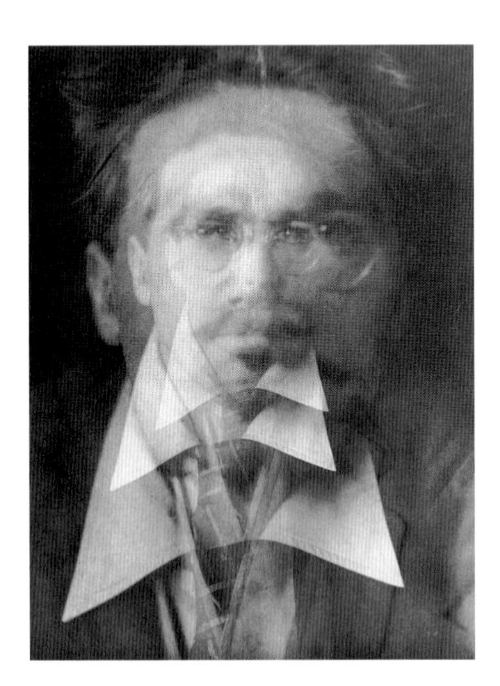

10.43 Alvin Langdon Coburn, *Portrait of Ezra Pound*, 1916. Photograph. Strongly influenced by Cubism, the diversely talented photographer Coburn produced this multiple image of the poet Ezra Pound. Courtesy George Eastman House, Rochester, NY.

painting after Cubism). Two other Cubists of note were Fernand Léger (1881–1955), another French artist, and Juan Gris (1887–1927), a Spaniard like Picasso. Léger and Gris developed individual form qualities within the Cubist idiom that set them apart as important creators in their own right. Inspired by the impact of industry on society, Léger took the machine as his central motif (see fig. 4.28). Gris, on the other hand, stayed close to nature, treating material masses as decorative shape patterns suggestive of recognizable objects, but without aiming to merely imitate appearances (see fig. 4.8).

There were also some photographers who worked within the Cubist idiom, such as Paul Strand (1890–1976) and the Englishman Alvin Langdon Coburn (1882–1966), who were members of Stieglitz's Photo-Secession group in New York (figs. 10.42 and 10.43). They either worked with close-up camera shots from above a subject or used overlapping multiple effects to produce decoratively formal photographic images. These photographers later explored more abstract imagery, with Coburn going through a Futurist phase as well.

Futurism

Futurism was a movement in art and literature that refashioned Cubism in light of its own desire to glorify the dynamic character of the twentieth-century machine age. Certain Italian artists training in Paris during the excitement caused by Cubism formed Futurism between 1909 and the end of World War I. Like Cubism, Futurism remained a submovement within the overall field of abstraction. Among the most important of these Italian artists was Gino Severini (1883–1966), who was instrumental in getting a French journal (*Figaro,* Paris) to publish the poet-critic Tommaso Marinetti's "Futurist Manifesto," which initiated the movement in 1909.

The most important artists in this movement, besides Severini (see fig. 8.53), were Giacomo Balla (1871–1958) and Umberto Boccioni (1882–1916). Balla was the oldest Futurist (fig. 10.44) and seems to have inspired the others to follow his style (fig. 10.45; see fig. 8.52). The Futurist painters tried to express the ceaseless activity of modern machinery, the speed and violence of contemporary life, and the psychological effects of this ferment on humanity by using sheaves of lines, faceted planes, and multiple brilliant colors. The activity and beauty of modern machinery at work appealed to them, as well as attempts to interpret contemporary incidents of violence—such as riots, strikes, and wars—and their effects for the future. These representations of forms in motion influenced many painters, including Marcel Duchamp (1887–1968). Futurism also counterinfluenced Cubism and had an impact on Russian Constructivism.

Arguably, however, the fervor of the Futurists does not really match up to their artistic contributions. They merely energized the somewhat static geometry of Cubism and brought back richer coloring. Perhaps the group's attention to the machine was its most important contribution, making other artists and the public more aware of the growing mechanization of society for good or bad. Again it appears that photography and the other graphic arts had a mutual impact on one another. In Italian Futurism, for example, the influence of early photographers such as the Englishman Eadweard Muybridge is implicit, not only on painters such as the Frenchman Marcel Duchamp (1887–1968) and the Italian Giacomo Balla (see figs. 8.51 and 8.52), but on Italian photographers like Anton Giulio Bragaglia (1889–1963) (fig. 10.46).

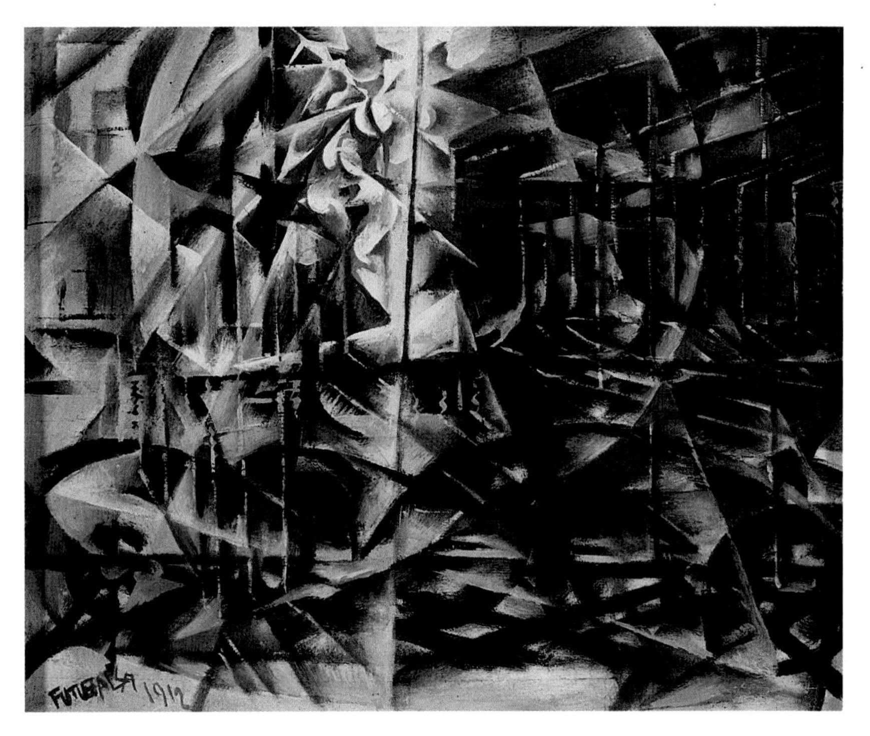

10.44 Giacomo Balla, *Speeding Automobile,* 1912. Oil on wood, 21⅞ × 27⅛ in. (55.6 × 68.9 cm). This artist's handling of the image of a speeding machine is characteristic of the Futurist idiom. Incorporated into the dynamic form is a sense of the hysteria, violence, and sheer tension in modern life. © 2005 Artists Rights Society (ARS), New York/SIAE, Rome. The Museum of Modern Art, New York, NY. U.S.A. Purchase. Digital image © The Museum of Modern Art/Licensed by SCALA/Art Resource, NY.

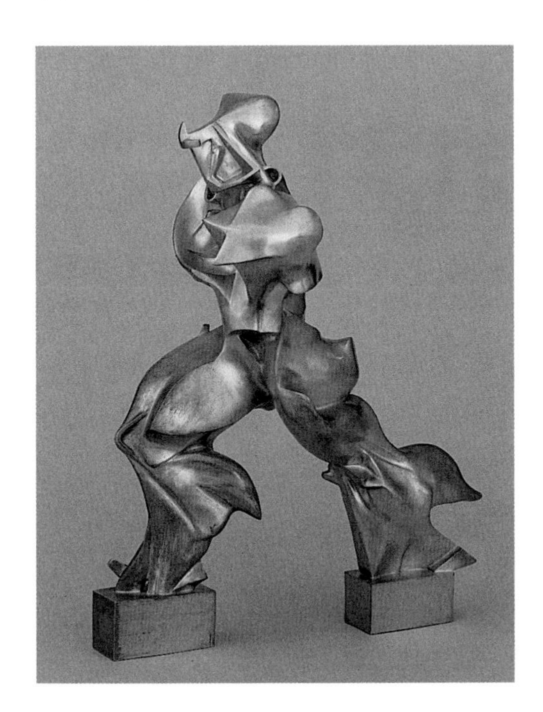

10.45 Umberto Boccioni, *Unique Forms of Continuity in Space,* 1913. Bronze (cast 1931), 43⅞ × 34⅞ × 15¾ in. (111.4 × 88.6 × 40 cm). Boccioni was a leading founder and member of the Futurist group. An accomplished painter and sculptor, he was preoccupied for much of his career with the dynamics of movement. Acquired through the Lillie P. Bliss Bequest. (231.1948) The Museum of Modern Art, New York, NY. U.S.A. Digital image © The Museum of Modern Art/Licensed by SCALA/Art Resource, NY.

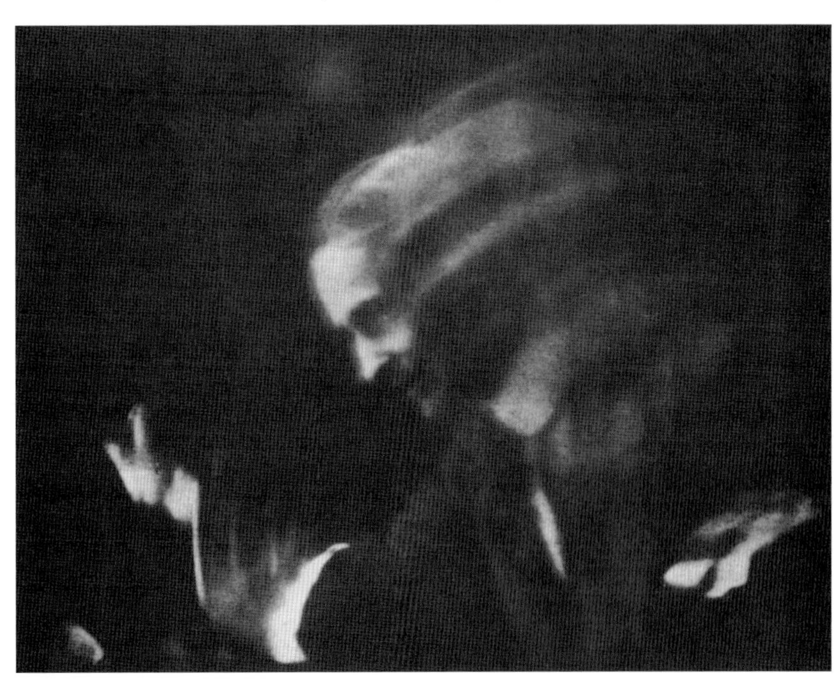

10.46 Anton Giulio Bragaglia, *Salutando* (*Greeting*), 1911. Fotodinamica. From Fotodinamismo Futurista Sedici Tavole, 1911. Within the milieu of Italian Futurist painting, Bragaglia made this time exposure of a man in the midst of greeting someone with a broad gesture. He coined the term *photo-dynamic* to describe pictures of this kind. Centro Studi Bragaglia, Rome. Collection of Antonella Vigiliani Bragaglia. © 2005 Artists Rights Society (ARS), New York, SIAE, Rome.

Abstract Art

Abstract Art in Europe

During the period from 1910 to 1918, the chief motivation of many artists throughout Europe was to completely eliminate nature from art. When abstract art began, however, the starting point still referred to visible matter, and nature was still the primary inspiration for the Fauves and Cubists, particularly Picasso. As artists ventured more and more toward totally nonrepresentational form, they took two main directions. Some, like the Russian Wassily Kandinsky (1866–1944) in his early abstractions, preferred an emotional, sensuous, expressionist quality (which later influenced American Abstract Expressionist painting). Perhaps Kandinsky's best works were these early abstractions with their powerful rhythms, biomorphic shapes, and sense of spontaneity (fig. 10.47). In 1919, however, after Kandinsky joined the German Bauhaus as a faculty member, his style became more geometrically abstract and more reserved in feeling.

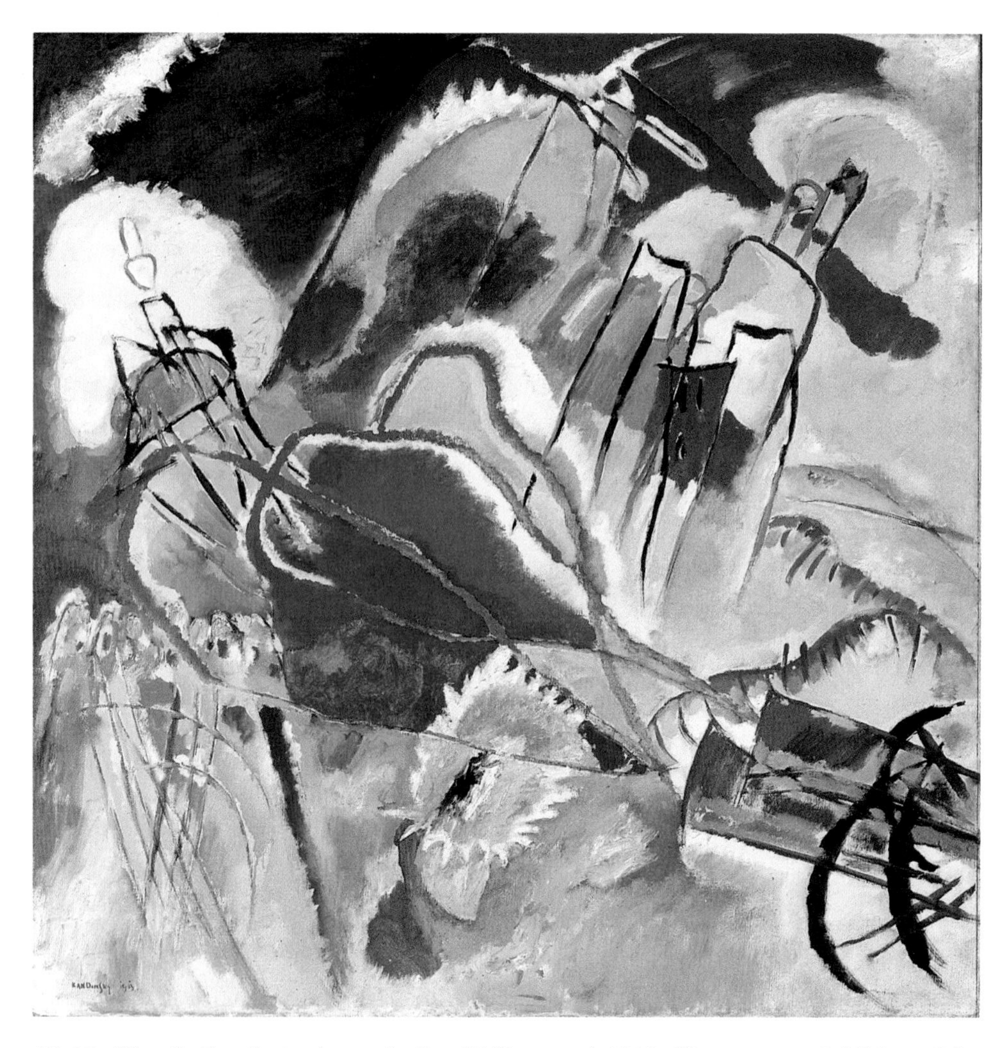

10.47 Wassily Kandinsky, *Improvisation 30 (Cannons),* 1913. Oil on canvas, 3 ft 7 in. × 3 ft 7¼ in. (1.09 × 1.10 m). About 1910, the Russian Wassily Kandinsky began to paint freely moving biomorphic shapes in rich combinations of hues. His characteristic early style can be seen in this illustration. Such an abstract form of expression was an attempt to show the artist's feelings about object surfaces rather than to describe their outward appearances. Art Institute of Chicago. Arthur Jerome Eddy Memorial Collection, 1931.511. Photo © 1998 Art Institute of Chicago. All rights reserved. © 2005 Artists Rights Society (ARS), New York, ADAGP, Paris.

Others, like Piet Mondrian (1872–1944), the leader of the Dutch Abstract group **De Stijl,** preferred Geometric Abstraction with its colder precision and reserve (which inspired Hard-Edge Abstraction in the United States later). He was the most representative exponent of Geometric Abstraction in the early stages of abstract art (fig. 10.48). While starting from nature like Kandinsky, Mondrian eventually dealt with the most basic elements of form; but, unlike Kandinsky, he purged his work of perceivable emotional qualities (see figs. 1.3–1.6). In such work, meaning or content is inherent in the precise arrangement of horizontal and vertical lines bounding rectilinear shapes of primary colors. This direction seemed sterile and shallow to other artists and critics when it first appeared. That it was, instead, momentous and rich in possibilities has been proven by its impact on hundreds of artists since then. Believers were soon finding metaphysical and mystical content in the purely optical harmonies of Geometric Abstraction, and the critics ridiculing Mondrian's art were soon in the minority.

The abstract art discussed so far in this chapter originated from nature. There is another aspect to abstraction called *nonobjective art,* in which the form originates from the artist's imagination. The difference between these two approaches to abstraction is of theoretical interest only, so today the term *abstract* is used for all nonfigurative and nonrepresentational art. The use of the elements of form, unencumbered by recognizable objects, became the basis for the work of hundreds of artists. As with other styles of art, a certain amount of abstract art lacks originality, of course, because although it is easy to produce synthetic (or academic) abstract art as an end in itself, this art may truly have no meaning. However, where abstraction is a genuine part of the creative process, great powers of thought and expression are required of the artist.

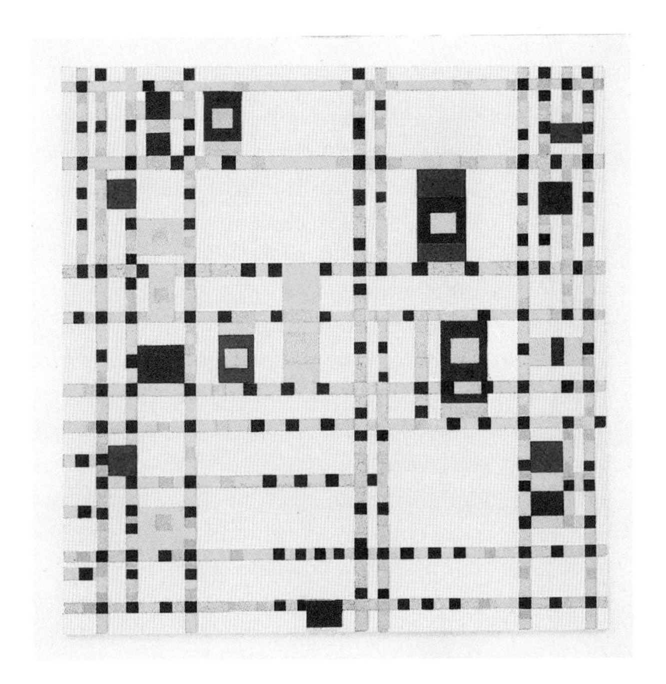

10.48 Piet Mondrian, *Broadway Boogie Woogie,* 1942–43. Oil on canvas, 50 × 50 in. (127 × 127 cm). Though some may consider Mondrian's style sterile, this work with its bright colors and sometimes unexpected shape placements probably reflects the artist's interest in popular music.

10.49 Kasimir Malevich, *White on White,* 1918. Oil on canvas, 31¼ × 31¼ in. (79.4 × 79.4 cm). The "suprematist" Malevich was possibly the first Geometric Abstract or nonobjective painter. He had begun with a black square drawn on a white ground in 1913. This later painting followed his earlier drawing, reversing the square to white on white.

Many elements of the twentieth-century world derived their character from the continuing influence of abstraction. Modern architects and designers readily assimilated abstract theories of form in buildings (the International Style of architecture), furniture, textiles, advertising, and machines, for example. The gap between fine art and art of a commercial or industrial nature gradually narrowed. This may be because abstract art developed out of an environment where the operation of the machine had become both an implicit and a conscious part of life. In a sense, the abstract artist created a machine-age aesthetic. From the late 1900s into the new millennium, artists have frequently sought a more humanized content, or expression, again.

The outstanding representatives of the nonobjective concept were the Russian **Constructivists,** artists who were part of a movement founded by Vladimir Tatlin between 1913 and 1922 devoted to Geometric Abstraction. Because Constructivism is primarily associated with three-dimensional spatial concepts, or sculpture, it is discussed in the section "Abstract Sculpture." There were Russian painters at the time with constructivist leanings worth mentioning, however. Principal among these was Kasimir Malevich (1878–1935), who called himself a Suprematist. In 1913 he exhibited a pencil drawing of a black square on a white ground. This appears to have been the first Geometric Abstract artwork (compare fig. 10.49).

In Weimar, Germany, the Bauhaus (an architectural training school) also favored Constructivism. Among the faculty, including painters and sculptors, was the abstract painter Joseph Albers (1888–1976), one of many who were forced to come to the United States with the closing of the Bauhaus by the Nazis in 1933 (see fig. 4.25).

Abstract Art in the United States

Abstract art was slow in coming to America. The New York Armory Show in 1913 revealed to American audiences for the first time many of the important avant-garde artists of Europe. Some of the Americans who were to create an American Abstract movement, out of which others would sprout, were also exhibited. Meanwhile, between 1905 and 1917, primarily under the aegis of Alfred Stieglitz, the New York–based 291 Fifth Avenue gallery became a meeting place for American and international pioneers of avant-garde photography, painting, and sculpture. Among the

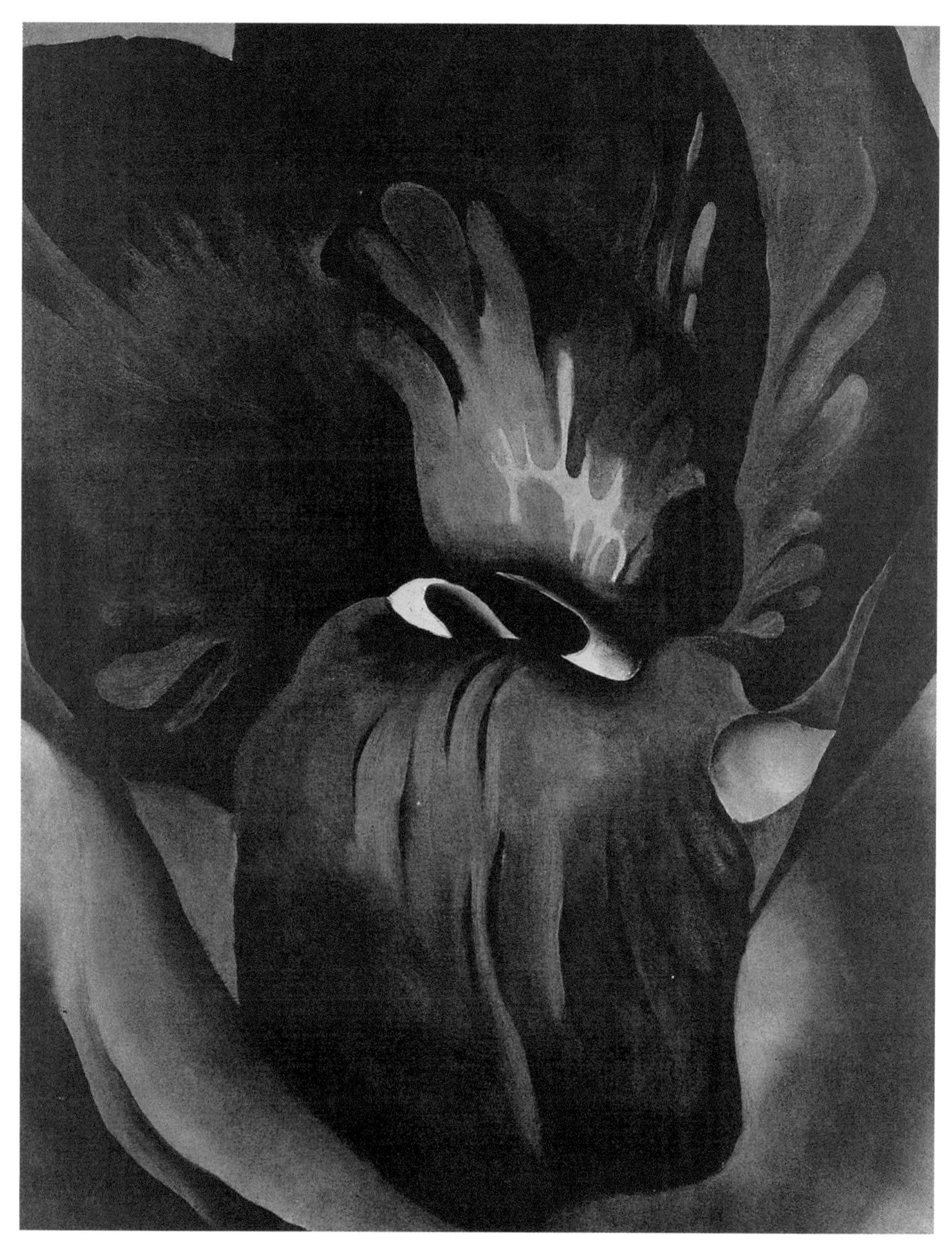

10.50 Georgia O'Keeffe, *Canna Red and Orange,* 1922. Oil on canvas, 10 × 16 in. (50.8 × 40.6 cm). Inspired by light, this "Precisionist" artist stripped away most features of reality to create her colorful, semi-abstract images. Private Foundation.

European painters and sculptors introduced by the gallery were Cézanne, Rodin, Matisse, Toulouse-Lautrec, Constantin Brancusi, Picasso, and Marcel Duchamp, along with American artists such as John Marin and Georgia O'Keeffe (whom Stieglitz married). These events encouraged the earliest experiments of Americans with abstraction. Shortly after World War I, a coterie of pioneer abstractionists appeared. Some, like Marin, Weber, and Burchfield, remained close to Expressionism (see figs. 8.43 and 4.24); others, called the Precisionists, kept a representational form while stripping away detail so that the impact of their forms is nearly abstract. The founders and principal artists in the group include Georgia O'Keeffe (1887–1986) and Charles Sheeler (1883–1965). O'Keeffe and Sheeler both felt the influence of photography. While O'Keeffe painted buildings, flowers, and cow skulls in a semi-abstract manner that was notable for its clarity, poise, and harmony, Sheeler concentrated mainly on different kinds of buildings in a somewhat similar style (fig. 10.50; see figs. 1.11, 4.26, and 8.25).

It took a while longer before total abstraction gathered momentum in the United States, evolving in the 1930s but not maturing until the 1940s. European emigré artists were an important influence in this development. Most outstanding among these artists were Hans Hofmann (1880–1966) and Joseph Albers. Albers was active at the Bauhaus before coming to the United States, and Hofmann taught in his own school in Germany before leaving for the United States in the 1930s. Hofmann's teaching in this country and his loose, abstract, brilliantly colorful style helped establish the **Abstract Expressionist** style (see fig. 8.44). Albers was a student and teacher at the Bauhaus before he came to America, where he became an important teacher and early exponent of Bauhaus ideas. He was also a Constructivist. His signature work experiments with color relations within a constructivist grid (see fig. 4.25).

Abstract Sculpture

Picasso's Cubist collages and constructions of 1912–14 opened the way for a wide range of abstract sculptural forms. The most important early abstract sculptor was the Franco-Romanian Constantin Brancusi (1867–1957). As early as 1913, he chose to free sculpture from mere representation. Such works as the *Bird in Space* of 1928 reveal an effective and sensuous charm through their flowing, geometrical poise and emphasis on beautifully finished materials. Brancusi usually preferred to work in a semi-abstract mode but always considered the shape, texture, and handling of materials to be more significant than the representation of subject (fig. 10.51).

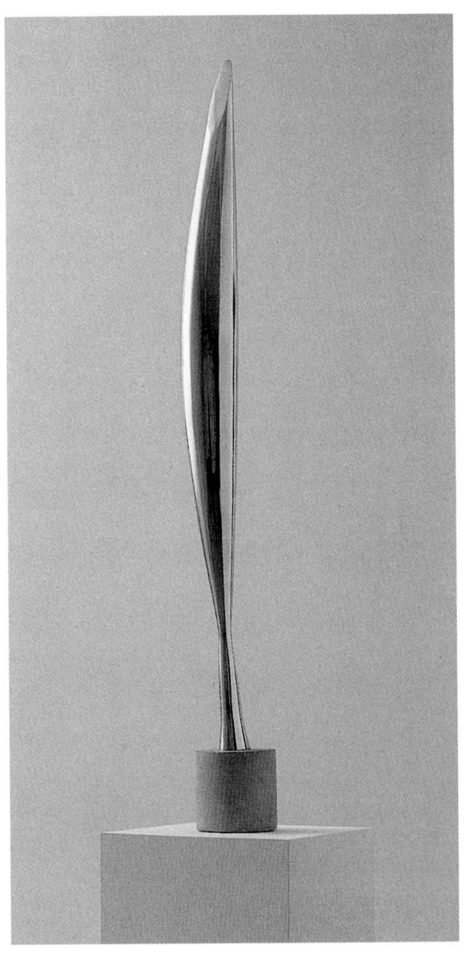

10.51 Constantin Brancusi, *Bird in Space,* 1928. Bronze (unique cast), 54 × 8½ × 6½ in. (137.2 × 21.6 × 16.5 cm). Brancusi abstracted down to essential forms and showed great concern for the properties of his medium. © 2005 Artists Rights Society (ARS), New York/ADGP, Paris. The Museum of Modern Art, New York, NY. U.S.A. Given anonymously. Digital image © The Museum of Modern Art/Licensed by SCALA/Art Resource, NY.

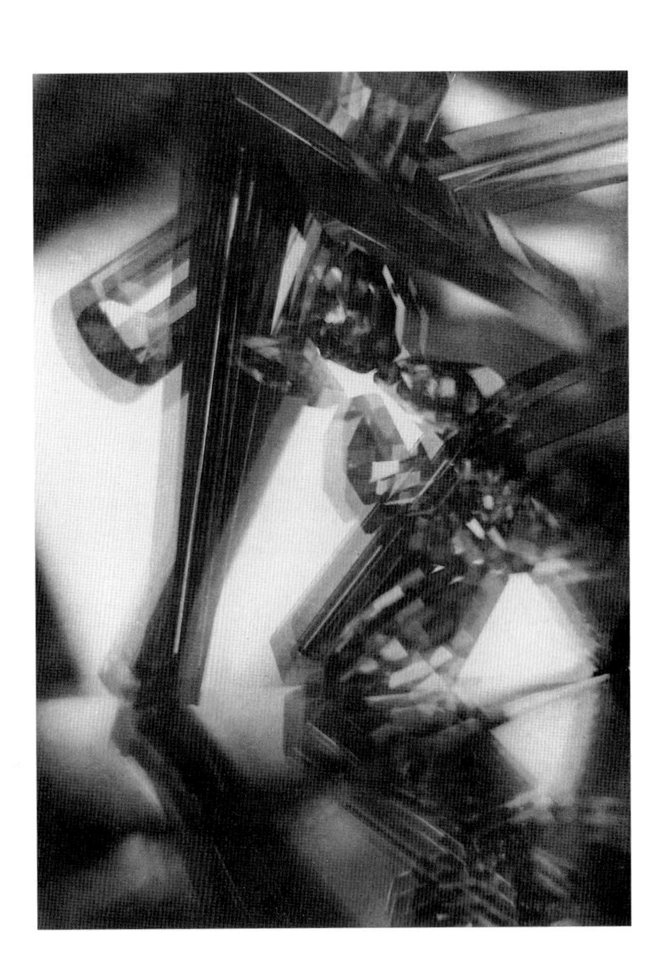

10.52 Alvin Langdon Coburn, *Vortograph #1,* 1917. Gelatin silver print, 7⅞ × 5¾ in. (20 × 14.6 cm). As was already evident in *Portrait of Ezra Pound* (fig. 10.43), before coming to his pure-abstract "vortographs" Coburn had invented a method of recording multiple images of people. In the vortographs, the image was recorded from the manifold refractions of objects from three mirrors, which were arranged in an open triangle around the objects. Gift of the photographer. The Museum of Modern Art, New York, NY. U.S.A. Digital image © The Museum of Modern Art/ Licensed by SCALA/Art Resource, NY.

Another pioneer Abstract sculptor, the Russian-born Alexander Archipenko (1887–1964), like Brancusi, belonged to the so-called School of Paris during the Cubist period of Picasso and Braque. His significant contribution was the use of negative space (the void) in sculpture, as in *Woman Doing Her Hair* (in which a hollow replaces the face) (see fig. 9.23). Archipenko also explored the use of new materials and technology, occasionally incorporating machine-made parts into his work.

The same Cubist intellectual and artistic ferment that led Archipenko to explore human-made materials and Brancusi to pioneer the use of power tools also led the Russian brothers Naum Gabo (1890–1977) and Antoine Pevsner (1882–1962) to develop their important Constructivist concepts. The Constructivist movement, although founded by Vladimir Tatlin, is most closely associated with these brothers due to their proclamation in a 1920s manifesto that total abstraction was the new realism in art. Gabo was the more exciting of the two, inventing both nonobjective and nonvolumetric forms (three-dimensional forms that do not enclose space but interact with it). Pevsner worked with solid masses, nearer to sculpture of a traditional kind. The common denominator in the work of all Abstract sculptors during the period of 1900–30 was an approach that emphasized materials and blurred the division between the fine arts and the functional arts. This was essentially the point of view held by both the Constructivists and the Bauhaus movement.

Abstract and Realist Photography

Abstract art was also making its influence felt in the experimental work of photographers. So photography, too, began to be freed from its former role as a recorder of reality and to explore a whole new language of patterned design. We saw this process beginning to some extent with photographers inspired or stimulated by Cubist and Futurist painting, such as Paul Strand (see fig. 10.42) and Alvin Langdon Coburn (see fig. 10.43). These artist-photographers had been determined to work in the Realist or Straight tradition without manipulating focus, negatives, or the process of development. Coburn's image in figure 10.52 illustrates how he

10.53 Alfred Stieglitz, *Equivalent*, 1929. Chloride print, 3⅝ × 4⅝ in. (9.2 × 11.6 cm). Stieglitz reacted to the criticism that he could only create powerful portraits by producing completely straight abstract images of cloud patterns, anticipating Abstract Expressionist painting of the 1940s. Art Institute of Chicago. The Alfred Stieglitz Collection, 1949.791. Photo © Art Institute of Chicago. All rights reserved.

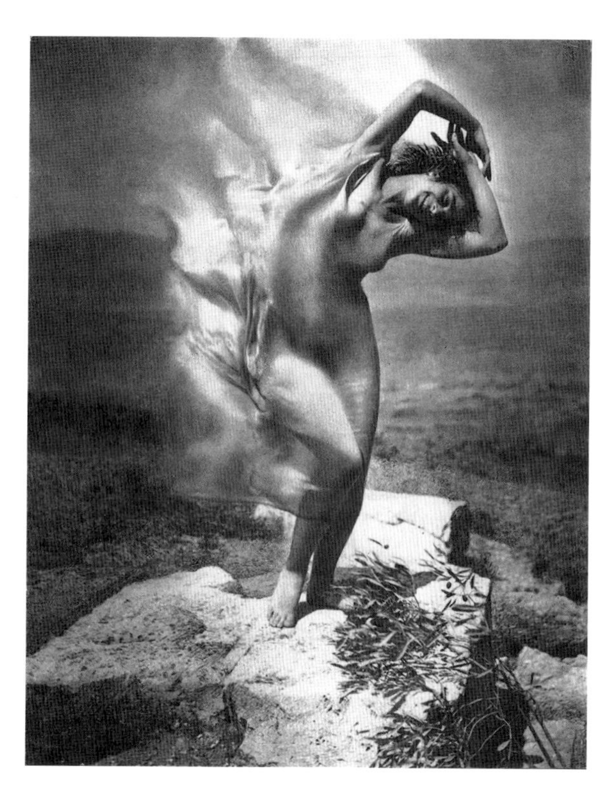

10.54 Edward Steichen, *Wind Fire (Thérèse Duncan)*, 1921. Gelatin silver print, 16 9/16 × 13⅝ in. (42 × 34.6 cm). This magnificent portrait of the dancer Thérèse Duncan, daughter of Isadora Duncan, is one artist's tribute to another. Steichen, in Athens to photograph Isadora's dance troupe, wrote about the garments flickering like flames in the wind when he took this photograph. Photo courtesy of George Eastman House. Reprinted with permission of Joanna T. Steichen.

achieved his more abstract manner by inventing a system of multiple, three-mirror image reflections of his subjects. Under the backing of Stieglitz, we have also seen how European and American artists were often first exhibited in this country at 291 Fifth Ave., New York. Among the earliest group of photographers exhibited at 291 were Edward Steichen, A. L. Coburn, and Stieglitz's protégé Paul Strand. In the early 1930s, Edward Weston, Imogen Cunningham, Ansel Adams, and others were added to these early exhibitors. The exhibits of these photographers were significant in gaining respect for photography; it could no longer be dismissed as not being an art form. At the same time, American photographers were far more respected in Europe than were American artists working in other media. They seemed to be more inventive than their European counterparts and often took the prizes in photographic exhibits during the first two decades of the twentieth century.

Despite some lingering Pictorialism, Stieglitz had become an exponent of Straight (or Realist) photography. In later years, probably under the influence of his wife, Georgia O'Keeffe (see fig. 10.50), Stieglitz presented some cloud-pattern photographs that were very abstract and evocative, predicting American Abstract Expressionist painting in the 1940s. They were titled *Songs of the Sky*, but Stieglitz called them Equivalents (fig. 10.53), intended to be seen not merely as clouds alone but as gateways to profound emotional experiences.

Edward Steichen, Stieglitz's ingenious compatriot, came to the United States in 1880. He helped form 291 and promoted the introduction of avante-garde painting and sculpture into the United States. A Pictorialist by persuasion, under Stieglitz's influence and due to his experiences as an aerial photographer during World War I Steichen became a Straight photographer. With the closing of 291 in 1917, he turned to fashion photography, becoming chief photographer for *Vogue* and *Vanity Fair*. Steichen again served in World War II as director of the U.S. Navy's Photographic Institute. After the war, he became head of photography at the Museum of Modern Art in New York, where he mounted the famous international photographic exhibit *The Family of Man* in 1955. Steichen was also an accomplished painter (fig. 10.54).

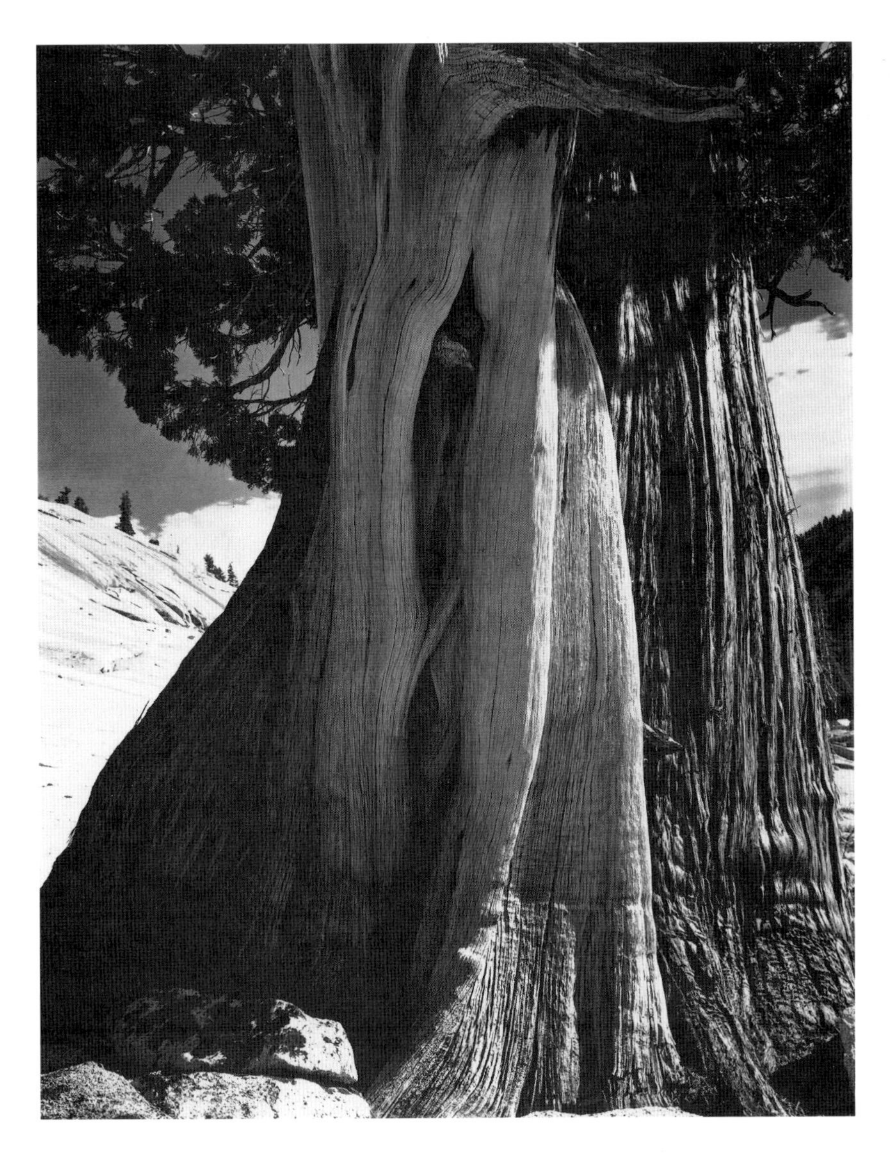

10.55 Edward Weston, *Juniper, Lake Tenaya,* 1937 (Yosemite National Park). Gelatin silver print. The hypnotic play of dark and light values and the contrast between the textures of bark, stone, and clouds are indicative of Weston's artistic accomplishments. © 1981 Center for Creative Photography, Arizona Board of Regents.

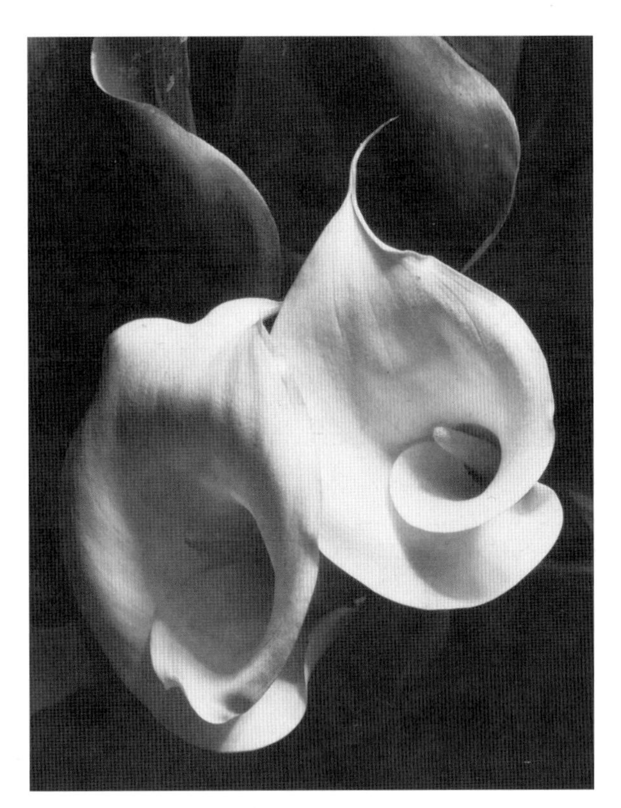

10.56 Imogen Cunningham, *Two Callas,* c. 1929. Photograph. As a member of the F-64 group of western photographers, Cunningham created precisionist flowers in photography similar to the way that O'Keeffe crafted them in paintings. © The Imogen Cunningham Trust.

Paul Strand, Stieglitz's young protégé, was a practitioner of Straight photography. He was noted for his studies of ordinary New Yorkers, landscapes, and other natural objects that became abstract in handling. Like Steichen, he served during World War II, as an X-ray technician for a medical team. After the war, Strand made movies for a time before returning to photography to create an album of photographs on life and scenery in Mexico (see fig. 10.42).

In 1932 a photographic group calling themselves F-64, because they used the smallest aperture (the f-64) to provide good depth of field, was established in the western United States. Charter members of the group were Edward Weston (1886–1958), Imogen Cunningham (1883–1976), and Ansel Adams (1902–1984). Edward Weston was born in Illinois, but he moved to California, where he opened a studio and achieved international fame for his soft-focused, Pictorialist portraits of Hollywood personalities. Later, after meeting Stieglitz and winning a Guggenheim fellowship, Weston became noted for his beautifully detailed studies of nudes, nature, and structures typical of "the American scene" (fig. 10.55). In this respect, he shared the preoccupations of Regionalist painters like Grant Wood. After soft-focused beginnings, Imogen Cunningham also changed to Realist photography. She produced enlarged studies of plants with precisionist lighting and details that are the counterpart in photography of Georgia O'Keeffe's floral studies in painting (fig. 10.56; see also fig. 10.50).

Another photographer carrying on the Stieglitz credo after World War II was Ansel Adams. Like the other members of F-64, Adams changed from earlier Pictorialist imagery to Straight and was influenced by Paul Strand. By 1936, Adams had become so well known for his scenes of the West with their dramatic dawn or sunset lighting that Stieglitz exhibited his work at the American Place, a new gallery opened to replace the earlier 291 (see fig. 1.23). Adams was also important as a teacher, as a publisher of technical books (particularly for his "zonal system," used to translate the values of nature to those of the photographic image), and for starting college photography departments. Adams also worked for periods as a commercial photographer and served as an advisor to the Polaroid Company.

Fantastic Art

Fantasy was the third major direction of twentieth-century art. Fantasy as a trend began to be apparent in about 1914, at the beginning of World War I, although it has always been an undercurrent in the human psyche. Its two important directions, or styles, were **Dadaism** (1916–23) and Surrealism (1924–c. 1940). The focus on fantasy by writers, poets, and artists at this time was impelled by the war, its horrors, and a gathering sense of alienation from society in an age of technology. These artists felt that individual freedoms might actually be destroyed and that the machine cult in Futurism and abstract art promoted war and alienation and thus needed countering. As a kind of antidote, they began to extol the emotional, intuitive side of creativity. From World War I through the mid-1920s, Picasso too set an example by his interest in Fantastic directions. Moving away from the monumental style of early Cubism, he made experiments that were to become a partial basis for Dadaism and Surrealism. A suggestion of this direction in Picasso's art can be found in the example from 1914 (fig. 10.57). The **Fantastic** movement thus widened the range of early twentieth-century experimentation, and Picasso continued to lead and influence many artists.

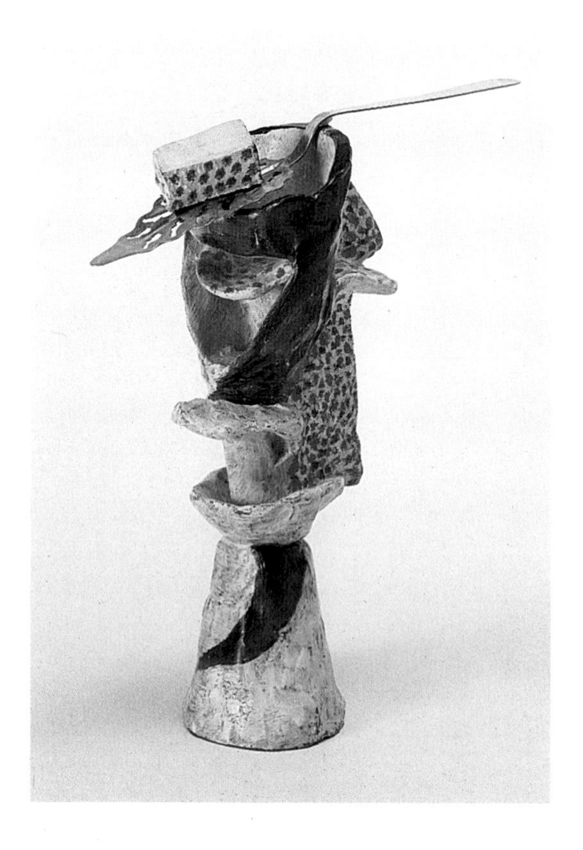

10.57 Pablo Picasso, *Glass of Absinth*, spring 1914. Painted bronze with absinth spoon, 8½ × 6½ × 3⅜ in. (21.6 × 16.4 × 8.5 cm); diameter at base, 2½ in. (6.4 cm). In constructions such as this, which were produced during the same period as his Cubist paintings, Picasso opened the door for many developments in the plastic arts, such as assemblage and "found" art.

Dadaism

Dadaism was the earliest style of Fantastic art to appear in the 1900s. The terrible bloodshed and destruction of World War I fostered both disillusionment with the role of reason and fascination with the irrational side of human behavior. Dada was founded in Zurich, in neutral Switzerland, in 1916 by Tristan Tzara, a Romanian poet, and the sculptor Jean Hans Arp (1887–1966), among other poets, writers, artists, and entertainers. There this motley group met in the Café Voltaire and developed their antiwar, anti-aesthetic multimedia program to undermine traditional mores by deriding all of society's most firmly held beliefs. All that had formerly been thought to be important, noble, or beautiful in the visual and literary arts was openly and playfully mocked and ironically protested against in public exhibits. The name Dada, ostensibly chosen at random from a French language dictionary, meant either "hobby horse" or one of a baby's earliest sounds. In principle, although there was no limit to the disorder that might be unleashed on painting, poetry, and general social behavior, what Dada really accomplished was to open modern art to a new freedom of humorous expression and creative imagination. The Dada movement lasted until about 1923 in Europe and the United States, when it formed the foundation for the Surrealist movement.

Artists like Marcel Duchamp (1887–1968) and Max Ernst (1891–1976) fashioned machinelike forms that depicted humans as unthinking robots, by way of deriding the machine-age aesthetic behind abstract art. Later, they created biomorphic images that discredited Kandinsky's romanticized abstract art (fig. 10.58; see fig. 10.47). Their inventions intended disrespect toward all the

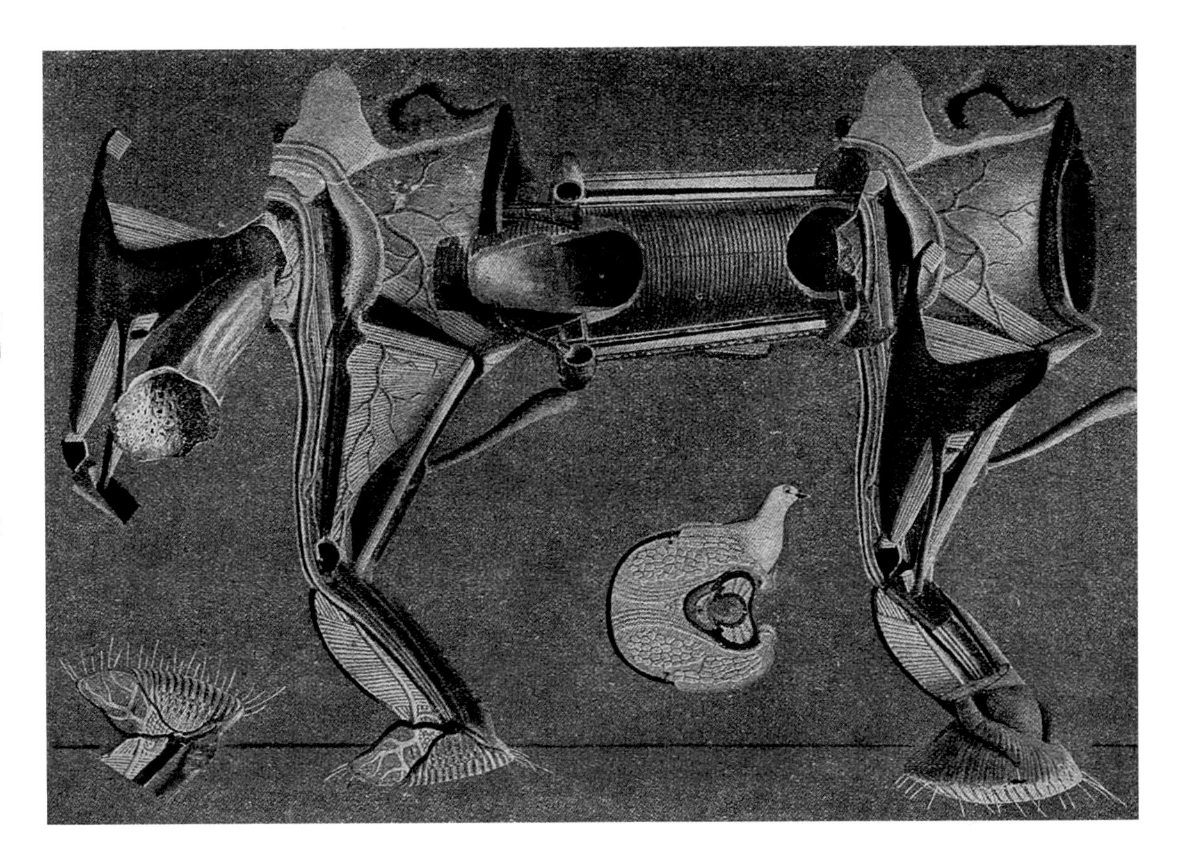

10.58 Max Ernst, *The Horse, He's Sick,* 1920. Pasted photoengraving and pencil on paper, 5¾ × 8½ in. (14.6 × 21.6 cm). As part of the Dadaists' debunking of all twentieth-century art forms, a natural organism is here turned into a mechanical absurdity. At the same time, the use of pasted photoengravings is a nonsensical twist of the collage technique first invented by Braque.

other relatively new art forms, such as Expressionism, Cubism, Futurism, and Abstraction, and to shock a public already discomfited by that visual revolution. Marcel Duchamp, one of the most complex and intelligent of the Dadaists, was already well known for his Futurist *Nude Descending a Staircase, No. 2* (see fig. 8.51). He established a form of Dada that was to have an impact on the rest of the century by pioneering "ready-mades" or "found art," as illustrated by *Bicycle Wheel* (fig. 10.59). In this form of Dadaism, commonplace items were given an "artistic" value when they began to be exhibited and were bought by museums and collectors, even though they were intended to satirize all conventional aesthetic values and laugh them out of existence.

Dada, while thus providing its adherents with an intellectual license to attack the old social and artistic order, had a different significance for many succeeding aspects of twentieth-century art.

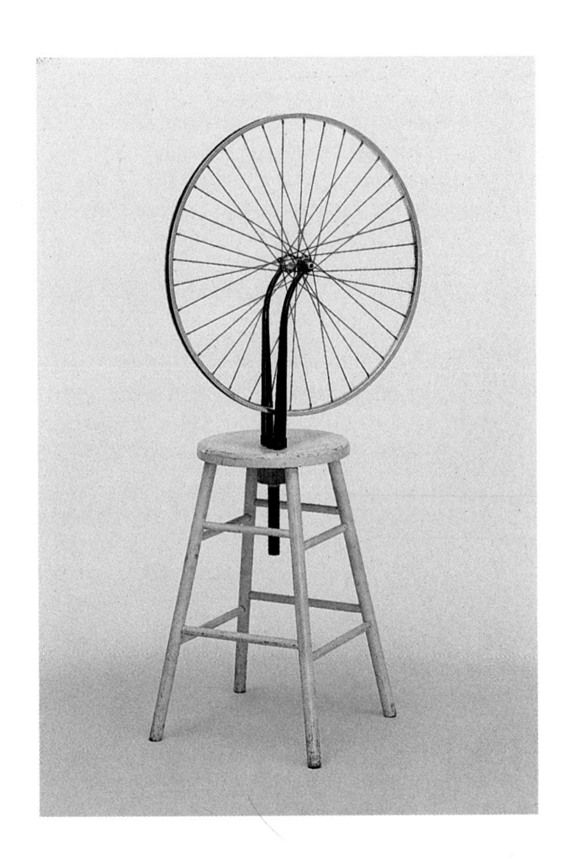

10.59 Marcel Duchamp, *Bicycle Wheel,* 1951 (third version, after lost original of 1913). Assemblage, metal wheel, 25½ in. (63.8 cm) in diameter, mounted on painted wood stool 23¾ in. (60.2 cm) high; overall, 50½ × 25½ × 16⅝ in. (128.3 × 63.8 × 42 cm). Duchamp was one of the most complex and inventive of the Dadaists. After having become disillusioned with Cubism and Futurism, he was forever questioning the aesthetic viability of art. With this piece he gave birth in 1913 to the concept of "ready-made" art, which was to be a profound influence.

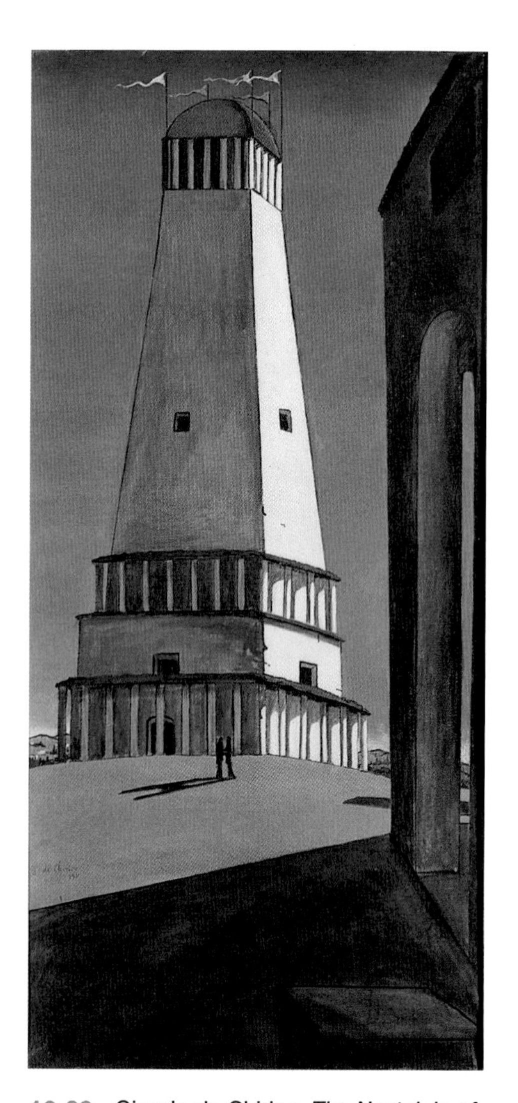

10.60 Giorgio de Chirico, ***The Nostalgia of the Infinite,*** **1913–14? (date on painting is 1911). Oil on canvas, 53¼ × 25½ in. (135.2 × 64.8 cm).** Giorgio de Chirico often used shadow effects, strong contrasts of value, and stark shapes to enhance the lonely, timeless nostalgia that is so much a part of his poetic expression. © ARS, NY. Purchase. (87.1936) The Museum of Modern Art, New York, NY. U.S.A. Digital image © The Museum of Modern Art/Licensed by SCALA/Art Resource, NY.

While the annoying side of Dada originally created a backlash among critics and the public against modern art, this increase in attention eventually gave opportunity for Dada's "inner message" to become more understandable. Dada's main value today is historical, because it was the principal source of Surrealism and a liberator of expressive freedom.

Individual Fantasists

Fantasy was a general tendency in western European art during the early 1900s, as well as in the paintings of certain artists who were not part of the Dada or Surrealist movements. The Italian painter Giorgio de Chirico (1888–1978), between 1909 and 1915, for example, painted melancholy, vaguely classic, shadowed plazas (fig. 10.60), often containing strangely incongruous imagery. These silent city squares inhabited by vestiges of an unknown people seem to be comments on the modern world. Their quiet enchantment also evokes a certain nostalgia for a mysterious past. The dreamlike paintings of the Surrealists seem to owe at least part of their origin to de Chirico.

The Swiss artist Paul Klee (1879–1940), who was strongly influenced by children's art, created an idiom using witty, abstract imagery based on Expressionism and Cubism. His work pokes gentle but penetrating fun at the cult of the machine and smiles shyly at human pretensions. Klee seems to imply that there is more to intuitive perception than our practicality wants us to believe (fig. 10.61).

Marc Chagall (1887–1985) was Russian born but a resident of Paris for

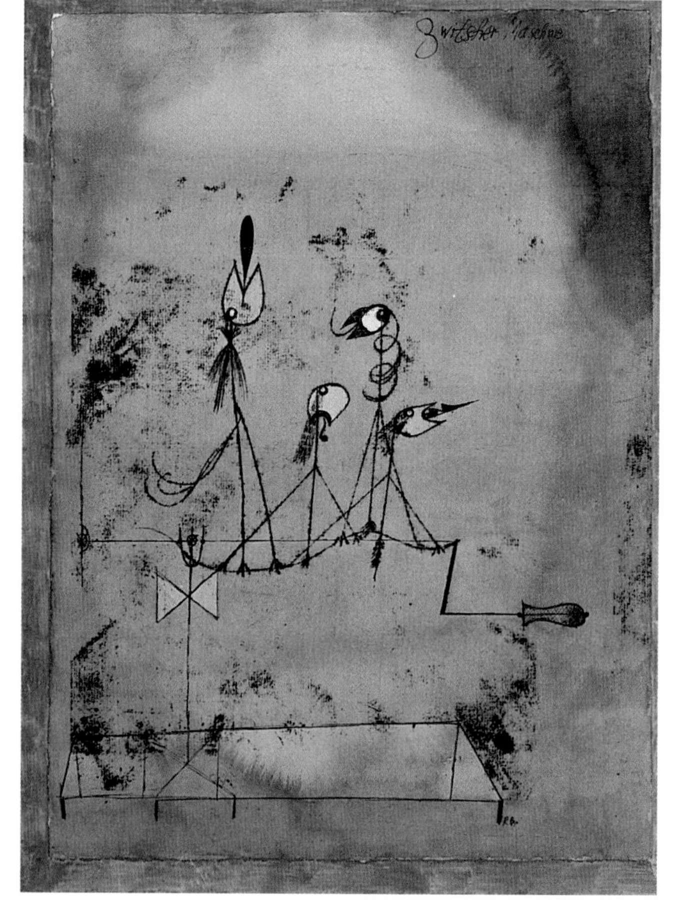

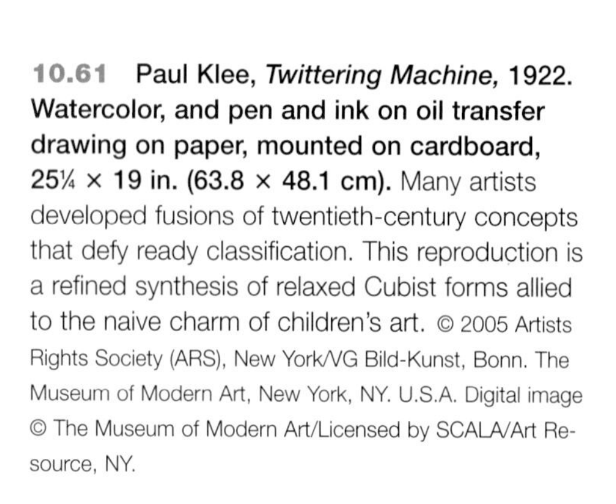

10.61 Paul Klee, ***Twittering Machine,*** **1922. Watercolor, and pen and ink on oil transfer drawing on paper, mounted on cardboard, 25¼ × 19 in. (63.8 × 48.1 cm).** Many artists developed fusions of twentieth-century concepts that defy ready classification. This reproduction is a refined synthesis of relaxed Cubist forms allied to the naive charm of children's art. © 2005 Artists Rights Society (ARS), New York/VG Bild-Kunst, Bonn. The Museum of Modern Art, New York, NY. U.S.A. Digital image © The Museum of Modern Art/Licensed by SCALA/Art Resource, NY.

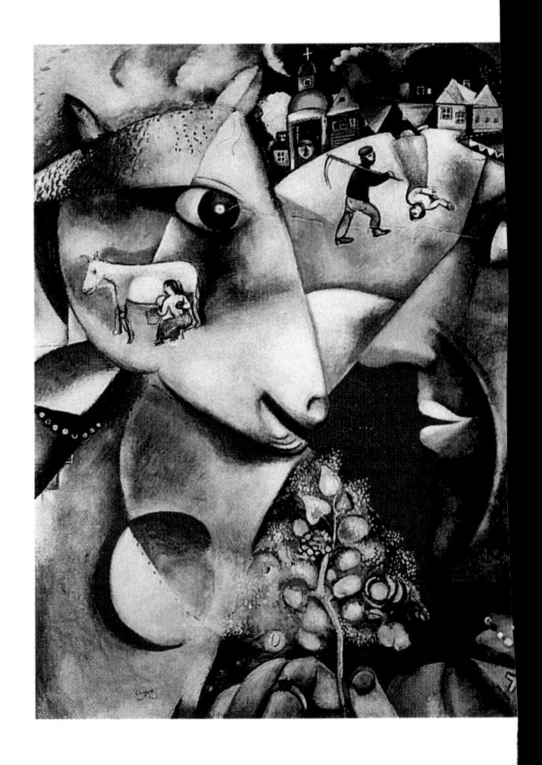

a time before moving to the United States during World War II. While still in Russia, Chagall worked in an Expressionist manner, but his life in France brought him within the sphere of Cubism. His style gradually became more dreamlike as he merged Expressionist with Cubist effects to create a fantasy world of warmth and humanity. Floating people, often loving couples, reveal Chagall's romantic, poetic soul (fig. 10.62).

Surrealist Painting

Primarily a literary movement, Surrealism was introduced in 1924 by the French writer and former Dadaist André Breton (1896–1966), when he published the first of three manifestos. As a style it emerged from the art of the Dadaists, while its theories, as set forth by Breton, became a way of life for its members. With the end of World War I came a semblance of stability, and the public became complacent about the ills of modern society. The Surrealists reacted to this by following a nonnegative Dadaist program designed to preserve the life of the imagination against the pressures and tensions of the world.

Whereas the Dadaists had tried to debunk meaning in art as the remnants of a stale tradition propped up by a corrupt society, the Surrealists tried to create a new art mythology by fusing conscious with unconscious levels of the mind. Generally speaking, both Dadaism and Surrealism were continuations of the counterattack, begun by the Romantics in the nineteenth century, against an increasingly mechanized and materialistic society. Sigmund Freud's theories of dreams and their meanings lent strong credence to Surrealist beliefs, and Surrealist writers and artists tried to create a new pantheon of subconscious imagery, which they claimed to be more real than those generated by activities and behavior on the conscious level. The Surrealists believed that only in dreams, which arise in the mind from below the conscious level, could humans retain their personal liberties. In their art, the Surrealists cultivated images that arose ostensibly unbidden from the mind. They recorded these images through

invented several devices in exploring his fantastic concepts (see fig. 10.58). His Frottages (invented around 1925) employed the Surrealist technique of shutting off the conscious mind. Frottages were rubbings made on rough surfaces with crayon, pencil, or similar media. In the resulting impressions, the artist would search for a variety of images while in a state of feverish mental intoxication. A process bordering on self-hypnosis was embraced to arrive at this heightened state. The Spanish painter Salvador Dalí affected a creative fever similar to that of Ernst while creating his improbable, weird, and shocking images, using meticulous, naturalistic technique to give them authenticity (fig. 10.63).

Yves Tanguy, a French merchant seaman who took up painting after seeing a work by Giorgio de Chirico, the Italian Fantasist, employed a method similar to that of Ernst. Allowing his hand to wander in free and unconscious doodlings, he created strange landscapes consisting of nonfigurative objects that suggested life. Tanguy's pictorial shapes have the appearance of perceptive, alien organisms living in a mystical twilight land (fig. 10.64). There were many Surrealists, but Ernst, Dalí, and Tanguy were the most influential, thanks to their unflagging invention of arresting images.

René Magritte (1898–1967) was the hidden artist among the Surrealists, always preferring anonymity to fame. Like Tanguy, he was so shocked by the sight of a painting by de Chirico that he also embraced the Surrealist style. Magritte based his approach on slightly changing the ordinary in order to make it strangely evocative and extraordinary. Born in Brussels, he could not stand the frenetic and polarized atmosphere of Paris art circles and returned to his birthplace in 1930 for the rest of his career. In spite of his being out of the mainstream, his style of Magic Realism, as it was known in the 1940s, began to slowly be widely recognized. His *Portrait* of 1935 shows a realistic glass, bottle of wine, silverware, and plate, all everyday in appearance; but an eye peers up at us from the food on the plate. This captures the essence of Magritte's style in juxtaposing commonplace objects with ele-

10.63 **Salvador Dalí, *Persistence of Memory*, 1931. Oil on canvas 9½ × 13 in. (24.1 × 33 cm).** A naturalistic technique combined with strange abstractions gives a nightmarish mood to this painting. The limp watches may be a commentary on the unreliability of our sense of time. © 2005 Salvador Dali, Gala-Salvador Dali Foundation/Artists Rights Society (ARS), New York. The Museum of Modern Art, New York, NY. U.S.A. Given anonymously. Digital image © The Museum of Modern Art/Licensed by SCALA/Art Resource, NY.

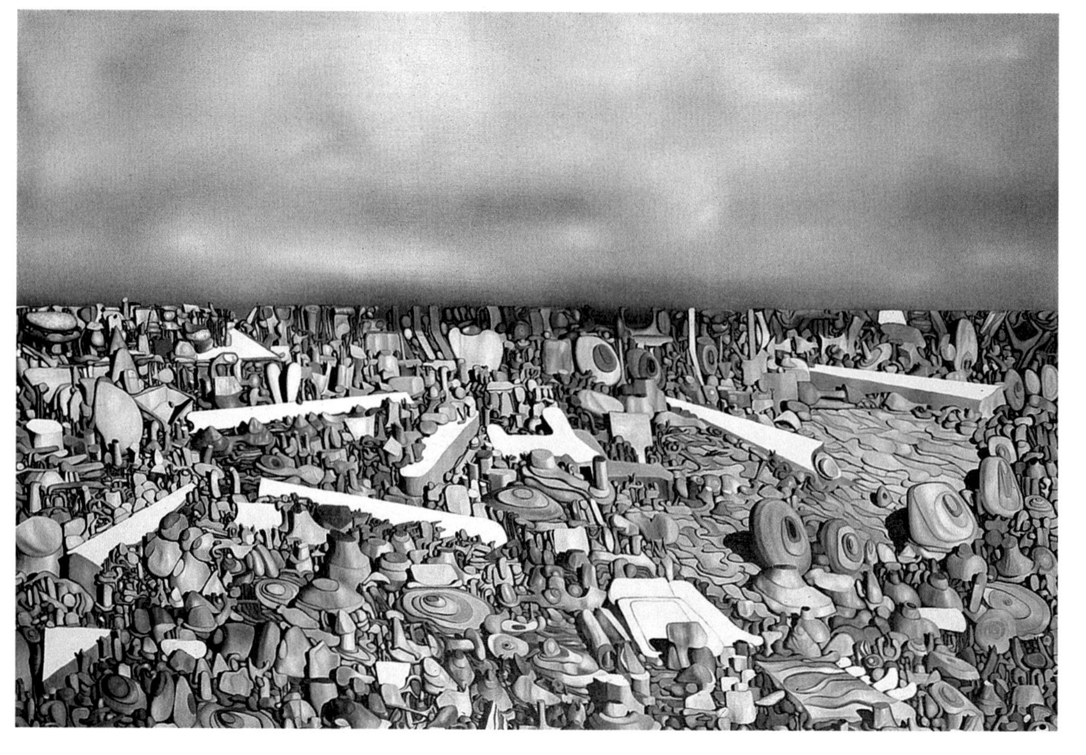

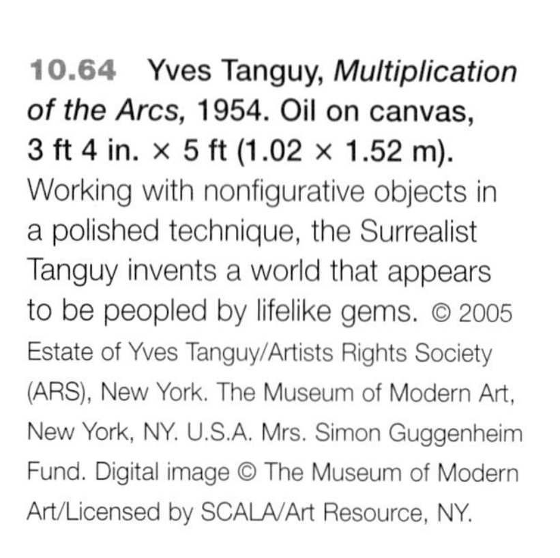

10.64 **Yves Tanguy, *Multiplication of the Arcs,* 1954. Oil on canvas, 3 ft 4 in. × 5 ft (1.02 × 1.52 m).** Working with nonfigurative objects in a polished technique, the Surrealist Tanguy invents a world that appears to be peopled by lifelike gems. © 2005 Estate of Yves Tanguy/Artists Rights Society (ARS), New York. The Museum of Modern Art, New York, NY. U.S.A. Mrs. Simon Guggenheim Fund. Digital image © The Museum of Modern Art/Licensed by SCALA/Art Resource, NY.

ments or situations that are abnormal (see fig. 8.45).

Even when other artists did not hold with the strictures of André Breton's *Surrealist Manifesto,* they fell under the sway of its ideas. But among those so influenced were some who began to merge it with more Expressionist and Abstract directions already prevalent during the early part of the 1900s.

Surrealist Sculpture

The effect of Surrealism on the work of many artists was variable. Certainly, not many twentieth-century sculptors were pure Surrealists when we consider the character of their work. Generally, however, the trends of the first two decades merged to such an extent that classification into specific categories is rarely possible. This tendency increased after the middle of the century and led to the complex, interwoven movements of the second half of the twentieth century.

Alberto Giacometti (1901–1966), a Swiss sculptor and painter who spent much of his career in France, was one of the great Surrealist artists of the century. The evolution of his personal style was affected as well by the diverse influences of Expressionism, Cubism, and Constructivism. Giacometti was fascinated not only by the effects of material on form but also by the effects of light and space. After World War II, he reached his mature style of elongated, slender figures pared away until almost nothing substantial remained. In their arrested poses, these figures suggest poignant isolation (fig. 10.65). Giacometti's indirect method of approaching content came from Surrealism and was related to the stream-of-consciousness theories proposed by early-twentieth-century psychologists.

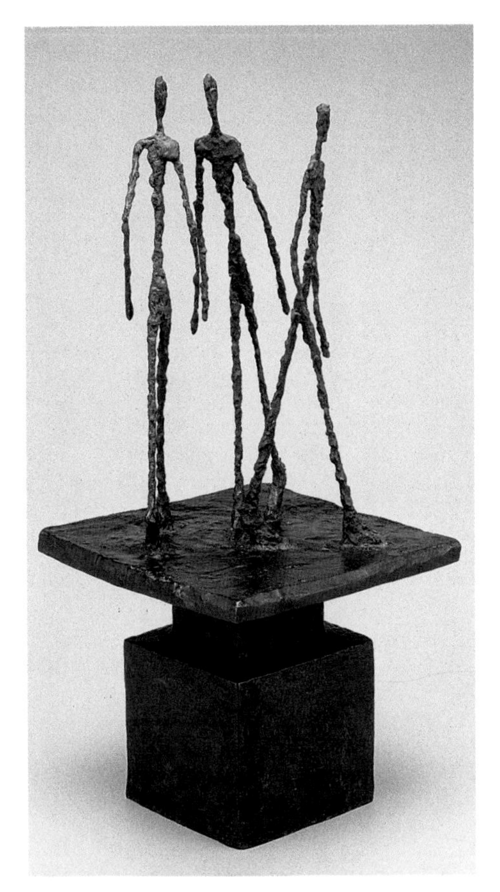

10.65 Alberto Giacometti, *Three Walking Men,* 1948/49. Bronze, 29½ in. (74.9 cm) high. Giacometti emphasizes the lonely vulnerability of humanity by reducing his figures to near invisibility and by emphasizing the spaces between them. Art Institute of Chicago. Edward E. Ayer Endowment in memory of Charles L. Hutchinson, 1951.256. Photo © Art Institute of Chicago. All rights reserved. © 2005 Artists Rights Society (ARS), New York/ADAGP, Paris.

Another Surrealist, the Spaniard Julio González (1876–1942), was the first sculptor to explore direct metal sculpture, or welding. In the late 1920s, under the influence of Picasso, González began to substitute outlines for masses and planes, even allowing tendrils of metal to stop short so that they were completed by implication alone. This dematerialization of form is similar to Giacometti's but is touched with a humor that teeters on the edge of the subconscious. González's work influenced Picasso's sculptural experiments of the 1930s and was influenced in return as well (fig. 10.66).

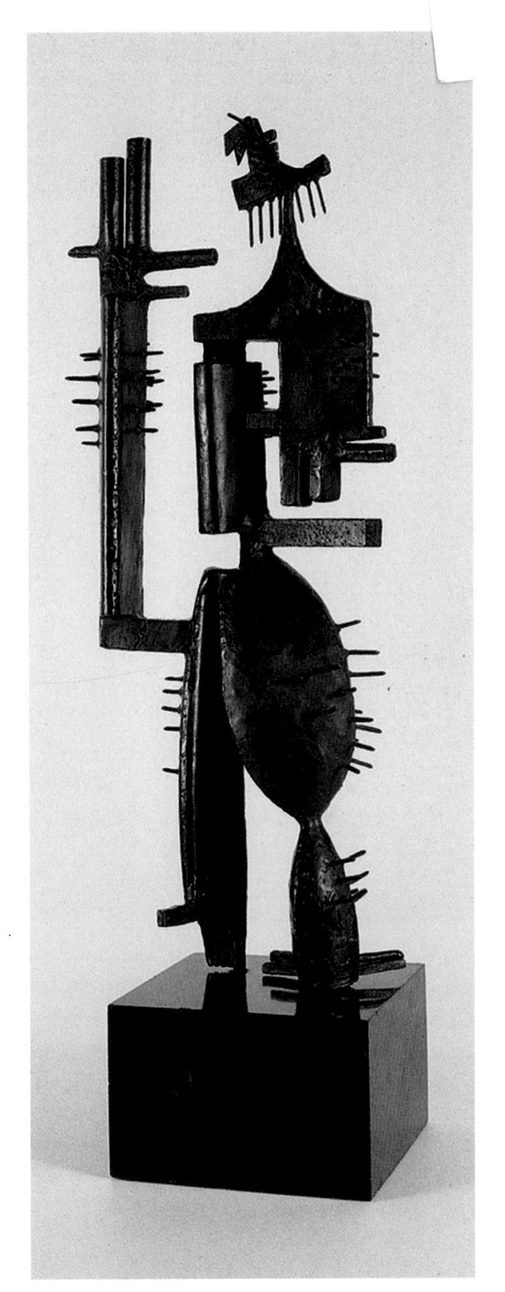

10.66 Julio González, *Cactus Man No. 1,* 1939–40. Bronze, 30¾ × 10⅝ × 7⅞ in. (78 × 27 × 20 cm). Expressively textured surfaces appealed greatly to this Spanish artist, who was the earliest modern sculptor to introduce welding as part of his repertoire. Collection of the Montreal Museum of Fine Arts. Purchase, Horsley and Annie Townsend Bequest. Photo: Montreal Museum of Fine Art. © 2005 Artists Rights Society (ARS), New York/ADAGP, Paris.

The cofounder of Dada, Jean Hans Arp, also explored the Surrealist preoccupation with preconscious suggestion and the effect of the unexpected, or surprising, form. Before this shift of

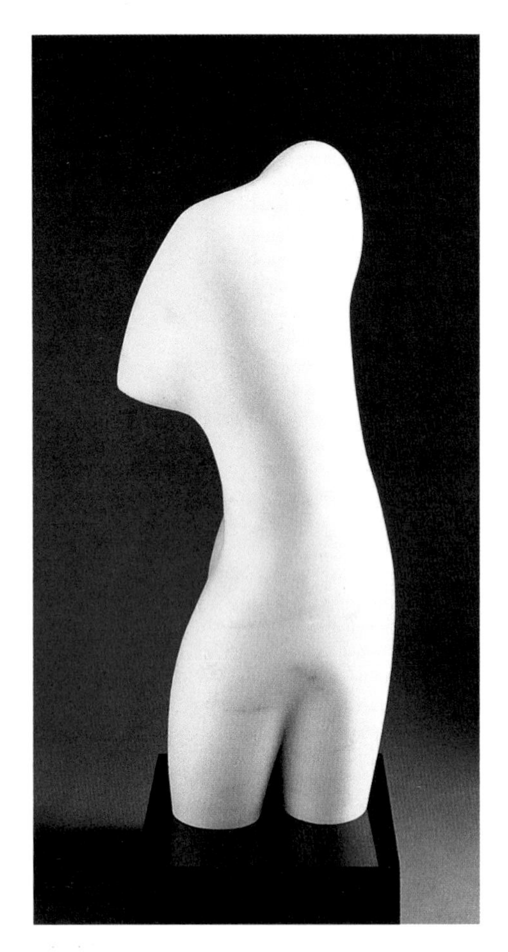

10.67 Jean Hans Arp, *Torso,* 1953. Marble, 31 × 14 × 13⅜ in. (79.4 × 36.8 × 33.9 cm). Arp shows his affinity with biomorphic shapes that suggest organic life in this highly simplified and polished marble. Smith College Museum of Art, Northampton, Massachusetts. Gift of Mr. and Mrs. Ralph F. Colin, 1956. © 2005 Artists Rights Society (ARS), New York/VG Bild-Kunst, Bonn.

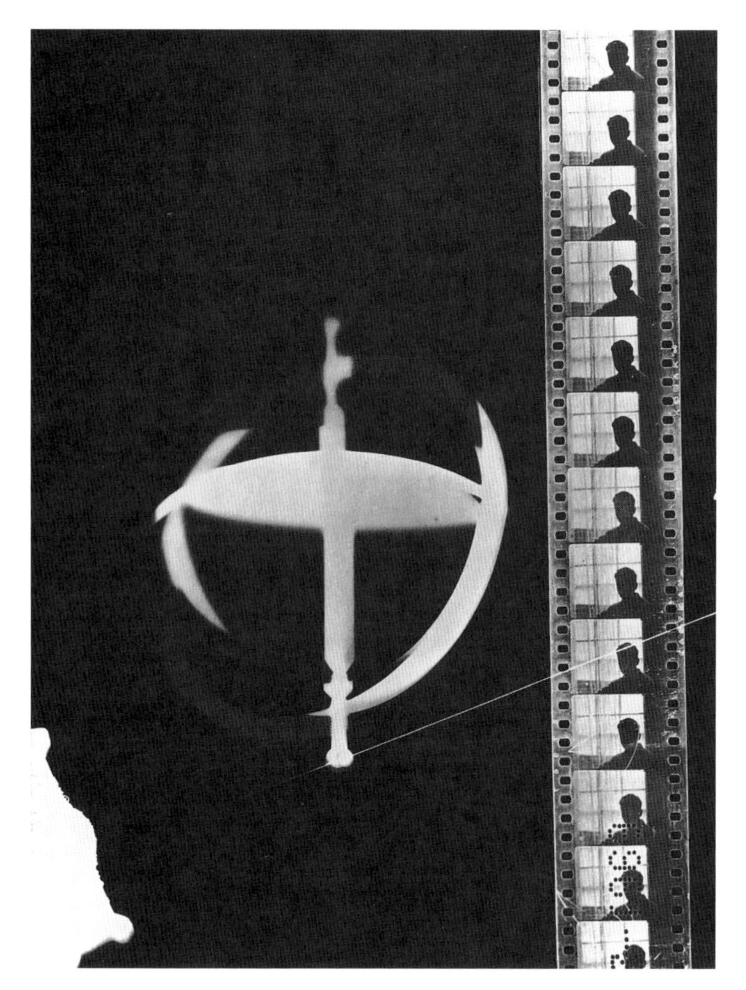

10.68 Man Ray, *Rayograph,* 1924. This photograph involves the technique, developed by Man Ray, of placing objects on sensitized paper that is then exposed to light. Courtesy of the International Museum of Photography at George Eastman House, Rochester, NY. © 2005 Man Ray Trust/Artists Rights Society (ARS), New York/ADAGP, Paris.

direction, Arp had explored most of the avant-garde movements of the early twentieth century: Cubism, the Blaue Reiter, and Constructivism, besides co-founding Zurich Dada with the poet Tristan Tzara. He was known for his abstract collages and reliefs, arranged according to the laws of chance, such as *Mountain Table Anchor Navel* of 1925, before turning to ovoid sculptural forms in the 1930s. These later works reveal the influence of Brancusi and the prehistoric sculpture of the Cycladic Islands. In fact, Arp's ovoid shapes became so famous that all kinds of rounded, organic shapes were called "Arp shapes" for a time (fig. 10.67).

Surrealism and Photography

While only a few Dadaists and Surrealists seemed to use photography as a source for their images, the medium's power to distort reality proved a way for some to free themselves from traditional image-making. Arp, for example, may have taken the cut-and-paste method he used for creating accidental arrangements from photography, where it is known as photomontage. This technique, arguably invented by George Grosz, descended from the Cubist *papier collé*, or collage, techniques. While Dalí profoundly admired the Dutch Baroque painter Jan Vermeer (1632–1675) (see fig. 2.22), and the nineteenth-century Romantic-Naturalist Jean Louis Ernest Meissonier (1815–1891), he called his weirdly delineated paintings "hand-painted dream photographs," hinting that he was much influenced by that medium. Along with Spanish director Luis Buñuel (1900–1983), he created

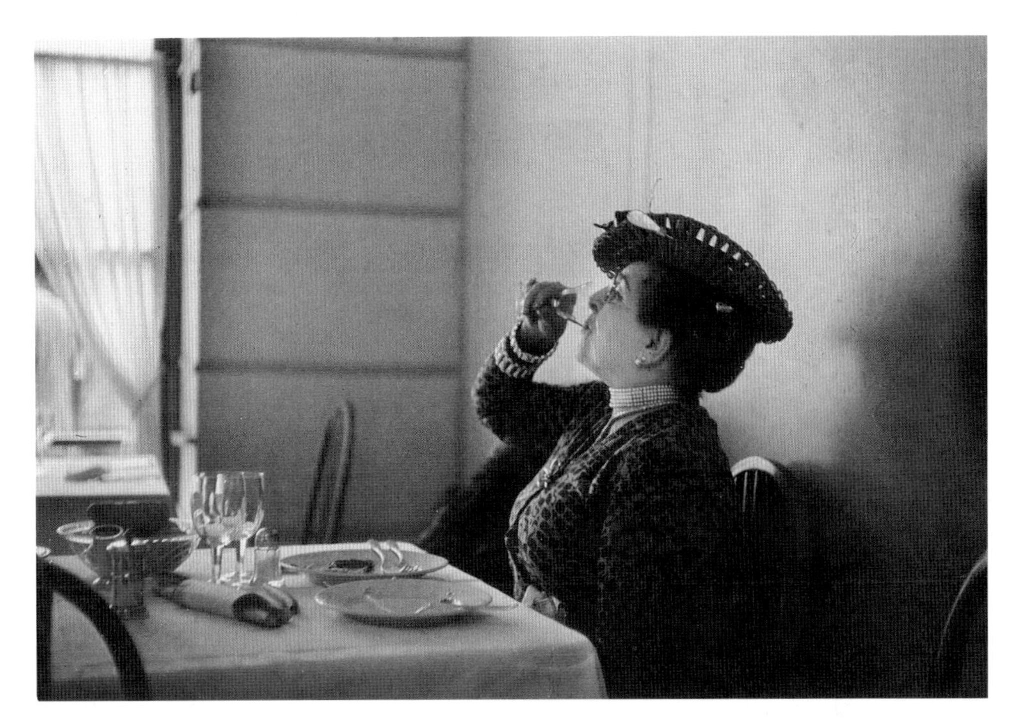

10.69 Henri Cartier-Bresson, *An Old Customer, San Remo, Italy,* 1953. Photograph. This "chance" photograph of a genteel woman, caught at the moment of downing the last of her drink, was typical of this great photographer's semisurreal "accidental" images. © Henri Cartier-Bresson/ Magnum.

two Surrealist art movies, *Un Chien Andalou* and *L'Age d'Or,* using the advantages of the medium to create memorable Surrealist effects.

Two photographers liberated by Surrealism were the American Man Ray and the Frenchman Henri Cartier-Bresson (1908–2004). Duchamp and Man Ray were invited to exhibit at 291 by Stieglitz and were important for introducing Dada and Surrealism to New York. Man Ray took up photography at Stieglitz's instigation and had a long, successful career. He is credited with inventing a photographic technique, independent of cameras, which he called the *Rayograph*. This consisted of placing objects on or near sensitized paper that was then exposed to light, thereby creating "chance" or "automatic" photographic images (fig. 10.68). This technique has been popular ever since. Man Ray was also a painter; in 1922, his *Aerographs* were made with the first spray techniques used in the medium. Similarly, he was able to create unearthly halo effects in his photographic *Solarizations,* which were made by exposing the film to light halfway through the development time to fog it. Around 1920, Man Ray went to Paris, where he resided, photographing artists, art, and fashions, until he died.

Henri Cartier-Bresson was famous for his "chance" photographs of people engaged in their day-to-day activities. His pictures attempted to seize the moment, and his aim was "to 'trap' life . . . as it unrolled itself before his eyes." Although he was basically a photojournalist, his images have a character that goes far beyond the mere record of an incident and are creative in terms of their organization and dramatic lighting. He was also among the first to use the recently introduced 35-millimeter Leica, a format that became the most popular among professionals and amateurs alike. Cartier-Bresson later returned to painting after dabbling with it in his youth (fig. 10.69).

LATE-TWENTIETH-CENTURY ART

Abstract Expressionist Painting

Beginning in about 1940, a host of artists began mixing aspects of the major movements of the early twentieth century. By the late 1940s, this new stylistic category was being called Abstract Expressionism, a name derived from Alfred Barr's description in 1929 of the more romantic versions of Kandinsky's early abstractions. (Barr was the first curator of the Museum of Modern Art in New York City, which also opened in 1929.)

Generally speaking, the artists grouped as Abstract Expressionists had found pure abstraction too impersonal, mechanical, and dehumanizing. On the other hand, they felt that Surrealism neglected the desire for order that was traditionally fundamental to most art. Thus, Abstract Expressionism was a coalescence of the three major movements that had peaked by the 1930s: Expressionism, Abstraction, and Surrealism. Some deeper roots can also be traced to the influence of Post-Impressionism.

The leaders of Abstract Expressionism were Europeans, some of whom (Albers, Hofmann, and Mondrian) we met under abstract art. Others, such as Arshile Gorky (1905–1948) of Armenia, Joan Miró (1893–1983) of Spain, and Willem de Kooning (1904–1997) of Holland, had a more Surrealist Abstract or Expressionist inclination (figs. 10.70, 10.72; see fig. 4.5). These artists helped to pioneer what seemed to be the first wholly American art movement but is now interpreted by some critics as fundamentally derived from Europe due to the arrival of these émigré artists in the late 1930s and early 1940s.

Two Latin American artists important to the movement in its early stages were Rufino Tamayo (1899–1991) of

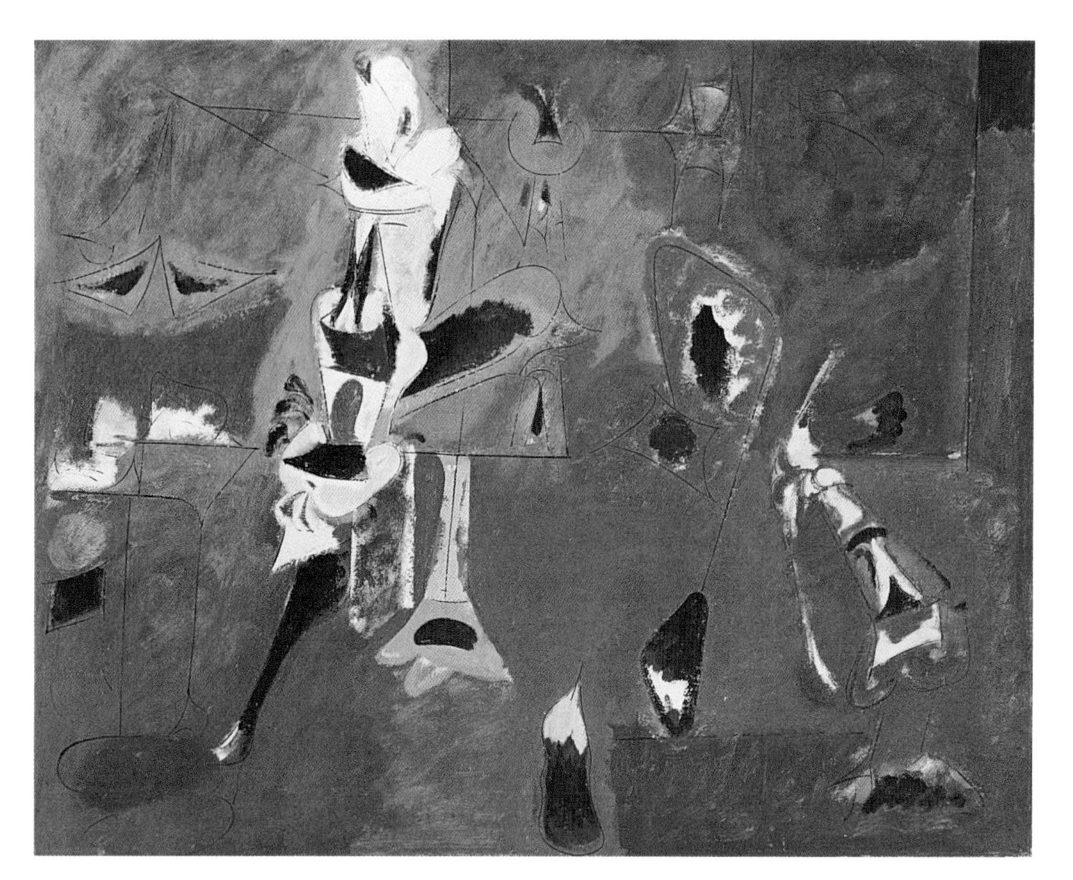

10.70 Arshile Gorky, *Agony*, 1947. Oil on canvas, 3 ft 4 in. × 4 ft 2½ in. (1.02 × 1.28 m). A combined engineering and artistic background in his student days, plus the stimulation of Surrealism's unconscious imagery, led this artist into the emotionalized phase of Abstract Expressionism. Gorky's career followed a downward spiral of bad luck and tragedy, which seems to be mapped out in his work. His early paintings are precise and stable, gradually becoming more unsettled and unsettling in the later work. Gorky was an important influence on the younger generation of American Abstract Expressionists. The Museum of Modern Art, New York. A. Conger Goodyear Fund. Photo: The Museum of Modern Art/SuperStock. © 2005 Artists Rights Society (ARS), New York.

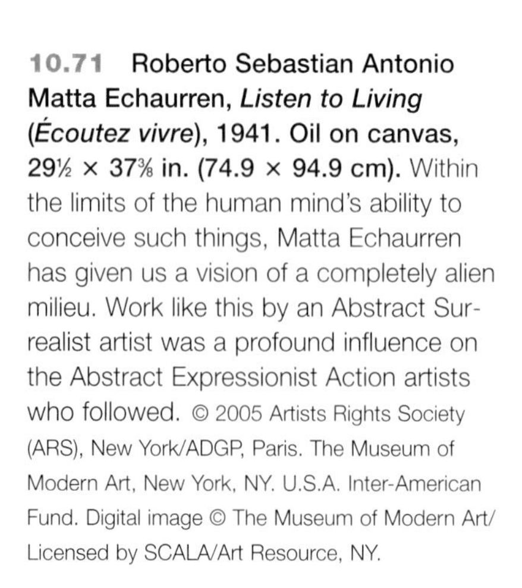

10.71 Roberto Sebastian Antonio Matta Echaurren, *Listen to Living* (*Écoutez vivre*), 1941. Oil on canvas, 29½ × 37⅜ in. (74.9 × 94.9 cm). Within the limits of the human mind's ability to conceive such things, Matta Echaurren has given us a vision of a completely alien milieu. Work like this by an Abstract Surrealist artist was a profound influence on the Abstract Expressionist Action artists who followed. © 2005 Artists Rights Society (ARS), New York/ADGP, Paris. The Museum of Modern Art, New York, NY. U.S.A. Inter-American Fund. Digital image © The Museum of Modern Art/ Licensed by SCALA/Art Resource, NY.

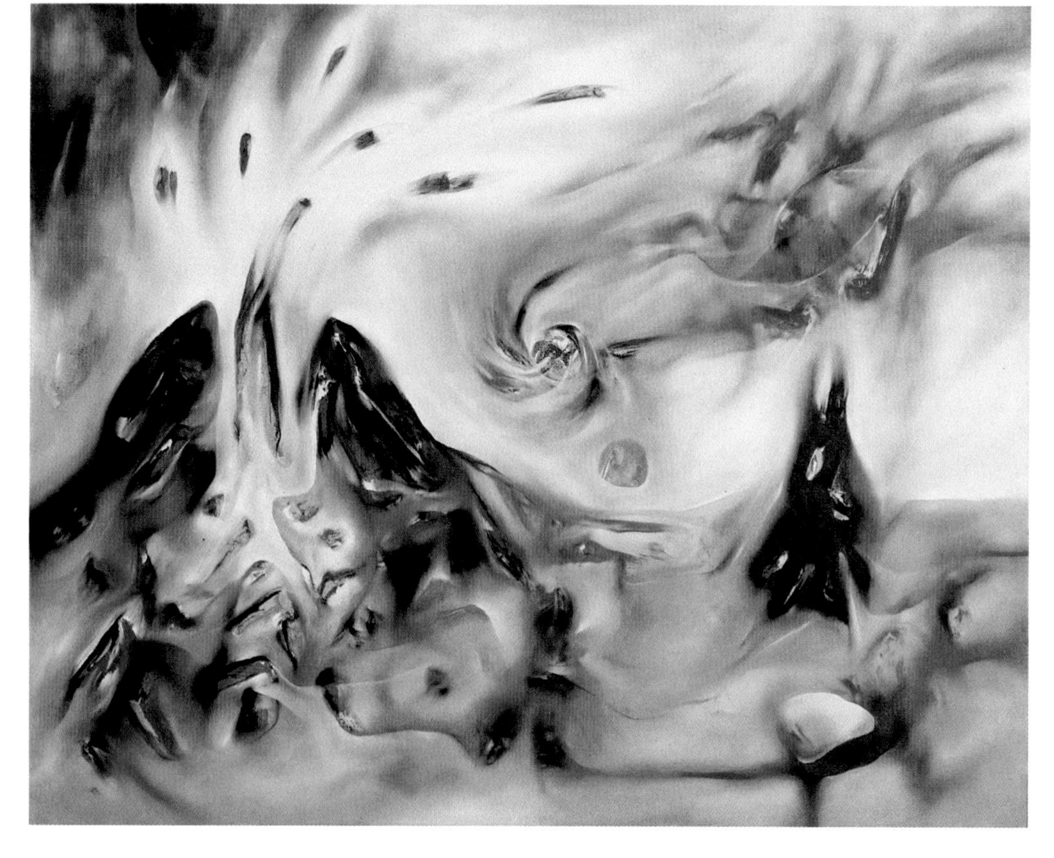

Mexico and Roberto Matta Echaurren (Roberto Sebastian; 1912-2002) of Chile (fig. 10.71; see fig. 4.1).

Essentially, the Abstract Expressionists wanted to express their individual emotional and spiritual state of being without necessarily referring to representational form, but it should also be stressed that Abstract Expressionism was a movement without a common style: Each artist expressed his or her experiences independently. With the exhibit in 1951 of *Abstract Painting and Sculpture in America,* at New York's Museum of Modern Art, the arrival of the new movement was made official. Although the founders of Abstract Expressionism were primarily concentrated in New York City at first and were, therefore, often referred to as the New York School, by the mid-1950s there were artists working in this manner throughout the United States, Latin America, and Western Europe. As the movement developed, it divided roughly into two groups with some overlapping between them. The "Action" or "Gestural" group achieved a generally active, external expression of their emotions by spontaneous drippings, splashings, sprayings, and rolling of paint on the canvas. Most of them had gone through earlier phases of their careers as Expressionists, Dadaists, or Surrealists. They tended to find their origins in the works of such artists as van Gogh (see figs. 1.16 and 10.24), and Matisse (see figs. 4.7 and 10.28), and Kandinsky (see fig. 10.47) and in the "automatic" techniques of the Dadaists and Surrealists. All felt the influence of Picasso and the dream imagery of the Surrealists.

The second group, usually called the "Color Field" painters, was more closely allied to pre–World War II Geometric Abstraction. Their overriding influences came from artists such as Piet Mondrian (see fig. 1.3), Hans Hofmann (see fig. 8.44), and Joseph Albers (see fig. 4.25). This group was indifferent to the impromptu looseness or

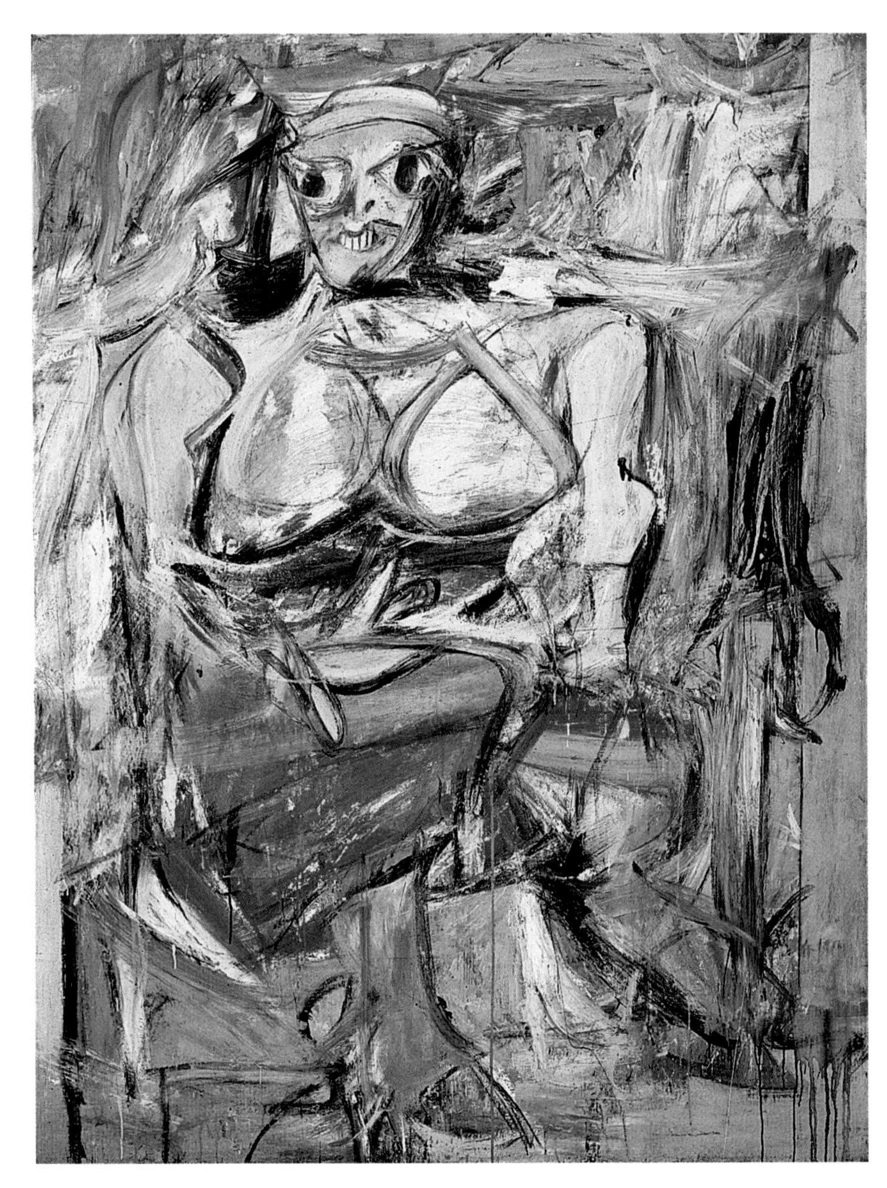

10.72 Willem de Kooning, *Woman, I,* 1950–52. Oil on canvas, 6 ft 2⅞ in. × 4 ft 10 in. (1.90 × 1.47 m). This artist summarized most aspects of the Romantic, or Action, group of Abstract Expressionism: revelation of the ego through the act of painting; neglect of academic or formal organization in favor of bold, direct, free gestures that are instinctively organized; and willingness to explore unknown and indescribable effects and experiences. Even though de Kooning's subject was ostensibly the figure, its representational value was subordinated to the motivating activity of pure painting.

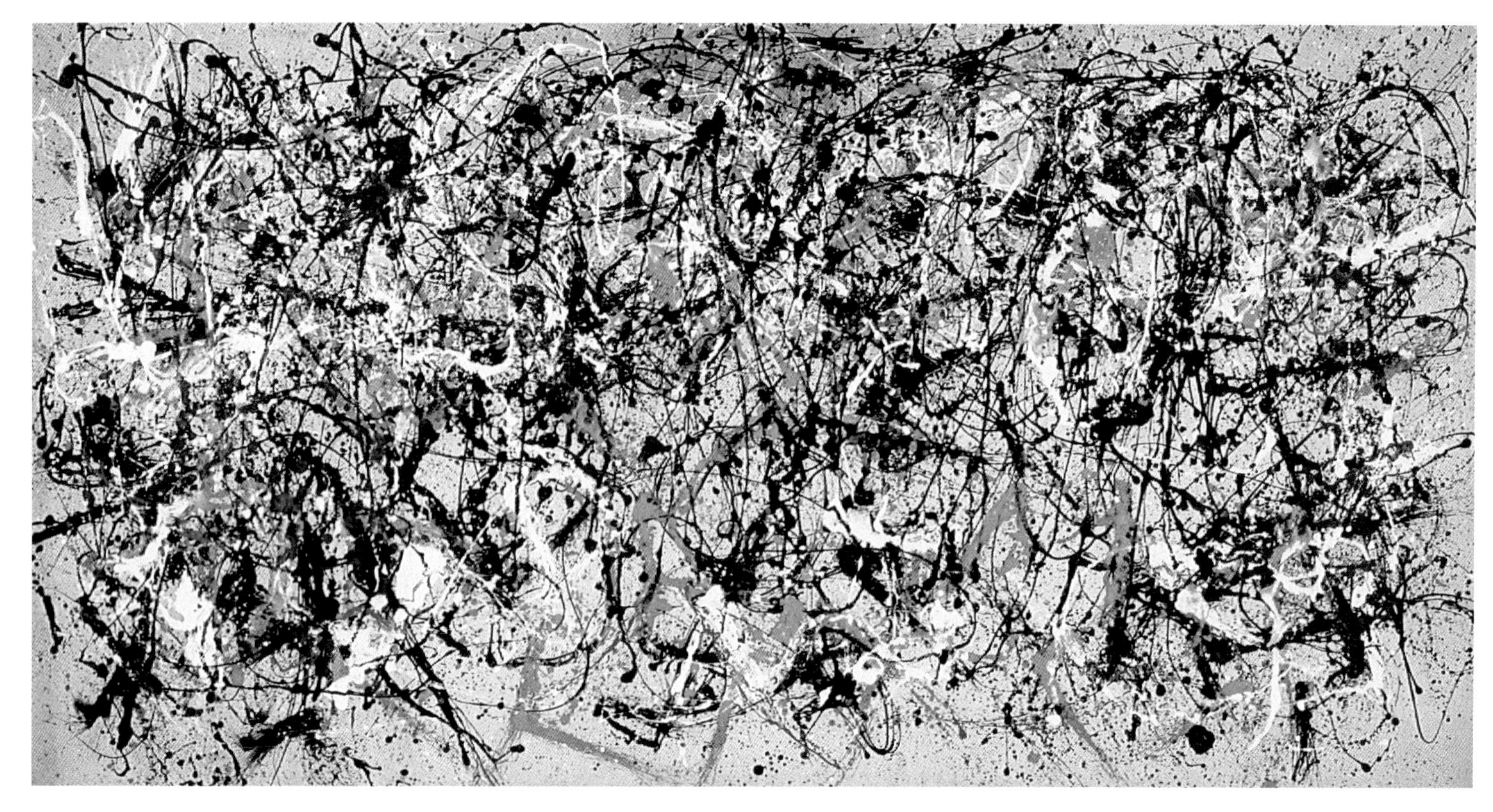

10.73 **Jackson Pollock, *Autumn Rhythm,* 1957. Oil on canvas, 8 ft 9 in. × 17 ft 3 in. (2.67 × 5.26 m).** This artist is considered the prime example of youthful Abstract Expressionist Action painters in the late 1940s. He is noted primarily for creating swirling nonrepresentational images in linear skeins of fast-drying paint that are dripped directly onto canvases through controlled gestures of his tools. The Museum of Modern Art, New York. George A. Hearn Fund, 1957. © 2005 The Pollock-Krasner Foundation/Artists Rights Society (ARS), New York.

"painterliness" of the Action painters, preferring large, flat planes painted in a more traditional manner, and therefore are sometimes labeled the **Post-Painterly Abstractionists.**

Jackson Pollock (1912–1956), Franz Kline (1910–1962), and Helen Frankenthaler (b. 1928) are some of the significant artists of the Abstract Expressionist Action group. Not only did they work in a way that was reminiscent of Surrealism and Kandinsky's pre–World War II biomorphic expressionism, but their techniques of painting also remind people of Impressionism. Confusion, fear, and uncertainty about humanity's place in a world threatened by thermonuclear annihilation may have led such painters to reject most previous forms of twentieth-century art. As a kind of personal catharsis, they seemed to want to express their belief in the "value of doing" at the expense of more traditional forms of expression. Pollock, for example, originated the "gesture," or the use of arm and hand movements to drop fast-drying pigments directly on the canvas in linear skeins. This is the technique on which **Action painting** was founded. (Navajo sand painting is also said to have been a strong influence on Pollock's technique.) The swirling, nonrepresentational images Pollock created in this manner expressed, through the direct act of creation, the reality of self or what the artist was experiencing as he worked (figs. 10.73 and 10.74).

Franz Kline followed a slightly different course but with a similar intention of expressing himself through direct contact with the forms created. His drawings were made with brush gestures on newsprint, then cut up and reassembled to provide a sense of power, movement, and an intensified personal rapport. Kline used these "sketches" as guides and enlarged them with loaded brushes on large canvases without directly copying them. Applied with a housepainter's brush, his slashings in black and white, or sometimes color, became monumental projections of inward experiences (fig. 10.75).

Helen Frankenthaler, a younger Abstract Expressionist, is still actively at work. She developed a method of staining unprimed canvas with pure, thinned layers of acrylic paint, utilizing the bright colors and fast-drying nature of these

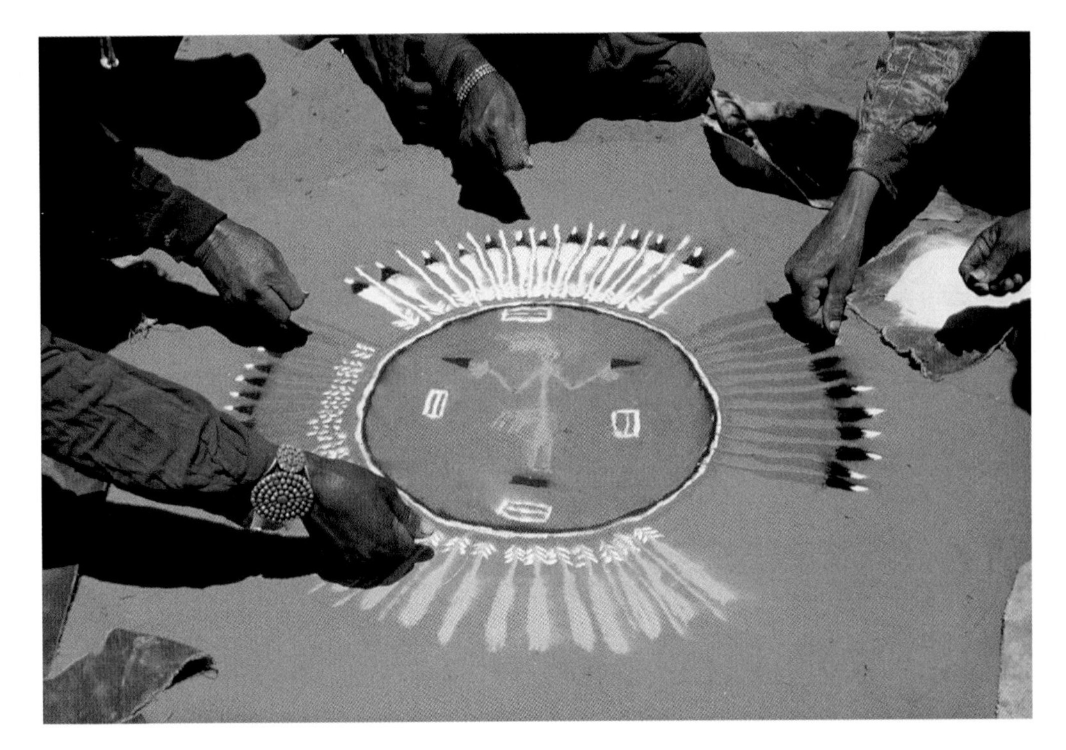

10.74 Navajo dry or sand painting, July 1957. Photograph. This kind of painting used by the Navajo for religious and symbolic healing powers is said to have influenced the gestural style of Jackson Pollock. Medicine men and their helpers crushed sandstone, pollen, and charcoal. The works are temporary, needing to be destroyed by sunset to avoid evil spirits. This example depicts the sun god and the sacred eagle. © Charles W. Herbert/ National Geographic Image Collection.

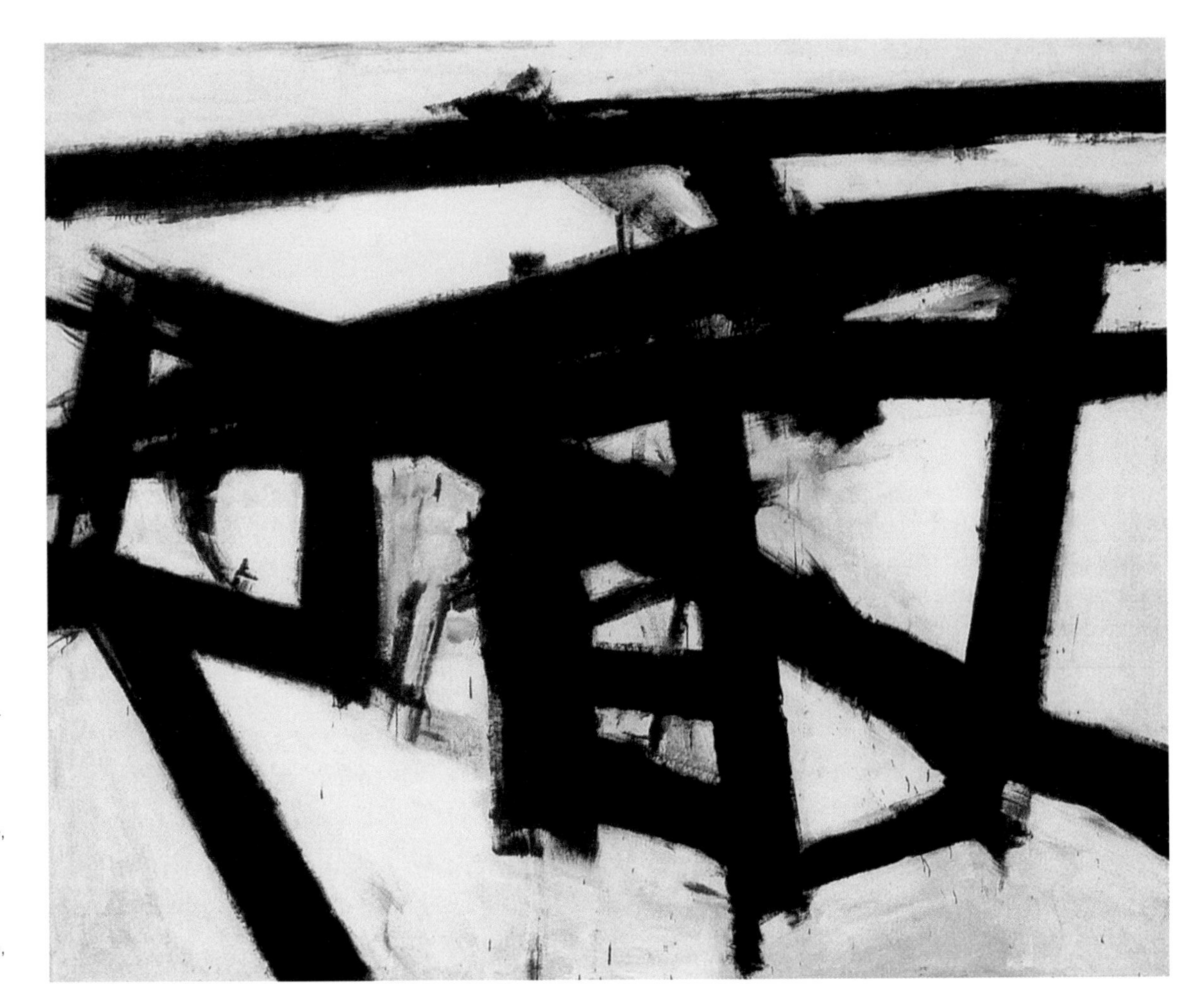

10.75 Franz Kline, *Mahoning,* 1956. Oil and paper collage on canvas, 6 ft 8 in. × 8 ft 4 in. (2.03 × 2.54 m). The artist was more interested in the actual physical action involved in this type of expression than in the character of the resulting painting. Collection of the Whitney Museum of American Art, New York. Purchase, with funds from the Friends of the Whitney Museum of American Art. 57.10. © 2005 The Franz Kline Estate/Artists Rights Society (ARS), New York.

10.76 **Barnett Newman, *Covenant,* 1949. Oil on canvas, 3 ft 11¾ in. × 4 ft 11⅝ in. (1.21 × 1.51 m).** This example is characteristic of Newman, an early Color Field painter. Such works generally feature carefully placed stripes superimposed on a flat color. Hirshhorn Museum and Sculpture Garden, Smithsonian Institution, Washington, D.C. Gift of Joseph H. Hirshhorn, 1972. Photo: Lee Stalsworth. © 2005 Barnett Newman Foundation/Artists Rights Society (ARS), New York.

recently innovated synthetic pigments to achieve the brilliant density and depth of her paintings. Some of her paintings seem to become planar, moving closer to the Color Field category. Frankenthaler is said to have been influenced, in developing her novel staining approach, by witnessing Jackson Pollock pour thinned black paint on raw canvas. She used oil paint in this technique until acrylics became popular (see fig. 4.27).

The second category of Abstract Expressionist painting, mentioned above, called the **Color Field,** was contemporary with the Action group. This group was also sometimes referred to as Hard-Edge painters, since they all owed a debt to early-twentieth-century Geometric Abstract works, particularly those of Josef Albers. His series called *Homage to the Square* (see fig. 4.25) had a particularly strong influence. In this series, Albers expressed his interest in Gestalt psychology through the effects of optical illusion. He created passive, free-floating square shapes that had just enough contrast in value, hue, and intensity with surrounding colors to be able to emerge slightly from the background. Albers's successors, Color Field painters like Barnett Newman (1905–1970) and Ellsworth Kelly (b. 1923), stress definition of edges or shapes that are set off more explicitly than others in the color field (fig. 10.76; see also fig. 7.14). The paintings of this band were generally more restrained than those of the Action painters. They painted large-scale, unified color fields of personally

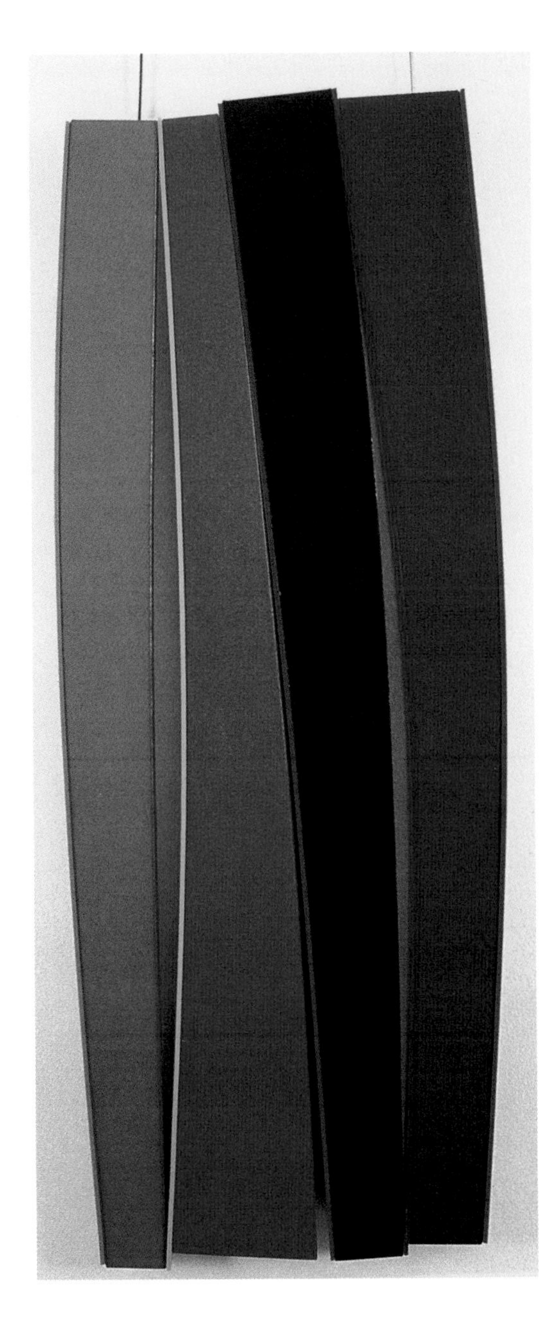

10.77 Kenneth Noland, *Flares: Storm Gray,* 1991. Acrylic on canvas mounted on canvas, with Plexiglas, 61¾ × 24⅜ in. (156.8 × 61.9 cm). Along with Newman, Kelly, and other Color Field painters, Noland conceived shapes or signs meant to evoke emotional response. But their approach seems more cerebral than that of the Action or Gestural Group. The size of such works of the 1960s and 1970s has a riveting impact. More recently, in the 1990s, Noland turned to shaped canvases.

10.78 Mark Rothko, *Number 10,* 1950. Oil on canvas, 7 ft 6⅜ in. × 4 ft 9⅛ in. (2.30 × 1.45 m). Using apparently simple masses of color on a large scale, the artist is able to evoke emotional sensations in the observer. Rothko was one of the American artists who worked in the pure abstract idiom.

conceived shapes concerned primarily with evoking sensations of ritual, tragedy, and mythology.

Other noteworthy Color Field painters were Kenneth Noland (b. 1924) (fig. 10.77) and Frank Stella (b. 1936). Stella is of interest because of the excitement caused by his early large shaped canvases (see fig. 2.3). Later, he also turned to large-scale sculpture. Most of the Color Field painters used stripes or bands of color moving in different directions, like Noland and Stella, while others used spots and shapes of various kinds—specific combinations of these were trademarks of their individual styles. Many, like Stella, from either branch of Abstract Expressionism have changed their styles or mediums in more recent times. One of the most interesting of the Color Field painters, Mark Rothko (1903–1970), is said to have been inspired by the emotional and spiritual qualities he found in primitive and archaic art. He also believed in the flatness of the picture plane and large rectangular shapes to express "complex ideas simply" (fig. 10.78). Rothko is known for his color fields of softly blurred looming shapes, which became increasingly more melancholic and expressive of his feelings of social and artistic rejection.

As contemporaries, Action and Color Field painters shared similar goals, such as wanting to enwrap the spectator as a part of the painting through shared sensation. This goal was carried further by the styles that succeeded them after 1960.

Abstract Expressionist Sculpture

Many sculptors worked in forms allied to Surrealism but with a greater degree of formality. These ranged from the organic figures of the Englishman Henry Moore (1898–1986) to the built-up, open-wire, and welded sculptures prefigured by the forms of González and Picasso in the 1930s. Among those influenced by wire or linear sculpture was the maker of mobiles Alexander Calder (1898–1976). González, as the pioneer of welded sculpture, must also be credited with influencing a younger generation of sculptors, most important of whom was David Smith (1906–1965).

Henry Moore merged the vitality and expressive potential of González and Arp with such older traditions as Egyptian, African, and pre-Columbian sculpture, which he had discovered as a student. Moore's objective over the years was to create lively, though not lifelike, forms. His sculptures emphasize the natural qualities of the selected materials; only secondarily do they resemble human forms. In this respect, his frequently repeated theme of the reclining nude seems to retain in stone a geologically inspired character and in wood a sense of organic growth and an emphasis on the natural grain. Moore was primarily responsible for reestablishing British art on the international scene and laid a basis for the renewed confidence British art showed in the twentieth century (fig. 10.79).

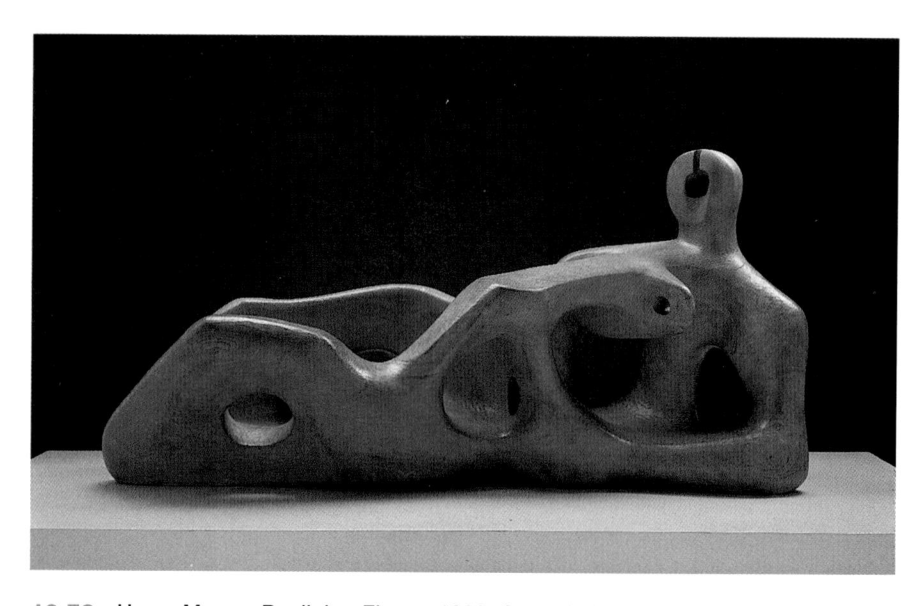

10.79 Henry Moore, *Reclining Figure,* 1939. Carved elm wood, 37 × 79 × 30 in. (94 × 201 × 76 cm). Moore's work is a synthesis of influences from primitive sculpture, Surrealism, and a lifelong study of the forms of nature. Detroit Institute of Arts. Founders Society Purchase with funds from the Dexter M. Ferry, Jr., Trustee Corporation. Reproduced by permission of the Henry Moore Foundation.

The Latvian sculptor Jacques Lipchitz (1891–1973), who worked in France before World War I and was strongly influenced by Cubism at the time, began to be concerned with the Surrealist idiom in the 1930s (see fig. 9.21B). He developed a robust style of freely flowing, knotted, and twisted masses that evoke, at times, the agonies of birth, death, and psychic torment, and, at other times, he depicted nameless new monsters. The horrors of the Jewish Holocaust were in the minds of many of the artists after World War II. From Surrealism, Lipchitz had also gleaned the semi-automatic principle, kneading his favorite sketching medium of clay into shapeless blobs without forethought. Then, through the accident of suggested form, he would construct the finished piece (fig. 10.80). Lipchitz, whose fame became international, came to the United States in 1941, where he influenced a younger generation of American Abstract Surrealist sculptors.

Certainly one of the most significant American pioneers of Surreal Abstract sculpture was Philadelphia-born Alexander Calder. Calder's father was a sculptor working in a conservative nineteenth-century Realist style. At first, Calder reacted to this academic conservatism by training as an engineer. However, he was soon ensconced at the Art Students League in New York and, in 1926, he left for Paris. There he began to create wire sculptures of animals that won him almost immediate recognition. In the late 1920s, he was mingling in Dada, Surrealist, and Abstract circles, meeting people like Miró, Duchamp, Mondrian, Arp, and González. These new associations led him to drop figurative work for free-form abstract shapes of sheet metal and wire, and, by 1930, he had created the first of his mobiles. His earlier kinetic (moving) forms had been powered by motors and pulleys; but the delicate balance and perfect engineering of the mobiles needed only air currents to create rhythmic, varied motion, producing ever-new compositions and relationships of shapes in space (see fig. 9.34). Thus, Calder was able to express the fourth dimension of time and movement in space, which artists had been trying to accomplish with implied kinetics since the beginnings of

Impressionism. Calder evolved three basic types of kinetic objects:

1. The *stabiles* were usually attached to a base, could rest on the ground, and did not move in earlier examples; but later some were made with moving parts.
2. The *mobiles* hung in the air, usually from a ceiling.
3. The *constellation* was a form of mobile that was usually suspended on one or more arms from a wall.

Mobiles are probably one of the most popular forms of modern art, and Calder is thus considered by many as among the most important American artists of the twentieth century. From 1933 until his death in 1976, Calder divided his time between farms in Connecticut and France, where he created, toward the end of his career, monumental stabiles and stabile-mobiles of welded iron, some of which were architectural in scale (fig. 10.81).

The promising career of David Smith, an Ohio native who studied at the Art Students League in New York during the late 1920s and early 1930s, was cut short by a fatal automobile accident in 1965. In the 1930s, pictures of González's and Picasso's Surrealist sculptures awoke Smith's interest in creating similar Surreal Abstract forms. Their influence helped him to originate welded sculpture, and he was reportedly the earliest American artist to employ this technique. Smith usually investigated linear sculptures and volumetric shape systems at the same time. Smith's use of such materials as welded sheets of wrought iron and steel gives his sculptures an undeniable power, reminiscent of both Cubism and Constructivism and the Action painting of Franz Kline. The slashing diagonals of his linear forms and metal cubes, in particular, remind one of Kline's black diagonals against their flat white-canvas surfaces. Smith's last cubic style before his death influenced the

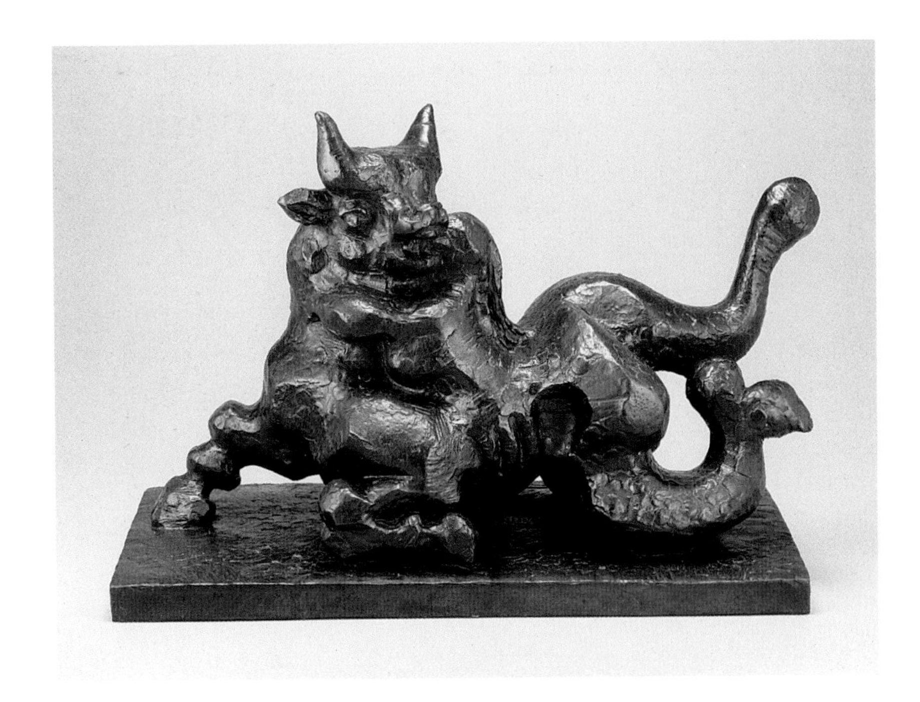

10.80 Jacques Lipchitz, *Rape of Europa*, 1938. Bronze, 16 × 23 in. (40.6 × 58.4 cm). After an early exposure to Cubism, Lipchitz developed his unique sculptural shapes and personal symbolism, but his Cubist background always served as a disciplinary force. Art Institute of Chicago. Gift of an anonymous donor. 1943.594. Photo: Robert Hashimoto/Art Institute of Chicago.

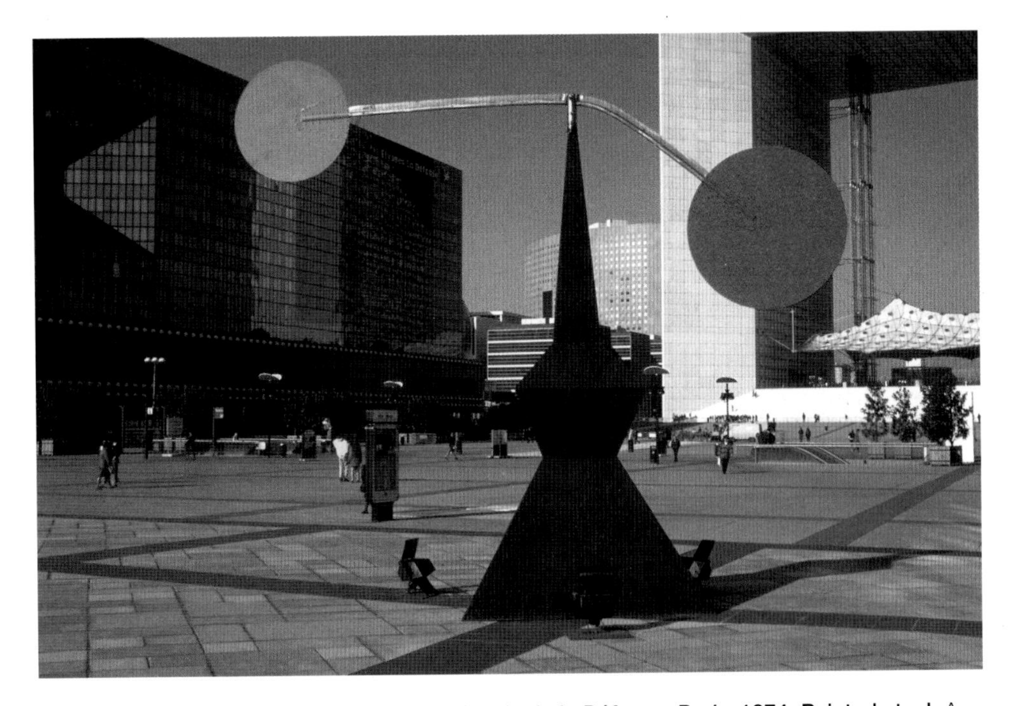

10.81 Alexander Calder, *Totem, on the Parvis de la Défense, Paris*, 1974. Painted steel. A late work by the famous inventor of movable sculpture combines portions of moving (mobile) and static (stabile) forms. Alexander Calder, Sache, 1974. Painted Steel. Photo Art on File/CORBIS. © 2005 Estate of Alexander Calder/Artists Rights Society (ARS), New York.

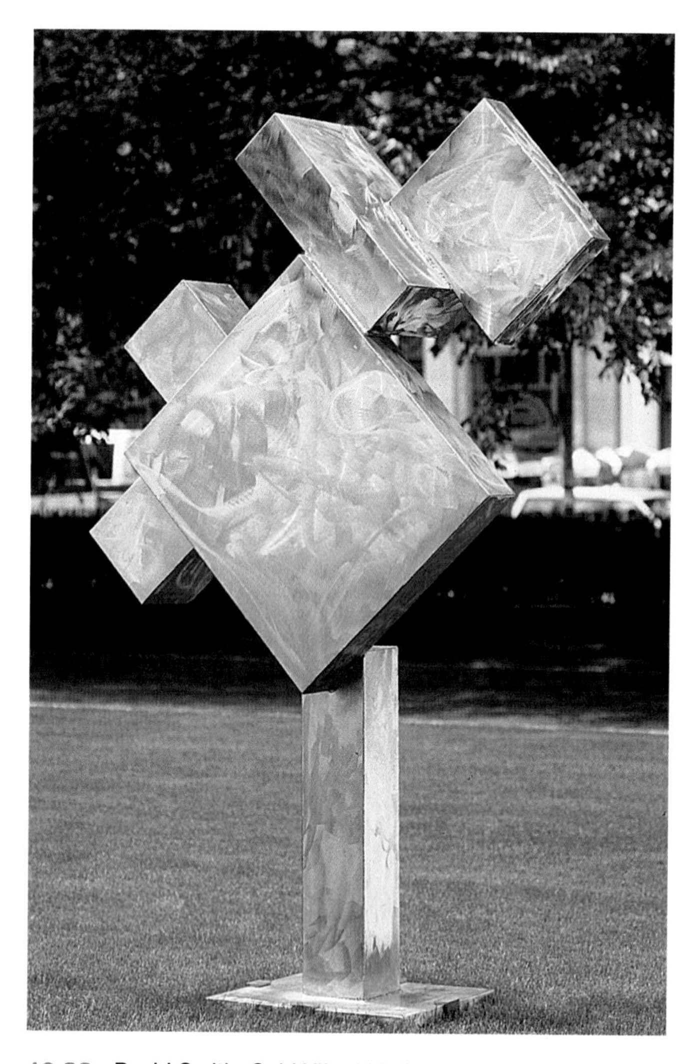

10.82 David Smith, *Cubi VII,* 1963. Stainless steel, 9 ft 3⅜ in. (2.83 m) high. Smith was rarely concerned with likeness to natural objects. Instead, he used nonobjective forms and tried to give them a life of their own through his animated arrangement. Art Institute of Chicago. Grant J. Pick Purchase Fund, 1964.1141. Photo © Art Institute of Chicago. All rights reserved. © Estate of David Smith/Licensed by VAGA, New York, NY.

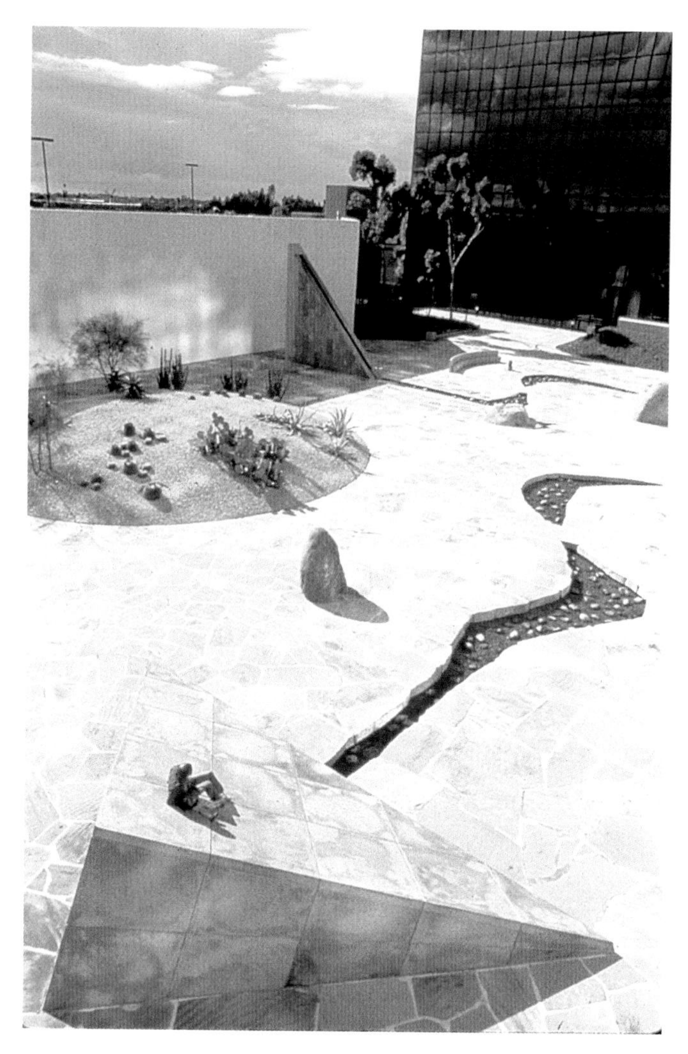

10.83 Isamu Noguchi (and Shoji Sadao), *California Scenario,* located at Two Town Center, Costa Mesa, California, 1981–82. The work of the great Japanese American sculptor Isamu Noguchi ranged from pure abstract through Surreal Abstract and Minimalist styles, but he is equally well known for his architecturally oriented plazas in various parts of the world. © 2005 The Isamu Noguchi Foundation and Garden Museum, New York/Artists Rights Society (ARS), New York. Photograph © Gary McKinnis.

next generation of sculptors, who, like their counterparts in painting, broke away from the metaphysical subjectivism of Abstract Expressionism (fig. 10.82).

Another distinguished international sculptor was the Japanese American Isamu Noguchi (1904–1988), who started his career studying with the academic sculptor Gutzon Borglum (1867–1941) before studying further in New York, Japan, and France. He was in Paris on a Guggenheim fellowship at the height of Cubist and Surrealist domination. Noguchi's study with Brancusi was particularly important; he also became acquainted with Calder while in France. His first exhibit of Constructivist-like sculpture took place in New York in 1929. Noguchi was soon widely recognized as an important sculptor, but throughout his career he also pursued interests in architectural landscape, furniture, and theatrical design. Always aware of both his Asian heritage and Western origins, his sculpture, with a sense of grace and elegance, makes use of a kind of Surreal Abstract biomorphics. Noguchi's style ranged from near Surrealism to something approaching Minimalism (see fig. 9.1). One of Noguchi's distinguished landscape designs and sculptures can be seen in the plaza at Costa Mesa, California (fig. 10.83). Perhaps through his association with Brancusi, Noguchi has always shown an inclination for a complete

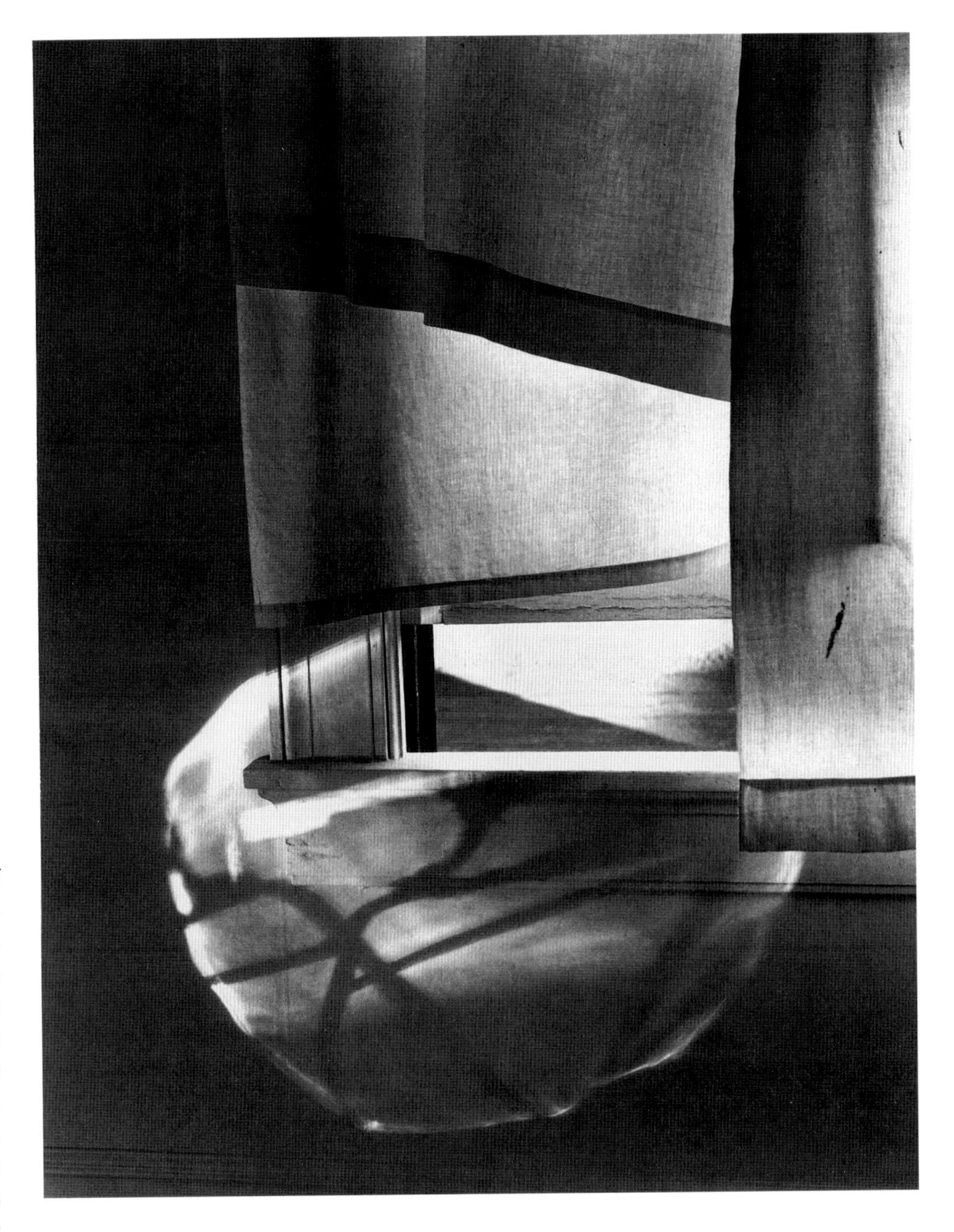

10.84 Minor White, *Windowsill Daydreaming*, 1958. Photograph. A follower of Stieglitz's Straight photography, White applied his knowledge of religion and psychology to his photography. His study of early-morning sunlight pouring through a window has an almost mystical sensitivity. Reproduction courtesy of the Minor White Archive, Princeton University, NJ.

mastery of craft, which entails the use of beautiful materials. His preferred taste was for stone, which shows how Noguchi cherished natural materials. The inherent color and character of natural material add inestimable integrity to sculpture, whether the works are small or very large.

Abstract Expressionism and Photography

In the years after World War II, at least two photographers continued to show the Straight photographic influence of Stieglitz and his group while also sharing affinities with the Abstract Expressionist painting then developing. The most important of these photographers was Minor White (1908–1976). His background of psychology and religious studies provided a basis for the sensitivity seen at work in his photography. White also wrote poetry and sometimes used it in conjunction with photographs to enhance their meaning. Although he generally created Straight images of a Realist kind (see fig. 1.19), White often favored two forms tending toward abstraction—the Equivalents, based on the photography of Stieglitz (fig. 10.84), and the Sequences, which he invented. The Sequences appear to draw on organic natural forms and, while often obscure in form and meaning, generally seem to concern White's own feelings, as do the Equivalents. His photographs were often metaphysical, expressive of the fears and tensions of his time, and were probably a form of personal catharsis. White's imagery was masterly and beautiful in its use of detail, texture, and value relationships or luminosity. The reasons for White's importance as a force in creative photography are multiple. The frequent exhibits of his work; his association as a staff member of the George Eastman House; his editing of the influential journal *Aperture;* his teaching and workshops, held at technological institutes across the country—all contributed to his respected position.

A second post–World War II photographer whose work sometimes seems similar to Abstract Expressionist painting was Harry Callahan (1912–1999). Early in his career, he became interested in pattern and design, creating images reminiscent of Paul Strand and Edward Steichen. Callahan's main source of inspiration was the second generation of

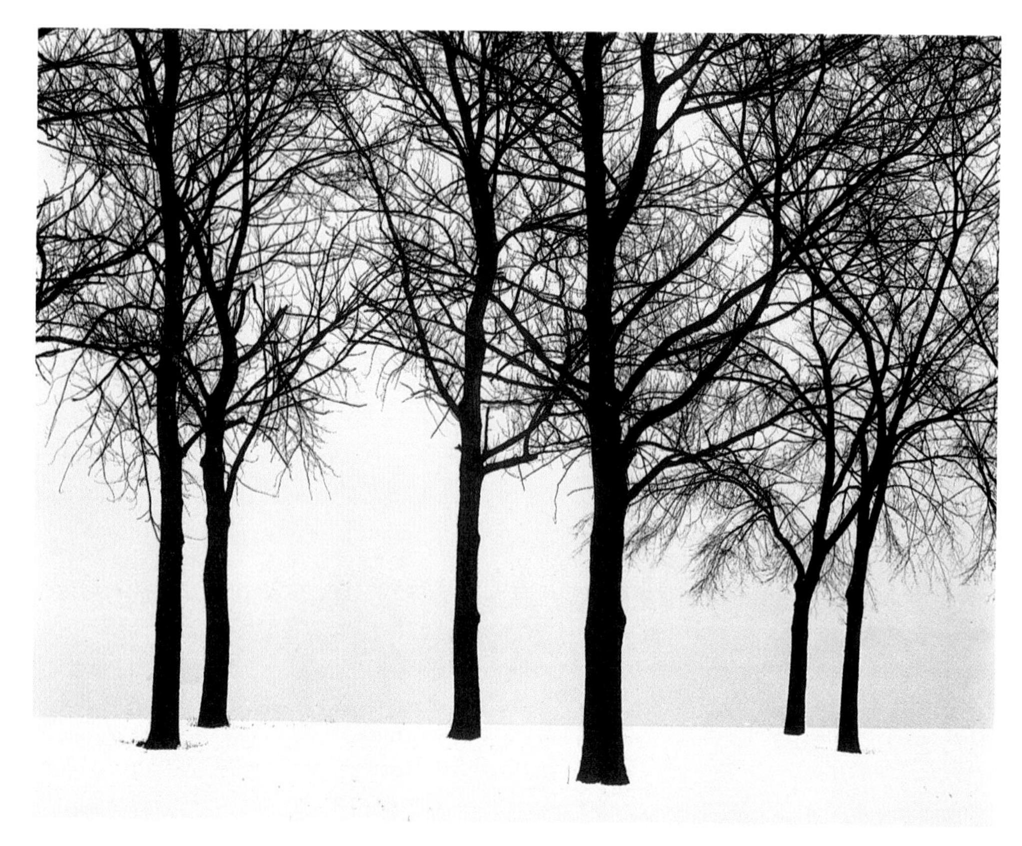

10.85 Harry Callahan, *Chicago*, 1950. Photograph. Callahan's work always reveals a concern with pattern and is notable for its strong values, sparse realism, and poetic simplicity. The linear starkness of the trees superimposed on an almost featureless background is reminiscent of the Color Field Abstract Expressionists. © The Estate of Harry Callahan, courtesy Pace/MacGill Gallery, New York.

Stieglitz-influenced photographers—Ansel Adams and Edward Weston. To some degree, he also emerged from the Bauhaus tradition of Moholy-Nagy (1895–1946) at the Chicago Institute of Design (sometimes called the American Bauhaus). From the 1940s forward, Callahan worked in a multitude of styles that always showed his interests in form; his subjects ranged from nudes and street life to multiple-exposure abstractions. Callahan's more abstract works are often akin to those of the Color Field painters; even the realistic trees of *Chicago* (1950) can conjure up the stark lines of a Newman or Noland against a single-color ground (fig. 10.85). It is this range from dark to light, this sparse realism and lyrical simplicity, that make Callahan's work notable. Like White, Callahan was a teacher, organizing the admired and popular program at the Chicago Institute of Design.

Kinetic Sculpture

As we have seen with Calder's kinetic objects, kinetic forms of art are those that create movement. Although they are derived from Calder's motor-driven wire and wood circus of the 1920s and later mobiles, they also owe their origins to Dadaism and Op Art. Dadaists, under the aegis of their antitraditional and destructive credo, created the first examples of actual movement or kinetics in art. The earliest examples can be found in the work of Marcel Duchamp. For a short period in the 1920s, he became fascinated by the swirling designs produced by phonograph turntables or disks driven by other rotating means. Duchamp soon lost interest in movement, but Calder did not.

Many kinetic artworks use a mechanical means to make the art object move, as in the example by Pol Bury (b. 1922) (fig. 10.86). Others use not only a mechanical or electronic means but also random wind currents to achieve their ends. One of the early kineticists, Jean Tinguely (1925–1991), created large, slack, junky contrivances that sometimes moved about but more often merely stood and shook, as if they were about to scatter the gears and cogs that ran them. In fact, Tinguely's most famous kinetic construction of this kind, called *Homage to New York,* did just that, destroying itself in 1960 in the garden of the Museum of Modern Art in New York.

George Rickey's (1907–2002) pieces use wind to produce motion, as did those of Calder. Nonetheless, Rickey's style is distinct from Calder's and is distinguished in its own right (fig. 10.87). While kinetics owes a tribute to abstract sculpture, it does not appear to have the underlying revelation of the psyche that came over from Surreal Abstract sculpture into Abstract Expressionist art and therefore is discussed here as a separate category. Kinetic sculpture is thus another form deriving from a concern with space and time that began with elements of Impressionism in the late nineteenth century and continued with Futurism, Dadaism, and Calder's Surreal Abstract mobiles in the early twentieth century.

Pop Art and Assemblage

The movement named **Pop Art** originated in England with the artist Richard Hamilton's (b. 1922) small collage titled *Just What Is It That Makes Today's Homes So Different, So Appealing?* when it was exhibited in an art show in 1956 (fig.

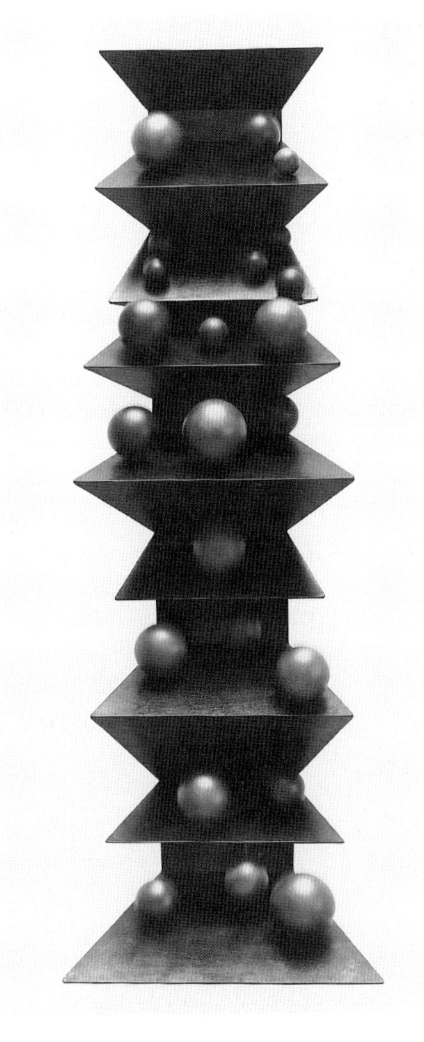

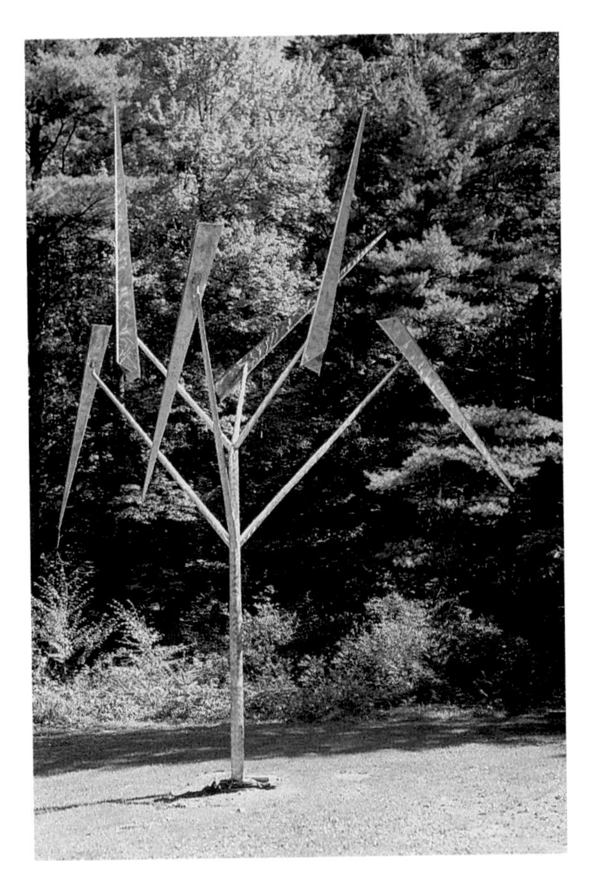

10.87 George Rickey, *Six Random Lines Excentric,* 1993. Stainless steel, 28 ft high × 31 ft wide, blades 12 ft long (8.52 m high × 9.43 m wide, blades 3.65 m long). Many of Rickey's works are kinetic, having been constructed to make use of the wind to provide constantly changing views of the parts. Photograph courtesy Gerald Peters Gallery, Santa Fe, NM. © The Estate of George Rickey/Licensed by VAGA, New York, NY.

10.88 Richard Hamilton, *Just What Is It That Makes Today's Homes So Different, So Appealing?* 1956. Collage on paper, 10¼ × 9¼ in. (26 × 23.5 cm). Hamilton's painting was the progenitor of art to be called "Pop." The subjects were familiar images that the artist hoped to show in a new light. Kunsthalle, Tübingen, Germany/The Bridgeman Art Library. © 2005 Artists Rights Society (ARS), New York/DACS, London.

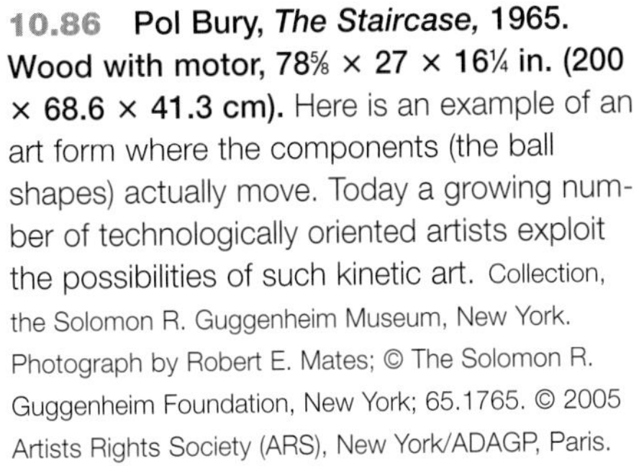

10.86 Pol Bury, *The Staircase,* 1965. Wood with motor, 78⅝ × 27 × 16¼ in. (200 × 68.6 × 41.3 cm). Here is an example of an art form where the components (the ball shapes) actually move. Today a growing number of technologically oriented artists exploit the possibilities of such kinetic art. Collection, the Solomon R. Guggenheim Museum, New York. Photograph by Robert E. Mates; © The Solomon R. Guggenheim Foundation, New York; 65.1765. © 2005 Artists Rights Society (ARS), New York/ADAGP, Paris.

10.88). An English critic, on seeing it, coined the term *Pop Art;* however, in the 1960s, this type of art found a natural home in the United States. The term *Pop Art* stands for "popular art," which was prompted by the dissatisfaction that younger artists were having with their position or prospects in relation to the

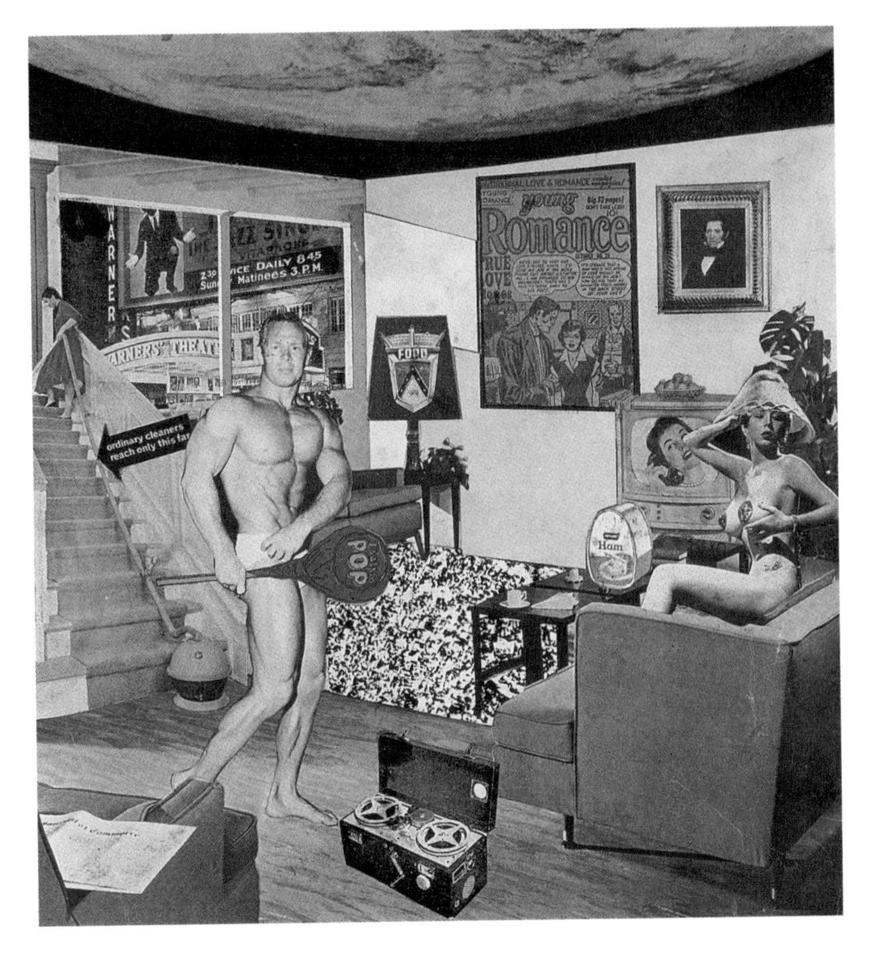

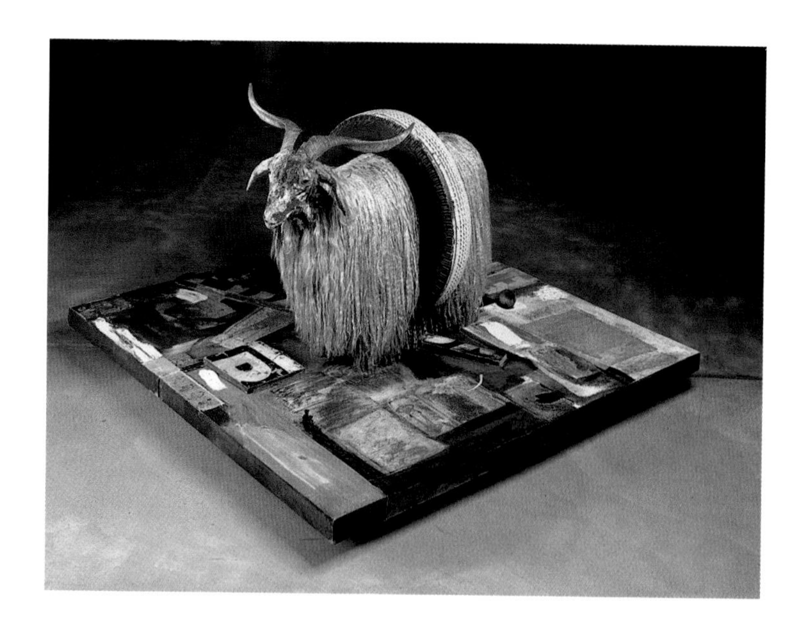

10.89 Robert Rauschenberg, *Monogram,* 1955–59. Construction (freestanding combine), 3 ft 6 in. × 5 ft 3¼ in. × 5 ft 4½ in. (1.07 × 1.61 × 1.64 m). In this combine-painting that merges into three-dimensional assemblage, one can witness the drift away from the pure painting of the 1950s. Such work provided a platform for the Pop Art movement that followed shortly. Moderna Museet, Stockholm, Sweden. Photo: Per Anders Allsten. © Robert Rauschenberg/Licensed by VAGA, New York, NY.

10.90 Louise Nevelson, *American Dawn,* 1962. Painted wood, 18 × 14 × 19 ft (5.49 × 4.27 × 3.05 m) in situ. This example of the assemblage concept in today's art is by a well-known sculptor. She utilized separate columnar shapes that build up in a unified but dynamic overall form. The shapes are a change from the more frequently used boxlike screens that enclose smaller sculptural units in other works. Art Institute of Chicago, Grant J. Pick Purchase Fund 1967.387. Photo: Jerry L. Thompson, Art Institute of Chicago. All rights reserved. © 2005 Estate of Louise Nevelson/Artists Rights Society (ARS), New York.

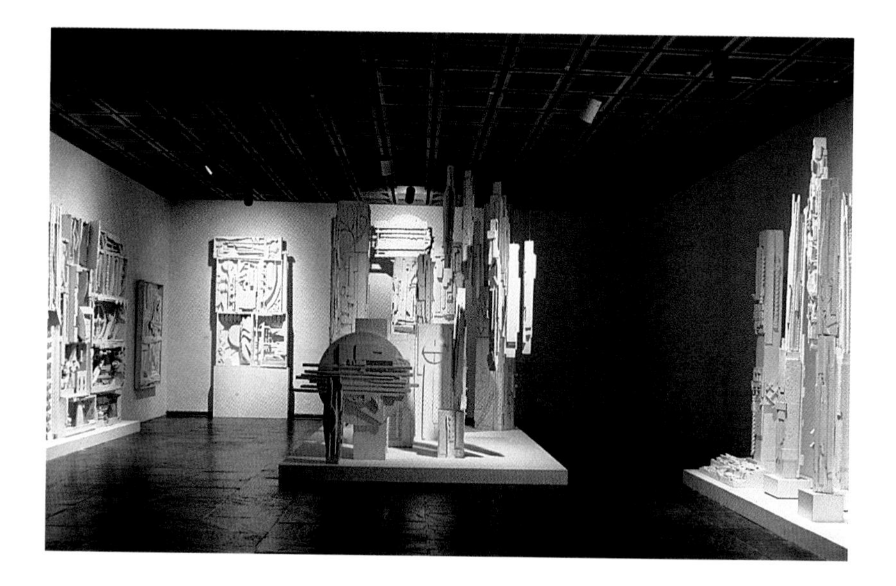

dominance of abstract art. The return to realism by the young artists associated with the Pop movement was predicted by two artists: Robert Rauschenberg (b. 1925) and Jasper Johns (b. 1930), between about 1955 and 1960. But before moving into an analysis of Pop Art, the art of *assemblage* needs to be discussed.

During periods of technological innovation, artists have at times reflected the desire for change by neglecting to observe the separate categories of painting and sculpture, instead merging the two in assemblages. This mixture of hitherto separate disciplines has its closest parallel in Baroque art of the seventeenth century, during which a similar intermingling of traditionally separate media and disciplines took place. Some artists have explored film, video, dance, theater, and computer-generated art. A fusion of computer technology with video, particularly, has been of great significance recently.

Robert Rauschenberg was one of the first to drift away from pure Abstract Expressionism. Such objects as Rauschenberg's *Monogram* (fig. 10.89), with its combination of pure, fluid brushwork from Abstract Expressionism and foreign three-dimensional materials, indicate his departure from Abstract Expressionist painting. Rauschenberg called his new form of art *combines,* but others began to prefer the term *assemblage* (a term invented by Marcel Duchamp in 1950). By the 1960s, this term was applied synonymously to Rauschenberg's early work and to any type of object assembled from various normally unrelated parts, whether stationary or kinetic. He continued to use objects in later assemblages such as mattresses, wireless sets, and photographic images, as well as stuffed animals, like the ram in Figure 10.89, attached to a surface (see fig. 6.10). The prototypical assemblages can be seen in Dadaist "found objects," particularly those of Marcel Duchamp (see his *Bicycle Wheel,* fig. 10.59), and in certain of Picasso's work from about 1914 on (see figs. 4.16, 6.7, and 10.57). Ultimately, all forms of assemblage stem from Picasso's and Braque's experiments with collage in the early part of the century. There is a satire implicit in the use of found and ready-made materials in combination with paintings because, in a sense, they were the detritus of an overly affluent and wasteful society.

Another practitioner of assemblage who came out of Abstract Sculpture was Louise Nevelson (1900–1988). Early in her career, Nevelson used smooth abstract shapes comparable to those of Henry Moore. In about 1960 she became enthused by "junk," or cast-off materials, to move toward assemblage. Nevelson developed her own distinct style by fitting together ready-made wooden shapes, such as knobs, bannisters, moldings, and posts gleaned from demolished houses and old furniture. These fragments were put into boxlike compartments—various-sized rectangles and squares that became large screens or freestanding walls. These pieces were usually painted a uniform color, which unified a relationship between the parts. Nevelson's forms and methods seem in keeping with the trend toward Process Art, but her results seem less contrived than those of the Minimalists, who emphasized process over content (fig. 10.90).

In Jasper Johns, we have a second artist who established innovations that Pop artists were frequently to use. Like Rauschenberg, Johns was an American artist, but he was even more satirical in his approach than Rauschenberg in the use of symbols, signs, and objects of mass culture such as the U.S. flag, maps, targets, and the like (see figs. 7.22 and 8.1).

Like Rauschenberg and Johns, the Pop artists were against the "high art" connotations given by critics, galleries, and museums to abstract art in general and Abstract Expressionism in particular. As a counteraction, they glorified images from mass-media advertising, comic strips, and everyday objects (such as soft-drink bottles, beer cans, and supermarket products). They presented these in bizarre combinations, distortions, and exaggerations of size, in both painted and assembled forms. The original pop icon was always rendered faithfully, however. Works such as Andy Warhol's (1928–1987) Campbell's soup cans and Roy Lichtenstein's (1923–1997) grotesquely magnified comic-strip paintings are typical subjects in Pop Art.

Pop Art startled viewers by presenting banality in a new context (figs. 10.91, 10.92; see also 6.13). As with Abstract Expressionism, the observer was intended to be involved directly in the work of art, in this case due to the familiarity of these mundane items in commonplace settings. Pop's source was partly in Dada, but while Dada was nihilistic, frenetic, and satirical, Pop Art encouraged an ironic reaction to the new sensations provided by elevating everyday objects out of their normal context. Pop Art retained only a bit of the satirical vein from Dada, featuring more of a deadpan enthusiasm for the images and objects of American culture.

Claes Oldenberg (b. 1925) and George Segal (1924–2000) were the leading sculptors in Pop Art (figs. 10.93 and 10.94). Oldenberg, one of the most imaginative of the Pop artists, has gone through various phases of good-humored work, playing with commonly accepted reality. He began by making edibles in painted plaster and presenting them at his street-front studio called The Store. Later, he also re-created telephones, toilets, engines, and other objects as flaccid, soft sculptures in stuffed canvas. Finally, he has made colossal monuments of lipstick tubes, clothespins, and the like, in metal. These strange icons are featured in numerous public places (see fig. 2.47). The environmental concept was an important development in the 1960s. We shall see it continued into the 1970s and '80s with renewed vigor.

In the late '50s and '60s, at about the same time as the tongue-in-cheek humor of Pop Art's new look at consumerism in the United States, came another

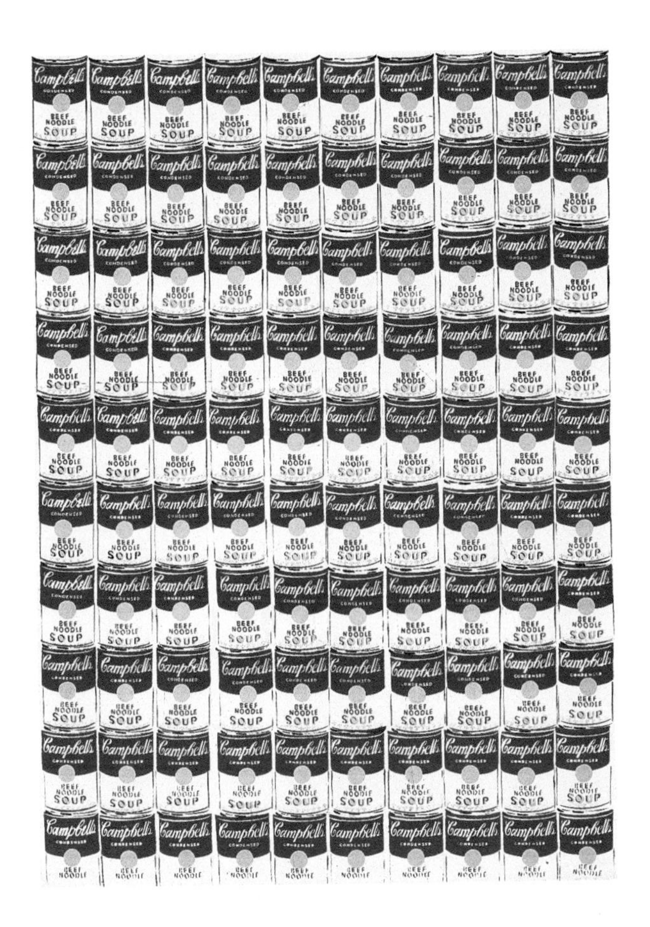

10.91 Andy Warhol, *100 Cans*, 1962. Oil on canvas, 6 ft × 4 ft 4 in. (1.83 × 1.32 m). Warhol's *100 Cans* beats a repetitive visual tattoo whose power derives from the insistence of similar commercial imagery in our daily lives. Repetition of a more or less monotonous kind was one of the principles of form exploited first by the Pop artists. Albright-Knox Art Gallery, Buffalo, NY. Gift of Seymour H. Knox, 1963. © 2005 Andy Warhol Foundation for the Visual Arts/Artists Rights Society (ARS), New York.

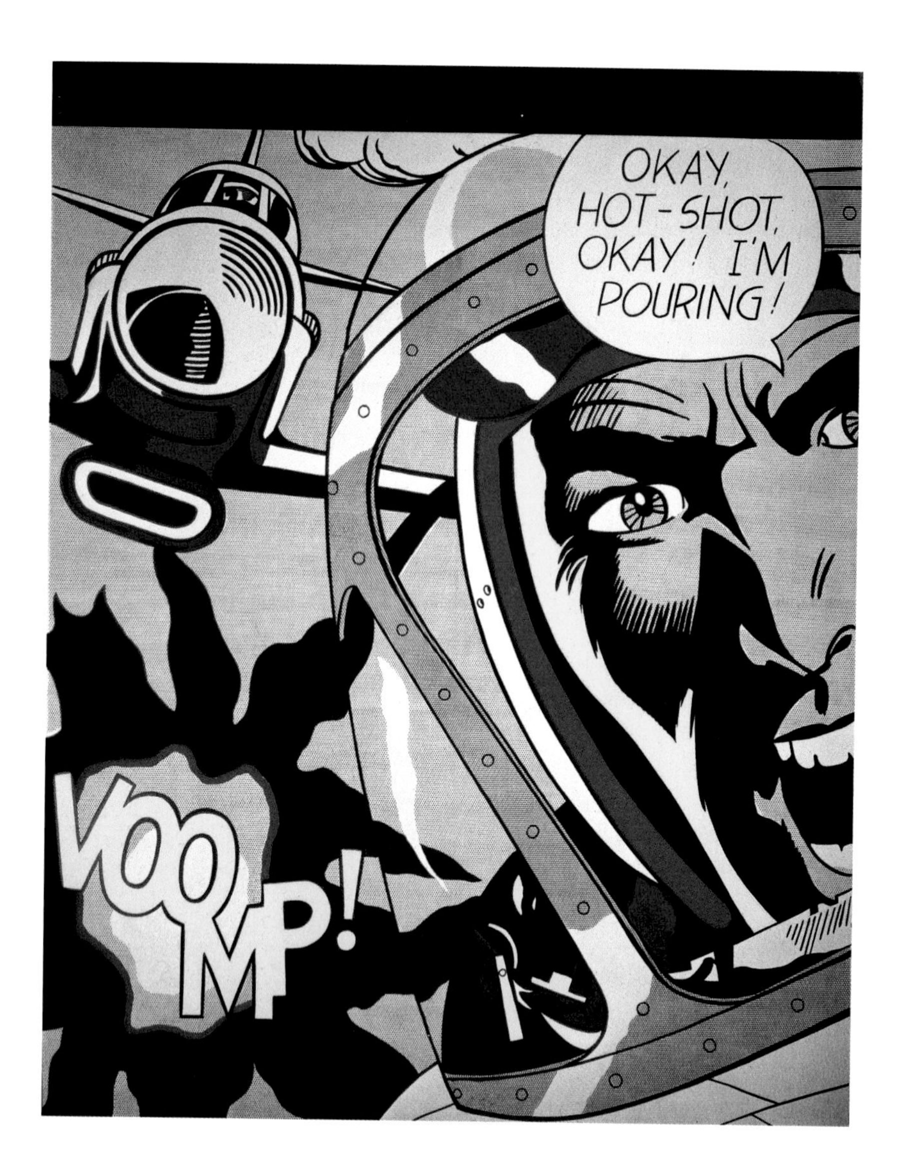

10.92 Roy Lichtenstein, *Okay, Hot Shot,* 1963. Oil and magna on canvas, 80 × 68 in. (203.2 × 172.7 cm). Lichtenstein's use of magnified comic-strip heroes and heroines was typical of Pop Art's playful treatment of popular culture.

unique way of looking at American life through photography. It was introduced by a Swiss-born American, Robert Frank (b. 1924), in his photographic journal titled *The Americans* (1959). Created in a style reminiscent of the social commentary of the Farm Security Administration photographers during the Great Depression, the journal is a photographic record of Frank's automobile travels throughout the country on a Guggenheim fellowship. Frank apparently took candid shots of the mundane that seem to say, "This is life." Sometimes rough, sometimes sad, in empty rooms and uninhabited landscapes, with vacant expressions, and from all walks of life, his subjects suggest their isolation from one another. Frank influenced a new generation of social realist photography, later epitomized by the work of Gary Winogrand (1928–1984) (fig. 10.95) and Lee Friedlander (b. 1934) (fig. 10.96).

Happenings and Performance or Action Art

The blurring between art and life in Pop Art is even more pronounced in the Pop-originated Happenings. **Happenings** were a form of participatory art in which spectators, as well as artists, were engaged. They have been defined as an

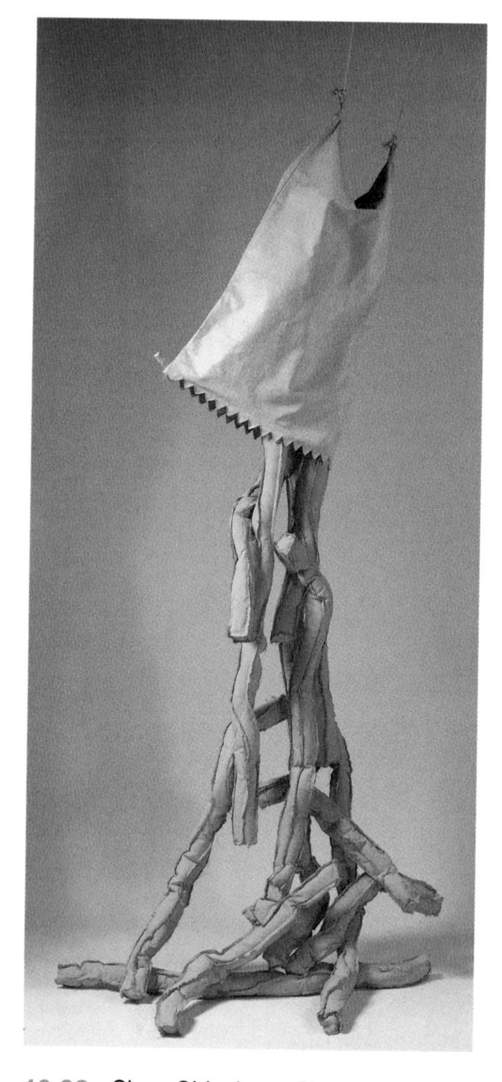

10.93 Claes Oldenberg, *Shoestring Potatoes Spilling from a Bag,* 1966. Canvas, kapok, glue, acrylic, 9 ft × 3 ft 10 in. × 5 ft 6 in. (2.74 × 1.17 × 1.67 m). Pop artists generally disregarded all form considerations, which they believed created a barrier between the observer and the everyday objects that served as subjects. Pop Art was an art rooted in the present. Collection of the Walker Art Center, Minneapolis, MN. Gift of the T. B. Walker Foundation, 1966.

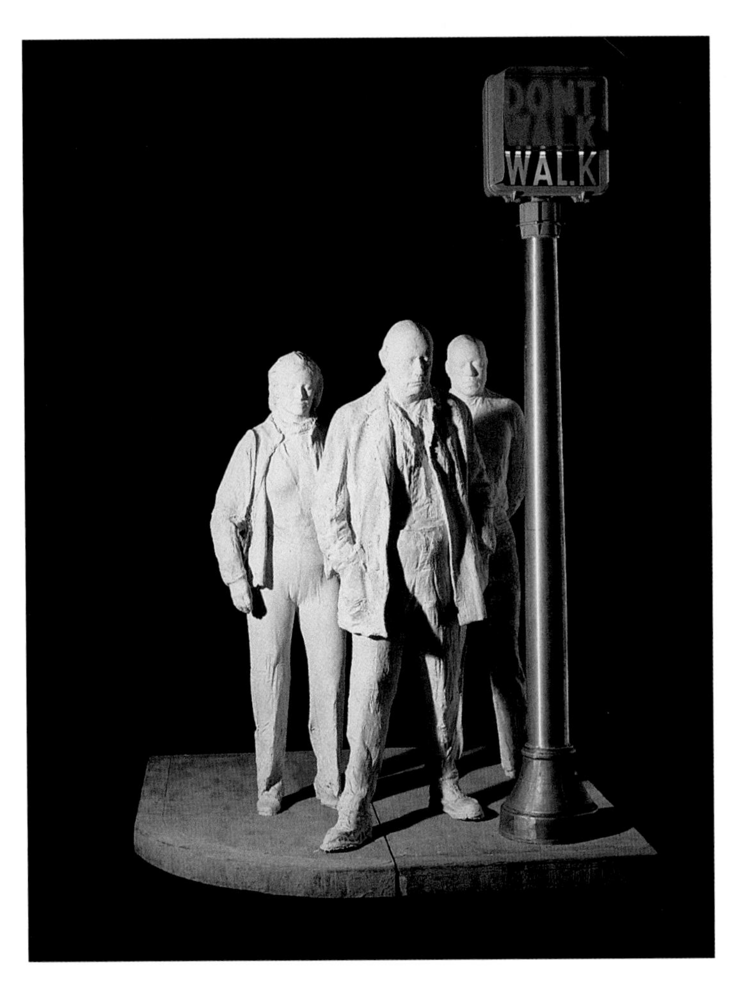

10.94 George Segal, *Walk, Don't Walk,* 1976. Plaster, cement, metal, painted wood, and electric light, 8 ft 8 in. × 6 ft × 6 ft (2.64 × 1.83 × 1.83 m). In 1961, this artist began to win fame for his plaster casts of living people. Dressing them in ordinary clothing and placing them in everyday situations, Segal was able to break down the barriers between life and art—a familiar preoccupation with Pop artists. Collection of the Whitney Museum of American Art, New York. Purchased with funds from the Louis and Bessie Adler Foundation, Inc., Seymour M. Klein, President, the Gilman Foundation, Inc., the Howard and Jean Lipman Foundation, Inc., and the National Endowment for the Arts. 79.4. Photograph © 2001 Whitney Museum of American Art. © The George and Helen Segal Foundation/Licensed by VAGA, New York, NY.

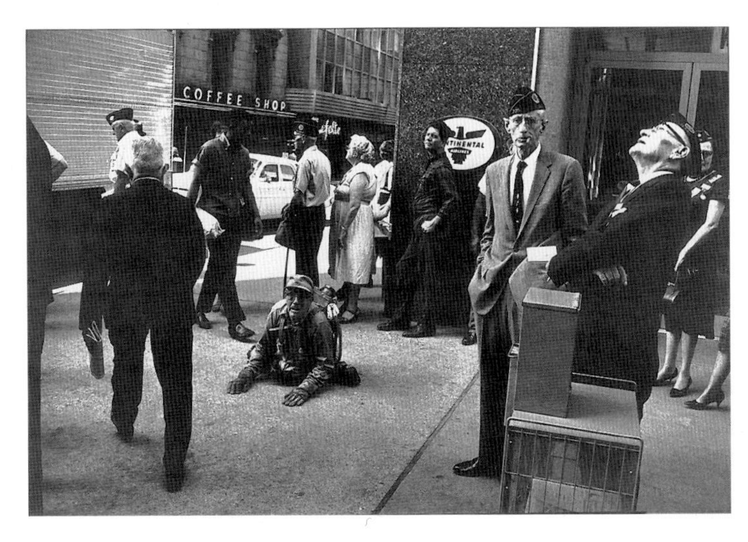

10.95 Garry Winogrand, *American Legion Convention,* Dallas, Texas, 1964. Gelatin silver print. In the 1960s, Garry Winogrand chose to photograph the moment glimpsed before or after an important event. An earlier generation of photographers, in the tradition of Henri Cartier-Bresson (see fig. 10.69), would have searched for a scene showing the precise moment of an occurrence of apparently deeper significance. © The Estate of Garry Winogrand, courtesy Fraenkel Gallery, SF.

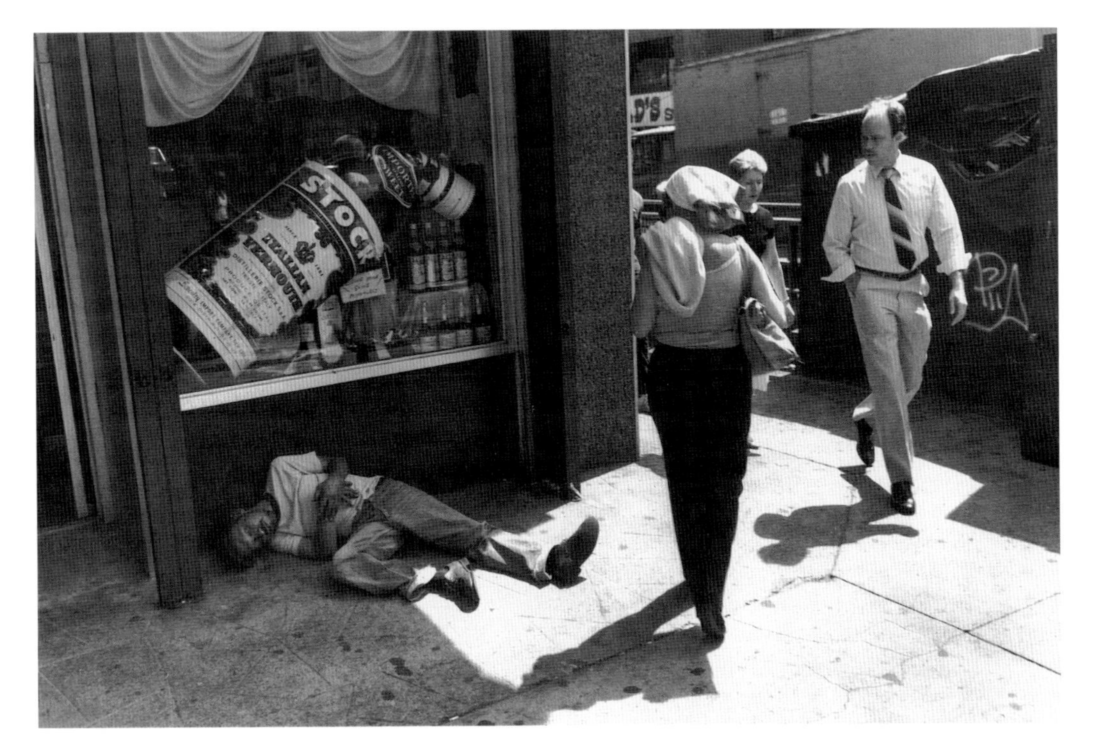

10.96 Lee Friedlander, *New York City,* 1983. Photograph. Running a gamut from street photography to nature and nudes, this photographer is another of the innovative "social land-scapists" that appeared in the 1950s and '60s. Friedlander, like the others in this group, captures unusual aspects of life events caught in a happened-upon moment. Courtesy of Fraenkel Gallery, SF.

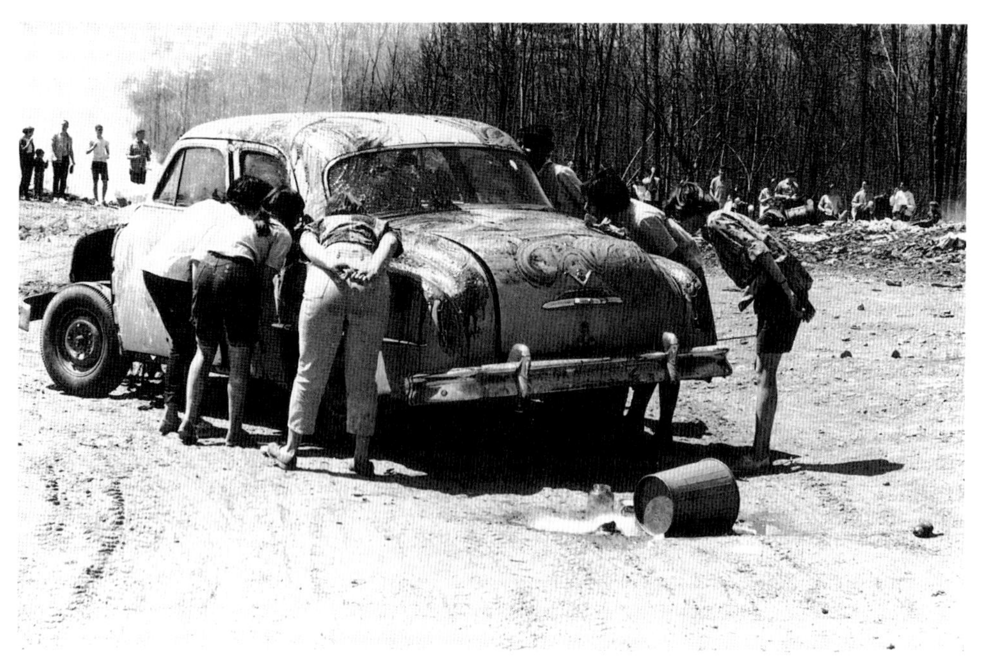

10.97 Allan Kaprow, *Household,* May 1964. One photograph of a series taken of a Happening commissioned by Cornell University, Ithaca, NY. There were no spectators at the event. Those taking part in it attended a preliminary meeting where the Happening was discussed and parts distributed. In Scene V, shown, women go to the car and lick jam. Courtesy of the artist, Allan Kaprow. Photograph © Sol Goldberg.

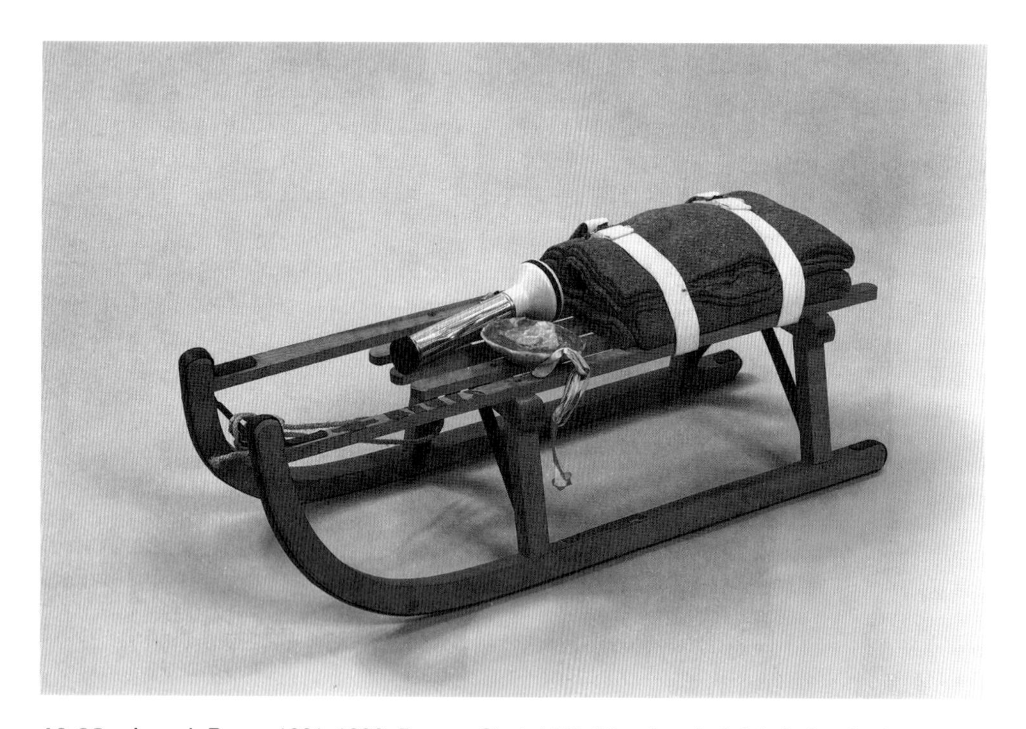

10.98 Joseph Beuys 1921–1986, *Rescue Sled,* 1969. Wooden sled, felt, belts, flashlight, fat and rope, 35 × 90 × 35 cm). Process artists such as Joseph Beuys believe that the ideas behind and the production of an artwork are more important than its medium or form. Beuys's commonplace objects often entail a complex symbolism springing from personal experiences. Twentieth Century Purchase Fund, 1973.56. Photograph by Bob Hashimoto. Reproduction, The Art Institute of Chicago. © 2005 Artists Rights Society (ARS), New York/VG Bild-Kunst, Bonn.

"assemblage on the move," bringing in the basic concepts of motion, time, and space. More recently this type of art has been called **Performance** or Action Art, an expanded category that can include theater, dance, music, cinema, video, and computer. Both Happenings and Performances are based on the concept of drawing spectators into the heart of a work of art so that they can experience the work more directly. This concept reached an earlier climax in Baroque art of the seventeenth century, when religious iconography, the church building itself, and the churchgoers' participation were intermingled in an artistic fabric.

Happenings were pioneered by Allan Kaprow (b. 1927), who gave his first happenings in John Cage's classes for experimental music at the New School for Social Research in New York in 1957. Usually, these performances were initiated by the artist with a particular setting in mind. Kaprow's Happenings exploited human or group activities. His art materials were everyday materials, often junk found on the street, as well as sounds, lights, and odors (fig. 10.97). These performances inspired other artists, and soon Happenings became popular events that spread from the United States to Europe. Kaprow, however, chose to avoid such publicity and has carried out his experiments more or less among friends to date.

Joseph Beuys (1921–1986), a German artist who was shot down by the Russians in World War II while flying for the Nazis, was associated with Performance Art after the war. In his Düsseldorf school, established at that time, Beuys put on performances that had a ritualistic or spiritual quality based on his rescue during the war, which he saw as a kind of resurrection. Beuys, however, did not think of these art projects as Happenings or Performances, preferring to call them "Action Sculptures," which he believed were a direct means of affecting his audiences. Beuys also created many drawings, paintings, and mixed-media assemblages to express his views of life and the world. His *Rescue Sled* of 1969 (fig. 10.98) is a reference to his war rescue by nomadic Tartars who wrapped him in animal fat and felt blankets to save his life.

Op Art

The "Op" in **Op Art** is an abbreviation for "optical." This form of art is primarily graphic, although it can merge into three-dimensionality when used in paintings that include an element of relief. Op Art is an extension and modification of earlier twentieth-century Geometric Abstraction. Even while some artists were opposing the relative obscurity of meaning in modern abstraction—such as, most notably, the Pop artists—others chose to send abstract art in yet another direction. Among the artists who chose to do this were the kinetic and light sculptors, the Minimalist sculptors, and the Op artists: Victor Vasarely (1908–1997), Richard Anuszkiewicz (b. 1930), and Bridget Riley (b. 1931) (fig. 10.99; see also figs. 2.25 and 7.23). Flourishing in the mid-1960s, these artists employed precise shapes and lines (sometimes wavy, as in Bridget Riley's work) or concentric patterns that have a direct impact on the physiology and psychology of vision (fig. 10.100; see also fig. 2.14). They explored the kinds of abstract patterns that seem dedicated as much to the investigation of vision as to its evocative expression in art.

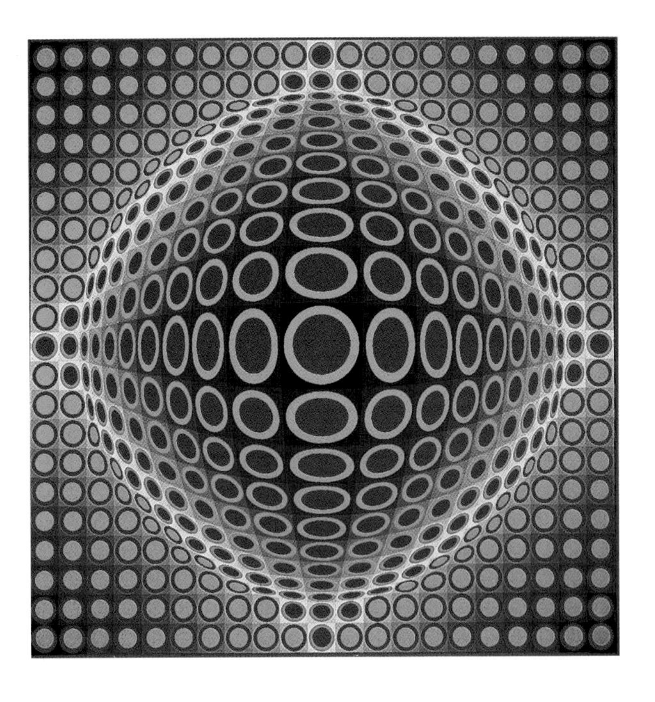

10.99 Victor Vasarely, *Vega Per,* 1969. Oil on canvas, 64 × 64 in. This painting is typical of Op Art in its predilection for creating unusual visual effects. In this case, Vasarely is obviously concerned with a three-dimensional illusion. Honolulu Academy of Arts. Gift of the Honorable Clare Boothe Luce, 1984 (5311.1). © 2005 Artists Rights Society (ARS), New York/ADAGP, Paris.

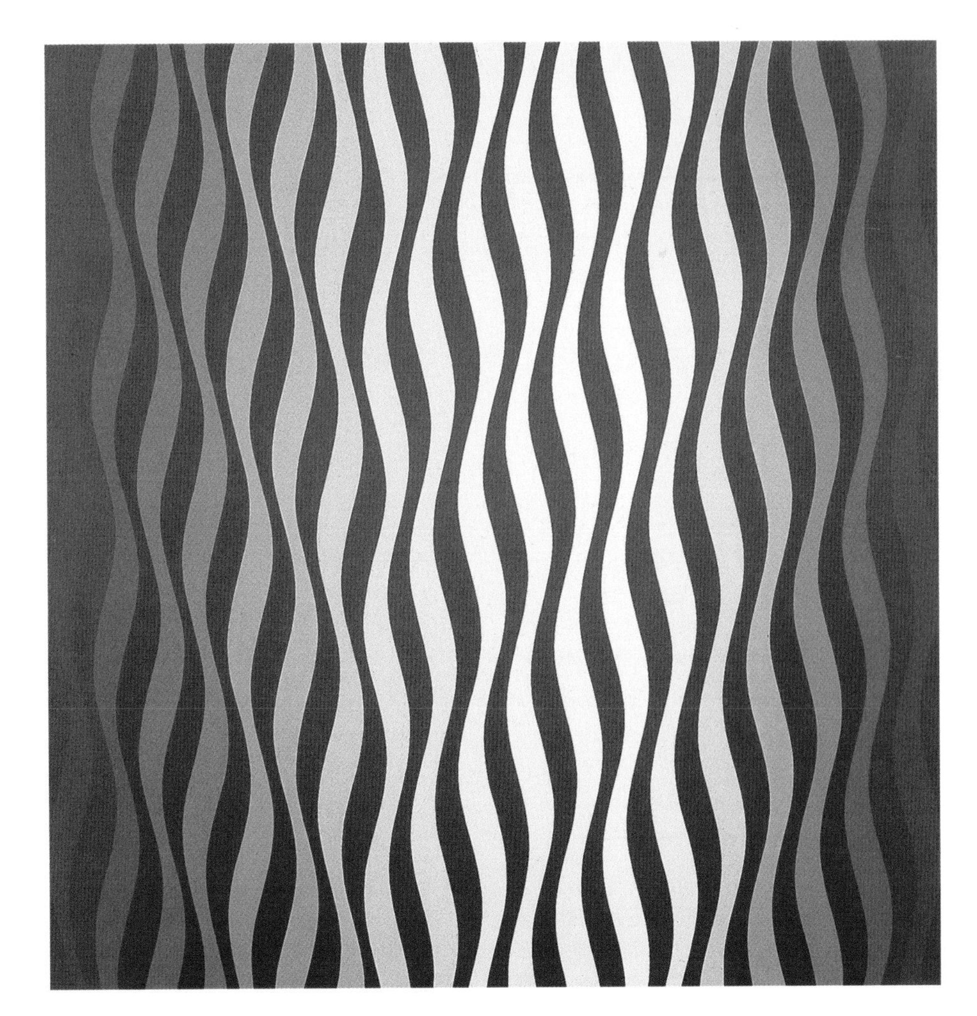

10.100 Bridget Riley, *Drift No. 2,* 1966. Acrylic on canvas, 7 ft 7½ in. × 7 ft 5½ in. (2.32 × 2.27 m). Op artists generally use geometric shapes, organizing them into patterns that produce fluctuating, ambiguous, and tantalizing visual effects very similar to those observed in moiré patterns, such as in door or window screens. Albright-Knox Art Gallery, Buffalo, NY. Gift of Seymour H. Knox. 1967.

10.101 Ad Reinhardt, Abstract Painting, *Blue 1953,* 1953. Oil on canvas, 50 × 28 in. (127 × 71.1 cm). This Reinhardt work is an example of Minimalist painting, in which the values are so close that only intense scrutiny can reveal differences of shape within. Collection of the Whitney Museum of American Art, New York. Gift of Susan Morse Hilles 74.22, © 2005 Estate of Ad Reinhardt/Artists Rights Society (ARS), New York.

10.102 Agnes Martin, *Untitled #9,* 1990. Synthetic polymer and graphite on canvas, 6 × 6 ft. A Canadian artist who studied in the United States, Martin worked with people like Reinhardt and Albers. Her early work was usually in the form of a linear grid in graphite revealing metaphysical meanings. More recently, in the 1990s, she replaced the grids with bands of color. She remained close to the Minimalist attitude in most of her work. Whitney Museum of American Art. Gift of the American Art Foundation 92.60. Photograph © 2001 Whitney Museum of American Art.

Minimalism

The **Minimalists** were a group of painters and sculptors who appeared in art circles from the 1960s to the 1970s, although the movement also included music, dance, poetry, and fiction. In painting there were precedents for the style in early-twentieth-century nonobjective abstraction. In fact, the painting branch grew out of Color Field paintings by such artists as Noland, Newman, and Rothko. The painters Ad Reinhardt (1913–1967) and the Canadian Agnes Martin (1912–2004) were key figures of the late 1950s in predicting the arrival of Minimalism on the scene in the 1960s. Reinhardt, a Color Field painter influenced by Constructivist painters like the Russian Malevich (see 10.49), painted pictures in such close values that only with intense concentration can the spectator determine that any shapes or lines or other elements of form are present at all (fig. 10.101). Martin in turn was influenced by the Color Field painters to present pure forms, relying only on the basic elements for meaning—without any trace of the artistic process—that became the goal of Minimalism. She had also absorbed much from the spirit of Paul Klee and old Chinese landscape painting (fig. 10.102).

Among important Minimalist sculptors were Donald Judd (1928–1994), Larry Bell (b. 1939), and Dan Flavin (1933–1996). They transformed the late mechanomorphic cubes of David Smith into blunt sculptures of simplified geometric volumes that seem stripped of all psychological or symbolic content. For their minimal presentation of nonobjective forms, the Minimalist sculptors were sometimes labeled Primary Structurists and ABC artists. Sometimes they shunned metal and welding, preferring materials hitherto uncommon in sculpture, such as cardboard, masonite, plywood, plastics, and glass. Donald Judd constructed repeated sequences of plastic and sheet-metal boxes hung on a wall, relief fashion (see fig. 9.41). Later he turned to making identical large, open-centered concrete boxes. Whether in the same or in different materials, Judd's and other Minimalists' sculptures were often repeated in rows or stacked up vertically. When a considerable number of such "repeats" were laid out on the floor of galleries, museums, warehouses, or other open spaces large enough to contain them, they were labeled siteworks or Site Art, terms that more recently have been replaced by the term **Installations.** This subject will be discussed later in the chapter.

While a few artists preferred the appearance of at least an abstract mass or solid, most of the Minimalists actually wanted to obliterate the core, creating

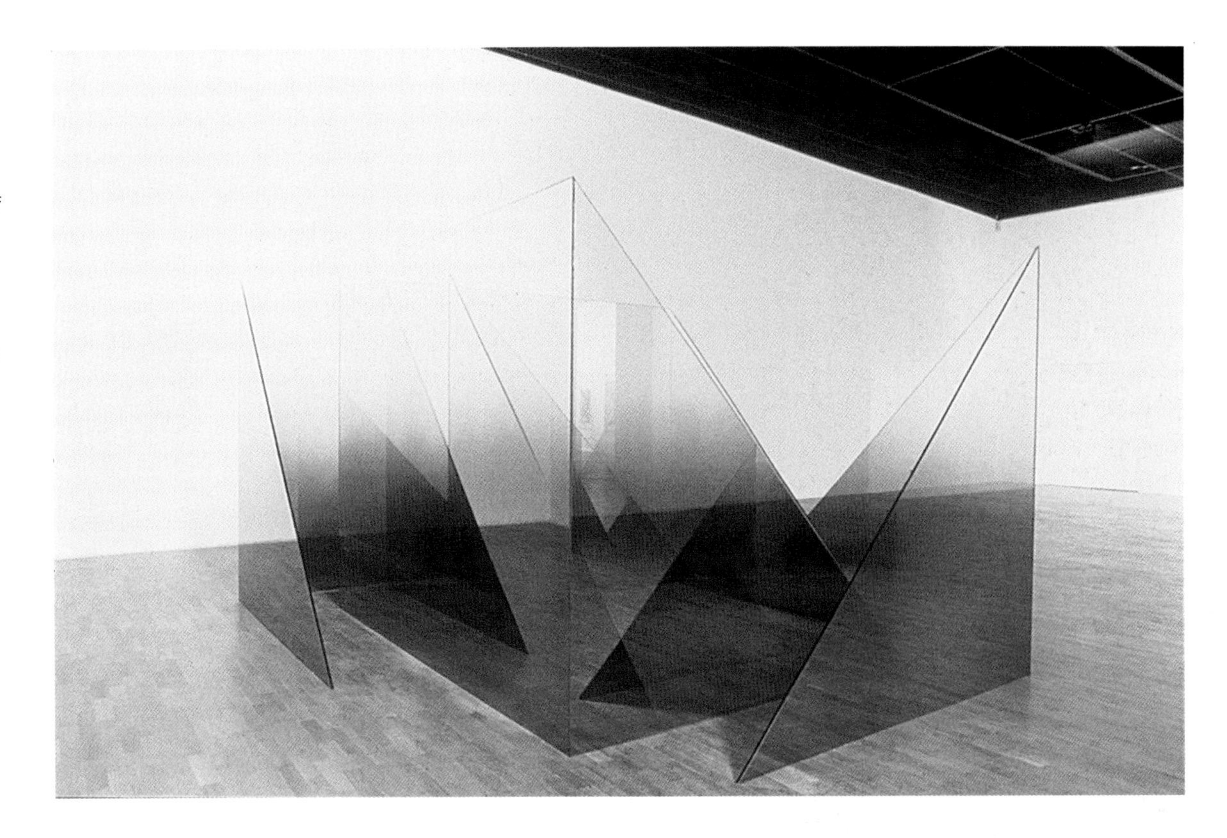

10.103 Larry Bell, *First and Last,* 1989. Two glass rectangles, 6 × 8 ft, eight glass triangles, 6 × 6 ft, coated: nickel-chrome. The Minimalists make use of simple monumental forms exploiting a wide variety of materials. Musée d'Art Contemporain, Lyon, France. © Larry Bell. Photograph courtesy of the artist.

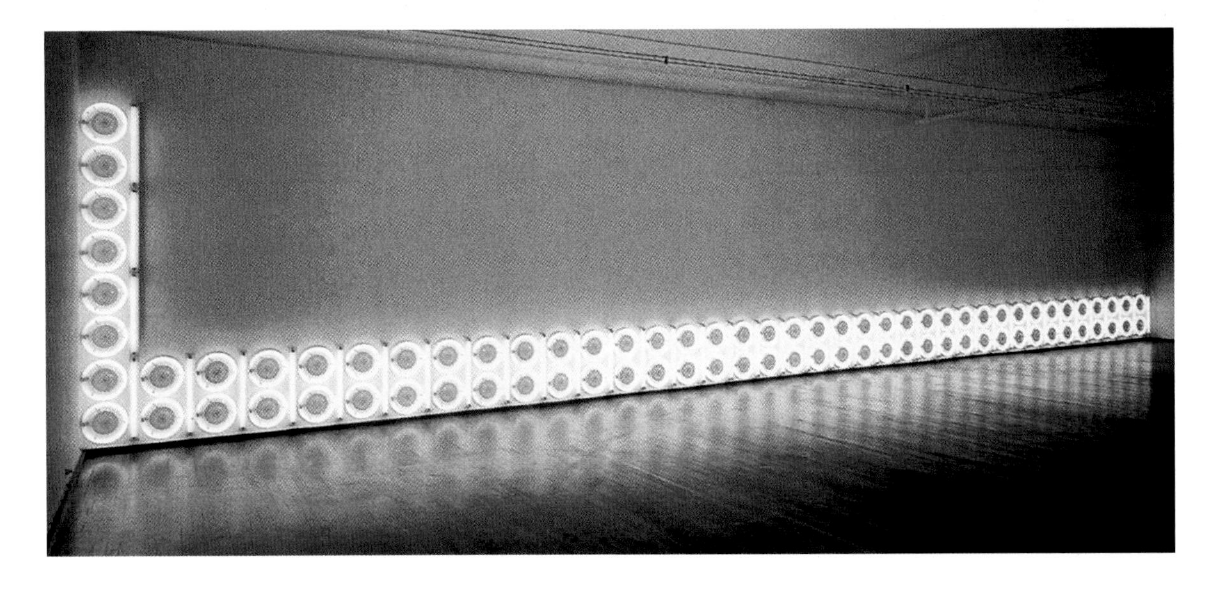

10.104 Dan Flavin, *Untitled* (in memory of my father, D. Nicholas Flavin), 1974. Daylight fluorescent light (edition of three), 8 × 48 ft (2.44 × 14.63 m). One of the Minimalist artists who devoted much of his career to light sculptures or assemblages, Flavin represents a branch of artists working with static assemblies of fluorescent lights. Courtesy Leo Castelli Gallery, New York. © 2005 Estate of Dan Flavin/ Artists Rights Society (ARS), New York.

simple volumes of enclosed space or opening up numerous voids. Some of these pieces are simply boxes of gigantic size. (Large size is a characteristic of much twentieth-century sculpture and painting.)

Some, like Larry Bell, used hard sheet plastic (Plexiglas) or tinted glass to create transparent volumes that enclose space (fig. 10.103). Dan Flavin made light sculptures, often by arranging groups of fluorescent fixtures in large room installations (fig. 10.104). Sometimes artists combine lighted objects with movement and electronically produced sounds to create kinetic fantasies. Artists who create light sculptures often use neon light in their assemblages.

There are some Minimalists who preferred to produce open spatial forms creating large simplified voids, which might look closed from one point of view and open from another. Examples of this can be found in Lila Katzen's

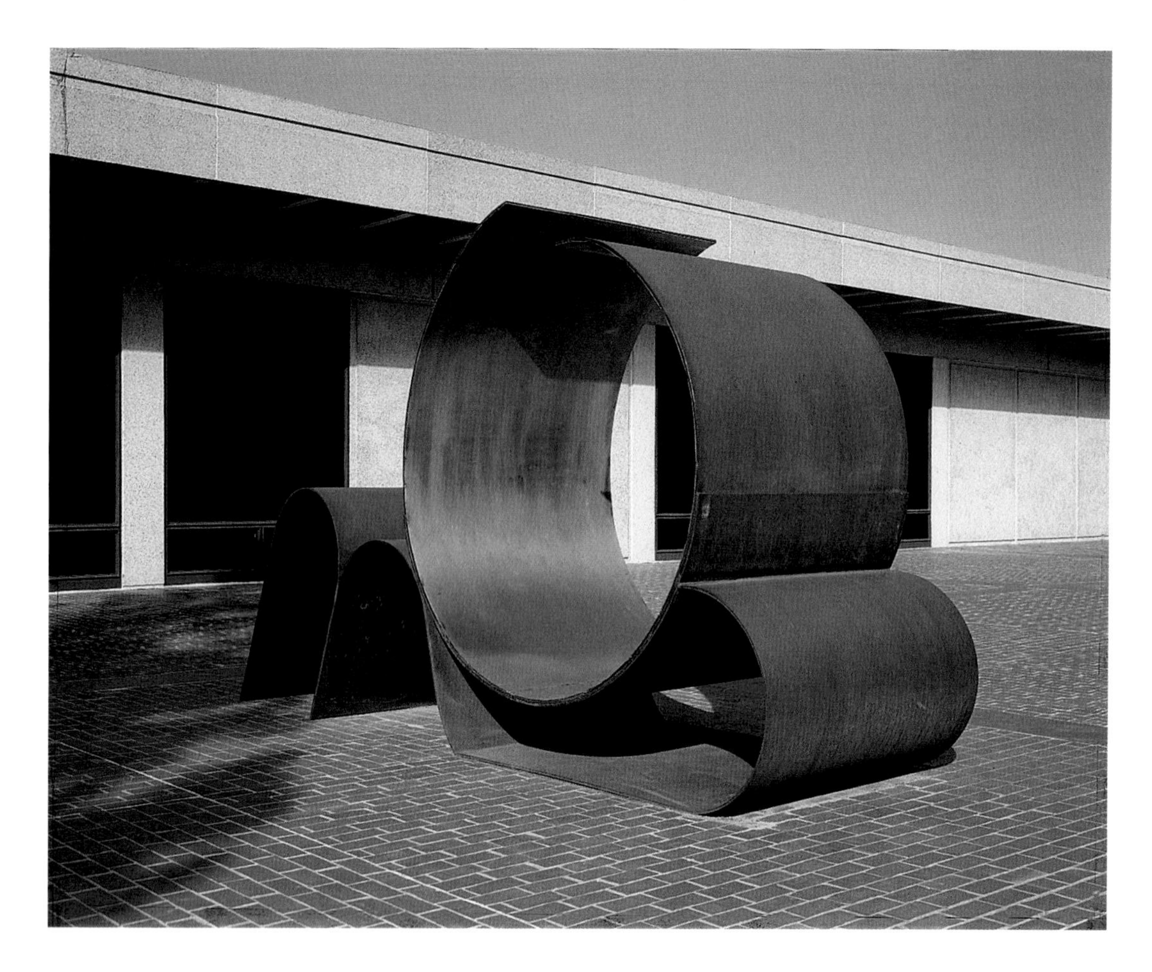

10.105 Lila Katzen, *Oracle*, 1974. Corten and stainless steel, 11 × 17 × 5 ft (3.35 × 5.18 × 1.52 m). These flowing sheet-metal forms, set in outdoor space, are typical of the works of Katzen. University of Iowa Museum of Art, Gift of Phillip Katzen (1978.69) © The University of Iowa. © Philip Katzen and Lila Katzen Living Trust/Licensed by VAGA, New York, NY.

(b. 1932) large, open-rolled, sheet-metal forms (fig. 10.105). A few of the open boxes, and occasionally some of the enclosed rectilinear sculptures, stress brightly colored surfaces, while others are neutral or devoid of color. These monumental forms can make a powerful impact on the observer as they are encountered in public places, but they also transmit a message of monotony.

Gradually, Minimalism seemed to lack content to the generation of artists coming to maturity in the 1960s and 1970s. Minimal forms began to be rejected in favor of realism and observable meanings. On the one hand, the lack of content in Minimalist art had been a reaction to the psychologically suggestive meanings found in Abstract Expressionist art. On the other hand, the rejection of Minimalism's reductionism was in line with the reaction that had brought about Pop Art a bit earlier.

Environmental Art and Installations

Environmental Art and Installations tend to take their names from their locations, outdoors or indoors. Both forms are meant to surround viewers and make them a part of the experience. The artwork is completed by the spectators' participation in the details of the created forms. Both types of art came out of Pop, Assemblage, Performances, and Minimalism. Installation artists believe that spectators engage in works of art with not only their vision but also their whole bodies, including the senses of touch, smell, and hearing. Kurt Schwitters (1887–1948), a German artist who created his own version of Dadaist works called "Merz," and Marcel Duchamp created the first twentieth-century Installations. The Pop artists can be credited with renewing the Installational form of art in the 1960s and 1970s. While Lucas Samaras (b. 1936) was primarily a Pop artist, his *Mirrored Room* is also a good example of an Installation (fig. 10.106), due to its indoor location and space-filling size.

When Installations were first exhibited in the 1960s, being arranged on the floors or walls or from the ceilings of a gallery or another large inside location, they were named Scatterworks, Floorworks, Siteworks, or by the general term Environments. With the growing popularity of such artworks, however, these categories seem to require separate emphases, particularly pertaining to the

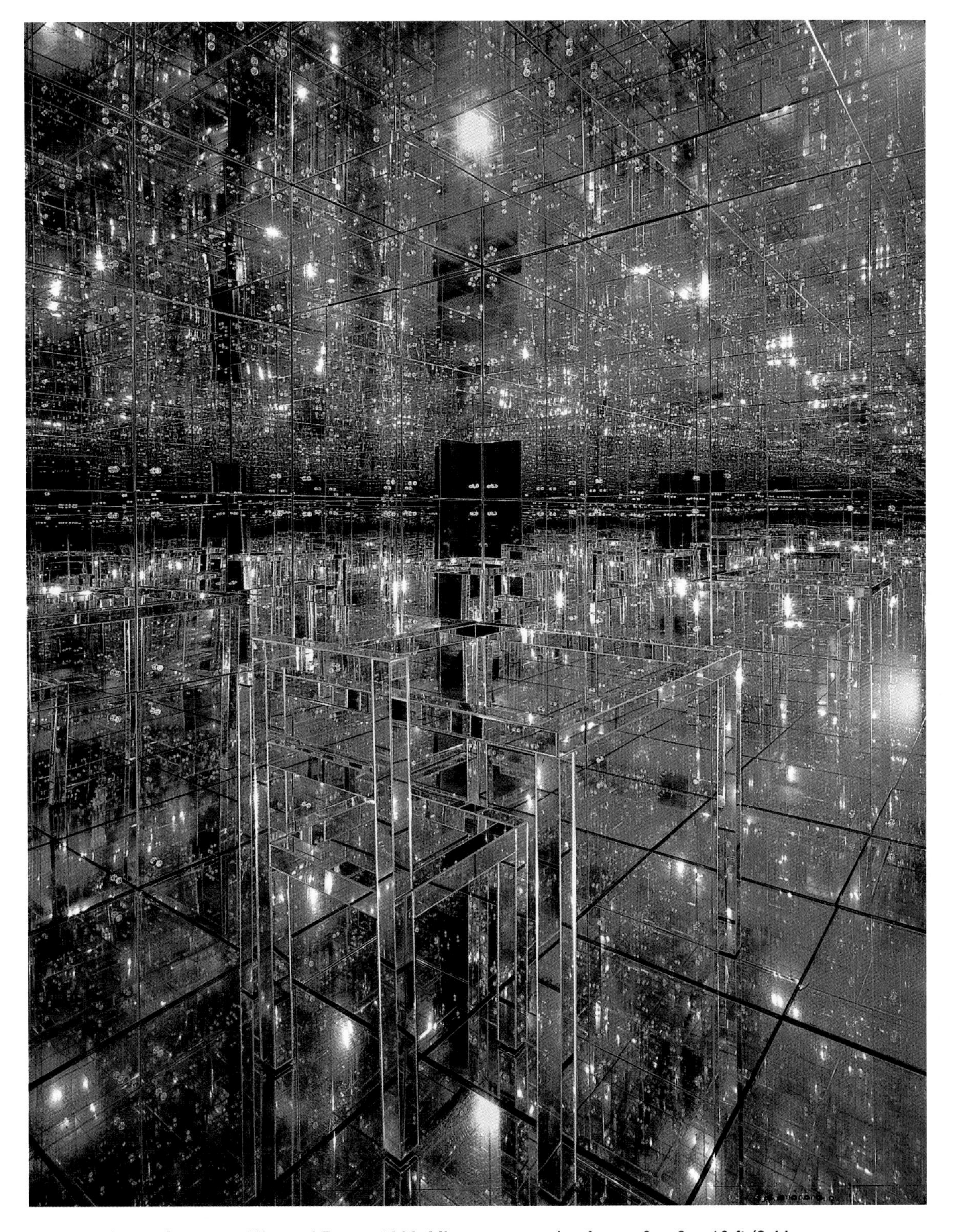

10.106 Lucas Samaras, *Mirrored Room,* 1966. Mirrors on wooden frame, 9 × 9 × 10 ft (2.44 × 2.44 × 3.05 m). This is an example of Environmental Art, which, by its size and structure, may actually enclose the observer within the form of the work. Albright-Knox Art Gallery, Buffalo, NY. Gift of Seymour H. Knox, 1966.

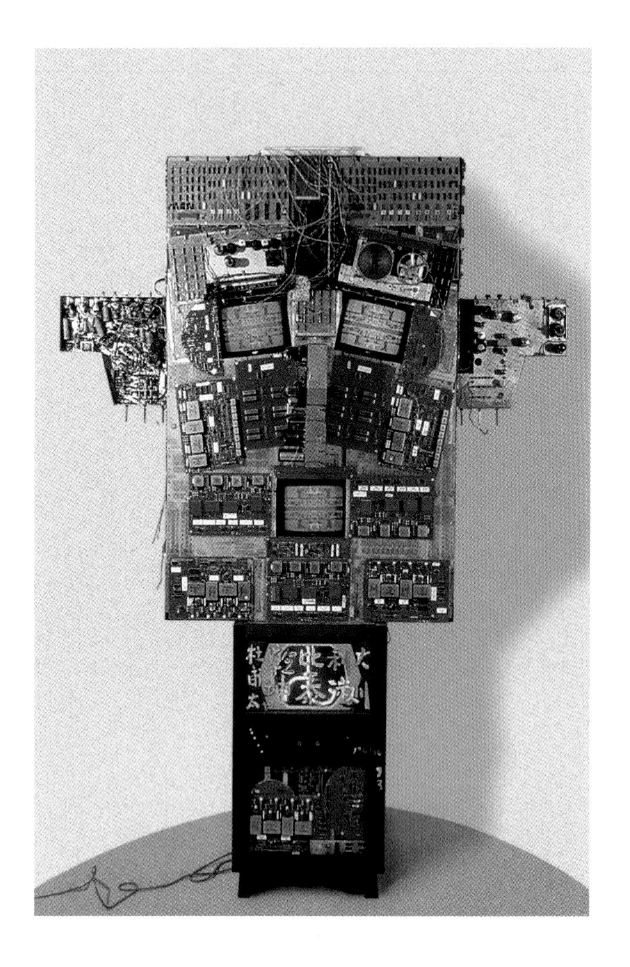

10.107 Nam June Paik, *Descartes in Easter Island,* 1993. Video sculpture, 94 × 68 × 30 in. Process, Conceptual, and Performance Art are closely related and often overlapping art forms. The Korean American artist Nam June Paik, who mostly produces video installations—which he pioneered—bridges the slight differences between the forms. He has several followers who also explore the impact of technology on modern society. Courtesy of the artist.

10.108 Judy Pfaff, *Deepwater,* Installation view, 1980. Organic matter (roots and branches), balsa and veneer plywood, wire, various plastics, oil and latex paint. As can be seen from this illustration, Installations can be composed of virtually any kind of material. Courtesy of the artist.

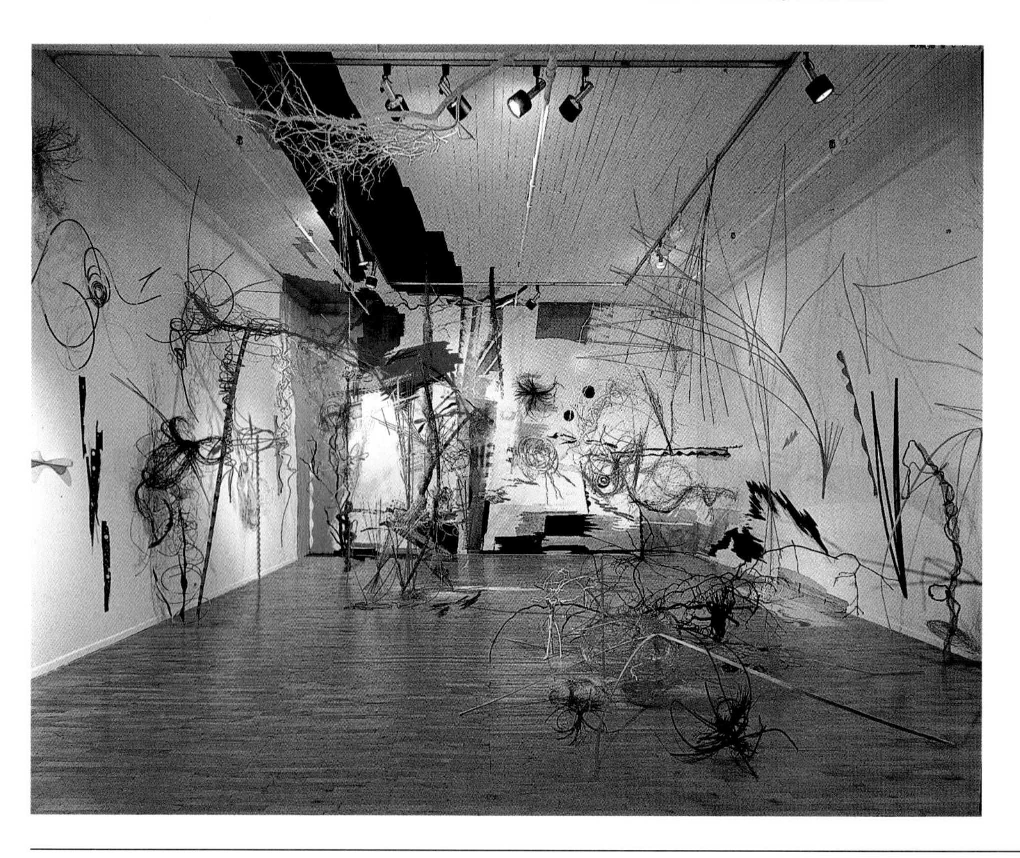

location of each. The term *Installations* can be used to designate interiors where the intention is to transform a fairly large volume of space with sculpture or assemblage. The term *Environments,* on the other hand, can be used to indicate an all-encompassing assemblage, usually in an outdoor location.

An artist producing a different kind of lighted, sculptural Installation is the Korean-born artist Nam June Paik (b. 1932), who began his art career in Germany as an electronic musician and composer and then recognized the possibilities of video assemblage. Video gave him the ability to express ideas about the mass media directly. He thus became famous as the first artist to display video ensembles (fig. 10.107; see also fig. 8.58). He now has several followers, although it is difficult to be original after Paik's example.

Judy Pfaff (b. 1946), an English artist who was trained in the United States, is an example of an Installation artist in the locational sense, since she makes her creations site-specific. She began as an Abstract Expressionist painter of huge canvases but turned to experimenting with small sculptural Installations in the 1970s. She is now primarily known for huge, rambling, and soaring Installations in materials such as wires, glass, plastics, and metals (fig. 10.108).

Ann Hamilton (b. 1956), an American artist from Ohio who trained at the University of Kansas and the Yale School of Art, is an Installation artist of imaginative, strangely moving, sensuous forms (fig. 10.109). She appears to be concerned with the direct bodily sensations provided by experiencing her works. This aspect of her content is found in the strange world of copper, animal pelts, or penny-covered floors (among other materials) that she creates with numerous assistants. The walls and ceilings are also often subtly modified but are unified with the building or fabric of the location. Barely audible sounds from the outside and recordings usually accompany the Installation, becoming a part of the total experience. An attendant, often Hamilton herself, is seen seated at a table burning paper, sewing, erasing, or chewing some substance. This presence is meant to make attendees feel as though they are participants as well as spectators of the experience. Hamilton's strange interior worlds cause the observer to respond to sensations that are now lost to modern society and that may account for various ills afflicting the society.

Another Installation artist who has been making a name for herself is Sandy Skoglund (b. 1947). From New England, she trained at Smith College and later at the University of Iowa. Some observers believe that her neon-hued animal hordes, consisting of cats, dogs, and squirrels romping in normal household interiors, provide a sense of healing and conflict resolution through their whimsical imagery. Others interpret her content to be like a child's imagery gone awry, evoking haunting fears (see fig. 9.44).

Environments are now more concerned with that branch of art in which the artist transforms an outdoor location on a gigantic scale. The Pop Art concept of bombarding the spectator with mundane images from the everyday world by taking the most commonplace items in our culture out of their normal context and giving them the legitimacy of fine art was of considerable importance in the evolution of both Installations and Environments. But like Minimalists, these artists also seem to avoid connotations other than the look of human intervention. With Installations and Environmental Art, spectators become involved in the principle of space/time—the action involved in either creating or looking at art—that involves the fourth dimension. A leading pioneer of Environmental Art was the sculptor Robert Smithson (1938–1973), whose *Spiral Jetty,* created at Great Salt Lake, Utah, in 1970, played an important part in introducing such large-scale Environments (fig. 10.110).

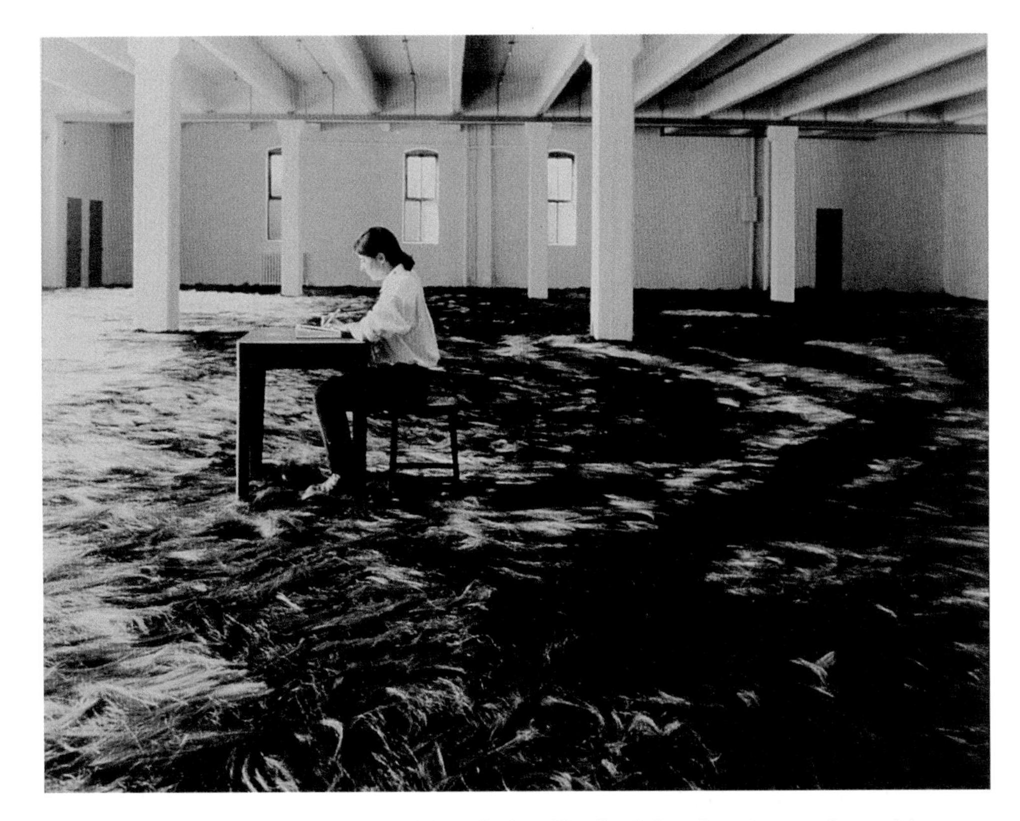

10.109 Ann Hamilton, *tropos,* 1993 Installation. Hamilton's installments seem to provide an imaginative, strangely moving, sensuous world beyond verbal or logical apprehension. They offer a direct bodily sensation or experience that is at the core of human instincts, as the title of this work implies. Courtesy of Sean Kelly Gallery, New York. Photo courtesy of Dia Center for the Arts. Photographer Thibault Jenson.

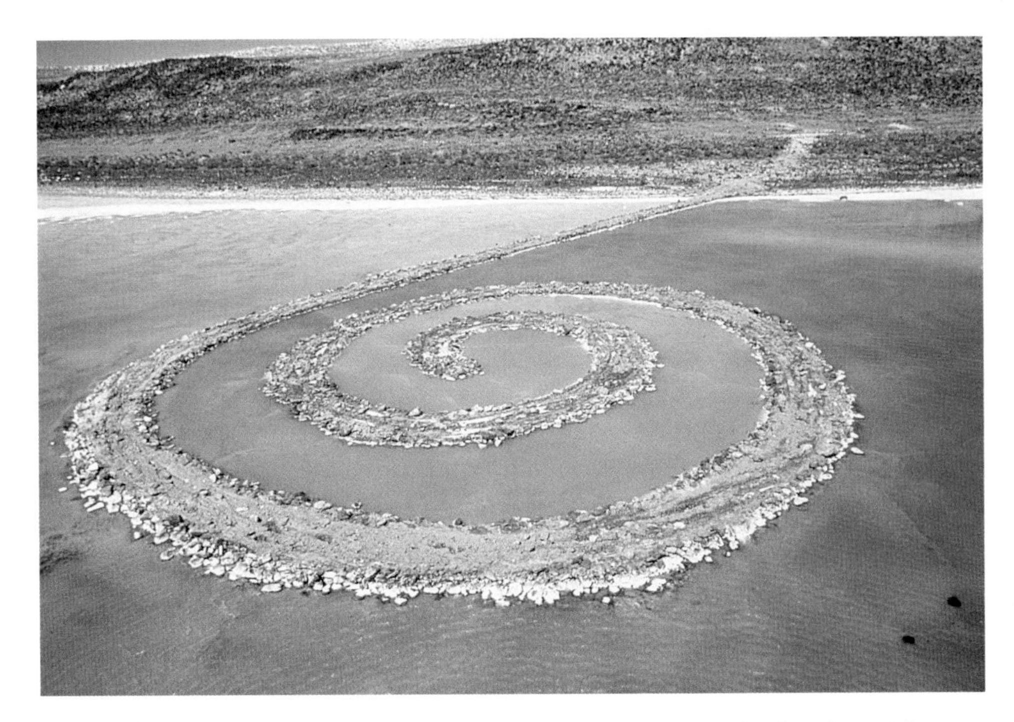

10.110 Robert Smithson, *Spiral Jetty,* Great Salt Lake, Utah, 1970. Rock, salt crystals, earth, algae, coil, 1,500 ft (457 m). Students of art must be willing to concede the possible validity of many unfamiliar forms of individual expression. © Estate of Robert Smithson/Licensed by VAGA, New York, NY.

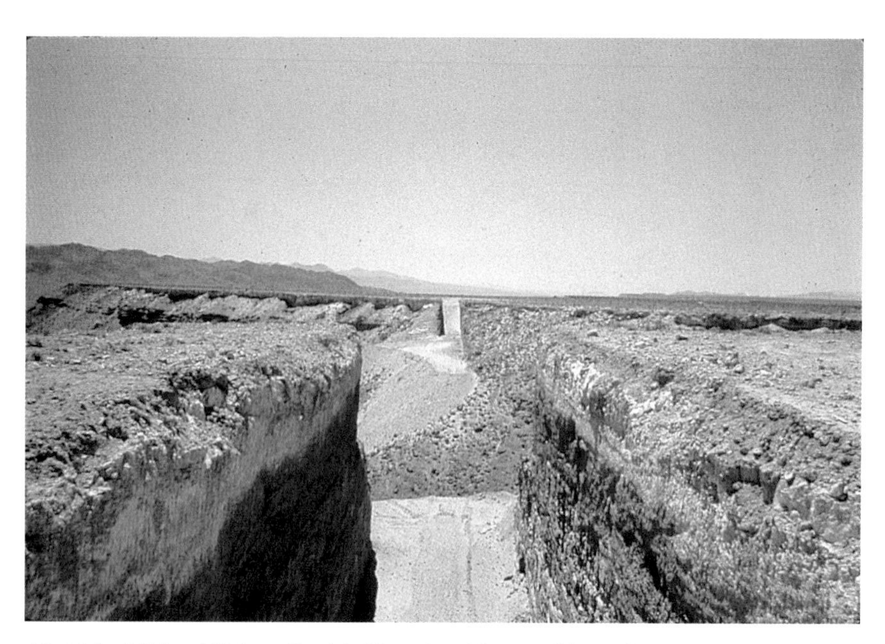

10.111 Michael Heizer, *Double Negative,* Mormon Mesa, Overton, Black Rock Desert, Nevada, 1969. 240,000-ton displacement in rhyolite and sandstone, 1,500 × 50 × 30 ft (457 × 15 × 9 m). Some of the artists producing Environments—in this case, an earthwork—were looking to escape the high-pressure commercial world of galleries and museums. Antecedents for Environments are found in landscape architecture and painting, while the modern desire for works on a monumental scale also played a part. © Michael Heizer. Photograph courtesy of the artist.

Christo (b. 1935) and Jeanne-Claude (b. 1935) are among the artists who currently produce Environmental Art. Known for their international activity, Christo and Jeanne-Claude have continuously explored the environment, from 1968 in the great 280-foot-high balloons suspended by cables that were featured at the Whitney Museum, to the *Wrapped Reichstag* (the German parliament), which they encapsulated in polypropylene fabric in 1995 (see fig. 1.17). Most recently, in 2005 they have been constructing a procession of gateways with fabric hangings in New York City's Central Park. All their enormous environmental works are preceded by copious plans consisting of drawings, paintings, and working models. These are sold to raise funds for the materials and helpers required to carry out their monumental conceptions.

The displacement of land and space necessary for the setting or exhibiting of large-scale public Environments drew attention to the question of the actual location where they are situated. Soon, some artists recognized that the manipulation of the setting, or natural environment itself, was a significant artwork in its own right. The exact origins of earth-displacement Environments is difficult to pinpoint, although roots existed in landscape painting, sculptural monuments, and landscape or park design for at least three centuries. As a movement in modern times, Earth Art developed in the late 1960s. In 1967, for example, Claes Oldenberg dug holes in New York City's Central Park and called them "invisible sculptures." Michael Heizer (b. 1944) dug five trenches that he lined with wood in the Black Rock Desert of Nevada in 1969 (fig. 10.111). The concept of "bigger is better" also soon took hold in such earthworks, because cranes and power shovels had to be used by the artist-directors to produce their works.

Part of the reason artists took their work outdoors was to escape from the dominance of the studio as a place to make art and from the reverential hype of the galleries marketing avant-garde artists' works (usually meaning abstract art of various kinds). Ironically, in spite of the desire to escape institutional domination, almost all Installations are now found in museums and galleries. On the other hand, the fashion of making earthwork Environments seems to have ended, probably because of the works' isolation, lack of public attendance, and cost.

People continue to see and enjoy the environments of Christo and Jeanne-Claude, due to their public, rather than isolated, locations. But their work, like most of the Installation works, is temporary. On the other hand, the popularity of Installations, marked by their increase in numbers in the late 1990s and into the 2000s, seems to be growing.

Postmodernism

Throughout history, new generations of artists become dissatisfied with the path taken by their predecessors and strike out in new directions. The feeling that inherited methods and media have reached a state of perfection or exhausted their possibilities seemed especially keen among artists of the twentieth century and increasingly so after midcentury. **Postmodernism** is the term given by critics to the recent art that circumvents all so-called **modern art** as passé. The particular catalyst for Postmodernism in painting and sculpture was the severe limitation posed by Minimalism on finding new directions. During the modern period, figurative art had been placed in the shadow of formal abstraction, of which Minimalism was the most pronounced form.

Postmodernism first gained prominence in architecture, as a reaction to the stripped-down boxes of the International style, which had resulted from the theory that "form follows function," and the teachings of the German Bauhaus. Just as the new Postmodernist artists began to question whether "progress" was important and to appropriate elements of earlier artistic styles, so did architects begin to take the ornamentation and manner of former architectural periods and combine them in contemporary materials.

Certain aspects of American culture unconnected directly to the arts affected the rise of Postmodernist art. The growing desire to "clean the slate and start over again" has been discernible from about the 1960s but has been accompanied by the feeling that society is exhausted, out of new ideas, and unable to solve its problems. Wars, forced migrations, attempts at genocide, and the consequent upheavals suggest the depth of the turmoil that artists witnessed. Racial prejudice, the unequal treatment of women, the uneven distribution of income, and bitter partisanship in politics were still with us as we entered the new millennium, and, as a reflection of our world, all the arts are affected. All art of the past forty years in which artists appear to be looking for a new means of expression or a new kind of form can be said to embody the Postmodern condition. Some critics see Postmodernism as part of a normal rejection of the pedantic "control" of the arts that always accompanies the approved forms or styles in the past, not a radically new phase of art (or of history). For centuries such control was wielded by religion, then by government academies, and since the nineteenth century by galleries, critics, museums, and, in our country, governing bodies or officials, once again.

Most of Postmodern art is individualistic. Yet some artists reject individualism and want to return art to the anonymity that prevailed before the Renaissance. In today's context this seems unlikely. Other characteristics of Postmodernism are the reintroduction of decoration, such as can be found in Islamic manuscripts; a diversity of novel techniques, as required by new media; and a return to literary sources, as was adopted by the nineteenth-century Romantics. Since early modernism the constant switching back and forth between styles and media has made it difficult to coin specific names for groups or categories of artists. Because of this, it makes no sense to say that Postmodernism implies that the practices of modernism have been abandoned; thus, the term is used loosely to encompass the styles that have come into being as reactions to Abstract "dogmas." In some cases, Postmodernists have returned to abstraction, to sample from it as they might sample from other historical styles. In these cases, Postmodernism has taken on a new or different meaning. Postmodernist artists try to present their forms in such a way that a reference to content beyond or in back of the work seems apparent. At all events, Postmodernism does not depend on a "worship" of total form "for its own sake."

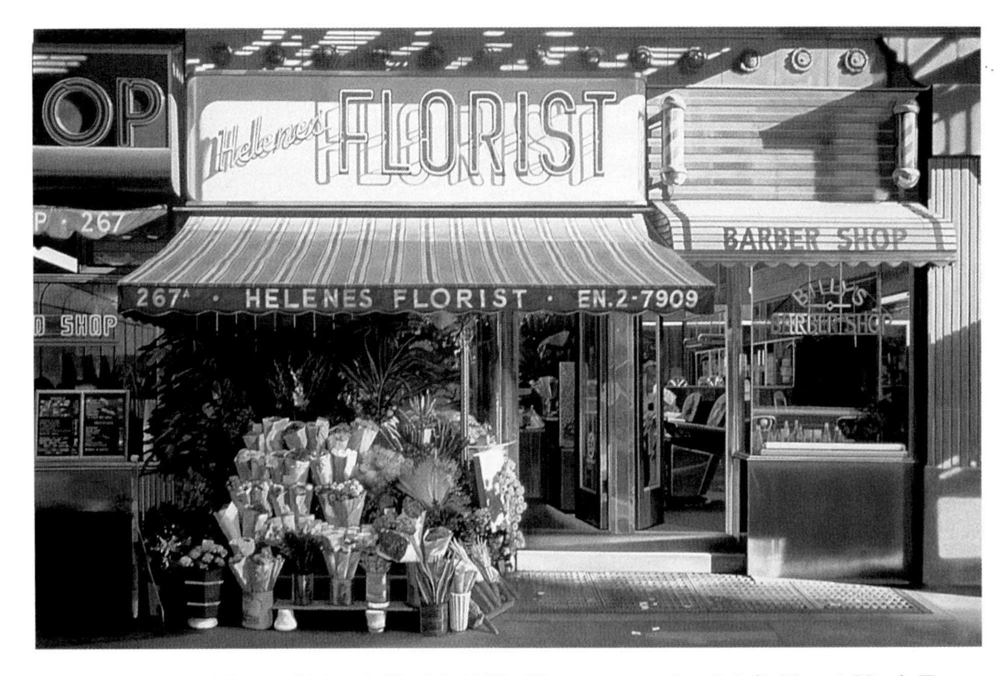

10.112 **Richard Estes, *Helene's Florist*, 1971. Oil on canvas, 4 × 6 ft (1.22 × 1.83 m).** The meticulously rendered images of Richard Estes attempt to reach the degree of reality found in photography. Toledo Museum of Art, Toledo, OH. © Richard Estes/Courtesy Marlborough Gallery, NY.

New Realism (Photorealism)

New Realism was the first art to emphasize the human figure and portraiture extensively since the early part of the twentieth century. As a trend during the 1960s and '70s, it was, in a sense, a new kind of Pop Art that strove for a matter-of-fact kind of verisimilitude, but without the sly humor of Pop. For most of the century, representation had been anathema to abstract artists. Their values had been based on the rejection of anything suggesting an objective mapping of reality. But now representation, or realism, returned with a vengeance in painters such as Richard Estes (b. 1936), Chuck Close (b. 1940), and Philip Pearlstein (b. 1924) (figs. 10.112 and 10.113; see also fig. 2.11). The example by Duane Hanson (1925–1996) (fig. 10.114) indicates how New Realism extended into sculpture.

The New Realists were also sometimes referred to as New Illusionists,

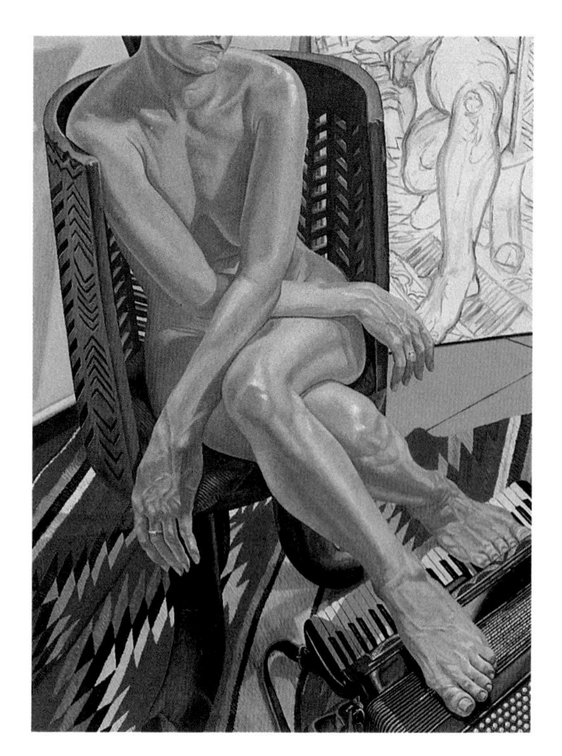

10.113 Philip Pearlstein, *Chevrons #2,* 1996. Oil on canvas, 48 × 36 in. (121.9 × 91.4 cm). This New Realist painter uses a kind of descriptive lighting to represent human figures.

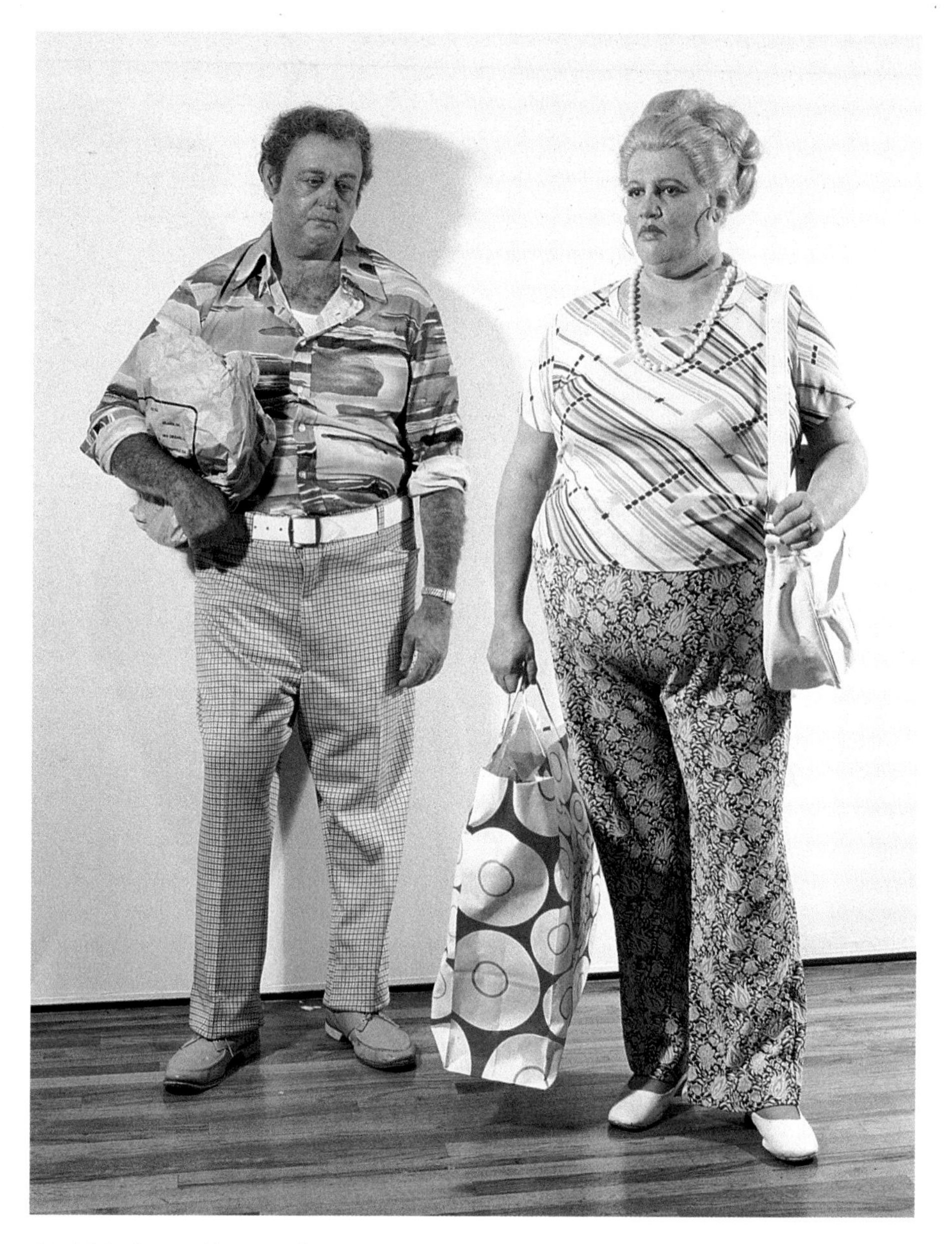

10.114 Duane Hanson, *Couple with Shopping Bags,* 1976. Polyvinyl/polychromed in oil, life size. This work belongs in the context of photorealist painting, but it incorporates more illusions than any painting could. Hanson's three-dimensional, lifelike, life-size figures are cast in colored polyester resin and fiberglass to look like real skin and are clothed in real garments. His human reproductions are so meticulously detailed that one reacts to them first as real people and only later as sculpture.

Photorealists, and Superrealists. Most depended on photography to gain their meticulous artistic ends, although some, like Pearlstein, maintain that they do not paint from projected images, or photographs, but rely on painstaking observation of their models. By and large, however, the New Realists show average people involved in everyday activities, with little or no evocative content. Many feature photolike renditions of city streets, storefronts, and similar structures.

The New Realists were preceded, clearly, by the continuing high level of interest in realistic art throughout the twentieth century, particularly in the United States. This can be witnessed not only in the unabated popularity of Andrew Newell Wyeth (b. 1917) but also in the perennial interest in artists like Edward Hopper (1882–1967), Charles Sheeler (1883–1965), and Ben Shahn (1898–1969) from the earlier part of the century (see figs. 1.11, 2.30, 4.26, 6.2, 8.24, and 8.25). On occasion, nineteenth-century Realism—from the Pre-Raphaelites (a nineteenth-century English Realist movement based on Proto-Renaissance and early Renaissance "primitives" before Raphael) to the Impressionists—has returned to favor. Even Picasso, that towering genius of the century, in the midst of all his Expressionist, Abstract, and Surrealist explorations, continually revisited realistic idioms.

The New Realist sculptors refined the styles of Segal and Oldenberg and made even more lifelike images in fiber-

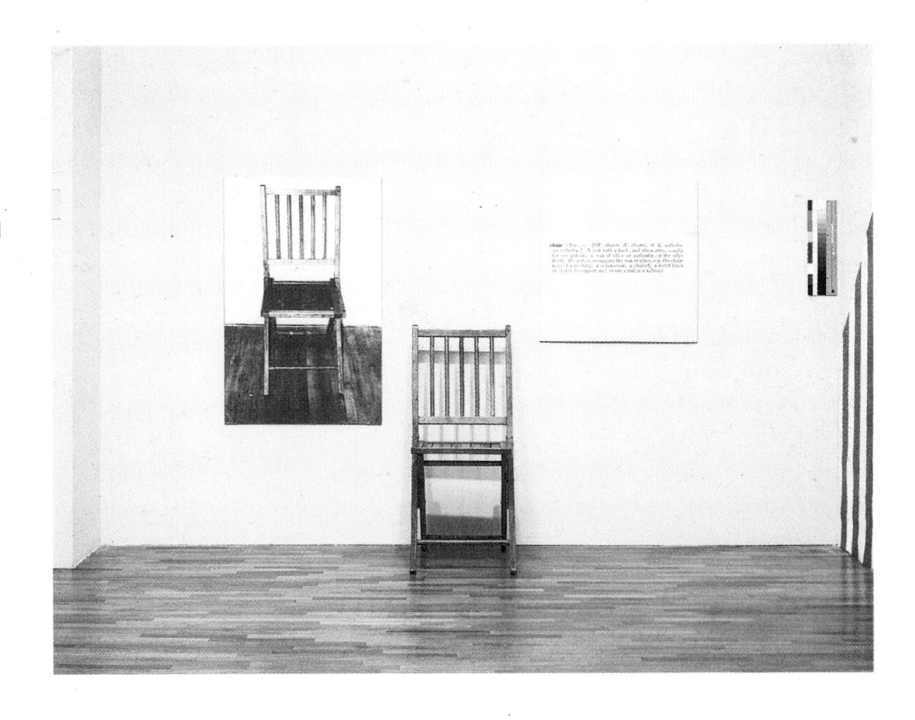

10.115 Joseph Kosuth, *One and Three Chairs,* 1965. Wooden folding chair, photographic copy of a chair, and photographic enlargement of dictionary definition of a chair; chair, 32⅜ × 14⅞ × 207 in. (82 × 37.8 × 53 cm); photo panel, 36 × 24⅛ in. (91.5 × 61.1 cm); text panel, 24 × 24⅛ (61 × 61.3 cm). In this example of Conceptual Art, the idea of one actual or "ready-made" chair is triplicated by a photograph of a chair and a dictionary definition of a chair.

glass and resins. Trompe l'oeil verisimilitude reached a new level of virtuosity in such three-dimensional illusions.

Process and Conceptual Art

As we have found, the Minimalists of the 1960s and '70s emphasized purity of form in simple volumes with obscure content (which the faithful saw as transcendental). As the Postmoderns saw it, the Abstract Expressionists had promoted this lack of content by raising in importance the creative act over the form of the finished artwork. In these movements, artists had expended a great deal of energy toward exploring the creative process and the conception of ideas. The forms called Process and Conceptual Art are the results of this kind of thinking carried to a logical conclusion, where the "process" or "idea" becomes an end in itself. To Postmoderns, at least, both forms seem to conceal artistic expression, which had served as the goal in early modern art. The Process artists believed that art is experienced primarily in the act of physically producing. The interpretations given to the final form do not seem important to them, as is suggested by, for example, the exposure of their artworks to the natural effects of the weather or to the natural effect of aging and decomposing. Process and Conceptual Art are, therefore, transitional between earlier forms like Minimalism and full-blown Postmodernism. One of the strongest postminimal Process artists was the German-born Eva Hesse (1936–1970), who died tragically after a short life and career. Had she lived longer, she might have expanded her role as one of the first feminist artists, opposing the male-dominated code of monumentality in Minimalism by her preference for techniques of wrapping, sewing, and lacing. Hesse's childhood was disrupted by having to flee Nazi persecution in Germany. Her sense of insecurity must have been increased by feelings of abandonment and loneliness when her mother committed suicide after moving with Hesse to New York. Hesse's use of binding materials may have expressed her desire to find a means to bind to something stable in life (see fig. 2.4).

The most significant concern of Conceptual Art is the idea that creates it. For many artists, the show called *Information* at the Museum of Modern Art in 1970 marked the decline of the formalist aesthetic. Conceptual artists believed that neither the act of making nor the act of completing an art object was as important as the idea, or concept, that lay behind it. The most extreme representatives of this point of view, and an early indication of how idea would dominate form eventually, were the artists who conceived of filling the air with oxygen or steam vapor in the early 1960s—most significant of whom was, perhaps, Robert Morris (b. 1931). They called it "universal art," because the vapors would expand endlessly into the universe. Today this form of art, like Process Art, often involves action by the artist alone but more often involves helpers and/or an audience, since it was partly influenced by Happenings and Performance Art. In a sense, Christo's siteworks can be considered Conceptual forms of art since they require a "director" who has conceived of the work and assistants who participate in realizing the idea in whatever form it may take. However, most Conceptual Art was on a smaller scale and began to take on the respectable veneer of "fine art" once it was exhibited in galleries.

An early example of Conceptual Art is found in Joseph Kosuth's (b. 1945) *One and Three Chairs* of 1965 (fig. 10.115). Kosuth took a ready-made or "found" object, in this case a chair, added a photograph of the chair, and next to that placed a dictionary definition of a chair. During the late 1960s and early 1970s, similar items were being exhibited and given the status of art. When they were put on display, it was much to the discomfiture of the artists involved, because their intentions had been to squash the idea of art-as-precious-object and the control exerted over artists by galleries, museum officials, and private owners. Many Conceptual works were just displays of typed or handwritten words, explaining theories of art, the sciences, topology, or anything else that might make the idea positive. Some Conceptual artists' methods and attitudes were probably influenced by commercial advertising. Photographs, plus cinematic and video images, were frequently used to record these concepts or to get them across in some way. The Minimalist sculptor Sol Lewitt (b. 1928), who may have coined the term *Conceptualism,* once wrote to the effect that Conceptual works were only as good as the idea behind them.

One common denominator in works of art from the 1970s forward has been a desire to bring back recognizable content and meaning to works of art. Attempts to name this new concern for a more representational approach flounder because of the diversity of manners prevalent today. Good examples of this diversity can be found in the work of single artists because, quite often, artists shift styles or combine different stylistic effects.

Another indicator of differences between the 1980s and 1960s in the arts was the increasing use of a wide variety of media and techniques. For example, where acrylic painting fairly dominated the pictorial arts in the 1960s, the 1980s saw a return to the use of conté crayon, charcoal, pastels, and graphite. Some of the media were new, requiring new techniques, and very often a single format displayed a wide diversity of media. Some of the media that appeared new were older media in a new form, such as oil paint sticks and oil pens, while other materials were new, for paintings particularly, such as fabrics, ceramics, powdered metallics, sheet metal, and even straw. Collage, assemblage, and the temporal materials of Process Art were undoubtedly antecedents influencing the use of such media.

Oils, acrylics, and watercolors in their traditional form are still being used, however, and sometimes combinations of these media appear in the same work of art. In the realm of printmaking, this juxtaposition of media is duplicated by the combining of techniques. Lithography, silk screen, etching, and engraving are often employed in the same image along with India ink, graphite, and other materials. Some of these "combo-techniques" descended from history, of course, but not as great a variety of techniques were put together in the past. Newer-appearing media and techniques are photoprinting and the use of plastic for engraving. Zinc plates came into use years ago, although copper remains a favorite for etching and engraving.

Although it was difficult to predict the exact form much of the newer art of representation would take, since the late 1980s one direction has become clearer: A great deal of the new art reflects a dramatic reaction to the momentous social and political changes that have taken place in recent decades. Reacting to the sexual, political, social, and environmental violence of the times, younger artists have tended to reject not only the works of their predecessors but also the philosophical beliefs that accompany them. These artists respond to what they think are the deceptions fed to them by mass communication and advertising. They question not only the originality of art and what is presented as authentic but also the concept of originality as a worthwhile goal. Thus, these artists even question their own individuality. Much of what they see seems largely untruthful to them, conveying a partial view of the world. Yet the sources for these artists' works are often to be found in the media, which they parody or satirize by exposing the structures through which entertainment and information are disseminated.

Reality is in question again! What is real? The media portrayals of "ordinary" people in their beautiful apartments and designer clothes, or those people found in tenements, or "everyday" working women or men? Are the handsomely staged street scenes of Hollywood as real as those decaying inner-city streets all over America?

Neo-Expressionism

The strongest movement of new figurative art in the past quarter-century has been that of the **Neo-Expressionists.** Their work seemed to fulfill the widespread desire in the early 1980s among the general populace for a return to figurative art and for a more personalized expression. The roots of Neo-Expressionism were deep, and the values it expressed were genuinely being sought by a new generation. Neo-Expressionists satisfied the growing appetite for recognizable images and meaningful content by producing monumental dramatic figures with broad gestures, painted in broad brush strokes.

Both the social conditions and the failure of modernism raised questions responsible for the work of artists representing Neo-Expressionism, such as the Italian Enzo Cucchi (b. 1950), the American Julian Schnabel (b. 1951), and the German Anselm Kiefer (b. 1945). Enzo Cucchi and Anselm Kiefer were chief among the European Neo-Expressionists, while the Texan Julian Schnabel was the first American to take up the style. The common denominator of style was the reawakening of the emotional fervor of early-twentieth-century Expressionism, updated with modern techniques and themes. Late

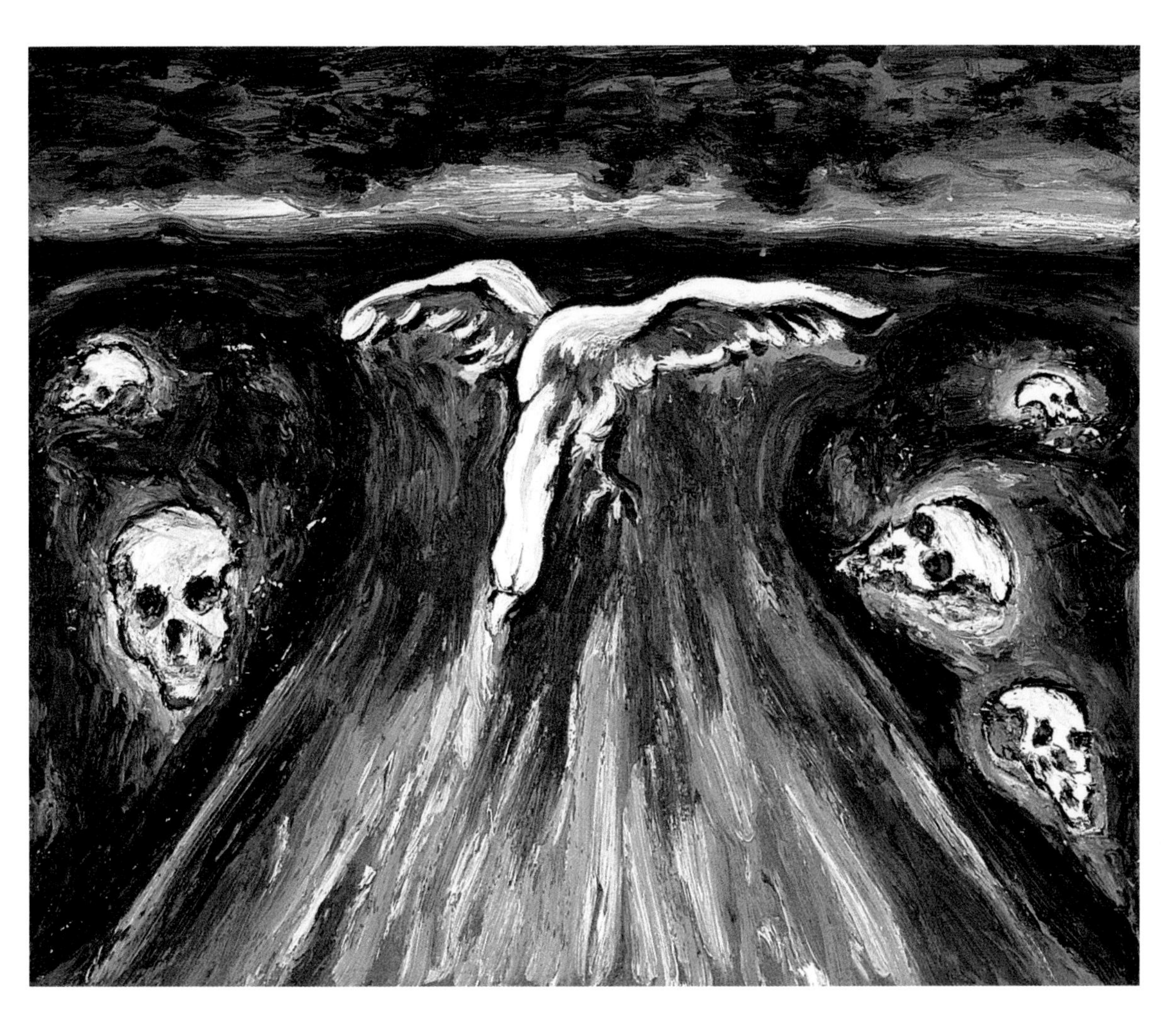

10.116 **Enzo Cucchi, *Paesaggio Barbaro,* 1983. Oil on canvas, 4 ft 3 in. × 5 ft 2¾ in. (1.30 × 1.59 m).** The Italian Neo-Expressionist Enzo Cucchi paints heavily pigmented canvases contrasting living creatures with symbols of death, abandonment, and decay. Private Collection. Photograph courtesy of the Sperone Westwater Gallery, New York. Courtesy Gallery Bruno Bischofberger, Zurich.

Renaissance Mannerism, the later phases of Giorgio de Chirico's classicizing style, and the more representational styles of Picasso were all sources for the Neo-Expressionists.

Enzo Cucchi (fig. 10.116) lives on his native soil near the seaport of Ancona on the east coast of Italy. It is a land of sudden landslides. The animal and human life on his family farm and the abruptness with which death can appear have fed his art. Cucchi's heavily pigmented canvases, sometimes mixed with powdery materials like earth and coal dust, express through their contrasts of living creatures and bony skulls his sense of death, abandonment, and decay.

Anselm Kiefer, who was born during the last gasps of Hitler's regime at the end of World War II, has given Germany a new, monumental, dramatically mythic style. He expresses, by symbolic means, an apology for Germany's crimes against humanity while providing more hopeful signs for the future by recalling the country's more noble, courageous, and heroic moments. Like Cucchi, Kiefer uses materials formerly considered inappropriate for painting, including old photographs, metal, and straw. The far-reaching symbolic meanings in this artist's works are difficult to completely explore in so few words. He is well worth further study. In the painting *Osiris and Isis,* for example, Kiefer asks whether modern technology can reunite a world torn asunder, just as Isis, the sister-wife of Osiris, was able to reassemble Osiris's body parts after he was slain and dismembered by his brother Set. Modern technology is symbolized by the circuit board at the top of the pyramid, from which wires emanate, while the reference to Osiris and Isis comes from Egypto-Roman mythology and suggests the pyramid and desert sky. Pyramids are sacred mountains built to improve communication with the heavens.

Though Schnabel is a commentator on modern life, many of his themes are gleaned from the Old and New Testaments. A notable feature of his work, like that of the other Neo-Expressionists, is the use of unusual materials and methods, ranging from canvases made of

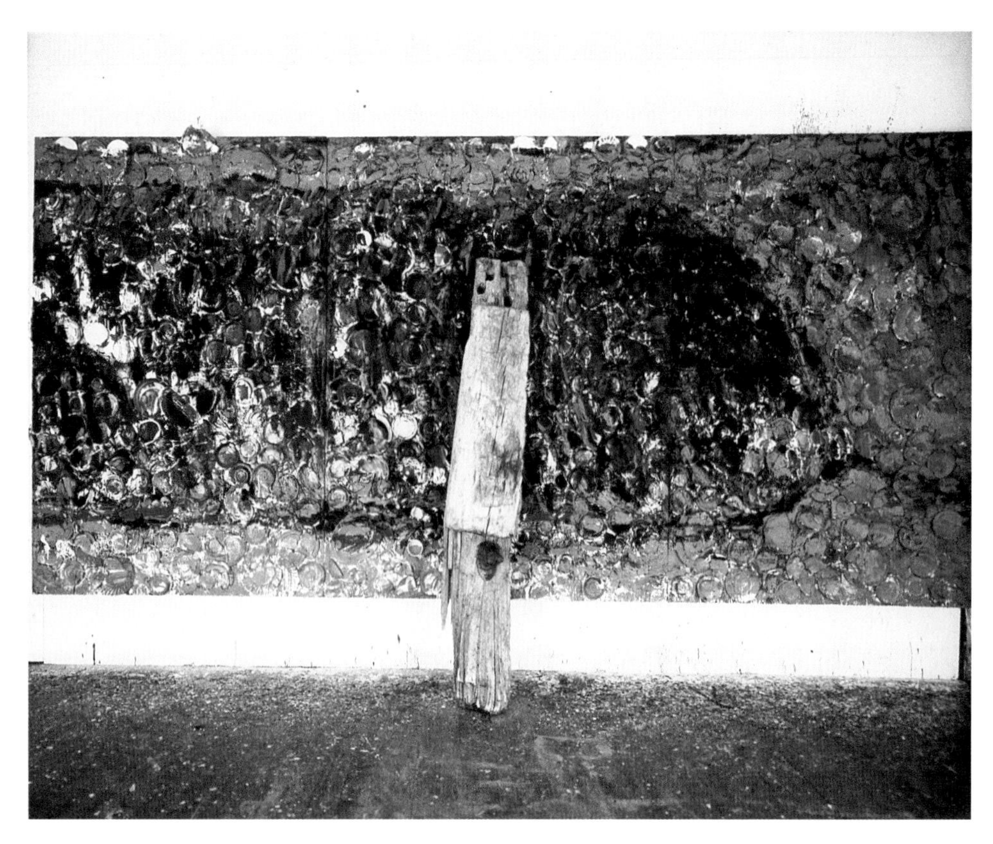

10.117 Julian Schnabel, *Affection for Surfing*, 1983. Oil, plates, wood, and bondo on wood, 108 × 228 × 24 in. (274.3 × 579.1 × 61 cm). Schnabel, one of the Neo-Expressionists of the early 1980s, uses size and bulky collage to symbolize the discarded materials of a dying civilization. Courtesy of Pace Wildenstein.

velvet to picture planes comprising broken china (fig. 10.117). By and large, these Neo-Expressionists were rejecting what the mainstream avant-garde establishment had dictated as acceptable art in the modern age.

Feminist Art

While there have always been female artists, the significance and extent of their contributions were often suppressed by male domination of social behavior, taste, and value. So, although individual women have contributed to the history of art, their accomplishments have usually suffered undeserving neglect. Today, of course, women artists are accepted and recognized in all media by the quality of their creations. An early phase of this recognition took the form of appreciating women's domestic arts on the same level with the graphic, sculptural, and architectural arts. Exhibits in museums, galleries, and private spaces helped to establish the recognition of domestic arts as "fine art." Judy Chicago (née Cohen) (b. 1939) and Miriam Schapiro (b. 1923) cofounded the Feminist Art Movement (1960s) in San Diego. Also we should note here that the African American artist Faith Ringgold (b. 1934) not only brought recognition to women's domestic arts with her narrative quilts but also brought more attention to the artistic creations of African Americans (fig. 10.118).

Miriam Schapiro was a New York–based Abstract Expressionist Field painter before she moved to Southern Califor-

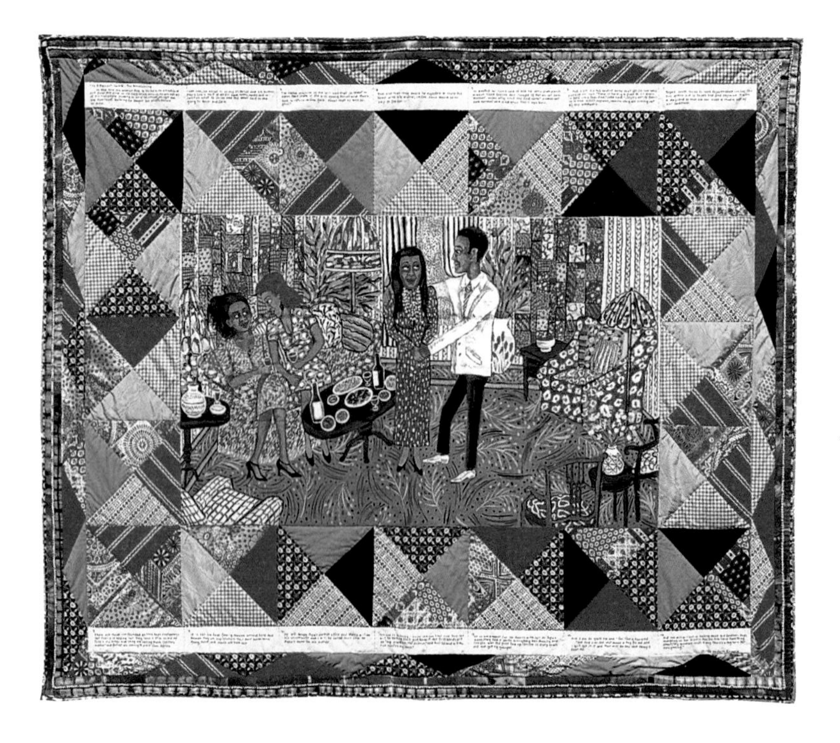

10.118 Faith Ringgold, *The Bitter Nest, Part V: Homecoming*, 1988. Acrylic on canvas with pieced fabric border, 76 × 96 in. (193 × 243.8 cm). This African American artist, through her narrative painting/quilts, helped to bring women's domestic arts to the level of "high" or "fine" art recognition. This also brought about a consequent renewed appreciation of all African American art from the period of slavery to the present. Courtesy of the artist.

nia in the late 1960s to teach art at the University of California, San Diego. While she and Judy Chicago were teaching there, they helped female students to restructure an old house into a completely feminine environment. Their interests had been aroused by the long history of beautiful, intricate designs in women's domestic handiwork, such as sewing, weaving, and crocheting. Wanting to bring attention to this long-neglected artistic tradition, Schapiro began to make abstract and semirepresentational collages of women's craft and needlework materials. She called these *femmages* (fig. 10.119). These works may be interpreted as symbols of the long-devalued role of women's arts in general. Schapiro continued through the 1980s and '90s to create lively, colorful images, usually with discernible but sometimes ambiguous content. Many are related to searches for self-identity and melancholy at the gradual dissolution of the Women's Movement using metaphorical images of other female artists, such as Mary Cassatt, Berthe Morisot, and the Mexican artist Frida Kahlo, along with her own.

Judy Chicago meanwhile went in a somewhat more assemblage or sculptural direction in her art to emphasize specific female meanings. Chicago's landmark work expressing these views is *The Dinner Party* installation of 1974–79, in which she used painted ceramics, embroidery, needlepoint, and other women's crafts to form symbolic place settings at a giant triangular table for famous women of history and the arts (fig. 10.120). The place settings depict women's genitalia, while the triangular shape of the table is also symbolic of women. Chicago has continued to bridge the dichotomy between women's crafts and fine art. She has written many books on these themes, four alone on *The Dinner Party.* She also brings knowledge about the significance of women's art to the general public through her group projects. One of Chicago's most

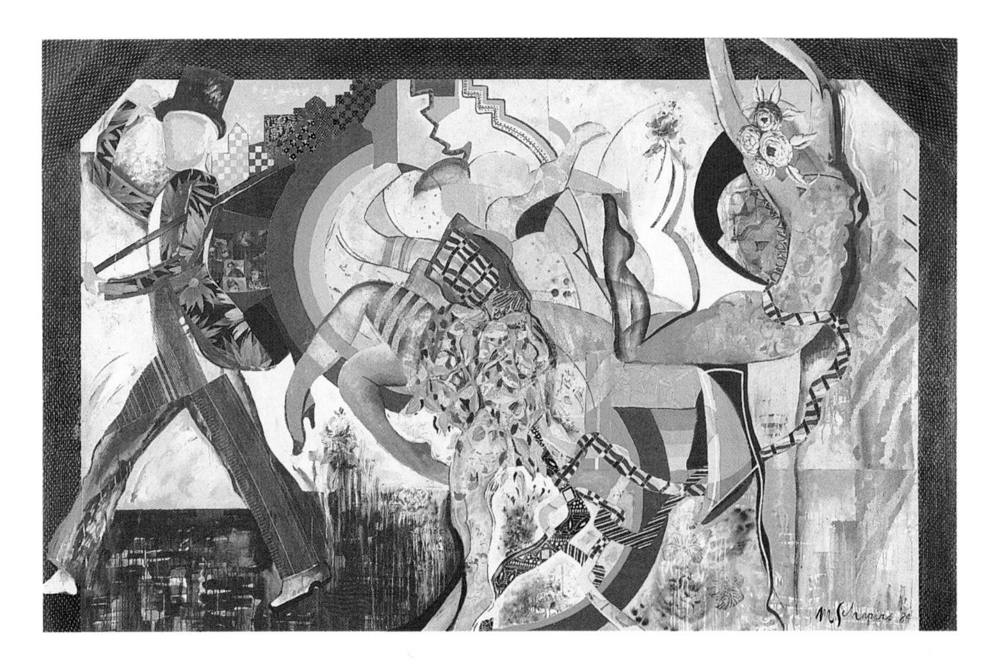

10.119 Miriam Schapiro, *I'm Dancin' as Fast as I Can,* 1985. Acrylic and fabric on canvas, 7 ft 6 in. × 12 ft (2.29 × 3.66 m). This artist became well known in the late 1960s for her *femmages,* which incorporate collage, sewing, and quilting materials and techniques. Using the same basic techniques, she has recently propelled her work in a figurative direction, though the content remains disturbing and ambiguous. Her work is a good example of recent Postmodernist directions in art. Bernice Steinbaum Gallery, Miami, FL.

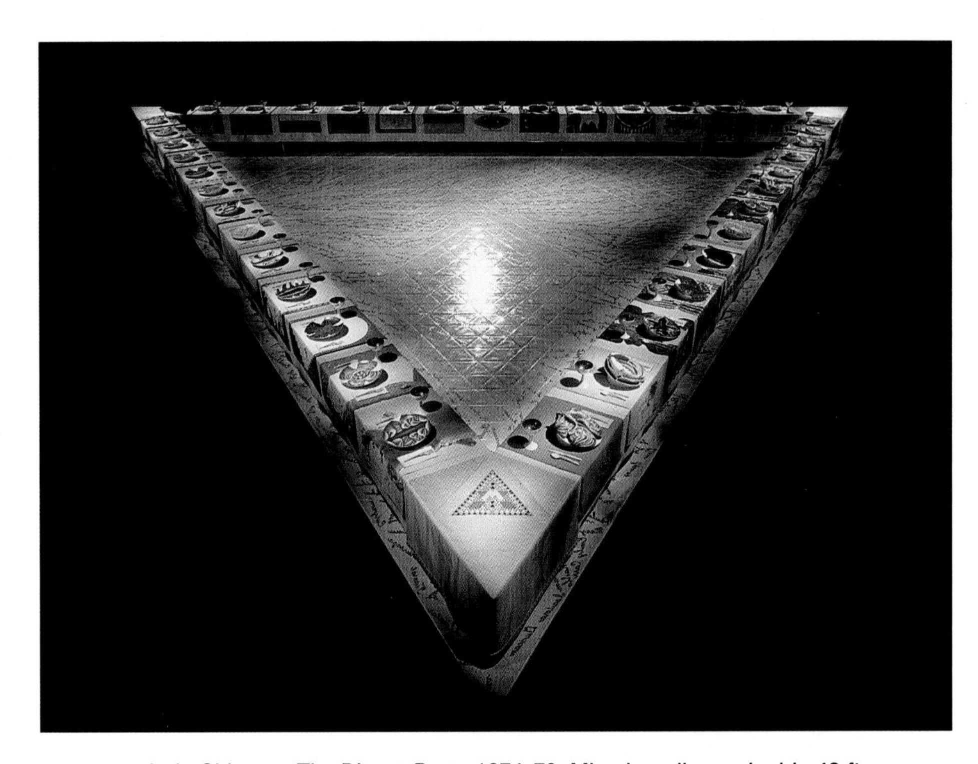

10.120 Judy Chicago, *The Dinner Party,* 1974–79. Mixed media, each side 48 ft (14.63 m). Created by one of the important founders of the feminist movement in art, this work is undoubtedly one that well expresses the movement's and artist's views. Chicago required the assistance of many others to create this sculpture or assemblage dedicated in shape and through the use of place settings to famous women of history and the arts. © 2005 Judy Chicago/Artists Rights Society (ARS), New York. Collection of the Brooklyn Museum of Art; Gift of the Elizabeth A. Sackler Foundation. Photo © Donald Woodman.

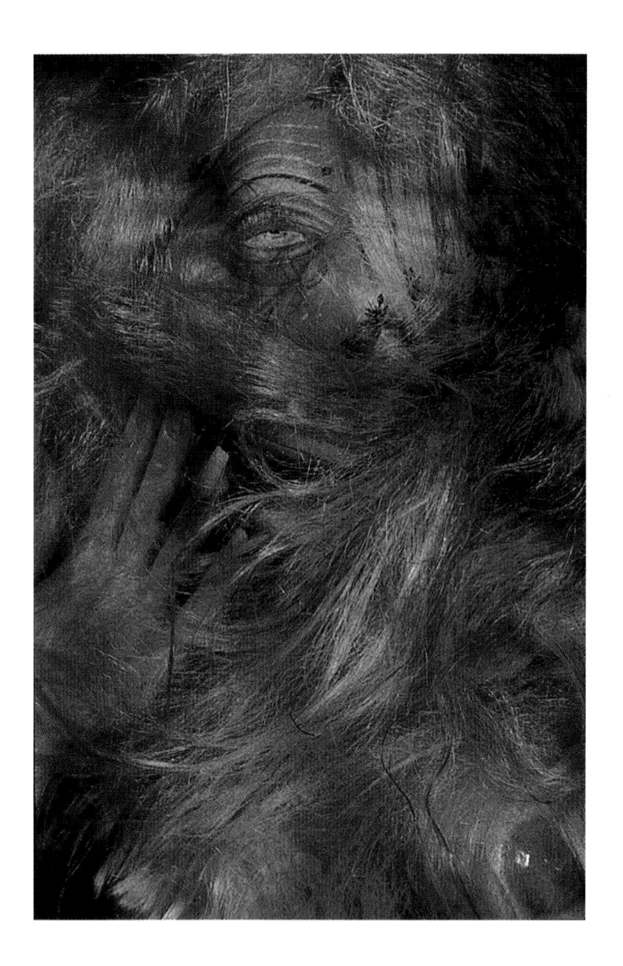

10.121 Cindy Sherman, *Untitled,* 1989. Color photograph, 7 ft 6 in. × 5 ft (2.29 × 1.52 m). Sherman, like other Postmodernist artists, focuses her creative energies on many of the environmental and social problems of our times. She deals, in particular, with the various trite ways in which women are viewed by society and through the visual media. Her photographs generally take the form of theatrical self-portraits that parody female stereotypes. Courtesy of the artist and Metro Pictures.

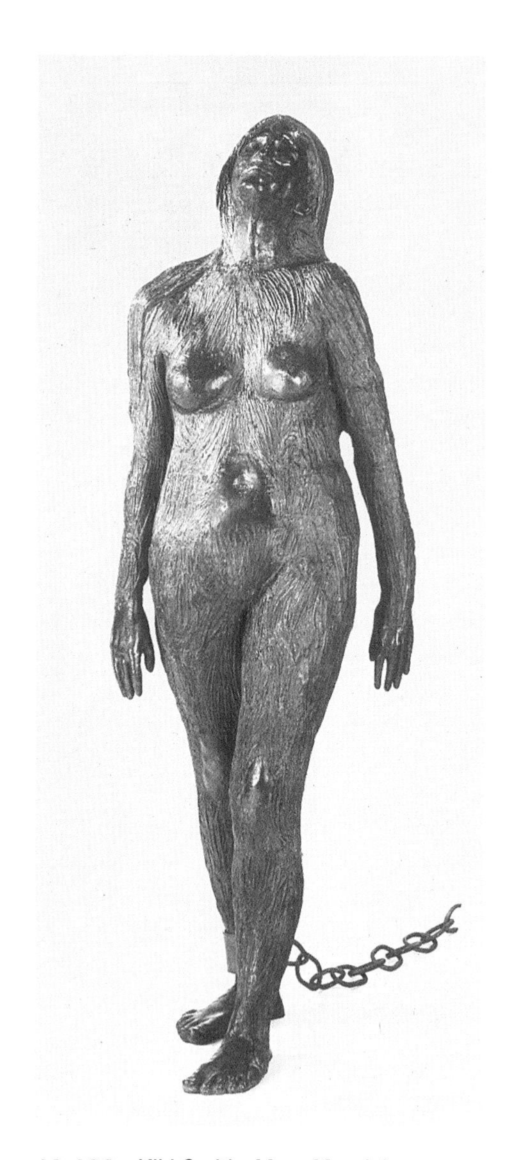

10.122 Kiki Smith, *Mary Magdalene,* 1994. Silicon bronze and forged steel, edition 2 of 4, 59⅞ × 20½ × 21⅝ in. (152 × 52 × 55 cm). Smith is a sculptor who has expressed through her Body Art a unique content often specializing in feminine concerns with the prevalence of AIDS, gender, battered women, origins, and rape. Courtesy Anthony d'Offay Gallery, London.

recent cooperative projects, called *Resolutions (for the millennium), A Stitch in Time,* consisting of needlepoint, embroidery, appliqué, and acrylic paint, opened in May 2000 at the New York City American Craft Museum.

Cindy Sherman (b. 1954), originally a photographer working in a Neo-Expressionist idiom, is well known for her self-portraits. These show her dressed in all kinds of costumes, modern and historical, and serve to suggest how the images we project of ourselves are in some way staged fables. Sherman's signature work replicates the visual clichés that the motion-picture industry has used to stereotype women. In the late 1980s, her work became more abstract, grotesque, and sinister, decrying the power man has held over woman because of her physical and sexual vulnerability (fig. 10.121). This message has become even more obvious in recent work, where she uses mannequin parts to dramatize rape and violence.

Kiki Smith's (b. 1954) sculptural forms of "body art" appear to owe influences partly to precedents in Happenings and Performance Art but are addressed with particular reference to concerns such as AIDS, battered women, and racial origins. Her particular concern with such feminist social issues led to her own unique iconography using the female body. Sometimes Smith shows the inner workings of women on the surface. In other sculptures, often with historical associations, as in the bronze *Mary Magdalene* (of which she created three versions), she may refer to the mistreatment of women, either physically or mentally (fig. 10.122).

Other Trends: Neo-Abstraction, Film Stills, Photography

Neo-Abstraction

At the same time that the Neo-Expressionists were making themselves known in the 1980s and beyond, other artists were retaining a more abstract style. Even some Neo-Expressionists were showing this tendency in the late 1980s. None of these artists is exactly alike, so, again, any abstract work created through the 1990s and in the first years of the twenty-first century should be seen as a part of the flux of many styles. Art today seems to comprise loose affiliations of individual artists working together but not as part of any particularly distinct movement. Hence, **Neo-Abstraction** is just one of the many trends in the arts of recent times.

Susan Rothenberg (b. 1934) became known for her heavily impastoed, monochromatic horse paintings in the 1970s. These retained a sense of the flat painting surface through the use of a slashing diagonal or vertical across the canvas, which split the shallow space and horse into two uneven, but visually balanced, parts. By the mid-1980s she was painting other subjects, including the human figure, that were partially blurred into the deeper space provided. Her images of this kind became increasingly Expressionist and abstract (fig. 10.123; see fig. 3.16).

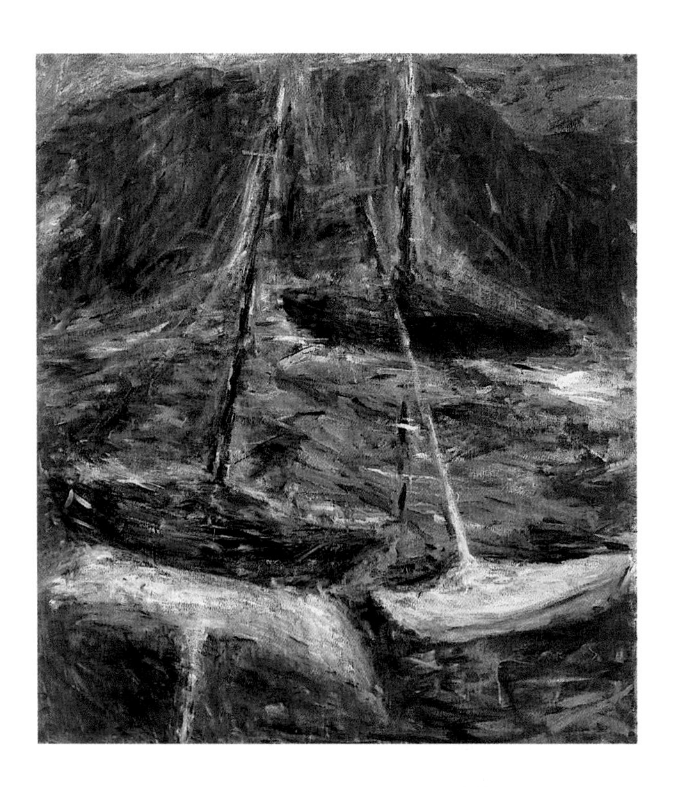

10.123 Susan Rothenberg, *Reflections,* 1981. Oil on canvas, 3 ft 8 in. × 3 ft 4 in. (1.12 × 1.02 m). The Postconceptual work of this artist has run the gamut from simple, heavily pigmented canvases of horses to expressionistic and abstract seascapes, such as this. Collection of Mr. and Mrs. Robert Lehrman, Washington, D.C. Photograph courtesy of the Greenberg Gallery, St. Louis, MO. Courtesy of Sperone Westwater, New York on behalf of the artist. © 2005 Susan Rothenberg/Artists Rights Society (ARS), New York.

Lynda Benglis (b. 1941) was trained as a painter but began to be fascinated by sculpture in the early 1970s, when she was considered a Process artist. She developed a method of adding beautiful colors to different plastics in their molten state. After allowing the plastics to flow freely onto the floor, she shaped them into large insectlike creatures, which were then usually mounted on a wall. She has also created videos and mock advertisements of herself, aiming to satirize the hackneyed representations of women in the media and society. In later work, Benglis has turned to shaping knots, bows, and pleated sculptures in shiny metal (fig. 10.124).

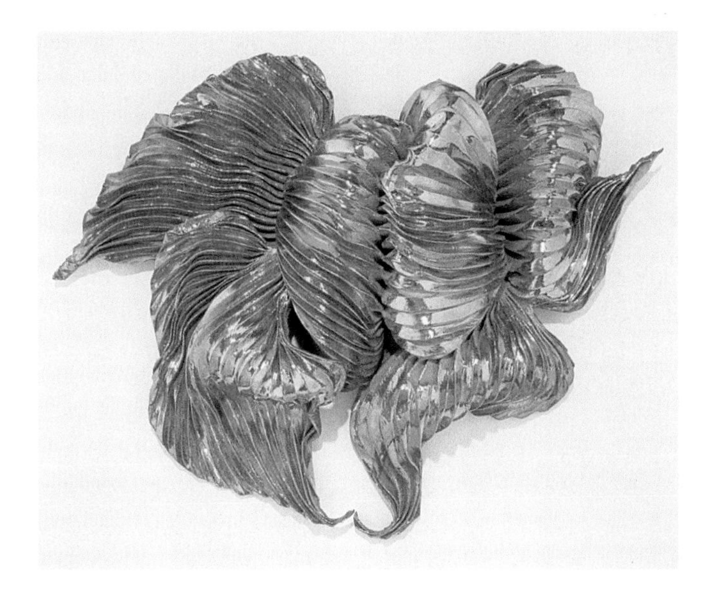

10.124 Lynda Benglis, *Tossana,* 1995–96. Stainless steel, wire mesh, zinc, aluminum, and silicone bronze, 49 × 63 × 14 in. (1.24 × 1.6 × .36 m). This artist began as a painter, then moved over to Process Art using heated, free-flowing plastics that were shaped before the material had set. Recently she has switched to working in shiny metals, forming knots, bows, and insectlike pleated sculptures. © Lynda Benglis/Licensed by VAGA, New York, NY.

Another example of abstraction is found in the art of the African American Martin Puryear (b. 1941). Born in Washington, D.C., Puryear began as a Realist but discovered the "magic" or "sense of life" evoked by primitive African forms while serving with the Peace Corps in Sierra Leone during the mid-1960s. He became particularly fond of making sculpture in wood, which he

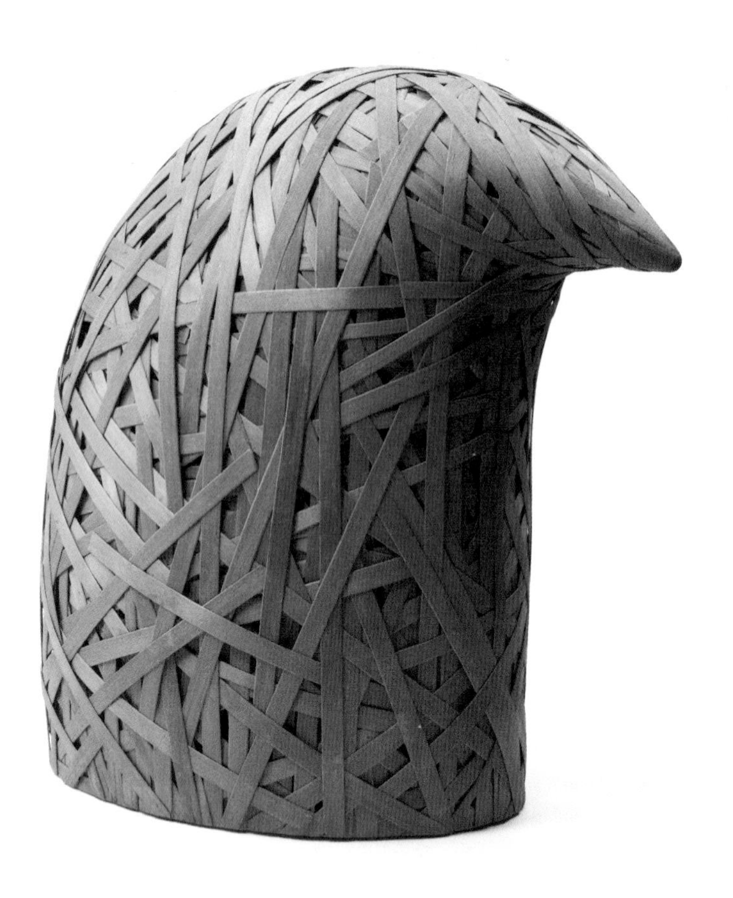

10.125 **Martin Puryear, *Old Mole,* 1985. Red cedar, 61 × 61 × 34 in.** This African American artist demonstrates the influences that African tribal art and his worldwide study of woodcraft techniques had in the development of his mature work. Purchased with gifts (by exchange) of Samuel S. White, 3rd and Vera White, and Mr. and Mrs. Charles C. G. Chaplin and with funds contributed by Marion Boulton Stroud, Mr. and Mrs. Robert Kardon, Gisela and Dennis Alter, and Mrs. H. Gates Lloyd. Photo: The Philadelphia Museum of Art/Art Resource, NY.

studied in Scandinavia and Japan as well as in Africa. From this background, Puryear developed an organic abstract style that goes beyond some Minimalist leanings. His works are marked by a heightened sensitivity to craft and a quiet animation of meaning. Some works flow and stretch, as though filled with nature. Others have a tension, as though wanting to project into space while remaining rooted to the ground. All embody refined craftsmanship and attention to detail, reflecting Puryear's study of cabinetmaking, joinery, boat building, and traditional Japanese carpentry (fig. 10.125).

Finally, in concluding our survey of the Neo-Abstract style, we look at a painter who represents her own kind of Geometric Abstraction: Dorothea Rockburne.

Canadian-born Dorothea Rockburne (b. 1934) had her training at Black Mountain College in North Carolina, where she met modern artists like Rauschenberg, Kline, and Guston. She also studied dance with Merce Cunningham and knew the highly inventive American composer John Cage. She began to find her style, a vibrant color palette dominated by reds, yellows, blues, and greens translucently filling overlapping geometric shapes, in the late 1960s. Rockburne's abstractions have always maintained a continuity of shape, from her earliest near-Minimalist abstract monochromes to the present diagonals used in large murals. Another continuous quality is the lack of emotion in her forms. But unlike Minimalist art, Rockburne's paintings have a metaphysical quality that links past and present in a way that makes her audience search for meaning beyond their presence. Her shapes, colors, and looping arabesques especially add a feeling of lightness, almost joyfulness, to the otherwise hard-edge geometry (see figs. 3.10 and 4.29).

Film Stills

The idea that photography should be Straight, or a one-to-one copy of reality and not staged or manipulated to obtain better results in a Pictorialist sense, has been a long-standing theory in photography. This theory, like those in other art disciplines, is undergoing a revision, especially in this computer age. Among Straight photographers there is a fear that their photographic art will be superseded by computers, digital cameras, scanners, and so forth that can reproduce and alter any photographic image on any scale, while twisting and tweaking an image to eliminate undesirable features or improve the photograph. The notion that photographs should not be staged or manipulated in any way has not held sway throughout history. From the beginning of photography, when long poses were necessitated by the available cameras, chemicals, and surfaces, staged scenes have been employed. Oscar Rejlander's *The Two Ways of Life* of

1857 (see fig. 10.9) shows how certain artists could defy the notion that photographs should portray only unadulterated reality. More recently, as with Cindy Sherman's parodies of media stereotypes, photographers have been using elaborate staging techniques for their pictures. Using specialized lighting, staged sets, or natural settings given eerie effects by lighting and film alteration, they are creating surrealistic photographs of all sorts of phantasmagoria. Some of these film-still photographers act as directors and hire lighting and staging specialists and actors and actresses to play parts in their photographs. Others may play the part of actor, as well as director/producer, dressing in costume or employing special locations, or staging, for their creations.

Photography

During the past decade, there has been a surge in interest in photography as an artistic medium, and it is widely acknowledged that much of the significant artwork being made now is photo based. A good example of this development is the work of Bernd and Hilla Becher (b. 1931 and 1934) and the generation of younger objectivist photographers whom they have taught. The Bechers, a husband and wife team, have spent their careers photographing extensive catalogs of large-scale industrial building types (fig. 10.126). Their photographs are intentionally bland: frontal views taken in even light, with the subject occupying the center of the shot, and an absence of human figures. This look requires painstaking timing, attention to weather conditions, and camera placement, as well as research of subject matter and location. The Bechers have also become famous for their numerous outstanding students. One of their students, Andreas Gursky (b. 1955), is both known for his impressive prints and precise detail, exemplifying the perfection of photographic technique on a monumental scale (fig. 10.127).

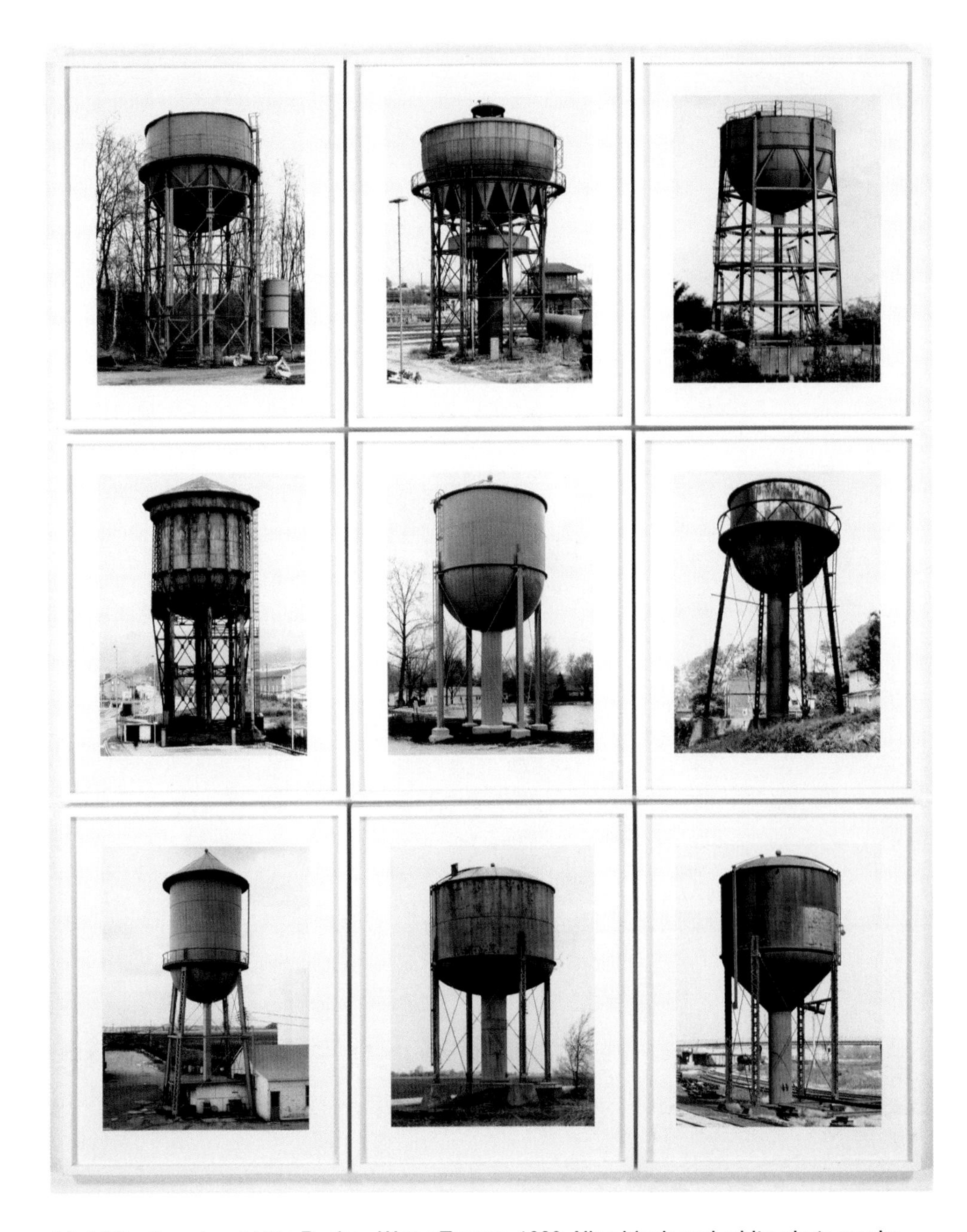

10.126 Bernd and Hilla Becher, *Water Towers,* 1980. Nine black-and-white photographs, mounted on board, Each: 15⅞ × 12 in.; Overall, approximately: 61¼ × 49¼ in. Careful photographic typologies of old industrial buildings emphasize the sculptural qualities of their structures. Solomon R. Guggenheim Museum, New York. Purchased with funds contributed by Mr. and Mrs. Donald Jonas, 1981, 81.2793.

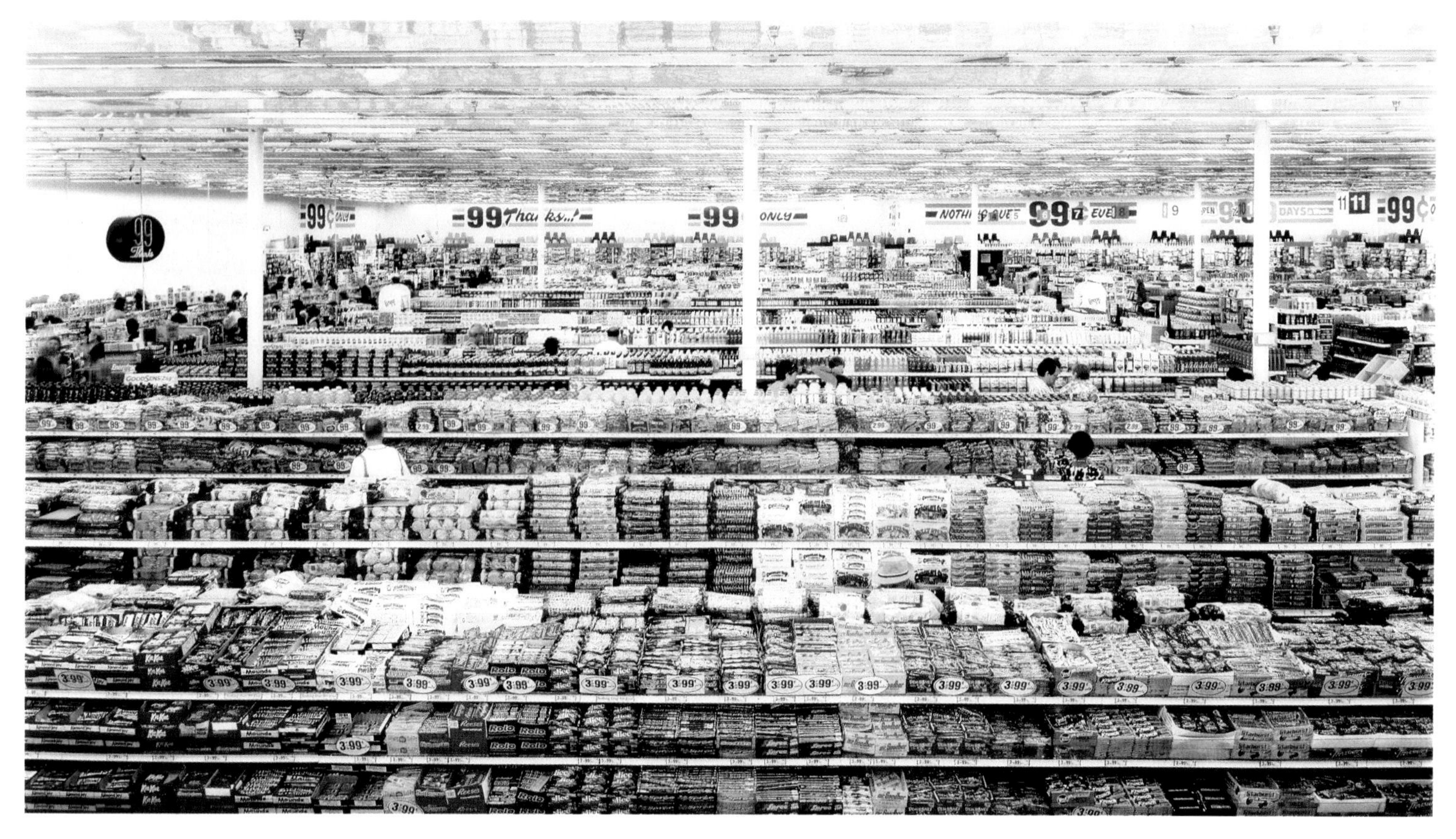

10.127 Andreas Gursky, *99 Cent,* 1999. Chromogenic color print, 6 ft 9½ in. × 11 ft (207 × 337 cm). Gursky's huge photographic prints are striking for their intense precision of detail. © ARS, NY. 99 c. 1999. Cibachrome print. Inv.: AM 2000-96. Photo: Philippe Migeat. Location: Musée National d'Art Moderne, Centre Georges Pompidou, Paris, France. Photo Credit: CNAC/MNAM/Dist. Réunion des Musées Nationaux/Art Resource, NY. Image Reference: ART156862.

At the other end of the technical spectrum, Vera Lutter (b. 1960) uses a pinhole camera technique to turn a room with a view of her subject into a camera obscura (fig. 10.128). She creates unique prints by exposing giant sheets of light-sensitized photographic paper. Some of her exposures can take weeks to make, and she is even known to have inhabited her camera during the interval. She displays her eerie prints just as they are made, her only concession being to rotate them so that they may be viewed right side up.

10.128 Vera Lutter, *Battersea Power Station, XIII: July 13, 2004,* Gagosian Gallery NYC. Unique gelatin silver print, 80¾ × 55¾ in. (205.1 × 141.6 cm). Lutter's prints help us imagine what it is like to be inside a camera, thus rendering a kinesthetic experience of photography. Courtesy Gagosian Gallery, New York. Photograph by Robert McKeever. © 2005 Vera Lutter/Artists Rights Society (ARS), New York.

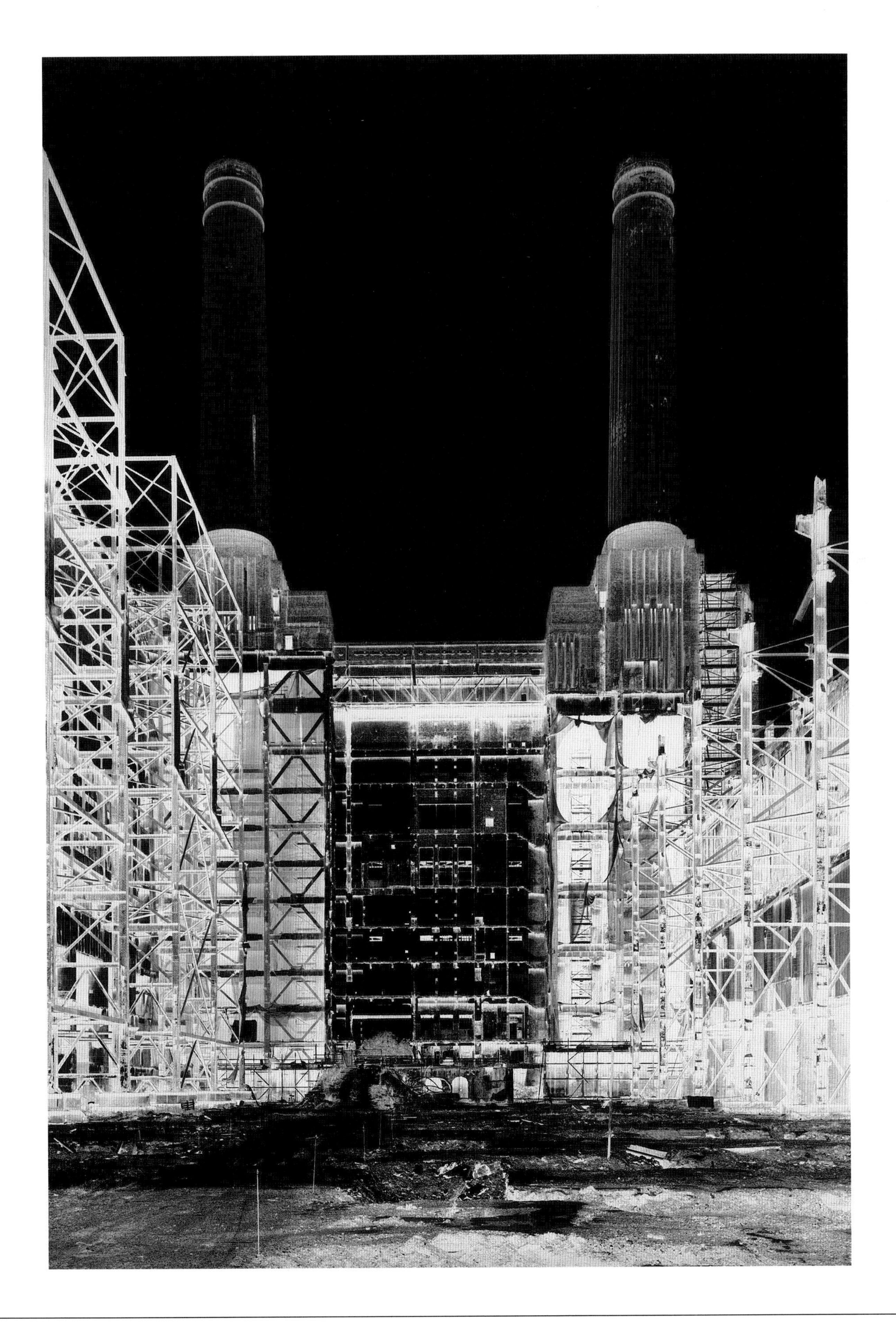

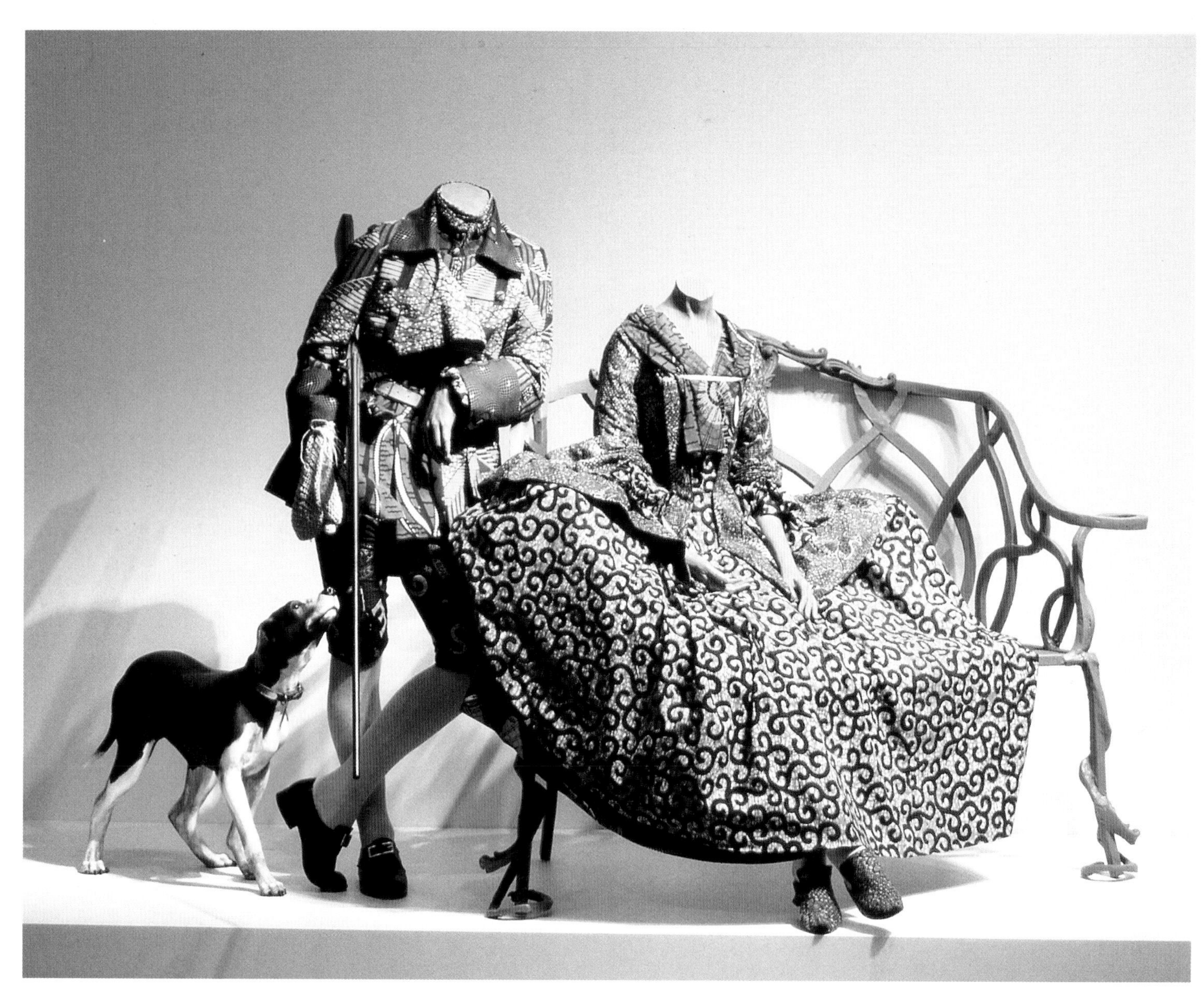

10.129 Yinka Shonibare, *Mr and Mrs Andrews without Their Heads,* 1998. Wax-print cotton costumes on armatures, dog, mannequin, bench, gun, 165 × 570 × 254 cm (65 × 224⅜ × 100 in.) (overall). Sometimes with humor and sometimes in anger, Yinka Shonibare addresses questions about multi-ethnic identity. Born to Nigerian parents in London and raised in the African city of Lagos, Shonibare considers himself a product of postcolonial culture. *Mr and Mrs Andrews without Their Heads* is based on a famous portrait by Thomas Gainsborough (1727–1788). Shonibare beheads the Andrewses, removes their privileged surroundings, and dresses them in "African" prints. Collection National Gallery of Canada, Ottawa, Canada. SHO 33. Courtesy of Stephen Friedman Gallery, London.

NEW GLOBAL ART

In the early 1980s, as we have noted, the Neo-Expressionists (see figs. 10.116 and 10.117) captured international attention. After a decade of cool, minimalistic abstraction, the Neo-Expressionists' messy, large figurative work and stormy feelings seemed like a sharp departure. The early Neo-Expressionists, who came from Italy and Germany in particular, gave the impression that they were expressing national feelings that had been bottled up ever since the end of

10.130 **Yayoi Kusama, *Infinity Mirror Room-Phalli's Field (or Floor Show),* 1965. Sewn stuffed fabric, plywood, mirrors, 2.5 × 5 × 5 m.** Mixing Pop, Op, Conceptual Art, and Abstraction, Yayoi Kusama's work seems as strange today as when it was first presented forty years ago. Enjoying something of a revival, she is now recognized as a forerunner of global art.

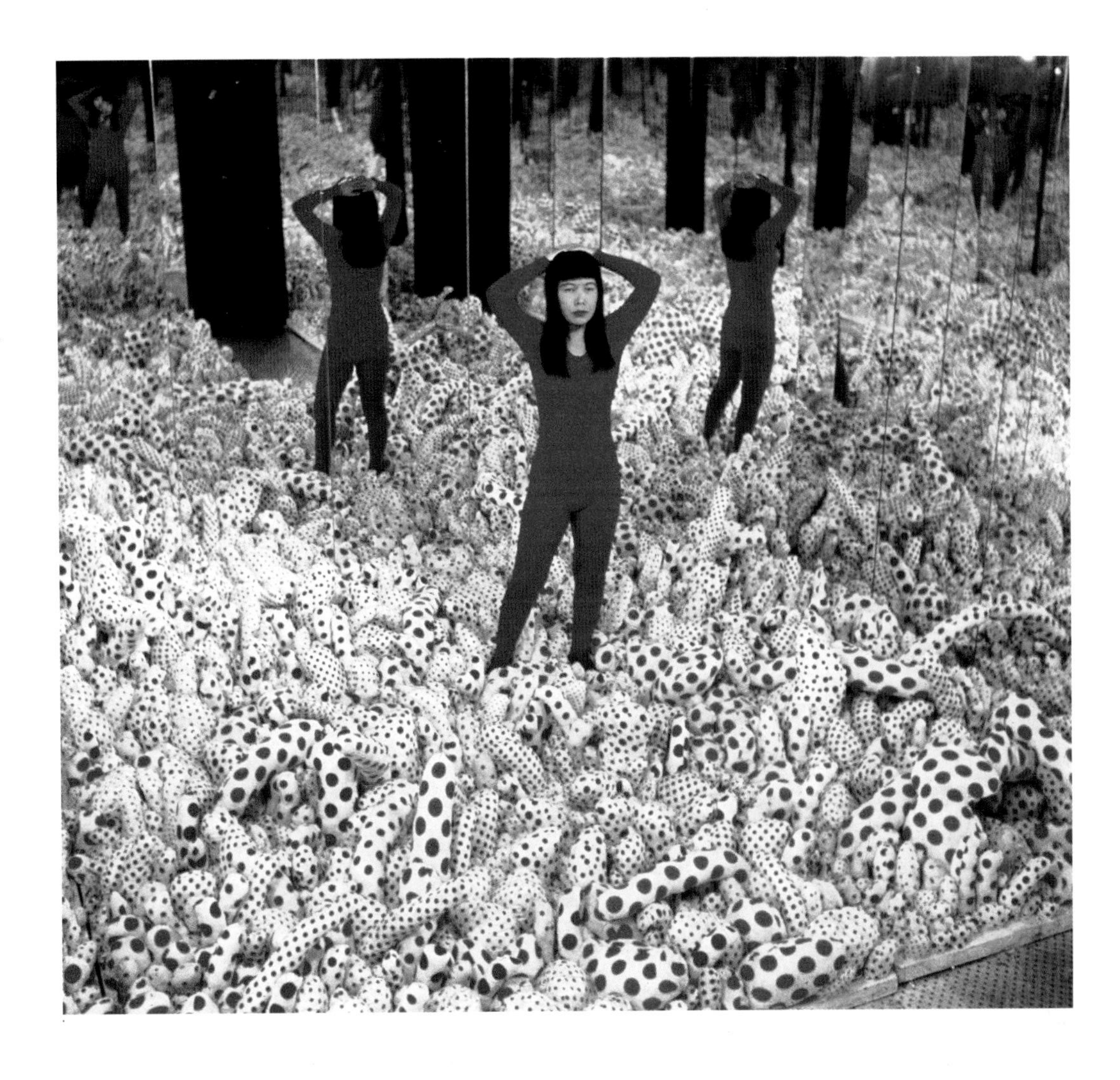

World War II. Their emergence also pointed to vital new centers of art activity beyond New York.

The gradual ascendance of global art since then, by artists from all over the world, gives a similar feeling, that we are hearing new voices expressing themselves in ways that seem unusual to us, with messages that we are not used to hearing. In some measure, these artists are coming to wider attention through the ever-proliferating phenomenon of international art expositions. The most established of these is the Venice Biennial, founded in 1895, encompassing national presentations, thematic exhibitions, and events throughout the city. Founded in 1951, the São Paulo Bienal is the premier visual arts event in South America and one of the largest in the world. The first Documenta took place in Kassel in 1955 and has been held about every five years since then. It is recognized as the most significant international forum for contemporary art. The Indian Triennale (since 1968) and the Biennale of Sydney (since 1973) highlight art from Asia and the Asia-Pacific. Biennials in Havana and Cairo (both since 1984) encompass the Caribbean and the African continent. Biennials and triennials also take place in Berlin, Buenos Aires, Dakar, Istanbul, Guangzhou, Kwangju, Liverpool, Lyon, Pusan, Shanghai, Sharjah (United Arab Emirates), Taipei, Tirana, Valencia, Vilnius, and Yokohama, with the nomadic Manifesta appearing in a different city every two years. These international events attract ambitious artists and curators from every part of the globe. The effect is multiplied by the advent of the Internet, which has made it possible to communicate new ideas around the globe instantaneously. For instance, one can readily learn about recent art events on the African continent from www.artthrob.co.za, the Web site of a South African art magazine. The wealth of information available in this way is truly mind-boggling. Equally astonishing is the breadth and depth of new art being made around the world today.

Today's global art is not a single stylistic movement. Quite the opposite; it is characterized by diversity and difference. But it does share one common

10.131 Cai Guo-Qiang, ***Cry Dragon/Cry Wolf: The Ark of Genghis Khan,*** **1996. 90 sheepskins, 3 Toyota car engines, branches, wooden paddles, rope, 350 × 1986 × 261 cm.** Cai was born in China in 1957, made his reputation in Japan, and now lives in New York City. His Installations address the cross-cultural experience of the global citizen and have instigated heated debates among intellectuals in his native land. The sheepskins are a reference to Ghengis Khan's Mongol horde, which used inflated skin rafts to cross rivers during its invasion of the West. The car engines refer to the contemporary invasion of consumer goods from Asia. Photo by Hiro Ihara, Courtesy Cai Guo-Qiang Studio.

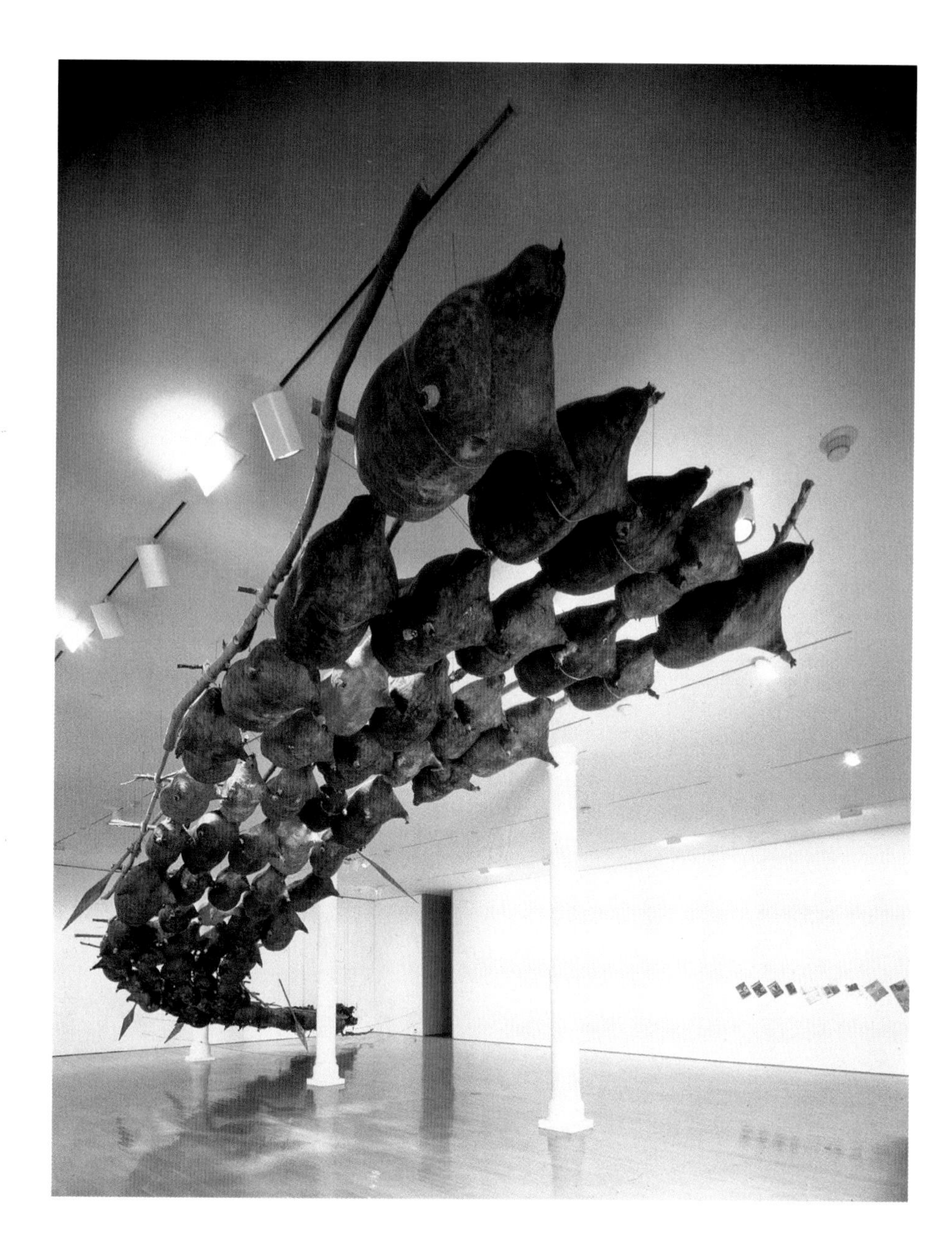

attribute: the sense that art addresses humanity as a whole, not just one national or ethnic group; and to this degree, global art has a kernel of political content, even while being highly personal (see fig. 10.129). In this way, global art emphasizes concept, linking intention and consciousness and action. Thus, it not only traces an ancestry to the internationalism of Neo-Expressionism but also points further back to the premises of Conceptual art (see fig. 10.130) but further once again to a kinship with the Dada (see fig. 10.131). As this family tree continues to recede into prehistory, we can begin to sense the interrelationship of all art that global art suggests.

INVESTIGATE THE CD-ROM **Questions to Ask Yourself**

The great artworks of the world have both meaning and character, content and style.

As you review this chapter on the CD-ROM, list all the artworks you particularly like, and answer these questions:

1. What do these artworks all have in common?
2. What qualities make them each unique and distinct from one another?
3. Are you particularly attracted to a certain era of art? To a certain style? To a certain medium? If so, why? If not, why not?
4. Are there eras, styles, or media that you just don't care for? Explain.
5. Imagine that you are about to begin your masterpiece. How will you begin? What will you do? What materials will you use? What will you express? How will you know when your work is done?

CHRONOLOGICAL OUTLINE OF **WESTERN ART**

PREHISTORIC ART (c. 35,000–3000 B.C.)

35,000 B.C.	**Upper Paleolithic: Late Old Stone Age.** Stone tool industries.
28,000	**Art begins:** Cave painting and fertility goddesses (Europe).
10,000	**Mesolithic: Middle Stone Age.** End of last Ice Age.
6000–3000	**Neolithic: New Stone Age.** Begins Middle East; spreads to Europe. Settled agricultural communities; pottery, architecture begins.

ANCIENT ART (c. 4000 B.C.–A.D. 146)

4000 B.C.	**Egyptian Art:** Old Kingdom.
3000	**Sumerian Art:** Iraq. Invention of writing.
2800	**Aegean Art:** Minoan I & II, Crete.
2300	**Akkadian Art:** Syria and Iraq.
2000	**Aegean Art:** Mycenaean Age, Greece. Minoan III, Crete.
1700	**Babylonian Art:** Syria and Iraq.
1600	**Egyptian Art:** New Empire.
1500	**Neolithic:** Ends in Europe.
1100	**Aegean Art:** Homeric Age, Greece, Turkey.
	Etruscan Art: Italy.
1000	**Egyptian Art:** Decadence.
900	**Assyrian Art:** Middle East.
750	**Greek Art:** Archaic Age, Greece and southern Italy.
	Etruscan Art: Northern Italy.
600	**Neo-Babylonian Art:** Middle East.
550	**Achaemenid Persian Art:** Iran, Middle East.
470	**Greek Art:** Classical Age, Greece.
330	**Greek Art:** Ptolemaic Age, Egypt.
320	**Greek Art:** Hellenistic Age, Greece and Middle East (Seleucid Empire).
280	**Roman Art:** Roman Republic, Italy.
140	**Graeco-Roman Art:** Italy to Greece and Middle East.
30 B.C.–A.D. 146	**Imperial Roman Art:** Italy, parts of Europe and Middle East.
30 B.C.?	**Jesus Christ born?**

EARLY CHRISTIAN AND MEDIEVAL ART (c. A.D. 200–1300)

500 B.C.–A.D. 400	**Migratory Period Art in Europe:** Celts, Goths, Slavs, Scandinavians.
200	**Iranian (Persian) Art:** Sassanid Empire.
	Late Imperial Roman Art and Early Christian Art: Italy and Europe.
330	**Early Byzantine Art:** Centers at Constantinople (Istanbul), Turkey, and part of Middle East.
	Coptic Christian Art: Egypt.
	Early Christian Art: Western Europe and Italy.
476	**Roman Art ends.**

493	**Early Byzantine Art:** Introduced at Ravenna and Venice.
570–632	**Mohammed founds Islamic religion.**
650	**Islamic Art:** Beginning in Syria, Palestine, and Iraq.
760	**Carolingian Art:** France, Germany, and northern Italy.
800	**Developed Byzantine Art:** Middle East, Greece, Balkans, and parts of Italy.
950	**Ottonian Art:** Mostly in Germany.
1000	**Romanesque Art:** France, England, northern Spain (Moslems in southern Spain), Italy, and Germany.
1150	**Gothic Art:** France, Italy, northern Spain, Germany, and England.

RENAISSANCE ART (c. 1300–1600)

NOTE: From here on, indicated artists are painters unless otherwise indicated in parentheses.

1300	**Proto-Renaissance Italy:** Duccio, Giotto, Pisano (sculptor).
1400	**Early Renaissance Italy:** Donatello (sculptor), Masaccio, Francesca, Fra Angelico, Fra Filippo Lippi, Brunelleschi (architect), da Vinci.
	Early Northern Renaissance: (modified by vestiges of Medievalism): *Netherlands:* van Eyck, van der Goes, van der Weyden; *France:* Limbourg brothers, Fouquet; *Germany:* Lochner, Moser, Witz, Pacher, Schongauer (printmaker).
1500	**High Renaissance Italy:** Giorgione, Titian, Raphael, Michelangelo (sculptor), Tintoretto.
	High Renaissance in Western Europe (affected by Italy): *Netherlands:* Bosch, Breughel; *Germany:* Dürer (printmaker), Grünewald; *France:* Master of Moulins; *Spain:* El Greco.
1520	**Mannerism and Early Baroque Italy:** Caravaggio, Bernini (sculptor).

BAROQUE AND ROCOCO ART (c. 1600–1800)

1600	**Baroque Art in Europe:** *Netherlands (Belgium, Holland):* Rubens, van Dyck, Hals; *France:* Poussin, Claude; *Spain:* Ribera, Velázquez.
	Early Colonial Art in the Americas: Primarily limners (or primitive portraitists) in English colonies. Church or cathedral art in Latin Americas.
1700	**Rococo Art:** Primarily French, but spreads to other European countries: *France:* Watteau, Boucher, Chardin, Fragonard; *Italy:* Canaletto, Guardi, Tiepolo; *England:* Gainsborough, Hogarth, Reynolds.
	Colonial Arts and Early Federal Art in United States: Copley, Stuart, West.

NINETEENTH-CENTURY ART (c. 1780–1900)

c. 1780	**Neoclassicism:** *France:* David, Ingres; *Italy:* Canova (sculptor).
1820 **1826**	**Romanticism:** *France:* Barye (sculptor), Delacroix, Géricault, Niépce (first permanent camera image), Daguerre (photographic process), Rejlander (painter and photographer); *Spain:* Goya, *England:* Turner, Fox Talbot (photographic process); *United States:* Ryder.
1850	**Realism (and Naturalism):** *France:* Daumier, Courbet, Rodin, Camille Claudel (Romantic/Realist sculptors); *England:* Constable; *United States:* Eakins, Homer, Brady, Gardner, Jackson and O'Sullivan (photographers).
1870	**Impressionism:** *France:* Monet, Pissarro, Renoir, Degas (some sculpture), Morisot; *England:* Sisley; *United States:* Cassatt, Hassam, Twachtman, Muybridge (Anglo-American photographer); *Italy:* Medardo-Rosso (sculptor).
1880	**Post-Impressionism:** *France:* Cézanne, Gauguin, Seurat, Toulouse-Lautrec; *Holland:* van Gogh.
	Symbolism: *France:* Bonnard.

EARLY-TWENTIETH-CENTURY ART (1900–c. 1955)

†NOTE: Artists often change styles and mediums, so some names appear under more than one category. Note Pablo Picasso particularly!

1900 — **Sculpture in the Early 1900s:** *France:* Maillol; *United States:* Lachaise; *Germany:* Lehmbruck, Kolbe.

1902–1907 — Stieglitz and Steichen found **291 Gallery** in New York City to advance acceptance of photography and avant-garde art.

Expressionism: *France:* **Les Fauves** (Wild Beasts): Dufy, Matisse, Modigliani **(Italian)**, Vlaminck, Rouault, Utrillo, Picasso (**Spanish**: Blue, Rose, and Negro periods).

1902–1913 — **German Expressionism: Die Brücke (The Bridge):** Kirchner, Munch **(Norwegian)**, Nolde, Schmidt-Rotluff; **Der Blaue Reiter (The Blue Rider):** Jawlensky, Kandinsky†, Macke, Kuehn (photography).

c. 1918/19–1924 — **Die Neue Sachlichkeit (The New Objectivity):** Dix, Grosz, Heckel, Schlemmer, Sander (photographer); **Independent German Expressionists:** Beckmann, Kokoschka† **(Austrian)**.

1906 — **Cubism:** *France:* Picasso† (**Spanish** painter, sculptor, potter), Braque, Léger, Gris **(Spanish)**.

Futurism: *Italy:* Balla, Severini, Carra, Boccioni (painter & sculptor), Bragaglia (photographer); *France:* Duchamp†.

1910–1920 — **Abstract Art:** *Germany:* Albers†, Hofmann†, Kandinsky† **(Russian)**, Archipenko (**Russian** sculptor), Feininger **(American)**.

1913–1922 — **Constructivism:** *Russia:* Tatlin, Malevitch, Larionov, Gabo, and Pevsner (sculptors); *Holland:* Mondrian; *France:* Delaunay, Brancusi (**Romanian** sculptor), Arp† (**French** sculptor); *England:* Nicholson; *United States:* Dove, Marin, O'Keeffe, Sheeler, Davis, Stieglitz (photographer), Steichen (**German** photographer), Strand (photographer), Coburn (**English** photographer).

Fantasy in Art—Individual Fantasists: *France:* Chagall **(Russian)**, Rousseau (primitive painter); *Italy:* de Chirico; *Germany:* Schwitters†, Klee **(Swiss)**.

1913 — **Armory Show, New York:** Helps introduce avant-garde art to United States.

1914 — **Dadaism:** *France:* Arp†, Duchamp†, Picabia; *Germany:* Schwitters†, Ernst†; *United States:* Man Ray (photographer, painter).

c. 1920–1930 — **Later Expressionism:** *France:* Soutine, Buffet, Balthus, Dubuffet; *United States:* Avery, Baskin, Broderson, Lawrence, Levine, Shahn, Weber; *Mexico:* Kahlo, Orozco, Rivera, Siqueiros†.

1924 — **Surrealism:** *France:* Arp† (sculptor), Cartier-Bresson (photographer), Delvaux, Magritte **(Belgian)**, Masson, Miró **(Spanish)**, Picasso **(Spanish)**, Tanguy, Gonzáles (**Spanish** sculptor); *Switzerland:* Giacometti (sculptor, painter); *England:* Bacon; *Germany:* Ernst†; *United States:* Dalí (**Spanish** painter; Surrealist cinemas with Luis Buñuel), Man Ray (photographer, painter).

1930–1940 — **Realist Painting and Photography (Straight) in United States:** Wyeth, Wood, Benton, Burchfield; **F-64 Group of photographers:** Weston, Adams, Cunningham.

LATE-TWENTIETH-CENTURY ART

c. 1951–1965 — **Abstract Expressionist Painting**

Action or Gestural Group (predecessors from abroad): Albers† **(German)**; de Kooning **(Dutch)**; Gorky **(Turkish)**; Hoffmann **(German)**; Matta **(Chilean)**; Mondrian† **(Dutch)**; Tamayo **(Mexican)**.

U.S. New York School: Frankenthaler, Kline, Louis, Mitchel, Pollock, White (photographer).

Color Field Painting Group (Hard-Edge): *United States:* Diebenkorn, Callahan (photographer), Kelly, Newman, Noland, Stella, Rothko **(Russian)**.

Painters elsewhere similar to Abstract Expressionism: *France:* Mathieu, Manessier, Soulages; *Portugal:* Vieira da Silva; *Spain:* Tapies; *Japan:* Okidata.

Surreal Abstract or Abstract Expressionist Sculpture: *England:* Moore, Hepworth, Chadwick; *France:* Richier, Lipchitz (Latvia); *United States:* Calder†, Smith, Noguchi.

1920s–1950s — **Kinetics and Light Sculpture** (early 1900s examples): *France:* Duchamp† (1920s); *United States:* Calder† (U.S. Wire Circus, c. 1928), Wilfred (Clavilux color organ, 1930–63).

1960s–1970s — **United States:** Rickey, Bury (Polish); Chryssa, Flavin, Lippold (English); Samaris and Takis (Greek); Tinguely (Swiss 1930–63).

c. 1958–1965 — **Pop Art and Assemblage:**

Predecessors: *England:* Tom Hamilton; *United States:* Johns, Rauschenberg†, Chamberlain (assembler), Dine, Frank (Swiss photographer), Friedlander (photographer), Hockney (English), Indiana, Kienholz (assembler), Kitaj (English), Lichtenstein, Marisol (Venezuelan—sculptor or assembler), Nevelson (sculptor or assembler), Oldenberg† (sculptor or assembler), Samaras† (Greek—assembler), Segal (sculptor), Stankiewicz (assembler), Warhol, Wesselman, Winogrand (photographer).

c. 1958–1970 — **Happenings, Performance or Action Art:** *United States:* Kaprow (earliest Happening 1958), most POP artists involved; *Germany:* Beuys.

c. 1964–1970s — **Op Art:** (Extremely limited abstract style depending primarily on the observer's visual perception for content. Derives from earlier scientific investigations into color theory). *France:* Vasarely; *United States:* Anuskiewicz; *England:* Riley.

c. 1964–1975 — **Minimalism:** (Climax of abstract/nonobjective art, informed by Color Field painting and all types of abstract sculpture). *United States:* Bell (sculptor assembler), Flavin† (light sculptor assembler), Judd (sculptor), Katzen (sculptor), Lewitt (painter), Martin (sculptor), Pepper (sculptor), Reinhardt†, di Suvero (sculptor), Caro and Smith (English—sculptors).

1965–1990s — **Environmental and Installation Art**

1920s — **Forerunners:** Schwitters† (German) and Duchamp† (French).

Environmental Art: *United States:* Christo and Jeanne-Claude, Oldenberg†, Smithson, Heizer, Samaras† (Greek).

Installation Art: Paik (Korean), Pfaff (English), Hamilton, Skoglund.

c. 1965–1990s — **Postmodernism:** Reactions to abstract art and dogma (especially to Minimalism and the International Style in architecture), the increasing financial disparity between rich and poor, cynicism about politics and society (some of which resulted from the Vietnam War and Watergate), etc., in art resulted in the reintroduction of the human figure, decoration, literary subjects, the appropriation of earlier artists' work or parts thereof, the reuse of older media, and mixed techniques along with newer methods. Introduction of Computer Art in the 1980s.

1960s–1980s — **New Realism (Photorealism):** *United States:* Estes, Fish, Pearlstein, Close, Hanson (sculptor).

c. 1965–1980s — **Process and Conceptual Art:** *Germany:* Beuys†; *United States:* Hess (German), Early exemplars—1965: Kosuth, Morris.

1960s–1980s — **Feminist Art Movement:** Historical precedents. Begins in acknowledgment of women's domestic arts as significant art achievements. Role of Chicago and Schapiro. Ringgold (African American achievements), Sherman's influence.

1980s–1990s — **Neo-Expressionism:** *Germany:* Kiefer, Baselitz, Fetting; *Italy:* Cuchi, Chia; *United States:* Schnabel, Rothenberg†, Sherman† (photographer-painter).

1980s–2000s — **Other Trends**

c. mid-1980s–2000s — **Neo-Abstraction:** *United States:* Benglis (sculptor-painter), Graves (sculptor), Marden (sculptor-painter), Puryear (sculptor), Jensen, Scully (Irish), Rockburne (Canadian), Rothenberg†.

Late 1990s–2000s

Film Stills (Pictorialism in Photography): Use of staging, including special lighting effects, with photographic artists often acting and directing. Strong influence of movies and Sherman†. Photographic method.

Photography: Exploration of objectivity by making precise photographs on a very large scale.

New Global Art Related to Neo-Expressionist Art of the 1980s: Uses multimedia and art installation to express human diversity and differences while addressing humanity as a whole.

New-New Painters: Use of synthetic materials to produce three-dimensional paintings. Information unavailable yet. No historical perspective established.

GLOSSARY

abstraction
1. The selection, simplification, and/or rearrangement of the representation of natural appearance. 2. Nonrepresentational work arranged simply to satisfy artists' needs for organization or expression. In varying degrees, abstraction is present in all works of art.

abstract texture
A texture derived from the appearance of an actual surface but rearranged and/or simplified by the artist to satisfy the demands of the artwork.

academic
Art that conforms to the traditions and conventions practiced in art academies. Academic art stresses standards, set procedures, and rules.

accent
Any stress or emphasis given to elements of a composition that makes them attract more attention than the other features around them. Accent can be created by a brighter color, darker tone, greater size, or any other means by which a difference is expressed.

achromatic
Relating to differences of light and dark; the absence of hue and its intensity.

actual shape
A clearly defined or positive area (as opposed to an implied shape).

actual texture
A surface that can be experienced through the sense of touch (as opposed to a surface visually simulated by the artist).

addition
A sculptural term that means building up, assembling, or putting on material.

additive color
Color created by superimposing light rays. Superimposing the three primary color lights—red, blue, and green—produces white. The secondaries are cyan, yellow, and magenta.

aesthetic, aesthetics
Traditionally a branch of philosophy concerned with the theory of the "beautiful," aesthetics is now a compound of the philosophy, psychology, and sociology of art. As such, aesthetics is no longer solely confined to determining what is beautiful in art, but attempts to discover the origins of the art experience and the relationship between art and other aspects of culture. In this book, the term *aesthetics* refers to the concern with artistic qualities of form, as opposed to descriptive form or the mere recording of facts.

allover pattern
The repetition of design units in a recognizably systematic arrangement over an entire surface.

amorphous shape
A shape without clear definition: formless, indistinct, and of uncertain dimension.

analogous colors
Colors that are closely related in hue. They are usually adjacent to each other on the color wheel.

approximate symmetry
The use of similar imagery on both sides of a central axis. The imagery on one side resembles that on the other but is varied to prevent monotony.

assemblage
A technique that combines actual items in a display.

asymmetry
Having unlike, or noncorresponding, appearances—"without symmetry." An example: a two-dimensional artwork that, without any necessarily visible or implied axis, displays an uneven distribution of parts throughout.

atectonic
Characterized by considerable amounts of space; open, as opposed to massive (or tectonic), and often with extended appendages.

atmospheric perspective
The illusion of depth produced in graphic works by lightening values, softening details and textures, reducing value contrasts, and neutralizing colors in objects as they recede.

balance
A sense of equilibrium achieved through implied weight, attention, or attraction, by manipulating the visual elements within an artwork.

Bauhaus
Originally a German school of architecture that flourished between World War I and World War II. The Bauhaus attracted many leading experimental artists of both two- and three-dimensional fields.

biomorphic shape
An irregular shape that resembles the freely developed curves found in living organisms.

calligraphy
Elegant, decorative writing. Lines in artworks that possess qualities found in writing may be called "calligraphic" and are generally flowing and rhythmical.

casting
A sculptural technique in which liquid materials are shaped by being poured into a mold.

cast shadow
The dark area that occurs on a surface as a result of something being placed between that surface and a light source.

chiaroscuro
1. Distribution of light and dark in a picture. 2. A technique of representation that blends light and shade gradually to create the illusion of three-dimensional objects in space or atmosphere.

chroma
1. The purity of hue or its freedom from white, black, or gray. 2. The intensity of hue.

chromatic value
The relative degree of lightness or darkness demonstrated by a given color.

closed-value composition
Composition in which values are limited by the edges or boundaries of shapes.

closure
A concept derived from Gestalt psychology describing the mental relationships that develop while incomplete information is grasped as a complete, unified whole; the artist provides visual suggestions, which the observer brings to final recognition.

collage
A technique of picturemaking in which real materials possessing actual textures are attached on the picture plane surface, often in combination with painted or drawn passages.

color
The visual response to different wavelengths of sunlight identified as red, green, blue, and so on; having the physical properties of hue, intensity, and value.

color tetrad
Four colors, equally spaced on the color wheel, containing a primary and its complement and a complementary pair of intermediates. This has also come to mean any organization of color on the wheel forming a rectangle that could include a double split-complement.

color triad
Three colors spaced an equal distance apart on the color wheel, forming an equilateral triangle. The twelve-color wheel is made up of a primary triad, a secondary triad, and two intermediate triads.

complementary colors
Two colors directly opposite each other on the color wheel. A primary color is complementary to a secondary color, which is a mixture of the two remaining primaries.

composition
The total arrangement of all the elements in an artwork. Sometimes interchangeable with the terms *design* and *form*.

concept
1. A comprehensive idea or generalization. 2. An idea that brings diverse elements into a basic relationship.

content
The essential meaning and significance of a work of art. Content refers to the sensory, subjective, psychological, or emotional properties a work of art contains, as opposed to its descriptive aspects alone.

contour
The line that defines the edges of an object or a drawn or painted shape. The "outline" contours also may be marked by the variations of tones, textures, or colors.

craftsmanship
Aptitude, skill, or quality workmanship in the use of tools and materials.

cross-contour
A line that defines the surface undulations between, or up to, the outermost edges of shapes or objects.

Cubism
The name given to the painting style invented by Pablo Picasso and Georges Braque between 1907 and 1912, which incorporates multiple views of objects to simulate their three-dimensionality while acknowledging the two-dimensional surface of the picture plane. Signaling the beginning of abstract art, Cubism is a semi-abstract style that continued a trend away from representational art initiated by Cézanne in the late 1800s.

curvilinear
Stressing the use of curved lines, as opposed to **rectilinear,** which stresses straight lines.

decorative
Ornamenting or enriching but, more importantly in art, emphasizing the two-dimensional nature of an artwork or any of its elements. Decorative art emphasizes the essential flatness of a surface.

design
The underlying plan on which an artwork is based. In a broader sense, design may be considered synonymous with the term **form.**

dominance
The principle of visual organization that certain elements are more important than others in a particular composition or design. Some features are emphasized, and others are subordinated.

economy
The distillation of the image to the basic essentials for clarity of presentation.

elements of art
Line, shape, value, texture, and color—the basic ingredients the artist uses to produce imagery. The use of these elements produces the visual language of art.

equivocal space
A condition, usually intentional on the artist's part, in which the viewer may, at different times, see more than one set of relationships between art elements or depicted objects.

expression
1. The manifestation of thought, emotion, or quality of meaning in artistic form. 2. In art, expression is synonymous with the term **content.**

form
1. The organization and arrangement of visual elements that develop unity in an artwork. 2. The total appearance or organization of an artwork.

four-dimensional space
An imaginative treatment of forms that gives a sense of intervals of time or motion.

fractional representation
A pictorial device (used notably by the Egyptians) in which several spatial aspects of the same subject are combined in the same image.

genre painting
Picture subjects that concern everyday life, domestic scenes, family relationships, and the like.

geometric shape
A shape that appears related to geometry; usually simple, such as a triangle, rectangle, and circle.

Gestalt (Gestalt psychology)
A German word for "form"; an organized whole in experience. Around 1912, the Gestalt psychologists promoted the theory that explains psychological phenomena by their relationships to total forms, or Gestalten, rather than by their parts.

glyptic
1. The quality of an art material like stone, wood, or metal that can be carved or engraved. 2. An art form that retains the color and the tensile and tactile qualities of the material from which it was created. 3. The quality of hardness, solidity, or resistance found in carved or engraved materials.

golden mean, golden section
1. Golden mean—"perfect" harmonious proportions that avoid extremes; the moderation between extremes. 2. Golden section—a traditional system for harmonious proportion expressed by dividing a line or an area into two sections such that the smaller part is to the larger as the larger is to the whole. The ratio developed is 1:1.6180, or roughly 8:13.

graphic art
1. Two-dimensional art forms, such as drawing, painting, and printmaking. 2. The two-dimensional use of the elements of art. 3. May also refer to the techniques of commercial art as used in the layout and production of newspapers, books, magazines, and Web pages.

harmony
The pleasing quality achieved by different elements of a composition interacting to form a whole. Harmony is often accomplished through repetition of the same or similar characteristics.

hatching
Repeated strokes of an art tool producing clustered lines (usually parallel) that create values. In "cross-hatching," similar lines pass over the hatched lines in a different direction, usually resulting in darker values.

high-key color
Any color that has a value level of middle gray or lighter.

high-key value
A value that has a level of middle gray or lighter.

highlight
The portion of an object that, from the observer's position, receives the greatest amount of direct light.

hue
Designates the common name of a color and indicates its position in the spectrum or on the color wheel. Hue is determined by the specific wavelength of the color in a ray of light.

implied line
Implied lines (subjective lines) are those that dim, fade, stop, and/or disappear. The missing portion of the line is implied to continue and is visually completed by the observer as the line reappears.

implied shape
A shape that does not physically exist but is suggested by dots, lines, areas, or their edges. (See **Gestalt.**)

infinite space
Pictorial space in which the picture frame acts as a window through which objects can be seen receding endlessly.

installations
Interior or exterior settings of media created by artists to heighten the viewers' awareness of the environmental space.

intensity
The saturation, strength, or purity of a hue. A vivid color is of high intensity; a dull color is of low intensity.

intermediate color
A color produced by a mixture of a primary color and a secondary color.

interpenetration
The interlocking movement of planes, objects, or shapes within a specified area of space.

intuitive space
The illusion of space that the artist creates by instinctively manipulating certain space-producing devices, including overlapping, transparency, interpenetration, inclined planes, disproportionate scale, fractional representation, and the inherent spatial properties of the art elements.

invented texture
A created texture whose only source is in the imagination of the artist. Generally a decorative pattern, it should not be confused with **abstract texture.**

isometric projection
A technical drawing system in which a three-dimensional object is two-dimensionally presented; starting with the nearest vertical edge, the horizontal edges of the object are drawn at a 30-degree angle and all verticals are projected perpendicularly from a horizontal base.

kinetic art
From the Greek word *kinesis,* meaning "motion," art that includes the element of actual movement.

line
The path traced by the point of a tool, instrument, or medium as it moves across an area. A line is visible when it contrasts in value with its surroundings. Three-dimensional lines may be made using string, wire, tubes, solid rods, and the like.

linear perspective
A system used to depict three-dimensional images on a two-dimensional surface; it develops the optical phenomenon of diminishing size by treating edges as converging parallel lines. They extend to a vanishing point or points on the horizon (eye level) and recede from the viewer (see **perspective**).

local (objective) color
The color as seen in the objective world (green grass, blue sky, red barn, and the like).

local value
The relative lightness or darkness of a surface, seen in the objective world, that is independent of any effect created by the degree of light falling on it.

low-key color
Any color that has a value level of middle gray or darker.

low-key value
Any value that has a level of middle gray or darker.

manipulation
The sculptural technique of shaping pliable materials by hands or tools.

mass
1. In graphic art, a shape that appears to stand out three-dimensionally from the space surrounding it or that appears to be a solid body of material. 2. In the plastic arts, a physical bulk of material. (See **plastic art, three-dimensional,** and **volume.**)

medium, media (pl.)
The materials and means used to bring an artwork into existence.

mobile
A three-dimensional moving sculpture.

modeling
The sculptural technique of shaping a pliable material.

monochromatic
Having only one hue; the complete range of value of one color from white to black.

motif
A design unit that is repeated often enough in the total composition to make it a significant or dominant feature. Motif is similar to a theme in a musical composition.

movement
Eye travel directed by visual design in a work of art.

naturalism
The approach to art that attempts a description of things as they appear in nature. Pure naturalism would contain no personal interpretation introduced by the artist.

natural texture
Texture created as the result of nature's processes.

negative area
The unoccupied or empty space in an artwork defined by the positive elements created by the artist. (See **positive area.**)

neutralized color
A color that has been grayed or reduced in intensity by being mixed with any of the neutrals or with a complementary color.

neutrals
1. The inclusion of all color wavelengths will produce white, and the absence of any wavelengths will be perceived as black. With neutrals, no single color is noticed—only a sense of light and dark or the range from white through gray to black. 2. A color altered by the addition of its complement so that the original sensation of hue is lost or grayed.

nonobjective art
A type of art that is entirely imaginative and not derived from anything visually perceived by the artist and, consequently, not associated by the observer with any previously experienced natural object.

nonrepresentational art
Artwork encompassing nonrecognizable imagery, ranging from pure abstraction (nonrecognizable but derived from a recognizable object) to nonobjective art (not a product of abstraction, but derived from the artist's mind).

objective art
Art that is based on physical actuality, optical perception, and the appearance of things as they are. Such art tends to appear natural or real.

oblique projection
A technical drawing system in which a three-dimensional object is two-dimensionally presented, the front and back sides of the object are parallel to the horizontal base, and the other planes are drawn as parallels coming off the front plane at a 45-degree angle.

open-value composition
Composition in which values cross over shape boundaries into adjoining areas.

optical perception
Things as seen through the eye.

organic unity
A condition in which the components of an artwork—that is, subject, form, and content—form an interdependent whole.

orthographic drawing
Graphic representation of two-dimensional views of an object, showing a plan, vertical elevations, and/or a section.

paint quality
The textural character of applied paint. Interest is created by the ingenuity in handling paint for its intrinsic character.

papier collé
A visual and tactile technique in which scraps of paper are pasted to the picture surface. In addition to the texture of the paper, the use of printed matter can add richness and pattern similar to an artist's invented texture.

patina
1. A natural film, usually greenish, that results from the oxidation of bronze or other metallic material. 2. Colored pigments and/or chemicals applied to a sculptural surface.

pattern
1. Any artistic design serving as a model for imitation. 2. A repeated element and/or design that is usually varied and produces interconnections and obvious directional movements.

perspective
Any graphic system used in creating the illusion of three-dimensional images and/or spatial relationships on a two-dimensional surface. There are several types of perspectives—atmospheric, linear, and projection systems.

picture frame
The outermost boundary of the picture plane.

picture plane
The actual flat surface on which the artist executes a pictorial image. In some cases, the picture plane acts merely as a transparent plane of reference to establish the illusion of forms existing in a three-dimensional space.

pigments
Color substances that give their color property to another material by being mixed with it or covering it. Pigments, usually insoluble, are added to liquid vehicles to produce paint and ink. Colored substances dissolved in liquids that give their coloring effects by being absorbed or staining are referred to as dyes.

planar
Having to do with planes.

plane
1. An area that is essentially two-dimensional, having height and width. 2. A flat or level surface. 3. A two-dimensional surface having a positive extension and spatial direction or position.

plastic art
1. The use of the elements of art to create the illusion of the third dimension on a two-dimensional surface. 2. Three-dimensional art forms, such as architecture, sculpture, and ceramics.

positive area(s)
The portion of an artwork in which the art elements (shape, line, etc.), or their combination, produce the subject—nonrepresentational or recognizable images. (See **negative area.**)

primary color
The preliminary hues that cannot be broken down or reduced into component colors. The basic hues of any color system that in theory may be used to mix all other colors.

principles of organization
Seven principles that guide the use of the elements of art in achieving unity: harmony, variety, balance, proportion, dominance, movement, and economy.

proportion
The comparative size relationship between the parts of a whole. For example, the size of the Statue of Liberty's hand relates to the size of her head. (See **scale.**)

radial
Emanating from a center.

realism, Realism (art movement)
The style of art that creates an impression of visual actuality without going to extremes of detail, while attempting to relate and interpret universal meanings that lie beneath surface appearances. As a movement, it relates to painters like Honoré Daumier in nineteenth-century France and Winslow Homer in the United States in the 1850s.

rectilinear shape
A shape whose boundaries consist of straight lines.

relief sculpture
An artwork, graphic in concept but sculptural in application, utilizing relatively shallow depth to establish images. The space development may range from very limited projection, known as "low relief," to more exaggerated space development, known as "high relief." Relief sculpture is meant to be viewed frontally, not in the round.

repetition
The use of the same visual effect a number of times in the same composition. Repetition may produce dominance, harmony, pattern, or rhythm.

representational art
A type of art in which the subject is presented through the visual art elements so that the observer is reminded of actual objects. (See **naturalism** and **realism.**)

rhythm
A sense of movement achieved by the repetition of visual units; the use of measured accents.

scale
Size relative to human dimensions or another standard unit of measure. For example, the Statue of Liberty's scale is apparent when she is seen next to an automobile. (See **proportion.**)

sculpture
The art of expressive shaping of materials that are three-dimensional. "Man's expression to man through three-dimensional form" (Jules Struppeck; see Bibliography).

secondary color
A color produced by a mixture of two primary colors.

shadow, shade, shading
The darker value on the surface of an object that gives the illusion that a portion of it is turned away from or obscured by the source of light.

shallow space
The illusion of limited depth. With shallow space, the imagery appears to move only a slight distance back from the picture plane.

shape
An area that stands out because of a defined or implied boundary or because of differences of value, color, or texture.

silhouette
The area between or bounded by the contours, or edges, of an object; the total shape.

simulated texture
A convincing copy or translation of an object's texture in any medium.

simultaneous contrast
When two different colors come into direct contact, the contrast intensifies the difference between them.

space
The interval, or measurable distance, between points or images.

spectrum
The band of individual colors that results when a beam of white light is broken into its component wavelengths, identifiable as hues.

split-complement(s)
A color and the two colors on either side of its complement.

style
A specific artistic character or dominant trend of form noted during a period of history or during an art movement. Style also refers to the expressive use of media that gives an artwork individual character.

subject
The persons, things, signs, or ideas represented in an artwork that express the artist's inspiration or intention.

subjective
That which is derived from the mind, reflecting a personal viewpoint, bias, or emotion.

substitution
In sculpture, replacing one material or medium with another (see also **casting**).

subtraction
A sculptural term meaning the carving or cutting away of material.

subtractive color
The sensation of color that is produced when wavelengths of light are reflected back to the viewer after all other wavelengths have been subtracted and/or absorbed.

Surrealism
A style of art, influenced by Freudian psychology, that emphasizes fantasy and is said to be revealed by the subconscious through the use of automatic techniques (rubbings, doodles, blots, cloud patterns, and the like). Originally a literary movement that grew out of Dadaism, Surrealism was established by a literary manifesto written by André Breton in 1924.

symmetry
The mirrorlike repetition of appearances on both sides of an imaginary central axis.

tactile
A quality that refers to the sense of touch.

technique
The manner with which an artist uses tools and materials to achieve an expressive effect.

tectonic
The quality of simple massiveness; lacking any significant extrusions or intrusions.

tenebrism
A technique of painting that exaggerates or emphasizes the effects of **chiaroscuro.** Larger amounts of dark value are placed close to smaller areas of highly contrasting lights—which change suddenly—in order to concentrate attention on important features.

tertiary color
Color resulting from the mixture of all three primaries in differing amounts or two secondary colors. Tertiary colors are characterized by the neutralization of intensity and hue. They are found on the color wheel on the inner rings of color leading to complete neutralization.

texture
The surface character of a material that can be experienced through touch or the illusion of touch. Texture is produced by natural forces or through an artist's manipulation of the art elements.

three-dimensional
Possessing a dimension of depth, in addition to having the dimensions of height and width.

transparency
A visual quality in which a distant image or element can be seen through a nearer one.

trompe l'oeil
Literally, "deceives the eye"; a painting technique that copies nature with such exactitude as to be mistaken for the real thing.

two-dimensional
Possessing the dimensions of height and width.

unity
The result of bringing the elements of art into the appropriate ratio between harmony and variety to achieve a sense of oneness.

value
1. The relative degree of light or dark. 2. The characteristic of color determined by the quantity of light reflected by the color.

value pattern
The arrangement or organization of values that control compositional movement and create a unifying effect throughout a work of art.

variety
Differences achieved by opposing, contrasting, changing, elaborating, or diversifying elements in a composition to add individualism and interest; the counterweight of **harmony** in art.

void
1. An area lacking positive substance and consisting of negative space. 2. A spatial area within an object that penetrates and passes through it.

volume
A measurable area of defined or occupied space.

ADAM, MICHAEL. *Womankind*. New York: Harper and Row, 1979.
ADAMS, LAURIE SCHNEIDER. *Art across Time*. 2 vols. New York: McGraw-Hill (College), 1999.
AGOSTON, GEORGE A. *Color Theory and Its Application in Art and Design*. Berlin, Heidelberg, New York: Springer Verlag, 1987.
ALBERS, JOSEF. *Interaction of Color*. New Haven, Conn.: Yale University Press, 1963.
ANDERSON, MAXWELL L., et al. *2000 Biennial Exhibition*. New York: Harry N. Abrams, 2004.
ARMSTRONG, TOM. *200 Years of American Sculpture*. Catalog for Whitney Museum of American Art. Boston: The Godine Press, 1976.
ARNASON, H. H. *History of Modern Art*. Englewood Cliffs, N.J.: Prentice-Hall, 1986.
ARNHEIM, RUDOLPH. *Art and Visual Perception*. Berkeley: University of California Press, 1966.
ART IN AMERICA (periodical). 575 Broadway, New York City, N.Y.
ART NEWS (periodical). W. 38th Street, New York City, N.Y.
BATCHELDER, ANN, and ORBAN, NANCY. *Fiberarts Design Book Five*. Asheville, N.C.: Lark Books, 1995.
BATES, KENNETH F. *Basic Design: Principle and Practice*. New York: Funk & Wagnalls, 1975.
BETHERS, RAY. *Composition in Pictures*. New York: Pitman Corporation, 1956.
BETTI, CLAUDIA, and SELE, TEEL. *A Contemporary Approach: Drawing*. New York: Holt, Rinehart & Winston, 1980.
BEVLIN, MARJORIE E. *Design through Discovery*. New York: Holt, Rinehart & Winston, 1980.
BINDMAN, DAVID. *William Blake*. New York: Thames and Hudson, 1982.
BIRREN, FABER. *Color Perception in Art*. New York: Van Nostrand Reinhold, 1976.
———. *Creative Color*. New York: Van Nostrand Reinhold, 1961.
———. *Principles of Color*. New York: Van Nostrand Reinhold, 1969.
BLOCK, JONATHAN, et al. *Understanding Three Dimensions*. Englewood Cliffs, N.J.: Prentice-Hall, 1987.
BLOOMER, CAROLYN M. *Principles of Visual Perception*. New York: Van Nostrand Reinhold, 1976.
BRO, L.V. *Drawing: A Studio Guide*. New York: W. W. Norton, 1978.
BUENDIA, J. R., et al. *Paintings of the Prado*. Boston: Little, Brown, 1994.
CANADAY, JOHN. *What Is Art?* New York: Alfred Knopf, 1980.
CARPENTER, JAMES M. *Visual Art: An Introduction*. New York: Harcourt Brace Jovanovich, 1982.
CHADWICK, WHITNEY. *Women Artists and the Surrealist Movement*. New York: Thames and Hudson, 1991.
CHAET, BERNHARD. *The Art of Drawing*. New York: Holt, Rinehart & Winston, 1970.
CHEATHAN, FRANK R.; CHEATHAN, JANE HART; and OWENS, SHERYL HATER. *Design Concepts and Applications*. Englewood Cliffs, N.J.: Prentice-Hall, 1983.
CHEVREUL, M. E. *The Principles of Harmony and Contrasts of Colors and Applications to the Arts*. New York: Van Nostrand Reinhold, 1981.
CHILVERS, IAN; OSBORNE, HAROLD; and FARR, DENNIS. *The Oxford Dictionary of Art*. New York: Oxford University Press, 1988.
CLEAVER, DALE G. *Art: An Introduction*. New York: Harcourt Brace Jovanovich, 1972.
COLEMAN, RONALD. *Sculpture: A Handbook for Students*. Dubuque, Iowa: Wm. C. Brown, 1990.
COLLIER, GRAHAM. *Form, Space and Vision*. Englewood Cliffs, N.J.: Prentice-Hall, 1972.
COMPTON, MICHAEL. *Pop Art*. London: Hamlyn, 1970.
CRAWFORD, WILLIAM. *The Keepers of the Light: A History and Working Guide to Early Photographic Processes*. New York: Dobbs Ferry, 1979.
DANOT, ARTHUR C., and SWEET, CHRISTOPHER. *Mark Tansey: Visions and Revisions*. New York: Harry N. Abrams, 1992.
DANTZIC, CYNTHIA MARIS. *Design Dimensions*. Englewood Cliffs, N.J.: Prentice-Hall, 1990.
DAVIS, PHIL. *Photography*. Dubuque, Iowa: Wm. C. Brown, 1990.
DIAMOND, DAVID G. *Art Terms*. Boston: A Bulfinch Press Book; Little, Brown, 1992.
EDWARDS, BETTY. *Drawing on the Right Side of the Brain*. Los Angeles: Tarcher, 1979.
ELIOT, ALEXANDER. *Myths*. New York: McGraw-Hill, 1976.
ELSEN, ALBERT E. *Origins of Modern Sculpture*. New York: George Braziller, 1974.
ENSTICE, W., and PETERS, M. *Drawing*. Englewood Cliffs, N.J.: Prentice-Hall, 1996.
FAINE, BRAD. *The Complete Guide to Screen Printing*. Cincinnati: Quartu Publishing, 1989.
FAULKNER, RAY; SMAGULA, HOWARD; and ZIEGFELD, EDWIN. *Today: An Introduction to the Visual Arts*. New York: Holt, Rinehart & Winston, 1987.
FINE, RUTH E., et al. *Contemporary American Realist Drawings*. Manchester, Eng.: Hudson Hills Press, 2000.
GARDNER, HELEN, revised by Tansey, Richard G., and Kleiner, Fred S. *Art through the Ages*. Vol. II, *Renaissance and Modern Art*. New York: Harcourt Brace, 1996.
GETLEIN, MARK. *Living with Art*. New York: McGraw-Hill (College), 2005.
GILBERT, RITA, and MCCARTER, WILLIAM. *Living with Art*. New York: Alfred Knopf, 1988.
GOLDSTEIN, NATHAN. *The Art of Responsive Drawing*. Englewood Cliffs, N.J.: Prentice-Hall, 1977.
HAMMACHER, ABRAHAM MARIE. *The Evolution of Modern Sculpture*. New York: Harry N. Abrams, 1969.
HARLAN, CALVIN. *Vision and Invention: A Course in Art Fundamentals*. Englewood Cliffs, N.J.: Prentice-Hall, 1970.
HELLER, NANCY. *Women Artists: An Illustrated History*. New York: Abbeyville Press, 1981.
HIBBARD, HOWARD. *The Metropolitan Museum of Art*. New York: Harper & Row, 1980.
HOPTMAN, LAURA; TATEHATA, AKIA; and ZELEVANSKY, LYNN. *Love Forever: Yayoi Kusama, 1958–1968*. Los Angeles County Museum of Art, 1998.
HUNTER, SAMUEL. *American Art of the 20th Century*. New York: Harry N. Abrams, 1972.

ITTEN, JOHANNES. *The Art of Color.* New York: Van Nostrand Reinhold, 1970.

———. *Design and Form.* New York: Van Nostrand Reinhold, 1975.

JENKINS, DONALD. *Images of a Changing World.* Portland, Ore.: Portland Art Association, 1983.

KISSICK, J. *Art Context and Criticism.* Madison, Wis.: Brown and Benchmark, 1993.

KNAPPE, KARL-ADOLF. *Dürer.* New York: Harry N. Abrams, 1965.

KNOBLER, NATHAN. *The Visual Dialogue.* New York: Holt, Rinehart & Winston, 1980.

KUEPPERS, HARALD. *The Basic Law of Color Theory.* New York: Barron's Educational Series, 1982.

———. *Color Atlas.* New York: Barron's Educational Series, 1982.

LANE, R. *Images from the Floating World.* Secaucus, N.J.: Cartwell Books, 1978.

LAUER, DAVID. *Design Basics.* New York: Wadsworth, 2004.

LERNER, ABRAM, et al. *The Hirshhorn Museum and Sculpture Garden.* New York: Harry N. Abrams, 1974.

LEWIS, R. L., and LEWIS, S. I. *The Power of Art.* Orlando, Fla.: Harcourt Brace, 1994.

LOCKER, J. L. *The World of M. C. Escher.* New York: Harry N. Abrams, 1971.

LOWE, SARAH M. *Frida Kahlo.* New York: University Publishing, 1991.

LUCIE-SMITH, EDWARD. *Late Modern: The Visual Arts since 1945.* New York: Praeger, 1969.

———. *The Thames and Hudson Dictionary of Art Terms.* New York: Thames and Hudson, 1984.

MACAULAY, DAVID. *The New Way Things Work.* Boston: Houphton Mifflin/Walter Lorraine Books, 1988.

MEISEL, L. K. *Photorealism since 1980.* New York: Harry N. Abrams, 1993.

MENDELOWITZ, DANIEL M., and WAKEMAN, DUANE A. *A Guide to Drawing.* Orlando, Fla.: Harcourt Brace Jovanovich, 1993.

MYERS, JACK FREDRICK. *The Language of Visual Art.* Orlando, Fla., New York: Holt, Rinehart & Winston, 1989.

NATIONAL GALLERY OF ART. *Johannes Vermeer.* Washington, D.C., 1995.

POIGNANT, R. *Oceanic Mythology.* London: Paul Hamlyn, 1967.

PREBLE, DUANE. *Art Forms.* New York: Prentice-Hall, 2004.

———. *Art Forms.* New York: Harper & Row, 1989.

RICHARDSON, J. A. *Art: The Way It Is.* Englewood Cliffs, N.J.: Prentice-Hall/Harry N. Abrams, 1986.

RICHARDSON, JOHN ADKINS, et al. *Basic Design.* Englewood Cliffs, N.J.: Prentice-Hall, 1984.

RUBIN, W. *Primitivism in 20th Century "Art."* 2 vols. New York: Museum of Modern Art, 1984.

RUSSELL, STELLA PANDELL. *Art in the World.* Orlando, Fla.: Holt, Rinehart & Winston, 1989.

SAFF, DONALD, and SACILOTTO, DELI. *Printmaking.* New York: Holt, Rinehart & Winston, 1978.

SIMMONS, SEYMOUR, III, and WINER, MARC S. A. *Drawing: The Creative Process.* Englewood Cliffs, N.J.: Prentice-Hall, 1977.

SMITH, BRADLEY. *Mexico—a History in Art.* New York: Doubleday, 1968.

SMITH, B., and WENG, W. *China—a History in Art.* New York: Harper & Row, 1972.

SPARKE, PENNY; HODGES, FELICE; DENT, EMMA; and STONE, ANNE. *Design Source Book.* Secaucus, N.J.: Chartwell, 1982.

STRUPPECK, JULES. *The Creation of Sculpture.* New York: Henry Holt, 1952.

SUTTON, P. *Dreamings: The Art of Aboriginal Australia.* New York: George Braziller, 1988.

TERUKAZU, AKIYAMA. *Japanese Painting.* New York: Rizzoli International Publications, 1977.

THORP, R. L. *Son of Heaven: Imperial Arts of China.* Son of Heaven Press, Seattle, 1988.

TOWNSEN, CHRIS. *The Art of Bill Viola.* New York: Thames and Hudson, 2004.

VERITY, ENID. *Color Observed.* New York: Van Nostrand Reinhold, 1980.

WALKER ART CENTER. *Painting and Sculpture from the Collection.* Walker Art Center and Rizzo International Publications, Inc., 1990. Subsequent editions probable.

WAX, CAROL. *The Mezzotint.* New York: Harry N. Abrams, 1996.

WEISS, HILLARY. *The American Bandanna.* San Francisco, Calif.: Chronicle, 1990.

WILLIAMS, RICHARD L. Series Editor, *Life Library of Photography.* New York: Time-Life, 1971.

WINGLER, M. HANS. *The Bauhaus.* Cambridge, Mass.: M.I.T. Press, 1986.

WONG, WUCIUS. *Principles of Color Design.* New York: Van Nostrand Reinhold, 1987.

———. *Principles of Form and Design.* New York: Van Nostrand Reinhold, 1993.

———. *Principles of Three-Dimensional Design.* New York: Van Nostrand Reinhold, 1977.

YENAWINE, PHILIP. *How to Look at Modern Art.* New York: Harry N. Abrams, 1991.

ZELANSKI, PAUL, and FISHER, MARY PAT. *Shaping Space.* New York: Wadsworth, 1995.

A

abstract art, 278–281, *278, 279, 280*
color in, 156, 279
and Cubism, 90, 275
and Fantastic art, 284
photography, 281–282
and Pop Art, 305
and Post-Impressionism, 263, 264
and Postmodernism, 317
sculpture, 279, 280–281, *281*
shape in, 94–95
space in, 181–182
subject in, 11
United States, 279–280
See also Abstract Expressionism; abstraction; Neo-Abstraction
Abstract Expressionism, 280, 291–302
Action painting, 293–296, *294, 295*
Color Field painting, 293–294, 296–297, *296, 297,* 302, 310
origins of, 291–293, *292, 293*
and photography, 282, 301–302, *301, 302*
and Pop Art, 304, 305
and Process/Conceptual Art, 319
and sculpture, 298–301, *298, 299, 300*
abstraction
and content, 12–13
and creative process, 12–13, 19
defined, 4, 90
and economy, 65, 66
and texture, 128, 134–136
See also abstract art
Abstraction, Porch Shadows, Twin Lakes, Conn. (Strand), *276*
Abstract Painting and Sculpture in America (Museum of Modern Art), 293
abstract texture, 128, 134–135
academic art
color in, 156
defined, 28, 142
and nineteenth-century art, 248–249
accents, 128, 135, 171
achromatic values, 112, 142, 148
Action painting, 293–296, *294, 295*
actual shapes, 90, 93
actual texture, 128, 131–133
Adams, Ansel, 21, 282, 283–284, 302
Banner Peak and Thousand Island Lake, 21
addition, 220, 229–230, *230*
additive color, 142, 144–145, *144*
Aerographs (Man Ray), 291
aesthetics, 4, 6
Affection for Surfing (Schnabel), *322*
Africa (Motherwell), *25*
African art, 268, 269, 274–275, *274*. *See also* primitive art
Age d'Or, L', 291
Agony (Gorky), *292*
Albers, Joseph
and Abstract Expressionism, 291, 293, 296
and American abstract art, 280
and color wheel evolution, 163
and Constructivism, 279
Homage to the Square, 106, 296
White Line Square IX, 106
Alf, Martha
Pears Series 11 #7, 111, 113
alla prima painting, 259
allover pattern, 28, 34, 35
American Dawn (Nevelson), *304*
American Legion Convention (Winogrand), *307*
amorphous shapes, 90, 92, 93
analogous colors, 142, 154, *154,* 207
Analytical Cubism, 275
Ancestors of Tehemana (Gauguin), *25*
Ancestral Figure from House Post (Maori), *132*
Andalusian Dog, The (Un Chien Andalou), 214, 291
Andreas, George
Energy, 65
angular lines, 74
Annunciation (Botticelli), *188, 189*
Anuskiewicz, Richard, 309
Injured by Green, 159
Apartment Houses (Hopper), *193*
Aphrodite (Coffey), *224*
Apple Face (Haskins), *44*
applied arts, 54–55
approximate symmetry, 28, 53–54
Archipenko, Alexander, 281
Woman Doing Her Hair, 232, 281
architecture
and abstract art, 279
Bauhaus, 220, 224
overlapping in, 239
and Postmodernism, 316–317
radial balance in, 54–55
recent innovations, 225
texture in, 139
Arman
Lava Bike, 213
Armchair (Wright), *224*
Arp, Jean Hans, 284, 287, 289–290, 298
Mountain Table Anchor Navel, 290
Torso, 290
art
appreciation of, 15, 17
basic components of, 10–15
definitions of, 5–6
Artemis, Acrobats, Divas and Dancers (Spero), *62*
Artistic Painting, The (Lasker), *77*
Asian art
and Expressionism, 268
and Impressionism, 259–260
line in, 75
rhythm in, 38
space in, 179, 180, 200, 201
symmetry in, 54
value in, 121
assemblage, 128, 133, 237, 284, 304–305
asymmetry, 28, 55–56, 190, 240
atectonic qualities, 220, 238
atmospheric perspective, 128, 138–139, 178, 181, 182
At the Point of Waking (Frank), *125*
automatic techniques, 287, 293, 298
Autumn Rhythm (Pollock), *294*
Avenger, The (Barlach), *243*
Avery, Milton, 65
Seated Blonde, 66

B

balance, 50–56, *51*
asymmetry, 55–56
and color, 168, 170
defined, 28
and dominance, 63
and gravitational forces, 50, *50*
radial, 28, 51, 54–55, 240
and shape, 101
symmetry, 28, 29, 52–54, 240
in three-dimensional art, 240
and value, 114, 116
Balancing Act with Stone II (Yasami), *54*
Balla, Giacomo, 276, 277
Dynamism of a Dog, 211
Speeding Automobile, 277
Bamboo in the Wind (Wu Zhen), *75*
Banner Peak and Thousand Island Lake (Adams), *21*
Barden, Brice
Study for the Muses, 78
Barlach, Ernst
Avenger, The, 243
Barlow, Clarence
Im Januar am Nil, 217
Baroque Art, 119, 308
Barr, Alfred, 291
Barye, Antoine Louis, 253, 255, 265
Tiger Devouring an Antelope, 253
Bathers (Chase-Riboud), *10*
Battersea Power Station, XIII (Lutter), 328, *329*
Bauhaus
and Abstract Expressionism, 302
and Albers, 280
and Constructivism, 279
defined, 220
and Kandinsky, 278
and Postmodernism, 317
and streamlining, 224
Beal, Jack, 116
Still Life with Tools, 118
Bearded Captive, The (Michelangelo), *223*
Bearden, Romare
Family Dinner, 171
beauty, 6
Becher, Bernd, 327
Water Towers, 327
Becher, Hilla, 327
Water Towers, 327
Beckmann, Max, 175, 180, 270
Departure, 271
Bell, Larry, 310, 311
First and Last, 311
Benglis, Lynda, 325
Tossana, 325
Bernini, Giovanni Lorenzo, 265
Bertelli, Renato
Continuous Profile of Mussolini, 212
Beuys, Joseph, 308–309
Rescue Sled, 308, 309
Biblical subjects, 250, 268, 269
Bicycle Wheel (Duchamp), *285,* 304
Bierstadt, Albert, 181
View from the Wind River Mountains, Wyoming, 181
Big Egypt (De Woody), *238*
Big Springs (Jaudon), *53*
Bing, Ilse
My World, 132
biomorphic shapes, 90, 94
Birchman, Fred
Plum, 104
Bird Blast (Tomaselli), *55*
Bird in Space (Brancusi), 280, *281*
bird's-eye view, 194–195
Birren, Faber, 163
Bitter Nest, The, Part V: Homecoming (Ringgold), *247, 322*
Blaue Reiter, Der (The Blue Rider), 269
Blue Rider, The (*Der Blaue Reiter*), 269
Blue Window Brick Vine (Ward), *236*
Boccioni, Umberto, 276
Unique Forms of Continuity in Space, 277
Bochner, Mel
Vertigo, 76
Bodio, Gene
New City, 194
Borglum, Gutzon, 300
Botticelli, Sandro, 181
Annunciation, 188, 189
Bouchel, Clouret
Fight or Flight, 76
Passing Through, 44–45, *45*
Braden, Michael
Nurse Log, 237
Brady, Mathew, 257
Bragaglia, Anton Giulio, 277
Salutando (Greeting), 277
Brancusi, Constantin, 280, 290, 300
Bird in Space, 280, *281*
Braque, Georges
and collage, 132, 304
and Cubism, 267, 275–276
and shape, 90, 95
Still Life with Fruit and Stringed Instrument, 101
Breakfast (González), *95*
Breton, André, 90, 287, 289
Breznik, Eta Sadar
Space, 219, 227
Briar (Kelly), *73*
Bridge, The (*Die Brücke*), 269–270, 273
Britton, David, 217
Broadway Boogie Woogie (Mondrian), *279*
Broken Star (Nierman), *183*
Bronze with Two Squares (Kendrick), *228*
Brown, Roger
Giotto and His Friends (Getting Even), 210
Land of Lincoln, 202
Brücke, Die (The Bridge), 269–270, 273
Brunelleschi, Filippo, 186
Brussels Construction (Rivera), *232*

Builders in the Workshop (Lawrence), *63*
Bullfight, The (Goya), *105*
Buñuel, Luis, 214, 290–291
Burchfield, Charles, 272, 280
  Night Wind, The, 106, 107
Burghers of Calais, The (Rodin), *265*
Burial at Ornans (Courbet), *256*
Burial of Pierrot, The (Matisse), *89, 95*
Burnham, Sheriann Ki-Sun
  Nomad, 216
Bury, Pol, 303
  Staircase, The, 203
Bust of Maria van Reygersberg (Verhulst), *130*
B/WX (Held), 99, *205*
Byron, George Gordon (Lord), 250

C

Cabinet Makers (Lawrence), *180*
Cactus Man No. 1 (González), *289*
Cage, John, 308, 326
Cai Guo-Qiang
  Cry Dragon/Cry Wolf: The Ark of Genghis Khan, 332
Calder, Alexander
  and Abstract Expressionism, 298–299, 300
  and line, 73
  and movement, 242
  and rhythm, 39
  Spinner, The, 238
  Totem, on the Parvis de la Defense, Paris, 299
California Scenario (Noguchi), *300*
Callahan, Harry, 301–302
  Chicago, 302
calligraphy, 70, 74, *74*
Callot, Jacques
  Great Fair at Imprunita, The, 182
camera obscura, 255
Camera Work, 266–267
Campo di Rialto (Canaletto), *177, 191*
Canaletto, Antonio
  Campo di Rialto, 177, 191
Canna Red and Orange (O'Keefe), *280*
canon, 57, 58, 59
Canova, Antonio
  Perseus with the Head of Medusa, 250
Caprichos, Los (Goya), 253
Caravaggio (Michelangelo Merisi)
  David Victorious over Goliath, 119
Carnival (Stepovich), 39, *124*
Caro, Anthony
  Odalisque, 93
Cartier-Bresson, Henri, 291, 307
  Old Customer, An, San Remo, Italy, 291
Cassatt, Mary
  Jeune Fille, La, 262
casting, 220, 230. *See also* substitution
cast shadows, 112, 114, 204
cave paintings, 5
Celmins, Vija
  Drypoint–Ocean Surface, 129
ceramics, 55, 139, 227
Cézanne, Paul, 262, 263–264
  and color, 156, 206
  and Cubism, 264, 274, 275
  Mount Sainte-Victoire, 264
  and space, 185, 208, 209
  and Stieglitz, 280
  Still Life with Apples, 156
  Still Life with Basket of Fruit (The Kitchen Table), 208, 263
Chagall, Marc, 286–287
  I and the Village, 287
  Le Pont de Passy et la Tour, 55
character
  of lines, 77
Chase-Riboud, Barbara
  Bathers, 10
Cheney, Sheldon, 4
Chevreul, M. E., 156–157
Chevrons #2 (Pearlstein), *318*
chiaroscuro, 112, 114, 116–118
Chicago, Judy, 322, 323–324
  Dinner Party, The, 323
  Resolutions (for the millennium), A Stitch in Time, 324
Chicago (Callahan), *302*
Chien Andalou, Un (The Andalusian Dog), 214, 291
Chihuly, Dale
  Lakawanna Ikebana, 226
Chilikat blanket (Tlingit), *53*
Christ Mocked by Soldiers (Rouault), 268, *269*
Christo, 316, 319
  Wrapped Reichstag, 16, *16,* 316
Christ Presented to the People (Rembrandt), *19*
chroma, 142, 150
  See also intensity
chromatic qualities, 142, 148
chromatic values, 112, 113, 142, 149
cinema, 114, 211, 213–214, 290–291
Circus Sideshow (La Parade) (Seurat), 59, *60*
Civil War, 257
classical art, 253
Claudel, Camille
  Maturity (L'Age Mûr), 266
Clayton, David
  One Dead Tern Deserves Another, 229
Close, Chuck, 36, 37, 317
  John, 62, *63*
  Paul III, 36
closed composition, 238
closed-value compositions, 112, 124, 125
closure
  defined, 28
  and harmony, 40–41, *40*
  and shape, 91, 92, 93
  in three-dimensional art, 239
Cobblestone House, Avon, New York (White), *17*
Coburn, Alvin Langdon, 276, 281–282
  Portrait of Ezra Pound, 276
  Vortograph #1, 281
Coffey, Michael
  Aphrodite, 224
collage, 128, 131, 132, 133, 275, 285, 304
Collins, Dan
  Of More Than Two Minds, 212
color, 18, 142–175
  in abstract art, 156, 279
  additive, 142, 144–145, *144*
  analogous/monochromatic relationships, 154, *154*
  balance in, 168, 170
  color wheel evolution, 163–168
  complementary/split-complementary relationships, 152–153, *153*
  and composition, 150, 168, 169
  and emotion, 81, 143, 161, 168
  in Expressionism, 162, 174, 175, 268, 269
  in Futurism, 277
  and harmony, 170–171
  in Impressionism, 156, 157, 160, 259, 260
  and light, 143, *143, 144,* 148
  and line, 81
  mixing, 146–148, *146, 147*
  in photography, 166–167, *167,* 258, 273
  physical properties of, 148–152, *148,* 159
  plastic, 155–156, 157, 206–207
  in Post-Impressionism, 156, 157, 262, 263
  in printmaking, 120
  and psychology, 161–163
  in Romanticism, 251
  simultaneous contrast, 142, 156–161
  and space, 155–156, 206–207
  subtractive, 143, 145–146, 165–166, *165, 166*
  temperature of, 154–155
  tetradic relationships, 154, *154*
  in three-dimensional art, 237
  triadic relationships, 153–154
  and variety, 171–175
  vocabulary list, 142–143
  See also value of color
Color Field painting, 293–294, 296–297, *296, 297,* 302, 310
color tetrads, 142, 154, *154*
color triads, 142, *146,* 147, 153–154, 163
commercial products, *9, 34*
complementary colors
  and color relationships, 152–153, *152, 153*
  defined, 142, 147
  evolution of, 163
  in Expressionism, 269
  in Impressionism, 259
  and intensity, 150, 151, *152*
  and simultaneous contrast, 159
  and variety, 173–174
composition
  and color, 150, 168, 169
  defined, 28
  and form, 30
  in Impressionism, 259–260, 261
  in Neoclassicism, 249
  in Romanticism, 251
  and texture, 135, 137–138
  and value, 112, 121, 123–125
Composition around Red (Pennsylvania) (Sheeler), *11*
Composition in an Oval (Slobodkina), *23*
Composition (Mondrian), *8*
Composition with Red, Blue, Yellow, Black, and Gray (Mondrian), *8*
computer art, 215–216
computer technology, 215–217
  and color, 144, 167
  computer art, 215–216
  and kinetic art, 242–243
  multimedia, 216–217
concept, defined, 28
Conceptual art, 319–320, *319*
  and aesthetics, 6
  content in, 13
  and global art, 332
conceptual perception, 4, 15
Concert for Anarchy (Horn), *245*
consistency, 67, 104
constellations, 299
Constructivism
  and abstract art, 279, 280, 281
  and Abstract Expressionism, 299, 300
  and Futurism, 276
  and Minimalism, 310
  and three-dimensional art, 237
content
  defined, 4, 10, 12–15, 248
  and expression, 70
  and shape, 104–109
  See also stylistic movements
Continuous Profile of Mussolini (Bertelli), *212*
Continuous Ship Curves, Yellow Ochre (Rockburne), *76*
Contour Drawing (Tovish), *80*
contours, 70, 79–80, 211, 231
contrast
  and color, 171–173
  and dominance, 62–63, 103
  simultaneous, 142, 156–161
  and variety, 48
converging parallels, 185–186, *186,* 200, 201
Cook, Lia
  Point of Touch: Bathsheba, 155
cool colors, 154–155
Couple with Shopping Bags (Hanson), *318*
Courbet, Gustave, 255–256
  Burial at Ornans, 256
Covenant (Newman), *296*
craftsmanship
  defined, 4
creative process, 18–20, 22
  and content, 12–13, 14–15
  and form, 29
Crimean War, 257
cross-contours, 70, 79, *79*
cross-hatching, 70, 82
Cry Dragon/Cry Wolf: The Ark of Genghis Khan (Cai), *332*
Csuri, Charles
  Wondrous Spring, 141
Cubism, 274–276, *274, 275, 276*
  and Abstract Expressionism, 298, 299
  defined, 90
  and Expressionism, 270, 271, 272
  and Fantastic art, 286, 287

and Futurism, 276
naming of, 267, 275
and photography, 276, *276,* 281
and Post-Impressionism, 264
sculpture, 275, 280
shape in, 95, 183
space in, 209, 275
texture in, 133
and three-dimensional art, 237
value in, 121
Cubist Still Life with Playing Cards (Lichtenstein), *135*
Cubi VII (Smith), *300*
Cucchi, Enzo, 320, 321
Paesaggio Barbaro, 321
Cunningham, Imogen, 282, 283
Two Callas, 283
Cunningham, Merce, 326
Currin, John
Moved Over Lady, The, 24
curved lines, 74
curvilinear shapes, 90, 96–97
"Cybernetic Serendipity," 215

D

Dadaism, 284–286, *285*
and Abstract Expressionism, 293
and kinetic art, 302
and Pop Art, 304, 305
and Surrealism, 90, 287
Daguerre, Louis J. M., 255, 258
Dalí, Salvador, 287, 288
and cinema, 214, 291
Persistence of Memory, 288
and photography, 290–291
Damascus Gate Stretch Variation (Stella), *31*
Danaide (Rodin), 265
dance, 11
Dante Alighieri, 250
da Silva, Marilyn
Golden Pair, The, 226
Daumier, Honoré, 255
Street Show, 69, 86
Uprising, The, 256
David, Jacques-Louis, 249
Oath of the Horatii, The, 249
David and Goliath (Unknown), *210*
David Victorious over Goliath (Caravaggio), *119*
da Vinci, Leonardo. *See* Leonardo da Vinci
Davis, Ron
Parallelpiped Vents #545, 99
Day and Night (Escher), *43,* 48
Dead Toreador, The (Manet), *122,* 258
Death by Violence (Manzu), *235*
Death of Sardanapalus, The (Delacroix), *251*
de Chirico, Giorgio, 286, 287, 288, 321
Nostalgia of the Infinite, The, 286
decorative art
defined, 4, 18
and Postmodernism, 317
shape in, 90, 96
space in, 178, 179
value in, 112, 121, 122
decorative space, 178, 179
decorative value, 112, 121, 122
Deepwater (Pfaff), *314*
definitions. *See* vocabulary lists
Degas, Edgar, 213, 258, 260, 262
Four Dancers, 261
de Kooning, Willem, 291
Woman, I, 293
Delacroix, Eugène, 157, 251
Death of Sardanapalus, The, 251
Delmonico Building (Sheeler), *194*
Demoiselles d'Avignon, Les (Picasso), *274*
Denial of St. Peter, The (Rembrandt), *120*
Departure (Beckmann), *271*
depth illusions. *See* space; three-dimensional effects
Descartes in Easter Island (Paik), *314*
descriptive art, 4, 15, 113–114
design, 4, 28, 30
design principles. *See* principles of organization
De Stijl, 9, 278
detail, 181–182
De Woody, James
Big Egypt, 238
Diana and the Nymphs (Vermeer), *46*
Diebenkorn, Richard
Ocean Park #9, 56
dimension. *See* space; three-dimensional effects
Dinner Party, The (Chicago), *323*
direction, 74, 76, 101
Disasters of War (Goya), *253*
discord, 31
di Suvero, Mark
For Veronica, 241
Dix, Otto, 269, 270, 273
Dr. Mayer-Hermann, 271
Dog and Cock (Picasso), *138*
dominance, 62–63
and color, 170
defined, 28
and shape, 103
and texture, 137
Donatello, 265
Doryphoros (Polyclitus of Argos), 57, *58,* 59
Dos Personajes Atacados por Perros (Tamayo), *91*
Double Fugue (Sunshine), *173*
Double Negative (Heizer), 316, *316*
Draftsman Drawing a Nude (Dürer), *190*
drawing. *See* graphic art
dream imagery, 287, 293
Drift No. 2 (Riley), *309*
Dr. Mayer-Hermann (Dix), *271*
Drypoint–Ocean Surface (Celmins), *129*
Dubuffet, Jean
Urgence, 83
Duchamp, Marcel
and Abstract Expressionism, 298
and assemblage, 304
Bicycle Wheel, 285, 304
and Dadaism, 284, 285
and Futurism, 276, 277
and Installations, 312
and kinetic art, 302
Nude Descending a Staircase, 210–211, *211,* 285
and Stieglitz, 280
and Surrealism, 291
Dürer, Albrecht, 255
Draftsman Drawing a Nude, 190
Dykmans, Anne, 114
Trois Fois, 115
Dynamic Hieroglyphic of the Bal Tabarin (Severini), *212*
Dynamism of a Dog (Balla), *211*

E

Earth Art, 316
Eastman, George, 257
economy, 28, 65–66, 241–242
Ecriture No. 940110 (Park), *131*
edges
and content, 106–107
extended, 45, 46
shared, 41–43, 43
Effect of Light on Objects (McKnight), *122*
Egyptian art, ancient, 184–185, *185*
Eiso (Manes), *33*
elaboration, 48–49
electromagnetic spectrum, *149*
elements of art, 4, 18
El Greco
Madonna and Child with Saint Martina and Saint Agnes, 23
emotion
in Abstract Expressionism, 297
and color, 81, 143, 161, 168
in Expressionism, 267, 270, 271
and Geometric Abstracion, 278
and line, 85
in Post-Impressionism, 264, 265
in Romanticism, 250–251, 253, 255
and shape, 109
Energy (Andreas), *65*
engraving, 21
Entombment of Christ, The (Titian), *118*
Environmental Art, 312–316, *313, 314, 315, 316*
Equivalent (Stieglitz), *282*
equivocal space, 90, *98,* 99
Ernst, Max, 284, 287, 288
Horse, The, 285
Escher, M. C.
Day and Night, 43, 48
Rippled Surface, 34
Waterfall, 199
Estes, Richard, 114
Helene's Florist, 317
et in Arcadia Ego (Shepherds of Arcadia) (Poussin), *18*
Euclid, 57
Evoë 1 (Riley), *39*
expression, 70
defined, 4
and line, 78–79
and shape, 104
and subject, 11
and value, 114, 116–121
See also content
Expressionism, 267–273, *268, 269, 270*
and abstract art, 280
color in, 162, 174, 175, 268, 269
and Fantastic art, 286, 287
Fauvism, 264, 267–268, *268,* 272, 273, 274
German, 268–270, *269, 270, 271*
Mexican, 272–273, *272*
and Neo-Expressionism, 320
and photography, 273
and Post-Impressionism, 264–265, 267
and sculpture, 270, 272
United States, 272
extensions, 45–47, 239

F

F-64, 283
Family Dinner (Bearden), *171*
Family of Man, The (Steichen), 282
Family of Saltimbanques (Picasso), *56*
Fang tribal mask from Gabon, 274–275, *274*
Fantastic art, 284–287
individual artists, 286–287, *286, 287*
See also Dadaism; Surrealism
fantasy, 91. *See also* Fantastic art
Fauvism, 267–268, *268,* 272
and photography, 273
and Picasso, 274
and Post-Impressionism, 264
faux surface treatments, 134
feelings. *See* emotion
Feininger, Lyonel
Hopfgarten, 203
feminist art, 321–324, *321, 322, 323, 324*
femmages, 323
fiberwork, 227
Fibonacci, Leonardo, 59
Fibonacci Series, 58, 59
field, 24. *See also* positive areas
Fight or Flight (Bouchel), *76*
figure, 24. *See also* positive areas
film, 114, 211, 213–214, 290–291
film stills, 326–327
First and Last (Bell), *311*
Fischdampfer (Fishing Boat) (Nolde), *83*
Fit for Active Service (Grosz), *271*
Flags (Johns), *158*
Flares: Storm Gray (Noland), *297*
Flavin, Dan, 310, 311
Untitled, 311
folk art, 270
Forest Devil (Snelson), *239*
form, 28–67
balance, 50–56
and content, 13
defined, 4, 11–12
dominance, 62–63
economy, 65–66
and line, 78
and medium, 19
movement, 63–65
proportion, 56–62
and space, 66–67
and subject, 10, 11

in three-dimensional art, 221
variety, 47–50
and visual ordering, 29–31
vocabulary list, 28–29
See also harmony
For Veronica (di Suvero), *241*
found objects, 284, 285, 304–305
Four Dancers (Degas), *261*
fourth dimension
and Calder, 298–299
defined, 178
and Installations/Environmental art, 315
and movement in time, 207, 210–215
and space, 178, 207
and three-dimensional art, 237–238
Fox Games (Skoglund), *244*
Fox Talbot, William Henry, 255
Nicole & Pullen Sawing and Cleaving, 254
Fra Angelico, 116
fractional representation, 178, 184–185, 209
Fragonard, Jean Honoré, 262
Frank, Mary
At the Point of Waking, 125
Frank, Robert, 306
Americans, The, 306
Frankenthaler, Helen, 294, 296
Madame Butterfly, 107
freestanding sculpture (sculpture in the round), 235
French Revolution, 249
French Royal Academy of Arts and Letters, 248–249
Freud, Sigmund, 287
Fridge, Brian
Vault Sequence No. 10, 136
Friedlander, Lee, 306
New York City, 307
frog's-eye view, 194–195
frontality, 53
Frottage, 287
Futurism, 276–277, *277*
and Fantastic art, 284
and kinetic art, 302
movement in, 211, 212, 277
overlapping in, 44
and photography, 277, 281
"Futurist Manifesto" (Marinetti), 276

G

Gabo, Naum, 281
Gagnon, Pauline
Secret Little Door, 32
Gainsborough, Thomas, 330
Ganson, Arthur, 242
Machine with Chair, 243
Gardner, Alexander
Lincoln Meeting McClellan after the Battle of Antietam, 257
Gate, The (Hofmann), *206*
Gates of Hell, The (Rodin), *236*, 265
Gauguin, Paul, 262, 264
Ancestors of Tehemana, 25
and color, 156, 157
Siesta, The, 157
and space, 180
Gehry, Frank
Model for a New Guggenheim Museum in New York City, 225
General Motors
Pontiac Protosport concept car, *223*
genre painting, 128, 134
Geometric Abstraction, 109, 278, 279, 293, 296, 309
geometric shapes, 90, 95
Geostructure 1 (Jonas), *48*
German Expressionism, 268–270, *269, 270, 271*
Gerzso, Gunther, 41
Personage in Red and Blue, 42
Gestalt psychology
and Abstract Expressionism, 296
and Cézanne, 263
and closure, 40
defined, 28
and shape, 91, *92*, 93, 98
gestural drawing, 86, 87
Giacometti, Alberto, 289
Three Walking Men, 289
Giotto, 116, 117
Kiss of Judas, The, 117
Giotto and His Friends (Getting Even) (Brown), *210*
glass design, 226
Glass of Absinth (Picasso), *284*
global art, 330–332, *330, 331, 332*
glyptic materials, 220, 221
Goethe, Johann Wolfgang von, 163, 250
Goforth, John W.
Untitled, 222
Going Forth by Day (Viola), *215*
golden mean, 28. *See also* golden section
Golden Pair, The (da Silva), *226*
golden section, 28, 57–60, *57, 58*
Golub, Leon, 162
Prometheus II, 162
González, José Victoriano (Juan Gris)
Breakfast, 95
Portrait of Max Jacob, 85
González, Julio, 289, 298, 299
Cactus Man No. 1, 289
Gordon, George, 250
Gorky, Arshile, 291
Agony, 292
Goya, Francisco, 251, 253
Bullfight, The, 105
Caprichos, Los, 253
Disasters of War, 253
Third of May, The, 252
Grand Odalisque, La (Ingres), *250*
graphic art, 4, 15, 19, 112–113
graphic design, 47
Graves, Nancy
Perfect Syntax of Stone and Air, 49
Unending Revolution of Venus, Plants, and Pendulum, 240
gravitational forces, 50
Gray, Thomas, 250
Gray Tree, The (Mondrian), *3, 7*
Great Depression, 272
Great Fair at Imprunita, The (Callot), *182*
Greek art, ancient, 210, 222, 237, 249, 250
Gris, Juan. *See* González, José Victoriano
Gris, Juan, 276
Grosz, George, 269, 270, 290
Fit for Active Service, 271
ground, 24. *See also* negative areas
ground plane, 188
Guardian Angels (Tanning), *94*
Guernica (Picasso), *100*
Guggenheim Museum (Bilbao, Spain), 225
Gursky, Andreas, 327
99 Cent, 328
Guston, Philip, 326

H

halftones, 166
Hamilton, Ann, 245, 314–315
Tropos, 315
Hamilton, Richard
Just What Is It That Makes Today's Homes So Different, So Appealing?, 303
Hamlet Robot (Paik), 214–215, *214*
Handball (Shahn), *27, 52*
Hanson, Duane, 317
Couple with Shopping Bags, 318
Happenings, 306, 308–309, *308*
Hard-Edge Abstraction, 278
See also Color Field painting
harmony, 31–47
and closure, 40–41
and color, 170–171
defined, 28
repetition, 31, 32–39
rhythm, 39
and shape, 104
in three-dimensional art, 238–240
vs. variety, 29, 47–48
and visual linking, 41–47
Harris, Morris, 163
Haskins, Sam
Apple Face, 44
hatching, 70, 81, 82
Haverfield, Tom
Kerosene Lamp, 209
Kerosene Lamp II, 209
Haystack at Sunset (Monet), *259*
Heizer, Michael
Double Negative, 316, *316*
Held, Al
B/WX, 99, 205
Quattro Centric XIII, 184
Helene's Florist (Estes), *317*
Helmholtz, Hermann von, 168
Hesse, Eva, 319
Repetition 19 III, 32
hierarchical scaling, 61–62
high-key colors, 142, 149–150, 171
high-key values, 112, 113
highlights, 112, 113
Hill, Thomas
Yosemite Valley (from below Sentinel Dome as Seen from Artist's Point), 139
Hilty, Thomas
Meditation, 20
Hiroshige, Utagawa
Kintaikyo Bridge at Iwakuni (No. 52), 259–260, *260*
History of the Art of the Ancients, The (Winckelmann), 249
Hofmann, Hans, 206–207, 280, 291, 293
Gate, The, 206
Hokusai, Katsushika
Under the Wave off Kanagawa, 38
Holocaust, 298, 319
Homage to New York (Tinguely), 302
Homage to the Square (Albers), *106,* 296
Homer, Winslow
Returning Fishing Boats, 182
Hopfgarten (Feininger), *203*
Hopper, Edward, 272, 318
Apartment Houses, 193
horizon line, 182–183, *183,* 188, 189–190, 192
horizontal lines, 76
Horn, Rebecca
Concert for Anarchy, 245
Horse, The (Ernst), *285*
Horse's Motion Scientifically Considered, A (Muybridge), *213*
Household (Kaprow), *308*
hue, 142, 148, 149, *149*
Hugo, Victor, 15
Hunwick, Uwa, 162–163
Lya-Ibeji, 162

I

I and the Village (Chagall), *287*
Image Location (Winters), *204*
I'm Dancin' as Fast as I Can (Schapiro), *323*
Im Januar am Nil (Barlow), *217*
implied lines, 70, 73, 93
implied shapes, 90
Impressionism, 258–262, *258, 259, 260, 261, 262*
and Abstract Expressionism, 294
color in, 156, 157, 160, 259, 260
and kinetic art, 302
and New Realism, 318
and photography, 266
and Turner, 253
Impression—Sunrise (Monet), 259
Improvisation 30 (Cannons) (Kandinsky), *278*
incised lines, 236–237
Industrial Revolution, 248, 253, 255
infinite space, 178, 180–181
Infinity Mirror Room-Phalli's Field (or Floor Show) (Kusama), *331*
Information (Museum of Modern Art), 319
Information Wall (Paik), 214
Ingres, Jean-Auguste-Dominique, 249–250
Grand Odalisque, La, 250
Injured by Green (Anuskiewicz), *159*
Inner Sanctum Waterfall (Steir), *71*

Installations, *313, 314, 315, 316*
defined, 220
and Minimalism, 310
overviews, 243–245, 312–316
and video, 214–215
intaglio printing, 119
intensity, 142, 148, 150–152, *151, 152,* 171
intermediate colors, 142, 146–147, *146*
International style, 279, 316–317
interpenetration, 44–45
defined, 28, 178
and space, 184, *184*
in three-dimensional art, 239–240
intuitive space, 65, 101, 178, 200, 202, 203
invented texture, 128, 135–136
I Remember Being Free (Lawe), *130*
isometric projections, 178, 200
Itten, Johanness, 163

J

Jackson, William Henry
Scenes along the Line of the Denver and Rio Grande Railway, 257
Jacquette, Yvonne
Lower Manhattan—Lower Brooklyn Bridge View II, 92
James, Michael
Rhythm/Color: Spanish Dance, 35
Jane Avril (Toulouse-Lautrec), *73*
Japanese art. *See* Asian art
Jaudon, Valerie
Big Springs, 53
Jeanne-Claude, 316
Wrapped Reichstag, 16, 316
Jeff Davies (Witkin), *61*
Jefferson Westward Expansion Memorial (St. Louis), 225
Jeune Fille, La (Cassatt), *262*
jewelry, 54, 139, 225–226
John (Close), 62, *63*
Johns, Jasper, 304, 305
Flags, 158
White Numbers, 179
Jonas, Franklin
Geostructure 1, 48
Judd, Donald, 65–66, 310
Untitled, 242
Judy Trying on Clothes (Wesselmann), *66*
Juniper, Lake Tenaya (Weston), *283*
Just What Is It That Makes Today's Homes So Different, So Appealing? (Hamilton), *303*

K

Kahlo, Frida, 273
Still Life with Parrot, 168
Kahn, Louis I.
National Assembly Building at Shere-e-Bangla Nagar (Dhaka, Bangladesh), *225*
Kanarek, Yael
World of Awe, 215–216, *216*
Kandinsky, Wassily, 278
and Abstract Expressionism, 291, 293, 294
and Cubism, 275
and Dadaism, 284
and German Expressionism, 269
Improvisation 30 (Cannons), 278
Kaprow, Allan, 308
Household, 308
Karan, Khem
Prince Riding an Elephant, 121
Katzen, Lila, 311–312
Oracle, 312
Kelly, Ellsworth, 65, 296
Briar, 73
Spectrum, 153
Kendrick, Mel
Bronze with Two Squares, 228
White Wall, 231
Kennedy Center (Washington, D.C.), 225
Kerosene Lamp (Haverfield), *209*
Kerosene Lamp II (Haverfield), *209*
Keyhole (Murray), *23*
Kiefer, Anselm, 320, 321
Osiris und Isis/Bruch und Einung, 186, 321
kinetic art, 232, 302, *302*
and Abstract Expressionism, 298–299
defined, 90
recent innovations, 21–22, 242–243
shape in, 96
and time, 65
King, Tony
Map: Spirit of '76, 205
Kintaikyo Bridge at Iwakuni (No. 52) (Hiroshige), 259–260, *260*
Kirchner, Ernest Ludwig
Street, The, 269
Kiss of Judas, The (Giotto), *117*
Klee, Paul, 286, 287, 310
Twittering Machine, 286
Kline, Franz, 294, 299, 326
Mahoning, 295
Kokoschka, Oskar, 270
Self-Portrait, 270
Kosuth, Joseph
One and Three Chairs, 319–320, *319*
Kraut, Susan
Unitled, 114
Kuehn, Heinrich
Malschirm, Der, 273
Kusama, Yayoi
Infinity Mirror Room-Phalli's Field (or Floor Show), 331

L

Lakawanna Ikebana (Chihuly), *226*
Land of Lincoln (Brown), *202*
Lascaux cave paintings, *5*
Lasker, Jonathan
Artistic Painting, The, 77
Last Supper, The (Nolde), *174*
La Tour, Georges de
Payment of Taxes, The, 116
Lava Bike (Arman), *213*
Lawe, Gary
I Remember Being Free, 130
Law of Simultaneous Contrast of Colors (Chevreul), 157
Lawrence, Jacob, 272
Builders in the Workshop, 63
Cabinet Makers, 180
Le Blon, J. C., 163
Léger, Fernand, 276
Three Women (Le Grand Déjeuner), 108
Leonardo da Vinci, 15, 116, 117
Mona Lisa, 64, 117
Proportions of the Human Figure, 59
Lewitt, Sol, 320
Liang Kai
Sericulture, 201
Liberation of the Peon, The (Rivera), *30*
Lichtenstein, Roy, 305
Cubist Still Life with Playing Cards, 135
Okay, Hot Shot, 306
light, 113–114
and color, 143, *143, 144,* 148
and Expressionism, 273
in Impressionism, 259, 260, 261
See also value
Light and Dark (McKnight), *115*
light primaries, 167–168
light sculptures, 311
Lincoln Center for the Performing Arts (New York), 225
Lincoln Meeting McClellan after the Battle of Antietam (Gardner), *257*
line, 18, 70–87
and color, 81
defined, 70
expressive qualities of, 78–79
extensions of, 45–46
physical characteristics of, 74–77
and representation, 84–87
and shape, 79–81, 91
and space, 84, 202, 204
and texture, 81, 83
in three-dimensional art, 73–74, 236–237
and value, 81, *81,* 82
vocabulary list, 70
linear perspective, 178, 186–200
applications of, 195–198, *196, 197, 198, 199*
define, 178, 186
development of, 186–189
disadvantages of, 198–199
one-point, 189–191, *190*
three-point, 194–195, *194, 195*
two-point, 191–194, *191, 192*
Line No. 50 (Sykora), *84*
Linked Ring, 266
Lipchitz, Jacques, 298
Man with Mandolin, 231
Rape of Europa, 299
Lippi, Fra Filippo, 116
Lippold, Richard, 73, 236
Variations within a Sphere, No. 10, the Sun, 233
Listen to Living (Écoutez vivre) (Matta Echaurren), *292*
literature, 15, 250, 317
lithography, 21, 120
Livingstone, Joan
Seeped, 222
local (objective) color, 142, 168, 259
local value, 112, 113
Long, Richard, 245
Lorraine, Claude, 253
Los Angeles City Hall and Civic Center, 225
Louis, Morris
and economy, 65
Lower Manhattan—Lower Brooklyn Bridge View II (Jacquette), *92*
low-key colors, 142, 149–150, 171
low-key values, 112, 113
Lunar Image I (Shin), *123*
Luncheon of the Boating Party (Renoir), 260, *261*
Lutter, Vera, 330
Battersea Power Station, XIII, 328, *329*
Lya-Ibeji (Hunwick), *162*

M

Machine with Chair (Ganson), *243*
Madame Butterfly (Frankenthaler), *107*
Madonna and Child with Saint Martina and Saint Agnes (El Greco), *23*
Madonna of Mercy (Piero della Francesca), *62*
Madonna of Mt. Carmel and the Souls in Purgatory (Tiepolo), *64*
Magada, Steve
Trio, 87
Magic Realism, 288–289
Magritte, René, 288–289
Portrait, 288–289
Unmasked Universe, The, 207
Mahoning (Kline), *295*
Maillol, Aristide, 270, 272
Montagne, La, 272
Malevich, Kasimir, 310
White on White, 279
Malschirm, Der (Kuehn), *273*
Manes, Paul
Eiso, 33
Manet, Edouard, 121, 213, 258–259
Dead Toreador, The, 122, 258
Olympia, 258
Races at Longchamps, The, 258, 259
manipulation, 220, 229, *229*
Mannerism, 321
Man Ray, 287, 291
Aerographs, 291
Solarizations, 291
Man with a Violin (Picasso), *275*
Man with Mandolin (Lipchitz), *231*
Manzu, Giacomo, 237
Death by Violence, 235
Map: Spirit of '76 (King), *205*
Marca-Relli, Conrad
Picador, The, 105
Marchesa (Martin), *233*
Marin, John, 162, 206, 272, 280
Sun Spots, 206
Marinetti, Tommaso, 276
Marisol

Women and Dog, 237
Marrey, Gilles
1997, 169
Martin, Agnes, 310
Untitled #9, 310
Martin, Julie Warren
Marchesa, 233
Mary Magdalene (Smith), *324*
Masaccio, 116, 186
Trinity with the Virgin, St. John and Donors, 187
Mason, Emily
Upon a Jib, 155
mass
defined, 4, 18, 90
and shape, 97
in three-dimensional art, 220, 221
materials, 228–229, 320
Matisse, Henri
and Abstract Expressionism, 293
Burial of Pierrot, The, 89, 95
and economy, 65
Odalisque with Tambourine (Harmony in Blue), 268
and shape, 95
and space, 180
and Stieglitz, 280
Matta Echaurren, Roberto Sebastian Antonio, 293
Listen to Living (Écoutez vivre), 292
matting, 50
Maturity (L'Age Mûr) (Claudel), *266*
Maxwell, James Clerk, 168, 258
McKnight, Russell F.
Effect of Light on Objects, 122
Light and Dark, 115
Shadows, 115
measure, 74
media, 4, 19
Medieval art, 121, 180, 210, 264, 269–270
Meditation (Hilty), *20*
Meeting of Saint Anthony and Saint Paul, The (Sassetta), *103,* 104
Megatron (Paik), 214
Meissonier, Jean Louis Ernest, 213, 290
metalwork, 225–226
Mexican Expressionism, 272–273, *272*
Michelangelo Buonarroti, 265
Bearded Captive, The, 223
Minimalism, 310–312
and Abstract Expressionism, 300
economy in, 65–66, 241–242
and Pop Art, 305
and Postmodernism, 316
and Process/Conceptual Art, 319
and sculpture, 310–312, *311, 312*
Miró, Joan, 287, 291, 298
Painting, The, 94, 107
Mirrored Room (Samaras), 312, *313*
Mitchell, Joan
Untitled, 172, 173
mobiles, 220, 223, 233, 238. *See also* kinetic art
Model for a New Guggenheim Museum in New York City (Gehry), *225*
modeling, 220, 222
Modern Art, 316
Modigliani, Amadeo, 180, 268
moments of force, 52
Mona Lisa (Leonardo da Vinci), 64, *117*
Mondrian, Piet, 278
and Abstract Expressionism, 291, 293, 298
Broadway Boogie Woogie, 279
Composition, 8
Composition with Red, Blue, Yellow, Black, and Gray, 8
and Cubism, 275
Gray Tree, The, 3, 7
influence of, 9
styles of, 7–8
Tree, 7
Trees by the River Gein, 96
Monet, Claude
Haystack at Sunset, 259
Impression—Sunrise, 259
Waterloo Bridge, Grey Weather, 160
Waterloo Bridge, Sunlight Effect, 160
monochromatic color, 142, 154
Monogram (Rauschenberg), *304*
Montagne, La (Maillol), *272*
Moore, Henry, 232
Reclining Figure, 298
Morisot, Berthe, 260, 262
Young Girl by a Window, 262
Morris, Robert, 319
Motherwell, Robert
Africa, 25
motif, 34, 36, 37, 39
motifs
defined, 28
motion pictures, 211, 213–214, 290–291
Mountain Table Anchor Navel (Arp), 290
Mount Sainte-Victoire (Cézanne), *264*
Moved Over Lady, The (Currin), *24*
movement, 63–65
defined, 28
in Futurism, 211, 212, 277
in Impressionism, 260
and line, 202
and texture, 137–138
in three-dimensional art, 242–243
and time, 207, 210–215
See also fourth dimension; space
movement (actual), 21–22, 242–243. *See also* kinetic art
Mozart and Mozart Upside Down and Backward (Rockburne), *108*
Mr. and Mrs. Andrews without Their Heads (Shonibare), *330*
multimedia, 216–217
Multiplication of the Arcs (Tanguy), *288*
Munch, Edvard, 270
Scream, The (The Cry), 270
Muniz, Vik
Raft of the Medusa, The, 138
Munsell, Albert, 163
Munsell color system, 163, *164,* 165
Murray, Elizabeth
Keyhole, 23
music, 11, 31, 37, 39, 48
Muybridge, Eadweard, 213, 258, 259, 277
Horse's Motion Scientifically Considered, A, 213
My World (Bing), *132*

N

Nadar (Gaspard-Félix Tournachon), 259
Napoleonic regime, 249, 250
Nathan Admonishing David (Rembrandt), 77
National Assembly Building at Shere-e-Bangla Nagar (Dhaka, Bangladesh) (Kahn), *225*
Native American art, 53, 294, *295*
Naturalism, 4, 255, 256
Natural System of Colours, The (Harris), 163
natural texture, 128
nature, 58, 94, 97
Navajo sand painting, 294, *295*
Nebamun hunting birds (Egypt), *185*
Nees, George, 215
negative areas, 25
closure in, 40–41
defined, 4
and shared edges, 43
and unity, 22, 24
voids, 220, 232, 281
Neo-Abstraction, 108, 325–326, *325, 326*
Neoclassicism, 248–250, *249, 250*
Neo-Expressionism, 320–322, *321, 322*
and global art, 330–331, 332
Neshat, Shirim
Untitled (Rapture), 37
Neue Sachlichkeit, Die (The New Objectivity), 269, 270
neutralized colors, 146, 147, 151–152, 159, 161, 175
neutrals, 142, 148, 151, 175, 204. *See also* neutralized colors
Nevelson, Louise, 305
American Dawn, 304
New City (Bodio), *194*
New Illusionism, 317
Newman, Barnett, 65, 296, 310
Covenant, 296
New Objectivity, The (*Die Neue Sachlichkeit*), 269, 270
New Realism, 317–319, *317, 318*
Newton, Sir Isaac, 163
New York Armory Show (1913), 279
New York City (Friedlander), *307*
Nicole & Pullen Sawing and Cleaving (Fox Talbot), *254*
Niépce, Joseph N., 255
Nierman, Leonardo
Broken Star, 183
Night Wind, The (Burchfield), *106,* 107
1997 (Marrey), *169*
99 Cent (Gursky), *328*
nineteenth-century art, 248. *See also* stylistic movements
Nix, Patricia
La Primavera, 17
Noguchi, Isamu
California Scenario, 300
Stone Within, The, 221
Noland, Kenneth, 310
Flares: Storm Gray, 297
Nolde, Emil, 269–270
Fischdampfer (Fishing Boat), 83
Last Supper, The, 174
Nomad (Burnham), *216*
nonobjective art, 4, 11, 13, 90, 278, 279
nonrepresentational art, 4, 90, 94, 105
Nostalgia of the Infinite, The (de Chirico), *286*
Nude Descending a Staircase (Duchamp), 210–211, *211,* 285
Number 10 (Rothko), *297*
Nurse Log (Braden), *237*

O

Oath of the Horatii, The (David), *249*
objective art, 4, 90, 93
objective (local) color, 142, 168, 259
oblique projections, 178, 200
occult balance. *See* asymmetry
Oceanic art. *See* primitive art
Ocean Park #9 (Diebenkorn), *56*
Odalisque (Caro), *93*
Odalisque with Tambourine (Harmony in Blue) (Matisse), *268*
Of More Than Two Minds (Collins), *212*
Okay, Hot Shot (Lichtenstein), *306*
O'Keeffe, Georgia, 280, 282, 283
Canna Red and Orange, 280
Old Customer, An, San Remo, Italy (Cartier-Bresson), *291*
Oldenberg, Claes, 305, 316, 318
Shoestring Potatoes Spilling from a Bag, 306
Spoonbridge and Cherry, 61
Olympia (Manet), 258
One and Three Chairs (Kosuth), 319–320, *319*
One Dead Tern Deserves Another (Clayton), *229*
100 Cans (Warhol), *305*
one-point perspective, 189–191, *190*
Op Art, 309, *309*
color in, 159
and kinetic art, 302
line in, 85
space in, 205
open-value compositions, 112, 125
optical perception, 4, 15
Oracle (Katzen), *312*
ordering, visual, 29–31
organic unity, 4, 13, 19–20
Orion (Vasarely), 48–49, *48*
Orozco, José Clemente, 273
Zapatistas, 272
orthogonals, 188
orthographic drawing, 178, 200, 209
Osiris und Isis/Bruch und Einung (Kiefer), *186,* 321
Ostwald, Wilhelm, 163
Ostwald color system, 163
overlapping, 44, 183, *183,* 239
Ox, Jack, 217

P

Pacific (Price), *231*
Paesaggio Barbaro (Cucchi), *321*
Paik, Nam June, 314
Descartes in Easter Island, 314
Hamlet Robot, 214
Information Wall, 214
Megatron, 214
Painting, The (Miró), *94,* 107
paint quality, 128, 131
Pair o' Dice (Smith), *133*
Paisley pattern, *34*
papier collé, 128, 131, 132, 133, 275
Parallelpiped Vents #545 (Davis), *99*
Park, Seo-Bo
Ecriture No. 940110, 131
Passing Through (Bouchel), 44–45, *45*
Past and Present (Pomalaza), *171*
patina, 220, 237
patronage, 248
pattern
allover, 28, 34, 35
defined, 28, 128
and repetition, 32, 34, 136
and texture, 133, 136–137, *136, 137*
Paul III (Close), *36,* 37
Payment of Taxes, The (La Tour), *116*
Pearlstein, Philip, 114, 317, 318
Chevrons #2, 318
Pears Series 11 #7 (Alf), *111, 113*
Pedestal Piece (Soldner), *227*
Pepper, Beverly, 65–66, 242
Thel, 242
perception, 4, 15
Perfect Syntax of Stone and Air (Graves), *49*
Performance Art
and Conceptual Art, 319
and feminist art, 324
Happenings, 306, 308–309, *308*
Perseus with the Head of Medusa (Canova), *250*
Persistence of Memory (Dalí), *288*
Personage in Red and Blue (Gerzso), *42*
perspective, 90, 100, 178
atmospheric, 128, 138–139, 178, 181, 182
See also linear perspective
Pevsner, Antoine, 281
Pfaff, Judy, 314
Deepwater, 314
photography
abstract, 281–282
and Abstract Expressionism, 282, 301–302, *301, 302*
appreciation of, 15
color in, 166–167, *167,* 258, 273
and Conceptual Art, 320
Cubist, 276, *276,* 281
early, *254,* 255, 256–258, *257*
early twentieth-century, 273
and film stills, 326–327
and Futurism, 277, 281
late nineteenth-century, 21, 266–267, *267*
motion and, 213
and New Realism, 318
and nineteenth-century art, 248, 255, 258, 259, 260
and Pop Art, 306, *307*
recent developments, 327–330, *327, 328, 329*
and Surrealism, 290–291, *291*
value in, 114, 283, 284
photojournalism, 257–258
photomontage, 290
Photorealism, 318
Photo-Secessionism, 266, 267, 276
phyllotaxy, *58,* 59
Picador, The (Marca-Relli), *105*
Picasso, Pablo
and Abstract Expressionism, 293, 298, 299
and assemblage, 304
and Cubism, 90, 280
Demoiselles d'Avignon, Les, 274
Dog and Cock, 138
and economy, 65
Family of Saltimbanques, 56
and Fantastic art, 284
Glass of Absinth, 284
Guernica, 100
Man with a Violin, 275
and Neo-Expressionism, 321
and papier collé, 131, 132
and realism, 318
and space, 185, 206
and Stieglitz, 280
Still Life with Chair Caning, 132
and Surrealism, 287, 289
Pictorialism, 255, 256, 266–267, 282
picture frame, 4, 22, *22,* 23
picture plane, 4, 18, 22, *22*
picture stories, 15, 18
Piero della Francesca
Madonna of Mercy, 62
pigments, 142, 145, 149
Pisarro, Camille
Place du Théâtre Français, La, 259–260, *260*
Place du Théâtre Français, La (Pisarro), 259–260, *260*
planar shapes, 90, 96
planes, 5, 18, 90, 96, 98, *98*
plastic art, 15
color in, 155–156, 157, 206–207
defined, 5
shape in, 93
and space, 178, 180–181, 208, 209
value in, 112, 114
See also three-dimensional art; three-dimensional effects
plastic shapes, 90, 93
plastic space, 178, 180–181
plastic value, 112, 114
pleasure, 6
plein air painting, 259
Plum (Birchman), *104*
Pointillism, 59, *60,* 263, 273
Point of Touch: Bathsheba (Cook), *155*
Pollock, Jackson, 294, 296
Autumn Rhythm, 294
Polyclitus of Argos
Doryphoros, 57, *58,* 59
Pomalaza, Fernando
Past and Present, 171
Le Pont de Passy et la Tour (Chagall), *55*
Pontiac Protosport concept car (General Motors), *223*
Pontormo, Jacopo, 255
Pop Art, 237, 302–306, *303, 304, 305, 306, 307*
and Installations/Environments, 312, 315
and New Realism, 317
and photography, 306, *307*
and sculpture, 305, *307*
Portrait (Magritte), 288–289
Portrait of Ezra Pound (Coburn), *276*
Portrait of Max Jacob (González), *85*
position, 182–183, *183*
positive areas, 5, 22, 24, 25, 40
Post-Impressionism, 262–266, *263, 264, 265, 266*
and Abstract Expressionism, 291
color in, 156, 157, 262, 263
and Expressionism, 264–265, 267
space in, 209
Postmodernism, 316–317, 323
Post-Painterly Abstractionists, 294. *See also* Action painting
Poussin, Nicolas, 251
et in Arcadia Ego (Shepherds of Arcadia), 18
Rape of the Sabines, 123
Pousttchi, Bettina
Vera Naturelle, 145
Prang, Louis, 163
Precisionism, 280
prehistoric art, 5–6, *5, 6*
Pre-Raphaelites, 318
Price, Ken
Pacific, 231
primary colors, 142, *146,* 147, 152, 163
Primary Structurism, 241–242, 310. *See also* Minimalism
La Primavera (Nix), *17*
primitive art
and Abstract Expressionism, 297, 298
color in, 161
and Cubism, 274–275
and definitions of art, 5, 6
and Expressionism, 268, 269
form in, 12
and Neo-Abstraction, 325, 326
and Post-Impressionism, 264
and Surrealism, 290
texture in, 132
Prince Riding an Elephant (Karan), *121*
principles of organization, 28, 100–104. *See also specific principles*
printmaking, 21, 113, 119–121, 120, 139
Process Art, 6, 13, 305, 319–320
process color system, 165–166, *165, 166*
product design, 223, 227, 279
Prometheus II (Golub), *162*
proportion, 56–62
defined, 28
and picture frame, 22
and space, 182
in three-dimensional art, 240–241
Proportions of the Human Figure (Leonardo da Vinci), *59*
psychology
and color, 161–163
and Expressionism, 269–270
and Romanticism, 253
and shape, 107–108
and texture, 138
See also Gestalt psychology
Puryear, Martin, 325–326
Thicket, 326

Q

Quattro Centric XIII (Held), *184*
quilts, 35, 37

R

Races at Longchamps, The (Manet), *258,* 259
radial balance, 28, 51, 54–55, 240
Raft of the Medusa, The (Muniz), *138*
Ragamala
Salangi Raga (Three Females under a Tree), 54
Rain, Steam, and Speed—The Great Western Railway (Turner), *252,* 253
Rape of Europa (Lipchitz), *299*
Rape of the Sabines (Poussin), *123*
Raphael
and Ingres, 250
Rauschenberg, Robert, 304, 305, 326
Monogram, 304
Rayographs, 291
ready-made art, 285
Realism, 255–256, *256*
content in, 12
defined, 5
and New Realism, 318
and photography, 255, 266, 281, 282
Reclining Figure (Moore), *298*
rectilinear shapes, 90, 95, 96, 97
Red/Blue Chair (Rietveld), *9*
Reflections (Rothenberg), *325*
Regionalism, 272, 283
Reinhardt, Ad, 65, 310
Rejlander, Oscar G., 255
Two Ways of Life, The, 254, 326–327
relief sculpture, 220, 234–235, 240
Rembrandt Harmenszoon van Rijn, 119, 181
Christ Presented to the People, 19
Denial of St. Peter, The, 120
Nathan Admonishing David, 77
Renaissance art
and Neoclassicism, 250
and photography, 255
space in, 180, 186–189, 207, 210
Renoir, Pierre-Auguste, 258, 260
Luncheon of the Boating Party, 260, *261*
repetition, 31, 32–39
defined, 28
and motif, 34, 37, 39

and pattern, 32, 34, 136
in Pop Art, 305
and radial balance, 54
in three-dimensional art, 242
Repetition 19 III (Hesse), *32*
representational art
color in, 143
content in, 13
defined, 5, 70
and line, 84–87
and shape, 93–94
Rescue Sled (Beuys), *308*, 309
Resolutions (for the millennium), A Stitch in Time (Chicago), 324
Returning Fishing Boats (Homer), *182*
rhythm, 31, 38, 39
defined, 28
and dominance, 63
and shape, 101
in three-dimensional art, 239, 242
and value, 123
Rhythm/Color: Spanish Dance (James), *35*
Rickey, George, 242, 303
Six Random Lines Excentric, 303
Rietveld, Gerrit
Red/Blue Chair, 9
Rietveld-Schröder House, 9
Rietveld-Schröder House (Rietveld and Schröder), *9*
Riley, Bridget
Drift No. 2, 309
Evoë 1, 39
Ringgold, Faith, 322
Bitter Nest, The, Part V: Homecoming, 247, 322
Rippled Surface (Escher), *34*
Rivera, Diego, 273
Liberation of the Peon, The, 30
Rivera, José de, 236, 242
Brussels Construction, 232
Rockburne, Dorothea, 326
Continuous Ship Curves, Yellow Ochre, 76
Mozart and Mozart Upside Down and Backward, 108
Rococo style, 249, 251
Rodin, Auguste, 280
Burghers of Calais, The, 265
Danaide, 265
Gates of Hell, The, 236, 265
Rolling Power (Sheeler), 106, *107*
Roman art, ancient, 249, 250
Romanticism, 250–255, *251, 252, 253*
and Expressionism, 267
and Postmodernism, 317
and Surrealism, 287
Rothenberg, Susan, 325
Reflections, 325
United States, 80
Rothko, Mark, 310
Number 10, 297
Rouault, Georges, 175, 268, 273
Christ Mocked by Soldiers, 268, *269*
Rousseau, Jean-Jacques, 250
Rubens, Peter Paul, 251
Rueda, Ismael Rodríguez
El Sueño de Erasmo, 103
Ruisdael, Jacob van, 181
Runge, Philipp Otto, 163
Running Horse Attacked by Arrows (Paleolithic cave painting), *5*

S

Salangi Raga (Three Females under a Tree) (Ragamala), *54*
Salutando (Greeting) (Bragaglia), *277*
Samaras, Lucas, 312
Mirrored Room, 312, *313*
São Paulo Biennial, 331
Sassetta, workshop of
Meeting of Saint Anthony and Saint Paul, The, 102, 103
saturation. *See* intensity
scale, 28, 56, 62, 182. *See also* proportion
Scenes along the Line of the Denver and Rio Grande Railway (Jackson), *257*
Schactman, Barry
Study after Poussin, 123, *124*
Schapiro, Miriam, 322–323
I'm Dancin' as Fast as I Can, 323
Schnabel, Julian, 320, 321–322
Affection for Surfing, 322
School of Paris, 281
Schröder, Truus
Rietveld-Schröder House, 9
Schumer, Gary
Simulation, 134
Schwitters, Kurt, 312
Scott, Sir Walter, 250
Scream, The (The Cry) (Munch), *270*
screen printing, 120–121
sculpture, 222–223
abstract, 279, 280–281, *281*
and Abstract Expressionism, 298–301, *298, 299, 300*
Cubist, 275, 280
defined, 220
economy in, 65–66
and Expressionism, 270, 272
form in, 11–12
Impressionist, 260
kinetic, 65, 302, *302*
lines in, 73–74
and Minimalism, 310–312, *311, 312*
and Neo-Abstraction, 325–326
and New Realism, 317, 318–319, *318*
nineteenth-century, 248, 260, 265–266
and Pop Art, 305, *307*
and Surrealism, 289–290, *289, 290*
texture in, 129, 131, 139
See also three-dimensional art
sculpture in the round (freestanding sculpture), 235
Seated Blonde (Avery), *66*
Sebastian
Variacion Nuevo Mexico, 239
secondary colors, 142, *146,* 147
Secret Little Door (Gagnon), *32*
Seeley, J.
Stripe Song, 85
Seeped (Livingstone), *222*
Segal, George, 305, 318
Walk, Don't Walk, 307
Self-Portrait (Kokoschka), *270*
Self-Portrait (van Gogh), *264*
Sellers, Coleman, 213
Sericulture (Liang Kai), *201*
serigraphy, 21
Serra, Richard
Tilted Arc, 244
Seurat, Georges, 59, 262, 273
Circus Sideshow (La Parade), 59, *60*
Sunday Afternoon on the Island of La Grande Jatte, 263
Severini, Gino, 276
Dynamic Hieroglyphic of the Bal Tabarin, 212
sfumato, 117
shading, 112
shadows, 112, 113, 114, 233
Shadows (McKnight), *115*
Shahn, Ben, 272, 318
Handball, 27, 52
Shakespeare, William, 250
shallow space, 65, 180, *180*
defined, 112, 178
and transparency, 183
and value, 121, 123
shape, 18, 90–109
and attention, 95–96
and content, 104–109
defined, 91–95, *92*
and design principles, 100–104
extensions of, 47
and form, 11–12
and line, 79–81, 91
and picture frame, 23
in three-dimensional art, 93, 220, 221, 230–232
and three-dimensional effects, 96, 97–100, *98,* 104, 204, *205*
two-dimensional, 96–97
vocabulary list, 90
shared edges, 41–43, *43*
Sheeler, Charles, 280, 318
Composition around Red (Pennsylvania), 11
Delmonico Building, 194
Rolling Power, 106, *107*
Sherman, Cindy, 324, 327
Untitled, 324
Shin, Jisik
Lunar Image I, 123
Shoestring Potatoes Spilling from a Bag (Oldenberg), *306*
Shonibare, Yinka
Mr. and Mrs. Andrews without Their Heads, 330
Siesta, The (Gauguin), *157*
silhouettes, 220, 233
simulated texture, 128, 133–134, *135*
Simulation (Schumer), *134*
simultaneity, 274, 275
simultaneous contrast, 142, 156–161
Six Random Lines Excentric (Rickey), *303*
size. *See* scale
Sketchpad, 215
Skoglund, Sandy, 245, 315
Fox Games, 244
sky plane, 188
Slobodkina, Esphyr
Composition in an Oval, 23
Smith, Alexis
Pair o' Dice, 133
Smith, David, 298, 299–300, 310
Cubi VII, 300
Smith, Kiki, 324
Mary Magdalene, 324
Smith, W. Eugene, 12
Spanish Wake, 12
Smithson, Robert, 315
Spiral Jetty, 315
Snelson, Kenneth, 73
Forest Devil, 239
social protest, 269, 270, 271, 272–273
Social Realism, 272, 273, 306
Solarizations (Man Ray), 291
soldering, 236
Soldner, Paul
Pedestal Piece, 227
space, 178–217
and color, 155–156, 206–207
and converging parallels, 185–186, *186,* 200, 201
in Cubism, 209, 275
defined, 5
and detail, 181–182
and form, 66–67
four-dimensional, 178, 207
and fractional representation, 178, 184–185, 209
importance of, 179
and interpenetration, 184, *184*
intuitive, 65, 101, 178, 200, 202, 203
and line, 84, 202, 204
and movement in time, 207, 210–215
and overlapping, 183, *183*
perception of, 179
in photography, 273
and picture frame, 22
and plastic art, 208, 209
and position, 182–183
projection systems, 178, 200
and scale, 182
and shape, 104, 204, *205*
and texture, 138–139, 206
in three-dimensional art, 234–235, *234, 235*
and transparency, 183
types of, 179–181
and value, 204
vocabulary list, 178
See also linear perspective
Space (Breznik), *219, 227*
Spanish Wake (Smith), *12*
spectrum, 142, 143, *143,* 149, *149,* 163
Spectrum (Kelly), *153*
Speeding Automobile (Balla), *277*
Spero, Nancy
Artemis, Acrobats, Divas and Dancers, 62
Spinner, The (Calder), *238*
Spinoza, Baruch, 255
Spiral Jetty (Smithson), *315*
spirals, *58,* 59
split-complements, 142, 152–153, *153*

Spoonbridge and Cherry (Oldenburg and van Bruggen), *61*
Spring Beauty (Wyeth), *127, 129*
stabiles, 299
stage lighting, 145
Staircase, The (Bury), *303*
Starry Night, The (van Gogh), *14*, 131
Steichen, Edward, 21, 266, 282, 301
Wind Fire (Thérèse Duncan), 282
Stein, Gertrude, 15
Steir, Pat
Inner Sanctum Waterfall, 71
Stella, Frank, 297
Damascus Gate Stretch Variation, 31
Stepovich, Andrew
Carnival, 39, *124*
stereoscopic vision, 179
Stieglitz, Alfred, 21, 266–267
and abstract art, 279–280, 282
and Cubism, 276
Equivalent, 282
and Surrealism, 291
Terminal, The, 266, *267*
and Weston, 283
Still Life with Apples (Cézanne), *156*
Still Life with Basket of Fruit (The Kitchen Table) (Cézanne), *208,* 263
Still Life with Chair Caning (Picasso), *132*
Still Life with Fruit and Stringed Instrument (Braque), *101*
Still Life with Parrot (Kahlo), *168*
Still Life with Tools (Beal), *118*
Stone Within, The (Noguchi), *221*
straight lines, 74
Straight photography movement, 255, 266–267, 281, 282–284, 301
Strand, Paul, 281, 282, 283, 284, 301
Abstraction, Porch Shadows, Twin Lakes, Conn., 276
streamlining, 224
Street, The (Kirchner), *269*
Street Show (Daumier), *69, 86*
Stripe Song (Seeley), *85*
Struppeck, Jules, 220
Struth, Thomas, 327
Study after Poussin (Schactman), 123, *124*
Study for Figure of Falsehood on the Ceiling of the Palazzo Trento-Valmarana, Vicenza (Tiepolo), *86*
Study for the Muses (Barden), *78*
style, 5, 6. *See also* stylistic movements
stylistic movements, 248–332
early photography, 255, 256–258
early twentieth-century photography, 273
Environmental Art/Installations, 214–215, 220, 243–245, 310, 312–316
Fantastic art, 284–291
feminist art, 321–324
film stills, 326–327
Futurism, 44, 211, 212, 276–277, 281, 284, 302
global art, 330–332
Happenings, 306, 308–309
late nineteenth-century photography, 21, 266–267
Minimalism, 65–66, 241–242, 300, 305, 310–312, 316, 319
Neo-Abstraction, 108, 325–326
Neoclassicism, 248–250
Neo-Expressionism, 320–322, 330–331, 332
New Realism, 317–319
Op Art, 85, 159, 205, 302, 309
Pointillism, 59, 263, 273
Pop Art, 237, 302–306, 312, 315, 317
Post-Impressionism, 156, 157, 209, 262–266, 267, 291
Postmodernism, 316–317, 323
Process/Conceptual Art, 6, 13, 305, 319–320, 332
Realism, 5, 12, 255–256, 266, 281, 282, 318
Romanticism, 250–255, 267, 287, 317
See also abstract art; Abstract Expressionism; Cubism; Expressionism; Impressionism; kinetic art; Surrealism
subject, 5, 10, 11, 78
subjective art, 5
subjective colors, 143, 168, 169
subjectivity, 15, 90, 93
substitution, 220, 230, *230*
subtraction, 220, 229, *229*
subtractive colors, 143, 145–146, 165–166, *165, 166*
El Sueño de Erasmo (Rueda), *103*
Sullivan, Louis, 223
Sunday Afternoon on the Island of La Grande Jatte (Seurat), *263*
Sunshine, Norman
Double Fugue, 173
Sun Spots (Marin), *206*
Superrealism, 318
Suprematism, 279
Surrealism, 287–291, *288*
and Abstract Expressionism, 292, 293, 294, 298
and de Chirico, 286
defined, 90
and motion pictures, 214
and photography, 290–291, *291*
and sculpture, 289–290, *289, 290*
and shape, 94, 95, 109
and texture, 136
Sutherland, Ivan, 215
Sykora, Zdenek
Line No. 50, 84
symbolism
and color, 161, 168
and Neo-Expressionism, 321
in photography, 266
and Post-Impressionism, 264
and shape, 106
and texture, 138
Symbols of Manifest Destiny (Victory), *64*
symmetry, 28, 29, 52–54, 240
synthetic design, 209

T

tachiste painting, 259
tactile qualities, 128, 129, *130*, 131, 134
Tamayo, Rufino, 291, 293
Dos Personajes Atacados por Perros, 91
Tanguy, Yves, 287–288
Multiplication of the Arcs, 288
Tanning, Dorothea
Guardian Angels, 94
Tansey, Mark
Triumph over Mastery II, 170
Tatlin, Vladimir, 279, 281
technical illustration, 200
technique
and aesthetics, 6
defined, 5
recent innovations, 320
three-dimensional art, 229–230
tectonic qualities, 220, 223, 238
television, 144, 214
temperature, 154–155
tenebrism, 112, 118, 119, 120
Terminal, The (Stieglitz), 266, *267*
terms. *See* vocabulary lists
Terrain 10 (Woods), *72*
tertiary colors, 143, 147, 151–152, 159, 161
texture, 18, 128–139
abstract, 128, 134–136
actual, 128, 131–133
and composition, 135, 137–138
defined, 129
in Expressionism, 271
invented, 128, 135–136
and line, 81, 83
and pattern, 133, 136–137, *136, 137*
in Post-Impressionism, 264
in Romanticism, 251
simulated, 128, 133–134, *135*
and space, 138–139, 206
tactile nature of, 129, *130*, 131, 134
in three-dimensional art, 236
vocabulary list, 128
theater, 145
Thel (Pepper), *242*
themes, 37, 39
Theory of Color, The (Prang), 163
Thicket (Puryear), *326*
Third of May, The (Goya), *252*, 253
Thomasos, Denyse
Urban Jewels, 84
three-dimensional art
areas of, 222–227
balance in, 240
color in, 237
and creative process, 18–19, 22
defined, 5
economy in, 241–242
harmony/variety in, 238–240
line in, 73–74, 236–237
materials, 228–229
movement in, 242–243
proportion in, 240–241
shape in, 93, 220, 221, 230–232
space in, 234–235, *234, 235*
techniques, 229–230, *229, 230*
texture in, 236
and time, 237–238
value in, 232–233
vocabulary list, 220
See also Installations; sculpture
three-dimensional effects
atmospheric perspective, 128, 138–139, 178, 181, 182
and color, 144, 155–156, 168, 206–207
computer models, 144
and converging parallels, 185–186, *186*, 200, 201
and creative process, 18
defined, 90, 178
infinite space, 178, 180–181
and interpenetration, 184, *184*
and line, 84, 202, 204
and overlapping, 183, *183*
and position, 182–183, *183*
and scale, 182
and shape, 96, 97–100, *98*, 104, 204, *205*
and shared edges, 41
and texture, 138–139, 206
and transparency, 183
and value, 112, 114, 204, *205*
See also linear perspective; space
three-point perspective, 194–195, *194, 195*
Three Walking Men (Giacometti), *289*
Three Women (Le Grand Déjeuner) (Léger), *108*
Tiepolo, Giambattista
Madonna of Mt. Carmel and the Souls in Purgatory, 64
Tiepolo, Giovanni Battista
Study for Figure of Falsehood on the Ceiling of the Palazzo Trento-Valmarana, Vicenza, 86
Tiger Devouring an Antelope (Barye), *253*
Tilted Arc (Serra), 244
time
and space, 207, 210–215
and three-dimensional art, 237–238
See also fourth dimension
Tinguely, Jean, 242, 302
Homage to New York, 302
Titian (Tiziano Vecellio), 116, 118
Entombment of Christ, The, 118
Toast, The (Zorn), *82*
Tomaselli, Fred
Bird Blast, 55
Torso (Arp), *290*
Tossana (Benglis), *325*
Totem, on the Parvis de la Defense, Paris (Calder), *299*
Toulouse-Lautrec, Henri de, 265, 280
Jane Avril, 73
Tovish, Harold
Contour Drawing, 80
transparency
defined, 29, 178
in Fantastic art, 287
and harmony, 44
and space, 183
in three-dimensional art, 239

Treatise on Painting (Leonardo da Vinci), 15
Tree (Mondrian), 7
Trees by the River Gein (Mondrian), *96*
Trinity with the Virgin, St. John and Donors (Masaccio), *187*
Trio (Magada), *87*
Triumph over Mastery II (Tansey), *170*
Trois Fois (Dykmans), *115*
trompe l'oeil, 128, 134, 228, 318, 319
Tropos (Hamilton), *315*
Trova, Ernest
  Untitled, from the series *Index, 106*
Turner, J. M. W., 253, 255
  Rain, Steam, and Speed—The Great Western Railway, 252
twentieth-century art. *See* stylistic movements
Twittering Machine (Klee), *286*
Two Callas (Cunningham), *283*
two-dimensional art, 18
  defined, 5
  media/techniques, 20–22
  shape in, 93
  space in, 179
two-dimensional effects, 90, 96–97, 178
two-point perspective, 191–194, *191, 192*
Two Ways of Life, The (Rejlander), *254,* 326–327
Tzara, Tristan, 284, 290

U

Uli figure, New Zealand, *12*
Under the Wave off Kanagawa (Hokusai), *38*
Unending Revolution of Venus, Plants, and Pendulum (Graves), *240*
Unique Forms of Continuity in Space (Boccioni), *277*
United States (Rothenberg), *80*
Unitled (Kraut), *114*
unity
  defined, 5, 29
  and form, 31
  organic, 4, 13, 19–20
  and positive/negative areas, 22, 24
  and space, 67
Unmasked Universe, The (Magritte), *207*
Untitled #9 (Martin), *310*
Untitled (Flavin), *311*
Untitled (Goforth), *222*
Untitled (Judd), *242*
Untitled (Mitchell), *172,* 173
Untitled (Rapture) (Neshat), *37*
Untitled (Sherman), *324*
Untitled, from the series *Index* (Trova), *106*
Upon a Jib (Mason), *155*
Uprising, The (Daumier), *256*
Urban Jewels (Thomasos), *84*
Urgence (Dubuffet), *83*

V

value, 18, 112–125, *113*
  compositional uses of, 112, 121, 123–125
  descriptive uses of, 113–114
  in Expressionism, 271
  expressive uses of, 114, 116–121
  and line, 81, *81,* 82
  in Minimalism, 310
  in photography, 114, 283, 284
  in Romanticism, 251
  and space, 204
  and texture, 137
  in three-dimensional art, 232–233
  vocabulary list, 112
  See also value of color
value of color, 113, 143, 148, 149–150, *150*
  and harmony, 171
  and intensity, 152
value patterns, 112, 123–125
value studies, 123–125
van Bruggen, Coosje
  Spoonbridge and Cherry, 61
van Gogh, Vincent, 162, 262, 264–265, 293
  Self-Portrait, 264
  Starry Night, The, 14, 131
vanishing points, 188, 190, 191, 192, 194–195
  multiple, 198, *199*
Variacíon Nuevo Mexico (Sebastian), *239*
Variations within a Sphere, No. 10, the Sun (Lippold), *233*
variety, 47–50
  and color, 171–175
  defined, 29
  and shape, 104
  in three-dimensional art, 238–240
Vasarely, Victor
  Orion, 48–49, *48*
  Vega Per, 309
Vault Sequence No. 10 (Fridge), *136*
Vauxcelles, Louis, 267, 275
Vega Per (Vasarely), *309*
Venice Biennial, 331
Venus of Lespugue, 6
Vera Naturelle (Pousttchi), *145*
Verhulst, Rombout
  Bust of Maria van Reygersberg, 130
Vermeer, Jan, 290
Vermeer, Johannes
  Diana and the Nymphs, 46
vertical lines, 76
Vertigo (Bochner), *76*
Victory, Poteet
  Symbols of Manifest Destiny, 64
video, 214–215, 314
viewer's location point, 188, 189
View from the Wind River Mountains, Wyoming (Bierstadt), *181*
Viola, Bill, 214–215
  Going Forth by Day, 215
visual grouping, 40–41
visual linking, 41–47, *41*
  and extensions, 45–47
  and interpenetration, 44–45
  and overlapping, 44
  and shared edges, 41–43, *43*
  and transparency, 44
visual ordering, 29–31
vocabulary lists
  color, 142–143
  form, 28–29
  introductory terms, 4–5
  line, 70
  shape, 90
  space, 178
  texture, 128
  three-dimensional art, 220
  value, 112
Vogel, Hermann, 258
voids, 220, 232, 281
volume
  in Cubism, 275–276
  defined, 5, 18–19, 90
  and shape, 97
  in three-dimensional art, 220, 221–222
Vortograph #1 (Coburn), *281*

W

Walk, Don't Walk (Segal), *307*
Wang Hsi-chih
  Three Passages of Calligraphy, *75*
Ward, Nari
  Blue Window Brick Vine, 236
Warhol, Andy, 37
  100 Cans, 305
warm colors, 154–155
Waterfall (Escher), *199*
Waterloo Bridge, Grey Weather (Monet), *160*
Waterloo Bridge, Sunlight Effect (Monet), *160*
Water Towers (Becher & Becher), *327*
Weber, Max, 272, 280
welding, *230,* 236, 289
Wertheimer, Max, 40
Wesselmann, Tom
  Judy Trying on Clothes, 66
Weston, Edward, 282, 283, 302
  Juniper, Lake Tenaya, 283
White, Minor, 301
  Cobblestone House, Avon, New York, 17
  Windowsill Daydreaming, 301
White Line Square IX (Albers), *106*
White Numbers (Johns), *179*
White on White (Malevich), *279*
White Wall (Kendrick), *231*
Winckelmann, Johann Joachim, 249
Wind Fire (Thérèse Duncan) (Steichen), *282*
Windowsill Daydreaming (White), *301*
Winogrand, Gary, 306
  American Legion Convention, 307
Winters, Terry
  Image Location, 204
Witkin, Jerome Paul
  Jeff Davies, 61
Woman, I (de Kooning), *293*
Woman Doing Her Hair (Archipenko), *232*
Women and Dog (Marisol), *237*
Wondrous Spring (Csuri), *141*
Wood, Grant, 272, 283
woodcut prints, 21, 119–120
Woods, Lebbeus
  Terrain 10, 72
World of Awe (Kanarek), 215–216, *216*
World War I, 284
Wrapped Reichstag (Christo and Jeanne-Claude), *16,* 316
Wright, Frank Lloyd
  Armchair, *224*
Wu Zhen
  Bamboo in the Wind, 75
Wyeth, Andrew Newell, 318
  Spring Beauty, 127, 129

Y

Yasami, Masoud
  Balancing Act with Stone II, 54
Yosemite Valley (from below Sentinel Dome as Seen from Artist's Point) (Hill), *139*
Young Girl by a Window (Morisot), *262*

Z

Zapatistas (Orozco), *272*
Zola, Émile, 255, 256
Zorn, Andres
  Toast, The, 82